Footprint
Peru, Bolivia

Ben Box, Geoffrey Groesbeck, Robert and Daisy Kunstaetter
2nd edition

"We need the tonic of wildness... At the same time that we are earnest to explore and learn all things, we require that all things be mysterious and unexplorable, that land and sea be infinitely wild, unsurveyed and unfathomed by us because unfathomable. We can never have enough of nature."

Henry David Thoreau, Walden

❶ Quito
World Heritage treasure trove of colonial art and architecture, page 448.

❷ Parque Nacional Cotopaxi
The snow-capped cone of one of the world's highest volcanoes, page 507.

❸ Quilotoa Circuit
An emerald-green crater lake and traditional villages and markets, page 509.

❹ Devil's Nose
Ride one of the most spectacular railways in the Andes, page 522.

❺ Vilcabamba
Fabled fountain of youth at the rainbow's end, an exceptionally scenic and tranquil resort, page 546.

❻ Galápagos
One of the world's foremost wildlife sanctuaries, page 605.

❼ Cañon del Pato
Thrill-a-minute bus ride through a spectacular narrow pass, page 222.

❽ Cordillera Blanca
Beautiful and terrifying, these mountains are the highest in Peru, page 205.

❾ Nazca Lines
Whales, spiders and humming birds, etched in the desert sand over 2500 years ago, page 197.

❿ Manu Biosphere Reserve
One of the largest protected areas of rainforest, home to jaguars and giant otters, page 288.

Peru, Bolivia & Ecuador Highlights

See colour maps at back of book

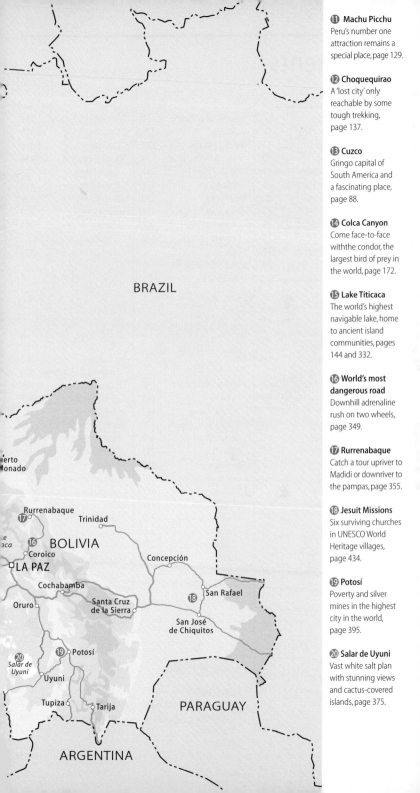

Contents

Two alpacas brave the cold in Sajama, Bolivia's oldest national park.

Worth its salt
The Salar de Uyuni in Bolivia is the world's largest salt lake, a vast and surreal expanse of arctic white nothingness.

A foot in the door

Imagine Peru, Bolivia and Ecuador and you automatically think of the Andes, the long, sinuous mountain chain that runs the full length of all three countries and forms the geographical and cultural spine of South America. Here, at over 12,000 feet, the first Incas rose from the freezing waters of Lake Titicaca. They named their capital Cuzco, 'Navel of the World', and built an empire that lasted until the Spanish came, saw, conquered and converted the natives.

But old habits die hard and today indigenous customs and beliefs are very much in evidence: in the beautiful and skilful *artesanía* (handicrafts); the spectacular festival costumes; the sacred temples and pyramids; or in the burying of a llama foetus under a new house to repel evil spirits. Often these ancient traditions were subsumed into the 'new' religion of the colonial masters.

It is the synthesis of ancient America and medieval Europe that is the essence of these countries. Thousands of years of empire-building, natural disasters, conquest, occupation and independence have all been played out, against the backdrop of those mighty mountains, the one constant in a continent of constant change.

Peru

Ever since the intrepid explorer Hiram Bingham first described Machu Picchu as a "wonderland", the fabled Inca city has become one of the most recognized images in the world. So much so that it virtually represents Peru, acting as a magnet for every visitor. But this is only the tip of the pyramid. Peru has more ancient archaeological sites than any other country in South America – hence its unofficial title 'Egypt of the Americas' – and more are being found all the time.

One such discovery, Caral, on the desert coast north of Lima, has turned the world of archaeology on its head and challenged accepted thinking on the entire theory of urban development. This long stretch of desert coast may sound uninhabitable, yet pre-Inca cultures thrived there. Around the northern towns of Trujillo and Chiclayo they welcomed gods from the sea and irrigated the soil to feed great cities of adobe bricks. In the south, they left their monuments in sculptures etched into the surface of the desert, most famously at Nazca.

There is much more to Peru than old stones, however. Of the 117 recognized life zones on the planet, Peru has 84, from mangroves to

Road to ruins
High above today's famous Sunday market, the Inca ruins at Pisac have a superb vantage point over agricultural terraces and the Urubamba valley.

cloudforest, mist-fuelled oases in the desert to glacial lakes. It also has 28 out of 32 climate types. Amazingly, 60% of the country is jungle, even though less than 6% of its population lives there. Because the physical barrier of the Andes has prevented Peru from integrating the tropical lowlands, much of its jungle remains intact. This vast green carpet is home to the greatest diversity of plants and wildlife on the planet. In the far south is Manu Biosphere Reserve, one of the largest protected areas of rainforest (over half the size of Switzerland) and arguably the most pristine conservation unit in the world, with much of it completely unexplored. This is, quite simply, the best place on earth for seeing jungle wildlife.

Peru is also a country of fiestas, and it would be an unlucky visitor who did not encounter at least one. Masks and costumes tell centuries-old stories and reveal an intense spirituality which enriches daily life. Christian saints are carried through the streets as if they were the Inca emperors' sacred remains. Pachamama – Mother Earth – is offered a drop of every drink and animal spirits and old combats come alive in masquerades.

Peru is a wonderland, indeed, with the uncanny knack of springing new surprises at every turn.

Paradise found
Giant otters, macaws, monkeys and hoatzin can be seen at tranquil Lago Sandoval, a popular destination in the Tambopata National Reserve.

1 *Revellers dress in traditional regalia at Oruro carnival, where dancing, music and water bombs all add up to lots of fun.* ▸▸ *See page 370.*

2 *The snowy peaks, valleys and ancient trails of the Cordillera Blanca never cease to attract trekkers and climbers.* ▸▸ *See page 205.*

3 *The squirrel monkey is one of countless rainforest species found in the Oriente jungle of Ecuador.* ▸▸ *See page 557.*

4 *The highest capital city on earth, La Paz leaves most visitors breathless – literally.* ▸▸ *See page 301.*

5 *Humpback whales visit the coast of Ecuador to mate and calve between June and September every year.* ▸▸ *See page 592.*

6 *The ruins of a Tiahuanaco-era fortress on Isla del Sol are set amongst the sapphire-blue waters of Lake Titicaca.* ▸▸ *See page 334.*

7 *Two thousand-year-old underground aqueducts near Nazca still provide water for local communities.* ▸▸ *See page 196.*

8 *The Peruvian jungle covers more than half the country but is largely uninhabited. Rivers are the highways and an essential form of transport.* ▸▸ *See page 643.*

9 *Beautifully engineered Inca stonemasonry was designed to withstand earthquakes as well as look remarkable.* ▸▸ *See page 628.*

10 *El Mercado de las Brujas – the witches' market – sells weird and wonderful concoctions to protect a dwelling from evil spirits.* ▸▸ *See pages 310.*

11 *Montañita is the most popular surfing beach in Ecuador and hosts a number of annual competitions.* ▸▸ *See page 586.*

12 *With its immense blue-dome cathedral, colonial Cuenca (Ecuador) is a UNESCO World Heritage Site.* ▸▸ *See page 531.*

Everything about this land-locked country in the heart of the continent is out of the ordinary. It's the kind of place where you start taking the strangest things for granted: like sitting next to an alligator on a bus or waiting behind a group of piglets at the check-in desk. In Bolivia, it seems, pigs really do fly.

The minute you arrive in the capital, La Paz, you realize this is no ordinary place. The airport, at 4000 m above sea level, is the highest in the world. So high, in fact, that incoming flights almost have to ascend to land. La Paz is one giant street market, where indigenous women in bowler hats and voluminous skirts will sell you everything you could possibly need – from a pair of black market designer jeans to a dried llama foetus. These grotesque objects are burned and used along with incense, bits of wool, grease and coca leaves in white magic ceremonies and to rid houses of evil spirits. Bolivia's strange curiosities are not confined to La Paz.

Only a few hours north is Lake Titicaca, the highest navigable lake in the world, which gave birth to the Inca empire. In the southwest of the country is the Salar de Uyuni, the world's highest and largest salt lake – 12,000 sq km of blinding white nothingness. South of the salt lake is a Salvador Dalí landscape of deserts, volcanoes, bizarre rock formations, bubbling geysers, peculiar green plants and a blood-red lake filled with flamingoes. East from here is a hollow silver mountain, dinosaur footprints, villages where annual festivities revolve around ritualized fights and national parks that are so remote no one has yet visited them.

"I am rich Potosí, treasure of the world. The king of all mountains, and the envy of all kings":
Cerro Rico looms behind the city of Potosí.

Bartolomé Island, set against the backdrop of Sullivan Bay, is the most visited and photographed spot in the Galápagos.

Ecuador

The phrase 'small is beautiful' could have been coined specifically with Ecuador in mind. By South American standards it is tiny – dwarfed by its neighbours Colombia and Peru. But it is this relative compactness that is one of its main attractions. Here, you can watch dawn break over the jungle canopy, have lunch high in the Andean mountains, then watch the sun slip into the Pacific Ocean – all in the same day.

Ecuador also boasts extraordinary biological diversity; a fact that did not escape the attention of 18th- and 19th-century scientists and explorers, who came, saw and compiled large volumes extolling its many virtues. The first to put Ecuador on the map was French savant, Charles-Marie de la Condamine, who determined the precise location of the equatorial line here and so helped to give the country its name. The early 19th-century explorer, Alexander Von Humboldt, was impressed by the snow-covered peaks running down the country's spine, dubbing it the 'Avenue of the Volcanoes'. And it was a young Englishman called Charles Darwin, who, in 1835, first brought the world's attention to the Galápagos Islands – Ecuador's premier attraction and the greatest wildlife show on Earth. Today, visitors to Ecuador can still write home about smoking volcanoes, weird and wonderful creatures, impenetrable jungles and exotic peoples. Two centuries of 'progress' have not diminished the keen sense of adventure that this country inspires.

Sound foundations
Calle Hatun Rumiyoc contains some of Cuzco's best surviving Inca stonework, which the Spanish used as the foundation for many colonial buildings.

Essentials

Planning your trip

Where to go

The variety that Peru, Bolivia and Ecuador can offer the visitor is enormous. The obvious attractions in Peru are Machu Picchu, the Nazca Lines and the jungle reserves of Manu and Tambopata; while in Ecuador the colonial heritage of the capital, Quito, and the wildlife extravaganza that is the Galápagos Islands are the major draws. Bolivia's main attraction for tourists, meanwhile, is its wild natural beauty; much of the country lies off the beaten track, a vast wilderness waiting to be explored and appreciated. The problem is, if you're on a tight schedule, how to fit it all in. Seeing much of these countries by bus in the space of a few weeks is a forlorn hope. So you'll either need to concentrate on a smaller area or consider taking internal flights.

Two weeks
The best option for a two week visit is to limit yourself to one or two countries. As Peru is sandwiched in the middle, it is logical to combine it with a visit to either Bolivia or Ecuador. In Peru there are certain places that fit neatly into seven days of travelling. **Southern Peru** offers a very rewarding short circuit covering the most important and popular sites in this part of the country. **Cuzco** and **Machu Picchu**, the crown jewels of the Inca Empire, require at least four days, more if you plan to hike the **Inca Trail**. Beautiful **Titicaca**, the highest navigable lake in the world, the elegant colonial city of **Arequipa**, nearby **Colca Canyon**, and the incredible **Nazca Lines** could all be combined with Cuzco into a 10-day tour using air, rail and road travel.

You could then head from Lake Titicaca across the border to the Bolivian capital, **La Paz**, which is fairly small and manageable and easy to explore on foot in a couple of days. Several interesting trips can be made from La Paz, including the ruins of the great pre-Inca city of **Tiahuanaco**. From La Paz you can mountain bike down the 'world's most dangerous road' to the little town of **Coroico**, a popular resort in the sub-tropical valleys of the **Yungas**.

An alternative to Bolivia would be to fly from Lima to the beautiful colonial city of **Quito**, in Ecuador. One of Ecuador's great attractions is its relative compactness and much of what you want to see is only a few hours by road from the capital. Just two hours north is **Otavalo**, home to one of the finest craft markets in all of Latin America and a few hours' south is the spectacular **Cotopaxi National Park**, the stunning **Quilotoa circuit** and **Baños**, a very popular spa town at the foot of an active volcano.

If you don't arrange a trip to the **Amazon jungle** from Cuzco (see below), it's relatively cheap and easy to arrange one from Quito to one of Ecuador's many jungle lodges. The alternative is to travel under your own steam to one of the main jungle towns and arrange a tour from there with a local agency. Tours can be arranged from Puyo, Tena, Misahuallí, Coca and Baños, which is on the road from the highlands to the Oriente. And then there's the **Galápagos Islands**, Ecuador's famed wildlife showcase. It's expensive to visit but well worth it. Galápagos tours range from four days up to 14 days, but seven days would be optimal, if you can afford it, to fully appreciate this once-in-a-lifetime experience.

One month
A month allows you the luxury of several further options for exploring more of Peru, Bolivia and Ecuador. With this amount of time you really should visit **Manu National Park** or the **Tambopata National Reserve** in Peru's southeastern jungle. These provide wonderful opportunities for watchers of birds, butterflies and animals and for plant

How big is your footprint?

During the past decade there has been a phenomenal growth in tourism that promotes and supports the conservation of natural environments and is also fair and equitable to local communities. This 'eco-tourism' segment is probably the fastest growing sector of the travel industry. Amongst the best known examples in the region are the **Kapawi Lodge** in southern Oriente (page 559) and **Chalalán Eco Lodge** in Bolivia (page 360). **Tourism Concern**, Stapleton House, 277-281 Holloway Rd, London N7 8HN, UK T0207-753 3330, www.tourismconcern.org.uk, promotes a greater understanding of the impact of tourism on host communities and environments. **Centre for Responsible Tourism (CRT)**, PO Box 827, San Anselmo, California 94979, USA, co-ordinates a North American network and advises on North American sources of information on responsible tourism. **Centre for the Advancement of Responsive Travel (CART)**, UK, T01732-352757, has a range of publications available as well as information on alternative holiday destinations. **CARE International UK**, 10-13 Rushworth St, London SE1 0RB, T0207-934 9334, www.careinter

national.org.uk, works to improve the economic conditions of people living in developing countries. They are currently involved in the development of the Che Guevara Trail in Bolivia.

→ Choose a destination, tour operator or hotel with a proven ethical and environmental commitment; if in doubt ask.
→ Spend money on locally produced (rather than imported) goods and services and use common sense when bargaining.
→ Stay in local, rather than foreign-owned, accommodation; the economic benefits for host communities are far greater.
→ Use water and electricity carefully; travellers may receive preferential supply while local communities are overlooked.
→ Learn about local etiquette and culture; consider local norms of behaviour and dress appropriately.
→ Protect wildlife and other natural resources.
→ Always ask before taking photographs or videos of people.
→ Rather than giving money or sweets to children, which encourages begging, consider donating to a recognized project, charity or school.

lovers. Trips to the southeastern jungle can be booked in Cuzco, which is the jumping off-point for flights or the 24-hour overland journey.

Another option in Peru is to head for **Huaraz**, in the **Cordillera Blanca**, seven hours by road from Lima and one of the world's top climbing and trekking destinations. A week spent exploring the Cordillera and neighbouring areas can easily be linked with the coastal archaeological sites near the colonial city of **Trujillo** and, further north, around **Chiclayo**. From Chiclayo you could venture to the more remote **Chachapoyas** region, which contains a bewildering number of prehispanic archaeological sites (spend at least a week if possible). North of Peru, there are several border crossings to the south of Ecuador. The easiest, from Piura to Loja, provides access to **Vilcabamba**, once a fabled fountain of youth, today the southern terminus of Ecuador's 'gringo trail'. Six hours north of here is **Cuenca**, a lovely colonial city and also a great place to buy Panama hats (yes, they're made in Ecuador!). There are good road links north from Cuenca to Riobamba, with its spectacular Devil's Nose train ride, and on to Baños and Quito.

Don't forget your toothbrush...

→ Pack light. Take clothes that are quick and easy to wash and dry. Loose-fitting clothes are more comfortable in hot climates and can be layered if it gets cooler.

→ You can easily, and cheaply, buy things en route, but musts are: good walking shoes, a money belt, a sun hat and sunglasses.

→ Other useful items are a Swiss Army knife, flip flops, a headtorch/flashlight, the smallest alarm clock you can find, a padlock, dental floss and a basic medical kit.

→ Pack photocopies of essential documents like passport, visas and traveller's cheque receipts just in case you lose the originals. Also leave a copy with someone at home.

→ Photographers should take all film and memory sticks required for the trip. Keep them in a waterproof bag.

→ Keep a stash of tissues with you.

→ Don't load yourself down with toiletries. They're heavy and can be bought everywhere. Items like contact lens solutions and tampons may be harder to find; stock up in major cities.

Alternatively, you could spend more time in Bolivia instead of visiting northern Peru. Those visiting during the dry season – April to October – would be strongly advised not to miss a trip to **Rurrenabaque**, from where you can take a jungle or pampas tour and experience the country's amazing diversity of wildlife. Rurre is also the starting point for the fantastic **Chalalán Eco-lodge**. Ecotourism with a capital 'E', it stands in the **Madidi National Park**, one of Bolivia's newest protected areas, and one that boasts a greater biodiversity than anywhere else on earth. The **Southern Altiplano** is one of the most remote corners of Bolivia and also one of the most fascinating. Old colonial **Potosí** is probably the most interesting of all Bolivia's cities and a visit to its former silver mines is a must. Nearby is the country's official capital, **Sucre**, with some stunning colonial architecture. Southwest from Potosí is **Uyuni**, the starting point for a three- to four-day tour to the **Salar de Uyuni**, a vast, blindingly white salt lake and one of the most spectacular sights in the entire country. South of the Salar, near the Chilean border, are deserts, volcanoes and multi-coloured soda lakes teeming with flamingos.

When to go

Peru's high season in the highlands is from May to September. At this time the days are generally clear and sunny, though nights can be very cold at high altitude. During the wettest months in the highlands, November to April, some roads become impassable. April and May, at the tail end of the highland rainy season, is a beautiful time to see the Peruvian Andes. On the coast, high seasons are September and Christmas to February. The summer months are from December to April, but from approximately May to October much of this area is covered with *la garúa*, a blanket of cloud and mist.

The best time to visit the jungle in **Peru** and **Bolivia** is during the dry season, from April to October. During the wet season, November to April, it is oppressively hot (40° C and above) and while it only rains for a few hours at a time, it is enough to make some roads virtually impassable. These are also the months when mosquitos and other biting insects are at their worst, so this is not a good time to visit the jungle. As for the rest of **Bolivia**, the Altiplano does not receive much rain, so timing is not so crucial here, although hiking trails can get very muddy during the wet season. During the winter months of June and July, nights tend to be clearer but even colder than at other times. These are the best months to visit the Salar de Uyuni, as the salt lake is even more impressive under clear blue skies.

Ecuador's climate is so varied and variable that any time of the year is good for a visit. In the highlands, temperatures vary more with altitude than they do with the seasons (which mainly reflect changes in rainfall). To the west of the Andes, June to September are dry and October to May are wet (but there is sometimes a short dry spell in December or January). To the east, October to February are dry and March through September are wet. There is also variation in annual rainfall from north to south, with the southern highlands being drier. In the Oriente, as in the rest of the Amazon basin, heavy rain can fall at any time, but it is usually wettest from March to September. The Galápagos are hot from January to April, when heavy but brief showers are likely. From May through December is the cooler misty season.

Overall June to September offers the best weather conditions, but this is also the high season when prices rise and accommodation and bus tickets are hard to come by. If you know when you will be travelling it's best to buy your ticket in advance and book hotel rooms, especially for more upmarket places. ▶▶ *See also Festivals and events, page 37.*

Activities and tours

The region has an incredibly varied climate and landscape, making it perfect for a multitude of outdoor activities. This is one of the very best parts of the world for a number of adventure sports, including trekking and climbing, whitewater rafting, mountain biking and surfing. Facilities for adventure tourism tend to develop in correlation with general tourist services so always make sure the infrastructure and equipment is adequate before signing up for a potential dangerous activity. Also check the experience and qualifications of operators and guides. Peru, Bolivia and Ecuador also offer probably the greatest wildlife viewing opportunities on the planet and Peru is unmatched anywhere for the sheer scale of its ancient ruins.

Birdwatching

Peru has nearly 20% of all bird species in the world and 45% of all neotropical birds. Bird-watching is possible all year round and the range to be seen is hugely rewarding for beginners and the more experienced. Ecuador is also one of the world's richest places for birds, see **Jocotoco Foundation** reserves, www.fjocotoco.org.

★ **Head for ...**
Paracas, page 203 (note that this area was affected by the 2007 earthquake). **Colca Canyon**, page 172. **Manu Biosphere Reserve**, page 288. **Tambopata National Reserve**, page 292. **Amboró**, page 427. **Mindo**, page 477. **Jungle lodges**, pages 283 and page 559. **Madidi**, page 358.

Climbing

There is excellent climbing throughout the region, with over a thousand peaks above 5000 m and several more above 6000 m. Peru has fantastic ice climbing while Ecuador has

something to offer both beginners and experts, with the magical opportunity to climb an active volcano by moonlight. Bolivia has some of the best mountaineering in the world but the infrastructure is not very developed, so do not expect to be rescued if you get into trouble. The climbing season runs May-Sep, with the best months being Jun-Aug. In Ecuador Dec-Feb can also be good. Proper technical equipment, experience and/or a competent guide are essential to cross glaciers and climb snow and ice safely. A number of summits are achievable by acclimatized beginners with a competent guide and the correct high-altitude climbing equipment.
Asocación Ecuatoriana de Guías de Montaña (**Aseguim**), Pinto 416 y JL Mera, p 2, Quito, T02-223 4109. They can be very hard to contact in an emergency, it is best to contact them through **Safari Tours** (page 469) or **Compañía de Guías de Montaña**, page 466).
Club Andino Boliviano, Calle Mexico 1638, La Paz, T/F02-2324682, is the national mountaineering club in Bolivia.
Peruvian Mountain Guide Association (**AGMP**), Casa de Guías, Huaraz, see page 208.

★ Five of the best adventure highs

Sandboarding down the world's highest sand dune, see page 203.
Climbing in the Cordillera Blanca, see page 208.
Whitewater rafting on the Río Blanco, see page 465.
Mountain biking down the volcanic cone of Chimborazo, see page 522.
Exploring the reefs and sea life of the Galápagos Islands, see page 618.

★ **Head for ...**
Cordillera Blanca, page 208. **La Paz**, page 322. **Sorata**, page 336. **Cotopaxi**, page 507. **Chimborazo**, page 522.

Cultural tourism

Cultural tourism is a rapidly growing niche market and includes rather more esoteric pursuits such as archaeology and mystical tourism. Several tour operators offer packages for special interest groups. PromPerú (see page 49), www.peru.info, has community-based tourism projects in archaeology, agro tourism, jungle trips, education, llama trekking, nature tourism and traditional medicine. Prodecos, www.prodecos.com, arranges for tourists to stay with local Ecuadorian families and take part in daily activities.

★**Head for ...**
Cuzco, page 88. **Trujillo**, page 232. **Chiclayo**, page 247. **Jesuit Missions**, page 434. **Quito**, page 451. **Runa Tupari**, page 490. **Pukyu Pamba**, page 500. **Kapawi Lodge**, page 559.

Cycling/mountain biking

Although the area is blessed with fantastic routes, views and a generally stable climate, cycling is yet to really take off. It is best to take a guide or join a tour group as most routes and trails remain unmapped. There are an increasing number of operators specializing in biking, many of the 'gravity assisted' type, with good equipment and back-up. One of the most thrilling rides in the continent is in Bolivia, down the 'world's most dangerous road', but there are many places for novices.

★ **Head for ...**
Cordillera Blanca, page 217. **Chacaltaya**, page 323. **La Paz to Coroico**, page 349. **Baños**, page 517. **Chimborazo**, page 522.

Diving and snorkelling

The Galápagos Islands are well known for their distinctive marine environments and offer more than 20 dive sites. Each island contains a unique environment and many are home to underwater life forms found nowhere else. There are several tour operators in Quito that offer diving and full instruction in their trips. Note that conditions in the Galápagos are difficult and for experienced divers only. Snorkelling is highly recommended, however, and you will come face-to-face with all manner of marine animals. A safer and easier option for novice divers is Machalilla National Park, on the coast of Ecuador.

★ **Head for ...**
Parque Nacional Machalilla, page 587. **Galápagos**, page 618.

Parapenting/hang gliding

Vuelo Libre (parapenting) has become popular in the last few years. Flying from the coastal cliffs is easy and the thermals are good. In Peru, the best area is the Sacred Valley of Cuzco which has excellent launch sites, thermals and reasonable landing sites. In Ecuador it can be done in several highland cities and in the coastal towns. The season in the Sierra is May-Oct (best Aug-Sep). Some flights in Peru have exceeded 6500 m.

★ **Head for ...**
Cuzco, page 113. **Huaraz**, page 209. **Quito**, page 465. **Crucita**, page 590. **Canoa**, page 592.

Rafting and kayaking

Peru and Ecuador are perfect for rafting and kayaking of all levels of experience. At the height of the Andes expect to find routes for only the most experienced, while lower down, the rivers calm to provide great conditions for beginners and those who are content to drift and admire some of the magnificent, untouched scenery. The Río Blanco, in Ecuador, is possibly the best of all, with 47 km of non-stop grade III-IV rapids and is offered by agencies in Quito.

★ **Head for …**
Cuzco, page 112. **Quito**, page 465.
Baños, page 517. **Tena**, page 561.

Sandboarding

If you've always fancied tearing down a massive sand dune on a wooden board, then the southern coastal desert in Peru is the place for you. As much fun as snowboarding but without the cold or required technical expertise, sandboarding is a growing sport amongst warm-weather thrill-seekers.

★ **Head for …**
Huacachina, page 203. **Nazca**, page 196.

Skiing

Without the aid of lifts, skiing in Peru is largely for the high-altitude enthusiast. Pastoruri, at 5000 m, has the only piste and holds a championship during **Semana del Andinismo** at the end of the Nov-Jun season. The extreme ski descent craze has hit the Cordillera Blanca in a big way and no peak is considered off limits. Bolivia boasts the world's highest ski run, at Chacaltaya (5345 m), but facilities are limited and you can only ski immediately after a fresh snowfall. **Club Andino Boliviano** (see above under Climbing) arranges trips to Chacaltaya.

★ **Head for …**
Cordillera Blanca, page 205. **Chacaltaya**, page 323.

Surfing and bodyboarding

Peru is internationally renowned for its surf spots. Point Break, Left and Right Reef breaks and waves up to 6 m high can be found. Sep-Feb is best on the north coast and Mar-Dec south of Lima. Ecuador also has excellent beaches for beginners and experts. Waves are generally best Dec-Mar. *Tablista* is a bimonthly surfing mag in Peru. Also look out for *X3*.

The website www.wannasurf.com has lots of good surfing information.

★ **Head for …**
Huanchaco, page 238. **Montañita**, page 586.

Trekking

The whole region has wonderful trekking opportunities, from easy 1-day hikes to more challenging treks through mountain ranges and jungle habitats. It is also possible to combine hikes and treks with visits to ancient ruins, the prime example being the 4-day hike to Machu Picchu. There are also a number of alternative trails to Machu Picchu that are much less crowded and equally spectacular. Bolivia is endowed with many excellent treks, some of them on existing Inca roads. Most of the popular treks begin around La Paz and cross the Cordillera Real, finishing in the sub-tropical Yungas, but many other parts of the country also offer excellent possibilities. Intrepid hikers could find themselves in isolation for days with only the occasional llama for company, passing through

campesino villages, where the inhabitants may have never seen a fleece jacket or pair of hiking boots.

Check out www.trekkinginecuador.com. Good trekking guidebooks are: *Trekking in Ecuador* by Robert & Daisy Kunstaetter (Mountaineers, Seattle, 2002) and *Trekking in Bolivia* by Yossi Brain by the same publisher. Also *The Andes A Trekking Guide* by John & Cathy Biggar (Andes).

★ Head for …
Cuzco and Sacred Valley, page 118, **Inca treks**, page 133. **Cordillera Blanca**, page 208. **La Paz**, page 322. **Sorata**, page 336. **Quilotoa**, page 510. **Vilcabamba**, page 544.

Wildlife watching

Peru, Ecuador and Bolivia have a huge range of diverse habitats that can now be easily visited through a number of good tour companies. The Galápagos is the outstanding area for seeing wildlife but this is a very expensive option. The southern Peruvian Amazon offers the opportunity to spot jaguar, giant river otters, over a dozen species of monkey and huge black caiman, to name but a few. In Bolivia, jungle or pampas tours run from Rurrenabaque and are very popular, though nothing can match the sheer splendour of Madidi, Amboró or Noel Kempff Mercado.

★ Head for …
Manu Biosphere Reserve, page 288. **Tambopata**, page 292. **Madidi**, page 358. **Amboró**, page 427. **Noel Kempff Mercado**, page 440. **Parque Nacional Machalilla**, page 587. **Cuyabeno**, page 567. **Galápagos**, page 603.

Getting there and away

Arriving by air

Most international flights to the region arrive at **Quito** (UIO, page 448), **Lima** (LIM, page 58) or **La Paz** (LPB, page 304), with the first two receiving by far the majority. One-way and return flights are available to all of these destinations. Also enquire about 'open jaw' flights (arriving at one airport and leaving from another). Most airlines offer different fare types such as fixed return, yearly return or student (under 26) fares. While student fares are often the most flexible they may not necessarily be the cheapest. Airpasses for South America are often bought in conjunction with International flights so ask when booking if you plan to use internal flights.

From the UK flights to Quito start at between £400-500 (in low season). Lima is more expensive (£500-600), higher still in July and at Christmas. **From the USA**, flights to Lima and Quito cost around US$325-510. Most airlines offer discounted fares on scheduled flights through agencies who specialize in this type of fare (see below). The busy seasons are 7 December-15 January and 10 July-10 September. If you intend travelling during those times, book as far ahead as possible. From February to May and September to November special offers may be available.

Flights from Europe

It is only possible to get regular flights direct to **Lima** or **Quito**, making these destinations the most useful entry/exit points with the widest range of options and prices. Direct flights are available from Madrid or Barcelona with **Iberia** and from Amsterdam with **KLM**. Most connecting flights in Europe are through these cities although it is possible to fly to the USA and get a connecting flight with one of the carriers shown below. It is also possible to fly direct to South American cities and then get a connecting flight onward to Lima, La Paz or Quito. Direct flights to **La Paz** from Europe are not offered by any airline, the best option here is to fly direct to Lima, Rio de Janeiro or São Paulo and catch a connecting flight. Alternatively, you can fly to Miami and connect from there.

Lima is the best served destination from the USA with Miami serving as the main gateway, together with Atlanta, Dallas, Houston, Los Angeles and New York. The main carriers available from these destinations are **American Airlines, Lan Chile/Lan Perú, Continental, Delta, Copa, Lacsa** and **AeroMéxico**. From Canada, there are only direct flights from Toronto with **Air Canada**, which flies three times a week. Flights from all other Canadian cities must fly via one of the above gateways.

Quito can be reached directly from Miami, Houston, Atlanta and New York with **American Airlines, LAN, Delta** and **Continental Airlines**. Flights from all other US and Canadian cities must go via these destinations. Cheaper fares may be available from **Copa Airlines** and **TACA**, although these go via Panama City and San José, Costa Rica.

There are daily direct flights from Miami to **La Paz** with a cotinuing service to **Santa Cruz** with **American Airlines** and **LAB**. **Continental Airways** also has a direct service from Miami to **Santa Cruz** three times a week. **Note** At the time of going to press, the future of **LAB** was uncertain; contact www.labairlines.co.uk for the latest information.

Discount flight agents

In the UK
Journey Latin America, 12-13 Heathfield Terr, London, W4 4JE, T020-8747 8315; also at 12 St Ann's Sq, Manchester, M2 7HW, T0161-832 1441, www.journeylatinamerica.co.uk.
STA Travel, 86 Old Brompton Rd, London, SW7 3LQ, T0870 160 0599, www.statravel.co.uk. They have 65 other branches in the UK, including many University campuses. Specialists in low-cost student/youth flights and tours, also good for student IDs and insurance.
Trailfinders, 194 Kensington High St, London, W8 7RG, T020-7938 3939, www.trail finders.com. They also have other branches in London, as well as in Birmingham, Bristol, Cambridge, Glasgow, Manchester, Newcastle, Dublin and Belfast.
Trips Worldwide, 14 Frederick Pl, Clifton, Bristol BS8 1JT, T0117-311 4400, www.tripsworldwide.co.uk.

North America
Air Brokers International, 685 Market St, Suite 400, San Francisco, CA94105, T01-800-883 3273, www.airbrokers.com. Consolidator and specialist on RTW and Circle Pacific tickets.
Discount Airfares Worldwide On-Line, www.etn.nl/discount.htm. A hub of consolidator and discount agent links.
Exito Latin American Travel Specialists, 108 Rutgers St, Fort Collins, CO 80525, T1800-655-4053; worldwide T970-482-3019, www.exito-travel.com.
STA Travel, 5900 Wiltshire Blvd, Suite 2110, Los Angeles, CA 90036, 1-800-781-4040, www.sta-travel.com. Also branches in New York, San Francisco, Boston, Miami, Chicago, Seattle and Washington DC.
Travel CUTS, in all major Canadian cities and on university and college campuses, T1-866-246-9762, www.travelcuts.com. Specialist in student discount fares, IDs and other travel services. Branches in other Canadian cities as well as California, USA.

Australia and New Zealand
Contours Travel, 310 King St, Melbourne, T3-9670 6900, www.contourstravel.com.au. **Flight Centre**, T133133, www.flight centre.com.au. With offices throughout Australia and other countries. **STA Travel**, T1300-360960, www.sta travel.com.au; 208 Swanston St, Melbourne, VIC 3000, T03-9639 0599. In NZ: 130 Cuba Street, PO Box 6604, Wellington, T04-385 0561, cuba@statravel.co.nz. Also in major towns and university campuses. **Travel.com.au**, T02 9249 6000, outside Sydney: T1300 130 482, www.travel.com.au. **Trailfinders**, 8 Spring St, Sydney, NSW 2000, T1300-780212, www.trailfinders.com.au.

Leaving Peru, Bolivia and Ecuador

When you buy your ticket, always check whether departure tax is included. International departure tax is US$30 in **Peru**, payable in dollars or soles, US$41 from Quito in **Ecuador** (US$25 from Guayaquil), and US$25 in **Bolivia**, payable in dollars or bolivianos; cash only. You will not be allowed to board the plane without proof of payment.

Getting around

Peru

Air Two main national carriers serve the major routes in Peru, these are **WayraPerú**, www.wayra.com.pe, and **Star Perú**, www.starperu.com. Prices range from US$66-99 for a one-way trip anywhere from Lima. Prices rise during holiday times and elections so try to book early to guarantee flights. **Lan**, www.lan.com, and **Grupo Taca**, www.grupo taca.com, also offer flights along the major routes. For the more remote highland and jungle areas try **Aerocóndor**, www.aerocondor.com.pe, and **LC Busre**, www.lcbusre.com.pe. Be aware that these areas are prone to long delays and constant timetable revision due to unpredictable weather. Time-keeping tends to be better early morning than later. Always allow an extra day between national and international flights, especially in the rainy season. Internal flight prices are fixed in US dollars (but can be paid in soles) and have 19% tax added. **Note** Flights must be reconfirmed in the departure town at least 24 hours in advance.

Bus Services along the coast to the north and south, as well as inland to Huancayo, Ayacucho and Huaraz, are good. There are varying degrees of comfort offered, ranging from the relative luxury of first class to packed, uncomfortable second class. First class (*ejecutivo*) buses have direct services to major centres. Many buses have bathrooms, movies and reclining seats (*bus cama*) but the price and quality varies depending on the journey. The companies thought to have the best services and the most routes are **Ormeño**, www.grupo-ormeno.com, **Cruz del Sur**, www.cruzdelsur.com.pe, and **CIVA**, www.civa.com.pe. Take blankets when travelling in the mountains or on an a/c bus. Avoid sitting at the back of the bus next to the toilets. Where buses stop it is possible to buy food on the roadside. On local buses watch your luggage and always carry your valuables with you. In addition, smaller *combis* operate between most small towns on one- to three-hour journeys. **Note** Prices of bus tickets are raised by 60-100%, two to three days before Semana Santa, 28 July (Independence Day) and Christmas; tickets will be sold out two to three days in advance and transport is hard to come by.

Car You must have an international driving licence to drive in Peru and be over 21 years old. If renting a car, your home driving licence will be accepted for up to six months; you must be over 25 to hire a car. Car hire rates tend to be very expensive but tourist offices and hotels should know of the cheapest companies. Always check that the vehicle comes with spare wheels etc. The **Touring y Automóvil Club del Perú**, www.touringperu.com.pe, offers advice to tourists. Some mountain roads can be impassable in the rainy season.

Essentials Planning your trip · Getting around

★ Five of the most spectacular journeys

Cuzco to Puerto Maldonado, see page 290.
La Paz to Coroico bike ride, see page 349.
Across the Salar de Uyuni, see page 375.
Devil's nose train ride, see page 522.
Baños to Río Verde bike ride, see page 528.

Availability of fuel varies around the country and the price depends on the octane rating. Unleaded is widely available along the Pan American Highway and in large cities but rarely in the highlands. Prices range from US$3.45-4.72 per gallon for gasoline and US$3.27 for diesel. Tolls are charged on most major paved roads and cost US$1.65-2.25.

Train The main railways are Puno-Juliaca-Cuzco, and Cuzco-Machu Picchu, administered by **PerúRail SA**, www.perurail.com, and Lima-Huancayo, with a continuation to Huancavelica in the Central Highlands. The Lima-Huancayo service is run by **Ferrovías Central Andina**, www.ferroviasperu.com.pe, at weekends. Trains run daily between Huancayo and Huancavelica.

Bolivia

Air Internal air services are run by **Aero Sur**, www.aerosur.com (the principal carrier), **Lloyd Aéreo Boliviano (LAB)**, www.labairlines.com.bo, and **Amazonas**, www.amazonas.com. **LAB** offers a 45-day domestic 'Vibolpass' for US$155-250 (three to five coupons) for four flights between the main cities. It must be bought outside Bolivia. **Amazonas** also offers a five-coupon airpass. Many flights radiate from La Paz, Santa Cruz or Cochabamba. Note that a 'through' flight may require a change of plane, or be delayed waiting for a connecting flight coming from elsewhere. Insure your bags heavily as they tend to get left around and **LAB** is reluctant to give compensation. If your internal flight is delayed keep your baggage with you and do not check it in until the flight is announced. There have been reports of theft. **Note** At the time of going to press, the future of **LAB** was uncertain; contact www.labairlines.co.uk for the latest information.

Bus Travelling by bus in Bolivia may be the cheapest way to get around but it can also be dirty, uncomfortable, extremely time-consuming and, at times, downright scary. As a rule of thumb, the newer carriers have the best amenities. Trying to actually find the bus you need can present serious problems. La Paz and the other major cities have central bus terminals, but not all buses leave from them and finding out when and where the others leave from can take as long as the journey. On top of this, bus times are regularly changed to take account of local, regional and national festivals and soccer matches. **Note** On election day no public transport runs whatsoever; only cars with a special permit may be on the road. During the wet season journey times can be increased by hours, even days, as roads get washed out and vehicles get stuck in the mud. Be prepared for delays from roadblocks. Inter-urban buses are called *flotas*, urban ones *micros*, and there are also minibuses and *trufis* (shared taxis). Bus companies are responsible for any luggage packed on the roof. Avoid travelling at night, and take food and toilet wipes on all journeys.

Car The awful condition of the roads, tolls, high altitudes, behaviour of other drivers (who almost never dip their headlights, drive drunk, or fall asleep at the wheel), and even people sleeping at the roadside, all conspire to make driving in Bolivia a very bad idea. Furthermore, regulations are tight and police checks frequent. Always carry your passport, a driving licence and an International Driving Permit. You can be fined or

⁝ Transport

Bus

→ For international service, it's cheaper to take a bus to the border, cross and then take another to your final destination.

→ Make sure you see your gear being stored on the correct bus, especially at busy terminals. 'Mistakes', intentional or innocent, are not uncommon.

→ In general, try to reserve and pay for a seat as far as possible in advance and arrive in good time, as buses often depart when full. Confirm that the bus leaves from same place that the ticket was purchased.

→ In the Peruvian highlands, don't just rely on buses to get from A to B. Ask where the *colectivos* leave from. They may be a bit more expensive, but they are quicker.

→ In the wet season, bus travel is subject to long delays and detours.

→ It is always possible to buy food on the roadside, as buses stop frequently, but make sure you have very small-denomination notes.

→ Always carry your valuables with you, even when leaving the bus at a meal stop.

→ On overnight trips, especially in the Andes, you will appreciate extra clothing or a blanket as many buses do not have any form of heating.

→ On all journeys take toilet paper. Toilet facilities on cheaper buses are almost non-existent but bus drivers are generally happy to stop anywhere.

→ If your bus has a VCR, don't expect to see any scenery by day, and don't expect to get any sleep at night.

→ Avoid the back seats at all costs. On unpaved roads you will spend more time airborne than seated, and the windows will be jammed open, causing you to cough your lungs up from the exhaust fumes and clouds of choking dust, as well as freeze to death at night in the mountains.

Car

→ When hiring a car check exactly what the insurance policy covers. In many cases it will only protect you against minor bumps and scrapes and not major accidents. Ask if extra cover is available. Beware of being billed for scratches that were on the vehicle before you hired it.

→ Never leave a car unattended except in a locked garage or guarded parking space. Street children will generally protect your car fiercely in exchange for a tip. Lock the clutch or accelerator to the steering wheel with a heavy, obvious chain or lock.

→ You cannot take a hire car across international borders.

imprisoned for not doing so, even though car rental companies only require your national driving licence. The minimum age for renting a car is 25 and hire rates are prohibitively high. Check with **Autómovil Club Boliviano**, Avenida 6 e Agosto y Arce, La Paz, T02-243 2231, for any special documents which may be required. Note that roads may be closed in the rainy season (November to March). Avoid driving at night.

There are two types of gasoline: *especial* (85 octane) US$0.50 per litre, and *premium* (92 octane) US$0.60 per litre; both contain lead. Diesel costs US$0.46 per litre. Road tolls cost US$0.25-1.25 for journeys up to 100 km; you receive a stamped receipt at the first toll, which is then stamped at subsequent toll posts.

Train There are passenger trains to the Argentine border at Villazón from Oruro, via Uyuni and Tupiza. Another line runs from Uyuni to Calama in Chile. The only other public railways of significance run from Santa Cruz to the Brazil border and southward. The new Santa Cruz terminal is amazingly efficient, and has connections with bus lines as well. Always check departure times in advance.

Air TAME, www.tame.com.ec, is the main internal airline, flying to all major airports and the Galápagos. Enquire locally for up-to-date routes and timetables. Smaller airlines include: **Aerogal**, www.aerogal.com.ec, **Icaro**, www.icaro.com.ec, and **VIP** www.vipec.com. Confirm and reconfirm all flight reservations frequently.

Bus Bus travel is generally more convenient and regular than in other Andean countries. Several companies use comfortable air-conditioned buses on their longer routes; some companies have their own stations, away from the main bus terminals, exclusively for these better buses; these include **Flota Imbabura, Transportes Ecuador** and **Transportes Esmeraldas. Note** Throughout Ecuador, travel by bus is safest during the daytime. » *For the main intercity routes see the bus timetable, page 470.*

Car If driving your own vehicle, obtaining temporary admission can be complex and time-consuming. A *carnet de passages* is an official requirement, but this rule is not consistently applied. Ask the motoring organization in your home country about the availability of the *carnet*. You must be 21 and have an international credit card to hire a car in Ecuador. Surcharges may apply to clients between age 21 and 25. An authorization for a charge of as much as US$5000 may be requested against your credit card account. Rental rates are expensive, a small car costs about US$500 per week including all taxes and insurance. A sturdier 4WD (recommended for the Oriente and unpaved roads) can be more than twice as much.

There are two grades of gasoline, 'Extra' (82 octane, US$1.48 per US gallon) and 'Super' (92 Octane, US$1.98). Both are unleaded. Diesel fuel (US$1.03) is notoriously dirty and available everywhere.

Train Sadly, the spectacular Ecuadorean railway system has all but ceased operations. In 2007, only a few tourist rides were still being offered: over the Devil's Nose from Riobamba to Sibambe and back, and the lowland route Huigra to Bucay is operating at weekends and holidays. A weekend excursion runs from Tambillo, south of Quito to the El Boliche station near Parque Nacional Cotopaxi.

Maps

Peru The **Instituto Geográfico Nacional** in Lima sells a selection of maps, see page 78. Lima 2000's *Mapa Vial del Perú* (1:2,200,000) is the best road map. **South American Explorers** can provide maps and give advice on road conditions. The **Touring y Automóvil Club del Perú** ⓘ *Av César Vallejo 699, Lince, Lima, T221 2432, www.touringperu.com.pe*, sells a very good road map at US$5 (Mapa Vial del Perú, 1:3,000,000, Ed 1980) and route maps covering most of Peru. The *Guía Toyota* (Spanish), which is published annually, is one of the best guides for venturing off the beaten track. A good tourist map of the Callejón de Huaylas and Cordillera Huayhuash, by Felipe Díaz, is available in many shops in Huaraz, including Casa de Guías. **Alpenvereinskarte Cordillera Blanca Nord 0/3a** and **Alpenvereinskarte Cordillera Blanca Süd 0/3b** at 1:100,000 are the best maps of that region, US$12, available in Huaraz and Lima, but best bought outside Peru.

Bolivia Instituto Geográfico Militar (www.igmsantacruz.com). IGM map prices for detailed political maps start at US$5 original, US$4 photocopy. IGM maps were prepared some 20 years ago and do not show trails or passes for trekking. **Liam P O'Brien** has a 1:135,000, full colour, shaded relief topographic map of the Cordillera Real, US$12.95 per copy (very hard to find, 2007), also a 1:2,200,000 full colour travel map of Bolivia (US$12.95) highlighting the National Parks from map distributors (**Bradt,**

Stanfords, etc). **Walter Guzmán Córdova** colour maps, 1:150,000, of Choro-
Takesi-Yunga Cruz, Mururata-Illimani, Huayna Potosí Oruro-Potosí-Salar de Uyuni,
Illampu-Ancohuma, Titicaca-Tiwanaku-Yungas, Nigruni-Condoriri, Department of La
Paz, Department of Santa Cruz, Sajama and Mapa Físico-Político-Vial (1:2,250,000,
road map), available from bookshops in La Paz (see Shopping), US$6.70-7.50. The
German Alpine Club (Deutscher Alpenverein) produces two maps of Sorata-
Ancohuma-Illampu and Illimani, but are not available in La Paz.

Ecuador Instituto Geográfico Militar (IGM) ① *Senierges y Telmo Paz y Miño, T02-
254 5090, www.igm.gov.ec.* sells country maps and topographic maps, in various
scales, US$2. Maps of border areas and the seacoast are 'reservado' (classified) and
not available for sale without a military permit (requires extra time). Buy your maps
here, they are rarely available outside Quito. If one is sold out you may order a
photocopy. Map and geographic reference libraries are located next to the sales
room. The *IGM* is on top of the hill to the east of El Ejido park. From 12 de Octubre,
opposite the *Casa de la Cultura*, take Jiménez (a small street) up the hill. After crossing
Av Colombia continue uphill on Paz y Miño behind the Military Hospital and then turn
right to the guarded main entrance; you have to deposit your passport or
identification card. There is a beautiful view from the grounds. A good series of road
maps, pocket maps and city guides by Nélson Gómez, published by **Ediguías** in
Quito, are available in book shops throughout the country.

Sleeping

There is no regulated terminology for categories of accommodation in South America,
but you should be aware of the generally accepted meanings for the following. *Hotel*
is the generic term, much as it is in English. *Hospedaje* means accommodation, of any
kind. *Pensión* and *residencial* usually refer to more modest and economical
establishments. A *posada* (inn) or hostal may be an elegant expensive place, while
hosterías or *haciendas* usually offer upmarket rural lodgings. It is advisable to book in
advance during school holidays and local festivals, see pages 37 and 47.

Peru
Accommodation is plentiful throughout the price ranges and finding a hotel room to
suit your budget should not present any problems, especially in the main tourist
areas and larger towns and cities. The exception to this is during the Christmas and
Easter holiday periods, Carnival, Cuzco in June and Independence celebrations at the
end of July, when all hotels seem to be crowded. By law there are now four types of
accommodation, each will have a plaque outside defining its status: *Hotel* (H), *Hostal*
(HS), *Hostal Residencial* (HR) or *Pensión* (P). Foreigners do not pay the 19% IVA (sales
tax) but luxury and first-class hotels also add a 10% service charge which is not
included in our prices. **I-Peru**, www.peru.info, has a list of all accommodation
registered with them.

Student discounts are rare but for information on **youth hostels** consult **Intej**,
www.intej.org, or the **Asociación Peruana de Albergues Turísticos Juveniles**,
www.limahostell.com.pe. Information is also available from **Hostelling International
Peru**, www.hostellingperu.com.pe.

Camping is easy in Peru, especially along the coast. There can be problems with
robbery when camping near a small village; ask permission to camp in a backyard or
chacra (farmland).

Essentials Planning your trip *Sleeping*

⁞ Room service

→ Always take a look at the room before checking in. Hotel owners will often attempt to rent out the worst rooms first – feel free to ask for a better room or bargain politely for a reduced rate if you are not happy.

→ In cities, rooms away from the main street will be less noisy.

→ Air conditioning (a/c) is only required in the lowlands and jungle. If you want an a/c room it will add approximately 30% to the price.

→ The electric showers in cheaper places should be treated with respect. Always wear rubber sandals to avoid an unwelcome morning shock.

→ Taller travellers (over 180 cm) should check out the length of beds, especially in the highland areas.

→ A torch or candles are advisable in more remote areas, where electricity may only be supplied during certain hours; they are essential in jungle lodges.

→ Upmarket hotels will usually have their own restaurant, while more modest places may only serve a simple breakfast.

→ Some hotels charge per room and not per bed, so if travelling alone, it may be cheaper to share with others.

→ The cheapest and nastiest hotels are found near bus and train stations and markets. In small towns, better accommodation can often be found around the main plaza.

→ And finally, be sure that taxi drivers take you to the hotel you want rather than the one they think is best.

Bolivia

Away from the main cities, high-class **hotels** are few and far between. Getting off the beaten track usually means sacrificing creature comforts, but not necessarily standards of hygiene. Prices are low in Bolivia, but not uniformly so. The eastern part of the country tends to be a bit more expensive, especially the city of Santa Cruz, which is geared more towards commerce than tourism and therefore has few good budget places to stay. Smaller places that see plenty of tourists, such as Coroico, Rurrenabaque, Sorata or Copacabana, on the other hand, are full of good-value budget accommodation. Even in La Paz, it is quite easy to find a clean, comfortable hotel room, without a private bathroom, for around US$4-5 per person. For those on a tight budget, a cheaper room can be found in a *hospedaje*, *pensión*, *casa familial* or *residencial*; they are normally to be found in abundance near bus and railway stations and markets. There are seasonal variations in hotel prices in resorts, and prices can rise substantially during public holidays and festivals. Hotels must display prices by law (prices listed in this book include 20% tax and service charge). The number of stars awarded each hotel is regulated by law as well and is a fairly accurate assessment of an establishment's relative status. Some hotels run a curfew that is strictly adhered to, in La Paz this is often at 2400 but can be 2130 in Copacabana so check.

Youth hostels are not necessarily cheaper than hotels: many middle range *residenciales* are affiliated to the HI. For information contact **Hostelling International Bolivia**, www.hostellingbolivia.org. At affiliated establishments, members usually receive a 10% discount. They also sell the HI card, US$40 and the ISIC card, US$20. Another website listing hostels is http://boliviahostels.com, but they are not necessarily affiliated.

Camping is safe almost anywhere except near settlements (unless unavoidable). Warm sleeping gear essential, even in the lowlands in the winter. Sleeping bags are also useful for keeping warm on buses in the Andes.

Hotel price codes

Prices given are based on two people sharing a double room with bathroom (shower and toilet), unless otherwise stated. If travelling alone, it's usually cheaper to share with others in a room with three or four beds. Prices are for high season (May-September, Christmas-February, Holy Week). During low season it may be possible to bargain the room rate down. **LL** (over US$200), **L** (US$151-200), **AL** (US$101-150) and **A** (US66-100). Hotels in these categories are usually only found in the capital cities and other main tourist centres. They should offer extensive leisure and business facilities, plus restaurants and bars. Most will provide a safe box in each room. Credit cards are usually accepted.

B (US$46-65) and **C** (US$31-45). The better-value hotels in this category should provide more than the standard facilities and a fair degree of comfort. Most will include breakfast and offer extras such as a TV, minibar and tea and coffee making facilities. They may also provide tourist information and their own transport. Service is generally good and most accept credit cards. At he top end of the range, some may have a swimming pool, sauna and jacuzzi.

D (US$21-30) and **E** (US$12-20) Hotels in these categories range from very comfortable to functional and there are some real bargains to be had. At these prices you should expect a reasonably sized, comfortable room with a/c (in tropical regions), your own bathroom, constant hot water, a towel, soap and toilet paper, TV and a restaurant. **F** (US$7-11) Usually in this range you can expect some degree of comfort and cleanliness, a private bathroom, possibly with hot water, and perhaps continental breakfast. Many of those catering for foreign tourists in the more popular regions offer excellent value for money and many have their own restaurant and offer services such as laundry, safe deposit box, money exchange and luggage store. **G** (US$6 and under) Rooms at the upper end of this category may have a private bathroom, though this tends to be the exception. Breakfast is rarely included. At the lower end of this price range rooms usually consist of little more than a bed and four walls, with barely enough room to swing a cat. If you're lucky you may have a window, a table and chair. Cheap places don't always supply soap, towels and toilet paper. In colder regions they may not supply enough blankets, so take a sleeping bag.

Ecuador

Ecuador has a good selection of **hotels**, with the most upscale options to be found in the larger cities and more popular resorts. Outside the provincial capitals, there are few higher-class hotels. but friendly and functional family-run lodgings can be found almost everywhere. At New Year, Easter and Carnival accommodation can sometimes be hard to find and prices are likely to rise. Many (even the cheaper places) now add a service of 10% and a tax of 12% to rates but check if this is included in the price quoted. Many hotel rooms have very low wattage bulbs, keen readers are advised to take a head torch. **Camping** is possible in protected natural areas; there are few organized campsites. It is not safe to pitch your tent at random near villages or on beaches.

⁞ How the other half lived

The great *haciendas* of Ecuador were founded shortly after the Spanish Conquest, either as Jesuit *obrajes* (slave workshops) or land grants to the conquistadors. When the Jesuits fell from favour and were expelled from South America, these huge land holdings passed to important families close to the Spanish royalty; notables such as the Marqués de Solanda and Marqués de Maenza, to name just two. They were enormous properties covering entire watersheds and most of the owners never even laid eyes on all their land. The earliest visitors to Ecuador, people like La Condamine and Humbolt, were guests at these haciendas.

The *hacienda* system lasted until agrarian reform in the 1960s. The much reduced land holdings which remained in the hands of wealthy families, frequently surrounding beautiful historic homes, were then gradually converted to receive paying guests. Cusín, by Lago San Pablo, La Ciénega, near Lasso, and Andaluza, outside Riobamba, were among the first to take in tourists. They have since become successful upscale *hosterías* and are listed under the corresponding geographic locations in the text. They are no longer working haciendas but are nonethe- less pleasant and comfortable places to stay. Prices are usually in our L range and up. See www.hacienda-ecuador.com, www.haciendaleito.com, www.zuleta.com, www.lacarriona.com, www.incahacienda.com.

Eating and drinking

Peru

Peru is the self-styled gastronomic capital of South America and some of the cuisine is very innovative. Along the **coast** the best dishes are seafood based with the most popular being *ceviche*: a white fish marinated in lemon juice, onion and hot peppers. The staples of corm and potatoes are prevalent in **highland** cooking and can be found in a large and varied range of dishes. There is also an array of meat dishes with *lomo saltado* (stir-fried beef) always found on the menu and *cuy* (guinea pig) featuring as a regional delicacy. **Tropical cuisine** revolves around fish and the common yucca and fried bananas.

Lunch is considered the main meal throughout Peru and most restaurants will serve one or two set lunches called the *menú ejecutivo* (US$2 or more for a three-course meal) or *menú económico* (US$1.50-2.50). A la carte meals normally cost US$5-8 but in the top class restaurants it can be up to US$80. There are many *chifas* (Chinese restaurants) all over the country which offer good reasonably priced food.

The traditional favourite beers such as **Cusqueña** and **Arequipeña** (both lager) have recently been taken over by the giant Bavaria brewery and many connoisseurs claim that they have lost much of their distinctive taste. **Trujillo Malta** is probably the best dark beer, a sweetish 'maltina' brown ale . The best wines are from Ica, Tacama and Ocucaje. **Gran Tinto Reserva Especial** and **Viña Santo Tomas** are reasonable and cheap. The most famous local drink is *pisco* which is a strong, clear brandy and forms the basis of the deliciously renowned *pisco sour*.

Bolivia

Standard international meals can be found at most good hotels and restaurants but local cuisine is normally extremely tasty and very hot. Among the most popular are, *sajta de pollo* (hot spicy chicken), *silpancho* (fried breaded meat) and *ají de lengua*

Restaurant price codes

The following price codes are used for restaurants and other eateries in this guide. Prices refer to the cost of a meal for one person, with a drink.

¶¶¶	over US$12
¶¶	US$7-12
¶	under US$6

(ox-tongue with chilli). Also worth trying are the *salteñas*: meat and vegetable soups or meat/chicken pasties, which are a national institution and eaten for elevenses. In the lowland regions, most meals come with yucca and cooked banana and it is common to find wild meats on the menu.

In any restaurant the *comida del día* is the best value meal and the cheaper restaurants normally offer a basic set lunch and dinner. Many restaurants do not open for breakfast but the markets in most towns provide good, cheap meals at this time of day. Avoid dishes cooked in the street. Llama meat contains parasites similar to those in pork, so make sure it has been cooked for a long time and is hot when you eat it. Be very careful of salads, which may carry a multitude of amoebic life and bacteria.

Local beers are predominantly lager based but good, **Paceña** and **Ducal** are the most popular and **El Inca** offers something a little different (it is like a stout). The best wine producing area is near Tarija at the La Concepción vineyard. The national spirit, *singani*, is distilled from grapes and is strong and cheap. It is usually drunk with Sprite and known as a *chuflay*. There are many brands of bottled water. Do not drink tap water unless it has been sterilized and never take ice in drinks, even in the most expensive restaurants.

Ecuador

As with much of South America, cuisine here changes with the region. In the **highlands** *locro de papas* (potato and cheese soup), *llapingachos* (fried potato and cheese patties), *cuy* (roast guinea pig) and *humitas* (tender ground corn steamed in corn leaves) are some of the most typical dishes. Seafood plays an important role on the **coast**, particularly in *empanadas de verde* (fried snacks) and *encocadas* (dishes prepared in coconut milk). Dishes in the **Oriente** usually consist of yucca and a range of river fish. Popular throughout the country is *ceviche* which is generally safe although *ceviche de pescado* (fish) and *ceviche de concha* (clams) can be hazardous as they are marinated raw. Most Ecuadorean food is not overly spicy but many restaurants accompany dishes with a small bowl of *ají* (hot pepper sauce). Upmarket restaurants add 22% to the bill, 12% tax plus 10% service. All other places add the 12% tax, which is also charged on non-essential items in food shops.

The main beers available are **Pilsener**, **Club** and **Biela** and in the major cities good Argentine and Chilean wines can be found. The most popular spirit is unmatured rum, called *aguardiente* (literally 'fire water'). With such an outstanding number of different fruits available, there are a number of excellent fruit drinks on offer. The best are *maracuyá* (passion fruit), *guanábana* (soursop) and *mora* (blackberry).

Shopping

Artesenía (handicrafts), like food, enjoy regional distinctiveness, especially in items such as textiles. Each region, village even, has its own characteristic pattern or style of cloth, so the choice is enormous. Throughout the Andes, weaving has spiritual

Essentials Planning your trip Shopping

Day of the Dead (All Soul's Day)

One of the most important dates in the calendar is 2 November, *Día de los Difuntos* or *Finados* (Day of the Dead). This tradition has been practised since time immemorial. In the Inca calendar, November was the eighth month and meant *Ayamarca*, or land of the dead. The celebration is an example of religious adaptation in which the ancient beliefs of ethnic cultures are mixed with the rites of the Catholic Church.

According to ancient belief, the spirit visits its relatives at this time of the year and is fed in order to continue its journey towards reincarnation. The relatives of the dead prepare for the arrival of the spirit days in advance. Among the many items necessary for these meticulous preparations are little bread dolls, each of which has a particular significance: horse-shaped breads provide transport for the soul in order to avoid fatigue.

Inside the home, the relatives construct a tomb supported by boxes over which a black cloth is laid. Here they put the bread, along with various other items important in the ritual. The tomb is also adorned with the dead relative's favourite food and drink. Most households also share a glass of *colada morada*, a syrupy, purple-coloured drink made from various fruits and purple corn. Once the spirit has arrived and feasted with its living relatives, the entire ceremony is then transported to the graveside in the local cemetery, where it is carried out again, along with the many other mourning families.

significance as well as a practical side. Reproductions of pre-Columbian designs can be found in pottery and jewellery and many people throughout the continent make delightful items in gold and silver. Musical instruments from Bolivia, Panama hats from Ecuador and all manner of ceramics are just some of the things you can bring home with you. Remember that handicrafts can almost invariably be bought more cheaply away from the capital, though the choice may be less wide. **Bargaining** is expected when you are shopping for handicrafts and souvenirs, but remember that most items are made by hand, and people are trying to make a living, not playing a game. You want a fair price, not the lowest one.

Peruvian crafts

Good items to buy are textiles, especially in Lima, Cuzco and Lake Titicaca. Equally common but well made are llama and alpaca wool products that include ponchos, rugs, hats, gloves, sweaters and coats. The *mate burilado* (engraved gourd) is one of the most genuine images of folk art in Peru. Interesting items are bags for coca leaves, belts and knitted conical hats, which can be found around Lake Titicaca. For gold and silver jewellery, Lima is the best place to look.

Bolivian crafts

All but the most hardened anti-shopping visitors to Bolivia should arrive with plenty of space in their rucksacks. Llama- and alpaca-wool knitted and woven items are at least as good as those from Peru and much cheaper. Among the many items you can buy are *mantas* (ponchos), bags, *chullos* (bonnets), gold and silverware and musical instruments such as the *charango* (a mandolin traditionally with armadillo-shell sound-box, now usually of wood) and the *quena* (Inca flute), and other assorted wooden items. Rurrenabaque, Asención de Guarayos and San Antonio de Lomerío are good places to buy well-made, colourful hammocks for around US$5.

★ Five of the best ancient ruins

Machu Picchu, see page 129.
Choquequirao, see page 137.
Huaca de la Luna, see page 235.
Kuélap, see page 266.
Tiahuanaco, see page 311.

Ecuadorean crafts

The huge markets at Otavalo and Saquisilí are the best places to head for to find wall-hangings, sweaters, blankets and shawls. Authentic Panama hats are made on the coast and around Cuenca, and are sold throughout the country at a fraction of the prices in Europe. Silver jewellery, ceramics and brightly painted carvings are all very well made and there is even the opportunity to promote the conservation of the rainforest through buying some of the beautiful items made from *tagua* nut, or vegetable ivory. Quito has plenty of *artesenías* that will package your goods to ensure that they return home in one piece.

Festivals and events

→ *For Public holidays, see page 47.*

One of the major considerations of deciding when to travel, apart from the weather, is the festival calendar. Fiestas are a fundamental part of life for most South Americans, taking place throughout the continent with such frequency that it would be hard to miss one, even during the briefest of stays. This is fortunate, because arriving in any town or village during these inevitably frenetic celebrations is one of the great travelling experiences.

Invariably, fiestas involve drinking – and lots of it. There's also non-stop dancing, which can sometimes verge on an organized brawl, and water throwing (or worse). This means that, at some point, you will almost certainly fall over, through inebriation or exhaustion, or both. After several days, you will awake with a hangover the size of the Amazon rainforest and probably have no recollection of what you did with your backpack.

Not all festivals end up as massive unruly parties, however. Some are solemn and elaborate holy processions, often incorporating Spanish colonial themes into predominantly ancient pagan rituals. Many of the major fiestas, such as Carnival (throughout February) and Semana Santa (March/April) take place during the wet season. Here is a brief list of the most important festivals in each country:

Peru

First two weeks of Feb La Virgen de la Candelaria, Puno and the shores of Lake Titicaca, masked dancers and bands compete in a famous festival in which local legends and characters are represented.
Mar/Apr Semana Santa, Arequipa and Ayacucho, both cities celebrate Holy Week with fine processions, but each has its unique elements: the burning of an effigy of Judas in Arequipa and beautiful floral

'paintings' in Ayacucho, where Easter celebrations are among the world's finest.
Jun Semana de Andinismo, Huaraz, international climbing and skiing week. In the same region, San Juan and San Pedro are celebrated in late Jun.
Jun There are several major festivals in and around Cuzco: Corpus Christi, on the Thu after Trinity; mid-Jun, Q'Olloriti, the ice festival at 4700 m on a glacier; 24th, Inti Raymi, the Inca festival of the winter solstice at Sacsayhuaman (this is

★ Five of the best festivals

Festival de la Primavera This celebration of the arrival of Spring is one of Peru's most important tourist events and features the famous *Caballos de Paso*, see page 242.

Phujllay One of Bolivia's wildest celebrations, with lots of dancing, colourful costumes, gallons of *chicha* (maize beer) and no sleep, see page 389.

Oruro Carnival Dancing, music, great costumes, lots of alcohol and hundreds of water bombs all add up to a lot of fun, see page 370.

Mama Negra A surrealistic scene in which a white man, painted black and dressed as a woman, rides a horse through the streets of Latacunga, see page 514.

Día de Quito A week of parades, bullfights, performances and music in the streets, and a great deal of drinking, with a day to sleep it all off, see page 463.

preceded by a beer festival and, one week later, the Ollanta-Raymi in Ollantaytambo). Also in mid-Jun is the **Wiracocha** dance festival at Raqchi.

Last week of Sep Festival de la Primavera, Trujillo, with beauty pageant, *caballos de paso* horse shows and events.

Bolivia

24 Jan to first week in Feb Alacitas Fair, La Paz, a celebration of Ekeko, the household god of good fortune and plenty.

2 Feb La Virgen de la Candelaria, Copacabana, processions, fireworks, dancing and bullfights on the shores of Lake Titicaca (also celebrated in many rural communities).

Feb/Mar La Diablada, Oruro, celebrations in the high Andes with tremendous masked dancers and displays. **Carnival** is also worth seeing in the lowland city of Santa Cruz de la Sierra.

Mid-Mar Phujllay, Tarabuco (Sucre), a joint celebration of carnival and the Battle of Jumbate (12 Mar 1816), with music and dancing. **Holy Week**, Jesuit Mission towns of the Chiquitania, colourful processions and now-rare native dances and sports last all week long.

May/Jun Festividad del Señor del Gran Poder, La Paz, thousands of dancers perform a in procession through the centre of the city.

Jun-Aug (movable) Masked and costumed dances are the highlight of the 4-day **Fiesta de la Virgen de Urkupiña** in Quillacolla, near Cochabamba.

Ecuador

Feb Fiesta de las Frutas y las Flores, Ambato, carnival with parades, festivities and bullfights; unlike other Andean carnivals, throwing of water and other mess is banned.

Jun Los San Juanes, the combined festivals of (21st) Inti Raymi; (24th) **San Juan Bautista**; and (29th) **San Pedro y San Pablo**, Otavalo and Imbabura province, mostly indigenous celebrations of the summer solstice and saints' days, music, dancing, bullfights, regattas on Laguna San Pablo.

Second week of Sep Yamor and Colla Raimi, Otavalo, lots of festivities and events to celebrate the equinox and the festival of the moon.

6 Dec Día de Quito, Quito, commemorating the founding of the city with parades, bullfights, shows and music. The city is busy right through Christmas up to the 31st, **Años Viejos**, the New Year celebrations which take place all over the country.

Christmas Cuenca, many parades, the highlight being the **Pase del Niño Viajero**, the finest Christmas parade in the country.

A to Z

Accident & emergency

Contact the relevant emergency service and your embassy (page 40). Make sure you obtain police/medical reports in order to file insurance claims.

Emergency services
Peru Police T01-475 2995, Ambulance (Lima) T01-225 4040, Fire T116. **Tourist police**, at Jr Moore 268, Magdalena at 28th block of Av Brasil, Lima, T01-460 1060. **Bolivia** T911, Police T110, Ambulance T118, Fire T119. **Tourist police**: Calle Hugo Estrada 1354, Plaza Tejada Sorzano, opposite the stadium, Miraflores, La Paz, T222 5016. **Ecuador** Police T911 in Quito and Cuenca, T101 elsewhere, Ambulance T131.

Children

Travel with children can bring you into closer contact with South American families and, generally, presents no special problems – in fact the path is often smoother for family groups. Officials tend to be more amenable where children are concerned and even thieves and pickpockets seem to have some traditional respect for families, and may leave you alone because of it.

People contemplating overland travel in South America with children should remember that a lot of time can be spent waiting for public transport. Even then, buses can often be delayed during the journey due to bad weather.

All civil airlines charge half fare for children under 12. Children's fares on **Lloyd Aéreo Boliviano** (see note page 28) are considerably more than half, and there is only a 7 kg baggage allowance. (LAB also checks children's ages on passports.) Note that a child travelling free on a long excursion is not always covered by the operator's travel insurance; it is advisable to pay a small premium to arrange cover.

Food can be a problem if the children are not adaptable. It is easier to take food such as biscuits, drinks and bread with you on longer trips.

In all **hotels**, try to negotiate family rates. If charges are per person, always insist that 2 children will occupy one bed only, therefore counting as one tariff. If rates are per bed, the same applies.

Customs & duty free

Peru
Those entering Peru are allowed 50 cigars or 400 cigarettes or 500g of tobacco as well as 3 litres of alcoholic drink. You are only allowed new items or gifts up to the value of US$300. On no account should any object of archaeological interest be removed and taken out of Peru.

Bolivia
The import allowance consists of 200 cigarettes, 50 cigars and 450g of tobacco. In addition one unopened bottle of alcohol.

Ecuador
Free of import duty are 300 cigarettes or 50 cigars or 250g of tobacco, one litre of spirits and a reasonable amount of perfume and gifts amounting to no more than US$200. If you are planning to bring unusual or valuable items (for example, professional video equipment), obtain special permits or be prepared to pay duty on those items. Reasonable amounts of climbing gear and a used laptop should not be a problem. Your luggage will always be sniffed by dogs when leaving and may also be inspected by security personnel. Do not attempt to take any archaeology, wild plants or animals or certain works of art out of Ecuador without a special permit.

Disabled travellers

In most of South America, facilities for the disabled are severely lacking. For those in wheelchairs, ramps and toilet access are limited to some of the more upmarket, or most recently built hotels. Visually or hearing-impaired travellers are similarly poorly catered for, but there are experienced guides in some places who can provide individual attention. Some travel companies outside South America specialize in holidays that are tailor-made for the individual's level of disability. **PromPerú** (see page 49) has initiated a programme to provide facilities at airports, tourist sites, etc and Quito's trolley buses are supposed to have wheelchair access, but they are often too crowded to make this practical. While disabled South Americans have to rely on others to get around, foreigners will find that people are generally very helpful. For general information, consult the **Global Access – Disabled Travel Network** website, www.globalaccessnews.com.

Useful organizations

Directions Unlimited, 123 Green Lane, Bedford Hills, NY 10507, T1-800-533-5343, T914-241 1700. A tour operator specializing in tours for disabled US travellers.
Disability Action Group, 2 Annadale Av, Belfast BT7 3JH, T01232-491011. Information about access for British disabled travellers.
Disabled Persons' Assemble, PO Box 27-524, Wellington 6035, New Zealand, T04-801-9100, gen@dpa.org.nz. Has lists of tour operators and travel agencies catering for the disabled.

Drugs

While illegal drugs are easily available, anyone caught in possession will automatically be assumed to be a drug trafficker. Drug use or purchase is punishable by up to 15 years' imprisonment in Peru (up to 16 years in Ecuador and Bolivia). If you are asked to have your bags searched, insist on having a witness present at all times; searching is only permitted if prior paperwork is done. Be aware of tricks to plant drugs on you at all times. Planting of drugs on travellers by both traffickers and police is not unknown in Bolivia but never answer offers by anyone selling drugs on the street as they may be a plain-clothes officer. In Ecuador, police drug-planting is rare, but those apprehended with drugs must run the gauntlet of a particularly corrupt and inefficient judicial system.

Electricity

Peru: 220 volts, 60 cycles (Arequipa 50 cycles). Most 4- and 5-star hotels have 110 volts AC. Plugs are either American flat-pin or twin flat and round pin combined.
Bolivia: Varies considerably. Generally 110 volts, 50 cycles AC in La Paz, but newer districts and buildings have 220 volts; 220 volts 50 cycles AC elsewhere, but check before using any appliance. Sockets usually accept both continental European (round) and US-type (flat) 2-pin plugs.
Ecuador: AC throughout, 110 volts 60 cycles. Sockets are for twin flat blades, sometimes with a round earth pin.

Embassies and consulates

Peruvian

Australia, 40 Brisbane Av Suite 8, Ground Floor, Barton ACT 2600, Canberra, PO Box 106 Red Hill, T61-2-6273 8752, www.emba peru.org.au. Consulate in Sydney.
Bolivia, F Guachalla 300, Sopocachi, La Paz, T02-2441250, embbol@caoba.entelnet.bo.
Canada, 130 Albert St, Suite 1901, Ottawa, Ontario K1P 5G4, T1-613-238 1777, emperuca@bellnet.ca. Consulates in Montréal, Toronto and Vancouver.
Ecuador, República de El Salvador 495 e Irlanda, edif Irlanda, T02-246 8410, embpeecu@uio.satnet.net.
New Zealand, Level 8, 40 Mercer St, Cigna House, Wellington, T64-4-499 8087, embassy.peru@xtra.co.nz.
UK, 52 Sloane St, London SW1X 9SP, T020-7235 1917, www.peruembassy-uk.com.
USA, 1700 Massachusetts Av NW, Washington DC 20036, T1-202-833 9860, www.peruemb.org. Consulates in Los Angeles, Miami, New York, Chicago, Houston, Boston, Denver, San Francisco.

Bolivian

Australia and New Zealand, 74 Pitt St, Level 6, Sydney, NSW 2000, T923-51858.
Canada, 130 Albert St, Suite 416, Ottowa, ON K1P 5G4, T613-236 5730, bolcan@ iosphere.net.
Peru, Los Castaños 235, San Isidro, Lima 27, T01-4228231, postmast@emboli.org.pe.

UK, 106 Eaton Sq, London SW1 9AD,
T0207-235 4248, http://bolivia.embassy
homepage.com.
USA, 3014 Massachusetts Av NW,
Washington DC 20008, T202-483 4410, or
211 East 43 Road St, Suite 702 New York, NY
10017, T212-499 7401, www.bolivia-usa.org.

Ecuadorean

Australia, 11 London Circuit, 1st floor,
Canberra ACT 2601, T6-6262 5282,
embecu@hotkey.net.au.
Canada, 50 O'Connor St No 316, Ottawa,
ON K1P 6L2, T613-563 8206,
mecuacan@rogers.com.
New Zealand (consulate), Peace Tower,
level 9, 2 St Martins Lane, Auckland, T09-377
4321, jmorlaconsulacuadorxtra.co.nz.
Peru, Las Palmeras 356, San Isidro (6th block
of Av Javier Prado Oeste), T01-440 9991,
embjecau@amauta.rcp.net.pe.
UK, Flat 3B, 3 Hans Cres, Knightsbridge,
London SW1x 0LS, T020-7584 1367,
embajada@ecuador.freeserve.co.uk.
USA, 2535 15th St NW, Washington, DC 20009,
T202-234 7200, embassy@ ecuador.org. Also
1101 Brickell Av, Suite M-102, Miami, Fl 33131,
T305-539 8214, consecumia@aol.com.

Gay and lesbian

Much of Latin America is still quite intolerant
of homosexuality. Rural areas tend to be more
conservative than cities. It is therefore wise
to respect this and avoid provoking a reaction.
For the gay or lesbian traveller, however, Lima
and Quito have active communities and there
are local and international organizations
which can provide information. Cuzco also
has a gay scene. Useful websites include:
Ecuador www.quitogay.net, in Spanish and
English; Peru http://lima.queercity.info/
index.html (in English, with lots of links and
information), www.deambiente.com/web
and www.gayperu.com (both in Spanish).

Health

See your GP or travel clinic at least 6 weeks
before departure for general advice on travel
risks and vaccinations. Try phoning a specialist
travel clinic if your own doctor is unfamiliar

with health in the region. Make sure you
have sufficient medical travel insurance, get
a dental check, know your own blood group
and if you suffer a long-term condition such
as diabetes or epilepsy, obtain a Medic Alert
bracelet/necklace (www.medicalalert.co.uk).

Vaccinations
The list of obligatory vaccinations is thin,
only Yellow Fever is a pre-requisite for
entering the region. Nonetheless, it is
advisable to vaccinate against Polio, Tetanus,
Typhoid, Hepatitis A and, if going to more
remote areas, Rabies. Malaria is a danger
throughout the lowland tropics and coastal
regions. Specialist advice should be taken on
the best anti-malarials to take before you
leave. Among the most common are
Chloroquine and Paludrine.

Health risks
The major risks posed in the region are those
caused by insect disease carriers such as
mosquitoes and sandflies. The key parasitic
and viral diseases are malaria, South
American tyrpanosomiasis (Chagas Disease)
and Dengue Fever. Be aware that you are
always at risk from these diseases, Dengue
Fever is particularly hard to protect against
as the mosquitoes can bite throughout the
day as well as night (unlike those that carry
malaria and Chagas disease); try to wear
clothes that cover arms and legs and also
use effective mosquito repellent. Mosquito
nets dipped in permethrin provide a good
physical and chemical barrier at night. Some
form of diarrhoea or intestinal upset is
almost inevitable, the standard advice is to
be careful with drinking water and ice; if you
have any doubts about the water then boil it
or filter and treat it. In a restaurant buy
bottled water or ask where the water has
come from. Food can also pose a problem,
be wary of salads if you don't know whether
they have been washed or not. There is a
constant threat of tuberculosis (TB) and
although the BCG vaccine is available, it is still
not guaranteed protection. It is best to avoid
unpasteurized dairy products and try not to
let people cough and splutter all over you.
One of the major problems for travellers in the
region is altitude sickness, it is essential to get

acclimatized to the thin air of the Andes before undertaking long treks or arduous activities. The altitude of the Andes means that strong protection from the sun is always needed, regardless of how cool it may feel.

Further information

www.btha.org British Travel Health Association.

www.cdc.gov US government site that gives excellent advice on travel health and details of disease outbreaks.

www.fco.gov.uk British Foreign and Commonwealth Office travel site has useful information on each country, people, climate and a list of UK embassies/consulates.

www.fitfortravel.scot.nhs.uk A-Z of vaccine/health advice for each country.

www.numberonehealth.co.uk Travel screening services, vaccine and travel health advice, email/SMS text vaccine reminders and screens returned travellers for tropical diseases.

Insurance

Always take out comprehensive insurance before you travel, including full medical cover, repatriation and extra cover for any activities (rafting, biking, riding etc) that you may undertake. Check exactly what's being offered, the maximum cover for each element and also the excess you will have to pay in the case of a claim. Keep details of your policy and the insurance company's telephone number with you at all times and get a police report for any lost or stolen items.

Internet

Internet cafés are becoming more and more common throughout the region, both in large and small towns. Rates and speed vary from place to place but you should generally expect to pay between US$0.50-2 in the major cities. Outside of these places connections are slower and prices higher.

Regional websites

www.andes.org Quechua language lessons, music, songs, poems, stories and resources.

www.latinworld.com/sur Links to individual Latin American countries.

www.lanic.utexas.edu The Latin American Network Information Centre: loads of information on everything.

www.southamericadaily.com Links to newspapers, plus environment, health, business and travel sites.

Language

Without some knowledge of Spanish you will become very frustrated and feel helpless in many situations. English, or any other language, is absolutely useless off the beaten track. Not all the locals speak Spanish; you will find that some *indígena* in the more remote highland parts of Bolivia and Peru, and lowland *indígena* in Amazonia, speak only their indigenous languages (Quichua in Ecuador, Quechua in Peru and Bolivia, also Aymara in southern Peru and Bolivia), though at least one person in each village usually speaks Spanish. Some initial study or a

Essentials A to Z

beginners Spanish course are strongly recommended, as is a pocket phrasebook and dictionary. Quito is a particularly good place to head for cheap language courses. **Amerispan**, 117 South 17th St, Suite 1401, Philadelphia, PA 19103, T1-800-879 6640 (USA & Canada), T215-751 1100 (Worldwide), www.amerispan.com. Programmes are offered in Sucre, Cuenca, Quito and Cuzco. In Ecuador, they also offer a discount card for use in hotels, restaurants and shops. **LanguagesAbroad.com** 317 Adelaide St West, Suite 900, Toronto, Ontario, Canada, M5V 1P9, T416-925 2112, toll free T1-800-219 9924, www.languagesabroad.com, offers Spanish and Portuguese programmes in all three countries. They also have language immersion courses throughout the world. **Spanish Abroad**, 5112N, 40th St, Suite 103, Phoenix, AZ 85018, USA, T602-778 6791 (Worldwide), www.spanishabroad.com, year round classes catering for small groups and individuals. Can arrange accommodation.

Media

Latin America has more local and community radio stations than virtually anywhere else in the world. A shortwave radio will allow you to absorb local culture, as well as pick up **BBC World Service** (www.bbc.co.uk/worldservice) or the **Voice of America** (www.voa.gov).

Peru
There are several main morning papers in Lima: *El Comercio* has good international news; *La República* has liberal-left views; and *Gestión* is the major business daily. Most provincial towns will have at least one widely read newspaper. *Rumbos* is a good bi-monthly magazine in Spanish and English that focuses on tourism and culture. For online news coverage, the following websites are the most useful: www.yachay.com.pe, www.peru.com.

Bolivia
The main cities and towns all have their own daily, in La Paz *Presencia* and *El Diario* are the most popular while in Santa Cruz it is *El Día* and *El Deber*. Sucre has a number of papers that are good for foreign coverage, among these are *El Correo*, *El Mundo* and *La Razón*. *The Bolivian Times* is an English language

weekly and is available in the big cities. Of particular use to travellers is the *Llama Express* which is a free monthly paper in English that covers many travel and cultural features as well as local news reports, it is available across the country. It is only possible to find some foreign national papers in La Paz.

Ecuador
The main newspapers in Quito are *El Comercio* and *Hoy* and in Cuenca *El Mercurio*. There are also many local and regional publications throughout the the country. Foreign papers can only be found in the luxury hotels and some speciality bookshops in Quito.

Money

Withdrawing cash from ATMs with a credit or debit card is by far the easiest way of obtaining money, but always have a back-up plan. ATMs are common, but cannot always be relied on and have been known to confiscate valid cards. The affiliations of banks to the Plus and Cirrus systems change often, so ask around. Always bring some US dollar bills, traveller's cheques, or both. A good strategy is to gradually convert your traveller's cheques to cash in the larger cities. US dollar notes are often worn and tatty in Ecuador, but will only be accepted in Peru and Bolivia if they are in good condition. Low-value US dollar bills are very useful for shopping: shopkeepers and *casas de cambio* give better exchange rates than hotels or banks. Banks and the better hotels will normally change traveller's cheques for their guests (often at a poor rate) although some may ask to see a record of purchase before accepting. Take plenty of local currency, in small denominations, when making trips off the beaten track. Frequently, the rates of exchange on ATM withdrawals are the best available but check if your bank or credit card company imposes handling charges. Credit card transactions are normally at an officially recognized rate of exchange but are often subject to a sales tax. **For lost or stolen cards** in Peru call Visa T108 and ask the operator for a collect call (por cobrar) to T410-902 8022 (English) or T581-0120/9754 or T420-937 8091; MasterCard T01-311 6000/T0800-307 7309; American Express T01-690 0900. Whenever possible, change money at a bank or *casa de cambio* rather than from money changers on the street. Change any local currency before you leave the country or at the border.

Cost of travelling

A realistic budget for the region is roughly US$35-50 per person per day, based on 2 people travelling together, sleeping in comfortable, mid-range accommodation and eating reasonably well. Those spending more time in large cities and main tourist centres and taking frequent flights between destinations could easily spend more than this, up to as much as US$100 a day. Of course, you could quite easily get by on less (US$25-30) without enduring any hardship, especially in Ecuador and Bolivia. In all 3 countries budget travellers can find a basic but clean hotel room for as little as US$5-10 per person, and a simple meal for only US$1.50-2, and travelling by bus is relatively cheap. For sleeping and eating categories, see page 33 and page 35.

Peru

The monetary unit is the sol (s/), in Oct 2007 the conversion rate was **US$1 = s/3.15**, although Euros can also be used Some prices are quoted in dollars in more expensive establishments, to avoid changes in the value of the sol. Visa, Maestro, MasterCard, American Express and Diners Club are all valid and widely accepted. There is often an 8-12% commission for all credit card charges. Most of the main banks accept American Express and Visa traveller's cheques but it can be very difficult in cashing them in the jungle and other remote areas. Banks are the most discreet places to change traveller's cheques into soles. Some charge commission from 1-3%, some don't. ATMs are widespread and usually give dollars if you don't request soles. There are no restrictions on foreign exchange, banks always give a lower exchange rate than *cambistas* or *casas de cambio*. For changing into or out of small amounts of dollars cash, the street changers give the best rates, avoiding paperwork and queuing, but they also employ many ruses to give you a bad deal. **Note** A large number of forged US dollar notes (especially US$20 and larger bills) are in circulation. There are also many forged soles coins and notes. Posters in public places explain what to look for.

Bolivia

The monetary unit is the boliviano (Bs), in Oct 2007 the conversion rate was **US$1 = Bs 7.74**. Bolivianos are often referred to as pesos; expensive items, including hotel rooms, are often quoted in dollars. When changing money, try to get notes in small denominations. Bs 100 notes are very difficult to change in La Paz and impossible elsewhere. Small change is still occasionally often given in forms other than money: eg, cigarettes, sweets, or razor blades. It is difficult to buy dollars at points of exit when leaving or to change bolivianos in other countries. It can be impossible to change traveller's cheques outside the major cities. Changing dollars cash presents no problems anywhere but it is not worth trying to change other currencies. All the larger *casas de cambio* will give dollars cash in exchange for traveller's cheques, usually with a commission. Credit/ debit cards are commonly used to obtain cash. American Express is not as useful as Visa or MasterCard. ATMs displaying the **Enlace** sign are the best, accepting both Visa, Visa Electron and MasterCard (and therefore pretty much every foreign card). You can usually take out US dollars or bolivianos. For credit card purchases an extra charge, up to 10%, may be made.

Ecuador

The US dollar is the only official currency of Ecuador. Only US dollar bills circulate, in the following denominations: US$1, US$2 (rare), US$5, US$10, US$20, US$50 and US$100. US coins are used alongside the equivalent size and value Ecuadorean coins for 1, 5, 10, 25 and 50 cents and US$1 (US-minted bronze dollar). It is best to bring US dollars cash, in small denominations, as this is universally accepted. All other currencies are hard to exchange and fetch a very poor rate. The most commonly accepted credit cards are Visa, MasterCard, Diners and, to a lesser extent, American Express. Some banks allow a cash advance but a surcharge (at least 10%) may be applied in some hotels and restaurants. Places with credit card stickers do not necessarily take them. Traveller's cheques (American Express is most widely accepted) are safe, but can only be exchanged for cash in the larger cities and up to 5% commission may be charged.

Opening hours

Peru

Banks are generally open 0930-1200 and 1500-1800 but those in Lima and Cuzco operate 0900/0945 to 1700/1800, Sat 0930-1200. Businesses are most open to the same hours while shops open 0900 or 1000-1230 and 1500 or 1600-2000. Supermarkets don't usually close for lunch and some in Lima are 24 hours. Government offices generally open Mon-Fri 0900-1230 and 1500-1700, but in Jan-Mar Mon-Fri 0830-1130, but hours vary.

Bolivia

Business hours are 0900-1200 (sometimes 1230 in La Paz and Santa Cruz) and 1400-1800 (sometimes 1900 in La Paz and Santa Cruz) with a half day on Sat. Many offices in La Paz and Santa Cruz are now open during siesta. Afternoon opening and closing hours in the provinces are often several hours later than in towns and cities. Banks open Mon-Fri 0900- 1600 (BCP 0800-1800), some also open Sat 0900-1200 or 1300.

Ecuador

Banks are open Mon-Fri 0900-1600. Government offices Mon-Fri variable hours but most close for lunch. Other offices 0900-1230, 1430-1800. Shops 0900-1900, close at 1200 in smaller towns, open until 2100 on the coast.

Police and the law

You may well be asked for identification at any time, and if you cannot produce it you will be jailed. In the event of a vehicle accident in which anyone is injured, all drivers involved are automatically detained until blame has been established, and this does not usually take less than 2 weeks. Never offer a bribe unless you are fully conversant with the customs of the country. Do not assume that an official who accepts a bribe is prepared to do anything else that is illegal. If an official suggests that a bribe must be paid before you can proceed on your way, be patient (assuming you have the time) and they may relent.

Post

All mail should be registered and it is worth checking whether your embassy will hold mail in preference to the poste restante service (*lista de correos*), although this is available at most major post offices. If mail is sent here, check under both your surname and your first name when collecting and be prepared to show your passport. In general, postal services are very slow and unreliable.

Peru

The postal service is named **Serpost** and sending mail and parcels is possible from any post office although the office the Plaza de Armas in Lima is best. Sending packages out of Peru is incredibly expensive and is not really worth it but letters are much more reasonable; rates are US$1 to anywhere in the Americas, US$1.50 to Europe and US$1.70 to Australia. It is possible to pay an extra US$0.55 (for the Americas) or US$0.90 (for the rest of the world) for an '*expresso*' service.

Bolivia

Airmail letters to and from Europe should take 5-10 days. Letter/postcard up to 20 g to Europe US$0.90, to North America US$0.75, rest of the world US$1; letter over 30 g to Europe US$2.20, to North America US$1.50, rest of the world US$2.30. Packages up to 2 kg can be posted from the ground floor of the main post office in La Paz between 1200-1430; to Europe a 2 kg parcel costs US$30, to North America US$20.30, to the rest of the world US$42. Surface mail parcels up to 2 kg cost US$16 to North America, US$19 to Europe and US$21 to the rest of the world.

Ecuador

Airmail up to 20 g are US$0.90 to the Americas, US$1.05 to the rest of the world. Registered mail costs an additional US$0.95 per item. In principle, parcels up to 30 kg, of maximum dimensions 70 x 30 x 30 cm, may be mailed from any post office. In practice, the branches listed above are best. A 2 kg parcel sent by air mail costs: to the Americas US$22.50, to Europe US$28.10, to the rest of the world US$34.80. There is no surface (sea)

⁝ Travel safe

→ Keep valuables out of sight.
→ Keep documents/money secure.
→ Split up your main cash supply and hide it in different places.
→ Lock your luggage together at bus or train stations.
→ At night, take a taxi between transport terminals and your hotel. Use the hotel safe deposit box and keep an inventory of what you have deposited.

→ Look out for tricks to distract your attention and steal your belongings.
→ Notify the police of any losses and make sure you get a written report for insurance claims.
→ Avoid hiking alone in remote areas.
→ Avoid travelling at night.
→ Avoid all political demonstrations.
→ Don't fight back – it is better to hand over your valuables rather than risk injury.

Essentials A to Z

mail from Ecuador, but a lower priority service is available for 10% less than air parcel post.

Public holidays

Aside from the national holidays listed below, local holidays are also taken during the main festivals (see page 37). Most businesses such as banks, airline offices and tourist agencies close for the official holidays while supermarkets and street markets may be open. This depends a lot on where you are so try to find out before you leave home. Sometimes holidays that fall during mid-week will be moved to the following Monday to make a long weekend, or some places will take a *dia del puente* (bridging day) taking the Fri or Mon as a holiday before or after an official holiday on a Thu or Tue.

Peru
1 Jan New Year's Day; **6 Jan** Bajada de Reyes; **Carnival Week** (Mon, Shrove Tue, Ash Wed); **Easter** (Maundy Thu, Good Fri and Sat); **1 May** Labour Day; **Corpus Christi** (moveable); **28-29 Jul** Independence (Fiestas Patrias); **8 Oct** Battle of Angamos; **2 Nov** All Souls' Day; **24-25 Dec** Christmas.

Bolivia
1 Jan New Year's Day; **Carnival** (Mon-Wed before Lent); **Easter** (Maundy Thu, Good Fri, Sat); **1 May** Labour Day; **Corpus Christi** (moveable); **16 Jul** La Paz Municipal

Holiday; **5-7 Aug** Independence; **2 Nov** All Souls' Day; **25 Dec** Christmas Day.

Ecuador
1 Jan New Year's Day; Carnival, Mon and Tue before Lent; **Easter** Holy Thu and Good Fri; **1 May** Labour Day; **24 May** Battle of Pichincha (Independence Day); **10 Aug** 1st attempt at independence; **9 Oct** Independence of Guayaquil; **2-3 Nov** Day of the Dead and Independence of Cuenca; **25 Dec** Christmas Day.

Safety

The region is generally safe but you should always take sensible precautions to protect yourself and your baggage. Be especially careful in Lima, La Paz and Quito, particularly on public transport, in and around markets and when handling money in public places. While the police presence in the major cities in **Peru** has been improved, there have been alarming increases in violent muggings along the Gringo Trail. Check with South American Explorers (see page 49) for updates and advice. **Bolivia** remains safe and hospitable with strikes and demonstrations being the major problem. However, Police advise tourists not to stray from the main road in the main coca- growing country around Villa Tunari. In **Ecuador**, the countryside and small towns are generally safe and tranquil but caution is required in Quito, Guayaquil and Cuenca. Intercity bus hold-ups are a hazard and it is safest to travel by daylight. The northern border provinces of Esmeraldas,

Carchi and especially Sucumbíos (including Parque Nacional Cuyabeno) call for special precautions; enquire locally before visiting areas on the Colombian frontier. See also Drugs, page 40 and Police and the law, page 46.

It is better to seek advice on security before you leave from your own consulate than from travel agencies. Also contact the **British Foreign and Commonwealth Office**, Travel Advice Unit, T0870-606 0290, www.fco. gov.uk/travel. Footprint is a partner in the 'Know before you go campaign'. The US State Department's **Bureau of Consular Affairs**, Overseas Citizens Services, T202-647 4000 (travellers' hotline T647 5225), www.travel. state.gov/travel_ warnings.html. **Australian Department of Foreign Affairs**, T+61-2-6261 3305, www.dfat.gov.au/ consular/advice/advices_mnu.html

Student travellers

If you are in full-time education you will be entitled to an **International Student Identity Card (ISIC)**, which is distributed by student travel offices and agencies in 70 countries. The ISIC gives you special prices on transport and access to a variety of other concessions and services, including an emergency helpline T020-8762 8110. Discounts are often extended to teachers, who are entitled to an **International Teacher Identity Card (ITIC)**. Both are available from www.isic.org.

Tax

VAT is known as IVA. Ask for an official receipt if you want it documented.
Peru: 19%; **Bolivia**: 13%; **Ecuador**: 12%.

Telephone

Peru
Country code +51
IDD prefix 00
All Peruvian phone numbers are made up of 6 digits except Lima which has 7, plus the area code. All area codes are given with each number in the text. If calling Peru from abroad, dial the international access code (00 from the UK), followed by the Peru country code (51) and then dial in the area code and number. Local, national and international calls can be made from public phone boxes with coins and the more common pre-paid phone cards. The most popular phone cards are issued by the main service provider, **Telefónica**, www.telefonica.com.pe, which has offices in all large and medium-sized towns. For collect calls (reverse charge), dial 108 to reach the international operator. You can also receive calls at many **Telefónica** offices at about US$1 for 10 mins. Growing in popularity are **net-phones**, especially in Lima. Rates may be cheaper than normal phones, particularly if calling the US.

There are 3 **mobile** networks: Telefónica Movistar, TIM and Bellsouth. It's best to buy a phone locally. Special offers with prepaid cards start from US$45. All mobile numbers are prefixed by 9.

Bolivia
Country code +591
IDD prefix 0010 (Entel), 1100 (AES Communications Bolivia), 0012 (Teledata), 0013 (Bolivaitel).
Bolivian phone numbers consist of 7 digits and all area codes are made up of 2 digits. To make a regional call, dial 0 before the regional code and the number. If dialling from a private phone, an access number of the service provider must be dialled between the 0 and area code; the providers are Entel (10), AES (11), Telecel (17) and Boliviatel (13). Coins and tokens have been phased out of use in public phones, pre-paid phone cards are currently the best option for local and long distance calls. Collect calls can be made by accessing the provider in the receiving country and asking for a collect call there. Such providers in the US are AT&T, T0800-1111; MCI, T0800 2222; Sprint, T0800 3333; and IDB (TRT), T0800 4444. In the UK, BT, T0800-0044.

Ecuador
Country code +593
IDD prefix 00
All phone numbers are 7 digits, including cell phones (should be preceded by area code 08 or 09). The country is divided between 3 regional state companies, **Andinatel** in the northern highlands and northern Oriente; **Pacifictel** on the coast, the southern highlands and southern Oriente; and **Etapa** in Cuenca. Many towns now have public cell phones provided by **Movistar**,

Porta and Alegro, while these services can be convenient (they are used where there are no other phones), they are expensive. The most convenient places to make local, national or international calls are the many centros de llamada (calling centres) located throughout cities and towns. Examples of current rates are US$0.25 per min to the USA, US$37 per min to Canada, US$0.65 to the UK and US$0.90 to Australia. International voice-over-IP calls can be made from many cyber-cafés for about half these rates or less.

Time

Bolivia is 4 hrs behind GMT while Peru and Ecuador are both 5 hrs behind. The Galápagos are 6 hrs behind GMT.

Tipping

Mid-range to expensive restaurants in Peru add up to 17% service charge to the bill while those in Ecuador will include up to 10%. You should give up to 10% service for good restaurants, cheaper establishments do not expect anything, although it is welcome. Taxi drivers in Peru or Ecuador do not expect a tip (bargain the price down then pay extra if the service is good); but give about US$0.50-1 to porters and cloakroom attendants. Car 'watch' boys expect US$0.20. In Bolivia, anyone that provides a service should be given Bs0.50-1 on top of the fee and up to 10% in restaurants, although Bolivians rarely leave more than a few coins.

Tourist information

Contact details for tourist offices and other information resources are given in 'Ins and outs' throughout the text. The internet is an invaluable source of information, with countless websites dedicated to each country. For tourist information on the region from outside, visit the respective embassies and consulates of each country (page 40). See also Ron Mader's website www.planeta.com, which contains masses of useful information on ecotourism, conservation, travel, news, links, language schools and articles.
South American Explorers (**SAE**), www.sa explorers.org, is a non-profit educational organization staffed by volunteers, widely recognized as the best place to go for information on South America. Highly recommended as a source for specialized information, with member-written trip reports, maps, lectures, library resources. SAE publishes a 64-page quarterly journal, helps members plan trips and expeditions, stores gear, holds post, hosts book exchanges, provides expert travel advice, etc. Annual membership fee is US$50 individual (US$80 couple) plus US$10 for overseas postage of its quarterly journal, The South American Explorer. The SAE membership card is good for many discounts throughout Ecuador and Peru. The clubhouses, in **Quito**, Jorge Washington 311 y Leonidas Plaza, T02-222 5228, quitoclub@ saeexplorers.org; **Lima**, Piura 135, Miraflores, T01-445 3306, limaclub@saeexplorers.org; and **Cuzco**, Choquechaca 188, T084-245484, cuscoclub@saeexplorers.org, are helpful and friendly. SAE will sell used equipment on consignment (donations of used equipment, unused medicines, etc are welcome). The SAE headquarters is located in the **USA**, 126 Indian Creek Rd, Ithaca, NY, 14850, T607 277 0488, ithacaclub@saexplorers.org. If signing up from the UK allow 4-6 weeks for receipt of membership card.

Peru

Idecopi, T01-224 7777 (Lima), T0800-44040 (rest of Peru), www.indecopi.gob.pe, is the government-run consumer protection and tourist complaint bureau; friendly and helpful. **PromPerú**, Edificio Mincetur, 13th floor, Calle Uno Oeste 50, Córpac, San Isidro, Lima, T01-224 3131, www.peru.info, handles tourism promotion and information. It runs a 24-hr information and assistance service, **i perú**, Jorge Basadre 610, San Isidro, Lima, T01-421 1627, iperulima@promperu.gob.pe, Mon-Fri 0830-1830 (24-hr service T01-574 8000). There is also a 24-hr office at Jorge Chávez airport as well as offices in the major cities across the country.

Bolivia

Viceministerio de Turismo, Av Mariscal Santa Cruz (El Prado) y Loayza, Edif Cámara de Comercio, 11th floor, T02-237 5129, www.turismobolivia.bo, Mon-Fri 0830-1630, handles tourism. They have information centres, **InfoTur**, at international arrivals in El Alto airport (T02-285 2543) and Viru

Viru (Santa Cruz, T03-336 9595), 0600-2200, English spoken.

For information on national parks contact: **Servicio Nacional de Área Protegidas (SERNAP)**, Loayza 178, Edif La Papelera, La Paz, T02-231 7742, www.sernap.gov.bo; and **Fundación para el Desarrollo del Sistema Nacional de Áreas Protegidas (FUNDESNAP)**, Prolongación Cordero 127, La Paz, T02-211 3364, www.fundesnap.org.

Ecuador

Ministerio de Turismo, Eloy Alfaro N32-300 y Carlos Tobar, Quito, T02-250 7559, www.vive cuador.com, local offices are listed in the text. Outside Ecuador, some tourist information can be obtained from Ecuadorean embassies.

National parks, of which Ecuador has an outstanding array, are controlled by the **Ministerio del Ambiente**, Ministerio de Agricultura y Ganadería building, 8th floor, Amazonas y Eloy Alfaro, Quito, T02-250 6337, www.ambiente.gov.ec. The ministry has less information than the park offices in the cities nearest the parks themselves.

Tour operators

In the UK

4starSouth America, T0871-711 5370 (UK), T1-800-747 4540 (USA), www.4starsouth america.com (tours), www.4starflights.com.

Amazing Peru, 9 Alma Rd, Manchester, M19 2FG, T0808-234 6805 (toll free), www.amazingperu.com. Peru, Bolivia and Ecuador tour specialists with local offices and hundreds of itineraries including small-group adventure and cultural tours.

Condor Journeys & Adventures, 2 Ferry Bank, Colintraive, Argyll PA22 3AR, T01700- 841318, www.condor journeys-adventures.com

Dragoman, Camp Green, Debenham, Suffolk IP14 6LA T0870-499 4475, www.dragoman.co.uk

Exodus Travels, Grange Mills, 9 Weir Rd, London SW12 ONE, T020-8675 5550, www.exodus.co.uk

Explore, 1 Frederick St, Aldershot, Hants GU11 1LQ, T01252 760100, www.explore.co.uk

Galapagos Classic Cruises, 6 Keyes Rd, London NW2 3XA, T020-8933 0613, www.galapagoscruises.co.uk. An experienced company with excellent service providing specialist and adventure tours for individuals and groups to meet personal requirements.

High & Wild Adventures, Compass House, Gate Lane, Wells, T01749-671777, www.highandwild.co.uk. Organizes a wide range of individual and group tours.

Intrepid Travel, T01373-826611, www.intrepidtravel.com; travel store at 76 Upper St, London, N1 0NU.

Journey Latin America, 12-13 Heathfield Terrace, London W4 4JE, T020-8747 8315, and 12 St Ann's Sq (2nd fl), Manchester M2 7HW, T0161-832 1441, www.journeylatinamerica.co.uk.

Latin American Travel Association, 46 Melbourne Rd, London SW19 3BA, UK, T020-8715 2913, www.lata.org.

Essentials A to Z

Oasis Overland, The Marsh, Henstridge, Somerset, BA8 0TF, T01963-363400, www.oasisoverland.com. Small-group trips in Peru and overland trips across South America.

Peruvian Secrets, Unit 4, Brynsiencyn Business Units, Brynsiencyn, Anglesey, LL61 6HZ, T01248-430621, www.peruvian secrets.co.uk. Tailor made tours to the Galapagos and Peru. Specializes in trips to Northern Peru.

Reef and Rainforest Tours, Dart Marine Park, Steamer Quay, Totness, Devon, TQ9 5AL, T01803-866965, www.reefandrainforest.co.uk.

Select Latin America (incorporating Galapagos Adventure Tours), 79 Maltings Pl, 169 Tower Bridge Rd, London SE1 3LJ, T020-7407 1478, www.selectlatinamerica.com. Quality tailor-made holidays and small group tours.

Travelbag, 3-5 High St, Alton, Hants GU13 1TL, T0870-814 4440, www.travelbag.co.uk.

Trips Worldwide, 9 Byron Pl, Clifton, Bristol BS8 1JT, T0117-311 4400, www.tripsworldwide.co.uk.

In North America

GAP Adventures, 355 Eglinton Av East, Toronto, Ontario M4P 1M5, T1-800-465 5600, www.gapadventures.com.

Lost World Adventures, 337 Shadowmoor Drive, Decatur, GA 30030, USA, T1-800-999 0558, www.lostworld.com.

Quasar Nautica, 7855 N.W. 12th St, Suite 221, Miami, Florida 33126, www.quasar expeditions.com. Tours to sights throughout Ecuador and Peru, including the Galápagos and Machu Picchu.

Tambo Tours, 4405 Spring Cypress Rd, Suite #210, Spring TX, 77388, USA, T1-888-2-GO-PERU (246-7378), T001-281 528 9448, www.2GOPERU.com. Long-established adventure and tour specialist with offices in Peru and the USA. Customized trips to the Amazon and archaeological sites of Peru and Ecuador.

Tropical Nature Travel, PO Box 5276, Gainsville, Fl 326270 5276, USA, T1-877-827-8350/919-380-0966, www.tropical naturetravel.com. Eco tour company with itineraries to Ecuador, Peru and Bolivia.

Visas and immigration

Peru

No visa is necessary for citizens of countries in the EU, Asia, North and South America, and the Caribbean, or for citizens of Andorra, Iceland, Liechtenstein, Norway, Switzerland, Australia, New Zealand and South Africa. A Tourist Card is free on flights arriving in Peru, or at border crossings for visits up to 90 days. Insist on getting the full 90 days. It is in duplicate, the original given up on arrival and the copy on departure. A new tourist card must be obtained for each re-entry or when an extension is given. If your tourist card is stolen or lost, get a new one at **Inmigraciones**, Av España 700 y Av Huaraz, Breña, Lima, Mon-Fri 0900-1330. You can also get extensions here (expect to pay about US$30) as well as in Cuzco, Puno, Puerto Maldonado, and Iquitos, but in the provinces it can take more time. For citizens of countries not listed above, tourist visas cost about US$38, for which you require a valid passport, a departure ticket from Peru (or a letter of guarantee from a travel agency), 2 colour passport photos, one application form and proof of funds.

All foreigners should be able to produce on demand some recognizable means of identification, preferably a passport. You must present your passport when reserving tickets for internal, as well as, international travel. Travellers arriving by air are not asked for an onward flight ticket at Lima airport. If you let your tourist visa expire you can be subject to a fine of US$20 per day.

For a full list of Peruvian embassies and consulates visit www.rree.gob.pe.

Bolivia

A passport only, valid for one year beyond date of visit, is needed for citizens of almost all Western European countries (except

Ireland, Liechtenstein and Malta), Israel, Poland, Czech Republic, Japan, South Africa, Canada, South American countries (except Venezuela), Australia and New Zealand. Many are granted 90 days on entry, others are entitled to only 30. Nationals of all other countries require a visa, including USA (as of Dec 2007, US$134 for a 30-day visa; can be extended up to 90 days). Some nationalities must gain authorization from the Bolivian Ministry of Foreign Affairs, which can take 6 weeks. Other countries which require a visa do not need authorization (visas in this case take 1-2 working days).

Note In 2007 the Bolivian authorities were reviewing **all** visa requirements. Do not leave home without checking with a Bolivian consulate, or your home country's embassy in Bolivia (checking online will not give the latest situation). According to **SAE**, tourists must now produce proof of economic solvency when entering the country and provide a list of hotel reservations for the entire planned visit. Alternatively, they must be able to show a notarized invitation from a Bolivian citizen as well as a small passport photo taken against a red background.

Visa extensions and costs vary depending on your nationality. Extensions are granted in immigration offices in La Paz, Cochabamba and Santa Cruz. There should be a statutory 72-hr period outside Bolivia before renewing a visa but 24 hrs is usually acceptable. On arrival ensure that visas and passports are stamped with the same, correct date of entry or this can lead to 'fines' later. If you outstay your visa the current fine is US$1.25 per day.

For a full list of Bolivian embassies and consulates, see www.rree.gov.bo/inimin.htm.

Ecuador

All visitors to Ecuador must have a passport valid for at least 6 months and an onward or return ticket, although this is rarely asked for.

Also required but rarely asked for is an international vaccination certificate. Citizens of the following countries do not require a visa to visit Ecuador as tourists: EU countries, North and South American countries (except Guyana, Suriname and Mexico), Australia, Israel, South Africa and Switzerland. New Zealanders apparently do need a visa, even though the Ministry of Foreign Relations website says they do not; check with an Ecuadorean consulate before arrival. Members of the Sikh faith, irrespective of nationality, may need a visa.

Tourists are entitled to visit Ecuador for up to 90 days during any 12 month period. This may be extended, at the discretion of the Policía Nacional de Migración, www.migracion.gov.ec. In practice, those travelling by land from Peru or Colombia are seldom granted more than 30 days on arrival, but this can usually be extended. When arriving at Quito or Guayaquil airport you will be asked how long you plan to stay. If you have no idea, ask for 90 days. If you overstay your visa, you will be fined US$200.

Upon entry all visitors must complete an international embarkation/disembarkation card, which is stamped along with your passport. Keep this card with your passport, losing it can cause problems when leaving the country. **Note** you are required by law to carry your passport at all times. Failure to do so can result in imprisonment and/or deportation. A photocopy certified by your embassy or the immigration police may be acceptable, but you should also have your original passport close at hand.

For a complete list of Ecuadorian embassies and consulates, visit www.mmrree.gov.ec.

Weights and measures

Peru, Bolivia and Ecuador all use the Metric system.

⁙ Footprint features

Introduction

The well-established cliché is to call Lima a city of contradictions, but it's difficult to get beyond that description. Here you'll encounter grinding poverty and conspicuous wealth in abundance. The hardships of the poor in this sprawling metropolis of eight million inhabitants are all too evident in the lives of those struggling to get by in the crowded streets and frantic bus lanes. The rubbish-strewn districts between the airport and city, and the shanty towns on the outskirts, emphasize the vast divisions within society.

Most visitors, though, have the option of heading for Miraflores, San Isidro or Barranco, where smart restaurants and elegant hotels rub shoulders with pre-Inca pyramids, and neat parks and the cliff-top Larcomar shopping centre overlook the ocean. Lima's image as a place to avoid or quickly pass through is enhanced by the thick grey blanket of cloud that descends in May and hangs around for the next seven months. Wait until the blanket is pulled aside in November to reveal bright blue skies and suddenly all Limeños descend on the city's popular coastal resorts. At this time, weekends become a raucous mix of sun, sea, salsa and *ceviche*.

Lima can also entertain, excite and inform. It boasts some of the finest historical monuments and museums in the country. The colonial centre, with its grand Plaza de Armas, fine churches and beautiful wooden balconies, is one of Peru's 10 UNESCO World Heritage sites and strenuous efforts are being made to refurbish the historical districts. The city's cuisine has earned it the title 'Gastronomic Capital of the Americas' and the bars, discos and *peñas* of Barranco and Miraflores ring to the sounds of everything from techno to traditional music. Scratch beneath that coating of grime and decay and you'll find one of the most vibrant and hospitable cities anywhere.

★ Don't miss ...

1 **Plaza de Armas** Step into the main square and try to imagine the days when it was the headquarters of Spain's South American empire, page 61.

2 **San Francisco** One of the city's original churches, with some beautiful decorations and a set of ghoulish catacombs, page 61.

3 **Larcomar** Looking for something contemporary? Here are shops, entertainment and watering holes carved out of the cliffs, page 66.

4 **Parque del Amor** One of Lima's most romantic places with its giant statue of lovers kissing and its view of the sea. If inspired to fly you can go parapenting nearby, page 66.

5 **Barranco** Another side of Lima and a must to visit for its nightlife and its fashionable modern art galleries, page 68.

6 **Pachacámac** Escape from the rush of the traffic at this vast pre-Columbian ceremonial centre, rescued from the desert sands. In the museum look for the statue that was the heart of the cult, page 68.

7 **Rosa Náutica** For the ultimate nostalgic dining experience, come to this restaurant on an old pier jutting into the Pacific, page 75.

8 **Petit Thouars market** Overload yourself with handicrafts in the largest concentration of ethnic goods in the country, page 78.

Lima

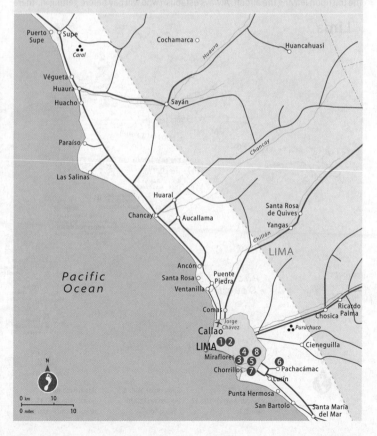

Ins and outs → *Phone code: 01. Colour map 2, C2. Population: 8,000,000.*

Getting there

Air All international flights land at **Jorge Chávez Airport** ① *16 km northeast of the centre, T01-511 6055, www.lap.com.pe.* Airport facilities include an ATM, *casa de cambio* and a bank (same end as the stairs to national Departures). There are public telephones and a **Telefónica del Peru** *locutorio*, daily 0700-2300. Internet facilities are more expensive than in the city. Information desks can be found in the national and international foyers. There is also a helpful desk in the international Arrivals hall, which can make hotel and transport reservations.

Transport into town is easy. *Remise* taxis (Mitsui or CMV) have representatives at desks outside Arrivals, US$11.75 to the city centre, US$7.25 to San Miguel, US$14.50 to San Isidro and Miraflores, US$17.50 to Barranco. This is the safest option, but also the most expensive. There are many regular taxis outside Arrivals with similar prices (more expensive at night). **Taxi Green**, T01-484 4001, www.taxigreen.com, has been recommended. Regular taxis do not use meters, so agree the price before getting in and insist on being taken to the hotel of your choice. If you are feeling confident, go to the car park exit and find a taxi outside the perimeter, by the roundabout. They charge US$3-6 to the city centre, US$6-8 to San Isidro/Miraflores. All vehicles can enter the airport for 10 minutes at no charge. After that, a fee is charged and taxis that have been waiting for more than the allotted free time will try to make the passenger pay the toll upon leaving the airport. Always establish who will pay before getting in. There

Lima Ins & outs

Lima

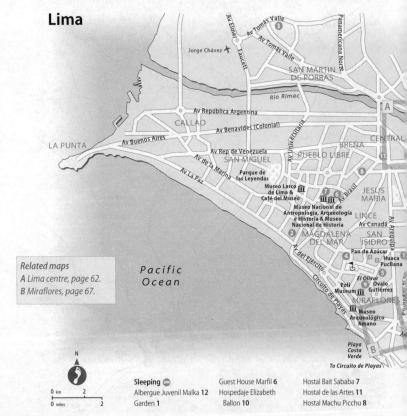

Related maps
A Lima centre, page 62.
B Miraflores, page 67.

Sleeping ●
Albergue Juvenil Malka **12**
Garden **1**

Guest House Marfil **6**
Hospedaje Elizabeth
Ballon **10**

Hostal Bait Sababa **7**
Hostal de las Artes **11**
Hostal Machu Picchu **8**

Arriving at night

Barring delays, there are usually no flight arrivals between 0100 and 0530. Money-changing facilities and information services stay open to meet all flights. There are few hotels in the vicinity of the airport, but taxis are available day or night. It's best to decide on a hotel before you even get to Lima. Many hotels will arrange to pick you up from the airport, either free as part of the room rate, or for a

fee of between US$12 and US$20 (depending on the category of hotel and how many people are in the vehicle). If you haven't arranged a room, don't leave the airport perimeter to find a public taxi or bus in the dark. The expensive *remise* services or the official taxis are the safest option. If you wish to stay in the airport until first light, the airport has seating areas and is safe.

is a bus service, **Urbanito** (T01-424 3650, urbanito@terra.com.pe) from the airport to the centre US$3, Pueblo Libre, San Isidro and Miraflores US$5; slow, calling at all hotels. The airport is the best and most cost-effective place to arrange car hire. The larger international chains – **Avis, Budget, Hertz, National** – are usually cheaper and tend to have better-maintained vehicles than local firms.

If arriving in Lima by **bus**, most of the recommended companies have their terminals just south of the centre, many on Avenida Carlos Zavala. Take a taxi to your hotel even if it's close, as this area is not safe. Some of the more upmarket bus companies have terminals in safer areas. ▶ *For further details, see Transport page 81.*

Hostal Mami Panchita **2**
Hostal Residencial Victor **3**
Libertador Hotels Peru **4**
Sofitel Royal Park **9**
Sonesta El Olivar **5**

Getting around

Downtown Lima can be explored on foot in the daytime, but take all the usual precautions. The central hotels are fairly close to the many of the tourist sites. At night taxis are a safer option. Many of the better hotels and restaurants are located in Miraflores and neighbouring San Isidro.

The Lima public transport system, at first glance very intimidating, is actually quite good. There are three different types of vehicle that will stop whenever flagged down: buses, *combis*, and *colectivos*. They can be distinguished by size; big and long, mid-size and mini-vans or cars, respectively. The flat-rate fare for buses and *combis* is US$0.35; *colectivos* cost a little more. For taxi fares, see Transport, page 82. On public holidays, Sunday and from 2400 to 0500 every night, a small charge is added to the fare. Always try to pay with the correct change. Routes on any public transport vehicle are posted on windscreens or written on the side. ▶ *For further details, see Transport page 81.*

⦂ The streets of Lima

Several blocks, with their own names, make up a long street, which is called a *jirón* (often abbreviated to Jr). You will be greatly helped by corner signs which bear the name of both the *jirón* and the block.

New and old names of streets are used interchangeably: remember that Colmena is also Nicolás de Piérola, Wilson is Inca Garcilaso de la Vega, and Carabaya is also Augusto N Wiese.

Best time to visit

Only 12° south of the equator, you would expect a tropical climate, but Lima has two distinct seasons. The winter is May-November, when a damp *garúa* (sea mist) hangs over the city, making everything look grey. At this time it is damp and cold, 8° to 15°C. However, the sun breaks through around November and temperatures rise as high as 30°C. Note that the temperature in the coastal suburbs is lower than in the centre because of the sea's influence. Protect yourself against the sun's rays when visiting the beaches around Lima, or elsewhere in Peru.

Tourist information

i perú has offices at **Jorge Chávez International Airport** ⓘ *T01-574 8000, daily 24 hrs*; at **Casa Basadre** ⓘ *Av Jorge Basadre 610, San Isidro, T01-421 1627, Mon-Fri 0830-1830*; and at **Larcomar shopping centre** ⓘ *Módulo 14, Plaza Gourmet, Miraflores, T01-445 9400, Mon-Fri 1200-2000*.

A full-service travel agency rather than a tourist office, but highly recommended nonetheless, is **Fertur Perú** ⓘ *Jr Junín 211, Plaza de Armas, T01-427 2626; also at Schell 485, Miraflores, T01-242 1900, www.fertur-travel.com, Mon-Sat 0900-1900; in USA: T1-877 247 0055.* Run by Siduith Ferrer de Vecchio, it not only offers up-to-date, correct tourist information on a national level, but also great prices on national and international flights, discounts for those with ISIC and youth cards and for **South American Explorers** members (of which she is one). Other services include flight reconfirmations, hotel reservations, transfers to and from the airport or bus stations and book exchange at the Junín branch.

South American Explorers ⓘ *Piura 135, Miraflores, T/F01-445 3306, www.sa explorers.org, Mon-Fri 0930-1700 (Wed until 2000) and Sat 0930-1300.* SAE is a non-profit educational organization which functions as a travel resource centre for South America and is widely recognized as the best place to get the most up-to-date information regarding everything from travel advice to volunteer opportunities. An annual membership is currently US$50 per person and US$80 per couple. Services include access to member-written trip reports, a full map room for reference, an extensive library in English and a book exchange. Members can store luggage and valuables in their very secure deposit space. SAE sells official maps from the **Instituto Geográfico Nacional**, SAE-produced trekking maps, used equipment and a wide variety of Peruvian crafts. They host regular presentations on various topics ranging from jungle trips to freedom of the press. Discounts are available for students, volunteers and nationals. If you're looking to study Spanish in Peru, hoping to travel down the Amazon or in search of a quality Inca Trail tour company, they have the information you'll need to make it happen. In addition to the services mentioned above, SAE is simply a great place to step out of the hustle and bustle of Lima and delight in the serenity of a cup of tea, a magazine and good conversation with a fellow traveller. SAE also has clubhouses in Cuzco and Quito (Ecuador). **SAE headquarters** ⓘ *126 Indian Creek Rd, Ithaca, NY, USA, 14850, T1-607 277 0488, www.saexplorers.org.*

Central Lima

The traditional heart of the city, at least in plan, is still what it was in colonial days. Although parts of it are run down, much of the old centre is undergoing restoration and many colonial buildings have been cleaned. It is worth visiting the colonial centre to see the architecture and works of art. Most of the tourist attractions are in this area. Churches open 1830-2100 unless otherwise stated. Many are closed to visitors on Sunday. Some museums are only open January to March 0900-1300, and some are closed in January.

Plaza de Armas

One block south of the Río Rímac lies the Plaza de Armas (also called Plaza Mayor since 1998), which has been declared a World Heritage Site by UNESCO. Running along two sides are arcades with shops: Portal de Escribanos and Portal de Botoneros. In the centre of the plaza is a bronze fountain dating from 1650. The **Palacio de Gobierno**, on the north side of the Plaza, stands on the site of the original palace built by Pizarro. The changing of the guard is at 1200. To take a tour register a day in advance (T01-311 3908), or at the office of public relations, Edificio Palacio 269, oficina 201 (ask the guard for directions). The free, 45-minute tours are in Spanish and English Monday- Friday, in the morning. The **cathedral** ① *T01-427 9647, Mon-Sat 0900-1630, US$1.50*, was reduced to rubble in the earthquake of 1746. The reconstruction, on the lines of the original, was completed in 1755. Note the splendidly carved stalls (mid-17th century), the silver-covered altars surrounded by fine woodwork, mosaic-covered walls bearing the coats of arms of Lima and Pizarro and an allegory of Pizarro's commanders, the 'Thirteen Men of Isla del Gallo'. The supposed remains of Francisco Pizarro lie in a small chapel, the first on the right of the entrance, in a glass coffin, though later research indicates that they reside in the crypt. There is a **Museo de Arte Religioso** in the cathedral, free tours (English-speaking guide available, give tip), ask to see the picture restoration room. Next to the cathedral is the **Archbishop's Palace**, rebuilt in 1924, with a superb wooden balcony.

Around the Plaza de Armas

Just off the plaza is the **Philatelic Museum** ① *central post office, daily 0815-1300, 1400-1800, free*, with an incomplete collection of Peruvian stamps and information on the Inca postal system. There is a stamp exchange in front of the museum every Saturday and Sunday, 0900-1300. Commemorative issues can be bought here. Nearby is the **Casa Aliaga** ① *Unión 224, Lima Tours has exclusive rights to include the house in its tours (T01-424 5110)*. It is still occupied by the Aliaga family but has been opened to the public. The house contains what is said to be the oldest ceiling in Lima and is furnished entirely in the colonial style.

The baroque church of **San Francisco** ① *1st block of Jr Lampa, corner of Ancash, a few blocks from the Plaza de Armas, T01-427 1381, daily 0930-1730, church and monastery US$1.50, US$0.50 children, only with guide, Spanish and English (recommended)*, was finished in 1674 and withstood the 1746 earthquake. The nave and aisles are lavishly decorated in Mudéjar style. The monastery is famous for the Sevillian tilework and panelled ceiling in the cloisters (1620). The catacombs under the church and part of the monastery are well worth seeing. The late 16th-century **Casa de Jarava** or **Pilatos** ① *Jr Ancash 390*, is opposite San Francisco church. Close by, **Casa de las Trece Monedas** ① *Jr Ancash 536*, still has the original doors and window grills.

The **Palacio Torre Tagle** (1735) ① *Jr Ucayali 363, Mon-Fri during working hours*, is the city's best surviving example of secular colonial architecture. Today, it is used by the Foreign Ministry, but visitors are allowed to enter courtyards to inspect the fine, Moorish-influenced wood-carving in balconies and wrought iron work. **Casa de la**

Rada, or **Goyoneche** ⓘ *Jr Ucayali 358*, opposite, is a fine mid 18th-century French-style town house, which now belongs to a bank. The patio and first reception room are open occasionally to the public. **Museo Banco Central de Reserva** ⓘ *Jr Ucayali at Jr Lampa, To1-613 2000 ext 2655, http://museobcr.perucultural.org.pe, Mon-Fri 1000-1630, Sat-Sun 1000-1300, free, photography prohibited*, is a large collection of pottery from the Vicus or Piura culture (AD 500-600) and gold objects from Lambayeque, as well as 19th and 20th-century paintings: both sections are highly recommended. **San Pedro** ⓘ *3rd block of Jirón Ucayali, Mon-Sat 0930-1145,*

Lima centre

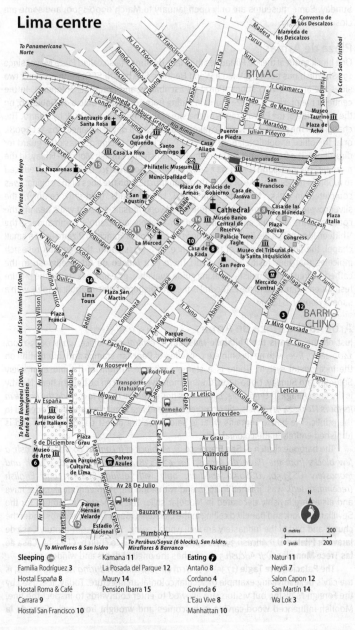

Sleeping

Familia Rodríguez 3
Hostal España 8
Hostal Roma & Café
Carrara 9
Hostal San Francisco 10

Kamana 11
La Posada del Parque 12
Maury 14
Pensión Ibarra 15

Eating

Antaño 8
Cordano 4
Govinda 6
L'Eau Vive 8
Manhattan 10

Natur 11
Neydi 7
Salon Capon 12
San Martín 14
Wa Lok 3

balconies, rich gilded-wood carvings in choir and vestry, and is tiled throughout. Several viceroys are buried here; the bell called *La Abuelita*, first rung in 1590, sounded the Declaration of Independence in 1821.

Between Avenida Abancay and Jr Ayacucho is **Plaza Bolívar**, where General José de San Martín proclaimed Peru's independence. The plaza is dominated by the equestrian statue of the Liberator. Behind lies the Congress building which occupies the former site of the Universidad de San Marcos; recommended. Behind the Congress is Barrio Chino, with many *chifas* and small shops selling oriental items. The **Museo del Tribunal de la Santa Inquisición** ① *Plaza Bolívar, Calle Junín 548, near the corner of Av Abancay, daily 0900-1700, free, students offer to show you round for a tip*, has good explanations in English. The main hall, with a splendidly carved mahogany ceiling, remains untouched. The Court of Inquisition was held here from 1584; between 1829 and 1938 it was used by the Senate. In the basement there is a recreation *in situ* of the gruesome tortures. A description in English is available at the desk.

The 16th-century **Santo Domingo church and monastery** ① *on the 1st block of Jr Camaná, T01-427 6793, monastery and tombs open Mon-Sat 0900-1230, 1500-1800; Sun and holidays morning only, US$0.75*, has a very attractive cloister, dating from 1603. The second cloister is less elaborate. Beneath the sacristy are the tombs of San Martín de Porres, one of Peru's most revered saints, and Santa Rosa de Lima (see below). In 1669, Pope Clement presented the alabaster statue of Santa Rosa in front of the altar. Behind Santo Domingo is **Alameda Chabuca Granda**, named after one of Peru's greatest singers. In the evening there are free art and music shows and you can sample foods from all over Peru. A few blocks away, **Casa de Oquendo** or **Osambela** ① *Conde de Superunda 298, 0900-1300*, stages art exhibitions. A few blocks west is **Santuario de Santa Rosa** ① *Av Tacna, 1st block, T01-425 1279, daily 0930-1300, 1500-1800, free to the grounds*, a small but graceful church and a pilgrimage centre. Here are preserved the hermitage built by Santa Rosa herself, the house in which she was born, a section of the house in which she attended to the sick, her well, and other relics. Nearby, **Casa La Riva** ① *Jr Ica 426*, has an 18th-century porch and balconies, and a small gallery with 20th-century paintings.

San Agustín ① *Jr Ica 251, T01-427 7548, daily 0830-1130, 1630-1900, ring for entry*, is west of the Plaza de Armas. Its façade (1720) is a splendid example of churriguer-esque architecture. There are carved choir stalls and effigies, and a sculpture of Death, said to have frightened its maker into an early grave. The church has been restored after the last earthquake, but the sculpture of Death is in storage. **Las Nazarenas church** ① *Av Tacna, 4th block, T01-423 5718, daily 0700-1200, 1600-2000*, is built around an image of Christ Crucified painted by a liberated slave in 1655. This, the most venerated image in Lima, and an oil copy of El Señor de los Milagros (Lord of Miracles), encased in a gold frame, are carried on a silver litter the whole weighing nearly a ton through the streets on 18, 19, and 28 October and again on 1 November (All Saints' Day). *El Comercio* newspaper and local pamphlets give details of times and routes.

Northeast of Plaza de Armas

From the Plaza, passing the Palacio de Gobierno on the left, straight ahead is the **Desamparados railway station** ① *free*, which now houses fascinating exhibitions on Peruvian themes. The **Puente de Piedra**, behind the Palacio de Gobierno, is a Roman-style stone bridge built in 1610, crossing the Río Rímac to the district of that name. On Jr Hualgayoc is the bullring in the **Plaza de Acho**, inaugurated on 20 January 1766, with the **Museo Taurino** ① *Hualgayoc 332, T01-482 3360, Mon-Sat 0800-1600, US$1, students US$0.50, photography US$2*. In addition to matador's relics, the museum contains good collections of paintings and engravings, including some by Goya. There are two bullfight seasons: October to the first week in December and during July. They are held in the afternoons on Sunday and holidays. The **Convento de Los**

Descalzos ① *on the Alameda de Los Descalzos in Rímac, T01-481 0441, daily 1000-1300, 1500-1800, except Tue, US$1, guided tour only, 45 mins in Spanish (worth it)*, was founded in 1592. It contains over 300 paintings of the Cuzco, Quito and Lima schools which line the four main cloisters and two ornate chapels. The chapel of El Carmen was constructed in 1730 and is notable for its baroque gold leaf altar. The museum shows the life of the Franciscan friars during colonial and early republican periods. The cellar, infirmary, pharmacy and a typical cell have been restored.

Cerro San Cristóbal dominates downtown Lima and can be visited in a one-hour **tour** ① *departing from in front of Santo Domingo, Jr Camaná, Sat-Sun 1000-2100; departures every 15 mins, US$1.50*, run by **Ofistur**. It includes a look at the run-down Rímac district, passes the Convento de los Descalzos (see above), ascends the hill through one of the city's oldest shanties with its brightly painted houses and spends about 20 minutes at the summit, where there is a small museum and café. There are excellent views on a clear day.

South of Plaza de Armas

Jirón de La Unión, the main shopping street, runs to the Plaza de Armas. It has been converted into a pedestrian precinct which teems with life in the evening. In the two blocks south of Jr Unión, known as Calle Belén, several shops sell souvenirs and curios. **La Merced** ① *Unión y Miró Quesada, T01-427 8199, 0800-1245, 1600-2000, Sun 0700-1300, 1600-2000; monastery daily 0800-1200 and 1500-1730*, is in Plazuela de la Merced. The first Mass in Lima was said here on the site of the first church to be built. The restored façade is a fine example of colonial baroque. Inside are some magnificent altars and the tilework on some of the walls is noteworthy. A door from the right of the nave leads into the monastery. The cloister dates from 1546. Jr de la Unión leads to **Plaza San Martín**, which has a statue of San Martín in the centre. The plaza has been restored and is now a pleasant place to sit and relax.

Museo de Arte ① *9 de Diciembre 125, T01-423 4732, http://museoarte.peru cultural.org.pe, Thu-Tue 1000-1700, US$3.65, free guide, signs in English*, is in the Palacio de la Exposición, built in 1868 in Parque de la Exposición (designed by Gustave Eiffel). There are more than 7000 exhibits, giving a chronological history of Peruvian cultures and art from the Paracas civilization up to the present day. It includes excellent examples of 17th- and 18th-century Cuzco paintings, a beautiful display of carved furniture, heavy silver and jewelled stirrups and also pre-Columbian pottery. The *Filmoteca* (movie club) on the premises shows films just about every night; see the local paper for details, or look in the museum itself. The **Gran Parque Cultural de Lima** ① *0800-2030*, is in the grounds. Inaugurated in January 2000, this large park has an amphitheatre, Japanese garden, food court and children's activities. Relaxing strolls through this green, peaceful and safe oasis in the centre of Lima are recommended.

The **Museo de Arte Italiano** ① *Paseo de la República 250, T01-423 9932, Tue-Fri 0900-1900, Sat-Sun 1100-1700, US$1*, is in a wonderful neoclassical building, given to Peru by the Italian colony on the centenary of its independence. Note the remarkable mosaic murals on the outside. It consists of a large collection of Italian and other European works of art and houses the **Instituto de Arte Contemporáneo**, which has many exhibitions.

San Borja

Museo de la Nación ① *Javier Prado Este 2465, T01-476 9933, Tue-Sun 0900-1800, closed public holidays, US$1.80; 50% discount with ISIC card*, in the huge **Banco de la Nación** building, is the museum for the exhibition and study of the art and history of the aboriginal races of Peru. It contains the **Museo Peruano de Ciencias de la Salud** ① *from Av Garcilaso de la Vega in downtown Lima take a combi with a "Javier Prado/Aviación" window sticker, get off at the 21st block of Javier Prado at Av Aviación; From Miraflores take a bus down Av Arequipa to Av Javier Prado (27th block), then take*

Guilt by inquisition

Established by Royal Decree in 1569, the Court of Inquisition proved to be a particularly cruel form of justice, even in the context of Spanish rule.

During its existence, the Church meted out many horrific tortures on innocent people. Among the most fashionable methods of making the accused confess their 'sins' were burning, dismemberment and asphyxiation, to name but a few. The most common form of punishment was public flogging, followed by exile and the not so appealing death by burning. Up until 1776, 86 people are recorded as having been burned alive and 458 excommunicated. Given that no witnesses were called except the

informer and that the accused were not allowed to know the identity of their accusers, this may have been less a test of religious conviction than a means of settling old scores. This Kafkaesque nightmare was then carried into the realms of surreal absurdity during the process of judgement. A statue of Christ was the final arbiter of guilt or innocence but had to express its belief in the prisoner's innocence with a shake of the head. Needless to say, not too many walked free.

The Inquisition was abolished by the Viceroy in 1813 but later reinstated before finally being proscribed in 1820.

a bus with a "Todo Javier Prado" or "Aviación" window sticker; taxi from downtown Lima or Miraflores US$2, which has a collection of ceramics and mummies, plus an explanation of pre-Columbian lifestyle. There are good explanations in Spanish and English on Peruvian history, with ceramics, textiles and displays of almost every ruin in Peru. It is arranged so that you can follow the development of Peruvian precolonial history through to the time of the Incas. A visit is recommended before you go to see the archaeological sites themselves. Guided tours in English/Spanish. There are displays of the tomb of the Señor de Sipán, artefacts from Batán Grande near Chiclayo (Sicán culture), reconstructions of the friezes found at Huaca La Luna and Huaca El Brujo, near Trujillo, and of Sechín and other sites. Temporary exhibitions are held in the basement, where there is also an **Instituto Nacional de Cultura** bookshop. The museum has a cafetería.

Lima suburbs

Pueblo Libre

The original museum of anthropology and archaeology is the **Museo Nacional de Antropología, Arqueología e Historia** ① *Plaza Bolívar (not to be confused with Plaza Bolívar in the centre), T01-463 5070, http://museonacional.perucultural.org.pe, Tue-Sun 0930-1700, US$3.35, students US$1, guides available for groups*. On display are ceramics of the Chimú, Nazca, Mochica and Pachacámac cultures, various Inca curiosities and works of art, and interesting textiles. The **Museo Nacional de Historia** ① *T01-463 2009*, in a mansion occupied by San Martín (1821-1822) and Bolívar (1823-1826) is next door. It exhibits colonial and early republican paintings, manuscripts and uniforms. Take any public transport on Avenida Brasil with a window sticker saying "Todo Brasil." Get off at the 21st block called Avenida Vivanco. Walk about five blocks down Vivanco. The museum will be on your left. From Miraflores take bus SM 18 Caraballyo-Chorrillos, marked "Bolívar, Arequipa, Larcomar", get out at block 8 of Bolívar by the Hospital Santa Rosa, and walk down Avenida San Martín five blocks until you see the 'blue line'; turn left. The 'blue line' marked on the pavement, very faded, links the Museo Nacional de Antropología, Arqueología e Historia to the Museo Larco (see below), 10 minutes' walk. Taxi from downtown US$2; from Miraflores US$2

The **Museo Larco de Lima** ① *Av Bolívar 1515, T01-461 1312, www.museolarco.org, 0900-1800; texts in Spanish, English and French, US$7.55 (half price for students), disabled access, photography not permitted*, is located in an 18th-century mansion, itself built on a seventh-century pre-Columbian pyramid. This museum has a collection which gives an excellent overview on the development of Peruvian cultures through their pottery. It has the world's largest collection of Moche, Sicán and Chimú pieces. There is a 'Gold and Silver of Ancient Peru' exhibition, a magnificent textile collection and a fascinating section on erotica. Don't miss the storeroom with its vast array of pottery, unlike anything you'll see elsewhere. It is surrounded by beautiful gardens. Take any bus to the 15th block of Avenida Brasil. Then take a bus down Avenida Bolívar. From Miraflores, take the SM 18 Carabayllo-Chorrillos to block 15 of Bolívar. Taxi from downtown, Miraflores or San Isidro, 15 minutes, US$2.50. Follow the 'blue line' marked on the pavement to the Museo Nacional de Antropología, Arqueología e Historia (see above), 10 minutes' walk.

San Isidro

To the east of Avenida La República, down Calle Pancho Fierro, is **El Olivar**, an olive grove planted by the first Spaniards which has been turned into a park. Between San Isidro and Miraflores, is **the Pan de Azúcar**, or **Huallamarca** ① *Calle Nicolás de Rivera 201 and Av Rosario, 0900-1700, closed Mon, US$1.75; take bus 1 from Av Tacna, or minibus 13 or 73 to Choquechaca, then walk*. An adobe pyramid of the Maranga culture, it dates from about AD 100-500. There is a small site museum. There are many good hotels and restaurants in San Isidro.

South of San Isidro is the rundown seaside resort of **Magdalena del Mar**, inland from which is **Pueblo Libre**, where many museums are located. **Parque las Leyendas** ① *T01-464 4282, daily 0900-1730, US$2*, is arranged to represent the three regions of Peru: the coast, the Sierra, and the tropical jungles of the Selva, with appropriate houses, animals and plants, children's playground. It gets very crowded at weekends. Take bus 23 or *colectivo* on Avenida Abancay, or bus 135. A or *colectivo* from Avenida La Vega, is reached from the 24th block of Avenida de La Marina in San Miguel: take Avenida Parque Las Leyendas to the entrance on Avenida La Mar.

Miraflores → *See Transport, page 81.*

Avenida Arequipa continues to the coast, to the most important suburb of Lima, with many hotels, restaurants and bars. Together with San Isidro and Barranco this is now the social centre of Lima. **Parque Kennedy**, the central park in Miraflores is located between Avenida Larco and Avenida Mcal Oscar Benavides (locally known as Avenida Diagonal). This extremely well-kept park has a small open-air theatre with performances Thursday to Sunday and an arts and crafts market most evenings. The house of the author **Ricardo Palma** ① *Gral Suárez 189, T01-445 5836, Mon-Fri 0915-1245, 1430-1700, small entrance fee*, is now a museum. At the end of Avenida Larco and running along the Malecón de la Reserva is the renovated **Parque Salazar** and the very modern shopping centre called **Centro Comercial Larcomar**. Here you will find expensive shops, hip cafés and discos, and a wide range of restaurants, all with a beautiful ocean view. The 12-screen cinema is one of the best in Lima and even has a 'cine-bar' in the 12th theatre. Don't forget to check out the Cosmic Bowling Alley with its black lights and fluorescent balls. A few hundred metres to the north is the famous **Parque del Amor** where on just about any night you'll see at least one wedding party taking photos of the newly weds.

The **Museo Arqueológico Amano** ① *Retiro 160, 11th block of Av Angamos Oeste, Miraflores, T01-441 2909, visits by appointment Mon-Fri in afternoons only, free (photography prohibited)*, has a collection of artefacts from the Chancay, Chimú and

Nazca periods, owned by the late Mr Yoshitaro Amano. It has one of the most complete exhibits of Chancay weaving, and is particularly interesting for pottery and pre-Columbian textiles, all superbly displayed and lit. Take a bus or *colectivo* to the corner of Avenida Arequipa y Avenida Angamos and another one to the 11th block of Avenida Angamos Oeste. Taxi from downtown US$2; from Parque Kennedy US$1.

Miraflores

Sleeping 🛏	Hostal El Patio **14** C2	Café Café **5** B2	Las Tejas **21** C2
Adventures House **36** A1	Hostal Esperanza **15** C3	Café de la Paz **6** B2	Madre Natura **39** A3
Albergue Turístico	Hostal La Castellana **17** C2	Café Tarata **25** C2	Pizza Street **23** B2
Juvenil	Hostal Señorial **19** D1	Café Voltaire **7** B3	Ricota **25** C2
Internacional **1** D3	Inka Lodge **13** A2	Café Zeta **27** B2	Rosa Náutica **11** D1
Albergue Verde **5** D2	José Antonio **21** C1	C'est Si Bon **35** A2	San Antonio **33** A3
Alemán **32** A3	Lion Backpackers **3** C3	Coco de Mer **9** B1	Sandwich.com **3** B2
Antigua Miraflores **2** B1	Loki Backpackers **20** B3	Dalmacia **38** D1	Sí Señor **28** B1
Casa Andina **43** D2	Miraflores Park **42** D1	Dino's Pizza **34** A2	Tapas Bar **46** B2
Casa de Baraybar **11** A1	Pensión Yolanda **33** B3	Dove Vai **10** B2	Vivaldi **29** B3
Eurobackpackers **39** C1	San Antonio Abad **28** D3	El Kapallaq **43** B3	Wa Lok **42** A3
Explorer's House **37** A1	Sipán **4** D2	El Parquetito **12** B2	Zugatti **30** C2
Flying Dog	Sonesta Posadas	El Señorío de Sulco **40** A1	
Backpackers **9** C2	del Inca **30** C2	Haiti **13** B3	**Bars & clubs** 🍸
Friend's House **10** C1	Stop & Drop **44** B2	Heladería 4D **14** A3	Barcelona **1** D1
Home Peru **38** A3	Wayruro's	Huaca Pucllana **8** A3	Media Naranja **31** B2
	Backpackers **45** A2	Il Postino **15** C3	Murphys **32** C2
		La Palachinke **17** B2	The Old Pub **45** B2
	Eating 🍴	Las Brujas de Cachiche **4** B1	Voluntarios Pub **24** B2
	Astrid y Gaston **2** C3	La Tiendecita Blanca **18** B3	

The **Poli Museum** ⓘ *Almte Cochrane 466, T01-422 2437, tours cost US$10 per person irrespective of the size of the group, allow 2 hrs, call in advance to arrange tours*, has one of the best private collections of colonial and pre-Columbian artefacts in Peru, including material from Sipán. At Borgoña, eighth block s/n, turn off Avenida Arequipa at 45th block, is **Huaca Pucllana** ⓘ *T01-445 8695, http://pucllana.perucultural.org.pe, US$2, 0900-1600, closed Tue*, a fifth to eigth-century AD, pre-Inca site which is under excavation. Guided tours are in Spanish only (give a tip). There is a small site museum, but with few objects from the site itself, and a handicrafts shop.

Barranco

This suburb further south was already a seaside resort by the end of the 17th century. Nowadays, a number of artists have their workshops here and there are several chic galleries. The attractive public library, formerly the town hall, stands on the plaza. Nearby is the interesting *bajada*, a steep path leading down to the beach. The **Puente de los Suspiros** (Bridge of Sighs), leads towards the Malecón, with fine views of the bay. Barranco comes alive at night, with many bars around the main plaza. Take a *colectivo* to Miraflores then another. Some run all the way to Barranco from Lima centre; check on the window or ask. The 45-minute walk from Miraflores to Barranco along the Malecón is nice in summer. The **Museo de Arte Colonial Pedro de Osma** ⓘ *Av Pedro de Osma 421, Barranco, T01-467 0915, open by appointment, US$3; only 10 visitors at any one time*, has a private collection of colonial art of the Cuzco, Ayacucho and Arequipa schools. Take bus 2, 54 or *colectivo* from Avenida Tacna.

Lima beaches

In summer (December-April) the city's beaches get very crowded at weekends and lots of activities are organized. Even though the water in the bay has been declared unsuitable for swimming, Limeños see the beach more as part of their culture than as a health risk. Do not camp on the beaches as robbery is a serious threat and, for the same reason, take care on the walkways. Don't take any belongings with you to the beach, only what is really necessary. The *Circuito de Playas*, which begins with **Playa Arica** (30 km from Lima) and ends with **San Bartolo** (45 km from Lima), has many great beaches for all tastes. If you want a beach that's always packed with people, there's **El Silencio** or **Punta Rocas**. Quieter are **Señoritas** or **Los Pulpos**. **Punta Hermosa** has frequent surfing and volleyball tournaments.

Pachacámac → *See Transport, page 81.*

ⓘ *T01-430 0168, http://pachacamac.perucultural.org.pe, and www.ulb.ac.be/philo/ychsma, 0900-1700, closed 1 May, US$1.65, includes the museum, guide US$6.*

When the Spaniards arrived, Pachacámac in the Lurín valley was the largest city and ceremonial centre on the coast. A wooden statue of the creator-god, after whom the site is named, is in the site museum. Hernando Pizarro was sent here by his brother in 1533 in search of gold for Inca emperor Atahualpa's ransom. In their fruitless quest, the Spaniards destroyed images and killed the priests. The ruins encircle the top of a low hill, whose crest was crowned with a **Temple of the Sun**, now partially restored. Hidden from view is the reconstructed **House of the Mamaconas**, where the 'chosen women' spun fine cloth for the Inca and his court. An impression of the scale of the site can be gained from the top of the Temple of the Sun, or from walking or driving the 3-km circuit (the site is large and it is expected that tourists will be visiting by car).

Puruchuco

ⓘ *End of Av Javier Prado Este, T01-494 2641, http://museopuruchuco.perucultural.org.pe, Tue-Fri 0830-1600, Sat-Sun 0900-1600, US$1.65.*

In the eastern outskirts of Lima, near La U football stadium, is Puruchuco, the reconstructed palace of a pre-Inca Huacho noble. There is a very good museum, **Jiménez**

Caral

In the far north of Lima Department, a few kilometres before the town of Barranca, is Caral, a city 20 km from the coast whose date (3200-3000 BC) and monumental construction indicate that it is easily the oldest city-state in South America. The dry, desert site lies on the southern fringes of the Supe Valley, along whose flanks and at whose mouth (Supe Puerto) there are many more unexcavated ruins.

Caral covers 66 ha and contains eight significant pyramidal structures. Of these, seven have been investigated, revealing a stone and mortar construction with a yellow and white wash being the most common finish, small areas of which remain visible. A viewpoint provides a panorama across the whole site. **Pirámide de Anfiteatro** (11 m high) is a large amphitheatre from which a series of ceremonial rooms rise. **Pirámide de la Huanca** (12 m high) is constructed in three tiers with a 23-step staircase leading up to the ceremonial platform. It takes its name from the large stone obelisk (*huanca*) in the centre of the plaza, which it overlooks. The residence of the elite, a complex of well-built adobe rooms, abuts the pyramid. **Pirámide de la Galería** (the gallery pyramid, 17 m high) has a nearly 7-m-wide stairway leading up to a room sunk into the ceremonial platform lined with huarango wood and containing eight huge whalebone vertebrate seats. **Pirámide Menor** (7.5 m high) is the smallest of the pyramids. **Pirámide Mayor** (the great pyramid, 153.5 by 110 by 28 m) is the largest pyramid with a sunken circular plaza on its south side. Two *lanzones* (obelisk-sized stones) frame the two entrances to the plaza and a further *lanzón* sits atop the pyramid which is reached by an impressive 9-m-wide stairway. **Pirámide de la Cantera** (the quarry pyramid, 13.5 m high) straddles a rock outcrop. A 4.2-m-wide stairway with 32 steps ascends to the summit, on which is a round, walk-in altar with an outer wall 8 m in diameter and an inner wall 3.7 m in diameter. In addition, there is a long building containing 18 internal niches along each facing wall. **El Templo de Altar Circular** (4 m high) consists of at least 13 rooms in at least two groupings. Some later adobe ruins fringe the site. Detailed, illustrated Spanish/English information panels are located around the site.

Visitors report to the tourist post in the car park. US$3, US$1 with student card, plus US$6 per group for a guide (Spanish only). Contact Proyecto Especial Caral, Unión 1040, Lima 1, T01-332 5380, www.caralperu.gob.pe.

Many tour operators run trips. To get there by public transport, take a *colectivo* from Avenida Lima, 2 blocks from the market, in Barranca for the village of Caral from 0700, 1½ hrs, US$1.50. The ruins are 25 km along a rough road which runs up the Supe valley. A path leads from the road across the valley to the ruins, 30 mins. Colectivos can also be picked up in Supe or at the signposted turn-off to the ruins on the Panamericana at Km 185. A taxi in Barranca or Supe will charge US$20, including a two-hour wait at the ruins.

Borja, with ceramics and textiles from the lower Rímac or Lima valley. This is also the site of a major archaeological find (2002): under a shanty town called Túpac Amaru, over 2000 intact mummy bundles have been uncovered in an Inca cemetery known as **Puruchuco-Huaquerones**. The quantity and completeness of the mummies, plus the tens of thousands of accompanying objects, should reveal a wealth of information about the last century of Inca society before the Spanish conquest. To see the tombs, ask the guards on Saturday morning if you can visit the archaeologists at work.

Lima Lima suburbs

◉ Sleeping

Central Lima is not as safe at night as the more upmarket areas of Miraflores, San Isidro and Barranco. If you are only staying a short time and want to see the main sites, it is convenient, but do take care. San Isidro is the poshest district while Miraflores has a good mix of places to stay, great ocean views, bookstores, restaurants and cinemas. From here you can then commute to the centre by bus (30-45 mins) or by taxi (20-30 mins). Barranco is a little further out. All hotels in the upper price brackets charge 19% state tax and service on top of prices. In hotels foreigners pay no tax and the amount of service charge is up to the hotel. Neither is included in the prices below, unless otherwise stated. All those listed below have received good recommendations.

Near the airport *map p58*
B-D Hostal Residencial Victor, Manuel Mattos 325, Urb San Amadeo de Garagay, Lima 31, T01-569 4662, hostalvictor@terra.com.pe. 5 mins from the airport by taxi, or phone or email in advance for free pick-up, large comfortable rooms, with bath, hot water, cable TV, free luggage store, free internet and 10% discount for Footprint book owners, American breakfast, evening meals can be ordered locally, mall with restaurants, fast food and gym nearby, very helpful, owner Víctor Melgar has a free reservation service for Peru and Bolivia.

Central Lima *p61, maps p58 and p62*
B Maury, Jr Ucayali 201, T01-428 8188, http://ekeko2.rcp.net.pe/hotelmaury. Fancy, secure, breakfast included, most luxurious hotel in the historical centre.
B-C Kamana, Jr Camaná 547, T01-426 7204, www.hotelkamana.com. Rooms with TV, comfortable, safe, French and some English spoken, very helpful staff.
C La Posada del Parque, Parque Hernán Velarde 60, block 1 and 2 Av Petit Thouars, Santa Beatriz, T01-433 2412, T01-332 0909, www.incacountry.com. Attractively furnished Peruvian mansion, rooms with private bath, hot water, cable TV. Free internet, breakfast US$3

extra, airport transfer 24 hrs for US$14 for up to 3 passengers, no credit cards. English spoken.
D Hostal Roma, Jr Ica 326, T/F01-427 7576, www.hostalroma.8m.com. With bath, **E** without bath, hot water all day, safe to leave luggage, basic but clean, often full, internet extra but good, motorcycle parking (**Roma Tours**, helpful for trips, reservations, flight confirmations, Errol Branca speaks English).
E-F Hostal de las Artes, Jr Chota 1460, Breña, T01-433 0031, http://arteswelcome. tripod.com. **F** without bath (no singles with bath), **G** pp in dormitory, Dutch owned, English spoken, safes in rooms and safe luggage store, nice colonial building, solar hot water system, book exchange, airport transfer US$12.
F Hostal San Francisco, Jr Azángaro 127, T01-426 2735, hostalsf@lanpro.com.pe. Dormitories with and without bathrooms, new, safe, Italian/Peruvian owners, good service, internet and cafeteria.
G pp Familia Rodríguez, Av Nicolás de Piérola 730, p 2, T01-423 6465, jotajot@terra.com.pe. With breakfast, popular, some rooms noisy, will store luggage, also has dormitory accommodation with only one bathroom (same price), transport to airport US$10 pp for 2 people, US$4 pp for 3 or more, good information, secure.
G Hostal España, Jr Azángaro 105, T01-427 9196, www.hotelespanaperu.com. **F** with bath (3 rooms), **G** pp in dormitory, fine old building, hot showers, English spoken, internet service, motorcycle parking, luggage store (free) and lockers, laundry service, don't leave valuables in rooms, roof garden, good café, can be very busy.
G Pensión Ibarra, Av Tacna 359, p 14-16, T/F01-427 8603 (no sign), pensionibarra@ekno.com. Breakfast US$2, discount for longer stay, use of kitchen, balcony with views of the city, very helpful owner, hot water, full board available (good small café next door).
G pp Hostal Machu Picchu, Av Juan Pablo Fernandini 1015 (block 10 of Av Brasil), Breña, T01-9794 4257. Family run, shared bath, hot water, kitchen facilities, cable TV, laundry service, excellent value.

● *For an explanation of sleeping and eating price codes used in this guide, see inside the* ● *front cover. Other relevant information is found in Essentials, see pages 31-35.*

Pueblo Libre *p65, map p58*

C **Hostal Mami Panchita**, Av Federico Gallessi 198, towards the suburb of San Miguel and the sea, T01-263 7203, www.mamipanchita.com. Dutch-Peruvian owned, many languages spoken, includes breakfast, comfortable rooms with bath, hot water, living room, bar, patio, email service, book exchange, **Raymi** travel agency (good service), 15 mins from airport, 20 mins from historical centre.

F pp **Guest House Marfil**, Parque Ayacucho 126, at the 3rd block of Bolívar, T01-261 1206, cosycoyllor@yahoo.com. English spoken, breakfast, kitchen, free laundry, internet, Spanish classes arranged, family atmosphere.

G **Hostal Bait Sababa**, Av San Martín 743, near the hospital, T01-261 4990, baitsababa@hotmail.com. The home of a Jewish family who speak Spanish, English and Hebrew, very helpful, Fri evening meal provided, restaurants, laundry, internet and phone nearby.

San Isidro *p66, map p58*

LL **Sonesta El Olivar**, Pancho Fierro 194, T01-712 6000, www.sonestaperu.com. Excellent, one of the top 5-star hotels in Lima, modern, many eating options, bar, garden, swimming pool, quiet, popular.

L **Libertador Hotels Peru**, Los Eucaliptos 550, T01-421 6666, www.libertador.com.pe (reservations: Las Begonias 441, office 240, T01-442 1995). Golden Tulip hotel, overlooking the golf course, full facilities, fine service, comfortable rooms, good restaurant. A combination of Peruvian hospitality and culture with hotels throughout Peru.

L-AL **Sofitel Royal Park**, Av Camino Real 1050, T01-215 1616, www.sofitel.com.

Excellent rooms, charming, part of the French group, prices can be negotiated.

A **Garden**, Rivera Navarrete 450, T01-442 1771, reservas@gardenhotel.com.pe. Includes breakfast, good beds, small restaurant, ideal for business visitors, convenient, free internet.

D-E **Hospedaje Elizabeth Ballon**, Av del Parque Norte 265, San Isidro, T01-9800 7557, http://chezelizabeth.typepad.fr. Family house in residential area 7 mins' walk from Cruz del Sur bus station. Shared or private bathrooms, TV room, laundry, luggage storage, breakfast extra, airport transfers US$12.

Youth hostels

F **Albergue Juvenil Malka**, Los Lirios 165 (near 4th block of Av Javier Prado Este), San Isidro, T01-442 0162, hostelmalka@terra.com.pe. Youth hostel, 20% discount with ISIC card, dormitory style, 4-8 beds per room, English spoken, cable TV, laundry, kitchen, climbing wall, nice café.

Miraflores *p66, map p67*

LL **Miraflores Park**, Av Malecón de la Reserva 1035, T01-242 3393, www.mira-park.com. An **Orient Express** hotel, excellent service and facilities, beautiful views over the ocean.

AL-A **Antigua Miraflores**, Av Grau 350 at Calle Francia, T01-241 6116, www.peru-hotels-inns.com. Small hotel in a quiet, central location, with gym, cable TV, good restaurant.

AL-A **Sonesta Posadas del Inca**, Alcanfores 490, T01-241 7688, www.sonestaperu.com. Part of renowned chain of hotels, convenient location, cable TV, a/c, restaurant.

A **Casa Andina**, Av 28 de Julio 1088, T01-241 4050, www.casa-andina.com. One of a recommended chain, all with similar facilities

and decor. Very neat, with many useful touches, comfortable beds, internet access and Wi-Fi, a/c, fridge, safe, laundry service, buffet breakfast, other meals available.

A José Antonio, 28 de Julio 398 y Calle Colón, T01-445 7743, www.hotelesjoseantonio.com. Good in all respects, restaurant, huge rooms, jacuzzis, internet, swimming pool, business facilities, helpful, some English spoken.

B Alemán, Arequipa 4704, T01-445 6999, www.hotelaleman.com.pe. No sign, quiet, comfortable, garden, excellent breakfast included, laundry, smiling staff, free internet.

B Hostal Esperanza, Esperanza 350, T01-444 2411, http://barrioperu.terra.com.pe/htlesperanza. Modern, convenient, hot water, very helpful, café, bar, secure, good value.

B Hostal La Castellana, Grimaldo del Solar 222, T01-444 4662, lacastellan@terra.com.pe. Pleasant, good value, nice garden, safe, expensive restaurant, laundry, English spoken, special price for SAE members.

B San Antonio Abad Hotel, Ramón Ribeyro 301, T01-447 6766, www.hotelsanantonio abad.com. Secure, quiet, helpful, tasty breakfasts, 1 free airport transfer with reservation, justifiably popular.

B-C Hostal El Patio, Diez Canseco 341, T01-444 2107, www.hostalelpatio.net. Includes breakfast, reductions for long stays, good suites and rooms, comfortable, English and French spoken, convenient, *comedor*, gay-friendly.

C Hostal Señorial, José González 567, T01-445 9724, senorial@viabcp.com. Includes breakfast, comfortable, nice garden.

C Sipán, Paseo de la República 6171, T01-447 0884, www.hotelsipan.com.pe. Breakfast and tax included, very pleasant, in a residential area, TV, fridge, security box, internet access. Free airport transfers available.

D Casa de Baraybar, Toribio Pacheco 216, T01-441 2160, www.casadebaraybar.com. One block from the ocean, extra long beds, breakfast included, TV, 24-hr room service, laundry, airport transfers free for stays of 3 nights. Bilingual staff, internet.

D-E Home Peru, Av Arequipa 4501 (no sign), T01-241 9898, www.homeperu.com. In a 1920s mansion with huge rooms, with breakfast, **E-F** pp with shared bath, group discounts, very welcoming and helpful, use of kitchen, luggage store, English spoken, laundry service, internet, safe, near Plaza Vea hypermarket. Can help with bus and plane tickets, connected to other *hostales* in Peru.

D-E Lion Backpackers, Grimaldo del Solar 139, T01-447 1827, www.lionbackpackers.com. Doubles and dormitories, 3 blocks from Parque Kennedy, nice atmosphere, safe, breakfast, very helpful.

E pp Inka Lodge, Elias Aguirre 278, T01-242 6989, www.inkalodge.com. Also with dorms (**F** pp), convenient, excellent breakfast included, internet, laundry, very helpful.

E Pensión Yolanda, Domingo Elias 230, T01-445 7565, pensionyolanda@hotmail.com or erwinpension@yahoo.com. Price includes breakfast, English and French spoken, family house, quiet, safe, laundry, book exchange, luggage store. They have travel information and can reserve flights and hotels.

E-F pp Eurobackpackers, Manco Cápac 471 (look for the cat with the world on his stick), T01-791 2945, www.eurobackpackers.com. Dormitory, also doubles, breakfast included, family atmosphere, comfortable, safe, internet. Good reputation although rooms downstairs are not as airy as those on first floor.

F pp Adventures House, Jr Cesareo Chacaltana 162, T01-241 5693, www.adventures

house.com. Rooms for up to 4 people, with bath and hot water, free internet access, national calls, pleasant, quiet, a short walk from all main facilities, airport transfer, use of kitchen, bike rental US$15/day. Associated with **Fly Adventures**, see Paragliding, below.

F pp Albergue Verde, Grimaldo del Solar 459, T01-445 3816, www.albergueverde.com. Nice small hostel, comfortable beds, **C pp** in double, friendly owner, Arturo Palmer, breakfast included, airport transfers US$15.

F pp Explorer's House, Av Alfredo León 158, by 10th block of Av José Pardo, T01-241 5002, explorers_house@yahoo.es. No sign, but plenty of indications of the house number, with breakfast, dormitory with shared bath, or double rooms with bath, hot water, use of kitchen, laundry service, Spanish classes, English spoken, very welcoming.

F pp Flying Dog Backpackers, Diez Canseco 117, T01-445 6745, www.flyingdog.esmart web.com. Dormitories or private rooms, shared bath (**D-E** in en suite), very popular so reserve online, central, comfortable, hot water, secure, free internet and local calls, book exchange, kitchen. Books onward tickets.

F Friend's House, Jr Manco Cápac 368, T01-446 6248, friendshouse_peru@yahoo.com.mx. Dormitories with hot water, cable TV, use of kitchen, includes breakfast, very popular with backpackers, near Larcomar shopping centre, plenty of information. Highly recommended. Another branch at José Gonzales 427, T01-446 3521. **E pp** with bath, same facilities, but private rooms and more like a family home.

F pp Loki Backpackers (formerly Incahaus), Av Larco 189, T01-242 4350, www.loki hostel.com. Restored house built in the 1920s, with period details but modern facilities. The capital's sister to the party hostel of the same name in Cuzco, **D** in double room, good showers, with breakfast (cooked breakfast extra), Fri barbecues, use of kitchen, free internet, lockers, airport transfer extra.

F pp Stop and Drop, Berlín 168, p2, T01-243 3101, www.stopandrop.com. **D** double rooms with private bath. Backpacker hotel and guest house, also Spanish school. Bar, kitchen facilities, luggage store, laundry, TV, movies, internet, games, comfortable beds, safe, hot showers 24 hours, adventure sports and volunteer jobs. Airport pick up US$17.

F Wayruro's Backpackers, Enrique Palacios 900, T01-444 1564, www.wayruros.com.

B&B, comfortable dorms, kitchen facilities, free tea and coffee, cheap bar, 24-hr hot water, laundry service, luggage storage, internet, TV, airport pick-up.

Youth hostel

F pp Albergue Turístico Juvenil Internacional, Av Casimiro Ulloa 328, San Antonio, T01-446 5488, www.limahostell.com.pe. Dormitory rooms or **D** doubles, basic cafeteria, travel information, laundry facilities, extra charge for use of kitchen, swimming pool often empty, safe, situated in a nice villa; 20 mins walk from the beach. Bus No 2 or *colectivos* pass Av Benavides to the centre; taxi to centre, US$2.50.

Barranco *p68*

C Domeyer, Calle Domeyer 296, T01-247 1413, domeyerhostel@peru.com. Hot water 24 hrs, laundry, secure, welcomes gay-friendly.

D-E La Quinta de Alison, Av 28 de Julio 281, T01-247 1515. Breakfast extra, modern, lovely rooms with TV and bath, hot water, some rooms with jacuzzi, excellent value, parking.

E Safe in Lima, Alfredo Silva 150, T01-252 7330, www.safeinlima.com. Quiet, Belgian-run hostal with family atmosphere in new premises, with breakfast, very helpful, airport pick-up US$14, good value, reserve in advance, lots of information for travellers.

F pp Barranco's Backpackers Inn, Malecón Castilla 260, T01-247 1326, www.barranco backpackers.com. All rooms shared, with lockers, hot water in bathrooms, breakfast included. **D** for double room, kitchen, laundry service, internet access, modern.

F pp Mochileros Hostal, Av Pedro de Osma 135, 1 block from main plaza, T01-447 4506, backpackers@backpackersperu.com. Beautiful house, English-speaking owner, huge shared rooms with lockers, gay friendly, use of kitchen, good pub on the premises, a stone's throw from Barranco nightlife.

F pp The Point, Malecón Junín 300, T01-247 7997, www.thepointhostels.com. Doubles and dormitories, all with shared bath, very popular with backpackers (book in advance at weekends), breakfast included, internet, cable TV, laundry, kitchen, gay-friendly, party atmosphere, **The Pointless Pub** open 2000 till whenever, weekly barbecues, therapeutic massage next door, can arrange bungee jumping, flight tickets and volunteering.

🍴 Eating

19% state tax and 10% service will be added to your bill in middle and upper class restaurants. Chinese *chifas* are often the cheapest at around US$5 including a drink.

Central Lima p61, map p62

Just behind the Municipalidad de Lima is Pasaje Nicolás de Rivera el Viejo, which has been restored and is now a pleasant place to hang out, with several good cafés with outdoor seating. There are many highly recommended *chifas* in the district of Barrios Altos (China town).

🍴 **Antaño**, Ucayali 332, opposite the Torre Tagle Palace, T01-426 2372. Good, typical Peruvian food, nice patio. Recommended.

🍴 **L'Eau Vive**, Ucayali 370, also opposite the Torre Tagle Palace, T01-427 5612. Run by nuns, Mon-Sat, 1230-1500, 1930-2130, fixed-price lunch menu, Peruvian-style in interior dining room, or à la carte in either of dining rooms that open onto patio, excellent, profits go to the poor, Ave Maria is sung at 2100.

🍴 **Manhattan**, Jr Miró Quesada 259, Mon-Fri 0700-1900, low end executive-type restaurant, local and international food US$5-10, good.

🍴 **Wa Lok**, Jr Paruro 864, Barrios Altos, T01-427 2656. English spoken, very friendly. Another branch at Av Angamos Oeste 703, T01-447 1280, good food in a tasteful, modern setting, 🍴🍴-🍴.

🍴-🍴 **San Martín**, Av Nicolás de Piérola 890, off Plaza San Martín. Typical Peruvian food from both coast and highlands, good value, reasonably cheap.

🍴 **Centro de Medicina Natural**, Jr Chota 1462, next door to *Hostal de las Artes*. Very good vegetarian.

🍴 **Cordano**, Jr Ancash 202. Typical old Lima restaurant/watering hole, slow service and a bit grimy but full of character. Definitely worth the time it takes to drink a few beers.

🍴 **Govinda**, Av Garcilaso de la Vega 1670, opposite Gran Parque de Lima. Vegetarian, also sells natural products, good.

🍴 **Natur**, Moquegua 132, 1 block from Jr de la Unión, T01-427 8281. Vegetarian, the owner, Humberto Valdivia, is also president of the South American Explorers' board of directors, good for food and casual conversation.

🍴 **Neydi**, Puno 367, daily 1100-2000. Good, cheap seafood, popular.

🍴 **Salon Capon**, Jr Paruro 819, Barrios Altos. Very good. Has another branch in Larcomar shopping centre, Miraflores, which is 🍴🍴🍴, elegant.

Cafés

🍴 **Café Carrara**, Jr Ica 330, attached to Hostal Roma, daily until 2200, multiple breakfast combinations, pancakes, sandwiches, nice ambience, good.

Pueblo Libre p65

🍴🍴🍴-🍴🍴 **Café del Museo** at the Museo Larco, Av Bolívar 1515, T01-461 1312, www.cafedelmuseo.com, daily 0900-1800. Seating inside and on the terrace. Specially designed interior, selection of salads, fine Peruvian dishes, pastas and seafood, a tapas bar of Peruvian foods, as well as snacks, desserts and cocktails. Highly regarded.

🍴🍴-🍴 **Antigua Taberna Quierolo**, Av San Martín 1090, 1 block from Plaza Bolívar. Atmospheric old bar with glass-fronted shelves of bottles, marble bar and old photos, owns bodega next door. Serves simple lunches, sandwiches and snacks, good for wine, does not serve dinner.

San Isidro p66

🍴🍴🍴 **Alfresco**, Santa Lucía 295 (no sign), T01-422 8915. Best known for its tempting seafood and *ceviche*, also pastas and rice dishes, expensive wines.

🍴🍴🍴 **Antica Pizzería**, Av Dos de Mayo 728, T01-222 8437. Very popular, great ambience, excellent food, Italian owner. Also Antica Trattoria in Barranco at Alfonso Ugarte 242, and an excellent bar, Antica Taberna, with a limited range of food at Conquistadores 605, San Isidro, very good value, fashionable, get there early for a seat.

🍴🍴🍴 **Asia de Cuba**, Conquistadores 780, T01-222 4940. Popular, with a mix of Asian, Cuban and Peruvian dishes. It also has a reputation for its bar and nightclub; try the martinis.

🍴🍴🍴 **Matsuei**, Calle Manuel Bañon 260, T01-422 4323. Sushi bar and Japanese dishes, very popular, among the best Japanese in Lima.

🍴🍴🍴 **Valentino**, Manuel Bañon 215, T01-441 6174. One of Lima's best international restaurants, formal, look for the tiny brass sign.

🍴🍴 **Chez Philippe**, Av 2 de Mayo 748, T01-222 4953. Pizza, pasta and crêpes, wood oven, rustic decor.

¶¶ **Segundo Muelle**, Av Conquistadores 490, T01-421 1206, and Av Canaval y Moreyra (aka Corpac) 605. Excellent *ceviche* and seafood dishes, popular with the younger crowd.

Cafés

Café Olé, Pancho Fierro 115 (1 block from Hotel El Olívar). Huge selection of entrées and desserts, very smart with prices to match.
Café Positano/Café Luna, Miguel Dasso 147. Popular with politicians, café and bistro.
News Café, Av Santa Luisa 110. Great salads and desserts, popular and expensive.

Miraflores *p66, map p67*

Calle San Ramón, known as 'Pizza Street' (across from Parque Kennedy), is a pedestrian walkway lined with outdoor restaurants/bars/discotheques open until the small hours of the morning. It's very popular, with good-natured touts trying to entice diners and drinkers with free offers.

¶¶¶ **Astrid y Gaston**, Cantuarias 175, T01-444 1496. Exceptional local/Novo Andino and international cuisine, one of the best in Lima, owners are Gastón Acurio and his wife Astrid. Also has a bar.
¶¶¶ **Café Voltaire**, Av Dos de Mayo 220. International cuisine with emphasis on French dishes, beautifully-cooked food, pleasant ambience, good service, closed Sun.
¶¶¶ **Coco de Mer**, Av Grau 400, T01-243 0278, www.cocodemerlima.com, daily 1200 till whenever. Run by English Lucy Ralph, popular, Mediterranean and Peruvian dishes, cocktails, events.
¶¶¶ **El Kapallaq**, Av Petit Thouars 4844, T01-444 4149, Mon-Fri 1200-1700. Prize-winning Peruvian restaurant specializing in seafood and fish, excellent *ceviches*.
¶¶¶ **El Señorio de Sulco**, Malecón Cisneros 1470, T01-441 0183, http://senoriode sulco.com. Overlooking a clifftop park, with ocean views from upstairs. Forget the Footprint grading, this is a '5-fork' restaurant which some believe is the best in Lima, all Peruvian food, à la carte and buffet, piscos, wines, piano music at night.
¶¶¶ **Huaca Pucllana**, Gral Borgoña cuadra 8 s/n, alt cuadra 45 Av Arequipa, T01-445 4042. Facing the archaeological site of the same name, contemporary Peruvian fusion cooking, very good food in an unusual setting, popular, caters for groups, has live music and dancing.

¶¶¶ **Las Brujas de Cachiche**, Av Bolognesi 460, T01-447 1883. An old mansion converted into bars and dining rooms, traditional food (menu in Spanish and English), best Lomo Saltado in town, live *criollo* music.
¶¶¶ **Las Tejas**, Diez Canseco 340, daily 1100-2300. Good, typical Peruvian food, recommended for ceviche.
¶¶¶ **Rosa Náutica**, T01-445 0149, www.larosa nautica.com, daily 1230-0200. Built on old British-style pier (Espigón No 4), in Lima Bay. Delightful opulence, finest fish cuisine, experience the atmosphere by buying an expensive beer in the bar at sunset.
¶¶¶ **Sí Señor**, Bolognesi 706, T01-445 3789, www.sisenor.org. Mexican food, cheerful, interesting decor, huge portions.
¶¶ **Café Tarata**, Pasaje Tarata 260. Good atmosphere, family-run, good varied menu.
¶¶ **Dalmacia**, San Fernando 401. Spanish-owned, casual gourmet restaurant, excellent.
¶¶ **Il Postino**, Colina 401, T01-446 8381. Great Italian food.
¶¶ **La Palachinke**, Av Schell 120 at the bottom of Parque Kennedy. Recommended pancakes.
¶¶ **Ricota**, Pasaje Tarata 248. Charming café on a pedestrian walkway, huge menu and big portions.
¶ **Dino's Pizza**, Av Cdte Espinar 374 and many other branches. Great pizza at a good price, delivery service.
¶ **El Parquetito**, Diez Canseco 150. Good cheap menu, serves breakfast, eat inside or out.
¶ **Madre Natura**, Chiclayo 815. Natural foods shop and eating place, very good, closes 2100.
¶ **Sandwich.com**, Av Diagonal 234. Good, cheap sandwiches with interesting combinations of fillings.

Cafés

Café Café, Martin Olaya 250, near the Parque Kennedy roundabout. Very popular, good atmosphere, over 100 different blends of coffee, good salads and sandwiches, very popular with 'well-to-do' Limeños. Also in Larcomar.
Café de la Paz, Lima 351, middle of Parque Kennedy. Good outdoor café right on the park, expensive, great cocktails.
Café Zeta, Mcal Oscar R Benavides 598 y José Gálvez. American owned, excellent Peruvian coffee, teas, hot chocolate, and the best homemade cakes away from home, cheap too.

C'est Si Bon, Av Cdte Espinar 663. Excellent cakes by the slice or whole, best in Lima.

Dove Vai, Diagonal 228. A bright *heladería* in this block of eating places; try the *encanto* with lumps of chocolate brownie.

Haiti, Av Diagonal 160, Parque Kennedy. Open almost round the clock daily, great for people watching, good ice cream.

Heladería 4D, Angamos Oeste 408. Open 1000-0100 daily, Italian ice cream, at other locations throughout Lima.

La Tiendecita Blanca, Av Larco 111 on Parque Kennedy. One of Miraflores' oldest, expensive, good people-watching, very good cakes, European-style food and delicatessen.

San Antonio, Av Angamos Oeste 1494, also Vasco Núñez de Balboa 770, Rocca de Vergallo 201, Magdalena del Mar and Av Primavera 373, San Borja. Fashionable *pastelería* chain, good, not too expensive.

Tapas Bar, Manuel Bonilla 103, T01-242 7922. Expensive but very good tapas bar behind huge wooden doors, the tapas are a meal in themselves, extensive wine list, reserve a table at weekends.

Vivaldi, Av Ricardo Palma 260, 1 block from Parque Kennedy. Good, expensive, reminiscent of a gentlemen's club. Also **Vivaldi Gourmet**, Conquistadores 212, San Isidro, an international restaurant.

Zugatti, Av Larco 361, across from Parque Kennedy. Good Italian gelato.

Barranco *p68*

♦♦♦ **La Costa Verde**, on Barranquito beach, T01-441 3086, daily 1200-2400. Excellent fish and wine, expensive but recommended as the best by Limeños, Sun buffet.

♦♦♦ **Manos Morenas**, Av Pedro de Osma 409, T01-467 0421, open 1230-1630, 1900-2300, creole cuisine with shows some evenings (cover charge for shows).

♦♦♦ **Ñaylamp**, Av 2 de Mayo 239, T01-467 5011. Good seafood and *ceviche*, a fashionable restaurant.

♦♦ **El Hornito**, Av Grau 209, corner of main plaza, T01-477 2465. Pizzería and creole food.

♦♦ **Festín**, Av Grau 323, T01-247 7218. Huge menu, typical and international food.

♦♦ **Las Mesitas**, Av Grau 341, open 1200-0200. Traditional tea rooms-cum-restaurant, serving creole food and old sweet dishes which you won't find anywhere else.

♦ Bars and clubs

Central Lima *p61, map p62*

The centre of town, specifically Jr de la Unión, has many discos. It's best to avoid the nightspots around the intersection of Av Tacna, Av Piérola and Av de la Vega. These places are rough and foreigners will receive much unwanted attention.

For latest recommendations for gay and lesbian places, check out www.gayperu.com, www.deambiente.com and http://lima.queer city.info/index.html.

El Rincón Cervecero, Jr de la Unión (Belén) 1045. German pub without the beer, fun.

Estadio Futbol Sports Bar, Av Nicolás de Piérola 926 on the Plaza San Martín, T01-428 8866. Beautiful bar with a disco on the bottom floor, international football theme, good international and creole food.

Piano Bar Munich, Jr de la Unión 1044, (basement). Small and fun.

San Isidro *p66*

Palos de Moguer, Av Emilio Cavenecia 129, T01-221 8363. Brews 4 different kinds of beer, typical bar food.

Punto G, Av Conquistadores 512. Very popular, really small.

Miraflores *p66, map p67*

Barcelona, in Larcomar, T01-445 4823. One of the best pubs in the city.

Media Naranja, Schell 130, at the bottom of Parque Kennedy. Brazilian bar with typical drinks and food.

Murphys, Schell 627. Great Irish pub, "a must", also doing food such as fish'n'chips.

The Old Pub, San Ramón 295 (Pizza Street). Cosy, with live music most days.

Voluntarios Pub, Independencia 131, T01-445 3939, www.voluntariospub.org. All staff are volunteers from non-profit organizations which benefit by receiving 90% of the profits made by the pub. Good atmosphere, music and drinks, nice to know that while you are partying other people are benefiting.

Barranco *p68*

Barranco is the capital of Lima nightlife. The following is a short list of some of the better bars and clubs. Pasaje Sánchez Carrión, off the main plaza, used to be the heart of it all. Watering holes and discos line both sides of this pedestrian walkway, but crowds and noise are driving people elsewhere. Some places have been closed for safety reasons. Av Grau, just across the street from the plaza, is also lined with bars. Many of the bars in this area turn into discos as the evening goes on.

Bosa Nova, Bolognesi 660. Chilled student-style bar with good music.

El Dragón, N de Piérola 168, T01-797 1033, dragoncultural@hotmail.com. Popular bar and venue for music, theatre and painting.

El Grill de Costa Verde, part of the *Costa Verde* restaurant on Barranco beach. Young crowd, packed at weekends.

Juanitos, Av Grau, opposite park. Barranco's oldest bar, and perfect to start the evening.

La Noche, Bolognesi 307, at Pasaje Sánchez Carrión. A Lima institution and high standard, live music, Mon is jazz night, kicks off around 2200 (also in Central Lima).

La Posada del Angel, three branches on Pedro de Osma between 164 and 222. These are popular bars serving snacks and meals.

Sargento Pimienta, Bolognesi 755. Live music, always a favourite with Limeños. Opposite is the relaxed **Trinidad**.

⊕ Entertainment

Lima *p55, maps p58, p62 and p67*
Cinema

The newspaper *El Comercio* has cinema listings in the section called *Luces*. Most charge US$2 in the centre and around US$4-5 in Miraflores; 2 tickets for the price of one often offered on Tue. The cultural institutions (see Directory, below) usually show films once a week. Most films are in English with Spanish subtitles.

Peñas

De Cajón, Calle Merino 2nd block, near 6th block of Av Del Ejército, Miraflores. Good *música negra*.

Del Carajo, San Ambrosio 328, Barranco, T01-241 7977. All types of traditional music.

La Candelaria, Av Bolognesi 292, Barranco, T01-247 1314, Fri-Sat from 2130. A good Barranco *peña*.

La Estación de Barranco, Pedro de Osma 112, T01-477 5030. Good, family atmosphere.

Las Brisas de Titicaca, Pasaje Walkuski 168, at 1st block of Av Brasil near Plaza Bolognesi, T01-332 1881, www.brisasdeltiticaca.com. A Lima institution.

Peña Poggi, Av Luna Pizarro 578, Barranco, T01-247 5790/885 7619. Over 30 years old, traditional.

Sachun, Av Del Ejército 657, Miraflores, T01-441 0123. Great shows on weekdays as well.

Theatre

There are many theatres in the city, some of which are related to cultural centres (see Directory, below). The press gives details of performances. Theatre and concert tickets booked through **Teleticket**, T01-610 8888, Mon-Fri 0900-1900, www.e-teleticket.com.

⊛ Festivals and events

Lima *p55, maps p58, p62 and p67*
18 Jan Founding of Lima. Semana Santa (Holy Week) has colourful processions.
28-29 Jul Independence, with music and fireworks in the Plaza de Armas on the evening before.
Oct The month of **Our Lord of the Miracles**; see Las Nazarenas church, page 63.

⊙ Shopping

Lima *p55, maps p58, p62 and p67*
Bookshops

Crisol, Ovalo Gutiérrez, Av Santa Cruz 816, San Isidro, T01-221 1010, Below **Cine Planet**. Large bookshop with café, titles in English, French and Spanish.

Ibero Librerías, Av Diagonal 500, T01-242 2798, Larco 199, T01-445 5520, and in Larcomar, Miraflores. Stocks Footprint guides as well as a wide range of other titles.

Special Book Services, Av Angamos Oeste 301, Miraflores, T01-241 8490, www.sbs.com.pe. Stocks books in several languages. Branches in San Isidro and Surquillo.

Camping equipment

It's better to bring all camping and hiking gear from home. Camping gas (in small blue bottles) is available from any large hardware store or bigger supermarket, about US$3.

Alpamayo, Av Larco 345, Miraflores at Parque Kennedy, T01-445 1671, Mon-Fri 0800-1330, 1430-2000, Sat 1000-1400. Sleeping mats, boots, rock shoes, climbing gear, water filters, tents, backpacks etc, very expensive but top quality equipment. The owner speaks fluent English and offers good information.

Camping Center, Av Benavides 1620, Miraflores, T01-242 1779, Mon-Fri 0800-1330, 1430-2000, Sat 1000-1400. Tents, backpacks, stoves, camping and climbing gear.
Minex, Gral Borgoño 394, Miraflores, T01-445 3923 (ring bell). Quality camping gear for all types of weather, made to order products.
Todo Camping, Av Angamos Oeste 350, Miraflores, near Av Arequipa, T01-447 6279. Sells 100% deet, bluet gas canisters, lots of accessories, tents, crampons and backpacks.

Handicrafts

Many artisans have come to Lima and it is possible to find any kind of handicraft in the capital. Miraflores is a good place for high quality, expensive handicrafts; there are many shops on and around Av La Paz.
Agua y Tierra, Diez Canseco 298 y Alcanfores, Miraflores, T01-444 6980. Fine crafts and indigenous art.
Alpaca 111, Av Larco 671, Miraflores, T01-447 1623, www.alpaca111.com. High-quality alpaca, baby alpaca and vicuña items.
Artesanía Santo Domingo, Plaza Santo Domingo, by the church of that name, in Lima centre, T01-428 9860. Good Peruvian crafts.
Da Capo, Aramburú 920, dpto 402, San Isidro, T01-441 0714. Beautiful alpaca scarves and shawls in new designs.
Dédalo, Paseo Sáenz Peña 295, Barranco, T01-477 0562. A labyrinthine shop selling furniture, jewellery and other items, as good as a gallery. Nice coffee shop and cinema.
Ilaria, Av 2 de Mayo 308, San Isidro, T01-221 8575. Jewellery and silverware with interesting designs. There are other branches in Lima, Cuzco and Arequipa. Recommended. On Calle La Esperanza, Miraflores, dozens of shops offer gold and silverware at reasonable prices.
Kuntur Wasi, Ocharan 182, Miraflores, T01-444 0557. English-speaking owner very knowledgeable about Peruvian textiles, often has exhibitions of fine folk art and crafts.
La Casa de la Mujer Artesana, Juan Pablo Ferandini 1550 (Av Brasil cuadra 15), Pueblo Libre, T01-423 8840, www.casadelamujer artesana.com. A cooperative run by the Movimiento Manuela Ramos, excellent quality work mostly from *pueblos jóvenes*.
Las Pallas, Cajamarca 212, 5th block of Av Grau, Barranco, T01-477 4629, Mon-Sat 0900-1900. Very high quality handicrafts.

Luz Hecho a Mano, Berlín 399, Miraflores, T01-446 7098, www.luzhechoamano.com. Lovely hand made handbags, wallets and other leather goods including clothing that last for years and can be custom made.

Maps

Instituto Geográfico Nacional, Av Aramburú 1190, Surquillo, T01-475 3030, ext 119, www.ignperu.gob.pe. Topographical maps of the whole country, mostly 1:100,000, political and physical maps of all departments and satellite and aerial photographs. It also has a new series of tourist maps for trekking, eg of the Cordillera Blanca, Cuzco area, at 1:250,000.
Lima 2000, Av Arequipa 2625, Lince (near the intersection with Av Javier Prado), T01-440 3486, www.lima2000.com.pe. Excellent street map of Lima (the only one worth buying), US$10, or US$14. Provincial maps and a country road map. Good for road conditions and distances, perfect for driving or cycling.

Markets

All are open 7 days a week until late.
Av Petit Thouars, Miraflores, blocks 51-54 (near Parque Kennedy, parallel to Av Arequipa). A crafts market area with a large courtyard and lots of small flags. This is the largest crafts arcade in Miraflores. From here to Calle Ricardo Palma the street is lined with crafts markets.
Parque Kennedy, the main park of Miraflores, hosts a daily crafts market from 1700-2300.
Polvos Azules, on García Naranjo, La Victoria, just off Av Grau in the centre of town. The 'official' black market, sells just about anything; it is generally cheap and very interesting; beware pickpockets.

Supermarkets

Lima's supermarkets are well stocked and carry a decent supply of imported goods.

▲▲ Activities and tours

Lima *p55, maps p58, p62 and p67*
Cycling
Best Internacional, Av Cdte Espinar 320, Miraflores, T01-446 4044, Mon-Sat 1000-1400, 1600-2000. Sells leisure and racing bikes, also repairs, parts and accessories.
Biclas, Av Conquistadores 641, San Isidro, T01-440 0890. Knowledgeable staff, tours,

good selection of bikes, repairs and accessories, cheap airline boxes for sale.

BikeMavil, Av Aviación 4023, Surco, T01-449 8435. Rental service, repairs, excursions, selection of mountain and racing bicycles.

Casa Okuyama, Manco Cápac 590, La Victoria, T01-330 9131. Repairs, parts, try here for 28-in tyres, excellent service.

Perú Bike, Parque Nueva Castilla, Calle A, D-7, Surco, T01-449 5234, www.perubike.com. Experienced in leading tours, professional guiding, mountain bike school and workshop.

Willy Pro (Williams Arce), Av Javier Prado Este 3339, San Borja, T01-346 4082, Mon-Sat 0800-2000. Selection of specialized bikes, helpful.

Mountaineering

Asociación de Andinismo de la Universidad de Lima, Universidad de Lima, Javier Prado Este s/n, T01-437 6767. Meetings on Wed 1800-2000, offers climbing courses.

Club de Montañeros Américo Tordoya, Francisco Graña 378, Magdalena, T01-460 6101, http://es.geocities.com/clubamerico tordoya. Meetings Thu 2000, contact Gonzalo Menacho. Climbing excursions ranging from easy to difficult.

Trekking and Backpacking Club, Jr Huáscar 1152, Jesús María, Lima 11, T01-423 2515, 9987 4193 (mob), www.angelfire.com/mi2/ tebac. Sr Miguel Chiri Valle, treks arranged, including in the Cordillera Blanca.

Paragliding

Fly Adventure, Cesareo Chacaltana 162 (Hogar del Mochilero), Miraflores, T01-241 5693, www.flyadventuresperu.com. US$40 for 15-min tandem flight, 1-day course US$80, 7-day course US$450. Recommended.

Surfing

Focus, Leonardo Da Vinci 208, San Borja, T01-475 8459. Shaping factory and surf boards, knowledgeable about local spots and conditions, rents boards.

Klimax, José González 488, Miraflores, T01-447 1685. Sells new and second-hand boards, knowledgeable.

Segundo, T9902 7112, or write to segundodurangarcia@hotmail.com. Contact in advance to buy Australian-made boards.

Wayo Whiler, Av 28 de Julio 287, Barranco, T01-247 6343, www.wayowhilar.com.pe. Makes all kinds of boards, sells clothing and materials, rentals and repairs, email in advance to have a board ready for when you arrive, can also organize excursions and runs a surf school with his brother (US$100 per month).

Tour operators

Do not conduct business anywhere other than in the agency's office and insist on a written contract. Bus offices or the airport are not the places to arrange and pay for tours. You may be dealing with representatives of companies that either do not exist or which fall far short of what is paid for.

Most of those in Lima specialize in selling air tickets, or in setting up a connection tour agencies around the country. It is cheaper to use a travel agent in the town closest to the place you wish to visit. Shop around and compare prices; check information carefully.

The MITINCI certify guides and can provide a list of private guides. Most are members of AGOTUR, La Venturosa 177, Surco, T01-448 5167, agoturlima@ yahoo.com. Book in advance. Most guides speak a language other than Spanish.

Andean Tours, Schell 319 oficina 304-305, Miraflores, T01-444 8665, www.andean-tours.com. Recommended for bespoke tours.
AQP, Los Castaños 347, San Isidro, T01-222 3312, www.saaqp.com.pe. Comprehensive service, tours offered throughout Peru.
Aracari Travel Consulting, Av Pardo 610, No 802, Miraflores, T01-242 6673, www.aracari.com. Regional tours of Peru, also 'themed' and activity tours. Good reputation.
Class Adventure Travel (CAT), San Martin 800, Miraflores; also Centro Comercial Sol Plaza, Av El Sol 948, Office 311, Cuzco, T1-512 535 5263, www.cat-travel.com, . Dutch-owned and run, one of the best, with 11 years experience of tailor-made travel solutions throughout the continent.
Coltur, Av Reducto 1255, Miraflores, T01-615 5555, www.coltur.com.pe. Very helpful, experienced and well-organized tours.
Dasatariq, Jr Francisco Bolognesi 510, Miraflores, T01-447 7772, www.dasatariq.com. Also in Cuzco. A well-organized company with a good reputation and helpful staff.
Domiruth Travel Service S.A.C, Jr Rio de Janeiro 216-218, Miraflores, Lima 18, T01-610 6000, www.domiruth.com.pe. Tours all over Peru, from the mystical to adventure travel. American Express travel service.
Explorandes, Calle San Fernando 320, T01-445 0532, www.explorandes.com. Award-winning company. Offers a wide range of adventure and cultural tours throughout the country. Also offices in Cuzco and Huaraz.
Fertur Perú, see Ins and outs, page 60.
InkaNatura Travel, Manuel Bañon 461, San Isidro, T01-420 2022, www.inkanatura.com. Also in Cuzco and Chiclayo, offers good tours with knowledgeable guides, special emphasis on sustainable tourism and conservation.

Lima Tours, Jr Belén 1040, Lima centre, T01-619 6900, www.limatours.com.pe. Recommended for tours in the capital and around the country.
Masi Travel Sudamérica, Porta 350, Miraflores, T01-446 9094, www.masitravel.com. Tours throughout Peru, helpful website. Contact Verónika Reategui for efficient service.
Peru Expeditions, Av Arequipa 5241-504, Lima 18, T01-447 2057, www.peru-expeditions. com. Specializing in expeditions in 4WD vehicles and Andes crossings.
Peru For Less, ASTA Travel Agent #900144402, US office: T1-877-269 0309; UK office: T0203-002 0571; Peru (Lima) office: T01-272 0542, www.peruforless.com. Will meet or beat any published rates on the internet from outside Peru.
Roma Tours, Jr Ica 330, next to Hostal Roma, T/F01-427 7572, dantereyes@hotmail.com. Good and reliable. Administrator Dante Reyes is very friendly and speaks English.
Rutas del Peru SAC, Av Enrique Palacios 1110, Miraflores, T01-444 5405, www.rutasdelperu.com. Tailor-made trips and overland expeditions in trucks.
Viajes Pacífico (Gray Line), Av La Mar 163, Miraflores, T01-610 1900, www.graylineperu.com. Expanded service with tours throughout Peru and within South America.
Victor Travel Service, Jr de la Unión (Belén) 1068, T01-433 5547, 24 hr line 9335 0095/ 9958 3303, victortravelservice@terra.com.pe. Hotel reservations, free maps of Lima and Peru, Mon-Sat 0900-1800, very helpful.
Viracocha, Av Vasco Núñez de Balboa 191, Miraflores, T01-445 3986, peruviantours@viracocha.com.pe. Very helpful for flights and adventure, cultural and birdwatching tours.

🅐 Transport

Lima *p55, maps p58, p62 and p67*

Air

For airport information, see Ins and outs, page 58. At the customs area, explain that you are a tourist and that your personal effects will not be sold in Peru; items such as laptops, cameras, bicycles, climbing equipment are exempt from taxes if for personal use.

There are internal services to most destinations there are daily flights (most options are given in the text) but flights may be cancelled in the rainy season.

Airline offices
Domestic Aero Cóndor, Calle Juan de Arona 781, San Isidro, T01-614 6000. **Lan**, Av José Pardo 513, Miraflores, T01-213 8200. **LC Busre**, Los Tulipanes 218, Lince, T01-619 1300. **Star Perú**, Av José Pardo 485, Miraflores, T01-705 9000. **Taca Perú**, Av Cdte Espinar 331, Miraflores, T01-511 8222. **International** Air France-KLM, Av Alvarez Calderón 185, p 6, San Isidro, T01-213 0200, Reservations.Peru@klm.com. **American Airlines**, Av Canaval y Moreyra 390, San Isidro, and in Hotel Las Américas, Av Benavides y Av Larco, Miraflores, T01-211 7000. **Continental**, 147 Via Principal 110 of 101, Edificio Real 5, San Isidro, and in the Hotel Marriott, Av Larco 1325, Miraflores, T01-712 9230, or 0800-70030. **Delta**, Víctor Belaúnde 147, San Isidro, T01-211 9211. **Iberia**, Av Camino Real 390, p 9, San Isidro, T01-411 7800. **Lloyd Aéreo Boliviano**, Av José Pardo 231, Miraflores, T01-241 5210. **Lufthansa**, Av Jorge Basadre 1330, San Isidro, T01-442 4455, lhlim@terra.com.pe. **Tame**, Av La Paz 1631, Miraflores, T01-422 6600.

Bus
Local See Ins and outs, Getting around, page 59, for city transport.

Buses to **Miraflores**: Av Arequipa runs 52 blocks between the downtown Lima area and Parque Kennedy in Miraflores. Public transport has "Todo Arequipa" on the windscreen. When heading towards downtown from Miraflores the window sticker should say "Wilson/Tacna". To get to Parque Kennedy from downtown look on the windshield for "Larco/Schell/Miraflores," "Chorrillos/ Huaylas" or "Barranco/ Ayacucho". On Vía Expresa,

buses can be caught at Avs Tacna, Garcilaso de la Vega, Bolivia and Ugarte (faster than Av Arequipa, but watch for pickpockets). The main stop for Miraflores is Ricardo Palma, 4 blocks from Parque Kennedy.

To get to **Pachacámac**, from the Pan American Highway (southbound) take a *combi* with a sticker in the window reading "Pachacámac/ Lurín" (US$0.85). Let the driver know you want to get off at the ruins. A taxi will cost approximately US$4.30, but if you don't ask the driver to wait for you (an extra cost), finding another to take you back to Lima may be a bit tricky. For organized tours contact one of the tour agencies listed in Tour operators, above.

Long distance There are many different bus companies, but the larger ones are better organized, leave on time and do not wait until the bus is full. For prices, frequency and duration of trip, see destinations.
Note In the weeks either side of 28/29 Jul (Independence), and of the Christmas/New Year holiday, it is practically impossible to get bus tickets out of Lima, unless you book in advance. Bus prices double at these times.

Cruz del Sur, Jr Quilca 531, Lima centre, T01-431 5125, www.cruzdelsur.com.pe. This terminal has routes to many destinations in Peru with *Ideal* service, quite comfortable buses and periodic stops for food and bathroom breaks, a cheap option with a quality company. They go to: **Ica**, **Arequipa**, **Cuzco**, **Puno**, **Chiclayo**, **Trujillo**, **Chincha**, **Pisco** and **Juliaca**. The other terminal is at Av Javier Prado Este 1109, San Isidro, T01-225 6163. This terminal offers the *Imperial* service (luxury buses), more expensive and direct, with no chance of passengers in the aisle, and *Cruzero* service (super luxury buses). They go to: **Tumbes, Sullana, Huancayo, Piura, Chiclayo, Trujillo, Huaraz, Arequipa, Cuzco** and **La Paz** (change buses in Arequipa). *Imperial* buses stop at the central terminal when going north and *Ideal* buses stop at the Javier Prado terminal when going south.

The following buses are all owned and operated by **Ormeño**: *Expreso Ancash* (routes to the **Huaraz area**), *Expreso Continental* (routes to **the north**), *Expreso San Cristóbal* (to **the southeast**), and *Expreso Chinchano* (to the **south coast** and **Arequipa**). These depart from and arrive to: Av Carlos Zavala 177, Lima centre, T01-427 5679; also

Av Javier Prado Este 1059, Santa Catalina, T01-472 5000, www.grupo-ormeno.com. **Ormeño** also offers *Royal Class* and *Business Class* service to certain destinations. These buses are very comfortable with bathrooms, hostess, etc. They arrive and depart from the Javier Prado terminal, but *Business* buses stop at both terminals. Javier Prado is the best place to buy any Ormeño ticket.

Other companies include: **Transportes Atahualpa**, Jr Sandia 266, Lima Centre, T01-428 7732. Direct to **Cajamarca** continuing on to **Celendín**. CIVA, Paseo de La República 569-571, La Victoria, T01-330 4080, www.civa.com.pe. To all parts of the country. Has various levels of service, but mixed reports about this company. **Ittsa**, Paseo de la República 815, T01-423 5232. Good service to the north. **Línea**, José Gálvez 999, Lima Centre, T01-424 0836, www.transporteslinea.com.pe. To destinations in **Northern Peru**. **Móvil Tours**, Av Paseo de La República 749, Lima Centre near the national stadium, T01-332 0024 (has a second terminal at Los Olivos, very close to the airport, good for those who are short in time for a bus connection after landing in Lima). To **Huaraz** by *bus cama*, and Chachapoyas. **Oltursa**, Bauzate y Meza 644, T01-431 2395 and Aramburu 1160, Surquillo, T01-225 4499, www.oltursa.com.pe. A reputable company offering top end services to **Arequipa** and destinations in **northern Peru**, mainly at night. **PerúBus/Soyuz**, Av México 333, T01-266 1515, www.soyuz.com.pe. To **Ica** every 8 mins, well-organized. **Rodríguez**, Av Roosevelt 393, Lima Centre, T01-428 0506. **Huaraz, Caraz, Yungay, Carhuaz**. Recommended to arrive in Huaraz and then use local transport to points beyond. Good. Various levels of bus service. **Tepsa**, Javier Prado Este 1091, La Victoria, T01-470 6666, www.tepsa.com.pe, also at Lampa 1237-41, Lima 1, T01-477 5642. Services to the north and the south. Also has Terminal Delta Norte on the Panamericana Norte, with **Cruz del Sur** and **Línea**, at Av Alfredo Mendiola 5100, Urb Industrial Infantas, Los Olivos, T01-593 9000. **Wari**, Av Luna Pizarro 343, La Victoria, and Av Los Héroes 811, San Juan de Miraflores, T01-330 3543, www.expreso wari.com.pe. To **Ayacucho** and **Cuzco** via **Abancay**. **International buses** Ormeño, Av Javier Prado 1059, Santa Catalina, T01-472 1710.

To **Guayaquil** (29 hrs with a change of bus at the border, US$50), and **Quito** (38 hrs). A maximum of 20 kg is allowed. Depending on the destination, extra weight penalties range from US$1-3 per kg. **Note** International buses are more expensive than travelling from one border to another on national buses.

Warning The area around the bus terminals is very unsafe; thefts and assaults are more common in this neighbourhood than elsewhere in the city. You are strongly advised either to take a bus from a company which has a terminal away from the Carlos Zavala area (eg **Cruz del Sur**, Ormeño, CIVA), or to take a taxi to and from your bus. Make sure your luggage is well guarded and put on the right bus. It is also important not to assume that buses leave from the place where you bought the tickets. Finally, check you change very carefully when paying in cash.

Car rental

Most rental companies have an office at the airport, where you can arrange everything and pick up and leave the car. Ask to test-drive before signing the contract as quality varies. It can be much cheaper to rent a car in a town in the Sierra for a few days than to drive from Lima. Cars can be hired from: **Avis Rent A Car**, Av Javier Prado Este 5235, T01-434 1111, www.avis.com. **Budget Car Rental**, Canaval y Moreyra 569, San Isidro, T01-442 8703, www.budget.com. **Hertz** (Inka's), Av Cantuarias 160, Miraflores, T01-445 5716, www.hertz.com.pe. **National**, Av Costanera 1380, San Miguel, T01-578 7878, www.nationalcar.com. **Paz Rent A Car**, Av Diez Canseco 319, of 15, Miraflores, T01-446 4395, pazrent@latinmail.com. Prices range from US$40-60. Make sure that your car is in a locked garage at night.

Taxi

The following are taxi fares for some of the more common routes, give or take a sol. From downtown Lima to: Parque Kennedy (Miraflores), US$2.25. Museo de la Nación, US$2.25. South American Explorers, US$2.25. Archaeology Museum, US$2. Immigration, US$1.15. From Miraflores (Parque Kennedy) to: Museo de la Nación, US$2.25. Archaeology Museum, US$3. Immigration, US$2, Barranco, US$3. From outside airport terminal to centre US$3-6, San Isidro/Miraflores US$6-8.

Whatever the size or make, yellow taxis are usually the safest since they have a number, the driver's name and radio contact. A large number of taxis are white, but as driving a taxi in Lima (or for that matter, anywhere in Peru) simply requires a windshield sticker saying "Taxi", they come in all colours and sizes. Licensed and phone taxis are safest and, by law, all taxis must have the vehicle's registration number painted on the side. There are several reliable phone taxi companies, which can be called for immediate service, or booked in advance; prices are 2-3 times more than ordinary taxis; eg to the airport US$15-20, to suburbs US$7-8. Some are **Taxi América**, T01-265 1960; **Moli Taxi**, T01-479 0030; **Taxi Real**, T01-470 6263; **Taxi Tata**, T01-274 5151; **TCAM**, run by Carlos Astacio, T01-9983 9305, safe, reliable. If hiring a taxi for over 1 hr agree on price per hour beforehand. Recommended, knowledgeable drivers: **César A Canales N**, T01-436 6184, T9687 3310 (mob) or through **Home Perú**, only speaks Spanish, reliable. **Hugo Casanova Morella**, T01-485 7708 (he lives in La Victoria), for city tours, travel to airport, etc. **Mónica Velásquez Carlich**, T01-9943 0796 (mob), vc_monica@hotmail.com. For airport pick-ups, tours, speaks some English, receives many recommendations. **Note** Drivers don't expect tips; give them small change from the fare.

Train

Service on the Central Railway to Huancayo has been revived as a tourist route. Details are given under Huancayo, page 187.

ⓘ Directory

Lima *p55, maps p58, p62 and p67*
Banks ATMs are easy to find at main branches of all major banks, **BCP, Banco de Comercio, BBVA Continental, Banco Financiero, Banco Santander Central Hispano (BSCH), Interbank** and **Scotiabank**. **Citibank**, in all *Blockbuster* stores, and at Av 28 de Julio 886, Av Benavides 23rd block and Av Emilio Cavenecia 175, Miraflores, Av Las Flores 205 and branch in Centro Comercial Camino Real, Av Camino Real 348, San Isidro. **Blockbuster** branches open Sat-Sun 1000-1900. **Exchange houses** A repeatedly recommended *casa de cambio* is **LAC Dolar**,

Jr Camaná 779, 1 block from Plaza San Martín, p 2, T01-428 8127, also at Av La Paz 211, Miraflores, T01-242 4069, Mon-Sat 0930-1800, good rates, very helpful, safe, fast, reliable, 2% commission on cash and TCs (Amex, Citicorp, Thomas Cook, Visa). Another recommended *casa de cambio* is **Virgen P Socorro**, Jr Ocoña 184, T01-428 7748, daily 0830-2000, safe, reliable and friendly. There are many *casas de cambio* on and around Jr Ocoña off the Plaza San Martín. Changing money on the street should only be done with official street changers wearing an identity card with a photo. Around Parque Kennedy and down Av Larco in Miraflores are dozens of official *cambistas* with ID cards and, usually, blue, sometimes green vest. **American Express**, *Travex SA*, Av Santa Cruz 621, Miraflores, T01-710 3900, info@travex.com.pe, Mon-Fri 0830-1730, Sat 0900-1300. Replaces lost or stolen Amex cheques of any currency in the world. Or branches of **Viajes Falabella**, eg Jr Belén 630, T01-428 9779, or Av Larco 747-753, Miraflores, T01-444 4239, lgutierrez@viajesfalabella.com.pe. **Master Card**, Porta 111, p 6, Miraflores, T01-311 6000. **Cultural centres** Alianza Francesa, Av Arequipa 4595, Miraflores, T01-446 5524, www.alianza francesalima.edu.pe. Various cultural activities, library. **British Council**, Torre Parque Mar, p 22, Av José Larco 1301, T01-617 3060, www.britishcouncil.org/peru.htm. **CCPUCP** (cultural centre of the Universidad Católica), Camino Real 1075, San Isidro, T01-616 1616, http://cultural.pucp.edu.pe. Excellent theatre, European art films (US$1.45 Mon-Wed), galleries, good café and a bookshop selling art and literature titles. Recommended. **Goethe Institute**, Jr Nazca 722, Jesús María, T01-433 3180, www.goethe.de/hn/lim/deindex.htm. **Instituto Cultural Peruano-Norteamericano**, Jr Cuzco 446, Lima Centre, T01-428 3530, with library. Central office at Av Angamos Oeste 120, Miraflores, T01-242 6300, www.icpna. edu.pe. Theatre, dance, Spanish lessons and more. **Embassies and consulates** During the summer, most embassies only open in the morning. **Australia**, Av Víctor Andrés Belaúnde 147, Vía Principal 155, Ed Real 3, of 1301, San Isidro, Lima 27, T01-222 8281, info.peru@ austrade.gov.au. **Bolivian Consulate**, Los Castaños 235, San Isidro, T01-442 3836, postmast@emboli.org.pe (0900-1330), 24 hrs for visas. **Canada**, Libertad 130, Casilla

18-1126, Lima, T01-444 4015, lima@ dfait-maeci.gc.ca. **Ecuadorean Consulate**, Las Palmeras 356, San Isidro (6th block of Av Javier Prado Oeste), T01-440 9991, embjecua@amauta.rcp.net.pe. **France**, Arequipa 3415, San Isidro, T01-215 8400, france.embajada@computextos .com.pe. **Germany**, Av Arequipa 4202, Miraflores, T01-212 5016, emergency number 9927 8338. **Israel**, Natalio Sánchez 125, p 6, Santa Beatriz, T01-433 4431. **Netherlands Consulate**, Torre Parque Mar, Av José Larco 1301, p 13, Miraflores, T01-213 9800, info@ nlgovlim.com, Mon-Fri 0900-1200. **New Zealand Consulate**, Av Camino Real 390, Torre Central, p 17 (Casilla 3553), San Isidro, T01-221 2833, reya@nzlatam.com, Mon-Fri 0830-1300, 1400-1700. **Spain**, Jorge Basadre 498, San Isidro, T01-212 5155, open 0900-1300. **Switzerland**, Av Salaverry 3240, Magdalena, Lima 17, T01-264 0305, embsuiza@correo.tnet com.pe. **UK**, Torre Parque Mar, p 22, T01-617 3000, www.britishembassy.gov.uk/peru, open 1300-2130 (Dec-Apr to 1830 Mon and Fri, and Apr-Nov to 1830 Fri). **USA**, Av Encalada block 17, Surco, T01-434 3000, for emergencies after hrs T01-434 3032, http://lima.usembassy.gov. **Internet** Lima is completely inundated with internet cafés, so you will have absolutely no problem finding one regardless of where you are. An hour will cost you S/2-3 (US$0.60-0.90).

Language schools Conexus, Av Paseo de la República 3195, of 1002, San Isidro, T01-421 5642, www.conexusinstitute.com. Reasonably priced and effective. **Instituto Cultural Peruano-Norteamericano**, see Cultural centres, above. Classes Mon-Fri 0900-1100, US$80 per month. **Instituto de Idiomas (Pontífica Universidad Católica del Perú)**, Av Camino Real 1037, San Isidro, T01-442 8761. Classes Mon-Fri 1100-1300, private lessons possible. Recommended. **Esit Idiomas**, Av Javier Prado Este 4457, Lima 33, T01-434 1060, www.esit-peru.com. **El Sol School of Languages**, Grimaldo del Solar 469, Miraflores, T01-242 7763, www.elsol. idiomasperu.com. US$15 per hr for private tuition, small groups US$11 per hr. Also family homestay and volunteer programmes. Independent teachers can be contacted thorugh peruidiomas@latinmail.com.

Recommended are: **Sra Lourdes Gálvez**, **Sra Georgelina Sadastizágal**, **Sr Mariano Herrera** and **Sr Dante Herrera**. Also try **Srta Susy Arteaga**, T01-534 9289, susyarteaga@ hotmail.com, or susyarteaga@ yahoo.com. Recommended. **Srta Patty Félix**, T01-521 2559, patty_fel24@yahoo.com. **Luis Villanueva**, T01-247 7054, www.acspanish classes.com. Flexible, reliable, helpful.

Medical services Contact your consulate for recommendations. **Hospitals: Instituto de Medicina Tropical**, Av Honorio Delgado near the Pan American Highway in the Cayetano Heredia Hospital, San Martín de Porres, T01-482 3903. Good for check-ups after jungle travel. Recommended. **International Health Department**, at Jorge Chávez airport, T01-517 1845. Open 24 hrs a day for vaccinations. **Backpackers Medical Care**, T01-9735 2668, backpackersmc@yahoo.com. The `backpackers' medic', Dr Jorge Bazán, is recommended, US$13 per consultation. **Pharmacy:** Pharmacy chains are modern, well-stocked and very professional. They can be found throughout the city, often in or next to supermarkets. **Post office** The central post office is on Jr Camaná 195 in the centre of Lima near Plaza de Armas, Mon-Fri 0730-1900 and Sat 0730-1600. In Miraflores the main post office is on Av Petit Thouars 5201 (same hours). There are many small branches but they are less reliable. For express service: **EMS**, next to central post office in downtown Lima, T01-533 2020. **Telephone** Easiest to use are the many independent phone offices, *locutorios*, all over the city. They take phone cards, which can be bought in *locutorios*, or in the street nearby. There are payphones all over the city. Some accept coins, some only phone cards and some both. **Useful addresses** Tourist Police, Jr Moore 268, Magdalena at the 38th block of Av Brasil, T01-460 1060, open 24 hrs. For public enquiries, Jr Pachitea at the corner of Belén (Jr de la Unión), Lima, T01-424 2053. They are friendly and very helpful, English spoken. Visit them if you have property stolen. **Immigration:** Av España 700 y Jr Huaraz, Breña, open 0900-1330. For visa extensions. Provides new entry stamps if passport is lost or stolen. **Intej**, Av San Martín 240, Barranco, T01-477 2846, extends student cards and can change student flight itineraries.

Cuzco and the Sacred Valley

✽ Footprint features

Introduction

Cuzco stands at the head of the Sacred Valley of the Incas and is the jumping-off point for the Inca Trail and famous Inca city of Machu Picchu. It's not surprising, therefore, that this is the prime destination for the vast majority of Peru's visitors. In fact, what was once an ancient Inca capital is now the 'gringo' capital of the entire continent. And it's easy to see why. There are Inca ruins aplenty, as well as fabulous colonial architecture, stunning scenery, great trekking, river rafting and mountain biking, beautiful textiles and other traditional handicrafts – all within easy reach of the nearest cappuccino or comfy hotel room.

The Spaniards transformed the centre of a magnificent Inca civilization into a jewel of colonial achievement. Yet the city today is not some dead monument; its history breathes through the stones. The Quechua people bring the city to life, with a combination of prehispanic and Christian beliefs, and every visitor is made welcome.

Starting your visit to the Cuzco region outside the city has many advantages. Staying a day or two in the valley of the Urubamba river will give you time to acclimatize to the shortage of oxygen at these altitudes. And, as nowhere is very far from the city, you can easily nip into town for any necessities. At Ollantaytambo and Pisac you will see Inca ruins and terraced hillsides without the overlay of the Spanish conquest. Then, when you are fit and ready, you can make your own assault on Cuzco and all its churches, museums, pubs, clubs and shops, not to mention the many festivals that are held throughout the year. If city life is not for you, there is no shortage of adventure. The huge influx of visitors has encouraged the opening of new trails, some for walking, some for biking, the latest hot spot being the 'lost city' of Choquequirao.

★ Don't miss …

1 **Church of San Blas** The carved pulpit is remarkable and you can get your fill of traditional crafts in the surrounding streets, page 93.

2 **Inca stonework** The Stone of 12 Angles on Calle Hatun Rumiyoc is the best example, page 94.

3 **Pisac** Walk up to the ruins; it's a stiff climb, but not only are the Inca ruins worth the effort, as you go higher the views of the Urubamba valley just get better and better, page 118.

4 **Moray** In the hills above the Urubamba, three large depressions, converted into terraced crop laboratories show to perfection the Incas' thorough understanding of their environment, page 120.

5 **Andahuaylillas** Visit the Sistine Chapel of the Andes and, nearby, the equally remarkable church at Huaro. For the best view, take a strong torch as they are poorly lit, page 127.

6 **Machu Picchu** Find the time to peer into corners, investigate angles of stones, the weight of lintels and the outlook of windows. See how rocks and openings align themselves with peaks across the valley, page 129.

7 **Choquequirao** The newest addition to the 'lost cities trail', is only reached by adventurous trekking, page 137.

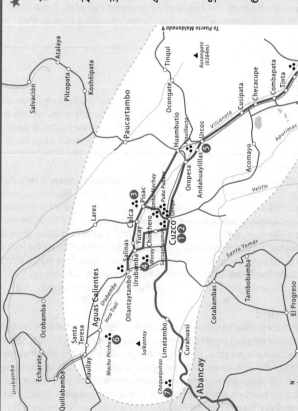

Cuzco city

→ *Colour map 2, C4. Altitude 3310 m.*

The ancient Inca capital is said to have been founded around AD 1100. According to the central Inca creation myth, the Sun sent his son, Manco Cápac, and the Moon sent her daughter, Mama Ocllo, to spread culture and enlightenment throughout the dark, barbaric lands. They emerged from the icy depths of Lake Titicaca and began their journey in search of a place where they could found their kingdom. They were ordered to head north from the lake until a golden staff they carried could be plunged into the ground for its entire length. They had to travel as far as the valley of Cuzco, on the mountain of Huanacari, until they found the sign they were looking for and the soil was suitably fertile. They named this place Cuzco, meaning 'navel of the earth'.

Today, the city's beauty cannot be overstated. It is a fascinating mix of Inca and colonial Spanish architecture: churches, monasteries and convents and pre-Columbian ruins are interspersed with hotels, bars and restaurants. Almost every central street has remains of Inca walls, arches and doorways and many are lined with Inca stonework, now serving as the foundations for more modern dwellings.

Cuzco has developed into a major commercial centre of 275,000 inhabitants, most of whom are Quechua. Despite its growth, the city is still laid out much as it was in Inca times. The Incas conceived their capital in the shape of a puma and this can be seen from above, with the Río Tullumayo forming the spine, Sacsayhuaman the head, and the main city centre the body. The best place for an overall view of the Cuzco Valley is from the hill of Sacsayhuaman. ▶▶ *For Sleeping, Eating and other listings, see pages 97-117.*

Ins and outs

Getting there

Most travellers arriving from Lima will do so by air. There are regular daily flights and none arrive at night. The **airport** ① *Quispiquilla, near the bus terminal, 1½ km southeast of the centre, T084-222611/601*, has a post office, phone booths, restaurant and cafeteria. Many hotel representatives operate at the airport and offer a free transfer. A taxi to and from the centre costs US$1-2 (US$3.50 by radio taxi). *Colectivos* cost US$0.20 and are found outside the airport car park.

All long-distance buses arrive and leave from the **Terminal Terrestre** ① *Av Vallejo Santoni, near the Pachacútec statue in Ttio district.* A *colectivo* from centre costs US$0.20; taxi US$0.60-0.85. Platform tax US$0.30. Transport to your hotel is not a problem as bus company representatives are often on hand.

There are two train stations in Cuzco. Trains from Juliaca and Puno arrive at **Estación Wanchac** ① *Calle Pachacútec, T084-221992.* A tourist bus meets the train to take visitors to hotels whose touts offer rooms on the train. Trains from Machu Picchu arrive at **Estación San Pedro** ① *opposite the Santa Ana market, T084-221313.*
▶▶ *For further details, see Transport, page 114. For trains to Machu Picchu, see page 138.*

Getting around

The centre of Cuzco is small and easily explored on foot. Remember that at this altitude walking up some of the city's steep cobbled streets may leave you out of breath, so take your time. *Combis* run 0500-2200, US$0.15, to all parts of the city, but are not allowed within 2 blocks of Plaza de Armas. Stops are signed and the driver calls out the names of stops. Taxis are cheap and recommended when arriving by air, train or bus. If you wish to explore on your own, *Road Map (Hoja de ruta) No 10* is excellent. You can get it from the **Automóvil y Touring Club del Perú.** ▶▶ *For further details, see Transport, page 115.*

⁝ Just the ticket

A combined entry ticket, called **Boleto Turístico General (BTG)**, is available to most of the main sites historical and cultural interest in and around the city, and costs 70 soles (US$21) for all the sites and valid for 10 days. One-day tickets cost 40 soles (US$12) for either the churches and museums in the city; or Qenqo, Qenqo, Puka Pukara and Tambo Machay; or Pisac, Ollantaytambo, Chinchero, Tipón and Piquillacta.

Tickets can be bought at the **OFEC** Casa Garcilaso, Plaza Regocijo, corner with Calle Garcilaso, T084-226919, Mon-Sat 0800-1600, Sun 0800-1200; Av Sol 103, T084-227037, Mon-Fri 0800-1800, Sat 0830-1230, or at any of the sites included in the ticket. There is a 50% discount for students with a green ISIC card, which is only available at the OFEC office upon

presentation of the ISIC card. Take your card when visiting the sites, as you may be asked to show it. Photography is not allowed in the churches, and museums.

Entrance tickets for the Santo Domingo/Qoricancha, the Inka Museum (El Palacio del Almirante) and La Merced are sold separately, while the cathedral and churches of El Triunfo, La Sagrada Familia, La Compañia and San Blas and the Museo de Arte Religioso del Arzobispado are included on a new religious buildings ticket which costs 36 soles (US$10) and is valid for 10 days. Machu Picchu ruins and Inca trail entrance tickets are sold at the **Instituto Nacional de Cultura (INC)** San Bernardo s/n, between Mantas y Almagro, T084-236061, Mon-Fri 0900-1300, 1600-1800, Sat 0900-1100.

Tourist information

Official tourist office ① *Portal Mantas 117-A, next to La Merced church, T084-263176, daily 0800-2000.* **i perú** ① *at the airport, T084-237364, daily 0600-1300; also at Av Sol 103, of 102, Galerías Turísticas, T084-234498, daily 0830-1930.* **Dircetur** ① *Av de la Cultura 734, 3rd floor, T084-223701, Mon-Fri 0800-1300*, gives out a good map. See box, above, for **OFEC** and **INC** offices. **South American Explorers** ① *Choquechaca 188, No 4, T084-245484, www.saexplorers.org, Mon-Fri 0930-1700, Sat 0930-1300*, is an excellent resource, only a couple of minutes' walk from the Plaza de Armas. It has great information on the Cuzco area, along with an extensive English-language library, expedition reports, maps, weekly events, flight confirmations, free internet for members, phone and mail service, equipment storage and a comprehensive recycling centre. It also has practical advice on responsible tourism and a volunteer resource centre. Its leaflet *Enjoy Cuzco Safely* is invaluable. There is also a branch in Lima, see page 58.

Safety

Police patrol the streets, train and bus stations, but one should still be vigilant. On no account walk back to your hotel after dark from a bar or club, as muggings do occur. For safety's sake, pay the US$1 taxi fare, but not just any taxi. Ask the club's doorman to get a licensed taxi for you (see Taxis, page 115). Other areas in which to be careful include Santa Ana market, San Cristóbal and at out-of-the-way ruins. If you need a *denuncia* (a report for insurance purposes, available from the Banco de la Nación), the **tourist police** ① *Calle Saphi 510, T084-249665/221961, or Ovalo de Pachacútec, T084-249654*, will type it out. Always go to the police when robbed, even though it will take a bit of time. The tourist protection bureau, **Indecopi** ① *Av Manco Inca 209, Wanchac, T084-252987/ T0800-44040, jpilco@indecopi.gob.pe*, protects the consumer rights of all tourists and helps with any problems or complaints. It can be helpful in dealing with tour agencies, hotels or restaurants.

⦂ Highlights

There are so many sights in Cuzco, that not even the most ardent tourist would be able to visit them all. For those with limited time, must-sees include: the combination of Inca and colonial architecture at Qoricancha; the huge Inca ceremonial centre of Sacsayhuaman; the paintings of the Last Supper and the 1650 earthquake in the cathedral; the main altar of La

Compañía de Jesús; the pulpit of San Blas; the high choir at San Francisco; the monstrance at La Merced; and the view from San Cristóbal. If you have the energy, catch a taxi up to the White Christ and watch the sunset as you look out upon one of the most fascinating cities in the world. If you visit one museum make it the Museo Inka; which has an excellent collection.

Sights

Plaza de Armas and around

The heart of the city in Inca days was *Huacaypata* (the place of tears) and *Cusipata* (the place of happiness), divided by a channel of the Río Saphi. Today, Huacaypata is the **Plaza de Armas** and Cusipata is **Plaza Regocijo**. This was the great civic square of the Incas, flanked by their palaces. Each territory conquered by the Incas had some of its soil taken to Cuzco to be mingled symbolically with the soil of Huacaypata, as a token of its incorporation into the empire. As well as the many great ceremonies, the plaza has seen many executions, among them the last Inca, Túpac Amaru, the rebel conquistador, Diego de Almagro the Younger, and the 18th-century indigenous leader, Túpac Amaru II.

On the northeast side of the square, the 17th-century baroque **cathedral** ① *daily 0500-1000 for worshippers, Quechua Mass at 0500-0600, tourists may visit Mon, Tue, Wed, Fri, Sat 1000-1130, 1400-1730, Thu and Sun 1400-1730*, forms part of a three-church complex: the cathedral itself, **Iglesia Jesús y María** (1733) on the left as you look at it and **El Triunfo** (1533) on the right. There are two entrances; the cathedral doors are used during Mass but the tourist entrance is on the left-hand side through Iglesia Jesús y María. The cathedral itself was built on the site of the Palace of Inca Wiracocha (*Kiswarcancha*) using stones from Sacsayhuaman.

The gleaming, renovated gilded main altar of the **Iglesia Jesús y María** draws the eyes to the end of the church. However, take the time to look up at the colourful murals which have been partially restored. The two gaudy, mirror-encrusted altars towards the front of the church are also hard to miss.

Walking through into the cathedral's transept, the oldest surviving painting in Cuzco can be seen. It depicts the 1650 earthquake. It also shows how, within only one century, the Spaniards had already divided the main plaza. *El Señor de los Temblores* (The Lord of the Earthquakes) can be seen being paraded around the Plaza de Armas, while fire rages through the colonial buildings with their typical red-tiled roofs. Much of modern-day Cuzco was built after this event. The choir stalls, by a 17th-century Spanish priest, are a fine example of colonial baroque art (80 saints and virgins are exquisitely represented), as is the elaborate pulpit. On the left is the solid-silver high altar. At the far right-hand end of the cathedral is an interesting local painting of the Last Supper, which depicts Jesus about to tuck into a plate of *cuy*, washed down with a glass of *chicha*!

Entering **El Triunfo** there is a stark contrast between the dark, heavy atmosphere of the cathedral and the light, simple structure of this serene church. Built on the site of *Suntur Huasi* (The Roundhouse), El Triunfo was the first Christian church in Cuzco. The fine granite altar of El Triunfo is a welcome relief from the usual gilding. Here, the statue of the Virgin of the Descent resides and, above her, is a wooden cross known as the Cross of Conquest, said to be the first Christian cross on Inca land brought from Spain.

On the southeast side of the plaza is the beautiful church of **La Compañía de Jesús**, built on the site of the *Amarucancha* (Palace of the Serpents), the residence of Huayna Cápac. The original church was destroyed in the earthquake of 1650 and the present building took 17 years to construct. The altarpiece is resplendent in gold leaf: it stands 21 m high and 12 m wide. It is carved in baroque style, but the indigenous artists felt that this was too simple to please the gods and added their own intricacies.

Around Plaza de Armas

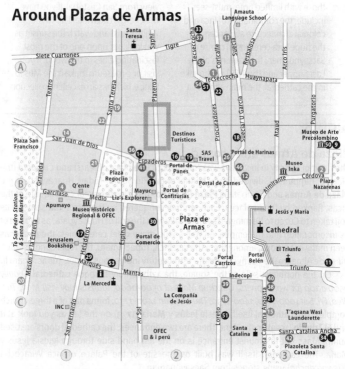

Plateros detail

Sleeping
Casa Andina Catedral 15 *C3*
Casa Andina Plaza 10 *C2*
El Procurador del
    Cusco 1 *A2*
Hostal Q'Awarina 11 *A2*
Hostal Resbalosa 13 *A3*
Hostal Royal
    Frankenstein 14 *B1*
Hostal Turístico Plateros 7
    Plateros detail
Inkaterra Cusco 2 *B3*
Marqueses 4 *B1*
Pensión Loreto 18 *C2*
Picoaga 19 *A1*
Royal Inka I 21 *B1*
Royal Inka II 22 *A1*
Sonesta Posadas
    del Inca Cusco &
    Inkafe Restaurant 8 *B2*
The Point 20 *C1*
Tumi I 24 *A1*

Eating
Al Grano 1 *C3*

Amaru 2 *Plateros detail*
A Mi Manera 11 *C3*
Ayllu 3 *B3*
Café Halliy 5
    Plateros detail
Cicciolina 11 *C3*
El Encuentro 34 *C3*
El Fogón 47 *Plateros detail*
Fallen Angel 9 *B3*
Incanto & Greens
    Organic 21 *C3*
Inka Grill 16 *B2*
Kapaj Ñan 22 *A2*
Kintaro 17 *B1*
Kusikuy 18 *B3*
La Bondiet 29 *C1*
La Retama 19 *B2*
MAP Café 50 *B3*
Pucará 28
    Plateros detail
Real McCoy 52
    Plateros detail
Trotamundos 30 *B2*
Tunupa 31 *B2*
Tupananchis 53 *C1*

Varayoc 14 *B2*
Víctor Victoria 33 *A2*
Witches Garden 51 *C2*
Yaku Mama 51 *A2*

Bars & clubs
Big Blue Martini 54 *A2*
Blueberry Lounge 12 *B3*
Corruption 55 *A2*
Cross Keys Pub 4 *B2*
El Garabato Video
    Music Club 41 *B2*
Extreme 46 *B3*
Kamikaze 36 *B2*
Los Perros 37 *A2*
Mama Africa 26 *B2*
Norton Rat's
    Tavern 9 *C2*
Paddy Flaherty's 40 *C3*
Rosie O'Grady's &
    Sky Travel 42 *C3*
Ukuku's 44 *Plateros
    detail*
Uptown 38 *C3*

0 metres 50
0 yards 50

Palacio del Almirante, just north of the Plaza de Armas, is one of Cuzco's most impressive colonial buildings and houses the interesting **Museo Inka** ① *Cuesta del Almirante 103, T084-237380, Mon-Sat 0800-1730, US$2.40*, which exhibits the development of culture in the region from pre-Inca, through Inca times to the present day. The museum has a good combination of textiles, ceramics, metalwork, jewellery, architecture, technology, photographs, three-dimensional displays and a section on coca. There is an excellent collection of miniature turquoise figures and other objects made as offerings to the gods. The display of skulls, deliberately deformed by trepanning is fascinating, as is the full-size tomb complete with mummies stuck in urns. Note the pillar on the balcony over the door, showing a bearded man from inside and a naked woman from the outside. During the high season, local Quechuan weavers can be seen working and selling in the courtyard. The weavings are for sale; expensive but high quality.

Two blocks northeast of Plaza de Armas, the **Palacio Arzobispal** was built on the site of the palace occupied in 1400 by the Inca Roca and was formerly the home of the Marqueses de Buena Vista. It contains the **Museo de Arte Religioso** ① *Hatun Rumiyoc y Herrajes, Mon-Sat 0830-1130, 1500-1730*, which has a fine collection of colonial paintings, furniture and mirrors. The collection includes the paintings by the indigenous master, **Diego Quispe Tito**, of a 17th-century Corpus Christi procession that used to hang in the church of Santa Ana. The throne in the old dining room is 300 years old and was taken up to Sacsayhuaman for the Pope to sit on when he visited in 1986.

In the Casa Cabrera, on the northwest side of the plaza, is the beautiful **Museo de Arte Precolombino** ① *Plaza de las Nazarenas 231, T084-233210, 0900-2200, US$6, US$3 with ISIC card; under same auspices as the Larco Museum in Lima*. Set around a spacious courtyard, it is dedicated to the work of the great artists of pre-Colombian Peru. Within the expertly lit and well-organized galleries are many superb examples of pottery, metalwork (largely in gold and silver) and wood carvings. There are some vividly rendered animistic designs, giving an insight into the way Peru's ancient peoples viewed their world and the creatures that inhabited it. Most of the pieces originate from the Moche, Chimú, Paracas, Nazca and Inca empires, with explanations in English and Spanish. The museum has shops, such as **Alpaca 111** and **H Stern**, and the **MAP Café**, see Eating, page 104.

San Blas

The San Blas district, called **Tococache** in Inca times, has been put on the tourist map by the large number of shops and galleries which sell local carvings, ceramics and paintings. Even though it's a bit of climb from the Plaza de Armas, it has become a popular place to stay and eat, with lots of choice and good-value options. The **church of San Blas** ① *Carmen Bajo, 0800-1130, 1400-1730, closed Thu mornings*, is a simple rectangular adobe building whose walls were reinforced with stone after the 1650 and 1950 earthquakes. It houses one of the most famous carvings in the Americas, a beautiful mestizo pulpit made from a single cedar trunk.

East and southeast of the Plaza de Armas

The magnificent church, convent and museum of **Santa Catalina** ① *Arequipa at Santa Catalina Angosta, Sat-Thu 0900-1200, 1300-1700, Fri 0900-1200, 1300-1600, entrance with BTG visitor ticket, guided tours by English-speaking students (tip expected), church daily 0700-0800*, is built upon the foundations of the *Acllahuasi* (House of the Chosen Women), whose nobility, virtue and beauty permitted them to be prepared for ceremonial and domestic duties – some were chosen to bear the Inca king's children. Today the convent is a closed order where the nuns have no contact with the outside world. The church has an ornate, gilded altarpiece and a beautifully carved pulpit. The museum has a wonderful collection of Cuzqueño school paintings spanning the decades of Spanish rule.

Much original Inca stonework can be seen in the streets, particularly in the **Callejón Loreto**, running southeast past La Compañía de Jesús from the main plaza. The walls of the *Acllahuasi* are on one side, and of the *Amarucancha* on the other. There are also Inca remains in Calle San Agustín, east of the plaza. The famous **Stone of 12 Angles** is in Calle Hatun Rumiyoc, halfway along its second block, on the right-hand side going away from the plaza. The finest stonework is in the celebrated curved wall beneath the west end of Santo Domingo. This was rebuilt after the 1950 earthquake, when a niche that once

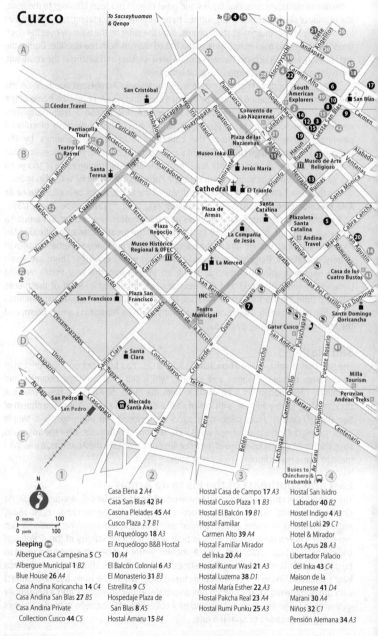

Cuzco

To Sacsayhuaman & Qenqo

To Sacsayhuaman & Qenqo

Buses to Chinchero & Urubamba

```
N
0  metres        100
0  yards         100
```

Sleeping
Albergue Casa Campesina **5** *C5*
Albergue Municipal **1** *B2*
Blue House **26** *A4*
Casa Andina Koricancha **14** *C4*
Casa Andina San Blas **27** *B5*
Casa Andina Private
  Collection Cusco **44** *C5*

Casa Elena **2** *A4*
Casa San Blas **42** *B4*
Casona Pleiades **45** *A4*
Cusco Plaza 2 **7** *B1*
El Arqueólogo **18** *A3*
El Arqueólogo B&B Hostal
  10 *A4*
El Balcón Colonial **6** *A3*
El Monasterio **31** *B3*
Estrellita **9** *C5*
Hospedaje Plaza de
  San Blas **8** *A5*
Hostal Amaru **15** *B4*

Hostal Casa de Campo **17** *A3*
Hostal Cusco Plaza 1 **1** *B3*
Hostal El Balcón **19** *B1*
Hostal Familiar
  Carmen Alto **39** *A4*
Hostal Familiar Mirador
  del Inka **20** *A4*
Hostal Kuntur Wasi **21** *A3*
Hostal Luzerna **38** *D1*
Hostal María Esther **22** *A3*
Hostal Pakcha Real **23** *A4*
Hostal Rumi Punku **25** *A3*

Hostal San Isidro
  Labrador **40** *B2*
Hostel Indigo **4** *A3*
Hostel Loki **29** *C1*
Hotel & Mirador
  Los Apus **28** *A3*
Libertador Palacio
  del Inka **43** *C4*
Maison de la
  Jeunesse **41** *D4*
Marani **30** *A4*
Niños **32** *C1*
Pensión Alemana **34** *A3*

contained a shrine was found at the inner top of the wall. Excavations have revealed Inca baths below here, and more Inca retaining walls. Another superb stretch of late-Inca stonework is in **Calle Ahuacpinta**, outside Qoricancha, to the east or left as you enter. True Inca stonework is wider at the base than at the top and features ever-smaller stones as the walls rise. Doorways and niches are trapezoidal. The Incas clearly learnt that the combination of these four techniques helped their structures to withstand earthquakes. This explains why, in two huge earthquakes (1650 and 1950), Inca walls stayed standing while colonial buildings tumbled down.

Related maps
A Around Plaza de Armas, page 92

Qoricancha at Santo Domingo

ⓘ *Mon-Sat 0800-1700, Sun 1400-1600 (closed holidays), US$1.50 (not included in the BTG visitor ticket). Guides charge US$2-3.*

This is one of the most fascinating sights in Cuzco. Behind the walls of the Catholic church are remains of what was once the centre of the vast Inca society. The Golden Palace and Temple of the Sun was a complex filled with such fabulous treasures of gold and silver it took the Spanish three months to melt it all down. The Solar Garden contained life-sized gold sculptures of people, animals, insects and flowers, placed in homage to the Sun God. On the walls were more than 700 gold sheets weighing 2 kg each. The conquistadors sent these back intact to prove to the King of Spain how rich their discovery was. There would also have been a large solar disc in the shape of a round face with rays and flames. This disc has never been found.

The first Inca, Manco Cápac, is said to have built the temple when he left Lake Titicaca and founded Cuzco with Mama Ocllo. However, it was the ninth Inca, Pachacútec, who transformed it. When the Spaniards arrived, the complex was awarded to Juan Pizarro, the younger brother of Francisco. He in turn willed it to the Dominicans who ripped much of it down to build their church.

Walk first into the courtyard then turn around to face the door you just passed through. Behind and to the left of the paintings (representing the life of Santo Domingo Guzmán) is Santo Domingo. This was where the Temple of the Sun stood, a massive structure 80 m wide, 20 m deep and 7 m high. Only the curved wall of the western end still exists and will be seen (complete with a large crack from the 1950 earthquake), when you later walk left through to the lookout over the Solar Garden. Still in the baroque cloister, close by and facing the way you came in, turn left and cross to the remains of the

Cuzco & the Sacred Valley Cuzco city

Eating
Café Cultural Ritual 12 *B4*
Café Manu 2 *E6*
Chocolate 14 *B4*
El Encuentro 23 *B4*
Granja Heidi 3 *B4*
Inka...fe 19 *B4*
Inkanato 5 *C4*
Jack's Café 15 *B4*
La Bodega 6 *A4*
Los Toldos 7 *D3*
Macondo 8 *A4*
Moni 20 *C4*

Mundo Hemp 22 *A4*
Pachapapa 9 *B4*
Panadería El Buen Pastor 10 *A4*
The Muse 17 *A4*
Velluto 4 *A3*
Yanapay 13 *B4*

Bars & clubs
Bar 7 16 *A3*
Km 0 (Arte y Tapas) 18 *A4*
Mandela's 11 *B3*
Siete Angelitos 21 *A4*

Temple of the Moon, identifiable by a series of niches. Beyond this is the so-called Temple of Venus and the Stars. Stars were special deities used to predict weather, wealth and crops. In the Temple of Lightning on the other side of the courtyard is a stone. Stand on this and you will appreciate how good the Incas were as stonemasons: all three windows are in perfect alignment.

South and southwest of the Plaza de Armas

Originally built in 1534, the church of **La Merced** ① *Calle Márquez, monastery and museum 1430-1700, church Mon-Sat 0830-1200, 1530-1730, US$0.85*, was razed in the 1650 earthquake and rebuilt by indigenous stonemasons in the late 17th century. The high altar is neoclassical with six gilded columns. There are a further 12 altars. Inside the church are buried Gonzalo Pizarro, half-brother of Francisco, and the two Almagros, father and son. Attached is a very fine monastery. The first cloister is the most beautiful, with its two floors, archways and pillars.

Museo Histórico Regional ① *Casa Garcilaso, Calle Garcilaso y Heladeros, daily 0730-1730, entrance with BTG visitor ticket, guide recommended,* shows the evolution of the Cuzqueño school of painting. It also contains Inca agricultural implements, a mummy from Nazca, complete with 1-m-long hair, colonial furniture and paintings, a photographic exhibition of the 1950 earthquake and mementos of more recent times.

Three blocks southwest of the Plaza de Armas, the austere church of **San Francisco** ① *Plaza San Francisco, daily 0600-0800, 1800-2000*, reflects many indigenous influences, but it has a wonderful monastery, cloister and choir. Its monastery is being rebuilt and may be closed. The cloister is the oldest in the city, built in the Renaissance style, but with diverse influences. The ground floor has several crypts containing human bones. The high choir contains 92 carvings of martyrs and saints.

West and northwest of the Plaza de Armas

Above Cuzco, on the road up to Sacsayhuaman, is the church of **San Cristóbal**, built to honour his patron saint by Cristóbal Paullu Inca. The church's atrium has been restored and there is access to the Sacsayhuaman Archaeological Park (see below). North of San Cristóbal, you can see the 11 doorway-sized niches of the great Inca wall of the **Palacio de Colcampata**, which was the residence of Manco Inca before he rebelled against the Spanish and fled to Vilcabamba. **Cristo Blanco**, arms outstretched and brilliantly illuminated at night, stands over the town and is clearly visible if you look north from Plaza de Armas. He was given to the city as a mark of gratitude by Palestinian refugees in 1944.

Sacsayhuaman → *Colour map 4, C3.*

① *Daily 0700-1730 (you can get in earlier if you wish; definitely try to get there before 1200 when the tour groups arrive. Entrance by BTG visitor ticket. Free student guides available, but give them a tip. The site is illuminated at night. To get there from the town centre: walk up Pumacurco from Plaza de las Nazarenas (30 mins). Taxi US$1.50. It is even possible to walk up to Sacsayhuaman, but a better idea is to take a combi to Tambo Machay and walk back downhill to town via Qenqo and Sacsayhuaman.*
There are some magnificent Inca walls in the ruined ceremonial centre of Sacsayhuaman, on a hill in the northern outskirts. The Inca stonework is hugely impressive. The massive rocks weighing up to 130 tons are fitted together with absolute perfection. Three walls run parallel for over 360 m and there are 21 bastions.

Sacsayhuaman was thought for centuries to be a fortress, but the layout and architecture suggest a great sanctuary and temple to the Sun, rising opposite the place previously believed to be the Inca's throne – which was probably an altar, carved out of the solid rock. Broad steps lead to the altar from either side. Zigzags in the boulders round the 'throne' are apparently 'chicha' grooves', channels down which maize beer flowed during festivals. Up the hill is an ancient quarry, the *Rodadero*, now used by children as a rock slide. Near it are many seats cut perfectly into the smooth rock.

unopposed in 1533 and lived safely at Sacsayhuaman, until the rebellion of Manco Inca, in 1536, caught them off guard. The bitter struggle that ensued became the decisive military action of the conquest, for Manco's failure to hold Sacsayhuaman cost him the war, and the empire. The destruction of the hilltop site began after the defeat of Manco's rebellion. The outer walls still stand, but the complex of towers and buildings was razed to the ground. From then until the 1930s, Sacsayhuaman served as a kind of unofficial quarry of pre-cut stone for the inhabitants of Cuzco.

Other sites near Cuzco

Along the road from Sacsayhuaman to Pisac, past a radio station at 3600 m, is the temple and amphitheatre of **Qenqo**. These are not exactly ruins, but are the finest examples of Inca stone carving *in situ*, especially inside the large hollowed-out stone that houses an altar. The rock is criss-crossed by zigzag channels that give the place its name and which served to course *chicha*, or perhaps sacrificial blood, for purposes of divination. The open space that many refer to as the 'plaza' or 'amphitheatre' was used for ceremonies. The 19 trapezoidal niches, which are partially destroyed, held idols and mummies.

Known as an Inca fortress, **Puka Pukara** ① *about 6 km from Qenqo*, whose name translates as 'Red Fort', was more likely to have been a *tambo*, a kind of post-house where travellers were lodged and goods and animals were housed temporarily. It is worth seeing for the views alone.

A few hundred metres up the road is the spring shrine of **Tambo Machay**, still in excellent condition. There are many opinions as to the function of this place. Some say it was a resting place for the Incas and others that it was used by Inca Yupanqui as a hunting place. There are three ceremonial water fountains built on different levels. It is possible that the site was a centre of a water cult. Water still flows via a hidden channel out of the masonry wall, straight into a rock pool, traditionally known as the Inca's bath.

Taking a guide to the sites mentioned above is a good idea and you should visit in the morning for the best photographs (take your BTG ticket). You can visit the sites on foot. It's a pleasant walk through the countryside requiring half a day or more, though remember to take water and sun protection, and watch out for dogs. An alternative is to take the Pisac bus up to Tambo Machay (which costs US$0.35) and walk back. Another excellent way to see the ruins is on horseback, arranged at travel agencies. An organized tour (with guide) will go to all the sites for US$6 per person, not including entrance fees. A taxi will charge US$15-20 for three to four people. Some of these ruins are included in the many city tours available (see page 109).

⬛ Sleeping

In Jun and other busy times, double-booking occurs so double-check reservations. Book more expensive hotels well in advance, particularly for the week or so around Inti Raymi, when prices are greatly increased. Prices given are for the high season in Jun-Aug. When there are fewer tourists hotels may drop their prices by as much as half. Always check for discounts. Train passengers are approached by unlicensed hotel agents for medium-priced hotels who are often misleading about details; their local nickname is *jalagringos* (gringo pullers), or *piratas*. Taxis and tourist minibuses meet the train and (should) take you to the hotel of your choice for US$0.75-1, but be insistent. Since it is cold here and many hotels have no heating, ask for an *estufa*, a heater which some places will provide for an extra charge.

Perurooms SAC, Las Acacias 502, Lima 18, T01-447 4630, www.perurooms.com. Helps travellers to select and book hotel rooms (3- to 4-star) in Cuzco and throughout Peru.

⬤ *For an explanation of sleeping and eating price codes used in this guide, see inside the*
● *front cover. Other relevant information is found in Essentials, see pages 31-35.*

Plaza de Armas and around *p91, map p92*

AL Picoaga, Santa Teresa 344 (2 blocks from the Plaza de Armas), T084-252330, www.pico agahotel.com. Includes buffet breakfast. Originally the home of the Marqués de Picoaga, this beautiful colonial building has large original bedrooms set around a shady court-yard and a modern section, with a/c, at the back. Cable TV, minibar and safe. Pleasant staff.

AL Sonesta Posadas del Inca Cusco, Portal Espinar 108, T084-227061, www.sonesta peru.com. Includes buffet breakfast, warmly decorated rooms with heating and cable TV, safe, some rooms on 3rd floor with view of plaza, very helpful, English spoken, restaurant with Andean food, excellent service.

A Casa Andina Plaza, Portal Espinar 142, T084-231733, www.casa-andina.com. 1 block from the plaza, this hotel has 40 rooms with cable TV, bath, safe, heating, duvets on the beds, Wi-Fi internet, ATM, restaurant and all the features common to this bright, cheerful chain. Equally recommendable are: **Casa Andina Koricancha**, San Agustín 371, T084-252633, the **Casa Andina Catedral**, Santa Catalina Angosta 149, T084-233661, and **AL Casa Andina San Blas**, Chihuampata 278, San Blas, T084-263694, all in the same vein (but the last 3 do not have an ATM).

A Royal Inka I, Plaza Regocijo 299, T084-231067, royalin@speedy.com.pe. Price includes buffet breakfast. Bedrooms, with cable TV and heating, are set in a colonial house around a shady central patio. Tranquil atmosphere, bar, restaurant with set menu.

A Royal Inka II, Santa Teresa, same phone and email as above. More modern and expensive but the price includes buffet breakfast, sauna and jacuzzi. Free bus for guests to Pisac at 1000 daily, returning 1800.

A-C Marqueses, Garcilaso 256, T084-264249, marqueses@sastravelperu.com. Recently restored in Spanish colonial style, with 16th-to 17th-century style religious paintings and 2 lovely courtyards. Rooms have heavy curtains and some are a little dark; luxury rooms have bath. Buffet breakfast.

C Pensión Loreto, Pasaje Loreto 115, Plaza de Armas (same entrance as **Norton's Rat** pub), T084-226352, www.hloreto.com. Great location. Price includes continental breakfast and a heater for the spacious rooms with original Inca walls. Laundry service, organizes travel services including guides and taxis.

D Hostal Q'Awarina, at the top of Suecia 575, T084-228130. Price includes continental breakfast, heating US$2, TV extra. Rooms are good, ask for those with a view. Lovely living room with views across the city; the breakfast area upstairs is even better. Good value.

D-E Hostal Turístico Plateros, Plateros 348, T084-236878, plateroshostal@hotmail.com. Includes continental breakfast. Good-value *hostal*, great location, pleasant communal area, cable TV. The best rooms overlook the street.

E Hostal Resbalosa, Resbalosa 494, T084-224839. Breakfast US$1.45; laundry US$0.75 per kg. Superb views of the Plaza de Armas from a sunny terrace. Hospitable owner. Best rooms have a view (US$1.45 extra), others may be pokey. The electric showers aren't brilliant, but it is very popular and often full.

E Hostal Royal Frankenstein, San Juan de Dios 260, 2 blocks from the Plaza de Armas, T084-236999, ludwig_roth@hotmail.com. This unforgettable place, with its ghoulish theme, has good services: fully equipped kitchen (US$0.30 a day), cable TV in the living room, safe, laundry facilities, excellent mattresses but few rooms have outside windows. German owner.

E-F El Procurador del Cusco, Coricalle 440, Prolongación Procuradores, at the end of Procuradores, T084-243559. **G** pp without bathroom, price includes use of basic kitchen (no fridge) and laundry. Basic rooms, upstairs is better. Staff are very helpful, good value.

F The Point, Mesón de la Estrella 172, T084-252266, www.thepointhostels.com. Price is per person in dormitory, also has doubles (**E**), includes breakfast, free internet, good beds, hot showers, clean, nice atmosphere.

F Tumi 1, Siete Cuartones 245, 2 blocks from Plaza de Armas, T084-244413. Price includes use of the kitchen and laundry area; free book exchange, laundry service US$0.85. Colonial house, clean rooms around a sunny courtyard, all with shared bath. Basic, you have to pay for more than one shower a day, popular, good value; bargain for longer stays.

North and northeast of the Plaza de Armas *p93, maps p92 and p94*

LL Inkaterra Cusco, Plazoleta Las Nazarenas 113, T084-245314, www.inkaterra.com. A new (2007), private, colonial-style boutique hotel in a converted 16th-century mansion. 11 exclusive suites, all facilities, concierge

⁞ Budget buster

LL El Monasterio, Palacios 136, T084-241777, www.monasterio-orient-express.com. This 5-star hotel is quite simply the best in town for historical interest; it has tranquil courtyards, charming cloisters and an excellent collection of religious paintings. Rooms have all facilities, including cable TV, some offer an oxygen-enriched atmosphere to help clients acclimatize (US$25 extra). Staff, who all speak English, are very helpful and attentive. The price includes a great buffet breakfast (US$19 to non-residents) which will fill you up for the rest of the day. The restaurant serves lunch and dinner à la carte.

Built in 1595 on the site of an Inca palace, it was originally the **Seminary of San Antonio Abad** (a Peruvian National Historical Landmark). One of its most remarkable features is the baroque chapel, constructed after the 1650 earthquake. If you are not disturbing mealtimes, check out the dining room. This is where the monks used to sing – ask at reception if you can have a wander. The **Convento de las Nazarenas**, on Plaza de las Nazarenas, is now an annex of El Monasterio hotel. You can see the Inca-colonial doorway with a mermaid motif, but ask permission to view the lovely 18th-century frescos inside.

service with activities and excursions (prices US$500-1000).

A El Arqueólogo, Pumacurco 408, T084-232522, www.hotelarqueologo.com. Price includes buffet breakfast. Services include oxygen canisters, a library and hot drinks. A colonial building on Inca foundations, with rustic but stylish decor. Lovely sunny garden with comfy chairs and a small restaurant that serves interesting Peruvian food and fondue. French and English spoken. Also has a B&B hostal (**C-D**), Carmen Alto 294, T084-232760. **Vida Tours**, Ladrillo 425, T084-227750, www.vidatours.com. Traditional and adventure tourism.

B Hostal Rumi Punku, Choquechaca 339, T084-221102, www.rumipunku.com. An Inca doorway leads to the sunny, tranquil courtyard. 20 large, clean, comfortable rooms (**C** low season), helpful staff, safe.

D Casa Elena, Choquechaca 162, T084-241202, www.geocities.com/casa_elena. French/Peruvian hostel with a good reputation, very comfortable and friendly, breakfast included.

D Hostal María Esther, Pumacurco 516, T084-224382. Price includes continental breakfast; heating extra. This very helpful place has a lovely gardens and a variety of rooms. There is also car parking.

E El Balcón Colonial, Choquechaca 350, T084-238129, balconcolonial@hotmail.com.

Continental breakfast extra, use of the kitchen US$1 per day and laundry US$0.70 per kg. Accommodation for 11 people in this family house. Basic rooms with foam mattresses. Exceptional hospitality. Free airport pickup.

San Blas *p93, map p94*

A Casa San Blas, Tocuyeros 566, just off Cuesta San Blas, T/F084-237900, www.casa sanblas.com. A 'boutique' hotel with bright, airy rooms decorated with traditional textiles. Breakfast and internet are included. Pleasant balcony with good views, attentive service.

A Hotel and Mirador Los Apus, Atocsaycuchi 515, corner with Choquechaca, T084-264243, www.losapushotel.com. Price includes buffet breakfast and airport pickup; full of character, very smart, central heating, good views, disabled facilities. Swiss-owned.

B Hostal Casa de Campo, Tandapata 296-B (at the end of the street), T084-244404, www.hotelcasadecampo.com. Price (10% discount for Footprint readers) includes continental breakfast and free airport/rail/bus transfer with reservations. Bedrooms have fabulous views but it's quite a climb to get to them! Safe deposit box, laundry service, meals on request and a sun terrace. Dutch and English spoken; take a taxi there after dark.

B-C Casona Pleiades, Tandapata 116, T084-506430, www.casona-pleiades.com. Small San Blas guesthouse in renovated colonial house, cosy and warm, generous hosts, hot water, cable TV, Wi-Fi, roof terrace, video lounge and book exchange, café, free airport pickup, lots of information.

C Hostal Amaru, Cuesta San Blas 541, T084-225933, www.cusco.net/amaru, (**E** without bathroom). Price includes breakfast and airport/train/bus pickup. Services include oxygen, kitchen for use in the evenings only, laundry and free book exchange. Rooms around a pretty colonial courtyard, good beds, pleasant, relaxing, some Inca walls. Rooms in the first courtyard are best. Recommended. Also has **C Hostal Amaru II** at Chihuampata 642, San Blas, www.amaruhostal.com, and **E Hostería de Anita**, with bath, safe, quiet, good American breakfast.

C Marani, Carmen Alto 194, T084-249462, www.hostalmarani.com. Breakfasts available. Book exchange and information on Andean life and culture. Large rooms with heaps of character, set around a courtyard. The **Hope Foundation** (www.stichtinghope.org) is run from here: Walter Meekes and his wife, Tineke, have built 20 schools in poor mountain villages and *barrios*, established a programme to teach teachers and set up a 30-bed burns unit in Cuzco general hospital. Good value and a great cause.

C Pensión Alemana, Tandapata 260, T084-226861. Price includes American breakfast; laundry and heating extra. Car parking available. Swiss-owned, modern European decor with a comfy lounge, free internet, lovely garden with patio furniture.

D Hostel Indigo, Atocsaycuchi 594, T084-223012, www.cusco-peru.de. With continental breakfast, hot water, cable TV. A charming hotel, in traditional style, spacious and clean, some shared bathrooms, books in English, German and French, videos to watch, free internet, tours arranged, discounts at neighbouring language school.

D Hostal Kuntur Wasi, Tandapata 352-A, T084-227570. **F** without bath, services include a safe, use of the kitchen (US$0.60 a day) and laundry. Great views from the terrace where you can breakfast. Very welcoming, helpful owners; a pleasant place to stay.

E Hostal Pakcha Real, Tandapata 300, T084-237484, pakcharealhostal@hotmail.com. Price includes airport/train/bus pickup; rooms with bath; breakfast, heaters and use of kitchen extra. Family-run with the comforts of home. Laundry service, spotless rooms, relaxed, confirm booking if arriving late.

E-F Hospedaje Plaza de San Blas, Plazoleta San Blas 630, T084-235358, psanblas@corihuasi.com. Colourful, welcoming and a great location. Price includes continental breakfast. The 4-bed family room has a balcony and overlooks the *plazoleta*.

E-F Hostal Familiar Mirador del Inka, Tandapata 160, off Plaza San Blas, T084-261384, miradordelinka@latinmail.com. Stylish, with Inca foundations and white colonial walls. Bedrooms with bath are spacious and some have great views; no hot water after dark. Use of kitchen. The owner's son Edwin runs trekking trips and has an agency on site.

F Hostal Familiar Carmen Alto, Carmen Alto 197, first on the right down steps (no sign), T084-504658, carmencitadelperu@hotmail.com. If there's no answer, ask at the shop next door, it's run by the same family. Basic rooms with great character (in one case, constructed around a huge tree). Tranquil, family-run, use of kitchen and washing

machine. Very good breakfast US$2. All rooms with shared bath, electric showers.
G pp The Blue House, Kiskapata 291 (there are 2 Kiskapatas – this one runs parallel to and above Tandapata), T084-242407. Snug little *hostal*, excellent value, reductions for longer stays. Breakfast included, DVD room, shared kitchen. Great views with a small park in front.

East and southeast of the Plaza de Armas *p93, map 94*

LL Libertador Palacio del Inka, Casa de los Cuatro Bustos, Plazoleta Santo Domingo 259, T084-231961, www.libertador.com.pe, (reservations: Las Begonias 441, of 240, San Isidro, Lima 27, T01-442 1995). This splendid 5-star, award-winning hotel is built on Inca ruins (the walls can be seen) and is set around courtyards. It has 254 well-appointed rooms; the attention to detail is so great there are even Nazca Lines drawn in the sand of the ashtrays. The excellent **Inti Raymi** restaurant has Andean music/dance. Recommended.
AL Casa Andina Private Collection Cusco, Plazoleta de Limacpampa Chico 473, T084-232610, www.casa-andina.com. In a 16th-century mansion with 3 courtyards, this hotel is one of the recommended Casa Andina chain's upmarket establishments, with even higher standards of services and comfort than those listed above. It has all the main facilities, plus a gourmet restaurant serving local cuisine and a bar with an extensive *pisco* collection.
D-E Maison de la Jeunesse (affiliated to Hostelling International), Av Sol, Cuadra 5, Pasaje Grace, Edificio San Jorge (down a small side street opposite Qoricancha), T084-235617, hostellingcusco@hotmail.com or maisondelajeunesse@hotmail.com. Price includes breakfast. With a selection of dormitories and private rooms, TV and video room, cooking facilities and very hot water.
F Albergue Casa Campesina, Av Tullumayo 274, T084-233466, ccamp@apu.cbc.org.pe. Price includes breakfast, shared bathrooms only. A lovely place, set up to support the work of **Casa Campesina** (www.cbc.org.pe/casacamp), which is linked to local *campesina* communities. On the same site is the **Store of the Weavers** (see Shopping, page 108). Profits go to this good cause. There is a 23% discount for **SAE** members.

F **Estrellita**, Av Tullumayo 445, parte Alta, 15-min walk from the centre, T084-234134. Price includes breakfast and free tea and coffee. TV, video and old stereo in the tiny communal sitting area, basic kitchen. Rooms are dorms with shared bath, plus 2 with private bath. Basic but excellent value. When you arrive ring the bell several times and wait; you will be given your own keys when you register. Safe parking for cars and bikes.

West and northwest of the Plaza de Armas *p96, map 94*

A **Cusco Plaza 2**, Saphi 486, T084-263000, www.cuscoplazahotels.com. The 24 nicely decorated rooms are set around 3 charming covered patios. Price includes American breakfast, and all rooms have cable TV and heating. Under same management as A-B **Hostal Cusco Plaza 1**, Plaza Nazarenas 181 (opposite **El Monasterio**), T084-246161.
B **Hostal El Balcón**, Tambo de Montero 222, T084-236738, balcon1@terra.com.pe. Price includes breakfast. Lovingly restored 1630 colonial house with rooms set around a beautiful garden, homely atmosphere. Ask for a TV if you want one. Restaurant and kitchen for guests, laundry service.
C **Hostal San Isidro Labrador**, Saphi 440, T084-226241, labrador@qnet.com.pe. Continental breakfast included in the price. Very pleasant 3-star hotel with elegant but simple decor, colonial arches and lovely patios. Plenty of hot water and heating.
C **Niños Hotel**, Meloc 442, T084-231424, www.ninoshotel.com. Excellent breakfast, costs US$1.70-2.50 extra. Services include the cafeteria and laundry (US$1.15 per kg). Spotless, beautiful rooms in a 17th-century colonial house funding a fantastic charity established by Dutch Jolanda van den Berg. Also has **Niños 2**, on Calle Fierro, a little further from the centre, 20 nicely decorated, clean and airy rooms, surrounding the central courtyard, and AL-C **Niños Hacienda** in the village of Huasao, so mins from Cuzco, with bungalows, rooms, pool, horse riding.
D **Hostel Loki**, Cuesta Santa Ana 601, T084-243705, www.lokihostel.com. G pp. Huge, funky hostel in a restored viceroy's residence on the steep Cuesta Santa Ana, dorms and rooms set around a beautiful courtyard, comfortable beds, hot water, free internet. A great meeting place.

F **Albergue Municipal**, Kiskapata 240, near San Cristóbal, T084-252506, albergue@ municusco.gob. Private rooms with double beds and dormitories in this very clean, helpful youth hostel. Nice communal area with cable TV and video. No rooms have bath. Great views, cafeteria and laundry facilities (laundry service US$0.75 per kg). Showers are electric, but there is no kitchen.
F **Hostal Luzerna**, Av Baja 205, near San Pedro train station (take a taxi at night), T084-232762. Price includes breakfast. A nice family-run *hostal*, hot water, good beds, clean, safe to leave luggage.

⊘ Eating

Plaza de Armas and around *p91, map p92*
Calle Procuradores, (or 'Gringo Alley' as the locals call it) leading off the northwest side of the Plaza de Armas, has good-value places, including Mexican, Italian, Spanish and Turkish. Parallel with Gringo Alley, **Calle Plateros** also has good-value eateries. It is also lined with a great many tour operators, so you can wander along checking out the deals.
₶₶₶ **Cicciolina**, Triunfo 393, 2nd floor, T084-239510, cicciolinacuzco@yahoo.com. Sophisticated restaurant focusing largely on Italian/Mediterranean cuisine. It also has a tapas bar and a boutique bakery, impressive wine list from across the globe. Good atmosphere, fine decor and great for treat.
₶₶₶ **Incanto**, Santa Catalina Angosta 135, T084-254753, daily 1100-2400. Under same ownership as **Inka Grill** and with the same standards, serves pastas, grilled meats, pizzas, desserts, extensive wine list. There is also a Peruvian delicatessen on the premises. Upstairs is **Greens Organic** (formerly in San Blas), exclusively organic ingredients in fusion cuisine and a fresh daily buffet.
₶₶₶ **Inka Grill**, Portal de Panes 115, T084-262992, www.inkagrillcusco.com, daily 1100-2300. According to many the best food in town is served here, specializing in *novo andino* cuisine, also home-made pastas, wide vegetarian selection, live music, excellent coffee and home-made pastries 'to go'.
₶₶₶ **La Retama**, Portal de Panes 123, 2nd floor, T084-226372. Excellent *novo andino* food and service. There is also a balcony, an enthusiastic music and dance group and art exhibitions.

♥♥♥ **Tunupa**, Portal Confiturías 233, 2nd floor (same entrance as **Cross Keys**). One of the finest restaurants on the plaza (often used by tour groups) with a long glassed-in balcony. International, traditional and *novo andino* food. The buffet for US$15 includes a *pisco sour* and a hot drink. In the evenings there is an excellent group playing 16th- and 17th-century style Cuzqueñan music and dance.

♥♥♥ **Tupananchis**, Portal Mantas 180, T084-976 4494, tupananchis_rest_cusco@ hotmail.com. Tasty, beautifully presented *novo andino* and fusion cuisine in a smart, sophisticated atmosphere. Café next door.

♥♥ **A Mi Manera**, (Culturas Peru), Triunfo 393, T084-222219, www.culturasperu.com. Imaginative *novo andino* dishes with open kitchen. Great hospitality and atmosphere.

♥♥ **Al Grano**, Santa Catalina Ancha 398, T084-228032, Mon-Sat 1000-2100. Lunchtime menu US$2.15; evening serves 5 authentic Asian dishes for US$5.50. Without doubt some of the best coffee in town, vegetarian choices and breakfasts, including 'Full English'.

♥♥ **Kapaj Ñan**, Procuradores 398, kapajnan@ hotmail.com. Attentive service, an interesting mix of Peruvian, Asian and Italian cuisine in a cosy hole-in-the-wall, quite different from the Gringo Alley standard.

♥♥ **Kintaro**, Heladeros 149, Mon-Sat 1200-2200. Excellent home-made food, set menu (1200-1500) particularly good value at US$3, run by its Japanese owner.

♥♥ **Kusikuy**, Suecia 339, T084-292870, Mon-Sat 0800-2300. Some say this serves the best *cuy* (guinea pig, US$10.90) in town. Many other typical Cuzco dishes on the menu. Set lunch is unbeatable value at only US$2. Good service, live music.

♥♥ **Pucará**, Plateros 309. 1230-2200, closed Sun. Peruvian and international food, good US$2 set lunch, pleasant atmosphere.

♥♥ **The Real McCoy**, Plateros 326, p 2, T084-261111, therealmccoycafelounge@ yahoo.com. A retreat for homesick Brits and Aussies. The equal best greasy-spoon brekkie in town (the other being **Jack's Café**). On offer for dinner are some English classic main courses and puddings.

♥♥ **Varayoc**, Espaderos 142, T084-232404, daily 0800-2400. Swiss-owned, dishes made with Peruvian ingredients (the only place in Cuzco that serves cheese fondue). Also has a variety of pastas, good desserts; 'tea time' beverage

and pastry US$2.80 accompanied by Andean harp music. Pleasant, literary atmosphere.

♥♥ **Witches Garden**, Loreto 125, T084-244077, www.witchesgarden.net. Bar, restaurant and lounge, good *novo andino*, Quebecois and international cuisine, good atmosphere.

♥♥-♥ **Yanapay**, Ruinas 415, p 2, T084-255134. A good café serving breakfast, lunch and dinner. It is run by a charity which supports children's homes; head office at Av Alta 466, T084-245779, www.aldeayanapay.org. They welcome volunteers.

♥ **El Encuentro**, Santa Catalina Ancha 384, T084-247977, and Choquechaca 136, T084-225496. One of the best-value eateries, 3 courses of good vegan food and a drink for US$1.35, very busy at lunchtime.

♥ **El Fogón**, Plateros 365. Huge local *menú del día* for US$1.80, good solid food at reasonable prices. Very popular.

♥ **Víctor Victoria**, Tecsecocha 466, T084-252854 (not to be confused with similar-sounding name at old address on Tigre). Israeli and local dishes, highly recommended for breakfast, good value.

Cafés, delis and panaderías

Amaru, Plateros 325, 2nd floor, T084-246976. Unlimited coffee, tea, great bread and juices, even on non-buffet breakfasts (from US$1.15). Colonial balcony; also a pub serving pizzas etc.

Ayllu, Portal de Carnes 208. One of the oldest cafés in Cuzco, serves breakfasts, sandwiches, coffee and wonderful apple pastries. Classical and folk music. Superb service.

Café Halliy, Plateros 363. Popular meeting place, especially for breakfast, good for comments on guides, has good snacks and *copa Halliy* (fruit, muesli, yoghurt, honey and chocolate cake), also serves vegetarian dishes.

La Bondiet, corner of Av Márquez and Heladeros. Clean, simple and inexpensive café with a huge selection of sweet and savoury pastries and decent sandwiches. Good juices and the coffee's OK.

Trotamundos, Portal Comercio 177, 2nd floor, Mon-Sat 0800-2400. Very pleasant, if a bit pricey. Balcony overlooks the plaza, warm atmosphere especially at night with its open fire. Good coffees and cakes, safe salads, *brochetas*, sandwiches and pancakes; internet.

Yaku Mama, Procuradores 397. Good for breakfast; unlimited fruit and coffee.

North and northeast of the Plaza de Armas *p93, map p94*

¶¶¶ **Fallen Angel**, Plazoleta Nazarenas 320, T084-258184, www.fallenangelincusco.com, Mon-Sat 1100 till whenever (bar closes at 2400, kitchen at 2300), Tue and Sun opens at 1500. Like nowhere else. The menu features steaks and some innovative pasta dishes. Cocktails are excellent. Live DJs. Regular parties/fashion shows are always events to remember. Free Wi-Fi internet. Always phone to reserve.

¶¶¶ **MAP Café**, Plaza de las Nazarenas 231, a glass structure in the **Museo de Arte Precolombino**, T084-242476, www.map-cafe.com. Operates as a café 1000-1830; from 1830-2200, serves excellent Peruvian-Andean and international cuisine, with an innovative children's menu. It has a very good list of wines and *piscos*.

¶ **Café Cultural Ritual**, Choquechaca 140. Good value and tasty vegetarian *menú*, including decent Indian dishes, for US$2.20.

Cafés, delis and panaderías

Chocolate, Choquechaca 162, T974 9343 (mob). Good for coffee and cakes but the real highlights are the fresh gourmet chocolates (up to European standards).

San Blas *p93, map p94*

¶¶ **Jack's Café**, Choquechaca y San Blas, T084-806960, opens at 0630 for great-value English breakfast. Excellent menu with generous portions, all in a light and relaxed atmosphere. Fabulous American-style pancakes and freshly ground local coffee. Lunchtime gets very busy.

¶¶ **La Bodega**, Carmen Alto 146. Snug Dutch- and Peruvian-owned café/restaurant serving hot chocolate by candlelight in the afternoons, evening meals with salad bar, American breakfast and a US$1.50 lunch menu.

¶¶ **Macondo**, Cuesta San Blas 571, T084-229415. Bit pricier than others in this range but fantastic. A casual, cosy, arty and comfortable restaurant serving an exotic menu with jungle and *novo andino* food. It also has an art gallery. Popular.

¶¶ **Pachapapa**, Plazoleta San Blas 120, opposite church of San Blas, T084-241318, open 1130-2200. A beautiful patio restaurant in a colonial house, with resident harp player. Under same ownership as **Inka Grill**. Very good Cuzqueña dishes. At night, diners can sit in their own private colonial dining room.

¶¶-¶ **Mundo Hemp**, Qanchipata 596, www.mundohemp.com. Foccacia bread, interesting savoury pancakes, quiche and good fresh juices. Nice atmosphere with a sunny courtyard, a colourful place, great for chilling out. Also a shop selling hemp products.

¶ **Granja Heidi**, Cuesta San Blas 525, T084-238383. US$3 gets you a 3- or 4-course *menú del día* in a clean and relaxed environment. There are usually vegetarian options.

¶ **Inkafe**, Choquechaca 131-A, T084-258073. Good coffee, set breakfasts and good-value lunch menus. Range of sandwiches in French bread and good desserts.

Cafés, delis and panaderías

The Muse, Tandapata 682, Plazoleta San Blas. Funky little café with a cosy feel and great views over the plaza. Fresh coffee, good food and the best smoothies in town. There's often live music in the afternoons/evenings with no cover charge. English owner Claire is very helpful. Will refill water bottles for a small charge in an attempt to minimize plastic waste.

Panadería El Buen Pastor, Cuesta San Blas 579. Very good bread and pastries, the proceeds from which go to a charity for orphans and street children. Very popular with backpackers. Recommended.

Velluto, Tandapata 700, T084-240966. A great place for sweet or savoury crêpes, huge variety of fillings, good drinks and hot chocolate.

East and southeast of the Plaza de Armas *p93, map p94*

¶¶ **Inkanato**, San Agustín 280, T084-222926, www.perou.net. Good food, staff dressed in Inca outfits and dishes made only with ingredients known in Inca times, calls itself a 'living museum'.

¶¶ **Los Toldos**, Almagro 171 y San Andrés 219. Grilled chicken, fries and salad bar. Also a *trattoria* with home-made pasta and pizza, delivery T084-229829.

South and southwest of the Plaza de Armas *p96, map 94*

Cafés, delis and panaderías

Café Manu, Av Pardo 1046. Good liqueur coffees and food, jungle decor.

Moni, San Agustín 311, T084-231029, www.moni-cusco.com. Peruvian/English-owned, good fresh food and breakfast, British music, magazines, bright, clean and comfy.

🔆 Bars and clubs

Plaza de Armas and around *p91, maps p92 and p94*

Big Blue Martini, Tecseccocha 148, T084-248839. Sophisticated, split-level sofa bar with good cocktails, food and a lively music scene. Jazz sessions on Thu; guest DJ on Sat.

Blueberry Lounge, Portal de Carnes 235, T084-249458. Dark, moody and sophisticated, with a good menu, featuring American gourmet fast food.

Cross Keys Pub, Portal Confiturías 233 (upstairs), 1100-0130. Darts, cable sports, pool, bar meals, happy hours 1830-1930 and 2130-2230, plus daily half-price specials Sun-Wed, great *pisco sours*, very popular, loud and raucous, great atmosphere.

Los Perros Bar, Tecseccocha 436, open 1100-0100. Great place to chill out, comfy couches, excellent music, welcoming, good coffee, tasty meals (including vegetarian), book exchange, magazines, board games.

Mandela's Bar, Palacios 121, 3rd floor, T084-222424. Bar/restaurant with an African theme, good atmosphere and lots of space to relax. Serves breakfast, lunch and drinks in the evening, also Sun barbecues and events through the year. Great 360° panorama from the rooftop. South Africans welcome.

Norton Rat's Tavern, Loreto 115, 2nd floor (same entrance as **Hostal Loreto**), T084-246204, nortonrats@yahoo.com. Pleasant pub with a pool table, dart board, cable TV and lots of pictures of motorbikes. The owner can provide information for bikers. The balcony offers great views of the Plaza de Armas. Also has a juice bar serving Amazonian specials. Happy hour 1900-2100 with daily specials.

Paddy Flaherty's, Calle Triunfo 124, corner of the plaza, open 1300-0100. An Irish theme pub, deservedly popular. Good seating and great food – the jacket potatoes, shepherd's pie and baguettes are highly recommended.

Rosie O'Grady's, at Santa Catalina Ancha 360, T084-247935, open 1100-late (food till 2400, various happy hours). Good music, tasty food.

Clubs

Before your evening meal don't turn down flyers being handed out around the Plaza de Armas. Each coupon not only gives you free entry, it is worth a *cuba libre*. Sadly, the free entry-and-drink system doesn't appear to apply to Peruvians who are invariably asked to pay, even if their tourist companions get in for free. This discrimination should be discouraged. Also note that free drinks are made with the cheapest, lowest quality alcohol; always watch your drink being made and never leave it unattended. If you fancy learning a few Latin dance steps before hitting the dancefloor, many of the clubs offer free lessons.

Corruption, Tecseccocha, just below **Los Perros** on the same side of the street. Varied music, a good alternative to the plaza scene.

El Garabato Video Music Club, Espaderos 132, 3rd floor, daily 1600-0300. Dance area, lounge for chilling, bar, tastefully decorated in a colonial setting, with live shows 2300-0300 and a large screen showing music videos.

Extreme, Suecia. An old Cuzco staple. Movies are shown late afternoon and early evening, but after 2400 this place really gets going with an eclectic range of music, from 1960s and 1970s rock and pop to techno and trance.

Kamikaze, Plaza Regocijo 274, T084-233865. *Peña* at 2200, good old traditional rock music, candle-lit cavern atmosphere, entry US$2.50.

Mama Africa, Portal de Harinas, 2nd floor. Cool music and clubbers' spot. Good food, happy hour till 2300, good value.

Ukuku's, Plateros 316. US$1.35. Different to the other clubs as every night there is a live band that might play anything from rock to salsa. The DJ then plays a mix of Peruvian and international music. Happy hour 0730-0930.

Uptown, Portal Belén 115, 2nd floor. Formerly **Mama América**, with a dancefloor and a large video screen. The music is middle of the road, from local music through 1970s classics to the latest releases.

San Blas *p93, map p94*

Bar 7, Tandapata 690, San Blas, T084-506472. Good food and drinks in a trendy bar which specializes in local ingredients.

Km 0 (Arte y Tapas), Tandapata 100, San Blas. Lovely Mediterranean-themed bar tucked in behind San Blas. Good snacks and tapas, live music every night from 2200. Lots of acoustic guitar, etc.

Siete Angelitos, Siete Angelitos 638. Tiny hole in the wall bar, but spectacular cocktails and good food, friendly owner, Walter, and a great atmosphere when things get going. Often hosts guest DJs, ranging from Latin to trance. Happy hour 2000-2200.

🎭 Entertainment

Cuzco *p88, maps p92 and p94*
Centro Qosqo de Arte Nativo, Av Sol 604, T084-227901. Nightly folklore show 1900-2030, entrance on the BTG visitor ticket.
Teatro Inti Raymi, Saphi 605. Music nightly at 1845, US$4.50 entry and well worth it.
Teatro Municipal, Calle Mesón de la Estrella 149 (T084-227321 for information 0900-1300 and 1500-1900). This is a venue for plays, dancing and shows, mostly Thu-Sun. Also music and dance classes Jan-Mar, great value.

❋ Festivals and events

Cuzco *p88, maps p92 and p94*
20 Jan A procession of saints in the San Sebastián district of Cuzco.
Feb/Mar Carnival in Cuzco is a messy affair with flour, water, cacti, rotten fruit and manure thrown about in the streets. Be prepared.
Mar/Apr Easter Mon sees the procession of **El Señor de los Temblores** (Lord of the Earthquakes), starting at 1600 outside the cathedral. A large crucifix is paraded through the streets, returning to the plaza de Armas around 2000 to bless the tens of thousands of people who have assembled there.
2-3 May The **Vigil of the Cross** takes place at all mountaintops with crosses on them, is a boisterous affair.
Jun **Corpus Christi**, on the Thu after Trinity, when all the statues of the Virgin and of saints from Cuzco's churches are paraded through the streets to the cathedral. This is a colourful event. The Plaza de Armas is surrounded by tables with people selling *cuy* (guinea pig) and a mixed grill called *chiriuchu* (*cuy*, chicken, tortillas, fish eggs, water-weeds, maize, cheese and sausage) and lots of *Cusqueña* beer.
Early Jun 2 weeks before Inti Raymi (see below) is the highly recommended **Cusqueña Beer Festival**, held near the rail station, which boasts a great variety of Latin American music. Well-organized and great fun.
Jun is **Qoyllur Rit'i** (Snow Star Festival), held at a 4700-m glacier north of Ocongate (Ausangate), 150 km southeast of Cuzco. It has its final day 58 days after Easter Sun. Several agencies offer tours.
10 Jun The annual rebuilding of the grass Inca bridge at **Qeswachaka**, southeast of

Cuzco. The footbridge has been rebuilt every year for the past 400 years during a 3-day festival which is celebrated by the communities who use it. Agencies offer tours.
24 Jun **Inti Raymi**, the Inca festival of the winter solstice (see box, opposite), where locals outnumber tourists, is enacted at the fortress of Sacsayhuaman. The spectacle starts at 1000 at the Qoricancha (crowds line the streets and jostle for space to watch), then proceeds to the Plaza de Armas. From there performers and spectators go to Sacsay-huaman for the main event, which starts at 1300. It lasts 2½ hrs and is in Quechua. Locals make a great day of it, watching the ritual from the hillsides and cooking potatoes in pits in the ground. Tickets for the stands can be bought in advance from the **Emufec** office, Santa Catalina Ancha 325 (opposite the Complejo Policial), and cost US$35. Standing places on the ruins are free but get there at about 1030 as even reserved seats fill up quickly, and defend your space. Travel agents can arrange the whole day for you, with meeting points, transport, reserved seats and packed lunch. On the night before **Inti Raymi**, the Plaza de Armas is crowded with processions and food stalls. Try to arrive in Cuzco 15 days before Inti Raymi. The atmosphere in the town during the build up is fantastic and something is always going on.
8 Sep **Day of the Virgin**, when there's a colourful procession of masked dancers from the church of Almudena, at the southwest edge of Cuzco, near Belén, to the Plaza de San Francisco. There is also a fair at Almudena, and a bull fight the following day.
8 Dec **Cuzco Day**, when churches and museums close at 1200.
24 Dec **Santuranticuy**, 'the buying of saints'. Huge celebration of Christmas shopping with a big crafts market in the Plaza de Armas, which is very noisy until the early hours of the 25th.

⬢ Shopping

Cuzco *p88, maps p92 and p94*
Arts and crafts
Cuzco has some of the best craft shopping in Peru. In and around Plaza San Blas, authentic Cuzco crafts still survive and woodworkers can be seen in almost any street. A market is held on Sat. The main market for artisans'

The festival of Inti Raymi

The sun was the principal object of Inca worship and at their winter solstice, in June, the Incas honoured the solar deity with a great celebration known as Inti Raymi, the sun festival. The Spanish suppressed the Inca religion, and the last royal Inti Raymi was celebrated in 1535.

However, in 1944, a group of Cuzco intellectuals, inspired by the contemporary 'indigenist' movement, revived the old ceremony in the form of a pageant, putting it together from chronicles and historical documents. The caught the public imagination, and it has been celebrated every year since then on 24 Jun, now a Cuzco public holiday. Hundreds of local men and women play the parts of Inca priests, nobles, chosen women, soldiers (played by the local army garrison), runners, and the like. The coveted part of the Inca emperor Pachacuti is won by audition, and the event is organized by the municipal authorities.

It begins around 1000 at the Qoricancha (page 95) – the former sun temple of Cuzco – and winds its way up the main avenue into the Plaza de Armas, accompanied by songs, ringing declarations and the occasional drink of *chicha*. At the main plaza, Cuzco's presiding mayor is whisked back to Inca times, to receive Pachacuti's blessing and a lecture on good government. Climbing through Plaza Nazarenas and up Pumacurcu, the procession reaches the ruins of Sacsayhuaman at about 1400, where scores of thousands of people are gathered on the ancient stones.

Before Pachacuti arrives the *Sinchi* (Pachacuti's chief general) ushers in contingents from the four *Suyus* (regions) of the Inca empire. Much of the ceremony is based around alternating action between these four groups of players. A *Chaski* (messenger) enters to announce the imminent arrival of the Inca and his *Coya* (queen). Men sweep the ground before him and women scatter flowers. The Inka takes the stage alone and has a dialogue with the sun. Then he receives reports from the governors of the four *Suyus*. This is followed by a drink of the sacred *chicha*, the re-lighting of the sacred fire of the empire, the sacrifice (faked) of a llama and the reading of auguries in its entrails. Finally the ritual eating of *sankhu* (corn paste mixed with the victim's blood) ends the ceremonies. The Inca gives a last message to his assembled children, and departs. The music and dancing continues dark. See Festivals and events, page 106.

stalls is at the bottom of Av Sol (the **Cholitas de los Andes** stall, No 96, sells textiles made by unsupported mothers). There are also small markets dotted around the city which offer goods made from alpaca or modern materials.

Cuzco is also the weaving centre of Peru and excellent textiles can be found at good value; but watch out for sharp practices when buying gold and silver objects and jewellery.
Agua y Tierra, Plazoleta Nazarenas 167; also at Cuesta San Blas 595, T084-226951. Quality crafts from lowland rainforest communities.

Alpaca 111, Plaza Regocijo 202, T084-243233. High-quality alpaca clothing, with shops also in hotels **Monasterio**, **Libertador** and **Machu Picchu Sanctuary Lodge**, the Museo de Arte Precolombino and at the airport.
Arte Vivo del Cusco al Mundo, on the right-hand side in Capilla San Ignacio, Plaza de Armas. The outlet for 2 weaving cooperatives.
Calas, Siete Angelitos 619-B, San Blas. Hand-made silver jewellery and alpaca goods from the Pitumarca community.
Carlos Chaquiras, Triunfo 375 y Portal Comercio 107, T084-227470, www.carlos

chaquiras.com. Upmarket jewellery, with lots of Inca figures, enhanced with semi-precious stones and shells. Also in Urubamba.

Center for Traditional Textiles of Cusco, Av Sol 603, T084-228117, www.textiles cusco.org. A non-profit organization that promotes the weaving traditions of the area. Weaving classes and tours of workshops. Excellent quality. 50% of profits go to the weaver. Recommended.

Ilaria, Portal Carrizos 258, T084-246253, and in hotels **Monasterio**, **Libertador** and at the airport. Recommended jewellery and silver.

Inkantations, Choquechaca 200. Radical baskets made from natural materials in all sorts of weird and wonderful shapes.

Josefina Olivera, Portal Comercio 173, Plaza de Armas. She sells old ponchos and antique *mantas* (shawls), without the usual haggling. Her prices are high, but it is worth it to save pieces being cut up to make other items.

Mullu, Triunfo 120, T084-229831. Contemporary silver jewellery with semi-precious stones; also cotton clothing.

Pedazo de Arte, Plateros 334B. A tasteful collection of Andean handicrafts, many designed by Japanese owner Miki Suzuki.

Primitiva, Hatun Rumiyoc 495, T084-260152, San Blas, www.coscio.com. Excellent Peruvian contemporary art gallery, largely featuring the work of Federico Coscio.

Spondylus, Cuesta San Blas 505 y Plazoleta San Blas 617, T084-226929, spondyluscusco@ mixmail.com. Interesting jewellery in gold and silver, using semi-precious stones and shells.

Store of the Weavers (Asociación Central de Artesanos y Artesanas del Sur Andino Inkakunaq Ruwaynin), Av Tullumayo 274, www.cbc.org.pe/tejidosandinos. Run by 6 local communities; all profits go to the weavers. Fine quality *mantas* and other textiles. Well worth a visit.

Taki Museo de Música de los Andes, Hatunrumiyoq 487-5. Shop and workshop selling and displaying musical instruments, the owner is an ethnomusicologist.

Books

Jerusalem, Heladeros 143, T084-235408. English books, guidebooks, music, postcards, book exchange (3 for 1).

The Sun, Plazoleta Limacpampa Chico 471. Café/restaurant with best book exchange.

Camping equipment

Several places on Plateros rent out equipment but check it carefully for missing parts. Average daily costs: tent US$3-5, sleeping bag US$2 (down), US$1.50 (synthetic), stove US$1. A deposit of US$100 is asked, plus credit card, passport or plane ticket. Check stoves carefully. White gas (*bencina*) costs US$1.50 per litre and can be bought at hardware stores. Stove spirit (*alcohol para quemar*) is available at pharmacies. Blue gas canisters, costing US$5, can be found at some hardware stores and at shops which rent gear. You can also rent equipment through travel agencies.

Edson Zuñiga Huillca, Mercado Rosaspata, Jr Abel Landeo P-1, T084-802831, 993 7243 (mob). 3 mins from Plaza de Armas. Repairs camping equipment and footwear, rents equipment, open 24 hrs a day, 7 days a week.

Soqllaq'asa Camping Service, Plateros 365 No 2F, T084-252560. Recommended for equipment hire, from down sleeping bags (US$2 per day) to gas stoves (US$1 per day) and ThermaRest mats (US$1 per day); pots, pans, plates, cups and cutlery are all provided. Also camping gear and alpaca jackets.

Tatoo, Calle del Medio 130 , T084-254211, www.tatoo.ws. High-quality hiking, climbing and camping gear, European prices, brand names include Colombia, Gore-Tex and Polartec. The house brand, Tatoo, produces good trousers, thermals, fleeces and jackets.

Food

Casa Ecológica Cusco, Triunfo 393, www.casaecologicacusco.com. Organic foods, wild honey, coffee, granola, natural medicines, indigenous art and weavings.

La Cholita, Portal Espinar 142-B and at airport. Extra-special chocolates, local ingredients.

Markets

San Jerónimo, just out of town, is the wholesale Sat morning fruit and vegetable market, but food just as good can be bought at the markets in town: **Huanchac**, Av Garcilaso (not Calle Garcilaso), or **Santa Ana**, opposite Estación San Pedro, which sells a variety of goods. The best value is at closing time or in the rain. Take care after dark. Sacks to cover rucksacks are available in the market for US$0.75. Both Huanchac and Santa Ana open every day from 0700.

▲ Activities and tours

Cuzco *p88, maps p92 and p94*

There are a million and one tour operators in Cuzco, most of whom are packed into the Plaza de Armas. The sheer number and variety of tours on offer is bewildering and prices vary dramatically. Only deal directly with the agencies and ask people returning from trips for the latest information. Agencies listed below are included under the field in which they are best known and for which they receive consistent recommendations. City tours cost about US$6 and last 4 hrs; check what sites are included (usually too few) and that the guide is experienced. Beware of tours which stop for long lunches at pricey hotels. Check if there are cancellation fees. Students often receive a discount with an ISIC card.

Inca Trail and general tours

Only a restricted number of agencies are licensed to operate Inca Trail trips. A full list will be found on www.inc-cusco.gob.pe: click on Sistema de Reservas RCI. (INRENA, Av José Gabriel Cosio 308, Urb Magisterial, 1 etapa, T084-229297, www.inrena.gob.pe, will verify operating permits.) Other agencies sell Inca Trail trips, but pass clients on to the operating agency in a pooling system. This can cause confusion and booking problems at busy times.

Inclusion in our list does not guarantee that the company is licensed to operate the Inca Trail. All those listed below have been recommended for their services. Many agencies, and the alternatives they offer, can be found in the trip reports in the **South America Explorers'** clubhouse at Choquechaca 188 (for members only).

Amazing Peru, Av Tullumayo 213, T084-262720 (9 Alma Rd, Manchester M19 2FG, T0808-2346805), www.amazingperu.com. Professional and well-organized, "perfect tour", knowledgeable guides.

Andina Travel, Plazoleta Santa Catalina 219, T084-251892, www.andinatravel.com. Specializes in trekking and biking, notably the Lares Valley, working with traditional weaving communities.

Apu Expediciones, T084-969 8311, www.geocities.com/thetropics/cabana/4037. Operator with many years experience in adventure and cultural travel. Deals with customers mostly on-line.

Big Foot, Triunfo 392 (of 213), T084-238568, www.bigfootcusco.com. Specialists in tailor-made hiking trips to remote corners of the Vilcabamba and Vilcanota mountains. Also the more conventional Inca Trail routes.

Ch'aska, Plateros 325, 2nd floor, T084-240424, www.chaskatours.com. Dutch-Peruvian company offering cultural, nature, adventure and esoteric tours. They specialize in the Inca Trail, but also llama treks to Lares and trips to Choquequirao and beyond.

Cóndor Travel, Calle Saphi 848-A, T084-225961, www.condortravel.com.pe. A high-quality, exclusive agency that organizes trips throughout Peru. Has a specialized section for adventure travel and are an excellent port of call if looking for international flight tickets.

Destinos Turísticos, Portal de Panes 123, of 101-102, Plaza de Armas, T084-228168, www.destinosturisticosperu.com. The owner speaks many languages and specializes in package tours for all budgets. Offers advice on everything from jungle trips to renting mountain bikes. Very informative and helpful.

Ecotrek Peru, Totorapaccha 769, T084-247286, T084-972 7237 (mob), www.ecotrekperu.com. Environmentally friendly tour agency run by long-time Cuzco resident Fiona Cameron. Wide range of adventures offered through their excellent website, specializing in little visited areas such as the Pongo de Mainique and Espíritu Pampa/Vilcabamba Vieja. Fiona's partner, David, offers tailor-made mountain biking trips; great fun.

Enigma, Jiron Clorinda Matto de Turner 100, Magisterial 1a etapa, T084-222155, www.enigmaperu.com. Adventure tour agency. Excellent reputation for well-organized and innovative trekking expeditions. Also offers cultural tours to weaving communities, Ayahuasca therapy and can arrange climbing and biking trips.

Explorandes, Av Garcilaso 316-A (not to be confused with Calle Garcilaso in the centre), T084-238380, www.explorandes.com. Experienced high-end adventure company. Their main office is in Lima, but trips arranged from Cuzco. Vast range of trips available in both Peru and Ecuador. Also arranges tours for lovers of orchids, ceramics or textiles. Award-winning environmental practices.

Gatur Cusco, Puluchapata 140 (a small street off Av Sol 3rd block), T084-223496, www.gaturcusco.com. Esoteric, ecotourism, and general tours. Owner is knowledgeable in Andean folk traditions. Excellent conventional tours, guides speak many languages, very helpful. They can also book internal flights.

Hiking Peru, Portal de Panes 109, office 6, T084-247942/965 1414 (mob), www.hikingperu.com. Licensed for the Inca Trail but concentrates on the less-beaten paths, eg 8-day treks to Espíritu Pampa, 7 days/6 nights around Ausangate, Lares Valley Trek.

Inca Explorers, Ruinas 427, T084-241070, www.incaexplorers.com. Specialist trekking agency with a good reputation for small group expeditions. Environmentally and socially responsible. More adventurous trips include a 2-week hike in the Cordillera Vilcanota (passing Nevado Ausangate), and Choquequirao to Espíritu Pampa.

Liz's Explorer, Medio 114B, T084-246619, www.lizexplorer.com. For the Inca Trail and other trips. Down sleeping bags are US$2.50 per day extra, fibre bags US$2. If you need a guide who speaks a language other than English let Lis know in advance. Also city tours and the Sacred Valley. Feedback on trip is good, less so for the office.

Machete Tours, Tecseccocha 161, T084-224829, www.machetetours.com. Founded by born-and-bred jungle hand Ronaldo and his Danish partner Tina. Innovative trekking trips such as a 9-day traverse of the Cordillera Vilcabamba from the Apurímac Canyon and Choquequirao across the range to Machu Picchu. Also expeditions to Espíritu Pampa and Ausangate. They have a rainforest lodge on the remote Río Blanco, south of the Manu Biosphere Reserve. Not all of the guides speak English so check beforehand. Eric is a recommended guide for Choquequirao.

Oropéndola Tours, Calle 7 Cuartones, 284 interior 3-D, T084-9668 5990, www.oropendolaperu.org. English-, Spanish- and Japanese-speaking guides specializing in Manu National Park, as well as birdwatching, nature and cultural experience tours.

Peruvian Andean Treks, Av Pardo 705, T084-225701, www.andeantreks.com. Manager Tom Hendrickson has 5-day/4-night Inca Trail for US$500 using high-quality equipment and satellite phones. His 7-day/6-night Vilcanota

Llama Trek to Ausangate includes a collapsible pressure chamber for altitude sickness. Also extended trekking itineraries.

Peru Treks and Adventure, Calle Garcilaso 265, office 11, 2 blocks from main square, T084-505863, www.perutreks.com. Trekking agency set up by Englishman Mike Weston and his wife Koqui González. They pride themselves on good treatment of porters and staff and are consistently recommended for professionalism and customer care, a portion of profits go to community projects. Treks offered include Salkantay, the Lares Valley and Vilcabamba Vieja. Mike also runs the **Andean Travel Web**, www.andeantravelweb.com.

Q'ente, Garcilaso 210, int 210b, T084-222535, www.qente.com. Their Inca Trail service is recommended. Also private treks to Salkantay, Ausangate, Choquequirao, Vilcabamba and Q'eros. Horse riding to local ruins costs US$35 for 4-5 hrs. Very good, especially with children.

SAS Travel, Portal de Panes 143, T084-237292, www.sastravel.com. Discount for SAE members and students. Inca Trail includes the bus down from Machu Picchu to Aguas Calientes and lunch on the last day. SAS have their own hostel in Aguas Calientes. Offers alternatives to the classic Inca Trail, including Salkantay and Santa Teresa. Also mountain bike, horse riding and jungle tours. All guides speak some English. Internal flights booked at cheaper rates than from overseas. Solid reputation for equipment and food on the trail, but reports increasingly mixed.

Sky Travel, Santa Catalina Ancha 366, interior 3-C (down alleyway next to Rosie O'Grady's pub), T084-261818, www.skyperu.com. English spoken. General tours of the city and Sacred Valley. Inca Trail with good-sized double tents and a dinner tent (choice of menu before departure). Other trips include Vilcabamba and Ausangate (trekking).

Tambo Tours, 4405 Spring Cypress Rd, Suite #210, Spring, TX, 77388, USA, T1-888-2-GO-PERU (246 7378), T1-281-528 9448, www.2GOPERU.com. Long-established adventure and tour specialist with offices in Peru and USA. Customized trips to the Amazon and archaeological sites of Peru, Bolivia and Ecuador.

Trekperu, Ricaldo Palma N-9, Santa Mónica, T084-252899, www.trekperu.com. Experienced

trek operator as well as other adventure sports and mountain biking. Offers 'culturally sensitive' tours. Cuzco Biking Adventure includes support vehicle and good camping gear (but providing your own sleeping bag).

United Mice, Plateros 351y Triunfo 392, T084-221139, www.unitedmice.com. Inca Trail and alternative trail via Salkantay and Santa Teresa, including entrance to Machu Picchu. Good English-speaking guides; Discount with student card, good food and equipment. City and Sacred Valley tours and treks to Choquequirao. Cheaper than most.

Wayki Trek, Procuradores 351, Plaza de Armas, T084-224092, www.waykitrek.net. Budget travel agency, recommended for the Inca Trail service. Owner Leo grew up near Ollantaytambo and knows the area well. Treks to several almost unknown Inca sites and interesting variations on the 'classic' Inca Trail with visits to porters' communities. Also treks to Ausangate, Salkantay and Choquequirao.

Mountain biking and rafting

Cuzco offers rides to suit all abilities. It's best to take a guide as its very easy to get lost. Moreover, the Cuzco region is probably the 'rafting capital' of Peru, with more whitewater runs than anywhere else in Peru. When looking for an operator consider more than just the price. Competition is intense and price wars can lead companies to compromise safety and cut corners. Bargaining the price down will have the same effect. A one-day trip should cost a minimum of US$30, and a 3-day trip to the Apurímac not less than US$250. Ask about the quality of safety equipment (lifejackets, etc) and the number and experience of rescue kayakers and support staff. On a large and potentially dangerous river like the Apurímac and when any of the rivers is high, this can make all the difference. Fatalities have occurred.

Amazonas Explorer, Av Collasuyo 910, Miravalle, T084-252846 T084-976 5448 (mob), www.amazonas-explorer.com. Experts in rafting, hiking and biking. English owner Paul has great experience, but most bookings are from overseas (T01437-891743 in UK). He may be able to arrange a trip for travellers in Cuzco. Rafting includes Río Apurímac and Río Tambopata, with all transfers from Lima. Also 5-day/4-night Inca Trail trip of the highest quality, and alternatives to the Inca Trail and Choquequirao to Vitcos. Excellent variation of the Ausangate Circuit, features an extension to the Laguna Singrenacocha and the chance for ice-climbers to tackle the remote Campa Peak. Activity and family trips are a speciality. At the higher end of the market.

Apumayo, Av Garcilaso 316, Wanchaq, T084- 246018, www.apumayo.com. Urubamba and Apurímac rafting; Inca Trail trekking. Also mountain biking, eg Maras and Moray in Sacred Valley, or 5-day epic biking from Cuzco to Quillabamba. This company also offers tours for disabled people, including rafting.

Camp Expeditions, Av Manco Capac 414, of 403, T084-431468, www.campexpedition.net. All sorts of adventure tours, but specialists in climbing, for which they are recommended as most reliable, and trekking.

Eric Adventures, Plateros 324, T084-234764, www.ericadventures.com. Popular company specializing in adventure activities: rafting, kayaking, canyoning, hydrospeed, mountain biking, plus the Inca Trail. Also rents motor-cross bikes. Huge discounts sometimes available if you go to the office in person.

Land of the Inkas, Av de la Cultura 1318, Wanchaq, T084-233451, www.landofthe inkas.com. Run by the very experienced Juan and Benjamín Muñiz, this company now largely operates through web-based bookings, arranging both multi-week expeditions and shorter adventures for those already in the Cuzco area. **Instinct** offers activities as diverse as surf safaris on Peru's north coast to multi-day horse-riding tours in the Sacred Valley.

Manu Expeditions, Humberto Vidal Unda G-5, 2a Etapa, Urb Magisterial, T084-226671, www.manuexpeditions.com. As well as Manu trips (see page 288), also runs tailor-made bird trips in cloud- and rainforest around Cuzco and Peru, as well as butterfly watching, and has horse riding and a 9-day/8-night trip to Machu Picchu along a different route from the Inca Trail, rejoining at Sun Gate. Horse- supported treks to Choquequirao from Huancacalle.

Mayuc Ecological Tourism Adventure Travel, Portal Confiturías 211, Plaza de Armas, T084-232666, www.mayuc.com. One of the longest-running river rafting adventure companies in Cuzco. Rafting on the Ríos Urubamba and Apurímac. **Mayuc** now have a permanent lodge, **Casa Cusi**, on the upper Urubamba, which forms the basis of 2-day, Class III-IV trips in the area. Other tours include Inca Trail and Salkantay.

The Medina Brothers, contact Christian or Alain Medina on T084-225163 or T084-965 3485/969 1670 (mob). Family-run rafting company with good equipment and plenty of experience. They usually focus on day rafting trips in the Sacred Valley, but services are tailored to the needs of the client. Reasonable prices dependent on numbers.

Swissraft-Peru, Plateros 369, T084-264124, www.swissraft-peru.com. This company runs rafting tours on the Apurímac and Urubamba rivers. Equipment is of good quality.

Terra Explorer Peru, T084-237352, www.terra explorerperu.com. Offers a wide range of trips from high-end rafting in the Sacred Valley and expeditions to the Colca and Cotahuasi canyons, trekking the Inca Trail and others, mountain biking, kayaking (including on Lake Titicaca) and jungle trips. All guides bilingual.

Paragliding and ballooning

Magnificent scenery, soaring close to snow-capped mountains makes this an awesome experience. 45 km from Cuzco is **Cerro Sacro** (3797 m) on the Pampa de Chincheros with 550 m clearance at take-off. It is the launch site for cross-country flights over the Sacred Valley, Sacsayhuaman and Cuzco. Particularly good for parapenting is the **Mirador de Urubamba**, 38 km from Cuzco, at 3650 m, with 800-m clearance and views over Pisac. Note that the Sacred Valley offers exciting but challenging paragliding so if wind conditions are bad, flights may be delayed till the following day. Beware pilots offering suspiciously cheap flights; their experience and equipment is unlikely to be appropriate for the Sacred Valley's conditions.

Globos de los Andes, Av de la Cultura 220, suite 36, T084-232352, www.globosperu.com. Hot-air ballooning in the Sacred Valley and expeditions with balloons and 4WD.

Richard Pethigal, T084-993 7333 (mob), www.cloudwalkerparagliding.com. A condor's-eye view of the Sacred Valley. May-Sep he runs half-day tandem paraglider flights from Cuzco. He is a very experienced pilot, the only one with an international licence in Cuzco. He charges US$70 for a 15-30 min flight. Longer cross-country flights and flights from El Misti (Arequipa) arranged.

Among the many forms of spiritual tourism offered in the Cuzco region, one that attracts much attention is shamanic and drug experiences. (The following list is not restricted to this type of tourism.) San Pedro and Ayahuasca have been used since before Inca times, mostly as a sacred healing experience. The plants are prepared with special treatments for curative purposes; they have never been considered a drug. If you choose to experience these incredible healing/ teaching plants, only do so under the guidance of a reputable agency or shaman and always have a friend with you who is not partaking. If the medicine is not prepared correctly, it can be highly toxic and, in rare cases, severely dangerous. Never buy tours off the streets, never buy from someone who is not recommended and never try to prepare the plants yourself.

Another Planet, Triunfo 120, T084-229379, www.anotherplanetperu.net. Run by Lesley Myburgh (who also runs **Casa de La Gringa**, Pasñapacana y Tandapata 148, San Blas, T241168, T965 2006 (mob), sleeping in **E** range), who operates all kinds of adventure tours and conventional tours in and around Cuzco, but specializes in jungle trips anywhere in Peru. Lesley is an expert in San Pedro cactus preparation and she arranges San Pedro journeys for healing at physical, emotional and spiritual levels in beautiful remote areas.

Milla Tourism, Av Pardo 689 y Portal Comercio 195 on the plaza, T084-231710, www.millaturismo.com, Mon-Fri 0800-1300, 1500-1900, Sat 0800-1300. Mystical tours to Cuzco's Inca ceremonial sites such as Pumamarca and the Temple of the Moon. Also private tours arranged to Moray agricultural terracing and Maras salt mines in Sacred Valley. Guide speaks only basic English. They also arrange cultural and environmental lectures and courses.

Eleana Molina, T084-975 1791, misticanativa@ yahoo.com. For Ayahuasca ceremonies.

Mystic Inca Trail, Unidad Vecinal de Santiago, bloque 9, dpto 301, T084-221358, ivanndp@terra.com.pe. Specializes in tours of sacred Inca sites and the study of Andean spirituality. This takes 10 days but it is possible to have shorter 'experiences'.

114 Tours to Manu Biosphere Reserve

There are many operators in Cuzco offering trips to Manu. For full details of these operators and the tours on offer, see page 297.

Private guides

As most of the sights do not have information or signs in English, a good guide can really improve your visit. Either arrange this before you set out or grab one of those hanging around the sights' entrances (much easier in low season). A tip is expected at the end of the tour. All of those listed are bilingual. Set prices: City tour US$15-20 per day; Urubamba/Sacred Valley US$25-30, Machu Picchu and other ruins US$40-50 per day.
Boris Cárdenas, boriscar@telser.com.pe. Esoteric and cultural tours.
José Cuba and Alejandra Cuba, Urb Santa Rosa R Gibaja 182, Urb Santa Rosa R Gibaja 182, T084-226179, T968 5187 (mob), ale17ch1@yahoo.com. English, German and French spoken; very good tours.
Miguel Angel Jove Mamani, T084-245670, 974 0143 (mob), miguelj24@hotmail.com. Recommended by South American Explorers.
Percy Salas Alfaro, c/o Munditur, T084-240287, T962 1152 (mob), smunditur@hotmail.com. Serious, friendly, English spoken.
Roger Valencia Espinoza, José Gabriel Cosio 307, T084-251278, 977 0973 (mob), vroger@qenqo.rcp.net.pe. Adventure trips.
Victoria Morales Condori, T084-224877, kuntur01@yahoo.com.mx.

◎ Transport

Cuzco *p88, maps p92 and p94*
Air
There is a Tourist Protection Bureau desk at the airport, which can be very helpful if your flight has not been reconfirmed (not uncommon). Do not forget to pay the airport tax at the appropriate desk before departure.
To **Lima**, 55 mins, daily flights with Taca, Star Perú and Lan. Flights are heavily booked in school holidays (May, Jul, Oct and Dec-Mar) and national holidays. Sit on right side of the aircraft for the best view of the mountains when flying Cuzco-Lima; check in 2 hrs before flight. Reconfirm 48 hrs before your flight. Flights may be delayed or cancelled during the wet season. Planes may leave early if the weather is bad.

To **Arequipa**, 30 mins with Lan. To **Puerto Maldonado**, 30 mins, with Lan. To/from **La Paz**, LAB but not daily. See note about LAB on page 28.
Airline offices Aero Cóndor, at the airport, T084-252774. LAB, Santa Catalina Angosta 160, T084-222990. Lan, Av Sol 627-B, T084-225552. Star Perú, Av Sol 679, of 1, T084-234060. Taca, Av Sol 602, T084-249921, good service.

Bus
To **Pisac**, buses leave from Calle Puputi on the outskirts of town, near the Clorindo Matto de Turner school and Av de la Cultura. 32 km, 1 hr, US$0.85. *Colectivos*, minibuses and buses leave when full, 0600-1600; also trucks and pickups. Also buses to **Calca** (18 km beyond Pisac).

To **Chinchero**, *combis* and *colectivos* leave from 300 block of Av Grau, 1 block before crossing the bridge (23 km, 45 mins, US$0.60); they continue to **Urubamba** (a further 25 km, 45 mins, US$0.45). Direct to **Urubamba**, US$1.10, or US$1.20 for a seat in a *colectivo*) from Av Tullumayo 800 block, Wanchac.

To **Ollantaytambo**, there is a direct bus service from Av Grau at 0745 and 1945 (or catch a bus to Urubamba from Av Grau), from where there are regular *colectivos*.
Long-distance Buses leave from the Terminal Terrestre. Daily direct buses to **Lima** (20-24 hrs) go via **Abancay**, 195 km, 5 hrs (longer in the rainy season), and **Nazca**, on the Panamerican Highway. This route is paved, but floods in the wet season can damage sections of the highway. If prone to car sickness, be prepared on the road to Abancay, there are many bends, but the scenery is magnificent (it's also a great route for cycling). At Abancay, the road forks, the other branch going to **Andahuaylas**, a further 138 km, 10-11 hrs from Cuzco, and **Ayacucho** in the Central Highlands, another 261 km, 20 hrs from Cuzco. On both routes at night, take a blanket or sleeping bag to ward off the cold.

Molina has 3 services a day to **Lima** via **Abancay** and **Nazca**, and one, at 1900, to **Abancay** and **Andahuaylas**. Wari has 4 a day to **Abancay**, **Nazca** and **Lima**. Cruz del Sur has a cheaper *Ideal* service to **Lima** via Abancay, and 2 more comfortable *Imperial* services, all in the afternoon. San Jerónimo and Los Chankas have buses to **Abancay**,

Andahuaylas and Ayacucho. Turismo
Ampay, Turismo Abancay, Expreso
Huamanga and Bredde all have buses
daily to Abancay. Fares to Abancay US$3.65,
Andahuaylas US$6, Ayacucho US$12, Nazca
US$17-20, Lima US$20 (Cruz del Sur, *Ideal*
class) to US$32 (Cruz del Sur, *Imperial* class).

To Juliaca (near Lake Titicaca), 344 km,
6 hrs, US$3-4. The road is paved, but after
heavy rain buses may not run. From Juliaco
to Puno, 44 km, US$4.50-6; there is a good
service with Ormeño at 0900, US$10, 6 hrs,
which continues to La Paz (Bolivia). First Class,
Av Sol 930, have a service at 0730, calling at
Andahuaylillas church, Raqchi and Pucará en
route (lunch included, but not entrance tickets),
arrives Puno 1700, US$25. Travel agencies sell
this ticket. Other services are run by Tour Perú
and Libertad (at night), US$8.60, 6½-8 hrs.
Note We have received many reports of
robbery on night buses on the Juliaca-
Puno-Cuzco route; travel by day, or by train.

To Arequipa, 521 km, Cruz del Sur use the
direct paved route via Juliaca and have an
Imperial service at night, 10 hrs, US$23.
Ormeño's fare is US$18. Other buses join
the new Juliaca–Arequipa road at Imata,
10-12 hrs, US$7.75 (eg Carhuamayo, 3 a day).

Car hire
Avis, Av El Sol 808 and at the airport,
T084-248800, avis-cusco@terra.com.pe.
Touring y Automóvil Club del Perú, Av Sol
349, T084-224561, cusco@touringperu.com.
pe. Information on motoring, car hire and
mechanics (membership is US$45 per year).

Taxi
Taxis have fixed prices: in the centre
US$0.60 (US$0.90 after dark); to the suburbs
US$0.85-1.55 (touts at the airport and train
station will always ask much higher fares).
In town it is advisable to take municipality-
authorized taxis which have a blue sticker on
the windscreen. Safer still are licensed taxis,
which have a sticker with a number in the
window and a chequerboard pattern on the
sides. These taxis are summoned by phone
and are more expensive, in the centre
US$1-1.25 (Ocarina T084-247080, Aló Cusco
T084-222222, radio taxi T084-222000).

Taxi trips to Sacsayhuaman cost US$10; to
the ruins of Tambo Machay US$15-20 (3-4
people); a whole-day trip costs US$40-70.

To organize your own **Sacred Valley**
transport, the following taxi drivers are
recommended by South America Explorers:
Manuel Calanche, T084-227368, T969 5402
(mob); Carlos Hinojosa, T084-251160;
Ferdinand Pinares, Yuracpunco 155,
Tahuantinsuyo, T084-225914, T968 1519
(mob), speaks English, French and Spanish;
Eduardo, T084-231809, speaks English.
Also recommended are: Angel Marcavillaca
Palomino, Av Regional 877, T084-251822,
amarcavillaca@yahoo.com, helpful,
patient, reasonable prices; Movilidad
Inmediata, T962 3821 (mob), runs local tours
with an English-speaking guide. Angel Salazar,
Marcavalle I-4 Huanchac, T084-224679 (to
leave messages), is English-speaking and
arranges good tours, very knowledgeable and
enthusiastic; Milton Velásquez, T084-222638,
T968 0730 (mob), is also an anthropologist
and tour guide and speaks English.

Train
Peru Rail administers the main railways for
Puno–Juliaca–Cuzco and Cuzco–Machu
Picchu, www.perurail.com; see the website
for train services out of Cuzco. Trains for
Aguas Calientes for Machu Picchu leave
from Estación San Pedro, opposite the Santa
Ana market (T084-221313), see page 138.

Trains to Juliaca and Puno run from
Estación Wanchac (see Ins and outs, page
88). The ticket office is open Mon-Fri 0800-
1700, Sat 0900-1200. The train leaves at
0800, on Mon, Wed and Sat, arriving in Puno
at 1730 (sit on the left for the best views).
The train makes a stop to view the scenery
at La Raya. Tourist/ backpacker class, US$19
(drinks and snacks extra), 1st class US$130,
includes lunch, afternoon tea, entertainment,
luxury seating (recommended); look out for
promotional offers. Tickets sell out quickly
and there are queues from 0400 before
holidays in the dry season. In the low season
tickets to Puno can be bought on the day of
departure. You can also buy tickets through
a travel agent, but check the date and seat
number. Meals are served on the train.
Always double check whether the train is
running, especially in the rainy season, when
services might be cancelled. Tickets can be
bought up to 5 days in advance, cash only
(dollars accepted). For trains from Puno to
Cuzco, see page 156.

ⓘ Directory

Cuzco *p88, maps p92 and p94*

Banks All the banks along Av Sol have ATMs from which you can withdraw dollars or soles. There can be long queues. Most banks are closed 1300-1600. **BCP**, Av Sol 189. Gives cash advances on Visa and changes Tcs to soles with no commission, 3% to dollars. It also handles Amex. **Interbank**, Av Sol y Puluchapata. Charges no commission on TCs. Next door is **Banco Continental**, which charges up to US$4 commission on TCs. **BSCH**, Av Sol 459. Changes Amex TCs at reasonable rates. **Scotiabank**, Maruri between Pampa del Castillo and Pomeritos. Gives cash advances on MasterCard and Visa, in dollars. As well as the ATMs in banks, there are ATMs on the Plaza de Armas at the entrance to Inka Grill, Portal de Panes, Incanto (Santa Catalina Angosta 135, for Citibank), Supermercado Gato's, Portal Belén, and the entrance to Cross Keys and Tunupa, Portal de Confiturías. There are other ATMs on Av la Cultura, beside supermarkets. Many travel agencies and *casas de cambio* change dollars. Some of them change TCs as well, but charge 4-5% commission. There are many *cambios* on the west side of the Plaza de Armas and on the west side of Av Sol, most change TCs. **LAC Dólar**, Av Sol 150, T084- 257762, Mon-Sat 0900-2000, with delivery service to central hotels, cash and TCs, is recommended. The street changers hang around Av Sol, blocks 2-3, every day. Some of them will also change TCs. **Clinics and doctors** Clínica Panamericana, Av Infancia 508, Wanchac, T084-249494, T965 1552 (mob). 24-hr emergency and medical attention. Clínica Pardo, Av de la Cultura 710, T084-240387, www.clinicapardo.com. 24-hr emergency and hospitalization/medical attention, international department, trained bilingual personnel, handles complete medical assistance coverage with international insurance companies, free ambulance service, visit to hotel, discount in pharmacy, dental service, X-rays, laboratory, full medical specialization. The most highly recommended clinic in Cuzco. **Hospital Regional**, Av de la Cultura, T084-227661, emergencies T084-223691. **Dr Johanna Menke**, T084-971 4558 (mob, 24 hrs). European qualified, Peruvian registered doctor who speaks German, English

and some French, swift service. **Embassies and consulates** Belgium, Av Sol 954, T084-221098, Mon-Fri 0900-1300, 1500-1700. France, Jorge Escobar, Calle Micaela Bastidas 101, 4th floor, T084- 233610. Germany, Sra Maria-Sophia Júrgens de Hermoza, San Agustín 307, T084-235459, Casilla Postal 1128, Correo Central. Mon-Fri, 1000-1200. Ireland, Charlie Donovan, Santa Catalina Ancha 360 (Rosie O'Grady's), T084-243514. Netherlands, Sra Marcela Alarco, Av El Sol 954, T084-224322, marcela_alarco@yahoo.com, Mon-Fri 0900-1500. Spain, Sra Juana María Lambarri, T965 0106 (mob). UK, Barry Walker, Av Pardo 895, T084-239974, bwalker@ amauta.rcp.net.pe. US Agent, Dra Olga Villagarcía, Apdo 949, Cuzco, T084-222183, or at the Binational Center (ICPNA), Av Tullumayo 125, Wanchac. **Internet** There are internet cafés everywhere. Most have similar rates, around US$0.60 per hr. **Language classes** Academia Latinoamericana de Español, Av El Sol 580, T084-243364, www.latinoschools.com. Professionally run with experienced staff. Many activities per week, including dance lessons and excursions to sites of historical and cultural interest. Good for homestay. Private classes US$350 for 20 hrs, groups, with a maximum of 4 students US$265, again for 20 hrs: thorough if traditional tuition. Acupari, San Agustín 307, T084-242970, www.acupari.com. The German-Peruvian Cultural Association, Spanish classes are run here. Amauta, PO Box 1164, Suecia 480, T084-262345, www.amautaspanishschool.org. Spanish classes, individual or in small groups, also Quechua classes and workshops in Peruvian cuisine, dance and music, US$10.50 per hr individual, but cheaper and possibly better value for group tuition (2-6 people), US$98 for 20 hrs. They have pleasant accommodation on site, as well as a free internet café for students, and can arrange excursions and can help find voluntary work. They also have a school in Urubamba and can arrange courses in the Manu rainforest, in conjunction with Pantiacolla Tours. Amigos Spanish School, Zaguán del Cielo B-23, T084-242292, www.spanishcusco.com. Profits from this school support a foundation for disadvantaged children. Private lessons for US$8 per hr, US$108 for 20 hrs of classes in a group. Homestays available, many recommendations. **La Casona de la Esquina**, Purgatorio 395, corner with Huaynapata, T084-235830, www.spanishlessons.com.pe. US$5 per hr for one-to-one classes. Recommended. **Cusco Spanish School**, Garcilaso 265, oficina 6 (2nd floor), T084-226928, www.cuscospanishschool. com. US$175 for 20 hrs of private classes, cheaper in groups. School offers homestays, optional activities including dance and music classes, cookery courses, ceramics, Quechua, hiking and volunteer programmes. They also offer courses on a hacienda at Cusipata in the Vilcanota Valley, east of Cuzco. **Excel**, Cruz Verde 336, T084-235298, www.excel-spanishlanguageprograms-peru.org. Very professional, US$7 per hr for private one-to-one lessons. US$229 for 20 hrs with 2 people, or US$227 with homestay and one-to-one tuition for 20 hrs. **Mundo Verde**, Calle Nueva Alta 432-A, T084-221287, www.mundoverdespanish.com. Spanish lessons with the option to study in the rainforest or work on environmental and social projects while studying. US$250 for 20 hrs tuition with homestay. **San Blas Spanish School**, Tandapata 688, T084-247898, www.spanishschoolperu.com. Groups, with 4 clients maximum, US$90 for 20 hrs tuition; US$130 for the same thing one-to-one. **Laundry** There are several cheap laundries on Procuradores, and also on Suecia and Tecseccocha. **Adonai**, Choquechaca 216-A, San Blas. Good hole-in-the-wall laundry. **Dana's Laundry**, Nueva Baja y Unión. US$2.10 per kg. **Lavandería**, Saphi 578. Good, fast service, US$1 per kg. **Lavandería Louis**, Choquechaca 264, San Blas. US$0.85 per kg, fresh, clean, good value.

Lavandería T'aqsana Wasi, Santa Catalina Ancha 345. Same-day service, they also iron clothes, US$2 per kg. **Splendid Laundry Service**, Carmen Alto 195. Very good, US$0.75 per kg, laundry sometimes available only 3-4 hrs. **Massage and therapies Casa de la serenidad**, Pumacurco 636, T084-233670, www.shamanspirit.net. A shamanic therapy centre run by a Swiss-American healer and Reiki Master who uses medicinal 'power' plants. Also has a good B&B. **Healing Hands**, based at Loki Hostel. Angela is a Reiki, Shiatsu and CranioSacral Therapist. Very relaxing and recommended, faeryamanita@ hotmail.com. **Post office** Central office, Av Sol at the bottom end of block 5, T084-225232, Mon-Sat 0730-2000, 0800-1400 Sun and holidays. Poste restante is free and helpful. Sending packages from Cuzco is not cheap. **DHL**, Av Sol 627, T084-244167. For sending packages or money overseas. **Telephone** There are independent phone offices in the centre. **Telefónica**, Av del Sol 386, T084-241111. For telephone and fax, Mon-Sat 0700-2300, 0700-1200 Sun and holidays. **Useful addresses Immigration** Av Sol, block 6, close to post office, T084-222740. Mon-Fri 0800-1300. Reported as not very helpful. **ISIC-Intej office**, Portal de Panes 123, of 107 (CC Los Ruiseñores), T084-256367. Issues international student cards. **Perú Verde**, Ricaldo Palma J-1, Santa Mónica, T084-226392, www.peruverde.org. For information and free video shows about Manu National Park and Tambopata National Reserve. They are friendly and have information on programmes and research in the jungle area of Madre de Dios.

Sacred Valley

→ *Colour map 4.*

The Río Urubamba cuts its way through fields and rocky gorges beneath the high peaks of the Cordillera. Brown hills, covered in wheat fields, separate Cuzco from this beautiful high valley, which stretches from Sicuani (on the railway to Puno) to the gorge of Torontoi, 600 m lower, to the northwest of Cuzco. That the river was of great significance to the Incas can be seen in the number of strategic sites they built above it; Pisac, Ollantaytambo and Machu Picchu among them. Upstream from Pisac, the river is usually called the Vilcanota; downstream it is the Urubamba.

▶▶ *For Sleeping, Eating and other listings, see pages 122-126.*

Ins and outs

Getting there The road from Cuzco runs past Sacsayhuaman and on to Tambo Machay, climbs up to a pass, then continues over the pampa before descending into the densely populated Urubamba Valley. This road then crosses the Río Urubamba by a bridge at Pisac and follows the north bank to the end of the paved road at Ollantaytambo. It passes through Calca, Yucay and Urubamba, which can also be reached from Cuzco by the beautiful, direct road through Chinchero. ▶▶ *For further details see Cuzco Tour operators, page 109, and Transport, page 126.*

Getting around Paved roads, plentiful transport and a good selection of hotels and eating places make this a straightforward place to explore. Take your time: most organized tours are too fast. The area is best explored on foot, by bike or on horseback. Alternatively, using public transport and staying overnight in the Valley allows much more time to see the ruins and markets.

Best time to visit The high season is June to September, but the rainy season, December to March, is cheaper and pleasant enough. The best times to visit are April to May or October to November.

Pisac ⬛🚻🚼🚾 ▶▶ *pp122-126. Colour map 4, C3.*

Only 30 km north of Cuzco the little village of Pisac is well worth a visit for its superb Inca ruins, perched precariously on the mountain, above the town. They are considered to be among the finest Inca ruins in the valley. However, most visitors treat the ruins as second priority, preferring to concentrate on the Sunday morning market and the growing number of shopping outlets. Pisac can be visited as part of a tour from Cuzco but this allows only 1½ hours on site, not enough time to take in the ruins and splendid scenery.

Pisac village and market

The market contains sections for the tourist and for the local community. Traditionally, Sunday is the day when the people of the highlands come down to sell their produce (potatoes, corn, beans, vegetables, weavings, pottery, etc). These are traded for essentials such as salt, sugar, rice, noodles, fruit, medicines, plastic goods and tools. The market comes to life after the arrival of tourist buses from around 0800, and is usually over by 1700. Pisac has other, somewhat less crowded, less expensive markets on Tuesday and Thursday morning; in each case, it's best to get there before 0900.

On the plaza, which has several large *pisonay* trees, are the church and a small interesting **Museo Folklórico**. The town, with its narrow streets, is worth strolling around. There are many souvenir shops on Bolognesi.

Inca ruins

ⓘ *Daily 0700-1730. If you go early (before 1000) you'll have the ruins to yourself. Entry is by BTG visitors' ticket (see page 90). Guides charge US$5, but the wardens on site are very helpful and provide free information. Allow 5-6 hrs on foot. Horses available for US$3. Transport approaches from the Kanchiracay end (20 mins from town); combis US$0.60 pp; taxis US$3 one-way from near the bridge. Then you can walk back down, 30 mins (or negotiate a fare and pickup time with the taxi).*

The ruins of Inca Pisac stand on a spur between the Río Urubamba to the south and the smaller Chongo to the east. It provides an ideal vantage point over the flat plain of the Urubamba, the terraces below and the terraced hillsides. This is one of the largest Inca ruins in the vicinity of Cuzco and it clearly had defensive, religious and agricultural functions, as well as being an Inca country estate.

The walk up to the ruins is recommended for the views (one hour). The path begins from the plaza, passing the Centro de Salud and a control post, then goes through working terraces. The first group of buildings is **Pisaqa**, with a fine curving wall. Climb up to the central part of the ruins, the **Intihuatana** group of temples and rock outcrops in the most magnificent Inca masonry. Here are the **Reloj Solar** (Hitching Post of the Sun) – now closed because thieves stole a piece from it – palaces of the moon and stars, solstice markers, baths and water channels. From Intihuatana, a path leads around the hillside through a tunnel to **Q'Allaqasa** (military area). Across the valley at this point, a large area of Inca tombs in holes in the hillside can be seen. The end of the site is **Kanchiracay**, where the agricultural workers were housed. At dusk you will hear, if not see, the *pisaca* (partridges), after which the place is named.

Urubamba and around ⊖⊘⊘⊛▲⊟❶ ›› *pp122-126.*

Urubamba → *See map page 123. Colour map 4, C2. Altitude: 2863 m.*

Like many places along the valley, Urubamba has a fine setting, with views of the Chicón snow-capped peaks and glaciers, and enjoys a mild climate. The main plaza, with a fountain capped by a maize cob, is surrounded by buildings painted blue. Calle Berriózabal, on the west edge of town, is lined with pisonay trees. The large market square is one block west of the main plaza. The main road skirts the town and the bridge for the road to Chinchero is just to the east of town.

Seminario-Behar Ceramic Studio ⓘ *Calle Berriózabal 111, a right turning off the main road to Ollantaytambo, To84-201002, kupa@terra.com.pe, open daily, ring the bell,* founded in 1980, is located in the beautiful grounds of the former **Hostal Urpihuasi**. Pablo Seminario has investigated the techniques and designs of pre-Columbian Peruvian cultures and has created a style with strong links to the past. Each piece is handmade and painted, using ancient glazes and minerals, and is then fired in reproduction pre-Columbian kilns. The resulting pieces are very attractive. Reservations to visit the studio and a personal appointment with the artists (Pablo and Marilú) are welcomed.

Yucay → *Colour map 4, C2.*

A few kilometres east of Urubamba, Yucay has two large, grassy plazas divided by the restored colonial church of **Santiago Apóstol**, with its oil paintings and fine altars. On the opposite side from Plaza Manco II is the **adobe palace** built for Sayri Túpac (Manco's son) when he emerged from Vilcabamba in 1558.

Valle de Lares

To the north of Urubamba and Calca, beyond the great peaks that tower above the Sacred Valley, lies the valley of **Lares**, an area famed for its traditional Quechua communities and strong weaving traditions. The mountainous territory that lies between these two valleys and, indeed, the valleys themselves offers a great deal for the ambitious trekker.

A good example is the four-day trek from **Huarán** (6 km west of Calca) to **Yanahuara** (beyond Urubamba on the road to Ollantaytambo) via the village of Lares through ancient native forests and past some of the Cordillera Urubamba's greatest snow peaks. Halfway you can have a good soak in the hot springs at **Lares**. Many of the locals may offer to sell weavings or *mantas* along the route, at prices a fraction of those in Cuzco.

Lares is also a perfect example of Peru's fabulous mountain biking opportunities, suiting all levels of ability. Many Cuzco agencies offer trekking and cycling tours, often as an alternative to the Inca Trail. ⏵ *See Cuzco Activities and tours, page 109.*

Chinchero → *Colour map 4, C2. Altitude: 3762 m.*
ⓘ *Daily 0700-1730. Can be visited on the BTG visitor ticket (see page 90).*

Chinchero is northwest from Cuzco, just off a direct road to Urubamba. The streets of the village wind up from the lower sections, where transport stops, to the **plaza** which is reached through an archway. The great square appears to be stepped, with a magnificent Inca wall separating the two levels. Let into the wall is a row of trapezoidal niches, each much taller than a man. From the lower section, which is paved, another arch leads to an upper terrace, upon which the Spaniards built an attractive **church**. The ceiling, beams and walls are covered in beautiful floral and religious designs. The altar, too, is fine. The church is open on Sunday for Mass and at festivals. Opposite the church is a small local museum. Excavations have revealed many Inca walls and terraces.

Chinchero attracts few tourists, except on Sunday for the colourful **market** (try to arrive before the tour groups; it's on your left as you come into town). There's also a small handicraft market on Sunday, up by the church.

Salinas → *Colour map 2, C4.*

Five kilometres west of Urubamba is the village of **Tarabamba** (Km 77 on the Sacred Valley road), where a bridge crosses the Río Urubamba. If you turn right after the bridge you'll come to **Pichingoto**, a tumbled-down village built under an overhanging cliff. Just over the bridge and before the town to the left of a small, walled cemetery is a salt stream. Follow the footpath beside the stream and you'll come to **Salinas**, a small village below which are a mass of terraced pre-Inca **salt pans** ⓘ *US$1.80*, which are still in production after thousands of years. There are 3200 pools and 480 cooperative members. They only work the pans from May to October, during the dry season. These are now a fixture on the tourist circuit and can become congested with buses.

It's a 45-minute walk from Urubamba to the salt pans. The climb up from the bridge, on the right side of the valley, is fairly steep but easy, with great views of Nevado Chicón. The path passes by the cascade of rectangular salt pans, taking up to 1½ hours to the top. From the summit of the cliff above the salt pans, walk to **Maras**, about 45 minutes. Head towards the white, colonial **church** ⓘ *US$1.80*, and visit it when you get there; it has been beautifully renovated. Take water as it can be very hot and dry.

Moray → *Colour map 4, B2.*
ⓘ *US$1.80, students US$0.90; allow an hour for a full visit.*

This remote but beautiful site lies 9 km by road to the west of the little town of Maras. There are three 'colosseums', used by the Incas, according to some theories, as a sort of open-air crop nursery, known locally as the laboratory of the Incas. The great depressions do not contain ruined buildings, but are lined with fine terracing. Each level is said to have its own microclimate. It is a very atmospheric place, which, some claim, has mystical power. The scenery around here is absolutely stunning, especially in the late afternoon when the light is wonderful. The road eventually arrives at the guardian's hut, but the scale of the colosseums is hidden until you reach the rim.

The most interesting ways to get to Moray are on foot from Urubamba via the *salineras* (see above), or a day-long cycle trip, starting in Chinchero and ending at the foot of the *salineras* (a challenging descent).

Ollantaytambo ⬛🟡✳🟢🟤 ➤ pp122-126.

→ Colour map 4, B2. Altitude: 2800 m.

The attractive little town of Ollantaytambo, at the foot of some spectacular Inca ruins, is built directly on top of the original Inca town, or Llacta. The Inca *canchas* (blocks of houses) are almost entirely intact and can be clearly seen. It's an impressive sight and shouldn't be missed, even though many people only visit the ruins above the town.

Ollantaytambo can be reached by bus from Cuzco, Urubamba and Chinchero. It is also one of the principal stations for catching the train to Machu Picchu; see box page 138 for details. You won't be allowed on the station unless you have previously bought a ticket for the train; the gates are locked and only those with tickets can enter.

The fortress

ⓘ *Daily 0700-1730. Admission is by BTG visitor ticket (see page 90), which can be bought at the site. Guides at the entrance charge US$6.50. Allow 2-3 hrs. Try to arrive very early before the tour groups. On Sun, tours from Pisac descend in their hundreds.*
When Manco Inca decided to rebel against the Spaniards in 1536, he fell back to Ollantaytambo from Calca to stage one of the greatest acts of resistance to the conquistadors. Hernando Pizarro led his troops to the foot of the Inca's stronghold and, on seeing how well-manned and fortified the place was, described it as "a thing of horror". Under fierce fire, Pizarro's men failed to capture Manco and retreated to Cuzco, but Manco could not press home any advantage. In 1537, feeling vulnerable to further attacks, he left Ollantaytambo for Vilcabamba.

When you visit Ollantaytambo you will be confronted by a series of 16 massive, stepped terraces of the very finest stonework, after crossing the great high-walled trapezoidal esplanade known as *Mañariki*. Beyond these imposing terraces lies the so-called **Temple of Ten Niches**, a funeral chamber once dedicated to the worship of Pachacútec's royal household. Immediately above this are six monolithic upright blocks of rose-coloured rhyolite, the remains of what is popularly called the **Temple of the Sun**. The dark grey stone is embellished today with bright orange lichen.

You can either descend by the route you came up, or follow the terracing round to the left (as you face the town) and work your way down to the **Valley of the Patacancha**. Here are more Inca ruins in the small area between the town and the temple fortress, behind the church. Most impressive is the **Baño de la Ñusta** (Bath of the Princess), a grey granite rock, about waist high, beneath which is the bath itself. The front of the boulder, over which the water falls, was delicately finished with a three-stepped pyramid, making a relief arch over the pool.

The town

If you are visiting Ollantaytambo, begin your tour at the Centro Andino de Tecnología Tradicional y Cultural de las Comunidades de Ollantaytambo, known as **El Museo Catcco** ⓘ *Casa Horno, Patacalle, 1 block from plaza, T084-204024, www.ollantaytambo.org, daily 0900-1900, US$1.50 requested as a donation*, which houses a fine ethnographical collection. Its information centre gives tips on day-hikes, things to see and places to dine and stay. Local guides are available for tours of the town and surrounding areas. Outside the museum, **Catcco** runs non-profit cultural programmes, temporary exhibitions, concerts and lectures. Also on site is a ceramics workshop, a textile revitalization programme and an educational theatre project. Ceramics and textiles are sold in the museum shop. Note the canal down the middle of the street outside the museum.

A two-dimensional **'pyramid'** has been identified on the west side of the main ruins of Ollantaytambo. Its discoverers, Fernando and Edgar Elorietta, claim it is the real Pacaritambo, from where the four original Inca brothers emerged to found their empire (this alternative Inca creation myth, the Inn of Origin, tells of four brothers and four sisters emerging from a cave in a cliff). Whether this is the case or not, it is still a first-class piece of engineering with great terraced fields and a fine 750-m wall creating the optical illusion of a pyramid. The wall is aligned with the rays of the winter solstice, on 21 June. People gather at mid-winter dawn to watch this event. The mysterious 'pyramid', which covers 50 to 60 ha, can be seen properly from the other side of the river. This is a pleasant, easy one-hour walk, west from the Puente Inca, just outside the town. You'll also be rewarded with great views of the Sacred Valley and the river, with the snowy peaks of the Verónica massif as a backdrop.

● Sleeping

Pisac *p118*

A Royal Inca Pisac, Carretera Ruinas Km 1.5, T084-203064, www.royalinkahotel.com/hpisac.html. In the same chain as the **Royal Incas** in Cuzco. It is a short distance out of town, on the road that goes up to the ruins; the hotel has its own bus service, or take a taxi after dark. Price includes taxes and breakfast. Rooms are comfortable, in a number of blocks in the grounds of a converted hacienda. Pool, sauna and jacuzzi (US$7), tennis court, horse riding and bicycle rental. The restaurant is good and there is a bar. Staff are very helpful. A guide for the ruins can be provided.

D-E Pisaq, corner of Pardo on the Plaza, Casilla Postal 1179, Cuzco, T084-203062, www.hotelpisaq.com. Bright and charming local decor and a pleasant atmosphere, rooms with private and shared bathrooms, hot water, sauna and massage. Good breakfast, basic, clean and friendly. The restaurant uses local ingredients, café.

F Residencial Beho, Intihuatana 642, 50 m up the hill from the plaza, T/F084-203001. Ask for a room in the main building. They serve a good breakfast for US$1. The *hostal* has a shop selling local handicrafts including masks. The owner's son will act as a guide to the ruins at the weekend.

G pp Parador, on the plaza, T084-203061. All rooms share bathrooms, which have hot water. Breakfast is not included, but the restaurant serves other meals.

Urubamba and around *p119, map p123*

L Libertador Valle Sagrado Lodge, 5ieme paradero, Yanahuara, T084-961 3316, http://en.vallesagradolodge.com/about. Affiliated to the Libertador group, a colonial-style hotel with 16 rooms in extensive grounds.

AL Casa Andina Private Collection Sacred Valley, 5th *paradero*, Yanahuara, between Urubamba and Ollantaytambo, T084-976 5501, www.casa-andina.com. In its own 3-ha estate, with all the facilities associated with this chain, plus a gym, organic garden and restaurant with *novo andino* cuisine. Adventure activities can be arranged here. It also has a spa offering a range of massages and treatments, a gym and a planetarium and observatory, showing the Inca view of the night sky (US$10).

AL Inkaterra Urubamba Villas, in the hamlet of Higuspurco, between Urubamba and Yukay, www.inkaterra.com. Price is per person in one of two self-contained villas in spacious gardens, fully-equipped, breakfast and dinner included, lunch optional, courtesy bottle of wine, also has a bar, access to excursions and activities with car and driver available.

AL Sol y Luna, west of town, T084-201620, www.hotelsolyluna.com. Attractive bungalows set off the main road in lovely gardens, pool, excellent buffet in restaurant, French-Swiss owned. Has **Viento Sur** adventure travel agency, for horse riding, mountain biking, trekking and paragliding, www.aventurasvientosur.com.

AL Sonesta Posadas del Inca, Plaza Manco II de Yucay 123, Yucay, T084-201107, www.sonestaperu.com. A converted 300-year-old monastery is now a hotel which is like a little village with plazas, lovely gardens, a chapel and 84 comfortable, heated rooms. The price includes buffet breakfast, but not taxes. The restaurant serves an excellent buffet lunch. Lots of activities can be arranged, canoeing, horse riding, mountain biking, etc. There is a conference centre. Highly recommended.

A La Casona de Yucay, Plaza Manco II 104, Yucay, T084-201116, www.cusco.net/casonayucay/index.htm. This colonial house was where Simón Bolívar stayed during his liberation campaign in 1824. The price includes taxes and breakfast. The rooms have heating and, outside, there are 2 patios and gardens. **Don Manuel** restaurant is good, also has bar. Helpful staff.

A K'uychi Rumi, Km 73.5 on the road to Ollantaytambo, 3 km from town, T084-201169, www.urubamba.com. 6 cottages with 2 bedrooms (but can sleep up to 6), fully equipped, fireplace, terrace and balcony, surrounded by gardens. Price is for 1-2 people.

A San Agustín Urubamba, on the Cuzco- Pisac road, Km 69, T084-201444, www.hoteles sanagustin.com.pe. An upgraded hotel in a lovely setting just out of Urubamba, with suites and standard rooms, pool, sauna, massage and jacuzzi, **Naranjachayoc's** restaurant and bar. Also has **San Agustín Monasterio de la Recoleta**, Jr Recoleta s/n, T084-201666. In a converted monastery (the earliest in Cuzco), **San Isidro** restaurant.

D Las Tres Marías, Zavala 307, T084-201004 (Cuzco T084-225252). Beautiful gardens, hot water, welcoming. Recommended.

D-E Hospedaje Los Jardines, Jr Convención 459, T084- 201331, www.machawasi.com. An attractive guesthouse with comfortable rooms, non-smoking, delicious breakfast extra (vegans catered for), safe, lovely garden, laundry. **Sacred Valley Mountain Bike Tours** also based here.

E pp Las Chullpas, 3 km west of town in the Pumahuanca Valley, T084-201568, www.uhupi.comchullpas. Peaceful, includes excellent breakfast, vegetarian meals, English and German spoken, Spanish classes, natural medicine, treks, horse riding, mountain biking, camping US$3 with hot shower. Mototaxi US$0.85, taxi (ask for Querocancha) US$2.

G pp Capulí, Grau 222. With bath, hot water and TV. Cheaper with shared bath.

G Hostal Urubamba, Bolognesi 605. Basic but pleasant rooms with bath and cold water, cheaper without bath.

Urubamba

Río Urubamba

0 metres 100
0 yards 100

Sleeping
Capulí 1
Hospedaje Los Jardines 3
Hostal Urubamba 4
K'uychi Rumi 8

Las Chullpas 10
Las Tres Marías 2
San Agustín
    Urubamba 11
Sol y Luna 7

Eating
El Fogón 1
La Casa de la Abuela 5
Pintacha 3
Pizzonay 4

AL Pakaritampu, Calle Ferrocarril s/n, T084-204020, www.pakaritampu.com. The price includes breakfast and taxes. This modern, 3-star hotel has 20 rooms with bath and views. It is owned by a former Peruvian women's volleyball star. There is a TV room, restaurant and bar, internet service for guests, laundry, safe and room service. Adventure sports such as rafting, climbing, trekking, mountain biking and horse riding can be arranged. Meals are extra: buffet US$20, dinner US$17. Excellent quality and service.

A-B Ñustayoc Mountain Lodge and Resort, 5 km west of Ollantaytambo, just before Chillca and the start of the Inca Trail, T084-204098, www.nustayoclodge.com. Large and somewhat rambling lodge in a wonderful location with great views of the snowy Verónica massif and other peaks. Lovely flower-filled garden and grounds. Nicely decorated, spacious rooms, all with private bath. Price includes continental breakfast served in the large restaurant area.

B El Albergue Ollantaytambo, within the railway station gates, T084-204014, www.elalbergue.com. 8 rooms with shared bathrooms. Price includes breakfast; box lunch available, full dinner on request. The rooms are full of character and are set in buildings around a courtyard and lovely gardens. Great showers (24 hrs a day) and a eucalyptus steam sauna. The whole place is charming, relaxing and homely. See the office-cum-shop-cum-exhibition where interesting handicrafts can be bought. Also for sale is Wendy's digestif, *compuesto matacuy*. It's very convenient for the Machu Picchu train and good place for information. Private transport can be arranged to the salt mines, Moray, Abra Málaga for birdwatching and taxi transfers to the airport.

C-E KB, between the main plaza and the ruins, T204091, www.kbperu.com. Spacious, comfortable rooms, cheaper without bath, also has budget lodging (**G**), hot water, flower-filled garden, very good restaurant (♛). Also offers adventure tours.

D Albergue Kapuly, at the end of the station road, T084-204017. Prices are lower in the off season. A quiet place with spacious rooms, some with and some without bath. The garden is nice and the price includes a good continental breakfast.

D Hostal Munay Tika, on the road to the station, T084-204111, munaytika@latin mail.com. Price includes breakfast and bath. Dinner served by arrangement. Sauna costs US$5 with prior notice. Also has a nice garden.

F Hostal Chaskawasi, Chaupicalle (also Calle Taypi) north of the plaza, T084-208085, anna_machupicchu@hotmail.com. A *hostal* snuggled away in the small alleys behind the plaza. Owner Anna is very friendly.

F Hostal La Ñusta, Calle Ocobamba, T084-204035. Ask about accommodation in the shop/restaurant of the same name on the plaza or in the **Gran Tunupa** restaurant. This is a decent although uninspiring budget option. Proprietor Rubén Ponce loves to share his knowledge of the ruins with guests. You get a good view of the ruins from the balcony. See page 125, for the restaurant.

F Hostal Ollanta, on the south side of the plaza, T084-204116. Basic and clean, but with a great location. All rooms with shared bath.

F Las Orquídeas, near start of the road to the station, T084-204032. A good choice. Price includes breakfast, and meals are available; may be used by tour groups.

G Hostal Chuza, just below the main plaza in town, T084-204113. Very clean and friendly with safe motorcycle parking. They have a TV in the front room for guests and one of the rooms features a wonderful view of the ruins with the Nevado de Verónica behind.

⑦ Eating

Pisac *p118*

♛♛ **Miski Mijuna Wasi**, on the Plaza de Armas, T084-203266. Serves very tasty local food, typical and *novo andino*, also international dishes. Has a *pastelería* also.

♛♛ **Mullu**, Mcal Castilla 375, T084-208182. Tue-Sun 0900-1900. Café/restaurant related to the Mullu store in Cuzco, also has a gallery promoting local artists.

♛ **Doña Clorinda**, on the plaza opposite the church, doesn't look very inviting but cooks tasty food, including vegetarian options. A very friendly place.

Cafés

Bakery, Av Mcal Castilla 372, sells excellent cheese and onion *empanadas* for US$0.25, suitable for vegetarians, and good whole-meal bread. The oven is tremendous.

Ulrike's Café, Plaza de Armas 828, T084-203195, ulrikescafe@terra.com.pe. This comfortable café is renowned for its apple crumble with ice cream, to say nothing of great coffee, smoothies and a wide range of international cuisine. A good place to chill after a hard day exploring the market and ruins.

Urubamba *p119, map p123*

♯♯ **El Fogón**, Parque Pintacha, T084-201534. Traditional Peruvian food, large servings, nice atmosphere. Recommended.

♯♯ **La Casa de la Abuela**, Bolívar 272, 2 blocks up from the Plaza de Armas, T084-622975. Excellent restaurant with rooms grouped around a small courtyard. The trout is fantastic and food is served with baskets of roasted potatoes and salad. Recommended.

♯ **Pintacha**, Bolognesi 523. Pub/café serving sandwiches, burgers, coffees, teas and drinks. Games and book exchange, cosy, open till late.

♯ **Pizzonay**, Av Mcal Castilla, 2nd block. Pizzas, excellent spinach ravioli (not so good lasagne). Mulled wine served in a small restaurant with nice decor. Clean, good value. Recommended.

Ollantaytambo *p121*

♯♯ **Fortaleza**, 2 branches, one on Plaza Ruinas, the other on north side of the main plaza. Basic but good food, breakfasts, pizza and pasta – all the gringo favourites are on offer, as well as some more local dishes.

♯♯ **Il Cappuccino**, just before the bridge on the right-hand side. Offers the best cappuccino in town, great coffee generally. Good continental and American breakfasts. Slightly more sophisticated ambience and service in comparison with many other establishments in town. Also **Kusicoyllor**, Plaza Ruinas, for pizza, pasta and good coffee.

♯♯ **Mayupata**, Jr Convención s/n, across the bridge on the way to the ruins, on the left, T084-204083 (Cuzco). International and Peruvian dishes, desserts, sandwiches and coffee. It opens at 0600 for breakfast, and serves lunch and dinner. The bar has a fireplace; river view, relaxing atmosphere.

♯ **Alcázar Café**, Calle del Medio s/n, 50 m from the plaza, T084-204034, alcazar@ollantay tambo.org. Vegetarian restaurant, also offering fish and meat dishes, pasta specialities. Offers excursions to traditional Andean communities.

♯ **Bahía**, on the east side of the plaza. Very friendly, vegetarian dishes served on request.

♯ **Heart´s Café**, on Plaza de Armas, T084-977 8592. Brand new wholefood restaurant, including chicken and fish, owned by SAE member Sonia, whose expertise is in vegetarian food, due open 2007.

♯ **La Ñusta**, on the plaza, same owner as *hostal*. Popular, good food, snacks available.

✿ Festivals and events

Pisac *p118*
15 Jul A local fiesta in Pisac.

Urubamba *p119, map p123*
May-Jun Harvest months, with many processions following mysterious ancient schedules.
1st week of Jun Urubamba's main festival, El Señor de Torrechayoc.

Chintero *p120*
8 Sep Day of the Virgin.

Ollantaytambo *p121*
6 Jan Bajada de Reyes Magos (the Magi), with traditional dancing, a bull fight, local food and a fair.
End May-early Jun Pentecost, 50 days after Easter, is the Fiesta del Señor de Choquekillca, patron saint of Ollantaytambo. There are several days of dancing, weddings, processions, masses, feasting and drinking (the last opportunity to see traditional *cuzqueño* dancing).
29 Jun Following Inti Raymi in Cuzco, there is a colourful festival, the Ollanta-Raymi, at which the Quechua drama, *Ollantay*, is re-enacted.
29 Oct Aniversario de Ollantaytambo, a festival with dancing in traditional costume and many local delicacies for sale.

▲▲ Activities and tours

Urubamba *p119, map p123*
Agrotourism
Chichubamba, Casa de ProPerú, Jr Rejachayoc, Urubamba, T084-201562, www.agrotourismsacredvalley.com. A community tourism project which lets visitors take part in a number of traditional activities (culinary, horticulture, textiles,

ceramics, beekeeping, etc, US$3 pp, cheaper for groups), hiking US$10, lodging **E** pp and local meals. It's about 10 mins' walk from Urubamba; follow the signs.

Horse riding
Perol Chico, 5 km from Urubamba at Km 77, T01-9822 3297 (mob), office T054-284732, www.perolchico.com. Owned and operated by Eduard van Brunschot Vega (Dutch/ Peruvian), 1- to 14-day trips out of Urubamba, good horses, riding is Peruvian Paso style; 1-day trip to Moray and the salt pans costs US$110 (minimum 2 people, starting in Cuzco). Recommended.

Trekking
Haku Trek, contact Javier Saldívar or Yeral Quillahuman, T084-961 3001 (mob). A cooperative tourism project in the Chicón valley (the mountain valley above Urubamba), run by residents of the community. 3 different hiking trips are offered: two 1-day options (US$20 pp including food and lodging) and a third, 2-day hike up to the Chicón Glacier itself (US$45 all inclusive). Hikes are based at a simple, but beautifully located eco-lodge in the valley and profits are used to fund reforestation of native forest in the area.

⊖ Transport

To organize your own Sacred Valley transport, try one of the taxi drivers listed on page 115.

Pisac *p118*
Bus Buses to **Cuzco** are often full (32 km, 1 hr, US$0.85). There are also *colectivos*, minibuses and pick-up trucks. The last one back leaves around 2000. Taxis charge about US$20 for the round trip. Also buses to **Calca** (18 km beyond Pisac) and **Urubamba**.

Urubamba *p119, map p123*
Bus The bus and *combi* terminal is just west of town on the main road. To **Calca**, **Pisac** (US$0.80, 1 hr) and **Cuzco** (2 hrs, US$1.10), from 0530 onwards. Also buses to Cuzco via **Chinchero**, same price.

Colectivos to **Cuzco** can be caught outside the terminal and on the main road, US$1.20. *Combis* run to **Ollantaytambo**, 45 mins, US$0.30. There are also buses from here to **Quillabamba**.

Train See page 138 for the Sacred Valley Railway from Urubamba to **Aguas Calientes**.

Chinchero *p120*
Bus To **Cuzco**, there are *combis* and *colectivos*, 23 km, 45 mins, US$0.60. To **Urubamba** , 25 km, 45 mins, US$0.45.

To **Maras**, there is public transport until 1700-1800 (US$0.60-1) as well as regular pickup trucks. If you cannot get transport to Maras, take any *combi* going between Urubamba and Chinchero, get out at the junction for Maras and walk from there.

It's 4 km to Maras; once through the village, bear left a little, and ask directions to Moray. Hitching back to **Urubamba** is quite easy, but there are no hotels at all in the area, so take care not to be stranded.

Taxi Taxis wait at the Maras/Moray junction on the Urubamba/ Chinchero road. They charge US$20 to go to Salinas and then on to Moray, with a 1 hr wait at each.

Ollantaytambo *p121*
Bus There is a direct bus service to **Cuzco** at 0715 and 1945; the fare is US$2.85. *Colectivos* to **Urubamba** all day 1 block east of main plaza, leave when full.

Train See page 138. The station is 10- 15 mins walk from the plaza (turn left at the sign that says 'Centro de Salud' between the Plaza de Armas and the ruins). There are *colectivos* at the plaza for the station when trains are due. Also, a bus leaves the station at 0900 for **Urubamba** (US$0.30) and **Chinchero** (US$1).

⊕ Directory

Urubamba *p119, map p123*
Banks Banks in the centre on Comercio. ATM on the main road not far from the bridge. **Internet** Connections, corner of Av M Castilla and Av La Convención. **Post office** Serpost, Plaza de Armas. **Telephone** Several phone booths in the centre. The one outside Hostal Urubamba makes international calls.

Ollantaytambo *p121*
Banks ATM at Calle Ventiderio 248, between the Plaza and Av Ferrocarril. **Internet** Several places in town, US$0.30 for 30 mins.

Southeast of Cuzco

A paved road runs southeast from Cuzco to Sicuani, at the southeastern edge of the Department of Cuzco. It continues to Puno, on the shores of Lake Titicaca, then on to the border with Bolivia. Along or near this road are a number of archaeological sites, some fascinating colonial churches, beautiful lakes and the majestic Ausangate massif. Off this route is also the gateway to Peru's southeastern jungle in the Department of Madre de Dios. ▸▸ *For Sleeping, Eating and other listings, see page 128.*

To Huambutío and Paucartambo

The **Tipón ruins** ① *between Saylla and Oropesa, US$1.80, or BTG visitor ticket, see page 90*, are extensive and include baths, terraces, irrigation systems and a temple complex, accessible from a path leading from just above the last terrace. From Tipón village it's an hour's climb; or take a taxi. If you head to the left at the back of the ruins, there is a trail round to where you will see more small ruins. From there you will find an amazing Inca road with a deep irrigation channel, which can be followed to Cerro Pachatusan.

At **Huambutío**, north of Huacarpay, the road divides: northwest to Pisac and north to **Paucartambo**, on the eastern slope of the Andes. This once remote town, 80 km east of Cuzco, is on the road to Pilcopata, Atalaya and Shintuya. This is now the overland route used by tour companies from Cuzco into Manu Biosphere Reserve (see page 288). Consequently, it has become a popular tourist destination.

Piquillacta Archaeological Park → *Colour map 4, C3.*

① *Daily 0700-1730, US$1.80 or by BTG visitor ticket, see page 90. Buses to Urcos from Av Huáscar, Cuzco drop you at the north side entrance, though this is not the official entry.*
The Piquillacta Archaeological Park is 30 km southeast of Cuzco, with an area of 3421 ha. Its nucleus is the remains of a lake, the **Laguna de Huacarpay**, around which are many pre-Columbian archaeological remains. The lake is a favourite birdwatching destination and it's good to hike or cycle round it. The Huari ruins of **Piquillacta** ('City of Fleas') are large, with some reconstruction in progress. It was an administrative centre at the southern end of the Huari Empire. The whole site is surrounded by a wall, encompassing many enclosed compounds with buildings of over one storey; it appears that the walls were plastered and finished with a layer of lime.

The huge gateway of **Rumicolca** is on the right of the main road to Sicuani, shortly after the turn-off to Piquillacta. You can walk around it for free. This was a Huari aqueduct, built across this narrow stretch of the valley, which the Incas clad in fine stonework to create this gateway. If you look at the top you can see the original walls, four tiers high.

Andahuaylillas and Huaro → *Colour map 4, C3.*

Continuing southeast towards Urcos you reach Andahuaylillas, 32 km from Cuzco, with a fascinating 17th-century church. This is a simple structure, but it has been referred to as the Andean Sistine Chapel because of its beautiful frescoes, and internal architecture. Go in and wait for your eyes to adjust to the darkness, in order to see, on the right of the splendid door, the path to heaven, which is narrow and thorny, and, on the left, the way to hell, which is wide and littered with flowers. Above is the high choir, built in local wood, where there are two organs. The carved ceiling is painted, too. The main altar is gilded in 24-carat gold leaf and has symbols from both the Quechua and Christian religions. Ask for Sr Eulogio; he is a good guide, but speaks Spanish only.

At the quiet village of **Huaro**, the church on the ugly plaza is stunning inside. The walls are plastered with frescoes used to evangelize the illiterate. Grinning skeletons compete with dragons and devils ushering the living into the afterlife and punishing them thereafter. They are now mostly in a sad state of repair.

Beyond Huaro is **Urcos**, from where a road crosses the Eastern Cordillera. Some 82 km from Urcos is **Ocongate**, which has two hotels on the Plaza de Armas. It sits at the base of **Nevado Ausangate**, at 6384 m the loftiest peak in the Cordillera Vilcanota, impressive even from a distance of nearly 100 km. The small town of **Tinqui**, further east from Ocongate, is the traditional starting point for treks into the region. Forty-seven kilometres after passing the snow-line **Hualla-Hualla pass**, at 4820 m, the super-hot thermal baths of **Marcapata** ① *173 km from Urcos, US$0.10*, provide a relaxing break. Beyond this point, what is arguably the most spectacular road in Peru descends the eastern flank of the Andes towards Puerto Maldonado (see pages 291 and 290).

Raqchi → *Colour map 2, C5.*
① *Entry US$1.80. There is a basic shop at the site.*

About 120 km southeast of Cuzco, in a fertile tributary valley of the Vilcanota, is the colonial village of **San Pedro de Cacha**, which stands within one of the most important archaeological sites in Peru, Raqchi. A few hundred metres beyond the village are the principal remains, the once great **Temple of Viracocha**, the pan-Andean creator of all living creatures. This is one of the only remaining examples of a two-storey building of Inca architecture. It was 90 m long and 15 m high and was probably the largest roofed building ever built by the Incas. Above walls of finely dressed masonry 3-4 m high rise the remains of another 5-6 m high wall of adobe brickwork of which only isolated sections remain. Similarly, of the 22 outer columns, which supported great sloping roofs, just one or two remain complete, the others being in various states of preservation.

◉ Sleeping

Andahuaylillas *p127*
F **La Casa del Sol**, close to the central plaza on Garcilaso. Relaxing, clean and bright *hostal*. Well-decorated rooms set around a courtyard, this is excellent value. Owned by Dr Gladys Oblitas, the *hostal* funds her project to provide medical services to poor *campesinos*. While staying you can take a course or take part in workshops on natural and alternative medicine.

◉ Festivals and events

Paucartambo *p127*
15-17 Jul The Fiesta of the Virgen del Carmen is a major attraction and well worth seeing. Masked dancers enact rituals and folk tales in the streets.

Raqchi *p128*
24-29 Jun Start of the Wiracocha festivities in San Pedro and neighbouring San Pablo. Dancers come to Raqchi from all over Peru and through music and dance they illustrate everything from the ploughing of fields to bull fights. This leads into the feast of San Pedro and San Pablo on 29 Jun.

◉ Transport

Paucartambo *p127*
Private car hire for a round trip from Cuzco on 15-17 Jul costs US$30. Tour operators in Cuzco can arrange this. A minibus leaves for Paucartambo from Av Huáscar in Cuzco, every other day, US$4.50, 3-4 hrs; alternate days Paucartambo–Cuzco. Trucks and a private bus leave from the Coliseo, behind Hospital Segura in Cuzco, 5 hrs, US$2.50.

Andahuaylillas *p127*
To **Andahuaylillas** take a taxi, or the **Oropesa** bus from Av Huáscar in Cuzco, via Tipón, Piquillacta and Rumicolca.

Huaro and Urcos *p127*
Transportes Vilcanota depart from the terminal on Av de la Cultura, Cuzco, at the Paradero Hospital Regional (on a side street), and run to **San Jerónimo, Saylla, Huasao, Tipón, Oropesa, Piquillacta/ Huacarpay, Andahuaylillas** and on to **Urcos**. These buses run 0500-2100, fare US$0.75 to Urcos.

Raqchi *p128*
There are frequent *combis* to and from **Cuzco** on the Sicuani route.

Machu Picchu

There is a tremendous feeling of awe on first witnessing this incredible sight. The ancient citadel of Machu Picchu, 42 km from Ollantaytambo by rail, straddles the saddle of a high mountain with steep terraced slopes falling away to the fast-flowing Río Urubamba snaking its hairpin course far below in the valley floor. Towering overhead is Huayna Picchu, and green jungle peaks provide the backdrop for the whole majestic scene.

If you take the Inca Trail to Machu Picchu, following in the footsteps of its creators, you are making a true pilgrimage and the sweat and struggle is all worth it when you set your eyes on this mystical site at sunrise from the Inca sun gate above the ruins. That way you see Machu Picchu in its proper context. Afterwards you can recover in Aguas Calientes and soothe those aching limbs in the hot springs. ▸▸ *For Sleeping, Eating and other listings, see pages 131-133.*

Ins and outs

Getting there There are two ways to get to Machu Picchu. The easy way is by train from Cuzco, Ollantaytambo or Urubamba, with a bus ride for the final climb from the rail terminus at Aguas Calientes to the ruins (see Transport, page 133, for the timetables). The walk up from Aguas Calientes takes 1½ to two hours, following the Inca path. Walking down to Aguas Calientes, if staying the night there, takes between 30 minutes and one hour. The ruins are quieter after 1530, but don't forget that the last bus down from the ruins leaves at 1730.

The strenuous, but most rewarding way to Machu Picchu is to hike one of the Inca Trails, the 'classic' example of which is described in its own section (see page 133).

Tourist information Tickets for Machu Picchu must be purchased in advance from the **Instituto Nacional de Cultura** (**INC**) ① *Av Pachacútec cuadra 1, Aguas Calientes, www.inc-cusco.gob.pe, or in Cuzco (see page 90).* The INC website publishes the regulations and lists of licensed tour operators and guides (see Inca Trail and general tours, page 109). The agency officially responsible for the site is **Unidad Gestión de Machu Picchu** ① *Calle Garcilaso 223, Cuzco, T084-242103.* It is an excellent source of information on Machu Picchu and this is the place to which any complaints or observations should be directed. **i perú** ① *in the INC office, as above, of 4, T084-211104, can provide general information.*

Machu Picchu ruins 🖥 ▸▸ pp131-133.

→ *Altitude: 2380 m. Colour map 4, B2.*

① *Daily 0600-1730. Entry US$40, buy tickets in advance from INC, see above. It is possible to pay in dollars, but only clean, undamaged notes accepted. At the time of writing, an increase in the entry fee (even to US$100) was being considered. You cannot take backpacks into Machu Picchu; leave them at the entrance, US$0.50. Guides at the site are often very knowledgeable and worthwhile, and charge US$15 for 2½ hrs.*

For centuries Machu Picchu was buried in jungle, until Hiram Bingham stumbled upon it in July 1911. It was then explored by an archaeological expedition sent by Yale University. Machu Picchu was a stunning find. The only major Inca site to escape 400 years of looting and destruction, it was remarkably well preserved. Its inaccessible location above the Urubamba Gorge helped to keep its fine buildings hidden for so long, but once it came under the tourist spotlight the flow of visitors has grown to an upper limit of 2500 a day.

This represents big money and Machu Picchu's election to the "New Seven Wonders of the World" list in 2007 will keep the site in sharp focus. Whether its stones can support so much attention remains to be seen.

Once you have passed through the ticket gate you follow a path to a small complex of buildings which now acts as the **main entrance** to the ruins. It is set at the eastern end of the extensive **terracing** which must have supplied the crops for the city. Above this point, turning back on yourself, is the final stretch of the Inca Trail leading down from **Intipunku** (Sun Gate), see page 136. From a promontory here, on which stands the building called the **Watchman's Hut**, you get the perfect view of the city, laid out before you with Huayna Picchu rising above the furthest extremity. Go round the promontory and head south for the **Intipata** (Inca bridge), see below. The main path into the ruins comes to a **dry moat** that cuts right across the site. At the moat you can either climb the long staircase which goes to the upper reaches of the city, or you can enter the city by the baths and Temple of the Sun.

The more strenuous way into the city is by the former route, which takes you past quarries on your left as you look down to the Urubamba on the west flank of the mountain. Proceeding along this level, above the main plazas, you reach the **Temple of the Three Windows** and the **Principal Temple**, which has a smaller building called the **Sacristy**. The two main buildings are three-sided and were clearly of great importance, given the fine stonework involved. The wall with the three windows is built onto a single rock. In the Principal Temple, a diamond-shaped stone in the floor is said to depict the constellation of the Southern Cross.

Continue on the path behind the Sacristy to reach the **Intihuatana**, the 'hitching-post of the sun'. The name comes from the theory that such carved rocks (*gnomons*), found at all major Inca sites, were the point to which the sun was symbolically 'tied' at the winter solstice, before being freed to rise again on its annual ascent towards the summer solstice.

Climb down from the Intihuatana's mound to the **Main Plaza**. Beyond its northern end is a small plaza with open-sided buildings on two sides and on the third, the **Sacred Rock**. The outline of this gigantic, flat stone echoes that of the mountains behind it. From here you can proceed to the entrance to the trail to Huayna Picchu. Returning to the Main Plaza and heading southeast you pass, on your left, several groups of closely packed buildings which have been taken to be **living quarters** and **Workshops**, **Mortar Buildings** and the **Prison Group**, one of whose constructions is known as the **Condor Temple**. Also in this area is a cave called **Intimachay**.

A short distance from the Condor Temple is the lower end of a series of **ceremonial baths** or fountains. They were probably used for ritual bathing and the water still flows down them today. The uppermost, **Principal Bath**, is the most elaborate. Next to it is the **Temple of the Sun**, or Torreón. All indications are that this singular temple was used for astronomical purposes. Underneath the Torreón a cave-like opening has been formed by an oblique gash in the rock. Fine masonry has been added to the opposing wall, making a second side of a triangle, which contrasts with the rough edge of the split rock. But the blocks of masonry appear to have been slotted behind another sculpted piece of natural stone, which has been cut into a four-stepped buttress. Immediately behind this is a two-stepped buttress. This strange combination of the natural and the man-made has been called the Tomb or Palace of the Princess. Across the stairway from the complex which includes the Torreón is the group of buildings known as the **Royal Sector**.

The famous Inca bridge – **Intipata** – is about 30 minutes along a well-marked trail south of the Royal Sector. The bridge, which is actually a couple of logs, is spectacularly sited, carved into a vertiginous cliff-face. The walk is well worth it for the fine views, but the bridge itself is closed to visitors. Not only is it in a poor state of repair, but the path before it has collapsed.

ⓘ *Access daily 0700-1300, with the latest return time being 1500.*

Synonymous with the ruins themselves is Huayna Picchu, the verdant mountain overlooking the site. There are also ruins on the mountain itself, and steps to the top for a superlative view of the whole magnificent scene, but this is not for those with vertigo. The climb takes up to 90 minutes but the steps are dangerous after bad weather and you shouldn't leave the path. You must register at a hut at the beginning of the trail. The other trail to Huayna Picchu, down near the Urubamba, is via the Temple of the Moon: two caves, one above the other, with superb Inca niches inside, sadly blemished by graffiti. To reach the **Temple of the Moon** from the path to Huayna Picchu, take the marked trail to the left; it is in good shape. It descends further than you think it should. After the Temple you may proceed to Huayna Picchu, but this path is overgrown, slippery when wet and has a crooked ladder on an exposed part about 10 minutes before the top (not for the faint-hearted). It is safer to return to the main trail to Huayna Picchu, but this adds about 30 minutes to the climb. The round trip takes about four hours.

Aguas Calientes 🏠🚻🍴ℹ ➤ *pp131-133.*

➔ *Colour map 4, B2. Phone code: 084.*

Only 1.5 km back along the railway from Puente Ruinas, this is a popular resting place for those recovering from the rigours of the Inca Trail. It is named Aguas Calientes (or just Aguas) after the hot springs above the town. It is also called the town of Machu Picchu. Most activity is centred around the old railway station, on the plaza, or on Avenida Pachacútec, which leads from the plaza to the **thermal baths** ⓘ *10 mins' walk from town, daily 0500-2030. US$3.15.* They consist of a rather smelly communal pool, 10 minutes' walk from the town. You can rent towels and bathing costumes for US$0.65 at several places on the road to the baths. There are basic toilets and changing facilities and

‡ *The town of Aguas Calientes/Machu Picchu is twinned with Haworth, the birthplace of the Brontë sisters, www.haworth-village.org.uk.*

showers. Take soap and shampoo and keep an eye on your valuables. The new **Museo Manuel Chávez Ballon** ⓘ *Carretera Hiram Bingham, Wed-Sun 0900-1600, US$6,* displays objects found at Machu Picchu.

🛏 Sleeping

Machu Picchu ruins *p129*
Camping is not allowed at Intipunku or anywhere else at the site; guards may confiscate your tent. There is a free campsite beside the rail tracks at Puente Ruinas station.
L Machu Picchu Sanctuary Lodge, under the same management as the **Hotel Monasterio** in Cuzco, T084-211039, www.sanctuarylodge.net. This hotel, at the entrance to the ruins, has some environmentally friendly features and will accept American Express TCs at the official rate. The rooms are comfortable, the service is good and the staff helpful. Electricity and water are available 24 hrs a day. Food in the restaurant is well cooked and presented; the restaurant is for residents only in the evening, but the buffet lunch is open to all. The hotel is

usually fully booked well in advance; if struggling for a booking try Sun night as other tourists find Pisac market a greater attraction.

Aguas Calientes *p131*
Some hotels in Aguas Calientes have increased their prices in response to the rising costs of train services and excursions on the Inca Trail. Bargain hard for accommodation and book in advance from Cuzco.
L Inkaterra Machu Picchu, Km 110, T084-211122. Reservations: Jr Andalucía 174, Miraflores, Lima, T01-610 0404; in Cuzco at Plaza las Nazarenas 167, p 2, T084-245314, www.inkaterra.com. Beautiful colonial-style bungalows have been built in a village compound surrounded by cloudforest 5 mins' walk along the railway from the town. The

hotel has lovely gardens in which there are many species of birds, butterflies and orchids. There is a pool, an expensive restaurant, but also a campsite with hot showers at good rates. It offers tours to Machu Picchu, several guided walks on the property and to local beauty spots. The buffet breakfasts, included in price, are great. It also has the **Café Inkaterra** by the railway line. The hotel is involved in a project to rehabilitate spectacled bears and release them back into the wild. Recommended, but there are a lot of steps between the public areas and rooms.

A-B Rupa Wasi, Calle Huanacaure 180, T084-211101, http://perucuzco.com/rupawasi/lodge_english.htm. Rustic and charming 'eco-lodge', located up a small alley off Collasuyo. The lodge and its owners have a very laid-back, comfortable style, and there are great views from the balconies of the first-floor rooms. This lodge is slowly adding to its environmentally friendly credentials with purified water available (so you don't have to buy more plastic) and an organic garden and rainwater collector in the pipeline. Great breakfasts for US$3.

B Presidente, at the old station, T084-211034 (Cuzco T084-244598), presidente@terra.com.pe. Next to and under same ownership as **D Hostal Machu Picchu**, T084-211212. Both include breakfast and taxes. There seems to be only minimal difference between the 2 and **Machu Picchu** represents much better value for money: quiet, friendly, hot water, a nice balcony over the Urubamba, a grocery store and travel information is available.

C Gringo Bill's (Hostal Q'oñi Unu), Colla Raymi 104, T084-211046, gringobills@yahoo.com. Price includes bathroom and continental breakfast. An Aguas Calientes institution, it's friendly, relaxed, with a lot of coming and going, hot water, good beds, luggage store, laundry and money exchange. Good but expensive meals are served in **Villa Margarita** restaurant; breakfast starts at 0530 and they offer a US$4 packed lunch to take up to the ruins.

C Hostal Pachakúteq, up the hill beyond Hostal La Cabaña, T084-211061. Rooms with bathroom and 24-hr hot water. Good breakfast is included, quiet, family-run.

C La Cabaña, Av Pachacútec M20-3, T084-211048. Price includes bathroom and continental breakfast. Rooms have hot water. There is a café, laundry service and a DVD player and TV (with a good selection of movies) for clients in the lounge. The staff are helpful and can provide information on interesting local walks. The hotel is popular with groups.

D-E Jardín Real, Wiracocha 7, T084-211234, jardinrealhotel@hotmail.com. Modern, hot water, good value, same owner as **Pizzería Los Jardines** on Pachacútec.

E Hostal Wiracocha Inn, Calle Wiracocha, T084-211088. Rooms with bath and hot water. Breakfast included. There is a small garden at this helpful *hostal*. It's popular particularly with European groups.

E-F Hospedaje Las Bromelias, Colla Raymi, T084-211145. Just off the plaza before **Gringo Bill's**, this is a small place which has rooms with bath and hot water. Accommodation is cheaper without bath.

F Hostal Samana Wasi, Calle Túpac Inka Yupanki, T084-211170, quillavane@hotmail.com. Price includes bath and 24-hr hot water. There are cheaper rooms without bath at this friendly, pleasant place.

Camping

The only official campsite is in a field by the river, just below Puente Ruinas station. Do not leave your tent and belongings unattended.

❼ Eating

Aguas Calientes p131

Pizza seems to be the most common dish in town, but many of the pizzerias serve other types of food as well. The old station and Av Pachútec are lined with eating places.

♈♈♈ Café Inkaterra, on the railway, just below the **Inkaterra Machu Picchu**. US$15 for a great lunch buffet with scenic views of the river.

♈♈ Indio Feliz, Calle Lloque Yupanqui, T084-211090. Great French cuisine, excellent value and service, set 3-course meal for US$10, good *pisco sours*. Highly recommended.

♈♈ Inka's Pizza Pub, on the plaza. Good pizzas, changes money and accepts TCs. Next door is **Illary**, which is popular.

♈♈ Pueblo Viejo, Av Pachacútec, near the plaza. Good food in a spacious but warm environment. Price includes salad bar.

♈ Govinda, Av Pachacútec y Túpac Inka Yupanki. Vegetarian restaurant with a cheap set lunch. Recommended.

Transport

Aguas Calientes *p131*
Bus To **Machu Picchu** every 30 mins
0630-1300, US$12 return, US$6 single, valid
for 48 hrs. Buses return from the ruins 1200-
1730. It is also possible to take a bus down
0700-0900. The ticket office is opposite the
bus stop, 50 m from the railway station.
Tickets can also be bought in advance at
Consetur, Santa Catalina Ancha, Cuzco,
which saves queuing in Aguas Calientes.
Train See box, page 138.

Directory

Aguas Calientes *p131*
Banks There are several ATMs in town.
Internet Many internet shops, average
price US$1 per hr; slow connection.
Medical services Urgent Medical Center,
Av de Los Incas 119, T084-211005, 084-976
1314 (mob). Good care at affordable prices.
Telephone Oficina on Calle Collasuyo,
and there are plenty of phone booths
around town.

Inca Treks

The famous Inca Trail which leads to Machu Picchu, once a severe test for intrepid hikers, now a preferred route for charity challenges and the preserve of highly organized tour groups, has been a victim of its own success. Because of its outstanding character, everyone wants to do it and such pressure means that many more feet, and heavily-booted ones at that, are walking the route than ever the Incas intended. But as researchers learn more about the area around Machu Picchu and neighbouring sites they are understanding that the Inca Trail was not an isolated Via Sacra, but a tiny part of a vast, interlinking network of roads. Moreover, the introduction of new regulations for walking the Inca Trail in 2001 spurred the opening up of additional options for trekking to Machu Picchu, some shorter, some longer than the old route. So if you fancy widening the perspective of how the Incas walked to their sacred cities, ask your chosen tour operator to show you the alternatives. ➤➤ *For Sleeping, Eating and other listings see page 140.*

Inca Trail ➤➤ *p140.*

The wonder of Machu Picchu has been well documented over the years. Equally impressive is the centuries-old Inca Trail that winds its way from the Sacred Valley near Ollantaytambo, taking three to four days. What makes this hike so special is the stunning combination of Inca ruins, unforgettable views, magnificent mountains, exotic vegetation and extraordinary ecological variety. The government acknowledged all this in 1981 by including the trail in a 325-sq-km national park, the Machu Picchu Historical Sanctuary. Machu Picchu itself cannot be understood without the Inca Trail. Its principal sites are ceremonial in character, apparently in ascending hierarchical order. This Inca province was a unique area of elite access. The trail is essentially a work of spiritual art, like a Gothic cathedral, and walking it was formerly an act of devotion.

Ins and outs

Entrance tickets and tours An entrance ticket for the trail or its variations must be bought at the **Instituto Nacional de Cultura (INC)** office in Cuzco (see box page 90); no tickets are sold at the entrance gates. Furthermore, tickets are only sold on presentation of a letter from a licensed tour operator on behalf of the visitor. There is a 50% discount for students, but note that officials are very strict, only an ISIC card will be accepted as proof of status. Tickets are checked at Km 82, Huayllabamba and Wiñay-Wayna.

On all hiking trails (Km 82 or Km 88 to Machu Picchu, Salkantay to Machu Picchu, and Km 82 or Km 88 to Machu Picchu via Km 104) adults must pay US$120 (including

Cuzco & the Sacred Valley Inca Treks

entrance to Machu Picchu), students and children under 15 US$60. On the **Camino Real de los Inkas** from Km 104 to Wiñay-Wayna and Machu Picchu (see page 136) the fee is US$30 per adult, US$15 for students and children; Salkantay to Huayllabamba and Km 88 is US$30. The **Salkantay trek** (see page 136) is supposed to be subject to a charge of US$36, but a dispute between the INC and the mayor of Mollepata meant that it was not being collected in 2007. Do not assume that this will always be the case, nor that INC will not introduce charges on more trails.

Travel agencies in Cuzco arrange transport to the start, equipment, food, etc, for an all-in price. Prices vary from about US$350 to US$450 per person for a four-day, three-night trek (slightly lower prices are charged for the Salkantay trek). Remember that you get what you pay for, but also bear in mind that the cheaper the price the more corners may be cut and the less attention paid to the environment and the porters. This respect is, after all, the goal of the 2001 legislation.

There is a quota for agencies and groups to use the Trail, but some agencies make block bookings way in advance of departure dates. This makes it much harder for other agencies to guarantee their clients places on the Trail. Consequently, current advice is to book your preferred dates as early as possible, even up to a year in advance, then confirm nearer the time. There have been many instances of disappointed trekkers whose bookings did not materialize: don't wait till the last minute and always check your operator's cancellation charges.

You can save money by arranging your own transport back to Ollantaytambo in advance, either for the last day of your tour, or by staying an extra night in Aguas Calientes and taking the early morning train, then a bus back to Cuzco. If you take your own tent and sleeping gear, some agencies give a discount. Make sure your return ticket for the tourist train to Cuzco has your name on it, otherwise you have to pay for any changes.

Advice and information Although security has improved in recent years, it's still best to leave all your valuables in Cuzco and keep everything else inside your tent, even your shoes. Avoid the July/August high season and the rainy season from November to April (note that this can change, so check in advance). In the wet it is cloudy and the paths are very muddy and difficult. Also watch out for coral snakes in this area (black, red, yellow bands). Please remove all your rubbish, including toilet paper, or use the pits provided. Do not light open fires as they can get out of control. The **Annual Inca Trail Clean-up** takes place usually in September. Many agencies and organizations are involved and volunteers should contact **South American Explorers** in Cuzco (see page 90) for full details of ways to help.

Guidelines for the treatment of porters can be found on the website of the now defunct **Inka Porter Project**, www.peruweb.org/porters. If you feel that your porters have been neglected or abused on the trek, express this to your agency, inform the **South American Explorers** and please let Footprint know. We read all your letters and agencies who repeatedly mistreat porters will be removed from our publications.

Equipment It is cold at night and weather conditions change rapidly, so it is important to take strong footwear, rain gear and warm clothing (this includes long johns if you want to sleep rather than freeze at night): dress in layers. Also take food, water, water purification tablets, insect repellent, sunscreen, a hat and sunglasses, a supply of plastic bags, coverings, a good sleeping bag, a torch and a stove for preparing hot food and drink to ward off the cold at night. It is worth paying extra to hire a down sleeping bag if you haven't brought your own. A paraffin (kerosene) stove is preferable, as fuel can be bought in small quantities in markets.

A tent is essential, but if you're hiring one in Cuzco, check carefully for leaks. Caves marked on some maps are little better than overhangs and are not sufficient shelter to sleep in. You could also take a first-aid kit; if you don't need it, the porters probably will, given their rather basic footwear. It is forbidden to use trekking poles

⁞ Inca Trail regulations

→ All agencies must have a licence to work in the area.

→ Groups of up to seven independent travellers who do not wish to use a tour operator are allowed to hike the trail accompanied by an independent, licensed guide, as long as they do not employ support staff, such as porters or cooks.

→ A maximum of 500 people, including guides and porters, are allowed on the trail per day.

→ Operators pay US$12 for each porter and other trail staff to use the trail. A porter's wage should be US$50 (165.60 soles). Porters are not permitted to carry more than 20 kg.

→ Littering is banned. Plastic water bottles may not be carried on the trail; only canteens are permitted.

→ Pets and pack animals are prohibited; llamas are allowed as far as the first pass.

→ Groups have to use approved campsites; on the routes from Km 82, Km 88 and Salkantay, the campsites may be changed with prior authorization.

→ The Inca Trail is closed each February for maintenance.

→ Regulations change frequently so anyone wishing to trek any of the trails around Machu Picchu should contact the authorities or tour operators before setting out to avoid disappointment.

because the metal tips are damaging the trail. Instead, buy a carved wooden stick on sale in the main plaza in Ollantaytambo or at the trail head. Many will need this for the steep descents on the path.

All the necessary equipment can be rented in Cuzco, see page 108. Good maps of the trail and area can be bought from **South American Explorers** in Lima or Cuzco, see pages 60 and 90. If you have any doubts about carrying your own pack, porters/guides are available through Cuzco agencies. Always carry a day-pack, though, with water and snacks, in case you walk at faster or slower than the porters. Take around US$30 extra per person for tips and for a drink at the end of the trail.

The trek → Colour map 4, B2.
Day 1 The trek to the sacred site begins either at Km 82, **Piscacucho**, or at Km 88, **Qorihuayrachina**, at 2600 m. In order to reach Km 82, hikers are transported by their tour operator in a minibus on the road that goes to Quillabamba. From Piri onwards the road follows the riverbank and ends at Km 82, where there is a bridge. You can depart as early as you like and arrive at Km 82 faster than going by train. The Inca Trail equipment, food, fuel and field personnel reach Km 82 (depending on the tour operator's logistics) for the Inrena staff to weigh each bundle before the group arrives. When several groups are leaving on the same day, it is more convenient to arrive early. Km 88 can be only reached by train, subject to schedule and baggage limitations. The train goes slower than a bus, but you start your walk nearer to Llaqtapata and Huayllabamba.

The first ruin is **Llaqtapata**, near Km 88, the utilitarian centre of a large settlement of farming terraces which probably supplied the other Inca Trail sites. From here, it is an easy three-hour walk to the village of **Huayllabamba**. Note that the route from Km 82 goes via **Cusichaca**, the valley in which Ann Kendall worked, rather than Llaqtapata.

A series of gentle climbs and descents leads along the Río Cusichaca, the ideal introduction to the trail. The village is a popular camping spot for tour groups, so it's a better idea to continue for about an hour up to the next site, **Llulluchayoc** – 'three white stones' – which is a patch of green beside a fast-flowing stream. It's a steep climb but you're pretty much guaranteed a decent pitch for the night. If you're feeling

Cuzco & the Sacred Valley Inca Treks

really energetic, you can go on to the next camping spot, a perfectly flat meadow, called **Llulluchapampa**. This means a punishing 1½-hour ascent through cloudforest, but it does leave you with a much easier second day. There's also the advantage of relative isolation and a magnificent view back down the valley.

Day 2 For most people the second day is by far the toughest. It's a steep climb to the meadow, followed by an exhausting 2½-hour haul up to the first pass – aptly named **Warmiwañusqa** (Dead Woman) – at 4200 m. The feeling of relief on reaching the top is immense. After a well-earned break it's a sharp descent on a treacherous path down to the Pacamayo Valley, where there are a few flat camping spots near a stream if you're too weary to continue.

Day 2/3 If you're feeling energetic, you can proceed to the second pass. Halfway up comes the ruin of **Runkuracay**, which was probably an Inca *tambo* (post-house). Camping is no longer permitted here. A steep climb up an Inca staircase leads to the next pass, at 3850 m, with spectacular views of Pumasillo (6246 m) and the Vilcabamba range. The trail descends to **Sayacmarca** (Inaccessible town), a spectacular site over the Aobamba Valley. Just below Sayacmarca lies **Conchamarca** (Shell town), a small group of buildings standing on rounded terraces.

Day 3 A blissfully gentle two-hour climb on a stone highway, leads through an Inca tunnel and along the enchanted fringes of the cloudforest, to the third pass. This is the most rewarding part of the trail, with spectacular views of the entire Vilcabamba range. Then it's down to the extensive ruins of **Phuyupatamarca** (Cloud-level town), at 3650 m, where Inca observation platforms offer awesome views of nearby Salkantay (6270 m) and surrounding peaks. There is a 'tourist bathroom' here, where water can be collected, but purify it before drinking.

From here, an Inca stairway of white granite plunges more than 1000 m to the spectacularly sited and impressive ruins of **Wiñay-Wayna** (Forever Young), offering views of agricultural terraces at **Intipata** (Sun place). A trail, not easily visible, goes from Wiñay-Wayna to the terracing. There is a youth hostel at Wiñay-Wayna (see Sleeping, page 140) and there are spaces for a few tents, but they get snapped up quickly. After Wiñay-Wayna there is no water, and no place to camp, until Machu Picchu. A gate by Wiñay-Wayna is locked between 1530 and 0500, preventing access to the path to Machu Picchu at night.

Day 4 From Wiñay-Wayna it is a gentle hour's walk through another type of forest, with larger trees and giant ferns, to a steep Inca staircase which leads up to **Intipunku** (sun gate), where you look down, at last, upon Machu Picchu, basking in all her glory. Your aching muscles will be quickly forgotten and even the presence of the functional hotel building cannot detract from one of the most magical sights in all the Americas.

Camino Real de los Inkas
The Inca Trail from Km 104 This short Inca Trail is used by those who don't want to endure the full hike. It starts at Km 104, where a footbridge gives access to the ruins of **Chachabamba** and the trail ascends to the main trail at Wiñay-Wayna. Half way up is a good view of the ruins of **Choquesuysuy**. The first part is a steady, continuous three-hour ascent (take water) and the trail is narrow and exposed in parts. About 15 minutes before Wiñay-Wayna is a waterfall where fresh water can be obtained (best to purify it before drinking).

Salkantay treks → *Colour map 4, B2/3.*
Four hours' drive west of Cuzco is **Mollepata**, starting point for two major alternatives to the 'classic' Inca Trail. The road from Cuzco is good-quality tarmac until the turn off

steeply up to Mollepata. Both treks pass beneath the magnificent glacial bulk of **Salkantay**, at 6271 m the loftiest peak of the Vilcabamba range.

Santa Teresa trek The first four-day trek takes the northwestern pass under Salkantay, leading into the high jungles of the Santa Teresa valley and eventually down to the town of Santa Teresa itself at the confluence with the Río Urubamba, from where Aguas Calientes and Machu Picchu are accessible. **Cruzpata** (3100 m) is the starting point for the trek, which goes via **Soraypampa** and **Salkantay Pampa**, the 4500-m **Huamantay Pass**, the villages of **Chaullay** and **Colcanpampa** and the meeting of the Río Totora with the Quebrada Chalán to form the **Río Santa Teresa**. After the village of **La Playa** you can choose to go to the Hidroeléctrica railway station, via the ruins of **Patallacta**, or to the village of Santa Teresa. This trek may only be done with a registered agency.

High Inca Trail The second route, often referred to as the High Inca Trail, follows the same route up to the base of Salkantay before turning east across the **Inca Chiriasca Pass** at approximately 4900 m. This route then descends via **Sisaypampa**, from where you trek to **Pampacahuana**, an outstanding Inca ruin. The remains of an Inca road then go down to the singular Inca ruins of **Paucarcancha**. Paucarcancha is also an important camping site on the Ancascocha trek. On the third day you join the 'classic' Inca Trail at **Huayllabamba** (see page 135), before continuing to Machu Picchu. Because the route follows the Km 88 trail in its second half, permits are required and thus booking in advance is highly recommended. It is not possible to trek this route without a registered Peruvian guide. There is an obligatory change from animals to porters before you reach Huayllabamba.

If you don't want to join up with the classic Inca Trail, an alternative is to go to Huayllabamba, then down to Km 88, from where you can take the train to Aguas Calientes, or back to Cuzco. There is an entrance fee of US$30 for this hike, but it does not include the entrance to Machu Picchu. If you combine this route with the short Inca Trail from Km 104, you have to pay the US$30 trail fee (see above for full details on prices).

Inca Jungle Trail

This is offered by several tour operators in Cuzco: on the first day you cycle downhill from Abra Málaga to Santa María, four to five hours of beautiful, easy riding. The second day is a hard seven-hour trek from Santa María to Santa Teresa (see also box, page 138). It involves crossing three adventurous bridges and bathing in the hot springs at Santa Teresa (US$1.65 entry). The third day is the six-hour trek from Santa Teresa to Aguas Calientes and the final day is a guided tour of Machu Picchu.

Choquequirao ●● » *p140. Colour map 4, A2.*

① *Entry US$3.35.*
Choquequirao is another 'lost city of the Incas', built on a ridge spur almost 1600 m above the Apurímac. Its Inca name is unknown, but research has shown that it was built during the reign of Inca Pachacútec. Although only 30% has been uncovered, it is believed to be a larger site than Machu Picchu, but with fewer buildings. The stonework is different from the classic Inca construction and masonry, simply because the preferred granite and andesite are not found in this region. A number of high-profile explorers and archaeologists, including Hiram Bingham, researched the site, but its importance has only recently been recognized. And now tourists are venturing in there, too. The introduction of regulations to cut congestion on the Inca Trail promoted Choquequirao as a replacement for the traditional hike. At the time of writing the authorities had not increased the entry cost or imposed rules to prevent independent trekking.

⁝ Travelling by train to Machu Picchu

There are two classes of tourist train: **Vistadome** and **Backpacker**. Note that timetables and prices are subject to frequent change. Tickets for all trains should be bought at Wanchac station in Cuzco (see page 88), or via PerúRail's website, www.perurail.com. Services other than those listed here are run entirely at the discretion of PerúRail.

PerúRail trains leave from San Pedro station in Cuzco and pass through Poroy and Ollantaytambo en route to Aguas Calientes (the official name of this station is Machu Picchu).

From Cuzco

Vistadome (US$66 single, US$113 return) departs San Pedro station daily at 0600 and 0700, arriving Aguas Calientes (Machu Picchu) at 0940 and 1100. It returns from Machu Picchu at 1530 and 1700, reaching Cuzco at 1920 and 2125.

Backpacker (US$46 single, US$73 return) departs San Pedro station daily at 0615 reaching Aguas Calientes at 1015. It returns at 1555, getting to Cuzco at 2020. If you do not want to arrive in Cuzco in the dark, ask to get off the train at Poroy and take a bus from there. This saves about an hour.

Hiram Bingham (US$325 single Poroy-Machu Picchu, US$275 single Machu Picchu-Poroy, US$547 return) is a super-luxury train with dining car and bar. It leaves Poroy (west of Cuzco) at 0900 with brunch on board, reaching Aguas Calientes at 1230. It leaves Aguas Calientes at 1800, cocktails, dinner and live entertainment on board, arriving in Poroy at 2125 with a bus service back to Cuzco hotels. The cost includes all meals, buses and entry to the ruins.

From Urubamba

Sacred Valley Railway Vistadome (US$46 single, US$77 return) departs Urubamba at 0610, reaching Aguas Calientes at 0820. The return service leaves at 1645, reaching Urubamba at 1915. You must reserve seats 10 days in advance. Several hotels in Urubamba and Yucay offer free transport to/from the station in Urubamba. (Always check in advance that the train is running.)

Ollantaytambo Vistadome (US$46 single, US$77 return) leaves Ollantaytambo at 0705, 1030 and 1455, and returning from Aguas Calientes at 0835, 1320 and 1645; journey time 1 hr 20 mins. Tickets include food in

The main features of Choquequirao include the **Lower Plaza**, considered by most experts to be the focal point of the city. Three of the main buildings were two-storey structures. The **Upper Plaza**, reached by a huge set of steps or terraces, has what are possibly ritual baths. A beautiful set of slightly curved agricultural terraces run for over 300 m east-northeast of the Lower Plaza. The **usnu** is a levelled hilltop platform, ringed with stones and giving awesome 360° views. Perhaps it was a ceremonial site, or was used for solar and astronomical observations. The Ridge Group, still shrouded in vegetation, is a large collection of buildings some 50 to 100 m below the *usnu*. Unrestored, with some significant hall-like structures, this whole area makes for great exploring. The **Outlier Building**, isolated and surrounded on three sides by sheer drops of over 1.5 km into the Apurímac Canyon, possesses some of the finest stonework within Choquequirao. The significance of this building's isolation from other structures remains a mystery, like so many other questions regarding the Incas and their society. **Capuliyoc**, nearly 500 m below the Lower Plaza, is a great set of agricultural terraces, visible on the approach from the far side of the valley. These terraces enabled the Incas to cultivate plants from a significantly warmer climate in close geographical proximity to their ridge-top home. Recently uncovered are further terraces decorated with llamas in white stone; ask if they are open to the public.

the price. These trains have toilets, video, snacks and drinks for sale.
Ollantaytambo Backpacker Shuttle (US$57 return; no one-way tickets) only runs 1 Apr to 31 Oct, departing at 0905, arriving at 1100, returning from Aguas Calientes at 1620, reaching Ollantaytambo at 1800. Seats can be reserved even if you're not returning the same day.

There is also a cheap, unscheduled Backpacker train from Ollantaytambo (US$20 single, US$40 return), leaving at 2000, arriving in Aguas Calientes at 2120, returning from Aguas at 0545 the following morning and arriving in Ollantaytambo at 0740. Tickets can be bought 1-2 days in advance (and they sell out fast); but check on the train's existence at the time of travel as it is not included on regular timetables. Note that, if you use this service, you will have to spend two nights in Aguas Calientes if you want to see Machu Picchu.

Local trains
Tourists are not permitted to travel on the local train from Cuzco to Machu Picchu, but you can board the local train from the station at Hidroeléctrica.

This can be combined with local buses and walking for a cheap route to Machu Picchu as follows: take a bus from Cuzco towards Quillabamba at 1900, US$6. Get out at Santa María where minibuses wait to go to Santa Teresa, 2 hrs, US$2.10. You reach Santa Teresa by sunrise in time to buy breakfast. Walk 6 km to the Central Hidroeléctrica on a nice, flat road or hitch a ride on a workers' truck, US$0.60. From the Hidroeléctrica train station it's 40 mins on the local train to Aguas Calientes at 1520 (US$8 for tourists), or you can walk along the railway in 2-3 hrs. (At Km 114.5 along the track is G pp **Hospedaje Mandor**, with garden, about 2 km from the bridge to Machu Picchu.) To return, leave Aguas Calientes at 0600 to walk to Santa Teresa, where you catch the 1000 bus to Santa María, arriving at 1200. At 1300 take a bus to Cuzco, arriving around 1900-2000. Or take the local train from Aguas Calientes to Santa Teresa at 1210, stay in a hostal, then take the 1000 bus to Santa María. If using this route, don't forget to get your ticket for Machu Picchu in Cuzco, unless you want to buy it in Aguas Calientes.

Cachora to Choquequirao There are three ways to reach Choquequirao; none is a gentle stroll. The shortest way is from **Cachora**, a village in a magnificent location on the south side of the Apurímac, reached by a side road from the Cuzco–Abancay highway, near Saywite (see page 192). It is four hours by bus from Cuzco to the turn-off, then a two-hour descent from the road to Cachora (from 3695 m to 2875 m). *Combis* run from Abancay to Cachora. Accommodation, guides (Celestino Peña is the official guide) and mules are available in Cachora (about US$12 a day for guide and mule).

From Cachora take the road heading down, out of the village, through lush cultivated countryside and meadows. There are many trails close to the village; if uncertain of the trail, ask. After 15 minutes, a sign for Choquequirao points to a left-hand path, initially following the course of a small stream. Follow the trail and cross a footbridge to the other side of a large stream. From here the trail becomes more obvious, with few trails diverging from the main route. After 9 km, two to 2½ hours from the start of the trek, is the wonderful mirador (viewpoint) of **Capuliyoc**, at 2800 m, with fantastic vistas of the Apurímac Canyon and the snowy Vilcabamba range across the river (this also makes a great day-hike from Cachora). With a pair of binoculars it's just possible to recognize Choquequirao, etched into the forested hills to the west. Condors are sometimes seen in this area. Beyond Capuliyoc the trail begins to descend towards the river. Further down the valley lies **Cocamasana**, a rest spot with a rough covered roof. From this point the river is clearly visible. At Km 16 is **Chiquisca** (1930 m), a lovely wooded spot; if you don't want to continue any further on the first day, this is a good campsite, but ask permission of the local family. Another one-hour descent leads to the suspension bridge crossing the Río Apurímac. On the other side the path ascends very steeply for 1½ hours. **Santa Rosa**, a good area for camping, again near the property of a local family, is just after the Km 21 sign. Clean water is available. If this area is occupied, another larger site is available 10 minutes further up the hill. Ask residents for directions. From Santa Rosa continue uphill on a steep zigzag for two hours to the mirador of **Marampata**, from where the trail flattens out towards Choquequirao. After 1½ hours on this flatter trail you enter some beautiful stretches of cloudforest, before a final short climb and arrival at Choquequirao itself. If coming from Santa Rosa you should have the afternoon free to explore the complex, but you could easily allow an extra day here. To return to Cachora, simply retrace the route, possibly camping at Chiquisca, which would nicely break the two-day return trek.

● Sleeping

Inca Trail *p133*
G **Youth Hostel**, at Wiñay-Wayna, price per person, with bunk beds, showers and a small restaurant. It is often fully booked. You can sleep on the floor of the restaurant more cheaply, but it is open for diners until 2300. There are also spaces for a few tents, but they get snapped up quickly too. The hostel's door is closed at 1730.

Salkantay treks *p136*
G per person **Hospedaje Mollepata**, Mollepata, T084-832103/832045, or Cuzco 245449. Just above the plaza, behind the solid, elegant church. Hot water electric shower, nice courtyard with café and ÑanTika restaurant attached. Swings in the courtyard a real bonus!

Choquequirao *p137*
E-F pp **Los Tres Balcones**, Jr Abancay s/n, Cachora, www.choquequirau.com. New hostel designed as start and end-point for the trek to Choquequirao. Price includes

breakfast, more expensive rooms have roman bath. Comfortable rooms with hot showers, restaurant and pizza oven, camping. Shares information with the town's only internet café. They run a trek to Choquequirao, US$400, including transport from Cuzco, camping gear, mules and porters, all the meals, snacks, fruits, water, entrance ticket to the ruins, horses for riding, bilingual tour guide and lunch at the Hostel afterwards.
G pp **La Casona de Ocampo**, San M artín 122, Cachora, T084-237514, lacasonadeocampo@yahoo.es. With hot shower all day, free camping, owner Carlos Robles is very friendly and knowledgeable, rents camping equipment, organizes treks to Choquequirao and beyond.

● Transport

Choquequirao *p137*
From Cachora to **Abancay**, buses at 0630 and 1100, 2 hrs, US$1.50; also *colectivo* taxis.

Lake Titicaca and Arequipa

Introduction

Straddling Peru's southern border with landlocked Bolivia are the deep, sapphire-blue waters of mystical Lake Titicaca, everyone's favourite school geography statistic. This gigantic inland sea covers up to 8400 sq km and is the highest navigable lake in the world, at 3856 m above sea level. Its shores and islands are home to the Aymara and Quechua, who are among Peru's oldest peoples, predating the Incas by a thousand years. Here you can wander through old traditional villages where Spanish is still a second language and where ancient myths and beliefs hold true. The main town on the lake is Puno, where chilled travellers gather to stock up on warm woollies to keep the cold at bay. The high-altitude town is the departure point for the islands of Taquile and Amanataní, as well as the floating reed islands of Los Uros.

Arequipa stands in a beautiful valley at the foot of El Misti volcano, a snow-capped, perfect cone, 5822 m high. The distinctive volcanic sillar used in the building of Arequipa has given it its nickname of the 'White City'. Spanish churches, mansions and the 19th-century Plaza de Armas all shine with this stonework. In contrast, the city's most famous colonial legacy, the Santa Catalina convent, is painted in bright colours, a gorgeous little city within a city. But this is only one attraction in a region of volcanoes, deep canyons and terraced valleys, and ancient peoples. The famous Colca Canyon offers excellent trekking and riding on its vast terraces, but above all, Colca is the best place in the world to get a close up view of the majestic condor as it rises from the bottom of the canyon the morning thermals.

Lake Titicaca & Arequipa

★ Don't miss ...

1 Sillustani Wonder at the architectural quality of the funerary towers, emphasized by the barrenness of the surroundings, page 147.

2 Capachica Community tourism has made a great start at the charming villages on this peninsula, page 147.

3 Suasi Watch the sun set from the summit of this island hideaway, whose only building is a hotel, page 153.

4 Fiesta de la Virgen de Candelaria One of the best ways to immerse yourself in the region's extensive folklore, page 154.

5 Santa Catalina Convent One of the most fascinating sights in Arequipa, page 161.

6 Colca Canyon Join in a village festival to really experience the traditional way of life, page 172.

Puno and the islands

On the northwest shore of Lake Titicaca, at 3855 m, Puno is a major folklore centre and a great place to buy handicrafts, particularly those amazingly tactile alpaca jumpers and hats. It also has a rich tradition of music and dance and is a good place to enjoy a number of Andean festivals, some wild, some solemn. Puno is capital of its department and, while it isn't the most attractive of cities, it has a certain vitality, helped by the fact there is a large student population. ▶▶ *For Sleeping, Eating and other listings, see pages 151-158.*

Ins and outs

Getting there and around The nearest **airport** is at Juliaca. The **railway station** for trains from Cuzco is quite central and within walking distance of the centre, but if you've got heavy bags, it's a good idea to hire a three-wheel cycle cart, *trici-taxi*, which costs about US$0.35 per kilometre per person. The train halts for guests at the hotels **Libertador** and **Sonesta**. The **bus station** and the depots for local buses are southeast of the centre, between Avenida Simón Bolívar and the lake. There is a tourist office, snack bars and toilets, but *trici-taxis* and conventional taxis serve this area.

The centre of town is easy to walk around, but a *trici-taxi* can make life easier, even if this is not your first stop at high altitude. *Colectivos* (buses) in town charge US$0.20.

Puno

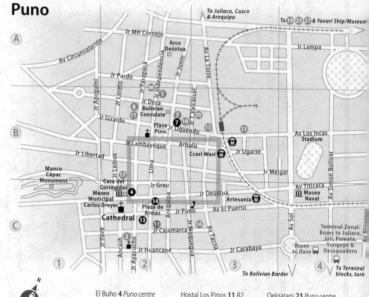

0 metres 200
0 yards 200

Sleeping
Balsa Inn **2** *C2*
Camino Real **1** *B2*
Casa Andina Plaza **17** *B2*
Casa Andina Private
  Collection Puno **27** *A4*
Casa Andina Tikarani **26** *B2*
Colón Inn **3** *Puno centre*

El Buho **4** *Puno centre*
Hospedaje Residencial
  Margarita **6** *B2*
Hostal Arequipa **7** *B2*
Hostal Don Julio **5**
  Puno centre
Hostal Europa **8**
  Puno centre
Hostal Hacienda **9**
  Puno centre
Hostal Illampu **15** *B3*
Hostal Imperial **20** *B3*
Hostal Italia **10** *B2*

Hostal Los Pinos **11** *B2*
Hostal Monterrey **12**
  Puno centre
Hostal Pukara **14**
  Puno centre
Hostal Q'oñiwasi **15** *B3*
Hostal Rubi
  'Los Portales' **16** *C3*
Libertador Isla
  Esteves **19** *A4*
Los Uros **20** *B3*
Ollanta Inn **13** *B3*
Plaza Mayor **22** *Puno centre*

Qelqatani **23** *Puno centre*
Sillustani **24** *Puno centre*
Sonesta Posadas
  del Inka **25** *A4*

Eating
Apu Salkantay **1**
  Puno centre
Cafetería Mercedes **3**
  Puno centre
Casa del Corregidor **4** *C2*
Chifa Fon Seng **5**
  Puno centre

Best time to visit Being so high up, Puno gets bitterly cold at night, especially in June-August, when the temperature can plummet to -25°C. Days are bright and the midday sun is hot, but the weather can change quickly. The first two weeks in February, when the **Fiesta de la Candelaria** takes place, and 4-5 November, the pageant of the emergence of the founding Incas, are good times to visit, but crowded.

Tourist information i perú ① *Lima y Deústua, T051-365088, near Plaza de Armas, daily 0830-1930*, is friendly and helpful, with free maps. Also try **Dircetur** ① *Ayacucho 682, T051-364976, puno@mincetur.gob.pe*. Puno is gaining a reputation for scams: don't be persuaded to change from the hotel of your choice by the offer of somewhere "better", and don't be fooled by changes to prices or menu items in restaurants, by claims that entry tickets have expired or that your return boat ticket is in fact a single. Do not be pressurized into taking a tour from your hotel. ▸▸ *See Tour operators, page 155.*

Puno ●▤⊘✦⊛⊡▲●● ▸▸pp151-158.

→ *Colour map 2, C5. Population: 113,700.*

Puno sits on a bay at the northwest end of the lake. The Bahía de Puno is only 3 m deep and a channel is dredged to the exit into the open water of Titicaca. The port and lakeside quarters are several blocks from the centre, whose focus is the Plaza de Armas. The impressive baroque exterior of the **cathedral** ① *0800-1200, 1500-1700*, completed in 1657, belies an austere interior. Just across the street from the cathedral is the famous **Balcony of the Conde de Lemos**, on the corner of Deústua and Conde de Lemos, where Peru's Viceroy stayed. Also here is the **Museo Municipal Carlos Dreyer** ① *Conde de Lemos 289, Mon-Fri 0730-1330, US$1*. The museum combines municipal collections with the private collection of pre-Columbian artefacts bequeathed to the city by their owner, Señor Carlos Dreyer. In the same block is the **Casa del Corregidor** ① *Deústua 576, T051-351921, www.casadelcorregidor.com.pe, Tue-Fri 1000-2200, closed for lunch on Sat*. One of Puno's oldest buildings, it has been converted into Puno's most important cultural centre, check for exhibitions. It also has a great café (see page 154).

A short walk up Independencia leads to the **Arco Deústua**, a monument to those killed in the battles of Junín and Ayacucho. Nearby, is a mirador giving fine views over the town, the port and also the lake beyond. The walk from Jirón Cornejo following the Stations of the Cross up a nearby hill, with fine views of Lake Titicaca, has been recommended, but be careful and don't go alone. The same applies to all the hills around Puno: Huajsapata is

Puno centre

⁝ Sacred lake

Lake Titicaca has played a dominant role in Andean beliefs for over two millennia. This, the highest navigable body of water in the world, is the most sacred lake in the Andes.

From the lake's profound, icy depths emerged the Inca creator deity, Viracocha. Legend has it that the sun god had his children, Manco Cápac and Mama Ocllo, spring from the its waters to found Cuzco and the Inca dynasty.

The name Titicaca derives from the word *titi*, an Aymara mountain cat and the Quechua word *caca* meaning rock. The rock refers to the Sacred Rock on the Isla del Sol (on the Bolivian side) which was worshipped by the pre-Inca people. The mountain cat inhabited the shores of the lake and is said to have visited the Isla del Sol.

The link between the rock and the cat comes from the legend that the ancient indigenous people saw the eyes of a mountain cat gleaming in the Sacred Rock and so named it Titicaca, or Rock of the Mountain Cat. It was this that gave rise to the idea of the sun having its home there.

The *titi* has characteristics – such as its aquatic ability and the brilliance of its eyes – that conceptually link it with a mythological flying feline called *ccoa*. The role of the *ccoa* was (and in some parts still is) important throughout the Andes. It is believed to have thrown lightning from its eyes, urinated rain, spit hail and roared thunder.

Among indigenous people today the *ccoa* is believed to be one of the mountain god's servants and lives in the mountains. It is closely involved in their daily life and is considered the most feared of the spirits as it uses lightning and hail.

known for music and folklore gatherings; Azoguine and Cancharani are higher, with good views and sacred associations. To get to Azoguine you go through Barrio Las Cruces, which is very dangerous.

On the way from the centre to the port is the **Museo Naval** ① *Av El Puerto y Av Sol, Mon-Fri 0900-1700, Sat-Sun 0900-1300*. Here you can find a small exhibit on navigating on Lake Titicaca. A new **Malecón Bahía de los Incas**, near the port, is a pleasant place for a stroll with views of the lake. The bay by Puno is noticeably polluted. There are plans for the construction of a badly needed sewage treatment plant.

The **MN Yavari** ① *0800-1715, illuminated till 2230 for 'Happy Hour' run by Hotel Posadas del Inca, entry free in daytime, donation of US$6 encouraged*, is the oldest ship on Lake Titicaca. It was restored in the port of Puno and turned into a museum in 2002. The iron-hulled ship, now painted in her original livery of black, white and red, was built in England in 1862 and, together with her twin, the *Yapura* (now the Peruvian Navy's Hospital ship and called the *BAP Puno*), was shipped in kit form to Arica in Chile. From Arica, the two ships went by rail to Tacna from where the 2766 pieces were carried by mule to Lake Titicaca. The journey took six years. The *Yavari* was eventually launched on Christmas Day 1870 and on 14 June 1871 sailed on her maiden voyage. Until 1975, she was operated as a passenger/cargo vessel by the London-based Peruvian Corporation. The ship was bought in 1987 and is being restored by an Anglo-Peruvian Association. Visitors are very welcome on board. The *Yavari* is berthed near the entrance to the **Sonesta Posadas del Inca Hotel**. You have to go through the hotel to get to the ship. To get there you can go by taxi, bus or *trici-taxi*, but the most charming way is by boat from the port, about US$2 return, including wait. **Project addresses** ① *61 Mexfield Rd, London, SW15 2RG, England, T44-20 8874 0583, info@ yavari.org; in Lima: Giselle Guldentops, T01-9998 5071, yavari.gulden@dwp.net; in Puno: Asociación Yavari, c/o Capitán Carlos Saavedra, T051-369329, carlosalberto@yavari.org*. For general information, volunteering, donations, etc, visit www.yavari.org.

Around Puno ⊕⊕ ⇢ pp151-158.

Sillustani

ⓘ US$1.65. It's best to take an organized tour, which lasts about 3-4 hrs and leaves at 1430, US$6.30. Or take a Juliaca bus to the Sillustani turn-off (US$0.35); from here a 15-km paved road runs across the altiplano to the ruins. Moto-taxis and some combis run to Atuncolla (4 km away with a lovely colonial church), US$0.40, or US$0.85 to Sillustani (out of season you may have to walk the 4 km from Atuncolla). A taxi from Puno costs about US$12, including wait.

A highly recommended trip is to the *chullpas* (pre-Columbian funeral towers) of Sillustani in a beautiful setting on a peninsula in **Lago Umayo** (3890 m), 32 km from Puno on an excellent road. According to expert John Hemming, these are burial towers of the Aymara-speaking Colla tribe and most of them date from the period of Inca occupation in the 15th century. As Hemming also states: "The engineering involved in their construction is more complex than anything the Incas built – it is defeating archaeologists' attempts to rebuild the tallest 'lizard' *chullpa*." Other Inca remains can be seen in the shape of square buildings, a temple of the Sun and a temple of the Moon. Underground burials at the site predating the Colla have been found from the Pukara and Tiahuanaco periods. There is a museum, and handicraft sellers in traditional costume wait at the exit. Guides are also available here. Photographers will find the afternoon light best, though this is when the wind is at its strongest and can kick up a mini-sandstorm. It's also best not to wear contact lenses. The scenery is barren, but nonetheless impressive.

Capachica Peninsula

The pretty farming villages of **Llachón**, **Santa María** and **Ccotos**, at the eastern end of the Península de Capachica, have become a focus of community-based tourism. The sandy beaches, pre-Inca terracing and trees and flowers dotted around, make the peninsula a charming place to visit. The peninsula is also good for hiking and mountain-biking and sailing boats can be hired. The sunset from the **Auki Carus** hill is reckoned to be better even than from Taquile. Neither Taquile nor Amantaní are far away. **Capachica** is the main town and crossroads of the peninsula. It has a colourful Sunday market, two very basic *hospedajes* and simple *comedores*. Throughout the peninsula the dress of the local women is very colourful, with four-cornered hats called *monteros*, matching waistcoats and colourful *polleras*.

There are currently six different community-tourism organizations, each with a dozen or more families and links to different tour operators in Puno, Cuzco or abroad. The atmosphere is pleasant and low key.

The islands ⊕⊘⊛▲⊕ ⇢ pp151-158.

Los Uros

ⓘ US$0.60. Take drinking water. Be careful where you walk; the surface can be unsteady.

Of the estimated 32 floating islands, only about 15 are regularly visited by tourists, and today we can talk about two kinds of Uros people; those close to the city of Puno and easily accessible to tourism, and those on islands which remain relatively isolated. The Uros' islanders fish, hunt birds and live off the lake plants, most important of which are the totora reeds they use for their boats, houses and the very foundations of their islands. On the more far-flung islands, reached via narrow channels through the reed beds, the Uros do not like to be photographed and continue to lead relatively traditional lives outside the monetary economy. They hunt and fish and still depend on trade with the mainland for other essentials.

A lasting tradition

One of the most enduring textile traditions in Peru is found among the people of Taquile. Each family possesses at least four different types of costume: for work, leisure, weddings and festivals.

For weddings, which all take place on 3 May, when the planet Venus – Hatun Chaska – is visible, the bridegroom wears a red poncho provided by the best man. As a single man he wore a half red, half white cap, but to signify his married status he wears a long red hat and a wide red wedding belt, or *chumpi*. His bag for coca leaves, *ch'uspa*, is also filled.

The bride wears a wide red hat (*montera*) and her hands are covered with a ritual cloth (*katana-oncoma*). A *quincha*, a small white cloth symbolizing purity, is hidden in her skirt. With her red wedding blouse, or *gonna*, she wears a gathered skirt or *pollera*, made from 20 different layers of brightly coloured cloth. She also wears a belt (*faja*) and black cloak known as a *chukoo*.

The wool used for weaving is usually spun by the women, but on Taquile men spin wool, as well as knitting their conical hats (*chullos*). In fact, only the men on Taquile know how to knit. By the age of 10, a boy can knit his own Chullo Santa María, which is white-tipped to show single status. When he marries, or moves in with a woman, he adopts the red-tipped *chullo*, which is exclusive to the island. Today, much of the wool for knitting is bought ready-spun from factories in Arequipa.

Visitors to the floating islands encounter more women than men. These women wait every day for the tour boats to sell their handicrafts. The few men one does see might be building or repairing boats or fixing their nets. The rest are to be found out on the lake, hunting and fishing. The Uros cannot live from tourism alone, and the extra income they glean from tourists merely supplements their more traditional activities.

Many tourists find that, although the people are friendly, they are very poor and a few subject visitors to a hard-sell approach for handicrafts. The islands visited by tour boats are little more than 'floating souvenir stalls'. All the same, this form of tourism on the Uros Islands is now well-established and, whether it has done irreparable harm or will ultimately prove beneficial, it takes place in superb surroundings.

Taquile

Isla Taquile, some 45 km from Puno, has numerous pre-Inca and Inca ruins, and Inca terracing. At the highest point is a ruin from which to view the sunset (the path is signed). The island is quiet and hospitable, but at the height of the season and at Sunday lunchtime it gets busy and touristy (about 50 boats a day in high season).

The island is only about 1 km wide and 6-7 km long. On the north side of the island is the warmest part of Lake Titicaca. Ask for the (unmarked) **museum of traditional costumes** ① *on the plaza, free,* and also where you can see and photograph local weaving. There is a co-operative shop on the plaza that sells exceptional woollen goods which are not cheap, but of very fine quality. They are cheaper in the market at Puno. You need to spend a night on Taquile to appreciate fully its beauty and, therefore, it may be better to travel independently and go at your own pace.

Every Sunday, the island's four *suyos* (districts) coordinate their activities with a reunion in the main plaza after Quechua mass. Numerous festivals take place on the island (see page 155), with many dances in between. Weddings are celebrated each May and August. The priest comes from Puno and there is a week-long party.

The influx of tourists unfortunately prompts persistent requests by children for sweets or to have their photo taken. They whisper, quite politely, *caramelo* (sweet) or *muña* (a herb used for infusions) for a sol. Recordings of traditional music have been made and are on sale as an additional source of income for the islanders. Buying their handicrafts is a way to help support the community. Gifts of fruit, sugar, salt, spices, torches/flashlights (there is no electricity), moisturizer or sun block (the children suffer sore cheeks) are appreciated.

You are advised to take with you some food, particularly fruit, bread and vegetables, water, plenty of small-value notes, candles and a torch/flashlight. Take precautions against sunburn and seasickness. If staying the night, take warm clothes, a sleeping bag and a hot water bottle. The same applies to Amantaní. Tourism to both islands is community based: the less you pay, the smaller the amount that goes to the islanders. Bear this in mind when you shop around for a good-value tour (there is not much variation at the lower end of the price range).

There are two main entry points. The Puerto Principal at the south end has a very steep climb up many steps; the northern entry is longer but more gradual (remember you are at 3800 m). Visitors pay US$0.60. There is plentiful accommodation in private houses and, on arrival, you are greeted by a *jefe de alojamiento*, who oversees where you are going to stay. You can either say where you are going, if you (or your guide) know where you want to stay, or the *jefe* can find you a room. ▸▸ *See Sleeping, page 153.*

Amantaní

Another island well worth visiting is Amantaní. It is very beautiful and peaceful, and many say is less spoiled, more genuine and friendlier than Taquile (about 10 boats visit a day in high season). Visitors pay US$0.60 to land. There are six villages and ruins on both of the island's peaks, **Pacha Tata** and **Pacha Mama**, from which there are excellent views. There are also temples and on the shore there is a throne carved out of stone, the **Inkatiana**. It is rather eroded from flooding. It's a 30-minute walk west of **El Pueblo**, the village on the north end. Turn right down the steep slope after the last house on the right.

Several festivals are celebrated on Amantaní (see page 155) and islanders arrange dances; visitors can dress up in local clothes and join in. Small shops sell water and snacks, but are more expensive than those in Puno.

The residents make beautiful textiles and sell them at the **Artesanía Cooperativa**, at the east end of El Pueblo. They also make basketwork and stoneware. The people are Quechua speakers, but understand Spanish.

Puno to Bolivia ⊟⊖❶ ▸▸ *pp151-158.*

The opposite shores of Lake Titicaca are quite different. Between Puno and Desaguadero at the lake's southeastern tip, the plain is intensively worked. The tin roofs of the communities glint everywhere in the sun. Heading north from Puno, the road crosses a range of hills to another coastal plain, which leads to Juliaca. North of Puno is the first sector (29,150 ha) of the Reserva Nacional del Titicaca. The smaller, Ramis sector (7030 ha) is northeast of Juliaca, at the outflow of the Río Ramis which floods in the wet season. The reserve protects extensive totora reed beds in which thousands of birds live. On the flat, windy altiplano between Juliaca and Huancané (see below) you will see small, square houses with conical roofs, all made of blocks of earth, *putukus de champa*. After Huancané, the lakeshore becomes mountainous, with cliffs, bays and fabulous vistas over the water.

The southwestern shore and into Bolivia

The road from Puno towards Bolivia runs along the western shore of Lake Titicaca, so the villages described below are easily reached by frequent public transport. Anybody interested in religious architecture should go from Puno to visit these villages.

Two routes cross the border here, both of which are fairly straightforward; both routes on the Peruvian side are paved. The route via **Yunguyo** and Copacabana, is far the more popular than that via **Desaguadero**. It is possible to cross the border by hydrofoil or catamaran as part of a tour (see Transport, page 158).

Chucuito

An Inca sundial can be seen near the village of Chucuito (19 km), which has an interesting church, **La Asunción**, and houses with carved stone doorways. Visits to Chucuito usually include the Templo de la Fertilidad, **Inca Uyo**, which boasts many phalli and other fertility symbols. The authenticity and original location of these objects is the subject of debate.

Juli and Pomata → *Colour map 2, C5*

The main road bypasses the little town of **Juli**, 83 km southeast, which has some fine examples of religious architecture in its churches. **San Pedro** on the plaza, designated as the cathedral, has been extensively restored. It contains a series of paintings of saints, with the Via Crucis scenes in the same frame, and gilt side altars above which some of the arches have baroque designs. **San Juan Letrán** ① *mornings only, US$1.15*, has two sets of 17th-century paintings of the lives of St John the Baptist and of St Teresa, contained in sumptuous gilded frames. San Juan is a museum. It also has intricate mestizo carving in pink stone. **La Asunción** ① *US$0.85*, is also a museum. The great nave is empty, but its walls are lined with colonial paintings with no labels. The original painting on the walls of the transept is fading. Its fine bell tower was damaged by earthquake or lightning. Outside is an archway and atrium which date from the early 17th century.

A further 20 km along the lake is Pomata (US$0.45 from Juli), whose church of **Santiago Apóstol** ① *0700-1200, 1330-1600, free, but give a donation and a tip to the*

To Bolivia via Yunguyo-Copacabana

Bolivian immigration at Kasani is open 0830-1930. It is 400 m from the Peruvian post, which is five minutes' drive from Yunguyo and is open 24 hours a day (see page 335). When leaving Peru you must get an exit stamp before crossing the border and a tourist visa on the other side. A 30 day visa is usually given. Bolivian time is one hour ahead of Peru.

Money Good rates are available for dollars or bolivianos at *casas de cambio* in the main plaza in Yunguyo. Travellers' cheques can be exchanged but rates are poor. There are good rates of exchange on the Bolivian side of the border and Peruvian soles can be changed in Copacabana.

Transport See page 157, for buses from Puno to La Paz.

To Bolivia via Desaguadero

The most direct road route continues 41 km beyond the turn-off to Yunguyo, and is paved for the 150 km to the border. Desaguadero is a scruffy, unscrupulous place, with poor restaurants and accommodation. There is no need to stop over here as all roads to it are paved and if you leave La Paz or Puno early enough you should be at your destination before nightfall.

Bolivian immigration and Peruvian immigration are at either end of the bridge. The Bolivian office is open 0830-1230 and 1400-2100, while Peru closes at 2000. A 30-day visa is normally given on entering Bolivia.

Money It is better to change money on the Peruvian side in Desaguadero.

Transport See Transport, page 158, for buses from Puno to Desaguadero.

guardian, is built of red sandstone (1532, started by the Jesuits, finished by the Dominicans). If the *colectivo* does not enter town, get out by the *cuartel* (barracks) and walk up. It stands on a promontory above the main road and has wonderful carvings in Andean mestizo baroque of vases full of tropical plants, flowers and animals in the window frames, lintels and cornices. The beautiful interior contains statues, painted columns, a Spanish tiled floor, paintings of the Cuzqueña school and a cupola decorated with figures whose florid, stylized bodies have linked arms.

Juliaca and the northeastern shore → *Colour map 2, C5. Altitude: 3825 m.*

Heading north and west, **Juliaca** is a major transport hub for paved roads to Cuzco and Arequipa and also has the only airport in the region. There is a border crossing at **Tilali**, however, transport along the north shore is less frequent. Tilali is the last settlement before the border, with a couple of basic, cheap *hospedajes*. There is no immigration service at the border here so you must get your exit stamp in Puno. From the border it is about 10 km to **Puerto Acosta**, Bolivia, where you must get a preliminary entry stamp at the police station on the plaza. Get the definitive entry stamp at Migración in La Paz.

▶▶ *For transport from Juliaca airport, see page 158; for the Puerto Acosta border crossing, see page 347.*

● Sleeping

Puno *p145, map p144*
Puno sometimes suffers from power and water shortages.

AL Libertador Isla Esteves, on an island linked by a causeway 5 km northeast of Puno (taxi US$3, or red *colectivo* No 16, or white Nos 24 and 33), T051-367780, www.liberta dor.com.pe. Built on a Tiahuanaco-period site, the hotel is spacious with good views. Bar, good restaurant, disco, good service, electricity and hot water all day, parking.

AL Casa Andi na Private Collection Puno, Av Sesquicentenario 1970, Huaje, T051-363992, www.casa-andina.com. A new addition in 2006 to this recommended chain, in its more luxurious range, on the lakeshore.

AL-A Sonesta Posadas del Inka, Av Sesquicentenario 610, Huaje, 5 km from Puno on the lakeshore (same transport as for **Libertador Isla Esteves**), T051-364111, www.sonestaperu.com. 62 large rooms with heating, similar to other hotels in this group but with local touches, such as the textile decorations and the Andean menu in the Inkafé restaurant. Disabled access, fine views, attractive, good service, folklore shows.

A Casa Andina Plaza, Jr Grau 270, T051-367520, www.casa-andina.com. Price includes breakfast and 10% service. One of this chain's modern hotels, a block from the plaza, rooms with bath, TV and heating, non-smoking rooms, clean, safe and central. Business centre with internet for guests, parking.

A Casa Andina Tikarani, Independencia 185, T051-367803, www.casa-andina.com. Similar in most respects to the **Casa Andina Plaza**, but further from the centre.

Lake Titicaca & Arequipa Puno & the islands Listings

A-B **Qelqatani**, Tarapacá 355, T051-366172, www.qelqatani.com. A hotel in colonial style, central, very clean, a good option.

B **Balsa Inn**, Cajamarca 555, T051-363144, www.hotelbalsainn.com. With breakfast (no other meals except for groups by arrangement). See the Nativity collection on display; comfortable lobby. Rooms are comfy, too, with big bathrooms, hot water, TV, safe, heating. Very helpful.

B **Colón Inn**, Tacna 290, T051-351432, www.coloninn.com. Price includes tax and buffet breakfast. Colonial style, good rooms with hot shower, good service, safe, internet for guests, restaurant **Sol Naciente** and pizzería **Europa**, the Belgian manager Christian Nonis is well known for his work on behalf of the people on Taquile island.

B **El Buho**, Lambayeque 142, T/F051-366122, www.hotelbuho.com. Breakfast included. Hot water, nicely decorated rooms with heaters, TV, restaurant, safe, special discount to Footprint readers, travel agency for excursions and flight reconfirmations.

B **Hostal Hacienda**, Jr Deústua 297, T/F051-356109, haciendahostal@hotmail.com. Price includes breakfast. Refurbished colonial house, comfortable rooms with bath and hot water, TV, café. Rooms facing the front have private balconies.

B **Plaza Mayor**, Deústua 342, T051-366089, www.plazamayorhotel.com. Price includes buffet breakfast. Comfortable and well appointed, very close to the plaza. Rooms have big beds, hot water and TV. Laundry, safe, restaurant has local and European food.

B **Sillustani**, Jr Lambayeque 195, T051-351881, www.sillustani.com. Price includes breakfast and taxes. Hot water, cable TV, safety deposit, heaters, internet, very good.

C **Camino Real**, Deza 328, T051-367296, www.caminoreal-turistico.com. Good central hotel, price includes buffet breakfast, cable TV, 24-hour room service, internet.

C **Hostal Italia**, Teodoro Valcarcel 122, T051-367706, www.hotelitaliaperu.com. 2 blocks from the station. With good breakfast, cheaper in low season. Good, safe, hot water, good food, free tea and coffee, small rooms, staff helpful, internet.

C **Hostal Pukara**, Jr Libertad 328, T/F051-368448, pukara@terra.com.pe. Includes good American breakfast. Popular, with bath, hot water and heating. English spoken, central, quiet, free coca tea in evening.

D **Hostal Imperial**, Teodoro Valcarcel 145, T051-352386, imperial_hostal_puno@yahoo.com. **E-F** (low season), breakfast extra, US$1.85 (good coffee). With good shower, hot water, helpful, stores luggage, comfortable if basic, safe, ask for extra blanket if cold.

D **Hostal Monterrey**, Lima 441, T051-351691, monterreytours@hotmail.com. Price includes breakfast and cable TV. **F** without bath, better rooms with showers, hot water, restaurant, laundry, secure, motorcycle parking US$0.50.

D-E **Hostal Don Julio**, Tacna 336, T051-363358, hostaldonjulio@hotmail.com. Very clean, hot water, price includes full breakfast, some staff speak English.

D-E **Hostal Rubi 'Los Portales'**, Jr Cajamarca 152-154, T/F051-353384, www.mancocapacinn.com. Breakfast US$2 extra, hot water, safe, TV, good, tours arranged.

E **Hospedaje Residencial Margarita**, Jr Tarapacá 130, T051-352820, hostalmargarita @hotmail.com. Large building, family atmosphere, hot water most of the day, stores luggage, tours can be arranged.

E **Los Uros**, Teodoro Valcarcel 135, T051-352141, huros@speedy.com.pe. Cheaper without bath. Hot water, plenty of blankets, breakfast available at extra cost, quiet at the back, good value. Small charge to leave luggage, laundry, often full, changes TCs.

E-F **Hostal Arequipa**, Arequipa 153, T051-352071, hotelarequipa@speedy.com.pe. With bath, hot water, will change TCs at good rates, stores luggage, secure, arranges tours to the islands, also has parking space.

E-F **Hostal Los Pinos**, Tarapacá 182, T/F051-367398, hostalpinos@hotmail.com. Cheaper without bath. Family-run, electric showers, clean, safe, luggage store, laundry facilities, helpful, cheap tours organized.

E-F **Hostal Q'oñiwasi**, Av La Torre 119, opposite the train station, T051-365784, qoniwasi@mundomail.net. **E** without bath and in low season. Heating extra, but hot water available all day, laundry, luggage store, breakfast extra, 0600-0900, safe, very helpful.

For an explanation of sleeping and eating price codes used in this guide, see inside the front cover. Other relevant information is found in Essentials, see pages 31-35.

• Budget buster

LL **Hotel Isla Suasi**, T051-962 2709, Casa Andina Private Collection hotel, www.casa-andina.com. Price includes full board, national drinks, entrance to island, land transfers, services and taxes. Facilities are spacious, comfortable and solar-powered. Rooms have bath and hot water and hot water bottles are put between your sheets at bedtime, very attentive service. The food is excellent and innovative, lots of vegetables, all locally produced. Sauna and massage room, internet access is a whopping US$20 per hour. For boat transport, contact Casa Andina. This is the only tourist project on the north shore. It is the only house on this tiny, tranquil island. The microclimate allows for beautiful terraced gardens, which are at their best from January to March. You can take a community rowing boat around the island to see birds (US$1.50) or paddle yourself in one of the hotel's canoes. The island has six vicuñas, a small herd of alpacas and various domestic animals. The sunsets from the highest point are out of this world.

E-F **Ollanta Inn**, Jr Ilo E-1, 2a cuadra Jr Los Incas, T051-366743. New, just behind station, hot water 24 hrs, pleasant, clean, helpful owner, fan heater and TV extra, breakfast also extra but is good.
F **Hostal Europa**, Alfonso Ugarte 112, near the train station, T051-353026, hostaleuropa @hotmail.com. Very popular, cheaper without bath, luggage may be stored, but don't leave your valuables in the room, hot water sometimes, garage space for motorcycles.
F **Hostal Illampu**, Av La Torre 137-interior 9, T051-353284, illampu97@hotmail.com. With bath and warm water, breakfast and TV extra. Has a café, laundry, safe, exchanges money, arranges excursions (ask for Santiago).

Around Puno *p147*
Llachón community phone T051-832323.
F **Primo Flores**, near church and bus stop in Llachón, T051-968 0040 (mob), primopuno@ yahoo.es. Rustic family accommodation, includes breakfast, other meals on request US$2.50, knowledgeable and friendly. Sr Flores is the head of one of the community tourism groups.
F **Valentín Quispe** is the organizer of tourism in Llachón. He offers lodging and meals (breakfast US$1.20, other meals US$2). To contact Don Valentín, T051-982 1392 (mob), llachon@yahoo.com, or visit www.titicaca-peru.com/capachicae.htm.
Another family is that of **Tomás Cahui Coila**, Centro Turístico Santa María Llachón, T051-992 3595 (mob). All hosts in Llachón can arrange boat transport to Amantaní. There is a campsite towards the end of the peninsula, mostly used by tour groups. See Transport, below.

The islands *p147*
Taquile
The average rate for a bed is US$3 pp, without any meals. Several families now have sizeable *alojamientos* (eg **Pedro Huille**, on the track up from the north entry, with showers, proper loos, no sign). Instead of staying in the busy part around the main square, the Huayllano community, on the south side of the island, is hosting visitors. Contact **Alipio Huata Cruz**, T051-966 8551/961 5239 (mob, you can leave a voicemail that he will retrieve from Puno as there is no reception on the island) or you can arrange a visit with **All Ways Travel** (see Tour operators, below).

Amantaní
Ask your boat owner where you can stay; families living close to the port tend to receive tour company business and more tourists. Accommodation is US$6 pp. This includes 3 meals of remarkable similarity and generally poor quality (take bread and fruit). It's good value for visitors, but the prices have been forced down to unrealistically low levels, from which the islanders benefit hardly at all. Some contacts for accommodation are:
Hospedaje Jorge Wasi, basic, but nice family, great view of lake from room.

Ambrosio Mamani, j.mamani.cari@eudora mail.com, skipper of the *Barco Atlántico*, good lodging and food.
Familia Victoriano Calsin Quispe, Casilla 312, T051-360220 (Irma) or T051-363320 (Puno contact).

Puno to Bolivia *p150*
G pp **Hostal Isabel**, San Francisco 110, Plaza de Armas, Yunguyo, T051-856019. Shared bathroom, hot water, good value, will change money and arrange transport.

🍴 Eating

Puno *p145, map p144*
Very cheap places on Jr Deústua serve lunch or dinner. There are many places on Lima, too many to list here, which cater for the tourist market, they usually have good atmosphere and very good food.
†† IncAbar, Lima 356-A. Open for breakfast, lunch and dinner, interesting dishes in creative sauces, fish, pastas, curries, café and couch bar, nice decor.
†† Internacional, Moquegua 201. Very popular, excellent trout, good pizzas, service variable.
†† La Plaza, Puno 425, Plaza de Armas. Good food, including fish.
†† Mojsa, Lima 635, p 2, Plaza de Armas, T051-363182. Good international and *novo andino* dishes, also has an arts and crafts shop. Recommended.
††-† Apu Salkantay, Lima 357 and in 400 block. Wide menu of meats, fish (more expensive), pastas, sandwiches, pizza, coffee, popular.
††-† Don Piero, Lima 360. Huge meals, live music, try their *pollo coca-cola*, slow service, popular, tax extra.
††-† La Caywa Andean Cuisine Bar, Jr Arequipa 410. T051-351490, open 1000-2200. Local and international. Recommended.
††-† Lago de Flores, Lima 357. Local dishes and pizza, very good food, open fire in the shape of a pizza oven keeps diners warm.
††-† Pizzería El Buho, Lima 349 and at Jr Libertad 386, open 1800 onwards. Excellent pizza, lively atmos- phere, pizzas US$2.35-3.
† Chifa Fon Seng, Arequipa 552. Good food, service and value, Chinese, popular.
† Chifa Nan Hua, Arequipa 167, 1 block from Plaza de Armas. Tasty, big portions of Chinese.
† Govinda, Deústua 312. Cheap vegetarian lunch menus, closes at 2000.

† Remembranzas, Jr Moquegua 200, open 0630-2200. Pizzas as well as local food.
† Vida Natural, Lambayeque 141. Open for breakfast, salads, fruits, yoghurts, helpful staff.

Cafés
Cafetería Mercedes, Jr Arequipa 351. Good *menú* US$1.50, breads, cakes, snacks, juices.
Casa del Corregidor, Deústua 576, aptdo 2, T051-355694. In restored 17th-century building, sandwiches, good snacks, coffee, good music, great atmosphere, nice surroundings with patio.
Ricos Pan, Jr Lima 424, Tue-Sat 0600-2300. Café and bakery, great cakes, excellent coffees, juices and pastries, good breakfasts and other dishes, reasonable prices, great place to relax. Branches of their *panadería* at Av Titicaca 155 and Moquegua 330.

The islands *p147*
On Taquile, there are many small restaurants around the plaza and on the track to the Puerto Principal (eg Gerardo Hualta's **La Flor de Cantuta**, on the steps; **El Inca** on the main plaza). Meals are generally fish (the island has a trout farm), rice and chips, tortilla and *fiambre* – a local stew. Meat is rarely available and drinks often run out. Breakfast consists of pancakes and bread. Shops on the plaza sell postcards, water, chocolate and dry goods. On Amantaní, there is one restaurant, **Samariy**.

🍸 Bars and clubs

Puno *p145, map p144*
Café Concert, Jr Lima 723. Open daily 2000-2300.
Pub Ekeko's, Jr Lima 355, p 2. Live music every night, happy hour 2000-2200.

🎉 Festivals and events

Puno *p145, map p144*
It is difficult to find a month in Puno without some sort of celebration.
Feb The very colourful **Fiesta de la Virgen de la Candelaria** takes place during the first 2 weeks in Feb. Bands and dancers from all the local towns compete in this *Diablada*, or Devil Dance, with the climax coming on Sun. The festival is famous for its elaborate and grotesque masks, which depict

characters in local legends as well as caricatures of former landowners and mine bosses. The festivities are better at night on the streets than the official functions in the stadium. Check in advance on the actual date because Candelaria may be moved if pre-Lenten carnival coincides with it. This festival is great fun and shouldn't be missed if you're in the vicinity around this time.

Mar/Apr On Good Fri there's a candlelit procession through darkened streets, with bands, dignatories and statues of Jesus.

3 May Invención de la Cruz, an exhibition of local art.

29 Jun San Pedro, is a colourful festival of with a procession at Zepita.

5 Nov There's an impressive pageant dedicated to the founding of Puno and the emergence of Manco Cápac and Mama Ocllo from the waters of Lake Titicaca. The royal couple sail from a point on the lake (it varies annually) and arrive at the port between 0900 and 1000. The procession from the lake moves up Av Titicaca to the stadium where a ceremony takes place with dancers from local towns and villages. If you buy an entrance ticket, US$0.60, you can watch from the top tier as the float carrying the Incas, followed by the local dancing groups, enters the stadium. Many of the groups continue dancing outside. This is not the best time to visit Taquile and Amantaní since many of their inhabitants are at the festival. This date coincides with the anniversary of the founding of Puno, celebrated with parades at night and a full military parade on the Sun.

The islands *p147*
Taquile
The principal festival days are: **Mar/Apr** (Semana Santa); **2 -7 Jun**; **Mid-Jul** (Fiesta de Santiago, held over 2 weeks); **1-2 Aug**.

Amantaní
15 Jan (or thereabouts) Fiesta de la Tierra Santa, or Pago a la Tierra is celebrated on both hills. The festivities have been reported as spectacular, very colourful, musical and hard-drinking.

9 Apr Aniversario del Consejo (of the local council), which might not be as boring as it sounds.

O Shopping

Puno *p145, map p144*
The markets between Av Los Incas and Arbulu (Ccori Wasi) and on the railway between Av Libertad and Av El Puerto are two of the best places in Peru (or Bolivia) for llama and alpaca wool articles, but bargain for a good price when buying in quantity (and you will!), especially in the afternoon. In the covered part of the market (bounded by Arbulu, Arequipa, Oquendo and Tacna) mostly foodstuffs are sold (good cheeses), but there are also model reed boats, attractive carved stone amulets and Ekekos (household goods). This central market covers a large area and on Sat it expands down to the stadium (mostly fruit and vegetables) and along Av Bolívar (potatoes and grains). You will be hassled on the street and outside restaurants to buy woollen goods, so take care.

Cooperación Artesanal Ichuña, Jr Libertad 113, www.ichunia.org. The outlet for a cooperative of about 100 women from Ichuña, 90 km southwest of Puno, selling handwoven textiles made of alpaca wool.

▲ Activities and tours

Puno *p145, map p144*
Agencies organize trips to the Uros floating islands and the islands of Taquile and Amantaní, as well as to Sillustani, and other places. Make sure that you settle all details before embarking on the tour. Alternatively, you can easily go down to the lake and make your own arrangements with the boatmen. Watch out for the many unofficial street tour sellers – or *jalagringos* – who offer hotels and tours at different rates, depending on how wealthy you look. Once you realize they have charged more than the going rate, they'll be gone. They are everywhere: train station, bus offices, airport and hotels. Ask to see their guide's ID card. Only use agencies with named premises and compare prices.

Tour operators
The following have been recommended as reliable and helpful and offer good value:
All Ways Travel, Tacna 234, T/F051-355552, www.titicacaperu.com. Also in Casa del Corregidor, Deústua 576. Very helpful, kind

and attentive to visitors' needs. Reliable, staff speak German, French, English and Italian. They offer a unique cultural tour to the islands of Anapia and Yuspique in Lake Wiñaymarka, beyond the straits of Tiquina, 'The Treasurer of Wiñaymarka', departures Thu and Sun. You can contribute to owner Víctor Lazo's educational project by donating children's books for schools. They also have a speed boat for 40 passengers. Also doing an alternative visit to Taquile where you go to the south of the island to visit the Huayllano community, this is a lot less touristy then the regular Taquile visit.

Edgar Adventures, Jr Lima 328, T/F051-353444 , www.edgaradventures.com. Run by Edgar Apaza and Norka Flórez who speak English, German and French, very helpful.
Käfer Viajes, Arequipa 179, T051-354742, www.kafer-titicaca.com. Efficient and helpful.
Kontiki Tours, Jr Melgar 188. T051-355887, www.kontikiperu.com. Receptive tour agency specializing in special interest excursions.
Nayra Travel, Jr Lima 419, of 105. T051-337934, www.nayratravel.com. Small but very helpful staff, offering local tours.
Peru Up to Date, Arequipa 340, T051-961 0810 (mob), www.peruuptodate.com. New, offers tours in the Puno and Titicaca area.
Pirámide Tours, Jr Rosendo Huirse 130, T051-366107, www.titikakalake.com. Unusual and classic tours, flexible, personalized service, modern fast launches, very helpful, but works only via internet and overseas clients.
Titikaka Explorers, Av La Torre 339-4, T051-355219, peru-titikaka@hotmail.com. Good service, helpful.

The Islands p147
Rene Coyla Coila, T051-974 3533, strippercc@hotmail.com. Official tourist guide for Los Uros, ask about guesthouses and community tourism on the Uros.

⊖ Transport

Puno p145, map p144
Air The nearest airport is at Juliaca (see page 158). **Lan**, Tacna y Libertad, T051-367227.
Boat Boats to the islands leave from the harbour; trici-taxi from centre, US$1.
Bus All long-distance buses, except some Cuzco services and buses to La Paz (see below), leave from the new Terminal

Terrestre Platform tax US$0.30. Bus prices to Cuzco and La Paz have seasonal variations.

Daily buses to **Arequipa**, 5-6 hrs via **Juliaca**, 297 km by paved road, US$4.50-6 (Cruz del Sur, Best Way, Destinos, Julsa, Señor de Milagros, or Sur Oriente, most have a morning and evening bus – better quality buses go at night). To **Lima**, 1011 km, 19 hrs, US$21-25, all buses go through **Arequipa**, bus cama (requires transfer in Arequipa) US$30; Ormeño T051-368176. Ormeño has a service to **La Paz** (Bolivia), as does Litoral (cheaper).

Small buses and colectivos for **Juliaca** and towns on the lake shore between Puno and Desaguadero, including **Yunguyo**, leave from Av Bolívar between Jrs Carabaya and Palma. To **Juliaca**, 44 km, 45 mins, US$0.85. For **Yunguyo** and the **Bolivian border**, see page 150.

To **Cuzco**, 388 km, 5 hrs. If you wish to travel by bus and cannot get on a direct bus, it is no problem to take separate buses to Juliaca, then to Sicuani, then to Cuzco, but obviously this takes longer. Do not take night buses to Cuzco: robberies occur. **Tour Perú**, 0830, 2000; **Libertad**, 4 a day, **Cisnes**, 2 a day, and others, US$4.50-6. **First Class** at 0830 arriving 1800, US$25, 10 hrs, daily. This service, while higher in price than the turismo train or other buses, leaves a little later and is comfortable, with a good lunch stop and visits to Pukará, La Raya, Raqchi and Andahuaylillas en route. This option is popular so book in advance, especially in high season.
Bus companies Cisnes, at Terminal, T051-368674. First Class, Jr Tacna 280, T051-365192, firstclass@terra.com.pe. Julsa, T051-369447. Libertad, at Terminal, T051-363694. Ormeño T051-368176. Sur Oriente, T051-368133. Tour Perú, T051-352991, tourperu@mixmail.com.

Train
The railway runs from Puno to **Juliaca** (44 km), where it divides, to **Cuzco** (381 km) and **Arequipa** (279 km; no passenger service). To **Cuzco** on Mon, Wed and Sat at 0800, arriving in Juliaca at 0910 and in Cuzco at about 1800 (try to sit on the right-hand side for the views). The train stops at **La Raya**. In the high season (Jun especially), tickets sell well in advance. In the wet season services may be cancelled; check www.perurail.com.
Puno-Cuzco fares: turismo/backpacker US$19; first class US$130 including lunch,

afternoon tea, entertainment and luxury seating (recommended). The ticket office is open daily 0630-1030. Tickets can be bought in advance, or 1 hr before departure if there are any left. The station is well-guarded by police and sealed off to those without tickets.

Around Puno *p147*
Only one weekly public boat from **Llachón** to Puno, Fri 0900, returning to Llachón Sat 1000. The daily 0800 boat from Amantantí can drop you off at **Colata** (at the tip of the peninsula), a 1-hr walk from Llachón, or a minibus ride to Capachica; confirm details in advance. Returning to Puno, you can try to flag down the boat from Amantaní which passes Colata between 0830 and 0930. All fares US$3 one way. *Combis* from Puno to **Capachica**, several departures 0700-1200, 1½ hrs, US$1; from Capachica to **Juliaca**, US$0.80, leave when full from the plaza (likewise to Puno). Capachica to Llachón, buses and *combis* leave plaza when full, 30 mins, US$0.80. Tour operators in Puno arrange visits, about US$25 per person staying overnight, in groups of 10-15.

The islands *p147*
Motorboats charge US$5 per person to take tourists to the **Uros** islands for a 2-hr excursion. Boats leave from the harbour in Puno about every 30 mins from about 0630 till 1000, or whenever there are 10 or more people to fill the boat. The earlier you go the better, to beat the crowds of tourists. Almost any agency going to the other islands in the lake will stop first at Los Uros. Just to Los Uros, agencies charge US$6.

Boats leave Puno harbour for **Taquile** daily at 0700 and 0800, returning 1430 and 1500, US$3 one way. The journey takes 3 hrs. This doesn't leave enough time to appreciate the island fully in one day. Organized tours can be arranged for about US$10-16 per person, but only give you about 2 hrs on the island. Make sure you and the boatman know exactly what you are paying for.

Boats for **Amantaní** from the harbour in Puno leave at 0800 daily, and return to Puno at 0800 the following day. The trip costs US$4.50 one way. The journey takes 4-5 hrs – take water. A 1-day trip is not possible as the boats do not always return on the same day. Several tour operators in Puno offer 2- to

3-day excursions to Amantaní, Taquile and a visit to the floating islands. These cost from US$12 per person upwards, including meals, depending on the season and size of group. This gives you 1 night on Amantaní and 3 or 4 hrs on Taquile. There is little difference in price visiting the islands independently or on a tour, but going independently means that the islanders get all the proceeds, with no commission paid to Puno tour companies, you can stay as many nights as you wish and you will be able to explore the islands at your own pace. When not taking a tour, do not buy your boat ticket from anyone other than the boat operator at the harbour, do not believe anyone who says you can only visit the islands on a tour and do not be pressurized by touts. If you wish to visit both Taquile and Amantaní, it is better to go to Amantaní first. From there boats go to Taquile at around 0800, costing US$2.50 per person. There is no regular service – boats leave if there are enough passengers. You can then take the 1430 or 1500 boat from Taquile to Puno.

Puno to Bolivia *p150*
Via Yunguyo
In Puno 3 companies sell bus tickets for the direct route from Puno to La Paz, taking 6-8 hrs (the fare does not include the Tiquina ferry crossing): **Colectur**, Tacna 221, T051-352302, 0730, US$6.50, combines with **Galería** in Bolivia; **Panamericano**, Tacna 245, T051-354001, 0730, US$7.35, combines with **Diana Tours**; **Tour Perú** (see bus companies page 156), 0800, US$8.75, combines with **Combi Tour** (fares rise at holiday times). They stop at the borders and 1 hr for lunch in Copacabana, arriving in La Paz at about 1700. Passengers change buses at Copacabana and it seems that the Bolivian bus may not be of the company indicated and may not be of the same standard as the Peruvian bus. This can cause discomfort and delays. Bus fare Puno-Copacabana US$4.40-5.80. There are minibuses and *combis* from the Terminal Zonal in Puno to Yunguyo 0600-1900, 2½ hrs, US$1.80. From Yunguyo to the border (Kasani), *colectivos* charge US$0.25 per person. From the border it is a 20-min drive to Copacabana. See border crossing, page 150. *Colectivos* and minibuses leave from just outside Bolivian immigration, US$0.50 per person. A taxi from Yunguyo to Copacabana

costs about US$1.50 per person. Entering Peru, don't take a taxi Yunguyo-Puno without checking its reliability first, the driver may pick up an accomplice to rob passengers.

Via Desaguadero
To Desaguadero, from Terminal Zonal in **Puno**, *combis* and minibuses hourly 0600-1900, 2½ hrs, US$1.80. The last bus from the border to Puno leaves at 1930. Taxis Puno–Desaguadero US$30, 1½ hrs. There are minibuses to **La Paz** (105 km from Desaguadero), 1½ hrs, US$1.50. The last one leaves at 1700, though buses may leave later if there are enough passengers. See Bolivia, page 347.

To La Paz by hydrofoil or catamaran
There are luxury services from Puno to La Paz by **Crillon Tours** hydrofoil and **Transturin**'s catamarans. See Activities and tours, pages 344 and page 346 for details.

Juli *p150*
Bus *Colectivos* from Puno to Juli cost US$1. They stop in the main plaza before going to the *paradero* outside market, at Ilave 349, from where they return to Puno.

Juliaca *p151*
Air There are daily flights to **Lima** (2¼ hrs) with Lan, via **Arequipa** (30 mins), or **Cuzco**, and **StarPerú** once a day via Arequipa. Tourist buses run direct from **Puno** to/from the airport, US$3.50 pp, 1 hr. **Rossy Tours** T051-366709, offers drop off/pick up at your hotel, US$3.50. A taxi from Juliaco airport to Puno costs US$11.75. If taking a public *colectivo* from Puno to Juliaca for a flight, allow plenty of time, as the drivers travel around town looking for more passengers.

Bus
The Terminal Terrestre is at Jr Mantaro y San Agustín: go down San Martín 10 blocks and cross Av Circunvalación. Lots of companies serve **Arequipa** (4 hrs, US$3) and **Cuzco** (6 hrs, US$3-4). Note that robberies have occurred on night buses to Cuzco). Also **First Class** tourist buses, see under Puno. To **Puno**, 44 km, 1 hr, US$0.60; small buses leave from Piérola y 18 de Noviembre. *Combis* to Puno leave from another Terminal Terrestre on Plaza Bolognesi, also US$0.85.

Train
The station at Juliaca is on the **Puno-Cuzco** line. See Puno (page 156) and Cuzco (page 115) for more information. No tickets are sold in Juliaca. You can get on the train in Juliaca but only if you must buy your ticket in Puno.

---

❶ Directory

Puno *p145, map p144*
Banks BCP, Lima 510. Changes TCs before 1300 without commission, cash advance on Visa and Visa ATM. Banco Continental, Lima 444-411, Visa ATM. **Scotiabank**, Lima with Deústua, MasterCard ATM. **Interbank**, Lima 444, changes TCs morning and afternoon, 0.5% commission, Visa ATM. For cash go to the *cambios*, the travel agencies or the better hotels. Best rates with money changers on Jr Lima, many on 400 block, and on Tacna near the market, eg Arbulu y Tacna. Check your Peruvian soles carefully. Exchange rates from soles to bolivianos and vice versa are sometimes better in Puno than in Yunguyo; check with other travellers.
Consulates Bolivia, Jr Arequipa 136, T051-351251. Issues a visa on the spot, US$10, Mon-Fri 0830-1400. **Internet** There are offices everywhere in the centre, upstairs and down. Average price is US$0.30-0.45/hr.
Laundry Don Marcelo, head office at Ayacucho 651, T051-352444, has agencies in several places in the centre, including on Lima 427, and will collect and deliver laundry. US$1.50 per kg, good service. Lavandería América, Moquegua 175, T051-351642. Also had a good service, US$1.50. **Post office** Jr Moquegua 267. **Telephone** Telefónica at Puno y Moquegua for local and international calls. Another phone office is at Lima 489. **Useful addresses** Immigration, Ayacucho 280, T051-357103. For renewing entry stamps, etc. The process is very slow and you must fill in 2 application forms at a bank, but there's nothing else to pay. Indecopi, Jr Lima 419, of 401, p 4, Edificio Multicentro, T051-363667, jpilco@indecopi.gob.pe. The office of the tourist protection bureau.

Puno to Bolivia *p150*
Consulates Bolivian Consulate, Jr Grau 339, T051-856032, near plaza, Yunguyo, Mon-Fri 0830-1500.

Arequipa

→ *Phone code: 054. Colour map 2, C5. Altitude: 2380 m.*

The city of Arequipa stands in a beautiful valley at the foot of El Misti volcano, a snow-capped, perfect cone, 5822 m high, guarded on either side by the mountains Chachani (6057 m), and Pichu-Pichu (5669 m). The city was re-founded on 15 August 1540 by an emissary of Pizarro, but it had previously been occupied by the Aymara and the Incas. It has since grown into a magnificent city – fine Spanish buildings and many old and interesting churches built of sillar, a pearly white volcanic material were almost exclusively used in the construction of Arequipa – exuding an air of intellectual rigour and political passion. Among its famous sons and daughters are former President Fernando Belaúnde Terry and the novelist and failed presidential candidate, Mario Vargas Llosa. Now, Arequipa is the main commercial centre for the south and its fiercely proud people resent the general tendency to believe that everything is run from Lima. ▶▶ *For Sleeping, Eating and other listings, see pages 163-172.*

Ins and outs

Getting there Rodríguez Ballón Airport ① *7 km from town, information T054-443464,* has two desks offering hotel reservations and free transport to town, a travel agency (**Domiruth**) and **Avis** car rental. A reliable means of transport to and from the airport to the hotel of your choice is with **King Tours** ① *T054-243357/283037, US$1.30 per person.* You need to give 24 hours' notice for the return pickup from your hotel. The journey takes 30 to 40 minutes depending on the traffic. Transport to the airport may be arranged when buying a ticket at a travel agency, for US$1 per person, but it's not always reliable. Local buses and *combis* go to about 500 m from the airport, look for ones marked 'Río Seco', 'Cono-Norte' or 'Zamacola'.

All buses use one of the two terminals south of the city centre; to get to the centre takes 15 minutes by *colectivo* US$0.30, or 10 minutes by taxi US$1. The older terminal is called **Terminal Terrestre**, which contains a tourist office, shops and places to eat. The newer terminal is **Terrapuerto**, the other side of the car park, also with a tourist office (which makes hotel reservations, with free transfers to affiliated hotels, and its own *hostal*, T054-421375). Theft is a serious problem in the bus station area. Take a taxi to and from the bus station (US$1 for an official taxi to the city centre from inside the terminal) and do not wander around with your belongings. No one is allowed to enter the terminal 2100-0500, so new arrivals cannot be met by hoteliers between those hours; best not to arrive at night. ▶▶ *For further information, see Transport, page 170.*

Getting around Arequipa is a compact city with the main places of interest and hotels within a few blocks of the Plaza de Armas. Take a bus or taxi if you want to the visit the suburbs. Taxis (can be shared) charge US$4-5 from the airport to the city. Fares around town are US$0.70-0.85.

Tourist information i perú ① *Casona Santa Catalina, Calle Santa Catalina 210, T054-221227.* Very helpful with lots of information. Also at the airport ① *2nd floor, T054-444564, daily 0630- 1730.* **Municipal tourist office** ① *Municipalidad, on the south side of the Plaza de Armas, No 112, T054-211021, www.arequipa-tourism.com.* **Indecopi** (tourist protection bureau) ① *Calle San Agustí 115, T054-212054, mlcornejo@ indecopi.gob.pe.* The **tourist police** ① *Jerusalén 315, T054-201258,* are very helpful for dealing with complaints or giving directions.

Security There has been an increase in street crime in Arequipa, with many reports of taxi drivers in collusion with criminals to rob both tourists and locals. Theft can be a problem in the market area, especially after dark, in the park at Selva Alegre and on Calles San Juan de Dios and Alvarez Thomas. Be very cautious walking south of the Plaza de Armas area at night. The police are conspicuous, friendly, courteous and efficient, but their resources are limited.

Climate Arequipa enjoys a wonderful climate, with a mean temperature before sundown of 23°C, and after sundown of 14°C. The sun shines on 360 days of the year. Annual rainfall is less than 150 mm.

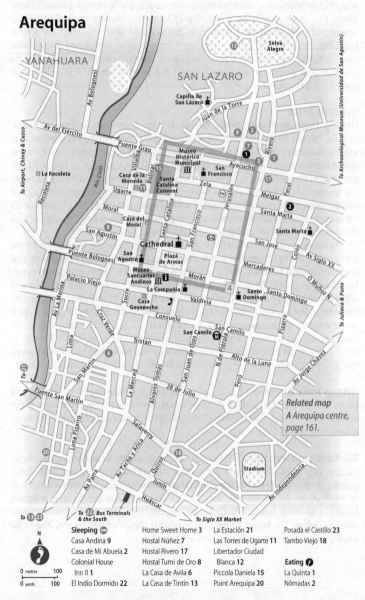

Arequipa

Related map
A Arequipa centre,
page 161.

N

| 0 metres | 100 |
| 0 yards | 100 |

Sleeping
Casa Andina 9
Casa de Mi Abuela 2
Colonial House
Inn II 1
El Indio Dormido 22

Home Sweet Home 3
Hostal Núñez 7
Hostal Rivero 17
Hostal Tumi de Oro 8
La Casa de Avila 6
La Casa de Tintin 13

La Estación 21
Las Torres de Ugarte 11
Libertador Ciudad
Blanca 12
Piccola Daniela 15
Point Arequipa 20

Posada el Castillo 23
Tambo Viejo 18

Eating
La Quinta 1
Nómadas 2

Sights

Santa Catalina Convent

ⓘ *Santa Catalina 301, T054-229798, www.santacatalina.org.pe, 0900-1600, US$7.25.*

By far the most interesting place to visit is the Santa Catalina Convent, opened in 1970 after four centuries of mysterious isolation. This is the most remarkable sight in Arequipa and a complete contrast to what you would expect from nuns who had taken vows of poverty. The convent has been beautifully refurbished, with period furniture, pictures of the Arequipa and Cuzco schools and fully equipped kitchens. It is a complete miniature walled colonial town of over 2 ha in the middle of the city. About 450 nuns lived here in total seclusion, except for their women servants.

The few remaining nuns have retreated to one section of the convent, allowing visitors to see a maze of cobbled streets and plazas bright with geraniums and other flowers, cloisters and buttressed houses. These have been restored and painted in white, orange, deep red and blue. There are tours of 1½ hours; there's no set price and many of the guides speak English (tip of US$2.85 expected). There is a good café, which sells cakes made by the nuns and a special blend of tea.

Around the centre

The elegant **Plaza de Armas**, beautifully laid out with palm trees, gardens and fountain, is faced on three sides by arcaded colonial buildings (rebuilt after an earthquake in 1863) with restaurants, and on the fourth by the massive **cathedral**. The cathedral was founded in 1612 and largely rebuilt in the 19th century. It is remarkable for having its façade along the whole length of the church and takes up one full side of the plaza. Inside is a fine Belgian organ and elaborately carved wooden pulpit. The entrance to the cathedral is on the plaza. Behind is an alley, Pasaje Catedral, with handicraft shops and places for tourists to eat.

A visit to the church and cloister of **La Compañía** at General Morán y Alvarez Thomas, is recommended. The main façade (1698) and side portal (1654) are striking examples of the Andean mestizo style. There are two adjoining cloisters now given over to attractive shops. Also of note is the royal chapel, **Capilla Real** ⓘ *Mon-Fri 0900-1130, 1500-1730, US$0.65*, to the left of the sanctuary, and its San Ignacio chapel with a beautiful polychrome cupola. The stark cloister is impressive.

Arequipa centre

0 metres 50
0 yards 50

Sleeping 🛏
Casa de Melgar **1**
Casablanca Hostal **7**
Colonial House Inn **2**
Hospedaje El
Caminante Class **4**
Hostal La Reyna **6**
Hostal Posada Santa
Catalina **10**
Hostal Regis **9**
Hostal Solar **11**
La Casa de Margott **3**
La Casita de Ugarte **12**
La Fiorentina **13**
La Posada del Cacique **19**
La Posada del Fraile **20**
Sonesta Posadas del Inca **18**

Eating 🍴
Ary Quepay **2**

Bóveda San Agustín **4**
Café Capriccio **5**
Café Manolo **7**
Café Valenzuela **1**
Cioccolata **8**
El Asador **18**
El Turko **13**
El Turko II **14**
Fez **9**
La Canasta **17**
La Casita de José Antonio **18**
Lakshmivan **19**
Mandala **21**
Pizzería Los Leños **22**
Salchichería Alemana **11**
Sonccollay **28**
Tacos y Tequila **12**
Zig Zag **25**
Zig Zag Crêperie **26**
Zun Zun **15**

Bars & clubs 🍸
Blue Margarita **33**
Farren's **34**
Forum **30**
Las Quenas **36**
Le Café Art Montreal **10**

Also worth seeing, west of the plaza, are the recently restored church of **San Agustín** ① *San Agustín y Sucre, Mon-Sat 0800-1200, 1700-1900*, and **La Casona Chávez de la Rosa** ① *San Agustín 104*, part of the Universidad San Agustín, which holds art and photography exhibitions.

Museo Santuarios Andinos ① *La Merced 110, T054-215013, www.ucsm.edu.pe/ santury, Mon-Sat 0900-1800, Sun 0900-1500, US$5*, contains the frozen mummies found on Ampato volcano. The mummy known as 'Juanita' is particularly fascinating (see page 175). From January to April, Juanita is often jetting round the world, and is replaced by other child sacrifices unearthed in the mountains. Admission to the includes a video of the discovery in English, followed by an hour-long tour (tip the guide).

Museo de Arte Textil ① *Patio del Ekeko, Mercaderes 141, Mon-Sat 1000-2030, Sun 1000-1530*, has an interesting collection of textiles and shows short documentaries about Arequipa. The 16th-century church of **San Francisco** also has a convent and library and opposite is the interesting **Museo Histórico Municipal** ① *Plaza San Francisco 407, Mon-Fri 0900-1700, US$0.50*, with much war memorabilia.

Arequipa is said to have the best-preserved colonial architecture in Peru, apart from Cuzco. Several fine seignorial houses with large carved tympanums over the entrances can be seen in the city centre. Thanks to their being one-storey structures, they have mostly withstood the earthquakes which regularly pound this city. They are distinguished by their small patios with no galleries, flat roofs and small windows, disguised by superimposed lintels or heavy grilles. One of the best examples is the 18th-century **Casa Tristán del Pozo**, better known as the **Gibbs-Ricketts house** ① *San Francisco 108, Mon-Sat 0915-1245, 1600-1800*, with its fine portal and puma-head waterspouts. It is now the main office of Banco Continental. Other good examples are the **Casa del Moral**, or **Williams house** ① *Moral 318 y Bolívar, Mon-Sat 0900-1700, Sun 0900-1300, US$1.80*, with a museum, in the Banco Industrial. **Casa de la Moneda** ① *Ugarte y Villalba*, is behind Santa Catalina convent. **Casa Goyeneche** ① *La Merced 201 y Palacio Viejo*, is now an office of the Banco Central de la Reserva. Ask to see the courtyard and fine period rooms.

The church of **Santo Domingo** ① *Santo Domingo y Piérola*, dates from the 17th century. In its fine door, an indigenous face can be seen amid the flowers and grapes. The central **San Camilo market** ① *between Perú, San Camilo, Piérola and Alto de la Luna*, is worth visiting, as is the **Siglo XX market**, to the east of the rail station.

La Recoleta
① *Jr Recoleta 117, T054-270966, Mon-Sat 0900-1200, 1500-1700, US$1.50.*
La Recoleta, a Franciscan monastery built in 1647, stands on the other side of the river. It contains several cloisters, a religious art museum, a pre-Columbian museum, two rooms dedicated to the Amazon rainforest, a library with 20,000 volumes including many rarities, and is well worth visiting.

San Lázaro
The oldest district in the city is San Lázaro, a collection of tiny climbing streets and houses quite close to the Hotel Libertador, where you can find the ancient **Capilla de San Lázaro**. At **Selva Alegre** there is a shady park in front of the **Hotel Libertador**, which is within easy walking distance of all the famous churches and main plaza (but see page 160). East of San Lázaro, the **archaeological museum** ① *Av Independencia between La Salle and Santa Rosa, apply to Dr E Linares, the Director, T054-229719, Mon-Fri 0800-1300, US$1*, is at the Universidad de San Agustín. It has a good collection of ceramics and mummies.

Northwest of Arequipa
Some 2 km northwest of the city is the district is **Yanahuara**, where there is a 1750 mestizo-style church (opens 1500), with a magnificent churrigueresque façade, all in

arches there is a fine view of El Misti with the city at its feet. There's live music at **Peña El Moro**, on Parque Principal. A score of *picanterías* specialize in piquant foods such as *rocoto relleno* (hot stuffed peppers), *cuy chactado* (seared guinea-pig), *papas con ocopa* (boiled potatoes with a hot spicy yellow sauce) and *adobo* (pork stew).

In the hillside suburb of **Cayma**, 3 km northwest of the city, is a delightful 18th-century **church** ① *open until 1700*, and many old buildings associated with Bolívar and Garcilaso de la Vega. Many local buses go to Cayma.

El Misti and Chachani
At 5822 m, **El Misti** volcano offers a relatively straightforward opportunity to scale a high peak. There are three routes for climbing the volcano; all take two days.

The northeast route starts from the Aguada Blanca reservoir, reached by 4WD, from where a four-hour hike takes you to the Monte Blanco camp at 4800 m. Then it's a 5½-hour ascent to the top. Two hours takes you back down to the trail. The southwest route involves taking a 4WD vehicle to the trailhead at Pastores (3400 m), followed by a hike of five to six hours to a camp at 4700 m. A five-hour climb takes you to the summit, before a three-hour descent to the trail. A southern route (Grau) also starts at 3400 m, with a camp at 4610 m, followed by a five-hour hike to the summit and a two-hour descent.

In all cases contact an experienced guiding agency in Arequipa. Be prepared for early starts and climbing on loose scree. Take plenty of water, food and protection against the weather. Favoured months are May to September.

In recent years climbing the peak of **Chachani**, just to the northwest of El Misti, has also become popular. In the January to April rainy season, when El Misti has a full covering of snow, they say he is wearing his poncho. But in recent years the sight of snow crowning El Misti's summit has become increasingly rare, especially in the drier winter months. Chachani, in contrast, still retains its icy covering, though this too is fast disappearing. The fact that Chachani tops the magic 6000-m mark (6057 m) has led to a growing number of climbers on the mountain.

Remember that both summits are at very high altitude and that this, combined with climbing on scree and sometimes ice, makes it hard going for the untrained; take your time to acclimatize. Proper equipment (crampons, walking pick, etc) is required on Chachani and recent reports of armed hold-ups make it inadvisable for you to climb alone; join a group or take a guide. Further information is available from travel agencies and professional guides; see Climbing page 169 for details.

◉ Sleeping

Arequipa *p159, maps p160 and p161*

L-AL Libertador Ciudad Blanca, Plaza Simón Bolívar, Selva Alegre, T054-215110, www.libertador.com.pe. Safe, large comfortable rooms, good service, swimming pool (cold), gardens, good meals, pub-style bar, cocktail lounge, squash court.
A Sonesta Posadas del Inca, Portal de Flores 116, T054-215530, www.sonesta peru.com. On the Plaza de Armas, all the services associated with this chain, **Inkafé** café and bar with good views, restaurant, tiny outdoor pool, business centre with internet. Price rises to **AL** at Christmas.
A-B Casa Andina, Calle Jerusalén 603, T054-202070, www.casa-andina.com.

Part of the attractive Casa Andina chain, with breakfast, comfortable and colourful, central, modern, good restaurant, safe, cable TV, phones, friendly staff, car parking.
C Casa de Mi Abuela, Jerusalén 606, T054-241206, www.lacasademiabuela.com. Very clean, friendly, safe, hot water, laundry, cable TV, swimming pool, rooms at the back are quieter and overlook the garden, **E** without bathroom, English spoken, internet access US$3 per hr, tours and transport organized (**Giardino**, T054-221345, www.giardino tours.com), which has good information, small library, breakfast or evening snacks on patio or in beautiful garden, parking, **B** for apartment for 4, lots of tour groups.

C Hostal Solar, Ayacucho 108, T/F054-241793, solar@star.com.pe. Nice colonial building, TV, bath, hot water, includes good breakfast served in nice patio, sun lounge on roof, very secure, quiet, helpful.

C-D Posada el Castillo, Pasaje Campos 105, Vallecito, T054-201828, www.posadael castillo.com. Newly built Dutch-owned hotel in colonial style 15 mins walk south of Plaza de Armas. Variety of rooms and suites, some with balcony and view of El Misti, free internet, TV, pool, wonderful breakfast, laundry.

D Casa de Melgar, Melgar 108, T/F054-222459, www.lacasademelgar.com. Excellent rooms, all different, delightful 18th-century building, with bathroom, hot water all day (solar panel), safe, clean, friendly, pleasant courtyard, good breakfast, café open 1730-2100, book exchange, luggage store. Can arrange good taxi tours with driver, Angel.

D La Casa de Avila, San Martín 116, T054 213177, www.casadeavila.com. All rooms with bathroom and hot water, price includes good breakfast, spacious, courtyard, guests' kitchen, internet, can arrange airport/bus station pickup, Spanish courses (which are recommended) and other activities.

D La Casa de Margott, Jerusalén 304, T054-229517, lacasademargotthostal @hotmail.com. Bright with a massive palm tree in patio, spotless, small bar/café, new, cable TV, phone, security box, bathroom.

D La Casa de Tintin, Urbanización San Isidro F1, Vallecito, T054-284700, www.hotel tintin.com. 15 mins' walk, 5 mins by taxi from the Plaza de Armas. Belgian/Peruvian owned, hot water, cable TV, garden, terrace, sauna, laundry service, restaurant, café, bar, internet, mountain bike hire, pleasant and comfortable, breakfast included.

D-E Casablanca Hostal, Puente Bolognesi 104, just off Plaza de Armas, T054-221327, www.casablancahostal.com. Super-stylish *hostal*, lovely minimalist rooms in a colonial building. Ambient lighting, most rooms with private bath (hot water) and balcony.

D-E La Posada del Fraile, Santa Catalina 103, T054-282006, posadadelfraile@hotmail. com. Cheaper without breakfast, with bath, clean, safe, well-furnished, very central.

D-G Tambo Viejo, Av Malecón Socabaya 107, IV Centenario, 5 blocks south of the plaza near the rail station, T054-288195, www.tambo viejo.com. Rooms vary and range from double

with bath to dormitory, quiet, English and Dutch spoken, walled garden, hot water, laundry service, cable TV, safe deposit, coffee shop, bar, book exchange, money exchange, tourist information for guests, internet, phone for international calls, bike rental, popular with young travellers, luggage store extra, tours and volcano climbs arranged. Free pick-up from bus station; US$5 from airport.

E Home Sweet Home, Rivero 509A, T054-405982, www.homesweethome-peru.com. Run by María and daughter Cathy, who runs a travel agency and speaks Spanish, English, Italian, French, very helpful, warm and inviting atmosphere, substantial fresh breakfast included. Private or shared bath, hot water all day, simple rooms.

E Hospedaje El Caminante Class, Santa Catalina 207-A, 2nd floor, T054-203444. With bathroom, cheaper without, hot water, TV, clean, laundry service and facilities, sun terrace, very helpful owners.

E Hostal Núñez, Jerusalén 528, T054-233268, hostal_nunez@terra.com.pe. With bathroom, cheaper without, hot water, small rooms but comfortable, TV, laundry, safe, good value, helpful, breakfast on roof terrace overlooking the city.

E Hostal Regis, Ugarte 202, T054-226111. Colonial house, French-style interior, clean, hot water all day, cooking and laundry service, sun terrace with good views, safe deposit, luggage store, video rental, tours arranged, but poor breakfast.

E Hostal Tumi de Oro, San Agustín 311A, 2½ blocks from the Plaza de Armas, T/F054-281319. With bathroom, French and English spoken, hot water, roof terrace, book exchange, tea/coffee facilities, safe.

E La Estación, Loreto 419, Umacollo, T054-273852, www.backpackerperu.com. Unusual dormitory accommodation in 2 train carriages, includes breakfast, hot water, restaurant next door, friendly, clean and fresh. 10 mins' walk from Plaza, ask directions for 'el Ovalo del Vallecito', English spoken.

E La Posada del Cacique, Puente Grau 219, T054-202170, posadadelcacique@yahoo.es. Old house with tall ceilings, teeny patio, sun terrace, friendly, good hot water, English spoken, family atmosphere, F without bath, also dorm accommodation, safe storage facilities, breakfast available, laundry service, will pick up from terminal.

E Las Torres de Ugarte, Ugarte 401-A, T/F054-283532, hostaltorresdeugarte@ star.com.pe. Next to Santa Catalina convent, occasional hot water, cable TV, roof terrace, laundry service, parking, safe, luggage store, helpful staff, price includes breakfast served in a sunny room.

F Colonial House Inn, Puente Grau 114, T/F054-223533, colonialhouseinn @hotmail.com. Hot water, quieter rooms at the back, laundry facilities and service, kitchen facilities, roof terrace, good choice of breakfasts, owners speak English. Same owners run **Colonial House Inn II**, Rivero 504, which is more modern and nicer.

F Hostal La Reyna, Zela 209, T054-286578, hostalreyna@yahoo.com. With or without bath, two more expensive rooms at the top of the house (very good), hot water 24 hrs, clean, can be noisy because of location, the daughter speaks English, laundry, breakfast for US$1.15, rooftop seating, can arrange Spanish classes, will store luggage and arrange trips to the Colca Canyon and volcanoes, especially Misti and Chachani (a bit chaotic, but recommended nonetheless). Do not believe taxi drivers who say the hotel is closed or full; ring the doorbell and check for yourself.

F Hostal Posada Santa Catalina, Santa Catalina 500, T054-243705. Comfortable rooms arranged around a courtyard, roof terrace with great views, charming and helpful staff. Can arrange trips and accommodation in other cities.

F Hostal Rivero, Rivero 420, T054-229266. Cheaper with shared bath, hot water, cable TV extra, medical assistance, laundry facilities, very helpful, good value.

F Piccola Daniela, Bolivar 400, T054-405727, piccoladanielaaqp@hotmail.com. Includes breakfast, **F** without bath, good value, cable TV, hot water, tiny patio, no English.

F pp The Point Arequipa, Av Lima 515, Vallecito, T054-286920, www.thepoint hostels.com. In a relaxed suburb, free airport/bus station pickup. Nice building with big garden, great place to meet other travellers, lots of services (free internet, laundry, DVDs etc) and a big party pad.

G pp El Indio Dormido, Av Andrés Avelino Cáceres B-9, T054-427401, the_sleeping_ indian@yahoo.com Close to bus terminal, free transport to centre, some rooms with bath, comfortable beds, **F**, TV, clean, very helpful.

G La Casita de Ugarte, Ugarte 212, T054-204363. English/Peruvian run, large basic rooms, colonial building, good value.

G La Fiorentina, Puente Grau 110, T054-202571. Cheaper without bath, hot water, comfortable, ask for a good room, family atmosphere, tours arranged, laundry facilities, use of kitchen extra.

🍴 Eating

Arequipa *p159, maps p160 and p161*
Several restaurants overlook the Plaza de Armas; their staff may pounce on you good-naturedly as you pass. For typical *Arequipeño* food, head to Av Arancota, in the Tingo District, by the Río Chili. La Cecilia is highly recommended. Typical Arequipeño food is also available at the San Camilo market. A good local speciality is Mejía cheese. You should also try the *queso helado*, which is frozen fresh milk mixed with sugar and a sprinkling of cinnamon. The local chocolate is excellent: La Ibérica, in Patio del Ekeko, Mercaderes 141, is top quality, but expensive. The toffee and the fruit drinks called *papayada* and *tumbada* are also local specialities in the market and restaurants. Try **Casa Tropical**, on the first block of Rivero for a huge selection.

♦♦♦ La Quinta, Jerusalén 522. Excellent, large portions of local food but limited menu, some vegetarian dishes, attentive service, quiet garden, aimed primarily at the tourist market.

♦♦♦ Zig Zag, Zela 210. In a colonial house, European and local dishes, excellent meats include ostrich and alpaca, top class.

♦♦ Ary Quepay, Jerusalén 502, open 1000-2400. Excellent local meat and vegetarian dishes, , very touristy, but fun.

♦♦ Café-Restaurante Bóveda San Agustín, Portal San Agustín 127-129, opens at 0700. Attractive, good value breakfasts and lunches, evening specials.

♦♦ El Turko II, San Francisco 315. Excellent Turkish, local and international food, has a lovely courtyard. Recommended.

♦♦ La Casita de José Antonio, Plaza San Francisco 401 y Zela. *Cevichería*, fish and seafood, lunchtime only.

♦♦ Nómadas, Melgar 306. Breakfasts, wide menu including vegetarian, sandwiches.

♦♦ Pizzería Los Leños, Jerusalén 407. Excellent, good atmosphere, evenings only, popular, especially with tourists.

♟ **Sonccollay**, Portal de San Agustin 149.
Serving 'Inca and Pre-Inca' dishes, this
restaurant gives a new twist to 'traditional'
food. Stone-cooked alpaca steaks and meats
are a speciality. Hosted by an entertaining
owner, plenty of home-made *chicha*.
♟ **Zig Zag Crêperie**, Santa Catalina 208.
Excellent crepes, good value set lunch,
also snacks, cocktails, coffee.
♟-♟ **El Asador**, Zela 200 block opposite Zig
Zag. Good value for alapca steaks, *parrillada*,
pleasant atmosphere, good music.
♟ **El Turko**, San Francisco 216. Kebabs, coffee,
breakfasts, good sandwiches, 0700-2200.
♟ **Fez**, San Francisco 229. Delicious falafel,
good vegetarian options, Middle Eastern fast
food and coffee, friendly, courtyard. Same
company as **El Turko**.
♟ **Lakshmivan**, Jerusalén 402. Vegetarian,
set lunch for US$1.25, pleasant courtyard,
good value and healthy, but slow service.
♟ **Mandala**, Jerusalén 207, mandala26@
correoweb.com. Good value vegetarian,
breakfast, 3 set menus for lunch, buffet,
dinner, friendly staff. Recommended.
♟ **Tacos y Tequila**, Ugarte 112. All the
Mexican regulars, tacos, burritos, enchiladas,
quesadillas, as vegetarian or carnivorous as
you like. Cheap, and you can even wear a big
hat and pretend to be in *The Good, the Bad
and the Ugly* – which one are you?

Cafés
Café Capriccio, Mercaderes 121. Not that
cheap, but excellent coffee, cakes etc.
Café Manolo, Mercaderes 107 and 113.
Great cakes and coffee, also cheap
lunches, pastas, sandwiches and juices.
Café Valenzuela, Moran 114. Fantastic
coffee, locals' favourite.
Cioccolata, Mercaderes 120. Among
the best for cakes, nicely decorated.
La Canasta, Jerusalén 115. Bakes excellent
baguettes twice daily, also serves breakfast
and delicious apple and brazil nut pastries.
Salchichería Alemana, San Francisco 137.
More sausages than you can wave a knack-
wurst at, plus some very good empanadas
and sandwiches. Good value and popular.
Zun Zun, San Francisco 304, T054-283086.
Best bagels (with cream cheese!) in town,
pastries, burritos and excellent coffee. Fresh
fruit juices and smoothies, very friendly
owner and staff. Free internet for customers.

❶ Bars and clubs

Arequipa *p159, maps p160 and p161*
There are many good dancing spots on
Av Ejército in Yanahuara, but most nightowls
head to Av Dolores, a short taxi ride away
(US$1), which can get rowdy. Try **Salsodromo**
for salsa, or **Cajuma** and **Siomama**.
Blue Margarita, Melgar 119. Large club
with several areas, good mix of music.
Déjà Vu, San Francisco 319-B. Café,
restaurant and bar, good food, relaxing
terrace, DJ evenings and live music, shows
movies, 2000-2400. Recommended.
Farren's, Pasaje La Catedral. Friendly Irish bar
with local and imported (expensive) beer.
Forum, San Francisco 317. Rock café, live
music Thu-Sat 1800-0400, disco, pool tables,
US$5 cover if band is playing, includes
1 drink, drinks US$1.50.
La Quinta, Jerusalén 522. For *peña* folklore
music, weekends mainly, US$1.50 cover.
Las Quenas, Santa Catalina 302. For *peña*
music, Mon-Fri 2100.
Le Café Art Montreal, Ugarte 210.
Atmospheric Canadian-run jazz/blues
restaurant/bar with live music Wed and Sat.

❷ Festivals and events

Arequipa *p159, maps p160 and p161*
10 Jan Sor Ana de Los Angeles y
Monteagudo, a festival for the patron
saint of Santa Catalina monastery.
2-3 Feb Fiesta de la Virgen de la
Candelaria is celebrated in the churches
of Cayma, Characato, Chiguata and Chapi
with masses, processions of the Virgin
through the streets, and fireworks.
3 Mar Fiesta de La Amargura is a movable
feast in Paucarpata, during which the Passion
Play is enacted in the main plaza. **Domingo
de Cuaresma**, in the district of Tiabaya, is also
dedicated to Jesus Christ. Residents gather in
the plaza and carry the cross from there up
to a nearby hilltop, crossing the Río Chili.
Mar/Apr Semana Santa celebrations in
Arequipa are carried out Sevillano style,
with the townsfolk turned out in traditional
mourning dress. There are huge processions
every night, culminating in the burning of
an effigy of Judas on **Easter Sun** in the main
plazas of Cayma and Yanahuara, and the
reading of his 'will', containing criticisms of

Lake Titicaca & Arequipa   Arequipa   Listings

the city authorities. Afterwards, people retire to the *picanterías* to partake of a little Adobo a la Antaño with some *pan de tres puntas*.

1 May Fiesta de la Virgen de Chapi is a great pilgrimage to the sanctuary of Chapi and one of the most important religious ceremonies in the region.

May Known as the **Month of the Crosses**, during May there are ceremonies on hilltops throughout the city.

15 May The popular fiesta of **San Isidro Labrador** takes place in Sachaca, Chuquibamba and other towns and villages in the valley, and lasts for 7 days.

29 Jun In Yanahuara, the **Fiesta de San Juan**, the local patron saint, is held with Mass and fireworks.

6-31 Aug Fiesta Artesanal del Fundo del Fierro, a sale and exhibition of artesanía from all parts of Peru, taking place near Plaza San Francisco. At the same time, 6-17 Aug is the celebration of the **city's anniversary**; various events are held, including music, dancing and exhibitions. On the eve of the actual day, the 15th, there is a splendid firework display in the Plaza de Armas and a decorated float parade. For a short time it feels like Rio Carnival with music everywhere, no space to move and parties continuing till morning. There is also a mass ascent of El Misti from the Plaza de Armas. It is virtually impossible to find a hotel room during the celebrations.

Nov In Arequipa, this is the month of the traditional *guaguas*, which are *bizcochos* (sponge cakes) filled with *manjar* (caramel made from boiling milk and sugar).

O Shopping

Arequipa *p159, maps p160 and p161*
Alpaca goods, textiles and clothing
Arequipa is an excellent place to buy top-quality alpaca knitwear.
Alpaca 21, Jerusalén 115, of 125, T054-213425. Recommended.
Colca Trading Company, Santa Catalina 300B, T054-242088 (Lima 01-254 1885), colcatradingperu@yahoo.com. Sells a wide variety of naturally coloured cotton and alpaca clothing for adults and children.
Millma's, Pasaje Catedral 117 and 112 opposite, millmas@hotmail.com. 100% baby alpaca goods, run by Peruvian family high quality, beautiful designs, good prices.

Mundo Alpaca, Alameda San Lázaro 101, T054-202525, www.michell.com.pe. Open daily 0830-1900. The shop, museum and gallery of **Michell y Cia** (Juan de la Torre 101), with alpacas and llamas in the grounds, demonstrations of sorting and weaving, exhibitions of paintings, museum of textile machinery and café. There is an outlet for Michell's excellent alpaca garments and other items, and a boutique of Michell's brand, **Sol Alpaca**, which has another shop at Santa Catalina 210, T054-221454, www.solalpaca.com, for its latest lines in contemporary clothing in alpaca and Pima cotton (branches also in Lima and Cuzco).
Patio del Ekeko, Mercaderes 141, T054-215861, www.patiodelekeko.com, is a shopping and entertainment and cultural centre. Shops include **Alpaca 111** for alpaca and vicuña (recommended for high-quality alpaca and wool products), **Ilaria** for fine jewellery and silverware, **La Ibérica** for chocolates and **Artesanías del Ekeko**. There is also the **Café del Ekeko**, which has internet, as well as sandwiches, desserts, coffee and a bar (**Centro del Pisco**), and **Museo de Arte Textil** (see Sights page 162).

Bookshops
For international magazines, look along San Francisco, between Mercaderes and San José.
Librería El Lector, San Francisco 221. Wide selection, book exchange in many languages.
Librerías San Francisco, Portal de Flores 138, San Francisco 102-106 and 133-135. Books on Arequipa and Peru, some in English.
SBS Book Service, San Francisco 125. Has a good selection of travel books etc.

Handicrafts
Arequipa is noted for its leather work. The main street of saddlers and leather workers is Puente Bolognesi. The handicraft shop in the old prison opposite San Francisco is particularly good for bags. There are markets which are good for general handicrafts. The covered market opposite the Teatro Municipal on Mercaderes is recommended for knitted goods, bags, etc. Also worth a try is the market around Valdivia and Nicolas de Piérola. The large **Fundo del Fierro** handicraft market behind the old prison on Plaza San Francisco is also worth a visit. Shop 14 sells alpaca-wool handicrafts from Callalli in the Colca Canyon.

▲▲ Activities and tours

Arequipa *p159, maps p160 and p161*

Climbing, cycling, rafting and trekking

Recommended climbing guides include **Julver Castro** at **Mountrekk**, T054-601833, julver_mountrekk@hotmail.com, an experienced guide, and **Jörg Krosel**, T054-997971, joergkrosel@hotmail.com.

Andina Travel Service, Jerusalén 309 - A402, T054-225082, andinatravelservice@hotamil.com. Good tours of Colca Canyon, guide Gelmond Ynca Aparicio is very enthusiastic.

Colca Trek, Jerusalén 401 B, T054-206217, www.trekinperu.com. Run by the English-speaking Vlado Soto, this company is recommended for climbing, trekking and mountain biking in the Colca Canyon. Vlado is one of the best guides for the Cotahuasi Canyon. He also rents equipment and has topographical maps. Recommended.

Cusipata, Jerusalén 408, T054-203966, www.cusipata.com. Recommended as the best local operator, run 6-day trips on the Río Colca. May-Dec, Río Chili 1-day kayak courses, also trekking and mountain bike tours.

Naturaleza Activa, Santa Catalina 211, T054-695793, naturactiva@yahoo.com. Experienced guides, knowledgeable, climbing and trekking. Good quality mountain biking and safety equipment. They also offer paragliding and rafting trips.

Peru Adventure Tours, Jerusalén 410, T054-221658, www.peruadventures tours.com. Downhill mountain biking, start at 0700 with 4WD 3-hr trip into Misti and Chachani mountains, stopping along the way for sightseeing. Cycle ride starts at Azufrero (5000 m), finishing in Arequipa at 1600. All equipment, oxygen and snack provided. English-speaking guide.

Sacred Tours, Jerusalén 400, T054-330408, sacred_road@hotmail.com. Arranges hiking and rock climbing in Colca Canyon, equipment available, experienced guides.

Selern Services, Urb Puerta Verde F13, José LB y Rivero, Arequipa, T054-348685, www.selernexpediciones.com. Trekking in Colca and Cotahuasi canyons, adventure tourism, volcano and rock climbing.

Volcanyon Travel, Calle Villalba 414, T054-205078, mario-ortiz@terra.com.pe. Trekking and some mountain bike tours in the Colca Canyon, also volcano climbing.

Carlos Zárate Aventuras, Santa Catalina 204, of 3, T054-202461/263107, www.zarate advenures.com. Run by Carlos Zárate of the Mountaineering Club of Peru. Good family-run business that always works with qualified mountain guides. A specialist in mountaineering and exploring, with a great deal of information and advice and some equipment rental. Carlos also runs trips to the source of the Amazon, Nevado Mismi, as well as trekking in the Cotahuasi canyon and climbing tougher peaks such as Coropuna.

Tour operators

These agencies have been recommended as helpful and reliable. Most run tours to the Colca Canyon (page 172). Many agencies on Jerusalén, Santa Catalina and around Plaza de Armas sell air, train and bus tickets and offer tours of Colca, Cotahuasi, Toro Muerto, Campiña and the city. Prices vary greatly so shop around. As a general rule, you get what you pay for, so check details of the cheapest of tours carefully and make sure that there are enough people for the tour to run. Many tourists prefer to contract tours through their hotel. If a travel agency puts you in touch with a guide, make sure he or she is official. It is not advisable to book tours to Machu Picchu here; make arrangements in Cuzco.

A I Travel Tours, Santa Catalina 203, Of 1, T054-222052, www.aitraveltours.com. Peruvian-Dutch tour operator offering cultural and adventure tours for groups or individuals, volunteer work and Spanish courses, large book exchange.

Eco Tours, Jerusalén 409, T054-202562, ecotours@terra.com.pe. Regular and adventure tours, recommended for Colca tours, Spanish lessons, accommodation arranged.

Pablo Tour, Jerusalén 400-AB-1, T054-203737, www.pablotour.com. Family-run agency that owns several *hostales* in Cabaconde (**Valle del Fuego** etc; page 177); they know the area well. Free tourist information, sells topographical maps, hotel and bus reservations. Son Edwin Junco Cabrera can usually be found in the office, T054-961 1241 (mob), he speaks fluent French and English. The family are keen to promote 'mixed adventure tours': several days exploring the region with combinations of biking (safety equipment provided), horse riding, trekking and rafting – many options available. Good for a challenge!

Santa Catalina Tours, Santa Catalina 219-223, T054-216994. Offer unique tours of Collagua communities in the Colca Canyon. Daily 0800-1900. Recommended.

Transcontinential Arequipa, Puente Bolognesi 132, oficina 5, T054-213843, transcontinental-aqp@terra.com.pe. Cultural and wildlife tours in the Colca Canyon.

⊖ Transport

Arequipa *p159, maps p160 and p161*
Air
Several flights daily to and from **Lima**, with **Lan**, **Aero Cóndor**, **Star Perú** and **Taca**. Lan also to **Juliaca** and **Cuzco**.

Airline offices Most tour agencies sell air tickets. Prices are quoted in dollars but payment is in soles so check exchange rate carefully. **Lan**, Santa Catalina 118-C, T054-201100. **Star Perú**, Santa Catalina 105a, T054-221896. **Taca**, Av Cayma 636 y Av Ejército, p 1 Scotiabank, T0800-18222.

Bus
For details of the terminals, see Ins and outs, page 159. A terminal tax of US$0.30 must be paid on entry to the platform. Check which terminal your bus will leave from as it may not depart from the terminal where you bought your ticket. All the bus companies have their offices in the **Terminal Terrestre** and several also have offices in **Terrapuerto**. Some tour operators also make bus reservations for a small fee.

To **Lima**, 1011 km, 16-18 hrs, 'normal' service US$8.70, 'imperial' US$17.40 (video, toilet, meals, comfortable seats, blankets), 'crucero' US$23-29 several daily. **Enlaces** (T054-430333, office only in Terrapuerto), **Tepsa** (T054-424135), **Cruz del Sur** (T054-217728) and **Ormeño** (T054-424187) are recommended (prices quoted are for Cruz del Sur). The road is paved but drifting sand may prolong the trip. Buses will stop at the major cities en route, but not always Pisco. The desert scenery is stunning.

To **Nazca**, 566 km, 9 hrs, US$7.25-10 (US$30 on Ormeño Royal service), several buses daily, mostly at night and most buses continue to Lima. Beware, some bus companies to Nazca charge the Lima fare.

To **Cuzco**, all buses go via Juliaca or Puno, US$15-23, 10 hrs. Most companies use double-decker buses (toilet, TV, hostess, etc), eg **Enlaces**, **Cruz del Sur**, **Cial** and **Ormeño**, running one morning and, some companies, one afternoon bus. The new paved road to **Juliaca**, via Yura and Santa Lucía, takes 4 hrs, US$3, and to **Puno**, 6 hrs, US$4.50-6. Most buses and *colectivos* continue to Puno. **Sur Oriente** and **Julsa** are recommended.

Car and taxi
Car hire **Avis**, Palacio Viejo 214, T054-282519, or at the airport T054-443576. **Genesis**, Jerusalén y Puente Grau, T054-202033. Rents 4WDs in good condition, can also arrange drivers. Owner of **Hostal Reyna**, see Sleeping, can arrange cars, vans and 4x4s with drivers. Recommended.

Radio taxis: Nova Taxi, T054-252511; Taxi 21, T054-212121; Telemóvil, T054-221515; Taxitur, T054-422323; Henry Málaga, T054-655095, Spanish-speaking only.

O Directory

Arequipa *p159, maps p160 and p161*

Banks ATM Globalnet cash machines everywhere, eg on the Plaza, at **i perú** offices. Many give cash in soles or US$ and they accept a wide range of cards: Visa, Plus, Diners Club, Amex, Maestro, Cirrus and many Peruvian cards. **Interbank**, Mercaderes 217. MasterCard representative, also Visa and AmEx, US$5 commission on TCs. **BCP**, San Juan de Dios 125, also at Santo Domingo y Jerusalén. Accepts Visa and gives good rates, no commission. Recommended. **BBV Continental**, San Francisco 108. US$12 commission on TCs. **BSCH**, Calle Jerusalén. Changes Visa and Citicorp TCs, low rates. **Scotiabank**, Mercaderes 410. Change money at cambios on Jerusalén and San Juan de Dios, and several travel agencies. **Sergio A del Carpio D**, Jerusalén 126, T054-242987, good rates for dollars. **Via Tours**, Santo Domingo 114, good rates. **Casa de Cambio**, San Juan de Dios 109, T054-282528, good rates. It is almost impossible to change TCs on Sat afternoon or Sun; try to find a sympathetic street changer. Better rates for cash dollars in banks and casas de cambio. **Consulates** Bolivia, Rivero 408, of 6, T054-213391. Mon-Fri 0900-1400, 24 hrs for visa (except those needing clearance from La Paz), go early. Chile, Mercaderes 212, p 4, Of 401-402, Galerías Gameza, T/F054-233556, entrance to lift 30m down passageway down Mercaderes on left. Mon-Fri 0900-1300, present passport 0900-1100 if you need a visa. Italy, La Salle D-5, T054-221444, 1130-1300; in the afternoon T054-254686 (home). Netherlands, Gonzales Prada 122, corner with Juana Espinoza, Umacollo, T054-252649, Mon-Fri 0900-1300, 1630-1830. Spain, Ugarte 218, p 2, T054-205747 (home T054-224915). Mon-Fri 1100-1300, Sat 0900-1300. Sweden, Av Villa Hermosa 803, Cerro Colorado, T054-259847. Mon-Fri 0830-1300, 1500-1730. Switzerland, Av Miguel Forga 348, Parque Industrial, T054-232723. UK, Mr Roberts, Tacna y Arica 156, T054-241340, gerencia@grupo roberts.com. Mon-Fri 0830-1230, 1500-1830, reported as very friendly and helpful. **Cultural centres** Alianza Francesa, Santa Catalina 208, T054-215579, www.afarequipa. org.pe. Instituto Cultural Peruano-Norte Americano, Casa de los Mendiburo, Melgar 109, T054-891020, www.ccpna.edu.pe, has an English library. Instituto Cultural Peruano Alemán, Ugarte 207, T054-218567, icpa@terra.com.pe. Instituto Nacional de Cultura, Alameda San Lázaro 120, T054-213171. **Internet** Internet cafés are everywhere, often charging less than US$0.50 per hr. Best services are constantly changing, so hunt around. **Language courses** Centro de Intercambio Cultural Arequipa (CEICA), Urb Universitaria G-9, T/F054-231759, www.ceica-peru.com. Individual classes US$6 per hr, US$4.50 for groups, rooms with families, with board (US$70 per week) or without (US$30), also excursions. Escuela de Español Ari Quipay (EDEAQ), T054-257358, 999 2995 (mob), www.edeaq.com. Peruvian-Swiss run, experienced, multilingual staff, recognized by Ministry of Education, in a colonial house near the Plaza de Armas, one-to-one and group classes, home stay available. Llama Education, Casabella, lote A6, Cerro Colorado, www.arequipaspanish.com/index.html. Professional, with personal attention, owner María Huaman is very helpful. Individual and small group tuition, home stays and cultural exchanges. Silvana Cornejo, 7 de Junio 118, Cerrito Los Alvarez, Cerro Colorado, T054-254985, silvanacornejo @yahoo.com. US$6 per hr, negotiable for group, recommended. Her sister Roxanna charges US$3 per hr. Liz and Edwin Pérez, T054-264068, edwinett@mixmail.com. US$5 per hr one-to-one tuition, will go to your hotel. Classes also available at the Instituto Peruano-Norte Americano (US$10 per hr) and Instituto Cultural Peruano Alemán (US$4 per hr). Cecilia Pinot Oppe, Jerusalén 406, and Zela 209, T054-996 1638, www.cepesmaidiomasceci.com. Good value lessons, held in a café which helps orphaned children. Carlos Rojas Núñez, Filtro 405, T054-285061, carlrojas@mixmail.com. Private or group lessons for all levels, encourages conversation, knowledgeable on culture and politics. Recommended. **Laundry** Don Marcelo, T054-421411 (morning), T054-229245 (afternoon). Delivery service. Lavandería Quick Laundry, Santa Catalina 312, T054-205503. Fast, reliable and friendly, clothes ironed and bagged. Magic Laundry, Jerusalén 404B and La Merced 125. Coin-operated, open daily. **Medical services** Central del Sur hospital, Filtro y Peral s/n, T054-214430 in emergency.

Lake Titicaca & Arequipa Arequipa Listings

Clínica Arequipa SA, esq Puente Grau y Av Bolognesi, T054-253424 /416. Fast and efficient with English-speaking doctors and all hospital facilities, consultation US$18, plus US$4 for sample analysis, around US$7 for a course of antibiotics. **Paz Holandesa**, Av Jorge Chávez 527, T/F054-206720, www.pazholandesa.com. Dutch foundation with a travel clinic for tourists. Dutch and English spoken, 24-hr service. Highly recommended. Pharmacies include: **Farmacia Libertad**, Piérola 108. Owner speaks English. **Post office** Central office is at Moral 118, opposite Hotel Crismar, Mon-Sat 0800-2000, Sun 0800-1400. DHL, Santa Catalina 115, T054-234288, for sending documents and money. Western Union representative. **Telephone** Alvarez Thomas y Palacio Viejo. *Locutorios* and internet cafés offer international calls from US$0.25 per min. **Useful addresses** Ambulance: San Miguel, T054-283330 (24 hrs).

Colca Canyon

→ *Colour map 2, C4.*

Twice as deep as the Grand Canyon and once thought to be the deepest canyon in the world (until the nearby Cotahuasi Canyon was found to be 163 m deeper), the Colca Canyon is an area of astounding beauty. Giant amphitheatres of pre-Inca terracing become narrow, precipitous gorges, and in the background looms the grey, smoking mass of Sabancaya, one of the most active volcanoes in the Americas, and its more docile neighbour, Ampato (6288 m). Unspoilt Andean villages lie on both sides of the canyon, inhabited by the Cabana and Collagua peoples. The Río Colca snakes its way through the length of this massive gorge, 3500 m above sea level at Chivay (the canyon's main town) falling to 2200 m at Cabanaconde, at the far end of the canyon. Visitors flock here for a close encounter with the giant Andean condor at the aptly named Cruz del Cóndor and for many, this is the final destination in the canyon. Rather than hurrying back to Arequipa, continue to Cabanconde, as good a base for exploring as Chivay, with many new options opening up. ➤➤ *For Sleeping, Eating and other listings, see pages 176-178.*

Ins and outs

Getting there and around Most buses from Arequipa take the new road via Yura and Cañahuas, following the railway, which is being developed as a route to Cuzco. This is longer, but quicker, than the old route through Cayma. In the rainy season it is better to travel by day as the road can get icy and slippery at night. Buses all leave from the main terminal in Arequipa (see page 159) but you can get your ticket the previous day at the bus company offices in Calle San Juan de Dios, or reservations through some of the tourist agencies on Santa Catalina and Jerusalén. Buses and *colectivos* run from Chivay to the villages in the canyon. ➤➤ *For further details, see Transport, page 178.*

Entry ticket A fee of US$10 is charged for a tourist ticket (usually valid for up to a week) granting entrance to the Cruz del Cóndor, trekking and tourist areas in the Colca and valley of the volcanoes. This cost is not included in agency prices and most visitors buy the ticket at a checkpoint before entering Chivay. Keep the ticket with you while in the Colca area

Best time to visit From January to April is the rainy season, but this makes the area green, with lots of flowers. This is not the best time to see condors. May to December is the dry, cold season when there is more chance of seeing the birds.

Chivay and around ⬣🔋✳️🔺🔘🔵 ➤ *pp176-178*.

Chivay is the gateway to the canyon and the overnight stopping point for two-day tours run by agencies in Arequipa. There is a road bridge over the river here (others are at Yanque and Lari).

Arequipa to Chivay → *Colour map 2, C4.*

From Arequipa there are two routes to Chivay, the first village on the edge of the Canyon: the old route, via the suburb of **Cayma**, and the new route following the railway, through **Yura**, which is longer but quicker. It can be cold, reaching 4825 m on the Pata Pampa pass, north of Cañahuas, but the views are worth it. Cyclists should use the Yura road, as it's in better condition and has less of a climb at the start.

The old dirt route runs north from Arequipa, over the *altiplano*. About an hour out of Arequipa is the **Aguada Blanca National Vicuña Reserve**. If you're lucky, you can see herds of these rare and timid camelids near the road. If taking a bus to the reserve to vicuña-watch, there should be enough traffic on the road to be able to hitch a ride back to Arequipa in the evening. This route affords fine views of the volcanoes Misti, Chachani, Ampato and the active Sabancaya.

Chivay → *Colour map 2, C4. Altitude 3600 m.*

There is a very helpful **tourist office** in the Municipalidad on the west side of the plaza which gives away a useful map of the valley. The tourist police, also on the plaza, can give advice about locally trained guides. A reconstructed *chullpa* on the hilltop across Puente Inca gives good views over the town. The **Maria Reiche Planetarium and Observatory** ① *Casa Andina hotel, 6 blocks west of the Plaza between Huayna Capac and Garcilazo (www.casa-andina.com), US$6, discounts for students*, makes the

Colca Canyon

AREQUIPA

most of the Colca's clear Southern Hemisphere skies with a powerful telescope and two 55-minute presentations per day at 1830 (Spanish) and 1930 (English).

The hot springs of **La Calera** ⓘ *US$3*, are 4 km from Chivay. To get there take one of the regular *colectivos* (US$0.25) from beside the market or it's a pleasant hour-long walk. There are several large hot pools and showers but only two pools are usually open to tourists. The hot springs are highly recommended after a hard day's trekking, with good facilities and a beautiful setting. A small cultural museum on site is included in the price. From La Calera you can trek through the Canocota canyon to Canocota (four to five hours); alternatively take a *colectivo* to Canocota and hike to La Calera; it's a beautiful trip, but ask directions.

From Chivay you can hike to **Coporaque** (1¾ hours) and **Ichupampa** (a further 1½ hours). Half an hour above Coporaque are interesting **cliff tombs** and, just beyond the village, are the Huari ruins of **Ullu Ullu**. West beyond Ichupampa are **Lari**, **Madrigal** (where a footbridge connects to Maca) and **Tapay** (connected by a footbridge to Cabanaconde). Between Coporaque and Ichupampa, foot and road bridges cross the river to **Yanque** (one hour), from where it's an 8-km hike back to Chivay. Follow the road or you'll end up lost in a maze of terraced fields. If you feel too tired to walk back to Chivay, catch a *colectivo* from the plaza in Yanque for US$0.25.

Chivay to Cabanaconde 🚌🏍✳🏔🚐 » pp176-178.

From Chivay, the main road goes west along the Colca Canyon. The first village, after 8 km, is **Yanque**, where there's an interesting church and a bridge to the villages on the other side (see page 174). Beside the renovated Inca bridge, a 20-minute walk from Yanque plaza, is a large, warm thermal **swimming pool** ⓘ *US$0.75*. The next village after Yanque is **Achoma**, 30 minutes from Chivay along the Cabanaconde road. There is an old settlement where you can camp. The road continues to **Maca**, which barely survived an earthquake in November 1991. Then comes the tiny village of **Pinchollo**, with a basic *hostal* on the plaza (a room full of beds and one shared bathroom). There are no restaurants but you can eat at the *comedor popular*. You can walk from here to the **Sabancaya** geyser in approximately seven hours. Boys will offer to guide you there. For information, ask for Eduardo, who acts as a guide. He lives next to the plaza.

Cruz del Cóndor → *See Ins and outs, page 172, for entry fees.*

From Pinchollo the road winds its way on to the Mirador, or Cruz del Cóndor at the deepest point of the canyon. The view from here is wonderful but people don't come for the view. This is where the immense Andean vulture, the condor, can be seen rising on the morning thermals. The reason this particular spot is so unique is that the condors swoop by in startling close up, so close, in fact, that you feel you can reach out and touch them. It is a breathtaking and very humbling experience.

The best time to arrive in the morning is a matter of some dispute, although the consensus is around 0900. Arrive by 0800 for a good spot, any earlier and you may be faced with a long, chilly wait; this may be unavoidable if you're travelling by public transport, as buses from Chivay stop here very briefly. To get to the Mirador from Cabanaconde, take one of the return buses which set off at around 0730, and ask to be dropped off at the Mirador, just in time for the morning performance. Or you can walk along the road, which takes about three hours. Horses can be hired to save you the walk; arrange the night before in Cabanaconde.

The condors fly off to look for carrion on the higher slopes of the surrounding peaks at 0900-1000. The condors can also be seen returning at around 1600-1800. Just below the Mirador is a rocky outcrop, which allows a more peaceful viewing but take great care on the loose scree. Binoculars are recommended. Snacks and drinks are available but camping here is officially forbidden.

⁝ Appeasing the gods

To the Incas, Nevado Ampato was a sacred god who brought life-giving water and good harvests and, as such, claimed the highest tribute: human sacrifice.

In September 1995, Johan Reinhard of Chicago's Field Museum of Natural History, accompanied by Peruvian climber, Miguel Zárate, whose brother, Carlos is a well-known mountain guide, were climbing Ampato when they made a startling discovery. At about 6000 m they found the perfectly preserved mummified body of an Inca girl, wrapped tightly in textiles. They concluded that she had been ritually sacrificed and buried on the summit.

Mummies of Inca human sacrifices had been found before on Andean summits, but the girl from Ampato, nicknamed Juanita, is the first frozen Inca female to be unearthed and her body may be the best preserved of any found in the Americas from pre-Columbian times. The intact tissues and organs of naturally mummified, frozen bodies are a storehouse of biological information. Studies reveal how she died, where she came from, who her living relatives are and even yield insights about the Inca diet.

Juanita's clothes are no less remarkable. The richly patterned, dazzling textiles will serve as the model for future depictions of the way noble Inca women dressed. Her *lliclla* – a bright red and white shawl beneath the outer wrappings – has been declared "the finest Inca woman's textile in the world".

Ampato was described as one of the principal deities in the Colca Canyon region. The Incas appeased the mountain gods with the sacrifice of children. The Cabana and Collagua people even bound their children's heads to make them look like the mountains from which they believed they were descended.

A subsequent ascent of Ampato revealed a further two mummies at the summit. One is a young girl and the other, though badly charred by lightning, is believed to be a boy. If so, it may mean that these children were ritually sacrificed together in a symbolic marriage.

Nowadays, villages in the Colca continue to make offerings to the mountain gods for water and good harvests, but thankfully the gods have modified their tastes, now preferring *chicha* to children.

Cabanaconde → *Colour map 2, B4* .

From the Mirador it is a 20-minute bus ride to this friendly village at 3287 m, the last in the Colca Canyon. To walk from the Mirador to Cabanaconde, follow the road until Cabanaconde is in sight, then turn off the road 50 m after a small reservoir down a walled track. After about 1 km turn left on to an old Inca road and continue down to rejoin the road into Cabanaconde.

The indigenous people of this part of the canyon are *Cabanas*. Cabanaconde plaza is brimming with life. Women squat on their haunches, selling bruised fruit and a few knobbly root crops. Their distinctive flower-patterned hats, voluminous skirts and intricately embroidered blouses bring a splash of colour to the uniform brown adobe buildings. Children tend sheep, goats and llamas; old men lead burdened mules while pigs laze in the sun and chickens peck at the ground. At dusk, large groups of animals wander back into the village to the corrals adjoining most houses.

The views into the canyon are excellent and condors can be seen from the hill just west of the village, a 15-minute walk from the plaza. From here, you'll also see the amazing terraces to the south of the village, arguably the most attractive in the valley. The hill is surrounded by a 2-km-long Huari wall, which is 6 m high and 4 m wide in places. It also encompasses the village football field where it is possible to see condors overflying a late-afternoon game.

Cabanaconde provides an excellent base for visiting the region. Interesting trekking and climbing lies all around the village, and local guides are beginning to see new opportunities for biking and horse riding in this amazing landscape. Many locals are keen to encourage respectful tourism in the area. There's a tourist information office attended by friendly locals willing to give plenty of advice, if not maps. It's a good place to find trekking guides and muleteers.

● Sleeping

Chivay and around *p173*
Ask if your hotel can provide heating. Many of the better hotels are used by tour groups. There are several other hotels and family homes where you can stay; ask around.
AL El Parador del Colca, T054-288440, colca@peruorientexpress.com.pe. 3½ km from Yanque, 10 km from Chivay. Built of local materials, with solar power, on an old estate, the hotel offers lots of activities; comfortable cabin-like suites, typical food and home-grown vegetables, meals extra. Closed for refurbishment until Jan 2008.
AL Estancia Pozo del Cielo, over the Puente Inca from Chivay amid pre-Inca terraces, T054-531041, www.pozodelcielo.com.pe. Very comfortable, friendly, warm rooms, good views, good service and restaurant.
A Casa Andina, Huayna Cápac s/n, T054-531020, www.casa-andina.com. Attractive cabins with hot showers and a cosy bar/dining area, another member of this recommended hotel chain, heating, internet, parking. Also here (not directly owned by Casa Andina) is the **Maria Reiche Planetarium and Observatory**; see page 173.
A Colca Lodge, between Coporaque and Ichupampa, T054-20258, www. colca-lodge.com. Very pleasant and relaxing, safe, heating, restaurant with good buffet, TV and DVD players. Beautiful hot springs by the river, trekking, cycling, riding, rafting, spend at least a day there to make the most of what's on offer. A good spot for families and children.
C Colca Inn, Salaverry 307, T054-531111, www.hotelcolcainn.com. A good mid-range option, modern, spick and span, hot water, with a decent restaurant.
D Hostal Posada Chivay, Salaverry 325, T054-531032, posadachivay@hotmail.com. Central, clean and friendly, good rooms, hot water, breakfast included.

D Tradición Colca, on main road, Yanque. Reservations: Calle Argentina 108, Urb Fecia JL Bustamante y Rivero, Arequipa, T054-424926, 935 7117 (mob), www.tradicioncolca.com. Price is per unit, **E** in low season and includes breakfast, with gardens, spa, restaurant, bar, games room, also backpackers' rooms; they also have a travel agency. Recommended.
D Wasi Kolping, 10 blocks south of the town, opposite the Plaza de Toros, T054-521076. Comfortable cabins with hot shower, very clean and quiet, good views.
E La Pascana, Calle Siglo XX 106, T054-531190, hrlapascana@hotmail.com. On the northwest corner of the Plaza. Excellent value with spacious en-suite rooms, spotless showers with hot water, most rooms overlooking a pleasant garden. Price includes breakfast, there is parking space and a good restaurant.
E-F Hospedaje Restaurant Los Portales, Arequipa 603, T054-521101. Good-value accommodation, though beds have rather floppy mattresses, breakfast included in the price. Clean restaurant downstairs.
F Hostal Anita, on the north side of the plaza, T054-531114. Clean, with bathroom, rooms look onto a small garden, friendly.
F La Casa de la Bella Flor, Cuzco 303, Yanque, T054-280454. Charming small lodge run by Sra Hilde Checca, flower-filled garden, tasteful rooms, good meals (also open to non-residents), Hilde's uncle, Gregorio, guides visitors to pre-Columbian sites.
G Hospedaje Jessy, Zarumilla 218, 1 block from market. Simple, clean, excellent showers, cheaper without bath, helpful, with parking.
G pp Rumi Wasi, Calle Sucre 714, 6 blocks from plaza (3 mins' walk), T054-531146. Good rooms, breakfast included, hot water, bike hire, helpful.

Cabanaconde *p175*
B Kuntur Wassi, Calle Cruz Blanca s/n, on the hill above the plaza, T054-812166, kunturwassi@terra.com.pe, or waltertinta @hotmail.com. Excellent 3-star hotel with parking, breakfast included and fine traditional meals on request. Creative design with rooms spaced between rock gardens and waterfalls. 'Viewing tower' and conference centre above. Good views of the valley everywhere, and owners Walter and María very welcoming. Recommended.
C Posada del Conde, Calle San Pedro a couple of blocks from the plaza, T054-440197, pdelconde@yahoo.com. Very smart, cheaper in low season, rooms with private hot shower, excellent value but can be a bit noisy, very good restaurant. Booking advised.
E-F Hostal Valle del Fuego, 1 and 2 blocks from the plaza on Calle Grau, T054-830032, www.pablotour.com. Good rooms with comfortable beds, all with private bath and hot water, plus free laundry facilities. They have 2 places, both with restaurants serving meals for around US$3. The Junco family, Pablo, Edwin and Jamil, among others, are a wealth of information having built up a small family 'empire', including the Arequipa agency **Pablo Tour**, the **Oasis Paradise** in Sangalle (discounts for clients of Valle del Fuego) and a new bar, the **Casa de Pablo Club** (see below) at the end of the street. They usually meet the incoming buses. Good value choice for backpackers, but keep in mind the 'family' nature of the business.
G Virgen del Carmen, 5 blocks from the plaza. Clean, hot showers, friendly, may offer you a welcoming glass of *chicha*. Recommended.

● Eating

Chivay and around *p173*
There are several good, attractively decorated restaurants in Chivay, both cosy and friendly. They serve good value set meals for around US$3 with a choice of dishes. Not all restaurants are open at night.
♥♥-♥ Fonda del Cazador, on the north side of the plaza, serves delicious alpaca steaks.
♥♥-♥ Lobos Pizzería, on the plaza. Good pizzas and pasta, fast service, bar, popular.
♥♥-♥ Los Sismos, by the petrol station. Also serves great alpaca steaks, often has live folklore shows.

♥♥-♥ Witete, Siglo XX 328. Good international food and some local dishes.
♥♥-♥ McElroy's Irish Pub, on the plaza. Bar run by a Peruvian and an Irishman, warm, friendly, good selection of drinks (including – sometimes – expensive Guinness), pizza, pasta, sandwiches and music. Mountain bikes for hire. Accepts Visa.

Cabanaconde *p175*
Both hotels **Posada del Conde** and **Kuntur Wassi** offer excellent food (♥♥), although they might need some advance notice. There are several basic restaurants around the plaza (♥).
♥♥-♥ Casa de Pablo Club, Calle Grau. Jamil Junco has now opened this comfortable bar just beyond **Valle del Fuego**. Excellent fresh juices and pisco sour, cable TV (football!), small book exchange and equipment hire.
♥ Don Piero, signposted just off main plaza. Excellent choice and good information.
♥ Limeño, just to the north of the Plaza. Excellent value breakfasts, friendly service.
♥ Rancho del Colca, on the plaza. Serves mainly vegetarian food.

✪ Festivals and events

Colca Canyon *p172*
20-25 Jan This is a region of wild and frequent festivals. El Día de San Sebastián is celebrated over 5 days in Pinchollo.
2-3 Feb Virgen de la Candelaria is celebrated in the towns of Chivay and Cabanaconde, with dancing in the plaza, and over 5 days in Maca and Tapay.
Mar/Apr Semana Santa is celebrated with particular gusto in the villages of the Colca Canyon.
27 Apr Celebration of the apostle Santiago.
Apr/May Many festivals are held in the Colca canyon at this time of year. La Cruz de Piedra is celebrated over 5 days in May in the main plaza in Tuti, near Chivay.
13 Jun San Antonio is celebrated in the villages of Maca, Callalli and Yanque.
14 Jun In Sibayo and Ichupampa the Fiesta de San Juan is held over 5 days.
21 Jun Anniversary of the district of Chivay in Cailloma.
14-17 Jul Fiesta de la Virgen del Carmen is held in Cabanaconde and Pampacolca, when folk dancing takes place in the streets. Of particular interest is the dance of **Los Turcos**,

which represents the indigenous peoples' struggle against the conquistadors. This fiesta is also held in the churches of Yura, Carmen Alto, Congata, Tingo Grande and the Convent of Santa Teresa in Arequipa city.

25 Jul Fiesta de Santiago Apostol in Coporaque and Madrigal, in the canyon.

26 Jul-2 Aug Various religious ceremonies, accompanied by dancing, are held in honour of the **Virgen Santa Ana** in Maca.

15 Aug In Chivay, fiesta of the **Virgen de la Asunta**, the town's patron saint, lasts 8 days.

Sep In Tisco, the fiesta of the **Virgen de la Natividad** is held over 5 days.

8 Dec The fiesta of the **Inmaculada Concepción** is held in Chivay and Yanque. Groups of musicians and dancers present the traditional dance, the **Witite**, lasting 5 days.

25 Dec In Yanque, the **Witite** lasts for 6 days.

▲ Activities and tours

Travel agencies in Arequipa (see page 169) arrange a one-day tour to the **Cruz del Cóndor** for US$20-25. They leave Arequipa at 0400, arriving at the Cruz del Cóndor at 0800-0900, followed by an expensive lunch stop at Chivay and back to Arequipa by 2100. For many, especially for those with altitude problems, this is too much to fit into one day (the only advantage is that you don't have to sleep at high altitude). It's also more dangerous since drivers get tired on the way back. Two-day tours start at US$25-30 per person with an overnight stop in Chivay; more expensive tours range from US$45 to US$90 with accommodation at the top of the range. You should allow at least 2-3 days, more if you are planning to do some trekking in the Colca Canyon.

Travel agents frequently work together in a 'pooling' system to fill buses (even the more expensive agencies may not have their own transport) and there are lots of touts. This can mean that a busload of tourists will come from different agencies, all paying different prices, but all expecting the same level of service. On occasion the company providing the transport may not have the same high standards as the operator through whom the tour was booked.

Note Don't forget that the compulsory entry ticket (see Ins and outs, page 172) is rarely include in agency prices.

Chivay and around *p173*

Ampato Adventure Sports, Plaza de Armas (close to **Lobos Pizzería**), Chivay, T054-531073, www.ampatocolca.com. Offer information and rent good mountain bikes.

Colca-Turismo, Av Salaverry 321, Chivay, 054-503368, and guide **Zacarías Ocsa Osca**, zacariasocsa@hotmail.com, offers a professional service.

Cabanaconde *p175*

Henry López Junco, is a guide in Cabanaconde, T054-280367. He charges US$7.15 per day for 2 people.

⊝ Transport

Chivay and around *p173*

Transportes Milagros, La Reyna (recommended) and **Andalucia** have 7 departures daily from Arequipa to **Chivay**, continuing to **Cabanaconde** (a further 75 km, 2 hrs, US$1). **La Reyna** has the quickest service at about 6 hrs, US$3.85; others US$3. Buy a ticket in advance to ensure a seat (many agencies can buy them for you for a fee). Buses return to **Arequipa** from the new bus station in Chivay, 3 blocks from the main plaza, next to the stadium. For **Cruz del Cóndor** catch the 0500 Cabanaconde bus from Chivay, which stops briefly at the Mirador at 0700 (if this doesn't seem likely, ask), US$0.75.

Combis and *colectivos* leave from the new terminal in Chivay to any village in the area including **Achoma** (every 30 mins), **Maca** (every hour), **Ichupampa** (every hour) and **Puente Callalli** (every hour); ask the drivers for details.

Cabanaconde *p175*

See under Chivay for buses on the Arequipa–Chivay–Cabanaconde route. **Milagros, Andalucía** and **La Reyna** buses leave Cabanaconde for **Arequipa** between 0730 and 1500, always from the Plaza de Armas, US$4.50 (usually a wait in Chivay).

⊕ Directory

Chivay and around *p173*

Banks TCs and credit cards are seldom accepted so take plenty of cash in soles, not dollars.

Introduction

A number of roads make it possible to move between the Pacific Coast, with its ramshackle fishing villages and brief flashes of green irrigated valleys, and the central highlands with their timeless Andean towns and villages. The Central Railway from Lima to Huancayo may only have an intermittent service but it is one of South America's outstanding train rides and a great way to reach this fascinating region. Huancayo itself is a little off the tourist compass, but the surrounding villages of the Mantaro Valley are famous for their handicrafts and fiestas. Ayacucho, further south, hosts one of the largest and most impressive Holy Week celebrations in Latin America and at that time becomes a real focus of attention.

Many bus hours and some truly fabulous landscapes lead from Cuzco to the coastal desert, where, etched on the plains, are one of Peru's most famous enigmas, the Nazca Lines, whose origin and function continue to puzzle scientists. More designs on the desert, plus tomb finds at neighbouring Palpa are casting new light on the mystery.

In August 2007, an earthquake of 8.0 on the Richter scale struck the coast of Peru south of Lima. Hardest hit was the province of Ica, but the effects were felt in many places inland, including in the Sierras. The city of Pisco was largely destroyed. At the time of writing, over 500 people were known to have been killed, over 1000 wounded and some 100,000 left without housing or services. Consequently, this section will not include information on the worst-hit zone between Cañete and Ocucaje as it will take many months for the area to recover and to be able to receive tourists. If your journey takes you south of Lima, enquire locally about what services are available.

★ Don't miss ...

1 **Mantaro Valley** Go shopping in this souvenir-hunter's paradise. Each village specializes in its very own variety of artesanía, page 184.

2 **Ayacucho** Don't miss the fine array of colonial churches, spectacular processions with carpets of flowers decorating the streets and the artists' quarter of Santa Ana, page 189.

3 **Nazca Lines** From a small plane, take a gods' eye view of the lines etched in the desert, one of the great archaeological enigmas, page 197.

4 **Huacachina** An oasis lake amid towering sand dunes, not far from Peru's pisco-producing bodegas, page 203.

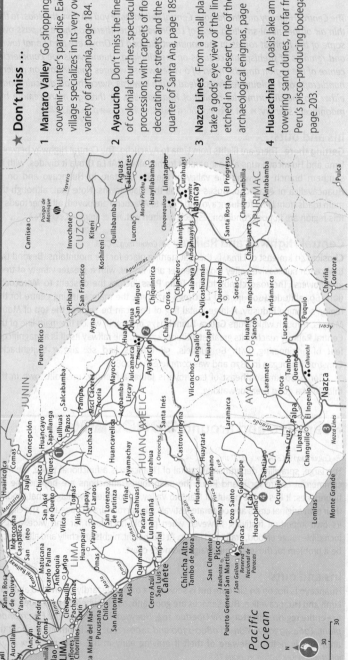

Central Highlands

The Central Highway and the famous Central Railway take you up from the coast to the thin air of the metal-smelting zone of La Oroya. To get there you have to pass over some of the highest routes in the continent. Beyond La Oroya are traditional towns and remains of prehispanic cultures on the altiplano. Huancayo is the commercial centre of the region and the heart of a valley whose villages concentrate on making handicrafts and holding festivals. Head south towards Ayacucho on difficult roads, either via the departmental capital of Huancavelica, or through more remote but magnificent scenery. ▸▸ *For Sleeping, Eating and other listings, see pages 185-188.*

Ins and outs

Getting there There are flights from Lima to Ayacucho. The Central Highway between Lima and Huancayo runs almost parallel to the railway. At La Oroya it divides, with its southern branch following the valley of the Río Mantaro to Huancayo and on to Huancavelica or Ayacucho. Buses serve all the main towns. Note that, although the main roads from Lima to Huancayo and Pisco to Ayacucho are paved, all other roads in this region are in poor condition, especially when wet. ▸▸ *See Transport, page 187.*

Central Highway and Railway → *Colour map 2, C2/3.*

Chosica, 40 km east of Lima, is the real starting place for the mountains. Beyond this town each successive valley looks greener and lusher, with a greater variety of trees and flowers. The road climbs to the **Ticlio Pass**, before the descent to **Morococha** (Km 169, altitude 4600 m) and **La Oroya** (3755 m), the main smelting centre for the region's mining industry. A large metal flag of Peru can be seen at the top of Mount Meiggs, through which runs **Galera Tunnel**, 1175 m long, in which the main line of the Central Railway reaches its greatest altitude, 4781 m. The railway itself is a magnificent feat of engineering, with 69 tunnels, 58 bridges and six zigzag switchbacks. Construction began in 1870 and was completed in 1908.

Some 80 km southeast of La Oroya is **Jauja**, a friendly, unspoilt town in the middle of a good area for walking.

Huancayo and around 🅑🅐🅕🅒🅧🅞🅐🅔🅒 ▸▸ *pp185-188.*

→ *Colour map 2, C3. Altitude: 3271 m.*

The large, sprawling departmental capital of Huancayo is a functional place, the main commercial centre for inland Peru. The main tourist attractions are beyond the city boundaries. It lies in the beautiful Mantaro Valley, surrounded by villages that produce their own original crafts and celebrate festivals all year round, see page 186. The city has its own important festivals, however, when people flock from far and wide with an incredible range of food, crafts and music. At this height, nights are chilly and altitude can be a problem for those arriving straight from the coast.

Ins and outs

Huancayo is not on an air route but is served, if a bit haphazardly, by train to and from Lima and Huancavelica. Bus services are good and, as elsewhere in the Andes, serve the entire region. **Dircetur** ⓘ *Av Libertad 204, Huayucachi, opposite the Electroandes plant, T064-433007, Mon-Fri 0800-1300 and 1400-1700,* has information about the area and is helpful. Beware of theft if arriving early in the morning. ▸▸ *For further information, see Transport, page 187.*

Sights

The Plaza de Armas is called **Plaza Constitución**. The main sights, though, as well as the Sunday market, are quite a way from the centre. The **Sunday market** gets going after 0900 every week and provides little taste of Huancayo at festival time. The stalls on Jirón Huancavelica, 3 km long, still sell typical clothes, fruit, vegetables, hardware, handicrafts and, especially, traditional medicines and goods for witchcraft. However, the market has been described as expensive and offering little choice; it is better to go to the villages for local handicrafts. There is also an impressive daily market behind the railway station.

Huancayo

Sleeping
Casa Alojamiento de
  Aldo y Soledad Bonilla 1 C2

Casa Hospedaje 2 B2
Confort 3 A2
El Marquez 5 A2
Hostal Baldeón 6 B3
Hostal Santo Domingo 8 B1
La Casa de la Abuela 9 B3
Peru Andino 10 A3
Presidente 11 C2
Pussy Cat 12 B3

Retama Inn 15 C2
Santa Felicita 13 B2
Turismo 14 B2

Eating
Berisso 1 B2
Café El Parque 2 B2
Chanchamayo 6 B2
Chez Viena 3 B3

Chifa El Centro 4 B2
El Paraíso 7 C2
El Pino 8 B2
ImaginArte 5 A2
La Cabaña 9 B3
Panadería Koky 11 B2
Pizzería Antojitos 12 B2

0 metres 100
0 yards 100

Parque de Identidad Wanka ① *Jr San Jorge, Barrio San Carlos, northeast of the city (35 mins' walk from plaza), free but donation appreciated*, is a fascinating mixture of surrealistic construction, interwoven with indigenous plants and trees and the cultural history of the Mantaro Valley. It can get crowded at weekends. Opposite are the **Misti Wasi** and **Pacaywasi** restaurants serving traditional meals; there are about six others.

Mantaro Valley

The main attraction in the area is the Mantaro Valley, which is rich in culture, music, local food, dances and handicrafts and plays host to numerous festivals. To the west of the Río Mantaro, 19 km from Huancayo, is **Viques**, which is known for the production of belts and blankets. **Sra María Magdalena Huzco**, Calle San Martín, two blocks from the Plaza Principal, offers **weaving lessons**, US$34 for 15 hours, plus the cost of materials. Other weavers may also give lessons. It's a worthwhile experience, not just for learning how to weave, but also for an insight into the life of this part of Peru. **Huayucachi**, 7 km away, organizes festivals with dancing and impressive costumes in January and February and also makes embroidery.

The ruins of **Warivilca** ① *15 km from Huancayo, daily 1000-1200 and 1500-1700, US$0.15; to get here take one of the micros for Chilca, which leave from Calle Real*, feature the remains of a pre-Inca temple of the Huanca culture. There is a museum in the plaza (open in the morning only), with deformed skulls, and modelled and painted pottery of successive Huanca and Inca occupations of the shrine. The ruins and museum are under the supervision of a local archaeologist and are slowly being restored.

The villages of **Cochas Chico** and **Cochas Grande**, 11 km from Huancayo on the east side of the river, are both well worth visiting. *Micros* leave from Plaza Hunamarco or by the market near the railway line, US$0.25. This is where the famous *mate burilado*, or gourd carving, is done. You can buy the gourds cheaply direct from the manufacturers, but ask around. There are beautiful views of the Valle de Mantaro and Huancayo.

In the village of **Hualhuas**, 12 km from Huancayo, you can find fine alpaca weavings, which you can watch being made. The weavers take special orders; small items can be finished in a day. Negotiate a price. One particularly recommended place to buy them is **Tahuantisuyo**, run by Familia Faustino Maldonado y Agripina, on a side road on the way to the San Jerónimo junction.

The town of **San Jerónimo** is renowned for the making of silver filigree jewellery, on sale at the Wednesday market. A major fiesta is held in the town on the third Saturday in August, when one of the two plazas is converted into a temporary bullring.

Huancavelica and around 🖬🕖❀🖬🌀 ‣ *pp185-188*.

→ *Colour map 2, C3. Altitude: 3660 m.*

Huancavelica, capital of the next department south, is a friendly and attractive town, surrounded by huge, rocky mountains. It's not really geared up for tourism, owing to its remoteness. Founded in the 16th century by the Spanish to exploit rich deposits of mercury and silver, Huancavelica has very few mines open now. It is predominantly an indigenous town, where people still wear traditional costume.

Ins and outs

Like Huancayo, Huancavelica is not on an air route and bus services are limited but, mechanical problems aside, the Huancayo–Huancavelica train service should run daily. Buses and *colectivos* serve the entire region. **Dircetur** ① *Victoria Garma 444, p 2, T067-452938, dircetur_hcv@hotmail.com, Mon-Fri 0800-1300, 1415-1730*, is very helpful and has useful information. Don't wander around the surrounding hills alone.

‣‣ *For further information, see Transport, page 188.*

Sights

The **cathedral** on the Plaza de Armas has an altar considered to be one of the finest examples of colonial art in Peru. Bisecting the town is the Río Huancavelica. South of the river is the main commercial centre. North of the river, on the hillside, are the **thermal baths** ① *0600-1500, US$0.10 for the public pool.* There are also hot showers but take a lock for the doors. The **handicraft sellers** congregate in front of the Municipalidad on M and the Biblioteco on the Plaza de Armas (V Toledo). The regional **INC office** ① *Plazoleta San Juan de Dios s/n, T067-453420, inc_huancavelica@yahoo.es,* is a good source of information on festivals, archaeological sites and history. The institute also runs courses on music and dancing, and hosts lectures some evenings. There is an interesting but small **Museo Regional** ① *Arica y Raimondi, Mon-Sat 1000-1300 and 1500-1900.*

● Sleeping

Huancayo and around *p182, map p183*
Prices may rise in Holy Week.
C **El Marquez**, Puno 294, T064-219026, www.elmarquezhuancayo.com. Rooms with bath and TV, free internet, good value and efficient, safe parking.
C **Presidente**, Calle Real 1138, T064-231275, same email address as **Turismo**. Rooms with bathroom, clean, helpful, safe, breakfast only.
C **Turismo**, Ancash 729, T064-231072, hotelhyo@correo.dnet.com.pe. In an old building. Rooms with bathroom, some rooms are small, quiet. Restaurant serves good meals for US$3.50.
D **Retama Inn**, Ancash 1079, T064-219193, retamainn73@hotmail.com. All amenities, comfortable beds, TV, café/bar, helpful, internet US$1.50 per hr, breakfast US$2.
D **Santa Felicita**, Giráldez 145, Plaza Constitución, T064-235285. With bathroom, hot water, good.
E pp **Casa Alojamiento de Aldo y Soledad Bonilla**, Huánuco 332, no sign, T064-232103. Prices is for full board, beautiful colonial house, owners speak English, laundry, secure, relaxing, nice courtyard, they can arrange local tours, book ahead to guarantee a room.
E **Hospedaje César Ada**, Pasaje Santa Teresa 294, El Tambo-3 Esquinas, Vilcacoto, 5 km from centre, T064-253646 for pickup, wadaycesar@hotmail.com. Quiet, shared bath, garden, meals available, use of kitchen, breakfast included.
E **La Casa de la Abuela**, Av Giráldez 691, T064-223303. G pp in dorms. Comfortable hostel with a warm atmosphere and plenty of services. Some rooms with antique beds, good hot showers, breakfast included, meals available, games room, internet, laundry services, sociable staff. Good place to meet

other backpackers. Free taxi pickup from the bus station if requested in advance.
F **Confort**, Ancash 231, 1 block from the main plaza, T064-233601. All rooms are good value with hot water, very clean, spacious, ask for a room not facing the street for peace and quiet, safe for bikes, car parking US$1.
F **Pussy Cat**, Giráldez 359, T064-231565. Not what the name might suggest, G with shared bathroom, hot water, safe, friendly, luggage stored, comfortable beds.
G pp **Casa Hospedaje**, Huamanmarca 125, T064-219980. Central, small, comfortable, hot water, family-run, nice atmosphere.
G pp **Hostal Baldeón**, Amazonas 543, T064-231634. Friendly, kitchen and laundry facilities, nice patio, good hot shower on request, basic rooms with poor beds, security-conscious.
G **Hostal Santo Domingo**, Ica 655, T064-235461. Set around 2 pleasant patios, clean, basic, good value.
G pp **Peru Andino**, Pasaje San Antonio 113-115, San Carlos, on Av Centenario go 3 blocks from 2 de Mayo to San José, then 3 blocks north (left), 10-15 min walk from the centre, T064-223956; if taking a taxi, stress that it's Pasaje San Antonio), www.geocities.com/ peruandino_1. Price includes breakfast, clean rooms with hot showers, some with private bathroom, safe area, cosy atmosphere, friendly. Trekking and mountain bike tours organized, Spanish classes, cooking and laundry facilities. Highly recommended.

Huancavelica and around *p184*
D **Presidente**, Plaza de Armas, T067-452760. Lovely colonial building, cheaper without bathroom, price includes breakfast and bath, very clean but not a warm building, hot water a 'hit and miss' affair, overpriced.

F **Camacho**, Jr Carabaya 481, T067-753298. Best of the cheap hotels, shared hot shower in morning and early evening, clean and well maintained, excellent value.

F **San José**, Jr Huancayo, at top of Barranca (past Santo Domingo), T067-752958. With bath, hot water 1700-1900, **G** without bath, clean, comfortable beds, helpful.

G **Santo Domingo**, Av Barranca 336, T067-953086. Cheap, very basic, with shared bath.

🍴 Eating

Huancayo and around *p182, map p183*

🍴 **La Cabaña**, Av Giráldez 652. Pizzas, ice-cream, *calentitos* and other dishes, roast New Zealand lamb, folk music at weekends (see Incas del Perú under Tour operators, below).

🍴 **Pizzería Antojitos**, Puno 599. Attractive, atmospheric pizzeria, live music some nights.

🍴 **Chifa El Centro**, Giráldez 245. Chinese food, good service, excellent value and atmosphere (waterfall and rainforest).

🍴 **El Pino**, Real 539. Serves typical food for about US$2-3 a dish, and fixed-price *menú*.

Cafés

Berisso, Giráldez 258. Good cakes, friendly.

Café El Parque, Giráldez y Ancash, main plaza. Smart place to take coffee and cake.

Chanchamayo, Puno 209. Good little family café, cheap, good for breakfast.

Chez Viena, Puno 125. Another up-market place for coffee and cakes.

El Paraíso, Arequipa 929. Very good vegetarian food, good value and service.

ImaginArte, Jr Ancash 260. An interesting contemporary art gallery, often displaying work based on ethnic Peruvian culture. Good coffee and cakes add to the appeal.

Panadería Koky, Ancash y Puno. Good for breakfasts and pastries, pricey.

Huancavelica and around *p184*

There are lots of cheap, basic restaurants on Calle Muñoz and Jr Virrey Toledo. All serve local food, mostly with a set menu for US$1.50. There area also *chifas* on Toledo.

🍴 **Mochica Sachún**, Av Virrey Toledo 303. Popular *menú* US$1.50, otherwise expensive.

🍴 **Cami**, Barranca y Toledo. No sign, small, lively, good set menus and juices.

🍴 **La Casona**, Jr Virrey Toledo 230. Good-value *menú* and *peña*.

🍸 Bars and clubs

Huancayo and around *p182, map p183*

All *peñas* have folklore shows with dancing, normally Fri, Sat and Sun 1300-2200. Entrance is about US$2 pp. Try **Ollantaytambo**, Puno, block 2, or **Taki Wasi**, Huancavelica y 13 de Noviembre. Most discos are open 2000-0200; some charge an entrance fee of US$3-4.

⊛ Festivals and events

Huancayo and around *p182, map p183*

19-31 Jan Festividad del Tayta Niño.

8 Sep Festividad de la Virgen de Cocharcas.

30 Sep Festividad San Jerónimo de Tunan.

Oct San Francisco de Asís, San Lucas. The culmination of month-long celebrations for El Señor de los Milagros.

16 Nov The beginning of Semana Turística de Huancayo.

Mantaro Valley *p184*

Practically every day of the year there is a celebration in one of the villages.

19-31 Jan Festividad del Tayta Niño, in Huayucachi.

Feb Carnival celebrations for the whole of the month, with highlights on 2, **Virgen de la Candelaria**, and 17-19, **Concurso de Carnaval**.

Mar/Apr Semana Santa is impressive throughout the valley, especially the Good Fri processions.

1 May Fiesta de la Cruz also takes place throughout the valley.

24-30 Jul Fiesta de Santiago.

8 Sep La Virgen de Cocharcas is held in Concepción, Jauja and, more famously, in Sapallanga, 8 km south of Huancayo.

Sep The Semana Turística del Valle del Mantaro is held on different dates.

Huancavelica and around *p184*

The whole area is rich in culture with many festivals and dances.

4-8 Jan Fiesta de Reyes Magos y Pastores.

2nd Sun in Jan Fiesta del Niño Perdido. Pukllaylay Carnavales.

20 Jan-mid Mar Celebration of the first fruits from the ground (harvest).

Mar/Apr Semana Santa, Holy Week.

End May-beginning Jun Toro Pukllay.

May and Aug Fiesta de Santiago.

22-28 Dec Los Laygas (scissors dance).

○ Shopping

Huancayo and around *p182, map p183*
All handicrafts are made outside Huancayo
in the many villages of the Mantaro Valley
(see page 184). The villages are worth
a visit to learn how the items are made.

Casa de Artesano, corner of Real and
Paseo La Breña, Plaza Constitución, has
a wide selection of good quality crafts.

There is also a large market between
Ancash and Real, block 7, offering a wide
selection of local handicrafts. Watch out for
pickpockets. There are 2 supermarkets on
Real between Breña and Lima.

▲ Activities and tours

Huancayo and around *p182, map p183*
Guides
Marco Jurado Ames, andinismo_peru
@yahoo.es. Organizes long-distance treks
on the 'hidden paths of Peru'. Many of these
include Huancayo, such as a two-week trip
from Lima to Machu Picchu via Huancayo,
the Amazon lowlands and Vilcabamba.

Tour operators
American Travel & Service, Plaza
Constitución 122, of 2 (next to the cathedral),
T064-211181, T932 5767 (mob), www.travel
tourshuancayo.com. Wide range of classical
and more adventurous tours in the Mantaro
Valley and in the Central Jungle. Transport
and equipment rental possible. Most group
based day tours start at US$8-10 pp.
Andina Tours, Calle Real 455, of 2, T064-
253434, T999 8168 (mob), andinatours_hyo
@hotmail.com. Professional tour organizer.
Incas del Perú, Av Giráldez 652, T064-
223303, www.incasdelperu.org. Associated
with the La Cabaña restaurant and
La Casa de la Abuela. Jungle, biking
and riding trips throughout the region,
as well as language and volunteer
programs. Very popular with travellers
in the region.
Peruvian Tours, Plaza Constitución 122,
p 2, of 1, T064-213069, T966 1044 (mob).
Next to the cathedral and American Travel
& Service. Classic tours of the Mantaro
Valley, plus day trips up to the Huaytapallana
Nevados above Huancayo, and long, 16-hr
excursions to Cerro de Pasco and Tarma.

○ Transport

Huancayo and around *p182, map p183*
Bus Local buses to the **Mantaro Valley**
leave from around the market area. Buses to
Hualhuas, **Cajas** and **Huamancaca** leave
from block 3 of Pachitea. Buses to **Cochas**
leave from Amazonas y Giráldez.

Long distance Most of the better bus
offices to Lima are 2-3 blocks north of the
main plaza, while the cheaper companies
are north of the Río Shullcas, a 10- to 15-min
walk from the centre. Bus companies to
destinations south of Huancayo, eg
Huancavelica and Ayacucho, are 4-5 blocks
south of the main plaza. A new bus terminal
for all buses to all destinations is being
planned, 3 km north of the centre. To **Lima**,
7 hrs on a paved road, US$10-13. Travel by
day for fantastic views and for safety. If you
must travel by night, take warm clothes.
Recommended are **Ormeño**, Av Mcal Castilla
1379, El Tambo; **Cruz del Sur**, Ayacucho 281,
T064-235650; **Turismo Central**, Jr Ayacucho
274, T064-223128 (double-decker *bus cama*),
and **Transportes Rogger**, Lima 561, T064-
212687, *cama* and *semi-cama* at 1300 and
2330, *comercial* at 2230.

To **Huancavelica**, 147 km, 5 hrs, US$2.85.
Many buses leave daily, eg **Transportes Yuri**,
Ancash 1220, 3 a day. The road is being
improved but takes longer when wet.
The scenery is spectacular.

To **Ayacucho**, 319 km , 9-10 hrs, US$6.65-
7.55. **Molina**, Calle Angaráes 334, T064-
224501, 3 a day, recommended. The road is
paved for 70 km, then in poor condition and is
very difficult in the wet. Take warm clothing.

Train There are 2 unconnected railway
stations. The **Central station** (Av Ferrocarril
461, T064-217724/216662) serves **Lima**,
via **La Oroya** (298 km). Service on this
railway is run by **Ferrocarril Centro Andino**,
T01-226 6363, ext 222, www.ferrocarril
central.com.pe (reservations by phone or
reservas@fcca.com.pe). Trains run 2-3 times a
month; see website for dates. The return fare
is US$50 *tren clásico* (older carriages with
non-reclining seats), US$78.75 *tren turístico*
(pullman cars with reclining seats, panoramic
views, bar, a/c); US$30.30 and US$48.50 one
way respectively. The train leaves Lima Fri
0700, arrives Huancayo 1800, returns Sun

1800, arrives Lima 0500; occasionally the return is 0700 Sun, or Mon or Tue. Both services have heating, restaurant, tourist information, toilets and nurse with first aid and oxygen.

From the small station in Chilca suburb (15 mins by taxi, US$1), trains run 128.7 km to **Huancavelica**, on a narrow gauge track (3 ft). There are 2 trains: the *autovagón* leaves at 1300 daily. It costs US$4 and has 1st class and buffet carriages. The journey takes 7 hrs, and is a spectacular one with fine views, passing through typical mountain villages. There are 38 tunnels and the line reaches 3676 m. Meals, drinks and snacks are served on the train, and vendors sell food and crafts at the village stations. The local train leaves at 0630 daily and takes 5 hrs. There are 1st, US$2.55, 2nd, US$2.20, and buffet, US$3.70, classes. Tickets can only be bought on the day of travel; get in the queue at 0600 at the latest. Services are often suspended, especially when rainy; the trains frequently suffer technical problems.

Huancavelica and around *p184*
Bus All bus companies are at the east end of town, around Parque M Castilla, on Muñoz, Iquitos, Tumbes and O'Donovan. To **Huancayo**, 147 km, 5 hrs, US$2.85, rough road. **Transportes Yuri** at 2200 and **Transportes Ticllas**, 6 a day. To **Lima** via Huancayo, 445 km, 13 hrs minimum, US$5.70. **Libertadores** buses to Huancayo at 1830 go on to Lima, also **Ticllas** at 1700.

The only direct transport from Huancavelica to **Ayacucho**, is 0430 Sat with **San Juan Bautista**, Plaza Túpac Amaru 107, T067-803062, US$5.70. On other days you have to catch a **San Juan Bautista** bus at 0430 to **Rumichaca** on the paved Pisco– Ayacucho road, just beyond Santa Inés, 4 hrs, then wait for a passing bus to Ayacucho, 1500, 3 hrs, US$2, or take a truck. (There's nothing in Rumichaca other than a couple of foodstalls and some filthy toilets.) From Rumichaca it's a spectacular but cold journey to Ayacucho on the paved road, which rarely drops below 4000 m for 150 km. The best alternative is to take a *colectivo* from Huancavelica to **Lircay**, and continue with the same company from Lircay Terminal Terrestre hourly from 0430 to **Julcamarca**, 2½ hrs, US$3. Minibuses run from Julcamarca plaza to Ayacucho, US$2, 2 hrs.

Train Just a little beyond the bus stations and about 500m from the Plaza de Armas is the train station. The *autovagón* leaves daily at 0630 for **Huancayo**. It tends to be very crowded. The local train leaves at 1300 daily. Sit on the left for the best views. For further details, see Huancayo Transport, page 187.

◑ Directory

Huancayo and around *p182, map p183*
Banks BCP, Real 1039. Changes TCs with no commission, cash advance on Visa. **Scotiabank**, Real casi Ica. ATM does not accept international cards, poor rates for TCs. **Interbank** and **Banco Continental** are on block 6 of Real. There are several *casas de cambio* on Ancash and on Av Lima between Ancash and Real. Street changers hang out in front of Hotel Kiya. **Hospital Daniel A Carrión**, Av Daniel A Carrión 1552, T064-222157. **Internet** Numerous places round Plaza Constitución on Giráldez, Paseo La Breña. Average price under US$0.75 per hr. **Language classes** Katia Cerna is a recommended teacher, T064-225332, katiacerna@hotmail .com She can arrange home stays; her sister works in adventure tourism. **Incas del Perú** (see page 187) organize Spanish courses for beginners, US$100 per week, 3 hrs a day, including 5 nights' accommodation at **La Casa de La Abuela** and all meals, also homestays, and classes in weaving, Quechua, traditional music and gourd carving. See also Peru Andino Lodging above. **Laundry** Good *lavandería* on Paseo La Breña behind Casa de Artesano. **Post office** On Plaza Huamanmarca. **Useful addresses** Police, Av Ferrocaril 555, T064-211653. **Tourist Police**, Av Ferrocaril 580, T064-219851.

Huancavelica and around *p184*
Banks BCP, Virrey Toledo 300 block, west of Plaza. There is a Multired ATM on M Muñoz in the arches of the Municipalidad. **Internet** Internet places open 0900-2100. There are places on V Toledo and M Muñoz. Also **Librería Municipal**, Plaza de Armas, US$0.60 per hr. **Post office** On Ferrua Jos, block 8 of M Muñoz. **Telephone** Carabaya y Virrey Toledo.

Ayacucho and around

→ *Colour map 2, C3. Population: 142,500. Altitude: 2748 m .*

The city of Ayacucho, the capital of its Department, is famous for its hugely impressive Semana Santa celebrations, its splendid market and, not least, a plethora of churches (33 of them no less) giving the city its alternative name La Ciudad de las Iglesias. It was here, on the Pampa de Quinua, on 9 December 1824, that the decisive Battle of Ayacucho was fought, bringing Spanish rule in Peru to an end. The Liberator, Simon Bolívar, decreed that the city be named Ayacucho, meaning 'City of Blood'. For much of the 1980s and early 1990s, this title seemed appropriate as the Shining Path terrorized the local populace, severely punishing anyone they suspected of siding with the military. Now, though, peace has returned to this beautiful colonial Andean city. A week can easily be spent enjoying Ayacucho and its hinterland. The climate is lovely, with warm, sunny days and pleasant balmy evenings. It is a hospitable, tranquil place, where the inhabitants are eager to promote tourism. It also boasts a large, active student population. ▶ *For Sleeping, Eating and other listings, see pages 193-196.*

Ins and outs

Getting there and around The **airport** ⓘ *east of the city, Av Castilla*, receives flights from Lima and Andahuaylas. A taxi to the centre costs US$2; or walk half a block from the airport to find a bus or *colectivo* to Plaza Mayor. Most of the **bus** offices are nearer the centre of town, in the north and northeast. This is a large city but the interesting churches and colonial houses are all close to Plaza Mayor. Barrio Santa Ana is further to the south and you may want to take a taxi to get to it (US$1; it's easy to walk back). Taxis are cheap and mototaxis are plentiful. ▶ *For further information, see Transport, page 195.*

Tourist information i perú ⓘ *Portal Municipal 48, on the Plaza, T066-318305, iperuayacucho@promperu.gob.pe, Mon-Sat 0830-1930, Sun 0830-1430*, is very helpful. Ask Smith Pariona Medina here for guides who work with the **Asociación de Guías e Turismo–Ayacucho (Agotur-A)**. There is a desk at the airport to meet incoming flights. **Dircetur** ⓘ *Asamblea 481, T066-312548. Mon-Fri 0745-1700*, is also friendly and helpful.

Sights

The construction of Ayacucho's many colonial religious buildings is said to have been financed by wealthy Spanish mine-owners and governors. Unfortunately many have fallen into disrepair and are closed to the public.

Plaza Mayor and north

Ayacucho is built round the Plaza Mayor in the centre of which is a statue of Independence hero Antonio José de Sucre. Facing onto the plaza are the cathedral, Municipalidad, the Prefectura and the Supreme Court, housed in fine colonial buildings within the Plaza's arcades. The **cathedral** ⓘ *1700-1900, Sun 0900-1700*, was built in 1612. The two towers are in green stone, while the portal is pink. It has three strong, solid naves of simple architecture, in contrast to the elegant decoration of the interior, particularly the superb gold-leaf altars. The cathedral is beautifully lit at night.

On the north side of the Plaza Mayor, on the corner of Portal de la Unión and Asamblea, are the **Casonas de los Marqueses de Mozobamba y del Pozo**, also called Velarde-Alvarez. The **Museo de Arte Popular Joaquín López Antay** ⓘ *Portal de la Unión 28, in the BCP building, museo@unsch.edu.pe, Tue-Fri 1030-1700, Sat 1030-1230*, displays local craft work. Leading north from the Plaza is Jr Asamblea, full of

Sleeping
Ayacucho Hotel Plaza 1
Florida 4
Grau 5
Hospedaje El Centro 7
Hostal El Marqués de Valdelirios 16
Hostal San Blas 10
Hostal Tres Máscaras 8
La Crillonesa 13
La Posada de Santa Inés 10
Marcos 2
San Francisco 15
Santa Rosa 12

Eating
Brasa Roja 12
Cabo Blanco 10
Café Dorado 11
Chifa Hua Lin 1
La Casona 3
Mía Pizza 4
Nino 5
Tradición 7
Urpicha 14

Transport
Combis to Vilcashuamán 10
Cruz del Sur 5
Libertadores 9
Los Chankas 8
Molina 6
Ormeño 3
ReyBus 4
Wari 1

eating places, internet cafés and discos. On a parallel street, one of the city's most notable churches is **Santo Domingo** (1548) ① *9 de Diciembre, block 2, open for Mass daily 0700-0800*. Its fine façade has triple Roman arches and Byzantine towers.

North of the centre, **Museo de Anfasep** ① *Prol Libertad 1226, www.dhperu.org/anfasep, 15 mins' walk from Mercado Artesanal Shosaku Nagase, donation*, provides an insight into the recent history of this region during the violence surrounding the Sendero Luminoso campaign and the government's attempts to counter it.

South of Plaza Mayor

A stroll down Jr 28 de Julio towards the prominent **Arco del Triunfo** (1910), which commemorates victory over the Spaniards, passes **La Compañía de Jesús** (1605) ① *open only for Mass*. It has one of the most important façades of Viceregal architecture. It is of baroque style and guarded by two impressive 18th-century towers. Its altar is covered in gold leaf and large paintings of saints adorn the nave.

Go through the arch to the church of **San Francisco de Asís** ① *28 de Julio, block 3, open daily for morning Mass and 1730-1830*. It dates from 1552 and has an elaborate gilt main altar and several others. It claims the largest bell in the city in its tower. Across 28 de Julio from San Francisco is the **Mercado de Abastos Carlos F Vivanco**, the packed central market. As well as all the household items, meat and other local produce, look for the cheese sellers, the breads and the section dedicated to fruit juices.

Santa Clara de Asís ① *Jr Grau, block 3, open for Mass*, is renowned for its beautifully delicate coffered ceiling. It is open for the sale of sweets and cakes made by the nuns (go to the door at Nazarenas 184). On the 5th block of 28 de Julio is the late 16th-century **Casona Vivanco**, which houses the **Museo Andrés A Cáceres** ① *Jr 28 de Julio 508, T066-812360, Mon-Sat 0900-1300, 1400-1800. US$1.25*. The museum has a collection of baroque paintings and colonial furniture, some republican and contemporary art, and exhibits on Mariscal Cáceres' battles in the War of the Pacific.

Further south still, on a pretty plazuela, is **Santa Teresa** ① *28 de Julio, block 6, open daily for Mass 1600*, with its monastery dating from 1683. It has magnificent gold-leafed altars, heavily brocaded and carved in the churrigueresque style. Opposite is tiny **San Cristóbal** ① *Jr 28 de Julio, block 6, rarely open*, with its single tower. This was the first church to be founded in the city (1540) and is one of the oldest in South America.

Back near the centre, the 16th-century church of **La Merced** ① *2 de Mayo, open for Mass*, is the second oldest in the city. The high choir is a good example of the simplicity of the churches of the early period of the Viceroyalty.

Barrio Santa Ana

For a fascinating insight into Inca and pre-Inca art and culture, a visit to Barrio Santa Ana is a must. Here, about 200 families have workshops making *artesanías*: textiles, *retablos*, ceramics and work in stone. Their work is distributed through many galleries; **Galería de Arte Latina** ① *Plazuela de Santa Ana 105, T066-528315, wari39@hotmail.com*, is recommended. The owner, Alejandro Gallardo Llacctahuamán, and his son are very friendly and have information on weaving techniques and the preservation of their culture. They plan to open a textile museum soon and work with local communities and orphans. Also visit **Wari Art Gallery** ① *Jr Mcal Cáceres 302, Santa Ana, T066-312529*, run by Gregorio Sulca and his family, who will explain the Quechua legends, weaving and iconography. Next door is the Sulcas' **Instituto de Cultura Quechua**, which affords wonderful views of the city and surrounding hills from its roof. The Gallardos and Sulcas are renowned internationally. A knowledge of Spanish will help appreciate the galleries.

Huari

A good road going 22 km north from Ayacucho leads to **Huari** ① *daily 0800-1700, US$0.90*, frequently spelt Wari, dating from the 'Middle Horizon' (AD 600-1000), when the Huari culture spread across most of Peru. This was the first urban walled centre in the Andes and was used for political, administrative, ceremonial and residential purposes. The huge irregular stone walls are up to 4 m high (although many are long and low) and rectangular houses and streets can be made out. There are large areas of flat stone, which may have been for religious purposes, and there are tomb complexes and subterranean canals and tunnels.

The most important activity here was artistic production. High temperature ovens were used to mass produce ceramics of many different colours. The Huari also worked with gold, silver, metal and alloys such as bronze, which was used for weapons and decorative objects. The ruins now lie in an extensive tuna cactus forest. There is a small museum at the site, but the few explanations are only in Spanish. Tombs of the Huari nobles are being excavated along the road from Ayacucho to Quinua.

Quinua → *Colour map 2, C4.*

This village, 37 km northeast of Ayacucho, has a charming cobbled main plaza and many of the buildings have been restored. There is a small market on Sunday. Nearby, on the Pampa de Quinua, a huge obelisk commemorates the battle of Ayacucho. The obelisk is 44 m high, representing 44 years of struggle for independence.

The village's handicrafts are recommended, especially ceramics, which range from model churches and nativity figures to humorous groups of musicians and gossiping women. The rich red local clay is modelled mainly by hand and decorated with local mineral earth colours. Traditionally, the model churches are set on the roofs of newly occupied houses to ward off evil spirits. Virtually every roof in the village has a church on it – including the church itself. **San Pedro Ceramics**, at the foot of the hill leading to the monument, and **Mamerto Sánchez**, Jr Sucre, are good places to find typical pieces.

Ayacucho to Cuzco → *Colour map 2, C3/4.*

About 261 km from Ayacucho, in a fertile, temperate valley of lush meadows, cornfields and groves of eucalyptus, alder and willow, stands **Andahuaylas** (2980 m). There is a good Sunday market, various places to eat and sleep and the surrounding scenery is beautiful. Nestled between mountains in the upper reaches of a glacial valley at 2378 m, the friendly town of **Abancay** is first glimpsed after about two hours on the bus from Andahuaylas. The last few kilometres are on the paved highway from Nazca, a relief after the rough, tortuous descent from the high sierra. The town is a functional, commercial centre, growing in importance now that the paved Lima–Nazca–Cuzco road passes through. It also hopes to benefit from the tourist trade to Choquequirao (see page 195); there is much investment in building hotels and generally improving the town. For information visit the **tourist office** ⓘ *Lima 206, T083-321664, open 0800-1430,* or **Dircetur** ⓘ *Av Arenas 121, p 1, T083-321664.*

One hour out of Abancay, at a place called **Carbonera**, a road to the left goes to **Huanipaca** (40 minutes, US$15.15 in car, lodging available, and guides). It continues to Ccenhualla, from where Choquequirao, is visible. You descend 1½ hours to **Hacienda San Ignacio** by the Río Apurímac, then climb 14 hours up to **Choquequirao** (much steeper than the Cachora route). Shortly after Carbonera is the turn to Cachora.

Three kilometres from the main road to Cuzco, at 3000 m, is the **Saywite stone** ⓘ *Km 49 from Abancay, well-signed, allow 1-2 hrs, US$3.* This large carved rock and its surroundings is a UNESCO World Heritage Site. The principal monolith is said to represent the three regions of jungle, sierra and coast, with the associated animals and Inca sacred sites of each. The holes around the perimeter suggest that it was covered in gold. It is said to have been defaced when a cast was made, breaking off many of the animals' heads; ask the guardian for a closer look. Six main areas spread away from the stone and its neighbouring group of buildings. Look out for a staircase beside an elegant watercourse of channels and pools; a group of buildings around a stone (split by lightning), called the Casa de Piedra (or Rumi Huasi), an *usnu* platform and another monolith, called the Intihuatana.

About 20 minutes from Saywite is **Curahuasi** (126 km from Cuzco), famous for its aromatic anise herb, which has several roadside restaurants and *hospedajes*. A good two-hour walk takes you up Cerro San Cristóbal to **Capitán Rumi**, a huge rock overlooking the Apurímac canyon. The views are staggering, particularly if Salkantay and its snowy neighbours are free of cloud. Ask for directions, especially at the start.

● Sleeping

Ayacucho *p189, map p190*
B **Ayacucho Hotel Plaza**, 9 de Diciembre 184, T066-312202, hplaza@derrama.org.pe. Lovely colonial building but the rooms don't match up to the splendour of the reception. Some rooms overlook the plaza, comfortable, TV.
D **Marcos**, 9 de Diciembre 143, T066-316867. A comfortable, modern hotel in a cul-de-sac ½ block from the Plaza. It's quiet, clean and rooms have bath, hot water and TV. The price includes breakfast in the cafetería.
D **Santa Rosa**, Jr Lima 166, T066-314614, www.hotel-santarosa.com. Beautiful colonial courtyard in the Casona Gutiérrez (1630); the Monja Alferez lived here for a while. It served as the press HQ during the terrorist years. There is a roof terrace. Rooms are very clean and warm, hot water all day, friendly, attentive staff, car parking, good restaurant.
E **Hostal El Marqués de Valdelirios**, Alameda Bolognesi 720, T066-318944. Go through the arch below Santa Teresa to the broad Alameda for this colonial-style mansion, beautifully furnished, with blue flower pots, pickup from the airport for US$3, reserve 24 hrs ahead. Price includes breakfast, hot water, bar.
E **Hostal Tres Máscaras**, Jr 3 Máscaras 194, T066-314107, hoteltresmascaras@yahoo. com. New rooms with bath are better, but with less character, than the old ones, some of which have shared bathroom (F), in this nice colonial building, which has a deep red patio with plants and caged parrots. Clean, basic rooms, hot water, breakfast extra, car park.
E **San Francisco**, Jr Callao 290, T066-312353, www.sanfranciscohotel.cjb.net. Rather like an old museum with a nice patio, this is a friendly hotel and a popular choice. Breakfast is extra (US$1), hot water, TV, comfortable rooms and some suites. Recommended.
E-F **Florida**, Jr Cuzco 310, T066-312565, F316029. Small and pleasant: a leafy courtyard leads to a modern block with clean, quiet rooms with bath and TV, electric showers.
F **Hospedaje El Centro**, Av Cáceres 1048, T066-313556. Rooms without bath and TV

are G, large rooms, hot water, very clean, good value, but on a busy avenue.
F **Grau**, Jr San Juan de Dios 192, T066-312695. On the 3rd floor, by the markets. With bath (G without, but with TV), hot water in all bathrooms, clean, clothes washing facilities and laundry service, good value, safe, friendly, noisy, breakfast extra.
G **Hostal San Blas**, Jr Chorro 167, T066-312712. Special tourist price, good value, nice rooms with bath (cheaper without), hot water all day, clean, friendly, kitchen facilities and laundry service, cheap meals available, bicycles to lend, tourist information.
G **La Crillonesa**, El Nazareno 165, T066-312350, hotelcrillonesa@hotmail.com. A big blue and white building just up from Santa Clara and the market, with colourful, locally made decorations and excellent services. The price, set specially for tourists, includes bath, hot water in the basins as well as the shower, 1-hour free internet, kitchen and laundry facilities, discount for longer stay, great views from roof terrace. English and Italian spoken, clean, friendly, lots of tourist information. Carlos will act as a local tour guide and knows everyone.
G **La Posada de Santa Inés**, Jr Chorro 139, T066-319544, posada_staines@hotmail.com. Opposite Mercado 12 de Abril, with bath, hot water morning and evening, TV, terrace with small swimming pool (ask in advance for it to be cleaned), clean, very good value.

Ayacucho to Cuzco *p192*
Abancay
C-D **Turistas**, Av Díaz Bárcenas 500, T083-321017, hotursa@terra.com.pe. With bathroom, breakfast included. The original building is in colonial style, rooms (D) a bit gloomy, breakfast not included. Newer rooms on top floor (best) and in new block (C), including breakfast. Good restaurant (♥♥), enjoy a pisco sour over a game of billiards in the wood panelled bar. Internet (US$0.60 per hour), parking space.

E Imperial, Díaz Bárcenas 517, T083-321538. Rooms are around the central parking space in this hospitable, efficient and spotless hotel. Rooms have great beds, TV and hot water (also in the shared bathrooms). The price of rooms without bath does not include breakfast. Helpful and good value.

● Eating

Ayacucho p189, map p190
Those wishing to try cuy should do so in Ayacucho as it's a lot cheaper than Cuzco. Also try mondongo, a soup made from intestines, maize and mint. Many restaurants include this and puca picante (beef in a thick spicy sauce, rather like Indian curry) on their Fri lunch menu. You can also find mondongo at the central market in the Sección Comidas in the main building, or at Pasajes 2 and 3 outside; make sure the food is piping hot.

For a cheap, healthy breakfast try maca, a drink of maca tuber, apple and quinoa. It is sold opposite **Santa Clara** 0600-0800. There are countless small, unnamed eateries in the centre. Few vegetarian options, so if required, buy food in the market and prepare it yourself in hostales such as **La Crillonesa** or **San Blas**.

♥♥ Tradición, San Martín 406. A popular place for local food, also has a good cheap menú.

♥♥ Urpicha, Jr Londres 272. Recommended for typical food. The dish called urpicha includes something of everything.

♥♥-♥ La Casona, Jr Bellido 463, open 1200-2200. Dining under the arches and in dining room, regional specialities, try puca picante and cuy, and a wide menu. Recommended for food, service and cleanliness.

♥♥-♥ Nino, Jr 9 de Diciembre 205, on small plaza opposite **Santo Domingo** church, T066-814537. Open Sun evening, very nice dining rooms with pleasant decor, terrace and garden (look for the owls in the trees); chicken, pastas and pizzas, including take-away, friendly.

♥ Brasa Roja, Jr Cuzco block 1. Relatively upmarket chicken place with food cooked a la leña, salads, very good.

♥ Cabo Blanco, Av Maravillas 198, close to **Shosaku Nagase** market. Ceviches, seafood and fish, small, with friendly personal service.

♥ Café Dorado, Jr Asamblea 310. Excellent value set menu and chicken dishes in a long, cavernous dining room, mirrors and wood oven.

♥ Chifa Hua Lin, Asamblea 257. Very popular Chinese, said to be the best in town.

♥ Mía Pizza, San Martín 420-424. For pizzas, pastas and karaoke (also has a bar to get you in the mood for singing).

Ayacucho to Cuzco p192
Abancay
♥ Focarela Pizzería, Díaz Bárcenas 521, T083-322036. Simple but pleasant decor, fresh pizza from a wood-burning oven, popular.

♥ Pizzería Napolitana, Diaz Barcenas 208. Wood-fired clay oven and lots of toppings.

● Festivals and events

Ayacucho p189, map p190
This area is well known for its festivals. Almost every day there is a celebration in the area.
6 Jan Bajada de Reyes, when people pay to take gifts from an adorned Baby Jesus.
Feb and Mar Festival Internacional de la Tuna y Cochinilla (date varies, lasts for 15 days), for real 'dye' hards.
Feb/Mar Carnival has a respectable side and a riotous side, the comparas urbanas and the comparsas rurales; ask Carlos at Hotel La Crillonesa about taking part.
Mar/Apr Ayacucho is famous for its **Semana Santa** which begins on the **Fri before Holy Week**. There once one of the world's finest Holy Week celebrations, with candle-lit nightly processions, floral 'paintings' on the streets, daily fairs, horse races and contests among peoples from all over central Peru. All hotels are booked for months in advance. Many people offer beds in their homes during the week. Look out for notices doors.
30 Aug One of the main festivals in **Barrio Santa Ana**, with processions and bull running in the plaza.

● Shopping

Ayacucho p189, map p190
Ayacucho is a good place to buy local crafts including filigree silver, which often uses mudéjar patterns. Also look out for little painted altars which show the nativity scene, carvings in local alabaster, harps, or the pre-Inca tradition of carving dried gourds. The most famous goods are carpets and retablos. In both weaving and retablos, scenes of recent political strife have been added to more

traditional motifs. Even the newspaper stands on the Plaza, along with the Coca Cola emblems, are painted like *retablos*. For carpets, go to Barrio Santa Ana, page 191.

Centro Turístico Cultural San Cristóbal, Jr 28 de Julio 178. Complex with a quiet courtyard, art galleries, shops and restaurants.

Familia Pizarro, Jr San Cristóbal 215, Barrio Belén. Good-quality textiles, masks for Carnaval and *piedra de huamanga* (alabaster).

Shosaku Nagase, Mercado Artesanal y Centro de Capacitación, on Jr Quinua. Some of the same goods can be found in the **Mercado Carlos Vivanco** (see Sights, above).

▲ Activities and tours

Ayacucho *p189, map p190*
Tours to Vilcashuamán with agencies include Intihuatana, full day US$13, but they only run with 8 passengers. Trips to Huari, Quinua village and the battlefield with travel agencies, US$7.55 pp, minimum 4 people.
Adán Castillo Rivera, T066-315789, T970 1746 (mob), castilla68@hotmail.com. An archaeologist who guides tours to local sites and the city, very knowledgeable.
Orlando Román, T066-960-1982, orlandoyabish@starmedia.com. English-speaking guide, also gives Spanish classes (at **La Crillonesa** if you wish), reliable.
Urpillay Tours, Portal Independencia 62, T066-315074, urpillaytours@terra.com. All local tours and flight tickets.
Wari Tours, Portal Independencia 70, T066-311415. Local tours. Also handles Ormeño bus tickets and Western Union.
Warpa Picchu, Portal Independencia 66, T066-315191. Tours with an ecotourism angle.
Willy Tours, Jr 9 de Diciembre 107, T066-314075. Personal guide, flight/bus tickets.

Ayacucho to Cuzco *p192*
Abancay
Tours from US$28, depending on numbers.
Apurimak Tours, at **Hotel Turistas**, see Sleeping. Run local tours and 1- and 2-day trips to Santuario Nacional de Ampay: 1-day, 7 hrs, US$40 pp for 1-2 people (cheaper for more people). Also 3-day trip to Choquequirao including transport, guide, horses, tents and food, bring sleeping-bag, US$60 pp.
Carlos Valer, guide in Abancay – ask for him at **Hotel Turistas** – very knowledgeable.

⊖ Transport

Ayacucho *p189, map p190*
Air To **Lima**, with **Aero Cóndor**, Tue, Thu, Sun, 55 mins, via **Andahuaylas**, 30 mins. **LC Busre** daily from **Lima**.
   Airline offices Aero Cóndor, 9 de Diciembre 123, T066-313060, daily 0900-2100. LC Busre, Jr Lima 178, T066-316012. Most travel agents also sell tickets.

Bus
Local *Combis* to **Vilcashuamán** run from Av Ramón Castilla, daily 0400-1500 when full, 4 hrs, US$3. From Vilcashuamán to **Vischongo** costs US$0.45. The return journey from Vischongo to Ayacucho takes 4 hrs, US$2.70. *Combis* to **Huari**, 40 mins, US$0.75, and **Quinua**, a further 25 mins (US$0.50, US$1 from Ayacucho) leave from Paradero below the Ovalo de la Magdalena, at the corner of Jr Ciro Alegría and Jr Salvador Cavero, when full from 0700. Ask the driver to go all the way to the Obelisco in Quinua for an extra 50 ¢, then walk back to town. *Combis* and cars to **Huanta** leave from the same place, US$1.35.
Long-distance To **Lima**, 9-10 hrs, via **Ica** (7 hrs). For **Pisco**, 332 km, you have to take a Ica/Lima bus and get out at San Clemente, 10 mins from Pisco, and take a bus or *combi* (same fare to San Clemente as for Ica). Companies include **Wari**, Pasaje Cáceres 177, US$5.15, and **ReyBus**, Pasaje Cáceres 166 (opposite **Wari**), US$5.80. More expensive are **Cruz del Sur**, Av Mcal Cáceres 1264, US$15.15 to Lima, **Libertadores**, Tres Máscaras 493, and **Ormeño**, Jr Libertad 257, (ticket office at Asamblea 354), US$7.55 to Lima at 0730 and US$12 at 2030, meal stops, US$6.65 to San Clemente for Pisco; also to Ica at 2100, 7 hrs, US$7.55. **Following the August 2007 earthquake, there may be disruption to these services.**
   To **Huancayo**, 319 km, 9-10 hrs, US$6.65-7.55, with **Molina**, Jr 9 de Diciembre 458, T066-312984, 3 a day. The road is paved as far as **Huanta**, thereafter it is rough, especially in the wet season, but the views are breathtaking.
   For **Huancavelica**, take an **Ormeño** 0730 bus as far as **Rumichaca**, US$2, where *combis* wait at 1030 for Huancavelica, 4 hrs.
   To **Andahuaylas**, 261 km, 10-11 hrs (more in the rainy season), the road is unpaved but good when dry. Daytime buses stop for lunch

South Central Peru Ayacucho & around Listings

at **Chumbes** (4½ hrs). Departures are **Wari** at 0400, **ReyBus** at 1830 (not Sun), and **Los Chankas**, at 0630 and 1900, all US$6.

Although you still have to change buses in Andahuaylas, **Los Chankas'** 1900 service has a direct connection (no waiting) through to **Cuzco**, US$12. To get to **Abancay**, a further 138 km, 5 hrs, you must change buses and then go on to Cuzco, a further 195 km, 5 hrs. It takes 24 hrs to Cuzco. Road conditions are quite good, but landslides are common in the wet season. The scenery is stunning.

Ayacucho to Cuzco *p192*
Ayacucho to Andahuaylas
All buses on the **Lima–Nazca–Cuzco** route pass through Abancay at about midnight. Abancay–Lima bus companies such as **Wari** reserve a few seats for **Nazca**, 464 km, US$7.50, if you wish to break the journey. The journey to **Cuzco** takes 4½ hrs, US$3.65. The scenery is dramatic, especially as it descends into the Apurímac Valley. The road is paved and in good condition. (From Cuzco, after the pass it takes 1 hr to zig-zag down to Abancay.)

Buses to **Cachora** (for Choquequirao) depart from the terminal at Jr Prado Alto,

between Huancavelica and Núñez (5 blocks uphill from Díaz Bárcenas; it's not the first Jr Prado you come to), daily 0500 and 1400, 2 hrs, US$1.50. Cars from Curahuasi terminal on Av Arenas, next to the Wari office, US$10.

⊙ Directory

Ayacucho *p189, map p190*
Banks BCP, Portal Unión 28. Interbank, opposite Hotel Ayacucho, Jr 9 de Diciembre 183. Many street changers and *casas de cambio* at Portal Constitución Nos 2, 3 and 5 on the plaza; good rates for cash. **Internet** Many in the centre, US$0.60 per hr, some charge US$0.90 at night. **Post office** Asamblea 293. **Telephone** Many phone offices in the centre. **Useful addresses** Tourist Police at 2 de Mayo y Arequipa.

Ayacucho to Cuzco *p192*
Abancay
Banks BCP, Jr Arequipa 218, has ATM. Several *cambios* on Jr Arequipa, opposite Mercado Central. **Internet** The town is full of internet places. Some have phone cabins. **Post office** Junín y Arequipa.

Nazca and around

→ *Colour map 2, C3. Phone code: 056. Population: 21,100. Altitude: 598 m.*
Set in a green valley surrounded by mountains, Nazca would be just like any other anonymous desert oasis (the sun blazes for much of the year by day and the nights are crisp) were it not for the 'discovery' of a series of strange lines etched on the plains to the north. Tourists in their thousands now flock to the town to fly over the famous Nazca Lines, whose precise purpose still remains a mystery. Overlooking the town, 10 km southeast, is Cerro Blanco (2078 m), the highest sand dune in the world; it's popular for sandboarding and paragliding. Fortunately, the Nazca Lines were not damaged by the 2007 earthquake. ▶ *For Sleeping, Eating and other listings, see pages 199-202.*

Ins and outs
Getting there and around There is no central bus station in Nazca, but offices are at the western end of town, close to the Panamericana Sur after it has crossed the Río Tierras Blancas. Most of the hotels are on Jirón Lima and around the Plaza de Armas, within easy walking distance of the bus stations. A taxi to the airport for sightseeing flights costs US$1.35; bus, US$0.10. Do not pay attention to people selling tours or hotel rooms on the street, especially near bus stations; head straight to a hotel and find an official agency to handle your flights and tours. Taxi drivers usually act as guides, but most speak only Spanish. It is not dangerous to visit the outlying sites with a trustworthy person but do not take just any taxi on the plaza, as they are unreliable and can lead to robbery. Taxis charge from US $4-6 per hour to wait for you at the sites and bring you back to the city. ▶ *see Activities and tours, page 201, and Transport, page 202.*

As most of Nazca's attractions lie on the outskirts, the town itself is quite functional. The large **Museo Antonini** ⓘ *Av de la Cultura 600, eastern end of Jr Lima, ring the bell, T056-523444, cahuachi@terra.com.pe, daily 0900-1900, US$3 including local guide, US$1.50 to use a camera*, is worth a visit for a perspective on the area. It is a 10-minute walk from the plaza, or a short taxi ride. It houses the discoveries of Professor Orefici and his team from the huge pre-Inca city at Cahuachi (see page 199), which, Orefici believes, holds the key to the Nazca Lines. Many tombs survived the *huaqueros* and there are displays of mummies, ceramics, textiles, amazing *antaras* (panpipes) and photos of the excavations and the Lines. Recommended.

The **Maria Reiche Planetarium** ⓘ *Hotel Nasca Lines, T056-522293, shows at 1900 and 2100, US$6*, was opened in May 2000 in honour of the German expert who dedicated her life to uncovering and studying the lines. She died in 1998, aged 95. Stimulating lectures are given every night, based on Reiche's theories, which cover archaeology and astronomy. The show lasts about 45 minutes (commentary in English), after which visitors are able to look at the moon, planets and stars through sophisticated telescopes.

Nazca Lines

Cut into the stony desert are large numbers of lines, not only parallels and geometrical figures, but also a killer whale, a monkey, birds (one with a wing span of over 100 m), a spider and a tree. The lines, which can best be appreciated from the air, are above the Ingenio valley on the Pampa de San José, about 22 km north of Nazca, and across the Ingenio river, on the plain around Palpa. The Pan-American Highway passes close to, even through, the Lines.

Viewing and understanding the Nazca Lines
In 1976 Maria Reiche had a 12-m **Mirador** put up at her own expense, 17 km north of Nazca. From here three of the huge designs can be seen – the Hands, the Lizard and the Tree, although some travellers suggest the view from the hill 500 m back to Nazca

Nazca

Sleeping 🛏
Casa Andina 17
Hostal Alegría 4
Hostal Internacional 7
Hostal Las Líneas 5
Hotel Alegría 1
Maison Suisse 8
Majoro 2

Mirador 9
Nasca 10
Nasca Lines 11
Nido del Cóndor 12
Paredones Inn 3
Posada Guadalupe 13
Sol de Nasca 15
Walk On Inn 16

Eating 🍴
Chifa Guang Zhou 2
Concordia 3
El Portón 1
El Puquio 4
Kañada 6
La Carreta 13
La Choza 15

La Púa 7
La Taberna 8
Los Angeles 9
Picante's 14
Plaza Mayor 12
Rico Pollo 10

Drawing conclusions from the lines

Since the Nazca Lines were first spotted from the air 70 years ago, their meaning, function and origin have tormented scientists around the world. The greatest contribution to our awareness of the lines is that of Maria Reiche, who lived and worked on the *pampa* (plain) for over 50 years. Her meticulous measurement and study of the lines led her to the conclusion that they represented a huge astronomical calendar that not only recorded celestial events but also had a practical day-to-day function such as indicating the times for harvest, fishing and festivals. Maria Reiche died in June 1998.

There are many competing theories as to the function of the Nazca lines. One of the most far-fetched was that of Erich Von Daniken, who believed that the lines were an extraterrestrial landing strip. This idea, however, only succeeded in drawing to the site thousands of sci-fi freaks who tore across the lines on motorbikes, four-wheel drives, horses and whatever else they could get their hands on, leaving an indelible mark.

The most recent theory regarding the true purpose of the Nazca lines is results of six years' work by Peruvian archaeologist Johny Isla and Markus Reindel of the Swiss-Liechtenstein Foundation. It ties together some of the earlier ideas and discredits both the astronomical calendar and extraterrestrial theories. They have deduced that the lines on the Nazca plains are offerings dedicated to the worship of water and fertility. These two elements were vital to the coastal people in this arid environment and they expressed their adoration not only in the desert, but also on their ceramics and on the engraved stones of the Paracas culture. This new research proposes the theory that the Nazca culture succumbed not to drought, but to heavy rainfall, probably during an El Niño event.

is better. The Mirador is included on some arranged tours but enquire with your agency to be sure. If you're travelling independently, go early as the site gets very hot; better still, take a taxi (US$4-6 per hour) and arrive at 0745 before the tour buses; make sure it will wait for you and take you back.

In January 1994 Maria Reiche also opened a small **museum** ① *5 km from Nazca, Km 416, US$1; take micro from in front of Ormeño terminal, US$0.70.* Viktoria Nikitzhi, a colleague of Maria Reiche, gives one-hour lectures about the Nazca Lines at **Dr Maria Reiche Center** ① *Av de los Espinales 300, 1 block from Ormeño bus stop, T056- 969 9419, viktorianikitzki@hotmail.com.* She also organizes tours in June and December to see the sun at the solstice striking the Lines (phone in advance to confirm times) and has many original documents and objects; see also the Planetarium, page 197. ▶▶ For details of aerial tours over the Lines, see Activities and tours, page 201.

Around Nazca ⊕ ▶▶ p201.

Palpa → *Population: 15,000.*
Known as the 'Capital de la Naranja' (the Capital of Oranges), Palpa is a hospitable town 43 km northwest of Nazca, 97 km south of Ica. The climate is hot and dry (average annual temperature 21.4°C). On the Plaza de Armas is the **Municipal Museum** ① *daily 0900-1700, free,* which contains aerial photos of the area, models and ceramics. Information is displayed in English and Spanish.

On the desert near Palpa there are drawings similar to those found at Nazca: a sun dial, the Reloj Solar, measuring 150 m, a whale (35 m), a pelican (45 m), the so-called

Familia Real, a man, woman and child (30 m tall) and another 1000 or so lines and figures. Two Nazca culture centres have been excavated at **La Muña**, which has the largest Nazca tombs, and **Los Molinos**. Ceramics, necklaces, spondylus sea shells and gold objects have been found, despite earlier sacking by grave robbers. Los Molinos is a monumental complex where more burials have been uncovered. For information, visit the Consejo Municipal in Palpa or ask tour agencies in Nazca, see page 201.

Cemeteries and other sites

The Nazca area is dotted with over 100 cemeteries and the dry, humidity-free climate has preserved perfectly invaluable tapestries, cloth and mummies. A good cemetery, with mummies still to be seen, is in the valley of **Jumana**, one hour west of Nazca in the river bed. Gold mining is one of the main local industries and a cemetery tour usually includes a visit to a small family processing shop where old-fashioned techniques are still used. Some tours also include a visit to the studio of local potter, Señor Andrés Calle Benavides, who makes Nazca reproductions. He is very friendly and takes time to explain the techniques he uses, although his small gallery is a bit on the expensive side. Anyone interested in pre-Columbian ceramics is welcome to make an appointment to visit him independently. He is very knowledgeable on the coastal desert cultures.

West of the Nazca Lines, **Cahuachi** comprises some 30 pyramids and is believed to have been a sacred centre for the exclusive use of artists and priests whose symbols were given expression in the lines on the desert. A site called 'El Estaquería', with a series of wooden pillars, is thought to have been a place of mummification, where dead bodies were dried. Tours of the ruins of Cahuachi cost US$10 per person, minimum two people; some include a visit to the **Museo Antonini** (see page 197).

The ruins of **Paredones** ① *just east of Nazca on the Puquio road, US$3, ticket also includes Acueducto Ocongalla, Cantalloc, El Telar and Las Agujas, taxi US$10 round-trip or tour US$10 per person*, also called Cacsamarca, are Inca on a pre-Inca base. They are not well-preserved but the cool, underground aqueducts, or *puquios*, built 300 BC to AD 700, still provide water for the local people: 33 aqueducts irrigate 20 ha each and, to this day, local farmers have the job of cleaning the section for which their group has been responsible for as long as they can remember. The aqueducts are beautifully built and even have S-bends to slow down the flow of water.

Up to one hour on foot from Paredones, through Buena Fe, are markings on the valley floor at **Cantalloc**. These consist of a triangle pointing to a hill and a *tela* (cloth) with a spiral depicting the threads; climb the mountain to see better examples. There are also aqueducts here. Visits to Catalloc are best done with a guide, or by car. A round-trip by taxi (with a wait at the site) will cost US$7; arranged tours cost US$10 per person, minimum two people.

Some 30 km south of Nazca on the Panamericana Sur, then a further 12 km left off the highway (unsigned) is the cemetery site of **Chauchilla**. Grave-robbing *huaqueros* have ransacked the tombs and left remains all over the place: bones, skulls, mummies and pottery shards litter the desert. A tour is worthwhile and takes about two hours. It should cost about US$10 per person, plus the cost of entrance to the cemetery, with a minimum of two people. The area has been cordoned off and has clean bathrooms.

◉ Sleeping

Nazca *p197, map p197*

When arriving by bus you may be told your hotel is closed or full. Find out for yourself.
AL-A Maison Suisse, opposite the airport, T05-522434, www.aeroica.net. Comfortable, safe car park, expensive restaurant, pool, suites with jacuzzi, shows video of Nazca Lines. Also has camping facilities. Ask for packages, including flights over Nazca Lines.
A Casa Andina, Jr Bolognesi 367, T056-523563, www.casa-andina.com. Part of chain of hotels, offering standardized services in distinctive style. Bright, modern decor, clean, a/c, pool, friendly staff, TV, internet, restaurant.

A **Nasca Lines**, Jr Bolognesi, T056-522293, reservanasca@derramajae.org.pe. Large remodelled hotel with a/c, comfortable, rooms with private patio, hot water, peaceful, price includes American breakfast, restaurant, expensive meals, safe car park, pool (US$4.50 for non-guests, or free if having lunch), they can arrange package tours which include 2-3 nights at the hotel plus a flight over the lines and a desert trip: enquire about the price.

B **Majoro**, Panamericana Sur Km 452, T056-522490, www.hotelmajoro.com. A charming old hacienda at Majoro about 5 km from town past the airstrip, beautiful gardens, pool, restaurant, quiet and homely, attentive service, arrangements for flights and tours.

B **Nido del Cóndor**, opposite the airport, Panamericana Sur Km 447, T056-522424, contanas@terra.com.pe. Large rooms, hot water, good restaurant, bar, shop, videos, swimming pool, camping US$3, parking, English, Italian German spoken, free pickup from town, reservation advised.

C-D **Hotel Alegría**, Jr Lima 166, T056-522702, www.nazcaperu.com. Continental breakfast and tax included. Rooms with bathroom, carpet and a/c, rooms with shared bath G pp, hot water, cafeteria, pool, garden, many languages spoken, laundry facilities, safe luggage deposit, book exchange, email US$2 per hr, very popular. Efraín Alegría also runs a tour agency (see page 201), flights and bus tickets arranged. Don't listen to anyone who says that Alegría is closed, or full, and no longer runs tours; if you phone or email the hotel they will pick you up at the bus station free of charge (1 hr free internet to those who email in advance).

D **Paredones Inn**, Jr Arica 115, T056-522181, paredoneshotel@terra.com. One block from the Plaza de Armas, nice, ample rooms with cable TV, clean bathrooms, modern, great views from rooftop terrace, laundry service, bar, suites with jacuzzi, helpful staff. Good.

E **Hostal Internacional**, Av Maria Reiche 112, T056-522744, hostalinternacional @hotmail.com. With bathroom, hot water, garage, café and very nice bungalows.

E **Hostal Las Líneas**, Jr Arica 299, T056-522488. Cheaper without bath, clean, spacious, restaurant, ask for a room away from the street.

E **Mirador**, Tacna 436, main plaza, T056-523121. Comfortable rooms with shower,

cheaper with shared bath, hot water, good breakfast, TV downstairs, modern, clean.

E **Nasca**, Calle Lima 438, T/F056-522085.
F without bathroom, hot water, noisy, clean, nice lawn area, new annex at the back, clothes washing facilities, luggage store, safe motorcycle parking.

F **Hostal Alegría**, Av Los Incas 117, opposite Ormeño bus terminal, T056-522497. More basic than Alegría (not related), F without bathroom, hot water, clean, nice gardens, hammocks, camping permitted, restaurant.

F **Posada Guadalupe**, San Martín 225, T056-522249. Family-run, basic rooms, G without bath, hot water, good breakfast, relaxing (touts who try to sell tours are nothing to do with hotel).

F **Sol de Nasca**, Callao 586, T056-522730. Rooms with and without hot showers, TV, also has a restaurant, pleasant, don't leave valuables in luggage store; tours booked here are expensive.

F **The WalkOn Inn**, JM Mejía 108, 3 blocks from Plaza de Armas, T/F056-522566, www.walkoninn.com. Rooms with bathroom, hot water, family feel, small swimming pool, TV room, excellent and cheap restaurant on top floor for breakfast and salads, very helpful staff, internet, luggage store, works with **Nasca Trails** for flights and tours, information given. Under new management

⦿ Eating

Nazca p197, map p197
There are many restaurants near the Plaza de Armas and along Bolognesi as well.

♥♥-♥ Concordia, Lima 594. Good, also rents bikes at US$1 an hr.

♥♥-♥ El Portón, Moresky 120, in front of **Hotel Nasca Lines**. A popular stopover with tours, and well worth the visit. Specializes in Peruvian food, has a great indoor/outdoor setting with wood decor.

♥♥-♥ El Puquio, Bolognesi 50 m from plaza. Good food, especially pastas, pleasant atmosphere, good for drinks, popular.

♥♥-♥ La Carreta, Bolognesi, next door to **Los Angeles**. New, look for *novo andino* dishes using traditional Andean ingredients, rustic, lively atmosphere, stage for live music. Good.

♥♥-♥ La Choza, Bolognesi 290. Nice atmosphere with woven chairs and thatched roof, all types of food, live music at night.

La Taberna, Jr Lima 321, T056-521411. Excellent food, live music, popular with gringos, it's worth a look just for the graffiti on the walls.

Plaza Mayor, on the Plaza. Specializes in barbecue of all types, roasted chicken, steaks, anticuchos and great salads. Large portions, nice staff. Highly recommended.

Chifa Guang Zhou, Bolognesi 297, T056-522036. Very good Peruvian/Chinese food.

Kañada, Lima 160, nazcanada@yahoo.com. Cheap *menú*, excellent *pisco sours*, nice wines, popular, display of local artists' work, email service, English spoken, owner Juan Carlos Fraola is very helpful.

La Púa, Jr Lima, next to **La Taberna**. Great espresso, also serves pizzas, pastas and sandwiches, good, courtesy *pisco sour*.

Los Angeles, Bolognesi 266. Good, cheap, try *sopa criolla*, and chocolate cake.

Rico Pollo opposite **Hotel Alegría**. Good local restaurant with great chicken dishes, cheap.

Picante's, Av Bolognesi 464. Delicious real coffee and cakes. Owner, Percy Pizzaro, is knowledgeable about the Nazca Lines.

✪ Festivals and events

Nazca *p197, map p197*
29 Aug-10 Sep Festival de la Virgen de la Guadelupe.

Palpa *p198*
Mar/Apr Fiesta de la Ciruela y Vendimia (plum and wine harvest festival).
30 Jul-17 Aug Fiesta de la Naranja is part of tourist week; 15 Aug is the main day.

✪ Shopping

Nazca *p197, map p197*
There is a market at Lima y Grau; the **Mercado Central** is between Arica and Tacna.

▲ Activities and tours

Nazca *p197, map p197*
All guides must be approved by the Ministry of Tourism and should have an official identity card. More and more touts (*jaladores*) operate at popular hotels and the bus terminals using false ID cards and fake hotel and tour brochures. They are all rip-off merchants who overcharge and mislead those who arrive by bus. Only conduct business with agencies at their office, or phone or email the company you want to deal with in advance. Some hotels are not above pressurizing guests to buy tours at inflated prices.

Aerial tours
Flights over the Nazca Lines last 30-40 mins and are controlled by air traffic personnel at the airport, just south of town. Small planes take 3-5 passengers. The price for a flight is US$40 per person. You also have to pay US$3 airport tax. It is best to organize and reserve a flight direct with the airlines at the airport rather then through an agency or tout. The companies listed below are well-established and recommended; there are others.

Flights are bumpy and many people are airsick, so it may be best avoid food and drink. Best times to fly are 0800-1000 and 1500-1630 when there is less turbulence and better light (assuming there is no fog, in which case chaos may ensue).

Aero Ica, in Jr Lima and at the airport, T01-446 3026 (Lima), www.aeroica.net. Make sure you clarify everything before getting on the plane and ask for a receipt. Also offers full-day packages from Ica and Lima with lunch at **Maison Suisse** plus flight over the lines, but book 48 hrs in advance.

Aerocóndor, based at Hostal Nido del Cóndor, Panamericana Sur Km 447, T056-521168, www.aerocondor.com.pe. They offer flights over the lines in a 1-day tour from Lima with lunch in Nazca.

Alas Peruanas, T056-522444, www.alasperuanas.com. (experienced pilots fluent in English). Often include other features in their 35-min flight over the Lines, such as the spiral ventilation holes of the aqueducts. Also 1-hr flights over the Palpa and Llipata areas (US$75 per person, minimum 3). All flights include the BBC film. Can be booked at **Hotel Alegría** (see Sleeping, page 200).

Tour operators
Air Nasca Travel, Jr Lima 185, T056-521027, guide Susi recommended. Very helpful and friendly, very competitive prices. Offers tours around Nazca, Ica, Paracas and Pisco.
Alegría Tours, Lima 168, T056-522444 (24 hrs), www.nazcaperu.com. Run by Efraín Alegría (see Sleeping, page 200). Inclusive

tours to Palpa, Puerto Inca, Sacaco and the San Fernando Reserve, also to Chauchilla, Cantalloc, Ica, Paracas and the Ballestas Islands. Often recommended. Guides with radio contact and maps can be provided for hikes to nearby sites. They have guides who speak many languages. Birdwatching in the high Andes, visits to Pampas Galeras vicuña reserve, the village of Andamarca and downhill mountain biking trips. Also sandboarding on Cerro Blanco. Alegría runs a bus from Nazca to Pisco daily 1000 (from Pisco's, Plaza de Armas), via Ica, Huacachina and *bodegas*. Bus and flight tickets can be arranged, as well as packages to other parts of Peru. Ask Efraín Alegría to arrange a taxi for you to one of the sites outside Nazca (eg US$50 to Sacaco, 30 mins at site).
Félix Quispe Sarmiento, El Nativo de Nazca, Fedeyogin5@hotmail.com. He has his own museum, **Hantun Nazca**, Panamericana Sur 447 and works with the Instituto Nacional de Cultura. Tours off the beaten track, can arrange flights, knowledgeable, ask for him at **Kañada** restaurant.
Fernández family, who run the **Hotel Nasca**, also run local tours. Ask for the hotel owners and speak to them direct. They will arrange taxis to outlying sites.
Jesús Erazo Buitrón, Juan Matta 1110, T056-523005. Very knowledgeable. He speaks a little English and his Spanish is easy to follow.
Nanasca Tours, Jr Lima 160, T/F056-522917, 962 2054 (mob), nanascatours@yahoo.com. Very helpful.
Nasca Trails, Bolognesi 550, T056-522858, nascatrails@terra.com.pe. Juan Tohalino Vera speaks English, French, German and Italian.

Transport

Nazca *p197, map p197*
Bus
Local To **Palpa**, *colectivos* leave when full, 20 mins, US$0.75. *Colectivos* to **Chala**, 2 hrs, daily in the morning, US$3.50 per person.
  Long distance To **Ica**, 2 hrs, US$1.50, 4 daily, with both **Ormeño** and **Flores**.
To **Pisco**, 210 km, with **Ormeño**, 3 daily, 3 hrs, US$5, also Royal Class via **Paracas**, 2¾ hrs, 1330, US$12. Note that all buses going north may be subject to changes following the August 2007 earthquake.

To **Lima** (446 km), 6 hrs, several buses and *colectivos* daily. Recommended companies include: **Ormeño**, T056-522058, Royal Class from Hotel Nasca Lines, Jr Bolognesi, at 0530 and 1330, US$21.50, normal service from Av Los Incas, 6 a day, US$12.50; **Civa**, Av Guardia Civil, T056-523019, normal service at 2300, US$6; **Cruz del Sur**, Av Guardia Civil 290, T056-523713, 4 daily, US$6 (Cruzero US$20). Note that **Ormeño's** Royal Class arrives in Santa Catalina, a much safer area of Lima.
  To **Arequipa**, 565 km, 9 hrs, with **Ormeño**, 1530, 2000, 2400, from Av Los Incas, US$10, or with Royal Class at 2100, US$20, 8 hrs; **Cruz del Sur** has 4 buses daily 1900-2400, US$10-US$27; **Civa**, at 1100, US$20, 8 hrs. Delays are possible out of Nazca because of drifting sand across the road or mudslides in the rainy season. Travel in daylight.
  To **Cuzco**, 659 km, 14 hrs, via **Chalhuanca** and **Abancay**, with **Expreso Wari**, 6 daily on the Lima–Nazca–Abancay–Cuzco route, normal US$17, or Imperial US$20 (bus may run if not enough passengers). Their offices are at the exit from Nazca on the road to Puquio. Nazca to **Puquio**, *combis*, 4 hrs, US$3, and *colectivos*, 3 hrs, US$4.50. Most depart, in both directions, in the early morning from the market. They will drop visitors off at the **Pampas Galeras** vicuña reserve en route, 2 hrs, US$1.50 by *combi*, or 1½ hrs, US$2.50 by *colectivo*. Also buses to Cuzco via Arequipa with **Ormeño**, US$27, and **Cruz del Sur**, 2015 Imperial and 2100 Ideal, US$27.

Directory

Nazca *p197, map p197*
Banks BCP, Lima y Grau, changes cash and Visa TCs at decent rates, also cash advance on Visa, Visa ATM. Some street changers will change TCs, but at 8% commission.
Hospital Callao entre Morsesky y Castillo. Open 24 hours. **Internet** Many places on Jr Bolognesi. Facilities at Hotel Alegría and Casa Andina. **Post office** Fermín de Castillo 379, T056-522016. Also at Hotel Alegría.
Police Av Los Incas, T056-522105, T105 emergencies. **Telephone** Telefónica for international calls with coins on Plaza Bolognesi. Also on Plaza de Armas and at Lima 359.

Ica to Lima

Before the earthquake of August 2007, the coast between Ica and Lima had much to offer the visitor, the wine bodegas at Ica, the oasis at Haucachina, the marine wildlife at the Paracas National Reserve and the Ballestas Islands and the beach resorts south of Lima. At the time of writing it was reported that the area from Cerro Azul, near Cañete, to Ocucaje, south of Ica, was seriously affected, but that services in Ica itself were soon back in operation. Also, the Panamerican Highway was reported open, despite heavy damage in parts. By the time the book is in use, things may well be getting back to normal (we hope so), but readers are encouraged to make local enquiries about what it is prudent to do and where to go. Contact i perú, T01-574 8000, for the latest information on the situation. ≫ *For Sleeping, Eating and other listings se page 204.*

Ica and Huacachina → *Colour map 2, C3. Phone code: 056. Altitude: 410 m*

Ica, 70 km southeast of Pisco, is Peru's chief wine centre and is famous for its *tejas*, a local sweet of *manjarblanco*. For information contact **Dircetur** ⓘ *Av Grau 148, T056-238710, ica@mincetur.gob.pe.* Ask here about which services are open. Some tourist information is available at travel agencies. The **Museo Regional** ⓘ *southwest of the centre, take bus 17 from the Plaza de Armas (US$0.50),* has mummies, ceramics, textiles and trepanned skulls from the Paracas, Nazca and Inca cultures; a good, well-displayed collection of Inca counting strings (*quipus*) and clothes made of feathers. Behind the building is a scale model of the Nazca lines with an observation tower; a useful orientation before visiting the lines. The kiosk outside sells copies of motifs from the ceramics and textiles. Also ask locally which wine bodegas are open to visitors. Among the best known are: **El Carmen**, **El Catador**, **Bodega Alvarez** and the **Ocucaje** winery, 30 km south of Ica. There is a wine harvest festival in early March.

About 5 km from Ica, round a palm-fringed lake and amid amazing sand dunes, is the oasis and summer resort of **Huacachina** ⓘ *take a taxi from Ica for under US$1,* an increasingly popular gringo spot to warm up after the Andes. Its green sulphur waters are said to be curative and thousands of visitors come to swim here. There are lots of eating places and bars with music around the lake. Sometimes the water and shore get dirty and polluted. **Sandboarding** on the dunes is a major pastime here; board hire US$1.50 per hour. **Note** For the inexperienced, sandboarding can be dangerous on the big dunes. **Dune buggies** also do white-knuckle, rollercoaster tours for US$12, or you can hire a buggy and scare yourself for US$6 per person for three to four hours.

Pisco to Cañete → *Colour map 2, C3.*

Pisco was christened San Clemente de Macera by the Spanish in 1640, but unofficially named after the famous local brandy, was the largest port between Callao and Matarani, 237 km south of Lima. The majority of buildings were destroyed in the earthquake.

Fifteen kilometres down the coast from Pisco is the bay of **Paracas** sheltered by the Paracas Peninsula. It is named after the Paracas winds – sandstorms that can last for three days, especially in August. The wind peaks at around 1500 every afternoon. The whole peninsula, a large area of coast to the south and the Ballestas Islands are part of the **Paracas National Reserve**, created in 1975, which covers a total of 335,000 ha on land and sea. It is one of the most important marine reserves in the world, with the highest concentration of marine birds. Reports in August 2007 indicate that the marine wildlife largely survived the earthquake, but the famous cliff formation, El Catedral, was destroyed. The **Ballestas Islands**, dubbed the poor man's Galápagos by many, are spectacular in their own right and well worth visiting. They are eroded into numerous arches and caves, hence their name – *ballesta* means bow, as in archery. These arches provide shelter for thousands of seabirds, some of which are very rare, and sea lions.

North of Pisco, **Chincha Alta** (Colour map 5, A2) was a fast-growing town, the heart of Peru's negro/criollo culture. Like Pisco, most of its buildings were destroyed in the earthquake.

⊜ Sleeping

Ica p203

A Las Dunas, Av La Angostura 400, T056-256224, www.lasdunashotel.com. Service not included, 20% cheaper on weekdays. Highly recommended, in a complete resort with restaurant, swimming pool, horse riding and other activities, it has its own airstrip for flights over Nazca, 50 mins.

D-E Hostal Siesta I, Independencia 160, T056-233249. Hot water, hospitable owner, noisy. Siesta II, T056-234633, similar.

E Princess, Urb Santa María D-103, T056-215421, www.geocities.com/hotel_princess. Taxi from plaza, small rooms, hot water, TV, pool, tourist information, helpful, peaceful, very good.

E-F Arameli, Tacna 239, T056-239107. A good choice, cable TV, 1 block from plaza, clean.

Huacachina p203

Don't be bullied by taxi drivers: insist on going to the hotel of your choice.

B Mossone is at the east end of the lake, T056-213660, reserva@derrama.org.pe. Elegant, hacienda-style, full board available, lovely patio, pool, bicycles and sandboards for guests' use. Recommended.

C Hostería Suiza, Malecón 264, T056-238762, hostesuiza@terra.com.pe. Overlooking lake, lovely grounds, quiet, includes breakfast, safe parking. Recommended.

F Casita de Arena, T056-215274, casadearena@hotmail.com. Basic rooms, **G** without bath, bar, small pool, laundry facilities, board hire, popular with backpackers, check your bill carefully, don't leave valuables unattended.

F Hostal Rocha, T222256. Hot water, **G** without bath, family run, kitchen and laundry facilities, board hire, small pool, popular with backpackers, but a bit run-down.

G Hostal del Barco, Balneario de Huacachina 180. A very relaxed place with hammocks on the front terrace, basic rooms, bar, use of kitchen, can arrange tours.

G Hostal Salvatierra, T056-232352. A grand old place being renovated, not on waterfront, charming, pool, relaxing courtyard, rents sandboards, good value.

G Hostal Titanic, T056-229003. Small rooms, pool and café, clothes washing, board hire, good value for lodging and set meals.

⑦ Eating

Ica p203

†† -† Chifa Karaoke Central, Urb Los Viñedos de Santa María E-25. Excellent Chinese.

†† -† El Otro Peñoncito, Bolívar 255. Set lunch (US$6) in a pleasant atmosphere, good toilets.

†† -† Las Brujas de Cachiche, Cajamarca 118. Serves local dishes.

†† -† Pizzería Venecia, Lima 252. Best pizzas in town.

▲ Activities and tours

Ica p203

Ica Desert Trip, icadeserttrip@yahoo.es. Roberto Penny Cabrera (speaks Spanish and English) offers 1- to 3-day trips off-road into the desert, archaeology, geology, etc. US$50 pp per day, 4 people maximum, contact by email in advance. Take toilet paper, warm clothes, a long-sleeved loose cotton shirt for daytime and long trousers. Recommended, but "not for the faint-hearted".

⊜ Transport

Ica p203

Bus All bus offices are on Lambayeque blocks 1 and 2 and Salaverry block 3. Beware of thieves when changing buses and around the Plaza de Armas. To **Lima**, 302 km, US$5-10, several daily including **Soyuz** (Av Manzanilla 130, every 8 mins 0600-2200), **Flores** and **Ormeño** (at Lambayeque 180). To **Nazca**, 140 km, several buses (US$1.50) and colectivos (US$3.75) daily, including Ormeño, Flores, 4 daily, and Cueva (José Elias y Huánuco), hourly on the hour 0600-2200. To **Arequipa** the route goes via Nazca.

Cordillera Blanca

‣ Footprint features

Introduction

The Cordillera Blanca is a region of jewelled lakes and sparkling white mountain peaks that attracts mountaineers, hikers, cyclists and rafters in their thousands. Here stand the highest mountains in South America, with some 30 snow-crested peaks of over 6000 m, including Huascarán, the highest mountain in Peru at 6768 m. From the region's main centre, Huaraz, several of these giants can be seen. This area contains the largest concentration of glaciers found in the world's tropical zone: a source of both beauty and danger.

The turquoise-coloured lakes (*cochas*) which form in the terminal moraines are the jewels of the Andes and you should hike up to at least one during your stay. Laguna Churup is a day's walk from Huaraz, Lago Parón is close to Caraz, while the beautiful twin lakes of Llanganuco are within easy reach of Yungay and are on the route of the long-distance Santa Cruz trek. The tranquility of these glacial lakes masks a frightening history. They have caused much death and destruction when dykes have broken, sending tons of water hurtling down the canyons, wiping out everything in their path. The levels of some have been artificially lowered for flood control and to feed the huge Cañón del Pato dam. Earthquakes, too, have scarred the high valleys and the mass grave which was once the old town of Yungay is a very humbling place.

Even the archaeologist is catered for here in the shape of the ruins of Chavín de Huantar. This fortress-temple belonged to one of the earliest and most influential cultures in pre-Inca Peru and it has some fine carvings and stonework.

Cordillera Blanca

★ **Don't miss …**

1 **Yungay** Besides its typical market on a Thursday, Yungay's *campo santo* is a poignant memorial to the devastating power of the mountains, page 220.

2 **Llanganuco lakes** Take time to study the bark of the *quenoal* trees, like shreds of the finest paper, against the blue of the water, page 221.

3 **Cañon del Pato** The bus ride through this spectacular narrow pass will keep the adrenaline pumping, page 222.

4 **Puya Raimondi** There are many plants in the mountains, but keep an eye out for these remarkable bromeliads with their century-long lifespan, page 223.

5 **Llanganuco to Santa Cruz trek** To visit the Cordillera Blanca without doing just one of the fantastic treks would be missing the point, page 223.

6 **Chavín de Huantar** Don't leave without visiting the 2500 year-old fortress temple; either take a tour, or hike three days from Olleros, page 224.

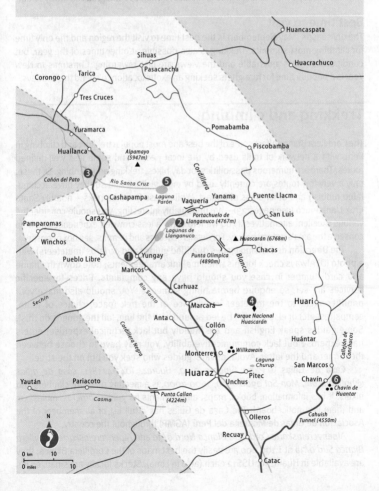

Cordillera Blanca

Ins and outs → *Colour map 2, B2.*

Getting there

There are three main routes to reach the Cordillera Blanca. The easiest is the paved road which branches east off the Pan-American Highway north of Pativilca, 187 km from Lima. The road goes via Chasquitambo, climbs to a pass at 4080 m and then passes Laguna Conococha. The road then descends to Catac and the junction of the road to Chavín; Huaraz is 36 km from Catac. Further north on the coast, a second route is via the Callán pass (4224 m) from Casma to Huaraz, a rough but beautiful trip through the heart of the Cordillera Negra. Few buses take this route, which is best done in daylight. The third alternative is from Chimbote to Caraz via the Cañón del Pato, also a very scenic journey, with magnificent views of this spectacular canyon.
➤ *For further details, see Transport, page 219.*

Getting around

In the Cordillera Blanca minibuses run between most of the towns on a regular basis, while more remote places have less frequent services. Several roads are being improved to cope with mining traffic. Of course, on some routes, you can always walk.

Best time to visit

The dry season (May-September) is the best time to visit the region and the only time for climbing most summits. Trekking is also possible at other times of the year, but conditions are less amenable and the views are less rewarding. Christmas to New Year is a popular time for foreigners seeking an exotic location to spend the holidays.

Trekking and climbing

The Cordillera Blanca offers some of the best and most popular trekking and climbing in Peru, with a network of trails used by the local people and some less well-defined routes. There are numerous possibilities for day hikes, trekking and climbing. Of these, only a very few routes are currently used by most visitors, and so they have accumulated rubbish and other signs of impact. While these favourite treks – notably Santa Cruz-Llanganuco (see page 223) – are undeniably interesting, you should consider the various excellent alternatives if you want to enjoy a less-crowded experience and help conserve the area's natural beauty. For details of access and permits, see box opposite.

The **Dirección de Turismo** issues qualified guides and *arrieros* (muleteers) with a photo ID. Always check for this when making arrangements; note down the name and card number in case you should have any complaints. Prices for specific services are set, so enquire before hiring someone. You should also make your priorities clear to the muleteer in advance of the trek (pace, choice of route, campsites, etc) or else you will be led around with the line, 'all the gringos do this'. Some guides speak English and are friendly but lack technical expertise; others have expertise but lack communicative ability. You may have to choose between the former and the latter. Avoid 'private' guides who seek you out on the street.

Casa de Guías ① *Plaza Ginebra 28-g, Huaraz, T043-421811, casa_de_guias @hotmail.com, Mon-Sat 0900-1300, 1600-2000,* is a meeting place for climbers and hikers. It has information, books, maps, arrangements for guides, *arrieros*, mules etc and there is a noticeboard. The Casa de Guías has a full list of all members of the **Asociación de Guías de Montaña del Perú (AGMP)** throughout the country.

Alpenvereinskarte Cordillera Blanca Nord 0/3a and *Alpenvereinskarte Cordillera Blanca Süd 0/3b* at 1:100,000 are easily the best maps of the Cordillera Blanca; they are available in Huaraz for US$12 each (also in Lima). Stocks locally are small, so it's

Huascarán National Park

Established in July 1975, the park encompasses the entire Cordillera Blanca above 4000 m. It covers a total area of 3400 sq km: 180 km from north to south and 20 km from east to west. It is a UNESCO World Biosphere Reserve and part of the World Heritage Trust. The park's objectives are to protect the unique flora, fauna, geology, archaeological sites and extraordinary scenic beauty of the Cordillera. Please make every attempt to help by taking all your rubbish away with you when camping; there have been numerous complaints that campsites are dirty and toilet pits foul.

Park administration is at Jirón Federico Sal y Rosas 555, by Plazuela Belén, Huaraz, T043-422086, open Monday-Friday 0830-1300, 1430-1700. Fees for visiting the national park are collected at rangers posts at **Quebrada Llanganuco** and **Huascarán** for the Llanganuco to Santa Cruz trek, at **Collón** on the way up the Quebrada Ishinca and at **Pitec**. It costs US$1.25 for a day visit. For visits of up to seven days (ie for trekking and climbing trips) a permit costing US$20 must be bought. If you stay longer than seven days, you will need another permit.

In September 2006 **INRENA** (the National Institute for Natural Resources, www.inrena.gob.pe) announced new regulations governing the national park. Similar to rules governing the Inca Trails at Machu Picchu, local guides will be mandatory for everywhere except designated 'Recreation Zones' (areas accessible by car) and climbers attempting difficult climbing routes will have to be accompanied by a local climbing guide. At the time of writing these regulations had not been instituted, nor the cost of permits announced, but anyone wishing to trek or climb independently should make enquiries before setting out.

best to get it before you arrive. **Instituto Geográfico Nacional** has mapped the area with its 1:100,000 topographical series. These are more useful to the mountaineer than hiker, however, since the trails marked are confusing and inaccurate. **South American Explorers** (see page 49) publishes a good map with additional notes on the popular Llanganuco to Santa Cruz loop.

The **Policía Nacional de Perú** ① *T043-393333, usam@pnp.gob.pe*, has a 35-member rescue team in Yungay, with 24-hour phone service and vhf/uhf radio dispatch.

Huaraz and around

→ *Colour map 2, B2. Phone code 043.*

The main town in the valley, with a population of 82,800, Huaraz is expanding rapidly as a major tourist centre but it is also a busy commercial hub, especially on market days (Monday and Thursday). The region is both a prime destination for hikers and international climbers, as well as a vacation haven for Peruvian urbanites seeking clean mountain air and a glimpse of the glaciers. School groups flock to the city from mid-September to mid-December. The city was half destroyed in the earthquake of May 1970 so don't expect red-tiled roofs or overhanging eaves. What the reconstructed city lacks in colonial charm, it makes up for with its spectacular setting at 3091 m between the mountains of the cordilleras Blanca and Negra. The peaks of Huamashraju, Churup, Rima Rima and Vallunaraju loom so close as to seem almost a part of the architecture while, in the distance, the giants Huascarán and Huandoy can be seen. ►► *For Sleeping, Eating and other listings, see pages 212-219.*

Getting there and around There is a new **airport** at Anta 21 km north of Huaraz. The bus offices are in the centre of town, conveniently close to many of the hotels and hostels. The city is small enough to get around by foot, providing sensible precautions are taken, especially at night (see below).

Related map
A Huaraz centre, page 213.

Huaraz

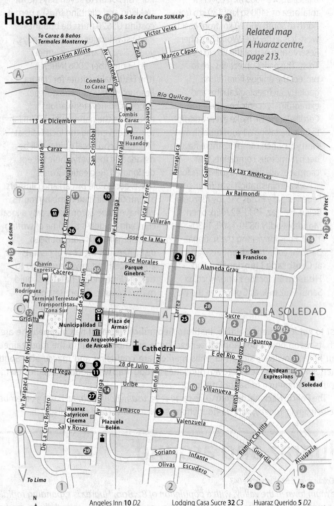

N

0 metres 100
0 yards 100

Sleeping
Albergue Churup **1** C3
Alojamiento El Jacal **2** C3
Alojamiento Marilia **4** C3
Alojamiento Nemy's **5** C3
Alojamiento Norma **6** D2
Alojamiento Soledad **7** C3
Andino Club **9** D3

Angeles Inn **10** D2
Apu Wasi **8** D3
Backpackers **11** B1
Casa de Jaimes **12** C1
Casa Jansy's **13** C2
Edward's Inn **15** B1
Hatun Wasi **16** A1
Hostal Colomba **18** A2
Hostal Estoico **20** C1
Hostal Quintana **26** C1
Jo's Place **29** A2
La Cabaña **30** C3
La Casa de Zarela **31** C3
Lazy Dog Inn **17** B3

Lodging Casa Sucre **32** C3
Lodging House Ezama **21** A3
Olaza Guesthouse **33** D3
San Sebastián **14** B3
Steel Guest House **22** D3
Way Inn Hostel **23** C3
Way Inn Lodge **24** B3

Eating
Bistro de los Andes **2** C2
Café El Centro **3** C1
Cafetería y Jugería **25** C2
California Café **6** C1
Fuente de Salud **4** B1

Huaraz Querido **5** D2
Las Puyas **7** B1
Pachamama **9** C1
Panadería La Alameda **26** B1
Panadería Montserrat **27** D1
Pepe's Place **10** B1
Pizza Bruno **11** D1
Siam de Los Andes **12** C2

Bars & clubs
Chacraraju/Chill-out **28** C2
Extreme **14** D1
La Cascada **29** D1

Tourist information i perú ⓘ *Luzuriaga, Plaza de Armas, T043-42 8812, iperuhuaraz @promperu.gob.pe, Mon-Sat 0800-1830, Sun 0800-1400.* On the second floor of same building, **Policía de Turismo** ⓘ *T043-421341, ext 315, Mon-Fri 0900-1300, 1600-1900, Sat 0900-1300*, is the place to report all crimes and mistreatment by tour operators, hotels. Huaraz has its share of crime, especially since the arrival of mining in the area and during the high tourist season. Take a taxi at night. On no account should women go to surrounding districts and sites alone. ▸▸ *For safety while trekking or climbing, see page 208.*

Sights

The **Plaza de Armas** has been rebuilt, with a towering white statue of Christ, and a new cathedral is being constructed. **Museo Arqueológico de Ancash** ⓘ *Instituto Nacional de Cultura, Plaza de Armas, daily 0800-2000, US$1.80*, contains stone monoliths and *huacos* (pottery artefacts) from the Recuay and other cultures. The exhibits are well displayed and labelled. The **Sala de Cultura SUNARP** ⓘ *Av Centenario 530, Independencia, T043-421301, Mon-Fri 1700-2000, Sat 0900-1300, free*, often has interesting art and photography exhibitions by local artists.

The main thoroughfare, **Avenida Luzuriaga**, is bursting with travel agencies, climbing equipment hire shops, restaurants, cafés and bars. Within a block or two you can find a less frantic ambience, but a good alternative for those seeking peace and quiet is the **La Soledad** neighbourhood, six blocks uphill from the Plaza de Armas on Avenida Sucre. Here, along Sucre as well as Jirón Amadeo Figueroa, every second house seems to rent rooms, most without signs. There are several decent neighbourhood eateries nearby, plus many shops, internet cafés and other facilities.

Around Huaraz ● ▸▸ *p212-219.*

Willkawain → *Colour map 2, B2.*

ⓘ *8 km northeast of Huaraz. Entrance to the site is US$1.50. Take a combi from 13 de Diciembre y Comercio, US$0.55 direct to Willkawain. Alternatively, the purple city bus (line 2B) will take you to Marian, a 15-min walk from the ruins.*

The Willkawain archaeological site near Huaraz dates from AD 700-1000. This was the second and imperial phase of the Huari empire, when Huari influence spread north from the city of the same name near Ayacucho. The Huari empire was remarkable for the strong Tiahuanaco influence (see page 314) in its architecture and ceramics, and for introducing the concept of a great walled urban centre.

The site consists of one large three-storey structure with intact stone slab roofs and several small structures. The windowless inner chambers can be explored as electric light has been installed. All the rooms are accessible and a few have been opened up to reveal a sophisticated ventilation system and skilful stone craftsmanship. About 500 m past Willkawain is **Ichiwillkawain** with several similar but smaller structures.

Even if you're not an archaeology buff, the trip is worth it for a fascinating insight into rural life in the valley. Taking a *colectivo* up to the ruins and then walking back down to Huaraz is thoroughly recommended. If walking up, go past the **Hotel Huascarán**. After crossing a small bridge, take a second right (well-signposted), from where it's about a two-hour uphill walk. Ask frequently as there are many criss-crossing paths. Beware of dogs en route (and expect begging children). A good grasp of Spanish will greatly enhance the pleasure of this experience as the locals are very welcoming.

Baños Termales Monterrey → *Colour map 2, B2.*

ⓘ *6 km along the road to Caraz. Lower pool US$0.85, upper pool US$1.35 (closed Mon), individual tubs US$1.35 for 20 mins. Buses from Av Luzuriaga, US$0.22. Taxi US$2-3.*

North of Huaraz, Monterrey makes a good day trip or an alternative place to stay for those seeking peace and quiet, although it gets crowded at weekends and holidays.

The baths are run by the **Hotel Baños Termales Monterrey** and, owing to the high iron content, the water is dark brown but usually not too dirty. The upper pool is the nicest. There are also individual and family tubs.

Laguna Churup → *Colour map 2, B2.*

ⓘ *US$20 payable to local cooperative in Pitec, only for groups with pack animals. Colectivo from Caraz y Comercio early in the morning to Llupa, 40 mins, US$0.60.*

To the east of Huaraz, off the road between Unchus and Pitec is a trail to Laguna Churup, which makes a good one-day excursion from Huaraz. The trail starts at **Llupa**, from where it's a one-hour hike to the National Park ranger post at **Pitec**. From there, it's a further three hours up to the lake, which is surrounded by high mountains. The last part involves scrambling over rocks (dangerous when raining). It's about three hours back to Llupa, where *colectivos* run until about 1800.

From **Pitec** there are three-day hikes up the Quebrada Quillcayhuanca to Cayesh or to Lagunas Tullpacocha and Cuchilacocha. From the latter you can cross a pass to the Cojup Valley (see below) and descend to Llupa (a further two days). You have to pay a national park entrance fee in Pitec to do these treks.

Quebrada Ishinca → *Colour map 2, B2.*

A good place for acclimatization and trekking at high altitude is the Ishinca hut at 4350 m in the Quebrada Ishinca. To get there, take a bus towards Paltay and then a *colectivo* to **Collón**; a taxi from Huaraz costs US$20. From Collón it's a nice four-hour walk to the hut; donkeys can be arranged in Collón, ask for Lorenzo. To sleep at the hut costs US$10, breakfast and dinner are US$10 each; you can also camp here. It's very popular with climbers. The easiest nearby climbs are Urus, 5420 m, and Ishinca, 5530 m. It is also possible to make a circuit back to Huaraz via Quebrada Cojup in three days, going over 5000 m. This is a good trek with great views.

● Sleeping

Huaraz *p209, maps p210 and p213*
Hotels are plentiful (far more than listed) but all fill up rapidly during May-Sep, and during public holidays and special events (such as the Semana de Andinismo in Jun) when prices rise. Lodging in private homes is common during these periods. Avoid touts at bus stations offering rooms and tours.

AL Andino Club, Pedro Cochachín 357, some way southeast from the centre (take a taxi after dark), T043-421662, www.hotel andino.com. Good international standard hotel with restaurant, free internet, lift, safe parking, friendly. Many rooms have balconies and views of Huascarán. Newly built section has suites and an apartment, which boast personal saunas (more expensive).

A Hostal Colomba, Francisco de Zela 278, on Centenario across the river, T043-421501, www.huarazhotelcolomba.com. Lovely old hacienda, family-run, fabulous garden, safe car parking, gym and well-equipped rooms with cable TV, comfortable beds and internet access. All bathrooms have tub and jacuzzi.

B San Sebastián, Jr Italia 1124, T043-426960, www.hotelhuaraz.com. Elegant, modern hotel, comfortable beds with duvets, parking available, internet connection in rooms. Very helpful, buffet breakfast included, good views.

C Steel Guest House, Alejandro Maguiña 1467, T043 429709, www.steelguest.com. Comfortable guesthouse under new management. Excellent view of the major peaks from the roof terrace, although it's a fair walk from the centre; taxi recommended at night. Small but comfortable rooms with TV and private bathroom, a sauna, kitchen, internet access, good value. Table football, a full size pool table, plus a TV lounge with DVDs make this a good place to recuperate after a tough adventure in the mountains.

D Albergue Churup, Jr Figueroa 1257, T043-422584, www.churup.com. Price includes breakfast and bath, **F** in dorm without breakfast, hot water, nice fire in the attractive sitting room, Wi-Fi access in private rooms, cafeteria, use of kitchen, sauna and massage room, roof terrace, lots of information, luggage store, laundry, book exchange, English spoken, Spanish classes, very helpful.

D **Apu Wasi**, Jr Federico Sal y Rosas 820, T043-426035, h_apuwasi@yahoo.com. Modern but simple hotel. All rooms have TV, private bathrooms and very comfortable beds. Standard price includes a basic breakfast. Discounts for longer stays.

D **Hostal Montañero**, Plaza Ginebra 30-B, T/F043-426386, www.trekkingperu.com. Price includes breakfast. Hot water, comfortable,

clean, friendly and a good contact point for quality mountain and trekking guides. Also climbing equipment rental and sales.

D **Olaza Guesthouse**, J Argüedas 1242, T043-422529, www.andeanexplorer.com. Recently upgraded with minimalist but very comfortable rooms. Safe, stylish, luggage stored, nice terrace with views, breakfast included. Pickup from bus station with room reservation. Downstairs there's an office for **Mountain Bike Adventures** (see page 217), run by Julio Olaza. They have a second office closer to the centre at Jr Lúcar y Torre 530.

D-E **Alojamiento Soledad**, Jr Amadeo Figueroa 1267, T043-421196, ghsoledad @hotmail.com. Price includes breakfast and bath, some hard beds, hot water, kitchen, use of internet, family-run and friendly, secure, trekking information given.

D-E **Monte Blanco**, José de la Mar 620, T043-426384, http://monteblancohotel.com. Very comfortable, good showers, cable TV, helpful staff (no English spoken), great value, breakfast, roof terrace with superb views.

E **Angeles Inn**, Av Gamarra 815, T043-422205, solandperu@yahoo.com. No sign, look for **Sol Andino** travel agency in same building (www.solandino.com). Kitchen and laundry facilities, small garden, hot water. Owners Max and Saul Angeles are official guides, helpful with trekking and climbing, equipment hire.

E **Edward's Inn**, Bolognesi 121, T/F043-422692, www.edwardsinn.com. Cheaper without bath, clean, nice garden, laundry, friendly, insist on proper rates in low season, popular. Edward speaks English and has 30 years' experience trekking, climbing and guiding in the area. He also rents gear.

E **La Casa de Zarela**, J Argüedas 1263, T043-421694, www.lacasadezarela.com. With bath, hot water, breakfast available, use of kitchen, laundry, owner speaks English and organizes tours, very knowledgeable. Luggage store, pleasant terrace.

E-F **Hatun Wasi**, Jr Daniel Villayzán 268, T043-425055, www.hatunwasi.net. Clean, spacious rooms with private bathroom and hot water. Pleasant roof terrace, ideal for breakfasts, with great views of the Cordillera.

E-F **The Way Inn Hostel**, Jr Buenaventura Mendoza 821, near Parque Fap, www.the wayinn.com. Dorms and private rooms; orthopaedic mattresses. Kitchen (including oven and fridge), video library, laundry

Cordillera Blanca Huaraz & around Listings

Huaraz centre

N

0 metres 20
0 yards 20

facilities, camping equipment for hire, information on treks, sauna and steam room. Mixed reports.

F Alojamiento Marilia, Sucre 1123, T043-428160, alojamaril@latinmail.com. Good views, modern, clean rooms with bath, **G** without bath, also dormitories, hot water, breakfast available, kitchen facilities, luggage store, knowledgeable, friendly owners.

F Alojamiento Nemy's, Jr Figueroa 1135, T043-422949. Secure, hot shower, breakfast US$2.40, good for climbers, luggage store.

F Alojamiento Norma, Pasaje Valenzuela 837 (Hostal 'NG' on the sign), near Plaza Belén, T043-421831, www.residencialng.com. **G** pp, includes breakfast, cheaper without bathroom, hot water, good value, friendly.

F Familia Meza, Lúcar y Torre 538, T043-426367, familiameza_lodging@hotmail.com. Shared bath, hot water, use of kitchen and laundry facilities, terrace with view, popular with trekkers, mountaineers and bikers.

F Hostal Estoico, San Martín 635, T043-422371. Cheaper without bathroom, friendly, clean, safe, hot water, laundry, good value.

F Hostal Gyula, Parque Ginebra 632, opposite the Casa de Guías, T043-421567, hostal_gyula_inn@yahoo.com. With bathroom, hot water, cheaper in dorm-style rooms, very friendly and helpful, information on tours, stores luggage. Noisy at weekends.

F Hostal Quintana, Jr Mcal A Cáceres 411, T043-426060, www.geocities.com/hostal_quintana. Cheaper without bathroom, hot shower, laundry, clean, basic, stores luggage, breakfast extra, friendly, popular with trekkers. **Mountclimb** rental agency next door is owned by the same family.

F Hostal Tany, Lúcar y Torre 468A, T043-422534. With bathroom, cheaper without, hot water, clean, friendly but rather old fashioned, money exchange, tours, café/restaurant.

F Jo's Place, Jr Daniel Villayzan 276, T043-425505, www.josplacehuaraz.com. Safe, hot water at night, kitchen facilities, mountain views, garden, terrace, warm atmosphere, Good source of information with plenty of advice on trekking and climbing in the area. Popular meeting point for climbers.

F La Cabaña, Jr Sucre 1224, T043-423428, www.huaraz.com/lacabana. Shared and double rooms, hot showers, cable TV, small breakfast included, laundry, kitchen, computer, DVD, very friendly, popular, safe for parking, bikes and luggage, English and French spoken, very good value.

F Lodging Caroline , Urb Avitentel Mz D – Lt 1, T043-422588, 978 6727 (mob). Price includes breakfast, 20-min walk from centre, free pickup from bus station (phone in advance), hot water, kitchen facilities, tourist information and guides, laundry, very helpful.

F Lodging Casa Sucre, Sucre 1240, T043-422264, filibertor@terra.com.pe. Private house, with bath, kitchen, laundry facilities, friendly, clean, hot water, English, French and German spoken. Mountaineering guide, Filiberto Rurush, can be contacted here.

F Oscar's Hostal, La Mar 624, T/F043-422720, cvmonical@hotmail.com. With bathroom, hot water, cheap breakfast next door, good beds, helpful, cheaper in low season.

F-G Alojamiento El Jacal, Jr Sucre 1044, T043-424612, reservaseljacal@yahoo.es. With or without shower, hot water, nice family, use of kitchen, internet, garden, luggage store, laundry, good value, popular.

F-G Casa Jansy's, Jr Sucre 948. Hot water, meals, laundry, owner Jesús Rivera Lúcar is a mountain guide. Recommended.

F-G pp Cayesh Guesthouse, Jr Julián de Morales 867, T043-428821, www.cayesh.net. Comfortable new hostel with good location, efficient solar hot water system, kitchen and TV lounge with over 250 DVDs. Owner is an enthusiastic climber and happy to provide advice on potential routes in the Cordilleras.

G pp Casa de Jaimes, Alberto Gridilla 267, T043-422281, www.casajaimes.com. Friendly and cheap. 1 hr free internet use per day, laundry facilities, maps and books, equipment rental, use of kitchen, popular with Israelis. Noisy but recommended.

G pp Backpackers, Av Raimondi 510, T043-429101, http://huaraz.com/backpackers. Breakfast not included. Spacious, hot showers, good views, very friendly, a real bargain.

G pp Lodging House Ezama, Mariano Melgar 623, Independencia, T043-423490, 15 mins' walk from Plaza de Armas (US$0.50 by taxi). Light, spacious rooms, hot water, safe, helpful.

● For an explanation of sleeping and eating price codes used in this guide, see inside the
● front cover. Other relevant information is found in Essentials, see pages 31-35.

Youth hostels

G pp **Alojamiento Alpes Andes**, at Casa de Guías, Plaza Ginebra 28-g, T043-421811, casa_de_guias@hotmail.com. Member of the Peruvian Youth Hostel Association, dorms with 14 beds or 6 beds, hot water, with very good restaurant, laundry, free luggage store, the owner Sr López speaks English, French and German and is very helpful, he is the mountain guides administrator.

Around Huaraz *p211*

A-C The Lazy Dog Inn, 3.1 km past the town of Marian, close to the Quebrada Cojup and the boundary of Huascarán National Park, T043-9789330, www.thelazydoginn.com. Eco-tourism lodge built with local materials, manpower and support. Actively involved in community projects. Beautifully designed in warm colours, each room with its own design. The lodge is constructed with adobe bricks and features water recycling systems and composting toilets. Great location gives access to several fabulous, little-visited mountain valleys. Friendly owners Wayne and Diana can organize horse-riding and hiking trips into the mountains. Excellent home cooking on request. 30 mins' drive from Huaraz (US$8-10 by taxi).

B El Patio, Av Monterrey, 250 m downhill from the Monterrey baths, T043-424965, www.elpatio.com.pe. Very classy, with lovely gardens and comfortable rooms, some with balconies; also a couple of bungalows (A). Meals on request, bar, friendly, colonial-style.

D The Way Inn Lodge, www.thewayinn.com. Close to the border of Huascarán National Park, at 3712 m. Dorm rooms and camping **F** and **G** respectively, including breakfast. Vegetables grown on site. Many activities available, from paragliding to yoga classes and mountain biking. Mixed reports.

● Eating

Huaraz *p209, maps p210 and p213*
For local dishes, such as *pachamanca*, go to Calle José Olaya at the weekend, where stalls are set up.

♔♔♔ **Crêperie Patrick**, Luzuriaga 422. Tasty crêpes, fish, quiche, spaghetti and good wine.
♔♔♔ **Huaraz Querido**, Bolívar 981. Excellent *cevichería*.

♔♔♔ **Monte Rosa**, J de la Mar 661. 1000-2300. Pizzería, also fondue and other Swiss dishes. Swiss owner is Victorinox representative, offering knives for sale and repair also Suunto (altimeters, GPS), mountain gear and excellent postcards. Rents snowboards and skis and has climbing and trekking books.
♔♔♔ **Pizza Bruno**, Luzuriaga 834. 1600-2300. Excellent pizzas, crêpes and pastries, good service. French owner Bruno Reviron also has a 4WD with driver for hire.
♔♔♔ **Siam de Los Andes**, Gamarra corner J de Morales. Authentic Thai cuisine, not cheap, but tasty and with a wide range of dishes, as mild or spicy as you desire. Nice fireplace.
♔♔ **Bistro de los Andes** 823 and Plaza de Armas 2nd floor, T/F043-426249 /429556. Good food, owner speaks English, French and German. Plaza branch has a nice panoramic view of the plaza. Very wide range of dishes including breakfasts, meats, pastas and curries.
♔♔ **Chilli Heaven**, Parque Ginebra, just up from the Casa de Guías. Great curries, Indian, Thai, or otherwise and filling burritos, chillies – the works. In fact anyone who appreciates a bit of spice will enjoy this snug new, very popular restaurant and its wares. Good pizza and the desserts are mouth-watering as well.
♔♔ **El Horno, Pizzería Grill**, Parque del Periodista, T043-424617. Good atmosphere, fine grilled meats and nice location overlooking the Parque del Periodista.
♔♔ **El Rinconcito Minero**, J de Morales 757. Breakfast, good value at lunchtime (including vegetarian), coffee and snacks, popular for good food and service, video bar.
♔♔ **Fuente de Salud**, J de la Mar 562. Vegetarian, also meat and pasta dishes, good soups, excellent fruit salads and smoothies, breakfasts. Recommended.
♔♔ **Pachamama**, San Martín 687. Bar, café and restaurant, concerts, art gallery, garden, nice place to relax, good toilets, pool table and table-tennis, information on treks, Swiss-owned. Recommended.
♔♔ **Pepe's Place**, Raimondi 624, good pizza, chicken, meat, warm atmosphere, run by Pepe from Residencial Cataluña.
♔♔ **Piccolo**, J de Morales 632. Pizzería, very popular with gringos.
♔♔ **Pizza B&B**, La Mar beside laundry of same name. Pizza is excellent, as is their dessert specialty *tarte flambée*, wood oven,

pleasant decor and atmosphere, attentive service. Recommended.

♥♥ **Pizzería Landauro**, Sucre, on corner of Plaza de Armas. Good for pizzas, nice vibe.

♥♥ **Sabor Salud**, Luzuriaga 672, upstairs. Restaurant and pizzería specializing in vegetarian and Italian food.

♥♥-♥ **Chifa Jim Hua**, Luzuriaga 645, upstairs. Large, tasty portions, *menú* US$1.15 and a wide variety of Peruvian-Chinese dishes.

♥♥-♥ **Encuentro**, Parque Ginebra, off Luzuriaga cuadra 6. Opens 0700 for breakfast, serves good lunches and dinners, very busy, try the fillet mignon. Recommended.

♥ **El Querubín**, J de Morales 767. Clean, friendly, good breakfast and set meals (high season only), also vegetarian, snacks and à la carte, very good, decorated with nice regional paintings. Recommended.

♥ **Las Puyas**, Morales 535. Popular with gringos, serves an excellent *sopa criolla* and very good trout, also serves breakfast.

Cafés

Café Andino, Lúcar y Torre 538, T043-421203, cafeandino@hotmail.com. American-run café and book exchange, great coffee and food, extensive library, great atmosphere and a good meeting place. The café's owner, Chris, organizes treks in cordilleras Blanca and Huayhuash, lots of advice offered.

Café El Centro, 28 de Julio 592. Good breakfast for US$1.30-2, great chocolate cake and apple pie.

Cafetería y Juguería, Sucre 806. Cheap, just above plaza. Excellent yogurt/honey drinks.

California Café, Jr 28 de Julio 562, T043-428354. A rival to **Café Andino** in all but the view. Perhaps the best breakfast in town, great coffee and chocolate cake. Book exchange, library, games, comfortable sofas.

Las Tulpas y Chimichurri, J de Morales 756, between Luzuriaga y Bolívar. Open 0730-2300, nice garden. Good breakfasts and good value lunchtime menu, keen to promote Peruvian cuisine with Western standards of presentation. Good fish, excellent *lomo saltado*. Recommended.

Panadería La Alameda, Juan de La Cruz Romero 523 near market. Excellent bread.

Panadería Montserrat, Av Luzuriaga 928, T043-426260. Bakery and café, pleasant atmosphere, lots of cakes and *empanadas*, sausage rolls etc. Good for a snack.

⊕ Bars and clubs

Huaraz *p209, maps p210 and p213*

13 Buhos Bar, José de la Mar 2nd floor, just above Makondo's. Funky, popular bar with good range of tunes, snacks and plenty of games. Owner, Lucho, has a big personality and a hat like Indiana Jones.

Amadeus, Parque Ginebra, bar-disco.

Chacraraju/Chill-out Bar, Jr Sucre 959, next of the agency of the same name. Good pizzas and atmosphere, occasional DJs.

Extreme, Jr Gabino Uribe near Luzuriaga. Upstairs bar, popular with gringos. 1900-0200.

La Cascada, Luzuriaga 1276, disco tavern.

Makondo's, José de la Mar opposite Cruz del Sur bus station. Disco, bar and nightclub, safe, popular.

Monttrek Disco, Sucre just off Plaza de Armas, in a converted cinema, reasonable prices.

Taberna Tambo, José de la Mar 776, daily 1000-1600 and 2000 till late. Folk music and disco. Full-on, non-stop dance mecca. Very popular with both locals and gringos.

Vagamundo, J de Morales 753. Popular bar with snacks and football tables.

⊕ Entertainment

Huaraz *p209, maps p210 and p213*

Huaraz Satyricon, Luzuriaga 1036, T043-9557343. American-run café and movie theatre, big screen, comfortable sofas, chocolate chip cookies and falafel sandwiches, US$1.20. Movies range from 1960s' classics to cutting-edge Latin American, plus occasional showings of *Touching the Void*, the film set and partially shot in the Huayhuash.

⊛ Festivals and events

Huaraz *p209, maps p210 and p213*

Mar/Apr Semana Santa (Holy Week) is widely celebrated and always colourful and lively.

3 May El Señor de la Soledad, the town's patron saint's day, marks the start of a week of parades, music, fireworks and much drinking.

Jun Semana del Andinismo is an international climbing and skiing week.

Last week of Jun San Juan and San Pedro are celebrated throughout the region. On the eve of San Juan fires are lit throughout the valley to burn the chaff from the harvest. The following day the valley is thick with smoke.

O Shopping

Huaraz *p209, maps p210 and p213*

Climbing and trekking equipment

For equipment hire, see trekking, below.
Tatoo, on Parque Ginebra, T043-422966,
www.tatoo.ws. Good shop for climbing and
outdoor clothes and gear, locally produced
and international brands.

Food and drink

The central market offers a wide variety of
canned and dry goods, including nuts and
dried fruit, as well as fresh fruit and vegetables.
Be sure to check expiry dates. Also be sure
to leave all valuables in a safe place when
shopping in the market; pickpockets abound.
Ortiz, Luzuriaga 401 corner Raimondi.
A well-stocked supermarket with a good
selection of items, but expensive.

Handicrafts

Local sweaters, hats, gloves, ceramics and
wall hangings can be bought from stalls on
Pasaje Mcal Cáceres just off Luzuriaga, in the
stalls off Luzuriaga between Morales and
Sucre, on Bolívar cuadra 6 and elsewhere.
Andean Expressions, Jr J Arguedas 1246,
near La Soledad church, T043-422951,
olaza@qnet.com.pe, 0800-2200.
Recommended for hand-printed T-shirts
and sweatshirts with unusual motifs.

▲ Activities and tours

Huaraz *p209, maps p210 and p213*
Huaraz is overflowing with agencies and
quality varies. Try to get a recommendation
from someone who has just returned from a
tour or climb. All agencies run conventional
tours to Llanganuco, Pastoruri (US$10 pp,
both very long days) and Chavín (8-10 hrs,
US$6-10 pp), entry tickets not included. Many
rent equipment and offer climbing/trekking
tours and ski instruction. **Note** Tour agencies
shouldn't recommend Pastoruri as a first trip.
It's best to go to Llanganuco first to acclimatize.

Horse riding

Sr Robinson Ayala Gride, T043-423813.
Contact him well in advance for half-day
trips (enquire at **El Cortijo** restaurant).
Posada de Yungar, Yungar (20 km on the
Carhuaz road), T043-421267, T967 9836

(mob). Ask for José Flores or Gustavo Soto.
US$4.50 per hr on nice horses; good 4-hr trip
in the Cordillera Negra with fabulous views.

Mountain biking

Mountain Bike Adventures, Lúcar y Torre
530, T043-424259, julio.olaza@terra.com.pe.
Contact Julio Olaza. US$20 for 5 hrs. Julio
speaks excellent English and sells topo maps
and climbing books. Recommended for the
excellent standard of equipment.

Mountain guides

For further information, visit the **Casa de
Guías** (see page 208). The guides listed
below are not necessarily members of **AGMP**
but are recommended for their expertise.
Aritza Monasterio, through **Casa de Guías**.
Speaks English, Spanish and Euskerra.
Augusto Ortega, Jr San Martín 1004,
T043-424888. The only Peruvian to
have climbed Everest.
Filiberto Rurush Paucar, Lodging Casa
Sucre, Sucre 1240, T043-422264. Speaks
English, Spanish and Quechua.
Hugo and César Sifuentes Maguiña, Siex
(Sifuentes Expeditions), Jr Huaylas 139,
T043-426529, www.siexperu.org. César
speaks English and a little French.
Koky Castañeda, La Casa de Zarela,
T043-421694 (or through **Café Andino**).
Speaks English and French, AGMP certified.
Ted Alexander, Skyline Adventures,
T043-427097, www.sladventureschool.com.
American Outward Bound instructor, very
knowledgeable, lots of information.

River rafting and canoeing

Ario Ferri, T043-961 3058, T963 5920 (mob),
www.yurakyaku.com, or contact through
Café Andino. Multilingual rafting guide and
certified kayak instructor. Also a well-
regarded climbing and hiking guide.

Trekking and climbing

For general trekking information, see page
210. Trekking tours cost US$40-70 pp per day;
climbing US$90-140 pp per day. Ask tour
agencies, independent guides and the **Casa
de Guías** about rock-climbing courses at
Monterrey (behind **Hotel Baños Termales
Monterrey**), Chancos, Recuay and Huanchac
(30 mins' walk from Huaraz), and about
ice climbing on Vallanaraju and Pastoruri

218

Cordillera Blanca Huaraz & around Listings

(for example). Jatun Machay in the Cordillera Negra is another fabulous spot for rock climbing and bouldering, be it at beginner level or if you are an experienced climber looking for a serious challenge.

For equipment hire, the following are recommended: **Casa de Guías** (see page 208), **Andean Kingdom**; **Andean Sport Tours**; **Galaxia Expeditions**, **Monttrek**; **Kallpa**. Also try **Skyline**, T043-427097, www.sladventureschool.com; **Montañero**, Parque Ginebra 30-B, T043-426386, andeway@terra.com.pe, and **MountClimb**, Jr Mcal Cáceres 421, T043-426060, mountclimb@yahoo.com.

Active Peru, Av Gamarra 699, T043-423339, www.activeperu.com. Friendly, offers the classic treks, climbing, plus tours to Chavín, Pastoruri and Llanganuco.

Andean Kingdom, Jr San Martín 613, p 2, T043-425555, www.andeankingdom.com. Free information, maps, climbing wall, rock and ice climbing, multi-day courses, treks, equipment rental, very helpful, can be very busy. The company is building a lodge near the excellent rock climbing site of Hatun Machay in the Cordillera Negra.

Andean Sport Tours, Luzuriaga 571, T043-421612. Have a basic practice wall behind the office. They also organize mountain bike tours, ski instruction and river rafting.

Andeno Viaggio, Av Luzuriaga 627, T043-428047, www.andenoviaggio.com. The usual range of day tours (Llanganuco, Pastoruri, Chavin) plus trekking and climbing, reputable.

Andescamp, Malecón Sur 310 (Río Quillkay), T043-428214, www.andescamp.com. Popular, especially with budget travellers. Only qualified guides used for climbing trips. Variety of treks from the 9-12 day Huayhuash circuit to Olleros to Chavín over 3 days, plus rafting, paragliding and more.

Chacraraju Expeditions, Jr José de Sucre No.959, T043-426172, www.chacraraju expedition.com. Tours and equipment for hire, plus a small climbing wall and the aptly named **Chill-out Bar** next door.

Cordillera Blanca Adventures, T043-424352. Experienced, quality climbing and trekking trips, good guides and equipment.

Explorandes, Av Centenario 489, T043-421960, postmast@exploran.com.pe.

Galaxia Expeditions, Jr Mariscal Cáceres 428, T043-425691, galaxia_expeditions @hotmail.com. Reputable agency with the usual range of tours, equipment hire.

Huascarán, Jr Figueroa 1257 (below Albergue Churup), T043-424504, peru huascaran@yahoo.com. Contact Pablo Tinoco Depaz. 4-day Santa Cruz trip recommended. Good food and equipment, professional and friendly service, free loan of waterproofs and *pisco sour* on last evening. Recommended.

Kallpa, José de la Mar y Luzuriaga, p 2, T043-427868, www.peruviantrek.com. Organizes treks, rents gear, arranges *arrieros* and mules, very helpful.

Montañero, Parque Ginebra 30-B, T043-426386, www.trekkingperu.com. Run by veteran mountain guide Selio Villón, German, French and English spoken.

Monttrek, Luzuriaga 646, upstairs, T043-421124. Good trekking/climbing advice and maps, ice and rock climbing courses, tours to Laguna Churup and the 'spectacular' Luna Llena tour; also hires out mountain bikes, ski instruction and trips, and river rafting. Conscientious guides. Next door in the Pizzería is a climbing wall. For new routes and maps contact Porfirio Cacha Macedo, 'Pocho', at **Monttrek** or at Jr Corongo 307, T423930.

Peruvian Andes Adventures, José Olaya 532, T043-421864, www.peruvianandes.com, www.perutrekkingclimbing.com. Run by Hisao and Eli Morales, with an agency in New Zealand, professional, registered mountain and trekking guides. All equipment and services for treks of 3-15 days, climbing technical and non-technical peaks, or just day walks. Vegetarians catered for.

Trekking guides
Christopher Benway, La Cima Logistics, T043-421203, cafeandino@hotmail.com. Chris is the owner of **Café Andino**, so usually easy to track down, plus very friendly and helpful.

Genaro Yanac Olivera, T043-422825. Speaks good English, also a climbing guide.

Max and Saul Angeles, T043-422205 (**Sol Andino** travel agency), speaks some English.

Tjen Verheye, Jr Carlos Valenzuela 911, T043-422569, is Belgian and speaks Dutch, French, German and reasonable English, runs trekking and conventional tours and is knowledgeable about the Chavín culture.

Vladimiro and Máximo Hinostrosa, at **Mountain Shop Chacraraju**, T043-969 2395, trekking guides with good knowledge.

Tour operators

It is difficult and pricey to purchase airline tickets in Huaraz. Best to do so in Lima. **Chavín Tours**, Luzuriaga 502, T043-421578, F424801. Local tours, long-standing agency. **Pablo Tours**, Luzuriaga 501, T043-421142. Local tours, with many years of operation.

⊖ Transport

Huaraz p209, maps p210 and p213
Air LC Busre flies daily to/from **Lima** (50 mins). Office: Av Toribio de Luzuriaga 904, Belén, T043-424734.

Bus Many bus companies have offices selling tickets in the centre, but buses leave from the edge of the centre. Several buses and minivans run daily, 0500-2000, to **Caraz**, 1¼ hrs, US$1.35, stopping at all the places in between. They depart from the parking area under the bridge on Fitzcarrald and from the open space beside the bridge on the other side of the river (beware of thieves here).

To **Chavín**, 110 km, 2 hrs (sit on left side for best views), US$3. Service provided by **Chavín Express**, Mcal Cáceres 338, 3 a day, Sun 1500, and by **Trans Río Mosna**, Tarapacá 576, daily 0700 and 1300. Both have buses that go on to **Huari**, 6 hrs, US$5.

To **Chacas** (US$3.75) and **San Luis** (US$5.75), at 0700 with **Virgen de Guadalupe**, Caraz 607. **Renzo**, Raimondi 821, runs to Chacas and San Luis (Mon-Sat 0615, Sun 0645), **Yanama, Piscobamba** and **Pomabamba** (0630, best). **Los Andes**, same office as Yungay Express, daily 0630 to **Yungay**, US$0.75, **Lagunas de Llanganuco**, US$3.45, **Yanama**, US$3.45, **Piscobamba**, US$5.20 and **Pomabamba**, US$6 (8 hrs). This route also served by **Copa**, J de Morales y Lúcar y Torre, daily 0630 and 1430; **Transvir**, Caraz y Comercio, daily 1400, and **La Perla de Alta Mayo**, daily 0630, 8 hrs to Pomabamba, US$6.

Colectivos to **Recuay**, US$0.45, **Ticapampa** and **Catac**, US$0.55, leave daily 0500-2100, from Gridilla, just off Tarapacá (Terminal Terrestre Transportistas Zona Sur).

To **Lima**, 420 km via Pativilca, 7-8 hrs, US$6-14. The road is in good condition. There is a large selection of buses to Lima, both ordinary service and luxury coaches, with departures throughout the day. Many of the companies have their offices along Av Raimondi and on Jr Lúcar y Torre. Some recommended companies are: **Cruz del Sur**, Bolívar y José de la Mar; **Transportes Rodríguez**, Tarapacá 622; Civa, Morales opposite Lúcar y Torre; **Móvil Tours**, Bolívar 452; **Empresa 14**, Fitzcarrald 216, terminal at Bolívar 407.

To **Casma** via the Callán pass and Pariacoto, 150 km, 7 hrs, US$6, the lower section of the road is very poor, landslides and closures are common (sit on the left for best views, as long as you don't mind precipices): **Transportes Huandoy**, Fitzcarrald 261 (terminal at Caraz 820), daily 0800, 1000 and 1300; **Yungay Express**, Raimondi 744, 3 a day, continuing to **Chimbote**, 185 km. To **Chimbote** via Caraz and the Cañón del Pato (sit on the right for the most exciting views), with **Yungay Express**, daily, US$7, 10 hrs. Other companies go to **Chimbote**, US$6, 7 hrs, via **Pativilca**, 160 km, 4 hrs, US$3.50, and most continue to **Trujillo**, 8-9 hrs, US$8.60; all buses depart at night: **Chinchaysuyo**, J de Morales 650; **Línea**, Simón Bolívar 450; **Empresa 14** and Móvil Tours, addresses above.

Taxi

The standard fare for a taxi in town is about US$0.60, US$0.70 at night. The fare to Monterrey or Huanchac is US$1.45. Radio taxis T043-421482 or T043-422512.

① Directory

Huaraz p209, maps p210 and p213
Banks BBVA, on the Plaza de Armas, cash withdrawals in soles and US$. **BCP**, on the Plaza de Armas, good rates, 2 ATMs (Visa). Interbank, on Plaza de Armas, cash and TCs (no commission into soles), MasterCard ATM. Scotiabank, Sucre 766, changes cash and cheques. **Casa de Cambio Oh Na Nay**, across the street from Interbank, good rates for US$. There are several other *casas de cambio* and many street changers (be careful) on Luzuriaga. **Internet** Ubiquitous, US$0.30 per hr. **Laundry** B & B, La Mar 674. US$1.20 per kg, special machine for down garments and sleeping bags. Recommended. Also many others. **Post office** Serpost is on Luzuriaga 702, daily 0800-2000. **Telephone** Telefónica, Sucre y Bolívar, corner of Plaza de Armas. National and international phone and fax, daily 0700-2300. Private calling centres along Luzuriaga. Many coin phones.

North and east of Huaraz

The road north out of Huaraz goes through the beautiful Callejón de Huaylas, giving access to some wonderful treks which go up into, or over the mountains of the Cordillera Blanca. Caraz, the focus of the northern end of the valley, is less hectic than Huaraz, but is just as good a place to stay. It is definitely worth spending some time in this area. ▶▶ *For Sleeping, Eating and other listings, see pages 225-228.*

Huaraz to Caraz 🚌🚲🌀🚍 ▶▶ *pp225-228. Colour map 2, B2.*

There are frequent buses running up and down the Callejón from Huaraz and between the towns en route. The main road north from Huaraz through the **Callejón de Huaylas** goes to **Taricá**, where there is a home pottery industry, and **Marcará**, 26 km from Huaraz (one hour, US$0.45), where there are a couple of hotels, basic restaurants and shops.

Carhuaz → *Colour map 2, B2.*
Carhuaz, a friendly, quiet mountain town with a pleasant plaza with tall palm trees and lovely rose bushes is 7 km further on from Marcará. There is very good trekking in the neighbourhood, for instance up the Ulta valley to Yanama, to the Baños de Pariarca hot springs and, beyond, to Laguna 513. There's a market on Wednesday and another larger market on Sunday, when *campesinos* bring their produce to town. Good peaches are grown locally, among other crops. The locals are renowned for their lively celebrations, hence the town's nickname, '*Carhuaz alegría*'.

Mancos and around → *Colour map 2, B2.*
From Carhuaz it is a further 14 km to Mancos, at the foot of Huascarán. (From here, climbers can go to **Musho** to reach the base camp.) You can also do a strenuous 30-km, one-day walk from Mancos which gives great views of Huascarán. Follow the road east and take the branch for Tumpa, about 13 km away; ask directions. Continue north to Musho for about 1 km, then descend via Arhuay to **Ranrahirca**, which is between Mancos and Yungay on the main road. There are daily *colectivos* from Mancos to Musho; transport to Ranrahirca and Arhuay is on Wednesday and Sunday only.

Yungay → *Colour map 2, A2. Altitude 2500 m.*
Yungay is 8 km north of Mancos on the main road. The original town of Yungay was completely buried during the 1970 earthquake by a massive mudslide, caused when a piece of Huascarán's glacier was prised loose by the quake and came hurtling towards the town. It was a hideous tragedy in which 20,000 people lost their lives. The earthquake and its aftermath are remembered by many residents of the Callejón de Huaylas and the scars remain part of the local psyche.

The original site of Yungay, known as **Yungay Viejo** ① *off the Huaraz–Yungay road, officially open daily 0800-1800, US$0.75,* has been consecrated as a *camposanto* (cemetery). It is a haunting place, with flower beds and paths covering the eight to 12 m of soil under which the old town lies. Of the four palm trees from the old Plaza de Armas that protrude through the landslide, only one remains alive. Five pine trees and a monument mark the site where five policemen died. Nearby, on top of a hill, is the old cemetery with a large statue of Christ, where a handful of residents managed to escape the disaster. Many of the town's children also escaped as they were in the stadium watching the circus. There are a few monuments marking the site of former homes. There's a café, toilets and shops at the main entrance.

The **new settlement** is on a hillside just north of the old town, and is growing gradually. It has a pleasant modern plaza and a concrete market, busiest on Wednesday and Sunday, which is good for stocking up on supplies for hiking. The predominant colour in the town is *celeste* (sky blue). One part of town is called the **Barrio Ruso**, where typical, Russian wooden houses, erected temporarily in the 1970s as a gift from the USSR, are still in use. For information, visit the **tourist office** ① *on the corner of the Plaza de Armas, Mon-Fri 0800-1300, 1400-1800*.

Around Yungay

Laguna 69 can be visited on a day-trip from Yungay. Take a *combi* from Yungay past the Llanganuco lakes (see below; US$2.45-3). After about 1½ hours get off the bus at a bend called Curva Pisco. Keep to the right of the river along the valley bottom. You will see the gentle zigzags going up to the right to a col with a small lake. Pass this and you come to a large plateau: keep to the right-hand side. There is a signpost in the middle pointing right to a glacier and straight ahead to Laguna 69, heading to a large wall of rock. The path zigzags steeply up to the left of this rock face to the lake, near glaciers and the snow line. It takes three to four hours for the 7-km hike and 750-m climb and some two to three hours to walk back down to the road. There are superb views of waterfalls, glaciers and Huascarán. A new trail now leads from Laguna 69 to the Refugio Perú or Pisco Base Camp, taking about two to three hours. Ask the *combi* to return for you at about 1630, the latest time to get back to Yungay for a *combi* back to Huaraz.

Lagunas de Llanganuco

The Lagunas de Llanganuco are two lakes nestling 1000 m below the snowline beneath Huascarán and Huandoy. From Yungay, the first you come to is **Laguna Chinancocha** at 3850 m, followed by **Laguna Orconcocha** at 3863 m. A nature trail, **Sendero María Josefa** (sign on the road), leads for 1½ hours to the western end of Chinancocha where there is a control post, descriptive trail and boat trips on the lake (a popular area for day trippers). Walk along the road beside the lake to its far eastern end for peace and quiet among the *quenoal* trees. These trees (polylepis, or paper bark) are the symbol of the Huascarán national park and provide shelter for 75% of the birdlife found in the park. The lakes themselves are superb areas for observing water birds, with yellow-billed, blue and mountain ducks commonly seen, as well as Andean geese, puna ibis and a variety of gulls. Hunting birds such as caracas and American kestrels make an appearance. If you're lucky, you may even catch a glimpse of the rare torrent duck, swimming up grade V rapids in classic style.

> ‡ This trek can also be done as a day trip from Huaraz by taking the 0700 combi to Yungay.

Caraz and around 🖥️🚲🛶❄️⛰️🎫🍴 ⇥ *pp225-228.*

→ *Colour map 2, B2. Altitude: 2290 m.*

The pleasant town of Caraz is a good centre for walking and the access point for many excellent treks and climbs. It is increasingly popular with visitors as a more tranquil alternative to Huaraz. In July and August the town has splendid views of Huandoy and Huascarán from its lovely plaza, which is filled with jacarandas, rose bushes and palms. In other months, the mountains are often shrouded in cloud. Caraz has a milder climate than Huaraz and is more suited to day trips. The sweet-toothed will enjoy the locally produced *manjar blanco*, from which the town derives its nickname, '*Caraz dulzura*'. Market days are Wednesday and Sunday. The **tourist office** ① *Plaza de Armas, T043-391029, Mon-Fri 0745-1300, 1430-1700*, has limited information.

The ruins of **Tunshukaiko** are 1 km from the Plaza de Armas, in the suburb of Cruz Viva. This is a poor area so be discreet with cameras etc. There are seven platforms from the Huaraz culture, dating from around 2000-1800 BC, between the Galgada and Chavín periods. Recent excavations have uncovered structures 300 m in diameter, 25 m high. They are on a promontory with a panoramic view of the farms, fields, eucalyptus and other trees between the Cordilleras Blanca and Negra. To get there, from the plaza in Caraz follow San Martín uphill, turn left on 28 de Julio, continue about 400 m past the bridge over the Río Llullán. Look for a wide track between houses on your left (about 300 m before the turnoff for Lago Parón); ask the way.

Cañón del Pato

The road out of the Callejón de Huaylas heads north from Caraz, en route to Chimbote on the coast. After some 30 km the road enters the very narrow and spectacular **Cañón del Pato**. You pass under tremendous walls of bare rock and through nearly 40 tunnels, but the flow of the river has been greatly reduced by the hydroelectric scheme based at Huallanca, which takes the water into the mountain at the Bocatoma. After the paved road in the Callejón de Huaylas, the road through the canyon is a track, very bumpy, stony and dusty (hard driving). The road goes between barren hills and passes poor mining camps. The geology is fantastic, with ravines, whorls, faults and strata at all angles to each other. The varying colours of the rock are also amazing. At Chuquicara, some 60 km after Huallanca, the road is paved for the three hours to Chimbote. There is accommodation at Yuramarca and Huallanca and places to eat en route.

The canyon can be visited on a half-day trip from Caraz. Take a *micro* from near the market towards Yuramarca, see Transport page 228. Sit in the front or on the right for great views. Get off at Huallanca and get on the next bus going back. Ask the driver to drop you off at the yellow footbridge where the canyon is narrowest (ask for Cañón del Pato). Walk back north through one small tunnel. In the second tunnel, take the first side tunnel to the right that leads to a very precarious footpath that goes along the edge of the canyon at its narrowest point. Walking back south you come to a dam and the hydroelectric plant with water pouring over the dam wall. Pick up another bus going back to Caraz. Take great care on the path in the canyon and in the tunnels as they are narrow and have no places to retreat if a large vehicle comes through. Take a torch. The trip is best at midday when the sun shines directly into the gorge.

Treks from Caraz in the Cordillera Blanca

A good day hike with good views of the Cordillera Blanca is to **Pueblo Libre** (about four hours round trip, or you can take a *colectivo* back to Caraz). A longer day walk of six to seven hours in total with excellent views of Huandoy and Huascarán follows the foothills of the Cordillera Blanca, from Caraz south. It ends at Puente Ancash on the Caraz–Yungay road, from where transport goes back to Caraz.

A large stand of **Puya Raimondi** can be seen in the Cordillera Negra west of Caraz. Beyond Pueblo Libre the road which continues via Pamparomas and Moro joins the coastal highway between Casma and Chimbote. After 45 km (two hours) are the Puya Raimondi plants at a place called **Winchos**, with views of 145 km of the Cordillera Blanca and to the Pacific. The plants are usually in flower May or October. Take warm clothing, food and water. You can also camp near the puyas and return the following day. The most popular way to get there is to rent a bike (US$15 a day), go up by public transport (see below), and ride back down in four to five hours. Or form a group (eg via the bulletin board at **Pony's Expeditions**, see page 227) and hire a car which will wait for you (US$50 for eight, including guide). From Caraz, a *combi* for Pamparomas leaves from Grau y Ugarte between 0800 and 0900, US$2, two hours. From the pass (El Paso) or El Cruce it is a short walk to the plants. Return transport leaves between 1230 and 1300. If you miss the bus, you can walk back to Pueblo Libre in four hours, to Caraz in seven hours, but it is easy to get lost and there are not many people to ask for directions.

A blooming century

The giant Puya Raimondi, named after Antonio Raimondi, the Italian scholar who discovered it, is a rare species and one of the oldest plants in the world.

Often mistakenly referred to as a cactus, it is actually the largest member of the bromeliad family and is found in only a few isolated areas of the Andes. One of these areas is the Huascarán National Park, particularly the Ingenio and Queshque gorges, the high plateaus of Cajamarquilla, along the route leading to Pastoruri in the Pachacoto gorge and by the road from Caraz to Pamparomas.

At its base, the Puya forms a rosette of long, spiked, waxy leaves, 2 m in diameter. The distinctive phallic spike can reach a height of 12 m during the flowering process. This takes its entire lifespan – an incredible 100 years – after which the plant withers and dies.

As the final flowering begins, usually during May for mature plants, the spike is covered in flowers. As many as 20,000 blooms decorate a single plant. During this season, groups of Puya Raimondi will bloom together, creating a spectacular picture against the backdrop of the Cordillera Blanca.

Laguna Parón From Caraz a narrow, rough road goes east 32 km to Laguna Parón, in a cirque surrounded by several, massive snow-capped peaks, including Huandoy, Pirámide Garcilazo and Caraz. The water level has been lowered to protect Caraz, and the water from the lake is used for the Cañón del Pato hydroelectric scheme. The gorge leading to it is spectacular. It is a long day's trek for acclimatized hikers (25 km) up to the lake at 4150 m, or 4½-hour walk from the village of Parón, which can be reached by *combi*. Camping is possible next to the Duke Energy refuge.

Santa Cruz Valley One of the finest treks in the area is the four- to five-day route over the path from the Santa Cruz valley, by **Mount Huascarán** to the **Lagunas de Llanganuco** (see page 221). The most popular place to start the trek is from Cashapampa in the Santa Cruz valley. It takes four to five days over the pass of Punta Unión, 4750 m, to Vaquería or the Llanganuco lakes. Many recommend this 'anticlockwise' route as the climb is gentler, giving more time to acclimatize, and the pass is easier to find. You can hire an *arriero* and mule in Cashapampa. Campsites are at Llamacorral and Taullipampa before Punta Unión, and Quenoapampa (or Cachina Pampa) after the pass. You can end the hike at Vaquería on the Yanama–Yungay road, or, a day later with a night at the Paccha Pampa campsite, at the Llanganuco lakes, from where cars go back to Yungay.

Cordillera Negra

Pueblo Libre

A good day-hike (four-hour round-trip) is from Caraz to Pueblo Libre, with views of the Cordillera Blanca. Follow Jirón D Villar west across the Río Santa bridge and turn south to **Tunaspampa**, a desert area with cacti and hummingbirds. Continue through the villages of Shingal, Tocash and Rinconada to **Pueblo Libre**.

Winchos

Beyond Pueblo Libre, the road continues via Pamparomas and Moro to join the coastal highway between Casma and Chimbote. After 45 km (two hours) a large stand of Puya Raimondi (see box, above) can be seen at a place called **Winchos**, with views stretching 145 km, east to the Cordillera Blanca and west to the Pacific. The flowers are usually in bloom in May or October. 'Wincho' is the local name for the giant hummingbird, Patagona gigas, which has an 18-cm wingspan.

There are two possible routes by public transport from Caraz to the puyas at Winchos: Caraz–Huata–El Cruce (from where it's a 2-km walk to the puyas), continuing to Pamparomas; or Caraz–Pueblo Libre–Huashtacruz–El Paso (from where it's a 15-minute walk to the puyas), continuing to El Cruce and **Pamparomas**. On the return to Caraz, you will have to walk 2 km to El Cruce to be sure to catch the returning transport between 1230 and 1300. This will not give you too much time at the puyas. Increasingly popular alternatives are to rent a bicycle (US$15), which you can take on public transport to the *puyas* (departing at 0900; see Transport, page 228) and then ride back to Caraz in about four to five hours. Or form a group and hire a car which will wait for you; a board at **Pony's Expeditions** (see page 227) has offers of shared transport.

Chavín de Huantar ●❂❸❹❺ ▸▸ *pp225-228. Colour map 2, B2.*

ⓘ *Daily 0800-1700; some areas are closed to visitors. US$3, US$5 for a group with Spanish-speaking guide; recommended if you want to see the tunnels properly. All galleries open to the public have electric lights. There is a small museum at the entrance, with carvings and some Chavín pottery.*

A trip to Chavín de Huantar is a must if you are in the area, as it is one of the most important archaeological sites in the country. The ruins lie just to the south of the town of Chavín. This fortress temple, built about 800 BC, is the only large structure remaining of the Chavín culture which, in its heyday, is thought to have held influence in a region between Cajamarca and Chiclayo in the north to Ayacucho and Ica in the south. In 1985, UNESCO designated Chavín a World Heritage Site.

The site is in good condition despite the effects of time and nature. The easternmost building was damaged in 1993, when the Río Mosna burst its banks, while, in 1945, a major landslide along the Río Huachecsa completely covered the site with mud. It took many years to remove the rubble and some structures remain hidden. Ongoing investigations suggest an extensive tunnel system beyond the boundaries of the current site, which has yet to be excavated. The Huaraz road, which cuts across this area, may have to be moved to the other side of the valley some time in the future in order for excavations to continue.

The main attractions are the marvellous carved stone heads, the designs in relief of symbolic figures and the many tunnels and culverts which form an extensive labyrinth throughout the interior of the structures. The carvings are in excellent condition, though many of the best sculptures are in Huaraz and Lima. The famous Lanzón dagger-shaped stone monolith of 800 BC is found inside one of the temple tunnels. Excavations in 2001 uncovered 20 *pututos* (wind instruments) dating from the site's origins.

Day tours from Huaraz are offered by many agencies; it's a long but worthwhile trip, but check how many hours you get at the site. In high season, the site is busy with tourists all day through. You will receive an information leaflet in Spanish at the entrance. The guard also sells other reference material including *Chavín de Huantar* by Willhelm and Nancy Hoogendoorn, an English/Spanish guide to the ruins which includes a description of each building and an historical overview.

Chavín → *Colour map 2, B2. Altitude: 3160 m.*

The town of Chavín is the commercial centre for the nearby potato- and corn-growing area. The local fiesta takes place 13-20 July. It has a pleasant plaza with palm and pine trees, and several good, simple hotels and restaurants. The shops are well stocked with basic supplies, and carved stone replicas are produced for the tourist trade. There is also a small market. Gasoline is available at the north end of town but there is nowhere to change money. Now that the road from Huaraz is fully paved, the trip to Chavín takes about two hours, short enough for a day trip. Sadly, perhaps because it has been flooded by tour groups, Chavín has become increasingly uncomfortable for gringos, with

The stone gods of Chavín

Archaeologists have learnt very little about the Chavín culture, whose architecture and sculpture had a strong influence on the cultural development of a large part of the coast and central highlands of Peru. Based on physical evidence from the study of this 7-ha site, the temple of Chavín de Huantar is thought to have been a major ceremonial centre.

What first strikes visitors is the quality of the stonework. The sculptures have three functions: architectural, ornamental and cultist. Examples include the Lanzón, the Tello obelisk and the Raimondi stela; the latter two are in the Museo Nacional de Antropología, Arqueología e Historia in Lima (see page 65).

At 5 m high, the **Lanzón** is the crowning glory of the Chavín religion and stands at the heart of the underground complex. Its Spanish name comes from the lance-, or dagger-like shape of the monolith which appears to be stuck in the ground. Carved into the top of the head are thin, grooved channels;

some speculate that animals, or even humans, may have been sacrificed to this god. Others suggest that the Lanzón was merely the dominant figure for worship.

Named after the Peruvian scientist, Julius C Tello, the **Tello obelisk** belongs to the earliest period of occupation of Chavín (circa 100 BC). It represents a complex deity – perhaps a caiman-alligator – connected with the earth, water and all the living elements of nature. Carved on the body are the people, birds, serpents and felines that the divine beast has consumed.

The **Raimondi stela** was named after the Italian naturalist, who also gave his name to the famous plant (see box page 223), not to mention many of the streets in the region. It shows a feline anthropomorphic divinity standing with open arms and holding some sort of staff in each hand.

Together, the figures carved on the stones at Chavín indicate that the resident cult was based principally on the feline, or jaguar, and secondarily on serpents and birds.

overcharging, begging and hostile stares. The **Baños Termales de Chavín** ① *Quercos, Km 68, 2 km south of Chavín, US$0.60*, are hot sulphur baths, consisting of one small, quite cool pool and four individual baths in a pleasant setting by the Río Mosna. You may have to queue and clean the bath yourself. Camping is possible here.

● Sleeping

Carhuaz *p220*
B-C **El Abuelo**, Jr 9 de Diciembre y Tumbes, T043-394149, www.elabuelohostal.com. Modern, 3-star, comfortable, with cafeteria and parking. Knowledgeable owner, Felipe Díaz, is the publisher of a useful map of the *cordilleras* Blanca and Huayhuash.
C pp **Casa de Pocha**, 1½ km out of town towards Hualcán, T043-961 3058, lacasadepocha@ yahoo.com. Book in advance. Price includes breakfast and dinner, solar- and wind-powered electricity, hot water, sauna, pool, home-produced food, horses for hire, many languages spoken. Good base for hiking.

F **Hostal Señor de Luren**, Buin 549, 30 m from Plaza de Armas. Hot water, TV, safe motorcycle parking, very friendly.
G **Hostal La Merced**, Ucayali 724, T043-394241 (in Lima T01-442 3201). 'Like going back to the 1950s', clean, friendly, hot water, some rooms with private bath, luggage store.

Hospedajes
Four family-run *hospedajes* (F) have been built as part of a community development project. All have private bath and hot water. The better 2 are the modern **Hospedaje Robri**, Jr Comercio 935, T043-394505, and

Alojamiento Las Torresitas, Jr Amazonas 603, T043-394213. The latter is good, with friendly *señora* and pretty courtyard. Rooms with TV and bath. Breakfast negotiable.

Yungay *p220*

F pp **Comtury**, Complejo Turístico Yungay, Prolongación 2 de Mayo 1019, 2½ km south of the new town, 700 m east of the main road in Aura, the only part of old Yungay that survived, T043-969 1698 (mob). Bungalows with space for up to 10, in a pleasant country setting, hot water, fireplace, friendly, restaurant with regional specialities, camping possible.

F **Hostal Gledel**, Av Arias Grazziani, north past the plaza, T043-393048, rugamboa@ viabcp.com. Hospitable, good food, very clean but tiny rooms, shared bathroom, warm water, no towels or soap, cheap meals prepared on request, nice courtyard.

F **Hostal Sol de Oro**, Santo Domingo 07, T043-393116. Private bath, hot water, comfortable and good value. Best in town.

G **Hostal Mery**, 28 de Julio s/n. Simple, hot water, the rooms at the front can be noisy.

Caraz and around *p221*

B-C **O'Pal Inn**, 3 km south of Caraz, T/F043-391015, www.opalsierraresort.com. Scenic hotel outside town, set back from road. Bungalows and rooms, which have private bath, in a country setting, swimming pool.

D **Chamanna**, Av Nueva Victoria 185, 25-min walk from centre, T043-978 4841, T953 5279 (mob), www.chamanna.com. Clean *cabañas* in a beautiful garden, hot water, safe, excellent international cuisine in pricey restaurant.

D-F **Los Pinos**, Parque San Martín 103, 5 blocks from plaza, T043-391130, lospinos @apuaventura.com. Hot water, airy and comfortable, garden, camping US$2.50, internet US$0.50 per hr, use of kitchen US$3, laundry, clean, safe, book exchange, information and travel agency **Apu-Aventura** (see page 227). Breakfast and dinner are available, bar with movies every night.

E **La Alameda**, Av Noé Bazán Peralta 262, T043-391177, jtorres@viabcp.com.pe. Hot water, good rooms, breakfast, parking, gardens.

E **Caraz Dulzura**, Sáenz Peña 212, about 10 blocks from the town centre, T043-391523, hostalcarazdulzura@hotmail.com. Modern building in an old street, 6 double rooms, hot water, with bathroom and TV, comfortable,

very helpful owner, clean and airy rooms, breakfast included, very good food available.

E **La Perla de los Andes**, Plaza de Armas 179, T/F043-392007. Comfortable rooms with bath, hot water, TV, helpful, fair restaurant. Has a large new, cheaper annex on San Martín.

F **Chavín**, San Martín 1135 just off the plaza, T043-391171, hostalcahvin66@hotmail.com. With bathroom, warm water, good service but a bit grubby and dark, breakfast extra, guiding service, tourist information, owner can arrange transport to Lago Parón.

F **Regina**, Los Olivos s/n y Gálvez, south end of town, 1 block west of road to Yungay, T043-391520. Modern, with bathroom, hot water, clean, quiet, good value.

G **Alojamiento Caballero**, D Villar 485, T043-391637, or ask at **Pony's Expeditions** . Shared bathroom, hot water, washing facilities, stores luggage, basic, family run.

G **Hostal La Casona**, Raimondi 319, 1 block east from the plaza, T043-391334. Most rooms without bathroom; a couple of more expensive rooms have bath, hot water, clean, lovely little patio, basic but good.

Chavín *p224*

E **La Casona**, Wiracocha 130, Plaza de Armas, T043-454048, lacasonachavin@peru.com. In an old house with attractive courtyard, private bathroom, cheaper with shared bath, insufficient hot water, friendly, one room with a double bed, motorcycle parking.

E **R'ickay**, on 17 de Enero 172N (north), T043-454027, T01-9657 4013 (mob). Set around 2 patios, modern, pricey, all rooms with private bathroom and TV, hot water, restaurant.

F **Hostal Chavín**, Jr San Martín 141-151, half a block from the plaza, T/F043-454055. Set around a pleasant courtyard, G without bath, hot water, provides breakfast for groups, best of the more basic hotels, friendly and helpful, but poor beds.

E **Inca**, Wiracocha 160, T043-454021. In a renovated house, garden, friendly.

Camping at Chavín de Huantar is possible for vehicles, with permission from the guard.

🍴 Eating

Carhuaz *p220*

🍴 **El Abuelo**, Plaza de Armas, T043-394149. Local and international fare. Produce from their garden, including natural ice cream.

La Bicharra, just north of Carhuaz on main road, T043-978 0893 (mob). Innovative North African/Peruvian cooking, lunch only, busy at weekends, check if they are open Mon-Fri.

Yungay *p220*
Alpamayo, Av Arias Grazziani s/n, northern entrance to town. Best in town, excellent value local dishes such as trout, *cuy*, *tamales* and *pachamanca* at weekends. Lunch only.
Café Pilar, on the main plaza. Good for juices, cakes and snacks.

Caraz and around *p221*
La Punta Grande, D Villar 595, 10 mins' walk from centre. Best place for local dishes, good, open for lunch only till 1700.
Esmeralda, Av Alfonso Ugarte 404. Good set meal, breakfast, friendly, recommended.
Heladería Caraz Dulzura, D Villar on the plaza, next to **Perla de los Andes**. Excellent home made ice cream, good value meals, pastries.
Jeny, Daniel Villar on the plaza between cathedral and phone office. Good food at reasonable prices, also *pollería*.

Cafés
Good *manjar blanco* is sold by the Lúcar family, Villa Luisa brand, in a house next to the phone office on Raimondi.
Café de Rat, Sucre 1266, above **Pony's Expeditions**. Breakfast, some vegetarian dishes, pizzas, travel books, nice vibe.
El Turista, San Martín 1117. Small, popular for breakfast; ham omelettes and ham sandwiches are specialities.
Establo La Alameda, D Villar 420. Excellent *manjar blanco*, cakes and sweets.
Panificadora La Alameda, D Villar y San Martín. Very good bread and pastries.

Chavín *p224*
Specialities include rabbit stew, trout *ceviche* and *llunca*, a solid, wheat-based soup.
R'ickay, see Sleeping, above. Pasta and pizza dishes in the evenings.
Chavín Turístico, 17 de Enero. Overpriced *menú*, but good à la carte, delicious apple pie, clean, nice courtyard. Beware overcharging.
La Portada, 17 de Enero. In an old house with tables set around a garden.
La Ramada, 17 de Enero. Regional dishes, also trout and set lunch.

Bars and clubs

Caraz and around *p221*
Taberna Disco Huandy, Mcal Cáceres 119. Reasonable prices, good atmosphere, young crowd, Latin music. Fri and Sat only.

Festivals and events

Carhuaz *p220*
14-24 Sep Fiesta in honour of the Vírgen de las Mercedes, rated as the best in the region.

Yungay *p220*
28 Oct The anniversary of the founding of the town: parades, fireworks and dances.

Caraz and around *p221*
20 Jan Virgen de Chiquinquirá.
Mar/Apr Semana Santa (Holy Week), processions and streets carpeted with petals.
Last week in Jul Semana Turística, with sports and folkloric events.

Activities and tours

Caraz and around *p221*
Apu-Aventura, based at Hotel Los Pinos (see page 226), www.apuaventura.com. Adventure sports and equipment rental.
Pony's Expeditions, Sucre 1266, near the Plaza de Armas, T/F043-391642, www.pony expeditions.com. English, French and Quechua spoken, reliable information about the area. Owners Alberto and Aidé Cafferata are very knowledgeable about treks and climbs. They arrange local tours, trekking and transport (US$30 for up 4 people) for day excursions, maps and books for sale, also equipment for hire, mountain bike rental (US$15 for a full day). Possible to pay for services with Visa. Highly recommended.

Trekking
Mariano Araya is a trekking guide who is also keen on photography and archaeology. Ask at the municipality.

Transport

Carhuaz *p220*
Bus All transport leaves from the main plaza, 0500-2000. To **Huaraz**, *colectivos* and buses US$0.75, 40 mins. To **Caraz**, US$0.75, 1 hr.

Bus Most transport leaves from Jr 28 de Julio. Buses, *colectivos* run all day to **Caraz**, 12 km, US$0.30, and to **Huaraz**, 54 km, 1½ hrs, US$1. To **Lagunas Llanganuco**, *combis* leave when full, 0700-0900, from Av 28 de Julio 1 block from the plaza, 1 hr, US$1.50; otherwise US$9 to hire a vehicle (or US$12 with 2 hrs wait). To **Yanama**, via the Portachuelo de Llanganuco Pass, 4767 m, 3½ hrs, US$3; stopping at María Huayta, after 2 hrs, US$2. To **Pomabamba**, via Piscobamba, Trans Los Andes, daily 0700-0730 (this is the only company with a ticket office in Yungay); **Transvir** and **La Perla de Altamayo** buses from Huaraz, 0730, stop if they have room, 6-7 hrs, US$6. After passing the Llanganuco lakes and crossing the Portachuelo the buses descend to Puente Llacma, where it is possible to pick up buses and *combis* heading south to San Luis, Chacas and Huari.

Caraz and around *p221*
Local To **Huaraz**, frequent *combis* 0400-2000, 1¼ hrs, US$1.35, the road is in good condition. They leave from a terminal on the way out of town, where the south end of Sucre meets the highway. By *combi* to **Yungay**, 12 km, 15 mins, US$0.30. To the village of **Parón** (for trekking in Laguna Parón area) *combis* leave from the corner Santa Cruz and Grau by the market, Mon-Sat 0400 and 1300, Sun 0300 and 1300, 1 hr, US$1.20; they return from Parón at 0600 and 1400. To **Cashapampa** (Quebrada Santa Cruz) buses from Santa Cruz y Grau, hourly 0600-1530, 2 hrs, US$1.50; taxis charge US$7.55. To **Huallanca** (Caraz) and **Yuramarca** for the Cañón del Pato, *combis* and cars leave from Córdova y La Mar, 0700-1730, US$1.50. To **Huata** for the Cordillera Negra, *combis* and cars leave from the Parque del Maestro (Córdova y Santa Cruz), 0700, 1000, 1200, 1 hr. For the Puya Raimondi at **Winchos**, take a *combi* from Grau y Ugarte around 0900 to **Pamparomas**, 2 hrs, US$2, or hire a *combi* for US$42.50 for 8 people, plus US$7.20 for a guide.

Long distance Most Lima–Huaraz buses continue to Caraz. To **Lima**, 470 km, via Huaraz and Pativilca; several companies on D Villar and Jr Córdova, daily, 10-11 hrs, US$7: **El Huaralino**, **Expreso Ancash**, T043-391509, **Móvil**, **Rodríguez**, T043-391184.

To **Chimbote**, with Yungay Express (D Villar 318), via Cañón del Pato, 0830, US$6.60, 8 hrs; sit on the right for best views.
Note If you take this route to the coast, to change buses here for Trujillo, do not walk the 4 km from Chimbote bus station to the city centre. This is an extremely unsafe area and most unwelcoming. Never get off a bus in the city centre, always go to the terminal even though there are no hotels nearby: a *colectivo* to town costs US$0.30, taxi US$1. Try to avoid staying overnight in Chimbote.

Chavín *p224*
Bus To Huaraz, 110 km, 2 hrs, US$3. **Chavín Express** passes through around 1200, 1600 and 1700 daily; **Río Mosna** around 0430, 1600, 1800, 2000, and 2200 daily. All schedules are subject to change during road construction and improvements in the area.

To **Lima**, 438 km, 12 hrs, US$9, with **Trans El Solitario** and **Perú Andino** daily. Most companies use older, uncomfortable buses and many locals prefer to travel first to Huaraz and then take one of the more reputable companies from there (see page 219).

To other destinations in the Callejón de Conchucos it is necessary either to use buses coming from Huaraz or Lima, or to hop on and off *combis* which run between each town. *Combis* to **San Marcos**, every 20 mins from the Plaza de Armas, 25 mins, US$0.50; to **Huari**, 2 hrs , US$1.50. There are buses during the day from Lima and Huaraz, which go on to Huari, with some going on to **San Luis**, a further 3 hrs.

Directory

Caraz and around *p221*
Banks BCP, D Villar /217, cash and TCs at good rates. **Importaciones América**, Sucre 721, good rates and service. For large amounts of cash, however, it is better to exchange in Huaraz. **Internet** Many places around the plaza, US$0.30. **Post office** At San Martín 909. **Telephone** Phone and fax service at Raimondi and Sucre. Also several others, eg at Sucre y Santa Cruz, and on Plaza de Armas.

Chavín *p224*
Internet At Librería Aquarius, 17 de Enero y Túpac Yupanqui, US$1 per hr. **Post office** At 17 de Enero 365N (north). 0630-2200. **Telephone** Pay phones all over town.

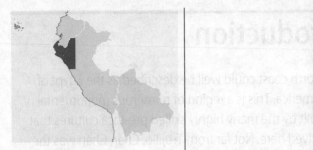

Introduction

Peru's north coast could well be described as the Egypt of South America. This is a region of numerous monumental ruins, built by the many highly skilled pre-Inca cultures that once thrived here. Not far from Trujillo, Chan Chán was the capital of the Chimú Kingdom; its crumbling remains still represent the largest adobe city in the world. The Huaca de la Luna of the Moche empire is revealing fabulous, multicoloured friezes of gods from the first millennium AD. Further north, near Chiclayo, the adobe brick pyramids of Túcume, Sipán and Sicán rise massively from the coastal plains. The wealth from some of their tombs is now displayed in new, state-of-the-art museums. The northern Highlands, too, contain some of Peru's most spectacular pre-Columbian ruins, with fantastic archaeological treasures in the Chachapoyas region, whose mysteries are just being uncovered. There are fortresses, cities and strange burial sites replete with mummies and giant sarcophagi.

But it's not all pyramids and tombs. The elegant city of Trujillo is one of the finest examples of colonial architecture in the country. Cajamarca, where the Inca Atahualpa was captured by the Spanish, has a pleasant colonial centre with comfortable hotels and good restaurants. On the seaboard there are charming towns such as Huanchaco, with its bizarre-looking reed-fishing rafts, quaint ports and a rain-free climate, ideal for bathing and surfing on Peru's finest beaches.

★ Don't miss...

1 **Huaca de la Luna** Recent discoveries tell a remarkable story of the beliefs of the Moche people, page 235.
2 **Huanchaco** Ride the waves on the totora-reed boats-cum-surfboards, known as 'little horses', page 238.
3 **Sicán** An excellent new museum and an ancient carob-tree forest show the culture and home of the Sicán people, page 250.
4 **Máncora** Great beaches, good surfing, a lively party scene at weekends, just the place for a break on the long haul up the Panamericana, page 256.
5 **Marca Huamachuco** For an out-of-the-way archaeological experience, go to this ancient site, in its strategic location overlooking all the surrounding valleys, page 264.
6 **Kuélap** Hike up to the vast fortress of the Chachapoyans. Seeing it in sunshine gives the clearest view, but on a misty day the Cloud People's citadel is truly atmospheric, page 266.

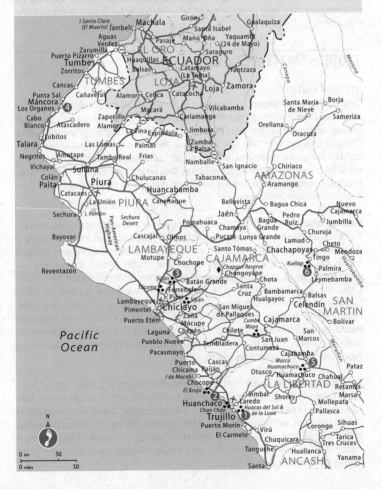

Northern Peru

Trujillo and around

→ *Colour map 2, B2. Phone code: 044. Population: 642,500.*

Trujillo, capital of the Department of La Libertad, disputes the title of second city of Peru with Arequipa. Founded by Diego de Almagro in 1534 as an express assignment ordered by Francisco Pizarro, the city was named after the latter's native town in Spain. There is enough here to hold the attention for several days. The area abounds in pre-Columbian sites, there are beaches and good surfing within easy reach and the city itself still has many old churches and graceful colonial homes, built during the reigns of the viceroys.

Perhaps Trujillo's greatest attractions are the impressive, varied Pre-Inca ruins that surround it: the Moche pyramids of Huaca del Sol and de la Luna, Chan Chán and the more distant El Brujo. All can be reached by public transport, but if that sounds complicated, there are many tours available. You need at least an hour to gain a full explanation of Chan Chán and Huaca La Luna, but many tours only allow 20 minutes each. If you are all ruined-out, just a few minutes up the coast from Trujillo is the seaside town of Huanchaco, long a favourite of travellers for surfing, watching the fishermen on their reed boats and just hanging out. ▸▸ *For Sleeping, Eating and other listings, see pages 238-246.*

Trujillo 🏨🍴🎒ℹ️✳️⬛🔺⬛📷🍷 ▸▸ *pp238-246.*

Ins and outs

Getting there The **airport** is to the west of town. You will enter town along Avenida Mansiche. There is no central bus terminal and none of the bus stations is in the centre. They are spread out on three sides the city, beyond the inner ring road, Avenida España. Plenty of taxis and *colectivos* can be found at the terminals to get you to your hotel. Insist on being taken to the hotel of your choice. Taxi drivers constantly say your hotel is too far/close, expensive/cheap, noisy/boring. They want to take you to the most distant/ expensive/remote place to increase fare/commission/overcharging possibilities.
▸▸ *See Transport page 244 for more details.*

Getting around With its compact colonial centre and mild, spring-like climate, Trujillo is best explored on foot. However, should you need a taxi, there are plenty of them. Always use official taxis, which are mainly yellow. Note that the very centre of Trujillo has confusing double street names; the smaller printed name is the one generally shown on maps, and in general use. The major sites outside the city, Chan Chán, the Moche pyramids and Huanchaco beach are easily reached by public transport or taxi/*colectivo*, but care is needed when walking to or from bus stops. Beware of overcharging, check fares with locals. A taxi can be hired from in front of the **Hotel Libertador** for US$7 an hour about the same rate as a tour with an independent guide or travel agent for one to two people. A number of recommended guides run expert tours to these and other places.

Tourist information i perú ① *Municipalidad, Pizarro 402, p 2, Plaza Mayor, T044-294561, iperutrujillo@promperu.gob.pe, Mon-Sat 0800-1900, Sun 0800-1400.* Take care anywhere beyond the inner ring road, Avenida España, as well as obvious places around bus stops and terminals, and at ATMs. Tourists may be approached by vendors selling *huacos* and necklaces from the Chimú period. The export of these items is strictly illegal if they are genuine, but they almost certainly aren't. Also take care if visiting the beaches south of Trujillo.

The focal point is the pleasant and spacious **Plaza Mayor**. The prominent sculpture represents agriculture, commerce, education, art, slavery, action and liberation, crowned by a young man holding a torch depicting liberty. Fronting it is the **cathedral**, dating from 1666, with its museum of religious paintings and sculptures next door. Also on the Plaza are the **Hotel Libertador**, the colonial style Sociedad de Beneficencia Pública de Trujillo and the Municipalidad. The **Universidad de La Libertad**, second only to that of San Marcos at Lima, was founded in 1824. Two beautiful colonial mansions on the plaza have been taken over. The first is the **Banco Central de Reserva**, in the colonial-style **Casa Urquiaga (or Calonge)** ⓘ *Pizarro 446, Mon-Fri 0900-1500, Sat-Sun 1000-1330, free 30-min guided tour, take passport*, which contains valuable pre-Columbian ceramics. The other is **Casa Bracamonte (or Lizarzaburu)** ⓘ *Independencia 441*, with occasional exhibits. Opposite the cathedral on Independencia, is the **Casa Garci Olguín** (*Caja Nor Perú*), recently restored but boasting the oldest façade in the city and Moorish-style murals. The buildings that surround the Plaza, and many others in the vicinity, are painted in bright pastel colours. Street lamps are on brackets, adding to the charm of the centre.

A couple of blocks north of Plaza Mayor is the church of **San Francisco** ⓘ *corner of Gamarra and Independencia, 0800-1200, 1600-2000*, which has a pulpit that survived the earthquake of Saint Valentine's Day in 1619 and three golden altars. **Casa Ganoza Chopitea** ⓘ *Independencia 630, opposite San Francisco, Mon-Fri 0915-1230, 1430-1630*, is architecturally the most representative house in the city and considered the most outstanding of the viceroyalty. It combines baroque and rococo styles. Continuing north you come to the **Museo del Juguete** ⓘ *Independencia 705 y Junín, Mon-Sat 1000-1800, US$0.85*, the toy museum, which contains examples from prehistoric times to 1950. At the northend end of Pizarro is **Plazuela El Recreo**, which was known as El Estanque during the colonial period as it housed a pool from which the city's water was distributed. A marble fountain by Eiffel now stands in the square.

Heading back towards Plaza de Armas, is the spacious 18th-century **Palacio Iturregui**, now occupied by the **Club Central** ⓘ *Jr Pizarro 688, daily 1100-1800*. To enter the patio is free, but to see more of the palace and the ceramics collection costs US$1.45. This exclusive social centre of Trujillo houses a private collection of ceramics. **Casa de la Emancipación** ⓘ *Jr Pizarro 610, Banco Continental, Mon-Sat 0915-1230, 1600-1830*, is where independence from Spain was planned and was the first seat of government and congress in Peru. There are exhibits on the life of the poet César Vallejo (1892-1938) and Bishop Martínez Compañón (1737-1797), whose circuits took him all around northern Peru. Before you arrive back at the plaza you come to the 17th-century church of **La Merced** ⓘ *Pizarro 550, 0800-1200, 1600-2000, free*, with picturesque moulded figures below the dome, has been restored. It has a mock rococo organ above the choir stalls and *retablos* from the 17th century which, unusually, are still visible, painted on the walls, from the time before free-standing altars were used.

If you leave the plaza on Orbegoso, the **Casa del Mariscal de Orbegoso** ⓘ *Orbegoso 553, daily from 0930, free, take passport*, is at the first junction. It was named after the ex-president, General Luis José de Orbegoso, and is owned by Banco de Crédito. It holds temporary exhibitions and cultural events most Thursday evenings. Turn up Bolívar and go one block right for the **Museo de Arqueología** ⓘ *Casa Risco, Junín 682 y Ayacucho, T044-249322, www.unitru.edu.pe/cultural/arq (mainly Spanish), Mon 0900-1445, Tue-Fri 0900-1300, 1500-1900, Sat-Sun 0930-1600. US$1.50, guided tours in Spanish available*. It houses a large collection of thematic exhibits from prehispanic cultures of the area. Further up Bolívar is the church and monastery of **El Carmen** ⓘ *Colón y Bolívar, church and pinacoteca open Mon-Sat 0900-1300, US$0.85, the church is open for Mass Sun 0700-0730*. Described as the 'most valuable jewel of colonial art in Trujillo', El Carmen has five gilt altars, balconies and religious paintings. Next door is the Pinacoteca Carmelita, with more paintings. It includes a room on picture restoration.

Northern Peru Trujillo & around

Trujillo

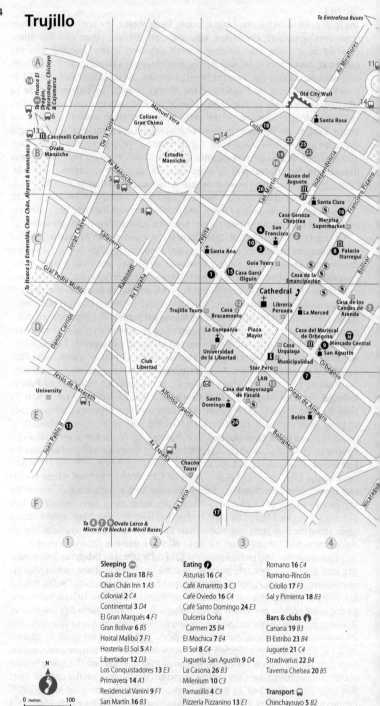

To Emtrafesa Buses

N

0 metres 100
0 yards 100

Sleeping

Casa de Clara 18 *F6*
Chan Chán Inn 1 *A5*
Colonial 2 *C4*
Continental 3 *D4*
El Gran Marqués 4 *F1*
Gran Bolívar 6 *B5*
Hostal Malibú 7 *F1*
Hostería El Sol 5 *A1*
Libertador 12 *D3*
Los Conquistadores 13 *E3*
Primavera 14 *A1*
Residencial Vanini 9 *F1*
San Martín 16 *B3*
Turismo 10 *D5*

Eating

Asturias 16 *C4*
Café Amaretto 3 *C3*
Café Oviedo 16 *C4*
Café Santo Domingo 24 *E3*
Dulcería Doña
  Carmen 25 *B4*
El Mochica 7 *E4*
El Sol 8 *C4*
Juguería San Agustín 9 *D4*
La Casona 26 *B3*
Milenium 10 *C3*
Parnasillo 4 *C3*
Pizzería Pizzanino 13 *E1*
Rincón de Vallejo 15 *C3*

Romano 16 *C4*
Romano-Rincón
  Criollo 17 *F3*
Sal y Pimienta 18 *B3*

Bars & clubs

Canana 19 *B3*
El Estribo 23 *B4*
Juguete 21 *C4*
Stradivarius 22 *B4*
Taverna Chelsea 20 *B5*

Transport

Chinchaysuyo 5 *B2*
Cial 2 *A5*

Heading northwest from plaza, you pass **Santa Ana** ⓘ *2nd block of Mcal Orbegoso*, one of the three 'iglesias menores' (lesser churches). The others were San Lorenzo and Santa Rosa. The street becomes Avenida Mansiche which leads to the routes out of town. The basement of the **Cassinelli** garage ⓘ *on the fork of the Pan-American and Huanchaco roads, 0900-1300, 1500-1900, US$1.50*, contains a collection of Mochica and Chimú pottery and is highly recommended.

Around Trujillo
 » *pp238-246.*

Huacas del Sol and de la Luna
ⓘ *0830-1600 (last entry, but site open till sunset), US$3.50 including guide. A booklet in English or Spanish costs US$2.85. See Proyecto Huaca de la Luna, Jr Junín 682, Trujillo, T044-297430, www.huacadelaluna .org.pe; also www.huacas.com.*

A few kilometres south of Trujillo a new 3-km access road leads to the huge Moche pyramids, the Huaca del Sol and Huaca de la Luna. The **Huaca del Sol** was once, before the Spanish diverted the nearby river and washed a third of it away in a search for treasure, the largest man-made structure in the Americas, reaching a height of 45 m. It consisted of seven levels, with 11 or 12 phases of construction over the first six centuries AD. Built from 143 million adobe bricks, it was the political centre of the site. The ceremonial platforms have been further eroded by the weather and visitors, but climbing on them is now prohibited. Today, about two-thirds of the pyramid has been lost.

The **Huaca de la Luna**, 500 m away, was a 'religious pyramid'. It received relatively little attention compared to its larger neighbour until more than 8000 sq m of remarkable mural paintings and reliefs were uncovered since 1990. The yellow, white, blue, red and black paint has faded little over the centuries and many metres of the intricate geometric patterns and fearsome feline deities depicted are virtually complete. It has now been established that the pyramid once consisted of six levels, each possibly pertaining to a different ruler-priest. When each priest died he was buried within the *huaca* and a new level was built covering up

Colectivos to Huaca del Sol
y de la Luna **3** *D6*
Combi A to Huanchaco,
Chan Chán **4** *E2, E5*
Combis A & B & Micros B, H
& H Corazón to Chan Chán
& Huanchaco **13** *B1*
Combi A & Micro H to Chan
Chán & Huanchaco **1** *E1*
Combi B & Micro B to
Chan Chán &
Huanchaco **14** *A5, B3*
El Dorado **6** *B1*
Ittsa **8** *B2, C2*
Oltursa & Flores **10** *A5*

Ormeño **11** *A5*
Turismo Díaz & Horna **9** *B1*

Masters of sculpture

One of the most remarkable pre-Inca civilizations was that of the Moche people, who evolved during the first century AD and lasted until around AD 750. Though these early Peruvians had no written language, they left a vivid artistic record of their life and culture in beautifully painted ceramics.

Compared with the empires of their successors, the Chimú and Inca, the realm of the Moche was very small, covering less than 250 miles of coast from the valleys of Lambayeque to Nepeña, south of present-day Chimbote. Though a seemingly inhospitable stretch of coast, the Moche harnessed the water from rivers from the Andean cordillera, channelling it into a network of irrigation canals. This resulted in plentiful crops, which, along with fish from the sea, gave the Moche a rich and varied diet. With the leisure allowed by such abundant food, Moche craftsmen invented new techniques to produce their artistic masterpieces.

These masters of sculpture used clay to bring to life animals, plants and anthropomorphic deities and demons. They recreated hunting and fishing scenes and elaborate sexual ceremonies. They depicted the power of their rulers as well as the plight of their sick and invalid. Ritual combat is also a common theme in their work; prisoners of war are apparently brought before congregations where their throats are cut and their blood offered to those present. Decapitation and dismemberment are also shown.

Moche potters were amazingly skilled at reproducing facial features, specializing in the subtle nuances of individual personality. They were skilled at low relief work. Among the most popular scenes are skeletal death figures holding hands while dancing to the accompaniment of musicians. The potters also developed a technique of fineline painting scenes on ceramic vessels. Over a period of several centuries the painters became increasingly skillful at depicting complex and lively scenes with multiple figures. Because of their complexity and detail, these scenes are of vital importance in reconstructing Moche life.

The early introduction of moulds and stamps brought efficiency to the production of Moche ceramics. By pressing moist clay into the halves of a mould, it was possible to produce an object much more rapidly than by hand. Similarly, the use of stamps facilitated the decoration of ceramic vessels with elaborate designs. Mould-making technology thus resulted in many duplications of individual pieces. Since there were almost no unique ceramic objects, elaborate ceramics became more widely available and less effective as a sign of power, wealth and social status of the élite.

Although among the most sophisticated potters in Spanish America, the Moche did not use ceramics for ordinary tableware and their ceramics do not depict everyday activities, such as farming or cooking. This is because Moche art expresses the religious and supernatural aspects of their culture and little of everyday life is illustrated for its own sake.

entirely the previous level. The number of levels suggests that there were six ruler-priests over a period of approximately 600 years. The highest mural is a 'serpent' which runs the length of the wall, beneath it there are repeated motifs of 'felines' holding decapitated heads of warriors, then repeated motifs of 'fishermen' holding fish against a bright blue background and, next, huge spider/crab motifs. The bottom two levels show dancers or officials grimly holding hands and, below them, victorious warriors following naked prisoners past scenes of combat and two complex scenes, similar to those at Huaca Cao Viejo at El Brujo (see page 238). Below the bottom end of the north/south ramp, the second level shows a 5-m-long reptile approaching a lifesize human figure aparently defending human figures holding hands. Combined with intricate, brightly painted two-dimensional motifs in the sacrificial area atop the *huaca*, Huaca de la Luna is now a truly significant site well worth visiting. Between the two *huacas* lie the remains of a once sizeable settlement of an estimated 20,000 people, now mainly lost beneath the sands, though excavations are taking place.

The **visitor centre** ① *T044-834901*, has a video/lecture hall, decent toilets, a patio with craftsmen selling replicas based on authentic designs and a souvenir shop. Books and videos are sold at the ticket office. Food is available at the nearby town of Moche.

Chan Chán

① *US$3.50 for 2-day entrance to the Chan Chán, museum, Huaca El Dragón and Huaca La Esmeralda; tickets can be bought at any of the sites, except La Esmeralda. A guide costs US$5.80 per hr; recommended. Map and leaflet in English for US$0.75. Robberies have occurred on the dirt track from turn-off to the site (20 mins). It is best to go in a group. If alone, contact the Tourist Police in Trujillo to arrange for a policeman to accompany you (there should be no charge). On no account walk the 4 km to the site, or on Buenos Aires beach, near Chan Chán.*

This crumbling imperial city of the Chimú is the largest adobe city in the world and lies about 5 km from Trujillo. Heavy rain and flooding in 1925 and 1983 damaged much of the ruins and, although they are still standing, eight palaces are closed to visitors. Money donated by UNESCO has gone towards protection work and conservation.

The ruins consist of nine great compounds built by Chimú kings. The 9-m-high perimeter walls surrounded sacred enclosures with usually only one narrow entrance. Inside, rows of storerooms contained the agricultural wealth of the kingdom, which stretched 1000 km along the coast from Guayaquil, in Ecuador, to beyond Paramonga.

Most of the compounds contain a huge walk-in well which tapped the ground water, raised to a high level by irrigation higher up the valley. Each compound also included a platform mound which was the burial place of the king, with his women and his treasure, presumably maintained as a memorial. The Incas almost certainly copied this system and transported it to Cuzco where the last Incas continued building huge enclosures. The Chimú surrendered to the Incas around 1471 after 11 years of siege and threats to cut the irrigation canals.

The dilapidated city walls enclose an area of 28 sq km containing the remains of palaces, temples, workshops, streets, houses, gardens and a canal. Canals up to 74 km long kept the city supplied with water. What is left of the adobe walls bears well-preserved moulded decorations showing small figures of fish, birds and various geometric motifs. Painted designs have been found on pottery unearthed from the debris of a city ravaged by floods, earthquakes and *huaqueros*.

The **Ciudadela of Tschudi** ① *daily 0900-1630 (but it may be covered up if rain is expected); arrive well before 1600 as you need more than 30 mins to see the site and will not be allowed in much after that*, is a 20-minute walk from the main road and has been restored. The site museum on the main road, 100 m before the turn-off, has a son-et-lumière display of the growth of Chan Chán as well as objects found in the area. Sometimes a singer waits in the Plaza Principal of the Ciudadela to demonstrates the perfect acoustics of the square (she expects a tip).

Huaca El Dragón

The partly restored temple, **Huaca El Dragón** ① *daily 0900-1630*, dating from Huari to Chimú times (AD 1000-1470), is also known as **Huaca Arco Iris** (rainbow), after the shape of friezes which decorate it. It is on the west side of the Pan-American Highway in the district of La Esperanza. Take a *combi* from Avenida España y Manuel Vera marked 'Arco Iris/La Esperanza', from the Ovalo Mansiche, or, if on the east side of the city, from Huayna Cápac y Avenida Los Incas; a taxi costs US$2.

A popular alternative to staying in Trujillo is the fishing and surfing town of Huanchaco, which is full of hotels, guesthouses and restaurants, but has little nightlife. It has great beaches to the south; to the north are reed beds good for birdwatching. The town is famous for its narrow pointed fishing rafts, known as *caballitos* (little horses), made of totora reeds and depicted on Salinar, Gallinazo, Virú, Moche, Lambayeque and Chimú pottery. These are a familiar sight in places along the northern Peruvian coast. Unlike those used on Lake Titicaca, they are flat, not hollow, and ride the breakers rather like surfboards. You can see the reeds growing in sunken pits at the north end of the beach. Fishermen offer trips on their *caballitos* for US$1.50, be prepared to get wet (groups can contact Luis Gordillo, El Mambo, T044-461092). Fishermen give demonstrations for US$2.85 (groups should give more). You can see fishermen returning to shore in their reed rafts about 0800 and 1600 when they stack the boats upright to dry in the fierce sun.

The town, now developed with beach houses, is overlooked by a huge **church**, one of the oldest in Peru (1535-1540), from the belfry of which are extensive views. The **pier** ⓘ *US$0.20*, also gives good views. Drivers should note that the municipality charges US$0.55 per vehicle to enter town in summer; in winter it is very quiet.

El Brujo

ⓘ *US$3.50, students half price, see www.xanga.com/elbrujoperu.*

Sixty kilometres north of Trujillo, is considered one of the most important archaeological sites on the entire north coast. The complex, covering 2 sq km, consists of Huacas Prieta, Cortada and Cao Viejo. This complex is collectively known as El Brujo and was a ceremonial centre for perhaps 10 cultures, including the Moche.

Huaca Cortada (or El Brujo) has a wall decorated with high-relief, stylized figures. **Huaca Prieta** is, in effect, a giant rubbish tip dating back 5000 years, which once housed the very first settlers to this area. **Huaca Cao Viejo** has extensive friezes, polychrome reliefs up to 90 m long, 4 m high and on five different levels, representing warriors, prisoners, sacrificer gods, combat and more complex scenes, with a total of seven colours in reliefs. The mummy of a tattooed woman, La Señora de Cao, dating from AD 450, has also been found. Her mausoleum, with grave goods, can be visited. In front of Cao Viejo are the remains of one of the oldest Spanish churches in the region. It was common practice for the Spaniards to build their churches near these ancient sites in order to counteract their religious importance. The excavations will last many years at the site, which was opened to the public in 2006. Photography is allowed. There are exhibitions in the Chan Chán site museum and Museo de la Nación in Lima.

⬤ Sleeping

Trujillo *p232, map p234*

AL Libertador, Independencia 485 on Plaza de Armas, T044-232741, trujillo@libertador. com.pe. Price includes tax, pool (can be used by non-guests if they buy a drink), cafeteria and restaurant, continental breakfast US$5, excellent buffet lunch on Sun. Recommended.
A El Gran Marqués, Díaz de Cienfuegos 145-147, Urb La Merced, T/F044-249366, www.elgranmarques.com. Price includes tax and breakfast, modern, free internet connection in rooms, pool, sauna, jacuzzi, restaurant. Recommended.

A Los Conquistadores, Diego de Almagro 586, T044-203350, losconquistadores@ viabcp.com. Price includes tax and American breakfast, bar, restaurant, garage and internet connection, very comfortable.
B Gran Bolívar, Bolívar 957, T044-222090, www.granbolivarhotel.net. Price includes breakfast, airport transfer and welcome drink, in converted 18th-century house, internet, café, bar, gym and parking.
C Hostal Malibú, Av Larco 1471-1474, T044-284811, www.hostalmalibu.com. Variety of rooms, restaurant, room service,

Huanchaco

To 🔟 🔟

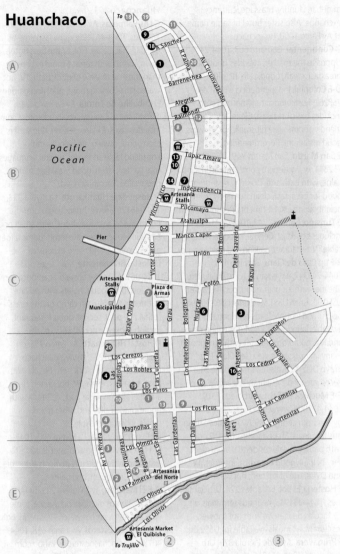

Pacific Ocean

Northern Peru Trujillo & around Listings

N

| 0 metres | 100 |
| 0 yards | 100 |

Sleeping 😴
Caballito de Totora **6** *D1*
Casa Hospedaje
  Los Ficus **13** *D2*
Cherry's **16** *D2*
El Malecón **3** *E1*
Golden Club **4** *D1*
Hospedaje El
  Boquerón **20** *A2*
Hospedaje Huankarute **2** *E1*
Hospedaje My Friend **1** *D2*
Hostal Bracamonte **5** *E2*
Hostal Huanchaco **7** *C2*
Hostal Ilablo **14** *E2*
Hostal Los Esteros **8** *B2*
Hostal Solange **9** *D2*

Hostal Sol y Mar **10** *D2*
Huanchaco Inn **15** *D2*
Huanchaco's
  Garden **11** *A2*
Las Brisas **12** *A2*
Las Palmeras **18** *A2*
Ñaylamp **19** *A2*

Eating 🍴
Big Ben **1** *A2*
Casa Tere **2** *C2*
Chelita **3** *C3*
Club Colonial **4** *D1*
El Mochica **14** *B2*
El Mococho **7** *B2*
Estrella Marina **10** *B2*

La Barca **11** *A2*
La Charapita **6** *C2*
Lucho del Mar **13** *B2*
Otro Cosa **9** *A2*
Piccolo **16** *D3*
Sabes? **18** *A2*

Bars & clubs 🍸
La Tribu **19** *D2*
Nutrias **20** *D1*
Xeros **20** *D1*

mini-bar, laundry, massage, currency exchange. Also sister hotel of same name at Av Larco 1000, Huanchaco.

D Continental, Gamarra 663, T044-241607. Opposite the market, includes good buffet breakfast, clean, good, safe, helpful.

D-E Colonial, Independencia 618, T044-258261, hostcolonialtruji@hotmail.com. Price includes basic breakfast. Clean, attractive, friendly, rooms are a bit small, hot showers, good restaurant. Recommended.

E San Martín, San Martín 749, T/F044-252311, www.deperu.com/sanmartin. Good value, with bath and TV, small restaurant, good for breakfast, clean but noisy from neighbouring establishments. Recommended.

E Turismo, Gamarra 747, T044-244181. Price includes breakfast. Central, good services, cable TV, restaurant, parking and travel agency.

E-F pp Casa de Clara, Cahuide 495, T044-243347, www.xanga.com/TrujilloPeru. Cheaper without bath, good food (breakfast US$0.90, lunch US$1.50, dinner US$2.10), very helpful and friendly, loads of information available, laundry US$1.50/kg, meeting place and lots going on, internet with broadband, many languages spoken (see **Clara Luz Bravo Díaz**, Activities and tours page 244). Recommended. Restaurants nearby.

E-F Mochica's B&B, La Arboleda E-19, T044-422006, www.mochicas.com. 5 mins by taxi from centre near Av América Sur and bus terminals. Shared rooms for 1, 2 or 4 with bath, in a safe residential area, quiet, very helpful, good breakfast, internet, TV and DVDs, use of kitchen, hot water.

F Hostería El Sol, Brillantes 224, Urb Santa Inés, T044-231933, near bus terminals on Av Nicolás de Piérola. With hot shower, restaurant, all meals available for US$2.60.

F Primavera, Av N de Piérola 872, Urb Primavera, T044-231915. With bathroom, hot water, restaurant, bar, pool.

F Residencial Vanini, Av Larco 237, T044-200878, enriqueva@hotmail.com. Youth hostel in a converted private house, a good option but not in the centre, some rooms with bath, others with shared shower.

G pp Chan Chán Inn, Av Ejército 307, T/F044-294281, mocheperu@hotmail.com. Close to several bus terminals so noisy, price includes breakfast (cheaper without), popular with backpackers, luggage store, café, laundry, internet, money exchange and information.

Huanchaco *p238, map p239*

C Las Palmeras, Av Larco 1150, sector Los Tumbos, T044-461199, www.laspalmeras dehuanchaco.com. One of the best hotels in town, rooms with terrace more expensive than those with view of pool; bath, TV, hot water, small dining room, pool and gardens.

D Caballito de Totora, Av La Rivera 219, T/F044-461154, www.caballitodetotora.com. Includes taxes, **E** in low season, **G** in surfers' room, pool, owners are friendly and knowledgeable and speak several languages, nice garden, clean, good breakfast, parking, good value. Recommended.

D Hospedaje Huankarute, La Rivera 233, T044-461705, www.huanchaco.com/huankarute. On the seafront, with small pool, bar, sun terrace, friendly; some rooms larger, more luxurious and more expensive.

D Hostal Bracamonte, Los Olivos 503, T044-461162, www.hostalbracamonte.com. Comfortable, good (chalets with private bathroom **C**), you can camp on the grass (US$4.25), pool, secure, good restaurant, English spoken, internet US$0.65/hr.

D Hostal Huanchaco, Av Larco 287, on plaza, T044-461272, www.huanchaco hostal.com. Half a block from beach. With bath, breakfast extra, TV, hot water, clean and friendly, pool, car park, cafeteria with home-made cakes and other good meals, video, pool table.

D Hostal Sol y Mar, La Rivera 400, T044-461120, www.ctsolymar.cjb.net. Breakfast extra, expanding, friendly owner is a doctor. With pool, restaurant and garden.

D-E El Malecón, Av La Rivera 225, T044-461275. Rooms overlooking the sea, some with terrace, clean, hot water, TV, café, friendly.

E Hostal Los Esteros, Av Larco 618, T044-461300, huanchacoesteros@yahoo.com. Bathroom, hot water, cable TV, restaurant, friendly, safe car and motorcycle parking, can arrange surfing and *caballitos de totora* trips.

E Huanchaco Inn, Los Pinos 528, T044-461158, www.huanchacoinn.com. Rooms with and without bath, new and still expanding, hot water, cable TV, internet cabins, use of kitchen, laundry service, small pool.

E Las Brisas, Raimondi 146, T044-461186, lasbrisas@hotmail.com. 20 rooms with bathroom, hot water, cafeteria, cable TV, comfy.

F Ñaylamp, Prolongación Víctor Larco 1420, northern end of the seafront in El Boquerón,

T044-461022, www.hostalnaylamp.com.
Rooms set around a courtyard, a little
more expensive in the new wing, dorms
too (**G** pp), hammocks, nice garden, kitchen,
very clean, with bath, hot water 24 hrs,
camping US$2.45 with own tent, US$3
with hired tent, laundry facilities, safe,
good views of the sunset from the
campsite and terrace restaurant,
Italian food, good breakfasts.

G Casa Hospedaje Los Ficus, Los Ficus 516,
T044-461719, www.huanchaco.net/losficus.
With bath, breakfast and laundry extra.
Family-run, hot water, use of kitchen.

G pp **Cherry's**, Los Pinos 448, T044-461837,
juancarlos160@yahoo.es. Owner speaks
English, cheaper without bath, hot water,
use of kitchen, it has a shop, bar, internet
with good machines, small swimming pool.

G pp **Golden Club**, Av La Rivera 217,
T044-461306. Popular with surfers, 5 rooms,
gym, pool, laid-back atmosphere, excellent
value, rooms available for monthly
rent (US$300).

G Hospedaje El Boquerón, R Palma 330,
T044-461968, maznaran@hotmail.com.
One block from beach, a modern house
with shared bathrooms, hot water, fully
equipped kitchen, laundry facilities and
service, clean, friendly landlady
speaks French.

G Hospedaje My Friend, Los Pinos 533,
T044-461080, magowave@hotmail.com.
Popular new place with surfers and
foreigners, good for meeting others
and for a meal in the restaurant (closed
1500-1900), with bath and hot water,
TV room. Tours arranged.

G Hostal Ilablo, La Orquídeas 339,
T044-9579753. Hot water, roof terrace,
popular with backpackers.

G Hostal Solange, Los Ficus 484, 1 block
from the beach, T044-461410, hsolange@
yahoo.es. With bathroom, hot water,
good food, laundry facilities, limited
use of kitchen, very helpful.

G pp **Huanchaco's Garden**, Av
Circunvalación 440, El Boquerón, T044-
461194, www.huan chacogarden.com.
Family-run, bungalows, cable TV, also
camping, hot water, use of kitchen, free
luggage store, friendly and helpful, garden
with 2 pools (1 for children), internet
US$0.65, parking, laundry.

🍴 Eating

Trujillo *p232, map p234*

A speciality is *shambar*, a thick minestrone
made with gammon, served on Mon. There
are 5 cheap seafood restaurants at Plazuela
El Recreo, at the end of Pizarro. For really
cheap meals try the central market at Grau y
Ayacucho. Avoid street sellers' hamburgers
and their sauces (very unsanitary).

🍴 **El Mochica**, Bolívar 462. Typical restaurant
with a good reputation, the food is good
and, on special occasions, there's live music.
There is another branch on the road to Las
Delicias beach and another in Huanchaco.

🍴 **Pizzería Pizzanino**, Av Juan Pablo II 183,
Urb San Andrés, opposite the university.
Great for pizzas, pasta, meats and desserts

🍴 **Romano**, Pizarro 747. International food,
good *menús*, breakfasts, coffee, milkshakes
and cakes, good service.

🍴 **Romano-Rincón Criollo**, Estados Unidos
162, Urb El Recreo, a 10-min walk from the
centre. Specializes in northern Peruvian
cuisine and has a good-value lunch menu
for US$2 in smart surroundings.

🍴 **Asturias**, Pizarro 741. Pleasant café with
set meals better than à la carte, excellent
desserts, good juices and snacks.

🍴 **Café Oviedo**, Pizarro 737. Vegetarian
options, good salads, helpful.

🍴 **Café Santo Domingo**, Av Larco 268.
Popular with locals in the morning.

🍴 **El Sol**, Pizarro 660. The original and best
vegetarian, cheap set meals and other dishes.

🍴 **Juguería San Agustín**, Bolívar 526. Good
juices and good *menú*, popular, excellent value.

🍴 **La Casona**, San Martín 677. Their set lunch
menu is popular with locals.

🍴 **Milenium**, Gamarra 316. Value vegetarian.

🍴 **Parnasillo**, Gamarra 353, T/F044-234715.
Hotel and restaurant school, good set menu
US$1.70 and US$2.25, but small portions.

🍴 **Rincón de Vallejo**, Orbegoso 303. Good
set menu, typical dishes, crowded at times.

🍴 **Sal y Pimienta**, Colón 201. Very popular for
lunch, US$1 and US$1.85, close to buses for
Huanchaco and Chan Chán.

Cafés

Café Amaretto, Gamarra 368. Best selection
of coffees, brilliant cakes, snacks and drinks.

Dulcería Doña Carmen, San Martín 814.
Serves local 'sweet' specialities.

Northern Peru Trujillo & around *Listings*

There are about 30 restaurants on the beach-front. Many close in low season and at night.
¶¶¶ Big Ben, Av Larco 836, near A Sánchez, T044-461869, daily 1130-1730.. Seafood and international menu, à la carte only, most expensive but very good.
¶¶¶ Club Colonial, La Rivera 171, on the beachfront, T044-461015. A smart restaurant and bar, open in the evenings, Belgian owner.
¶¶¶ El Mochica, Av Larco 552, T044-293441, daily 0900-1800. Same owners as in Trujillo, very pleasant dining area and panorama.
¶¶¶ El Mococho, Bolognesi 535. Said to be one of the best for seafood, expensive.
¶¶ Estrella Marina, Av Larco, next door to Lucho del Mar. Great value for fish.
¶¶ La Barca, Raimondi 111, T044-461855. Very good seafood, well-run, popular, but loud music or TV usually playing.
¶¶ Lucho del Mar, Av Larco. On seafront road, serves excellent sea food.
¶¶ Sabes?, Av Larco 920, T044-461555, ysabes@yahoo.com. Pub with food, internet café, popular, owned by an American tour guide.
¶¶-¶ Otra Cosa, Av Larco 921, T044-461346, www.otracosa.info, Wed-Sun 0900-2000. A vegetarian restaurant overlooking the sea (fair trade and organic produce), with Dutch owners, also has a volunteering agency, internet, massage, Spanish lessons, book exchange, movies, tourist information and surfing services. Recommended.
¶ Casa Tere, Av Larco 280, Plaza de Armas. For best pizzas in town, also pastas, burgers and breakfasts.
¶ Chelita, Deán Saavedra 270. Good-value *menú*, fish dishes are best, very popular.
¶ La Charapita, Huáscar 162. Modest but very popular restaurant serving large portions.
¶ Piccolo, Los Abetos 142, 5 blocks from the plaza. Cheap, friendly, live folk music week-end evenings, excellent, surf and art shop.

❶ Bars and clubs

Trujillo *p232, map p234*
Bar/Café Juguete, Junín y Independencia, open till 2400. An old-style café, good coffee.
Bar/Café Stradivarius, Colón 327. An attractive café with sofas, evenings only.

Canana, San Martín 788, T044-232503. Bars and restaurant, disco, live music at weekends (US$1.50-3 depending on the show), video screens (also has travel agency). Recommended, but take care on leaving.
El Estribo, San Martin 380. A new club playing a wide genre of sounds and attracting a mixed crowd.
Taverna Chelsea, Estete 675, T044-257032. Bar, restaurant, live salsa at weekends (US$4 entry), exclusive and lively. Recommended.

Huanchaco *p238, map p239*
On Av La Rivera, block 5, there are several lively bars with music such as **Nutrias** and **Xeros**. They open late in the summer.
La Tribu, Los Pinos 540. Galería, café and bar, opens 1900, unpretentious and popular, live music Thu. The owner is a sculptor, his workshop is worth seeing.

⊛ Festivals and events

Trujillo *p232, map p234*
End Jan The **National Marinera Contest** lasts 2 weeks and sees hundreds of couples competing in 6 categories, from children to seniors. This event is organized by the Club Libertad and has taken place since 1960.
18 Jun Festival de la Música.
Last week of Sep Festival Internacional de la Primavera, www.tuprimaveraentrujillo.com. Organized by the Club de Leones, it is a celebration of the arrival of spring and has become one of Peru's most important tourist events. The final parade (*corso*) has plenty to enjoy, with many local dancers, dog owners' clubs, schools parades and so on. Those who are opposed to beauty pageants may want to give it a miss as there are floats with beauty queens from South and North America. Other days feature cultural events (some charitable), and, above all, Trujillo's famous **Caballos de Paso**, a fine breed of horses with a tripping gait that has made them renowned worldwide. These horses, a Spanish legacy, have been immortalized in Peruvian waltzes. Riders still compete in their own form of the Marinera dance and buyers from around the world congregate to see them at the Spring Festival. See www.rcp.net.pe/rcp/caballos.

● *For an explanation of sleeping and eating price codes used in this guide, see inside the*
● *front cover. Other relevant information is found in Essentials, see pages 31-35.*

Huanchaco *p238, map p239*
There are also surf competitions and **Carnival** and **New Year** are especially popular.
1st week of May Festival del Mar, a celebration of the disembarkation of Taycanamo, the leader of the Chimú period. A procession is made in *totora* boats.
30 Jun San Pedro, patron saint of fishermen. His statue is taken out to sea on a huge *totora*-reed boat.

◎ Shopping

Trujillo *p232, map p234*
Bookshops
Librería Adriatica, Jr Junín 565, T044-291569, libreria@adriaticaperu.com. A very good bookshop, stocks Footprint.
Librería Peruana, Pizarro 505, just off the Plaza Mayor. Has the best selection of books in town, ask for Sra Inés Guerra de Guijón.

Handicrafts
APIAT, Av España near Zela, open daily 0900-2300, Sun 0900-1400. The largest crafts market in Trujillo, selling ceramics, woodcarvings, totora boats, etc, and kiosks selling shoes and leather goods at competitive prices.

Markets
Mercado Central, Gamarra, Ayacucho and Pasaje San Agustín.
Mercado Mayorista between Sinchi Roca and Av Los Incas (not a safe zone).
Merpisa, Junín y Pizarro and Av Larco y Los Angeles. A supermarket, the best choice for food at competitive prices.

Huanchaco *p238, map p239* **243**
The main *artesanía* market, **El Quibishe**, is at the entrance to Huanchaco at the southern end of the beach and is divided into handicraft stalls and a food section. Some stalls also on the seafront adjoining the Municipalidad, **El Erizo**, and in Av Larco, block 2, **Takaynamo. Artesanías del Norte**, Los Olivos 504, www.artesaniadelnorte.com. Sells items mostly to the owner, Mary Cortijo's design using traditional techniques. Food in the shops is a bit more expensive than Trujillo. There is a small fresh food market on Pilcomayo, ½ block from Deán Saavedra.

▲ Activities and tours

Trujillo *p232, map p234*
Tour operators
Prices vary and competition is fierce so shop around for the best deal. Average tour costs per person are: to **Chan Chán**, **El Dragón** and **Huanchaco**, 3 hrs, US$8.50, not including entrances. To **Huaca del Sol** and **Huaca de la Luna**, 2 hrs for US$7. To **El Brujo**, US$25. **City tours** cost US$5.65 (minimum 2 people; discounts for 4 or more). Few agencies run tours on Sun and often only at fixed times on other days. Check exactly which sites are included in the tour and whether guides speak anything other than Spanish.
Chacón Tours, Av España 106-112, T044-255212. Open Sat afternoon and Sun morning. Recommended.
Guía Tours, Independencia 580, T044-234856, guiatour@amauta.rcp.net.pe. Also Western Union agent. Recommended.

Northern Peru Trujillo & around *Listings*

Michael White & Claro Bravo: English, Español, Français, Deutsch, Italiano
World Heritage Sites of Chan Chan and Colonial Trujillo. Tours & Transfers.
Temples of the Rainbow (Dragon), Sun, Moon and El Brujo.
Museums, colonial houses, churches, markets, Huanchaco.
Sipán, Sicán and Brüning Museums, Túcume, Batán Grande
Kuntur Wasi, Cajamarca, Kuelap, Sectín, Huaraz.
Caballos de Paso, Marinera, peñas, folklore.

Casa de Clara: family guest house, cable TV, internet
Cahuide 495, Urb. Santa María - Trujillo - Perú
24 hrs: Tel (044) 243347 / 299997. Mobile (044) 9662710
Maps and photo album: http://groups.msn.com/TrujilloPeru
E-mail: microbewhite@yahoo.com Web: www.xanga.com/TrujillPeru

Tesores del Perú, Pizarro 575, of 03, T044-582381, oscarcampos10@hotmail.com. Oscar Campos Santa María organizes custom-made tours at affordable prices to archaeological sites, as far as Lambayeque.
Trujillo Tours, San Martín y Almagro 301, T044-257518, ttours@pol.com.pe. Work with **Lima Tours**.

Tour guides
Many hotels work on a commission basis with taxi drivers and travel agencies. If you decide on a guide, make your own direct approach. The tourist police (see Directory, below) has a list of official guides; average cost is US$7 per hr. Beware of cowboy outfits herding up tourists around the plazas and bus terminals for rapid, poorly translated tours. Also beware of scammers offering surfing or salsa lessons and party invitations.
Clara Luz Bravo Díaz, Cahuide 495, Urb Santa María, T044-243347, www.xanga.com/trujillo peru. An experienced tourist guide, who speaks Spanish, German and understands Italian. She takes tourists on extended circuits of the region and is very knowledgeable (archaeological tour US$16 for 6 hrs, city tour US$7 pp, US$53 per car to El Brujo, with extension to Sipán, Brüning Museum and Túcume possible). Clara works with Michael White (microbewhite@yahoo.com) who is English but speaks many languages. He is very knowledgeable. They run tours any day of the week. They can also arrange tours to see and possibly ride *caballos de paso*.
Laura Durán, T044-281590, lauraduran@yahoo.com. Speaks English, German and some Hebrew, very informative and helpful.
Oscar and Gustavo Prada Marga, Miguel Grau 169, Villa del Mar, or at Chan Chán.
Jannet Rojas Sánchez, Alto Mochica Mz Q 19, Trujillo, T044-934 4844, jannarojas@hotmail.com. Speaks English, enthusiastic, works independently and for **Guía Tours**.
Celio Eduardo Roldán, celioroldan@hotmail.com. Helpful and informative taxi driver.
José Soto Ríos, Atahualpa 514, dpto 3, T044-251489. He speaks English and French.

Huanchaco *p238, map p239*
Surfing
Piccolo, Los Abetos 142. Instruction, rent wet suits and boards, owner is a local champion.

The Wave, Av Larco 525. Staff speak English.
Un Lugar, Bolognesi 457, T044-957 7170, unlugarsurfingschool@hotmail.com. Ask for English-speaking Juan Carlos. Yenth Ccora, Av Larco 468, T044-940 3871, ycc_mar@hotmail.com. Surf school and surf equipment manufacture, repair and rental.
Yenth Ccora, Av Larco 468, T044-940 3871, ycc_mar@hotmail.com. Surfing equipment manufacture, repair, rental and surf school.

⊖ Transport

Trujillo *p232, map p234*
Air
Airport T044-464013. There are daily flights to and from **Lima** with **Lan** and **Star Perú** (also to **Chiclayo**). Taxi to airport costs US$4; or take a bus or *colectivo* to Huanchaco, get out at airport turn-off then walk 2 km (US$0.25).
 Airline offices Lan, Pizarro 340-42, T044-221469. **Star Perú**, Almagro 539, of 102, T044-293392, 0900-1930.

Bus
Local *Micros* (small buses with 25 or more seats) and *combis* (up to 15 passengers), on all routes, cost US$0.15-0.30; *colectivos* (cars carrying 6 passengers), US$0.25, tend to run on main avenues starting from Av España. None is allowed inside an area bounded by Av Los Incas in the east to Ovalo Mansiche in the west and the north and south perimeters of Av España.
Long distance Concentrations of companies are around Avs Ejército/Amazonas/Túpac Amaru; on Av Nicolás de Piérola, blocks 10-13 for northbound buses; and on Av La Marina, between Ovalos Grau and La Marina, for southbound buses. The better bus companies maintain their own terminals. To and from **Lima**, 561 km on a good road, 8 hrs in the better class buses, average fare US$14.30-18.50 in luxury classes, 10 hrs in the cheaper buses, US$7.15-11.50. There are many bus companies doing this route, among those recommended are: **Ormeño**, 3 levels of service, 5 daily; **Cruz del Sur**; **Turismo Días**, leaves at 2230; **Línea**, 13 daily, 3 levels of service, recommended, also to **Chimbote**, US$2.20, hourly, **Huaraz**, 2100, 9 hrs, US$8.65, Cajamarca 5 a day, US$4.25-10, **Chiclayo**, US$3.35, and **Piura**, 2300, US$7.

Also **Flores**, **Ittsa** and **Móvil Tours**. **Oltursa** offers a *bus cama* service to Lima, with full reclining seats, a/c, heating, meals and drinks, depart at 2200, with connection at Lima for Arequipa. Small **Pakatnamú** buses leave when full, 0400-2100, from Av N de Piérola 1092, to **Pacasmayo**, 102 km, 1¼ hrs, US$2.

To **Chiclayo**, another 118 km, 3 hrs from Trujillo, US$3.35, several companies. Among the best are **Emtrafesa**, on the half-hour every hour; to **Piura**, 278 km beyond Chiclayo, 6 hrs, US$7 (Ittsa's 1330 bus is a good choice); and **Tumbes**, a further 282 km, US$8.50, 8 hrs. Other companies include: **Transportes El Dorado**, leave at 1245, 2220 to **Piura** and **Sullana**, US$4.30/5.75; and **Olano**, **Civa**, **Ormeño**, US$8.60; Ormeño also has US$14.35 (2215) and US$8.65 (1915) services to Tumbes. Móvil's **Lima-Chiclayo-Chachapoyas** service passes through Trujillo at 1600 and Chiclayo at 2000 (US$11.50).

Direct buses to **Huaraz**, 319 km, via Chimbote and Casma (169 km), with **Móvil** and **Línea**, 8 hrs, US$8.60 special. Also **Chinchaysuyo**, at 2030, 10 hrs. There are several buses and *colectivos* to **Chimbote**, with **América Express** from Av La Marina (Panamericana Sur), 135 km, 2 hrs, US$2.20, departures every 30 mins from 0530 (ticket sales from 0500); then change at Chimbote. Leave Trujillo before 0600 to make a connection with the 0830 Cañón del Pato service; **Línea**'s 0600 bus also makes the connection. Ask Clara Bravo and Michael White (see Tour guides, page 244) about transport to Caraz avoiding Chimbote (a worthwhile trip via the Brasileños road and Cañón del Pato). To **Cajamarca**, 300 km, 7-8 hrs, US$4.55-10: with **Línea**, best at 1030; **Emtrafesa**, at 2200, and **Tur Díaz** 4 a day. To **Huamachuco**, 170 km, 6 hrs, US$4.55-5.50, **Trans Gran Turismo**, 4 a day; **Trans Horna**, 4 a day; **Turismo Negreiros**, 0900, 1300, recommended. To **Jaén**, Ejetur, at 1600, US$7.50.

Bus companies América Express, Av La Marina/Panamericana Sur. **Cruz del Sur**, Amazonas 437 near Av Ejército, T044-261801. **Ejetur** Av N de Piérola 1238, T044-222228. **Emtrafesa**, Av Túpac Amaru 285, T044-471521. **Flores**, Av Ejército 350, T044-208250. **Ittsa**, Av Mansiche 145, T044-251415; No 431 for northern destina-

tions, T044-222541. **Línea**, Av América Sur 2857, T044-297000 (ATM in terminal, video surveillance), ticket office at Orbegoso 300, T044-255181. **Móvil Tours**, Av América Sur 3959 – Ovalo Larco, T044-286538. **Oltursa**, Av Ejército 342, T044-263055. **Ormeño**, Av Ejército 233, T044-259782. **Pakatnamú**, Av N de Piérola 1092, T044-206564. **Trans Garrincha**, Prolongación Vallejo 1250, T044-214025. **Trans Gran Turismo**, Prolongación Vallejo 1368, T044-425391. **Trans Horna**, Av N de Piérola 1279, T044-294880. **Transportes El Dorado**, Nicolás de Piérola (Av América Norte) opposite Díaz, T044-291778. **Turismo Díaz**, Nicolás de Piérola 1079 on Panamericana Norte, T044-201237. Turismo Negreiros, Prolongación Vallejo block 13.

Taxi

Taxis charge US$0.55 within Av España and US$0.70 within the Av América ring road (drivers may ask for more at night). To Chan Chán US$3 per car, to the airport is US$4; to Huanchaco, US$3-5.

Huacas del Sol and de la Luna *p235*
The road to the site is paved. A taxi to the site costs US$2 (there are plenty at the site for the return). *Colectivos* (blue and yellow) every 15 mins to the visitors' centre, US$0.30. They are most safely caught at the Ovalo Grau; less safe stops at Huayna Cápac blocks 5 and 6, southeast of Av Los Incas, and Suárez y Los Incas. On the return go to Ovalo Grau for onward connections, or you can get out at Huayna Cápac y Los Incas. If you want a walk take any Moche *colectivo* or bus and ask to get off at the turn-off to the Huacas. It's about an hour's interesting walk through farmland beside irrigation canals, but don't walk after dusk.

Chan Chán *p237*
Take any transport between Trujillo and Huanchaco (see next paragraph) and ask to get out at the turn-off to Chan Chán, US$0.25. A taxi is US$3 from Trujillo to the ruins, US$0.85 from museum to ruins, US$1.85 to Huanchaco.

Huanchaco *p238, map p239*
Two *combi* routes (A and B) run between Trujillo and Huanchaco. 3 *micros* run between Trujillo and Huanchaco: **micro B** (also known

as Mercado Mayorista), **micro H** (UPAO) and **micro H-Corazón** (with red heart, Mercado Hermelinda). *Combis* run 0500-2030, *micros* 0630-2030, every 5-10 mins. Fare is US$0.35 for the 20-min journey. The easiest place to pick up any of these *combis* or *micros* is Ovalo Mansiche, 3 blocks northwest of Av España in front of the Cassinelli museum. In Trujillo, **combi A** takes a route on the south side of Av España, before heading up Av Los Incas. **Combi B** takes the northerly side of Av España. From Huanchaco to the **Línea**, **Móvil Tours** and southern bus terminals, take **micro H**. It also goes to Ovalo Grau where you can catch buses to the **Huacas del Sol y de la Luna**. For Cruz del Sur, Ormeño, Flores, Oltursa, etc, take *combi* or **micro B** from Huanchaco. There are also *colectivos* and taxis Trujillo-Huanchaco, minimum fare US$3, more likely US$4-5.

El Brujo *p238*
The complex can be reached by taking one of the regular buses from **Trujillo** to **Chocope**, US$0.55, and then a *colectivo* (every 30 mins) to **Magdalena de Cao**, US$0.45, then a mototaxi or taxi to the site, including wait, US$4.50, or a 5-km walk to the site. Alternatively take a tour with an agency from Trujillo.

❶ Directory

Trujillo *p232, map p234*
Banks BCP, Gamarra 562. No commission on cash into soles, but US$12 fee on TCs or changing into dollars, cash advance on Visa card. **Interbank**, Pizarro y Gamarra. Good rates for cash, no commission on Amex TCs into soles, reasonable rate, Visa cash advance, quick service (doesn't close for lunch). **Scotiabank**, Pizarro 314, Casa de Mayorazgo de Facalá. Good rates for Amex TCs, 2% commission into soles or dollars. **BBV Continental**, Pizarro 620. Amex TCs and Visa card accepted, US$10 commission up to US$500. Note that banks close 1300-1615. There is little difference between the rates for cash dollars given by banks and street changers, *casas de cambio* and travel agencies. There are many *casas de cambio* and street changers on the plazoleta opposite the Casa de Condes de Aranda and all along the 600 block of Bolívar.

Cultural centres Alianza Francesa, San Martín 858-62, T044-231232, www.ucv.edu.pe/ alianzafrancesa-trujillo. Instituto de Cultura Peruano Norte-americano, Av Venezuela 125, Urb El Recreo, T044-232512, www.elcultural.com.pe.
Consulates UK, Honorary Consul, Mr Winston Barber, Jesús de Nazareth 312, T044-235548, winstonbarber@terra.com.pe, Mon-Fri 0900-1700. **Hospitals** Hospital Belén, Bolívar 350, T044-245281, emergency entrance from Bolognesi. Clínica Peruano Americana, Av Mansiche 702, T044-231261. English spoken, good.
Immigration Av Larco 1220, Urb Los Pinos, Mon-Fri 0815-1230, 1500-1630. Gives 30-day visa extensions, US$20 (proof of funds and onward ticket required), plus US$0.80 for *formulario* in Banco de la Nación (fixers on the street will charge more).
Internet There are internet offices all over the centre, mostly on Pizarro blocks 1 and 6, and Av España blocks 1 and 8. **Laundry** American dry cleaners, Bolognesi 782, US$1.45 wash only, ironing extra, 24-hr service. Aquarelas, Bolívar 355, laundry and dry cleaner. Lavandería y Tintorería Luxor, Grau 637, cheap, next day service. **Post office** Independencia 286 y Bolognesi, 0800-2000, Sun 0900-1300, stamps only on special request. **Telephone** Telefónica, head- quarters at Bolívar 658. Private call centre at Pizarro 561, Ayacucho 625, Gamarra 450, others on 5th block of Orbegoso and Av España 1530. **Tourist police** Orbegoso 652, T044-291705, policia_turismo_tru@ hotmail.com, Mon-Sat 0800-2000. They provide useful information.
Useful addresses Gobierno Regional de La Libertad, Los Brillantes 650, Urb Santa Inés, T044-231791. For information on rural tourism in the department. Instituto Nacional de Cultura, Independencia 572. Indecopi, tourist complaints office, Jr Bolivia 251, Urb El Recreo, T044-295733, sobregon@indecopi.gob.pe.

Huanchaco *p238, map p239*
Banks BBV ATM just south of pier next to Municipalidad. **Health** Centro de Salud, Jr Atahualpa 128, T044-461547. **Internet** Many places on Los Pinos, Deán Saavedra and La Rivera, as well as in hostales. **Post office** Grau y Manco Capac, Mon-Sat 1300-1800.

Chiclayo and around

→ *Colour map 2, B1. Phone code: 074. Population: 471,500.*

Sandwiched between the Pacific Ocean and the Andes, Lambayeque is one of Peru's principal agricultural regions. Chiclayo is the major commercial hub of the zone, but also boasts distinctive cuisine and musical tradition (Marinera, Tondero and Afro-Peruvian rhythms), a famous witchdoctors' market and an unparalleled archaeological and ethnographic heritage. The area is also growing in importance as a birdwatching destination. Chiclayo is dubbed 'The Capital of Friendship', and while that tag could equally apply to most of the north coast of Peru, there is an earthiness and vivacity about its citizens that definitely sets it apart. ▸▸ *For Sleeping, Eating and other listings, see pages 251-254.*

Chiclayo

Sleeping 🛏
América 2 *B2*
Costa del Sol 3 *C3*
El Sol 4 *B1*
Europa 5 *B2*
Garza 6 *C3*
Gran Hotel Chiclayo 7 *B1*
Hostal Santa Victoria 9 *C3*
Hostal Sicán 10 *C2*
Inca 11 *B2*
Kalu 12 *A3*
Mochicas 13 *C2*
Paracas 14 *A3*
Paraíso 15 *A3*
Pirámide Real 19 *C3*
Sol Radiante 18 *C2*

Eating 🍴
Boulevar 1 *B2*
Café Astoría 2 *C2*
El Huaralino 4 *C1*
Govinda 7 *B3*
Hebrón 8 *C3*
Kaprichos 9 *A3*
La Parra 11 *C3*
La Plazuela 12 *B1*
Las Américas 13 *B3*
Mi Tía 14 *B2*
Roma 15 *C3*
Romana 16 *C3*
Tradiciones 17 *C3*

Transport 🚌
Brüning Express to
  Lambayeque 1 *B1*
Civa 2 *C3*
Colectivos to
  Lambayeque 3 *A2*
Cruz del Sur 7 *C3*
Emtrafesa 8 *C3*
Flores/Cial 9 *C3*
Línea 10 *C2*
Oltursa 11 *B1*
Tepsa 12 *C2*
Transportes Chiclayo 13 *B1*

Northern Peru Chiclayo & around

Getting there and around José Abelardo Quiñones González airport is 1 km from the centre; taxi US$2. Piura also has an airport for national flights. There is no bus terminal; most **buses** stop outside their offices, many on or around Bolognesi, south of the centre. Confusingly many of the buses leaving for the surrounding area are north of the centre. Most bus offices are on blocks 11-13 of Avenida Sánchez Cerro, northwest of the centre.

Calle Balta is the main street of Chiclayo, but the markets and most of the hotels and restaurants are spread out over about five blocks from the Plaza de Armas. Mototaxis are cheap. They cost US$0.50 anywhere in city, but are not allowed in the very centre. The surrounding area is well served by public transport.

Tourist information Centro de Información Turística ① *Sáenz Peña 838, Chiclayo, T074-238112.* There are kiosks on the plaza and outside **El Rancho**. For information on birdwatching sites, visit www.darwinnet.org/VICNO/birding_main.htm.

Sights

On the Plaza de Armas is the 19th-century neoclassical **cathedral**, designed by the English architect Andrew Townsend, whose descendants can still be identified among the town's principals. The **Palacio Municipal** is at the junction of Avenida Balta, the main street and the plaza; it was burnt down by protesters in 2006. The private **Club de la Unión** is on the plaza at the corner of Calle San José. Where Avenida Balta meets Bolognesi, a **Paseo de Las Musas** has been built, with pleasant gardens, statues of the Greek muses and imitation Greek columns. A similar **Paseo de Los Héroes** is at the opposite end of town. Another newish plaza is **Parque Leonardo Ortiz**, with a statue of Ñaylamp, buildings in the Lambayeque style and fountains.

Around Chiclayo 💿 ⏵⏵ *pp251-254.*

Sipán → *See Transport, page 253.*

① *Site is open 0800-1600 and the museum 0800-1700. Entrance for the tombs and museum is US$2. A guide at the site costs US$2.85 (may not speak English). Small boys also offer to guide you. Allow about 3-4 hrs. Take mosquito repellent.*

At this imposing twin-pyramid complex 35 km southeast of Chiclayo, excavations since 1987 in one of the three crumbling pyramids have brought to light a cache of funerary objects considered to rank among the finest examples of pre-Columbian art.

The Peruvian archaeologist Walter Alva, leader of the dig, continues to probe the immense mound that has revealed no less than 12 royal tombs filled with 1800-year-old offerings worked in precious metals, stone, pottery and textiles of the Moche culture (circa AD 1-750). In the most extravagant Moche tomb discovered, **El Señor de Sipán**, a priest was found clad in gold (ear ornaments, breast plate, etc), with turquoise and other valuables. A site museum was opened in 1992 featuring photos and maps of excavations, technical displays and replicas of some finds (it is due for redevelopment).

In another tomb were found the remnants of what is thought to have been a priest, sacrificed llama and a dog, together with copper decorations. In 1989 another richly appointed, unlooted tomb contained even older metal and ceramic artefacts associated with what was probably a high-ranking shaman or spiritual leader, called 'The Old Lord of Sipán'. A new find in July 2007 revealed a further élite burial.

Three tombs are on display, containing replicas of the original finds. Replicas of the Old Lord and the Priest are awaited. You can wander around the previously excavated areas of the Huaca Rajada to get an idea of the construction of the burial mound and adjacent pyramids. For a good view, climb the large pyramid across from the excavated Huaca Rajada. There is a path, but it looks as though it should be closed off to prevent erosion of the pyramid.

❚ Old Lord of Sipán

The excavations at Sipán by the archaeologist Walter Alva have already revealed a huge number of riches in the shape of 'El Señor de Sipán'. This well-documented discovery was followed by an equally astounding find dating from AD 100. The tomb of the 'Old Lord of Sipán', as it has come to be known, predates the original Lord of Sipán by some 200 years, and could well be an ancestor of his.

Some of the finest examples of Moche craftsmanship have been found in the tomb of the Old Lord. One object in particular is remarkable; a crab deity

with a human head and legs and the carapace, legs and claws of a crab. The piece is over 50 cm tall – unprecedented for a Moche figurine. This crab-like figure has been called Ulluchu Man, because the banner on which it was mounted yielded some of the first samples yet found of this ancient fruit.

The ulluchu fruit usually appears in scenes relating to war and the ritual offering of a prisoner's blood. One theory is that the ulluchu is part of the papaya family and has anticoagulant properties which are useful to prevent clotting before a man's blood is offered.

Chaparrí → *Colour map 2, B1.*

A minor road runs to **Chongoyape**, a pleasant old town 70 km to the east. Nearby are the vast Taymi and Pampa Grande pre-Columbian and modern irrigation systems. In the district of Chongoyape is the 34-sq-km **Chaparrí** private ecological reserve. Visitors can go for the day (T074-433194, US$3) or stay at the Chaparrí EcoLodge (see Sleeping, page 251); entry costs US$10 if intending to stay overnight. All staff and guides are locals. There are no dogs or goats in the area so the forest is recuperating. The variety of habitats, including dry desert forest, harbours many bird and mammal species, some of which are extremely rare. Notable birds are the white-winged guan and the Peruvian plantcutter, while there are also spectacled bears, Sechuran fox, puma and other cats. The Tinajones reservoir is good for birdwatching.

Lambayeque → *Colour map 2, B1. See Transport, page 253.*

About 12 km northwest from Chiclayo is the quiet town of Lambayeque. Its narrow streets are lined by colonial and republican houses, many retaining their distinctive wooden balconies and wrought-iron grille-work over the windows. For some fine examples, head along Calle 8 de Octubre: at No 410 is the opulent **Casona Iturregui Aguilarte** and, at No 328, **Casona Cuneo** is the only decorated façade in the town. Opposite is **Casona Descalzi**, perhaps the best preserved of all. Calle 2 de Mayo is also a good source of colonial and republican architecture, especially **Casa de la Logia o Montjoy,** whose 64-m balcony is said to be the longest in the colonial Americas. Also of interest is the 16th-century **Complejo Religioso Monumental de San Pedro** and the baroque church of the same name which stands on the Plaza de Armas.

The reason most people come to visit is to see the two museums. The **Brüning Archaeological Museum** ① *daily 0900-1700, US$3.50, guide US$2.85,* specializes in Mochica, Lambayeque/Sicán and Chimú cultures, and has a fine collection of Lambayeque gold. A board outside shows Peruvian cultures in relation to each other.

Three blocks east, the **Museo de las Tumbas Reales de Sipán** ① *T074-283978, http://sipan.perucultural.org.pe, Tue-Sat 0900-1700, US$9, enthusiastic multilingual guides,* is shaped like a pyramid. The magnificent treasure from the tomb of 'The Old Lord of Sipán', found at Sipán in 1987, and a replica of the Lord of Sipán's tomb are displayed here. A ramp from the main entrance takes visitors to the third floor, from where you descend, mirroring the sequence of the archaeologists' discoveries. This museum is frequently recommended and is judged to be one of the best in the world.

ⓘ *Daily 0800-1600 (the site stays open till 1700), US$2; guides charge US$2.85.*

About 35 km north of Chiclayo, beside the old Panamericana to Piura, lie the ruins of this vast city built over 1000 years ago. A short climb to the two *miradores* on **Cerro La Raya** (or **El Purgatorio**) offers the visitor an unparalleled panoramic vista of 26 major pyramids, platform mounds, walled citadels and residential compounds flanking a ceremonial centre and ancient cemeteries. One of the pyramids, Huaca Larga, where excavations were undertaken from 1987-1992, is the longest adobe structure in the world, measuring 700 m long, 280 m wide and over 30 m high. There is no evidence of occupation of Túcume previous to the Sicán, or Lambayeque people who developed the site AD 1000-1375 until the Chimú conquered the region, establishing a short reign until the arrival of the Incas around 1470. The Incas built on top of the existing structure of **Huaca Larga** using stone from Cerro La Raya. Among the other pyramids which make up this huge complex are: **Huaca El Mirador** (90 m by 65 m, 30 m high), **Huaca Las Estacas**, **Huaca Pintada** and **Huaca de las Balsas** which is thought to have housed people of elevated status such as priests. (Do not climb the fragile adobe structures.)

Excavations at the site, which were once led by the late Norwegian explorer-archaeologist Thor Heyerdahl of *Kon-Tiki* fame, challenged many conventional views of ancient Peruvian culture. Some suspect that it will prove to be a civilization centre greater than Chan Chán. A **site museum** (same entrance as site), contains architectural reconstructions, photographs and drawings. No excavations are visible at the site, where there is little shade. There is a good, new hostel (F), built of traditional materials, next to the huacas.

The town of Túcume is a 10-15 minute walk from the site. On the plaza is the interesting **San Pedro church**. The surrounding countryside is pleasant for walks and swimming in the river. *Fiesta de la Purísima Concepción*, the festival of the town's patron saint, is eight days prior to Carnival in February, and also in September.

Ferreñafe and Sicán → *Colour map 2, B1. See Transport, page 253.*

The colonial town of Ferreñafe, 18 km northeast of Chiclayo, is worth a visit, especially for the **Museo Nacional Sicán** ⓘ *T074-286469, http://sican.perucultural.org.pe, Tue-Sun 0900-1700, US$2.40, students US$1, plus US$4 per guide (Spanish only), café, handicraft shop.* This excellent new museum is designed to house objects of the Sicán (Lambayeque) culture from near Batan Grande: fascinating exhibits on food, climate, architecture, metal work and ceramics. It includes life-sized reproductions of the Sicán burials. The museum also has a botanical garden. There is a helpful **Mincetur tourist office** ⓘ *T074-282843, citesipan@mincetur.gob.pe*, on the Plaza de Armas.

The entrance to **El Santuario Histórico Bosque de Pómac** ⓘ *free, visitor centre, T9807 2291, dalemandelama@gmail.com, 0900-1700, a guide (Spanish only) can be hired with transport, US$3, horses for hire US$6,* which includes the ruins of **Sicán**, lies 20 km beyond Ferreñafe along the road to Batán Grande (there is another entrance from the Panamericana near Túcume). Visiting the sanctuary is not easy because of the arid conditions and distances involved: it is 10 km to the nearest huaca (pyramid). At the visitor centre food and drinks are available and camping is permitted. The guide covers a two-hour tour of the area which includes at least two huacas, some of the most ancient carob trees and a mirador (viewpoint), which affords a beautiful view across the emerald green tops of the forest with the enormous pyramids dramatically breaking through. Sicán has revealed several sumptuous tombs dating to AD 900-1100. The ruins comprise some 12 large adobe pyramids, arranged around a huge plaza, measuring 500 by 250 m, with 40 archaeological sites in total. The city, of the Sicán (or Lambayeque culture) was probably moved to Túcume (see above), 6 km west, following 30 years of severe drought and then a devastating El Niño related flood in AD 1050-1100. These events appear to have provoked a rebellion in which many of the remaining temples on top of the pyramids were burnt and destroyed.

The site lies within the largest intact *algarrobo* (carob) forest in the world, containing trees up to 1000 years old. Despite the dry, scrubby terrain the tree tops shimmer emerald green and there is prolific birdlife (47 species) as well as numerous reptiles and mammals, including an endangered species of wild cat.

● Sleeping

Chiclayo *p247, map p247*
There are several cheap hotels on Av Balta, near the bus offices, which range from basic to hygienically challenged. Most have only cold water. There are other cheap hotels near the Mercado Modelo, especially on Arica.
A Gran Hotel Chiclayo, Villareal 115, T074-234911, www.granhotelchiclayo.com.pe. Refurbished to a high standard, includes taxes and breakfast, pool, jacuzzi, restaurant, safe car park, changes dollars, casino.
A-B Garza, Bolognesi 756, T074-228172, www.garzahotel.com. Excellent bar and restaurant, a/c, pool, car park, tourist office in lobby provides maps, information in English, vehicle hire. Very good all round; it is close to the bus stations so there is activity at all hours.
A-C Inca, Av L González 622, T074-235931, www.incahotel.com. Recently refurbished, with TV and a/c, more expensive with jacuzzi, restaurant, garage, comfortable and helpful.
B Costa del Sol, Balta 399, T074-227272, www.costadelsolperu.com. Smart, TV, minibar, non-smoking rooms, small pool, sauna, jacuzzi. **Páprika** restaurant, good value Sun buffets US$7.50, vegetarian options.
D América, Av L González 943, T074-229305, americahotel@latinmail.com. Comfortable, friendly, breakfast included, restaurant, good value (except for the expensive laundry).
D Hostal Santa Victoria, La Florida 586, Urb Santa Victoria, T074-225074. Hot water, restaurant, free parking, dollars exchanged, very good, 15-20 mins' walk from the centre.
D-E El Sol, Elías Aguirre 119, T074-232120, hotelvicus@hotmail.com. Includes taxes, big rooms with bath, hot water, restaurant, pool by the car park, TV lounge, clean, good value.
E Kalu, Pedro Ruiz 1038, T/F074-228767, hotelkalu@hotmail.com. Near the Mercado Modelo. Comfortable, with bath and TV, laundry, safe, good.
E Mochicas, Torres Paz 429, T074-237217, mochcas1@hotmail.com. Fan, TV, helpful.
E Paracas, Pedro Ruiz 1046, T074-221611. Near the Mercado Modelo. With bathroom, TV, good value.

E Paraíso, Pedro Ruiz 1064, T/F074-222070, hparaiso@terramail.com.pe. Also near the Mercado Modelo, also comfortable and well appointed, but can be noisy.
E Pirámide Real, MM Izaga 726, T074-224036. Compact but spotless, good value, very central.
E-G Europa, Elías Aguirre 466, T074-237919, hoteleuropachiclayo@terra.com.pe. With bath (cheaper without; single rooms can be small), hot water, restaurant, good value.
F Hostal Sicán, Izaga 356, T074-237618. With breakfast, bath, hot water, cable TV, clean, comfortable but some rooms are gloomy, welcoming and trustworthy.
F Sol Radiante, Izaga 392, T074-237858, robertoiza@mixmail.com. With bath and TV, comfortable, pleasant, but noisy at the front.

Chaparri *p249*
A-C EcoLodge Chaparrí, T074-868 5626 or 074-453471, www.chaparrilodge.com. A delightful oasis in the dry forest, 6 beautifully decorated cabins, built of stone and mud, nice and cool, solar power. Price is for all-inclusive package (except horse-hire). First-class food. Sechuran foxes in the gardens; hummingbirds bathe at the pool. Recommended.

● Eating

Chiclayo *p247, map p247*
Local specialities include *ceviche* and *chinguirito* (a *ceviche* of strips of dried guitar fish, which is chewy but good). For delicious and cheap *ceviche*, go to the Nativo stall in the Mercado Central, a local favourite. *Cabrito* is a spiced stew of kid goat. *Arroz con pato* is a paella-like duck casserole. *Humitas* are *tamal*-like fritters of green corn. *King kong* is a baked pastry layered with candied fruit and milk caramel, appealing to those with a very sweet tooth (San Roque is the best brand). *Chicha* is the fermented maize drink with delicious fruit variations.
♈ El Huaralino, La Libertad 155, Santa Victoria. Serves a wide variety of international and creole dishes.

¶¶ **Hebrón**, Balta 605. For more upmarket than average chicken, but also local food, salads and *parrilla*. Also does an excellent breakfast and a good buffet at weekends.

¶¶ **Kaprichos**, Pedro Ruiz 1059. Chinese, delicious, huge portions.

¶¶ **Las Américas**, Aguirre 824, daily 0700-0200, good service. Recommended.

¶¶ **Roma**, Izaga 706. Wide choice of dishes.

¶¶ **Romana**, Balta 512. First-class food, good breakfast, popular with locals.

¶¶ **Tradiciones**, 7 de Enero Sur 105, daily 0900-1700. Good variety of local dishes, including *ceviche*, and drinks, nice atmosphere and garden, good service.

¶ **Boulevar**, Colón, between Izaga and Aguirre. Good, friendly, *menú* and à la carte.

¶ **Govinda**, Balta 1029. Good vegetarian.

¶ **Café Astoria**, Bolognesi 627. Breakfast, and a good-value *menú*.

¶ **La Parra**, Izaga 752. Chinese and creole, *parrillada*, very good, large portions.

¶ **La Plazuela**, San José 299, Plaza Elías Aguirre. Good food, seats outside.

¶ **Mi Tía**, Aguirre 650, just off the plaza. Huge portions, great-value *menú*, very popular at lunchtime, poor breakfasts, otherwise good.

⊛ Festivals and events

Chiclayo *p247, map p247*

6 Jan Among the many festivals held in and around the city is **Reyes Magos** in Mórrope, Illimo and other towns. This is a recreation of a medieval pageant in which pre-Columbian deities become the Wise Men.

4 Feb Túcume devil dances.

Feb Túcume celebrates the **Fiesta de la Purísima Concepción**, the town's Patron Saint, 8 days prior to Carnival, with music, dancing, fireworks, cockfights, sports events and much eating and drinking.

Mar/Apr Holy Week, many villages have traditional Easter celebrations and processions.

Dec At Christmas and New Year, processions and children dancers (*pastorcitos* and *seranitas*) can be seen in Ferreñafe.

⊙ Shopping

Chiclayo *p247, map p247*

Mercado Modelo, 5 blocks north of the main plaza on Balta. This is one of northern Peru's liveliest and largest daily markets.

Don't miss the colourful fruits, handicrafts stalls (see Monsefú) and the section of ritual paraphernalia used by traditional curers and diviners (*curanderos*), just off Calle Arica on the south side. It is filled with herbal medicines, folk charms, and exotic objects used to cure all manner of illnesses. The stallholders are friendly and will explain the uses of such items as monkey claws, dried foetuses and dragon's blood. As in all markets, take good care of your belongings.

Paseo de Artesanías, 18 de Abril at the end of Colón. Stalls sell woodwork, basketwork and other handicrafts in a quiet, peaceful, custom-built open-air arcade.

▲ Activities and tours

Chiclayo *p247, map p247*

Expect to pay US$18-25 pp for a 3-hr tour to Sipán, and US$25-35 pp for Túcume and Lambayaque (5 hrs). Brüning Museum, Sipán and Túcume, however, can easily be done by public transport. Sicán, which has less frequent public transport, is US$45-55 pp for a full-day tour including Ferreñafe and Pómac. Prices are based on 2 people.

Indiana Tours, Colón 556, T074-222991, www.indianatoursperu.com. Daily tours to nearby archaeological sites and museums and a variety of other daily and extended excursions with 4WD vehicles, as well as reservations for national flights and hotels. English and Italian spoken and Footprint users welcome. Recommended.

Inkanatura Travel, Gran Hotel Chiclayo, see page 251, T074-209948, www.inka natura.com,. Archaeological and cultural programmes, wildlife tours, catamaran trips and jungle walks.

Peruvian Treasures Explorer, Balta 398, T074-233435. Archaeological tours, helpful.

Horse riding

Rancho Santana, in Pacora, T074-968 7560 (mob), rancho_santana_peru@ yahoo.com. Relaxing tours on horseback in Santuario Histórico Bosque de Pómac, trips from 2 hrs (US$8) to full day (US$25), Swiss run (Andrea Martin), good Paso horses, free camping possible at the ranch, or lodging in E range. Andrea also takes tours to archaeological sites, etc. Frequently recommended.

◎ Transport

Chiclayo p247, map p247

Air

Flights to and from **Lima** and **Piura** with Lan, daily, and **Star Perú**, except Sun (Av Bolognesi 316, T074-271173).

Bus

To **Lima**, 770 km, US$12 and US$22 for bus cama: Civa, Cruz del Sur (bus cama; has the only daytime service at 0800, US$22); Ormeño, especial and bus cama (US$20); Línea, especial and bus cama service (recommended); Móvil; Oltursa, full range of services; Tepsa, Transportes Chiclayo. Most companies leave from 1900 onwards. To **Trujillo**, 209 km, with Línea and Emtrafesa, almost hourly from 0530-2015, US$3.35. Direct bus to **Cajamarca**, 260 km, 6 hrs; with Línea, 1315, US$5.65, 2200, US$8.45, bus cama at 2245 US$7.60; many others from Tepsa terminal, eg El Cumbe, 4 a day, Días, 3 a day, Mendoza, 2 a day, all US$4.55. To **Chachapoyas**, 230 km, US$6-10.60: with Civa at 1730 daily, 10-11 hrs; Móvil at 2000; Turismo Kuélap, in Tepsa station, 1830 daily. To **Jaén**, US$4.35-6.15: with Línea at 1300 and 2300, 8 hrs; Móvil, 1400 and 2300 daily; Turismo Jaén, in Tepsa station, 7 a day.

To **Piura**, US$3.65, Línea and Trans Chiclayo leave hourly throughout the day; also Emtrafesa and buses from the Cial/Flores terminal on Bolognesi 751. To **Sullana**, US$4.35. To **Tumbes**, US$5.75, 9-10 hrs; with Cial, or Transportes Chiclayo; Oltursa has an overnight service which leaves at 2015 and arrives at 0530 (this is a good bus to take for crossing to Ecuador the next day), seats can be reserved, unlike other companies which tend to arrive full from Lima late at night.

To Ecuador Many buses go on to the Ecuadorean border at **Aguas Verdes**, while Ormeño goes direct to **Guayaquil** (daily 0200) and **Quito** (Tue 0100). It's possible to get a substantial discount on the fare to the border: go to the Salida on Elías Aguirre (mototaxi drivers know where it is), be there by 1900. All buses stop here after leaving their terminals to try and fill empty seats. Bear in mind that the cheapest buses may not be the most secure.

Bus companies Civa, Av Bolognesi 714, T074-223434; Cruz del Sur, Bolognesi 888,

T074-225508; Días, T074-224448; Ejetur, Bolognesi 536, T074-209829; El Cumbe, T074-272245; Emtrafesa, Av Balta 110, T074-234291; Flores, T074-239579; Línea, Bolognesi 638, T074-222221; Móvil, Bolognesi 195, T074-271940; Oltursa, ticket office at Balta e Izaga, T074-237789, terminal at Vicente de la Vega 101, T074-225611; Ormeño, Haya de la Torre 242 (2 blocks south of Bolognesi), T074-234206; Tepsa, Bolognesi 504-36 y Colón, T074-236981; Transportes Chiclayo, Av L Ortiz 010, T074-237984.

Around Chiclayo p248

Buses to **Sipán** leave from Terminal Este Sur-Nor Este on Calle Nicolás de Piérola, east of the city (take a taxi, US$1; the area can be dangerous), US$0.45, 1 hr. Colectivos leave from 5-6 blocks east of Mercado Modelo (take care here, too). The way to the village is well signed through fields of sugar cane. Once at the village, the signs end: turn left, then right and go through the village to get to the site.

Buses from Chiclayo to **Chongoyape** leave from the corner of Leoncio Prado and Sáenz Peña; US$1, 1½ hrs. Then take a mototaxi to **Chaparrí**, US$7.50.

For **Lambayeque**, colectivos from Chiclayo; US$0.45, 25 mins. They leave from Pedro Ruiz at the junction with Av Ugarte. Also Brüning Express combis from Vicente de la Vega between Angamos and Av L Ortiz, every 15 mins, US$0.20.

For **Túcume** combis go from Chiclayo, Angamos y Manuel Pardo, US$0.70, 45 mins. A combi from Túcume to the village of **Come** passes the ruins hourly. You cannot miss the town of Túcume with its huge sign. Soon after the sign take a right turn on the paved road which leads to the museum and site. Don't be fooled by the pyramid close to the sign; it's part of the group, but some distance from the entrance. A combi from Túcume to **Lambayeque** is US$0.35 and takes 25 mins.

Colectivos from Chiclayo to **Ferreñafe** leave every few mins from 8 de Octubre y Sáenz Peña, 15 mins, U$0.30, but only run to Ferreñafe town centre so take a mototaxi on to the museum, 5 mins, US$0.50. Alternatively, combis for Batan Grande depart from the Terminal Nor-Este, in Av N de Piérola in Chiclayo, and pass the museum every 15-20 mins, 20 mins, US$0.50.

❻ Directory

Chiclayo *p247, map p247*
Banks Banks open 0915-1315, 1630-1830, Sat 0930-1230. It's much quicker and easier to use the ATMs. Beware of counterfeit bills, especially among street changers on the 6th block of Balta, on Plaza de Armas and 7th block of MM Izaga. **BCP**, Balta 630, no commission on Amex TCs for US$100 or more (US$12 commission if less), cash on Visa. Opposite, at Balta 625, is **Scotiabank**, changes Amex TCs, cash advance on Visa card. **Banco Santander**, Izaga y Balta, changes Amex TCs. **Interbank**, on the Plaza de Armas, no commission on TCs, good rates for cash, Visa cash advance. **Cultural centres** Alianza Francesa, Cuglievan 644, www.universidad peru.com/alianza- francesa-de-chiclayo.php. Instituto de Cultura Peruano-Norte--americana, Av MM Izaga 807, T074-231241,

icpnachi@mail.udep.edu.pe.
Instituto Nacional de la Cultura, Av L González 375, T074-237261. Has occasional poetry readings, information on local archaeological sites, lectures, etc. **Internet** Lots of places, particularly on San José and Elías Aguirre, average price US$0.60 per hr.
Medical services Ambulance: Max Salud, 7 de Enero 185, T074-234032, maxsalud@ telematic.edu.com. **Post office** On the 1st block of Aguirre, 6 blocks from the plaza.
Telephone Telefónica, at Aguirre 919; bank of phone booths on 7th block of 7 de Enero behind cathedral for international and collect calls. **Tourist police** Av Sáenz Peña 830, T074-236700, ext 311, 24 hrs a day, are very helpful and may store luggage and take you to the sites themselves. **Useful addresses** Indecopi, Elías Aguirre 770, T074-206223, mguzman@indecopi.gob.pe, for complaints and tourist protection.

North to Ecuador

From Lambayeque, the old Pan-American Highway heads north to the peaceful town of Olmos (90 km), where the Festival de Limón is celebrated at the end of June. At Olmos, a road runs east over the Porculla Pass for Jaén and Bagua. The old Pan-American Highway then continues from Olmos to Cruz de Caña and on to Piura. The new Pan-American Highway branches off the old road at Lambayeque and heads 190 km to Piura, straight across the Sechura Desert, a large area of shifting sands.
▸▸ *For Sleeping, Eating and other listings, see pages 257-261.*

Piura ⬤⬤⬤⬤⬤ ▸▸ *pp257-261. Colour map 2, A1.*

A proud and historic city, 264 km from Chiclayo, Piura was founded as San Miguel at Tangarará in 1532, three years before Lima, by the conquistadors left behind by Pizarro. It was relocated, first as Pirwa, then with its current name, in 1534. There are two well-kept parks, Cortés and Pizarro (with a statue of the conquistador, also called Plaza de las Tres Culturas), and public gardens. Old buildings are kept in repair and new buildings blend with the Spanish style of the old city. The winter climate, May to September, is very pleasant although nights can be cold and the wind piercing, while December to March is very hot. It is extremely difficult to find a room in the last week of July because of Independence festivities. The city suffers from water shortages.

Ins and outs → *Phone code: 073. Population: 361,000.*
Capitán Guillermo Concha airport ⓘ *Castilla, 10 mins from the centre by taxi*, receives daily flights from Lima and Cuenca. It has gift shops and two car rental agencies. A taxi to the centre costs US$1.85 by day, more by night. Taxis in town charge US$1, mototaxis US$0.50. **Radio Taxis,** T073-324509 or T073-324630. Information is available from the **tourist office** ⓘ *Ayacucho 377, T073-310772, daily 0900-1900*. The website www.munipiura.gob.pe/turismo, has lots of information in Spanish.

Sights

Standing on the **Plaza de Armas** is the **cathedral**, with gold-covered altar and paintings by Ignacio Merino. The church of **María Auxiliadora** stands on a small plaza on Libertad, near Avenida Sánchez Cerro. Across the plaza is the **Museo de Arte Religioso. San Sebastián**, on Tacna y Moquegua, is also worth seeing. The birthplace of Admiral Miguel Grau, hero of the War of the Pacific with Chile, is **Casa Museo Grau** ⓘ *Jr Tacna 662, opposite the Centro Cívico, Mon-Fri 0800-1300, 1530-1800, free*. It has been opened as a museum and contains a model of the *Huáscar*, the largest Peruvian warship in the War of the Pacific, which was built in Britain. It also contains interesting old photographs.

The **Museo Municipal Vicús** ⓘ *Sullana, near Huánuco, Mon-Sat 0800-2200, Sun 0800-1200*, includes 60 gold artefacts from the local Vicus culture. It also has an art section. Local craftwork is sold at the **Mercado Modelo**. The market on Sánchez Cerro is good for fruit.

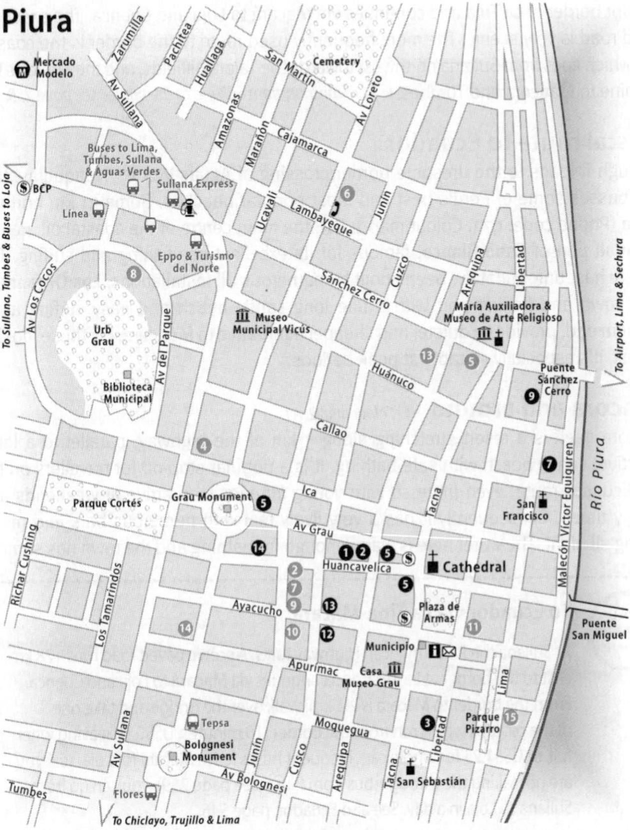

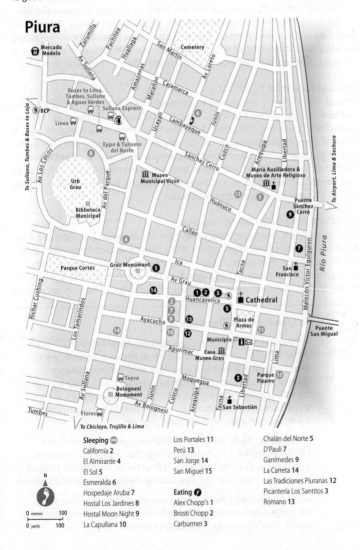

Sleeping
California 2
El Almirante 4
El Sol 5
Esmeralda 6
Hospedaje Aruba 7
Hostal Los Jardines 8
Hostal Moon Night 9
La Capullana 10
Los Portales 11
Perú 13
San Jorge 14
San Miguel 15

Eating
Alex Chopp's 1
Brosti Chopp 2
Carburmer 3
Chalán del Norte 5
D'Pauli 7
Ganímedes 9
La Carreta 14
Las Tradiciones Piuranas 12
Picantería Los Santitos 3
Romano 13

Routes to Ecuador ⬤🚲🚌🄲 ⟫ *pp257-261. Colour map 2, A1.*

Taking one of the inland routes from Piura to Ecuador, either to Loja or Vilcambamba, or the Jaén to Vilcabamba road (see page 269), is greatly preferable to the coastal highway via Tumbes, although the latter does have the advantage of beaches for chilling or surfing. The Highland crossings are more relaxed, with less traffic and fewer hassles.

Sullana to La Tina → *Colour map 2, A1. Population: 177,500.*

Sullana, 39 km north of Piura, is built on a bluff over the fertile Chira valley and is a busy, modern place. Avenida José de Lama, once a dusty, linear market, has a green, shady park with benches. Many of the bus companies have their offices along this avenue. Although the city is safer than it once was, you should still take great care by the market. Do not arrive in the town after dark.

From Sullana the Pan-American Highway forks. To the east it crosses the Peru-Ecuador border at **La Tina** and continues via Macará to Loja and Cuenca. The excellent paved road is very scenic. The more frequently used route to the border is the coastal road which goes from Sullana northwest towards the Talara oilfields, and then follows the coastline to Máncora and Tumbes. ⟫ *For Transport from Sullana to the border, see page 259.*

Coastal route to Ecuador

Although it leads to the tiresome border crossing of Aguas Verdes/Huaquillas, this road passes some of Peru's best and most popular beaches. Some 31 km north of **Talara** (Phone code: 073. Colour map 1, B1), the main centre of the coastal oil area, is the small port of **Cabo Blanco**, famous for its excellent sea-fishing and surfing. The scenery has, unfortunately, been spoilt by numerous oil installations. **Los Organos**, a small town and fishing port with a fine long sandy beach and easy surfing at its southern end, provides a quieter and cheaper alternative to Máncora. For those looking to relax, it's especially suitable at peak periods.

Máncora and around → *Colour map 2, A1.*

Máncora itself is a resort stretching along 3 km of the highway, parallel to a long, attractive, sandy beach with safe bathing. It is a popular stop-off for travellers on the Peru-Ecuador route, even more so with young *limeños* who arrive at weekends and holiday times. Consequently it has a very lively feel with numerous bars and music playing all night. The water here is warm enough for bathing and the town has some of

---

To Ecuador via La Tina-Macará

At Sullana the Pan-American Highway forks. A scenic paved road runs 128 km east to the border at **La Tina**, and continues via **Macará** to Loja and Cuenca. From the border to Macará is 2½ km: walk over the bridge and take one of the pickups which run from the border (10 minutes, US$0.30 leaving when full, or US$1.25 for whole car). Frequent buses leave Macará for Loja, so if you are not taking the through-bus from Piura (see page 259), you can go from Sullana to Loja in a day. See also Ecuador, page 546.

Immigration The border crossing is problem-free, open 24 hours and officials are helpful. Go to **Peruvian immigration** at the end of the bridge, get a stamp, walk across and then go to **Ecuadorean immigration**. There are no customs searches (vehicles, including *colectivos*, are subject to full searches).

At the border, there is one *hospedaje* and several eateries on the road to the bridge. There are banks at each side for changing cash only, open during the week; rates are a little better in Macará.

the friendliest local surfers on the planet. Surfing is best November to March (boards and suits can be hired from several places along the southern blocks of Avenida Piura, US$1.50 each per hour).

Tumbes → *Colour map 2, A1. Phone code: 072. Population: 92,000.*

Tumbes, 265 km north of Piura, is the most northerly of Peru's provincial capitals. It is not the most beautiful, but it does have some interesting historic wooden buildings, particularly on Calle Grau. The long promenade, the **Malecón Benavides**, gives good views of the river. Tumbes is a garrison town, so watch where you point your camera. Mosquito repellent is a must. Information is available from the **Centro Cívico** ① *Bolognesi 194, on the plaza, T072- 524940, irntum@yahoo.com, 0730-1300, 1400-1630.*

● Sleeping

Piura *p254, map p255*

A **Los Portales**, Libertad 875, Plaza de Armas, T073-321161, www.hoteleslosportales.com. Price includes breakfast, tax and cocktail. Attractively refurbished and is the city's social centre, elegant, a/c, hot water, pleasant terrace and patio, nice pool.
D **Esmeralda**, Loreto 235, T/F073-331205, www.hotelesmeralda.com.pe. With bathroom, hot water, fan (**C** with a/c and breakfast), clean, comfortable, good, restaurant.

D **San Miguel**, Lima 1007, Plaza Pizarro, T073-305122. Modern, comfortable, bath, TV, café.
E **El Almirante**, Ica 860, T/F073-335239. With bathroom, fan, clean, modern, owner is knowledgeable about the area.
E **El Sol**, Sánchez Cerro 411, T073-324461. With bathroom, hot water, small pool, snack bar, parking, accepts dollars cash or TCs.
E **Perú**, Arequipa 476, T073-333919. With bathroom and fan, clean, safe, friendly, laundry service, cold water, small rooms.

To Ecuador via Aguas Verdes–Huaquillas

Many buses run along the coast road from Lima to Tumbes (frequent road tolls, US$0.75), continuing on to Machala or Guayaquil in Ecuador. From Tumbes *colectivos* run 27 km to the border (see Transport, page 260).

Immigration For those those leaving Peru, immigration is at **Zarumilla**, at an office 4 km before the international bridge; for those entering Peru, immigration is at the western end of the bridge, at **Aguas Verdes** (see Ecuador, page 584). PNP is on the east side. The border is open 24 hours a day and passports can be stamped on either side of the bridge at any time. There are virtually no customs formalities for passengers crossing on foot, but spot-checks may take place. Having obtained your exit stamp, proceed across the bridge into **Huaquillas**. Passports are stamped 3 km north of town on the road to Machala.

Immigration formalities are reportedly trouble-free. However, this border has a terrible reputation for scams. Porters on either side of the border charge exorbitant prices; don't be bullied. Taxi drivers try to rip passengers off, or rob them. People offer to expedite formalities for US$20, without saying how they will help you. Money changers give out fake currency. And so on. Travelling on a through bus such as **Ormeño** or **CIFA** seems to involve less hassle, but it is much better to use the La Tina-Macará border crossing (see opposite page).

Aguas Verdes is a small place with basic facilities. Money can be changed on either side of the border. Ecuador uses the dollar as currency. Get rid of all your *soles* here as they are difficult to exchange further inside Ecuador. Do not change money on the minibus in Aguas Verdes, very poor rates. Do your own arithmetic, count your change carefully and watch out for counterfeit bills. Especially avoid those changers who chase after you.

E **San Jorge**, Jr Loreto 960, T073-327514. With bathroom and fan, cheaper without cable TV, hot water, clean but a little overpriced.

F **La Capullana**, Junín 925, T073-321239. With bath, some cheaper single rooms, welcoming.

F **Hostal Los Jardines**, Av Los Cocos 436, T073-326590. With bath, hot water, TV, laundry, parking, good value.

F-G **Hostal Moon Night**, Junín 899, T073-336174. Comfortable, modern, spacious, cheaper without bath/TV, clean, good value.

G pp **California**, Junín 835, upstairs, T073-328789. Shared bath, own water tank, mosquito netting on windows, roof terrace, clean, brightly decorated, friendly owner.

G **Hospedaje Aruba**, Junín 851, T073-303067. Small rooms but clean and comfortable, shared bath, fan on request, very friendly.

Sullana *p256*

B-C **Hostal La Siesta**, Av Panamericana 400, T/F073-502264, at the entrance to town. Hot water, fan, cable TV, cheaper with cold water, pool, restaurant, laundry.

E **El Churre**, Tarapacá 501, T/F073-507006. With bath, TV, laundry, café, good choice.

F **Hostal Lion's Palace**, Grau 1030, T073-502587. With bathroom, fan, patio, pleasant, quiet, no breakfast.

F-G **Hospedaje San Miguel**, Calle J Farfán 204, T073-502789. Cheaper without bathroom, all rooms open off a central passage-way, basic, helpful, good showers, cafeteria.

Máncora and around *p256*

All places to stay are to be found along the Panamericana between the main plaza at the north end of Máncora town and the bridge at the south end. The better hotels are at the southern end of Máncora. Prices can double in high season (Dec-Mar).

D pp **Hospedaje El Bucanero**, at entrance to Playa Punta Sal, set back from the beach, T072-381125, www.elbucaneropunta sal.com. Popular with travellers, great view.

D **Los Delfines**, near the beach at the entrance to Playa Punta Sal, T072-617804, angelicaborja@hotmail.com. Clean rooms, meals available, Canadian-run, very friendly.

D pp **Sunset Punta Sal**, 500 m south along the beach, T072-807702, puntasunset@ hotmail.com. B in high season, full board, wonderful place overlooking the sea, small, with pool, restaurant, popular with travellers.

E **Huá**, on beach, by the entrance to Playa Punta Sal, T072-540023, www.huapunta sal.com. C in high season. A rustic wooden building, pleasant terrace overlooking ocean, camping permitted on the beach by the hotel.

E **Hostal Casa Azul del Turista**, Av Piura 224, Máncora, T073-258126. Clean, friendly, family-run, with bath and TV, and roof terraces giving sea views. Recommended (but not at weekends or holiday times due to its proximity to the Sol y Mar disco).

Tumbes *p257*

The water supply is poor. There are many cheap hotels by the market. At holiday times it can be very difficult to find a vacant room.

B **Costa del Sol**, San Martín 275, Plazuela Bolognesi, T072-523991, ventastumbes@ costadelsolperu.com. Clean, hot water, mini-bar, fan, front rooms noisy, good restaurant, parking extra, has nice garden with swimming pool, racquetball court, provides information.

Eating

Piura *p254, map p255*

Piura's special dishes include *majado de yuca* (manioc root with pork); *seco de chavelo* (beef and plantain stew); and *carne seca* (sun-dried meat). Its best-known sweet is the delicious *natilla*, made mostly of goats' milk and molasses. The local drink is *pipa fría*, chilled coconut juice drunk from the nut with a straw.

♦♦♦ **Carburmer**, Libertad 1014, T073-332380. Very good lunches and dinners, also pizza.

♦♦♦ **Picantería Los Santitos**, in the same precinct and same phone as **Carburmer**. Lunch only, wide range of traditional dishes in a renovated colonial house.

♦♦ **Alex Chopp's**, Huancavelica 538. A la carte dishes, seafood, fish, chicken and meats, beer, popular for lunch.

♦♦ **Brosti Chopp**, Arequipa 780. Similar to Alex Chopp's, but lunch menu for US$1.45.

♦♦ **La Carreta**, Huancavelica 726. One of the most popular places for roast chicken.

♦♦ **Las Tradiciones Piuranas**, Ayacucho 579. Regional specialities, also an art gallery.

♦♦ **Romano**, Ayacucho 580. Popular with locals, extensive menu, excellent set meal for US$1.55. Highly recommended.

♦ **Ganímedes**, Lima 440. A good vegetarian restaurant, popular set lunch, à la carte is slow but worth it. Excellent yoghurt and fruit.

Cafés

Chalán del Norte, Tacna 520, Plaza de Armas, Grau 173 and 452 (Chalán de la Grau). Several branches of this popular chain, for good sweets, cakes and ice cream.
D'Pauli, Lima 541. Also for sweets, cakes and ice cream, good.

Máncora and around *p256*
There are many small restaurants and surprisingly trendy bars lining the Panamericana. Among the good ones are **La Espada** and **Don Pedro**, on the highway, both offer excellent value lobster dishes.
⊮ Laguna Camp, 100 m from the sea near the new breakwater, T9401 5628, www.vivamancora.com/lagunacamp. Thatched roofs, hammocks, delicious food, breakfast, lunch and dinner, pizza and barbeque nights, has cabins sleeping up to 6 people, helpful. Recommended.

Tumbes *p257*
There are cheap restaurants on Plaza de Armas, Paseo de la Concordia and near the markets.

⊖ Transport

Piura *p254, map p255*
Air Airport tax US$3.50. There are 2 daily flights with **Lan** (T073-302145) to **Lima** via Chiclayo. **Icaro** inaugurated flights between Piura and **Cuenca** (Ecuador) in Jan 2007.

Bus To **Lima**, 1038 km, 14-16 hrs, from US$7 (eg **Tepsa**), on the Panamericana Norte. Most buses stop at the major cities on route; **Flores**, **Ittsa**, US$17.15 on top floor, US$21.50 on lower floor, **Línea**. To **Chiclayo**, 190 km, 3 hrs, US$3.65, several buses daily. To **Trujillo**, 7 hrs, 487 km, US$7, several daily. To travel by day change in Chiclayo. To **Talara**, US$2, 2 hrs, with **Eppo**. To **Máncora**, US$3.15, 3 hrs, with **Eppo**. To **Tumbes**, 282 km, 4½ hrs, US$4.80, several daily, eg **Cruz del Sur** (also to Lima), **Cial** and **Emtrafesa** (also to Chiclayo and Trujillo); also *colectivos*, US$5.75. For **Chulucanas** *combis* from Piura charge US$1.50.

To border at La Tina **Trans Loja** and **Unión Cariamanga** both run to **Loja** (Ecuador) via **Sullana** and **La Tina** and **Macará**, 8 hrs, US$8. There are connecting *colectivos* to **Vilcabamba** from Loja.

To border at Aguas Verdes CIFA to **Machala** US$6, 6 hrs, and **Guayaquil** US$10, 9 hrs, via **Tumbes**, 4 a day from 1100. Otherwise go to Tumbes and travel on from there for the Aguas Verdes crossing to Ecuador.

Bus companies Most companies are on Av Sánchez Cerro, blocks 11, 12 and 13, www.munipiura.gob.pe/turismo/transporte.s html. There are some hotels in this area, but for central ones take a taxi. **Cial**, Bolognesi 817, T073-304250. **CIFA**, Los Naranjos y Sánchez Cerro (cuadra 11-12), T073-305925. **Cruz del Sur**, La Libertad 1176, T073-337094. **Emtrafesa**, Los Naranjos 235, T073-337093. **Eppo**, T073- 331160. **Flores**, Av Libertad 1210, T073-306664 (helpful). **Ittsa**, Sánchez Cerro 1142, T073-333982. **Línea**, Sánchez Cerro 1215, T073-327821. **Tepsa**, Loreto 1195, T073-323721. **Trans Dora**, Sánchez Cerro 1391. **Trans Loja**, Sánchez Cerro 1480, T073-309407. **Unión Cariamanga**, Sánchez Cerro y Av Vice, Urb Santa Ana, T073-990 0135 (mob).

Car hire At the air port: **Servitours**, T073-342008, www.servitourspiura.com; **Vicús**, T073-342051, www.vicusrentacar.com. US$50 per day for a small vehicle; they also provide transfers to Punta Sal US$80.

Sullana *p256*
Bus There are frequent buses to **Piura**, 38 km, 30 mins (US$0.45), **Eppo, Sullana Express** and **Turismo del Norte**, all on 1100 block of Sánchez Cerro, Piura; also *colectivos* (US$1). Try not to arrive in Sullana or Piura after dark.

To **Lima**, 1076 km, 14-16 hrs, US$9-18, several buses daily, most coming from Tumbes or Talara. A luxury overnight bus via Trujillo with **Ittsa** (T073- 503705) is US$18; also with **Cruz del Sur** and **Ormeño**.

To border at La Tina From Sullana to the border *combis* leave from Terminal Terrestre La Capullana, off Av Buenos Aires, several blocks beyond the canal, to the international bridge. They leave when full, US$2.85 per person, 1¾ hrs. It's best to take a taxi or mototaxi to and from the terminal.

To border at Aguas Verdes There are several daily buses to **Tumbes**, 244 km, 4-5 hrs US$5, from where there is onward transport to the border.

Taxi Mototaxis in Sullana charge US$0.30 in town. **Radio Taxis**, T073-502210/504354.

Bus To **Sullana** and **Piura** with EPPO, Grau 470, 1 block north of plaza, and **Dorado** both offer hourly service, just over 3 hrs, US$4, and just under 3 hrs, US$5, respectively. Other buses stop en route from Tumbes in the main plaza. To **Tumbes** (and points in between), *combis* tour the length of Av Piura all day as far as the bridge until full, US$1.50, 2 hrs.

Taxi A taxi from Máncora is the quickest and easiest way to get to Punta Sal Grande, 20 mins, US$9. Mototaxis are also prepared to make the trip, 40 mins, US$6.

Tumbes *p257*

Air There are regular flights to **Lima**. A taxi to the airport costs US$4, 20 minutes. *Combis* charge US$1.50. Taxis meet flights to take passengers to the border for US$7-9.

Bus Daily buses to and from **Lima**, 1320 km, 18-20hrs, US$12 (normal service), US$25 (**Cruz del Sur**), US$34 (**Cruz del Sur** VIP service). Most bus companies have offices on Av Tumbes. Cheaper buses usually leave 1600-2100, and more expensive ones 1200-1400. Except for luxury service, most buses to Lima stop at major cities en route. Tickets to anywhere between Tumbes and Lima sell quickly, so if arriving from Ecuador you may have to stay overnight. Piura is a good place for connections in the daytime. To **Talara**, 171 km, US$3.50, 3 hrs. To **Sullana**, 244 km, 3-4 hrs, US$4.50, several buses daily. To **Piura**, 4-5 hrs, 282 km, US$4.50; with Trans Chiclayo, Cruz del Sur, El Dorado, also to Máncora and Trujillo) 8 a day. Comité **Tumbes/Piura** *colectivos* costs US$5.75, fast cars, leave when full, 3½ hrs. To **Chiclayo**, 552 km, 6 hrs, US$5.75, several each day with Cruz del Sur, El Dorado. To **Trujillo**, 769 km, 10-11 hrs, US$8.50-14.35, Ormeño, Cruz del Sur, El Dorado and Emtrafesa. To **Chimbote**, 889 km, 13-14 hrs, US$10.

To border at Aguas Verdes
Colectivos leave from block 3 of Av Tumbes, US$1 pp or US$6 to hire the car, and wait and the immigration office before continuing to the border, 30-40 mins. *Colectivos* can cross the bridge, taxis cannot (so don't hire a Peruvian taxi to take you into Ecuador). Make sure that the drive takes you all the way to the border and not just as far as the comlex 4 km south of the bridge.

CIFA runs through-buses to **Machala** and **Guayaquil** in Ecuador, 6 a day, luxury bus at 1000, US$6, 5 hrs to Guayaquil, recommended for crossing the border.

Bus companies Civa, Av Tumbes 518, T072-525120. Comité Tumbes/Piura *colectivos*, Tumbes 308, T072-525977. **Cruz del Sur**, Tumbes Norte 319, T072-896163. El Dorado, Piura 459, T072-523480. Emtrafesa, Tumbes 596, T072-522894. Ormeño, Av Tumbes s/n, T072-522228. Tepsa, Av Tumbes 195-199, T072-522428. Trans Chiclayo, 466, T072-525260.

❶ Directory

Piura *p254, map p255*

Banks BCP, Grau y Tacna. Cash and Visa and Amex TCs (US$12 commission), cheques changed in the mornings only. Banco Continental, Plaza de Armas. Changes Amex TCs with US$10 commission. Interbank, Grau 170, changes Visa TCs. *Casas de cambio* are at Arequipa 600 block and 722, and Ica 366, 456 and 460. Street changers can be found on Grau outside BCP. **Consulates** Honorary British Consul, c/o American Airlines, Huancavelica 223, T073-305990. Honorary German Consul, Jutta Moritz de Irazola, Las Amapolas K6, Urb Miraflores, Casilla 76, T073-332920. **Internet** Several in the centre. 10 machines in the Biblioteca Municipal, Urb Grau, US$0.60 per hr, clean. **Laundry** Lavandería Liz-to, Tacna 785. Charges by weight. **Post office** Corner of Libertad and Ayacucho on Plaza de Armas is not too helpful, Mon-Sat, 0800-1600. Hotel Los Portales is better. **Telephone** Loreto 259, national and international phone and fax. Also at Ovalo Grau 483. **Useful addresses** Dirección Regional de Turismo, Av Fortunato Chirichigno, Urb San Eduardo, T073-308229, at the north end of town. Indecopi, Ayacucho y Libertad, Plaza de Armas, T073-308549, dnavarro@indecopi.gob.pe, helpful for problems.

Máncora and around *p256*

Banks Tienda Marlón, Piura 613. Changes US$ cash at poor rates. **Internet** Several internet cafés on the highway. **Telephone** Piura 509, opposite the church.

Tumbes *p257*

Banks BCP, Paseo de los Libertadores 261, for cash only, poor rates. **Banco Continental**, Bolívar 121, changes cash and Amex TCs only, US$5 commission. **Cambios Internacionales**, Av Bolívar 161, Plaza de Armas. Cash only, good rates. Money changers on the street (on Bolívar, left of the cathedral), some of whom are unscrupulous, give a much better rate than the banks or *cambios*, but don't accept the first offer you are given. Street changers don't change cheques. All banks close for lunch. Rates offered at the airport are bad. If you are travelling on to Ecuador, it is better to change your soles at the border as the rate is higher. **Consulates** Ecuadorean Consulate, Bolívar 129, Plaza de Armas, T072-521739, consultum@speedy.com.pe, Mon-Fri 0900-1300, 1400-1630. **Internet** Widely available in many cheap cafés and major hotels. **Laundry** Lavandería Flash, Piura 1000. Pay by weight. **Post office** San Martín 208, on Paseo de la Concordia. **Telephone** San Martín 210, on Paseo de la Concordia. **Useful addresses** Pronaturaleza, Av Tarapacá 4-16, Urb Fonavi, T072-523412.

Northern Highlands

This vast area stretches from the western foothills of the Andes across the mountains and down to the fringes of the Amazon jungle. It contains Peru's most spectacular pre-Columbian ruins, some of them built on a massive scale unequalled anywhere in the Americas. A good road rises from the coast to the beautiful colonial city of Cajamarca, where the Inca Atahualpa was captured by the Spanish. Only one Inca building remains, the so-called Ransom Chamber, but the city has a pleasant colonial centre with comfortable hotels and good restaurants. Change is coming fast as a huge gold mine is bringing new investment, but also conflict, to the area. Close by are the hot springs where Atahualpa used to bathe, still very much in use today, and a number of pre-Inca sites. Beyond Cajamarca, a tortuous road winds its way east to the functional town of Chachapoyas. This is a friendly place, opening its doors to visitors as it lies at the centre of a region full of fantastic archaeological treasures whose mysteries are just being uncovered. There are fortresses, mysterious cities and strange burial sites replete with mummies and giant sarcophagi. ▶▶ *For Sleeping, Eating and other listings see pages 269-276.*

Cajamarca and around 🏨🍴❄️⬜🔺🚌ℹ️ ▶▶ *pp269-276.*

→ *Colour map 2, B2. Phone code: 076. Population: 122,500. Altitude: 2750 m.*

Before Cajamarca became an Inca religious centre and favoured haunt of the nobility in 1456, it had been at the heart of a culture known as Caxamarca, which flourished from AD 500 to 1000. The violent events of 1532-1533, when the conquistador Pizarro ambushed, captured and executed Atahualpa, the Inca emperor, marked the first showdown between the Spanish and the Incas. Despite their huge numerical inferiority, the Spanish emerged victorious and moved on to overthrow the entire Inca empire.

In addition to its historical associations, Cajamarca is best known for its dairy industry, textiles and intricately worked mirrors. It sits at the edge of a green valley which is ideal for dairy farming. Around the Plaza de Armas are many fine old houses, which are being converted into tasteful hotels, restaurants and galleries to cater for engineers and incomers from the adjacent Yanacocha mining project. The airport has likewise been expanded. The mine, now that it is fully operational and looking to expand, has provoked opposition from farmers and created worries over pollution and intrusion on the provincial calm of the city. It remains, though, a great place to buy handicrafts. Outside town are several good haciendas which offer bed, board and rural pursuits, while at the Baños del Inca, just up the road, you can unwind as the steam from the thermal waters meets the cool mountain air.

Getting there The **airport** ① *3 km northeast of town (take the Cerillo road)*, receives regular flights from Lima. Taxi to the centre US$1.50, mototaxi US$0.75. The **bus** offices are to the southeast of the centre, on the Baños del Inca road past La Recoleta church; a 20-minute walk from the Plaza de Armas. Cajamarca can be reached from the coast, directly northeast from Trujillo on an improving road, or via a much faster road, from the port of Pacasmayo, midway between Trujillo and Chiclayo. The paved 180-km road branches off the Pan-American Highway soon after it crosses the Río Jequetepeque at Madre de Dios. However, it still takes a couple of days by bus via Huamachuco and Cajabamba, as opposed to seven hours on the paved road from either Trujillo or Chiclayo. The old road is more interesting, passing through sierra towns and over the bare puna before dropping into the Huamachuco Valley, where the archaeological site of Marca Huamachuco is one of the main attractions.

Getting around All the main sights are clustered around the Plaza de Armas. With its many old colonial buildings it is an interesting town to wander around although the climb up Santa Apolonia hill is quite demanding. The district around Plaza Francia (Amazonas y José Gálvez), the market area and east of Amazonas are not safe at night (prostitution and drugs). Buses in town charge US$0.15. Taxis US$0.60 within city limits. Mototaxis US$0.30. *Combis* run to the main places outside town, like Baños del Inca. Others, like Cumbemayo, are best reached on a tour, while still others make good day walks.

Best time to visit Cajamarca has a pleasant climate, with warm days and chilly nights. The wettest months are December-March. During October-November there are numerous school trips to this area, so most of the budget hotels are full at this time.

Tourist information Dirección Regional de Turismo and **Instituto Nacional de Cultura** ① *Belén 631, T076-362997, www.inccajamarca.org, Mon-Fri 0730-1300, 1430-1800*; **University tourist school's office** ① *Del Batán 289, T076-361546, Mon-Fri 0830-1300, 1500-2200, donation*. The **Circuito Turístico Nororiental**, which is opening up the Chiclayo-Cajamarca-Chachapoyas tourist route, is becoming firmly established.

Sights

The main **Plaza de Armas**, where Atahualpa was executed, has a 350-year-old fountain, topiary and gardens. The impressive **cathedral**, opened in 1776, is still missing its belfry, but the façade has beautiful baroque carving in stone. The altar is covered in original gold leaf. On the opposite side of the plaza is the 17th-century **San Francisco Church**, older than the cathedral and with more interior stone carving and elaborate altars. A side chapel has an ornate ceiling. **Museo de Arte Colonial** ① *Mon-Sat 1430-1800, US$0.85, entrance is unmarked on far left corner of church*. Tickets are sold from an unmarked office on the right of courtyard as you walk towards the church. Attached to San Francisco, the museum is filled with colonial paintings and icons. The guided tour of the museum includes entry to the church's spooky catacombs.

The **Complejo Belén** ① *Mon-Sat 0900-1300, 1500-1730, Sun 0900-1230, US$1.20; tickets also valid for the Cuarto de Rescate; Spanish guide US$2.85 (US$5.75-8.50 for other languages)*, comprises the **tourist office** and **Institute of Culture**, a beautifully ornate church, considered the city's finest, and two museums. The arches, pillars and walls of the nave of Belén church are covered in lozenges (*rombos*), a design picked out in the gold tracery of the altar. Take a look at the inside of the dome, where eight giant cherubs support an intricate flowering centrepiece. The carved pulpit has a spiral staircase and the doors are intricately worked in wood. In the same courtyard is the **Museo Médico Belén**, which has a collection of medical instruments. Across the street is a maternity hospital from the colonial era, now the **Archaeological and Ethnological Museum** ① *Junín y Belén*. It has ceramics from all regions and civilizations of Peru.

The **Cuarto de Rescate** ⓘ *entrance at Amalia Puga 750, Mon-Sat 0900-1250, 1500-1750, Sun 0900-1250*, is not the actual ransom chamber but in fact the room where Atahualpa was held prisoner. A red line on the wall is said to indicate where Atahualpa reached up and drew a mark, agreeing to have his subjects fill the room to the line with gold treasures. The chamber is roped off and can only be viewed from the outside. Pollution and weather have had a detrimental effect on the stone.

Also worth seeing are **La Recoleta Church** ⓘ *Maestro y Av Los Héroes*, and **San Pedro** ⓘ *Gálvez y Junín*. The city has many old colonial houses with garden patios, and 104 elaborately carved doorways: see the **Bishop's Palace** across the street from the cathedral; the **Palace of the Condes de Uceda** ⓘ *Jr Apurímac 719*, now occupied by BCP bank; and the **Casa Silva Santiesteban** ⓘ *Junín y 2 de Mayo*.

Museo Arqueológico Horacio H Urteaga ⓘ *Del Batán 289, Mon-Fri 0700-1445, free, donation*, of the Universidad Nacional de Cajamarca, has objects of the pre-Inca Cajamarca and other cultures. The university maintains an experimental arboretum and agricultural station, the **Museo Silvo-agropecuario** ⓘ *Km 2.5 on the road to Baños del Inca*, with a lovely mural at the entrance.

You can also visit the plaza where Atahualpa was ambushed and the stone altar set high on **Santa Apolonia hill** ⓘ *US$0.60*. To get there, take bus marked Santa Apolonia/Fonavi, or *micro A* or *combis* on Sabogal or Tarapacá. Here the Inca is said to have reviewed his subjects. There is a road to the top or, if you are fit, you can walk up from Calle 2 de Mayo, using the stairway. The view from the top, over red-tiled roofs and green fields, is worth the effort, especially very early in the morning for the beautiful sunrises.

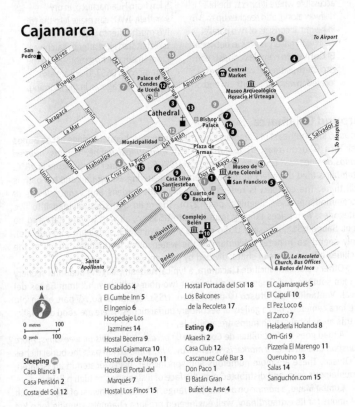

Cajamarca

Sleeping 😴
Casa Blanca 1
Casa Pensión 2
Costa del Sol 12
El Cabildo 4
El Cumbe Inn 5
El Ingenio 6
Hospedaje Los
 Jazmines 14
Hostal Becerra 9
Hostal Cajamarca 10
Hostal Dos de Mayo 11
Hostal El Portal del
 Marqués 7
Hostal Los Pinos 15
Hostal Portada del Sol 18
Los Balcones
 de la Recoleta 17

Eating 🍴
Akaesh 2
Casa Club 12
Cascanuez Café Bar 3
Don Paco 1
El Batán Gran
 Bufet de Arte 4
El Cajamarqués 5
El Capulí 10
El Pez Loco 6
El Zarco 7
Heladería Holanda 8
Om-Gri 9
Pizzería El Marengo 11
Querubino 13
Salas 14
Sanguchón.com 15

Marca Huamachuco

The Marca Huamachuco ruins rank in the top 10 archaeological sites in Peru. It is an extensive site, 3 km long, dating back to at least 300 BC though many structures were added later. It seems likely that Marca Huamachuco existed for many centuries as the centre of an autonomous religious cult, separate from the activities of the Chachapoyans to the north and east. The site was used as both a ceremonial centre and for defence. Its most impressive features are: **El Castillo**, a remarkable circular structure with walls up to 8 m high located at the highest point of the site. This and other structures are the oldest-known buildings in Peru to extend to more than two storeys and may have reached five storeys. The outer defensive wall, which is accessible where it bisects the hill halfway along, also reaches up to 8 m in height. It consists of two parallel walls with gallery rooms in between. **El Convento** complex consists of five circular structures of varying sizes located towards the northern end of the hill. These are later constructions dating back to AD 600-800. The largest one has been partially reconstructed and provides an interesting insight into how they must have appeared. It has been suggested that these buildings housed the privileged members of an elite class.

Ins and outs No entry fee. Allow two to four hours to explore. Carry all food and drink with you. The nearest town is Huamachuco (bus from Trujillo six hours, US$5; from Cajamarca take a *combi* to Cajabamba, three hours, US$3.50, and another *combi* from there), where there are hotels and restaurants. Access is along a poor vehicle road, off the road to Sanagorán. There is an archway at the turn-off, 5 km from Huamachuco. In dry weather, 4WDs can make it to the top. It is much faster to walk on the mule trail that starts just after the archway. From Huamachuco a mototaxi to the turn-off costs US$2. There are also *combis* to Sanagorán in the morning.

Around Cajamarca

About 6 km southeast of Cajamarca are the sulphurous thermal springs of **Los Baños del Inca** ① *0500-1945, T076-348385, www.inkatermas.com.pe, combis marked Baños del Inca cost US$0.20, 15 mins, taxi US$1.80*. The water temperature is 78°C. Atahualpa tried the effect of these waters on a festering war wound and his bath is still there. The complex is renewed regularly, with gardens and various levels of accommodation (see Sleeping, page 270). The main baths are divided into five categories, with prices ranging from US$1 to US$1.50, all with private tubs and no pool. Sauna US$3, massage US$6-9 (take your own towel; soaps are sold outside). Only spend 20 minutes maximum in the water; obey instructions; many of the facilities allow bathers in shifts, divided by time and/or sex.

Other excursions include **Llacanora**, a typical Andean village in beautiful scenery (13 km southeast of Cajamarca; a pleasant two-hour walk downhill from Baños del Inca). **Ventanillas de Otusco** ① *0800-1800, US$1, combi US$0.15*, part of an old pre-Inca cemetery, has a gallery of secondary burial niches. There are good day walks in this area; local sketch maps are available.

A road goes to **Ventanillas de Combayo** ① *occasional combis on weekdays; more transport on Sun when a market is held nearby, 1 hr*, some 20 km past the burial niches of Otusco. These are more numerous and spectacular, being located in an isolated, mountainous area, and distributed over the face of a steep 200 m high hillside.

Cumbe Mayo, a *pampa* on a mountain range, is 20 km southwest of Cajamarca. It is famous for its extraordinary, well-engineered pre-Inca channels, running for 9 km across the mountain tops. It is said to be the oldest man-made construction in South America. The sheer scale of the scene is impressive and the huge rock formations of Los Frailones ('big monks') and others with fanciful names are strange indeed. On the way to Cumbe Mayo is the Layzón ceremonial centre. There is no bus service; guided tours run 0900-1300 (recommended in order to see all the pre-Inca sites); taxi US$15. To walk up takes three to four hours (take a guide). The trail starts from the hill of Santa Apolonia (Silla del Inca), and goes to Cumbe Mayo straight through the village and up the hill; at the top of the mountain, leave the trail and take the road to the right to the canal. The walk is not difficult and you do not need hiking boots. Take a good torch. The locals use the trail to bring their goods to market.

The **Porcón** rural cooperative, with its evangelical faith expressed on billboards, is a popular excursion, 30 km northwest of Cajamarca. It is tightly organized, with a carpentry, bakery, cheese and yoghurt-making factory, a zoo and vicuñas. A good guide helps to explain everything. If visiting independently (ie not on a tour), contact **Cooperativa Agraria Atahualpa Jerusalén** ⓘ *Chanchamayo 1355, Fonavi 1, T/Fo76-825631, granjaporcon@yahoo.com*.

Some 103 km east of Pacasmayo is the mining town of Chilete, 21 km north of which on the road to San Pablo is **Kuntur Wasi**. The site was devoted to a feline cult and consists of a pyramid and stone monoliths. Extensive excavations are under way and significant new discoveries are being made (excellent site museum). There are two basic *hostales* in Chilete; very limited facilities.

Chachapoyas Region ⊙⦿🏍❋🛆🚌🄲 ↠ *pp269-276.*

Cajamarca is a convenient starting point for the trip east to the province of Amazonas, which contains the archaeological riches of the Chachapoyans, also known as Sachupoyans. Here lie the great pre-Inca cities of Vilaya (not yet developed for tourism), Cerro Olán and the immense fortress of Kuélap, among many others. The road is in terrible condition to Chachapoyas, and barely passable in the rainy season because of landslides. It follows a winding course through the north Andes, crossing the wide and deep canyon of the Río Marañón at Balsas. The road climbs steeply with superb views of the mountains and the valleys below. The fauna and flora are spectacular as the journey alternates between high mountains and low rainforest.

Celendín → *Colour map 2, B2.*
East from Cajamarca, this is the first town of note, with a pleasant plaza and cathedral. There is also an interesting local market on Sunday where you can buy cheap sandals and saddlebags. The **Museo Cultural Huauco** ⓘ *Bolívar 211, in the nearby village of Sucre, To76-552096*, is interesting for local history (friendly curator).

Leymebamba and around → *Colour map 2, B2.*
There are plenty of ruins around this pleasant town, many of them covered in vegetation. The **Comité Turístico** on the plaza is the place to go for all information on how to reach sites, including Laguna de los Cóndores (see below), for guides and horse hire. See www.leymebamba.org.

La Congona, a Chachapoyan site, is well worth the effort, with stupendous views. It consists of three hills: on the easterly, conical hill, the ruins are clustered in a small area, impossible to see until you are right above them. The other hills have been levelled. La Congona is the best preserved of three sites, with 30 round stone houses (some with evidence of three storeys) and a watch tower. Two other sites, El Molinete and Pumahuanyuna, are nearby. It's a brisk three-hour walk from Leymebamba along a clearly marked trail which starts at the end of the street with the hotels. All three sites can be visited in a day but a guide is advisable; ask in the Comité Turístico.

In 1996, a spectacular site consisting of six burial *chullpas*, containing 219 mummies and vast quantities of ceramics, textiles, woodwork, *quipus* and everyday utensils from the late Inca period, was discovered at **Laguna de los Cóndores**, a beautiful lake in a jungle setting south of Leymebamba. The trip to Laguna de los Cóndores takes 10 to 12 hours on foot and horseback from Leymebamba, nine hours return. All the material was moved to a new **museum** ① *San Miguel, 3 km south of Leymebamba: 30-40 mins' walk, take the footpath and ask directions, Tue-Sun 0930-1630, US$4.35, http://centromallqui.org.pe.* It is beautifully laid-out, very informative and has a café.

The road to Chachapoyas is paved and crosses the Utcubamba River, passing through **Palmira** before heading north. Before Puente Santo Tomás there is a turn-off which heads east beyond **Duraznopampa** to the small town of **Montevideo** (basic *hospedaje*). Another Chachapoyan site is **Cerro Olán**, reached by *colectivo* to San Pedro de Utac, a small village beyond Montevideo, then a 30 minute walk. From the Plaza a clear trail rises directly into the hills east of town to the ruins, which can be seen from the village. Here are the remains of towers which some archaeologists claim had roofs like mediaeval European castles.

Further north are the towns of **Yerbabuena** and **Puente Santo Tomás**, which is at the turn-off for the burial *chullpas* of **Revash**, of the Revash culture (AD 1250).

The attractive town of **Jalca Grande** (or La Jalca as it is known locally), at 2800 m, lies between Montevideo and Tingo, up on the east side of the main valley. In the town itself, one block west of the Plaza de Armas, is the interesting and well-preserved Chachapoyan habitation of **Choza Redonda**, which was inhabited until 1964. There is one very basic *hostal*, otherwise ask the mayor. Take a torch.

Tingo → *Phone code: 041. Colour map 2, B2. Altitude: 1800 m.*

Situated in the Utcubamba valley, 25 km from Leymebamba, 37 km south of Chachapoyas by road, much of this village was washed away in the floods of 1993. About 3½ km above Tingo in the hills is **Tingo Nuevo**. There is a petrol station here, the only one between Celendín and Chachapoyas.

Kuélap → *Altitude: 3000 m.*

① *0800-1700, US$3 (50% discount for students with ID).*

Kuélap is a spectacular pre-Inca walled city which was re-discovered in 1843. It was built over a period of 200 years, from AD 900 to 1100 and contained three times more stone than the Great Pyramid at Giza in Egypt. The site lies along the summit of a mountain crest, more than 1 km in length. The massive stone walls, 585 m long by 110 m wide at their widest, are as formidable as those of any pre-Columbian city. Some reconstruction has taken place, mostly of small houses and walls, but the majority of the main walls on both levels are original, as is the inverted, cone-shaped dungeon. The structures have been left in their cloud forest setting, the trees covered in bromeliads and moss, the flowers visited by hummingbirds. Guides are available; pay them what you think appropriate. A huge restoration programme was recently undertaken at Kuélap, with further funding destined for other Chachapoyan sites. A small **Centro de Interpretaciones** is open 0800-1630; it has a good model of the site. There is also a toilet block. The ruins are locked; the guardian, Gabriel Portocarrero, has the keys and accompanies visitors, and is very informative.

Chachapoyas → *Phone code: 041. Colour map 2, B2. Population: 25,000. Altitude: 2234 m.*

The capital of the Department of Amazonas, founded in 1538, was an important crossroads between coast and jungle until the 1940s. Archaeological and ecological tourism in the 1990s is slowly bringing in new economic benefits. The modern **cathedral** stands on the spacious Plaza de Armas. The **INC Museum** ① *Ayacucho 904, Mon-Fri 0800-1300, 1400-1645, free,* contains a small collection of artefacts and

mummies in display cases, with explanations in Spanish. For **tourist information**
contact **i perú** ⓘ *Jr Ortiz 588, Plaza de Armas, T041-477292, iperuchachapoyas@*
promperu.gob.pe, Mon-Sat 0800-1300, 1500-1900, or **Dirección Regional de**
Turismo ⓘ *Grau 640, T041-478355*, www.chachapoyasonline.com, www.regionamaz
onas.gob.pe. Another useful site is http://camayocperu.com/lerche.htm of the
German ethnologist, Doctor Peter Lerche.

Huancas ⓘ *colectivos leave from Jr Ortiz Arrieta y Libertad, 20 mins, US$0.60,*
0700-1800, which produces rustic pottery, can be reached by a two-hour walk on the
airport road. Walk uphill from Huancas for a magnificent view into the deep canyon of
the Río Sonche.

Levanto was built by the Spaniards and was their first capital of the area, directly
on top of the previous Chachapoyan structures. The church dates from 1538. Although
the capital was moved to Chachapoyas a few years later, Levanto retained its
importance for a while, but is now an unspoilt colonial village overlooking the massive
canyon of the Utcubamba River. Kuélap can, on a clear day, be seen on the other side of
the rift. There are two small bar-bodegas in the village. A 30-minute walk from Levanto
are the partly cleared ruins of **Yalape**, which seems to have been a massive residential
complex, extending over many hectares. The local people will guide you to the ruins. It
is due to be restored, as is the trekking route on prehispanic roads to Kuélap.

East of Chachapoyas
On the road to Mendoza via Pipus and Cheto are the pre-Inca ruins of **Monte Peruvia**
(known locally as Purunllacta), hundreds of white stone houses with staircases,

Chachapoyas

N

0 metres 200
0 yards 200

Sleeping 🛏
Belén **1** *A1*
Casa Vieja **2** *A1*
Casona Monsante **12** *B2*

Eating 🍴
Chacha **1** *B2*
Chifa Chuy Xien **3** *B2*
El Edén **5** *A2*

El Dorado **3** *A1*
Gran Vilaya **5** *B2*
Hostal El Danubio **7** *B1*
Kuélap **9** *B1*
Puma Urcu &
   Café Café **13** *B2*
Revash **11** *B2*

Kuélap **4** *B2*
Las Rocas **6** *A2*
La Tushpa **2** *B1*
Mari Pizza **10** *A2*
Matalache **8** *B2*
Panadería San José **9** *B2*

Transport 🚐
Cars to Bagua Grande **7** *A2*
Cars to Pedro Ruíz **2** *A2*
Colectivos to Huancas **1** *A2*
Combis to Leymebamba **4** *B2*

Comité Interprovincial
   Santo Tomás & Roller's **6** *A2*
San Juan de Luya
   Combis **8** *A2*
Trans Zelada **9** *A2*
Turismo Kuélap **10** *A1*
Virgen del Carmen **11** *A3*

Northern Peru Northern Highlands

temples and palaces. The ruins have been cleared by local farmers and some houses have been destroyed. The ruins are two-hour walk from Cheto. A guide is useful as there are few locals of whom to ask directions. If you get stuck in Pipus, ask to sleep at restaurant *Huaracina* or the police station next door. There are no hotels in Cheto but a house high up on the hill above the town with a balcony has cheap bed and board. The same family also has a house on the Plaza.

The road east from Chachapoyas continues on to **Mendoza**, the starting point of an ethnologically interesting area in the Guayabamba Valley, where there is a high incidence of fair-skinned people.

Northwest of Chachapoyas

On a turn-off on the road 37 km from Chachapoyas to Pedro Ruiz, is **Lamud**, which is a convenient base for several interesting sites, such as San Antonio and Pueblo de los Muertos. About 20 minutes' drive south of Lamud, on the same road, is the village of **Luya**. From here, more sites can be reached: **Chipuric** and **Karajía**, where remarkable, 2½-m-high sarcophagi set into an impressive cliff face overlook the valley (entry at Karajía US$1; mototaxi to sarcophagi US$1.65 round trip). In a lush canyon, 1½ hours' walk from the road to Luya is **Wanglic**, a funeral site with large circular structures built under a ledge. Nearby is a beautiful waterfall, a worthwhile excursion. Ask for directions in Luya. Best to take a local guide (US$3.50-5 a day). Buses and *combis* to Lamud and Luya are listed under Chachapoyas, Transport. The road is unpaved but in reasonable condition.

Chachapoyas to Ecuador ⊟⊟⊡❶ » *pp269-276.*

From Chachapoyas, the road runs via Pedro Ruiz and runs west for 65 km to Bagua Grande. It passes through a narrow gorge, the ridges covered with lush cloudforest, then along the broad and fertile lower Utcubamba valley. It then crosses the Marañón at Corral Quemado. From the confluence of the Marañón with the Río Chamaya, the road follows the latter, past bare cliffs covered by dry scrub, towering over the deep river canyons.

With the opening of a bridge at Balsas on the Peru-Ecuador border, this route is becoming a worthwhile route for those who do not want to leave the highlands. **Bagua Grande** (phone code 041), the first town of note heading west from Pedro Ruiz, is a hot and dusty place. Most hotels and restaurants are located along the sprawling main street, Avenida Chachapoyas. Bagua Grande is not very safe and suffers water shortages. If arriving late, ask to sleep on the bus until daybreak. Police may ask to see travellers' documents here. There are internet cafés by the Plaza de Armas. BCP changes cash and Amex traveller's cheques.

From Bagua Grande the main road continues northwest, then forks: southwest to **Chamaya** (50 km from Bagua Grande, one basic hostel, El Volante), for Jaén and the coast; and northeast to Sarameriza, the first port on the Marañón. From Chamaya it's 15 minutes to Jaén, the best place to break the journey from Chachapoyas or the jungle to Ecuador or Chiclayo and vice-versa.

Jaén to the border → *Phone code: 076. Colour map 2, A/B2. Population: 55,300. Altitude: 740 m.*

Although founded in 1536, **Jaén** retains little of its colonial character. It is a friendly place and there is a **Dircetur office** ① *Jr Zarumilla 1345, T076-431188,* for information. A colourful modern **cathedral** dominates the large plaza around which most services of interest to the visitor are clustered. A **museum** ① *Instituto 4 de Junio, Hermógenes Mejía s/n,* displays pre-Columbian artifacts from the Pakamuros culture.

A pleasant road runs north from Jaén through rice fields, then alongside the Río Chinchipe to Puerto Ciruelos, where the road leaves the river and climbs through forested hills to **San Ignacio** (phone code 076), near the border with Ecuador. It is a plesasant town, with steep streets and a modern plaza, in the centre of a coffee-growing area. The **Fiesta de San Ignacio Loyola** is celebrated on 30 July; the **Semana Turística** is the third week in September. You can take excursions to waterfalls, lakes, petroglyphs and ancient ruins in the nearby hills. From San Ignacio the narrow, unpaved road runs 45 km through green hills to **Namballe**. Just to the north a dirt road goes west to the **Santuario Tabaconas-Namballe** ⓘ *reserve office at San Martín 332, Jaén, To76-846166, snntabaconasnamballe@yahoo.es*, a 29,500-ha reserve, with an altitude of 1200-3800 m protecting several Andean ecosystems.

● Sleeping

Cajamarca *p261, map p263*

AL Posada del Puruay, 5 km north, T076-367928, postmast@p-puruay.com.pe. A 17th-century hacienda which has been converted into a 'hotel museum' with all rooms appointed to a high standard and containing beautiful pieces of colonial furniture. All rooms en suite.

A Costa del Sol, Cruz de la Piedra 707, Plaza de Armas, T076-343434, ventascajamarca@costadelsolperu.com. New hotel, part of a Peruvian chain, with breakfast, airport transfer, welcome drink; restaurant, café and bars, pool.

B-C El Ingenio, Av Vía de Evitamiento 1611-1709, T/F076-367121, www.elingenio.com. 1½ blocks from new El Quinde shopping mall. With bathroom, solar-powered hot water, spacious, very relaxed, internet in rooms, helpful, good restaurant, bar, parking.

C Casa Blanca, 2 de Mayo 446, Plaza de Armas, T/F076-822141. Includes breakfast. Room service, clean, safe, nice old building with garden, good restaurant. Disco-bar.

C El Cumbe Inn, Pasaje Atahualpa 345, T076-366858, www.elcumbeinn.com. Includes breakfast, ask for discount in low season. Comfortable, bright rooms, with bath, hot water, cable TV and internet connection, personal service, 2 patios, small gym, well kept, will arrange taxis and tours, restaurant.

C Hostal El Portal del Marqués, Del Comercio 644, T076-368464, portalmarques@terra.com.pe. Price includes breakfast. In an attractive converted colonial house, all rooms carpeted, en suite, with TV, internet, laundry, safe, parking, tourist restaurant **El Mesón Gourmet** also has lunchtime *menú*.

D El Cabildo, Junín 1062, T/F076-367025, cabildoh@latinmail.com. Includes breakfast. In a historic monument with patio and modern fountain, full of character, elegant, local decorations, comfortable, breakfast served, gym, massage if booked in advance.

D Hostal Cajamarca, 2 de Mayo 311, T076-362532, hostalcajamarca@hotmail.com.

To Ecuador via Namballe–La Balsa

Regular cars run from Jaén to **Namballe** (1¾ hours, see page 276), from where you can take a shared taxi (15 minutes) to the border at **La Balsa** (Ecuador). From La Balsa you can take a *ranchera* to **Zumba**, 1½ hours (at 1230 and 1730, US$1.75), from where buses run to **Vilcabamba** (six to seven hours) and **Loja**, an hour further. To get to Vilcabamba in one day, you need to leave Jaén by 0700, a tiring journey, athough the road is being improved. If it has not been raining and the road is passable, there is one bus that goes from La Balsa directly to **Loja** at 2030 (US$7.50, 8½ hours). There are military controls at Pucapamba, 20 minutes north of La Balsa and just north of Zumba; keep your passport to hand. See also Ecuador, page 547.

Immigration An exit stamp must be obtained from **Peruvian immigration** ⓘ *0800-1300, 1500-2000*, before entering Ecuador. Once through **Ecuadorean immigration** ⓘ *open 24 hrs, ask around if no-one is in sight*.

There are a few basic hotels at Namballe. On the Ecuadorian side there are a few shops selling drinks and basic items and there are money changers, but no lodgings.

Sizeable rooms in a colonial house, clean, hot water, food excellent in **Los Faroles** restaurant, **Cajamarca Tours** next door.

D **Los Balcones de la Recoleta**, Amalia Puga 1050, T076-363302, luchi9200@ yahoo.com.pe. A beautifully restored 19th-century house, with a pleasant courtyard full of flowers; some rooms with period furniture but all are en suite with internet access, breakfast extra, use of kitchen, helpful staff, some English spoken. Recommended.

D **Hostal Los Pinos**, Jr La Mar 521, T/F076-365992, pinoshostal@yahoo.com. Price includes small breakfast. Lovely colonial house with a new extension, comfortable and secure, helpful staff, expensive laundry, lunch menu available for US$3.

D **Hostal Portada del Sol**, Pisagua 731, T076-363395, PortadadelSol@terra.com.pe. Good rooms, tastefully decorated, with bath, hot water, comfortable beds, internet access. Also has **Portada del Sol Hacienda** at Km 6 on road to Cumbe Mayo (**C**). Good choice.

E **Hospedaje Los Jasmines**, Amazonas 775, T076-361812, hospedajelosjasmines@ yahoo.com. In a converted colonial house with a pleasant courtyard and café serving good cakes, 10 rooms with bath, 2 without, all funds go to disabled children, some staff are disabled, guests can visit the project's school and help. Also **Fundo Ecológico El Porongo** on the road to Baños del Inca, bunk beds, **G** pp.

E **Hostal Becerra**, Del Batán 195, T076-367867. With bath, hot water and TV, modern, pleasant, clean and friendly, but front rooms can be noisy, they'll let you leave your luggage until late buses depart.

F **Hostal Dos de Mayo**, 2 de Mayo 585, T076-362527. With bath, hot water, basic, quite dark, friendly and helpful, internet cabins, good-value menú in the restaurant.

F **Casa Pensión**, 2 de Mayo 712, T076-369888. Full board, shared rooms, some with bath.

Around Cajamarca p264

L-AL **Laguna Seca**, Av Manco Cápac 1098, Los Baños del Inca, T076-594600, www.laguna seca.com.pe. In pleasant surroundings with thermal streams (atmospheric misty mornings), private hot thermal baths in rooms, swimming pool with thermal water, good restaurant, bar, health spa with a variety of treatments (US$10-48), horses for hire.

B **Hostal Fundo Campero San Antonio**, 2 km off the Baños road (turn off at Km 5 from Cajamarca), T/F076-348237, jc_luna@ viabcp.com. An old hacienda, wonderfully restored, with open fireplaces and gardens, 15 mins' walk along the river to Baños del Inca. All rooms en suite. Price includes breakfast and a ride on the hotel's *caballos de paso*. Restaurant serves its own dairy produce, fruit and vegetables, catch y our own trout for supper; try the *licor de sauco* (elderberry).

B-E **Los Baños del Inca**, see page 264, T076-348385, www.inkatermas.com.pe. Various levels of accommodation: **B** bungalows for 2-4 with thermal water, TV, fridge; **E** pp **Albergue Juvenil**, not IYFH, rooms with 3 bunk beds, private bath, caters to groups, basic and overpriced. Camping possible.

Leymebamba p265

D **Hostal La Casona**, Jr Amazonas 223, Leymebamba, T041-830106, www.lacaso nadeleymebamba.com. With bath, hot water, breakfast available on request.

E **Hostal La Petaca**, Jr Amazonas 461, Leymebamba, opposite the church, T041-770288. With bath, hot water.

E **Laguna de los Cóndores**, Jr Amazonas 320, Leymebamba, half a block from plaza, T041-770208, www.chachapoyasperu.com. pe/hostallagunadeloscondores.htm. Cheaper without bath, warm water, a good choice.

Tingo and Kuélap p266

F pp **Albergue León**, Jr Saenz Peña s/n, Tingo, no sign, walk 50 m from the police checkpoint to the corner and turn left, it's the third house on the left (right-hand door), T041-999 9390. Basic, shared bathroom, cold water, friendly, run by Lucho León, who is very knowledgeable.

When walking up to Kuélap from Tingo, the last house to the right of the track (**El Bebedero**, just above a small spring) offers accommodation: bed, breakfast and evening meal for US$6; good meals, friendly and helpful. A bit further, on the left, 100 m below the ruins, is the **Instituto Nacional de Cultura** (INC) hostel. It's a clean dormitory with room for about 12 people, in a lovely setting, US$1.75 per person, no running water (please conserve the rainwater in the buckets), simple meals may be available from the caretaker for US$1. There is free camping outside the hostel.

Chachapoyas p266, map p267

C **Gran Vilaya**, Ayacucho 755, T041-477664, http://granhotelvilaya.com. The best in town, comfortable rooms, firm beds, parking, English spoken, all services. The proprietor is knowledgeable about happenings in and around Chachapoyas.

D **Casa Vieja**, Chincha Alta 569, T041-477353, www.casaviejaperu.com. In a converted old house, very nicely decorated, all rooms different, family atmosphere, hot water, cable TV, living room and *comedor* with open fire, continental breakfast, internet and library.

D **Casona Monsante**, Jr Amazonas 746, T041-477702, www.lacasonamonsante.com. Rooms in a converted colonial house, cable TV, patio, café, breakfast US$1.50.

E **Belén**, Jr Ortiz Arrieta 540, on plaza, next to the bank, T041-477830, www.hostalbelen. com.pe. With bath, hot water, well furnished.

E **Kuélap**, Amazonas 1057, T041-477136, www.hotelkuelap.com. With private bathroom, hot water and TV, cheaper with shared bathroom and cold water, parking.

E **Puma Urcu**, Jr Amazonas 833, T041-477871, hotelpumaurcu@peru.com. Carpeted rooms, hot water, cable TV, **Café Café** next door, both hotel and café receive good reports.

E **Revash**, Grau 517, Plaza de Armas, T041-477391. With private bathroom, plenty of hot water, patio, friendly, helpful, laundry, good local information, restaurant.

F **El Dorado**, Ayacucho 1062, T041-477047. With bathroom, hot water, clean, helpful.

G **Hostal El Danubio**, Tres Esquinas 193 y Junín 584, Plazuela Belén, some distance from centre, T041-477337. With private bathroom, hot water, cheaper with shared bath and cold water, clean, friendly, meals can be ordered in advance.

Chachapoyas to Ecuador p268

E-G **Mejía**, Mesones Muro 282 (perpendicular to Av Chachapoyas), Bagua Grande. With bath, reliable (cold) water supply, fan, nice spacious rooms in new section. Cheaper for small rooms with shared bath.

F **Iris**, Av Chachapoyas 2390, Bagua Grande, T041-774115. Cheaper with shared bath, cold water, fan, simple, clean.

C **El Bosque**, Mesones Muro 632, Jaén, T/F076-731184, hoteleraelbosque@speedy.com.pe. On main road by bus terminals, just below roundabout for turn to San Ignacio, not noisy because rooms are at the back in gardens, nice pool, good restaurant.

D **Prim's**, Diego Palomino 1341, Jaén, T076-731039. Good service, comfortable, hot water, a/c, friendly, small pool. Recommended.

D-E **Hostal Valle Verde**, Mcal Castilla 203, Plaza de Armas, T/F 076-732201, hostal valleverde@hotmail.com. Very clean and modern, large comfortable rooms and beds, a/c (cheaper with fan), hot water, frigobar, parking, includes breakfast. Recommended.

E **Cancún**, Diego Palomino 1413, Jaén, T076-733511. Clean and pleasant, with bath, hot water, fan, restaurant, pool. Recommended.

E **Hostal César**, Mesones Muro 168, Jaén, T076-731277, F731491. Spacious rooms, comfortable, fan, phone, TV, parking.

F **Hostal Diego**, Diego Palomino 1267, T076-8031225. Private bath, fan, TV, views over the river, good value.

G **Santa Elena**, Sánchez Carrión 142, T076-803020. Private bath, cold water, fan, simple, nice, good value.

🍴 Eating

Cajamarca p261, map p263

🍴🍴🍴 **El Batán Gran Bufet de Arte**, Del Batán 369, T076-366025, elbatanrestaurant@ yahoo.com.mx. International dishes and nou- velle cuisine, good wine list and wide choice of drinks, local dishes on non-tourist menu, live music on Sat, art gallery on the 2nd floor.

🍴🍴🍴 **Querubino**, Amalia Puga 589. Mediterra-nean-style decoration with American and French influence in the cooking, specializes in fish, but lots of choice, breakfasts, cocktails, coffees, expensive wines.

🍴🍴 **Casa Club**, Amalia Puga 458-A, T076-340198. Set menu, including vegetarian, and extensive selection à la carte, family atmosphere, slow but attentive service.

🍴🍴🍴 **Don Paco**, Amalia Puga 390, T076-362655. Opposite Sn Francisco. Typical, including *novo andino*, and international dishes, tasty food, desserts and drinks.

🍴🍴🍴 **El Cajamarqués**, Amazonas 770, T076-362128. Good value set menus after 1300, elegant colonial building with garden full of exotic birds, nice place for families.

♥♥ **El Pez Loco**, San Martín 333. Recommended for fish, also on road to Baños del Inca.

♥♥ **Om-Gri**, San Martín 360, near the Plaza de Armas. Good Italian dishes, small, friendly, French spoken, opens at 1300 (1830 Sun).

♥♥ **Pizzería El Marengo**, Junín 1201, T076-368045. Good pizzas and warm atmosphere.

♥♥ **Salas**, Amalia Puga 637, on the main plaza, T076-362867, daily 0700-2200. A Cajamarca tradition. Fast service but can get very busy, excellent local food (try their *cuy* frito), best *tamales* in town; also has a branch in Baños del Inca.

♥♥-♥ **El Zarco**, Jr Del Batán 170, T076-363421. Sun-Fri 0700-2300. Very popular with local residents, good vegetarian dishes, excellent fish, popular for breakfast.

♥♥-♥ **El Zarco Campestre**, off road to airport, open daily. Both El Zarco's use own produce, recommended for pork.

♥ **Natur's Center**, Amalia Puga 409. Good selection of vegetarian dishes.

Cafés

Akaesh, 2 de Mayo 334, T076-368108. Café with couches, bar, live music Fri night.

Cascanuez Café Bar, Amalia Puga 554, near the cathedral. Great cakes, extensive menu including *humitas*, breakfasts, ice creams and coffees. Recommended.

El Capulí, Jr Junín, in the Complejo Belén. Coffee, drinks, sandwiches and snacks. Lovely atmosphere for a quiet coffee, and planning your next activity.

Heladería Holanda, Amalia Puga 657, Plaza de Armas, T076-340113. Easily the best ice cream in Cajamarca, 50 flavours, try *poro poro*, *lúcuma* or *sauco*, also serves coffee. Has a branch in Baños del Inca.

Sanguchón.com, Junín 1137. Best burgers in town, sandwiches, also popular bar.

Leymebamba *p265*

♥ **Cely Pizza's**, Jr La Verdad 530, 2 blocks from Plaza de Armas, opposite the health centre. Good value, 2-course set meals for US$2.50, pizzas take 20 mins unless you book in advance, will cook vegetarian meals at 24 hrs notice, great for breakfast, very clean, has fridge for cold beer, friendly. Recommended.

♥ **El Sabor Tropical**, 16 de Julio. Good chicken and chips, friendly.

Kuélap *p266*

Kuélap, at the junction of the main road with the road on the south bank of the Río Tingo. Clean and OK. There are 2 other eating places in Kuélap.

Chachapoyas *p266, map p267*

♥♥-♥ **Chacha**, Grau 534, Plaza de Armas. Good quality, nice view and atmosphere.

♥ **Chifa Chuy Xien**, Jr Amazonas 848, opposite Hotel Puma Urcu. Authentic Chinese cooking, daily specials and à la carte.

♥ **El Edén**, Grau y Ayacucho. Very good vegetarian, large helpings, open by 0830, closed Sat afternoon/evening.

♥ **La Tushpa**, Jr Ortiz Arrieta 753. The best in town, excellent meat and *platos criollos*, very clean kitchen, attentive service, open for lunch and dinner.

♥ **Las Rocas**, Ayacucho 932 on Plaza. Popular, good local dishes, open daily (and Sun evening when many others are shut).

♥ **Kuélap**, Ayacucho 832. Good, friendly.

♥ **Mari Pizza**, Ayacucho 912. Good pizza.

♥ **Matalache**, corner of Amazonas and Grau. Good and very popular. Serves huge portions. After a hard trek, try the massive *bistec a lo pobre* (tenderized steak piled high with fried plantains, fries and egg).

♥ **Panadería San José**, Ayacucho 816, closed Sun. Does good breakfasts and other meals throughout the day, also regional snacks.

⊛ Festivals and events

Cajamarca *p261, map p263*

Feb Cajamarca is known as the Carnival capital of Peru. **Carnival week**, with many processions and dances, is a messy, raucous affair – the level of water, motor oil and paint-throwing would put Laurel and Hardy to shame. This is not for the faint-hearted. You have been warned!

24 Jun San Juan in Cajamarca, Chota, Llacanora, San Juan and Cutervo.

1st Sun in Oct Festival Folklórico.

2nd week Oct The city's 'Tourist Week'.

Around Cajamarca *p264*

22 Jul An agricultural fair, **Feria Fongal**, is held at Baños del Inca. It coincides with **Fiestas Patrias** and besides agricultural displays, has *artesanía* and *caballos de paso*.

7-8 Sep Fiesta de Huanchaco in Baños del Inca, organized by local *campesinos*.
Mar/Apr Domingo de Ramos (Palm Sun) processions in Porcón are worth seeing.

Chachapoyas *p266, map p267*
1st week of Jun Among the town's festivals are Semana Turística de Amazonas.
Aug Virgen Asunta.

O Shopping

Cajamarca *p261, map p263*
Food and drink
El Porcón, Cooperative Atahualpa-Jerusalén, Chanchamayo 1355 (1 block from Vía Evitamiento, 'Fonavi' *combis*, No 19, and *micros A* pass). It sells excellent *queso suizo*.
La Collpa, see page 264, has a shop at Romero 124, sells some of the best cheese and butter. Try the *queso mantecoso*, which is full-cream cheese, or sweet *manjar blanco*.
Los Alpes, Junín 965. Recommended for quality and variety, pricey but excellent.

Handicrafts
Cajamarca is famous for its gilded mirrors. The Cajamarquiña frames are not carved but decorated with patterns transferred onto pieces of glass using the silkscreen process. This tradition lapsed during the post-colonial period and present production goes back less than 20 years.

Cajamarca is also an excellent place to buy cheap, good-quality handicrafts. Specialities include cotton and wool saddlebags (*alforjas*), found at the San Antonio market, at the north end of Jr Apurímac. Handwoven woollen items can be made to order. Other items include painted ceramic masks and soapstone figures (including miners with power drills). The market on Amazonas is good for *artesanía*. There are stalls in the street on block 7 of Belén every day. There are several shops on 300 block of 2 de Mayo. All offer a good range of local crafts.

Supermarkets
El Quinde, Av Hoyos Rubio, blocks 6 and 7, Fonavi. This is a new shopping centre on the road to airport, which has a well-stocked supermarket.

▲ Activities and tours

Cajamarca *p261, map p263*
Several travel agencies around the Plaza de Armas offer trips to local sites and further afield (eg Kuntur Wasi, Kuélap), trekking on Inca and other trails, riding *caballos de paso* and handicraft tours. Average prices of local tours: city tour, US$7.55, Cumbe Mayo, US$7.55, Ventanillas de Otusco US$6, Porcón US$6, Combayo US$30 (full day), Kuntur Wasi US$30, Kuélap US$260 (3-5 days). Recommended tour operators include:
Asociación Civil para el Rescate del Ecosistema de Cajamarca (APREC), Av Manco Cápac 1098, Baños del Inca, T076-894600, www.aprec.org. The association, sponsored by Pro Aves Perú, Hotel Laguna Seca and Yanacocha mines, aims to "restore the ecological health" of the Cajamarca region. Four Inca trail loops have been made accessible to hikers, including one, to Sangal, which passes the endangered Grey-bellied Comet hummingbird's habitat.
Atahualpa Inca Tours, La Mar 435, T076-367014 (in Hostal El Mirador), www.nunura.com/elmirador.
Cajamarca Tours, 2 de Mayo 323, T/F076-362813 (also DHL, Western Union and flight reconfirmations).
Cumbemayo Tours, Amalia Puga 635 on the plaza, T076-362938, cumbemayotours@usa.net. Guides in English and French.
Socio Adventures, Ben Eastwood, Pje Chota 123, Dpto 1A, Urb Ramón Castilla, Cajamarca, T076-341118, www.socioadventures.com. They offer a Stove Trek Tour, where you donate materials and help a local family build a cooking stove while taking a 5-day, 5-night guided tour of the area. You stay at their lodge called the Blur Poncho near Chota, excellent food and accommodation.

Tingo and Kuélap *p266*
Leo Cobina, G Prada y 2 de Mayo, Leymebamba, recommended guide.
Lázaro Mostanza Lozano, San Martín y 2 de Mayo, or through Hotel Laguna de los Cóndores.
Rigolberto Vargas Silva, Kuélap, ask for him at the ticket office. Very knowledgeable.

Tours in the surrounding area include: city tour, Levanto, Yalape (0800-1530, US$8.65), Kuélap (see page 267), Karajía, La Jalca, Leymebamba (all full day, US$12-20, depending on distance and number of passengers, including guide and food), Revash (by vehicle to Santo Tomás, then 2-hr hike), Gran Vilaya or Laguna de los Cóndores (4-5 days each, depending on size of group), Mendoza (groups of 6 to 8).

Andes Tours, contact information same as **Hostal Revash**. Daily trips to Kuélap, other conventional tours to ruins and caves in the area and trekking trips to Gran Vilaya, Laguna de los Cóndores and other destinations. These trips combine travel by car, on horseback and walking.

Chachapoyas Tours SAC, Grau 534, Plaza de Armas, T041-478838 www.kuelapperu.com, or in the USA T(1) 866-396 9582, international T407-5836786. Reliable, English-speaking guide, good service. Related to this company is Charles Motley's **Los Tambos Chachapoyanos** (LTC) programme, www.kuelap.org, with the lodges at Levanto and Choctámal.

Vilaya Tours, c/o Gran Hotel Vilaya, Jr Grau 624, T041-477506, www.vilayatours.com. All-inclusive area treks throughout northern Peru catering to international clientele. Excellent guides. Robert Dover is one of the founders and is British, contact him through **Vilaya Tours**. They have a regular newsletter and also work in conjunction with community projects.

● Transport

Cajamarca *p261, map p263*
Air To **Lima** (about US$120) daily with Aero Cóndor, and LC Busre, Sun-Fri. Aero Cóndor, 2 de Mayo 323, T076-365674. LC Busre, Comercio 1024, T076-361098.

Bus To **Lima**, 856 km, 12-14 hrs, económico US$9-12, to US$21-24.25 on **Civa**'s double-deckers, to US$27-33.35 for **Cruz del Sur**'s luxury service (includes taxi to your lodging in Lima), several buses daily. To **Trujillo**, 296 km, 6½ hrs, US$4.55-10, regular buses 0900-2230 most continue to Lima. To **Chiclayo**, 260 km, 6 hrs, US$4.55-9, several buses daily; change buses to go on to Piura and Tumbes. To

Celendín, 112 km, 4 hrs, US$3, **Atahualpa** at 0700 and 1300, **Royal Palace**'s 0900 (poor minibuses). Also *combis* from Av Atahualpa cuadra 3, leave when full 0400-1800, 3½ hrs, US$3. The route follows a fairly good dirt road through beautiful country. **Perú Bus**, **Rojas** and others go to **Cajabamba**, 75 km, US$3, 4 hrs, several daily; also *combis*, US$3.50, 3 hrs.

Bus companies: Atahualpa, Atahualpa 299, T076-363060; Civa, Ayacucho 753, T076-361460; Cruz del Sur, Atahualpa 600, T076-361737; El Cumbe, Sucre 594, T076-363068; Emtrafesa, Atahualpa 299, T369663; Línea, Atahualpa 318, T076-363956; Rojas, Atahualpa 405, T076-340548; Royal Palace's, Atahualpa 339, T076-365855; Tepsa, Sucre 594, T076-363306. Turismo Días, Sucre 422, T076-368289.

Leymebamba *p265*
Buses from Chachapoyas to **Celendín** (see page 265) pass through Leymebamba 3½ hrs after departure and make a lunch stop here. There's no guarantee of a seat, but you might have a better chance if you purchase your ticket in advance in Chachapoyas, informing that you will get on in Leymebamba. *Combis* run direct to Celendín on Sun and Tue, 1100. *Combis* to **Chachapoyas** leave the plaza regularly. The road between Chachapoyas and Leymebamba takes 2½-3½ hrs by car, but both car and bus take longer in the rainy season.

To **Jalca Grande**, Comité Interprovincial Santo Tomás *combis* from Chachapoyas, see above for details. They return from La Jalca to Chachapoyas at 0500 daily.

Tingo *p266*
For transport from **Chachapoyas** to Tingo, see Chachapoyas, Transport. Several *combis* (from 0500) daily to Chachapoyas. Tingo to **Leymebamba** takes 2 hrs, US$1.75.

Kuélap *p266*
There are 4 options: 1) Take a tour from Chachapoyas. 2) Hire a vehicle with driver in Chachapoyas, US$35 per vehicle. 3) Take a *combi* from Chachapoyas to María or Quisongo, or to Choctámal, the mid-point on the 36 km tortuous road from Tingo to Kuélap (see under Chachapoyas for details). You can stay in Choctámal with a family or at the lodge (see above), then walk 19 km

(4-5 hrs) along the road to the site. In María there are several hospedajes, **G** pp with hot water. Alternatively, go early from Chachapoyas to Tingo, hike up to Kuélap then walk down to María (2-3 hrs) and spend the night there. 4) Take a *combi* from Chachapoyas to Tingo, spend the night, then take the 3½-4 hrs' strenuous walk uphill from Tingo; take waterproof, food and drink, and start early as it gets very hot. Only the fit should try to ascend and descend in one day on foot. In the rainy season it is advisable to wear boots; at other times it is hot and dry (take all your water with you as there is nothing on the way up).

Chachapoyas *p266, , map p267*
Air It is hoped that flights to Chachapoyas will resume in 2007, after improvements to the airport's radar.
Bus To **Chiclayo** with Móvil Tours, US$10.60, en route to Trujillo, 2000, US$12, and Lima, 1230, 22 hrs, US$24. **Civa**, to Chiclayo at 0600 daily, 11½ hrs (may be longer in the rainy season), US$9-10.60; to **Lima**1230, 24 hrs, US$16.65-27.25; Turismo Kuélap, at 1700 daily, US$9 to Chiclayo. Trans Zelada buses leave 1100 daily to Chiclayo, Trujillo and Lima, US$20. To **Celendín**, from which there are connections to Cajamarca: with **Virgen del Carmen**, Tue and Fri at 0600, 14-15 hrs (may be much longer in the rainy season, an unforgettable journey, take warm clothing, food and water), US$11. To **Pedro Ruiz**, for connections to Chiclayo, *combis* (US$2.15, 2 hrs, 0800-1800) and cars/*colectivos* – more common (US$3, 1¾ hrs) leave from Grau y Salamanca, also from Ortiz Arrieta y Libertad. To **Bagua Grande**, 0430-1800, cars US$6, 3 hrs, from Grau 355 y Libertad.
    For **Kuélap**, Roller's, *combis* or cars, at 0500 and 1400, from Kuélap to Chachapoyas at 1200 and 1700, US$3.65, 3 hrs; **Yumal** US$3.65, 3 hrs; **María** US$3, 2½ hrs; **Lónguita** US$2.42, 2 hrs; **Tingo** US$1.50, 1½ hrs. *Combis* to Tingo from Grau y Salamanca, US$2.25, 1½ hrs. To **Santo Tomás**, Comité Interprovincial Santo Tomás, 0800-1600, US$2.75, 3 hrs; **Cruce de Revash**, US$2.75, 2½ hrs; **Tingo** US$2.25, 1½ hrs. To **Leymebamba**, *combis* and small buses from 2 de Mayo y Libertad, 1200,

1600 (also from cuadra 8 of Libertad), US$3, 2½ hrs. To **Jalca Grande**, Comité Inter-provincial Santo Tomás, departures about 1300 onwards (few if any on Sat), US$3.65 (return in morning). To **Luya** and **Lamud**, from **San Juan de Luya**, Ortiz Arrieta 364, cars 0400-2000, US$2.25, 1 hr to Lamud, same price to Luya. Taxis may be hired from the plaza for any local destination.
    To **Levanto** is 2 hrs by truck. Trucks leave from the market in Chachapoyas most days at 0600, US$0.90, and there are trucks and *combis* (2 hrs, US$1) from outside **Bodega El Amigo** on Jr Hermosura at 1400. To walk to Levanto, see page 267.
    Bus companies Civa, San Juan de la Libertad 956, T041-478048. **Comité Interprovincial Santo Tomás**, Grau, by the cul-de-sac between Salamanca and Libertad. **Móvil Tours**, Jr Libertad 464, T041-478545. Roller's, Grau 302.Trans Zelada, Ortiz Arrieta 310. Turismo Kuélap, Ortiz Arrieta 412, T041-478128. Virgen del Carmen, Av Salamanca 650.

Chachapoyas to Ecuador *p268*
Bus Many buses pass through **Bagua Grande** en route from Chiclayo to Tarapoto and Chachapoyas and vice versa, by day or night. You can book for Lima (US$15.15-27.30) or Chiclayo (US$5.45), but for Chachapoyas (US$4.55) you must wait and see if there is space and they are often full. A better bet is to take a car or *combi*. Cars and *combis* to **Jaén** leave from Mcal Castilla y Angamos at the west end of town: to Jaén, cars US$1.80, 1 hr; *combis* US$1.50, 1¼ hrs. From Jr B Alcedo at the east end of town, cars (US$2.75, 1 hr) leave to **Pedro Ruiz**, to **Chachapoyas**, cars US$6, 3 hrs. Taking a mototaxi (US$0.30) between the 2 stops is a good alternative to walking in the heat.

Jaén to the border *p268*
Bus Arrange bus transport at Mesones Muro, block 4. Enquire which address the bus actually leaves from, some companies also have ticket offices in the centre of town. Eg **Móvil Tours**, Av Mesones Muro 422 (next to terminal with other bus companies); **Civa** has an office at the terminal on Mesones Muro block 4, in addition to an office Mcal Ureta 1300 y V Pinillos and terminal at Bolívar

936. To **Chiclayo**, Móvil *bus cama* at 1700, US$7.60, 5½ hrs; regular service at 2330, US$6.66. **Civa**, 1330 and 2230, US$4.55, 6 hrs. **Transcade**, 1000 and 2100, US$4.55, 6 hrs. In front of the bus terminal at Mesones Muro are cars to Chiclayo US$9, 5 hrs. To **Lima**, Móvil *bus cama* at 1700, US$21.20, 15½ hrs; regular service at 2330, US$18.20. **Civa**, 1700, US$18.20, 16 hrs. Service to Lima also goes through **Trujillo**. To **Piura**, Tarapoto Tours at 2200, US$7.60, 8 hrs. **Sol Peruano**, at 2230, US$7.60, 8 hrs. To **Pedro Ruiz**, US$4.55, 3hrs. To **Bagua Grande**, cars US$1.80, 1hr; *combis* US$1.50, 1¼ hrs. To **San Ignacio**, *combis* from Av Pinillos 638, 0400-1900, US$3.65, 3 hrs.

To border at Namballe Cars run to the border with Ecuador from Jr Santa Rosa corner Progreso: **Namballe** US$2.45 1¾ hrs; **La Balsa** US$3, 2 hrs (see page 269).

● Directory

Cajamarca *p261, map p263*
Banks BCP, Apurímac 719. Changes Amex TCs without commission, cash advance on Visa, MasterCard and Amex, 0.5% commission. **Scotiabank**, Amazonas 750. Accepts Amex TCs, 0.5% commission, cash advance. **Interbank**, 2 de Mayo 546, on plaza. Closed 1300-1600. Accepts Vias TCs without commission if paid in soles, US$5 for dollars. Dollars can be changed in most banks and travel agencies on east side of plaza, but euros are hard to change. Casa de cambio in **Casa del Artefacto** musical and electrical store at Amazonas 537. Good rates, cash only. Casas de cambio also at Jr del Comercio y Apurímac and at Amalia Puga 673. **Street changers** on Jr Del Batán by the Plaza de Armas and at Del Batán y Amazonas. **Hospitals** Clínica Limatambo, Puno 265, T076-364241. Private, recommended. Doctor Gurmandi speaks English. **Clínica San Francisco**, Av Grau 851, T076-362050. Private, recommended. Hospital at Av Mario Urteaga. **Internet** There are internet cabins everywhere; rates are US$0.35 per hr. **Laundry** Lavandería Dandy, Jr Amalia Puga 545. Pay by weight. **Lava Express**, Jr Belén 678. Good service, US$1.50 per kg. **Post office** Serpost, Jr Amalia Puga 778. 0800-2045. **Telephone** Public phone offices can be found all over the centre. **Useful addresses** Indecopi, Apurímac 601, T076-363315, mcastillo@indecopi.gob.pe. The place to go if you have a complaint about tourist services.

Chachapoyas *p266, map p267*
Banks BCP, Ortiz Arrieta 576, Plaza de Armas. Gives cash on Visa card, changes cash and TCs, ATM (Visa/Plus). There are 2 well-signed places on Ayacucho, Plaza de Armas, which change cash. **Internet** Many places around the plaza and elsewhere, US$0.45 per hr. **Laundry** Lavandería Speed Clean, Ayacucho 964 on plaza (ask at the appliance store at the same address), T041-777665. Clean, Amazonas 817. **Post office** Grau on Plaza de Armas. **Telephone** Ayacucho 926, Plaza de Armas. Also at Grau 608.

Northwest of Chachapoyas *p268*
Banks Banco de la Nación, in Pedro Ruiz, changes cash only. **Post office and telephone** Telephone on the main road in Pedro Ruiz between Casablanca and Policía Nacional.

Jaén to the border *p268*
Banks BCP, Bolívar y V Pinillos. Cash only; ATM (Visa/Plus, no MasterCard ATM). BBV **Continental**, Ramón Castilla y San Martín. Cash, US$5 commission for TCs. **Cambios Coronel**, V Pinillos 360 (*Coronel* across the street at 339). Cash only, good rates. Others on plaza, next to public phones. Cash only. **Internet** Foto center Erick, Pardo Miguel 425. US$1.15 per hr. **Post office** Pardo Miguel y Bolívar. **Telephone** V Pinillos, on the plaza.

Introduction

The immense Amazon Basin covers a staggering 4,000,000 sq km, an area roughly equivalent to three quarters the size of the United States. But despite the fact that 60% of Peru is covered by this green carpet of jungle, less than 6% of its population lives here, meaning that much of Peru's rainforest is still intact. The Peruvian jungles are home to a diversity of life unequalled anywhere on Earth. It is this great diversity which makes the Amazon Basin a paradise for nature lovers. The area is home to 10 million living species, including 2000 species of fish and 300 mammals. It also has over 10% of the world's 8600 bird species and, together with the adjacent Andean foothills, 4000 butterfly species. This incredible biological diversity, however, brings with it an acute ecological fragility. Ecologists consider the Amazon rainforest to be the lungs of the earth – producing 20% of the Earth's oxygen – and any fundamental change could have disastrous implications for our future on this planet.

The two major tourist areas in the Peruvian Amazon Basin are the northern and southern jungles. They share many characteristics, but the main difference is that the northern tourist area is based on the River Amazon itself, with Iquitos at its centre. Although it has lost its rubber-boom dynamism, the city is still at the heart of life on the river. There are jungle lodges upstream and down, none more than half a day away by fast boat. In the south, the Manu Biosphere Reserve and Tambopata National Reserve are far removed from the modern world. Most of Manu is in fact off limits to tourists but, where access is possible, there are unparalleled opportunities for wildlife spotting. Many lodges in the area are close to the river port of Puerto Maldonado and include local communities as part of the jungle experience.

★ Don't miss …

1   **Iquitos** Amid the buzz of a thousand motorcycle taxis, look at the Iron House, or any other old mansion, and try to imagine the days of the rubber barons, when this city was closer to Paris than Lima, page 280.

2   **Jungle lodges** Your days will be filled with brand new sights, smells and sounds, thanks to the sharp eyes of your guide, pages 284 and 293.

3   **Canopy walkways** Watch the bird and animal life in the forest canopy at first or last light from the highest possible level, at the Explornapo Lodge, page 285, or the Inkaterra Reserva Amazónica, page 295.

4   **Manu** Make an early start to visit a *collpa* (macaw lick) to see the multitude of macaws and parrots getting their essential minerals, page 288.

5   **Tambopata** Take your patience to an oxbow lake and hope to see giant river otters, page 292.

Northern Jungle

Standing on the banks of the River Amazon the city of Iquitos still retains something of a frontier feel. It became famous during the rubber boom of the late 19th century and is now the main tourist attraction in this part of the country. For jungle visits there are many lodges to choose from and the fine protected area of Allpahuayo-Mishana.

▸▸ *For Sleeping, Eating and other listings, see pages 283-287.*

Iquitos 🛏️🍴🎒❄️💻🛄📶🌐 ▸▸ *pp283-287.*

→ *Colour map 2, A4. Phone code: 065. Population: 346,500.*

Capital of the Department of Loreto and chief town of Peru's jungle region, Iquitos is 3646 km from the mouth of the Amazon. It is an urban oasis, completely isolated except by air and river, and yet it is a pleasant tropical city. Founded by the Jesuits in 1757 as the mission settlement of San Pablo de los Napeanos, Iquitos became in 1864 the first port of note on the great river. Rapid growth followed the rubber boom of the late 19th century, though the city's new-found wealth was short lived. By the second decade of the 20th century the rubber industry had left for the more competitive oriental suppliers. Remnants of the boom period can still be seen in the fine houses decorated with Portuguese tiles, lending an air of faded beauty to the river embankment. The main economic activities are logging, commerce and petroleum. It is also the main starting point for tourists wishing to explore Peru's northern jungle.

Ins and outs

Getting there and around Francisco Secada Vigneta airport ① *in the southwest, T065-260147*, receives daily flights from Lima. There are several **ports** in Iquitos, but the main one for all long-haul service in large vessels is Masusa, 2 km north of the centre. The rise and fall of the river is such that the islands off Iquitos are constantly moving. Iquitos is well spread out. Hotels are dotted about all over the place. The best way to get around is by motorcycle taxi. ▸▸ *See Transport, page 287.*

Tourist information i perú ① *Napo 232, Plaza de Armas, T065-236144, iperuiquitos @promperu.gob.pe, daily 0830-1930; also at the airport daily 0800-1300 and 1600-2000*. Staff at both offices are knowledgeable and helpful. If arriving by air, go first to the i perú desk. They will give you a list of clean hotels and a map, and tell you about the touts outside the airport. **Dircetur** ① *Ricardo Palma 113, p 5, T065-234609, loreto@mincetur.gob.pe, Mon-Fri 0730-1430*, also offers information. Some English is spoken in all three tourist offices. The local paper is *La Región*, www.diario laregion.com. The city is friendly and generally safe.

Sights

The incongruous **Casa de Hierro** (Iron House) ① *Plaza de Armas at Próspero y Putumayo*, was designed by Eiffel for the Paris exhibition of 1889. It is said that the house was transported from Paris by a local rubber baron, and it is constructed entirely of iron trusses and sheets, bolted together and painted silver. It now houses a restaurant upstairs. Also on the plaza, is the **Casa de Fitzcarrald** or **de Barro** (Clay House) ① *Napo 200-12*. Built entirely of adobe, with wooden balconies, this warehouse predates the rubber boom, but the famous *cauchero*, Carlos Fermín Fitzcarrald, used it as his house and office in the early years of the 20th century. This is now a **Cuaracao** appliance store; descendants of Fitzcarrald still live upstairs. Werner Herzog's film *Fitzcarraldo* is a cause célèbre in the town. Next door to the tourist office on the plaza is a **Museo Municipal** ⓘ *Napo 224, T065-234272, Mon-Fri 0700-1445,* **281** *free*, with stuffed animals and woodcarvings of local native peoples.

Also worth seeing is the old **Hotel Palace** ⓘ *on the corner of Malecón Tarapacá and Putumayo*, now the army barracks. Of special interest are the older buildings, faced with *azulejos* (glazed tiles). Many are along the Malecón. They date from the boom of 1890-1912, when the rubber barons imported the tiles from Portugal and Italy and ironwork from England to embellish their homes. **Museo Amazónico** ⓘ *on the corner of Malecón Tarapacá and Calle Morona, Mon-Fri 0830-1200, 1530-1800, free,* is housed in the renovated Prefectura palace. It has a lovely carved wooden ceiling. Amazon art and sculptures of local native peoples are on display. The *malecón* has been refurbished and is a nice place for a stroll, with great views around sunset.

Belén, the picturesque, friendly waterfront district, is lively, but not safe at night. Most of its huts were built on rafts to cope with the river's 10-m change of level during the year: it begins to rise in January and is highest from May to July. Now, the cabins are built on wooden or concrete stilts (floating houses can still be seen below the north end of Malecón Maldonado). The main plaza has a bandstand designed by

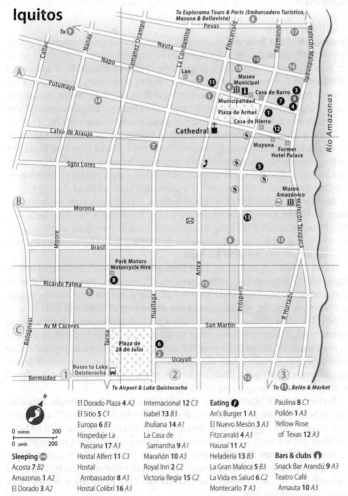

Iquitos

To Explorama Tours & Ports (Embarcadero Turístico, Masusa & Bellavista)

0 metres 200
0 yards 200

Sleeping
Acosta 7 *B2*
Amazonas 1 *A2*
El Dorado 3 *A2*
El Dorado Plaza 4 *A2*
El Sitio 5 *C1*
Europa 6 *B3*
Hospedaje La
  Pascana 17 *A3*
Hostal Alfert 11 *C3*
Hostal
  Ambassador 8 *A3*
Hostal Colibrí 16 *A3*
Internacional 12 *C3*
Isabel 13 *B3*
Jhuliana 14 *A1*
La Casa de
  Samantha 9 *A1*
Marañón 10 *A3*
Royal Inn 2 *C2*
Victoria Regia 15 *C2*

Eating 🍴
Ari's Burger 1 *A3*
El Nuevo Mesón 3 *A3*
Fitzcarrald 4 *A3*
Hausaí 11 *A2*
Heladería 13 *B3*
La Gran Maloca 5 *B3*
La Vida es Salud 6 *C2*
Montecarlo 7 *A3*
Paulina 8 *C1*
Pollón 1 *A3*
Yellow Rose
  of Texas 12 *A3*

Bars & clubs 🍸
Snack Bar Arandú 9 *A3*
Teatro Café
  Amauta 10 *A3*

Amazon Basin Northern Jungle

⁞ Androgynous Amazonians

The Amazon is the longest river in the world. It rises high up in the Andes as the Marañón, then joins the Ucayali and winds its way east to disgorge itself finally into the Atlantic, over 6000 km from its source. At its mouth, the Amazon is 300 km wide.

This mighty waterway was named by the Spaniard Francisco de Orellana during his epic voyage in 1542, following an encounter with a hostile, long-haired indigenous group which he took to be the fearsome women warriors of Greek legend.

Alexandre Gustave Eiffel. In the high-water season canoes can be hired on the waterfront (US$3 an hour) to visit Belén. The market at the end of the Malecón is well worth visiting, though you should get there before 0900 if you want to see it in full swing. On Pasaje Paquito, one of its side streets, vendors sell local medicinal herbs and potions.

Around Iquitos

Allpahuayo-Mishana Reserve ① *Instituto de Investigaciones de la Amazonía Peruana (IIAP), Av Quiñones on the way to the airport, 22 km south of Iquitos by road or 2-3 hrs by boat from Bellavista, T065-265515*, protects the largest concentration of white-sand jungle (*varillales*) in Peru. Part of the Napo ecoregion, biodiversity here is among the highest in the Amazon Basin, with 500 species of birds, including several endangered species including the Iquitos gnatcatcher or perlita de Iquitos (*Polioptila clementsi*) and five species new to science, two endangered primates and several endemic species.

There is a beach at **Bellavista**, a suburb of Iquitos, which is safe for swimming and very popular at weekends in summer. Boats can be hired from here to see the meeting of the Nanay and Amazon rivers, and to visit beaches and villages en route. There are lots of food stalls selling typical local dishes. Take a bus from Jirón Próspero to 'Bellavista Nanay'. It takes around 15 minutes and costs US$0.40.

Boats leave Iquitos for the village of **Indiana**. A road leads from Indiana to the village of Mazán through the secondary jungle. It's about a two-hour walk or a US$0.80 mototaxi ride. If the hotel in Indiana is full, ask at the mission or municipality for a tent for the night. From Indiana you can do several hikes of between two and four hours to little villages along the **Río Napo**.

Some 4 km south of the city, **Lake Quistococha** is beautifully situated in lush jungle, with a fish hatchery at the lakeside. On the lake, **Parque Zoológico de Quistococha** ① *0900-1700, US$1.30*, gives an insight into the local wildlife, though conditions are squalid. At the entrance are interesting pictures and texts of local legends. The ticket office will supply a map of the lake and environs. There's a good two-hour walk through the surrounding jungle on a clearly marked trail. Make sure you see the paiche, a huge Amazonian fish whose steaks (*paiche a la loretana*) can be found on menus in Iquitos' restaurants. There are also bars and restaurants on the lakeside and a small beach. Boats are for hire on the lake and swimming is safe but the sandflies are vicious, so take insect repellent.

On the road to Quistococha is the turn-off to the village of **Santo Tomás**. Take a left turn just before the airport, and then another left 300 m further on. Then it's about 4 km to the village. There are restaurants open on Sunday and dugout canoes can be hired. The village hosts a fiesta on 22-25 September. Trucks go there, taking passengers.

The **Pilpintuhuasi Butterfly Farm** ① *near the village of Padre Cocha, T065-232665, www.amazonanimalorphanage.org, Tue-Sun 0900-1600, US$5*, also has a small well-kept zoo, which is Austrian-Peruvian run. It is a 20-minute walk from Padre Cocha to the butterfly farm.

⬤ Sleeping

Iquitos *p280, map p281*

Around Independence Day (27 and 28 Jul) and Easter, Iquitos gets crowded. Prices rise at this time. At all times, hotels are more expensive than the rest of the country, but discounts can be negotiated in the low season (Jan-Apr). Taxi drivers and touts at the airport are paid commission by some hotels, insist on being taken where you want to go.

AL El Dorado Plaza, Napo 258 on main plaza, T065-222555, www.eldoradoplaza hotel.com. 5 stars, very good rooms and restaurant, excellent service, friendly, bar, internet access, prices include breakfast, welcome drink and transfer to/from airport. The hotel offers special 3-day/2-night packages from Lima in conjunction with some of the Amazon lodges.

A El Dorado, Napo 362, T065-232574, dorado@eldoradoplazahotel.com. Same ownership as El Dorado Plaza, pool (open to restaurant users), cable TV, bar and restaurant, prices include service and airport transfer.

A Victoria Regia, Ricardo Palma 252, T065-231983, www.victoriaregiahotel.com. Regarded as the second best in the city. Price includes breakfast and airport transfer, a/c, fridge, cable TV, free map of city, safe deposit boxes in rooms, good restaurant and pool. Has own internet next door.

C Acosta, Calvo de Araujo y Huallaga, T065-235974, www.hotelacosta.com. Price includes breakfast and airport transfer, a/c, fridge, cable TV, safety deposit boxes, good restaurant.

C Amazonas, Plaza de Armas, Arica 108, T065-242431. Modern, a/c, phone, fridge bar, TV.

C Europa, Próspero 494, T065-231123, rcpowerv@terra.com.pe. A/c, cable TV, phone and fridge in every room, pleasant café/bar, good views from 5th floor.

C Jhuliana, Putumayo 521, T/F065-233154. Includes tax and breakfast, friendly, nice pool, restaurant.

D Hostal Ambassador, Pevas 260, T065-233110, www.paseosamazonicos.com. Includes breakfast, a/c, transport to and from airport, member of Peruvian YHA, cafeteria, owns Sinchicuy Lodge.

D Internacional, Próspero 835, T/F065-234684. A/c, with bathroom, cable TV, fridge, phone, friendly, secure, medium-priced restaurant, good value.

D Marañón, Nauta 285, T065-242673, hotel maranon@terra.com.pe. Includes breakfast and airport transfers, small pool, a/c, frigobar, hot water, comfortable.

D Royal Inn, Aguirre 793, T065-224244, royalinn_casinohotel@terra.com. Includes breakfast, a/c, frigobar, hot water, bidet, modern and comfortable.

E Hospedaje La Pascana, Pevas 133, T065-233466, www.pascana.com. Cold shower, quiet and safe, helpful, English spoken, also has a tour operator which runs trips to nature reserves.

F El Sitio, Ricardo Palma 545 (no sign), T065-234932. With bathroom, very clean, fan, good value.

F Hostal Alfert, García Sanz 01, T065-234105. Hard beds, check fan, friendly, good views to the river, safe but in the market area, arranges jungle trips, but not an authorized operator.

F Hostal Colibrí, Nauta 172, T065-241737. One block from plaza and 50 m from river, new building, TV, fan, hot water, secure, good value, helpful, a/c rooms are more expensive.

G Isabel, Brasil 164, T065-234901. In 1910 building, with bathroom, basic, clean, but plug the holes in the walls, secure, often full.

G La Casa de Samantha, Jr Nauta 787, T065-231005. Shared bath, cold water, small place, family-run, friendly and helpful.

Jungle lodges

See Activities and tours, page 286, for general hints on booking tours. Note especially the advice on checking credentials.

Amazon Lodge and Safaris, Av La Marina 592A, T065-251078. 48 km downriver from Iquitos. Friendly and comfortable; 3 days/2 nights, US$200 pp for 2-4 people, US$50 pp for additional nights.

Amazon Wilderness Expeditions, Jr Putumayo 163, altos 202, T065-234565. Good tours to Emerald Forest Camp, on Río Yanayacu, 185 km from Iquitos, US$65 per day. Comfortable, simple accommodation (no shower – wash in river), clean, good food. Ask for guide Juan Carlos Palomino Berndt, T065-993 5472 (mob).

Amazon Yarapa River Lodge, Av La Marina 124, T065-993 1172, www.yarapariverlodge. com. On Río Yarapa, tributary of the Amazon, in a pristine location, this award-winning

Rubber barons

The conquest and colonization of the vast Amazon Basin was consolidated by the end of the 19th century with the invention of the process of vulcanizing rubber. Many and varied uses were found for this new product and demand was such that the jungle began to be populated by numerous European and North American immigrants who came to invest their money in rubber.

The rubber tree grew wild in the Amazon but the indigenous peoples were the only ones who knew the forests and could find this coveted tree. The exporting companies set up business in the rapidly expanding cities along the Amazon, such as Iquitos. They sent their 'slave hunters' out into the surrounding jungle to find the native labour needed to collect the valuable rubber resin. These people were completely enslaved, their living conditions were intolerable and they perished in their thousands, leading to the extinction of many indigenous groups.

One notable figure from the rubber boom was Fitzcarrald, son of an immigrant Englishman who lived on the Peruvian coast. He was accused of spying during the 1879 war between Peru and Chile and fled to the Amazon where he lived for many years among the indigenous people.

Thanks to Fitzcarrald, the isthmus between the basin of the Ucayali river and that of the Madre de Dios was discovered. Before this, no natural form of communication was known between the two rivers. The first steamships to go up the Madre de Dios were carried by thousands of native workers across the 8-km stretch of land which separated the two basins. Fitzcarrald, one of the region's richest men, died at the age of 36 when the ship on which he was travelling sank.

The rubber barons lived in the new Amazonian cities. Every imaginable luxury was imported for their use: latest Parisian fashions for the women; finest foreign liqueurs for the men; even the best musical shows were brought over from the Old World. But this period of economic boom came to a sudden end in 1912 when rubber grown in the French and British colonies in Asia and Africa began to compete on the world market.

lodge has a field laboratory in conjunction with Cornell University. It uses ecofriendly resources and local materials, and works with nearby villages. Flexible and responsible. **Cumaceba Lodge and Expeditions**, Putumayo 184 in the Iron House, T/F065-232229, www.cumaceba.com. Tours of 2-8 days to their lodges on the Amazon and Yarapa rivers, good birdwatching guides, 3 days/2 nights. Very good all round. **Explorama Tours**, by the riverside docks on Av La Marina 340, PO Box 446, T065-252530, www.explorama.com, are highly recommended as the most efficient and, with over 40 years experience, certainly the biggest and most established. The following 4 sites are run by them: **Ceiba Tops**, 40 km (1½ hrs) from Iquitos, is a resort providing 'an adventure in luxury', 75 a/c

rooms with electricity, hot showers, pool with hydromassage, beautiful gardens. The food is good and, as in all Explorama's properties, is served communally. There are attractive walks and other excursions, a recommended jungle experience for those who want their creature comforts, US$200 per person for 1 night/ 2 days, US$98 for each additional night (1-2 people). **Explorama Lodge** at Yanamono, 80 km (2½ hrs) from Iquitos, has palm-thatched accommodation with separate bathroom and shower facilities connected by covered walkways, cold water, no electricity, good food and service. US$285 for 3 days/ 2 nights and US$85 for each additional day (1-2 people). **Explornapo Lodge** at Llachapa on the Sucusai creek (a tributary of the Napo), is in the same style as Explorama Lodge, but is further away from Iquitos, 160 km (4 hrs), and is set in 105,000 ha of primary rainforest, so is better for seeing wildlife, US$820 for 5 days/ 4 nights (other packages are available). Nearby is the impressive canopy walkway 35 m above the forest floor and 500 m long, 'a magnificent experience and not to be missed'. It is associated with the Amazon Center for Tropical Studies (ACTS), a scientific station, only 10 mins from the canopy walkway. **Explor Tambos**, 2 hrs from Explornapo, offer more primitive accommodation, 8 shelters for 16 campers, bathing in the river, offers the best chance to see rare fauna. Close to Explornapo is the ReNuPeRu medicinal plant garden, run by a *curandero*. Members of South American Explorers are offered 15% discount. **Heliconia Lodge**, Ricardo Palma 242, T065-231959, www.amazonriverexpeditions.com. On the Río Amazonas, 1½ hrs from Iquitos, the lodge has hot water, electricity for 3 hrs a day, good guiding and staff; rustic yet comfortable, 3 days/2 nights trips. Same management as hotels **Victoria Regia** and **Acosta**, see above. They organize trips to Allpahuayo-Mishana with **Amazon Tours and Cruises**, see Activities and tours, page 287, and to the ACTS canopy walkway.

Jacamar Amazon Jungle Lodge, 5079 Mariana Lane, Tega Cay, SC 29708, USA, T1-803-548 6738, www.jacamarlodge.com. In the Reserva Comunal de Tamshiyacu-Tahuayo. Do as much or as little as you please, plenty of activities, remote, great food and attentive staff. Fully screened rooms, no electricity, flushing toilets, capacity for 24 guests.

Muyuna Amazon Lodge, Putumayo 163, T065-242858, T065 993 4424 (mob), www.muyuna.com. 140 km from Iquitos, on the Yanayacu, before San Juan village. Packages from 1-5 nights, 2 nights/3 days US$300; Footprint readers get a discounted price (similarly SAE members, 10%). All-inclusive. Good guides, accommodation, food and service, well organized and professional, flexible, radio contact, will collect passengers from airport if requested in advance. They offer a 7-day birdwatching trip, combining several areas including Allpahuayo-Mishana Reserve; also have a new underwater microphone for listening to dolphins.

Paseos Amazónicos Ambassador, Pevas 246, T/F065-231618, www.paseos amazonicos.com, operate the **Amazonas Sinchicuy Lodge**. The lodge is 1½ hrs from Iquitos on the Sinchicuy river, 25 mins by boat from the Amazon river. It consists of several wooden buildings with thatched roofs on stilts, cabins with bathroom, no electricity but paraffin lamps are provided, good food, and plenty of activities, disabled facilities, includes visits to local villages. Recommended. They also have **Tambo Yanayacu** and **Tambo Amazónico** lodges, organize visits to nature reserves and local tours.

Tahuayo Lodge, Amazonia Expeditions, 10305 Riverburn Dr, Tampa, FL 33647, toll free T+1 800-262 9669, www.perujungle.com. Near the Reserva Comunal de Tamshiyacu-Tahuayo on the Río Tahuayo, 145 km upriver from Iquitos, clean, comfortable cabins with cold shower, buffet meals, good food, laundry service, wide range of excursions, excellent staff. A 7-day programme costs US$1295, all inclusive, extra days US$100. Recommended. The lodge is associated with the **Rainforest Conservation Fund** (www.rainforestconser vation.org), which works in Tamshiyacu-Tahuayo, one of the world's richest areas for primate species and for amphibians (there is a poison dart frog management programme), birds, other animals and plants.

⊕ Eating

Iquitos *p280, map p281*
Try palm heart salad (*chonta*), or a *la loretana* dish; also try *inchicapi* (chicken, corn and peanut soup), *cecina* (fried dried pork), *tacacho* (fried green banana and pork, mashed into balls and eaten for breakfast or tea), *juanes* (chicken, rice, olive and egg, seasoned and wrapped in bijao leaves and sold in restaurants). Many jungle species such as deer and wild boar still figure prominently in Iquitos restaurants. Please be responsible. Try the local drink *chuchuhuasi*, made from the bark of a tree, which is supposed to have aphrodisiac properties but tastes like fortified cough tincture (for sale at Arica 1046), and *jugo de cocona*, the alcoholic *cola de mono* and *siete raíces* (aguardiente mixed with the bark of 7 trees and wild honey), sold at **Exquisita Amazónica**, Abtao 590. *Camu-camu* is an interesting but acquired taste, said to have one of the highest vitamin C concentrations in the world. Many private homes offer set lunch, look for the board outside.

Note Some places serve local specialities such as wild boar, alligator, turtle, tapir and other endangered species. these should be avoided.

₸₸₸ Fitzcarrald, Malecón Maldonado 103 y Napo. Smart, best pizza in town, also good pastas and salads.

₸₸₸ La Gran Maloca, Sargento Lores 170, opposite Banco Continental. A/c, high class.

₸₸₸ Montecarlo, Napo 140. Next to the casino, "best food in town".

₸₸ Ari's Burger, Plaza de Armas, Próspero 127. Fast food, good breakfasts, popular with tourists.

₸₸ Pollón, on the plaza next to Ari's Burger. For chicken and chips, open in the daytime.

₸₸ The Regal, in the Casa de Hierro, Plaza de Armas, Próspero y Putumayo, 2nd floor. Nice location, good set lunch for US$2.30, other meals more expensive.

₸₸ Yellow Rose of Texas, Putumayo 180. Run by the ex-director of the tourist office, Gerald W Mayeaux. Varied food, Texan atmosphere. Open 24 hrs so you can wait here if arriving late at night, huge breakfasts, lots of information, also has a bar, Sky TV and Texan saddle seats. Often recommended. Will arrange trips to nature reserves. Expeditions must be booked in advance, all equipment and food is provided, US$50 for each day in the park, plus US$33 transport and entry fee.

₸ Huasaí, Napo 326, daily 0730-1600. Varied and innovative menu, popular and recommended.

₸ La Vida es Salud, Aguirre 759 on Plaza 28 de Julio, open daily. Vegetarian, simple little place, good value.

₸ Paulina, Tacna 591. Good set lunch, popular with locals and tourists, very noisy.

Cafés
Heladería, Próspero 415. Excellent ice cream, several local flavours including *aguaje* and *camu-camu*. Highly recommended.

♪ Bars and clubs

Iquitos *p280, map p281*
Snack Bar Arandú, Malecón Maldonado. Good views of the Amazon river.
Teatro Café Amauta, Nauta 248, open 2200-2400. Live music, good atmosphere, popular, small exhibition hall.

⊛ Festivals and events

Iquitos *p280, map p281*
5 Jan Anniversary of the Founding of Iquitos.
Feb/Mar During Carnival you can see the local dance La Pandilla.
24 Jun Festival of San Juan, patron saint of Loreto. Also Tourist week, with regional music, in the Mercado Artesanal de San Juan.
8 Dec La Purísima, celebrated in Punchana, near the docks.

⊙ Shopping

Iquitos *p280, map p281*
Good hammocks in the markets in Iquitos cost about US$5.75. For crafts: **Amazon Arts and Crafts**, Napo block 100; **Artesanías de la Selva**, R Palma 190; **Mercado Artesanal de Productores**, 4 km from the centre in the San Juan district, on the road to the airport (take a *colectivo*). Cheapest in town with more choice than elsewhere.
Mad Mick's Trading Post, next to the Iron House. Hires out rubber boots for those going to the jungle.

▲ Activities and tours

Iquitos *p280, map p281*
See Sleeping above for jungle lodges and the trips that they offer. All agencies are under the control of the local Chamber of Tourism. They arrange 1-day or longer trips to places of interest with guides speaking some English. Package tours booked in Lima or abroad are much more expensive than those booked in Iquitos and personal approaches to lodge operators will often yield better prices than booking through an agency or the internet. Take your time before making a decision and don't be bullied by the hustlers at the airport (they get paid a hefty commission). You must make sure your tour operator or guide has a proper licence (the Municipalidad's *Iquitos Guía Turística* gives a full list). Do not go with a company which does not have legal authorization; there are many unscrupulous people about. Find out all the details of the trip and food arrangements before paying (a minimum of US$45 per day). Speed boats for river trips can be hired by the hour or day at the Embarcadero Turístico, at the intersection of Av de la Marina and Samánez Ocampo in

Punchana. Prices vary greatly, usually US$10-20 per hr, and are negotiable. In fact, all prices are negotiable, except **Muyuna**, who do not take commissions.

Take a long-sleeved shirt, waterproof coat and shoes or light boots on jungle trips and a good torch, as well as *espirales* to ward off the mosquitoes at night – they can be bought from pharmacies in Iquitos. Premier is the most effective local insect repellent. The dry season is from Jul-Sep (Sep is the best month to see flowers and butterflies).
Amazon Tours and Cruises, Requena 336, T065-231611, www.amazontours.net. An American-owned company offering a variety of cruises, many for nature watching, from 1-7 days on *Dawn of the Amazon I* and the luxury *Dawn of the Amazon III*. Also peacock bass fishing, trips to villages (including Pevas), jungle cabin at Llachama and more. Conscientious and efficient.
Blue Morpho, Centre for Shamanic Studies and Workshops, Calle Moore 144, T065-231168, www.bluemorphotours.com. For reservation information, schedule and pricing, see website.

⊖ Transport

Iquitos *p280, map p281*
Air
For airport information see Ins and outs, page 280. Iquitos flights are frequently delayed; be sure to reconfirm your flight in Iquitos, as they are often overbooked, especially over Christmas. Check times in advance as itineraries frequently change. A taxi to the airport costs US$2.85 per car (T065-241284). A *motocarro* (motorcycle with 2 seats) is US$2. To take a city bus from the airport, walk out to the main road; most bus lines run through the centre of town, US$0.20. Lan and Star Perú have daily flights to **Lima**.
Airline offices Lan, Napo 374, T065-232421, Mon-Sat 0900-1900, Sun 0900-1200. Star Perú, Próspero 428, T065-236208.

Bus
To get to **Lake Quistococha**, *combis* leave every hour until 1500 from Plaza 28 de Julio. The last one back leaves at 1700. Alternatively take a mototaxi there and back with a 1-hour wait, which costs US$6. Another option is to hire a motorbike and spend the day there.

287

Motorcycle hire
Park Motors, Tacna 579, T/F065-231688. The tourist office has details of other companies. Expect to pay US$2.50 per hr, US$25 for 24 hrs; remember that traffic in town is chaotic.

ⓘ Directory

Iquitos *p280, map p281*
Banks Don't change money on the streets. Visit the tourist office and obtain a list with the names of reliable money changers. BCP, Plaza de Armas. For Visa, also cash and TCs at good rates, has a Visa ATM around the corner on Próspero. BBV **Continental**, Sargento Lores 171, for Visa, 1% commission on TCs. **Banco de la Nación**, Condamine 478, good rates. **Scotiabank**, Próspero 282. **Banco del Trabajo**, Próspero 223, has Unicard ATM for Visa/Plus and MasterCard/Cirrus. *Casa de cambio* at **Tienda Wing Kong**, Próspero 312, Mon-Sat 0800-1300 and 1500-2000, Sun 0900-1200. **Western Union**, Napo 359, T065-235182. **Consulates** Britain, Casa de Hierro (Iron House), Putumayo 189, T065-22273 2, Mon-Fri 1100-1200. There is no Ecuadorean consulate. If you need a visa for Ecuador and plan to travel there from Iquitos, you must get the visa beforehand at home or in Lima. **Immigration** Mcal Cáceres 18th block, T065-235371, quick service. **Internet** There are internet places everywhere, US$0.80 per hr. **Laundry** At Ricardo Palma, blocks 4 and 5, and at Putumayo, block 1. **Medical services** Clínica Loreto, Morona 471, T065-233752, 24-hr attention. Recommended, but only Spanish spoken. Dr Héctor Navarro Mattos, Raymondi 211, T065-236708, T967 2291 (mob). Thorough and professional. **Police** Tourist police, Sargento Lores 834, T065-231851. Helpful with complaints against tour operators. In emergency T065-241000/241001. **Post office** On the corner of Calle Arica with Morona, near the Plaza de Armas, 0700-2000. **Telephone** Telefónica, Arica 276. Locutorio at Próspero 523, private cabins, cheap national and international calls, helpful staff. **Useful addresses** Indecopi, Calle Huallaga 325, T065-243490, ameza@indecopi.gob.pe, for the tourism protection service.

Amazon Basin Northern Jungle Listings

Southern Jungle

Both the Manu Biosphere Reserve and Tambopata National Park offer amazing wildlife spotting, large parts being remote and pristine, with such highlights as macaw clay licks and birdwatching on undisturbed lakes. The southern jungle is found mostly within the Department of Madre de Dios, created in 1902, and contains the Manu Biosphere Reserve, the Tambopata National Reserve and the Bahuaja-Sonene National Park. ▶▶ *For Sleeping, Eating and other listings, see pages 293-300.*

Manu Biosphere Reserve ●▲● ▶▶ *pp293-300. Colour map 2, C4.*

No other rainforest can compare with Manu for the diversity of its life forms. It is one of the world's great wilderness experiences, with the best birdwatching as well as offering the best chance of seeing giant otters, jaguars, ocelots and several of the 13 species of primate which abound in this pristine tropical wilderness. The more remote areas of the reserve are home to uncontacted indigenous tribes and many other indigenous groups with very little knowledge of the outside world. Covering an area of 18,810 sq km, Manu Biosphere Reserve is also one of the largest conservation units on Earth, encompassing the complete drainage of the Manu river, with an altitudinal range of 200-4100 m.

Ins and outs

Getting there and around   To visit Manu you must go as part of a tour leaving from Cuzco, either by road or by air. The frontier town of Puerto Maldonado is the starting point for expeditions to the Tambopata National Reserve and is only a 30-minute flight from Cuzco. ▶▶ *For details see Activities and tours, page 297 and Transport page 299.*

Best time to visit   The climate is warm and humid, with a rainy season from November to March and a dry season from April to October. A cool air mass descending from the Andes, called a *friaje*, is characteristic of the dry season, when temperatures drop to 15-16°C during the day, and 13°C at night. Always bring a sweater at this time. The best time to visit is during the dry season when there are fewer mosquitoes and the rivers are low, exposing the beaches. This is also a good time to see birds nesting and to view the animals at close range, as they stay close to the rivers.

Tourist information   **Manu National Park Office** ① *Av Micaela Bastidas 310, Cuzco, T084-240898, pqnmanu@terra.com.pe, casilla postal 591, 0800-1400.* They issue a permit for the former Reserved Zone, costing S/.150 per person (about US$40). This is included in package tour prices. For information on conservation issues: **Asociación Peruana para la Conservación de la Naturaleza (Apeco)** ① *Parque José Acosta 187, p 2, Magdalena del Mar, Lima 17, T01-264 0094, www.apeco.org.pe*; and **Pronaturaleza** ① *Av Alberto de Campo 417, Lima 17, T01-264 2736 and Jr Cajamarca, cuadra 1 s/n, Puerto Maldonado, T082-571585, www.pronaturaleza.org.* **Perú Verde** ① *Ricaldo Palma J-1, Santa Mónica, Cuzco, T084-226392, www.peruverde.org*, is a local NGO that can help with information and has free video shows about Manu National Park and Tambopata National Reserve. Staff are friendly and helpful and also have information on programmes and research in the jungle area of Río Madre de Dios.

The park areas

The biosphere reserve formerly comprised the **Manu National Park** (16, 921 sq km), where only government-sponsored biologists and anthropologists may visit with permits from the Ministry of Agriculture in Lima, the **Manu Reserved Zone** (2570 sq km), set aside for applied scientific research and ecotourism, and the **Cultural Zone** (920 sq km), containing acculturated native groups and colonists, where the locals still employ their traditional way of life. In 2003 the Manu Reserved Zone was absorbed into the Manu National Park, increasing its protected status. Ecotourism activities have been allowed to continue in specially designated tourism and recreational zones along the course of the Lower Manu River. These tourism and recreational areas are accessible by permit only. Entry is strictly controlled and visitors must visit the area under the auspices of an authorized operator with an authorized guide. Permits are limited and reservations should be made well in advance, though it is possible to book a place on a trip at the last minute in Cuzco. In the former Reserved Zone there are two lodges, the rustic **Casa Machiguenga** run by the Machiguenga communities of Tayakome and Yomibato with the help of a German NGO, and the upmarket **Manu Lodge**. In the Cocha Salvador area, several companies have tented safari camp infrastructures, some with shower and dining facilities, but all visitors sleep in tents. Some companies have installed walk-in tents with cots and bedding.

The Cultural and Multiple Use Zones are accessible to anyone and several lodges exist in the area. It is possible to visit these lodges under your own steam. Among the ethnic groups in the Multiple Use Zone (a system of buffer areas surrounding the core Manu area) are the Harakmbut, Machiguenga and Yine in the Amarakaeri Reserved Zone, on the east bank of the Alto Madre de Dios. They have set up their own ecotourism activities, which are entirely managed by indigenous people. Associated with Manu are other areas protected by conservation groups or local people, for example the Blanquillo reserved zone, a new conservation concession in the adjacent Los Amigos river system and some cloudforest parcels along the road. The **Nuhua-Kugapakori Reserved Zone** (4438 sq km), set aside for these two nomadic groups, is the area between the headwaters of the Río Manu and headwaters of the Río Urubamba, to the north of the Alto Madre de Dios.

Amazon Basin Southern Jungle

To Manu and Puerto Maldonado from Cuzco

▸▸ pp293-300. Colour map 2, C4.

The arduous trip over the Andes from Cuzco to Pilcopata takes about 16-18 hours by bus or truck (20-40 hours in the wet season). On this route, the scenery is magnificent.

Leaving Cuzco
From Cuzco you climb up to the Huancarani pass before **Paucartambo** (3½ hours), before dropping down to this picturesque mountain village in the Mapacho Valley. The road then ascends to the Ajcanacu pass (cold at night), after which it goes down to the cloudforest and then the rainforest, reaching **Pilcopata** at 650 m.

Atalaya → Colour map 2, B4.
After Pilcopata, the route is hair-raising and breathtaking. Even in the dry season this part of the road is appalling and trucks often get stuck. Travelling towards Atalaya, the first village on the Alto Madre de Dios river and about an hour away from Pilcopata, you pass **Manu Cloudforest Lodge**, **Cock of the Rock Lodge** and the **San Pedro Biological Station** (owned by Tapir Tours, visited in their Manu programmes). Atalaya consists of a few houses, and basic accommodation can be found here. Meals are available at the very friendly family home of Rosa and Klaus, where you can also camp. Boats here will take you across the river to **Amazonia Lodge**, see page 293. The village is also the jumping-off point for river trips further into the Manu. The route continues to **Salvación**, where a Manu Park office is situated. There are basic hostels and restaurants.

Shintuya and Itahuania → *Colour map 2, C5.*

The road now bypasses Shintuya, a commercial and social centre, as wood from the jungle is transported from here to Cuzco. There are a few basic restaurants and you can camp (beware of thieves). The priest will let you stay in the dormitory rooms at the mission. Supplies are expensive. There are two Shintuyas: one is the port and mission and the other is the indigenous village. The end of the road is **Itahuania**, the starting point for river transport. It won't be long before the port moves down river as the road is being built to Nuevo Edén, 11 km away, and there are plans to extend to Diamante by early 2007, with the road one day planned to reach Boca Colorado. **Note**: It is not possible to arrange trips to the Reserved Zone of the National Park from Itahuania, owing to park regulations; all arrangements must be made in Cuzco.

Boca Manu

Boca Manu is the connecting point between the rivers Alto Madre de Dios, Manu and Madre de Dios. It has a few houses, an airstrip and some well-stocked shops. It is also the entrance to the Manu Reserve and to go further you must be part of an organized group. The park ranger station is located in **Limonal**, 20 minutes by boat from Boca Manu. You need to show your permit here; camping is allowed if you have a permit.

To the Reserved Zone

Upstream on the Río Manu you pass the **Manu Lodge** (see page 293) on the Cocha Juárez, three to four hours by boat. You can continue to Cocha Otorongo, 2½ hours, and Cocha Salvador, 30 minutes, the biggest lake with plenty of wildlife where the **Casa Machiguenga Lodge** is located and several companies have safari camp concessions. From here it is one hour to **Pakitza**, the entrance to the National Park Zone. This is only for biologists and others with a special permit.

Boca Colorado

From Itahuania infrequent cargo boats sail to the gold-mining centre of Boca Colorado on the Río Madre de Dios, via Boca Manu, passing several ecotourism lodges including **Pantiacolla Lodge** and **Manu Wildlife Centre** (see page 293). The trip takes around nine hours, and costs US$15. Basic accommodation can be found here and is not recommended for lone women travellers. From Colorado you can take a *colectivo* taxi to Puerto Carlos, cross the river, than take another *colectivo* to Puerto Maldonado, 4¼ hours in all. Some lodges in the Manu area now use this route: flight to Puerto Maldonado, a vehicle to Boca Colorado and then a boat upstream to the lodge.

Between Boca Manu and Colorado is **Blanquillo**, a private reserve (10,000 ha). Bring a good tent with you and all food if you want to camp and do it yourself, or alternatively accommodation is available at the **Tambo Blanquillo** (full board or accommodation only). Wildlife is abundant, especially macaws and parrots at the macaw lick near Manu Wildlife Centre. There are occasional boats to Blanquillo from Shintuya, six to eight hours.

Puerto Maldonado ⊕🏨👤👥🏔️🚌🚉 → *pp293-300.*

→ *Colour map 2, C5. Phone code: 082. Population: 45,000. Altitude: 250 m.*

Puerto Maldonado is an important starting point for visiting the rainforest, or for departing to Brazil or Bolivia. Still, most visitors won't see much of the place because they are whisked through town on their way to a lodge on the Río Madre de Dios or the Río Tambopata. The city dwellers aren't too pleased about this and would like tourists to spend some time in town, which is a major timber, gold mining and tourism centre, expanding rapidly. It's a safe place, with *chicha* music blaring out from most street corners. **Dircetur tourist office** ① *Urb Fonavi, F20, Pasaje 12 de Septiembre, T082-571164, T970 3987 (mob), carloagpe@yahoo.com*. There is also an office at the airport.

Ins and outs

The road from Cuzco to Puerto Maldonado is being improved, with regular bus services. The road is passable in the wet season but takes a lot longer than in the dry. In its pre-upgrading state it was expertly described in Matthew Parris' book *Inka-Cola*. The road passes through Ocongate and Marcapata before reaching **Quincemil**, 240 km from Urcos, a centre for alluvial gold-mining. Quincemil marks the halfway point and the end of the all-weather road. Petrol is scarce here because most vehicles continue on 70 km to **Mazuko**, where it's cheaper. The journey is very rough, but the changing scenery is magnificent. This road is rarely passable in the wet season. Take warm clothing for travelling through the sierra. For an alternative route, see page 289.

Sights

Overlooking the confluence of the rivers Tambopata and Madre de Dios, Puerto Maldonado is a major logging and brazil-nut processing centre. From the park at the end of Jirón Arequipa, across from the Capitanía, you get a good view of the two rivers, the ferries across the Madre de Dios and the stacks of lumber at the dockside. The brazil-nut harvest is from December to February and the crop tends to be good on

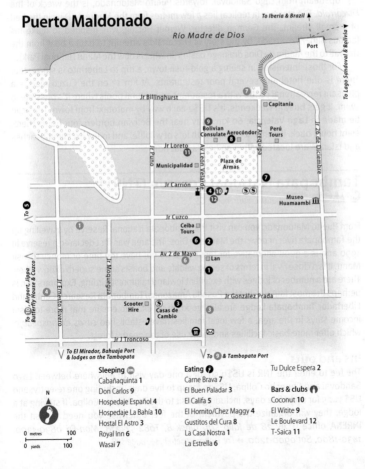

Puerto Maldonado

Río Madre de Dios

To Iberia & Brazil

Port

To Lago Sandoval & Bolivia

Jr Billinghurst

Capitanía

Bolivian Consulate   Aerocóndor
Perú Tours

Jr Loreto

Jr Puno

Municipalidad

Av León Velarde

Plaza de Armas

Jr Carrión

Museo Huamaambi

Jr Cuzco

Ceiba Tours

Av 2 de Mayo

Lan

Jr Moquegua

Jr Ernesto Rivero

To Airport, Jappa Butterfly House & Cuzco

Jr González Prada

Scooter Hire

Casas de Cambio

Jr J Troncoso

To El Mirador, Bahuaja Port & lodges on the Tambopata

To ⑨ & Tambopata Port

To ⑤

N

0 metres 100
0 yards 100

Amazon Basin Southern Jungle

Sleeping
Cabañaquinta 1
Don Carlos 9
Hospedaje Español 4
Hospedaje La Bahía 10
Hostal El Astro 3
Royal Inn 6
Wasai 7

Eating
Carne Brava 7
El Buen Paladar 3
El Califa 5
El Hornito/Chez Maggy 4
Gustitos del Cura 8
La Casa Nostra 1
La Estrella 6

Tu Dulce Espera 2

Bars & clubs
Coconut 10
El Witite 9
Le Boulevard 12
T-Saica 11

alternate years. Nuts are sold on the street, plain or coated in sugar or chocolate. **El Mirador** ① *at the junction of Av Fitzcarrald and Av Madre de Dios, Mon-Sat 0900-1700, Sun 1200-1700, US$0.60*, is a 47-m-high tower with 250 steps and three platforms giving fine views over the city and surrounding rainforest. There is also a toilet at the top – no curtains – from which there is an equally fine view over the city. **Museo Huamaambi** ① *26 de Diciembre 360, US$1*, contains photos and artefacts pertaining to the Harakmbut culture of central Madre de Dios. **Jippa Butterfly House** ① *adjoining the airport entrance (a 5-min walk from the terminal building), open 0800-1330, www.butterflyhouse.com.pe, US$3*, breeds butterflies as part of a sustainable development project and offers guided tours. Worth a visit if you arrive early for your flight or if it is delayed. **El Serpentario** snake house is next door.

Around Puerto Maldonado

The beautiful and tranquil **Lago Sandoval** ① *US$9.50, you must go with a guide (see page 297); this can be arranged by the boat driver*, is a one-hour boat ride along the Río Madre de Dios from Puerto Maldonado, and then a 5-km walk into the jungle. There is an interpretation centre at the start of the trail and a 35-m-high observation tower overlooking the lake. It is possible to see giant river otters early in the morning and several species of monkeys, macaws and hoatzin. There are two jungle lodges at the lake, see Sleeping. At weekends, especially on Sundays, the lake gets quite busy.

Upstream from Lago Sandoval, towards Puerto Maldonado, is the wreck of the *Fitzcarrald*. The steamer (a replica) lies a few metres from the Madre de Dios in the bed of a small stream. The German director, Werner Herzog, was inspired to make his famous film, *Fitzcarraldo*, by the story of Fitzcarrald's attempt to haul a boat from the Ucuyali to the Madre de Dios drainage basins (in what is now the Manu National Park).

For those interested in seeing a gold-rush town, a trip to **Laberinto** is suggested. There is one hotel and several poor restaurants. At Km 13 on the Cuzco road is a pleasant recreational centre with a restaurant and natural pools where it's possible to swim. It gets busy at weekends. It's US$2 each way by mototaxi from town. Trips can be made to **Lago Valencia**, 60 km away near the Bolivian border; four hours there, eight hours back. It is an oxbow lake with lots of wildlife, and many excellent beaches and islands are located within an hour's boat ride.

Tambopata National Reserve (TNR)

■▲● ▸ *pp293-300. Colour map 2, C5.*

From Puerto Maldonado you can visit the Tambopata National Reserve by travelling up the Tambopata river or down the Madre de Dios. The area was first declared a reserve in 1990 and is a good alternative for those who do not have the time or money to visit Manu. It is a close rival in terms of seeing wildlife and boasts some superb oxbow lakes. There are a number of lodges with excellent lowland rainforest birding. **Explorers' Inn** is perhaps the most famous, but the **Posada Amazonas/Tambopata Research Centre** and **Libertador Tambopata Lodge** are also good. In an effort to ensure that more tourism income stays in the area, a few local families have established *casas de hospedaje*, which offer more basic facilities and make use of the nearby forest.

Ins and outs

The fee to enter the TNR is US$9.50 for a one-day visit to anywhere between Lago Sandoval and Chuncho Collpa; US$20 for up to five days, including one re-entry; and US$31.25 for up to five days, including a visit to the Tambopata Collpa. If staying at a lodge, they will organize the payment of the fee, otherwise you need to visit the **INRENA office** ① *Av 28 de Julio s/n, block 8, T082-573278, Mon-Fri 0830-1300, 1430-1800, Sat 0900-1200.* ▸ *For Transport details, see page 300.*

The **Bahuaja-Sonene National Park** runs from the Río Heath, which forms the Bolivian border, across to the Río Tambopata, 50-80 km upstream from Puerto Maldonado. It was expanded to 10,914 sq km in August 2000, with the Tambopata National Reserve (2544 sq km) created to form a buffer zone. The park is closed to visitors though those visiting the *collpa* (macaw lick) on the Tambopata or river rafting down the Tambopata will travel through it.

● Sleeping

Manu Biosphere Reserve *p288*
Many of the following lodges are run by tour operators, see page 297.
Amazonia Lodge, in Cuzco at Matará 334, T/F084-231370, amazonia1@correo.dnet. com.pe. On the Río Alto Madre de Dios just across the river from Atalaya, an old tea hacienda run by the Yabar family, famous for its bird diversity and fine hospitality, a great place to relax, contact Santiago in advance and he'll arrange a pickup.
Casa Machiguenga, contact **Manu Expeditions** or the **Apeco NGO**, T084-225595. Near Cocha Salvador, upriver from Manu Lodge, Machiguenga-style cabins run by the local community of Tayakome with NGO help.
Cock of the Rock Lodge, run by the **Perú Verde** group. On the road from Paucartambo to Atalaya at San Pedro, at 1500 m, next to a Cock of the Rock lek, double rooms with shared bath and 7 private cabins with en suite bath.
Erika Lodge, contact **Aventuras Ecológicas Manu**, Plateros 356, Cuzco; or Ernesto Yallico, Casilla 560, Cuzco, T084-227765. On the Alto Madre de Dios, 25 mins from Atalaya. Like Amazonia Lodge, this is good place for birds. It offers basic facilities and is cheaper than the other, more luxurious lodges.
Manu Cloud Forest Lodge, owned by Manu Nature Tours. Located at Unión at 1800 m on the road from Paucartambo to Atalaya, 6 rooms with 4 beds.
Manu Lodge, run by **Manu Nature Tours** and only bookable as part of a full package deal with transport. Situated on the Manu river, 3 hrs upriver from Boca Manu towards Cocha Salvador, It's a fine location overlooking Cocha Juárez, an oxbow lake, which often plays host to a family of giant otters. The lodge has an extensive trail system, and stands of mauritia palms near the lake provide nesting sites for colonies of blue and yellow macaws.

Manu Wildlife Centre, book through **Manu Expeditions** or **InkaNatura**. 2 hrs down the Río Madre de Dios from Boca Manu, near the Blanquillo macaw lick. 22 double cabins, all with private bathroom and hot water. It also has a tapir lick and canopy tower for birdwatching.
Pantiacolla Lodge, book through **Pantiacolla Tours**. 30 mins downriver from Shintuya. Owned by the Moscoso family. This lodge is located at the foot of the Pantiacolla Mountains, which boasts vast biological diversity, particularly with birds. There are good trail system. Also managed by Pantiacolla is the **Yine Lodge**, see below, and the **Posada San Pedro Cloud Forest Lodge**, with 14 rooms, before Pilcopata.
Yanayaco Lodge, Procuradores 46, Cuzco, T084-248122, T960 6368 (mob), www.yanayacolodge.com. A relatively new lodge approximately 1 hr by boat above Diamante village on the southern bank of the Madre de Dios, close to a small parrot *collpa* (mineral lick); claims to offer frequent sightings of large mammals. Using local river transport to arrive at the lodge rates are very reasonable, US$35 including food and board in double room. The lodge also offers several different itineraries in Manu.

To Manu and Puerto Maldonado from Cuzco *p289*
Turismo Indígena Wanamei, T084-254033, T084-965 2520 (mob), or Av 26 de Diciembre 276, Puerto Maldonado, T082-572539, www.ecoturismowanamei.com. A new initiative of the Harakmbut indigenous people to introduce visitors to their ancestral lands, the Amarakaeri Communal Reserve, located between Manu and Tambopata. They offer 4- to 9-day trips starting and ending in Cuzco. Accommodation includes lodges, communities and camping. The trips aim to offer not only excellent wildlife

viewing opportunities but also an insight into the daily life of indigenous peoples in the early 21st century. To gain the most from this unusual experience you need to speak Spanish (or Harakmbut!). The 5-day/4-night trip costs US$200 and includes all transport, meals, lodging and a guide.

D **Boca Manu Lodge**, book through Emperadores Tours, Procuradores 190, Cuzco, T084-239987. Run by long-standing Manu resident Juan de Dios Carpio. Juan owns a general store in Boca, so if you're stranded in Boca Manu and you're looking for a reasonably priced place to stay this could be an option – just ask at the store.

G **Hospedaje Manu**, Boca Colorado, on street beside football field. Cell-like rooms, open windows and ceilings but comfortable mattresses and mosquito netting.

G **Hostal**, Boca Manu, run by the community. Basic accommodation.

G **The Mission**, Shintuya. The priest will let you stay in the dormitory rooms. There are a few basic restaurants and you can camp (beware of thieves). Supplies are expensive.

G **Sra Rubella**, Pilcopata. This unnamed place is very basic, but friendly.

Lodges

Yine Lodge, next to the airstrip, Boca Manu. A smart cooperative project between Pantiacolla Tours and the native Yine community of Diamante.

Puerto Maldonado *p290, map p291*
B **Wasai**, Billinghurst, opposite the Capitanía, T082-572290, www.wasai.com. Price includes breakfast, a/c, TV, shower. In a beautiful location overlooking the Madre de Dios, with forest surrounding cabin-style rooms which are built on a slope down to the river, small pool with waterfall, good restaurant if slightly expensive. Recommended, although service can be stretched if hotel is full. They run local tours and have a lodge on the Tambopata River (see page 292).

C **Cabañaquinta**, Cuzco 535, T082-571045, www.hotelcabanaquinta.com. With buffet breakfast, bathroom, a/c (cheaper rooms without a/c, cold water), free drinking water, internet, small pool, sauna, good restaurant, friendly, lovely garden, very comfortable, price includes airport transfer if needed. Recommended.

D **Don Carlos**, Av León Velarde 1271, T082-571029. Nice view over the Río Tambopata, a/c, restaurant, TV, phone, good.

E **Amarumayo**, Libertad 433, 10 mins from centre, T082-573860, residenciamarumayo @hotmail.com. Price includes breakfast. Comfortable, with pool and garden, good restaurant. Recommended.

E **Hospedaje Español**, González Prada 670, T082-572381. Garden setting, clean, friendly.

E **Hospedaje La Bahía**, 2 de Mayo 710, T082-572127. Cheaper without bath or TV, large rooms, clean. Best of cheaper options.

E **Royal Inn**, Av 2 de Mayo 333, T082-571048. Modern and clean, rooms at back are less noisy.

F **Hostal El Astro**, Velarde 617, T082-572128. Clean, safe, family-run.

Tambopata National Reserve *p292*
Most of the lodges in the Tambopata area use the term 'ecotourism', or something similar, in their publicity material, but it is applied pretty loosely. **Posada Amazonas'** collaboration with the local community is unique in the area, but fortunately no lodge offers trips where guests hunt for their meals. Prices are given only for standard 3-day/2-night packages which include all transport links, accommodation on a full-board basis and guiding. Lodges on the Tambopata are reached by vehicle to Bahuaja port, 15 km upriver from Puerto Maldonado, by the community of Infierno, then by boat. Some of the lodges mentioned above also offer guiding and research placements to biology and environmental science graduates. For more details send an SAE to **TReeS: UK**, c/o J Forrest, PO Box 33153, London NW3 4DR. Long-term visitors should be aware that leishmaniasis exists in this area.

Río Madre de Dios
C **Casa de Hospedaje Mejía**, book via Ceiba Tours in Puerto Maldonado (see Activities and tours, page 298). A small, family-run, rustic lodge close to Lago Sandoval, with 10 double rooms, none en suite. Canoes available to explore the lake. 3 days/2 nights costs US$70, one of the cheapest options. An English-speaking guide can be arranged.

Eco Amazonia Lodge, book through their office in Lima: Av 1083, of 408, Miraflores,

T01-242 2708; in Cuzco T083-225068, www.ecoamazonia.com.pe. On the Madre de Dios, 1 hr downriver from Puerto Maldonado. Accommodation for up to 80 in basic bungalows and dormitories, good for birdwatching with viewing platforms and tree canopy access, has a pool and its own Monkey Island with animals taken from the forest, US$160 for 3 days/2 nights.

El Corto Maltés, Billinghurst 229, Puerto Maldonado, T/F082-573831, cortomaltes @terra.com.pe. On the south side of the Madre de Dios river, one of the closest to Puerto Maldonado, halfway to Sandoval, the focus of most visits. Bungalows are very well spaced out and all have a river view. Hot water, huge dining room, well run, pool planned. Ayahuasca sessions can be arranged. US$180 for 3 days/2 nights.

Estancia Bello Horizonte, 20 km northwest of Puerto Maldonado, office in Puerto Maldonado, Loreto 258, T082-572748 (in **Heladería Gustitos del Cura**), www.estancia bellohorizonte.com. In a nice stretch of forest overlooking the Madre de Dios, a small lodge with bungalows for 25 people, with private bath, hammock and pool. 3 days/2 nights US$95-140, depending on the package. It is part of the scheme to train and employ young people. Suitable for those wanting to avoid a river trip.

Inkaterra Reserva Amazónica, 45 mins by boat down the Río Madre de Dios. To book: **Inkaterra**, Andalucía 174, Lima 18, T01-610 0400, Cuzco T084-245314, Puerto Maldonado T082-572283, www.inkaterra. com. A hotel in the jungle with 6 suites with electricity and hot water, and 38 rustic bungalows, solar power, good food. Caters mainly for large groups. Jungle tours available with multilingual guides, the lodge is surrounded by its own 100-sq-km reserve but most tours go to Lago Sandoval, US$345 pp (double occupancy) for a Superior Cabaña 2-night package, rising to US$1381 for 5 days/4 nights for a Suite Tambopata, a naturalists programme is also provided, negotiable out of season. Has the largest number of ant species recorded in a single location, 362. The lodge has a 350-m canopy walkway, two 30-m canopy viewing towers and a Monkey Island (Isla Rolín).

Sandoval Lake Lodge, to book, **InkaNatura**, Manuel Bañón 461, San Isidro, Lima, T01-440

2022, www.inkanatura.com. Also have an office in Cuzco. 1 km beyond Mejía on Lago Sandoval, usually accessed by canoe across the lake after a 3-km walk or rickshaw ride along the trail, this lodge, on a *cocha*, is part-owned by local brazil-nut collectors. It can accommodate 50 people in 25 rooms, bar and dining area, electricity, hot water. There is a system of trails nearby, guides are available in several languages. Price for 3 days/2 nights is US$215.

Río Tambopata

Casa de Hospedaje Picaflor, Casilla 105, Puerto Maldonado, picaflor_rc@yahoo.com. A small (4 rooms), family-run guesthouse with solar lighting, a good library, great cakes and fresh bread baked daily. It's located just downriver from **Libertador Tambopata Lodge**, guiding in English/ Spanish, good trail system, visits also made to Lake Condenados. Suited to birders and backpackers wanting a more intimate rainforest experience, US$20 per person per night plus TNR fee and transport. Special arrangements also for researchers and volunteers wanting to stay 4 or more weeks.

Casas de Hospedaje Baltimore, several families in the community of Baltimore on the banks of the Río Tambopata, 60 km upriver, www.baltimoreperu.com. They are developing accommodation for visitors (with EU funding), 4-12 tourists per home. They offer the opportunity to experience the forest close-up, and an insight into daily life in the forest at a more economical price. Prices vary depending on method of access: about US$120, 3 days/2 nights. Guiding in Spanish; English-speaking guide can be arranged. Researchers and volunteers also welcomed by arrangement.

Explorer's Inn, book through **Peruvian Safaris**, Alcanfores 459, Miraflores, Lima, T01-447 8888, or Plateros 365, T084-235342 Cuzco, www.peruviansafaris.com. The office in Puerto Maldonado is at Fonavi H15, T/F082-572078. The lodge is located adjoining the TNR, just before the La Torre control post, in the part where most research work has been done, 58 km from Puerto Maldonado. It's a 2½-hr ride up the Río Tambopata (1½ hrs return, in the early morning, so take warm clothes and rain gear), one of the best places in Peru for seeing jungle birds (more than 580 species have been recorded here), butterflies (more than 1230 species), also giant river otters, but you probably need more than a 2-day tour to benefit fully from the location. Offers tours through the adjoining community of La Torre to meet local people and find out about their farms (*chacras*) and handicrafts. The guides are biologists and naturalists from around the world who undertake research in the reserve in return for acting as guides. They provide interesting wildlife treks, including to the macaw lick (*collpa*), 5 days/4 nights costing US$450.

Libertador Tambopata Lodge, on the Río Tambopata, make reservations at Suecia 343, Cuzco, T084-245695, www.tambopata lodge.com. Associated with the **Libertador** hotel chain, the lodge has rooms with solar-heated water, accommodates 60. Good guides, excellent food. Trips go to Lake Condenado, some to Lake Sachavacayoc, and to the Collpa de Chuncho, guiding mainly in English and Spanish, package US$200 per person for 3 days/2 nights. Naturalists programme provided.

Posada Amazonas Lodge, on the Tambopata river, 2 hrs upriver from Puerto Maldonado. Book through **Rainforest Expeditions**, Aramburú 166, of 4B, Miraflores, Lima 18, T01-421 8347, or Portal de Carnes 236, Cuzco, T084-246243, www.perunature. com. A unique collaboration between a tour agency and the local community of Infierno. 24 large attractive rooms with bathroom, cold showers, visits to Lake Tres Chimbadas, with good birdwatching opportunities including the Tambopata Collpa. Offers trips to a nearby indigenous primary health care project where a native healer gives guided tours of the medicinal plant garden. Tourist income has helped the centre become self-funding. Service and guiding is very good. Recommended. Prices start at US$190 for a 3 day/ 2 night package.

They also offer 5 days/4 nights for US$690, staying at the **Tambopata Research Centre**. Rooms are smaller than those at the **Posada Amazonas**, shared showers, cold water. The lodge is 7 hrs upriver from Posada Amazonas Lodge, next to the famous Tambopata macaw clay lick. Tapir are often seen here on the bank opposite the *collpa*.

Refugio Amazonas, was opened in 2005 close to Lago Condenados, 2 hrs from Posada Amazonas Lodge. It is the usual stopover for those visiting the *collpa*. 3 bungalows accommodate 70 people in en suite rooms, large, kerosene-lit, open bedrooms with mosquito nets, well-designed and run, atmospheric. Prices as for **Posada Amazonas Lodge** (see above).

Wasai Lodge, on the Río Tambopata, 120 km (4½ hrs) upriver from Puerto Maldonado, T082-572290, 3 hrs return, same owners as **Hotel Wasai** in town; www.wasai.com. Small lodge with 7 bungalows for 40 people, 20 km of trails around the lodge, guides in English and Spanish. 3 days/2 nights costs US$300; including 1 night in **Hotel Wasai**; 5 days/ 4 nights costs US$400, including 1 night in the hotel and a visit to Collpa de Chuncho. See also Activities and tours, page 299.

Eating

Puerto Maldonado *p290, map p291*
The best restaurant in town is at the **Hotel Wasai**, the best lunchtime menu is at the Cabañaquinta.

††-† **Carne Brava**, on the Plaza de Armas. One of the smart new joints for a steak and chips. Similar, also on the Plaza, is Vaka Loca.

††-† **El Califa**, Piura 266. Often has bush-meat, mashed banana and palm hearts on the menu. Recommended.

††-† **El Hornito/Chez Maggy**, on the plaza. Cosy atmosphere, good pizzas, but pasta dishes are not such good value.

† **El Buen Paladar**, González Prada 365. Good-value lunch menu.

† **La Casa Nostra**, Av León Velarde 515. The best place for snacks and cakes.

† **La Estrella**, Av León Velarde 474. The smartest and best of the *pollo a la brasa* places.

Cafés

Gustitos del Cura, Loreto 258, Plaza de Armas. An ice cream parlour run by a project for homeless teenagers, offering delicious and unusual flavours such as *lúcuma* and brazil nut, only US$0.30 for a large cone!

Tu Dulce Espera, Av L Velarde 475. Good for evening juices and snacks.

🍸 Bars and clubs

Puerto Maldonado *p290, map p291*
Coconut, east side of the plaza. Disco.
El Witite, Av León Velarde 153. A popular, good disco, Latin music, open Fri and Sat.
Le Boulevard, behind **El Hornito**.
Live music, popular.
T-Saica, Loreto 335. An atmospheric bar with live music at weekends.

⛰️ Activities and tours

Manu Biosphere Reserve *p288*
The tour operators listed below are situated in Cuzco, the gateway to the reserve.
Amazon Trails Peru, Tandapata 660, San Blas, Cuzco, T084-437499, T084-974 1735 (mob), www.amazontrailsperu.com. Offers tours to Manu and to Blanquillo (macaw clay lick) and also operates trekking tours in the Cuzco area. Operated by ornithologist Abraham Huaman León who has many years' experience guiding in the region. Also runs **Amazon Hostal** next to the office. Well organized, recommended.
Bonanza Tours, Suecia 343, T084-507871, www.bonanzatoursperu.com. 3 to 8-day tours to Manu with local guides, plenty of jungle walks and camp-based excursions.
Expediciones Vilca, Plateros 363, T084-251872, www.cbc.org.pe/manuvilca/. Manu jungle tours: 8 days/7 nights, other lengths of stay are available. Will supply sleeping bags at no extra cost. Minimum 5 people, maximum 10 per guide. This is the only economical tour which camps at the Otorongo camp, which is supposedly quieter than Salvador where many agencies camp. There are discounts for students and **SAE** members. Very efficient, good service.
InkaNatura Travel, Gran Hotel Chiclayo (lobby), Chiclayo, T074-209948 (Plateros 361, Cuzco, T084-255255; Manuel Bañón 461, San Isidro, Lima, T01-440 2022), www.inkanatura. com. A non-profit organization with proceeds directed back into projects on sustainable tourism and conservation. Arranges trips to the Manu Reserved Zone, Manu Wildlife Centre, The Biotrip, 6 days/5 nights, which takes you through the Andes to lowland jungle, and **Sandoval Lake Lodge** in Tambopata. They sell a book called *Peru's Amazonian Eden – Manu*, US$80, proceeds go to the projects. The same title can be found in

other bookshops at a much inflated price. 10% discount on all trips for Footprint readers.
Manu Ecological Adventures, Plateros 356, T084-261640, www.manuadventures.com. Manu jungle tours, either economical tour in and out overland, or in by land and out by plane, giving you longer in the jungle. Other lengths of stay are available leaving on Mon and Tue. Options include a mountain biking descent through the cloudforest and 3 hrs of whitewater rafting on the way to **Erika Lodge** on the upper Río Madre de Dios. They operate with a minimum of 4 people and a maximum of 10 people per guide.
Manu Expeditions, Humberto Vidal Unda G-5, p 2, Urb Magisterial, T084-226671, www.manuexpeditions.com. English spoken. Run by ornithologist and British Consul Barry Walker of the **Cross Keys Pub**. 3 trips available to the reserve and Manu Wildlife Centre. 2 of the trips on 1st Sun of every month visit a lodge run by Machi-guenga people and cost an extra US$150.
Manu Nature Tours, Av Pardo 1046, T084-252721, www.manuperu.com. Owned by Boris Gómez Luna, English spoken. This company aims more for the luxury end of the market and owns 2 comfortable lodges in the cloudforest and Reserved Zone. Tours are very much based around these sites, thus entailing less travel between different areas. **Manu Lodge** has an extensive trail system and also offers canopy climbing for an additional US$45 per person. In the cloudforest zone a novel 'llama taxi' service is run by the local community of Jajahuana.
Oropéndola, Santa Teresa 379, interior p 2, T084-241428, www.oropendolaperu.org. Guide Walter Mancilla is an expert on flora and fauna. A new company for Manu, using lodges run by indigenous communities. Good reports of attention to detail and to the needs of clients.
Pantiacolla Tours SRL, Saphy 554, Cuzco, T084-238323, www.pantiacolla.com. Runs 5- to 9-day Manu jungle tours, includes transport. Prices do not include park entrance fee. Guaranteed departure dates regardless of number, maximum 10 people per guide. The trips involve a combination of camping, platform camping and lodges. All clients are given a booklet entitled *Talking About Manu*, written by the Dutch owner, Marianne van Vlaardingen, who is a

biologist. She is extremely friendly and helpful. Marianne and her Peruvian husband Gustavo run a community-based ecotourism project in conjunction with the Yine native community of Diamante in the Multiple Use Zone. Yine guides are used and community members are being trained in the various aspects of running the project.

Puerto Maldonado *p290, map p291*
The usual price for trips to Lago Sandoval is US$25 pp per day (minimum 2 people), and US$35 pp per day for trips lasting 2-4 days (minimum of 4-6). All guides should have a carnet issued by the Ministry of Tourism (**DIRCETUR**), which also verifies them as suitable guides for trips to other places and confirms their identity. Check that the carnet has not expired. Reputable guides are **Hernán Llave Cortez**, **Romel Nacimiento** and the **Mejía** brothers, all of whom can be contacted on arrival at the airport, if available. Also are recommended: **Víctor Yohamona**, T082-968 6279 (mob), victorguideperu@ hotmail.com. Speaks English, French and German. Boat hire can be arranged through the Capitanía del Puerto (Río Madre de Dios), T082-573003, about US$10 (beware overcharging).
Ceiba Tours, Av L Velarde 420, T082-573567, turismomejia@hotmail.com. Local trips, such as to their own lodge at Lago Sandoval.
Perú Tours, Loreto 176, T082-573244, peru toursytravel@hotmail.com. Runs local trips.
Wanamei, Av 26 de Diciembre 276, T082-572539 (Cuzco 084-965 2520), www.ecoturismowanamei.com. An indigenous ecotourism company run by Harakmbut people from the Amarakaeri communal reserve. Supported by the UNDP, 8 communities are engaged in sustainability projects, including tourism. Wildlife, cultural and mystical tours are offered.

Tambopata National Reserve *p292*
Peruvian Safaris, Plateros 365, T084-235342, www.peruviansafaris.com. For reservations for the **Explorer's Inn** – excluding park entrance fees and flights.
Tambo Tours, 4405 Spring Cypress Rd, Suite #210, Spring, TX, 77388, T1-888-2-GO-PERU (246-7378), T001-281 528 9448, www.2GOPERU.com. Long-established adventure and tour specialist with offices in Peru and USA. Customized trips to the Amazon.
Wasai Lodge and Expeditions, contact Las Higueras 257, Residencial Monterrico, La Molina, Lima 12, T01-436 8792, www.wasai.com. River trips. Wildlife observation, birdwatching, canoeing, volunteer work, etc. For lodge, see page 296.

⊖ Transport

Manu Biosphere Reserve *p288*
Air There is an airstrip at **Boca Manu**, but no regular flights from Cuzco. These are arranged the day before, usually by Manu tour operators, if there are enough passengers. If you want to arrange a private

flight this will set you back around US$750 one way (this cost can be divided between the number of passengers). Contact **Transandes**, T084-224638, or **Aerocóndor**, T084-252774. Both airlines have offices in the Cuzco airport terminal. Flights, which use small prop-engined aircraft, are sometimes delayed by bad weather.

Road From the Coliseo Cerrado in Cuzco 3 bus companies run to **Pilcopata** Mon, Wed, Fri, returning same night, US$10. They are fully booked even in low season. Trucks to Pilcopata run on same days, returning Tue, Thu, Sat, 10 hrs in wet season, less in the dry. Only basic supplies are available after leaving Cuzco, so take all your camping and food essentials, including insect repellent. Transport can be disrupted in the wet season because the road is in poor condition; paving is under way as part of the Carreterra Interoceánica (tour companies have latest details). *Camioneta* service runs between Pilcopata and **Salvación** to connect with the buses, Mon, Wed, Fri. The same *camionetas* run **Itahuania–Shintuya– Salvación**

Amazon Basin Southern Jungle Listings

regularly, when there are sufficient passengers, probably once a day, and 2 trucks a day. On Sun, there is no traffic whatsoever. To **Boca Manu** you can hire a boat in Atalaya, US$212 for a *peke peke*, or US$400 for a motorboat. It's cheaper to wait or hope for a boat going empty up to Boca Manu to pick up passengers, when the fare will be US$12.50 per passenger. Itahuania– Boca Manu in a shared boat with other passengers is US$6.25. A private chartered boat would be US$105. From Itahuania, cargo boats leave for **Boca Colorado** via Boca Manu, but only when the boat is fully laden; about 6-8 a week, 9 hrs, US$15. From **Boca Colorado** *colectivos* leave near football field for **Puerto Carlos**, 1 hr, US$5, ferry across river 10 mins, US$1.65; *colectivo* Puerto Carlos-**Puerto Maldonado**, 3 hrs, US$10, rough road, lots of stops (in Puerto Maldonado, **Turismo Boca Colorado**, Tacna 342, T082-573435, leave when full). Tour operators usually use their own vehicles for the overland trip from Cuzco to Manu.

Puerto Maldonado *p290, map p291*
Air To **Lima**, daily with **Lan** and **Aerocóndor**. Both fly via Cuzco. *Combis* to the airport run along Av 2 de Mayo, 10-15 mins, US$0.60. A mototaxi from town to the airport is US$2. If on the last flight of the day into Puerto Maldonado, usually **Lan**, don't hang around as most vehicles return to town quickly. A yellow fever vaccination is offered free, but check that a new needle is used.
    Airline offices Lan, Av León Velarde y 2 de Mayo, T082-573677. **Aerocóndor**, Loreto 222, T082-571733.

Bus There are daily buses from the Terminal Terrestre in **Cuzco** with **Transportes Iguazú** and **Mendivil** (both on Av Tambopata, blocks 3 and 5 in Puerto Maldonado), 19 hrs (potentially much longer in the wet), US$15, depart 1400 from Puerto Maldonado. Another option is to go from Cuzco to **Urcos**, 1 hr, US$2.25, then look for the **Transportes Juan Carlos** bus in Urcos' main plaza. This is a Volvo truck modified with seats and windows. In the dry season this takes 26 hrs to Puerto Maldonado, US$13; it leaves about 1500 daily. There are also daily buses from **Mazuko** to Puerto Maldonado with **Transportes Bolpebra** and **Transportes**

Señor de la Cumbre, 4 hrs, US$3. To **Laberinto**, combis take 50 mins, US$1.50, uncomfortable (return in the afternoon daily, see Around Puerto Maldonado, page 292). To **Juliaca**, **Transportes Madre de Dios**, Av Tambopata 1000, and **Transportes Tahuamanu**, Fizcarrald 609, daily services via San Gabán, at 1700 and 1900 respectively, 18 hrs, US$15.

Motorcycles/taxis Scooters and mopeds can be hired from **San Francisco**, and others, on the corner of Puno and G Prada for US$1.15 per hr or US$10 per day. No deposit is required but your passport and driving licence need to be shown. Mototaxis around town charge US$0.60; riding pillion on a bike is US$0.30.

Boat For **Boca Manu** and **Itahuania** take a *colectivo* to **Boca Colorado** (see above) and then take a cargo boat (no fixed schedule). From Itahuania there is transport to **Pilcopata** and **Cuzco** (see above under Manu Biosphere Reserve).

Tambopata National Reserve *p292*
Boat A river taxi makes 2 journeys a week, Mon and Thu upriver, Tue and Fri down, up to 10 hrs, US$5 to travel as far as **Wasai Lodge**. It leaves Puerto Maldonado between 0600 and 0900.

⊙ Directory

Puerto Maldonado *p290, map p291*
Banks BCP, cash advances with Visa, no commission on TCs (Amex only). **Banco de la Nación**, cash on MasterCard, quite good rates for TCs. Both are on the south side of the plaza. The best rates for cash are at the casas de cambio/gold shops on Puno 6th block, eg Cárdenas Hermanos, Puno 605. **Consulates** Bolivia, on the north side of the plaza. **Immigration** Peruvian immigration is at 26 de Diciembre 356, 1 block from the plaza, get your exit stamp here. **Internet** All over town, along Av León Velarde and most main streets. **Post office** Serpost, Av León Velarde 6th block. **Telephone** Telefónica, west side of plaza, adjoining the Municipalidad. A phone office on the plaza, next to **El Hornito**, sells phone cards for national/international calls.

Introduction

Few cities can boast such an impressive setting as La Paz, but architecturally the city is no beauty. Apart from Calle Jaén and a small area northeast of the centre, there are few surviving examples of colonial architecture. Furthermore, there is little in the way of classic tourist attractions – no great museums or art galleries. Yet La Paz is arguably the most fascinating 'capital city' in South America. What sets it apart are not only the sights, sounds and smells of the streets but the phenomenal views of the encircling mountains. As you stroll through the centre of the city, particularly towards dusk, a casual glance up will leave you awestruck as you catch sight of the triple-peaked Illimani, with its snow-capped summit ignited a blazing orange by the setting sun.

Huddled at the bottom of a huge canyon, the first view of La Paz is a sight that leaves most visitors breathless – literally – for La Paz stands at over 3500 m, making it the highest capital city in the world. Airborne visitors touch down at the highest commercial airport in the world, and can then play golf at the highest golf course in the world, or ski (just about) on the highest ski slope in the world.

Apart from its obvious highs, the other striking feature about La Paz is that it appears to be one gigantic street market. Every square inch of street space is taken up by Aymara women in traditional bowler hats and voluminous skirts squatted on their haunches yelling at passers-by to buy their wares. There is a vast array of handicrafts, entire markets devoted to fake designer labels, food and drink, bags of coca leaves – everything under the sun, in fact. There's also a Witches' Market, where you can find everything you need to put a spell on that crooked tour operator, or even buy dried llama foetuses to bury in the foundations of a new house in order to rid it of evil spirits.

★ Don't miss …

1 Museo Nacional de Arqueología Tiahuanaco mummies and Inca remains await to introduce you to ancient Bolivian history, page 310.

2 Browsing the markets Soak up the sights and sounds of the city's many and varied street markets where you can buy anything from imported Levi jeans to a dried llama foetus, page 307.

3 Valle de la Luna Wander round the weird rock formations, cactus gardens and perfect picnic spots, page 311.

4 Tiahuanaco ruins Step back in time and piece together the mysteries of one of South America's great ancient civilizations, page 311.

5 Takesi Trail Take a trek on the wild side on Bolivia's very own Inca highway, page 312.

6 Chacaltaya Visit the world's highest ski resort, from where you get stupendous views of Huayna Potosí and, on a clear day, all the way to Lake Titicaca, page 323.

Ins and outs → *Colour map 3, B2. Phone code: 02. Population: 1,004,440. Altitude: 3600 m.*

Getting there

Air The **La Paz airport** ① *El Alto, 10 km from the city, To2-281 0122*, is the highest commercial airport in the world, at 4058 m. It is connected to the city by motorway. A taxi between the airport and the city centre takes about 30 minutes and costs US$5. **Cotranstur** minibuses, white with 'Cotranstur' and 'Aeropuerto' written on the side and back, leave the airport every 10 minutes and run along the Prado to Plaza La Católica (US$0.60, 50 minutes). ▸▸ *For details of getting to the airport, see Transport, page 324.*

Airport facilities include an **Enlace** ATM that accepts Cirrus, Plus, Visa and MasterCard for taking out local cash when you arrive, as well as a bank that changes cash at reasonable rates (if the bank is closed, ask at the departure tax window). A small but helpful tourist office has some maps available, English spoken. There's an expensive bar/restaurant and a cheaper café/*comedor*, as well as a duty-free shop.

Bus Buses from Oruro, Potosí, Sucre, Cochabamba, Santa Cruz, Tarija, Villazón and all points south of La Paz arrive at the raucous **Terminal Terrestre** ① *1 km uphill from the centre, Plaza Antofagasta, To2-228 0551, 0700-2300*, as do international buses. *Micros* 2, M, CH or 130 run to the centre; a taxi should cost no more than US$1. The terminal has a post office, **Entel**, restaurant, luggage store, US$0.30 per bag (open 0530-2200). Buses from Sorata, Copacabana and Tiahuanaco arrive at the **cemetery district**, a transport hub, high up in the northwest of the city, with plenty of *micros* or taxis (US$1.20) to the centre. Buses from the Yungas and Rurrenabaque arrive at **Villa Fátima** in the far northeast of the city (*micros* or taxi US$1.20). ▸▸ *For onward travel, see Transport, page 324.*

Getting around

There are two types of city bus: *micros* (small, old buses), which charge US$0.15 per person in the centre, US$0.20 from outside centre; and the faster minibuses (small vans), US$0.20 in the centre, US$0.30 outside. *Trufis* are fixed route collective taxis, with a sign with their route on the windscreen, US$0.30 in the centre, US$0.40 outside. Prices vary with demand, they are slightly higher at rush hour. Taxis are often, but not always, white. There are three types: regular honest taxis, which may take several passengers at once; fake taxis, which have been involved in robberies (see below); and radio taxis, which take only one group of passengers at a time. Since it is impossible to distinguish between the first two, it is best to pay a bit more for a radio taxi, which has a sign and number on the roof and can be ordered by phone; note the number when getting in. Radio taxis charge US$1 in the centre, US$2 outside.

Orientation The city's main street runs from **Plaza San Francisco** as Avenida Mcal Santa Cruz, then changes to Avenida 16 de Julio (more commonly known as the Prado) and ends at **Plaza del Estudiante**. The business quarter, government offices, central university (UMSA) and many of the main hotels and restaurants are in this area. From Plaza del Estudiante, Avenida Villazón splits into Avenida 6 de Agosto which runs through **Sopocachi**, an area full of restaurants, bars and clubs, and Avenida Arce, which runs southeast towards the wealthier residential districts of **Zona Sur**. The latter is situated in a valley, 15 minutes south of the centre, and is home to the resident foreign community. It has international shopping centres, supermarkets with imported items and some of the best restaurants and bars in La Paz. Zona Sur begins after the bridge at La Florida beside the attractive Plaza Humboldt. The main road, Avenida Ballivián, begins at Calle 8 and continues up the hill to San Miguel on Calle 21 (about a 20-minute walk). Sprawled around the rim of the canyon is **El Alto**, now a city in its own right and one of the fastest growing in South America. Its population of almost one million consists mostly of indigenous immigrants from the countryside. El Alto is connected to

⁙ Arriving at night

Arriving in La Paz at night presents few problems beyond the usual issues of finding a hotel in the dark. It's certainly worth booking somewhere in advance and also checking that there will be someone to let you in.

The altitude is often a shock on first arriving, and stumbling around the city's dimly lit steep streets in the middle of the night looking for a hotel would be no fun. If you're flying in get a taxi from outside the airport, insist on being taken right to the door of the hotel and politely refuse when the driver offers to show you a better hotel run by his cousin.

La Paz by motorway (toll US$0.25, motorbikes and cycles free) and by a new road to Obrajes and the Zona Sur. Buses from Plaza Eguino and Pérez Velasco leave regularly for Plaza 16 de Julio, El Alto. Buses to and from La Paz always stop at El Alto in an area called *terminal*, off Av 6 de Marzo, where transport companies have small offices. If not staying in La Paz, you can change buses here and save a couple of hours. There is ample accommodation in the area.

Best time to visit

Because of the altitude, nights are cold all year round. In the day, the sun is strong, but the moment you go into the shade the temperature drops. In summer, December to March, it rains most afternoons, making it feel colder than it actually is. The city gets particularly busy during the festivals of **Alasitas** (end January/early February) and **Festividad del Señor del Gran Poder** (end May/early June). ▶▶ *See Festivals, page 320.*

Tourist information

The **Alcaldía Municipal de La Paz** ① *Plaza del Estudiante at the lower end of El Prado between 16 de Julio and México, T02-237 1044, Mon-Fri 0900-1900, Sat-Sun 0930-1300*, is very helpful, English and French spoken. There is also an office at the airport and small municipal kiosks in Zona Sur and along Calles Jaén and Sucre. See www.lapaz.bo/paginas/turismo. There is a private information office at Linares 932, which has a good selection of guide books for reference, purchase or exchange.

Safety

Fake police, fake narcotics police and fake immigration officers (usually plain-clothed but carrying a forged ID) have been known to take people to their 'office' and ask to see all their documents and money, they then rob them. Legitimate police do not ask people for documents in the street unless they are involved in an accident, fight, etc. If approached, try to walk away and seek assistance from as many bystanders as possible. Never get in a vehicle with the 'officer' nor follow them to their 'office'. Many of the robberies are very slick, involving taxis and various accomplices. Take only radio taxis, identified by their dome lights and phone numbers. Lock the doors and never allow other passengers to share your cab, the extra security is well worth the extra cost. If someone else gets in, get out at once. The scams often include a fake tourist who first shares the taxi; when the fake police officer arrives he shows his money and has it returned, all to reassure the real tourist who is then robbed. Also if smeared or spat-on, walk away, don't let the good Samaritan clean you up, they will clean you out instead. The worst areas for all the above are the cemetery neighbourhood where all the local buses arrive, and around Plaza Murillo. Other areas, eg Sopocachi, are generally safer. Warning for ATM users: scams to get card numbers and PINs have flourished, especially in La Paz. Make sure that nobody is watching or filming you from a distance. You have no obligation to show cards to anyone. The tourist police post warnings in hotels.

Sights

Around Plaza Murillo

Plaza Murillo, three blocks northeast of the Prado, is the traditional centre. Facing its formal gardens are the huge, modern, **cathedral** and **Palacio Presidencial**. The latter, usually known as the Palacio Quemado (Burnt Palace), is in Italian renaissance style and has twice been gutted by fire in its stormy 130-year history. On the east side of Plaza Murillo is the **Congreso Nacional**. In front of the presidential palace is a statue of former President Gualberto Villarroel who was dragged into the plaza by an angry mob and hanged in 1946.

Across from the Cathedral is the **Palacio de los Condes de Arana**, dating from 1775, with a beautiful exterior and courtyard, now the **Museo Nacional del Arte** ① *Calle Socabaya 432, T02-240 8600, www.mna.org.bo, Tue-Sat 0900-1230, 1500-1900, Sun 0900-1230, US$1.25*. The 18th-century baroque palace has a fine collection of colonial paintings including works by Melchor Pérez Holguín, one of the masters of Andean colonial art, and also exhibits the works of contemporary local artists.

The streets around Plaza Murillo are lined mostly by buildings dating from the late 19th and early 20th centuries. Running northwest to southeast across the plaza is Calle Comercio where you'll find most of the shops. Northeast of the plaza, on the corner of Calles Ingavi and Yanacocha, is the church of **Santo Domingo** (originally the cathedral), with its 18th-century façade. West of Plaza Murillo, in the palace of the Marques de Villaverde, is the **Museo Nacional de Etnografía y Folklore** ① *Ingavi 916, T02-240 8640, Tue-Fri 0900-1230, 1500-1700 Sat-Sun 0900-1300, US$1.25*. Undergoing renovation since 2005, various sections show the cultural richness of Bolivia by geographic region through textiles and other items. It has a *videoteca*.

Northwest of Plaza Murillo is **Calle Jaén**, a picturesque colonial street with a restaurant/*peña*, a café, craft shops, good views and four museums, known as the **Museos Municipales** ① *Plaza Riosinio, at the top of Jaén, Tue-Fri 0900-1230, 1500-1900, Sat-Sun 1000-1300, US$0.15 each*, housed in colonial buildings. **Museo Costumbrista** ① *T02-228 0758*, has miniature displays depicting incidents in the history of La Paz and well-known *Paceños*, as well as miniature replicas of reed rafts used by the Norwegian Thor Heyerdahl, and the Spaniard Kitin Muñoz, to prove their theories of ancient migrations. **Museo del Litoral Boliviano** ① *T02-228 0758*, has artefacts of the War of the Pacific, and interesting selection of old maps. **Museo de Metales Preciosos** ① *T02-228 0329*, is well set out with Inca gold artefacts in basement vaults, as well as ceramics and archaeological exhibits. **Museo Casa Murillo** ① *T02-228 0553*, the erstwhile home of Pedro Domingo Murillo, one of the martyrs of the La Paz independence movement of 16 July 1809, has a good collection of paintings, furniture and national costumes. In addition to the Museos Municipales is the private **Museo de Instrumentos Musicales** ① *Jaén 711 e Indaburo, T02-240 8177, Tue-Fri 0930-1230, 1530-1900, Sat-Sun 1000-1300, US$0.50*, in a nicely refurbished colonial house. **Museo Tambo Quirquincho** ① *Calle Evaristo Valle, south of Jaén, near Plaza Mendoza, T02-239 0869, Tue-Fri, 0930-1230, 1530-1900, Sat-Sun 1000-1300, US$0.50*, housed in a restored colonial building, displays modern painting and sculpture, carnival masks, silver, early 20th century photography and city plans, and is recommended.

Plaza San Francisco up to the cemetery district

At the upper end of Avenida Mariscal Santa Cruz is **Plaza San Francisco**, with the church and monastery of **San Francisco** ① *open for Mass Mon-Sat 0700, 0900, 1100 and 1900, Sun 0800, 1000 and 1200*, dating from 1549. This is one of the finest examples of colonial religious architecture in South America and is well worth seeing. Local weddings can often be seen on Saturday mornings between 1000 and 1200. The **Museo San Francisco** ① *in the church, Plaza San Francisco 503, T02-231 8472,* *www.centrocultural-museosanfrancisco.org, daily 0900-2100, US$2.50, allow 1½-2 hrs for visit, guides free but tip appreciated, some speak English and French,* offers access to various areas of the church and convent that were previously off limits, including the choir, crypt (open 1400-1730), roof, various chapels and gardens. Fine art includes religious paintings from the 17th, 18th and 19th centuries, plus visiting exhibits and a hall devoted to the works of Tito Yupanqui, the indigenous sculptor of the Virgen de Copacabana. There is a good but pricey café at the entrance.

Behind the San Francisco church a network of narrow cobbled streets rises steeply. Much of this area is a permanent street market. The lower part of **Calle Sagárnaga**, from Plaza San Francisco to Calle Illampu, is lined with shops and stalls selling handicrafts, clothes, guitar covers, silver and leatherware (you'll find the

La Paz centre

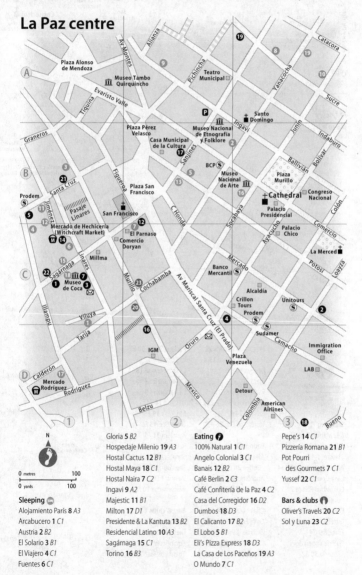

N

0 metres 100
0 yards 100

Sleeping 🛏
Alojamiento París **8** A3
Arcabucero **1** C1
Austria **2** B2
El Solario **3** B1
El Viajero **4** C1
Fuentes **6** C1
Gloria **5** B2
Hospedaje Milenio **19** A3
Hostal Cactus **12** B1
Hostal Maya **18** C1
Hostal Naira **7** C2
Ingavi **9** A2
Majestic **11** B1
Milton **17** D1
Presidente & La Kantuta **13** B2
Residencial Latino **10** A3
Sagárnaga **15** C1
Torino **16** B3

Eating 🍴
100% Natural **1** C1
Angelo Colonial **3** C1
Banais **12** B2
Café Berlin **2** C3
Café Confitería de la Paz **4** C2
Casa del Corregidor **16** D2
Dumbos **18** D3
El Calicanto **17** B2
El Lobo **5** B1
Eli's Pizza Express **18** D3
La Casa de Los Paceños **19** A3
O Mundo **7** C1
Pepe's **14** C1
Pizzería Romana **21** B1
Pot Pourri des Gourmets **7** C1
Yussef **22** C1

Bars & clubs 🍸
Oliver's Travels **20** C2
Sol y Luna **23** C2

La Paz

N

0 metres 100
0 yards 100

Sleeping
A la Maison **2** *F5*
Adventure Brew
  Hostel **1** *A2*
Alcalá Aparthotel **18** *F4*
Casa Grande **3** *F6*
Columbus Palace **7** *C5*
Continental **28** *A2*
El Rey Palace **29** *D4*
Estrella Andina **8** *B2*
Europa **9** *C4*
Galería Virgen de
  Rosario **30** *B2*

Hostal Copacabana **22** *B2*
Hostal República **13** *B4*
La Joya **16** *B1*
Plaza **20** *D4*
Radisson Plaza **21** *D5*
Residencial Sucre **23** *C3*
Rosario **24** *B2*
Tambo de Oro **26** *A2*

Eating
Alexander
  Coffee **28** *C4, E5*
Andrómeda **1** *D5*
Armonía **11** *E4*
Bistrot **3** *E5*
Chalet la Suisse **4** *F6*
Chifa Emy **5** *E5*
Club de la Prensa **2** *C4*
El Arriero **29** *E6*
Fridolín **6** *F6*

Kuchen Stube **30** *E5*
La Comedie **12** *E5*
La Quebecoise **18** *E5*
La Terraza **8** *C4*
La Tranquera **9** *F5*
Lu Qing **14** *E4*
Mongo's **19** *E5*
Olive Tree **15** *F6*
RamJam **31** *F5*
Reineke Fuchs **24** *E5*
Surucachi **13** *C4*
The Lounge **16** *F5*
Vienna **7** *D4*
Wagamama **10** *E6*

Bars & clubs
Deadstroke **27** *E5*
Diesel Nacional **26** *E5*
Equinoccio **21** *E4*
Thelonius Jazz **25** *E4*

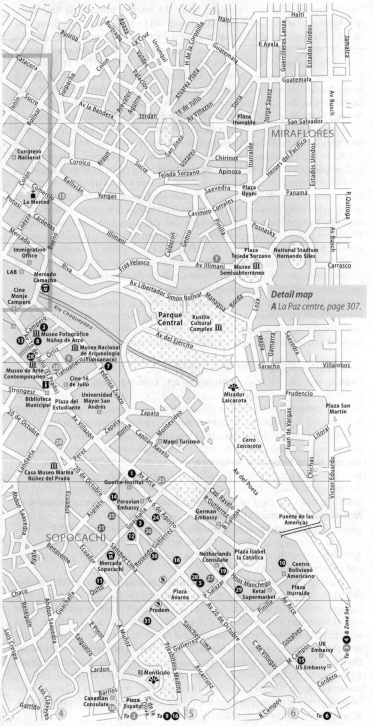

Detail map
A La Paz centre, page 307.

MIRAFLORES

SOPOCACHI

highest concentration of pickpockets here). The amazing **Mercado de Hechicería**, 'witchcraft market', on Calles Melchor Jiménez and Linares, which cross Santa Cruz above San Francisco, sells fascinating charms, herbs and more gruesome items like llama foetuses. Don't miss out on the highly recommended **Museo de Coca** ① *Linares 914, daily 1000-1900, US$1, shop with coca sweets for sale.* This fantastic and provocative little museum presents a historic and scientific explanation of the production and drug effects of this controversial plant, chewed for thousands of years by indigenous Bolivians. Signs are in English, French and German. In the same building as the Museo de la Coca is the **Museo de Arte Andino Boliviano** ① *Mon-Sat 1000-1930, Sun 100-1700, US$1*, a small collection of old traditional weavings (not to be confused with the larger Museo de Textiles Andinos Bolivianos in Miraflores).

Further up Sagárnaga turn right on Max Paredes, heading west, between Santa Cruz and Graneros, is the **Mercado Negro**, a bewildering labyrinth of stalls where you can pick up a cheap pair of Levi jeans, or almost anything else. Continuing west towards the cemetery district, Max Paredes meets **Avenida Buenos Aires**, one of the liveliest streets in the indigenous quarter, where small workshops turn out the costumes and masks for the **Gran Poder** festival (see page 321). This is the main market area and the streets are crammed with stalls selling every imaginable item – household goods, clothing, hats, food, festive goods. Do not expect to go anywhere in a hurry in this part of the city; just enjoy the atmosphere and the marvellous views of omnipresent Mount Illimani. Continuing west along Max Paredes, towards the **cemetery district**, the streets are crammed with stalls selling every imaginable item. See notes on Safety, page 305. Heading back southwards along Max Paredes, where it meets Calle Rodríguez and becomes Calle Zoilo Flores, is the **Mercado Rodríguez**, a riot of colour, fruit, vegetables and identifiable and unidentifiable parts of animals. The main market days are Saturday and Sunday mornings but there are stalls here every day.

The Prado, Sopocachi and Miraflores

Heading south on the Prado is **Museo de Arte Contemporaneo** ① *Av 16 de Julio 1698, T02-233 5905, Mon-Fri 0900-2100, US$1.* In an amazing old colonial building, strikingly decorated with glass roofs and iron fretwork, the museum itself is a missed opportunity. In three floors of contemporary art, Bolivian and international, the occasional interesting piece is swamped by some embarrassingly bad dross. A map and information room has some useful lists of La Paz attractions. The new **Museo Fotográfico Nuñez de Arco** ① *16 de Julio 1615, Mon-Fri 1000-1300, 1500-2000, Sat 1000-1300, US$1.90* has an interesting photo collection of the early excavations of Tiawanaku and old photos of La Paz and surroundings. Just off the Prado (go down the flight of stairs by the Hotel Plaza) is the **Museo Nacional de Arqueología Tiahuanaco** ① *Tiwanacu 93, between Bravo and F Zuazo, T02-231 1621, www.bolivian.com/arqueologia, Mon-Fri 0900-1200 and 1400-1800, US$1.25.* The museum contains good collections of the arts and crafts of ancient Tiwanaku and items from the eastern jungles. It also has a two room exhibition of gold statuettes and objects found in Lake Titicaca.

Running south from **Plaza del Estudiante** is Avenida Villazón which becomes Avenida Arce and heads southwards towards the suburbs of Zona Sur. Branching off to the right at the bridge is Avenida 6 de Agosto which leads to the district of Sopocachi with its many bars and restaurants. Due west of Plaza del Estudiante, Calle Landaeta leads to 20 de Octubre. Turn left (south) and it soon forks, with Calle Ecuador heading off to the right towards Sopocachi Alto. A short distance after the fork is the **Casa Museo Marina Núñez del Prado** ① *Ecuador 2034, T02-242 4175, www.bolivian.com/cmnp, daily 0930-1300, Tue-Fri 1500-1900 (may close afternoons and weekends), US$0.75, students US$0.30.* It houses an excellent collection of Marina Núñez's sculptures in the family mansion. At the southern end of Calle Ecuador, by Plaza España is **El Montículo**, a lovely park with great views of the city.

Back in the old centre, Avenida Libertador Simón Bolívar runs southeast, with Mount Illimani providing a backdrop. At its beginning, on the corner with Calle Bueno, is the Central Market, called **Mercado Camacho**. It's a colourful and raucous affair with the ubiquitous *cholas* haranguing passers-by with their cries of "Cómprame! Cómprame!" as they preside over their stalls. Outside the Hernan Siles national football stadium is the **Museo Semisubterráneo** ⓘ *Plaza Tejada Sorzano*, a sunken garden full of restored statues and other artefacts from Tiahuanaco, some of them badly eroded from traffic pollution. At Cerro Laicacota Hill, on Avenida del Ejército to the east of Avenida Arce, is the **Kusillo Cultural Complex** ⓘ *T02-222 6371, www.kusilloa.org, Tue-Sun 0930-1830, US$0.65, midweek US$1.25*, featuring interactive exhibits on Bolivian culture and textiles, craft shops, a Museum of Science and Play and the world's highest funicular railway. From the top you get great views of the city, especially at dusk, when all the lights begin to twinkle on the surrounding hillsides.

Further east is the residential district of **Miraflores** where you'll find **Museo de Textiles Andinos Bolivianos** ⓘ *Plaza Benito Juárez 488, T02-224 3601, Mon-Sat 0930-1200, 1500-1800, Sun 1000-1230, US$1.25*, with good displays of textiles from around the country, detailed explanations and a knowledgeable owner.

Zona Sur
ⓘ *In 'The Valley' 15 mins south of the city (US$0.50 by trufi or minibus – take any minibus marked Calacoto, San Miguel, Achumani or Chasquipampa from the centre.*
Home to the resident foreign community, the Zona Sur has developed into an important area in its own right. It has international shopping centres, a modern church that looks like a cockroach, supermarkets stocked with imported items and some of the smartest restaurants and bars in La Paz. The area begins after the bridge at La Florida where there is an attractive park, Plaza Humboldt, which has exhibitions of local art work on Sundays and a collection of kiosks selling cheap snacks. The main road, Avenida Ballivián, begins here at Calle 8 and continues up the hill to the shopping district of San Miguel on Calle 21 (about a 20-minute walk). The place comes alive in the evenings, when La Paz's affluent youth cram the streets in their parents' flashy cars and the city's expats visit national-themed cafés and bars to talk about home.

Around La Paz 🚌🚐 ↠ *pp314-328.*

South of La Paz → *For Transport to Valle de la Luna, see page 326.*
To the south of the city are dry hills of many colours, topped by the **Muela del Diablo**, a striking outcrop. Here is the **Valle de la Luna**, or 'Moon Valley', which has a nice terraced cactus garden worth walking through; the climate in this valley is always much warmer than in the city. About 3 km from the bridge at Calacoto the road forks. Get out of the minibus (see Transport, page 326) at the turning and walk a few minutes east to the Valle entrance, or get out at the football field which is by the entrance. Take good shoes and water. Just past the Valle de la Luna is **Mallasa** where there are several small roadside restaurants and cafés and the **Hotel Oberland** (see page 316). The **zoo** ⓘ *on the road to Río Abajo, entrance just past Mallasa after Valle de la Luna, daily 0900-1700, US$0.50, children US$0.25*, is in a beautiful, wide open park-like setting. Conditions for the animals and birds are relatively good and the public are allowed to feed the animals. Quad biking is available behind the zoo.

Tiahuanaco → *For Transport to Tiahuanaco, see page 326.*
ⓘ *The site is open 0900-1700, US$10 for foreigners, including entry to museums. Allow 4 hrs to see the ruins and village.*
This remarkable archaeological site, 72 km west of La Paz, near the southern end of Lake Titicaca, takes its name (often spelled as Tiwanaku) from one of the most

important pre-Columbian civilizations in South America. It is the most popular one-day excursion from La Paz, with facilities being improved as a result. Many archaeologists believe that Tiahuanaco existed as early as 1600 BC, while the complex visible today probably dates from the eight to 10th centuries AD. The site may have been a ceremonial complex at the centre of an empire which covered almost half Bolivia, south Peru, north Chile and northwest Argentina. It was also a hub of trans-Andean trade. The demise of the Tiahuanaco civilization, according to studies by Alan Kolata of the University of Illinois, could have been precipitated by the flooding of the area's extensive system of raised fields (*Sukakollu*), which were capable of sustaining a population of 20,000. The Pumapunka section, 1 km south of the main complex may have been a port, as the waters of the lake used to be much higher than they are today. The raised field system is being reutilized in the Titicaca area.

One of the main structures is the **Kalasasaya**, meaning 'standing stones', referring to the statues found in that part: two of them, the Ponce monolith (centre of inner patio) and the Fraile monolith (southwest corner), have been re-erected. In the northwest corner is the Puerta del Sol, originally at Pumapunku. Its carvings, interrupted by being out of context, are thought to be either a depiction of the creator God, or a calendar. The motifs are exactly the same as those around the Ponce monolith. The **Templo Semisubterráneo** is a sunken temple whose walls are lined with faces, all different, according to some theories depicting states of health, the temple being a house of healing; another theory is that the faces display all the ethnicities of the world. The **Akapana**, originally a pyramid (said to have been the second largest in the world, covering over 28,000 sq m), still has some ruins on it. At **Pumapunku**, some of whose blocks weigh between 100 and 150 tonnes, a natural disaster may have put a sudden end to the construction before it was finished. Most of the best statues are in the **Museo Tiahuanaco** (page 310) or the **Museo Semisubterráneo** (page 311) in La Paz. There is a small museum at the ticket office, the **Museo Regional Arqueológico de Tiahuanaco**, containing a well-illustrated explanation of the raised field system of agriculture. Next to the site museum is **La Cabaña del Puma** restaurant where lunch costs about US$2.

Useful **guidebooks** include: *Tiwanaku*, by Mariano Baptista (Plata Publishing Ltd, Chur, Switzerland), or *Discovering Tiwanaku* by Hugo Boero Rojo. *Guía Especial de Arqueología Tiwanaku*, by Edgar Hernández Leonardini, a guide who works on the site, recommended. Written material is difficult to come by; hiring a good guide costs US$10. A map of the site with explanations in English (published by Quipus) is sold at the ticket office, US$2.50. Locals sell copies of Tiahuanaco figures; cheaper than La Paz.

The nearby **Tiahuanaco village** still has remnants from the time of independence and the 16th-century church used pre-Columbian masonry. In fact, Tiahuanaco for a long while was the 'quarry' for the altiplano. For the festival on 21 June, before sunrise, there are dances and llama sacrifices. On the eighth day (Sunday) there is a colourful carnival. Souvenirs for sale, bargain hard, do not take photographs.

Trekking and climbing near La Paz → For Transport to the trails, see page 327.
Four so-called 'Inca trails' link the Altiplano with the Yungas, linking the high Andes to the sub-tropics, with dramatic changes in weather, temperature and vegetation. Each has excellent sections of stonework and they vary in difficulty from relatively straightforward to quite hard-going. In the rainy season going can be particularly tough.

Takesi Trail Start at Ventilla, walk up the valley for about three hours passing the village of Choquekhota until the track crosses the river and to the right of the road, there is a crumbling brick wall with a map painted on it. The Takesi and Alto Takesi trails start here, following the path to the right of the wall. The road continues to Mina San Francisco. In the first hour's climb from the wall is excellent stone paving which is Inca or pre-Inca, depending on who you believe, either side of the pass at 4630 m. There are camping possibilities at **Estancia Takesi** and in the village of Kakapi you can sleep at the G **Kakapi Tourist Lodge** (10 beds with good mattresses, solar shower and toilet). It is run by the local community and sponsored by Fundación Pueblo. It is also possible to camp. You also have to pass the unpleasant mining settlement of Chojlla, between which and Yanakachi is a gate where it is necessary to register and often pay a small 'fee'. Yanakachi has a number of good places to stay, several good hikes and an orphanage you can help at. The Fundación Pueblo office on the plaza has information. Buy a minibus ticket on arrival in Yanakachi or walk 45 minutes down to the La Paz-Chulumani road for transport. The trek can be done in one long day, especially if you organize a jeep to the start of the trail, but is more relaxing in two or three. If you take it slowly, though, you'll have to carry camping kit. Hire mules in Choquekhota for US$8 per day plus up to US$8 for the muleteer. A two- to three-day alternative is from Mina San Francisco to El Castillo and the village of Chaco on the La Paz-Chulumani road. This trek is called La Reconquistada and has the distinction of including a 200 m disused mining tunnel.

Choro Trail (La Cumbre to Coroico) Immediately before the road drops down from La Cumbre to start the descent to Las Yungas, there is a good dirt road leading up to the *apacheta* (narrow pass) where the trail starts properly. Cloud and bad weather are normal at La Cumbre (4660 m); you have to sign in at the Guardaparque post on the way to the pass. The trail passes Samaña Pampa (small shop, sign in again, camping US$0.60), Chucura (pay US$1.20 fee, another shop, camping), Challapampa (camping possible, US$0.60, small shop), the Choro bridge and the Río Jacun-Manini (fill up with water at both river crossings). At Sandillani it is possible to stay at the lodge or camp in the carefully-tended garden of a Japanese man, Tamiji Hanamura, who keeps a book with the names of every passing traveller. He likes to see postcards and pictures from other countries. There is good paving down to Villa Esmeralda, after which is Chairo (lodging and camping), then to Yolosa. It takes three days to trek from La Cumbre to Chairo, from where you can take a truck to Yolosa (it runs when there are enough people: US$2.25 each). From Yolosa it is 8 km uphill to Coroico with regular transport for US$1.20 per person. The Choro Trail has a reputation for unfriendliness and occasional robbery, take care.

Yunga Cruz (Chuñavi to Chulumani) The best, but hardest of the four 'Inca trails': from Chuñavi follow the path left (east) and contour gently up. Camping possible after two hours. Continue along the path staying on left hand side of the ridge to reach Cerro Khala Ciudad (literally, Stone City Mountain, you'll see why). Good paving brings you round the hill to join a path coming from Quircoma (on your right); continue, heading north, to Cerro Cuchillatuca and then Cerro Yunga Cruz, where there is water and camping is possible. After this point water and camping are difficult and normally impossible until you get down to Sikilini. The last water and camping possibilities are all within the next hour, take advantage of them. Each person should have at least two litres of water in bottles. For water purification, only use iodine-based preparations (iodine tincture, *iodo* in *farmacias* costs US$0.50: use five drops per litre.) There are some clearances on the way down but no water. *Colectivos* run from Sikilini to Chulumani. Starting in Chuñavi the trek takes three days. The Yunga Cruz trail is badly littered – clean up after yourself.

Huayna Potosí Huayna Potosí is normally climbed in two days, with one night camped on a glacier at 5,600 m. There is a *refugio* **Huayna Potosí**, which costs US$10 per night, plus food. Contact at Illampu 626, T/F02-245 6717, bolclimb@mail.megalink.com or La Paz agencies for further information. Average cost is US$140 for two-day tour including all equipment except sleeping bag. The starting point for the normal route is at Zongo, whose valley used to have a famous ice cave (now destroyed by global warming).
▸ *See Climbing, hiking and trekking, page 322, for details of guides.*

◐ Sleeping

Most of the budget accommodation is concentrated in 2 areas: in the streets which lead steeply up from behind San Francisco, especially Sagárnaga, Illampu and Santa Cruz; and around Plaza Murillo, in the triangle formed by the Prado, Calle Ingavi and Calle Loayza. Much of the upmarket accommodation can be found in Zona Sur and on the Prado, especially south of Plaza del Estudiante, around Av Villazón and Av Arce.

Around Plaza Murillo *p306, maps p307 and p308*

L-AL Presidente, Potosí 920 y Sanjines, near Plaza San Francisco, T02-240 6666, www.hotelpresidente-bo.com. 'The highest 5-star in the world' has great views from top floor and pool, gym and sauna, all open to non-residents. Some of the Las Vegas styling (mirrored ceilings and indoor waterfalls) feels out of place but it's comfortable and service is excellent.

B Gloria, Potosí 909, T02-240 7070, www.hotel gloria.com.bo. All rooms at this modern and central hotel have bathtubs and cable TV. The attached French-style **Café Pierrot** is good. There is also a canteen restaurant and a tour agency, **Gloria Tours** (www.gloria tours.com.bo) on site. Recommended.

D Hostal República, Comercio 1455, T02-220 2742, marynela@ceibo.entelnet.bo. **E** without bathroom. In the beautiful old colonial-era house of a former president, friendly República has attractive courtyards and a helpful travel information desk. The café, opposite reception, has free internet for hotel guests and serves good breakfasts. Book ahead.

E The Adventure Brew Hostel, Av Montes 533, T02-246 1614, www.theadventurebrew hostel.com. With solar-heated showers, **F** pp in dorm, on-site microbrewery, includes pancake breakfast, rooftop terrace with great views of the city and Illimani, nightly BBQs, use of kitchen, convenient for the bus station, associated with **Gravity Assisted Mountain Biking** (see Activities and tours, below).

F Alojamiento París, Av Sucre 949, T02-228 5029. Electric shower, **F-G** shared bath, good value.

F Ingavi, Ingavi 727, T02-232 3645. Pleasant rooms, not much hot water. Poor service but good value.

F Residencial Latino, Junín 857 y Sucre, T02-228 5463. With hot water, cheaper without bath, in a refurbished colonial house with patios, a pleasant simple hostel, good value.

F Tambo de Oro, Armentia 367, near the bus station, T02-228 1565. Hot showers, cable TV in rooms, clean, friendly, helpful, safe for luggage. Unlike many of the places near the bus station this is good value.

F Torino, Socabaya 457, T02-240 6003. An old colonial building near Plaza Murillo. Some of the older rooms are dingy, run-down and can be noisy. Newer rooms are better. There is a good restaurant next door for breakfast and good value lunch (weekdays 1200-1500), a free book exchange and a good (if pricey) internet café.

F-G Austria, Yanacocha 531, T02-240 8540, hotelaustria@aclerate.com. There are no private bathrooms and it can be gloomy (make sure you get a room with a window) but rooms are clean and staff are generally friendly. The 3 showers (for the 22 rooms) have hot water and there is also a safe deposit, laundry and TV lounge. Book in advance as it gets busy. Bus to Copacabana leaves from here 0800-0830.

F-G Hospedaje Milenio, Calle Yanacocha 860, T02-228 1263. Small, family-run place that makes guests feel at home. Good value and quiet, with kitchen.

Plaza San Francisco up to the cemetery district *p306, maps p307 and p308*

C Hostal Naira, Calle Sagárnaga 161, T02-235 5645, www.hostalnaira.com. Big, carpeted, fairly modern rooms are arranged around an internal courtyard with potted plants. Rooms at the front have balconies overlooking Sagárnaga; others lack much natural light. Staff are friendly but speak little English. Price includes a decent buffet breakfast downstairs at **Café Banais**. Try bargaining. Recommended.

C Rosario, Illampu 704, T02-245 1658, www.hotelrosario.com. Almost on the

---

● *For an explanation of sleeping and eating price codes used in this guide, see inside the*
● *front cover. Other relevant information is found in Essentials, see pages 31-35.*

doorstep of the Witches' Market, this very popular, attractive and modern 42-room, colonial-style hotel has a **Turisbus** travel agency downstairs (see page 324) as well as a fair trade shop. A 'Cultural Interpretation Centre' explains everything for sale in the nearby markets, from textiles to llama foetuses. All rooms have cable TV, safes and excellent showers – 2 have bathtubs. Price includes a huge buffet breakfast. There is also a family suite for up to 6, an excellent restaurant **Tambo Colonial** (see Eating) and a café with free internet. Stores luggage, friendly and helpful experienced staff. Highly recommended.

C **Sagárnaga**, Sagárnaga 326, T02-235 0252, www.hotel-sagarnaga.com. With red-jacketed bell boys and a smooth mirrored lift, Sagárnaga has pretensions to grandeur. Rooms come in 2 levels of quality – those higher up (**C**) have bigger, more comfortable beds and views, while those lower down are cheaper (**E**) and plainer. Hot water comes from solar panels on the roof and there is a cash machine and a regular *peña*.

D **Continental**, Illampu 626, T/F02-245 1176, hotelcontinental626@hotmail.com. F without bath, good rooms, stores luggage, member of **Hostelling International Bolivia**.

D **Galería Virgen de Rosario**, Santa Cruz 583, 4th floor, T02-246 1015, hgaleria@ceibo.entelnet.bo. Great rooms, all with private bathroom, cable TV and breakfast included. Slow and expensive internet access; friendly staff.

D **La Joya**, Max Paredes 541, near Buenos Aires, T02-245 3841, www.hotelajoya.com. In the heart of the market district, a modern and comfortable hotel with breakfast, cable TV and phone. Laundry, elevator, free transport to and from city centre and airport.

E **Arcabucero**, Calle Viluyo 307, Linares (close to Museo de Coca), T/F02-231 3473. Facing a small park, this helpful and good-value hotel in a converted colonial building has clean, pleasant new rooms with bathrooms. Breakfast costs extra.

E **Estrella Andina**, Illampu 716, T02-245 6421, juapame_2000@hotmail.com. Price includes breakfast, all rooms have a safe, English spoken, family run, comfortable, tidy, helpful, internet access, roof terrace, very pleasant.

D-E **Fuentes**, Linares 888, T02-231 3966, www.hotelfuentesbolivia.com. Cheaper

without bath, hot water, variety of rooms, includes breakfast, nice colonial style, comfortable, TV, internet, sauna, good value, family run, slow laundry service.

E **Hostal Copacabana**, Illampu 734, T02-245 1626, www.hostalcopacabana.com. The beds are very soft but the water is hot (**F** without bath), the price includes breakfast, and TCs can be changed. Jaded but good value. No sign of any showgirls called Lola but this is where Che Guevara stayed.

E **Hostal Maya**, Sagárnaga 339, T02-231 1970, mayahost_in@hotmail.com. Gloomy in places, some of its rooms have no windows and are horribly poky and mouldy, but the better ones have views over Sagárnaga and, as a whole, the place has more to offer than others nearby. Internet, money exchange, laundry, safe deposit, massage, will look after luggage. Cable TV in living room.

E **Majestic**, Santa Cruz 359, T/F02-245 1628. Rooms are simple and on the small side and there isn't much of a view, but there are private bathrooms, cable TV, and it's clean, breakfast offered.

E **Milton**, Illampu y Calderón 1124, T02-236 8003. A dated looking concrete block in the market district, Milton has private bathrooms, hot water, laundry, safe parking around the corner. Good views from roof, restaurant, friendly and clean. Rooms at the back are quieter.

E **Residencial Sucre**, Colombia 340, Plaza San Pedro, T02-249 2038. A friendly and helpful place with big rooms are set around a courtyard with a beautiful garden. There's a quiet area, warm water, it's clean and luggage is stored. Cheaper without bathroom.

F **El Viajero**, Illampu 807, T02-245 3465, www.viajero.lobopages.com. **F-G** without bath, **G** pp in dorm, a reasonable hostel, decorated with plants, dorm has lockers.

F-G **El Solario**, Murillo 776, T02-236 7963, elsolariohotel@yahoo.com. Central, good shared bathrooms, luggage store, use of kitchen, internet, international phone calls, laundry and medical services, taxi service, travel agency, good value.

F-G **Hostal Cactus**, Calle Jiménez 818 y Santa Cruz, T02-245 1421. Downstairs rooms are dark; those upstairs are better though still very simple. Kitchen, limited hot water, very peaceful, excellent position.

The Prado, Sopocachi and Miraflores *p310, map p309*

L **Europa**, Tiahuanacu 64, T02-231 5656, www.hoteleuropa.com.bo. Next to the Museo Nacional de Arqueología, excellent facilities and plenty of frills, internet in rooms, health club, several restaurants including a good café. Recommended.

L **Radisson Plaza**, Av Arce 2177, T02-244 1111, www.radisson.com/lapazbo. Formerly Hotel La Paz (and still referred to as the Sheraton), this 5-star hotel has 239 rooms, modern facilities, good views and an excellent buffet in its restaurant (see Eating, below).

AL **Plaza**, Av 16 de Julio 1789, T02-237 8311, www.plazabolivia.com.bo. A smart hotel with an excellent, good value restaurant (see Eating, below), *peña* show on Fri.

A **El Rey Palace**, Av 20 de Octubre 1947, T02-241 8541, www.hotel-rey-palace-bolivia.com. Including breakfast, large suites, excellent restaurant, stylish and modern. Top floors have good views.

B **Alcalá Aparthotel**, Sanjinés 2662 at Plaza España, Sopocachi, T02-241 2336, alcapt@ zuper.net. Pleasant, comfortable, spacious, furnished apartments, includes breakfast, 20% discount per month.

B-D **A La Maison**, Pasaje Muñoz Cornejo 15, Sopocachi, T02-241 3704, www.alamaison-lapaz.com. Apartment hotel, brightly decorated, with breakfast, laundry service, ADSL connection, TV, kitchens in the larger flats, meals and tourist services can be arranged, daily and monthly rates available.

C **Columbus Palace**, Illimani 1990 by Plaza Tejada Sorzano, Miraflores, T02-224 2444, www.hotel-columbus.com. Includes buffet breakfast, internet, comfortable modern rooms, restaurant with buffet lunch.

Zona Sur *p311*

AL **Casa Grande**, Av Ballivian 1000 y Calle 17, Calacoto, T02-279 5511, www.casa-grande.com.bo. Beautiful, top-quality apartments, includes buffet breakfast, Wi-Fi, airport pickup, restaurant, very good service, discounts for longer stays.

South of La Paz *p311*

A-B **Oberland**, Calle 2 y 3, Mallasa, PO Box 9392, 12 km from centre, T02-274 5040, www.h-oberland.com. A Swiss-owned, chalet-style restaurant (excellent, not cheap) and hotel (also good) with older resort facilities, gardens, *cabañas*, sauna, pool (open to public, US$2 very hot water), beach volley, tennis. Permits camping with vehicle.

A-C **Gloria Urmiri**, Urmiri, T02-237 0010, www.hotelgloria.com.bo. At hot springs 2 hrs from La Paz, price for weekend (wide range of choices depending on the type of tub), cheaper weekdays. Price includes full board shared bath, cheaper Mon-Fri. Transport US$5.60 pp return. Entry to pools: US$2.50 pp small pool, US$3.15 large pool, includes use of sauna. Massage available, camping US$1.50, reservations required.

C **Allkamari**, Pampa Koani in Valle de las Animas, 30 mins from town on the road to Palca, T02-279 1742, allkamari@ casalunaspa.com. Reservations required, cabins in a lovely valley between the Palca and La Animas canyons, a retreat with nice views of Illimani and Huayna Potosí, a place to relax and star-gaze, A cabin for up to 8, E pp in dorm, includes breakfast, solar heating, jacuzzi included, meals on request, use of kitchen, horse and bike rentals, massage, shamanic rituals. Taxi from Calacoto US$4.50, bus No 42 from the cemetery to

University (Mon-Fri 7 daily, Sat-Sun hourly), get off at Iglesia de las Animas and walk 1 km.

Tiahuanaco *p311*
There are a few places to sleep and eat in Tiahuanaco village, including: **F Tiahuanco**, rooms with bath, also restaurant. Market day is Sun; do not take photos.

🍴 Eating

Around Plaza Murillo *p306, maps p307 and p308*
♈♈ **La Casa de los Paceños**, Av Sucre 856, T02-228 0955. Near the Calle Jaen museums, this little restaurant offers very good Bolivian food, especially its *fritanga*. A la carte only.
♈ **Club de la Prensa**, Calle Campero 52. A long restaurant leading back to a pleasant garden, the limited menu is typically Bolivian (meat and fish only, in huge quantities) and the company is lively.
♈ **El Calicanto**, Sanjines 467, T02-240 8008. Good food including regional specialities, renovated colonial house, live music Sat-Sun.
♈ **Hotel Gloria**, Potosí 909, daily 1200-1500 and 1800-2230. Vegetarian restaurant, good *almuerzo* for US$3, also buffet breakfast, and dinner (US$2.15).
♈ **La Kantuta**, Hotel Presidente, Potosí 920. Excellent food and good service.

Cafés
Café Berlín, Mercado 1377 y Loayza and at Av Montenegro 5, Calacoto, daily 0800-2300. Coffee, sweets, omelettes, breakfast, popular with locals but smokey.
Café Confitería de la Paz, Camacho 1202, on the corner where Ayacucho joins Av Mcal Santa Cruz. Good albeit expensive tea room, traditional meeting place for businessmen and politicians, great coffee and cakes.

Plaza San Fancisco up to the cemetery district *p306, maps p307 and p308*
♈♈ **Casa del Corregidor**, Murillo 1040, T02-236 3633, Mon-Sat 1730-2300, *peña* from 2100. Centrally heated, Spanish colonial restaurant with mainly Bolivian dishes, excellent food, bar.
♈♈ **Tambo Colonial**, Hotel Rosario, Illampu 704, open from 0700. Huge buffet breakfast with fruit, yoghurt, pancakes and excellent wholemeal bread (there are even toasters).

In the evenings it becomes one of La Paz's best restaurants, with excellent local and international cuisine, including good llama steaks. Recommended.
♈-♈ **Pizzería Romana**, Santa Cruz 260. Good pizzas and pastas, good value.
♈ **100% Natural**, Sagárnaga 345, closed Sun. Good breakfasts and fantastic fresh juices and shakes. Service can be surly. More substantial sustenance is available in the form of burgers, llama, sandwiches and salads.
♈ **Angelo Colonial**, Linares 922. Fantastic, affordable food at candlelit tables in a ramshackle upstairs room overflowing with antiques. Good and plentiful vegetarian options and delicious steaks. Jazzy music with regular smatterings of The Beatles. One of the best central restaurants. Recommended.
♈ **El Lobo**, Santa Cruz 441. Up the hill on the corner with Illampu, El Lobo has a huge menu, huge portions, and is fairly cheap and very popular, especially with Israeli travellers. Great falafel on Wed night.
♈ **Pot Pourri des Gourmets**, Linares 906. In an attractive barrel-vaulted, wood and brick room, Pot Pourri offers an excellent value set lunch (US$2.20) with choice of soup, main course and dessert. Bolivian/French owners have produced a good mixture of local drinks and food combined with many international options. Exceptional value, great atmosphere and very friendly. Recommended.
♈ **Yussef**, Sagárnaga 380. Poorly signposted and well hidden on the right of Sagárnaga as you go up the hill, but well worth the effort for wonderful Lebanese food. Excellent vegetarian options as well as meaty choices. The mixed plate of *mezes* is a real feast, or you can mix and match individual portions. Friendly service, relaxed atmosphere. Highly recommended.

Cafés
Banais, Sagárnaga 161, same entrance as Hostal Naira. One of central La Paz's grooviest cafés, with wooden floors, laid-back music and especially good lemon meringue pie, salads and sandwiches. Downstairs there's a room of computers with internet access. The buffet breakfast (US$1.50) is simple but good, with delicious crusty bread and fruit salad.
O Mundo, Linares 906, open only until 1500, below Le Pot Pourri des Gourmets (see

above), from which you can order food, good range of drinks.

Pepe's, Pasaje Jimenez 894 (off Linares between Sagárnaga and Santa Cruz), T02-245 0788. Service can be a little slow but is invariably friendly in this chilled little café. Great all-day breakfasts range from US$1-3 and sandwiches and omelettes are also good. You can relax at an outside table in the sun after scouring the textiles and handicraft shops nearby, play with the provided cards or dominoes, or leaf through the guidebooks and magazines. The local pottery found in many cafés in the city is also for sale here.

The Prado, Sopocachi and Miraflores *p310, map p309*

Most of the top-class restaurants are in this part of town. Av 20 de Octubre has become the trendy place to eat and be seen eating, with new arty, funky cafés and restaurants springing up all the time. There are also several good *chifas* along Av 6 de Agosto offering tasty and cheap lunch menus.

♥♥ **El Arriero**, Av 6 de Agosto 2535 (Casa Argentina), Sopocachi. The best barbecue in the city with large portions.

♥♥ **Bistrot**, Fernando Guachalla 399, Sopocachi, in Alliance Française. Swish new restaurant with French menu, vegetarian options, sandwiches.

♥♥ **Chifa Emy**, Av 20 de Octubre 927, Plaza Avaroa, T02-244 0551, daily 1130-1430, 1800-2300, Fri-Sat till 0100. One of the best Chinese restaurants in town, with good service, over 170 dishes and a big screen TV. Accepts credit cards. Shows and concerts Wed-Fri at 2130.

♥♥ **High Lander's**, Final Sánchez Lima 2667, Sopocachi, T02-243 0023, Mon-Fri 1200-1500, 1700-2300, Sat 1800-2330. Very good Tex-Mex fare, nice atmosphere, good views from the end of the street.

♥♥ **La Comedie**, Pasaje Medinacelli 2234, Sopocachi, T02-242 3561. Branding itself as an 'art-café restaurant', La Comedie is a cool, terracotta-coloured, contemporary place with good salads, a predominantly French menu, round windows and plenty of candles. Also good for cocktails.

♥♥ **La Tranquera**, Capitán Ravelo 2123 next to **Hotel Camino Real**, T02-244 1103, daily 1200-1600, 1900-2300. Good international food, grill and salad bar.

♥♥ **The Lounge**, Presbitero Medina 2527, T02-241 0585. American/Bolivian run, chilled atmosphere, western and Latin food, art exhibitions, excellent toilets, popular.

♥♥ **Plaza Hotel**, Av 16 de Julio 1789). 2 restaurants: **Utama** on the top floor, with great views, 1700-2300, à la carte; and **Uma**, on the ground floor, for breakfast and lunch, buffet lunch US$6.15. Recommended.

♥♥ **Radisson Plaza Hotel**, Av Arce 2177, T02-244 1111, daily 1200-1500. Excellent buffet in 5-star setting, delicious, friendly to backpackers.

♥♥ **Reineke Fuchs**, Jáuregui 2241, Sopocachi. Many European beers and food in a German-style bar. Renovated in 2006.

♥♥ **Vienna**, Federico Zuazo 1905, T02-244 1660, www.restaurantvienna.com, Mon-Fri 1200-1400, 1830-2200, Sun 1200-1430. Frequently recommended. A smart, European-style restaurant with excellent German, Austrian and local food, excellent service, antique prints, a great atmosphere and huge, juicy steaks at moderate prices.

♥♥ **Wagamama**, just behind **Jalapeños**, Pasaje Pinilla 2557, T02-243 4911, Tue-Sat 1200-1430, 1900-2000. Huge plates of amazing sushi. Complimentary tea and excellent service. Popular with ex-pats – hardly a Bolivian in sight.

♥ **Andrómeda**, Av Arce 2116, T02-244 0726. Renowned for superb-value lunches. Recently reopened vegetarian restaurant and wine bar.

♥ **Armonía**, Ecuador 2286 y Quito, Mon-Sat 1200-1430. Nice vegetarian buffet lunch.

♥ **Eli's Pizza Express**, Av 16 de Julio 1400 block. English spoken, open daily including holidays (also at Comercio 914), very popular, maybe not the best pizza in La Paz, but certainly the largest omelettes.

♥ **La Quebecoise**, 20 de Octubre 2387, Sopocachi, T02-212 1682, Mon-Fri 1200-1500, 1900-2300, Sat 1900-2300. With an interior rather like a 19th-century French living room, this French-Canadian restaurant has an open fire and top-notch service.

♥ **Lu Qing**, 20 de Octubre 2090 y Aspiazu, T02-242 4188, Mon-Sat 1130-1500, 1830-2300, Sun 1100-1530. Chinese food, large choice of dishes, set meals on weekdays.

♥ **Mongo's**, Hermanos Manchego 2444, near Plaza Isabela la Católica, T02-244 0714, daily 1900-0300, live music Mon-Tue, club after 2400.

The most popular gringo spot in town. There's an open fire, cable TV for sports, set lunches which change every day and excellent food including fish and chips, great burgers, and Mexican dishes. Service can be slow for food but there's always the coldest beer in town to keep you going.

 The Olive Tree, Campos 334 y 6 de Agosto, Edificio Iturri, closed Sat evening and Sun. Good salads, soups and sandwiches.

 RamJam, Calle Presbitero Medina 2421, above Plaza Avaroa, T02-242 2295. Set up by some of the team that created **Mongo's**, this offers everything a homesick gringo could want, from coffee to curry, Sun roasts to cable TV. With the world's highest micro-brewery beer, expect some late nights and wobbly walks home.

 Surucachi, 16 de Julio 1598 (El Prado), T02-231 2135. Bolivian specialties, good-value set lunches on weekdays, plus à la carte.

Cafés

Many bars and restaurants operate as cafés during the day – **Mongo's** and **RamJam** (see above) are good examples, though both are a little out of the way. Many cafés are also good places to get light meals.

Alexander Coffee, Av 16 de Julio 1832, T02-231 2790, also at 20 de Octubre 2463 Plaza Avaroa, Av Montenegro 1336, Calacoto, and the airport. Usually referred to as 'Café Alex'. Excellent coffee, smoothies, muffins, cakes and good, salads and sandwiches, open 0730-0000. Recommended.

Dumbos, Av 16 de Julio, near **Eli's** and cinema. For meat and chicken *salteñas*, ice creams, look for the dancing furry animals outside.

Fridolin, Av 6 de Agosto 2415, T02-215 3188; also at Comercial La Chiwiña, San Miguel, Calacoto. *Empanadas, tamales*, savoury and sweet (Austrian) pastries, coffee, breakfast.

Kuchen Stube, Rosendo Gutiérrez 461, Sopocachi, Mon-Fri 0930-1230, 1500-1900. Excellent cakes, coffee and German specialities.

La Terraza, 16 de Julio 1615, T02-231 0701, 0630-2400; also at 20 de Octubre 2171 y Gutierrez, 0730-2400; and Av Montenegro y Calle 8, Calacoto, 0700-2400. A mini chain with wooden floors and chairs and a modern US feel. Pancakes and 1980s pop. You can make your own salad from a selection of ingredients on menu. Good range of coffee.

 Chalet la Suisse, Calle 23, on the main avenue, up the hill between calles 24 y 25, T02-279 3160. Expensive but highly recommended, with excellent fondue and steaks. Booking is essential on Fri evenings.

 El Arriero, Calle 17. Sister chain of the branch in Sopocachi. Excellent barbecues.

---

❶ Bars and clubs

Some cafés and restaurants stay open late and some have regular music. **Mongo's RamJam** and **La Comedie** are all good for a drink. Check fly-posters for details of gigs.

San Francisco up to the cemetery district *p306, maps p308 and p307*

Oliver's Travels, Murillo 1014. Fake English pub serving breakfasts, curries, fish and chips, pasta, sports channels, music, travel agency, very good book exchange, popular meeting place.

Sol y Luna, Murillo y Cochabamba, 1800-late. The best bar in the centre of town, and possibly in La Paz, Sol y Luna is warm, comfy and cosy. A Dutch-run place, it has stone walls and wooden floors, a good range of bottled beers, a travel book library, candles, and laid back grooves emanating from the music system. There are also different teas and coffees on offer, bar snacks and toasted sandwiches and a wide choice of cocktails including *Mojito Boliviano* (with coca leaves) and *Bolivia Libre* (with Singani instead of rum).

The Prado, Sopocachi and Miraflores *p310, map p309*

The epicentre for nightlife in La Paz is currently Plaza Avaroa in Sopocachi. Clubs are clustered around here and crowds gather Fri and Sat nights.

Deadstroke, Av 6 de Agosto 2460, 1700-late. US-style pub, café and billiards bar serving food and good value drinks.

Diesel Nacional, Av 20 de Octubre between Gutierrez and Guachalla. Top live music venue A hip, modern club with an industrial theme.

Equinoccio, Sánchez Lima 2191. Live music nearly every Thu, Fri and Sat.

Fak'n Tacos, Belisario Salinas opposite Presbitero Medina. Bizarre upstairs bar with a boxing ring for patrons' use (for those who

literally want to get smashed out their skulls), potent drinks, including the 'fishbowl'.
Ja Ron, 20 de Octubre, corner with Pasaje Medinacelli, Sopacachi, open till 0200. Bright bar with a bohemian feel, tree trunks for tables, potent cocktails, happy hour 1800-2100.
RamJam, Calle Presbitero Medina 2421, above Plaza Avaroa, Sopocachi, T02-242 2295, 1900-0300 or later. An energetic place aimed at gringos and upmarket locals, with coffee, curry, Sun evening roasts, micro-brewery beer and cable TV, dancing, packed Fri-Sat nights. Also much-needed oxygen bar.
Theolonius Jazz Bar, 20 de Octubre 2172, Sopocachi, T02-233 7806, Tue-Sat from 1700. Renowned for jazz, but expensive, with an extra charge to see the jazz. Did we mention there's jazz? Vies with **Mongos** for the most popular watering hole in the city.

Zona Sur *p311*
A vibrant nightlife has developed along Av Ballivián and through San Miguel.
The Britannia, Av Ballivián on the left between calles 15 y 16, Calacoto, T02-279 3070, Mon-Sat from 1700. Cosy, popular with expats, bar snacks, designed as English pub, now with an Asian restaurant.

⊙ Entertainment

La Paz *p301, maps p307 and p308*
For up-to-the-minute information on cinemas and shows, check *La Prensa* or *La Razón* on Fri, or visit www.laprensea.com.bo or www.la-razon.com. Best entertainment for visitors are the folk shows (*peñas*), which present the wide variety of local musical instruments.

Peñas
Bocaisapo, Indaburo 654 y Jaén, near Plaza Murillo. Live music in a bar; no cover charge.
Casa del Corregidor, see Eating above. Good dinner show Mon-Thu, no cover charge, Fri and Sat *peña* US$4, both 2100, good, colonial atmosphere, traditional music and dance.
El Calicanto. See Eating, above.
El Parnaso, Sagárnaga 189, above Plaza San Francisco, T02-231 6827, daily starting at 2030. Meals available, purely for tourists but a good way to see local costumes and dancing.

Marka Tambo, Junín 710, near Plaza Murillo, T02-228 0041. Wed-Sat 2000-0100, US$7 all inclusive, repeatedly recommended (also sells woven goods and serves lunch Mon-Sat 1200-1500).

Cinemas
Films mainly in English with Spanish subtitles. Expect to pay around US$3.15.

Theatre
Teatro Municipal Alberto Saavedra Pérez has a regular schedule of plays, opera, ballet and classical concerts, at Sanjines y Indaburo, T02-240 6183. The National Symphony Orchestra is very good and gives inexpensive concerts. Next door is the **Teatro Municipal de Cámara**, a small studio-theatre which shows dance, drama, music and poetry. **Casa Municipal de la Cultura 'Franz Tamayo'**, almost opposite Plaza San Francisco, hosts a variety of exhibitions, paintings, sculpture, photography, videos, etc, most of which are free. It publishes a monthly guide to cultural events, free from the information desk at the entrance. The **Palacio Chico**, Ayacucho y Potosí, in old Correo, operated by the Secretaría Nacional de Cultura, also has exhibitions (good for modern art), concerts and ballet, Mon-Fri 0900-1230, 1500-1900, closed at weekends, free. It is also in charge of many regional museums. Listings available in Palacio Chico.

⊛ Festivals and events

La Paz *p301, maps p307 and p308*
Jan-Feb Particularly impressive is the **Alasitas Fair** held from the last week of Jan to the first week of Feb, in Parque Central up from Av del Ejército, and Plaza Sucre/San Pedro.
May-Jun At the end of May/early Jun is the **Festividad de Nuestro Señor Jesús del Gran Poder** (generally known simply as the 'Gran Poder'), the most important festival of the year, with a huge procession of costumed dancers. Among the many dances is the *Waka Thokoris*, which derives from the disdain and reproach for the Spanish bullfight. The *Morenada* and *Diablada* are also featured. These 2 are more commonly associated with the Oruro carnival (see box page 370). *Los Caporales* originates in the Afro-Caribbean tradition of the Yungas and is a burlesque of the African slave bosses.

● Tiny treats

One of the most intriguing items for sale in Andean markets is *Ekeko*, the god of good fortune and plenty and one of the most enduring and endearing of the Aymara gods and folk legends.

He is a cheery, avuncular little chap, with a happy face to make children laugh, a pot belly due to his predilection for food and short legs so he can't run away. His image, usually in plaster of Paris, is laden with various household items, as well as sweets, confetti and streamers, food, and with a cigarette dangling from his lower lip. Believers say that these statues only bring luck if they are received as gifts.

The *Ekeko* occupies a central position in the festival of Alasitas, the Feast of Plenty, which takes place in La Paz every January. Everything under the sun can be bought in miniature: houses, trucks, buses, tools, building materials, dollar bills, suitcases, university diplomas, you name it, you can find it here. The idea is to have your mini-purchase blessed by a *Yatiri* (an Aymara priest) and the real thing will be yours within the year.

This dance is a recent addition to the **Gran Poder** and has spread to other parts of the country.
Jun Other festivals include **Corpus Christi**, usually in mid-Jun; and **San Juan** on 21 Jun, which is based on the Aymara New Year. People used to mark the passing of the old year by burning all their rubbish in the streets, especially old tyres; now it is mainly an excuse to let off fireworks.
Jul Fiestas de Julio, through Jul, is a month of concerts and performances at the Teatro Municipal and offers a wide variety of music, including the **University Folkloric Festival**.
6 Aug Independence Day is marked by a very loud gun salute at 0630 which can be heard all over the centre of the city.
8 Dec A festival is held around Plaza España. It's not very large, but very colourful and noisy.
31 Dec On **New Year's Eve** fireworks are let off and make a spectacular sight – and din – best viewed from a high vantage point.

● Shopping

La Paz *p301, maps p307 and p308*
Bookshops
Los Amigos del Libro, Mercado 1315, T02-220 4321; also Av Montenegro y Calle 18 (San Miguel); and at El Alto airport. Expensive, but they sell a few tourist guide books and will also ship books.
Gisbert, Comercio 1270, libgis@entelnet.bo. Books, stationery, will ship overseas.

Yachaywasi, just below Plaza del Estudiante, opposite **Hotel Eldorado**. Large selection, popular with students.

Camping equipment
Kerosene for pressure stoves is available from a pump in Plaza Alexander, Pando e Inca.
The Base Adventure Store, Av 16 de Julio 1490, Edif Avenida, basement. Camping gear and clothing, head lamps, no rentals.
Caza y Pesca, Edif Handal Center, No 9, Av Mcal Santa Cruz y Socabaya, T02-240 9209.

Handicrafts
Above Plaza San Francisco (see page 306), up Sagárnaga, by the side of San Francisco church (behind which are many handicraft stalls in the Mercado Artesanal), are booths and small stores with interesting local items of all sorts, best value on Sun morning when prices are reduced. The lower end of Sagárnaga is best for antiques. At Sagárnaga 177 is an entire gallery of handicraft shops. On Linares, between Sagárnaga and Santa Cruz, high-quality alpaca goods are priced in US$. Also in this area are many places making fleece jackets, gloves and hats, but shop around for value and service.
Artesanía Sorata, Linares 862 y Sagárnaga 311, Mon-Sat 0930-1900 (Sun high season), specializes in dolls, sweaters and weavings.
Ayni, Illampu 704, www.hotelrosario.com/ayni. Fair trade shop in **Hotel Rosario**, featuring Aymara work.

Comart Tukuypi, Linares 958, T/F02-231 2686. High-quality textiles from an artisan community association.

Comercio Doryan, Sagárnaga y Murillo, eg **Wari**, unit 12, Comercio Doryan. High-quality alpaca goods, will make to measure very quickly, English spoken, prices reasonable.

Kunturi, Nicolás Acosta 783, T02-249 4350. You will find wonderful handicrafts produced by the Institute for the Handicapped, including embroidered cards.

LAM on Sagárnaga. Quality alpaca goods.

Millma, Sagárnaga 225; also at Claudio Aliaga 1202, San Miguel, Zona Sur; closed Sat afternoon and Sun. Alpaca sweaters (made in their own factory) and antique and rare textiles.

Mother Earth, Linares 870. High-quality alpaca sweaters with natural dyes.

Toshy, Sagárnaga. Top quality knitwear (closed Sat afternoon).

Jewellery

Good jewellery stores throughout the city **Joyería King's**, Loayza 261, www.bolivia net.com/empresas/kings/index.html.

Torre Ketal, Calle 15, Calacoto, T02-277 2542. Gold and silver jewellery and souvenirs using native, Andean designs.

Maps

IGM, head office at Estado Mayor General, Av Saavedra 2303, Miraflores, T02-222 0513, igmsmg@unete.com; there is an office closer to the centre at oficina 5, Juan XXIII 100 (mud track between Rodríguez y Linares), Mon-Thu 0800-1200 and 1430-1800, Fri 0800-1400, will order maps from head office. Take passport.

Librería IMAS, Av Mcal Santa Cruz entre Loayza y Colón, T02-235 8234. Ask for the map collection and check what is in stock. Maps are also sold in the post office on the stalls opposite the poste restante counter.

Markets

In addition to those mentioned in the Sights section (see page 307), the 5-km sq **El Alto** market is on Thu and Sun (the latter is bigger). Take a Ceja bus from along the Prado to Desvío. At the toll plaza on the *autopista*, change buses for one marked 16 de Julio; most other passengers will be doing the same, follow them. Arrive around 1000 and stay to 1600. Goods are cheap. Don't take anything of value, just a bin liner to carry your purchases. **Mercado Sopocachi**, Guachala y Ecuador, a well-stocked covered market selling foodstuffs, kitchen supplies, etc.

Musical instruments

Many shops on Sagárnaga/Linares, for example **El Guitarrón**, Sagárnaga 303, corner with Linares, and **Marka 'Wi**, Sagárnaga 851. **Pasaje Linares**, the stairs off Calle Linares, has a number of shops selling just instruments. Note genuine *charrangos*, guitar-like instruments made from the carapace of an armadillo, may be legally confiscated by customs when leaving Bolivia.

Shopping malls and supermarkets

Hipermaxi, Cuba y Brazil, Miraflores. An out-of-centre mall.

Shopping Norte, Potosí y Socabaya. A modern mall with restaurants, expensive merchandise.

Supermercado Ketal, Calle 21, San Miguel, and Av Arce y Pinillo, near Plaza Isabel la Católica. Regular supermarket.

Supermercado Zatt, Av Sánchez Lima 2362 near Plaza Avaroa. Has the best selection of dried foods etc for trekking.

▲▲ Activities and tours

La Paz *p301, maps p307 and p308*

City tours

Sightseeing, T02-279 1440, daily except first Mon of each month. City tours on a double-decker bus, 2 circuits, downtown and Zona Sur with Valle de la Luna (one morning and one afternoon departure to each), departs from Plaza Isabel la Católica and can hop on at Plaza San Francisco, tour recorded in 7 languages, US$6 for each circuit.

Climbing, hiking and trekking

Guides must be hired through a tour company. For Maps, see Essentials, page 28 and Shopping, above. For books on trekking and climbing, see page 646.

Alberth Bolivia Tours, Illampu 773, T02-245 8018, alberthbolivia@hotmail.com. Good for climbing and trekking, good value, helpful, Juan speaks English, equipment rental.

Andean Summits, Aranzaes 2974, Sopocachi, T02-242 2106, www.andean summits.com. For mountaineering and other adventure trips off the beaten track.

Azimut Explorer, Sagárnaga 213, Galería Chuquiago, oficina 11, T02-233 3809. Guide Juan Villarroel is one of the best.
Bolivian Mountains, Murillo 929, T02-231 3197, www.bolivianmountains.com. A quality mountaineering outfit, with good equipment and experienced guides, not cheap.
Club Andino Boliviano (CAB), Calle México 1638, T02-231 0863, can provide a list of guides and works with the Bolivian association of mountain guides.
Iván Blanco Alba, Asociación de Guías de Montaña y Trekking, Chaco 1063.
Ricardo Albert, at Inca Travel, Av Arce 2116, Edif Santa Teresa.
Trek Bolivia, Calle Sagárnaga 392, T/F02-231 7106. Organizes expeditions in the Cordillera.

Football

Popular and played on Wed and Sun at the **Siles Stadium** in Miraflores (*micro A*), which is shared by both La Paz's main teams, *Bolívar* and *The Strongest*. There are reserved seats.

Golf

Mallasilla, the world's highest course, 3318 m. Non-members can play at Mallasilla on weekdays, when the course is empty, no need to book. Club hire, green fee, balls and a caddy (compulsory) costs US$37. The course is in good condition and beautiful (take water).

Skiing

At 5345 m, **Chacaltaya**, has the highest ski run in the world. It was also the first place in South America to get a ski lift, back in 1940. Unfortunately there has been little development since then and the lift is no longer working. Ski equipment is very limited and of poor quality (US$10 to hire). Another major problem is that the glacier is retreating 6-10 m a year; if this continues there will be nothing left in 30 years. The only time you can really ski now is immediately after a fresh snowfall. However, it's still fun to visit and take plastic bags to slide down. Be very wary of altitude sickness, see Essentials page 41.
Club Andino Boliviano, see above, is converting the old clubhouse into a plus *refugio* complete with all mod cons. This will appeal to serious hikers and mountain bikers, as the ride down the from the top is wonderful.

CAB organizes the cheapest regular transport to Chacaltaya; US$10 pp for the 2½-hr bus journey, leaving La Paz at 0800 on Sat and Sun, and returning about 1530. A taxi or minibus costs US$30 (whole car) for a half-day trip. Hiring a jeep and driver for the trip costs US$70. The trip can be hair-raising as buses do not have snow chains. Often the buses and tours only go halfway. Many agencies do day trips for US$12.50, often combined with Valle de la Luna.
   From the car park you can ascend the remaining 45 m on foot and legitimately claim to have climbed to the summit of a peak in excess of 5000 m!

Tour operators

Adventure Planet, Ramón Arias 100, Achumani, T02-271 0755, www.planetaven tura.com. Adventure travel, including trekking, mountaineering, climbing and 4WD tours.
America Tours SRL, Av 16 de Julio 1490 (El Prado), Edif Avenida, No 9, T02-237 4204, www.america-ecotours.com. Cultural and ecotourism trips to many parts of the country (including the renowned Chalalán Lodge near Rurrenabaque, the Che Guevara Trail and Parque Nacional Noel Kempff Mercado), rafting, trekking and horse riding, English spoken. Highly professional and recommended. Basic book exchange.
Bolivian Journeys, Sagárnaga 363, 1st floor, T/F02-235 7848. Camping, mountain bike tours, equipment rental (with large shoe sizes), maps, English and French spoken, very helpful.
Carmoar Tours, Calle Bueno 159, headed by Günther Ruttger T02-231 7202, carmoar@ zuper.net. Has information for the Inca Trail to Coroico, rents trekking gear.
Crillon Tours, PO Box 4785, Av Camacho 1223, T02-233 7533, www.titicaca.com. With 24-hr ATM for cash on credit cards. In USA, 1450 South Bayshore Dr, suite 815, Miami, FL 33131, T305-358 5353, darius@titicaca.com. A very experienced company. Joint scheduled tours with Lima arranged. Fixed departures to Salar de Uyuni and much more. Details of their Lake Titicaca services can be found on page 344.
Detour, Av Mariscal Santa Cruz, Edif Camara Nacional de Comercio, T02-236 1626. Good for flight tickets, very professional, English spoken.

Et-n-ic, A Villamil 5136, Obrajes, T7064 3566, www.visitabolivia.com. Overland tours throughout Bolivia, Swiss staff, good reports. English and German spoken.

Explore Bolivia, Sagárnaga 339, Galería Sagárnaga, oficina 1, T/F02-239 1810, explobol@ceibo.entelnet.bo. Adventure sports, good bikes (Trek).

Fremen, Edif Handal, Av Mariscal Santa Cruz y Socabaya, ground floor, oficina 13, T02-240 8200, www.andes-amazonia.com. They also have offices in Cochabamba, Santa Cruz, Uyuni, Trinidad and Atlanta (GA). They run the **Flotel Reina de Enín** on the Río Mamoré (US$423pp double occupancy for 5-day trip), **El Puente** hotel in Villa Tunari (C) and are involved with *Proyecto Tayka*, **Red de Hoteles de los Andes**, a chain of hotels in the Salar de Uyuni- Reserva Avaroa area (see page 379).

Gloria tours/Hotel Gloria, Potosí 909, T02-240 7070, www.hotelgloria.com.bo See Sleeping.

Gravity Assisted Mountain Biking, Av 16 de Julio 1490, Edificio Avenida, PB, oficina 10 (across the hall from, and part of, América Tours), T02-231 3849, www.gravity bolivia.com. A wide variety of mountain biking tours throughout Bolivia, including the world-famous downhill ride to Coroico (US$50). Also offers rides more challenging than the Coroico ride, including technical single-track and high-speed abandoned dirt roads, complete with coaching and all the safety equipment needed. Highly professional and recommended. Quality book exchange, sells new and used guidebooks, and gives a free T-shirt with every ride. Often full so worth booking on their website in advance.

Magri Turismo, Capitán Ravelo 2101, T02-244 2727, www.magriturismo.com. Amex representative, gives TCs against American Express card but doesn't change TCs, offers Amex emergency services and clients' mail. Recommended for tours and travel services.

Nuevo Continente, at Hotel Alem, Sagárnaga 344, T02-237 3423, quiquisimo@ mixmail.com. Recommended for trip to Zongo, Clemente is a good driver, cheap service to airport, very helpful.

Pachamama Tours, Sagárnaga 189 y Murillo Shopping Doryan, 2nd fl, oficina 35, T/F02-211 3179, www.magicbolivia.com. Cheap air fares within South America, very knowledgeable and professional for local tours, English spoken, also arranges cultural tours to indigenous

groups. Only tour agency in La Paz with English, French, Italian Spanish, Portuguese, German and Japanese speaking guides.

Tauro Tours, Mercado 1362, Galería Paladium Mezz, local 'M', T02-220 1846. Top end adventure tours, jeep trips, run by the highly experienced and trained Carlos Aguilar.

Toñito Tours, Sagárnaga 189, Comercio Doryan, oficina 18, T02-233 6250, www.bolivianexpeditions.com. Tours of the Salar de Uyuni, also book bus and train tickets, very helpful, hire out sleeping bags.

Topas Adventure Bolivia, Illampu 707, T02-211 1082, www.topas.bo. Joint venture of Akhamani Trek (Bolivia), Topas (Denmark) and the Royal Danish embassy, offering trekking, overland truck trips, jungle trips and climbing, English spoken, café and *pensión* to open, with permanent staff training.

Transturin, Calle Alfredo Ascarrunz 2518, Sopocachi, PO Box 5311, T02-242 2222, www.travelbolivia.com. Full travel services with this long-standing company, with tours ranging from La Paz to the whole country. Details of their Lake Titicaca services will be found on page 346.

Tupiza Tours, Av Tejada Sorzano 855, Edif Dica, between Puerto Rico and Costa Rica, Miraflores, T02-224 4282 (mob: T7206 0026, mob), hmitru@hotmail.com. For tours of La Paz or to the southwest from Uyuni or Tupiza.

Turisbus, Illampu 702, T02-245 1341, www.tur isbus.com. Helpful, trekking equipment rented, agent for PeruRail, tickets to Puno and Cuzco, also local and Bolivian tours. Recommended.

Turismo Balsa, Capitán Rvelo 2104, T02-235 4049, info@turismobalsa.com. City and tours throughout Bolivia (recommended). Also has deals on international flights.

⊖ Transport

La Paz *p301, maps p307 and p308*

Air

For airport information see page 304. To get to the airport: **Cotranstur** minibuses, white with 'Cotranstur' and 'Aeropuerto' written on the side and back, leave from Plaza Isabel La Católica or anywhere on the Prado and Av Mcal Santa Cruz, 0800-0830 to 1900-2000, US$0.50 per person, allow about 1 hr (it's best to have little luggage). *Colectivos* from Plaza Isabel La Católica charge US$3 per person and carry up to 4 passengers. Radio-taxi is US$5 to airport, US$6.50 from Zona Sur. The international departures hall is the main concourse, with all check-in desks, and is the hall for all domestic arrivals and departures.

Airline offices Aerolíneas Argentinas, Edif Petrolero, El Prado, Mezanine, oficina 13, T02-235 1624, F239 1059. **Aero Sur**, Av 16 de Julio 1616, p 11, T02-231 2244. **Amazonas**, Av Saavedra 1649, T02-222 0848. **American Airlines**, Av 16 de Julio 1440, Edif Herman, T02-235 5384, www.aa.com. **British Airways** and **Iberia**, Ayacucho 378, Edif Credinform p 5, T02-220 3885 (BA), T02-220 2869 (Iberia). **Lan**, Av 16 de Julio 1566, p 1, T02-235 8377, www.lan.com. **Lloyd Aéreo Boliviano (LAB)**, Camacho 1460, T02-236 7707. **KLM**, Plaza del Estudiante 1931, T244 1595. **Lufthansa**, Av 6 de Agosto 2512 y P Salazar, T02-243 1717, F243 1267. **TACA**, El Prado 1479, oficina 401, T02-231 3132, toll free T800-108222. **TAM** (Mercosur), Plaza del Estudiante 1931, T02-244 3442. **Transportes Aéreo Militar (TAM)**, Av Montes 738 esq Serrano, T02-212 1585, Mon-Fri 0830-1200 and 1430-1830.

Bus
Terminal Terrestre La Paz's main terminal, at Plaza Antofagasta, T02-228 0551, (*micros* 2, M, CH or 130) has agencies to Peru, such as **Turisbus**, **Diana** and **Vicuña**, which are cheaper here than their offices in town. Touts find passengers the most convenient bus and are paid commission by the bus company. Buses run to **Oruro**, **Potosí**, **Sucre**, **Cochabamba**, **Santa Cruz**, **Tarija**, **Villazón** and all points south of La Paz. Buses to **Chokilla** and **Yanachi** leave from a street just off Plaza 24 de Septiembre at 0800 and 1500, 3-4 hrs, US$2.75. See under each destination for details.

To **Copacabana**, several bus companies (tourist service) pick up travellers from their hotels (in the centre) and also stop at the main terminal; tickets from booths at the terminal (cheaper) or agencies in town. They all leave about 0800, 3½ hrs, US$2.50, return from Copacabana about 1100. When there are not enough passengers for each company, they pool them. Companies include: **Diana Tours**, T02-228 2809, **Nuevo Continente**, T02-228 5191, **Turisbus**, T02-245 1341 (more expensive). You can also book this service all the way to **Puno**, US$6.25. Open tickets are available so you

can break the journey in Copacabana and continue on from there.

Cemetery district To get to the cemetery district, take any bus or minibus marked 'Cementerio' going up Calle Santa Cruz (US$0.17). Buses and *micros* leave from different streets within the cemetery district.

Public buses to **Copacabana** leave from various offices on Calle Aliaga, opposite the cemetery (US$3 including lake crossing at Tiquina crossing). Several departures daily with **Manco Capac**, T02-245 3035, recommended, or **2 de Febrero**, T02-237 7181; both have offices on Plaza Reyes Ortiz, opposite the entrance to cemetery. Buy bus tickets as soon as possible as all buses are usually full by day of travel, especially Sun.

Minibuses to **Achacachi**, **Huatajata** and **Huarina**, and buses for **Sorata** (Trans Unificada Sorata, 0500-1600, 4½ hrs, US$1.65) leave from Av Bustillos a couple of blocks up the street. From the plaza, head up Av Kollasuyo and take the 2nd street on the right (Manuel Bustillos). Several *micros* (20, J, 10) and minibuses (223, 252, 270, 7) go up Kollasuyo; look for 'Kollasuyo' on the windscreen in most, but not all cases.

Villa Fátima Buses for **Coroico**, the **Yungas** and **Rurrenabaque** leave from here (25 mins from centre by *micros* B, V, X, K, 131, 135, or 136, or *trufis* 2 or 9, which pass Pérez Velasco coming down from Plaza Mendoza, and get off at the service station, Calle Yanacachi 1434). See Safety, page 305.

International buses From the Terminal Terrestre: to **Buenos Aires** (Argentina), US$85, Mon and Fri with **Ormeño**, 54 hrs. Alternatively, go to Villazón and change buses in Argentina. To **Arica** (Chile) via the frontier at Tambo Quemado and Chungará **Pullmanbus** at 0630 (good), **Cuevas** at 0700, **Zuleeta** at 0600, 1200 and 1300, **Nuevo Continente** at 0815, US$11.25-12.50. Connecting service for **Iquique** and **Santiago**. To **Cuzco**: *colectivos* and agencies to **Puno** daily with different companies, most easily booked through travel agencies, US$15, 10 hrs. **Note** Of the various La Paz-Puno services, only **Transturin** does not make you change to a Peruvian bus once over the border. International buses are run by **Ormeño** and **Litoral**. For luxury and other services to Peru see under Copacabana, page 346. To **Lima**, **Ormeño**, daily at 1630, **Nuevo Continente** at 0800, US$70, 26 hrs.

There's a car park on corner of Ingavi and Sanjines, US$1.35 for 24 hrs, safe and central. See Essentials page 28 for advice on car hire. Local companies include:

Imbex Rent A Car, Av Montes 522, T02-245 5432, www.imbex.com. Well-maintained Suzuki jeeps from US$60 per day, including 200 km free for 4-person 4WD. Highly recommended.

Kolla Motors, Rosendo Gutierrez 502, between Sánchez Lima and Ecuador, T02-241 9141, www.kollamotors.com. Well-maintained 6-seater 4WD Toyota jeeps, insurance and gasoline extra.

Petita Rent-a-car, Valentín Abecia 2031, Sopocachi Alto, T02-242 0329, www.renta carpetita.com. Swiss owners Ernesto Hug and Aldo Rezzonico. Recommended for well-maintained 4WD jeeps, etc, also offers adventure tours, German, French, English spoken, recommended, and arranges fishing trips. Ernesto also has garage for VW and other makes at Av Jaimes Freyre 2326, T02-241 5264. Highly recommended.

Taxi

Standard taxis charge US$0.75 pp for short trips within city limits. A *trufi* US$0.30 in the centre, US$0.40 per person beyond the centre. Taxi drivers are not tipped. At night, for safety, only take radio taxis (*radio móvil*), which are named as such, have a unique number and radio communication (e.g. **Alfa**, T02-241 2525, **Latino**, T02-231 1616). They charge US$1 in centre and US$2 in suburbs.

Also good value for tours for 3 people, negotiate price. **Adolfo Monje Palacios**, in front of Hotel El Dorado or T02-235 4384.

Highly recommended for short or long trips. **Eduardo Figueroa**, T02-278 6281, taxi driver and travel agent. Recommended. **Oscar Vera**, Simón Aguirre 2158, Villa Copacabana, T02-223 0453, specializes in trips to the Salar de Uyuni and the Western Cordillera, speaks English. Recommended.

South of La Paz *p311*

To get to **Valle de la Luna** from La Paz, take a minibus from the Prado. If you do not want to walk in the valley, stay on the bus to the end of the line and take a return bus, 2 hrs in all. Alternatively take *micro* No 11 ('Aranjuez' large, not small bus) from Calle Sagárnaga, near Plaza San Francisco, US$0.65, and ask driver where to get off.

Most of the local travel agents organize tours to the Valle de la Luna. These are very brief, 5 mins stop for photos in a US$15 tour of La Paz and surroundings; taxis cost US$6.

Tiahuanaco *p311*

To get to Tiahuanaco, **Cooperativa Turismo** has a tourist service with pick up from central hotels, or the terminal, at 0830, return at 1400, US$7.50. Otherwise take any *micro* marked 'Cementerio' in La Paz, get out at Plaza Félix Reyes Ortiz, on Mariano Bautista (north side of cemetery), go north up Aliaga, 1 block east of Asín to find Tiahuanaco *micros*, US$1, 1½ hrs, every 30 mins, 0600-1700. Tickets can be bought in advance. A taxi for 2 costs about US$20-25 return, with unlimited time at site (US$30-40 including Valle de la Luna).

To border at Desaguadero Some buses go on from Tiahuanaco to **Desaguadero**; virtually all Desaguadero buses stop at Tiahuanaco. Return buses (last back

1730-1800) leave from south side of the plaza in the Tiahuanaco village. Minibuses (vans) to Desaguadero, from José María Asín y P Eyzaguirre (cemetery district) US$1.25, 2 hrs, most movement on Tue and Fri when there is a market at the border.

Most tours from La Paz start at US$6.50 per person (not including site entrance or lunch) stopping at Laja and the highest point on the road before Tiahuanaco. Some tours include Valle de la Luna.
Note Watch belongings closely on all *micros* regardless of destination. When returning from Tiahuanaco (ruins or village) to La Paz, do not take a minibus if it has no other passengers. We have received reports of travellers being taken to El Alto and robbed at gun point. Wait for a public bus with paying passengers in it.

Takesi Trail *p312*
Take a Palca/Ventilla bus from outside *comedor popular* in Calle Max Paredes above junction with Calle Rodríguez, daily at 0530, US$1; or take any bus going to Bolsa Negra, Tres Ríos or Pariguaya (see Yunga Cruz below). Alternatively, take any *micro* or minibus to Chasquipampa or Ovejuyo and try hitching a lift with anything heading out of La Paz. If there isn't any transport, haggle with drivers of empty minibuses in Ovejuyo; you should be able to get one to go to Ventilla for about US$4. To **Mina San Francisco**: hire a jeep from La Paz; US$70, takes about 2 hrs. **Veloz del Norte** (T02-221 8279) leaves from Cocabaya 495 in Villa Fátima, 0900 and 1400; 3½ hrs, continuing to Chojlla. Buses to **Yanakachi** leave from a street just off Plaza 24 de Septiembre, La Paz, at 0800 and 1500, 3-4 hrs. Buses to **La Paz** (US$2.85) leave from Yanakachi at 0545 and 1245-1300 or 1400 daily.

Choro Trail *p313*
To the *apacheta* pass beyond La Cumbre, take a radio taxi from central La Paz for US$10, stopping to register at the Guardaparque hut. Or take a taxi to Villa Fátima in La Paz (US$1) then a bus to La Cumbre (US$1), 30 mins; make sure the driver knows you want to get off at La Cumbre.

Yunga Cruz Trail *p313*
Take the bus to **Pariguaya**, Mon-Sat 0730-0830 , from Calle Gral Luis Lara esq

Venacio Burgoa near Plaza Líbano, San Pedro, US$2, 6 hrs to Chuñavi, US$2.25; 6½ hrs to Lambate (3 km further on). Buses to **Tres Ríos** and **Barro Negro/Tabacaya** depart at same time but stop well before Chuñavi. It's not possible to buy tickets in advance, get there early (by 0700 at the latest) to procure them.

Huayna Potosí *p313*
The mountain can be reached by transport arranged through tourist agencies (US$70) or the refugio. *Camión* from Plaza Ballivián in El Alto early morning or midday Mon, Wed, Fri (return next day), taxi (US$30), or minibus in the high season. If camping in the Zongo Pass area, stay at the site maintained by Miguel and family near the white house above the cross.

🛈 Directory

La Paz *p301, maps p307 and p308*
Banks Amex, see *Magri Turismo* under Tour operators. **Banco Santa Cruz**, also known as BSCH (branch in Shopping Norte is open Sat afternoon), cash advance (in bols) on Visa. **Banco Mercantil**, Mercado 1190. **BCP**, Comercio y Yancocha, long hours Mon-Fri 0830-1800, Sat 0900-1200, US$ cash only. **Bisa**, Av Gral Camacho 1333, open 0830-1200, 1430-1800, Sat 1000-1300, good service, changes US$ cash. **Enlace** ATMs at many sites in the city. **Prodem**, Av Camacho esq Colón 1277, Illampu 784 y Santa Cruz, Sánchez Lima y Salinas and other branches, changes US$ cash. **Visa**, Av Camacho 1448, p 11 y 12, T02-231 8585 (24 hrs), for cancelling lost or stolen credit cards. *Casas de cambio* include: **Sudamer**, Colón 256 y Camacho, Mon-Fri till 1800, Sat till 1200. Good rates for cash, 2% commission on TCs. **Unitours**, Mercado y Loayza. Good rates for US$. Very few deal in Argentine and Chilean pesos. Street changers on corners around Plaza del Estudiante, Camacho, Colón and Prado, decent rates. **Cultural centres** **Alliance Française**, Guachalla 399 corner with Av 20 de Octubre, www.afbolivia.org, French-Spanish library, videos, newspapers, and cultural gatherings information. Call for opening hours. **Centro Boliviano Americano (CBA)**, Parque Zenón Iturralde 121 (10 mins walk from Plaza Estudiante down Av Arce),

www.cba.edu.bo. Has public library and recent US papers. **Goethe-Institut**, Av Arce 2708 esq Campos, www.goethe.de. Excellent library, recent papers in German, CDs and DVDS free on loan, German books for sale. **Embassies and consulates** Note that most embassies and consulates can no longer financially assist nationals needing to return home unexpectedly. **Canada**, Edif Barcelona p 2, Victor Sanjinez 2678, Plaza España, T02-241 5021, 0900-1200. **Denmark**, Av Arce 2799 and Cordero, Edif Fortaleza, p 9, lpbamb@um.dk, Mon-Fri 0800-1600. **France**, Av Hernando Siles y Calle 8 No 5390, Obrajes, amfrabo@ ceibo.entelnet.bo, *microbus* N, A or L down Av 16 de Julio, Mon-Thu 0800-1300, 1430-1730, Fri 0800-1230. **Germany**, Av Arce 2395, info@embajada-alemana-bolivia.org, Mon-Fri 0900-1200. **Netherlands**, Av 6 de Agosto 2455, Edif Hilda, p 7, T02-244 4040, nllap@caoba.entelnet.bo, open 0900-1200. **Peru**, F Guachalla 300, Sopocachi, embbol@caoba.entelnet.bo, Mon-Fri 0900-1600, visa US$10 in US$, issued same day if you go early. **Spain**, Av 6 de Agosto 2827 and Cordero, embespa@ceibo.entelnet.bo, Mon-Fri 0830-1500. **Sweden**, Pasaje Villegas s/n, entre 20 de Octubre y 6 de Agosto, T/F02-243 4943, open 0900-1200. **Switzerland**, Calle 13 No 455, Obrajes, T02-275 1001, vertretung@paz.rep.admin.ch, Mon-Fri 0900-1200. **UK**, Av Arce 2732, T02-243 3424, ppa@megalink.com, Mon-Thu 0830-1330, Fri 0830-1200, visa section 0900-1200 has a list of travel hints for Bolivia, doctors, etc. **USA**, Av Arce 2780 y Cordero, T02-216 8000, http://bolivia.usembassy.gov, Mon-Fri 0800-1730. **Internet** There are many internet cafés throughout all of La Paz, opening and shutting all the time. Cost US$0.40 per hr, fast connections, long hours, but many closed Sun. **Language schools** Alliance Française (see Cultural centres above). **Centro Boliviano Americano** (see Cultural centres above), US$140 for 2 months, 1½ hrs tuition each afternoon. **Instituto de La Lengua Española**, María TeresaTejada, Calle Aviador No 180, Achumani, sicbol@caoba.entelnet.bo, one-to-one lessons US$7 per hr. **Speak Easy Institute**, Av Arce 2047, between Goitia and Montevideo, just down from Plaza del Estudiante, speakeasy institute@yahoo.com,

US$6 for one-to-one private lessons, cheaper for groups and couples, Spanish and English taught, very good. **Medical services** For hospitals, doctors and dentists, contact your consulate or the tourist office for recommendations. Cruz Roja Boliviana: T02-222 7818. **Health and hygiene: Unidad Sanitaria La Paz**, on Ravelo behind Radisson Plaza hotel, yellow fever shot and certificate for US$12. **Ministerio de Desarollo Humano, Secretaría Nacional de Salud**, Av Arce, near Radisson Plaza hotel, yellow fever shot and certificate, rabies and cholera shots, malaria pills, bring own syringe (US$0.20 from any pharmacy). **Centro Piloto de Salva**, Av Montes y Basces, T02-236 9141, 10 mins walk from Plaza San Francisco, for malaria pills, helpful. **Laboratorios Illanani**, Edif Alborada p 3, oficina 304, Loayza y Juan de la Riva, T02-231 7290, open 0900-1230, 1430-1700, fast, efficient, hygienic, blood test US$4.75, stool test US$9.50. Tampons can be bought at most *farmacías* and supermarkets. The daily papers list chemists/pharmacies on duty (*de turno*). For contact lenses, **Optaluis**, Comercio 1089, is well-stocked. **Post office** **Correo Central**, Av Mcal Santa Cruz y Oruro, Mon-Fri 0800-2000, Sat 0830-1800, Sun 0900-1200. Another on Linares next to Museo de Coca, 0830-2000. Stamps are sold only at the post offices. *Poste restante* keeps letters for 2 months, no charge. Check the letters filed under both your first name and family name. For the procedure for sending parcels and for mailing prices, see Essentials page 46. To collect parcels costs US$0.15. Express postal service (top floor) is expensive. **DHL**, Av Mcal Santa Cruz 1297, T0800-4020, expensive and slow. **FedEx**, Rosendo Gutiérrez 113 esq Capitán Ravelo, T02-244 3537. **UPS**, Av 16 de Julio 1479, p 10. **Telephone** There are *cabinas* for competing phone companies everywhere. **Useful addresses** To renew a visa go to **Migración Bolivia**, Av Camacho 1433, T02-211 0960, Mon-Fri 0830-1600, go early. Drop passport and tourist card at the booth on the right as you walk into the office in the morning and collect in the afternoon, although an additional day is sometimes required. **Tourist police**, Calle Hugo Estrada 1354, Plaza Tejada Sorzano, opposite the stadium, Miraflores, next to Love City Chinese restaurant, T02-222 5016. Open 24 hrs, for insurance claims after theft, helpful.

Sorata, Yungas and Northern Amazon

Introduction

No visit to Bolivia would be complete without witnessing the sapphire-blue expanse of mystical Lake Titicaca and its beautiful islands. This gigantic inland sea – the largest on the continent – covers up to 8400 sq km and is the highest navigable lake in the world, at 3856 m above sea level.

In the mountains of the Cordillera Real, to the east of the lake, Sorata is a neglected old colonial town enjoying one of the most beautiful settings in the whole country, nestled at the foot of Mount Illampu with panoramic views over lush, alpine-like valleys. To the north of here the hills and mountains of the Cordillera Apolobamba are fantastic trekking and wildlife territory, while to the southeast the valleys drop steeply towards the Amazon Basin through the Yungas, where Coroico and Chulumani are good places for walking or chilling, especially if you've just cycled down the 'world's most dangerous road'.

★ Don't miss ...

1 **Isla del Sol** Take a boat trip to this charming island and spend a few days walking through tiny villages that seem to belong in another age, page 334.

2 **Area Protegida Apolobamba** Visit this remote area and see the graceful vicuñas grazing against a backdrop of spectacular snowy mountains, page 339.

3 **The word's most dangerous road** Brave the helter-skelter ride to Coroico by bus, truck or mountain bike, page 349.

4 **Rurrenabaque** Chill by the riverside and watch the world flow by in one of Rurrenabaque's great bars and restaurants, or in its spa, page 355.

5 **Eco-tourism opportunities** Go on a nocturnal search for jaguars at Chalalán or Mapajo eco-lodges, Latin America's 'greenest' tourist facilities, page 360.

Lake Titicaca and Sorata

The startlingly limpid waters of Lake Titicaca straddle Bolivia and Peru only a few hours from La Paz. This is an area of almost preternatural beauty and serenity, where the white-topped peaks of the Cordillera Real appear much closer than they are due to the thin altiplano air. Lake Titicaca is officially two lakes joined by the Straits of Tiquina. The larger, northern lake – Lago Mayor, or Chucuito – contains Isla del Sol, site of the Inca creation legend. You can spend a few days here relaxing and witnessing a way of life unchanged in centuries, or simply marvelling at the beauty of the lake's waters, reflecting the distant cordillera, mirroring the sky in the rarified air and changing colour when it is cloudy or raining. ▸▸ *For Sleeping, Eating and other listings, see pages 340-347.*

Copacabana 🏛️🛈🎵🍴✳️🍷🛏️ ▸▸ *pp340-347.*

→ *Phone code: 02. Colour map 3, B2.*

This attractive town with red-tiled roofs is nestled between two hills on the shores of Lake Titicaca. It is a popular stopping-off point on the way to or from Peru and definitely worth a brief visit. Its main plaza is dominated by the impressive and heavily restored Moorish-style cathedral. Every Sunday in front of the cathedral a line of cars, trucks, buses and minibuses, all decorated with garlands of flowers, waits to be blessed, as a spiritual form of accident insurance, see box opposite.

Ins and outs

A paved road runs northwest from La Paz across the Altiplano for 114 km to the village of San Pablo on the eastern shore of the **Straits of Tiquina**. It then continues from San Pedro, on the opposite side of the straits, for a further 44 km to Copacabana. By car from La Paz takes about four hours; take the exit to 'Río Seco' in El Alto. Public buses and *micros* run from La Paz or the Peruvian border arrive at Plaza Sucre (see Transport,

Copacabana

Lake Titicaca

Sleeping 🛏️
Ambassador **2**
Boston **3**
Chasqui de Oro **4**
Colonial del Lago **5**
Emperador **6**

Gloria **7**
Hostal La Luna **8**
Hostal La Sonia **1**
Kota Kahuaña **16**
La Cúpula **9**
Residencial Aransaya **11**

Residencial Sucre **13**
Rosario del Lago **14**
Utama **9**

Eating 🍴
Kála U'ta **1**

La Orilla **2**
Puerta del Sol **6**
Snack 6 de Agosto **3**
Sujma Wasi **5**

An answer to your prayers

In Copacabana all your dreams will come true. At least that's what the local people believe. And when you see them fervently blessing all manner of material goods on the Cerro Calvario perhaps you will start to believe it too.

On Sunday, a procession of the faithful makes its way up the steps to the summit of the Calvario to perform this ritual – a strange mix of the spiritual and the material. The believers climb the stairs past the 14 stations of the cross, pausing at each station to bless themselves and to enjoy a brief respite from the lung-bursting ascent. Once at the top, they find an array of stalls offering a veritable multitude of miniature items to pray for: cars, trucks, minibuses, houses (for the more optimistic), bricks and sacks of cement, cookers, wheelbarrows, tiny bags of pasta, suitcases stuffed with dollar bills, even mini certificates to ensure a successful graduation from university.

The devout take their pick before descending to a series of little altars where, for a small fee, they get a bag of incense to burn during the blessing of their desired object. Cars and money seem to be the favourite choices. These are carefully arranged before a miniature version of Copacabana's famous Virgen de la Candelaria.

The ceremony then begins, in either Latin or Aymara. Those electing the latter definitely get more value for money, with much chanting, dancing, histrionics and even flames emitting from a large cup. The alternative ceremony is an altogether more sedate affair. Only smoke instead of flames, a few lines of Latin, a song and some sprinkled flower petals. At a signal from the priest a *cholita* dutifully rushes over with a few bottles of beer which are shaken up and sprayed over the altar.

The ceremony over, the priest and his small congregation drink a toast to good fortune before the weekend pilgrims depart, happy in the belief that their heavenly benefactor will deliver the goods before the year is out.

page 346). There are also several agency buses that run between La Paz and Puno in Peru, all stopping at Copacabana for lunch. Day-trips from La Paz are not recommended as they allow only two hours in Copacabana. New arrivals may be pressurized into paying for 'entry' to the town; the fee is in fact for the sanctuary (see below). The **tourist information kiosk** ① *Plaza 2 de Febrero*, is helpful when open.

Sights

Dominating the main plaza is the huge **cathedral** ① *Mon-Fri, 1100-1200, 1400-1800, Sat-Sun 0800-1200, 1400-1800, only groups of 8 or more can visit, US$0.60,* with its gleaming white basilica, built between 1610 and 1620 to accommodate the huge numbers of pilgrims who flocked to the town when miracles began happening in the Sanctuary of Copacabana after the presentation of a black wooden statue of the Virgin Mary. The statue was carved in the late 1570s by Francisco Yupanqui, grandson of the Inca Túpac Yupanqui. The Virgin is known both as the Dark Virgin of the Lake, or the *Virgen de la Candelaria*, and is one of the three patron saints of Bolivia. Sunday vehicle blessings (which are supposed to bring good luck, and prevent accidents) outside the cathedral involve large quantities of fresh flowers and petals, garlands, firecrackers, beer scattered around and on the tyres and money tucked behind the steering wheel.

Don't miss the walk to the top of **Cerro Calvario**, up a long series of steps, especially at sunset, though you're unlikely to be alone. It's a steep climb up some rough steps but there are great views of the town and the lake from the top and on Sundays you can buy miniature items (cars, suitcases and money, plus a myriad of other things) and have them blessed. Head north and uphill from the centre of town.

Isla del Sol and around ⊕ ▸▸ pp340-347.

Though only a short distance by boat from Copacabana, Isla del Sol has an altogether different feel to it. It has a quiet, almost serene beauty making it the perfect place to relax for a few days. It is worthwhile staying overnight on the island for the many beautiful walks through villages and Inca terraces, some of which are still in use. A sacred rock at its northwestern end is worshipped as the birthplace of the first Incas, Manco Kapac and Mama Ocllo, son and daughter of Viracocha and the first Incas.

Isla del Sol is, by Bolivian standards, intensively inhabited (an estimated 5000 people live there) and cultivated, and so is covered in trails. The wilder west side has the highest point on the island. The most impressive ruins are at the far north at Chincana and the Labyrinth. It is possible to arrange a motor launch to take you there and then walk back across the island to be picked up at the Inca Steps at the other end, where there are a second set of ruins (much more visited) at Pilcocaina and the Inca Spring. Walking from one end of the island to the other takes four to five hours, so it's not really possible to see all the sites on the island and return to Copacabana in one day.

Ins and outs

Inca Tours and **Titicaca Tours** run motor boats to the island; both have offices on Avenida 6 de Agosto in Copacabana, as do other companies. Boats leave Copacabana at 0800, 1100 and 1300, US$1.20 per person. To hire a private boat for 12 costs US$70. Boats go to the north and south end: check on the day for return times. With the same ticket you can stay on the island and return another day. Other options are: half-day tours and tours which include north and south of Isla del Sol and Isla de La Luna in one day (not recommended, too short). Full-day tour US$4-5 per person (more if you stay overnight). Expensive express boats may also be taken to Isla del Sol from Yampupata, but none returns to Yampupata.

Isla del Sol

Around the island

Starting at the north end of the island is the village of **Challapampa**, not far from the **sacred rock of Titicaca** (after which the lake is named), the ruins of **Chincana**, and the **temple del Inca**, which have been restored by the National Institute of Culture. There is a good little **museum** ① *0800-1230, 1400-1800, US$1.45*, in Challapampa, containing artefacts from archaeological excavations at the nearby island of Koa, plus maps and pictures with excellent explanations in English. You will see hollow stones in which offerings were placed and dropped into the lake. These were retrieved by two American and Bolivian archaeologists working together.

About 1½ hours from Challapampa, in the middle of the island, is the friendly village of **Challa**, which is worth a stay. To get there from Challapampa walk past the northern beach (about an hour), then up a hill (20 minutes) to the open area where you'll see the village church. From here head down into the valley of southern Challa (another 20 minutes) and you'll reach the excellent little museum dedicated to the Aymara culture, the **Museo Comunitario de Etnografía** ① *daily 0900-1200, 1300-1800*,

---

To Peru via Copacabana–Yunguyo

There are two main routes into Peru from La Paz. The more common route leaves from Copacabana. An unpaved road leads to the Bolivian frontier at Kasani, 20 minutes away, then on to Yunguyo and from there to Puno. Note that Peruvian time is one hour behind Bolivian time. See also Peru, page 150.

Peruvian immigration is open 24 hours, but the Bolivian side, and therefore the border, is only open 0830-1930 (Bolivian time). Buses/*colectivos* stop at **Kasani** and on the Peruvian side; or you can walk between the two posts. There should be a statutory 72-hour period spent outside Bolivia before renewing a visa but 24 hours is usually acceptable. 30-day visas are often given on entering Bolivia, but there are no problems extending it in La Paz (see also Essentials, page 53); 90 days is normally given on entering Peru.

Money can be changed in Yunguyo, in Peru, at better rates than at the border. Coming into Bolivia, the best rates are given at the border, on the Bolivian side. Peruvian soles can be changed in Copacabana.

Transport Agency buses will take you from La Paz or Copacabana to Puno and stop for border formalities and to change money in Yunguyo. For details of these buses see under Copacabana Transport (see page 346), La Paz international buses (page 325) or La Paz Tour operators (page 323).

To Peru via Disaguadero

The less-used route takes the road to Tiahuanaco and goes along the west side of the lake to Guaqui, then on to Desaguadero on the border. The road heads west from La Paz 91 km to **Guaqui**, then crosses the border at **Desaguadero**, a dusty and dreary place (freezing cold at night) 22 km further west, and runs along the shore of the lake to **Puno**. The road is paved all the way to Peru. For bus services, see pages 326 and 347.

Bolivian immigration ① *0830-1230 and 1400-2030*, is just before the bridge in Desaguadero. A 30-day visa is normally given on entering Bolivia, so ask for more if you need it. Get your exit stamp, walk 100 m across the bridge, then get an entrance stamp on the other side. Both offices may also close for dinner around 1830-1900. Get a visa in La Paz if you need one.

Peruvian immigration opens same hours (Peruvian time) and has been known to give 90-day visas. Money changers just over the bridge on the Peruvian side give reasonable rates for bolivianos or dollars.

The sacred lake

Lake Titicaca has played a dominant role in Andean beliefs for over two millennia. This, the highest navigable body of water in the world, is the most sacred lake in the Andes.

Near Titicaca arose the population and ceremonial centre of Tiahuanaco, capital of one of the most important civilizations of South America. Tiahuanaco ceremonial sites were built along its shores, indicating that the lake was considered sacred at least 2000 years ago.

At the time of the Spanish conquest, one of the most important religious sites of the Inca empire was located on the Isla del Sol. From its profound, icy depths emerged the Inca creator deity, Viracocha. Legend has it that the sun god had his children, Manco Capac and his sister, Mama Ocllo, spring from the lake's azure waters to found Cuzco and the Inca dynasty. Legends about the lake abound. Among them are several which describe underwater cities, roads and treasures.

Titicaca was perceived by its ancient cultures to be an island sea connected to the ocean, mother of all waters. Today, people still believe that the lake is involved in bringing rain and that, closely associated with mountain deities, it distributes the water sent by them. The people who utilize the lake's resources still make offerings to her, to ensure sufficient totora reeds for the boats, for successful fishing, for safe passage across its waters and for a mild climate.

the sign on the door says 'Museo Templo del Sol', if it looks closed just wait for a few mins and someone will show you around, entry by donation. The interior is nothing to shout about, with bare concrete floors, but there are fascinating displays of traditional Aymara costumes worn for dances and in daily life, as well as artefacts from around the island. There are also excellent explanations in English. The museum is run by members of the community to commemorate and preserve their traditions.

From Challa it's about two hours southeast to **Yumani**, where there are a number of places to stay. Below Yumani is the jetty for **Crillon Tours'** hydrofoils and other boats (see page 344). A series of steep **Inca steps** leads up from the jetty to the **Fuente del Inca**, three natural springs said to aid in matters of love, health and eternal youth. A 2-km walk from the spring takes you to the main ruins of **Pilcocaina** ① *US$1.20*, a two-storey building with false domes and superb views. The Sun Gate from the ruins is now kept in the main plaza in Copacabana. There is accommodation by the ruins.

Isla de la Luna

Southeast of the Isla del Sol is the Isla de la Luna (or Coati), which can also be visited as part of a day tour, though this doesn't leave you enough time on Isla del Sol. The best ruins on Isla de la Luna are an Inca temple and nunnery, both sadly neglected.

Sorata and around ⊖⊘⊗⊙▲⊜⊙ ➤ pp340-347. Colour map 3, B2.

Northeast of Lake Titicaca and four hours from La Paz is the gorgeous little mountain town of Sorata. Locals believe that this was the original Garden of Eden and though that claim may be stretching the bounds of credibility somewhat, it would certainly be a sin to miss out on a visit. Sorata is the starting point for some of Bolivia's most spectacular treks, from the strenuous Illampu Circuit to the masochistic Mapiri Trail, the ultimate hardcore trekking challenge, which takes you from the slopes of the Andes to the depths of the rainforest.

Further north, near the Peruvian border, is the remote and beautiful Cordillera Apolobamba, a wild, remote and untamed land of incomparable beauty, home to the famed Kallawayas, Bolivia's ancient and wise medicine men. This part of Bolivia is so off-the-beaten-track it makes the middle of nowhere look busy. Here you'll hardly see another soul, and the few that you do will not speak Spanish as their first language. This is a vast wilderness where condors soar over the mountains, herds of rare vicuñas run free and even the perilously endangered spectacled bear makes an occasional appearance.

Ins and outs

There are several daily buses from the cemetery district in La Paz (see page 325) and the journey to takes about 4½ hours. The road from La Paz heads northwest to the shores of Lake Titicaca before branching off at Huarina towards the village of **Achacachi**, where there is a military checkpoint. Sometimes, all foreigners are required to get off the bus and register here, so remember to take your passport. Don't leave anything on the bus while registering. ▶▶ *See Transport, page 347.*

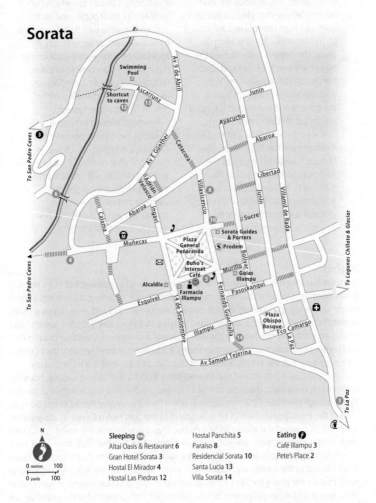

Sorata

0 metres 100
0 yards 100

⦂ A taste of their own medicine

When a Bolivian is ill, he or she is more likely to pay a visit to the local *curandero* (healer) than arrange an appointment with a doctor. In rural areas in particular, Western medicine is seen as a last resort. Every village or community in Bolivia has its own *curandero* who knows about the medicinal properties of plants.

Traditional medicine is an integral part of Andean culture and, unlike Western practices, takes into account the patient's own perceptions of his or her illness and emotional condition. Healers believe that physical illnesses originate from the soul and are caused by the *ajaya* (life force) leaving the body. The healer's job is to coax the ajaya back into the body and restore the mind/body equilibrium. In this way, the healer instills confidence in the patient and lowers psychological resistance to the purification process.

The pop stars of Bolivian traditional medicine are the Kallawayas, the famous travelling healers of the Andes. With their bag of herbs, roots, ointments and amulets, the Kalla-wayas travel the length and breadth of the Andes from Ecuador to Argentina, dispensing spiritual wisdom and natural remedies. Curiously, the Kallawayas all hail from the same region, a group of six small villages in the Apolobamba Mountains. Why this should be the case is something of a mystery, though one theory is that they are descendants of the Tiahuanaco culture. Something like a quarter of the residents of these villages are believed to possess considerable knowledge and healing powers. The Kallawayas' travels have given them access to and knowledge of as many as 1000 plants and herbs.

The Kallawayas pass their knowledge on to their sons, or occasionally apprentices. Women are traditionally not allowed to become Kallawayas, though they play an essential role as midwives and as healers of the female reproductive system.

Renewed interest in natural medicine has helped preserve the Kallawaya tradition, which was in danger of disappearing. Perhaps Western doctors will finally learn to accept herbal medicine as a valuable and well-researched science instead of dismissing it as some form of witchcraft.

Sights

The town has long been a centre for coca, quinine, and rubber growing, but more recently it has become a popular tourist destination. This is not surprising as it offers superb hiking and trekking as well as a great place to wander around and relax. It has a lovely atmosphere, with chickens and children playing in the narrow cobbled streets, and boasts an extremely comfortable climate. It's lower and noticeably warmer than La Paz, and higher and cooler than the Yungas towns. It has fewer swimming pools than Coroico (see page 349) but the setting is more spectacular, and the road is a lot less scary.

The town itself has little of real interest other than its spectacular setting. From the main plaza, on a clear day, you can see Illampu (on the left) and Ancohuma (on the right), though the view of the mountains is better from the smaller Plaza Obispo Bosque. One of the most popular walks near Sorata is to the **San Pedro Caves** ① *daily 0800-1700, US$1*, beyond the village of San Pedro. The caves, despite the warm (21°C) lake and nectar-sipping bats, are not much in themselves but the walk there and back (2½ hours each way) is worth it. Where the road splits after San Pedro take the lower road (signed to the caves) and look for the white building above. It is also possible to walk to the cave along the Río Cristóbal, but either way get clear directions and take at least one litre of water per person before setting out. For your entry fee the guardian will fire up a generator to light your eerie path into the depths; but take a torch in case the power fails. Continue past the cave for 30 minutes to reach a point on the ridge which gives great views over the surrounding valleys. You can camp here, too. Plans have been approved to spend enormous amounts of money on sprucing up the caves.

A good one-day walk is to **Cerro Istipata**. Either take a La Paz-bound bus to below the cross on Cerro Ulluni Tijja (US$0.40), and follow the ridge up and over Cerro Lorockasini and on to Cerro Istipata, or walk the whole way from Sorata. Follow the La Paz road until just before the YPFB garage opposite the Gran Hotel. Drop down right, cross the Río San Cristóbal and head up through the spread-out village of Atahuallani and then up to join the ridge between Cerro Lorockasini (on the right) and Cerro Istipata.

Trekking and climbing from Sorata

Sorata is the starting point for climbing **Illampu** and **Ancohuma** but all routes out of the town are difficult, owing to the number of paths in the area and the very steep ascent. Experience and full equipment necessary and it's best to hire mules (see Activities and tours, page 346). The two- to four-day trek to **Lagunas Chillata and Glaciar** is the most common route and gets busy during high season. Laguna Chillata can also be reached in a day-hike with light gear, but mind the difficult navigation and take warm clothing, food, water, sun protection, etc. Laguna Chillata has been heavily impacted by tourism (remove all trash, do not throw it in the pits around the lake) and many groups camp there. The Inka Marka ruins are on the back of the rock looking towards Illampu from Laguna Chillata. The structures nearest the lake are in a sad state and unfortunately many have been converted to latrines. The **Circuito Illampu**, an eight- to 10-day high-altitude trek (five passes over 4500 m) around Illampu, is excellent. It can get very cold and it is a hard walk, though very beautiful with nice campsites on the way. Some food can be bought in Cocoyo on the third day. You must be acclimatized before setting out. A more recent option is the **Trans-Cordillera trek**, 12 days from Sorata to Huayna Potosí, or 20 days all the way to Illimani at the opposite (south) end of the Cordillera Real. **Note** Laguna San Francisco, along the Illampu Circuit, has for many years been the scene of repeated armed holdups. This is the only place in the Sorata area not considered safe and guided trekking parties may pass though in the small hours of the night to avoid contact with the local population.

Cordillera Apolobamba → *Colour map 3, B2. See Transport, page 347.*

The beautiful Cordillera Apolobamba, northwest of Sorata, stretches north from Charazani north to Pelechuco and then on into Peru, and boasts many 5000 m-plus peaks, while the stunning 4837-sq-km **Area Protegida Apolobamba** protects herds of vicuña, huge flocks of flamingoes and many condors. Apolobamba is well known for its scenic beauty, owing to its impressive array of snow-capped mountains, crystal-clear lakes, and even glaciers (the impressive Chaupi Orcko is one of the largest intact glaciers on earth). The area is made up of several mini ecological zones, ranging from the mountainous and cold Cordillera Real to humid grasslands and finally to the jungle-like Yungas. It also boasts the cela rainforest, now one of the most intact anywhere in South America.

Apolobamba is increasingly popular with day-trippers because of its thermal springs and well-defined network of trails, which often parallel the park's rivers. There is much to see and do in the park. If you have your own transport, the wild vicuña herds can be observed at close range and followed cross country. During the day, especially in the dry season, the vicuñas graze in the marshy areas, in amongst the alpacas, but towards evening, when their domesticated cousins return home to their stone-walled corrals, the vicuñas wander off to more isolated pastures. It's a particularly beautiful sight to see these graceful animals grazing on the plains at dawn against a backdrop of snowy peaks. It is also a primary habitat for literally millions of flamingoes, and a few thousand condors, the national bird.

The terrain and altitude make it a trekker's paradise, and the five-day **Charazani to Pelechuco** mountain trek is one of the best in the country (see *Footprint Bolivia* for details). It passes traditional villages and the peaks of the southern Cordillera Apolobamba. **Charazani,** the main starting point, is the biggest village in the region (3200 m). Its three-day fiesta is around 16 July. There are some *alojamientos* (G), restaurants and shops. **Pelechuco** (3600 m) is a basic village, also *alojamientos* (G), cafés and shops. The reserve headquarters are at **La Cabaña,** 5 km outside the village of Ulla Ulla. There is basic but clean accommodation and food and visitors are very welcome. Orphaned vicuñas which would otherwise die are reared at La Cabaña. This allows you to get closer to them than anywhere else.

● Sleeping

Copacabana *p332, map p332*

B-C Rosario del Lago, Rigoberto Paredes, between Av Costanera and Av 16 de Julio, T02-862 2141, www.hotelrosario.com/lago. Same ownership as **Rosario** in La Paz (see page 314) and a similar modern colonial-style building. Excellent shared spaces with internet (US$0.75 per hr), views and free tea. Rooms all have good lake views but are small and lack much character. Bathrooms are good though, with powerful, hot showers. The restaurant, **Kota Kauhaña,** has good fish specialities and the price includes a generous buffet breakfast. Also has **Turisbus** office.

C Gloria, 16 de Julio, T/F02-862 2094, www.gloria-tours-bolivia.com. May look like a comprehensive school from the outside but inside is pleasing and warm, reminiscent of a seaside dance hall. Spacious, basic bedrooms have views over the lake, bar, café and restaurant, changes money.

C-D Chasqui de Oro, Av Costanera 55, T02-862 2343. Includes buffet breakfast and parking. Lakeside hotel, 50 rooms all with comfy beds, bathrooms and even some bathtubs. Café/breakfast room has great views, trips organized, also has video room.

C-E La Cúpula, Calle Michel Pérez 1-3, T02-862 2029, www.hotelcupula.com. A short and steep walk from the centre of town, La Cúpula is one of Bolivia's best hotels. There are fantastic views, the design is imaginative and innovative, and the attention to the needs of travellers is exceptional. The price depends on the room: of 17 bright and comfortable rooms 7 have private bathrooms and one has a kitchen. The honeymoon suite is so spectacular it might just make you propose. There's also a sitting room with DVD showings, a library, a garden with hammocks, a book exchange and a great restaurant (see

Eating, below). Run by German Martin Strätker. Very highly recommended.

E Hotel Utama, Michel Peréz and San Antonio (50 m from La Cúpula), T02-862 2013. Spotless rooms are arranged around an orange-coloured covered courtyard. Free oranges and *maté* on arrival. Good evening set meal. Book exchange. Price includes breakfast.

F Boston, Conde de Lemos, near the basílica, T02-862 2231. With bathroom, cheaper without, clean, helpful, quiet.

F Colonial del Lago, Av 6 de Agosto y Av 16 de Julio, T02-862 2270. A big hotel on the plaza, large comfortable rooms, books boats to the islands, breakfast included, garden, good restaurant and *peña.* Good value

F Residencial Sucre, Murillo 228, T02-862 2080. All rooms have private bathrooms with 24-hr hot water. Quiet and near the cathedral, there's a big courtyard and it's clean and friendly with good beds, parking, a good cheap breakfast and laundry (US$1.20), offers tours of the lake.

F-G Ambassador, Bolívar y Jauregiu, Plaza Sucre, T02-862 2216. This pink colonial building has big sunny shared spaces, rooms with balcony, a rooftop restaurant and great beds, 10% discount with an ISIC or YHA card. Heaters available for US$2 per day. Recommended.

G Emperador, Calle Murillo 235, T02-862 2083, behind the *basílica.* Very popular, breakfast served in room for US$2 if ordered the previous night, laundry service and facilities, shared hot showers 24 hrs, free clean kitchen, helpful for trips to Isla del Sol, cheap and friendly. Repeatedly recommended as great value.

G Hostal La Luna, Calle José P Mejía 260, T02-862 2051. The 28 rooms are set around a quiet courtyard at the back of town.

Bathrooms can be dirty, very basic but absurdly cheap, breakfast in room on request (US$1), discounts on trips to Isla del Sol.

G **Hostal La Sonia**, Calle Murillo 253, T7196 8441 (mobile). Most rooms have private bathrooms and big, light windows overlooking the town, though a couple of smaller rooms are a bit dark. There's a great roof terrace, a sink for laundry, a kitchen, and breakfast can be served in bed on request. Exceptionally friendly and helpful, and, at less than US$2 for a double room, the best value around.

G **Kota Kahuaña**, Av Busch 15. Hot showers 24 hrs, cheap, quiet and with kitchen facilities. Upstairs rooms have lake views, downstairs it's more poky, but quiet and recommended.

G **Residencial Aransaya**, Av 6 de Agosto 121, T02-862 2229. Simple, basic but clean. Comfortable and turquoise. Good restaurant and café.

Isla del Sol *p334, map p334*

It is worthwhile staying overnight for the many beautiful walks through villages and Inca terraces, some still in use. Rooms are offered by many families on the island. Apart from places to stay in Challapampa, Challa and Yumani, there are plenty of places to camp, especially on the western side of the island in a secluded bay. As dusk falls the lake stops lapping and you can take in the silence. If camping take all food and water (or water sterilizers) with you.

Yumani

Most of the dozen *posadas* on the island are at Yumani, on the south side near the Inca steps. They take advantage of the daily arrival of tourists, but do not always provide what they advertise (hot water, clean sheets). Shop around.

D **Puerta del Sol**, at the peak of the hill above the village. Very popular. (G without bath). Nearby is the owner's father's hostel, G **Templo del Sol**. Clean rooms, comfy beds, electric showers, good restaurant.

F **El Imperio del Sol**, on the hill. Peach-coloured house. Comfortable, no running water.

F **Inti Kala**, opposite **Templo del Sol**. Shared electric showers, fantastic views, great value, serves good meals.

Pilcocaina

G **Albergue Inca Sama**, next to Pilcocaina ruins. Beds are mattresses on the floor, good food, also camping in local-style tents (contact via **Hotel Playa Azul**, Copacabana, T02-862 2228, or La Paz T02-235 6566), Señor Pusari, offers a boat service from Copacabana and runs trips to the north of island.

Challa

G **Posada del Inca**, northeast coast, right on the beach. 8 double rooms, very basic outside toilets, no showers, contact Juan Mamani Ramos through **Entel** office, food is provided and beer or *refrescos* are for sale.

G pp **Qhumphuri**, mid-island on the east coast, 1 hr from the Inca Steps, 1 hr from the Inca ruins in the north. Simple but comfortable rooms with bath, local furniture, great views, restaurant serves all meals (extra cost), tasty food, cooking facilities, owner Juan Ramos Ticona interested in sustainable development.

Challapampa

Several places to stay around the plaza in Challapampa, at the north end of the island. Many places are owned by tour operators. **Crillon Tours** own La Posada del Inca, a restored colonial hacienda, only available as part of a tour (see below). **Magri Turismo** also owns a hotel on the island. See La Paz tour operators, page 323. See also **Transturin**'s overnight options on page 346.

G **Posada Manco Kapac**, one of 2 basic *hostales* owned by Lucio Arias and his father, Francisco (Lucio can also arrange boat tickets). Price depends on whether you have a shower or a bucket. Room for 35 people and a garden for camping, hot showers and views of Illampu. The second hostel has the same name but is further up the beach.

Sorata *p336, map p337*

E-F **Altai Oasis**, T02-7151 9856 (mobile), resaltai@hotmail.com. At the bottom of the valley, Altai's beautiful setting has a camping area by the river and cabins and rooms higher up. The cabins are thoughtfully designed and constructed, with fireplaces, kitchens and lots of wood and tiles. There are also outside areas for BBQs and fires. A bridge crosses straight over the river to the bottom of town but the path is steep and not recommended with heavy rucksacks or after a drink or two. The long way around, via one of the bridges further upstream, is easier. There is a good restaurant on site (see Eating). Transport is available to town, US$3 for 5. Camping US$1.25 per person, with showers and a basic kitchen. Double rooms with private bathrooms are G. Recommended.

E-F Gran Hotel Sorata, on the outskirts of town above the police checkpoint, T02-281 7378, call from plaza for free pick-up. Good value but marred by uncomfortable beds and its location. Built in the 1940s, it is spacious, though the bathrooms are a bit tired looking, large garden with great views and a swimming pool (open to non-residents for US$0.50), games room, restaurant. Accepts Visa, MasterCard, Amex.

G Hostal El Mirador, at the bottom of Calle Muñecas. Friendly, quiet and with great views down over the valley below. Hot showers, comfy beds and a terrace. Breakfast available.

G Hostal Las Piedras, just off Ascarrunz, T7191 6341 (mobile). There's a very good mellow feel to this new hotel, just off to the left on the way down to the cave. It's well designed, European run, very friendly, and gets its breakfast bread from **Café Illampu** (see Eating) across the river. Highly recommended.

G Hostal Panchita, on the corner of the plaza with Guachalla, T02-813 5038. All the rooms are large and have shared bathrooms. Clean and modern, there's a sunny courtyard with flowers and a sitting room. Hot water, good restaurant, **Entel** office. Very friendly, very good value. Recommended.

G pp Paraíso, Calle Villavicencio, T02-813 5043. Clean, pleasant, modern, all rooms with private bathroom and hot water, restaurant, American breakfast US$1.80.

G Residencial Sorata, on the corner of the main plaza and Villavicencio, T/F02-813 5218, resorata@ceibo.entelnet.bo. A huge, fascinating and ramblingly antique place with original fixtures, fittings and drawing room, and massive 18-20 ft long snake skins on the walls. The more expensive rooms overlook the beautiful internal garden. These have sepia prints and antique furniture but the beds are either saggy or lumpy and hard. Those in the modern section are not much better. Restaurant serves good lunch/dinner for US$2.75 and breakfast is US$2. Use of washing machine US$1.50, slow internet access US$3.60/hr. Run by French-Canadian Louis Demers, who is helpful and has lots of good trekking information.

G Santa Lucia, Ascarrunz, T02-213 6686, santa_lucia@yahoo.com. Modern, carpeted rooms, friendly owners and of pictures of horses and fast cars.

G Villa Sorata, F Guachalla, T02-213 5241. Large, well-furnished rooms, electric shower, terrace with lovely views, nice small courtyard, good value but the owner lives abroad and staff are often absent.

Cordillera Apolobamba *p339*
Pelechuco

There are a number of basic *alojamientos*:
G Rumillajta, behind the church; **G Pensión México**, on the main plaza; **G Chujlla Wasi**, on the main plaza.

🍴 Eating

Copacabana *p332, map p332*
Fantastic fresh fish is served from lots of beach shacks. In some you can choose your own fish before they're cooked and in all the food is cheap. It's hard to choose between them – pick by popularity or smell. There are many other restaurants offering decent cheap meals and good trout. Good breakfasts and other meals, especially fish, can be found in the market on Calle Abaroa. Very few places open before 0800.

ⓣ La Orilla, Av 6 de Agosto, close to lake, T02-862 2267, daily 1000-2200. One of the warmest, tastiest, most atmospheric places in town. Owners Lucas and Miguel are excellent hosts and have created a menu with great local and international combinations. The peppered steak is to die for and the stuffed trout superb. There's a terrace, an open fire, Cuban jazz, masks and dreamcatchers. Arachnaphobics should avoid looking up at the stuffed creatures in the ceiling. Main dishes cost around US$3. Highly recommended.

Kalá U'ta, Av 6 de Agosto, T02-015 73852. Run by same people as **Sujma Wasi**, below, warm atmosphere and good vegetarian food, organic coffee and chocolate and good music and fabrics. Recommended.

Puerta del Sol, 6 de Agosto. Excellent trout for around US$4. Very similar to several others along 6 de Agosto. Eat in or out.

Snack 6 de Agosto, 6 de Agosto, T02-862 2114. Good trout, big portions, some veggie dishes including range of omelettes, serves breakfast and has outside tables.

Sujma Wasi, Calle Jauregui 127, T02-862 2091, daily 0730-2300. Excellent food and lovely, warm atmosphere in the café/restaurant plus a very good collection of books on Bolivia in their *sala cultural*. Breakfasts are themed on a health/mountaineer/worldwide basis. A vegetarian lunch changes daily and there's a cobbled square courtyard with stone benches, plants and flowers. Recommended.

Sorata *p336, map p337*

There are several Italian restaurants on the plaza. These are much of a muchness and heavy on the cheese. A typical large pizza costs US$7.50, wine US$4.50 a bottle. The cheapest place to eat is the **Comedor Popular** in the market.

Altai Oasis, see Sleeping, above, open 0830-2200. Good breakfasts including porridge pancakes and fruit salad, great goulash and T-bone steaks, soy burgers and good coffee. Fresh vegetables are home-grown and honey comes from beehives in the garden.

Café Illampu, a 20-min walk from town via the short-cut, on the way to Gruta San Pedro. Open daily 0930-1830 except Tue when the owner walks his pet llamas around town. Closed Feb and Mar. Run by Swiss masterbaker Stefan, it's the best in Sorata for views of Illampu. Breakfasts include home-baked raspberry and strawberry cakes and yoghurts. Also sandwiches, hammocks and camping. There are basic mountain bikes for hire (US$4.50 per half day) which eases a trip to the caves, also camping (US$1 plus US$0.50 for tent hire).

Pete's Place, Esquivel y 14 de Septiembre, 2nd floor, Tue-Sat 0830-2200. On the corner of plaza, Pete's is the epicentre of gringo life in Sorata. Fantastic veggie and non-veggie food, great value breakfasts, set lunches and dinners. Very friendly and gets copies of the *Guardian Weekly* delivered weekly. Will change TCs for 3% commission if there is enough cash in the till. East Londoner Pete Good himself is a great source of local info (especially on trekking) and there's a good selection of books on Bolivia and maps to browse through. You may find it hard to leave.

⊙ Entertainment

Copacabana *p332, map p332*

Restaurant Mankha Uta, Av 6 de Agosto, towards the lake, is warm and has a Play Station and movies, although the set meals (US$1.25) are not up to much. Also has movies, video games and a big sound system and offers a selection of lunch boxes.

⊙ Festivals

Copacabana *p332, map p332*

Festivals in Copacabana are frequent and frantic and to be heartily recommended, especially to those who like drinking, dancing, eating and more drinking. See also page 37.

24 Jan, Alacitas, held on Cerro Calvario and Plaza Kolquepata, is when miniature houses, cars and the like are sold and blessed.

1-3 Feb, Virgen de la Candelaria a massive procession of the Dark Virgin takes place, this is a real highlight with much music, dancing, fireworks and bullfights.

End Feb/beginning Mar, Carnival.

Easter, during Semana Santa, there is a huge pilgrimage to the town.

2-5 May Fiesta del Señor de la Cruz, this is very colourful with dances in typical costumes.

5 Jun Anniversary of Manco Kapac.

12-13 Jun San Antonio.

23 Jun San Juan, this is also celebrated throughout the region and on Isla del Sol.

15-17 Jul Anniversary of La Paz department, a chance to share drinks and coca leaves with the locals, also marches and bullfights.

24-25 Jul Fiesta del Señor Santiago, dancing in typical costumes.

4-6 Aug La Virgen de Copacabana, the town fills with people, the plaza becomes a huge market and there are dancing and fireworks. During La Virgen de Copacabana and Semana Santa, petty crime rises massively. Otherwise the town is very safe.

Sorata *p336, map p337*
One week after Easter A major event is the **Fiesta Pascua** or San Pedro.
14 Sep Sorata's biggest bash is the **Fiesta Patronal del Señor de la Exaltación**.

O Shopping

Sorata *p336, map p337*
There are small shops all over the town. The stalls and shops in Calle Ingavi and *muñecas* (street vendors) cover just about everything available in Sorata – from packaged food, films and photocopying to machetes.

The market is just off the plaza, half a block down *muñecas* on the right. There are stalls selling fresh fruit and vegetables every day but market days are Thu, Sat and Sun, the latter being the biggest.
Artesanía Sorata, on the main plaza near the Transportes Unificado office, Mon-Sat 0900-2000, Sun 0900-1600. Sells postcards, handicrafts, jumpers, gloves and wall hangings. It also cashes TCs and accepts them as payment.
Centro de Medicina Natural Paya, Plaza Obispo Bosque. Sells natural foods and medicines.

▲▲ Activities and tours

Lake Titicaca *p332*
Crillon Tours (address under La Paz, Tour operators, page 323) runs a hydrofoil service on Lake Titicaca with excellent bilingual guides. Tours stop at their Andean Roots cultural complex at **Inca Utama**: the Bolivian History Museum includes a recorded commentary; a 15-min video precedes the evening visit to the Kallawaya (Native Medicine) museum. The **Inca Utama Hotel** (AL) has a health spa based on natural remedies; the rooms are comfortable, with heating, electric blankets, good service, bar, good food in restaurant, reservations through Crillon Tours in La Paz. Crillon is Bolivia's oldest travel agency and is consistently highly recommended. Also at **Inca Utama** is an observatory (*Alajpacha*) with 2 telescopes and retractable thatched roof for viewing the night sky, a floating restaurant and bar on the lake (**La Choza Náutica**), a 252-sq m floating island, a colonial-style tower with 15 deluxe suites, panoramic elevator and 2 conference rooms. Health, astronomical, mystic and ecological programmes are offered. The hydrofoil trips include visits to Andean Roots complex, Copacabana, Islas del Sol and de la Luna, Straits of Tiquina and past reed fishing boats. See **Isla del Sol** (Sleeping, above), for **La Posada del Inca**. Crillon has a sustainable tourism project with Urus-Iruitos people on floating islands by the Isla Quewaya. Trips can be arranged to/from Puno (bus and hydrofoil excursion to Isla del Sol) and from Copacabana via Isla del Sol to Cuzco and Machu Picchu. Other combinations of

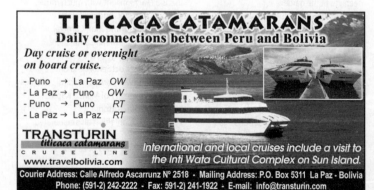
(side margin) Sorata, Yungas & Northern Amazon Lake Titicaca & Sorata Listings

hydrofoil and land-based excursions can be arranged (also jungle and adventure tours). All facilities and modes of transport connected by radio.

Transturin (see also La Paz tour operators, page 323) run catamarans on Lake Titicaca, either for sightseeing or on the La Paz-Puno route. The catamarans are more leisurely than the hydrofoils of *Crillon* so there is more room and time for on-board entertainment, with bar, video and sun deck. From their dock at Chúa, catamarans run day and day/night cruises starting either in La Paz or Copacabana. Puno may also be the starting point for trips. Overnight cruises involve staying in a cabin on the catamaran, moored at the Isla del Sol, with lots of activities. On the island, Transturin has the **Inti Wata** cultural complex which has restored Inca terraces, an Aymara house and the underground **Ekako** museum. There is also a 50-passenger *totora* reed boat for trips to the Polkokaina Inca palace. All island-based activities are for catamaran clients only. Transturin runs through services to Puno without a change of bus, and without many of the formalities at the border. **Transturin** offers last minute, half-price deals for drop-in travellers (24-48 hrs in advance, take passport): sold in Copacabana only, half-day tour on the lake, continuing to Puno by bus, or La Paz; overnight Copacabana-Isla del Sol-Copacabana with possible extension to La Paz. Sold in La Paz only: La Paz-Isla del Sol-La Paz, or with overnight stay (extension to Puno possible on request).

Turisbus (see La Paz tour operators, page 323 and **Hoteles Rosario**, La Paz, and **Rosario del Lago**, Copacabana) offer guided tours in the fast launches *Titicaca Explorer I* (28) and *Titicaca Explorer II* (8 passengers) to the Isla del Sol, returning to Copacabana via the Bahía de Sicuani for trips on traditional reed boats. Also La Paz-Puno, with boat excursion to Isla del Sol, boxed lunch and road transport, or with additional overnight at **Hotel Rosario del Lago**.

Sorata *p336, map p337*
Mountain biking
Hoodoo Tours, Plaza Gral Peñeranda, T02-7127 6685 (in La Paz, **Oliver's Travels**, Murillo y Tarija). Plenty of good routes, including multi-day trips (eg to Rurrenabaque) with emphasis on the fairly extreme.

Trekking
It is much cheaper to book trekking trips in Sorata than in advance with an agency in La Paz. Conversely, buy all your trekking food in La Paz as Sorata shops are poorly supplied.

Guiding associations include: **Asociación de Guías y Porteadores**, T02-213 6698; and **Asociación de Guías Illampu**, Murillo between Guachalla and Bolívar. Both offer similar services, quality and prices.

Louis at **Residencial Sorata** can arrange guides and mules. Guides cost from US$12 a day, porters and mules extra. Remember you also have to feed your guide/porter.

When trekking avoid drinking sedimented glacier melt water and treat all other water with iodine.

⊖ Transport

Copacabana *p332, map p332*
If arriving in Bolivia at Copacabana and going to La Paz, see Safety on page 305, for scams in the cemetery district, where public transport arrives.

Bus Buses and *micros* to **La Paz** leave regularly from Plaza Sucre (every 30 mins, 4 ½ hrs, US$3 including Tiquina crossing). Companies include: **Manco Capac**, T02-862 2234 or **2 de Febrero**, T02-862 2233.

Bus to **Huatajata**, US$2 and to **Huarina**, US$2.50. If travelling to **Sorata**, take a La Paz bus as far as Huarina and take a bus north from there (3 hrs, every 30 mins).

To get to the **Peruvian border**, it's possible to pick up one of the agency buses that run between La Paz and Puno stopping in Copacabana for lunch (see page 324); open tickets are offered so that you can break the journey. Buses leave Copacabana around 1200-1400 for the border at Kasani (stopping for immigration formalities and changing money – better rates in Copacabana or Puno), arriving **Puno** about 1700 (Copacabana-Puno 3½ hrs, US$2.50-4 depending on season). It's also possible to catch a tour bus to **Cuzco** (Peru), usually departing around 1400, US$17-20, change bus in Puno, tour company arranges connection.

Border with Peru *p335*
Via Copacabana
Bus In Peru, bus starts at **Yunguyo**. *Colectivo* Copacabana-Kasani US$0.50 pp, Kasani-

Yunguyo US$0.60 pp. Make sure, if arranging a through ticket La Paz-Puno, that you get all the necessary stamps en route, and find out if your journey involves a change of bus.
Note A common complaint is that through-services La Paz-Puno (or vice versa) deteriorate once the border has been crossed, eg smaller buses are used, extra passengers taken on, passengers left stranded if the onward bus is already full, drivers won't drop you where the company says they will.

Via Guaqui and Desaguadero
Bus Road paved all the way to Peru. Buses from La Paz to Guaqui and Desaguadero depart from same location as *micros* for Tiahuanaco (see above) every 30 mins, US$1.55, 1½-2 hrs. From Desaguadero to **La Paz** last bus departs 1700, buses may leave later if enough passengers, but charge a lot more.

Via Puerto Acosta
Bus Buses from **La Paz** (Reyes Cardona 772, Cancha Tejar, cemetery district, T02-238 2239), 5 hrs, US$3.75, daily 1400, more on Sun, run to **Puerto Acosta** on the east side of Lake Titicaca, 10 km from the Peruvian border. There are also frequent minivans to **Escoma**, 25 km south of Puerto Costa. The road is paved as far as Escoma then good until Puerto Acosta in the dry season (Oct-Mar).

Transport past Puerto Acosta only runs on market days, Wed and Sat, and is mostly cargo trucks. The road deteriorates and should only be attempted in the dry season. You should get an exit stamp in La Paz before heading to this border (only preliminary entrance stamps are given here). There is a Peruvian customs post 2 km from the border and 2 km before Tilali, but Pervuian immigration is in Puno.

Sorata *p336, map p337*
Bus Buses to the cemetery district in **La Paz** (see page 325) leave from the main plaza in Sorata every hour daily 0400-1400 (till 1700 Fri and Sun) or so through the day. To **Rurrenabaque**: jeeps run between Sorata and **Santa Rosa**, down the valley past Consata. From Santa Rosa transport can be arranged to Mapiri and all the way to Rurrenabaque (a very long rough ride with interesting vegetation and views). If travelling to or from **Peru**, change buses at **Huarina** for Copacabana.

Cordillera Apolobamba *p339*
Bus Buses to **Charazana** leave from Calle Reyes Cardona in the cemetery district of La Paz (daily, 10 hrs, US$4.40), very crowded. Buses to **Pelechuco** (also from Calle Reyes Cardona) leave Wed and Thu at 1100, returning Fri 2000 and Sat 1600 (US$6, 18-24 hrs).

Jeeps Jeeps from La Paz charge US$250 to **Charazani** and US$300 to **Pelechuco**.

ⓘ Directory

Copacabana *p332, map p332*
Banks Banco Unión, 6 de Agosto opposite Oruro, reasonable rates of exchange, TCs at US$2 commission, cash advance on Visa and MasterCard 3% commission. **Prodem**, Av 6 de Agosto entre Oruro y Pando, for cash advances on Visa or MasterCard only (no debit cards), 5% commission, changes US dollars cash. No ATM in town. Several *artesanías* on Av 6 de Agosto buy and sell US$ and Peruvian soles. **Internet** Alcadi, next to post office, opposite cathedral, US$2.40 per hr. **Alf@Net**, Av 6 de Agosto, next to Hostal Colonial, 0830-2200, US$2, has book exchange. In **Municipal building**, Plaza 2 de Febrero, US$2.95 per hr. **Ifa-Internet**, Av 16 de Julio y Jáuregui, Plaza Sucre. US$3.50 per hr. **Post office** Plaza 2 de Febrero, Tue-Sat 0900-1200, 1430-1830, Sun 0900-1500, *poste restante*. **Telephone** Entel, 0800-1230, 1330-2000, international phone and fax, accept US$.

Sorata *p336, map p337*
Banks Prodem, on main plaza, variable hours Tue-Sun, changes US$ cash at fair rates, 5% commission on Visa/MasterCard cash advances only (no debit cards). Nowhere in town to change TCs. **Internet** Buho's Internet Café, on the plaza, 0900-1800. US$3 per hr, very slow connection but a cosy place. **Medical services** Hospital: Villamil de Rada e Illampu. Has oxygen and X-ray. There is an adequately equipped pharmacy. **Post office** On the plaza, 0830-1230, 1500-1800, but La Paz Correo is more reliable. **Telephone** Several around the plaza, rates vary considerably from place to place, so shop around.

The Yungas

Only a few hours from La Paz are the subtropical valleys known as the Yungas. These steep, forested slopes are squeezed in between the high cordillera and the vast green carpet of jungle that stretches east, providing a welcome escape from the breathless chill of the capital as well as a convenient stopping point for those hardy souls travelling overland to the jungle.

The town of Coroico, in the northernYungas, is a firm favourite and the road that winds its tortuous way down from the high mountains has achieved near-legendary status in South American travelling lore as being at one time 'the most dangerous in the world'. Many tourists now opt for the relative safety of two wheels rather than four for the terrifying and spectacular 70-km downhill ride. The lovely little town of Chulumani, in the Sud Yungas, offers a less nerve-wracking but equally attractive alternative. Tipped to become a major tourist destination in its own right, today it's still a quiet backwater, where people quietly go about their business and where the secrets and rumours of Nazi war criminals lie buried in the local cemetery.

▶▶ *For Sleeping, Eating and other listings, see pages 352-355.*

La Paz to the Yungas → *Colour map 3, B2.*

The most commonly used route to the Yungas goes via **La Cumbre**, northeast of La Paz. The road out of La Paz circles cloudwards over La Cumbre pass at 4660 m; the highest point is reached in half an hour; all around are towering snow-capped peaks. Soon after **Unduavi** the paving ends, the road becomes 'all-weather' and drops over 3400 m to the green subtropical forest in 80 km. The roads to Chulumani and Coroico divide just after Unduavi, where there is a *garita* (check point), the only petrol station, and lots of roadside stalls.

To Coroico From Unduavi to Yolosa, the junction 8 km from Coroico, the road – once described as the world's most dangerous – corkscrews its way down to the Yungas. It is a breathtaking descent, through a series of steep, twisting turns. The road is disarmingly narrow in places and clings desperately to the side of the sheer cliffs; it's best not to look over the edge if you don't like heights. Its reputation for danger, however, is more than matched by the beauty of the scenery (and sections have recently been upgraded with IMF funding). A new road from La Paz, including a 2½-km tunnel, has been built to Coroico via Chuspipata and Yolosa. For the **Choro trail**, see page 313. **Gravity Assisted Mountain Biking** (see La Paz tour operators, page 324) runs bike tours from La Cumbre down to Yolosa with top-quality bikes (complete with hydraulic disc brakes), English-speaking guides, helmet, gloves and vehicle support throughout the day. It takes four hours to hurtle down to Yolosa, then there's transport to Coroico and free next-day transfer back to La Paz. Other companies also do this trip but quality varies; it's worth choosing a reputable company as the cheaper operators often have to cut corners. Many bike companies take riders back to La Paz the same day, but Coroico is worth much more of your time than that. Note that the road is especially dangerous mid-December to mid-February and many companies will not run downhill bike tours at this time.

To Chulumani The road to the Sud Yungas branches east just beyond Unduavi. Though less nerve-wracking than the road to Coroico, this is nevertheless a scenically rewarding trip as the road follows the steep-sided valley of the Río Unduavi. It also passes under a waterfall.

The most exhilarating road in the world

The journey from La Paz to Coroico must be the most impressive in all Bolivia. It's an absolute must for adrenalin junkies but a definite no-no for those of a more nervous disposition. Beginning at La Cumbre, a mountain pass above La Paz at 4700 m where there is often snow the bike ride drops more than 3600 m in around four hours and 64 km to the sub-tropical jungle of Yolosa, below Coroico. For most of this route the road is little more than a bumpy, rocky ledge carved into the rockface of the mountains, through streams and under waterfalls and often with a sheer drop of as much as 1000 m on the left hand side. Almost every turn of the road seems to be punctuated with crosses for those that have died there. Into this mix should be added Bolivian drivers who think nothing of the odd tipple or two before they set out and trucks who stop for nobody.

The claim that this counts as the most dangerous road in the world originally came from Inter-American Development Bank in 1995. Although it can no longer claim this distinction (a road in Tibet now has the dubious honour, according to the IMF), the biggest single road accident in history apparently happened here in the 1980s, when a lorry packed with almost 100 *campesinos* plunged over the edge.

The worrying accident rate can't be helped by the fact that, according to Bolivian road law, the vehicle going downhill should keep to the outside of the road, closest to the drop.

If you're travelling by bus, bear this in mind when you board in La Paz, and insist on a seat on the left for the best views. A few hours later you will regret this foolish act of bravado. The scenario is this: your driver rounds yet another bend to come face to face with yet another massive timber truck. He reverses back uphill, getting ever closer to the edge of the precipice until you look out the window and can see no part of the road, only the tops of the trees hundreds of metres below. This gets to you after a while.

Similarly, while hurtling downhill on two wheels trying not to look at the view, all your instincts will scream at you to keep away from the edge as a mammoth truck trundles up the road toward you. To date, six people have died cycling down this road and it's worth choosing a good tour company from among the 30 or so that now offer the trip.

But the dangers of the road to Coroico are far outweighed by the thrill of the journey. The views are magnificent as you descend from the snows of the cordillera to the humid sub-tropics. After a couple of days relaxing by the pool, enjoying a cold beer and the magnificent scenery, this trip won't seem so bad. Until of course, it's time to go back.

Sorata, Yungas & Northern Amazon The Yungas

Coroico 🖂🚲🏵🔺🚌ℹ️ ⏵ *pp352-355.*

→ *Phone code: 02. Colour map 3, B2. Altitude: 1760 m.*

The little town of Coroico has long been a favourite with visitors to Bolivia and residents of La Paz. It clings to the flanks of a steep, forested mountain amid orange and banana groves and coffee plantations, with stupendous views, particularly to the southwest, where you can see the distant snowy peaks of the Cordillera Real. Coroico isn't a place for the hyperactive. There's not a huge amount to do here, except lay by the hotel pool soaking up the sun and sipping ice-cold beer as you enjoy the views, swap travelling tales with your equally chilled-out fellow travellers and recover from that harrowing bus trip or thrilling bike ride.

Chulumani's dark secrets

In the late 1930s Chulumani was the very end of the road, a remote sub-tropical refuge surrounded by impenetrable forests. After the Second World War, this quiet, out-of-the-way town was home to Klaus Barbie, Adolf Eichmann and several other Nazi top-brass who had come here to escape justice. Stories abound of how the Nazis settled in Chulumani and locals recall with irony how they arrived to discover a group of Jews had beaten them to it by 12 years. Escaping the growing Nazi menace in Europe, the Jews had populated the mercado area. "The locals wondered why the gringos spat at each other," says guesthouse owner Xavier Sarabia. Barbie lived in relative tranquility in a house below the town, at Puente de Tablas (it is still in good repair), occasionally visiting La Paz to act as military consultant for the various Bolivian dictatorships. The whole subject of Chulumani's Nazis is shrouded in secrecy and still spoken of in hushed tones, especially as many top Bolivian industries are said to have been founded with Nazi money. The truth may lie buried in the cemetery (which has many German names on the gravestones). Even local carpenter, Hitler Mamani, knows little of the origin of his rather unusual name.

Ins and outs

There are several daily buses from the Villa Fátima district of La Paz. The journey takes three hours; sit on the left-hand side for the best views of the descent into the Yungas. Pick-ups from La Paz may drop you at Yolosa, 7 km from Coroico; there is usually transport from Yolosa to Coroico, US$1, or you can walk, uphill all the way, two hours. Buses, trucks and pick-ups also run to Yolosa from Caranavi, Guanay and Rurrenabaque. **Tourist information** ① *Cámera Hotelera on the plaza.* ▸▸ *See Transport, page 354 for more details.*

Walks around Coroico

There are a number of good walks around Coroico. One is down to the pools at the **Río Vagante**, 7 km away, off the road to Coripata. It takes about three hours to get there. Ask Fernando at **Hotel Esmeralda** for directions. Another good walk is up to the waterfalls, starting from **El Calvario**. Follow the Stations of the Cross by the cemetery, off Calle Julio Zuazo Cuenca, which leads steeply uphill from the plaza. Facing the chapel at El Calvario, with your back to the town, look for a path on the left, which soon becomes well-defined. It leads in one hour to the **Cascada y Toma de Agua de Coroico**, the source of the town's water supply. Walk beyond this to a couple of waterfalls further on which are better for swimming.

Possibly the best walk is up **Cerro Uchumachi**, the mountain behind El Calvario. The mountain is considered sacred and witchcraft is practised at various sites here. Once again, follow the stations of the cross but this time look for the (now faded) red and white antenna behind the chapel. From there it's about 1½ hours' very steep uphill walk. At the top of the mountain another trail continues to the right for about one hour to a campsite. The views from Uchumachi in the morning are spectacular but in the afternoon there can be fog. There's no water en route, so take your own and watch out for biting insects. Cerro Uchumachi is also good for birdwatching, in the elfin forest at the summit. There is horse riding with **El Relincho** ① *100 m past Hotel Esmeralda (a 15-minute walk up the hill from the plaza).*

Note There have been several incidents of women being raped or attacked on the trails around Coroico; do not hike alone.

From the road junction at Yolosa the lower fork follows the river northeast 75 km to Caranavi, an uninspiring town 156 km from La Paz. From here the road continues towards the settled area of the Alto Beni, at times following a picturesque gorge. Market days are Friday and Saturday. There is a range of hotels and *alojamientos* and buses from La Paz (Villa Fátima) to Rurrenabaque pass through. Beyond Caranavi, 70 km, is **Guanay** at the junction of the Tipuani and Mapiri rivers (basic lodging). From here there is river transport to Rurrenabaque.

Chulumani and around ⬛🚹❎🏨🚍🅲 » *pp352-355.*

→ *Colour map 3, B2.*

Chulumani is the capital of Sud Yungas. It's an attractive, relaxed and friendly little town, perched on the slopes of a hill with magnificent views across the valley to the forest of Apa Apa and the villages of Chicaloma and Irupana. Saturdays and Sundays are market days when Afro-Bolivians come dressed in traditional costume. The town throws a party, **Fiesta de San Bartolomé**, on 24 August. It lasts for 10 days but the first three are the best.

Ins and outs

Buses from La Paz all leave from Villa Fátima district; the journey takes about four hours. From Culumani, *micros* to other Yungas villages leave from the *tranca* (outdoor bus station by the side of road) 0500-1900 when full. There is a petrol station is at the entrance to the town, by the *tranca*. The **tourist office** ⓘ *centre of the main plaza, allegedly open Mon-Fri 0900- 1330, 1500-2200, Sat-Sun 0700-2200*, sells locally grown coffee, teas, jams and honey. ▶ *For details, see Transport, page 355.*

Sights

From Chulumani it is 1½ hours by bus to the old colonial village of **Irupana**, which hosts a fiesta on 5 August. Three hours beyond Irupana by truck (one leaves twice a week – check in advance for times) are the seldom-visited Inca ruins and terraces of **Pastogrande** with a beautiful river flowing below. Another road to Irupana goes via the ancient village of **Ocabaya** (2½ hours away), where the 1952 revolution began, also passing through the Afro-Bolivian community of **Chicaloma**, where the Saya, a traditional world-famous African dance, was born. This village hosts its **Santísima Trinidad** festival on 16 July and you can see the dancing at its Corpus Christi celebrations in late May. This road is less direct and used less often, and transport from the tranca in Chulumani is infrequent, so ask around.

The main road to Irupana passes the turn-off to Apa Apa, a protected forest area of 800 ha, 8 km from Chulumani. This is the last area of original subtropical Yungas forest with plenty of interesting wildlife, such as small deer, agoutis, hoachi, nocturnal monkeys and many birds including parrots and hummingbirds. Even porcupines, pumas and the rare Andean spectacled bear are seen here and there are many tree orchids. The flora includes the giant *leche-leche* trees, which have a small 'cave' in the trunk. A recent study revealed seven new types of tree and many new ferns in the park. At the time of writing only two trails are open for tourists – a three-hour hike through the lower part of the forest and a 4½-hour trip to the tip of the mountain.

Apa Apa forest is managed by Ramiro Portugal and his US-born wife, Tildi. Ramiro was born locally and knows the area well; he also speaks English. Their home is an 18th-century hacienda, which is a working dairy farm and provides accommodation. You can use their pool after the trek (three rooms, full-board available, and campsite with bathrooms, US$10 per tent). T02-213 6106 to arrange transport from town, taxi US$3 one way; or T02-279 0381 (La Paz), or write to Casilla 10109, Miraflores, La Paz.

Sorata, Yungas & Northern Amazon The Yungas

This tiny colonial village is the ideal place to really get away from it all and relax. It lies at the end of the Takesi Trail (see page 312), or can be reached by turning off the road to Chulumani at Florida and following the rough track (signposted). Yanakachi stands in a commanding position overlooking two major river valleys and there are great views over the village and surrounding areas from the bell-tower of the village church, one of the oldest in the Yungas, dating from the 16th century. Yanakachi also offers various activities and several small hiking trails. You can hike the three-hour trail down to the river and swim in one of the delightful pools below the waterfall. Or you can help out in the local **orphanage** for the day, which cares for 80-120 children. To find out where this is, ask at the office of **Fundación Pueblo** ① *on the plaza, daily 0800-1230, 1430-1830*, which also has maps and local information. The foundation itself is interesting for its work in preventing people migrating to the cities in search of better jobs. Programmes include boosting local services to tourism to create more jobs (they've rebuilt a refuge on the Takesi Trail), environmental education, better farming techniques and adult literacy classes. After chatting with the volunteers, you could go for a swim in the pool at **Alojamiento San Miguel**, 15 minutes' walk out of town on the road towards Florida.

There are some lovely walks in the area surrounding Yanakachi, with several out-of-the-way places to stay, making it the ideal alternative for those who like hiking but don't want to camp. From the northeast side of the village walk the one-hour pre-Hispanic trail down to Sakha Waya, and from there catch a passing bus up to La Paz or down to Chulumani, or Coripata. You can also hike the often-ignored final day of the Takesi Trail. From the bottom of the village, this pre-Hispanic trail continues on the south side of the ridge, past several small ruins and communities, and Villa Aspiazu, to the tiny settlement of **Puente Villa**, where there is a recommended hotel 30 minutes' walk upstream (see Sleeping, page 353). You can wait in town beside the Río Takesi for buses onwards to Chulumani, which leave 0900-2100. From the Unduavi bridge you can also take transport back to La Paz 0500-1000 and to Coripata at 1100 and 1200, from where are two daily buses to Arapata and on to Coroico.

● Sleeping

Coroico *p349*

For such a small town, Coroico has a good range of accommodation. Due to its popularity, however, the best hotels are booked up during holiday weekends when prices rise. Some private rooms are available, for rent, see language classes in Directory, below, for details.

C El Viejo Molino, a 20-min walk out of town on the road to Caranavi, T02-213 6004, valmar@waranet.com. Expensive option with a sauna, jacuzzi and pool.

C Gloria, Calle Kennedy, T02-213 6020, www.hotelgloria.com.bo. Full board with bath (**B-C** at weekend), cheaper Mon-Fri. Spacious, large pool and a kiddies' pool, breakfast extra, restaurant, internet, free transport from plaza.

C-E Esmeralda, reservations: Casilla PO Box 92 25, La Paz, T02-221 36017, www.hotelesmeralda.com. This large hotel is

worth the 15-min walk up the hill from the plaza. There's a great pool, a fantastic sauna and a lovely garden. Rooms at the front have great views and good hot showers; those at the back are cheaper. The owner Fernando speaks English, German and Spanish and is a good source of local information, he also arranges hikes, and tours by open-sided truck to coca fields and waterfalls. There's a free pick-up service (ring from **Totai Tours**) from the plaza and Visa and MasterCard are taken with no commission, also no commission on TCs. The excellent restaurant has a buffet, there's a terrace, a laundry service, high-speed internet access for US$1 per hr, Wi-Fi access, book exchange, cinema room, breakfast US$2, even welding facilities for overland drivers and an express van to La Paz on the new road. The only downside might be that sweaty bikers arrive en masse every day from the 'world's most dangerous road' groups and hog the showers. Highly recommended so be sure to book ahead.

D-G Sol y Luna, a 15-min walk beyond **Hotel Esmeralda**, T7156 1626 (or Maison de la Bolivie, 6 de Agosto 2464, Ed Jardines, La Paz, T02-244 0588, lamaisontour@ acelerate.com), www.solyluna-bolivia.com. A dreamily rustic set-up among verdant woods and flowery gardens, Sol y Luna is a sprawling fairytale place with winding paths connecting well designed wooden 'cottages', a swimming pool and hammocks with stunning views across the valley to the distant mountains. Meals are also available, try their superb Indonesian banquet. Camping US$2 pp by prior booking, shiatsu massage for US$15-20. Sigrid, the owner, speaks English, French, German and Spanish. Highly recommended.

E Bella Vista, Calle Heroes Chaco (2 blocks from main plaza), T7156 9237 (mob). **F** rooms without bath but much smaller. Modern, smart and clean rooms with beautiful views. 2 racquetball courts, pool, bikes for hire, restaurant.

E Don Quijote, a 10-min walk out of town on the road to Coripata, T02-213 6007, quijote@mpoint.com.bo. Restaurant, pool, gardens, TV in rooms, private bathrooms, quiet, English spoken.

E Hostal Kory, at the top of the steps leading down from the plaza. (**F** without bathroom), T02-243 1311. Bang in the middle of town, Kory offers discounts for stays any longer than a couple of days. There's a big pool, a lovely terrace good views, a video room and comfy beds in the smallish rooms. Recommended.

G pp El Cafetal, Miranda, T7193 3979 (mob). A 10-min walk from town, some of which is poorly lit, some of which is not lit at all. Soon after the road starts going downhill there is a turning off on the right, down steps. French-run, great views, clean rooms, friendly,. Also a fantastic restaurant (see Eating, below). Recommended.

G La Residencial Coroico, Calle F Reyos Ortiz. Cheap but worth bargaining further. All rooms share bathrooms. Dark rooms, sagging beds and no great views.

G Residencial de la Torre, Julio Zuazo Cuenca. Friendly and with a flowery courtyard but the clean sparse rooms could do with a lick of paint. No alcoholic drinks.

Chulumani p351

D Huayrani, near the *tranca* just off Calle Junín, T02-213 6351. Cabins for 1-8 people, includes breakfast, pleasant garden, pool, TV.

F Country House, 10 mins' walk southwest from the plaza towards the cemetery. The best backpackers' retreat and a real home-from-home experience, price includes breakfast. A great place to relax in the rustic charm of a family house, swimming pool fed by natural source, stock of 200 videos for hire (US$4.50), restaurant with tasty home cooking, home-grown coffee, jams etc, pool table and cold beer, good views, owner Xavier Sarabia has information on all hikes, arranges trips (see Tours operators below) and is great for a Nazi yarn or 2. No double beds otherwise highly recommended.

F Hostal Familiar Dion, Calle Alianza, just off the plaza, T02-213 6070. Spotless, modern and new rooms, roof terrace, includes breakfast, laundry facilities and use of kitchen. (**G** without bathroom and breakfast).

F Panorama, at top of the hill on Calle Murillo, T02-213 6109. Overpriced for basic rooms although some have views, garden, restaurant and small pool, friendly.

G Alojamiento Danielito, Bolívar. Hot water extra, laundry facilities, good views.

G El Mirador, Plaza Libertad, T02-213 6117. Basic but clean, the restaurant has a nice terrace with great views across to Apa Apa, noisy at weekends from disco, rooms at back without bathroom are cheaper.

Yanakachi p352

F Hotel San Carlos, at the junction entering the village (no sign), T02-223 0088 (La Paz). Rooms 5, 6 and 7 have great views across the valley, clean, hot showers, also offers full board in its restaurant, which is the best place to eat in town.

Puente Villa

D Tamampaya, at Puente Villa cross the Río Unduavi and 30 mins walk upstream, T02-270 6099 (La Paz). In a beautiful setting, this recommended hotel has attractive gardens and pool and birdwatching trails, good rooms with shower, good set meals and à la carte. The price includes breakfast. Camping is possible midweek.

🍴 Eating

Coroico *p349*

Cheap meals can be found at the market, near the plaza on the street beside the post office. Honey is sold throughout the town.

🍴 **Bamboo**, Iturralde. Good Mexican food in an atmospheric little restaurant. Live music some nights with a small cover charge; otherwise usually recorded reggae. Happy hour 1800-1900.

🍴 **El Cafetal**, Miranda, T02-7193 3979 (mob), see Sleeping for directions. French-run, with excellent French cuisine, though a fair walk from the centre of town. Laid-back jazz, good caipirinhas, menu includes pastas, savoury souffles, steak, llama and trout. *Copa cafetal* – ice cream of the house, with fruit, chocolate, cream and nuts. Good value. Recommended.

🍴 **Back-Stube**, next to **Hostal Kory**, T02-7193 5594 (mob), closed Tue. Excellent cakes and German breads, delicious vegetarian lasagne, lots of breakfast options, friendly atmosphere.

🍴 **Pizzeria Italia**, on the plaza. Possibly the best of an unexpected glut of mediocre Italian restaurants.

Cafés

Café de la Senda Verde, Plazuela Julio Zuzo Cuenca, T02-715 32703, daily 0630-1900. The home-roasted Yungas coffee is the highlight in this friendly café on the corner of **Hostal Kory**. Healthy breakfasts, oven-toasted sandwiches and cinnamon rolls also available.

Snack Hawaii, Plaza Manuel Victorio Garcia Lanza. This basic snack bar is open all day, serving breakfasts, sandwiches, burgers, steaks and juices etc. It also changes money.

Chulumani *p351*

🍴 **Chulumani**, overlooking the plaza is the very friendly, with a pleasant, breezy balcony and good *almuerzo*.

🍴 **El Mesón**, just off the plaza, open 1200-1330 only. Good cheap lunches, great views.

🍴 **La Hostería**, on Junin close to the *tranca*, Texan-run, good pizzas and hamburgers.

Yanakachi *p352*

Don Edgar, on the plaza facing the church, has good food and its owner unsurpassed knowledge of local history and hiking trails. See also **Hotel San Carlos**, under Sleeping.

🎉 Festivals

Coroico *p349*

19-22 Oct Colourful 4-day festival, accommodation is hard to find. It is great fun, but it might be an idea to wait a day or two before returning to La Paz, in order to give your driver time to recover.

Chulumani *p351*

Aug Fiesta de San Bartolomé, from 24 Aug for 10 days.

🏔 Activities and tours

Coroico *p349*

Cycling

CXC, Pacheco 79. Good bikes, US$20 for 6 hrs including packed lunch, a bit disorganized but good fun and helpful.

Horse riding

El Relincho, Don Reynaldo, T02-7191 3675/23814 (mob), 100 m past **Hotel Esmeralda** (enquire here, ask for Fernando), US$25 for 4 hrs with lunch.

Tour operators

Eco Adventuras and Inca Land Tours, both on the main plaza. Bala Tours, T03-892 2527, balatours@yahoo.com, and Enin Tours, T03-892 2487, enintours@yahoo.com, of Rurrenabaque, run tours to Guanay by 4WD then boat to Rurrenabaque, with 2 camps along the way, all inclusive, guide and cook, US$140 for 4-6 people.

🚌 Transport

Coroico *p349*

Bus *Micros* to **La Paz** arrive at Calle Yanacachi, beside YPFB station in the Villa Fátima. Companies include: **Turbus Totai** (T02-221 8385), US$2.25, 3 hrs, several daily 0730-1630; **Flota Yungueña** (T02-221 3513; on the plaza in Coroico); worth booking in advance. Extra services run on Sun. It can be difficult to book journeys to La Paz on holidays and on Sun evenings/Mon mornings (though these are good times for hitching).

To **Caranavi**, direct bus at 1300, continues to Rurrenabaque arriving at 0700 next day, US$8. Buses and pick-ups run from Yolosa to **Rurrenabaque** via Caranavi, daily at 1500 with **Yungueña**, except Sun at 1730, with **Turbus Totai**, US$8.75, 13-15 hrs, they will take you down to Yolosa to catch the bus from La Paz. To get to **Yolosa** from Coroico, take a pick-up from outside the market on Sagágnaga and run every 15 mins.

Chulumani *p351*
Bus Buses to the Villa Fátima district of **La Paz** leave from the San Bartolomé office on the plaza; *micros* from the *tranca*. **Trans San Bartolomé** (Virgen del Carmen 1750, Villa Fátima, La Paz, T02-221 1674), daily 0800-1600 or when full, 4 hrs, US$2.50. **Trans Arenas**, daily 0730-1800, US$2.25. **Trans 24 de Agosto** (15 de Abril 408 y San Borja, La Paz, T02-221 0607), 0600-1600, when full.

❶ Directory

Coroico *p349*
Banks Banco Mercantil, Central Plaza, Mon-Fri 0830-1230, 1430-1830, Sat 0900-1230, cash advances (no commission) on MasterCard and Visa. Prodem, J Suazo Cuenca, on main plaza, changes US$ cash,

cash advance on Visa or MasterCard only (no debit cards), 5% commission. **Internet** Carlos, who lives on Calle Caja de Agua, T/F02-213 6041, has an internet café, will exchange Spanish for English lessons. **Language classes** Siria León Domínguez, Julio Zuazo Cuenca 062, T02-7195 5431, siria_leon@yahoo.com.es. US$3.60 per hr, also has rooms for rent and makes silver jewellery, excellent English.
Medical services Hospital: T02-213 6002, the best in the Yungas, good malaria advice. **Police** East side of main plaza.
Post office on plaza. **Telephone** Entel, on Sagárnaga next to Flota Yungueña, for international and local calls. Cotel, next to church, phones, public TV.

Chulumani *p351*
Banks On Plaza Libertad, Banco Unión, changes US$100 or more only in cash and TCs (5% commission), Mon-Fri 0830-1200, 1430-1800. Cooperativa San Bartolomé, changes cash Mon-Fri 0800-1200, 1400-1700, Sat-Sun 0700-1200. **Internet** In tourist office, US$1.05 per hr.

Northern Amazon

The Bolivian Amazon accounts for over two-thirds of the country. This vast region, covered by steamy jungles and flat savannah lands, is bursting with all manner of wildlife. Beni Department alone has over half the country's birds and mammals. This natural paradise is also a prime target for corrupt and ruthless logging companies. But though destruction of forest and habitat is proceeding at an alarming rate, parts of the region are opening up to ecotourism and wildlife expeditions are becoming increasingly popular, most notably around Rurrenabaque, which can be reached from La Paz by road or air. Two of Bolivia's newest, and most authentic, ecotourism ventures are Mapajo, in the Reserva Biosferica Pilon Lajas, and Chalalán Ecolodge, in the neighbouring Parque Nacional Madidi. Both are owned and run by the indigenous population. Madidi, one of Bolivia's newest preservation areas, boasts the greatest biodiversity of any protected area on earth and a visit to Chalalán Eco-Lodge is now one of the country's top attractions. There are plans to extend the protection of Bolivia's precious tropical lowlands in the next decade and it is hoped that the influx of tourists will speed up the process. ▸▸ *For Sleeping, Eating and other listings, see pages 359-362.*

Rurrenabaque ●❷▲❸❶ ▸▸ *pp359-362.*

→ *Phone code: 03. Colour map 3, B2. Population: 10,000.*
Rurrenabaque, or 'Rurre' as the locals call it, is approximately 200 km northeast of La Paz, on the banks of the Río Beni, with San Buenaventura on the opposite bank. Rurre is an astonishingly beautiful place whatever your interests: whether it's the lush Amazon jungle, the savannah-like pampas, the sub-tropical lowlands, or the

wonderful eco-lodges upriver in the national parks, this is the logical starting point. In spite of the usually humid climate, the town has a charming quality, and even if your itinerary doesn't include one of the many tours around the area, just walking about the town itself is an unusual experience. It is with good reason that the settlement is considered the most picturesque in the Beni. The hotels almost all have hammocks, there are plenty of good bars and restaurants, an interesting **market**, and even a **spa**, complete with sauna. The local **swimming pool** is excellent and, although most come and go on tours fairly rapidly, it's also very easy to spend a few days here doing very little. The only real drawback is the occasional flooding of the Río Beni. It rarely overflows its banks, but when it does the place becomes a real mess.

Ins and outs

Getting there The new **airport** ① 1½ km from town, receives four daily flights from La Paz on **Amazonas**, and one from Trinidad. A motorcycle taxi into town costs US$1. Expect delays and cancellations in the dry season and severe delays in the rainy

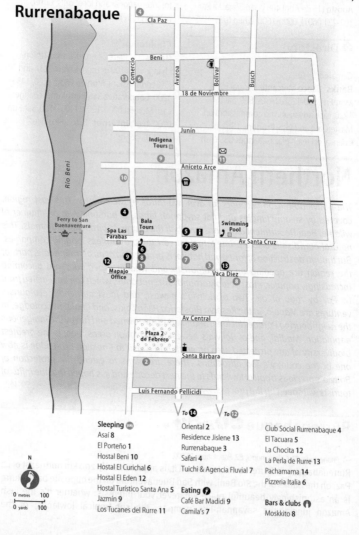

Rurrenabaque

Sleeping ⌂
Asaí 8
El Porteño 1
Hostal Beni 10
Hostal El Curichal 6
Hostal El Eden 12
Hostal Turístico Santa Ana 5
Jazmín 9
Los Tucanes del Rurre 11

Oriental 2
Residence Jislene 13
Rurrenabaque 3
Safari 4
Tuichi & Agencia Fluvial 7

Eating ●
Café Bar Madidi 9
Camila's 7

Club Social Rurrenabaque 4
El Tacuara 5
La Chocita 12
La Perla de Rurre 13
Pachamama 14
Pizzeria Italia 6

Bars & clubs ●
Moskkito 8

🝔 Rurre tours dos and don'ts

→ Insist that your tour be conducted in an environmentally sound manner.

→ Set the price in advance and make sure it includes all expenses.

→ Go with an established company as competition is forcing down prices and, consequently, quality and standards of guiding.

→ Most groups are of between five and 10 people – either find a group before choosing a tour agency or turn up and put yourself on the list. If you arrive early in the morning you probably won't have too much problem getting on a tour straight away, if you so wish.

→ The best season is July-October. Avoid trips during the rainy season; the humidity and insects will conspire to annoy even the most enthusiastic adventurer, and there are far fewer opportunities to see animals.

→ Take insect repellent – lots of it– to ward off sandflies and mosquitoes.

→ Pampas tours may involve wading through knee-deep water; wear appropriate shoes.

→ The tourist office can advise on the quality of tours.

→ It is cheaper to book tours in Rurrenabaque than La Paz and mosquito nets are much cheaper than in La Paz.

→ One-day trips are a waste of time as it takes three hours to reach the jungle.

season. All buses arrive and leave at Calle Junín. Buses from La Paz leave from the Villa Fátima district, on Calle Santa Cruz. ➤➤ *For details, see Transport, page 361.*

Getting around Unlike most Bolivian towns, the restaurants and offices in Rurre are not centred around the plaza (2 de Febrero), but instead are clustered together a few blocks north along Calle Vaca Diez and Santa Cruz. Just north of Calle Santa Cruz a small branch of the river effectively divides the town in half. The vast majority of businesses, including the many tour operators, are south of the estuary. Both of the town's markets are above it: the main market, on Calle Avaroa, between Anecito Arce and the old tributary; and the farmer's market, two blocks north and three blocks east

Tourist information Rurrenabaque's **tourist office** ① *Av Santa Cruz, at the corner of Bolivar, 0800-2000, and often later*, is probably the most helpful in the whole of Bolivia. The ranking system it has for tour companies has been a resounding success, meticulously quantifying customers' thoughts on every conceivable aspect of tours and charting the results in massive displays on the wall.

Tours from Rurre

Many agencies (see page 361) offer jungle tours from Rurrenabaque. Anyone wanting to join a tour should investigate carefully what the various companies are offering. The tourist office is a great place to start and, if you can, speak to people returning from tours. Tour prices have been set by the government. Jungle tours cost US$20-30 per person per day all inclusive, pampas tours US$25-35 per day. Acute competition means that some companies cut their prices to be even lower than this, but quality suffers. The usual minimum group size is three (four in the low season).

Pampas tours These are usually four days, three nights and involve a bumpy, dusty, four-hour jeep ride at either end. They also involve boat travel in long canoes, though this is a lot smoother and more enjoyable. The pampas is wetland savannah to the northeast of Rurre and there's little or no dry land at all – accommodation usually consists of wooden huts on stilts and most moving around is done in boats. It is an eerily beautiful and peaceful place, with watery wildlife sounds all around, fireflies at night. Expect to see caiman, monkeys, all sorts of birds and probably pink river dolphins. Anaconda are harder to see, and though you may be promised piranha-fishing, this will probably be a stop-off at a pond on the way home. Generally wildlife is easier to see here than in the denser vegetation of the jungle. However, there are also more mosquitoes and sandflies.

Jungle tours These offer the advantage of being able to leave Rurrenabaque in a boat and travel up the beautiful river Beni. Accommodation is either in special purpose-built, and relatively luxurious camps (such as **Mapajo** or **Chalalán**, page 360) or tents. Note that not all trips offer English-speaking guides and that accommodation is usually spartan (bring insect repellent, mosquito netting, toilet paper and a torch).

Pilón Lajas Biosphere Reserve and Indigenous Territory

ⓘ *Official headquarters are at the park's northernmost point, less than 1 km south of Rurrenabaque, US$6 pp. Contact Sernap's representative, Juan Carlos Miranda, Calle Campero, corner with Calle Busch, Rurrenabaque, T03-892 2245, www.sernap.gov.bo.*

Beyond the Beni River in the southeast runs the Pilón Lajas Biosphere Reserve and Indigenous Territory, home to several native groups. Together with Madidi, it constitutes approximately 60,000 sq km, one of the largest systems of protected land in the neotropics. Unfortunately, much of this land is under pressure from logging interests, and the government has allocated precious little resources to combat encroachment. The Pilón Lajas Biosphere Reserve and Indigenous Territory was set up under the auspices of UNESCO in 1977. The reserve has one of the continent's most intact Amazonian rainforest ecosystems, as well as an incredible array of tropical forest animal life. NGOs have been working with the people of La Unión, Playa Ancha, Nuevos Horizontes and El Cebó to develop sustainable forestry, fish farming, beekeeping, cattle ranching, *artesanía* and even fruit wines; tours are run by **Donato Tours**, which include lunch and transport. ▶▶ *See Activities and tours, page 361.*

Parque Nacional Madidi ⬤ ▶▶ *pp359-362. Colour map3, B2.*

Bolivia's Madidi National Park is one of the world's most important conservation areas, and is, along with Amboró and Noel Kempff to the east, possibly the most biodiverse of all protected areas on the planet's surface. Parque Nacional Madidi in the La Paz Department, is now roughly four times the size of Amboró, at 1,895,740 ha (almost half the size of Holland). A primary Amazonian watershed, like Amboró, it also contains a pristine ecosystem, one that is home to nearly 50% of all the mammal species known in the Western Hemisphere. It also provides shelter for more than a third of the known amphibian and bird species in the Americas. At last count, almost 1200 different species of bird had been identified, representing more than 90 % of all known types in Bolivia. It also has what may well be the largest number of plants anywhere in the world, with almost 6000 classified. By comparison the continental United States and Canada account for some 700 species. Birdlife ranges from minute hummingbirds to the Andean Condor, with a wingspan of 3 m, and the magnificent harpy eagle, the most powerful member of the raptor family. Mammals include: 10 species of primates, including the large spider and red howler monkeys; five species of cat, with healthy populations of jaguar and puma; giant anteaters and a myriad of lesser-known species. Reptiles are represented most spectacularly by the anaconda and the black caiman, which can reach lengths of 9 m and 6 m respectively. There are also several types of venomous snake, the most feared being the bushmaster and the fer de lance. Chances of encountering such snakes are very low, but caution is required.

There are lots of guides and tour agencies in Rurrenabaque offering tours to Madidi with widely varied and fluctuating standards. Most of these offer trips for small groups at US$25 per person per day. Beyond the usual three- to five-day jungle tour it's possible to arrange a customized itinerary for the same daily rate. It's hard to recommend agencies, other than the operation at **Chalalán Eco-Lodge,** as the standards vary between tours and between guides. Ask around when in Rurrenabaque and ask travellers recently returned from trips for recommendations.

⊖ Sleeping

Rurrenabaque *p355, map p356*
Most hotels in Rurrenabaque are safe, good and relatively inexpensive. Most offer laundry and breakfast (usually not included in the price), although only a few take credit cards. The better ones have ceiling fans, almost none have air conditioning. In high season hotels fill up very quickly.
C **Safari**, Calle Comercio, T03-892 2410, hotel-safari@hotmail.com. At the far north end of town, a 10-min walk along Calle Comercio from the centre, this relatively expensive but lovely hotel has a clean swimming pool sunk into immaculate and extensive green lawns. Palm trees create shade and all rooms have wooden floors and firm comfortable beds. Especially attractive family rooms have front doors that open onto the lawn, and double beds upstairs. The restaurant is good and the hotel accepts Visa. Prices include breakfast. Perfect for a small dose of luxury after a long hard tour. Recommended.
F **Asaí**, Calle Vaca Díez, T03-892 2439. Rooms have big bathrooms with electric showers, clean and quiet. There's a laundry area, a courtyard with chairs and tables. Breakfast is an extra US$2.50.
F **Hostal Beni**, Calle Comercio (near ferry), T03-892 2408. A big hotel on the other side of the stream, the colonial-style Beni has lots of stairs and landings, a/c and good big wooden beds. Accepts credit cards. Perhaps Rurre's quietest accommodation.
F **Hostal El Eden**, at the southern end of Calle Bolívar, T03-892 2452. All on the ground floor at the far southern end of town, El Eden is good value and has a good sandy area out the back with a few hammocks and tables. Rooms have fans, wardrobes and,

mostly, private bathrooms (**G** without). Price includes breakfast.
F **Oriental**, on Plaza 2 de Febrero, T03-892 2401. Oriental has a long courtyard leading into a garden strung with comfortable hammocks. Showers in private bathrooms are electric. A simple breakfast is included, but prices are higher than in other comparable hotels in town. However, it's very cheap (**G** pp) without bathroom or breakfast.
F **Rurrenabaque**, corner of Vaca Díez and Bolívar, T03-892 2481. Painted bright yellow and turquoise, Rurrenabaque, away from the riverfront, has a good veranda and comfortable rooms with private bathrooms and hot water, laundry and cooking facilities.
G **El Porteño**, Calle Comercio and Vaca Díez, T03-892 2558. This central hotel has an attractive courtyard with hammocks and a starfruit tree, from which, if you're lucky, you'll get a welcoming glass of *carambola* juice on arrival. Some rooms are especially big, with TV, private bathrooms, hot water, firm comfortable beds, ceiling fans and even wardrobes. The owner speaks no English and you may have to put up with the late night sounds of soft rock from **Moskkito Bar.**
G pp **Hostal El Curichal**, Calle Comercio 1490, T03-892 2647, elcurichal@hotmail.com. Nice courtyard, hammocks, laundry and small kitchen facilities, helpful staff, will change TCs and money.
G **Hostal Turístico Santa Ana**, 1 block north of the plaza on Avaroa, T03-892 2399. Fairly basic but adequate rooms look out onto a colourfully verdant garden courtyard. Beds have thin mattresses and the electric showers are not great. Laundry and parking both available. Mixed reports.

For an explanation of sleeping and eating price codes used in this guide, see inside the front cover. Other relevant information is found in Essentials, see pages 31-35.

Sorata, Yungas & Northern Amazon Northern Amazon Listings

G pp **Alojamiento Jislene**, Calle Comercio (north of Calle Aniceto Arce), T03-892 2526. Good basic cheap choice with hot water, fan, mosquito nets, free tea and coffee. Excellent breakfast of omelettes or pancakes with fruit (if booked in advance), and a great views over river. Friendly, popular with travellers but a fair way north of the centre.

G **Jazmín**, Calle Comercio between Aniceto Arce and Avaroa, T03-892 2337. Variety of rooms, some with bath, good value, fan, cold showers, hammock space. Recommended.

G pp **Los Tucanes del Rurre**, Aniceto Arce between Avaroa and Bolívar, http://hotel-tucanes.com. Rooms with electric fan and shower (hot water for 10 mins per guest), includes breakfast, clean, pleasant.

G **Tuichi**, Calle Avaroa and Santa Cruz, T7198 3582 (mobile). Cheaper without bath (shared bathrooms are dirty), cold showers, luggage storage, kitchen and laundry facilities, fan, a sad reflection of its former reputation.

Pilón Lajas *p358*

L **Mapajo**, Mapajo Ecoturismo Indígena, Calle Comercio, Rurrenabaque, T03-892 2317, www.mapajo.com. A community-run eco-lodge 2 hrs by boat from Rurrenabaque has 4 *cabañas* without electricity (take a torch and batteries), cold showers and a dining room serving traditional meals. Minimum stay 4 days/3 nights (from US$220). You can visit the local community, walk in the forest, go birdwatching, etc. Take insect repellent, long trousers and strong footwear. Recommended.

Parque Nacional Madidi *p358*

LL **Chalalán Ecolodge**, 5 hrs upriver from Rurrenabaque, San José de Uchupiamonas, www.chalalan.com. Reservations: Calle Sagárnaga 189, corner with Murillo, Edif Shopping Doryan, p 2, oficina 35, T/F02-231 1451; or in Rurrenabaque, Calle Comercio s/n, Zona Central (½ block from Plaza), T03-892 2419, info@chalalan.com. This is Bolivia's top ecotourism project, founded by the local community, Conservation International and the Interamerican Development Bank, and now has a well-deserved international reputation. Accommodation is in thatched cabins, and activities include fantastic wildlife-spotting and birdwatching, guided and self-guided trails, river and lake activities, and relaxing in pristine jungle surroundings.

A 5-day trip includes travel time from La Paz: tours cost about US$100 per person per night, 3-night stay US$290, discounts for larger groups or longer stays. Air fares US$110 extra.

A pp **Wizard's Mountain Jungle Lodge** (Cerro del Brujo), near Madidi and the Tacana community, T02-279 1742, www.bolivia mistica.com. Ecolodge offering jungle and pampas tours, wide range of therapies, shamanic rituals, and a good canopy walkway, price is for 2 days/1 night, many other options available, including community tourism at **Villa Alcira** in the Tacana community.

B **San Miguel del Bala**, 45-min boat trip up river from Rurrenabaque, T/F03-892 2394, www.sanmigueldelbala.com. 1- to 4-day itineraries based at Tacana community, living in private huts. A good choice.

🍴 Eating

Rurrenabaque *p355, map p356*
For a town of its size, Rurre has a large number of places to eat. Though none are 5-star, and only the pizza restaurant next door to the **Moskkito Bar** accepts credit cards, many are excellent and almost all are good value. There are also plenty of places offering chicken and the market, of course, is fantastic for fruit juices and good *almuerzos*. For the latter expect a lot of roasted chicken and to pay US$0.75-1.20. Otherwise, from the street stalls along Calle Aniceto Arce on Fri and Sat nights, join the locals scoffing *salchipapas* (a kind of hot dog) with fries and far too much mayonnaise and ketchup.

🍴🍴 **La Perla de Rurre**, corner of Bolivar and Vaca Diéz. With a big, walled courtyard under a large shady tree decked in coloured lights at night, La Perla is Rurre's smartest restaurant. Meaty and fishy menu.

🍴🍴 **Pizzeria Italia**, Calle Comercio, T03-892 2611. Next to Moskkito, the restaurant is open to the bar next door, so you can watch games of pool as you eat. 25 types of pizza, though many seem to have the same ingredients in a different order. 3 sizes, medium is about enough for one. A young atmosphere and a creatively translated menu.

🍴 **Camila's Restaurant**, Calle Santa Cruz and Avaroa. Good restaurant, next to Camilla's internet café. Lots of outside tables, plants, jungle murals and 1980s music. A big menu is good for fish dishes. Service can be slow.

There's a separate *heladeria* just down the road towards the river.

¶ **Club Social Rurrenabaque**, 1 block north of Calle Santa Cruz, on Calle Avaroa. A pleasant place to sip a cold beer whilst overlooking the river but don't miss their fishburgers and jugs of fruit juice.

¶ **El Tacuara**, Calle Santa Cruz. Opposite Camila's, in the middle of town. Good wide-ranging menu: soups, omelettes, pasta, meat and fish. Good for people-watching.

¶ **La Chocita**, just south of the ferry stop by the river, next to **La Cabaña**. A riverside fish restaurant with a few red-clothed tables outside under awning. Simple but popular, especially for the *almuerzo*.

Bars and cafés
Butterfly Pub, Calle Comercio. Good pasta and fish dishes, friendly atmosphere and bar outside.

Café Bar Madidi, Calle Comercio. Has little wooden tables under an awning almost opposite Mosskkito. 9 coffees, 11 juices and terrible MOR rock. Some vegetarian dishes.

Moskkito Bar, Calle Comercio. With rock music and pool tables (and now an attached t-shirt shop), the Mosskkito bar is a good place to drink away an evening in the company of new-found friends. Lots of beer and tales of large anacondas. You can also order in pizzas from the restaurant next door. Happy hour with half-price cocktails 1900-2100. Most popular gringo hangout in town.

Pachamama, Calle Avaroa Sud, T03-892 2620, open 1200-2230. At the southern end of town, a friendly café-bar run by an English/Bolivian couple with snacks, a balcony with a view over the river, a film room, playstation, internet, table football and a book exchange.

▲ Activities and tours

Rurrenabaque *p355, map p356*
Tour operators
Agencia Fluvial, Hotel Tuichi, T03-892 2372, runs jungle tours on the Río Tuichi, normally 4 days, US$100 (including food, transport and mosquito nets), but shorter by arrangement. Also 3-day 'Pampas Tours' on a boat to Río Yacuma, US$90. Tico Tudela has opened **Hotel de la Pampa** near Lago

Bravo, 2½ hrs from Rurrenabaque, as a base for visiting Lago Rogagua (birds) and Río Yacuma. Fully inclusive tours (meals and accommodation) US$40 per person per day.
Aguila Tours, Av Avaroa, T03-892 2478. Jungle and pampas tours. Can be booked **Eco Jungle Tours**, Calle Sagárnaga, La Paz.
Bala Tours, Av Santa Cruz, T03-892 2527, www.balatours.com. Arranges 'Pampas' and 'Jungle' tours, good base camp in the Pampas. Recommended.
Donato Tours, Calle A Arce, T03-892 2571, donatotours@hotmail.com. Regular tours and 'a day for the community' with trips to Pilón Lajas.
Indígena Tours, Abaroa s/n, T03-892 2091. Good value tours, food and lodging, helpful.
Mashaquipe Tours, Calle Comercio s/n between Santa Cruz and Vaca, T7113 8286, www.mashaquipe.com. Run by an indigenous, Tacana family, with a camp in Madidi, knowledgeable guides (some female), US$25 per day.
Turismo Ecológico Social (**TES**), Av Santa Cruz, next to tourist information office, T7128 9664 (mobile), turismoecologico social@hotmail.com. Day tours to 4 local communities and the Pilón Lajas buffer zone, US$25 including lunch and guides.

● Transport

Rurrenabaque *p355, map p356*
Air A motorcycle taxi to the airport costs US$1. Flights with **Amazonas** (Calle Santa Cruz, T03-892 2472), 3 daily to **La Paz** (US$62), also to **Trinidad, Santa Cruz, Riberalta, Guayaramerín, San Borja** and **Cobija**. Book all flights as early as possible and buy onward ticket on arrival. Check flight times in advance; they change frequently. Airport tax US$2.
Bus To/from **La Paz** via Caranavi daily at 1100 with **Flota Yungueña** and **Totai**; 18-20 hrs, US$8.20. Returns at 1100. **Flota Unificada** leaves La Paz (also from Villa Fátima) on Tue, Thu, Fri, Sat at 1030, same price. Continues to **Riberalta** and **Guayaramerín**; return departure time depends on road conditions. **Flota Yungueña** also has a 1030 bus which leaves Villa Fátima and continues to Riberalta and Guayaramerín. Rurrenebaque-**Riberalta** should take 14-16 hrs, but can take 6 days or

more in the wet. Take lots of food, torch and be prepared to work. To **Trinidad**, Tue, Thu, Sat, Sun at 2230 with **Trans Guaya** via **Yucumo** and **San Borja**, US$18.

⊙ Directory

Rurrenabaque *p355, map p356*
Banks Prodem, Av Comercio 21 between Vaca Díez and Santa Cruz, T03-892 2616. Changes US$ cash at fair rates, cash advance on Visa or MasterCard, 5% commission. Bala

Tours will give cash advance against credit cards at 7.5% commission. TCs can be used as payment for tours, but are difficult to cash. Try **Agencia Fluvial**, 5% commission. Most agencies accept credit cards for tours.
Internet Camila's, next to restaurant of same name on Santa Cruz, US$3 per hr.
Post office Next to taxi station on Calle Avaroa and Junín, open Sat. **Telephone** Entel, Calle Comercio, 2 blocks north of plaza; also at Santa Cruz y Bolívar. **Punto** Entel, Calle Avaroa and Campero.

Trinidad and southern Beni

The hot and humid capital of the lowland Beni Department, Trinidad has the look and feel of Santa Cruz some 40 years ago. Built as a Jesuit mission on the banks of the Río Ramoré, it was relocated in 1769 due to flooding and is now 14 km from it's original location. Rivers remain an important form of transport and cattle-ranching is the biggest regional industry. The main reason to come here is to visit the is to visit the smaller communities and remote jungle reserves, or as a stopover between Santa Cruz and Rurrenabeque. ▶ *For Sleeping, Eating and other listings, see pages 363-364.*

Trinidad → *Phone code: 03. Colour map 3, B3. Population: 60,000. Altitude: 327 m.*

Ins and outs The **airport** ⓘ *1 km northwest of town, T03-462 0678*; receives daily flights from La Paz, and also flights from Cochabamba and Santa Cruz. Motorcycle taxi US$1.20 to the centre. The **bus terminal** is on Rómulo Mendoza, between Beni and Victor Pinto, nine blocks east of the main plaza; motorbike taxis will take people with backpacks from the bus station to the centre for US$0.45. A motorbike taxi from Trinidad is US$1.30. Buses from San Ignacio de Moxos arrive and depart from their own terminal on Avenida Mamoré and Santa Cruz. For the hardy travellers it's also possible to arrive by cargo boat along the Río Mamoré from Guayaramerín. There are two **ports**, Almacén and Varador, check at which one your boat is docking. The **tourist office** ⓘ *Prefectural building, Joaquín de Sierra y La Paz, ground floor, T03-462 1305, ext 116,* is very helpful. ▶ *See Transport, page 364.*

Sights Trinidad vies with Iquitos in Peru as the motorcycle and scooter capital of South America. The plaza resembles a race track at night. Sometimes you'll see improbable numbers on one bike – entire families, including grandparents and distant cousins. In fact, the only people who walk here are the tourists. If you do manage to converse with the locals, on their way to or from their bikes, you'll find them open and friendly.

You can hire a motorbike or jeep to go to the **river**, which offers good swimming on the opposite bank. Boat hire costs US$5. Five kilometres from town is the **Laguna Suárez**, with plenty of wildlife. The water is very warm, and near the café with the jetty, where the locals swim, the bathing is safe. Elsewhere there are stingrays and caiman.

San Ignacio de Moxos → *Colour map 3, B3.*

San Ignacio de Moxos, 90 km west of Trinidad, is known as the folklore capital of the Beni Department. It's a quiet town with a mainly indigenous population; 60% are *Macheteros*, who speak their own language. San Ignacio still maintains the traditions of the Jesuit missions with big fiestas, especially during Holy Week and the **Fiesta del Santo Patrono de Moxos**, the largest festival in the lowlands, at the end of July.

Magdalena and Bella Vista → *Colour map 3, A4.*

A road from Trinidad heads northeast to **San Ramón** and then turns east to **Magdalena**, a charming little town on the banks of the Río Itonama. It was founded by Jesuit missionaries in 1719, made a city in 1911 and is now the capital of the province of Iténez. There is a 45-minute weekly flight with **TAM** from Trinidad. Beef is the main product of the region and the river is the means of transporting cattle and other agricultural produce. Some 7 km upriver is the **Laguna La Baíqui**, which is popular for fishing. There is an abundance of wildlife and birds in the surrounding area. The city's main festival, Santa María Magdalena, is held on 22 July and attracts many groups and visitors from all over Beni and beyond.

East of Magdalena on the Río Blanco, **Bella Vista** is considered by many to be one of the prettiest spots in northeast Bolivia. Lovely white sandbanks line the Río San Martín, which is 10 minutes by canoe from the boat moorings below town. Local boatmen will take you there, and collect you later by arrangement. The sandbanks are also accessible by motorcycle. Check that the sand is not covered by water after heavy rain. Other activities are swimming and canoeing in the Río San Martín, and the countryside is good for cycling. There are three well-stocked shops on the plaza, but none sells mosquito repellent or spray/coils. Bring your own as there are many mosquitoes at the beginning of the wet season (apply repellent before leaving the plane). There is no bank or Entel office. There are flights to Bella Vista from Magdalena or Trinidad, but no fixed schedule.

● Sleeping

Trinidad *p362*
B **Gran Moxos**, Av 6 de Agosto y Santa Cruz, T03-462 3305, F462 2240. Includes breakfast, a/c, fridge bar, cable TV, phone, good restaurant, accepts credit cards.
D-E **Hostal Aguahi**, Bolívar y Santa Cruz, T03-462 5570. A/c, fridge, comfortable, swimming pool in pleasant garden.
D-E **Monte Verde**, 6 de Agosto 76 and Av 18 de Noviembre, T03-462 2750. With or without a/c, fridge bar, includes breakfast, owner speaks English. Recommended.
E **Copacabana**, Calle Thomas Wellington and Vaca Díez, 3 blocks from plaza, T03-462 2811, copabeni@yahoo.com. Good value, though some beds uncomfortable, F pp without bath, helpful staff.
E-F **Hostal Jarajorechi**, Av 6 de Agosto y 27 de Mayo, T03-462 1716. With bath and breakfast, comfortable, ecotourism centre offers jungle trips, equipment and transport hire.
G **Paulista**, Av 6 de Agosto 36, T03-462 0018. Comfortable, good restaurant.

San Ignacio de Moxos *p362*
There are inexpensive *residencias* (F-G), all on and around the main plaza. The Hotel Plaza is perhaps the best of the lot, followed by the Hotel San Ignacio, Residencial Don Jaoquín and Residencial 22 de Agosto.

Magdalena *p363*
C **Internacional**, T03-886 2210, info@hwzinc.com. With breakfast, pools, beautiful setting. Also basic hotels.

Bella Vista *p363*
G **Hotel Pescador**, in the centre of the village. Owner Guillermo Esero Gómez very helpful and knowledgeable about the area, shared bath, provides meals for guests, offers excursions.
Hotel Tucunaré, T03-886 9100. Phone ahead for price. A new ecotourist spot along the banks of the Río San Martín, with gas- and electric-fitted *cabañas*. Offers local excursions. Children under 12 not admitted.

● Eating

Trinidad *p362*
There are several good fish restaurants in Barrio Pompeya, south of plaza across river.
♥♥ **Club Social 18 de Noviembre**, N Suárez y Vaca Díez on plaza. Good lunch for US$1.35, lively, popular with locals.
♥♥ **Pescadería El Moro**, Bolívar 707 y Natusch. Excellent fish.
♥ **La Casona**, Plaza Ballivián. Good pizzas and set lunch, closed Tue.

¶ **La Estancia**, Ibare, between Muibe and Velarde, Barrio Pompeya. Excellent steaks. **Heladería Oriental**, on plaza. Good coffee, ice-cream, cakes, popular with locals.

▲ Activities and tours

Trinidad *p362*
Most agents offer excursions to local *estancias* and jungle tours down river to Amazonia. Most *estancias* can also be reached independently in 1 hr by hiring a motorbike.
Amazonia Holiday, 6 de Agosto 680, T03-462 5732, F462 2806. Good service.
Fremen, Cipriano Barace 332, T03-462 2276, www.andes-amazonia.com. Run speed boat trips along the Mamoré and Ibare rivers and to Parque Nacional Isiboro Sécure, US$80 per day; their **Flotel Reina de Enin** offers tours of more than 1 day, US$80 per person per day, good food.
Moxos, 6 de Agosto 114, T03-462 1141, turmoxos@sauce.ben.entelnet.bo. Recommended.
Tarope Tours, 6 de Agosto 57, T/F03-462 1468. For flights.

⊙ Transport

Trinidad *p362*
Air Taxi to airport US$1.20. Daily flights with Amazonas (18 de Noviembre 267, T03-462 2426) to **La Paz, Rurrenabaque, San Borja, Riberalta, Guayaramerín, Cobija** and **Santa Cruz**. LAB (Santa Cruz 322, T03-462 1277) flies to **Cochabamba**. See note about LAB on page 28. TAM, Calle Bolivar and Av Santa Cruz, T4622 2363 (mob), flies to **La Paz** and **Santa Cruz**.

Bus Motorbike taxis run from the main plaza to the bus station, US$0.45. Several *flotas* daily to/from **La Paz** via San Borja and Caranavi, 20-21 hrs, depart 1730, US$17.50. To **Santa Cruz** (12 hrs in dry season, US$5.80) and **Cochabamba** (US$11.60), with Copacabana, Mopar and Bolívar at 1700, 1730 and 1800; irregular morning service (generally 0900). Trinidad to Casarabe is paved and Santa Cruz to El Puente; otherwise gravel surface on all

sections of unpaved road. To **Rurrenabaque** (US$18), **Riberalta** (US$21.15) and **Guayaramerín** (US$23), connecting with bus to **Cobija**; Guaya Tours Sun, Mon, Thu, Fri at 1030; road often impassable in wet season, at least 24 hrs to Rurrenabaque.

Ferry Cargo boats down the Río Mamoré to **Guayaramerín** take passengers, 3-4 days, assuming no breakdowns, best organized from Puerto Varador (speak to the Port Captain). *Argos* is recommended as friendly, US$22 pp, take water, fresh fruit, toilet paper and ear-plugs; only for the hardy traveller.

San Ignacio de Moxos *p362*
Bus Trinidad-San Borja bus stops at the **Donchanta** restaurant for lunch, otherwise difficult to find transport to **San Borja**. Minibus to **Trinidad** daily at 0730 from plaza, also *camionetas*, check times before.

Magdalena *p363*
Air TAM office on main plaza.

Road An unpaved road goes to Trinidad via San Ramón (pick-up US$10.50), passable only in the dry season. Magdalena to **San Ramón** takes 6 hrs on motorbike taxi, US$16.

Bella Vista *p363*
Bus There are daily buses to **Magdalena** (except in the rainy season), 2½ hrs, US$2.

⊙ Directory

Trinidad *p362*
Banks Banco Mercantil, J de Sierra, near plaza. Changes cash and TCs, cash on Visa. Banco Ganadero, Plaza Ballivián. Visa agent. Street changers on 6 de Agosto (US$ only). Banco Nacional de Bolivia, Plaza Ballivián. Banco Unión, Av Cipriano Barace. **Post office and telephone** In same building at Av Barace, just off plaza, daily till 1930. There are several *cabinas* on Av 6 de Agosto.

Magdalena *p363*
Banks Banco Union, Plaza Principal, no ATM.

Central and Southern Highlands

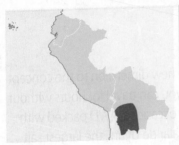

Footprint features

Introduction

Bolivia's extremities add a whole new dimension to the concept of remote. In the far southwest, you can travel for hours without seeing another soul, save for the occasional 4WD packed with tourists heading to or from the Salar de Uyuni, the largest salt lake in the world and biggest attraction in these parts. People also go out of their way to travel here for the dream-like landscapes, peppered with smoking volcanoes, kaleidoscopic lakes full of flamingos and belching geysers.

Equally surreal, but in a more sinister way, is the experience of burrowing down into the bowels of the aptly-named Cerro Rico (Rich Mountain), a pink-hued colossus that has, during its 400-plus years of silver mining, devoured many hundreds of thousands of indigenous slaves as well as turning Potosí into a booming, 17th-century version of Las Vegas, before the lodes wore thin and the city went bust. A few hours away is the distinctly soigné Sucre, famed for its whiter than white beauty and, nearby, is the greatest concentration of dinosaur footprints in the world, hundreds of them, all within the perimeter fence of the local cement factory.

Further south, Tarija is the country's wine centre in an isolated and little-visited area with a very agreeable climate. Tupiza is a mining town turned popular traveller's destination, in a verdant valley surrounded by a dramatic desert landscape. Nearby San Vincente is where Butch Cassidy and the Sundance Kid met their end.

★ Don't miss …

1 **Dancing with the devil**… and everyone else too at the Oruro Carnival, one of Latin America's greatest celebrations, page 370.

2 **The largest and highest salt lake in the world** Drive across the Salar de Uyuni on your way to kaleidoscopic soda lakes, erupting geysers and weird rock formations, page 375.

3 **The trail of the Wild West outlaws** Follow in the footsteps of Butch Cassidy and the Sundance Kid to their final resting place, page 383.

4 **Cerro Rico** Dig deep with the miners and explore the 16th century mine-workings here at 'Rich Mountain', which is said to have produced enough silver to pave a road all the way to Madrid, page 397.

5 **Torotoro National Park** Go wild in the country and explore the deep canyons, waterfalls and dinosaur tracks in the wonderfully off-the-beaten track reserve, page 410.

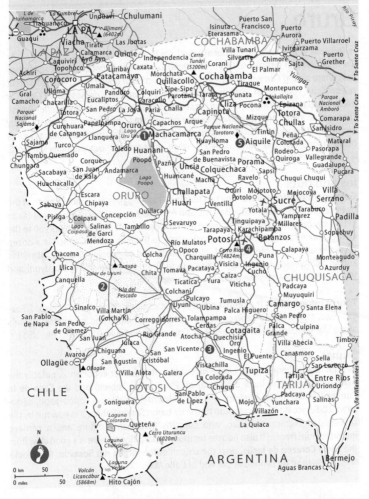

Southern Altiplano

The remote southwestern corner of Bolivia stretches from the mining centre of Oruro, south to the borders of Chile and Argentina. There would appear to be little to attract the tourist to this barren plateau sitting on the roof of the world. It's a bleak, windswept terrain of parched scrub, with the occasional tiny adobe settlement blending into the uniform brown landscape. But tourists do come to this starkly beautiful corner of Bolivia and are rewarded with some of the greatest visual delights that the country has to offer. In the far south is the Salar de Uyuni, the largest and highest salt lake in the world. You can take a tour and drive across this inconceivably vast expanse of blinding white nothingness. Further south is a Salvador Dalí landscape of bizarre rock formations, white-capped volcanoes, and sparkling soda lakes of jade and scarlet, filled with pink flamingoes and steaming geysers. To the east, in a dramatic desert landscape, is the former mining town of Tupiza, now a popular destination for travellers keen to track the final movements of famous outlaws, Butch Cassidy and the Sundance Kid.

Oruro

→ *Phone code 02. Colour map 3, B3. Population: 188,422. Altitude: 3706 m.*

The region's main settlement, Oruro, is nothing to write home about, unless you happen to be there during Carnival when it explodes into action in one of Latin America's great celebrations. Founded in 1606 as the Villa Real de San Felipe de Austria de Oruro, it became a famous mining centre and the second largest city in the Americas after Potosí. There are no longer any working mines of importance but Oruro remains a major railway junction and the commercial centre for the mining communities of the altiplano, as well as being a mightily cold place at night, when temperatures can plummet to -10°C.
▶▶ *For Sleeping, Eating and other listings, see pages 372-373.*

Ins and outs

Getting there and around The bus terminal, T02-525 3535, is 10 blocks north of the town centre at Avenida Raika Bakovic and Avenida Aroma, US$0.20 terminal tax to get on any bus. *Micro* No 2, or any one marked 'Plaza 10 de Febrero', takes you to the centre. Those saying 'Mercado' take you close to the train station, which is a dozen blocks south of the bus terminal, at the south end of Avenida 6 de Agosto (also known as 'Avenida Folklórico'). Trains run to Oruro from the south, via Uyuni and Villazón from the Argentine border. ▶▶ *See Transport, page 373.*

Tourist information The **tourist office** ① *Montes 6072, Plaza 10 de Febrero, T/F02-525 0144, Mon-Fri 0800-1200 and 1400-1800,* is very helpful and informative. There's also a kiosk outside **Entel** in Calle Bolívar. Colour map and guide (Spanish only) US$1.

Sights

Several fine buildings in the centre hint at the city's former importance, notably the baroque concert hall (now a cinema) on Plaza 10 de Febrero and the **Casa de la Cultura** (Museo Simón I Patiño) ① *Soria Galvarro 5755, Mon-Fri 0900-1200, 1400-1830, US$0.30.* Built as a mansion by the tin baron Simón Patiño, it is now run by the Universidad Técnica de Oruro, and contains European furniture and a carriage imported from France; it also houses temporary exhibitions. There is a good view from the **Cerro Corazón de Jesús**, near the church of the **Virgen del Socavón**, five blocks west of Plaza 10 de Febrero at the end of Calle Mier.

The **Museo Etnográfico Minero** ① *inside Virgen del Socavón, entry via the church 0900-1200, 1500-1800, US$0.50,* contains mining equipment and other artefacts from the beginning of the century as well as a representation of *El Tío* (in Catholic terminology the devil.) **Museo Antropológico** ① *Av España, Mon-Fri 0900-1200, 1400-1800, Sat-Sun 1000-2000, 1500-1800, US$0.50, take micro A heading south or any trufi going south,* has a unique collection of stone llama heads as well as impressive carnival masks. There are good guides to show you around. The **Museo Mineralógico** ① *part of the university, Mon-Fri 0800-1200, 1430-1700, US$0.60, take micro A south to the Ciudad Universitaria,* has over 5500 mineral specimens. **Casa Arte Taller Cardozo Velásquez** ① *Junín 738 y Arica, east of the centre, T02-527 5245, www.catcarve.org, Mon-Sat 0930-1200, US$0.45,* is the Cardozo Velásquez home – a family of seven artists. It displays contemporary Bolivian painting and sculpture.

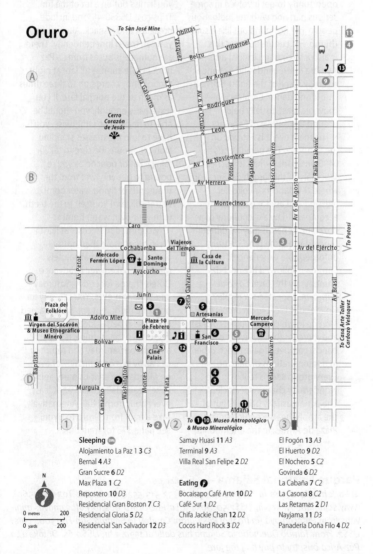

Oruro

Sleeping
Alojamiento La Paz **1** *C3*
Bernal **4** *A3*
Gran Sucre **6** *D2*
Max Plaza **1** *C2*
Repostero **10** *D3*
Residencial Gran Boston **7** *C3*
Residencial Gloria **5** *D2*
Residencial San Salvador **12** *D3*
Samay Huasi **11** *A3*
Terminal **9** *A3*
Villa Real San Felipe **2** *D2*

Eating
Bocaisapo Café Arte **10** *D2*
Café Sur **1** *D2*
Chifa Jackie Chan **12** *D2*
Cocos Hard Rock **3** *D2*
El Fogón **13** *A3*
El Huerto **9** *D2*
El Nochero **5** *C2*
Govinda **6** *D2*
La Cabaña **7** *C2*
La Casona **8** *C2*
Las Retamas **2** *D1*
Nayjama **11** *D3*
Panadería Doña Filo **4** *D2*

N

0 metres   200
0 yards   200

Oruro carnival

The normally cold, austere city of Oruro undergoes a complete transformation during its carnival. Over the week or so of celebrations the townsfolk go wild, so you can get hopelessly drunk with the locals, dance until you drop and, in the process, get soaked to the skin from a million water bombs. This is a rare opportunity to get involved in some serious partying with the indigenous people and not stand out like a sore thumb. For culture vultures this is also a fascinating insight into Aymara folk legends and a chance to enjoy some of the finest Bolivian music and dance. Carnival is a movable feast, usually held around the middle of February.

The main event is *Entrada* on the Saturday. The parade ends at 0400 on Sunday when it reaches the sanctuary of the Virgen del Socavón, where the dancers invoke her blessing and ask for pardon, accompanied by a cacophony of a dozen brass bands playing different tunes at the same time – a truly unforgettable experience. The Entrada is followed the next day (Sunday) by the *Gran Corso del Carnaval*, a spectacular display. On Monday is *El Día del Diablo y del Moreno* in which the *diablos* (devils) and *morenos* (black slaves), with their bands, compete against each other in demonstrations of dancing. Every group seems to join in the wonderfully chaotic spectacle. The action usually parades out of the amphitheatre, ending up at the Plaza de Armas. In the afternoon is

the *Despedida de la Virgen* (Farewell to the Virgin). At dusk dancers and musicians go their separate ways, serenading until the early hours.

Many agencies in La Paz organize day trips from La Paz for the Saturday parade. They leave at 0430, most will pick you up from your hotel. They return at round 1600-1700, so you'll miss out on a lot of the fun. Trips cost US$30-45, and include breakfast and a snack. Alternatively, you can travel independently. There are numerous buses from La Paz from before sunrise till late at night, though they charge up to three times as much as the normal fare. If you leave early enough, you should be able to find a seat. Otherwise, you'll have to join the masses standing along the route. Be sure to take a rain jacket or poncho as you're bound to get very wet from the thousands of flying water bombs. Better still, arm yourself to the teeth with your own water bombs.

Accommodation costs at least three times more than normal during Carnival and absolutely must be booked well in advance. Hotels charge for Friday, Saturday and Sunday nights. You can stay for only one night, but you'll be charged for three. A better idea, though, if you have the stamina, is to party all night on Saturday and return to La Paz by bus on Sunday – or even on Monday for serious party animals. Buses leave daily to La Paz at least every hour from 0400. Alternatively, take a train from Oruro to Uyuni, see page 373 for train times.

Parque Nacional Sajama → *Colour map 3, B2.*

ⓘ *Park headquarters in Sajama village, T0132-513 5526 (in La Paz T02-211 1360), www.sajamabolivia.com, US$2.50. Take a La Paz-Oruro bus to Patacamaya; mini-vans from Patacamaya (in front of Restaurant Capitol) to Sajama Sun-Fri 1300, 3 hrs, US$2. From Tambo Quemado to Sajama bus daily at 1530, 1 hr, US$0.65. Or take a La Paz-Arica bus, try to pay half the fare.*

Bolivia's oldest national park, established in 1939 and covering 100,517 ha, contains the world's highest forest, consisting mainly of the rare queñual tree (*Polylepis tarapacana*) which grows up to an altitude of 5200 m. The scenery is wonderful and includes views of three volcanoes (Sajama – Bolivia's highest peak at 6542 m – Parinacota and Pomerape). The road is paved and leads across the border into the Parque Nacional Lauca in Chile. You can trek in the park, with or without porters and mules, but once you move away from the Río Sajama or its major tributaries, lack of water is a problem. Visitors to the park can stay in Sajama village in one of the family-run *alojamientos* (G), which range from basic to very basic, especially the sanitary facilities, with no showers or electricity (solar power for lighting only). There are many small *comedores* but food supplies are limited. It can be very windy and cold at night, so a good sleeping bag, gloves and hat are essential (villagers sell alpaca woolen items). Crampons, ice axes and rope are needed for climbing the volcanoes and can be hired in the village. Local guides charge US$50 per day. Horses can be hired, US$8 per day including guide. There's good bathing in hot springs 7 km northwest of the village. Jeeps can be rented to visit for US$5-6.

Sleeping

Oruro *p368, map p369*

C Gran Sucre, Sucre 510, corner of 6 de Octubre, T02-527 6800, www.hotebol.com. Well refurbished old building, includes buffet breakfast, cheaper rooms on ground floor, heaters on request. Recommended.

C Max Plaza, Adolfo Mier, Plaza 10 de Febrero, T02-525 2561. Includes breakfast, comfortable carpeted rooms, good central location.

C Villa Real San Felipe, San Felipe 678 y La Plata, south of the centre, T02-525 4993, www.villarealsanfelipe.com. Quaint small hotel with nicely furnished but small rooms, heating, includes buffet breakfast, sauna and whirlpool, restaurant, tour operator, best hotel in town.

D Samay Huasi, Av Brasil 232 opposite the terminal, T02-527 6737. Modern, bright rooms,

---

To Chile via Tambo Quemado

The shortest and most widely used route from La Paz to Chile is the road to **Arica** via the border at Tambo Quemado (Bolivia) and **Chungará** (Chile). From La Paz take the highway south towards Oruro. Immediately before Patacamaya, turn right at green road sign to Puerto Japonés on the Río Desaguadero, then on to Tambo Quemado. Take extra petrol (none available after Chilean border until Arica), food and water. The journey is worthwhile for the breathtaking views.

Bolivian customs and immigration are at Tambo Quemado, where there are a couple of very basic places to stay and eat. Border control is open daily 0800-2000. Shops change bolivianos, pesos chilenos and dollars. From Tambo Quemado there is a stretch of about 7 km of 'no-man's land' before you reach the Chilean frontier at Chungará. Here the border crossing, which is set against the most spectacular scenic backdrop of Lago Chungará and Volcán Parinacota, is thorough but efficient; open 0800-2100. Expect a long wait behind lines of lorries. Drivers must fill in 'Relaciones de Pasajeros', US$0.25 from kiosk at border, giving details of driver, vehicle and passengers. Do not take any livestock, plants, fruit, vegetables, or dairy products into Chile.

Transport For details of buses between La Paz and Arica see International buses (page 325). There are also services from Oruro to Arica via Patacamaya and Tambo Quemado.

includes breakfast, hot water, internet, 30% discount for IYHF members. Recommended.
E Repostero, Sucre 370 y Pagador, T02-525 8001. Hot water, includes breakfast, renovated carpeted rooms are pricier but better value than the old rooms, secure parking.
F Bernal, Brasil 701, opposite bus terminal, T02-527 9468. Modern, good value, excellent hot showers, cheaper with shared bath, heaters on request, restaurant, tours arranged. Recommended.
F Residencial Gran Boston, Pagador 1159 y Cochabamba, T02-527 4708. Nicely refurbished house, internal rooms around a covered patio, electric shower, cheaper with shared bath, good value.
F Residencial San Salvador, V Galvarro 6325 near train station, T02-527 6771. Hot water, **G** with shared bath, electric shower, best in this area.
F Terminal, 21 de Enero y Bakovic, opposite the terminal, T02-527 3431. Modern, hot water, cheaper with shared bath.
G Alojamiento La Paz I, Cochabamba 180, T02-527 4882. Shared bath, basic, clean, hot shower extra.
G Residencial Gloria, Potosí 6059, T02-527 6250. In a 19th-century building, private toilet, shared electric shower, cheaper with shared toilet, basic but clean.

Sajama p370
A Tomarapi Ecolodge, north of Sajama in Tomarapi community, near Caripe, T02-241 4753, ecotomarapi@hotmail.com. Including full board (good food) and guiding service with climbing shelter at 4900 m, helpful staff, simple but comfortable, bath, hot water, heating.

🍴 Eating

Oruro p368, map p369
♥♥ La Cabaña, Junín 609, Sun-Mon 1200-1530. Comfortable, smart, international food, bar.
♥♥ Nayjama, Aldana, corner with Pagador. Best in town, huge portions.
♥♥-♥ Chifa Jackie Chan, Bolívar 615, corner with S Galvarro. Good Chinese.
♥♥-♥ El Fogón, Brasil y 21 de Enero. The best of a poor lot by the bus terminal.

The many greasy chicken places by the terminal are best avoided.
♥♥-♥ Las Retamas, Murguía 930 esq Washington. Excellent set lunch (♥), Bolivian and international dishes à la carte, very good pastries, pleasant atmosphere, out of the way but worth the trip. Recommended.
♥ Cocos Hard Rock, 6 de Octubre y Sucre. Set meals, local and international dishes.
♥ El Huerto, Bolívar 359, open Sun. Good, vegetarian options.
♥ Govinda, 6 de Octubre 6071, Mon-Sat 0900-2130. Excellent vegetarian.
♥ La Casona, Pres Montes 5970, opposite Post Office. A good pizzeria.

Cafés
Bocaisapo Café Arte, Calle Indaburo, almost at corner with Calle Jaén, south of the main plaza. *Cafetería*, bar, books to browse.
Café Sur, Arce 163, near train station, Tue-Sat. Live entertainment, seminars, films, good place to meet local students.
El Nochero, Av 6 de Octubre 1454, open 1700-2400. Good coffee.
Panadería Doña Filo, 6 de Octubre, corner of Sucre, closed Sun. Excellent savoury snacks and sweets, takeaway only.

🛍 Shopping

Oruro p368, map p369
Crafts
On Av La Paz the 4 blocks between León and Belzu, 48-51, are largely taken up by workshops producing masks and costumes for Carnival.
Artesanías Oruro, A Mier 599, corner of S Galvarro. Lovely selection of handicrafts produced by 6 rural community cooperatives; nice sweaters, carpets, wall-hangings.

Markets
Irupana, S Galvarra y A Mier. Good selection of natural foods and snacks.
Mercado Campero, V Galvarro esq Bolívar. Sells everything, also *brujería* section for magical concoctions.
Mercado Fermín López, Calle Ayacucho y Montes. Food and hardware. Calle Bolívar is the main shopping street.

⛰ Activities and tours

Oruro *p368, map p369*

Charlie Tours, Brasil 232 at Hotel Samay Huasi, T02-527 6737, charlietours@ yahoo.com. Regional tours including Salares de Coipasa and Uyuni, transport service.
Freddy Barrón, T02-527 6776, lufba@hotmail .com. Tours and transport, speaks German.
Viajeros del Tiempo, Soria Galvarro 1232, T02-527 1166, Mon-Fri 0900-1230, 1500-1930, Sat 0900-1200, phone in advance. Trips to the nearby mines, hot pools and other attractions.

⊖ Transport

Oruro *p368, map p369*

Bus Several companies run from Oruro terminal to **Challapata** (about every hour, US$1, 1¾ hrs) and **Huari**: (US$1.25, 2 hrs), last bus back leaves Huari about 1630. You can also take a bus to Challapata and a shared taxi from there to Huari, US$0.30.

There are daily services to **La Paz**, at least every hour 0400-2200, US$1.25-1.90, 3½ hrs;. To **Cochabamba**, US$2.50, 4 hrs, 9 daily with Copacabana, more with other companies. To **Potosí**, US$2.50 day bus, US$3.75 at night, 5 hrs, several daily, Copacabana *bus cama* at 2345 US$10. To **Sucre**, Bustillo at 1100 and 2000, US$5, **Copacabana** at 2230, *semi-cama* US$10, *bus cama* US$15, 10 hrs. To **Tarija**, Belgrano at 2030, US$7.50-10, 16 hrs. To **Uyuni**, several companies, all depart 1900-2100, US$2.50, US$3.75 on Wed, 7 hrs. To **Tupiza**, via Potosí, **Boquerón** at 1230, **Illimani** at 1630, US$9.75, 11-12 hrs, continuing to Villazón, US$10, 13-14 hrs. To **Santa Cruz**, Bolívar at 2000, US$7.50, *bus cama* at 2130, US$11.25, 11 hrs. To **Pisiga** (Chilean border, see box, opposite), **Trans Pisiga**, Av Dehene y España, T02-526 2241, at 2000 and 2030, or with Iquique bound buses, US$3.75, 4-5 hrs.

To Chile (US$2 to cross border). To **Iquique**, via Pisiga, several companies at 0100, **Interbus** at 0500 and 1200, **Bernal** at 1230, US$11.25, *bus cama* US$13.75, 10 hrs. To **Arica** via Patacamaya and Tambo Quemado (US$3.75, 4 hrs), several companies between 1200 and 1300, US$11.25, 10 hrs.

provide transport to regional attractions.

Train Trains run south from Oruro to Uyuni, Tupiza and Villazón, and on to the Argentine border. Check in advance which services are running, T02-526 0605. The ticket office is open 0700-1700, but it's best to be there early.

The 2 companies are: **Expreso del Sur**, Mon and Fri at 1530, arrives **Uyuni** 2200 (*Ejecutivo* US$10, *Salón* US$5.50, *Popular* US$3.75), **Tupiza** (US$20.75, US$10.25 and US$ 6.70 respectively), **Villazón** (US$23.30, US$11.60 and US$8.20). **Wara Wara del Sur** Sun and Wed at 1900, arriving in **Uyuni** at 0200 (*Ejecutivo* US$8.40, *Salón* US$4.25, *Popular* US$3.55); **Tupiza** (US$15.15, US$7.30 and US$ 6.10 respectively), **Villazón** (US$18.30, US$9.15 and US$7.30). For details of trains from Uyuni to Villazón and Uyuni to Oruro, see page 380.

Passengers with tickets Villazón-La Paz are transferred to a bus at Oruro. To check train times, T02-527 4605 (or La Paz T02-241 6545). In Nov-Jan and Jul you must have a lot of patience to get a ticket; demand is very high.

Sajama *p370*

Bus To **Patacamaya**, Mon-Fri 0600-0700, some days via **Tambo Quemado**, confirm details and weekend schedule locally.

❶ Directory

Oruro *p368, map p369*

Banks Banco Bisa, Bolívar at Plaza 10 de Febrero, fair rates for US$ cash, US$6 flat rate for TCs (max US$500), cash advances on Visa and MasterCard, Mon-Fri 0900-1600, Sat 0900-1300. BCP, Bolívar, corner with Montes at Plaza 10 de Febrero, fair rates for US$ cash, Visa and MasterCard ATM, Mon-Fri 0900-1800, Sat 0900-1300. *Casa de cambio* at the Terminal Terrestre, US$, euros, pesos, soles, cash only, fair rates, daily 0800-2000. **Internet** Many in town, rates US$0.30-0.35. **Post office** Presidente Montes 1456, half block from plaza. **Telephone** Many *cabinas* in town. **Useful addresses** Immigration, S Galvarro between Ayacucho and Cochabamba.

Uyuni

→ *Phone code 02. Colour map 3, C3. Population: 11,320. Altitude: 3,665 m.*

Hot in the sun, cold in the shade and bitterly cold in the wind and at night, Uyuni is a railway junction founded in 1889 and starting point for trips to Bolivia's most amazing scenery – the salt lake of the same name in the far southwest. Though once described as "a diamond encrusted in the shores of the Great Salar", Uyuni is no beauty. Once an important gateway to Argentina and Chile, the decline of the Bolivian railways had a knock-on effect on Uyuni. Despite the benefits of tourism, its functional architecture, wide, dust-blown streets and freezing winds, lend it a strange, post-apocalyptic feel.
▶▶ *For Sleeping, Eating and other listings, see pages 377-380.*

Ins and outs

Getting there and around Incoming (and outgoing) buses stop in Avenida Ferroviaria, between Arce and Bolívar. It is quite possible to spend your entire time in Uyuni within 150 m of this point. The majority of tour operators, hotels and restaurants and all the bus companies are in this area, with the station just to the south.

Tourist information There is a **tourist office** ① *Av Potosí 13, T02-693 2060, Mon-Fri 0830-1200, 1400-1830.* **Ranking Bolívia** ① *Potosí 9 y Arce, T02-693 2102, ranking bolivia@hotmail.com, daily 0830-2000,* was part of an internationally funded project, but since 2005 it has continued independently. It's a good source of local and regional information (English spoken), has a database of tour operators based on traveller's reports, a café, crafts and books for sale, a video room, a place to hang out while waiting for transport.

Uyuni

To Post Office & Bus Offices
To Colchani & El Salar de Uyuni

Av Acre
Av Colón
To 3 & Buses to San Cristóbal
To 7 9 & Todo Turismo Buses

Museo Arqueológico y Antropológico de los Andes Meridionales

Andes Salt Expeditions
Colque Tours
Bolívar
Clock Tower
Av Potosí
Sucre

To Cementerio de Trenes
Abaroa

Reli Tours
Plaza Arce
Prodem
Immigration

Kantuta Tours
Esmeralda Tours

Toñito Tours

Av Ferroviaria

To Tupiza

0 metres 20
0 yards 20

Sleeping
Avenida 1
Hostal Marith 10
Hostelling
  International 2

Jardines de Uyuni 9
Julia 11
Kory Wasy 3
Kutimuy 4
Los Girasoles 7

Mágia de Uyuni 6
Residencial Sucre 8
Toñito &
  Minuteman Pizza 5

Eating
16 de Julio 5
Arco Iris 2
Kactus 3
La Loco 1

Sights

Once you've sorted out your tour there's not much to do in Uyuni, but if you have some time check out the **Cementerio de Trenes** (train cemetery) just over 1 km from the centre following Avenida Ferroviaria and then the railway line. Rusting steam engines and carriages decay slowly into the barren landscape. Some agencies throw in a swift visit at the end of a tour, thereby saving you the walk. There is also a small museum, the **Museo Arqueológico y Antropológico de los Andes Meridionales** ① *Mon-Fri 1000-1200 and 1400-1800, Sat-Sun 0900-1300, US$0.35*, which has a well-labelled collection of deformed skulls, mummies, cloth and ceramics. A giant statue of an armed railway worker, erected after the 1952 Revolution, dominates Avenida Ferroviaria in front of the station, where there's also a British steam engine. Market days are Thursday, Friday and Sunday, and there's a fiesta on 11 July.

Salar de Uyuni ● ₩ *p378. Colour map 3, C2/3.*

The Salar de Uyuni is the highest and largest salt lake in the world at an altitude of 3650 m and covering roughly 12,000 sq km, making it twice as big as the Great Salt Lake in the United States. Driving across it is one of the strangest, most fantastic experiences you will have, especially during June and July when the bright blue skies contrast with the blinding-white salt crust. After particularly wet rainy seasons the lake is covered in water which adds to the surreal experience. A trip to this corner of Bolivia would not be complete without continuing to see two of Bolivia's most isolated marvels, the bright red Laguna Colorada and jade green Laguna Verde. These spectacular soda lakes lie 350 km southwest of Uyuni, across a Dali-esque desert landscape, and over unmarked, rugged truck tracks. Hundreds of pink flamingos standing in the midst of a shimmering salt lake is definitely a sight worth seeing.

Ins and outs

A four-day tour across the Salar and down to Laguna Colorada and Laguna Verde in Reserva Eduardo Avaroa on the Chilean border is not to be missed, but note that this is a region of harsh extremes of climate. Temperatures can reach 30°C at midday and minus 25°C at night. You'll need warm clothing and a good sleeping bag, and sunglasses are essential to avoid snowblindness. Many agencies in Uyuni will not send jeeps out when the Salar has reverted to a wet lake because the salt water destroys the engines; but shop around, someone will want your money.

Crossing the Salar

Some 20 km north of Uyuni is the tiny settlement of Colchani. A couple of minutes out of the village and you are on the salt. Workers from the village dig out piles of the stuff, which are then loaded onto trucks and taken back to the village to be ground and iodised before being sold. Next is **Hotel Playa Blanca** (see Sleeping, page 378), 34 km from Uyuni, which apart from the roof is completely made of salt.

It takes one to two hours from Hotel Playa Blanca (depending on the state of the Salar and your vehicle) to travel the 80 km to the cactus-studded **Isla del Pescado** (US$1), which has been developed to such an extent that there's even a branch of **Mongo's** there, as well as basic accommodation. That said, Isla del Pescado is the most impressive of the 60 or so islands in the Salar and there are stunning views across the huge white expanse of salt to the mountains shimmering on the horizon.

In the dry season, most tours then head south across the Salar to the Colcha K military post (also known as Villa Martín) and on to San Juan to spend the night in a basic but clean *alojamiento* with hot showers (electricity 1900-2100). Ask your driver to take you out on to the Salar for an unforgettable sunset. If the Salar is underwater, tours normally head back to Uyuni and continue south from there.

South of the Salar 🏠▲🌙 ➤ pp377-380.

Tours continue south from San Juan, via Chiguana (a rail station and military post) and its small Salar de Chiguana to Laguna Hedionda. Or from Uyuni they head south, crossing the 50-cm-deep Río Grande to Villa Alota, a military checkpoint five hours away, with a number of very cheap *alojamientos*. Then on through striking collections of eroded rocks surrounded by snow-capped mountains to Laguna Hedionda in another two hours. One of these mountains – Volcán Ollagüe – is actually an active volcano and wisps of smoke can usually be seen coming from just below its summit. It's possible to organise a five-day tour which includes a visit to the volcano.

Laguna Hedionda (literally, 'Stinking Lake', due to the sulphur) is popular with flamingos, which are mainly white as the algae that create the pink colour are not so numerous in this lake. Continuing south, the route climbs up through a red-brown rock and sand landscape to reach the **Siloli Desert** at 4600 m before dropping down to the bizarre **Arbol de Piedra** (rock tree), an improbably balanced piece of wind-eroded rock. It continues downwards and south to reach Laguna Colorada in around three hours from Laguna Hedionda.

Laguna Colorada and Laguna Verde
At 4278 m high and 60 sq km, Laguna Colorada gets its name from the effect of wind and sun on the micro-organisms that live in it. The shores of the lake are encrusted with borax, used for soap and acid, which provides an arctic-white counterpoint to the blood-red waters. Note that until midday the lake is a fairly normal colour, so it's best to visit in the afternoon. The pink algae provide food for the rare James flamingos (the population here is the world's biggest), along with the more common Chilean and Andean flamingos, and also gives them their pink colour. Of the places to stay at Laguna Colorada, the REA (park authorities) runs a clean, modern and comfortable 34-bed refuge with kitchen and friendly guardian. Insist that your agency books you in there, though they will probably charge an extra Bs 10. There is also a dirty, waterless shack for US$3 per person, which remains popular with Uyuni agencies for some reason. Be careful with water – there's not much of it about.

An unpleasantly cold and early start on day three gets you to the **Sol de Mañana**, a 50-m-high steam geyser, for dawn. You then continue to the 30°C thermal waters at the edge of **Laguna Chalviri**, 30 minutes from the geysers. It's a pleasant spot and the first (and last) chance for a wash. You continue for an hour through the barren, landscape of the **Pampa de Chalviri** at 4800 m, via a pass at 5000 m, to the wind-lashed jade waters of **Laguna Verde** (Green Lake) at 4400 m, the southernmost point of the tour. The stated causes of the lake's impressive colour range from magnesium, calcium carbonate, lead and arsenic. It covers 17 sq km and is at the foot of Volcán Licancábur (5868 m) which is on the border between Bolivia and Chile.

From Laguna Verde, tours start the 400-km-plus journey back to Uyuni. There are a number of options for routes back; check out what your agency is offering. It is possible to go through the village of Queteña, Laguna Celeste (not possible during the wet season) and the *bofedales* (wet grassy areas popular with wildlife), but most take the route through the bizarre and impressive **Valle de las Rocas** near Villa Alota. All the eastern routes give views of huge glaciated mountains including Uturuncu, at 6020 m, the highest in the area and the only one to exceed 6000 m.

An attractive option is to stop at **San Cristóbal**, which is being touted as an alternative base to Uyuni with the help of some sustainable tourism funding. The town is actually brand new, having been moved from its original location in order to build Bolivia's biggest mine. The 17th-century church and churchyard, however, are original, having been moved wholesale. With the emphasis on 'adventure travel', San Cristóbal offers a **Mongo's Mad Max** bar and restaurant built from an enormous water tank and hotel. There are condors in the area and lots of paths and bike tracks across the boulder fields with views across to the Salar. If you feel like getting off and not getting back in the jeep, you can buy tickets for onward travel from Uyuni here, and get the shuttle bus (US$2) to take you to the bus or train.

● Sleeping

Uyuni *p374, map p374*
Water is frequently cut off and may only be available between 0600 and 1200.
B Los Girasoles, Santa Cruz 155, 3½ blocks from clock tower, T02-693 3323, www.girasoleshotel.com. Buffet breakfast, bright and warm (especially 2nd floor), comfortable, nicely decorated, heaters available, best in town. Recommended.
C Jardines de Uyuni, Potosí 133, T02-693 2989. Includes breakfast, rustic style but comfortable, hot water, heaters available, open fire in lounge, parking.
D Kory Wasy, Av Potosí, between Arce and Sucre, T02-693 2670, kory_wasy@

hotmail.com. Overpriced but breakfast is included and generally good atmosphere, sunny lobby but many dark rooms, cheaper in low season, restaurant, tour agency.
D Mágia de Uyuni, Av Colón 432, T02-693 2541, Magia_Uyuni@yahoo.es. All rooms have bath, includes breakfast. Recommended.
D Toñito, Av Ferroviaria 60, T02-693 3186, www.bolivianexpeditions.com. Spacious rooms with good beds, good breakfast included, TV, solar-powered showers and new annex in 2007, **F** with shared bath and no breakfast, very helpful, laundry, internet, tours.
E-F Hostelling International, Potosí y Sucre, T02-693 2228. Hot water, cheaper without

To San Pedro de Atacama (Chile)

The easiest way is to go to San Pedro de Atacama as part of your jeep trip to the Salar and *lagunas* (see Tour operators, page 378). **Colque Tours**, as well as running a Salar and Lagunas tour that take you to San Pedro de Atacama, has a direct jeep leaving their office every day at 1900, US$25 per person, 16 hours. They also run two mini-buses daily from their camp near the ranger station at Hito Cajones to San Pedro de Atacama, departing 1000 and 1700, US$5, one hour, including stop at immigration. There is another vehicle from Hito Cajones to San Pedro de Atacama *tránsito público*), most days at about 1000, same price. At other times onward transport to San Pedro must be arranged by your agency, this can cost up to US$60 if it is not included in your tour. The ranger station may be able to assist in an emergency. The *tránsito público* leaves San Pedro for Hito Cajones at 0800 or 0830. It is usually booked through an agency in town. Occasionally it runs in the afternoon.

There is a train service to Calama leaving Uyuni Monday 0330, US$13.20. Tickets are sold Friday to Sunday. It should take 16 hours but involves a one-hour change of trains at Avaroa (arrives at Avaroa at 0800), then it's 40 minutes to Ollagüe, where Chilean customs take two to four hours. All passports are collected and stamped in the rear carriage and should be ready for collection after a couple of hours; queue for your passport, no names are called out. After that it is an uncomfortable eight hours to Calama. The train from Avaroa to Uyuni leaves Thursday 1200, arrives 1630. **Predilecto** has a bus to Calama, which leaves from the terminal (T02-694 2330) Wednesday and Sunday 0300, US$11, 15 hours (depending on border crossing).

Chile is one hour ahead of Bolivia from mid-October to March. Do not attempt to take coca leaves across the border; it is an arrestable offence. Chile does not allow dairy produce, tea bags (of any description), fruit or vegetables to be imported.

bath, kitchen facilities, modern and popular, discount for IYHF members.

E-F Julia, Ferroviaria 314 y Arce, T02-693 2134. Spacious comfortable rooms, unreliable hot water.

F Avenida, Av Ferroviaria 11, opposite train station, T02-693 2078. **G** with shared bath, basic, limited water and shower facilities, basic, quite old, frequently used by travellers, parking.

G pp Hostal Marith, Av Potosí 61, T02-693 2174. Good budget option (better value without private bath), hot showers from 0830, simple, sunny patio with laundry sinks.

G Kutimuy, Avaroa corner of Av Potosí, near market, T02-693 2391. Owned by **Colque Tours**, so often full of groups. Includes continental breakfast, warm rooms, electric showers, cheaper without bath.

G Residencial Sucre, Sucre 132, T02-693 2047, residencial.sucre.uyuni@gmail.com. Hot water, cheaper without bath, basic but adequate, very welcoming and warm though the 3 stars on the sign is optimistic.

Salar de Uyuni *p375*

These *hoteles de sal* are generally visited on tours, seldom independently.

AL Palacio de Sal, on the edge of the salar, near the ramp outside Colchani (book through **Jardines de Uyuni**, see above; operated by **Hidalgo Tours**, Junín, corner with Bolívar, T02-622 5186, Potosí, uyusalht@ ceibo.entelnet.bo). Price is half-board. Spacious, comfortable luxury salt hotel, decorated with large salt sculptures, heating, hot water, sauna, lookout on second storey with views of the salar. It was relocated from its original location on the salar.

A Luna Salada, north of Colchani near entrance to the salar, T2693 22423 (mob), rodri_lara@yahoo.com. Half-board, private bath, hot water. **A** (high season).

D Playa Blanca, on the Salar de Uyuni, about 10 km from the Colchani access and 70 km from Isla del Pescado, T02-693 2115 (Uyuni). **E** in low season, half-board, all furnishings made of salt blocks, shared bath, no showers, single beds only, all solid and liquid waste is removed in barrels. This is the only hotel left on the salar and it is not clear if it will remain here, hotels were asked to leave for environmental reasons. A stop for most tours, day visitors must

consume something in order to take photographs, use of toilet US$0.60.

Playa Blanca has a second salt hotel in Colchani, same price, half-board, private bath, no shower. See also **Tayka/Fremen** in Activities and tours, below.

South of the Salar *p376*
San Cristóbal

C Hotel San Cristóbal, Purpose-built, owned by the community. The bar is inside a huge oil drum, all metal furnishings. The rest is comfortable if simple, very hot water, good breakfast included, evening meal extra.

G pp Alojamiento, behind the internet office. Basic rooms with several beds, separate bath, hot water extra. Owners keep ñandúes.

G pp Alojamiento Ali. A bit more expensive, but not much difference, rooms with 3 beds, hot water extra.

🍴 Eating

Uyuni *p374, map p374*
There are plenty of small places serving *menú del día*. Avoid eating in the market; Uyuni is not a good place to get ill.

🍴-🍴 **16 de Julio**, Arce, between Ferroviaria and Potosí, opens 0700. Good-value breakfast and set lunch, à la carte in the evening, veggie options, meeting place.

🍴-🍴 **Kactus**, Arce y Potosí, p2. International food, homemade pasta, good pancakes, slow service.

🍴 **Arco Iris**, Plaza Arce. Good Italian food, pizza, and atmosphere, occasional live music.

🍴 **La Loco**, Av Potosí. Gringo food, with music and drinks till late, open fire, popular.

🍴 **Minuteman**, attached to Toñito Hotel (see above). Pizza restaurant , also good soups.

Cafés
Café Den Danske, Quijarro y Matos. Tiny Danish-run café with genuinely international cuisine, good reports. The owner speaks English as well.

🔺 Activities and tours

Uyuni *p374, map p374*
Tour operators
Andes Salt Expeditions, 55 Arce, Plaza, T02-693 2116, www.andes-salt-uyuni.com.bo. Recommended especially

⁝ Salar tours worth their salt

Organization of tours from Uyuni to the Salar is much improved, but even good companies, their guides or vehicles have their off days. Travel is in 4WD Landcruisers, cramped for those on the back seat, but the staggering scenery makes up for any discomfort. Always check the itinerary, the vehicle, the menu (vegetarians should be prepared for an egg-based diet), what is included in the price and what is not (accommodation is normally not included – add US$3-4.50 per person per night). Trip prices are based on a six-person group – it is easy to find other people in Uyuni, especially in high season, April-September. If there are fewer than six people you each pay more. Trips are the standard three- to four- day trip (Salar de Uyuni, Lagunas Colorada and Verde, back to Uyuni), the Uyuni-San Pedro de Atacama trip, including the Salar and lakes, and Uyuni to Tupiza via all the sights. Prices range from US$65-220 per person depending on agency, departure point and season. Agencies in Potosí and La Paz also organize tours, but in some cases this may involve putting you on a bus to Uyuni where you meet up with one of the Uyuni agencies and get the same quality tour for a higher price.

Tour tips
→ For the latest recommendations, speak to travellers who have just returned from a tour and choose from one of the agencies listed on these pages.
→ Take a good sleeping bag, sunglasses, sun hat, sun protection, lots of warm clothing, six litres of bottled water or water purification tablets or iodine tincture, lots of film or memory cards and your own CDs (or ipod). Snacks are a good idea too.
→ A good tip for freezing nights on the Salar or at Laguna Colorada is to fill a water bottle with hot water last thing at night, wrap it in a sock and use it as a sleeping bag warmer. If you're lucky it might still be luke-warm for washing with the next day.
→ If the tour seriously fails to match the contract and the operator refuses any redress, complaints can be taken to the tourism office in Uyuni (see page 374) and then to the **Director Regional de Turismo**, La Prefectura del Departamento de Potosí, Calle La Paz, Potosí, T02-622 7477.

for their tours of the salt flat salar and colour lagoons, but some mixed reports.
Andes Travel Office, Ayacucho 222, T02-693 2227. Good reports, run by Belgian Isabelle and Iver.
Colque Tours, Av Potosí 54, T/F02-693 2199, www.colquetours.com. Well-known but consistently mixed reports, has its own *hostales* on the edge of the Salar and by Laguna Verde and a branch in San Pedro de Atacama. Also rents vehicles (expensive).
Esmeralda, Av Ferroviaria esq Arce, T02-693 2130, esmeraldaivan@hotmail.com. Good, cheap tours (good laundry next door).
Kantuta, Av Arce y Av Potosí, T02-693 3084, kantutatours@hotmail.com. Run by 3 eager brothers, also volcano-climbing tours, good food.

Reli Tours, Av Arce 42, T02-693 3209, www.relitours.com. Reliable, good vehicles and food.
Tayka/Fremen, Sucre entre Uruguay y México, T02-693 2987, www.andes-amazonia.com. Proyecto Tayka, Red de Hoteles de los Andes, a chain of hotels being built in the Salar de Uyuni-Reserva Avaroa area, is a joint venture between Fremen, Fundación Prodem and 4 local communities. Hotels have 14 rooms with private bath, hot water, heating, restaurant, price in A range: **Hotel de Sal** at Tahua, just north of the Salar de Uyuni, west of Salinas de Garcimendoza, and **Hotel de Piedra** at San Pedro de Quemez south of the Salar, **Hotel del Desierto** at Ojo de Perdiz, Comunidad Soniquera, north of

Laguna Colorada, and **Hotel de los Volcanes** at Quetena Grande.

Toñito Tours, Av Ferroviaria 152, T02-693 3186, www.bolivianexpeditions.com. Offers a variety of good tours (also in La Paz, see page 323), with their own hotel at Bella Vista on the edge of the Salar.

South of the Salar *p376*

San Cristóbal

Llama Mama. 60 km of exclusive bicycle trails descending 2-3 or 4 hrs, depending on skill, 3 grades, US$200, all inclusive, taken up by car, with guide and communication.

Transport

Uyuni *p374, map p374*

Bus

Offices are on Av Arce, north of Colón. To **La Paz** with **16 de Julio**, daily at 2000 (La Paz-Uyuni, daily 1530), **Panasur** Wed and Sun at 1800 (La Paz-Uyuni Tue and Fri 1730), US$6.25, 12 hrs, or transfer in Oruro. Tourist buses with **Todo Turismo**, Calle Santa Cruz 155 next to Hotel Los Girasoles, T02-693 3337, www.touringbolivia.com, Tue and Sun at 2000, Fri at 2330, US$25, 11 hrs, 1 additional departure in high season (La Paz office, Plaza Antofagasta 504, Edif Paula, p1, opposite the bus terminal, T02-211 9418, depart Mon, Wed and Sat, 2100).

To **Oruro**, several companies 2000-2130, US$2.50-3.75; **Todo Turismo** (see above), US$20. To **Potosí** several companies 0930-1000 and 1900-2000, US$3.10, 6 hrs, spectacular scenery. To **Sucre** with **6 de Octubre** at 1900, or transfer in Potosí, US$5, 9 hrs. To **Tupiza** with **11 de Julio**, Wed, Fri and Sun 0900, US$4.40, 8 hrs, ramshackle buses. 6-8 passenger jeeps with **12 de Octubre** or **11 de Julio**, daily 0600, US$6.25, 5 hrs. For **Tarija** change in Potosí or Tupiza.

Regional services To **San Cristóbal**, from Av Potosí y Ayacucho, next to Hostal Marith, daily 1400, US$1.90, returns 0600. To **Vila Vila**, **San Cristóbal**, **Culpina K**, **Serena**, **Alota**, **Villa Mar**, **Soniquera**, **Quetena**, with **Trans Nor Lípez**, Sun 1000, US$5 to **Quetena**, 10 hrs, return Wed 0300. To **Alota** and **Colcha K**, 11 de Julio, Fri 1100, US$2.50,

return Wed 1100. To **Soniquera** (between Villa Mar and Quetena), Sun 1100, US$3.15, 5 hrs, return Wed 0700.

Road and train

A road and railway line run south from Oruro, through Río Mulato, to Uyuni (323 km). The road is sandy and, after rain, very bad, especially south of Río Mulato. The train journey is quicker and more scenic. Check services on arrival, T02-693 2153. **Expreso del Sur** leaves for **Oruro** on Tue and Fri at 0000, arriving 0630. **Wara Wara del Sur** service leaves on Mon and Fri at 0140, arriving 0840 (prices for both under Oruro). To **Atocha, Tupiza** and **Villazón**, **Expreso del Sur** leaves Uyuni on Mon and Fri at 2220, arriving, respectively, at 0045, 0315 and 0630. **Wara Wara** leaves on Mon and Thu at 0220, arriving 0500, 0810 and 1200. The ticket office opens at 0830 and 1430 each day and 1 hr before the trains leave. It closes once tickets are sold – get there early or buy through a travel agency.

Directory

Uyuni *p374, map p374*

Banks Banco de Crédito, Av Potosí, between Bolívar and Arce, changes cash occasionally. **Prodem**, Arce near Av Potosí, US$ cash at fair rates, Visa and MasterCard cash advances 5% commission, Mon-Fri 0830-1230 and 1430-1800, Sat 0830-1130. Several *casas de cambio* along Av Potosí, rates vary greatly, shop around, poor rates for TCs. **Internet** Many places in town, US$0.55 per hr. **Post office** Av Arce, corner with Calle Cabrera. **Telephone** Several offices in town. **Useful addresses** Immigration: Av Sucre 94, corner of Av Potosí, T02-693 2062, daily 0830-1200, 1400-1900 for visa extensions.

South of the Salar *p376*

San Cristóbal

Bank For exchange at weekends only. **Internet** By satellite, US$1.20 per hr. **Telephone** Public phone in entrance to Hotel San Cristóbal.

Tupiza

→ *Phone code: 02. Colour map 3, C3. Population: 20,000. Altitude: 2990 m.*

Tupiza, a rising star on Bolivia's 'Gringo Trail', lies in the narrow, fertile valley of the Río Tupiza, a beautiful and dramatic desert landscape of red, brown, grey and violet hills. Capital of Sud Chichas, a province of the Potosí Department, Tupiza is 200 km southeast of Uyuni. It's a pleasant town with a lower altitude and warmer climate than Uyuni, making it a good alternative for visits to the Reserva Nacional Eduardo Avaroa and the Salar. In the late 19th and early 20th centuries, the town was the base of the successful Aramayo mining dynasty. Such fantastic wealth attracted two Wild West outlaws going by the names of Butch Cassidy and the Sundance Kid (see page 383), who held up an Aramayo company payroll. It is this connection with the two famous outlaws that draws visitors who come to Tupiza to take one of the Butch Cassidy and the Sundance Kid tours offered by local operators. ▶▶ *For Sleeping, Eating and other listings see pages 384-385.*

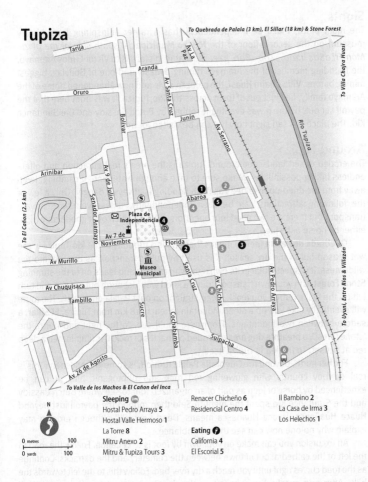

Tupiza

Sleeping	Renacer Chicheño 6	Il Bambino 2
Hostal Pedro Arraya 5	Residencial Centro 4	La Casa de Irma 3
Hostal Valle Hermoso 1		Los Helechos 1
La Torre 8	**Eating**	
Mitru Anexo 2	California 4	
Mitru & Tupiza Tours 3	El Escorial 5	

66 99 El Cañon has some superb rock formations – huge pinnacles of rock and soil, only a few inches thick, which seem to defy gravity …

Ins and outs

There is small, well-organized bus terminal at the south end of Avenida Pedro Arraya. The train station is more central (five blocks north of the bus station) and within two or three blocks of most hotels. Roads out are all fairly bad. The best (a two-way, dirt track, with a bridge over the Río Suipacha) runs south from Potosí and continues south to Villazón, but is still a washboard. The worst, a dry riverbed, is the route to Uyuni via Atocha; it is impassable during the wet season when (surprise) it turns into a river.

Sights

The main plaza, **Plaza de Independencia**, has a rather uninspiring local history museum on the second floor of the **Museo Municipal** ① *south side of the plaza, Mon-Fri 0800-1200, 1400-1800, free*. The statue in plaza is to Victor Carlos Aramayo, the founding member of the Aramayo mining dynasty and one of Bolivia's biggest mining barons. **Villa Chajra Huasi**, the palazzo-style and now abandoned home of the Aramayo family, lies just out of town across the Río Tupiza. It was from here that the payroll set out, before it was eventually robbed by Butch Cassidy and the Sundance Kid. The place is a sad sight now but can be visited for free.

Around Tupiza

The eroded desert landscape around Tupiza is the area's real attraction and offers endless hiking possibilities. Make sure to take enough water and, if camping, keep away from the dried-up river beds as flash flooding is always a danger. Only a few of the following attractions can be seen independently, unless you have private transport, but there are two good tour operators, both of which offer good-value trips, either by horse or by jeep. ▸▸ *See Tour operators, page 385.*

Quebrada de Palala (*palala* means 'barren') is a tributary of the Río Tupiza in the wet season but in the dry season it is used by public transport as a route into the wilderness. It is spectacular in its own right with red fins and leads on to the stunning **Stone Forest**. If in your own transport, drive a short way just north out of town and turn left up the first riverbed you reach. Keep straight on past Palala on the left. The route will eventually take you up a steep mountain to reach, 18 km from Tupiza, **El Sillar**, a saddle between two mountains. From here you'll see, to the right and north, the 'stone forest', a breathtaking area of eroded pinnacles of rock. It is illuminated a deep red at sunset. To the left is Tupiza itself.

Further north, beyond the Quebrada Palala turn-off, is some great scenery. This is real cowboy country with glowering red rock and photogenic hills. It can be experienced by horse or jeep as part of an organized tour to see where Butch Cassidy and the Sundance Kid spent the night in Salo then robbed the payroll just beyond **Huaca Huañasca**. Huaca Huañasca means 'Dead Cow Hill' although erosion may explain why no-one now can see the resemblance.

An excursion you can make on your own by foot is to **El Cañon**. Follow the road to the left of the cathedral out of town between the cemetery and the barracks. Continue as the road curves right until you reach a dry river bed. Follow this to the left towards the hills. After 200 m take the right fork in the river bed. Here are some superb rock

⦂ A tale of two outlaws

The movie Butch Cassidy and the Sundance Kid is based on a true story. Butch Cassidy, born Robert Leroy Parker in 1866, was the eldest of 13 children in a Mormon family in Utah. A cowboy named Cassidy and a stint as a butcher inspired his *nom de crime*. Sundance, born Harry Alonzo Longabaugh in 1867, was the youngest of five children in a Baptist family in Pennsylvania. He got his name by serving 18 months in jail at Sundance, Wyoming, for stealing a horse.

Butch and Sundance belonged to a gang dubbed the Wild Bunch. They held up trains, banks and mine payrolls in the Rocky Mountain West. With US$1000 rewards on their heads and the Pinkerton Detective Agency (later to become the FBI) on their tail, Butch and Sundance fled to South America in 1901, settling in Patagonia in Argentina, where they peacefully homesteaded a ranch, raising sheep, cattle and horses.

The peaceful life didn't last, however. Their names were linked to a bank robbery in Río Gallegos and the police issued an order for their arrest. In 1906, they found work at the Concordia Tin Mine in the central Bolivian Andes, but Butch still wanted to settle down as a respectable rancher. The bandits quit their jobs in 1908, soon after turning up in the mining centre of Tupiza, where they intended to rob a bank, perhaps to finance their retirement.

They soon turned their attention to the Aramayo mining company, after Butch learned that the local manager would be taking an unguarded payroll from Tupiza to Quechisla, a three-day journey to the northwest. So, on 3 November, the manager set off. As he made his way up Huaca Huañusca (Dead Cow Hill), near Salo, he was held up by two bandits.

Once the bandits had departed, the manager alerted his bosses and the alarm went out to local authorities, as well as to Argentine and Chilean border officials. With military patrols and armed miners (whose pay had been stolen) in pursuit, the pair headed north towards Uyuni. They followed the long, rugged trail to San Vicente, a tiny mining village set in an utterly barren landscape 4000 m up in the Cordillera Occidental.

At sundown on 6 November 1908, they rode into town and were given a room for the night. There they met Cleto Bellot, with whom they discussed their plans to head north to Uyuni. Bellot went straight to the home of a neighbour, where a four-man posse from Uyuni was staying. They had galloped in that afternoon and told Bellot to be on the lookout for two Yankees.

Accompanied by Bellot, they went to the house. A gunbattle ensued, then all went quiet. At dawn they entered the house, where they found the two bandits stretched out on the floor, dead, both with bullet holes in the head. Butch had shot his partner and then turned the gun on himself.

The outlaws were buried in the local cemetery that afternoon in unmarked graves, but their deaths were not widely reported in the United States until 1930. In the meantime, wild stories of their demise circulated. Some claim that the two outlaws killed in San Vicente were not actually Butch and Sundance and sightings of them were reported after the event. An exhumation at the San Vicente cemetery in 1991 failed to settle this long-running controversy. (Adapted from *Death in the Andes: The Last Days of Butch Cassidy and The Sundance Kid* by Daniel Buck and Anne Meadows, Washington DC.)

formations – huge pinnacles of rock and soil, only a few inches thick, which seem to defy gravity. The valley narrows rapidly but the path follows a stream bed for several hundred metres to a picturesque waterfall. The walk takes two hours; take water.

Another hike possible without a tour firm is to the **Valle de los Machos** and **El Cañon del Inca**. From Plaza El Castillin walk up 26 de Agosto and then between two hills. After a further 2 km you will see the **Door of the Devil** on your right-hand side, which resembles huge plates from the spine of a stegosaurus. Pass through these then turn right up a river bed. About 1½ km later take a right fork to arrive at a collection of phallic-like pinnacles, humourously named Valle de los Machos. Continue ahead to the start of El Cañon del Inca. Be prepared to climb what would be, in the rainy season, small waterfalls. You don't have to continue to the end of the canyon but if you do it is 28 km there and back. Again, take water and food.

San Vicente → *Colour map 3, C3.*

Tupiza is a good base from which to explore Butch Cassidy and the Sundance Kid country. The outlaws were supposed to have been killed here, in the tiny settlement of San Vicente, 103 km northwest of Tupiza, at 4500 m, on a good dirt road (it takes around four to six hours). It's a typically bleak Altiplano village, described by one correspondent as "a very sad place to die". The famous shoot-out site is off the main street – ask the locals. ▸▸ For tours to San Vicente, see page 385.

● Sleeping

Tupiza *p381, map p381*
E **Hostal Valle Hermoso**, Av Pedro Arraya 478, T02-694 2592, www.bolivia.free hosting.net. Good hot showers, breakfast included (**G** with shared bath and no breakfast), pleasant TV/breakfast room, breakfast extra, book exchange, tourist advice, *Butch Cassidy* video, firm beds, motorbikes can be parked in restaurant, accepts credit cards and TCs (5% extra). Second location (same price), **Valle Hermoso 2**, Av Pedro Arraya 585, T02-694 3441, near the bus station, refurbished house, 3 simple rooms with bath, several dorms for 6 or 8 with bunk beds, 10% discount for IYHF members in both locations.
E **Mitru**, Av Chichas 187, T/F02-694 3001, www.tupizatours.com. E in new rooms with bath, F in older rooms with bath or with shared bath (only 4 rooms left), B for suite with sitting room. All include breakfast. Very good, hot water, pool, games room, cable TV, parking, use of kitchen, luggage store, safes, book exchange, laundry (discount for hotel guests) and clothes-washing facilities, surcharge on credit card payments and TCs.
E-F **La Torre**, Av Chichas 220, T02-694 2633, latorrehotel@yahoo.es. **G** with shared bath, includes breakfast, lovely refurbished house,

comfortable rooms, good value, great service, use of kitchen. Recommended.
F **Hostal Pedro Arraya**, Av P Arraya 494, T02-694 2734, hostalarraya@hotmail.com. Convenient to bus and train stations, **G** with shared bath, hot water, includes small breakfast, modern comfortable rooms, use of kitchen, laundry, terrace. Check bill and confirm arrangements carefully.
F **Mitru Anexo**, Abaroa 20, T02-694 3002. **G** with shared bath, includes breakfast, restaurant, use of kitchen, use of pool and games room at **Hotel Mitru**.
G **Renacer Chicheño**, Barrio Ferroviario, Casa 18, T02-694 2718, hostalrenacer-ch@ hotmail.com. Cheaper with shared bath, includes basic breakfast, family home, kitchen.
G **Res Centro**, Av Santa Cruz 287, 2 blocks from station, T02-694 2705. Pleasant patio, parking, couple rooms with bath, most shared, basic but clean, hot water on request, parking, helpful owner, good value.

● Eating

Tupiza *p381, map p381*
Tupiza is famous for its *tamales*, a delicious scrap of spicy dried llama meat encased

● *For an explanation of sleeping and eating price codes used in this guide, see inside the*
● *front cover. Other relevant information is found in Essentials, see pages 31-35.*

in a ball of corn mash and cooked in the leaves of the plant.

A couple of places outside town serve speciality meals (♔-♔) in rural surrounds on weekends only: La Estancia, 2 km north in Villa Remedios, best on Sun, *picante de cabrito* (spicy goat); and La Campiña, in Tambillo Alto, 45 mins' walk north along the river, *cordero a la cruz* (lamb on the spit) and *lechón* (suckling pig).

♔ California, Cochabamba on main plaza, daily 0800-2300. Breakfast, pizza, vegetarian and regional dishes, popular with gringos.

♔ El Escorial, Chichas, corner with Abaroa. Good value set meal at midday, à la carte in the evening.

♔ Il Bambino, Florida y Santa Cruz, closed Sat and Sun evenings. Recommended, especially for *salteñas*

♔ Los Helechos, next door to Mitru Anexo on Abaroa, closed alternate Sun. Burgers and main courses, vegetarian options, good salad bar.

▲ Activities and tours

Tupiza *p381, map p381*
One-day jeep tours US$11-12; horse riding US$2-2.50 per hr; 2-day San Vicente plus colonial town of Portugalete US$55; Salar de Uyuni and Reserva Avaroa, 4 days with Spanish-speaking guide, US$85-100 low season, US$90-120 high season (tours out of Tupiza are more expensive than those out of Uyuni because of the additional 400 km travelled). Prices per person based on groups of 6, add US$10 per day for English-speaking guide. Some agencies include in their price entrance fees to Reserva Avaroa and Isla del Pescado.
Tupiza Tours, in Hotel Mitru (see Sleeping), are the most experienced and are at the higher end of the market. They have additional tours: 'triathlon' of riding, biking and jeep in the surroundings, US$22 pp (frequently recommended), and extensions to the Uyuni tour.
Valle Hermoso Tours, inside Hostal Valle Hermoso 1, T/F02-694 2592. Also recommended, offers similar tours, as do several new agencies. Most hotels listed have an agency.

⊖ Transport

Tupiza *p381, map p381*
Bus
To **Villazón** 0400, 1430, US$1.50, 2½ hrs. To **Potosí**, 1000, 2000, US$5.25, 7 hrs (change here for **Sucre**). To **Tarija**, 1930, 2000, US$5, 8 hrs (change here for **Santa Cruz**). To **Uyuni**, 11 de Julio, Mon, Thu, Sat at 1000, US$4.40, 8 hrs, poor vehicles; also 6-8 passenger jeeps daily at 0600 and 1030 (12 de Octubre) US$6.25, 5 hrs. To **Oruro**, 1200, 2030, US$6.25, 13 hrs (change here for **Cochabamba**). Expreso Tupiza has a direct bus to **La Paz** at 1000 (La Paz-Tupiza at 1930, 15 hrs), otherwise via Potosí, 17 hrs, US$7.50.

Train
Train station ticket office is open Mon-Sat 0800-1100, 1530-1730, and in the early morning half an hour before trains arrive. To **Villazón**: Expreso del Sur Tue and Sat 0330, arriving 0630; Wara Wara Mon and Thu at 0830, arriving 1200. To **Atocha**, **Uyuni** and **Oruro**, Expreso del Sur Tue and Fri at 1840; Wara Wara Mon and Thu at 1850. Fares are given under Oruro (see page 373).

⊙ Directory

Tupiza *p381, map p381*
Banks There is no ATM in town. Banco de Crédito, on main plaza, Mon-Fri 0830-1230, 1430-1700, fair rates for cash, US$5 commission for Visa/MasterCard cash advances. Prodem, Cochabamba on main plaza, Mon-Fri 0830-1230, 1430-1800, Sat 0900-1200, fair rates for cash, 5% commission for Visa/MasterCard cash advances (no debit cards). Cooperativa El Chorolque, Av Santa Cruz 300 y Abaroa, Mon-Fri 0900-1600, Sat 0900-1100, cash only. Cambios Latin America, Abaroa y Santa Cruz, open daily or knock on door (long hours), bargain for best cash rate, 6% commission for TCs. Tupiza Tours gives cash against Visa, MasterCard and TCs. **Internet** Many internet places, US$0.70 per hr. **Post office** On Abaroa, northwest of plaza, Mon-Fri 0830-1800, Sat 0900-1700, Sun 0900-1200. **Telephone** Several Entel offices, including one on the plaza and another across the street from the bus station.

Southern Highlands

Sucre and Potosí are the finest examples of Bolivia's colonial heritage and two of its main tourist attractions. Sucre exudes the assured confidence and charm befitting the country's official capital, legal centre and major university city. Its near neighbour, Potosí, is not only the highest city in the world, at over 4000 m, but was once the largest and wealthiest city in the Americas. All around are reminders of its silver-mining heyday, from the many crumbling colonial buildings, to the massive mint, where the silver was smelted into coins for the Spanish Crown. Towering over the city is Cerro Rico ('Rich Mountain') from which the silver was extracted, at an unimaginable human cost. Visitors can burrow into its bowels through a series of tunnels and shafts, meet the devil face to face, and experience what life was like many centuries ago for those who were forced to enter the 'Mouth of Hell'. Further south, Tarija is the country's wine centre in an isolated and little-visited area.

Sucre

→ *Phone code 04. Colour map 3, C3. Population: 131,769. Altitude: 2790 m.*

Sucre, Bolivia's official capital, is proud of its colonial legacy. Also known as 'La Ciudad Blanca' (the White City), owing to the fact that, by tradition, all the buildings in its centre are whitewashed every year (a tradition also observed in some towns in the Oriente), Sucre is not just a series of pretty façades but also a thriving university city and thousands of young students fill every street, plaza, bar and café. Surrounding this sparkling white colonial masterpiece is a hinterland of traditional weaving villages which burst into life during their frequent market days and festivals. Dinosaur-hunters are also making tracks for Sucre, with the discovery of many prehistoric footprints. Sucre enjoys a mild climate with an average daytime temperature of 24°C in July and August and 7°C at night . ▶▶ *For Sleeping, Eating and other listings see pages 389-394.*

Ins and outs

Getting there Flights arrive at **Juana Azurduy de Padilla airport** ① *5 km northwest of town, T04-645 4445.* The airport minibus goes from the entrance and will drop you off on Hernando Siles y Junín, in the centre. It returns from here, usually 1½ hours before flights leave; US$0.70, 20-30 minutes. A taxi from the centre is US$4-5. *Trufis* 1 and F go from the entrance to Hernando Siles y Loa, one block from the main plaza, US$0.55, 25 minutes. The **bus terminal** is on the northern outskirts of town, 3 km from centre on Ostria Gutiérrez, T04-645 2029. A taxi to and from the centre is US$0.75 per person inside the terminal compound or US$0.45 outside. Alternatively take *micro A* or *trufi 8* (going to the bus station, from Avenida H Siles, between Arce and Junín).

Getting around Sucre is a small, compact city and easy to explore on foot. Its busy narrow streets generally run uphill from the plaza eastwards and downhill west towards the train station. Taxis around town are around US$0.50 per person.

Tourist information The **tourist office** ① *Estudiantes 25, T04-644 7644, Mon-Fri 0900-1200, 1500-1830,* is very helpful, sells copies of town map, US$0.15; English and French spoken. There is also an office at the bus station, allegedly open Monday to Friday 1000-1230, 1500-1730, Saturday 0800-1200; and at the airport, to coincide with incoming flights. As in Potosí and La Paz, beware of fake police and immigration officials and gangs of youths by the market.

Sights

The city's heart is the spacious and elegant Plaza 25 de Mayo, on which stands the **Casa de la Libertad** ① *25 de Mayo 11, T04-645 4200, Tue-Fri 0900-1115, 1430-1745, Sat 0930-1115, US$1.50 with tour, US$1.50 photos, US$3 video*, where the country's Declaration of Independence was signed on 6 August 1825. The actual document is on display. Also among its treasures is a famous portrait of Simón Bolívar, said to be the most accurate. Also on the plaza is the beautiful 17th-century **cathedral** ① *entrance to the cathedral is through the museum, halfway down Calle Nicolás Ortiz, opposite La Vieja Bodega; if the door is locked wait for the guide, Mon-Fri 1000-1200,*

Sucre

0 metres 100
0 yards 100

Sleeping
Alojamiento La Plata 3 *C2*
Austria 4 *B3*
Avenida 17 *B1*
Backpackers Sucre
Hostel 2 *C1*
Casa de Huéspedes
Finita 22 *D3*
Casa de Huéspedes
San Marcos 1 *B2*
Colonial 6 *C2*
El Hostal de Su Merced 7 *D2*
Gloria 8 *B3*
Grand 9 *C2*
Hostal Colón 5 *D1*
Hostal Cruz de Popayán 2 *C1*
Hostal Libertad 10 *C2*
Hostal los Piños 11 *D1*
Hostal San Francisco 12 *B2*
Hostal Sucre 13 *D1*
La Posada 20 *D2*
Municipal Simón
Bolívar 14 *A1*
Paola Hostal 21 *D1*
Potosí 15 *B1*
Real Audiencia 16 *D3*
Residencial Bolivia 18 *C2*
Residencial Charcas 19 *B2*

Eating
Arco Iris 1 *D2*
Bibliocafé 2 *D2*
Café Hacheh 4 *B1*
Café Mirador 5 *D3*
El Germen 6 *C3*
Kultur-Café Berlin 10 *D3*
La Casona 11 *B3*
La Plaza 13 *C2*
La Repizza 14 *D2*
La Taverne 15 *C2*
La Tertulia 7 *C2*
Locot's Café
Aventura 3 *C3*
Penco Penquito 16 *C2*
Pizzería
Napolitano 13 *C2*
Salon de Té
Las Delicias 17 *C2*

Bars & clubs
Joy Ride Café 8 *D2*
La Luna 12 *D2*

1500-1700, Sat 1000-1200, US$1.50, which houses the famous jewel-encrusted Virgen de Guadalupe (1601), as well as works by the Italian Bernardo Bitti, the first great painter of the New World.

The church of **Santa Mónica**, at the corner of Arenales y Junín, is perhaps one of the finest gems of Spanish architecture in the Americas, but has been converted into a *salón multiuso* (multi-purpose space). Another one of Sucre's fine churches is the church of San Miguel (1130-1200). Completed in 1628, it has been restored and is very beautiful with Moorish-style carved and painted ceilings, pure-white walls and a gold and silver altar. In the Sacristy some early sculpture can be seen. Visitors are not allowed to wear shorts, short skirts or short sleeves. It was from San Miguel that Jesuit missionaries went south to convert Argentina, Uruguay and Paraguay. The church of **San Francisco** (1581) ① *Calle Ravelo, 0700-1200, 1500-1900,* has altars coated in gold leaf and 17th-century ceilings; the bell is the one that summoned the people of Sucre to struggle for independence.

The neoclassical church of **San Felipe Neri** ① *Azurduy y Ortiz, T04-645 4333, US$1 (extra charge for photos) with a free guide from Universidad de Turismo office on Plaza 25 de Mayo,* is officially closed but ask the guide nicely to gain access. The roof (note the penitents' benches), which offers fine views over the city, is only open for an hour between 1630 and 1800 (times change). The monastery is used as a school. Diagonally opposite is the church of **La Merced**, which is notable for its gilded central and side altars. A few blocks away, the **Museo Universitario Charcas** ① *Bolívar 698, Mon-Fri 0800-2000, Sat 0900-1200, 1500-1800, Sun 0900-1200, US$1.50, photos US$1.50,* has anthropological, archaeological and folkloric exhibits, and colonial collections and presidential and modern-art galleries.

Highly recommended for explanations of local indigenous groups and their distinctive textiles is the **Museo Textil-Etnográfico** ① *San Alberto 413 y Potosí, T04-645 3841, www.bolivianet.com/asur, Mon-Fri 0830-1200, 1430-1800, Sat 0930-1200 (Sat afternoon Jul-Sep), US$2, English, German and French-speaking guide,* run by **Antropológicas del Surandino** (**ASUR**). Their Jalq'a exhibit is perhaps the finest display of Bolivian ethnography now available. It includes superb examples of contemporary daily dress, as well as ritual costumes, a film of dances, live weaving demonstrations, photographs of earlier weavings and clear and full explanations of their history and descriptions of the iconography of the textiles. The knowledgeable, helpful staff can also arrange visits to the villages where the textile traditions have been revived. There's also a handicrafts shop downstairs which supports the project. There's a lot to see but tickets can be used again the following day.

Round the corner, the church of **San Lázaro** (1538) ① *Calvo y Padilla, daily for Mass 0630-0730, 1830-1930,* is regarded as the first cathedral of La Plata (Sucre). On the nave walls are six paintings attributed to Zurbarán, and there is fine silverwork and alabaster in the Baptistery.

Southeast of the city, at the top of Dalence, lies the Franciscan convent of **La Recoleta** with good views over the city and the **Museo de la Recoleta** ① *Calle Pedro de Anzúrez, Mon-Fri 0900-1130, 1430-1630, US$1.20 for entrance to all collections, guided tours only.* It is notable for the beauty of its cloisters and gardens; the carved wooden choir stalls above the nave of the church are especially fine (see the martyrs transfixed by lances). In the grounds is the Cedro Milenario, a 1400-year-old cedar. **Tanga Tanga** ① *Iturricha 297, La Recoleta, T04-644 0299, Tue-Sun 0900-1200, 1430-1800,* is an interactive children's museum with art, music, theatre, dance and books (the excellent **Café Mirador** is in the garden). Behind Recoleta monastery a road flanked by Stations of the Cross ascends an attractive hill, **Cerro Churuquella**, with large eucalyptus trees on its flank, to a statue of Christ at the top. In the cemetery are mausoleums of presidents and other famous people, boys give guided tours; take Calle Junín south to its end, about eight blocks from main plaza.

Around Sucre

About 5 km south on the Potosí road is the **Castillo de la Glorieta** ⓘ *daily 0830-1200, 1400-1800, US$1*, former mansion of the Argandoña family, built in a mixture of contrasting European styles with painted ceilings. Ask to see the paintings of the visit of the pope, in a locked room. Take any bus marked 'Liceo Militar' from the Plaza, or bus or *trufi* 4 or E. Some 7 km north of Sucre **Cal Orcko** ⓘ *at the Fanseca cement factory, T04-645 1863, guided tours at 1000 and 1230, tours in English are available for US$2*, is the site of the best-known and most accessible of the region's many dinosaur tracks. There are around 5000 footprints, making it possibly the world's largest paleontological site. The footprints are on the steep side of a rockface but it's not hard to imagine that once this was a flat muddy plain. One single set of footprints continues for 350 m. The tracks were discovered by the workers in 1994, but it took some time for them to be fully identified as those of a *Sauropdos*, or *Titanosauros*, *Anguilosaurios* and *Teropodos*. Access is through the factory, and you should be accompanied by a company employee. Tour agencies charge US$10 per person as do taxi drivers who have trained as guides (untrained drivers charge US$7); ask tourist office for approved drivers. Or take the fantastically cheesy **DinoTruck**, which leaves from the main plaza every day at 0930, 1200 and 1430, and costs US$4 (excellent explanations in good English). You'll ride in the back of a red and yellow lorry with a painted stegosaurus on its side.

One of the most interesting trips from Sucre is to the village of **Tarabuco**, 64 km southeast on a good road (see Transport, page 393). It is famous for its very colourful **market** on Sunday. The local people still wear their traditional dress of conquistador-style helmets, multi-coloured ponchos, *chuspas* (bags for carrying coca leaves) and the elaborate *axsu*, an overskirt worn by women. The market starts around 0930-1000 and could be described as a bit of a tourist trap, but many still find it an enjoyable experience. Those in search of a bargain should have an idea about the quality on offer before buying. Many of the sellers also come to Sucre through the week. Note the market is not held at Carnival (when all Tarabuco is dancing in Sucre), Easter Sunday or on the holiday weekend in November. In March, thousands of *campesinos* from the surrounding area join tourists and Securenses in the celebration of **Phujillay**, one of the best traditional festivals in the country. It is held in celebration of the Battle of Jumbata when the local people defeated the Spaniards on 12 March 1816. It is a very colourful and lively affair with great music, local food and the obgligatory chicha. No one sleeps during this fiesta so there are no accommodation problems. A good guide is Alberto from Sucre tourist office (see page 386), US$45 for a full day in a car for four people.

● Sleeping

Sucre *p386, map p387*

B Real Audiencia, Potosí 142, T/F04-646 0823, realaudiencia2000@hotmail.com. Modern, large rooms, excellent restaurant, heated pool. Recommended.

C El Hostal de Su Merced, Azurduy 16, T04-644 2706, sumerced@mara.scr.entelnet.bo. Beautifully restored colonial building, more character than any other hotel in the city, owner speaks fluent French and English (as do staff), good breakfast buffet, internet, sun terrace, restaurant. Recommended.

C La Posada, Audiencia 92, T04-646 0101, www.laposadahostal.com. A smart, central, colonial-style hotel with comfortable rooms with big beds and wooden

beams. There's also a good courtyard restaurant and ADSL internet.

C Paola Hostal, Calle Colón 138, T04-645 4978, paolahostal@pelicano.cnb.net. Smart, clean and helpful colonial house with modern rooms, some with bathtub, cable TV. Discount for 2 nights or more. Covered courtyard and small, green, sheltered garden, laundry, cafeteria for snacks, internet facilities, airport transfer, buffet breakfast included. Some good views from higher rooms.

C Refugio Andino Bramadero, 30 km from the city, details from Raul y Mabel Cagigao, Avaroa 472, T04-645 5592, bramader@ yahoo.com. Cabins or rooms, well-furnished, full board, drinks and transport included, excellent value, owner Raul is an astronomer and advises on hikes, book in advance. Recommended.

D Colonial, Plaza 25 de Mayo 3, T04-645 4079, hoscol@mara.scr.entelnet.bo. The Colonial is grander than its plain corridors and courtyard might suggest. Some rooms are noisy, the best room of all has a bathtub, an enormous bed and a great view overlooking the Plaza. Good continental breakfast included.

D Hostal Cruz de Popayán, Loa 881 y Colón, T04-644 0889, popayan@bolivia hostels.com. Comfy if rather dimly lit rooms around a sunny open courtyard with a tree. **F** without bath, also has dorms (**G** pp), use of kitchen, coffee shop, laundry service, book exchange, can arrange transport and language classes. Breakfast and internet are included but it's not as good value as they'd have you believe.

D Hostal Libertad, Arce y San Alberto, p 1, T04-645 3101. Clean and friendly with spacious comfortable rooms with cable TV and heating. Open stairs, well-equipped but characterless rooms, some with decent views.

D Hostal Sucre, Bustillos 113, T04-645 1411, hostalsucre@hotmail.com. A colonial place with rooms set around 2 courtyards with lots of winding stairs and corridors. Rooms have less character than the rest of the hotel but are comfortable, with TV, telephone and room service. Those at the back are quieter. Breakfast included.

D-E Municipal Simón Bolívar, Av Venezuela 1052, T04-645 5508 Including breakfast in patio, helpful and comfortable, restaurant.

E Austria, Av Ostria Gutiérrez 506, near bus station, T04-645 4202. Hot showers, redecorated, great beds and carpeted rooms, some cable TV, cafeteria, parking, **G** rooms available and, next door, **G** in the *alojamiento* (parking extra).

E Grand, Arce 61, T04-645 1704, granhot@mara.scr.entelnet.bo. Comfortable rooms with private bathrooms, hot showers and cable TV. There are lots of courtyards and plants and the price includes continental breakfast in room. Excellent central location, good value lunch in Arcos restaurant, laundry, safe, helpful. Recommended.

E Hostal los Piños, Colón 502, T04-645 4403, h-pinos@mara.scr.entelnet.bo. Comfortable but in need of a lick of paint. Carpets are shabby too but rooms have hot showers and cable TV, there's a great garden, a kitchen and free parking. It's also peaceful and friendly, though a bit away from the centre. Price includes breakfast.

E Residencial Charcas, Ravelo 62, T04-645 3972, hostalcharcas@latinmail.com. **F** without bath, good value breakfast, sunny roof terrace, friendly and helpful but some rooms need redecoration. Reasonable but overpriced. Runs bus to Tarabuco and back at 0730 on Sun.

F Casa de Huéspedes Finita, Padilla 233, T04-645 3220, delfi_eguez@hotmail.com. 2 rooms with bath, others without, breakfast included, hot water, heaters, **E** with full board for long stay, works with students studying Spanish.

F Hostal Colón, Colón 220, T04-645 5823, colon220@bolivia.com. Family-run colonial house, quiet, basic but clean, laundry US$1 per kg, helpful owner speaks excellent English and German. Rooms overlook a courtyard with a flowering tree and coffee room which opens out onto the street. Breakfast included. Small book exchange. Recommended.

F Hostal San Francisco, Av Arce 191 y Camargo, T04-645 2117, hostalsf@ cotes.net.bo. A pristine white hotel where rooms have private bathrooms, TV and phone. It's quiet and comfortable and rooms are centred around a large courtyard with a fountain. Breakfast is US$0.60 extra. Excellent value for money. Recommended.

F Residencial Bolivia, San Alberto 42, T04-6454346. (**F** without private bathroom). Big hotel with spacious rooms and hot water in good bathrooms. Breakfast included, large sunny courtyard with seats, very pleasant and clean. Rooms at back lighter and quieter, downstairs rooms a bit dark. Recommended.

G Alojamiento La Plata, Ravelo 32, T04-645 2102. Popular place with no private bathrooms. Wooden floors, bathrooms a bit dingy. Beds sink, but it's set back from road and is quiet. 3-hr laundry service.

G Avenida, Av Hernando Siles 942, T04-645 2387. Hot showers, breakfast US$1, laundry, helpful, small, family-run, use of kitchen.

G pp Backpackers Sucre Hostel,
Loa 891 y Colón, T04-644 0889, sucre@
boliviahostels.com. A good bet for travellers,
includes breakfast, safe, internet, laundry,
luggage store, travel information.
Recommended.

G Casa de Huéspedes San Marcos, Arce
223, T04-646 2087. Cheaper without bath.
Lovely flower-filled Spanish patio, kitchen,
friendly and quiet. Highly recommended.

G Gloria, Av Ostria Gutiérrez 438, T04-
645 2847. Opposite bus station. Clean,
great value.

G Potosí, Ravelo 262, T/F04-645 1975.
castro@sucre.bo.net. Set amongst the
lawyers and notaries on Ravello, basic rooms
are set around a courtyard with an enormous
palm tree. The paint is peeling, and rooms
are less than spotlessly clean but the tiled
floors add character and the place is very
good value.

Around Sucre p389

C Refugio Andino Bramadero, 30 km
from the city, details from Raul y Mabel
Cagigao, Avaroa 472, T04-645 5592,
bramader@yahoo.com. These fairy-tale
cabins are in the middle of some beautiful
countryside, with great walks from the front
door. Good food, candlelight, hot water. All
food and transport is included in the US$35
per person price. Family cottages or doubles
and a big house too. Recommended.

D Kantu Nucchu, 21 km southwest of
Sucre, T04-7244 7164, kantunucchu@
boliviahostels.com. Colonial hacienda,
with bath, kitchen, full board, **G pp**
without meals, peaceful, hiking,
swimming. Recommended.

Tarabuco

There are at least 2 budget hotels, including
G Residencial Florida, basic, cold and dirty,
but serves a good *almuerzo* in the garden,
with music and dancing, which is good fun.

🍴 Eating

Sucre p386, map p387

🍴 **Arco Iris**, Bolívar 567. Swiss restaurant,
good service and food, *peña* on Sat,
excellent *rösti*, live music some nights.

🍴 **El Huerto**, Ladislao Cabrera 86, T04-645
1538, Mon-Wed lunch only, Thu-Sun also

open for dinner until 2030. Reservation
advisable. International food with salad
bar, good *almuerzo*, in a beautiful garden.
Take a taxi there at night.

🍴 **La Casona**, Ostria Guitiérrez 401, near bus
terminal. Stylish, *platos típicos*, good value.

🍴 **El Germen**, San Alberto 231, Mon-Sat
0800-2200. Vegetarian, set lunches
(US1.80), excellent breakfast, US$1.05-
2.10, book exchange, selection of
German magazines. Recommended.

🍴 **Pizzería Napolitano**, Plaza 25 de Mayo 30,
open till 1700. Pizzas and pasta, home-
made ice cream, good lunch options.

🍴 **La Plaza**, Plaza 25 de Mayo 33, open
1200-2400. Good food, popular with
locals, set lunch US$2.10.

🍴 **La Repizza**, N Ortiz 78. Good-value
lunches, good pizzas in evening.

🍴 **La Taverne** of the **Alliance Française**,
Aniceto Arce 35, half a block from plaza,
closed Sun evening, *peñas* Fri-Sat in Jul
and Aug. Good French food, also regular
cultural events.

Cafés

Amanecer, Pasaje Junín 810-B, T04-645
1602, from 1530. Hard-to-find German
pastelería, run by social project supporting
disabled children. Has excellent biscuits
and cakes.

Bibliocafé, Nicolás Ortiz 50, near the plaza,
Mon-Sat 1100-0200, Sun 1800-0200. Good
pasta and light meals, crêpes, music.
Almuerzos, 1100-1600, for US$3. Atmospheric
but service can be slow. And despite the
name, there's a distinct shortage of books.

Café Hacheh, Pastor Sainz 233, open 1000-
0100. An unlikely but exceptionally good
café and cultural centre, well worth the walk
from the centre. The walls are adorned with
lots of sexy designer nakedness, Chomsky
and chess are laid out on tables, Pink Floyd
plays on the stereo, and a Freddie Mercury
lookalike stands behind the bar. Comfy
chairs, crêpes, good value juices, tasty
sandwiches, real fireplace. The 1970s
café of your dreams. Ring the bell to
be let in. Highly recommended.

Café Mirador, Plaza de la Recoleta, corner
of El Mirador, opposite Recoleta monastery.
T04-644 0299, Tue-Sun 1000-1800. Has the
best views of Sucre from its grassy terrace
below the plaza. Good juices, fantastic iced

cappuccino and equally good juices. Also omelettes, crêpes, pasta, cocktails. There's a book exchange too. The café is attached to the Tanga Tanga Museum (see page 382).

Kultur-Café Berlin, Avaroa 326. 0800-2400 (except Sun). A little slice of Germany. Part of a cultural centre (the Instituto Cultural Boliviano Alemán – ICBA) which includes a library and film room. Wooden tables, candles, arches, bar stools, wooden floor, black and white photos and letters, Sureña on tap, MTV on the telly. *Peña* every other Fri.

La Tertulia, Plaza 25 de Mayo 59, Italian and other dishes, could be great but let down by service. Good breakfasts.

Penco Penquito, Arenales 108. Excellent coffee and cakes, in a strange fungus design interior. Be warned that many of the cakes and the lemon meringue pie can only be purchased whole.

Salon de Té Las Delicias, Estudiantes 50, open 1600-1900. Great cakes and snacks, favourite student hangout.

🜲 Bars and clubs

Sucre *p386, map p387*

Joy Ride Café, Nicolás Ortiz 14, T04-642 5544, www.joyridebol.com, Mon-Sat 0730 until late (usually around 0200), weekends from 0900. Dutch-run. Good vibes and a popular night time haunt with great food and drink. 4 types of Belgian beer are among the drinks from the bar and if you're lucky you might even find some Guinness. Try the nachos, *pique a lo macho*, chilli con carne, or the 'hangover eggs' (eggs fried with cheese, ham, onion, tomato and a splash of chilli), which are talked about by travellers all over Bolivia. Good salads and a patio out the back with heating. Elegant and comfortable upstairs lounge with sofas has film showings Sun-Thu evenings. See also Tour operators, below, for details of their excellent biking and hiking trips. Highly recommended.

La Luna, at the back of Casa de la Cultura, Argentina 65. Popular video pub, sometimes with live music.

Mitsubanía, Av del Maestro corner with Av Venezuela. Currently the most happening place, popular with a local, young, fashionable crowd, mixture of music with lots of cumbia, US$3 for men, women get in free.

✺ Festivals and events

Sucre *p386, map p387*

Feb (dates change) Jueves de Compadres and Comadres, held 10 days and 3 days respectively before Carnival.

25 May Celebrates the first move towards independence, most services are closed.

End May A car rally starts and finishes in the city, closing many of the surrounding roads.

16 Jul Fiesta de la Virgen del Carmen, similar to Alasitas in La Paz (see page 319).

25 Jul Fiesta de Santiago Apostol, Mass and processions and traditional music.

16 Aug San Roque.

8 Sep Virgen de Guadalupe, a 2-day fiesta, followed by folkloric fiesta with dances and costumes from across Bolivia.

21 Sep Día del Estudiante: music and dancing around the main plaza.

Oct/Nov Festival Internacional de la Cultura, also held in Potosí, 2 weeks of cultural events.

Around Sucre *p389*

Mar Pujllay, in Tarabuco.

Apr Domingo de Ramos, also in Tarabuco.

⚙ Shopping

Sucre *p386, map p387*

Handicrafts

Antropológicos del Sur Andino (ASUR), in the Museo Arte Indígena, San Alberto 413, T04-642 3841 (see page 388), sells weavings from around Tarabuco and from the Jalq'a; their weavings are more expensive, but of higher quality than elsewhere.

Artesanía Bolivia, Argentina 31, has a variety of arts and crafts from Tarabuco.

Artesanías Calcha, Arce 103, opposite San Francisco Church, is recommended and the owner is very knowledgeable.

Chocolates Para Ti, San Alberto, just off the Plaza, T04-645 4260, www.chocolates-para-ti.com. Chocaholics should note that Sucre is the chocolate capital of Bolivia, and this is one of its best chocolate shops. Service can be a little unfriendly but there's a huge selection of handmade chocolates.

Fundación Aprecia, Raul F de Córdova 49, just off Colón, T04-642 4718. A workshop for blind weavers making beautiful rugs (they can make to order with advance notice).

Markets

Mercado Central is clean and colourful, with a wide variety of goods and many stalls selling *artesanía*. There are also lots of *artesanía* shops on the pedestrianized part of Junín between Ravelo and Hernando Siles. A bus from the central market will take you to the Mercado Campesino market on the outskirts of town, which is a vast, sprawling affair, selling local produce, second-hand clothing and some artesanía.

🚶 Activities and tours

Sucre *p386, map p387*
Bolivia Specialist, Bolívar 525, www.boliviaspecialist.com. Dutchman Dirk Dekker's agency for local hikes, horse riding and 4WD trips, tours throughout Bolivia and Peru, loads of information and connections.
Candelaria Tours, Audiencia No 1, Calle 322, T04-646 1661. Organizes excursions and also organizes Bolivian textile fashion shows, English spoken.
Joy Ride Bolivia, Calle Mendizabal 229, T04-642 5544, www.joyridebol.com. Speak to Gert or Hans at Joy Ride Café (see Eating). Recommended for top-quality bike trips and guided walks among the hills of Sucre's attractive surroundings. Includes full safety gear, insurance and experienced guides. Longer trips from 2-9 days can take in Uyuni, Tupiza and Santa Cruz; contact in advance. Prices are dependent on numbers but start at around US$18 per person per day. Put your name on the blackboard in the café if you're interested in making up a group.
Locot's Adventure, see Locot's Café Aventura under Eating, above. For many types of adventure sport.
Seatur, Plaza 25 de Mayo 24, T/F04-646 2425, seatur@latinmail.com. Local tours, English, German, French spoken. Lucho Laredo and his son at Calle Panamá final 127, corner with Comarapa, Barrio Petrolero, organize treks in the surrounding area. Recommended.
Sur Andes, Nicolás Ortiz 6, T04-645 3212, F645 2632. Organizes trekking from half-day to 5 days, including to pre-Columbian sites such as Pumamachay and the Camino Prehispánico. You must take a sleeping bag and good shoes, everything else is provided.

⊖ Transport

Sucre *p386, map p387*
Air
To get to the airport, a minibus picks up from Siles y Junín, 1½ hrs before flight (not always), US$0.70, 20-30 mins. Taxi US$4-5. *Trufis 1* and *F* go from H Siles y Loa, one block from main plaza to airport, US$0.55, 25 mins.

Aero Sur flies to La Paz, Santa Cruz and Tarija, LAB flies to Cochabamba (see note about LAB, page 28). Few flights are daily. Aero Sur, Arenales 31, T04-645 4895. LAB, Bustillos 121, T04-645 2666 (toll free T0800-3001).

Bus
Daily to/from La Paz at 1830-2000, 13 hrs, US$7.50-10 (Flota Copacabana and Trans Copacabana have *bus-cama*). To Cochabamba, several companies daily at 1830, arriving 0630, US$4.50-5.25 (Trans Copacabana *bus-cama*, US$7.50). To Potosí, 3 hrs on a paved road, frequent departures between 0630 and 1800, US$3. Silito Lindo taxis take 4 people to Potosí for US$3.75; T04-644 1014. To Tarija, several companies, 16hrs, US$5.25-6. To Uyuni, 0700 (Emperador), 0800 (Trans Capital), 9 hrs, US$5. Or catch a bus to Potosí and change; try to book the connecting bus in advance – see Trans Real Audencia, below. To Oruro, 1700 with Emperador via Potosí, arrives 0300, US$5 (*bus-cama*, US$15). To Santa Cruz: many companies go between 1600 and 1730, 15 hrs, US$6-7.50. To Villazón, at 1300 (Transtin Dilrey, direct) and 1400 (Villa Imperial, via Potosí) both 15 hrs, US$8.20. Trans Real Audencia, Arce 99 y San Alberto (same entrance as Hostal Libertad), T04-644 3119, for hassle-free bus tickets reservations to Potosí (US$3), Uyuni (US$6.70), Villazón and Tupiza (US$7.45), Tarabuco (Sun 0700 from outside office, US$3 return).

Car hire
Imbex, Serrano 165, T04-646 1222, www.imbex.com. Recommended.

Around Sucre *p389*
From Sucre to Tarabuco, buses (US$1.25) leave 0630 or when full from Plaza Huallparimachi, Av Manco Capac, or across the railway (take *micro B* or *C* from opposite

Mercado), 2½ hrs (or taxi, US$45). On Sun only, at least one bus will wait on Ravelo by the market for travellers, charging US$3 return to Tarabuco. Shared *trufi* taxis can be arranged by hotels, with pick-up service, starting at 0700, US$3.25 return. First bus back 1300; you must return on the bus you went on. **Andes Bus** run tourist services, departing 0800 (or when full), returning 1430, US$3, book at office, take food and drink. Transport more difficult on weekdays; take an early bus and return by truck.

❶ Directory

Sucre *p386, map p387*
Banks There are many **Enlace** 24-hr ATMs around town. **Banco Nacional**, España, corner with San Alberto, cash given on Visa and MasterCard US$3 commission, good rates for dollars, TCs changed, 5% commission. Diagonally opposite is **Banco Santa Cruz**, good rates for cash, advances on Visa, MasterCard and Amex, US$10 fee. Travel agencies' rates are good and at **España**, España 134, T04-646 0189, changes for TCs, 3% commission into US$, free into bolivianos, 9% commission on euro TCs. **Casa de Cambio Ambar**, San Alberto 7, T04-645 1339, good rates for TCs. Stalls at corner of Camargo and Arce buy and sell cash US dollars as well as Argentine, Chilean and Brazilian currency, but not as good rates as *cambios*. Many shops and street changers on Hernando Siles/Camargo buy and sell US dollars cash. **Cultural centres** Alianza Francesa, Aniceto Arce 35, T04-645 3599, www.af bolivia.org/_es/sucre.php, offers Spanish classes. **Casa de la Cultura**, Argentina 65, presents art exhibitions, concerts, folk dancing etc. **Centro Boliviano Americano**, Calvo 301, T04-644 1608, http://lapaz.us embassy.gov/cbasucre/cba.htm. Library open Mon-Fri 0900-1200, 1500-2000 (good for reference works). Recommended for language courses. The **Centro Cultural Hacheh** (see address for Café Hacheh, Eating), run by Felix Arciénega, Bolivian artist who organizes folk and jazz concerts, conferences, exhibitions and discussions, and is the editor of an art and poetry journal 'Hacheh'. **Centro Cultural Masis**, Bolívar 561, T04-645 3403, promotes the Yampara culture through textiles,

ceramics, figurines and music. Instruction in Quechua, traditional Bolivian music (3 hrs a week for US$15 a month, recommended) and handicrafts; stages musical events and exhibitions; items for sale. Open Mon-Sat 1430-2000 (knock if door closed); contact the director, Roberto Sahonero Gutierres at the centre Mon, Wed and Fri. The **Instituto Cultural Boliviano-Alemán** (Goethe Institute), Avaroa 326, T04-645 2091, www.icba-sucre.edu.bo, shows films, has German newspapers and books to lend (0930-1230 and 1500-2100), runs Spanish, German, Portuguese and Quechua courses and has the Kulturcafé Berlín (see Eating). Spanish lessons cost from US$6 for 45 mins for 1 person, with reductions the more students there are in the class. The ICBA also runs a folk music *peña* on Fri. **Embassies and consulates** Germany, Eva Kasewitz de Vilar, Rosendo Villa 54, T04-645 1369, ekvilar@mara.scr. entelnet.bo. Italy, Vice Consul, Martín Cruz 51, T04-645 5858. Paraguay, Plaza 25 de Mayo 28, T04-642 2999. Perú, Avaroa 472, T04-645 5592. **Internet** Many around town, generally slow connections, average US$0.60 per hr. **Language schools** Academia Latino-americana de Español, Dalence 109, T04-646 0537, www.latino schools.com. Professional, good extra-curricular activities, US$90 for 5 full days (US$120 for private teacher – higher prices if you book by phone or email). Bolivian Language School, Calle Kilómetro 7 250, T04-644 3841, www.bolivianspanish school.com. Near Parque Bolívar, pleasant school, good value, excellent teachers. Margot Macias Machicado, Olañeta 345, T04-642 3567, www.spanish-classes.8m.net. US$5 per hr. Recommended. Sofia Sauma, Loa 779, T04-645 1687, sadra@mara.scr. entelnet.bo. US$5 per hr. Private teachers advertise in bars etc. **Medical services** For hospitals, doctors and dentists, contact your consulate or the tourist office for recommendations. **Post office** Ayacucho 100 y Junín, open till 2000 (1600 Sat, Sun 1200), good service. *Poste Restante* is organized separately for men and women. **Telephone** Entel, España 252, 0730-2300. **Useful addresses** Immigration: Pastor Sáenz 117, T04-645 3647, Mon-Fri 0830-1630. Police patrol, T110 if in doubt about police or security matters.

Potosí

→ *Phone code 02. Colour map 3, C3. Population: 112,000. Altitude: 3977 m.*

Potosí is not only the highest city in the world, but also one of the most beautiful, saddest and fascinating places you'll ever experience. Towering over the city like a giant pink headstone is the 4824-m Cerro Rico. Silver from this mountain made Potosí the biggest city in the Americas and one of the richest in the world, rivalled only by Paris, London and Seville. But the 'Rich Mountain' also claimed the lives of countless thousands of indigenous slaves. This painful history still haunts the city and is as much a part of its colonial legacy as the many magnificent old buildings which led it to be declared Patrimony of Mankind by UNESCO in 1987. The Spanish still have a saying 'vale un Potosí' ('it's worth a Potosí') for anything incredibly valuable, but though Potosí's wealth is now only a distant memory, it remains one of Bolivia's greatest attractions and is certainly well worth a visit. ▸▸ For Sleeping Eating and other listings see pages 398-402.

Ins and outs

Getting there Vaca Guzmán airport ① *5 km out of town on the Sucre road*, is the world's highest. There are no scheduled flights. The **bus terminal** is on Avenida Universitaria below the rail station. It's a short taxi or *micro* ride to the centre of town, or a 20-minute uphill walk. There's an **Entel**, post office, police and US$0.10 terminal tax to pay. *Micros* within the city cost US$0.12. Taxis cost US$1. ▸▸ *For more detailed information see Transport, page 401.*

Tourist information The **tourist office** ① *Plaza 6 de Agosto, T02-622 7405, gobmupoi@cedro.pts.entelnet.bo, Mon-Fri 0800-1200, 1400-1800 (allegedly)*, is helpful and sells town maps for US$0.40 in English, French, German and Spanish; better than the glossy US$0.60 map (Spanish only). The police station by the *alcaldía* has a photo album showing common scams. Beware of fake 'plainclothes policemen', usually preceded by someone asking you for the time. The official police wear green uniforms and work in pairs. ▸▸ *See La Paz, page 305 for safety advice.*

Sights

Just wandering around the centre of Potosí is fascinating in itself and will take you past many colonial buildings. While Viceroy Toledo tried to bring order to the city's layout in 1574, the silver boom had led to fast and unplanned development which has left Potosí with a less-than-gridiron plan full of small streets with unexpected twists and turns which adds to the city's charm. There are lots of beautiful and ornate religious buildings well worth seeing but restoration work means buildings can be closed to visitors for months. Check with the tourist office if there is anywhere you particularly want to visit.

Below the main plaza, on Calle Ayacucho and Quijarro, is the huge and impressive Mint, the **Casa Nacional de Moneda** ① *Calle Ayacucho, T02-622 2777, Tue-Sat 0900-1200, 1400-1830, Sun 0900-1200, US$3, US$3 to take photos, US$3 for video, entry by 2-hr guided tour only (in English at 0900, usually for 10 or more people)*. Founded in 1572, rebuilt 1759-1773, it is one of the chief monuments of civil building in Hispanic America. Thirty of its 160 rooms are a museum with sections on mineralogy, and an art gallery in a splendid salon on the first floor. One section is dedicated to the works of the acclaimed 17th- to 18th-century religious painter Melchor Pérez de Holguín. Elsewhere are coin dies and huge wooden presses that made the silver strips from which coins were cut. The smelting houses have carved altar pieces from Potosí's ruined churches. You cannot fail to notice the huge, grinning mask of Bacchus over an archway between two principal courtyards, erected in 1865. Wear warm clothes when visiting as it is very cold inside.

Those who are into colonial architecture could do worse than begin in **Calle Quijarro**, one of Potosí's best-preserved streets. In colonial times it was known as Calle Ollería (potmakers) and Calle de los Sombreros (hats). At the bottom of Calle Ayacucho, on the corner with Chichas, is the **Convento y Museo de Santa Teresa** ① *T02-622 3847, daily 0900-1100 and 1500-1700, entry by guided tour in English or Spanish, US$3.15, US$1.50 to take photos, an extortionate US$25 to video.* The building was started in 1685 and has an impressive amount of giltwork inside. There is an eye-watering collection of flagellation tools (a must for sado-masochists), colonial paintings, religious architecture and furniture.

Potosí's first church, built in 1547, is the **Museo y Convento de San Francisco** ① *Calle Tarija y Nogales, T02-622 2539, Mon-Fri 0900-1200, 1430-1700, Sat 0900-*

Potosí

To Airport & Sucre

To Bus Terminal, Oruro & La Paz

Av Serrudo

Av Maestro

Av Cívica

Chayra

Museo Etno-indumentario

Omiste

Mercado Artesanal

Oruro

Ingavi

Bustillos

Quijarro

Junín

Sucre

Plaza del Estudiante

San Bernardo

Mercado Central

San Lorenzo

Av Camacho

Plaza la Católica

Héroes del Chaco

Mercado Central

San Agustín

Cerro Rico Travel

Simón Chacón

Bolívar

Matos

Plaza Vicuñas

Entel

Frías

Casa Nacional de Moneda

Cathedral

La Merced

Hoyos

Silver Tours

Compañía de Jesús

Amauta Expediciones

Koala Tours

Plaza 6 de Agosto

Andes Salt Expediciones

Immigration

Linares

Convento & Museo de Santa Teresa

Ayacucho

Chichas

Oruro

Bustillos

Plaza 10 de Noviembre

Plaza 25 de Mayo

Juan de la Cruz Tapia

Cobija

Carola Tours

Chuquisaca

C de Bolivia

A Palmero

La Paz

Castrillo

Nicolás Benino

Nogales

Padilla

Millares

Museo y Convento de San Francisco

Museo del Ingenio de San Marcos

Mejillones

Plazuela Colque

Cortes Periodista

Fanda

Tarija

N

0 metres 100
0 yards 100

To ⑦

66 99 The official shield of the city carries the words, "I am rich Potosí, the treasure of the world; the king of mountains, the envy of kings …"

1200, US$1.50, US$1.50 to take photos, US$3 video. The current building, begun in 1707 has the oldest surviving cloisters in Bolivia. It contains a museum of ecclesiastical art, with more than 200 paintings including one of Melchor Pérez de Holguín's best works, *The Erection of the Cross*. Don't miss going up on the roof, which provides one of the best viewpoints over the city.

There are a couple of other worthwhile museums. The **Museo del Ingenio de San Marcos** ① *Betanzos y La Paz, T02-622 2781, 1000-2300*, is a well-preserved example of the city's industrial past, with machinery used in grinding down the silver ore. It also has a restaurant, cultural activities and an exhibition of Calcha textiles. The **Museo Etno-indumentario** (also known as **Fletes**) ① *Av Serrudo 152, T02-622 3258, Mon-Fri 0900-1200, 1400-1800, Sat 0900-1200, US$1.10, includes tour in Spanish and German*, has a thorough display of the different dress and customs of the Department of Potosí.

Mine tours
Most people come to Potosí for the incredible experience of visiting one of the myriad mine workings of the infamous **Cerro Rico**. The state mines were closed in the 1980s and are now worked as cooperatives by small groups of miners. Cerro Rico was described by one Spanish chronicler in the mid-16th century as "the mouth of hell", and visitors should be aware that descending into its bowels is both physically and emotionally draining. The tour, as **Koala Tours** proclaim, is "not for wimps or woosies". The mine entrances are above 4000 m and you will be walking, or rather crouching, around breathing in noxious gases and seeing people working in appalling conditions in temperatures up to 40°C. You should be acclimatized, fit and not have any heart or breathing problems, such as asthma.

The standard price of a tour is US$14 per person, less in the low season. Make sure you are getting a helmet, lamp and protective clothing (but wear old clothes anyway). Tours follow a set itinerary. A full tour lasts four to five hours and does not give you time to join a tour of the Casa Nacional de Moneda afterwards. A trip to the thermal baths to clean up is a better option. The size of tour groups varies; some are as large as 20 people, which is excessive. Tours last from around 0800 to mid-afternoon, with around four hours inside the mines. Guided tours are conducted by former miners; by law all guides have to work with a travel agency and carry an ID card issued by the Prefectura.

The tour begins with a visit to **Mercado Calvario** where you are expected to buy gifts for the miners such as dynamite, coca leaves, meths, ammonium nitrate and cigarettes. Then it's up to the mine where you get kitted up and enter one of the tunnels. A tour will usually go down all the way to the fourth level, meeting and talking to working miners on the way. You will see how dynamite is used and also meet *El Tío*, the god of the underworld (Friday afternoon is the main day for making offerings to *El Tío*). A

● *The miners believe that the devil owns the minerals in the earth and, in order to appease*
● *him, every mine has its own statue of El Tío where the miners make offerings of cigarettes, coca or alcohol.*

A man's gotta chew

Apart from the dream of striking it rich, it is coca that keeps the miners going. The only real break they get down in the bowels of the earth is El Aculli, when they chew coca.

The sacred leaves are masticated with *lejía*, a paste moulded from plant ashes which activates with saliva to produce the desired effect from the coca. This numbs the senses and staves off hunger pangs and exhaustion. It is only by chewing coca that the miners can work at all. "No coca, no work", as one miner put it.

They spend several hours chewing the leaves every morning before entering the mine. Not only does the coca give the miners the energy to carry on working without food, they also believe that it acts as a filter of dust and toxic gases.

Although coca is also taken in a social context, workers used to deny this because, in the eyes of the priests and bosses, an increase in labour productivity was the only permissible reason for tolerating consumption of 'the devil's leaf'.

good guide will be able to explain mining practices, customs and traditions little changed since the Spanish left and enable you to communicate with the miners. Many tours also include some sort of dynamite pyrotechnics. A contribution to the miners' cooperative is appreciated as are medicines for the new health centre (*posta sanitaria*) on Cerro Rico.

Around Potosí

The thermal baths at **Tarapaya**, 25 km outside the city on the road to Oruro, are worth visiting to freshen up after crawling around in mine tunnels. There are public baths (US$0.30) and private (US$0.60); the private baths, higher up, may be cleaner. On the other side of the river from Tarapaya is a small 50-m-wide volcanic crater lake, with a temperature of 30°C. It's a pleasant enough spot **do not swim** in the lake. Several people have drowned here and though agencies in Potosí do not warn of the dangers. Nearby is **Balneario Miraflores** which also has swimming pools. Camping by the lake is possible and there's accommodation at Balneario Tarapaya. North of Balneario Miraflores is **Hacienda Mondragon**, set in a beautiful canyon, which is visited by most of the tour operators. Buses to Tarapaya and Miraflores leave from outside the Chuquimia market on Avenida Universitaria, up from the bus terminal, every 30 minutes or so (0700-1700, US$0.55, 30 minutes). A taxi costs US$7.50 for a group. The last bus back from Miraflores leaves at 1800.

Sleeping

Potosí *p395, map p396*
Hotels in Potosí have no heating, unless stated otherwise.
C **Claudia**, Av Maestro 322, T02-622 2242, claudia_ hotel@hotmail.com. This modern hotel is away from the centre. Helpful staff. Recommended.
C **Hostal Colonial**, Hoyos 8, T02-622 4809, F622 7146. A pretty colonial house near the main plaza, with heating and basic breakfast, TV, has names and telephone numbers of guides, very helpful, even if you're not

staying there, safe parking, best hotel in centre. Book in advance.
C **Hostal Libertador**, Millares 58, T02-622 7877, hostalib@cedro.pts.entelnet.bo. Central heating, quiet, helpful, comfortable, parking.
D **Hostal Cerro Rico**, Ramos 123 between La Paz and Millares, T/F622 3539. Very good rooms upstairs, heating, hot water, D without bath, cable TV, internet, helpful, parking.
D **Jerusalem**, Oruro 143, T/F02-622 2600, hoteljer@cedro.pts.entelnet.bo. Pleasant,

with breakfast, F without bath, helpful, *comedor*, parking, laundry, good value.
E **Hostal Compañía de Jesús**, Chuquisaca 445, T02-622 3173. Very friendly, old monastery. Some rooms are dark but beds are very comfortable and it's a nice old colonial building, which was once a monastery. Hot showers once the ice in the tank melts in the morning. Price includes a basic breakfast.
E **Hostal Felimar**, Junín 14, T02-622 4357. The price includes continental breakfast; it's US$3 cheaper to share a bathroom. 1st floor rooms have no exterior windows but are warm and quiet. There's one roof-top suite. Some of the ceilings were designed for people under 5 ft tall.
F **Carlos V**, Linares 42 on Plaza 6 de Agosto, T02-622 5121. With breakfast, G without bath, occasional hot water 0700-1200, luggage store, 2400 curfew.
F **El Turista**, Lanza 19, T02-622 2492, F622 2517. Also **LAB** office, helpful, hot showers, breakfast (US$1), great view from top rooms, good value. Recommended but poor beds.
F **Hostal Santa María**, Av Serrudo 244, T02-622 3255. Hot water, comfortable and friendly, though rooms have hospital beds and are on the dark side.
F **Koala Den**, Junín 56, T02-622 6467, see **Koala Tours**, below, but book separately. Refurbished, with heated dormitory (F) and shared showers, private rooms with bath and breakfast, TV and video and use of kitchen.
G pp **Backpackers Potosí**, Chuquisaca 460 y Padilla, T04-644 0889, potosi@ boliviahostels.com. Recent addition to the network of budget hostels.
G **Casa de María Victoria**, Chuquisaca 148, T02-622 2132. Built in the 17th century as accommodation for friars from Santo Domingo, all rooms open on to a stone courtyard, clean, stores luggage, popular with backpackers, travel agency offers cheap mine tours, breakfast in courtyard, owner speaks English, leave nothing unattended.
G **Posada San Lorenzo**, Calle Bustillos 967, opposite market. Colonial building, courtyard, no showers.
G **Res Copacabana**, Av Serrudo 319, T02-622 2712. Single or shared rooms, restaurant, separate hot showers, will change US dollars cash, safe car park.

G **Residencial Felcar**, Serrudo 345 y Bustillos, T02-622 4966. Shared bath, hot water 0800-1600, popular, nice patio garden.
G **Residencial Sumaj**, Gumiel 12, T02-622 2336, hoteljer@cedro.pts.entelnet.bo. Small rooms all without bath, double room on top floor with good views. There's a kitchen, a laundry and a TV lounge and it's popular with travellers. It's also friendly and helpful but it's a dark place apart from the central courtyard.
G **Tarija**, Av Serrudo 252, T02-622 2711. Clean and helpful, Tarija has no obvious sign but a big cobbled courtyard with free parking. The more expensive rooms are much nicer, with wooden beds and floors and good, newly tiled private bathrooms. Recommended.

---

❼ Eating

Potosí *p395, map p396*
Good value food in Mercado Central, between Oruro, Bustillos, Héroes del Chaco and Bolívar, breakfast from 0700, fresh bread from 0600.
❦❦-❦ **La Casona Pub**, Frías 34, T02-622 2954, Mon-Sat 1000-1230, 1815-2400. Good food (meat fondue and trout recommended) and beer, pleasant atmosphere and service.
❦❦-❦ **El Fogón**, Oruro y Frías, T02-622 4969, open 1200-1500, 1800-2400. Upmarket pub-restaurant, good food and atmosphere.
❦❦-❦ **Potocchi**, Millares 24, T02-622 2467, open from 0800. Great traditional food, with a *peña* most nights.
❦ **Chaplin**, Quijarro y Matos 10, closed 1200-1500 and Sun. Pleasant, good breakfasts and fast food, vegetarian options, great *tucumanos*.
❦ **Kaypichu**, Millares 24, Tue-Sun 0700-1300 and 1600-2100. Vegetarian, stylish, good breakfasts.
❦ **Sumaj Orcko**, Quijarro 46. Large portions, cheap set lunch, reasonably priced, very popular with travellers, heating.

Cafés
4060 Café, Hoyos between Padilla and Millares. Potosí's 'in' place, serving interesting food, more upmarket surroundings and pricier than others.
Café La Plata, Plaza 10 de Noviembre, corner with Linares, T02-622 6085, Mon-Sat 1500-2200, also for breakfast. A great place to relax over a coffee, wine or beer. The home-baked cookies are delicious and there

are games to play. Chic, warm and friendly, the owners speak English and French.

Café Tokyo, Oruro y Cobija. Good food, good value and service.

Candelaria Internet Café, Calle Ayacucho 5, daily from 0700. A part of the **Koala** mini empire, the slightly decrepit Calendaria is popular with travellers for its Bolivian food, balcony, book exchange, apple pie and travel guide library. Also has internet for US$0.75/hr.

Confitería Cherry's, Padilla 8, open from 0800. Good cakes (especially the apple strudel) and breakfast but the coffee is best avoided. Good value as long as you like loud 1980s pop and aren't too worried by painfully slow service.

⊛ Festivals and events

Potosí *p395, map p396*
Feb/Mar Carnival Minero is celebrated 2 weeks before the Oruro Carnival, on a Sat and is known locally as *Tata Ckascho*. The miners parade and dance down Cerro Rico from the church near the top, to Plaza El Minero, carrying their god, *El Tío*. This is his one and only annual appearance outside the mine. Another miners' festival, held 2 weeks before Carnival, is **Fiesta de los Compadres**, and 1 week later is **Fiesta de las Comadres**. During Carnival itself, Shrove Tuesday is celebrated as **Martes de Cha'lla**, when offerings to Pachamama are made at the doors of people's houses and drinks are offered to passers-by. Ash Wednesday throughout the region is **Carnival Campesina** which lasts for 5 days, ending with **Domingo de Tentación** (Temptation Sunday) in many small villages.
8-10 Mar San Juan de Dios, with music, dancing and parades.
Last Sun in May Fiesta de Manquiri, a festival when vehicles and miniatures are blessed in the village of Manquiri, 26 km northeast of the city. There's transport to Manquiri from Plaza Chuquimia. Also in May there's a **market** on Calle Gumiel every Sun, with lotteries, and items for sale.
May/Jun On 3 consecutive Sats llama sacrifices are made at the cooperative mines in honour of Pachamama.
Aug There are more llama sacrifices at the beginning of Aug: on the 1st day, **Chutillo**, people walk to the village of La Puerta, 5 km

from the centre on the Oruro road, to the church of San Bartolomé to pray and then climb the nearby hill. On day 2, **Majtillo**, indigenous people in costume from all over the department make their entrance into the city. Day 3 is **Thapuquillo**, when people from the city and invited groups from other parts of the country and abroad parade through the streets.
1st and 2nd Sun in Oct Virgen de La Merced and Virgen del Rosario, with processions through decorated streets and people throwing flower petals on passing religious images.
Oct/Nov Festival Internacional de la Cultura, when cultural events take place over 2 weeks in Potosí and Sucre.
10 Nov Fiesta Aniversario de Potosí, which celebrates the city's foundation.

○ Shopping

Potosí *p395, map p396*
Germán Laime, Sucre 38. Tailor, will make items (jackets, bags, etc) to customers' wishes.
Mercado Artesanal, at Sucre y Omiste, sells handwoven cloth and regional handicrafts. Some Fridays the merchants organize music, food and drink (*ponche*), not to be missed.
Mercado Central (see address above), sells mainly food and produce but silver is sold near the C Oruro entrance.

▲ Activities and tours

Potosí *p395, map p396*
Trips to the Salar de Uyuni, Laguna Colorada and Laguna Verde are expensive here. See page 375 for advice on booking a trip. The following have been recommended.
Amauta Expediciones, Ayacucho 17, T02-622 5515. For trips to Uyuni, the lagoons and the mines. Gerónimo Fuentes has been recommended and speaks English. 15% of income goes to the miners.
Andes Salt Expediciones, Plaza Alonso de Ibáñez 3, T02-622 5175, www.bolivia-travel .com.bo. Recommended guides. Run by Braulio Mamani, who speaks English. City tours, bus and flight tickets, also based in Uyuni.
Carola Tours, Lanza y Chuquisaca. Guide and owner Santos Mamani is recommended.
Cerro Rico Travel, Bolívar 853, T02-622 7044, jacky_gc@yahoo.com. Jaqueline

⁝ Fight for the right to party

A tradition peculiar to the Potosí Department is the *tinku* ritual fight. Basically, what happens is that two neighbouring communities meet up and beat the living daylights out of one another – literally. For death, though much less common these days, is always a possibility.

The *tinku* may look like a drunken Saturday night pub brawl, but it is loaded with symbolism and carries a deep spiritual significance. It is a meeting of equals and is not about winning, but of recognizing your rivals, respecting them and defining your territory. It symbolizes the need to co-exist with other people. It is also a celebration of forgiveness of family or personal enemies. In the tinku any problem is solved and all debts are paid.

Before the fight, the combatants meet and drink *chicha* and stronger alcohol. The alcohol is to give them courage for the impending battle. The fight begins with fists; each fighter wears rings of bronze adorned with claws to ensure the opponents guts are ripped out. For protection, the pugilists wear a leather helmet,

treated so that it is hard as steel, and a leather groin protector. Fighting is hand-to-hand and reaches a fever pitch of noisy violence. The losers begin to retreat and then stones rain down on both groups.

The winner of each fight then enjoys one year of dominance over his defeated opponent. The injured are respected for standing their ground and fighting bravely. The corpses, meanwhile, are buried as an offering to Pachamama, to ensure a good harvest.

There is no sexual discrimination here. Women also fight in the *tinku* and it is said that they fight more cruelly and with more honour. During the *tinku*, bands play continuously and those who are too scared, ill, old, or sensible to fight dance around in a circle.

Tourists are a relatively new phenomenon, so be discreet. Things can get ugly after few days' hard drinking and fighting, so it's wise to get out before the end. Some agencies, for example **Koala**, organize trips to the Macha *tinku* on 3 May and the Uncía *tinku* on 2 August.

---

knows the mines well and speaks good English. Also English and French guides for trips to village *artesanía* markets north of the city and to colonial haciendas, horse and mountain bike hire, treks, trips to Toro Toro including cave visits.
Hidalgo Tours, Junín y Bolívar 19, T02-622 5186, uyusalht@ceibo.entelnet.bo. Upmarket and specialized services within the city and to Salar de Uyuni. Efraín Huanca has been recommended for mine tours.
Koala Tours, Ayacucho 5, T/F02-622 2092, frontpoi@cedro.pts.entelnet.bo. Run by Eduardo Garnica Fajardo who speaks English and French. Excellent mine tours by former miners, Juan Mamani Choque and Pedro Montes Caria have been recommended. The company donates 15% of its fees to support on-site health-care

facilities. Frequently recommended. They also have a *hostal*, The Koala Den, see Sleeping, and an internet café.
Silver Tours, Quijarro 12, Edif Minero, T02-622 3600, www.silvertours.8m.com. One of the cheaper firms, guide Fredi recommended.

⊖ Transport

Potosí *p395, map p396*
Bus When you buy your ticket you check your luggage into the operator's office and it is then loaded directly onto your bus. Daily services to **La Paz**, 1830-1930, US$5, 10 hrs by paved road, *bus cama* with **Flota Copacabana** US$7.50 (all departures from La Paz 1830-2030). To travel by day, go to **Oruro**, 0700 and 1900, US$2.50, 5 hrs. To **Cochabamba**, 1830 and 1900, US$4.50, 12 hrs. To **Sucre**, 4 daily

0700-1800, US$3, 3 hrs. Cars also run to Sucre, taking 5 passengers, 2½ hrs, US$3.75 pp, drop-off at your hotel. To **Santa Cruz**, 1900 (change in Sucre or Cochabamba), US$12, 18 hrs. To **Villazón**, 0800, 1900, US$6, 10-12 hrs. To **Tarija**, 1800, US$6.70-7.45, 12 hrs, spectacular journey but crowded bus. Buses to **Uyuni** leave from either side of the railway line (uphill the road is called Av Antofagasta or 9 de Abril, downhill it is Av Universitaria), 5 daily 1030 to 1930, US$3.10, 6 hrs, superb scenery; book in advance.

Directory

Potosí *p395, map p396*

Banks There are ATMs around the centre. Banco Nacional, Junín 4-6. Exchange for US$ TCs and cash. **Banco Mercantil**, Sucre y Ayacucho. 1% commission on US$ TCs, no commission on Visa cash withdrawals. Almost opposite is **Casa Fernández** for cash exchange. **Banco de Crédito**, Bolívar

y Sucre. Cash withdrawals on Visa. **Prodem**, Bolívar y Junín. Cash advances on Visa and MasterCard, 5% commission, also changes US$ cash. Many shops on Plaza Alonso de Ibáñez and on Bolívar, Sucre and Padilla display 'compro dólares' signs. **Internet Café Candelaria**, see cafés above. Tuko's Café, Junín 9, p 3, T02-622 5489, tuco25@ hotmail.com. Open 0800-2300, 'the highest net café in the world'; US$0.75/hr, lots of information, English spoken, popular music, videos, good food. Another opposite bus terminal. **Post office** Lanza 3, Mon-Fri 0800-2000, Sat 0800-1800, Sun 0900-1200. **Telephone** Entel, on Plaza Arce at end of Av Camacho, T02-624 3496. Also at Av Universitaria near bus terminal, and on Padilla, opposite Confitería Cherys. **Useful addresses** Migración: Linares corner with Padilla, T02-622 5989, Mon-Fri 0830-1630, closed lunchtime, beware unnecessary charges for extensions. Police station: on Plaza 10 de Noviembre.

Tarija

→ *Phone code: 04. Colour map 3, C4. Population: 109,000. Altitude: 1840 m.*

Situated along the banks of the Río Guadalquivir, this tranquil agricultural and wine centre is linguistically and visually reminiscent of Spanish Andalucía. It is also culturally closer to Argentina than to the rest of Bolivia, something the native Tarijeños (or 'Chapacos' as they are also known) point to with pride. Tarija is blessed with plenty of sun and a spring-like climate almost all year-round. The city has a justly deserved reputation not only for its wonderful climate, but also for the easy-going nature of its inhabitants. Of all Bolivian cities, perhaps Tarija comes closest to capturing the ambience of a 'typical' post-colonial settlement, with its date and orange tree-lined plaza, wide streets and prominent churches. ▶▶ *For Sleeping, Eating and other listings see pages 405-407.*

Ins and outs

Getting there and around The **airport** ① *3 km east of town along Av Las Américas, T04-664 3135*, receives flights from La Paz, Cochabamba, Santa Cruz and Sucre. A taxi from the airport to the centre costs US$3.75; or take a *micro*, linea 'A' runs to the Mercado Central, US$0.25. Some hotels offer a free pick-up, but you may have to call them. On arrival at Tarija, reconfirm your next flight straight away. The **bus terminal** is in the outskirts on Avenida Las Américas, a 30-minute walk from the centre, on the way to the airport, T04-663 6508. **Note** All blocks west of Calle Colón have a small 'O' before the number (*oeste*), and all blocks east have an 'E' (*este*); blocks are numbered from Colón outwards. All streets north of Avenida Las Américas are preceded by 'N'.

Tourist information The **tourist office** ① *southwest corner of main plaza, in the Prefectura, T04-663 1000, Mon-Fri only, 0800-1200, 1430-1830*, is helpful, free city map and guide. Also at Sucre y Bolívar.

Sights

Tarija may be a pleasant enough place to hang out, but it is not over-endowed with cultural and historical sites. The most interesting church is the **Basílica de San Francisco** ① *corner of Av Daniel Campos and La Madrid, open for Mass Mon-Sat 0700-1000 and 1800-2000, Sun 0630-1200, 1800-2000.* Built in 1606, this is the oldest church in the city and it is beautifully painted inside, with praying angels depicted on the ceiling. Besides the stunning artwork, it contains two libraries, the old one containing some 15,000 volumes, and the new one a further 5000. A small museum boasts an outstanding collection of colonial books, including a 1501 edition of *The Iliad*, as well as numerous modern reference works and 19th-century photograph albums on Bolivia. To visit the libraries, you need permission from the Franciscan priests who maintain them. Ask for either Father Lorenzo or Maldini at the rectory, at Calle Ingavi 137.

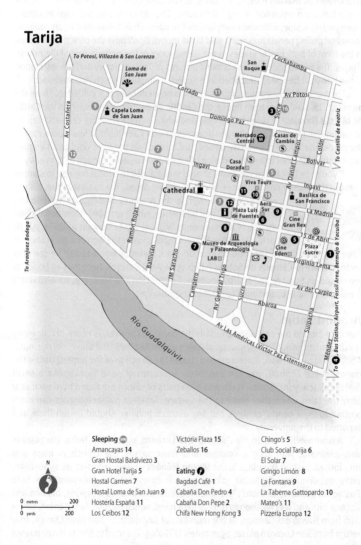

Tarija

Sleeping ⬤	Victoria Plaza **15**	Chingo's **5**
Amancayas **14**	Zeballos **16**	Club Social Tarija **6**
Gran Hostal Baldiviezo **3**		El Solar **7**
Gran Hotel Tarija **5**	Eating ⬤	Gringo Limón **8**
Hostal Carmen **7**	Bagdad Café **1**	La Fontana **9**
Hostal Loma de San Juan **9**	Cabaña Don Pedro **4**	La Taberna Gattopardo **10**
Hostería España **11**	Cabaña Don Pepe **2**	Mateo's **11**
Los Ceibos **12**	Chifa New Hong Kong **3**	Pizzería Europa **12**

0 metres 200
0 yards 200

The **Museo de Arqueología y Paleontología** ① *corner of Av General Trigo and Calle Virginio Lema, 1 block south of the main plaza, Mon-Fri 0800-1200 and 1500-1800, Sat 0900-1200, 1500-1800, free*, is part of Tarija's university. It contains a one-room paleontological collection, including dinosaur bones, fossils and the remains of several Andean elephants (one of which a family found under their patio following an earth tremor in 1999). Upstairs there are smaller mineralogical, ethnographic and anthropological collections. These are generally well presented and explained. There are two Spanish-only videos for sale (US$10 each); one about the culture of Tarija, the other about its fossilized heritage, both 25 minutes.

Two houses of the 19th-century merchant Moisés Navajas, one of Tarija's most prominent citizens, are also well worth a visit. The **Casa Dorada** ① *at the intersection of Av General Trigo and Calle Ingavi, entrance on Ingavi, Mon-Fri 0900-1200 and 1500-1800, Sat 0900-1200, entry by donation (US$0.30 minimum), guided tours in Spanish*, also known as **Maison d'Or**, is the city's official Casa de Cultura. Begun in 1886, the house has been repainted in original colours, silver and ochre on the outside, cerise, green and dark blue, with white trim, inside. The interior has Italian murals, art nouveau copies on ceiling panels and much gold in the rooms. Don't miss the crystal table lamps in the form of bunches of grapes in the dining room or the painted roof of the private chapel. The photography room contains pictures of Tarijan history and the restoration of the house. It has been described as a superb example of Kitsch decorative art.

For those who crave more of the same, it is possible to have a guided tour from the owner of Navajas' other town house, the **Castillo de Beatriz** (also known as the **Catillo de Moisés Navajas**). It resembles a blue-and-white, square wedding cake and can be found on Calle Bolívar, just after the intersection with Calle Junín, a few blocks east of the plaza. The house is privately owned, but a knock on the front door or an enquiry around the side door to the right during office hours is usually enough to gain entry.

If you're in Tarija then you really should make a visit to a local *bodega* to sample some of the local wines and to see how they are produced. The easiest to see, a short walk across the river, is the **Aranjuez Bodega**, at Avenida Los Sauces 1976. Their best white, which won an international silver medal, is a Chardonnay/Muscat '99 (a bargain at US$1.35). To visit, ask Señor Milton Castellanos at the Agrochemical shop at Trigo 789 (Monday-Friday 1000-1200, 1500-1730, Saturday 0900-1200); he can also arrange visits to **Campos de Solana** (shop 15 de Abril E-0259). Note that all *bodegas* are closed on Sunday. The nearby bodegas, Concepción and Köhlberg, are also worth a visit with ample opportunity to sample several wines.

❖ The best time to visit is from January, when the fruits are in season.

Around Tarija

The area around the city, and especially the banks of the river, is home to numerous fossils and dinosaur bones, several of which are on display in the university museum. About 5 km out of town, (take a *micro* or taxi in the direction of the airport) before the *garita* (police control), you can see lovely structures of sand looking like a small *barrancos* (canyon). Bones, teeth and even parts of spines are found here each year after the rains when they come to the surface. Amateur paleontologists can roam around to their hearts' content, but any unusual findings should be left there and reported to the university.

A worthwhile trip is to the village of **San Lorenzo**, 15 km from Tarija. The plaza is very pleasant, with palms, oranges and flowers, and the church is huge and unadorned. Just off the plaza is the **Museo Méndez** ① *daily 0900-1230, 1500-1830, entry by donation (US$0.30 minimum)*, the house of the Independence hero Eustaquio Méndez, 'El Moto'. The small museum exhibits his weapons, his bed and various bits and pieces, though not his right hand, which he lost. To get there, take a *trufi* from Barrio del Carmen, at the roundabout just north of San Juan Church, they return from San Lorenzo plaza; 45 minutes, US$0.45. The road to San Lorenzo passes

Tomatitas, 5 km from town, which is a popular swimming and picnic area. At lunchtime on Sunday, many courtyards serve very cheap meals.

In **El Valle de Concepción**, 36 km south of Tarija is the **Rugero Singani** *bodega*. To visit, an appointment must be made in Tarija with Inginiero Sergio Prudencio Navarro (Bodegas y Viñedos de la Concepción, La Madrid y Suipacha sin número. Alternatively call T04-664 3763). Inginiero Prudencio will show visitors round the vineyards and the *bodega*; try their highly recommended 1994 Cabernet Sauvignon Reserve or their Muscat. To visit the *bodegas* outside the city, it's best to join a tour (**VTB** is recommended). You can try it on your own, but be warned, it's easy to get lost. Take a *trufi* from Parada del Chaco every 20-30 minutes, US$0.75 (to get to Parada del Chaco catch any linea 'A' minibus from outside the Mercado Central). They return from the plaza in Concepción. The route takes the road past the airport. At the *garita* (guard post) the road forks left to Yacuiba/Pocitos or continues straight on to Bermejo. Take the latter and, 9 km later, turn right (the road is signposted to 'Concepción'). Then you pass the **Colonial** winery, the Santa Ana bridge and **Santa Ana Grande** vineyards and the **Centro Vitivinicola, Cooperación Española**, before reaching Concepción and its lovely plaza filled with bitter orange and ceibo trees.
▸ *See Activities and tours, page 407.*

Tarija to Villamontes → *Colour map 3, C4.*

A road runs east from Tarija, passing through Entre Ríos to Villamontes, where it branches north to Santa Cruz, south to Argentina and continues east to Paraguay. The road from Villamontes to Tarija is good all-weather surface, but there are a few bad patches in the mountains out of Entre Ríos due to landslides and rockfalls. The last 30 km into Tarija is paved, part of the new Tarija-Bermejo highway. The section from Entre Ríos to Villamontes is truly spectacular (sit on the left for the best views). The road is carved into the rockface high above the gorge of the Río Pilcomayo as it snakes its way down through densely forested slopes of the eastern cordillera.

The charming, sub-tropical little colonial town of **Entre Ríos** , with cobbled streets and a pretty plaza full of roses which give off a heady scent in the midday heat, lies halfway between Tarija and Villamontes. A giant statue of Christ towers over the town from a summit on the outskirts. There are great views from the top of the steps leading up to it. Also there's good walking in the surrounding hills. Some 10 minutes' walk away, at Rio Santa Ana you can swim when there is enough water; ask directions. You can also hike to a waterfall as well as hire horses; ask Beatrice at the excellent **Hotel Plaza** (see Sleeping, below). Some 51 km south of Entre Ríos, 6 km beyond the town of **Salinas**, is the village of **La Misión**, where the original wooden portal and porch of the Jesuit mission church survives. The road is not driveable beyond La Misión.

Villamontes, 280 km east of Tarija, is a friendly town on the edge of the Gran Chaco and is on the road and rail route from Santa Cruz to the Argentine border at Yacuiba. It is hot – very hot. The local Guarani make fine basketwork and cane furniture which is sold in shops outside the central market. The town is renowned for fishing and holds a **Fiesta del Pescado** in August. The main street runs west-east with the bus terminal and train station at the west end, 1½ km from the main square, Plaza 15 de Abril.

⬤ Sleeping

Tarija *p402, map p403*

AL Los Parrales Resort, Urb Carmen de Aranjuez Km 3.5, T04-664 8444 (ask for Lic Miguel Piaggio), parrales@mail.com. Stunning views of Río Guadalquivir. The only 5-star accommodation in southern Bolivia and

worth it, European-style amenities, can arrange city and vineyard tours and to Argentina, phone in advance for off-season discounts.

B Gran Hotel Tarija, Sucre N-0770, T04-664 4777. Modern, comfortable, parking, central.

B **Los Ceibos**, Av Víctor Paz Estenssoro y La Madrid, T04-663 4430, ceibhot@ cosett.com.bo. Including excellent buffet breakfast, large rooms, mini-bar, good restaurant, pool and cocktail bar.

B **Victoria Plaza**, Plaza Luis de Fuentes, T04-664 2600. Includes buffet breakfast in Café-Bar La Bella Epoca, 4-star, laundry service.

C **Hostal Loma de San Juan**, Bolívar s/n (opposite Capela Loma de San Juan), T04-664 4206. Comfortable, pool, sumptuous buffet breakfast included.

C **La Pasarela**, 10 km north of Tarija near the village of Coimata, T04-666 1333, info@ lapasarelahotel.com. Belgian-owned hotel/restaurant/bar, includes breakfast, country views, tranquil, family atmosphere, living room, jacuzzi, swimming pool, internet, mountain bikes, laundry and camping.

D **Gran Hostal Baldiviezo**, La Madrid O-0443, T/F04-663 7711, administracion@ghb.html planet.com. Central, good beds and facilities.

E **Hostal Carmen**, Ingavi O-0784 y R Rojas, T04-664 3372, vtb@olivo.tja.entelnet.bo. Shower, good value, F without cable TV, some ground floor rooms without exterior windows, good breakfast, transfer stand at airport, tour agency, book in advance.

F **Amancayas** (formerly **Res Rosario**), Ingavi 0-0777, residen_rosario@latinmail.com. F without bath, showers, cable TV, quiet, good value. Recommended but for the laundry.

F **Hostería España**, Alejandro Corrado O-0546, T04-664 1790. Hot showers, G without bath, pleasant.

F **Zeballos**, Sucre 0966, T04-664 2068. G without bath, includes breakfast, cable TV, quiet, safe, laundry, 5 mins from plaza. Good atmosphere.

🍴 Eating

Tarija p402, map p403
Many restaurants (and much else in town) close between 1400 and 1600.

🍴 **La Taberna Gattopardo**, on main plaza, daily 0700-0200. Pizza, *parrillada* with Argentine beef, local wines, snacks, excellent salads, good value.

🍴 **Cabaña Don Pedro**, Padilla y Av Las Américas. Good typical food.

🍴 **Cabaña Don Pepe**, D Campos N-0138, near Av Las Américas. Excellent steaks at moderate prices, *peña* at weekends with local folk music.

🍴 **Chifa New Hong Kong**, Sucre O-0235. Smart, Chinese, good service.

🍴 **Chingo's**, Plaza Sucre. Popular for cheap local food.

🍴 **Club Social Tarija**, east side of the plaza. Pleasant, old-fashioned, haunt of Tarija's business community, excellent *almuerzo* for US$1.80. Recommended.

🍴 **El Solar**, Campero y V Lema, Mon-Sat 0800-1400. Vegetarian, set lunch,

🍴 **Gringo Limón**, Trigo N-0345. Pay by weight, nothing special.

🍴 **Mateo's**, Trigo N-0610, closed 1530-1900 and Sun. Excellent *almuerzo* US$3 (includes salad bar), good value evening meals with a wide selection of local and international dishes, pasta a speciality.

🍴 **Pizzería Europa**, main plaza west side. Internet (US$0.90 per hr), good *salteñas*.

Cafés

Bagdad Café, Plaza Sucre. Also has live music at night.

La Fontana, La Madrid y Campos. Good for ice cream, snacks and coffee. For a cheap breakfast try the market. Try the local wines, eg Aranjuez, La Concepción, Santa Ana de Casa Real or Kohlberg, the *singani* (a clear brandy, San Pedro de Oro and Rugero are recommended labels), also local beer, Astra.

⚙ Festivals and events

Tarija p402, map p403
15 Mar The city is famous for its colourful *niño* (child) processions, **Día de Tarija**.
Mar/Apr A flower festival takes place in San Lorenzo.
Late Apr Exposur, held 20 km northwest of city; admission free; local and regional crafts, cuisine, and dances.
15 Aug La Virgen de Chaguaya, people walk from Tarija to Santuario Chaguaya, south of El Valle, 60 km south of the city. For less devoted souls, Línea P *trufi* from

● *For an explanation of sleeping and eating price codes used in this guide, see inside the*
● *front cover. Other relevant information is found in Essentials, see pages 31-35.*

Plaza Sucre, Tarija, to Padcaya, US$1; bus to Chaguaya and Padcaya from terminal daily, 0700, returns 1700, US$1.35.

1st Sun in Sep In the 3-day **San Roque** festival the richly dressed saint's statue is paraded through the streets; the people wear lively colours, cloth turbans and veils and dance before it. Women throw flowers from the balconies. Dogs are decorated with ribbons for the day.

2nd Sun in Oct A flower festival commemorates the **Virgen del Rosario** (celebrations in the surrounding towns are recommended, eg San Lorenzo and Padcaya).

Mid-Oct On 2 weekends there is a **beer festival** on Av de las Américas.

▲ Activities and tours

Tarija *p402, map p403*
Internacional Tarija, Sucre 721, T04-664 4446, F664 5017. Flights and tours, helpful.
Mara Tours, Gral Trigo N-739, T04-664 3490, marvin@olivo.tja.entelnet.bo. Helpful.
Viva Tours, Sucre 0615, T04-663 8325, vivatour@cosett.com.bo. Vineyard tours US$30 with lunch.
VTB, at **Hostal Carmen** (see Sleeping above). All tours include a free city tour; 4- to 6-hr trips including singani *bodegas*, US$19 pp; comprehensive 10-hr 'Tarija and surroundings in 1 Day', US$27; can also try your hand at an excavation with their palaeontology specialist.

◉ Transport

Tarija *p402, map p403*
Air
A taxi to the airport, T04-664 3135, from the centre of town costs US$3.75; or take a *micro A* from outside the Mercado Central which drops you 1 block away, US$0.25. **Aero Sur** flies to **La Paz**, **Sucre** and **Santa Cruz**. LAB (see note page 28) flies to **Cochabamba**. Schedules change frequently; also flights are frequently cancelled and/or delayed. Aero Sur office: 15 de Abril entre Daniel Campos y Colón, T04-663 0893. **LAB** office: Trigo N-0319, T04-644 2473.

Bus
Buses run daily on the 935-km route from **Potosí-Oruro-La Paz**, depart 0700 and 1700 (20 hrs, US$11.25; check which company operates the best buses, eg **San Lorenzo** has heating). To **Potosí** (386 km), daily at 1630, 12 hrs, US$6.70-7.45 with **AndesBus**, **San Lorenzo**, **San Jorge** and **Emperador**. To **Sucre**, direct with **AndesBus** (recommended), **Emperador** and **Villa Imperial**, depart 1600-1630, 17-18 hrs, US$5.25-6, check if you have to change buses in Potosí. To **Villazón**, several companies daily, depart morning and afternoon, 7 hrs, US$4.50, unpaved road. To **Santa Cruz**, several companies, US$10.45-12, 24 hrs over rough roads; the last 140 km from Abapó is paved; via Entre Ríos, Villamontes, Boyuibe and Camiri, between Entre Ríos and Villamontes is spectacular.

Trucks
Trucks to all destinations depart from Barrio La Loma, 10 blocks west of the market.

❶ Directory

Tarija *p402, map p403*
Banks Many ATMs accept foreign cards. **Banco Mercantil**, Sucre y 15 de Abril. Exchanges cash and gives cash against Visa and MasterCard (US$5 authorization charge). **Banco de Crédito**, Trigo N-0784, **Banco Nacional**, Av Trigo, all change TCs. US dollars and Argentine pesos can be changed at a number of casas de cambio on Bolívar between Campos and Sucre. **Embassies and consulates** Argentina, Ballivián N-0699 y Bolívar, T04-664 4273, Mon-Fri, 0830-1230. Germany, Campero 321 , T04-664 2062, methfess@olivo.tja.entelnet.bo, helpful. **Internet** Café Internet Tarija On-Line, Campos N-0488, US$0.75 per hr. Pizzería Europa (see above), US$0.90 per hr. Two on Plaza Sucre. **Language classes** Julia Gutiérrez Márquez, T04-663 2857, gringo108@hotmail.com. Recommended for language classes and information. **Post office** V Lema y Sucre. Also at bus terminal. **Telephone** Entel, on main plaza, at V Lema y D Campos and at terminal.

Cochabamba and around

→ *Phone code: 04. Colour map 3, B3. Population: 594,790. Altitude: 2570 m.*

Set in a bowl of rolling hills at a comfortable altitude, Cochabamba's unofficial title is 'City of Eternal Spring'. Its inhabitants enjoy a wonderfully warm, dry and sunny climate. Its parks and plazas are a riot of colour, from the striking purple of the bougainvillaea to the subtler tones of jasmin, magnolia and jacaranda. Bolivia's fourth largest city was founded in 1571. Today it is an important commercial and communications centre, while retaining a small-town feel. The fertile foothills surrounding the city provide much of the country's grain, fruit and coca. Markets, colonial towns and archaeological sites are all close by. Further afield, the dinosaur tracks and great scenery at Torotoro National Park are worth an exhausting trip. The lowland route to Santa Cruz de la Sierra, now preferred to the old road over the mountains, has great birdwatching and the animal refuge in Villa Tunari deserves your support. ▶▶ For Sleeping, Eating and other listings see pages 412-416.

Ins and outs

Getting there Flights arrive at **Jorge Wilstermann airport** ⓘ *a few kilometres southwest of town, T04-459 1820.* The airport bus, *Micro* B, runs to Plaza 14 de Septiembre, US$0.40; taxi to centre US$3.10. The city is 394 km from La Paz by road, now completely paved. The main **bus terminal** is on Avenida Ayacucho on the opposite side from Montes and Punata (T155); *trufis* C and 10 run to the centre.

Getting around *Micros* and *colectivos* cost US$0.20; *trufis*, US$0.30. Anything marked 'San Antonio' goes to the market. The city is divided into four quadrants based on the intersection of Avenida Las Heroínas running west to east, and Avenida Ayacucho running north to south. In all longitudinal streets north of Heroínas the letter 'N' precedes the four numbers. South of Heroínas the numbers are preceded by 'S'. In all perpendicular streets west of Ayacucho the letter 'O' (*Oeste*) precedes the numbers and all streets running east are preceded by 'E' (*Este*). The first two numbers refer to the block, 01 being closest to Ayacucho or Heroínas; the last two refer to the building's number. ▶▶ For more detailed information see Transport, page 415.

Tourist information The central **tourist office** ⓘ *Colombia E-0340, between 25 de Mayo y España, T04-422 1793, Mon-Fri 0830-1630,* is helpful and has an excellent city map and free guide. The tourist police are here for complaints, also at Jorge Wilstermann airport. **Note** Be wary of thieves at the markets and in Plaza San Antonio; you should not climb San Sebastián and La Coronilla hills because of robbery.

Sights

At the heart of the old city is the arcaded **Plaza 14 de Septiembre** with the **cathedral** dating from 1571. Nearby are several colonial churches: **Santo Domingo** ⓘ *Santiváñez y Ayacucho,* begun in 1778 and still unfinished; **San Francisco** ⓘ *25 de Mayo y Bolívar,* 1581, but heavily modernized in 1926; the **Convent of Santa Teresa** ⓘ *Baptista y Ecuador,* original construction 1760-1790; and **La Compañía** ⓘ *Baptista y Achá,* whose whitewashed interior is completely devoid of the usual riot of late Baroque decoration.

Museo Arqueológico ⓘ *Jordán, between Aguirre and Ayacucho, daily 0800-1700, US$2, student guides offer good 1½-hr tours (in Spanish, sometimes French or English), free,* is part of the Universidad de San Simón. The small but interesting display of artefacts includes Amerindian hieroglyphic scripts and pre-Inca textiles. **Casa de la Cultura** ⓘ *25 de Mayo y Av Las Heroínas, T04-425 9788, Mon-Fri 0800-1200, 1430-1830, free,* has a library and first editions of newspapers. Its **museum** ⓘ *Casona Santiváñez, Santiváñez O-0156,* exhibits colonial and modern paintings.

Cochabamba

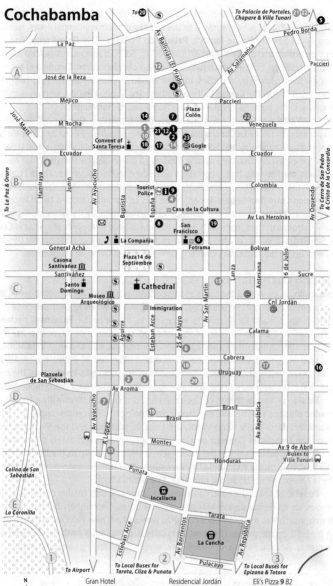

Central & Southern Highlands Cochabamba & around

N

0 metres   100
0 yards   100

Sleeping
Alojamiento Escobar 2 D2
Ambassador 1 B2
Americana 3 D2
Aranjuez 21 A3
Boston 4 B2
Cochabamba
  Backpackers 20 D2

Gran Hotel
  Cochabamba 22 A3
Hostal Buenos Aires 14 B2
Hostal Elisa 7 D1
Hostal Florida 8 D2
Hostal Ossil 11 D1
Hostería Jardín 9 B1
Ideal 10 B2
Maracaibo 11 D1
Regina 12 A2
Residencial Familiar 15 C2
Residencial Familiar
  Annexe 16 B2
Residencial Jordán 17 D3

Residencial Jordán
  Annexe 18 D2
Virgen de
  Copacabana 19 D2

Eating
Brazilian Coffee Bar 4 A2
Bufalo 5 A3
Café Express Bolívar 6 C2
Café Otoño 2 B2
Casablanca 23 B2
Comida Vegetariana 7 A2
Dumbo 8 B2
El Griego 21 B2

Eli's Pizza 9 B2
Gopal 11 B2
Habana Café 12 B2
La Cantonata 14 B2
Marco's 16 D3
Metrópolis &
  Metrópolis Pizza 17 B2
Picasso 18 B2
Snack Uno 19 B2
Souvenir 1 B2
Suiza 20 A2

Bars & clubs
Wunderbar 22 A3

From Plaza Colón, at the north end of the old town, the wide **Avenida Ballivián** (known as **El Prado**) runs northwest to the wealthy modern residential areas. North of Plaza Colón lies the Patiño family's **Palacio de Portales** ① *Av Potosí 1450, T04-424 3137, art gallery and gardens Mon-Fri 1700-1800, Sat-Sun 1000-1200, guided tours in Spanish, US$1.50*. Built in French renaissance style, furnished from Europe and set in 10 ha of gardens inspired by Versailles, the Patiño mansion was finished in 1927 but never occupied. It is now the **Centro Cultural Pedagócico Simón J Patiño**, with an excellent art gallery in the basement. Take *micro G* from Avenida San Martín.

South of the old town are some of the best markets in Bolivia; but beware of pickpockets. The huge **La Cancha market** ① *Punata, República y Pulacayo, San Martín*, is packed on Wednesday and Saturday with *campesinos* and well worth a visit. Woollen items are expensive but high quality (US$35-50 for an alpaca sweater). The nearby **Incallacta market** sells fruit, vegetables and some tourist souvenirs. There is also a Saturday market at Avenida América y Libertador, best before 0900. Overlooking the bus station **Cerro San Sebastián**; adjoining it is **La Coronilla**, topped by an imposing monument commemorating the defence of Cochabamba by its womenfolk against Spanish troops in 1812 (not safe to visit). At the east end of Avenida Heroínas is **Cerro de San Pedro** ① *cable car Mon-Sat 1000-1800, Sun 0900-1900, US$1 return; US$0.15 to climb inside the statue for viewpoint*, with a statue to Cristo de la Concordia.

Around Cochabamba

Quillacollo, 13 km west of the city, has a good Sunday market (but no tourist items, and the *campesinos* do not like being photographed) and a famous festival (see page 415). About 8 km beyond Quillacollo is a turn-off to the beautiful **Pairumani hacienda** ① *T04-426 0083, Mon-Fri 1500-1600, Sat 0900-1130, bus 7 or 38, or trufi 211 from Cochabamba*, centre of the Patiño agricultural foundation. Also known as **Villa Albina**, it was built 1925-1932, furnished from Europe and inhabited by Patiño's wife, Albina. Some 27 km west of Cochabamba, near Sipe-Sipe, are some **Inka-Rakay** ruins. The main attraction is the view from of the Cochabamba valley and the surrounding mountains.

Tarata, 33 km southeast of Cochabamba, is a colonial town with a traditional arcaded plaza on which stand the church, containing an 18th-century organ and other colonial artefacts (daily 0800-1300), the Casa Consistorial, and the Municipalidad. Inside the **Franciscan Convent** overlooking the town are the remains of the martyr, San Severino, patron saint of the town, more commonly known as the 'Saint of Rain'. A festival, held on the last Sunday of November, attracts thousands of people. Market day is Thursday (bus US$0.65, one hour, last return 1800).

Punata, 48 km to the east, has a very lively and colourful market on Tuesday. It is famous for its **Señor de los Milagros** festival on 24 September. Behind the main church, which has many baroque/mestizo works of art, new vehicles are lined up to be blessed by the priest. The local speciality is *garapiña*, a mixture of *chicha* and ice-cream. Beyond Punata, at Villa Rivera, woven wall hangings are produced.

Parque Nacional Torotoro 🌐⚡🔺 » *pp412-416.*

→ *Colour map 3, B3.*

Along with the Salar de Uyuni and Lake Titicaca, Torotoro National Park is one of the natural wonders of Bolivia. Set in a beautiful, arid rocky landscape, it is an isolated and relatively unexplored area, riddled with dinosaur tracks and punctuated by dizzying drop-offs into deep canyons. You can easily climb down into one of the canyons and clamber over boulders along the river until a sunny swimming hole appears next to a waterfall. Torotoro straddles the departments of Cochabamba and Potosí but is best reached from Cochabamba (130 km). It is highly recommended for the adventurous traveller. Torotoro covers an area of 16,570 ha and was declared a national park in 1989.

Although the park is just 130 km from Cochabamba, the road is horrendous and in the rainy season (end November to March) it is impassable. By far the easiest way in is to fly. Eugenio Arbinsona charges US$120 for up to five passengers in his Cessna, 25 minutes, T04-424 6289 or T0717-23779 (mob).

When the roads are open buses and trucks travel in convoy from Avenida República y 6 de Agosto at 0600 Sunday and Thursday, be there at 0530, US$4, eight hours on an improved dirt road via Aiquile, with stops at Cliza market and for lunch. Transport returns to Cochabamba Monday and Friday at 0600. Check bus schedules with Gonzalo Milán at **Comercial El Dorado**, Honduras 646, Cochabamba, T04-422 0207. Groups can arrange with Gonzalo to be picked up at a hotel. Alternatively, pay in advance and arrange to be picked up in Cliza where buses/trucks stop at 0800.

Entry to the park costs US$3, local guide US$5 per day plus their food. Information is available at the **park office**, open daily; ask here about tours, guides, etc. In Cochabamba, Parque Portales between Avenida G Villarroel y Trinidad 353, T04-448 6452, bichocu@hotmail.com. The climate is temperate all year round and in winter nights are fresh and the days are not too hot. Ideal in fact for walking or camping.

The park

Torotoro is actually a huge hanging valley at 2700 m surrounded by 3500-m-high mountains and criss-crossed by deep ravines. This is definitely an area of great scientific interest. Geologists, palaeontologists, archaeologists and botanists have all carried out studies here to investigate the discovery of dinosaur bones, fossils of turtles and sea shells, as well as archaeological ruins and pictographs. Other attractions include caves, canyons, waterfalls, and 80-million-year-old dinosaur tracks, which can easily be seen by the stream just outside the village. Condors and red-fronted macaws can also be spotted. Scattered throughout the valley are small traditional communities, which are friendly and welcoming.

The village of **Torotoro** lies at the head of the valley and is actually in the province of Potosí. It serves as a convenient starting point for all the hikes in the area and its people are very hospitable. There is no electricity, only a generator which runs in the evening until the village's one video cinema ends its screening, around 2130-2200.

A good one-day trip is to **Umajalanta Cave**, a cavern with many stalactites and a lake full of blind fish, about 8 km northwest of the village. Wearing a gas-powered headlamp, it's a tight crawl in places and definitely not for the claustrophobic. Many stalactites were taken by day-trippers before the area was declared a national park. A two-hour walk away are the **Pozas Bateas**, passing 1000-year-old rock paintings. Three hours away is **El Vergel** or 'Nariz de Vaca' (Cow's Nose), where two waterfalls pour out from the rockface and where you can swim in crystal clear water. A three-day trip from the village is to **Llamachaqui**, which are untouched pre-Columbian ruins in beautiful sub-tropical surroundings. It's 20 km each way to the ruins and a guide costs US$15 per person (with a minimum of two).

Umajalanta Cave, which has many stalactites and a lake with blind fish, is a 1½-hour walk northwest of Torotoro, with an hour's caving; a guide is necessary from the park office, US$5 per person in a group of two to five (take a head torch if possible). **El Vergel** waterfall can be reached without a guide, but you need good directions. The falls are fantastic, and the walk along the river bed is great fun if you like rock-hopping.

Siete Vueltas is an area of extensive fossils, 5 km from the village, but you need a guide; Mario Jaldín is recommended (see Activities and tours, page 415). There are also extensive areas of **dinosaur tracks**, and many rock paintings, close to the Torotoro river and on the many nearby walks. You can grab a clump of dead grass and be prepared to sweep out the dirt from tracks left 60-90 million years ago by meat-eating veloceraptors and eight-tonne vegetarian sauropods. Look very closely and you may even see where the mud splurged up between their toes.

Cochabamba to Santa Cruz 🚌🚆🚌 »» *pp412-416.*

The 465-km lowland road from Cochabamba to Santa Cruz is fully paved except for a 25-km stretch before Villa Tunari, almost at the end of the winding descent from the mountains, known as El Sillar. It's a beautiful trip, dropping from over 2500 m down to the lush, tropical lowland forests. The little town of **Villa Tunari**, four hours (166 km) from Cochabamba, is a relaxing place. Nestled between the San Mateo and Espíritu Santo rivers, it is Cochabamba's gateway to the tropics and the main tourist centre of the region. The two rivers are excellent for white-water rafting and kayaking. There's also good fishing and the town holds an annual **Fish Fair** on 5 and 6 August, with music, dancing and food.

‼ The road passes through the Chapare, Bolivia's main cocaine-producing region. While it's safe in the main towns, you should not stray too far off the beaten track.

Parque Ecoturístico Machía ① *just outside town, free, donations welcome*, is just outside town, on the left-hand side of the road after crossing the bridge towards Santa Cruz. The 36-ha park includes a well-signposted 3-km interpretive trail which explains the park's ecology and other good trails through semi-tropical forest. There are also panoramic lookouts and picturesque waterfalls as well as a wide variety of wildlife. Beside Parque Machía, by the riverside, 300 m outside Villa Tunari, heading for Santa Cruz (take the same entrance and then keep left), is the **Inti Wara Yassi** ① *T04-413 6572, www.intiwarayassi.org, donations welcome, camera US$2.25, video US$3.75*. This project rehabilitates animals back into the wild. Volunteering involves building rehabilitation facilities, and feeding and carrying out basic animal husbandry on a variety of monkeys, birds, wild cats and small land mammals. Living accommodation is basic, work is challenging but if you're lucky affords fascinating up-close encounters with native wildlife. A new park, **Parque Ambue Ari**, between Santa Cruz and Trinidad, consists of approximately 600 ha of jungle teeming with wildlife, rehabilitating pumas, monkeys, birds and bears. There is much to do and few volunteers, so lots of flexibility and opportunities for those interested. The routine is flexible to allow for yoga or a morning nap after the animals' breakfast! Delicious food is provided. »» *For transport from Cochabamba see page 415.*

The mountain road → *Colour map 3, B3/4.*

The 500 km road via the mountains and Epizana to Santa Cruz is not paved and the new lowland route is preferred by most transport. Before the Siberia pass, 5 km beyond Montepunco (Km 119), the 23 km road to Pocona and Inkallajta turns off. The Inca ruins of **Inkallajta** (1463-1472, rebuilt 1525), on a flat spur of land at the mouth of a steep valley, are extensive and the main building of the fortress is said to have been the largest roofed Inca building. There are several good camping sites. The Cochabamba Archaeological Museum has some huts where visitors can stay, free, but take sleeping bag and food. Water available at nearby waterfall. The mountain road continues to Epizana, the junction for the road to Sucre, and on to Samaipata (see page 587).

⬤ Sleeping

Cochabamba *p408, map p409*
There are many cheap and basic places to stay near the bus station, most are short-stay and the area is unsafe.
A **Aranjuez**, Av Buenos Aires E-0563, T04-428 0076, www.aranjuezhotel.com. 4-star, small, colonial style, good restaurant, jazz in the bar Fri-Sat night, small pool open to public (US$1). Recommended.

B **Ambassador**, España N-0349, T04-425 9001, ambassrv@comteco.entelnet.bo. Modern, central and reasonable, includes breakfast, good restaurant.
B **Gran Hotel Cochabamba**, Plaza Ubaldo Anze, 2 blocks from Los Portales at La Recoleta, T04-428 2551, cbbhotel@bo.net. Beautifully set in the north part of the city, with garden, swimming pool (US$3 for

non-guests) and tennis courts, popular with tour groups. Recommended.

C Americana, Esteban Arce S-788, T04-425 0554, americana@mail.infornetcbba.com.bo. Fan, helpful, lift, laundry, parking, *rodizio* grill next door, good service.

D Boston, Calle 25 de Mayo 0167, T04-422 8530, hboston@supernet.com.bo. Restaurant, quiet rooms at back, safe parking, luggage store. Recommended but cheaper rooms not so good.

D Ideal, España N-0329, T04-423 5175. Good-value and comfortable but can be noisy at weekends. Includes breakfast, TV, restaurant.

D Regina, Reza 0359, T04-425 7382, hregina@supernet.com.bo. Spacious, efficient, breakfast extra, restaurant.

F Alojamiento Escobar, Aguirre S-0749, T04-422 5812. Recently upgraded, good value (not to be confused with **Residencial** on Uruguay).

F Hostal Buenos Aires, 25 de Mayo N-0329, T04-425 4005. **G** without bath, pleasant, clean communal baths, breakfast US$1.35.

F Hostal Elisa, Agustín López S-0834, 2 blocks from bus station, T04-425 4404. **G** without bath, good showers, hot water, breakfast US$2.25, modern, garden, laundry service, popular with travellers, helpful owner, but small singles and area is a bit dodgy at night.

F Hostal Florida, 25 de Mayo S-0583, T04-425 7911, floridah@elsito.com. **G** without bath/cable TV, hot water, noisy, popular, laundry, safe deposit, internet, breakfast.

E Hostería Jardín, Hamiraya N-0248, T04-424 7844, jaguirre@latinmail.com. **F** without bath, garden, safe car and motorcycle parking, good breakfast included, basic but good value, in a nice area.

F Res Jordán, Calle Antesana S-0671, T04-422 9294. Youth hostel, **ABAJ** affiliate, modern, basic, with cable TV and small pool. Annex (F) at 25 de Mayo S-0651, T04-422 5010.

G pp Cochabamba Backpackers, Av Aroma E-437 between 25 de Mayo and San Martín, T04-425 7131, backpackers-cochabamba@boliviahostels.com. Close to bus station, a member of a network of Bolivian hostels.

G Hostal Ossil, Agustín López S-0915, close to bus terminal, T04-425 4476. New, good rooms, cooking facilities, helpful, good value.

G Maracaibo, Agustín López S-0925, T04-422 7110. Close to bus terminal, popular, safe.

G Res Familiar, Sucre E-0554, T04-422 7988. Pleasant, secure, good showers. Its annex at

25 de Mayo N-0234 (between Colombia and Ecuador), T04-422 7986. Pleasant, with a big courtyard, shared bath, hot water, comfortable.

G Virgen de Copacabana, Av Arce S-0875 y Brasil, T04-422 7929, near bus station. Electric showers, shared bath, good breakfast US$0.75, motorcycle parking, stores luggage, noisy TV, otherwise recommended.

Parque Nacional Torotoro *p410*

Several *hostales* have opened recently in Torotoro and there is electricity in some.

G Alojamiento Charcas, near bus terminal, with very good restaurant serving hot, filling meals, US$1 pp (order dinner in the morning).

G De Los Hermanos, very basic, running water, delightful owner, friendly pets.

Cochabamba to Santa Cruz *p412*
Villa Tunari

Several other hotels; also 2 internet cafés, **Entel** office and post office.

C Los Araras, across bridge on main road to Santa Cruz, T04-413 4116, hisc_marco@yahoo.com. **C** midweek, large rooms, nice gardens, good breakfast, HI affiliated.

C-D Las Palmas, T04-411 4103, 1 km out of town. With breakfast, pool and good restaurant, changes US$ cash, a bit run down.

D Bibosi, Plaza Principal, T04-428 0814. Pleasant, with gardens and pool.

D El Puente, Av de la Integración, 3 km from town, T04-425 9322 (book at **Fremen** travel agency). With breakfast and bath, cabins from 2 people to family-size, pool, tours to Carrasco National Park, the hotel has a stream and natural pools.

G La Querencia, Beni 700, T04-413 6548. Pleasant terrace on river front, avoid noisy rooms at front, good cheap food, clothes-washing facilities.

G Las Palmas 2, corner of plaza. With bath, breakfast, fan, swimming pool (not very clean).

G San Mateo, opposite *Baviera* restaurant, by the river. Shared bath, choice of beds (hard or soft), helpful.

● Eating

Cochabamba *p408, map p409*

The bars and restaurants centre around España, Ecuador and Colombia, Plaza Colón and Av Ballivián and north of Río Rocha near Av Santa Cruz. A few km north of the city, in the village of

Tiquipaya, are many *comida criolla* restaurants, eg El Diente, recommended.

♦♦♦ **La Cantonata**, España N-0409, T04-425 9222. Among the best Italian restaurants in Bolivia. Highly recommended.

♦♦♦ **Suiza**, Av Ballivián 820, T04-425 7103. Popular, recommended for international cuisine, good value.

♦♦ **Bufalo**, Torres Sofer, p 2, Av Oquendo N-0654. Brazilian *rodizio* grill, all-you-can-eat buffet for US$7.50, great service. Highly recommended.

♦♦ **Comida Vegetariana**, M Rocha E-0375. Good filling food, buffet lunch and breakfast, mostly soy-protein based dishes, but also serves chicken, closed Sun.

♦♦ **El Griego**, España N-0386. Good kebabs and lots of pasta dishes, colourful walls and modern art.

♦♦ **Habana Café**, M Rocha E-0348. Genuine Cuban food and drinks, can get lively at night, open 1200-last person leaves.

♦♦ **Marco's**, Av Oquenda between Cabrera and Uruguay, Sat-Sun 1200-1500. Good Peruvian *ceviche*.

♦♦ **Metrópolis**, España N-0299. Good pasta,, huge portions, good veggie options, noisy. Metrópolis Pizza next door is good value.

♦♦ **Picasso**, España 327, between Ecuador and Mayor Rocha. Good value Italian and Mexican.

♦ **Eli's Pizza**, 25 de Mayo N-0254 y Colombia. Son of the famous La Paz branch, great pizzas and serves Mexican fast food.

♦ **Gopal**, Calle España 250, Galería Olimpia. Harekrishna, 1200-1500 only, closed Sun. US$1.50 for vegetarian lunch, English spoken, very good.

♦ **Incallacta market** (see page 410) has excellent food for under US$1.

♦ **Snack Uno**, Av Heroínas E-0562. Good lunches and dinners including vegetarian.

Cafés

Brazilian Coffee Bar, Av Ballivián just off Plaza Colón. Upmarket, tables on pavement.

Café Express Bolívar, Bolívar, between San Martín and 25 de Mayo. Great coffee in a delightful old-fashioned café.

Café Otoño, 25 de Mayo y Mayor Rocha, T04-452 3903. Nicely decorated, simple but tasty dishes, good service.

Casablanca, 25 de Mayo between Venezuela and Ecuador. Next to Gogle internet café,

attractive, buzzing, good food and a wide selection of coffee, popular for wine and cocktails in the evening.

Dumbo, Av Heroínas 0440. Good ice-cream parlour, popular eating and meeting spot, also does cheap meals.

Souvenir, 25 de Mayo N-0391. *Salteñas*, crêpes and *confitería*, popular in the early evening.

Parque Nacional Torotoro *p410*

♦ **Salón de Té**, Torotoro. Lydia García provides good meals with prior notice, bakes bread and cakes, welcoming.

Cochabamba to Santa Cruz *p412*
Villa Tunari

♦♦ **El Bosque**, west end of town, 1 km past toll booth. German, run by botanists, with orchid garden, one of the best in town.

♦♦ **Surubi**, also known as Cuqui, 1 km west of town. A good restaurant with fish specialities, also has tents for camping.

♦♦-♦ **Baviera**, near bridge on main road. Good steak and fish, good value, tourist information, also has rooms to let with hot water.

♦♦-♦ **El Jazmín**, opposite Las Palmas. Gringo hangout serving good pizza.

◑ Bars and clubs

Cochabamba *p408, map p409*

Chilimania, M Rocha E-0333. Good for drinking and dancing.

D'Mons, Tarija y América, open 2300, US$4 including first drink. Mix of Latin, contemporary and classic American music, .

Lujos, Beni E-0330, open 2300, US$4 includes first drink. Good atmosphere. Mix of Latin, contemporary and classic American music,

Panchos, M Rocha E-0311, just off España. A lively dancing and drinking place.

Wunderbar, Venezuela E-0635, opens 1930. Cable TV sports on Mon, music, darts upstairs, ribs, wings, subs.

◉ Entertainment

Cochabamba *p408, map p409*
Peñas
Totos, M Rocha y Ayacucho, T04-452 2460. Fri night 2000-0300; may open on Sat. Free entry.

⚙ Festivals and events

Cochabamba *p408, map p409*
Feb/Mar Carnival is celebrated 15 days before Lent. Rival groups (*comparsas*) compete in music, dancing, and fancy dress, culminating in El Corso on the last Sat of the Carnival. **Mascaritas** balls also take place in the carnival season, when the young women wear long hooded satin masks.
14 Sep Day of Cochabamba.

Around Cochabamba *p410*
3 May Day of La Santa Cruz, with fireworks, a large procession and brass band
Jun-Aug (date varies) Fiesta de la Virgen de Urkupiña, in Quillacollo lasts 4 days with much dancing and religious ceremony. Lots of transport from Cochabamba, hotels all full. Be there before 0900 to be sure of a seat, as you are not allowed to stand in the street. The first day is the most colourful with all the groups in costumes and masks, parading and dancing in the streets till late at night. Many groups have left by the 2nd day and dancing stops earlier. The 3rd day is dedicated to the pilgrimage. (Many buses, *micros* and *trufis* from Heroínas y Ayacucho, 20 mins, US$0.30.)
24 Sep Punata, is famous for its Señor de los Milagros festival.
Last Sun in Nov Saint of Rain festival in Tarata, attracts thousands.

⦿ Shopping

Cochabamba *p408, map p409*
Fotrama, factory at Av Circunvalación 0413, T04-422 5468, outlet at Bolívar 0439. Co-operative for alpaca sweaters, rugs, alpaca wool (pricey).
Los Amigos del Libro, Ayacucho S-0156, T04-450 4150, in Hotel Portales, Av Pando 1271, and **Gran Hotel Cochabamba**, in the Torres Sofer shopping centre and at the airport. Good bookshop, stocks US/English magazines as well as *South American Handbook*. City map and guide in colour for US$2.50.

▲ Activities and tours

Cochabamba *p408, map p409*
Cochabamba is growing in popularity for parapenting, with several outfits offering tandem jumps and courses more cheaply

than other places, starting at US$30-35 and US$200-250 respectively; eg tornadojohn@hotmail.com (experienced, Spanish only – his brother speaks a bit of English).
AndesXtremo, La Paz 138 entre Ayacucho y Junín, T04-452 3392, www.andesxtremo.com. Adventure sports company offering parapenting, climbing, rafting, trekking and bungee jumps, good value, professional staff.
Todo Turismo, Jordán 280, T04-450 5384, www.touringbolivia.com. With offices in La Paz, Oruro and Uyuni. Many local tours, including Torotoro, tours to other parts of the country and reservations.
Vicuñita Tours, Av Ayacucho 350, T04-452 0194, vicunitatours@hotmail.com. Specializes in local and regional travel, also overseas reservations (T03-334 0591 Santa Cruz office).

Parque Nacional Torotoro *p410*
Mario Jaldín (Spanish-speaking only) is a knowledgeable guide. He lives 2 doors to the right of **Alojamiento Charcas**. He also leads a 4-day trek to see canyons, condors, orchids, many birds and, if lucky, the Andean bear and pumas; $80-100 per person, depending on the size of the group, includes camping gear and food, bring your own sleeping bag.

⊝ Transport

Cochabamba *p408, map p409*
Air To get to the airport take a *micro B* from Plaza 14 de Septiembre, US$0.40; taxis US$3.10. Reconfirm all flights and arrive early for international flights. Several flights daily to/from **La Paz** (35 mins) and **Santa Cruz** (45 mins) with LAB (see note page 28) and Aero Sur (book early for morning flights). LAB also flies to **Sucre**, **Trinidad** and **Tarija**. International flights to **Buenos Aires** with Aero Sur. LAB, Salamanca 675, open 0800, T04-423 0325. Aero Sur, Av Villarroel 105, corner with Av Oblitos (Pando), T04-440 0910.

Bus To **Santa Cruz**, 10 hrs, 0530-2200, US$3-4.50 (*buscama* US$7.50); only minibuses take the old mountain road via Epizana, from Av 9 de Abril y Av Oquendo, all day. See page 412. Many companies to **La Paz**, shop around for best times, services and prices (about US$2.50, *buscama* US$4.50-6), by night or day, 7 hrs on paved road. Bus to **Oruro**, US$2.50, 4 hrs, buses hourly. To **Potosí**, US$4.50-5.25

415

Central & Southern Highlands Cochabamba & around Listings

via Oruro, several companies 1830-2000. Daily to **Sucre**, US$4.50-5.25, 10 hrs, several companies 1930-2030 (**Flota Copacabana** and **Trans Copacabana** recommended; latter *buscama* US$8.90). To **Sucre** by day; take a bus to Aiquile, then a bus at 2400-0100 passing en route to Sucre. Local buses leave from Av Barrientos y Av 6 de Agosto, near La Coronilla for **Tarata**, **Punata** and **Cliza**. Av República y Av 6 de Agosto to **Epizana** and **Totora**. Av Oquendo y 9 de Abril (be careful in this area), to **Villa Tunari**, US$2.70, 4-5 hrs, several daily; **Chimoré**, US$5.75; **Eterazama**, US$5.75; **Puerto Villarroel**, US$4, 6-8 hrs (from 0800 when full, daily); **Puerto San Francisco**, US$6.50.

Taxi
US$0.50 from anywhere to the Plaza, more expensive across the river; double after dark.

Cochabamba to Santa Cruz *p412*
Inkallajta
Best to go Thu or Sat when *micros* leave when full from 0700 from 6 de Agosto y República, Cochabamba, passing the sign to the ruins, from where it's a 12 km walk. Otherwise take a micro to the checkpoint 10 km from Cocha-bamba, then a truck to Km 119 sign, walk towards Pocona or take a truck for 15 km, to where a large yellow sign indicates the trail. After 10 km the trail divides, take the downhill path and the ruins are a further 2 km.

◉ Directory

Cochabamba *p408, map p409*
Banks Visa and MasterCard at **Enlace** ATMs all over the town (especially on Av Ballivián) and next to the bus terminal. Cash on Visa or MasterCard from many banks; no commission on bolivianos. **Bisa**, Aguirre y Calama. Best rates for cash and Amex TCs, changes euro TCs at 5% commission. **Ef€c**, Plaza 14 de Septiembre S-0262, changes TCs into US$ 2% commission. Money changers congregate at most major intersections, especially outside **Entel**, and on Plaza Colón, poor rates. **Cultural centres** Centro Boliviano Americano, 25 de Mayo N-0365, T04-422 1288, www.cbacoch.org. Library of English-language books, open 0900-1200 and 1430-1900; also offers language classes. **Alianza Francesa**, Santiváñez O-0187, T04-422 1009, afcbba@afbolivia.org. **Instituto**

Cultural Boliviano-Alemán, Lanza 727, icbacbba@supernet.com.bo. Spanish classes. **Embassies and consulates** Argentina, F Blanco E-0929, T04-425 5859, consuladoar@ entelnet.bo. Visa applications 0830-1300. Brazil, Edif Los Tiempos Dos, Av Oquendo, p 9, T04-425 5860, cchbrvc14@ supernet.com.bo, open 0830-1130, 1430-1730. Germany, España, corner with Av Heroínas, Edif La Promotora, p 6, of 602, T04-425 4024, coricba@pino.cbb. entelnet.bo. Italy, Av Humboldt 932, T04-424 5809. Netherlands, Av Oquendo 654, Torres Sofer p 7, T04-423 0888, Mon-Fri 0830-1200, 1400-1630 . Paraguay, Av Gral Achá O-0107, Edif América p 6, T04-458 1801, Mon-Fri 0830-1230, 1430-1830. Peru, Pedro Blanco y Santa Cruz, edif Continental of 3H, T04-448 6157, conbba@acelerate.com, Mon-Fri 0800-1200, 1400-1800. Spain, Colombia O-655, T04-458 2281, Mon-Fri 0900-1200, 1430-1730. Sweden, Barquisimeto, Villa La Glorieta, T04-424 5358, arvidsson@comteco.entelnet.bo, Mon-Fri 0930-1200. USA, Av Oquendo, Torres Sofer p 6, T04-425 6714, open 0900-1200 (also attends to Britons and Canadians). **Internet** Many cyber cafés all over town, US$0.60 per hr. **Language classes** Sra Blanca de La Rosa Villareal, Av Libertador Simón Bolívar 1108, corner with Oblitas, T04-424 4298, US$5 per hr. Runawasi, J Hinojosa, Barrio Juan XXIII s/n, T/F04-424 8923, www.runawasi.org. Spanish and Quechua. Elizabeth Siles Salas, T04-423 2278, silessalas@latinmail.com. Reginaldo Rojo, T04-424 2322, frojo@supernet.com.bo. US$5 per hr. María Pardo, Pasaje El Rosal 20, Zona Queru Queru behind Burger King on Av América, T04-428 4615. US$5 per hr, also teaches Quechua. Carmen Galinda Benavides, Parque Lincoln N-0272, T04-424 7072. Maricruz Almanzal, Av San Martín 456, T04-422 7923, maricruz_almanza@hotmail.com. US$5 for 50 mins. Voluntarios Bolivia, Casilla 2411, www.volunteerbolivia.org, language classes, homestays and a recommended volunteer programme. **Medical services** For doctors, dentists and hospitals, contact your consulate or the tourist office for advice. **Post office** Av Heroínas y Ayacucho, Mon-Fri 0800-2000, Sat 0800-1800, Sun 0800-1200. **Telephone** Entel, Gral Achá y Ayacucho, fax, international phone (not possible to make AT&T credit card calls), open till 2300. **Useful addresses** Immigration office: Jordán y Arce, p 2, T04-422 5553, Mon-Fri 0830-1630.

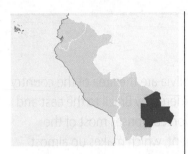

Eastern Lowlands

⚏ Footprint features

Introduction

The vast eastern lowlands of Bolivia are the area of the country richest in natural resources. Bordered by Brazil to the east and Paraguay to the south, this region comprises most of the enormous Santa Cruz Department, which makes up almost 34% of Bolivia's territory and, at 370,621 sq km, is larger than Germany.

The capital of the region, Santa Cruz (officially called Santa Cruz de la Sierra), is a booming modern city, more in tune with neighbouring Brazil and a world away from most people's image of Bolivia. The city is often ignored by tourists, or passed through quickly by travellers heading to or from Brazil, but that's their loss, for it stands on the threshold of one of the least-explored and most fascinating parts of Bolivia. To the northeast are the Jesuit Missions of Chiquitos, a string of seven dusty cattle towns, each boasting a Jesuit church more beautiful than the next. Only four hours west is Amboró National Park, one of the country's truly great natural experiences and an area containing a greater variety of plants and wildlife than almost anywhere else on earth.

One of the very few places that surpass Amboró is the remote and stunningly beautiful Noel Kempff Mercado National Park, in the far northeast of Santa Cruz Department. This is a place so beautiful and mysterious that it is thought to have been the inspiration for Sir Arthur Conan Doyle's famous book, *The Lost World*.

★ Don't miss ...

1 **El Fuerte** Bolivia's second most important archaeological sight as at El Fuerte, near the lovely town of Samaipata, page 427.

2 **Amboró National Park** Go for the full Indiana Jones experience in this national park, one of the most bio-diverse places on this planet, page 427.

3 **The Che Guevara Trail** Be a rebel with a cause and follow in the footsteps of the world's most famous revolutionary, page 429.

4 **The Jesuit churches** Your mission, should you accept it ... to visit the magnificent churches in the remote and dusty frontier towns north of Santa Cruz, page 434.

5 **Noel Kempff Mercado National Park** Discover a Lost World here, home to more rare wild beasts than you could shake a zoom lens at, page 440.

6 **Kaa-Iya del Gran Chaco** This enormous national park is the largest in the entire hemisphere, is the ultimate destination for the adventurer or ecotourist, and about as far off the beaten track as you can get, page 442.

Eastern Lowlands

Santa Cruz and around

→ *Phone code: 03. Colour map 3, B4. Population: 1,465,305. Altitude: 416 m.*

A little over 50 years ago, what is now Bolivia's largest city was a remote backwater. Rail and road links ended its isolation and the exploitation of oil and gas in the Department of Santa Cruz de la Sierra helped fuel the city's rapid development. Santa Cruz is far removed from most travellers' perceptions of Bolivia. Formerly a haven for narcotraficantes, it is now less opulent, although agribusiness is an important economic concern. The city centre still retains much of its colonial air and during the lunchtime hiatus when the locals (who like to call themselves cambas*) take refuge from the overwhelming heat, it can almost seem like its original self. Here, too, you can witness the incongruous sight of immigrant Mennonite farmers and their families, who fled persecution in the USA and Canada, going about their business in the presence of Bolivia's most open and laid-back population.* ➽ *For Sleeping, Eating and other listings, see pages 422-426.*

Ins and outs

Getting there The **international airport** ① *Viru Viru, 15 km north of the city, T181 for information*, has an emigration/immigration office, **Entel** office, luggage lockers, duty-free shops, coffee shops and a **Subway** sandwich shop. The bank is open 0830-1830 and changes cash and traveller's cheques, cash can be withdrawn using Visa and MasterCard. When the bank is closed try the **AASANA** desk, where you pay airport tax (US$25 for international departures). There's a **tourist Information kiosk** in the check-in hall (English spoken, free maps). The airport bus runs every 20 minutes to the centre (25 minutes, US$0.70, 0530-2030), also *colectivos*. A taxi costs US$7.50.

Long-distance buses arrive at the new combined bus/train terminal, the **Terminal Bimodal** ① *Av Montes, between Av Brasil and Tres Pasos al Frente, between the 2nd and 3rd anillos, T03-348 8382*. There's a bank, infirmary, luggage store and restaurants. Take bus No 12 to/from the centre, or a taxi (US$1.50 – catch it from outside the terminal, it's cheaper). *Trufis* from Buena Vista and Yapacani arrive near the old bus terminal, just south of the centre. *Trufis* from Samaipata arrive two blocks south of the **old terminal** ① *Av Omar Chávez y Solis de Olguín*. Buses from San Javier, Concepción and San Ignacio arrive at the various bus company offices. ➽ *See Transport, page 425.*

Getting around The city has 10 ring roads, referred to as *anillos* 1, 2, 3, 4, and so on. Equipetrol suburb, where many of the better hotels and bars are situated, is northwest of the city centre, between *anillos* 2 and 3; Avenida San Martin is one of its main streets. Local buses also use the new terminal. Taxis cost about US$1.15 inside the first *anillo* (US$1.50 at night), US$1.30 inside the third *anillo*, agree the fare in advance.

Tourist information The **tourist office** ① *in the Prefectura del Departamento, north side of the main plaza, T03-332 770, extension 144, daily 0800-1600*, has top-notch cultural and historical videos and exhibits, as well as a free and very useful city map (also available from many hotels and tour agents). The *Handbook of Santa Cruz* (English) and *Guía Turística Metropolitana de Santa Cruz* (English/Spanish) are useful local guidebooks; both are available in most *librerías* (stationers). Another excellent guide (Spanish) is *Santa Cruz Turístico*, published by APAC and available for US$5 in most *librerías*, also at **APAC**'s offices in Calle Beni 228 (T03-332 287/372 526).

Sights

The **Plaza 24 de Septiembre** is the city's main square, where people are so unhurried they would make the sloths who used to live in the trees here look uptight. Facing onto the plaza is the imposing brick-fronted **cathedral** ① *museum Tue, Thu, Sun 1000-1200,*

1600-1800, US$0.75, which is now technically a minor basilica after Pope John Paul II's visit in 1988. Its wonderfully cool interior features some interesting hand-wrought colonial silver and a museum containing what is considered the smallest book in the world, at only 7 sq mm. The city's **Casa de la Cultura** is also on the plaza. It hosts occasional exhibitions, an archaeological display, plays, concerts and folk dancing. Southwest of the plaza is the **Siete Calles** market, which takes up all of calles Isabel La Católica, Suárez de Figueroa, and Vallegrande and has all manner of goods.

Further south, the **Museo de Historia Natural Noel Kempff Mercado** ① *Av Irala 565, between Velasco and Independencia, T03-337 1216, www.museonoelkempff.org, Mon-Fri 0800-1200, Mon-Tue also 1500-1830, US$0.15*, has a video library. Contact them for trips to Noel Kempff Mercado National Park (see page 440).

Santa Cruz

N

0 metres 200
0 yards 200

Sleeping
Alojamiento Santa
  Bárbara 1 *B1*
Asturias 14 *D2*
Backpackers
  Santa Cruz 16 *D1*
Best Western House Inn 6 *D1*

Bibosi 2 *B1*
Colonial 3 *B2*
Copacabana 4 *B1*
Crismar 15 *C1*
Excelsior 5 *B2*
Jodanga 9 *D3*
Las Américas 7 *B2*
Posada El Turista 8 *B1*
Residencial 26
  de Enero 12 *C1*
Residencial Bolívar 10 *B2*
Residencial Sands 11 *B3*
Viru-Viru 13 *B1*

Eating
Capri 1 *D1*
El Boliche 2 *B2*
El Patito Pekín 3 *B2*
Fridolín 20 *B1*
Il Gatto 5 *B2*
Kivón 16 *B1*
La Buena Mesa 8 *A2*
La Casona 15 *B2*
La Esquina
  del Pescado 6 *B1*
Las Palmeras 7 *B1*
Michelangelo 9 *D2*
Pizzería Marguerita 10 *B2*

Rincón Brasil 17 *B2*
Sabor Brasil 11 *B1*
Santa Ana 4 *C2*
Shanghai 19 *B1*
Su Salud 18 *B3*
Tía Lía 12 *B2*
Vegetariano 13 *B1*
Yorimichi 21 *A2*

Bars & clubs
Café Irlandés 14 *B2*

An interesting area is the **Mercado Los Pozos**, which encompasses almost all of calles Quijarro, Campero, Suárez Arana, and 6 de Agosto. Here you'll see large numbers of Mennonites in their traditional clothing – the men in their high-crowned cowboy hats, checked shirts and dungarees, the women in dark, full-length dresses, shawls and full-brimmed hats. As in all busy markets, you need to be alert to the threat of bag-snatchers.

Around Santa Cruz

West of town, at the end of Avenida Roca Coronado, 10 minutes by bus from the centre of Santa Cruz, you can swim in the **Río Piraí** during the wet season, though at weekends it gets very crowded. Some huts on the beach sell local delicacies.

In the other direction, 10 km east of the city, on the road to Cotoca, are the new **Botanical Gardens**. Take a *micro* or *colectivo* from Calle Suárez Arana (15 minutes). A couple of kilometres later in **Cotoca** (20 minutes), the church has a statue of the Virgin Mary thought to perform miracles, associated with which is a religious handicraft tradition. Cotoca holds a fiesta on 8 December, where several hundred *cruzeños* making the trip on foot (with the more penitential on knees).

Eighteen kilometres south of Santa Cruz, off the road to Palmasola, are **Las Lomas de Arena del Palmar**, an area of huge sand dunes. In some parts are small lagoons where you can swim. **Note** Avoid the stagnant water in the nearest and most popular of the lagoons; head to the furthest ones where there's less chance of yeast infections. To get there take a 4WD from the bus terminal; in the wet season the river crossing can be difficult. It may also be possible to hitch at weekends. Windsurfing is popular here with the locals, but no rental facilities exist.

Los Espejillos (small mirrors) are a series of many small waterfalls, 41 km southwest of Santa Cruz, en route to Samaipata on the old Cochabamba highway. They're very popular at weekends and can be accessed by *micros* in the dry season.

⊜ Sleeping

Santa Cruz *p420, map p421*
Accommodation is relatively expensive in Santa Cruz and good value mid- and lower-range hotels are hard to find. Most of the budget hotels are near the old bus terminal.
L Los Tajibos, Av San Martín 455, in Barrio Equipetrol, T03-342 1000, www.lostajibos hotel.com. Set in 15 acres of lush vegetation, 5-star, a/c, El Papagayo restaurant is good (their *ceviche* is particularly recommended), business centre, art gallery, Viva Club Spa has sauna etc, pool for residents only.
AL Best Western House Inn, Colón 643, T03-336 2323, www.houseinn.com.bo. 5-star suites with computer in each room, unlimited internet use, price includes tax and breakfast, 2 pools, sauna, restaurant, a/c, parking.
B Las Américas, 21 de Mayo, corner with Seoane, T03-336 8778, lasamericas@ cotas.com.bo. Discount for longer stay, a/c, parking, arranges tours and car rental, restaurant, bar, 5-star service. Excellent value.
C Asturias, Moldes 154, T03-333 9611, www.hotelasturias.net. A/c, quiet, good pool and gardens, internet, bar, restaurant.

C Colonial, Buenos Aires 57, T03-333 3156. A/c, breakfast, restaurant, comfortable.
C Viru-Viru Junín 338, T03-333 5298. Includes breakfast, a/c, cheaper with fan, pleasant, central.
D Copacabana, Junín 217, T03-332 1843, hotelcopacabanascz@hotmail.com. TV, laundry, includes breakfast, restaurant, very good, popular with European tour groups.
D Excelsior, René Moreno 70, T03-334 0664, excelsior@cotas.net. Includes breakfast, good rooms, good lunches.
E Bibosi, Junín 218, T03-334 8548, htlbibosi@ hotmail.com. Cheaper with shared bath, breakfast included, internet. Recommended.
E Crismar, Vallegrande 285, between Pari and Camiri, by the 'Siete Calles' market (area not safe after 2100), T03-337 1918. **F** with fan or shared bath, breakfast served in rooms, basic but clean and good value.
E-F Jodanga, Calle El Fuerte 1380, Zona Parque Urbano, Barrio Los Chóferes, T03-339 6542, www.jodanga.com. Good new backpacker option 10 mins' walk from Terminal Bimodal, **G** in dorm, kitchen, bar,

swimming pool, billiards, DVDs, communal areas, internet, laundry, helpful owner, can arrange voluntary work.
E-F Res 26 de Enero, Camiri 32, T03-332 1818. **G** without bath, very clean.
F Res Sands, Arenales 749, 7 blocks east of the main plaza, T03-337 7776. Fantastic value, better than many expensive ones, cable TV, fan, very comfortable beds, pool.
F-G pp Res Bolívar, Sucre 131, T03-334 2500. Hot showers, some rooms with bath, others very small, lovely courtyard with hammocks, alcohol prohibited, excellent breakfast US$2.10. Recommended.
G Alojamiento Santa Bárbara, Santa Bárbara 151, T03-332 1817. Hot showers, shared bath, basic, helpful, popular, will store luggage, good value. Recommended.
G pp Backpackers Santa Cruz, Salvatierra 555 y Izozog, T03-312 0033, backpackers-santacruz@boliviahostels.com. Budget place, popular with backpackers.
G Posada El Turista, Junín 455, T03-336 2870. Small basic rooms, central, quiet.

🍴 Eating

Santa Cruz *p420, map p421*
Barrio Equipetrol is the area for upmarket restaurants and nightlife. Most restaurants close Mon. The bakeries on Junín, Los Manzanos and España sell local specialities.
ŸŸŸ El Boliche, Arenales 135. Good crêpes, fondues and salads.
ŸŸŸ Il Gatto, 24 de Septiembre 285. Bright and clean, good pizzas, US$2.25 lunch buffet.
ŸŸŸ Michelangelo, Chuquisaca 502. Excellent Italian option.
ŸŸŸ Yorimichi, Av Busch 548, T03-334 7717. Japanese, one of the city's best restaurants, could put some Tokyo restaurants to shame.
ŸŸ La Buena Mesa, Av Cristóbal de Mendoza 1401, T03-342 1248. Excellent barbecued steak.
ŸŸ Capri, Irala 634, "The best pizzas in town".
ŸŸ La Casa del Camba, Cristóbal de Mendoza 539, T03-342 7864. One of many barbecue places around the 2nd *anillo*, good sample the genuine *camba* culinary experience.
ŸŸ La Casona, Arenales 222. German-run, very good food
ŸŸ Mandarin 2, Av Potosí 793. Good Chinese.
ŸŸ Pizzería Marguerita, northwest corner of plaza, T03-337 0285. A/c, superb filet mignon, good service, coffee, bar, recommended.

ŸŸ Shanghai, Av 26 de Febrero 27, T03-352 3939. Another excellent Chinese restaurant.
Ÿ El Patito Pekín, 24 de Septiembre 307. Basic Chinese.
Ÿ La Esquina del Pescado, Sara y Florida. For fish, US$1.60 a plate.
Ÿ Las Palmeras, Ayacucho y Callali. Typical *camba* food, large portions. Also at Junín 381.
Ÿ Los Pozos market, taking up the whole block between 6 de Agosto, Suárez Arana, Quijarro and Campero, daily. Good for lunch, food aisles serve local and Chinese food.
Ÿ Rincón Brasil, Libertad 358. Brazilian-style *por kilo* place, popular, à la carte from 1800.
Ÿ Sabor Brasil, off Buenos Aires, between Santa Bárbara and España, No 20. Another popular Brazilian-style *por kilo* place.
Ÿ Santa Ana, Ingavi 164. Good value buffet lunch in a shady patio.
Ÿ Su Salud, Quijarro 115. Tasty vegetarian, filling lunch, huge portions. Recommended.
Ÿ Tía Lía, Murillo 40. Huge selection of salads, pasta and bean dishes. US$1.50 (US$2.25 weekends) for all the beef, chorizos, pork and chicken you want from a *parrillada*.
Ÿ Vegetariano, Ayacucho 444. Breakfast, lunch and dinner, good.

Cafés
There are lots of very pleasant a/c cafés and ice cream parlours, where you can get drinks, snacks and reasonably priced meals.
Alexander's Coffee, Av Monseñor Rivero 400, Zona El Cristo, T03-337 8653. For good coffee and people-watching.
Fridolin, Pari 254; also Av Cañoto y Florida. Two good places for coffee and pastries.
Kivón, Ayacucho 267. Recommended for ice cream; also Quijarro 409 in Mercado Los Pozos.

🍸 Bars and clubs

Santa Cruz *p420, map p421*
Bar Irlandés Irish Pub, 3o Anillo Interno 1216 (between Av Cristo Redentor and Zoológico). Irish-themed pub, food available.
Café Irlandés, Plaza 24 de Septiembre, Edificio Shopping Bolívar, No 157, over-looking main plaza, T03-333 8118. Live music Wed and Sat evening. Recommended.
M@D, Av San Martín 155, T03-336 0333. One of the best known and most popular clubs.
Moosehead, next to **Bar Irlandés** on 3rd *anillo*. Canadian bar/restaurant.

☺ Festivals and events

Santa Cruz *p420, map p421*
Cruceños are famous as fun-lovers and their music, the *carnavalitos*, can be heard all over South America.

Feb/Mar Carnival is renowned for riotous behaviour. It's celebrated for the 15 days before Lent: music in the streets, dancing, fancy dress and the coronation of a queen. The following day youths run wild with balloons filled with water – no one is exempt. The *mascaritas* balls also take place during the pre-Lent season at Caballo Blanco when girls have the right to demand that men dance with them, and wear satin masks.

Apr The Festival de Música Renacentista y Barroca Americana is held every other year (next in 2008) in Santa Cruz and the Jesuit mission towns of the Chiquitania (such as San Javier, Concepción). Organized by **Asociación Pro Arte y Cultura** (APAC), Beni 228, Santa Cruz, T03-333 2287, www.festivalesapac.com, it celebrates the wealth of sacred music written in the 17th and 18th centuries.

Mid-Apr Every other year in Santa Cruz and outlying towns APAC holds the **Festival Internacional de Teatro "Santa Cruz de la Sierra"**, next in 2009.

24 Sep is a departmental holiday, celebrated throughout all of Santa Cruz.

○ Shopping

Santa Cruz *p420, map p421*
Bookshops
International magazines and newspapers often on sale in kiosks on main Plaza, eg *Miami Herald*, after arrival of daily Miami flight.
El Ateno, Cañoto y 21 de Mayo, T03-333 3338. Books in English, access to internet.
Los Amigos del Libro, Igavi 14, T03-332 7937, Foreign language books and magazines.

Handicrafts
There are *artesanía* shops on Libertad and on Plaza 24 de Septiembre y Bolívar
Idepe Usaka, Suaréz de Figueroa near Independencia, Mon-Fri, 0900-1200, 1500-1800. Brilliant non-profit store specializing in colourful ceramics, fabrics, and mobiles.
Manos Indígenas, Cuéllar 16, T03-337 2042. For fabrics and weavings from a number of indigenous groups.

Museo de Historia, in the Casa de Cultura. Best local crafts; hours are sporadic, call ahead, T03-355 0611. All proceeds go to **La Mancomunidad**, a local outfit that supports indigenous craftsmen and their families.
Uniarte, Charagua 37 and 24 de Septiembre corner with Seoane, T03-330 2995, T7088-6942 (mob). Another first-rate non-profit store specializing in colourful ceramics, fabrics, and mobiles.
Vicuñita Handicrafts, Ingavi e Independencia, T03-333 4711. By far the best and biggest selection from altiplano and lowlands. Very honest, will ship.

Jewellery
RC Joyas, Bolívar 262, T03-333 2725. Jewellery and Bolivian gems, the manager produces and sells good maps of Santa Cruz city and department.

Markets
There is a fruit and vegetable market at Sucre y Cochabamba, and a large indigenous market on Sun near the bus terminal.
Bazar Siete Calles, mainly for clothing, but food and fruit is sold outside, main entrance is in 100 block of Isabel La Católica, also on Camiri and Vallegrande, past Ingavi.
Los Pozos, see Eating, daily. In summer it's full of exotic fruits. Beware of bag-snatching.

▲ Activities and tours

Santa Cruz *p420, map p421*
Fremen, Beni 79, T03-333 8535, F336 0265. Local tours, also jungle river cruises.
Forest Tour Operator, Cuéllar 22, T03-337 2042, www.forestbolivia.com. Environmentally sensitive tours to most national parks, Beni and Chiquitania. Works with local indigenous groups.
Jean Paul Ayala, jpdakidd@roble.scz. entelnet.bo. Recommended for birdwatching trips, speaks English.
Magri Turismo, Warnes esq Potosí, T03-334 5663, www.magri-amexpress.com.bo. American Express agent. Recommended.
Mario Berndt, T03-342 0340, tauk@em.daitec-bo.com. Does large-scale tailored tours off the beaten track, mostly to the Altiplano, requires approx 3 months notice, speaks English, German and Spanish and is very knowledgeable about the area.

Ruta Verde, 21 de Mayo 332, T03-339 6470, www.rutaverdebolivia.com. Dutch/Bolivian owned operator running tours to national parks (Amboró, Noel Kempff Mercado), Jesuit missions, Amazonian boat trips; well-organized, uses local guides, English, Dutch and German spoken, good value. A good new recommendation.

⊖ Transport

Santa Cruz *p420, map p421*
Air The airport bus runs from the centre to Viru Viru airport every 20 mins (25 mins, US$0.70, 0530-2030). **LAB** (see note page 28) flies at least twice daily to **La Paz** and **Cochabamba**. Aero Sur flies to **La Paz** (several daily), **Cochabamba**, **Sucre**, **Tarija** and **Puerto Suárez**. **International** Aero Sur flies to Madrid, Asunción, Buenos Aires, Lima, São Paulo and Miami. **Amazonas** flies to Trinidad for onward connections. International destinations include most South American capitals, as well as Salta, Tucumán and Córdoba, São Paulo and some US gateways and cities in Mexico and Central America.
   Airline offices Aerolíneas Argentinas, Edif Banco de la Nación Argentina, on main Plaza, T03-333 9776. **Aero Sur**, Irala 616, T03-336 4446. **Amazonas**, Aeropuerto El Trompillo, of 10, T03-357 8988. **American Airlines**, Beni 167, T03-334 1314. **LAB**, Warnes y Chuquisaca, T03-334 4596, or T901-10-5000.

Bus To **Samaipata**, *trufis* leave when full from the vicinity of the old bus station, at the junction of Av Omar Chávez Ortiz and Solís de Olguín: **Taxi Florida**, T03-333 5067, 2½ hrs, US$3.50. **Expreso Samaipata** minibus, Av Omar Chávez Ortiz 1111, T03-336 2312, US$2, at 1700. Other minibuses from Av Grigotá y Tercer Anillo, **Montenegro** daily 1630, **Rojas** 0415, but not Mon, Wed, Fri.
Long-distance Buses leave from the new combined bus/train terminal. Take a No 12 bus from the centre, or a taxi (US$1.50. Daily buses to **Cochabamba** (US$3-4.50, 10 hrs), many *flotas* leave between 0600-0900 and 1630-2100. Direct to **Sucre** daily between 1700-1800, 14 hrs, US$6-7.50. Some Sucre buses also stop in **Samaipata**. To **Oruro** and **La Paz** 17 hrs, US$10-12.50, between 1700-2200 (some are *buscama*); change in

Cochabamba for daytime travel. To **Camiri** (US$3.75), **Yacuiba** and **Tarija**, daily, several companies; 26-32 hrs to Tarija. To **Trinidad**, several daily, 12 hrs, US$4.50, all depart 1700 or 1900.

Car hire Aby's, 3rd *anillo* 1038, corner with Pasaje Muralto 1038 (opposite zoo), T03-345 1560. **Across**, 4th anillo, corner with Radial 27 (400 m from Av Banzer Oeste), T03-344 1717. US$70 per day for basic Suzuki 4WD (200 km per day) with insurance. **Barron's**, Av Alemana 50 y Tajibos, T03-342 0160, www.rentacar bolivia.com. Outstanding service, trustworthy; clean vehicles, fully equipped.

Train Trains to **Quijarro** on the Brazilian border go via **San José de Chiquitos** (8¾ hrs). **Expreso del Oriente** Pullman trains leave Santa Cruz Mon-Sat at 1530, arriving in Quijarro at 1000 the next day. Trains also run south to **Tacuiba**, for onward travel in Argentina.

⊙ Directory

Santa Cruz *p420, map p421*
Banks Enlace ATMs at airport and in town; also in Equipetrol. **Banco Mercantil**, René Moreno y Suárez de Figueroa. Cash advance on Visa, changes cash and TCs. **Medicambio**, Plaza 24 de Septiembre changes TCs into US$ at 3% commission. **Menno Credit Union**, 10 de Agosto 15, changes TCs, 1% commission. Street money changers on Plaza 24 de Septiembre and around bus terminal; they exchange guaraníes. **Cultural centres** See Asociación Pro Arte y Cultura, Festivals and events, above. **Centro Boliviano Americano**, Cochabamba 66, www.cba.com.bo. Library with US papers and magazines, English classes, some cultural events. **Centro Cultural Franco Alemán**, Av Velarde 200, www.ccfranco aleman.org. Joint cultural institute with language courses, cultural events, library (internet access). **Centro de Formación de la Cooperación Española**, Arenales 583, www.aeci.org.bo (concerts, films, art exhibitions, lectures, etc), very good. **Centro Simón I Patiño**, Independencia y Suárez de Figueroa 89, www.fundacionpatino.org/ fusip/fundacioni.htm. Exhibitions, galleries, and bookstore on Bolivian cultures.

Embassies and consulates Argentina, Edif Banco de la Nación Argentina, Plaza 24 de Septiembre, Junín 22, T03-332 8291, Mon-Fri 0800-1300. **Brazil**, Av Busch 330, Mon-Fri 0900-1500. It takes 24 hrs to process visa applications, reported as unhelpful. **Chile**, Av San Martín, Edif Equipetrol Tower, p 9, T03-353 1796. **Germany**, Ñuflo de Chávez 437, T03-332 4153, Mon-Fri 0800-1200. **Israel**, Av Banzer 171, T03-342 4777, hobsch@ infonet.bo. **Italy**, El Trompillo, Edif Honnen, p 1, T03-336 6113, Mon-Fri 0830-1230. **Netherlands**, Av Roque Aguilera 300, 3rd *anillo*, between Grigotá and Paraí, T03-353 8799, ludo@alke.net, Mon-Fri 0900-1230. **Paraguay**, Manuel Ignacio Salvatierra 99, Edif Victoria, of 1A, T03-336 7585. Colour photo required for visa, Mon-Fri 0730-1400. **Peru**,

Av La Salle 2327, T03-333 6344. **Spain**, Monseñor Santiesteban 237, T03-352 5200, Mon-Fri 0900-1200. **USA**, Güemes Este 6, Equipetrol, T03-335 4498, Mon-Fri 0900-1130 (very limited services offered; best to go to La Paz). **Internet** There are cyber cafés everywhere, US$0.40-0.80 per hr.
Medical services For hospitals, doctors and dentists, contact your consulate or the tourist office for advice. **Post office** Calle Junín 146. **Telephone** Entel, Warnes 36 (between Moreno and Chuquisaca), T03-332 5526, local and international calls and fax. Also small **Entel** office at Quijarro 267.
Useful addresses Immigration: 3rd *anillo* Interno, corner with Av Cronenbold, opposite zoo, T03-333 6442/2136, Mon-Fri 0830-1200, 1430-1800, service can be slow.

Samaipata and Amboró

In contrast to the highlands of the Andes and the gorges of the Yungas, eastern Bolivia is made up of vast plains stretching to the Chaco of Paraguay and the Pantanal wetlands of Brazil. Agriculture is well-developed and other natural resources are fully exploited, bringing prosperity to the region. The forested slopes of Parque Nacional Amboró support a great biodiversity, while historical interest lies in the pre-Inca ceremonial site at Samaipata and, of much more recent date, the trails and villages where Che Guevara made his final attempt to bring revolution to Bolivia. ▸▸ *For Sleeping, Eating and other listings see pages 430-433.*

Samaipata ⬛🚻⛰🚌🅲 ▸▸ *pp430-433.*

→ *Colour map 3, B4. Phone code 03. Altitude: 1650 m.*
From Santa Cruz the spectacular old mountain road to Cochabamba runs along the Piray gorge and up into the highlands. Some 120 km from Santa Cruz is Samaipata, a great place to relax midweek, with good lodging, restaurants, hikes and riding, and a helpful ex-pat community. This is no sleepy, laid-back little town, however. At the weekend it bursts into life when crowds of visitors from Santa Cruz come to escape the oppressive heat and party with a vengeance. Close by is El Fuerte, the easternmost capital of the Inca empire with the largest sculpted sacred rock in the whole of South America.

Ins and outs
Micros and *trufis* from Santa Cruz arrive at the main plaza; the journey takes about 2½ hours. The overnight bus from Santa Cruz to Sucre passes through Samaipata around 1800-2000. From Sucre, the overnight bus arrives in Samaipata 0500-0600 (set your alarm in case the driver forgets to stop for you), stopping in Mairana or Mataral for breakfast, about 30 minutes before Samaipata. ▸▸ *For full transport details, see page 433.*
There's no tourist office but tour operators offer free information. **Roadrunners**, (see page 433) are very helpful. They will arrange the purchase of bus tickets for buses heading to Sucre so you don't have to return to Santa Cruz; give them 24 hours notice. They also take bookings for *colectivos* to Santa Cruz. Also see www.samaipata.info.

The **Centro de Investigaciones Arqueológicos y Antropológicas Samaipata** ① *2 blocks east and 1 block north of the plaza, daily 0930-1230, 1430-1830, US$0.75 for museum only or US$4 including El Fuerte site, ticket valid 4 days,* provides a valuable introduction to the nearby pre-Inca ceremonial site known as El Fuerte (see below). There is also a collection of pre-Inca lowland ceramics with anthropomorphic designs dating from around AD 300 and a good mock-up of the cave near Mataral. English-speaking Olaf Liebhart of **Roadrunners** gives an enthusiastic tour of the museum included in his El Fuerte trip which really brings it to life.

El Fuerte → *Colour map 3, B4.*
① *9 km east of Samaipata, head 3 km along the highway, then 6 km up a rough, signposted road (taxi US$4.50); 2 hours' walk one way, or drive to the entrance.*
Often besieged by ferocious winds, El Fuerte is Bolivia's second-most visited pre-Columbian site after Tiahuanaco, and named '*Patrimonia de la Humanidad*' in 1998. Its chief attraction is a vast carved rock, a sacred structure which consists of a complex system of channels, basins and high-relief sculptures. Latest research on dates is conflicting. Some suggests that Amazonian people created it around 1500 BC, but it could be later. There is evidence of subsequent occupations and that it was the eastern outpost of the Incas' Kollasuyo (their Bolivian Empire). It is no longer permitted to walk on the rock, so visit the museum in Samaipata first to see the excellent model. Pleasant bathing is possible in a river on the way to El Fuerte.

Excursions from Samaipata
In addition to tours to El Fuerte, Amboró and the Che Guevara Trail (see page 429), many other tours are offered in the Samaipata area, in vehicles, on horseback, on foot or in combination. These include **Cuevas**, 20 km east of town, with waterfalls and pools; the beautiful landscape of the **Laguna Volcán** region, further east (turn off the Samaipata-Santa Cruz road near Bermejo); similar scenery of forest and sandstone mountains at **Bella Vista/Codo de los Andes**; the 40-m-high **La Pajcha** waterfall (40 km south), which can be combined with the **Cerro de los Cóndores**, where these magnificent birds can regularly be seen. Tour operators arrange trips, often with guides who specialize in wildlife watching.

Parque Nacional Amboró 🏞️🔺🚌 » *pp430-433. Colour map 3, B4.*

Bolivia's best-known protected area is Parque Nacional Amboró, a 6376-sq-km territory only three hours west of Santa Cruz, situated at the extreme northwest edge of Santa Cruz's Ichilo province. This is one of the last untouched wildernesses on earth and a place of special beauty. The park encompasses three distinct major ecosystems – those of the Amazon River basin, the foothills of the Andes mountains, and the Chaco plain – and 11 life zones. Nowhere else in the world do three such vast environments converge, and nowhere else can you see so many diverse ecological systems.

Those wishing to visit Amboró should bear in mind that although access is relatively easy, penetration into the park's more remote areas should always be undertaken with an experienced guide or as part of an organized tour. Much of the park is wet all year round and many of the routes are riverine or along poorly (if at all) marked trails. A good supply of food and water, insect repellent, a machete, good boots and long-sleeved shirts and long trousers are a must. The park's infrastructure is minimal: there are no hospitals, stores, telephones or any public facilities. Notwithstanding, a well-prepared two- to three-day trip into one or more of Amboró's ecosystems is an incredible experience. Keep in mind that most tours do not stretch beyond a week's stay and that great patience is needed actually to spot some of the more exotic creatures in the park. Particularly in the case of the larger game, nocturnal sightings are invariably more common than daylight ones. The best time of year to visit the park is during the May-October dry season.

Ins and outs

There are two places to base yourself: Samaipata and Buena Vista. The park is administered by **SERNAP** ① *head office Igmiri 210, Barrio Urbari, Santa Cruz , T03-355 5053, www.amboro-bo.org*. There are subsidiary offices in Samaipata and Buena Vista. Topographic maps of the area can be obtained at the **IGM** ① *Av Tres Pasos al Frente near the 3rd anillo, Barrio Petrolero Sur, Santa Cruz, T03-346 3040, 0830-1230, 1500-1800*. **Note** There are many biting insects so take repellent. ▸▸ *For Transport to Buena Vista see page 433.*

Access from Buena Vista Northwest of Santa Cruz by paved road is the sleepy town of Buena Vista. Most entrances to the park involve crossing the Río Surutú, which is usually in flood in the wet season (November-March). The most popular entrance to the park is Las Cruces, 35 km away, reached by a daily morning bus whose route runs alongside the Río Surutú for several kilometres. From Las Cruces, the trail leads directly to the settlement of Villa Amboró, in the park's buffer zone. Also in the buffer zone is Macañucú, 50 km from Buena Vista, which has the best services in the park, with horse riding, hiking trails, guides, camping, kitchens and showers (US$20 per person per day), radio contact with the park office. There is a **national park office** ① *just over a block from the plaza in Buena Vista, T03-932 2032 (permit free), closed Sun and siesta time*, which can help with guides and suggestions.

Access from Samaipata Many agencies in Samaipata offer excursions. If going on your own, access is via **Mairana**, 17 km by minibus from Samaipata over a bad, but beautiful road (several basic hotels and roadside eateries), the meal stop for long-distance buses is between Santa Cruz and Sucre; you can catch these if there are seats available. Shared taxis run from Santa Cruz to Mairana with **Cotrama** ① *Humberto Vásquez y 1st anillo, leave when full throughout the day, 3 hrs, US$3.50*, or take a minibus from Avenida Grigotá at Plaza Oruro. Shared taxis from Mairana to La Yunga, US$1.50 per person, more for an *expreso*. At **La Yunga** (US$2 entry fee), there are community-run cabins, E, with shared bath, no shower, basic, lovely views, meals available with advance notice. Guides from La Yunga charge US$15 per day to explore the buffer zone; take all your own trekking gear and provisions. Taxi Samaipata-La Yunga, 30 km, US$12 one way. The village of **Quirusillas** is 1½- to two hours by minibus from Mairana. As the area is close to the mountains, there is more rain than further east, with plenty of greenery and cloudforest. Quirusillas has two basic places to stay and a cemetery set on a hill overlooking a small valley. Lago Quirusillas is about 6 km away via a steep dirt road. There is a minibus service from Mairana to Vallegrande (see above) and overnight buses to Cochabamba along the old road with **Expreso Surumi** on Tuesday, Friday and Sunday, 1530, 12 hours, US$4.50 (passengers sleep in the locked bus in a Cochabamba market area until dawn).

Wildlife and vegetation

The park is home to a huge number of birds, including the nearly extinct blue-horned currasow, southern-horned currasows the very rare quetzal and cock-of-the-rock, blue-throated macaws, red and chestnut-fronted macaws, hoatzin and cuvier toucans. In total, 712 species of bird have been discovered. Most mammals native to Amazonia are also here. They include capybaras, peccaries, tapirs, several species of monkey such as howlers and capuchins, jungle cats like the jaguar, ocelot and margay, and the increasingly rare spectacled bear, the only bear found in South America. It is staggering to think that less than half of the area has been extensively researched. The park also

⁞ Paradise under threat

Parque Nacional de Amboró is potentially both Bolivia's greatest ecotourist attraction and its greatest ecological tragedy. Initially only covering 1800 sq km, in 1984 the reserve was proclaimed a national park, and six years later was expanded to 6300 sq km. However, intense settlement along its eastern borders led the government to establish the park's total area at its current size of 4300 sq km in 1995.

The government's action was seen by many observers as a concession to the illegal settlers, and led to vociferous opposition by conservation groups worldwide. Nonetheless, the 2000 sq km abandoned to the colonists was designated a 'multiple use area', ostensibly free from rampant development and theoretically to be opened up only under strict guidelines.

The reality is far different, however, and each year unchecked agricultural and mineral pursuits threaten the park's unique ecosystem. To make matters worse, Amboró lies between two of Bolivia's most heavily travelled roads: the old and the new Santa Cruz-Cochabamba highways, and is scarcely 25 km west of Santa Cruz itself. If encroachment is not halted soon, the entire area may one day fall prey to 'slash and burn' farming, its fragile ecosystem permanently damaged.

contains some recently discovered Inca and pre-Inca sites, not all of which have been excavated. Whatever a traveller's appetite, it is likely to be sated by a trip to the park. Whether you want to see large game or whether your tastes run to rare tropical or Andean birds, Amboró has it all. Only patience and, if possible, an experienced guide is needed. There are numerous tributaries of the Yapacani and Surutú rivers to explore, as well as numerous waterfalls and cool green swimming pools, moss-ridden caves and the fragile yet awe-inspiring virgin rainforest.

Che Guevara Trail ⬤🏍️🚌 → *pp430-433.*

In 2004 the **Ruta del Che** (Che Guevara Trail) was opened, following the route of Che and his band as they fled the Bolivian army. The entire 815-km circuit can be seen in three to six days. It winds its way along dirt roads in the sub-tropical area bordering the departments of Santa Cruz and Chuquisaca. Tourists travel by mule or on foot to the battlegrounds where the Cuban-backed revolutionary brigade clashed with Bolivian forces and includes the crossing by boat of the Río Grande at the Vado del Yeso, scene of the ambush that killed many of Che's group. The trail ends near the airstrip at Vallegrande, where Che's body was dumped in a secret grave. Nervous readers should rest assured, though, that the climax of the trail will not result in execution by firing squad. Accommodation along the route consists of basic lodges, cabins or campsites in order to keep the whole experience authentic. The trail is run by the Bolivian government, **CARE International** and local communities. Tour operators offer packages. See www.southamericanpictures.com/collections/che-guevara-trail/che-trail.htm.

Vallegrande and La Higuera → *Colour map 3, B/C4. See Transport, page 433.*
Those who prefer to pay their own tribute more privately can head 115 km south of the Santa Cruz-Cochabamba road to La Higuera, where Che Guevara was killed. On 8 October each year, people gather there to celebrate his memory. La Higuera is reached through the charming, unspoiled little colonial town of **Vallegrande** where, at

Hospital Nuestro Señor de Malta ① *no fee, but voluntary donation to the health station*, you can see the old hospital laundry building where Che's bullet-ridden body was laid out on public view for two days after his execution: dozens of journalists, as well as curious soldiers and civilians, filed in to see it. It's an evocative place, the walls covered in signatures and slogans scratched into the peeling plaster. One of the most poignant is actually on the adobe wall of the public telephone office. It reads: "Che – alive as they never wanted you to be". His body was shown to the international press on 9 October 1967. Near Vallegrande's air strip you can see the results of the excavations carried out in 1997, which finally unearthed his physical remains, ask an airport attendant to see the site. On the plaza in Vallegrande, there is an **archaeological museum** ① *in the Casa de Cultura, US$0.75.* Upstairs is the **Che Guevara Room** ① *US$0.30*, which has many photographs and a one-hour video in Spanish, which is fascinating for its original black-and-white footage. The schoolhouse in La Higuera, where Che was executed is now a museum. Another **museum** (T03-942 2003), owned by René Villegas, is open when he is in town. Guides, including Pedro Calzadillo, headmaster of the school, will show visitors to the ravine of El Churo, where Che was captured on 8 October 1967.

Camiri → *Colour map 3, C4.*

Camiri, a small oil town some 250 km to the south of the city of Santa Cruz, is the jumping-off point for the southern part of the Che Guevara Trail. Camiri is where Che's companion, the French journalist Regis Debray, was imprisoned and tried. It was also the Bolivian army's operational centre in hunting down Che's group. While here, try to see a display of the **Chaquerera**, possibly the most energetic dance of Bolivia. Camiri is the only place in the area where there are hotels. About 1½ hours northwest of Camiri is the village of **Lagunillas**, near to which Che had his base camp and from where provisions were bought. It's worth climbing the nearby Reducto for a panoramic view of the village and surrounding countryside. More interesting is a visit to Ñancahuasu where Che's group carried out their first and most successful ambush of the Bolivian Army. After about one hour's walk from the end of the road, you reach the river canyon where the attack was carried out; it's a beautiful but sad place if you remember the people who died there. Visitors wishing to follow the southern part of the Che Guevara Trail are advised that there is little tourist infrastructure. Much of the area where Che Guevara was active still has no roads and travel is by horse or mule.

● Sleeping

Samaipata *p426*
Rooms may be hard to find at weekends in high season. Most cabins listed have kitchen, bathroom, barbecue and hammocks. There are several other *cabañas* west of town, but all very expensive.
C **Campeche**, T7262 4762 (mob), www.campechebolivia.com. Cottages for 2-6 people, all self-catering, quiet, hot water, D midweek, E without kitchen.
D **Cabañas de Traudi**, across the road from La Víspera, T03-944 6094, traudiar@cotas.com.bo. Cabins for 2-8, also F lovely rooms (G with shared bathroom), heated pool US$1.50 for non residents, sitting area with open fire, TV and music system, ceramics shop, great place.

D **Landhaus**, Calle Murillo, T03-944 6033, www.samaipata-landhaus.com. The most central of all the *cabañas*, beautiful with a small pool, sun loungers, garden, hammocks, parking, internet and sauna (US$20 for up to 8 people), also rooms only with shared bathroom F pp; excellent restaurant and café.
C-D **La Víspera**, 1.2 km south of town, T03-944 6082, www.lavispera.org. Dutch-owned organic farm with accommodation in 4 cosy cabins, camping US$4-5, delicious local produce for breakfast, US$3 pp. Very peaceful; Margarita and Pieter know the local area very well and arrange excursions through their tour agency, **Bolviajes**. Highly recommended.

Band on the run

One of the most enduring, if exaggerated, images of youthful rebellion is that of Ernesto "Che" Guevara staring proud, implacable and defiant under that trademark black beret. It is an image that has graced many a student's wall. But how did this great 20th century icon come to die in a miserable little hamlet in the Bolivian wilderness?

Ernesto Guevara de la Serna, or "Che" as he became known, was born in Argentina on 14 June 1928 to wealthy middle-class parents. However, his eyes were soon opened to the plight of South America's poor during a journey around the continent on a beat-up old motorcycle, chronicled in *The Motorcycle Diaries*.

He met Fidel Castro in Mexico in 1956 and together they planned the overthrow of the harshly repressive dictatorship of Fulgencio Batista in Cuba. This was achieved in January 1959, after an extraordinary and heroic three-year campaign with a guerrilla force reduced at one point to 12 men.

Che worked tirelessly to create the ideal socialist model in Cuba as well as establish links with other, sympathetic nations, but his over-riding ambition had always been to spread the revolutionary word and take the armed struggle to other parts of the world. Bolivia seemed the obvious choice.

He left Cuba for Bolivia in November 1966, and, after a brief stay in La Paz, at the Hotel Copacabana, Che travelled to the guerrilla base at Ñancahuazú, a farm 250 km south of Santa Cruz where Che and his companions began their preparations. But their constant movements aroused suspicion and Che and his group were forced to go on the run from April 1967 when the army began looking for them. There was little sympathy from the Bolivian peasantry, as the government had successfully played on their patriotism in the face of this 'foreign invasion'.

Che and his band were now very much on their own and worse was to come. One of his men had been captured and, under interrogation, confirmed Che's presence in the country, contrary to the CIA belief that he had been killed a few years earlier in the Congo. The USA immediately despatched a group of Special Forces to create a counter-insurgency battalion known as the 'Bolivian Army Rangers', and stop Che gaining a foothold.

By August, Che was sick and exhausted, as were many of his dwindling force. On 31 August he lost one-third of them in an army ambush. The army had enlisted the help of local peasants to inform them of the guerrillas' movements, so they were ready and waiting when Che and his men made their way slowly north towards Vallegrande, the Argentine now crippled by his chronic asthma and travelling by mule.

They reached the tiny village of La Higuera, where they faced the US-trained Army Rangers in what would be their final battle. On 8 October the surviving guerrilla's were trapped in a ravine. A prolonged gun battle ensued during which a wounded Che was caught while trying to escape. He was held prisoner overnight in the village schoolhouse, under the supervision of a Cuban-American CIA agent, and executed the following day, 9 October, aged 39. Che's body was dumped in a secret grave, the precise whereabouts of which remained a mystery, until it was finally discovered in July 1997. He now lies in peace in his beloved Cuba.

E **Andoriña, Arte y Cultura**, Calle Campero
s/n facing El Deber, 2½ blocks from plaza,
T03-944 6333, www.andorinasamaipata.com.
G in dorm, C for cabin, includes breakfast with
fruit and juices, tastefully decorated, kitchen,
bar, public areas, garden, good views, picture
library, cultural events and films. Enthusiastic
owners Andrés and Doriña are very helpful
and knowledgeable, English spoken.

F **Hostería Mi Casa**, Bolívar, T03-944 6292.
Pretty flower patio, snack bar, G with shared
bath, 1 cabaña (D); renovated in 2006.

G **Alojamiento Vargas**, around the corner
from the museum. Clothes-washing facilities,
use of kitchen, breakfast, owner Teresa is
helpful. Recommended.

G **Aranjuez**, on the main road at the
entrance to town, T03-944 6223. Upstairs
terrace, area for washing clothes, food
available, includes breakfast, good value.

G **Don Jorge**, Bolívar, T03-944 6086. Cheaper
with shared bath, hot showers, good
beds, large shaded patio, good set lunch.

G **Paola**, western corner of plaza, T03-944
6093. Family-run, breakfast extra, good
beds, warm showers, use of kitchen, good
restaurant, can arrange guides to Amboró
and El Fuerte and book microbus to Santa
Cruz, rents mountain bikes US$1.25 per hr.

G **Residencial Kim**, near the plaza, T03-944
6161. Use of kitchen, cheaper with shared
bath, family-run, spotless, good value.
Recommended.

Parque Nacional Amboró p427

CARE has funded cabins on the far bank of the
Río Surutú just past Villa Aguiles on the road
from Buena Vista to the river. Good trails,
well located in the multiple-use area with
lots of flora and fauna.

AL **Flora y Fauna**, known as 'Doble F', Buena
Vista, T03-333 8118 (in Santa Cruz). Hilltop
cabins, viewing platforms for birdwatchers,
well-planned trails (same owner as **Café
Irlandés** in Santa Cruz).

C **Pozoazul**, on the bypass, Buena Vista,
T03-932 2091. A/c, kitchen, pool, good
restaurant, helpful, also camping US$14
including showers and pool.

E **Sumuqué**, Av 6 de Agosto 250, Buena
Vista, T03-932 2080. Cabins in pleasant
gardens, trails.

G **Nadia**, Buena Vista, T03-932 2049.
Central, small, family run.

Vallegrande and La Higuera p429

There is no formal accommodation in La
Higuera but you can camp at the school;
ask permission, US$0.30. The following
are in Vallegrande:

G pp **Alojamiento Teresita**, Escalante y
Mendoza. Good rooms.

G **La Sede de los Ganaderos**, 1 block from
plaza, T03-942 2176. Includes breakfast, hot
water, large rooms, comfortable, parking.

Camiri p430

Haciendas del Chaco, based in Camiri, T03-
952 4155, http://haciendasdelchaco.com.
A new group of 6 farms offering full board,
hot showers, activities such as horse riding,
cheese making, wildlife trails, trips to the
Ruta del Che and Guaraní communities.

Eating

Samaipata p426

There are several restaurants on and around
the plaza, most of which are cheap. Good
almuerzo (US$1.05) at **Media Vuelta**.

El Descanso en Los Alturas. Wide choice
including excellent steaks and pizzas.

Café Hamburg, Bolívar. Laid-back, bar,
food (including vegetarian), well-stocked
book exchange, internet US$2.25 per hr
(only after 1900), see **Roadrunners** tour
agency below.

Cafés

Café Baden, 1 km towards Santa Cruz.
Good for ice cream and tortes as well
as steak and schweizer würstsalat.

Chakana, daily 0900-late. Dutch-owned
bar/restaurant/café, relaxing, seats outside,
book exchange. Almuerzos for US$2.25,
good snacks and salads, cakes
and ice cream.

Panadería Gerlinde, near the Santa Cruz-
Cochabamba main road, daily 0700-2200.
Superb biscuits, bread, homemade pastas,
herbs, cheese, yoghurts and cold meats,
Swiss- run. Also has a weekend stall
in the market.

Vallegrande and La Higuera p429

Café Santa Clara, on the plaza. Decent
food and beer, Che-inspired decor,
helpful staff.

El Mirador. Huge portions of meat, good.

▲ Activities and tours

Samaipata *p426*
The following tour operators are all recommended and offer trips to similar destinations. Expect to pay US$10-12 pp in a group of 4, up to US$30 for smaller groups.
Amboró Tours, Bolívar 43, T/F03-944 6293, erickamboro@cotas.com.bo. Run by Erick Prado who speaks only Spanish.
Bolviajes, run by Margarita and Pieter of **La Víspera**, see Sleeping,
Gilberto Aguilera, T03-944 6050. Considered the most knowledgeable local guide, good value tours.
Michael Blendinger, Calle Bolívar opposite the museum, T03-944 6227, www.discoveringbolivia.com. German guide raised in Argentina who speaks English, runs fully-equipped 4WD tours, short and long treks, horse rides, specialist in nature and archaeology. Accommodation in cabins available, also inclusive packages.
Roadrunners, T03-944 6193, www.samaipata.info/roadrunners. Run by Olaf and Frank who are enthusiastic and speak English and German. Lots of information and advice, recommended tour of El Fuerte.

Parque Nacional Amboró *p427*
Amboró Adventures, on the plaza in Buena Vista, T03-932 2090. Excursions include guide and transportation, but not food.
Amboró Tours, near the park office in Buena Vista, T03-932 2093, T7163 3990 (mob), rodosoto@hotmail.com. Tours with very basic accommodation, simple food and include transport and guides, about US$50 pp per day, expensive for what's offered. Independent guides cost US$10 per day in Buena Vista.

⊖ Transport

Samaipata *p426*
Bus *Trufis* to **Santa Cruz** run to Av Omar Chávez Ortiz and Solís de Olguín, in the vicinity of the old bus station: Rojas, Montenegro (from **Heladería Dany** on the plaza; buy tickets here the day before), 3 hrs, US$2. Other companies include: Taxi Florida, T03-944 6133, 2½ hrs, US$3.50.

Expreso Samaipata minibus, T03-944 6199, US$2. *Colectivos* in Samaipata will pick you up from your hotel, or else take you from the petrol station. A minibus from **Mairana** passes through Samaipata daily at 0445 near **Residencial Kim**, and goes to Terminal Bimodal in **Santa Cruz**, T03-334 0772.
Long-distance It's possible to pick up one of the overnight buses that run between Sucre and Santa Cruz. Buses from Santa Cruz to **Sucre** pass through Samaipata between 1800 and 2000. Buses from Sucre to **Santa Cruz** pass through Samaipata at 0500-0600.

Parque Nacional Amboró *p427*
See Ins and outs, page 428, for getting to the park from Buena Vista or Samaipata. To get to **Buena Vista**, buses leave regularly from beside Santa Cruz terminal hourly 0500-1500 (also minibuses from Montero, US$1, and buses from Villa Tunari, US$5).

Vallegrande and La Higuera *p429*
Bus From Santa Cruz, **Trans Vallegrande** and other buses leave from Av Grigotá y 3rd *anillo*, daily at 0900, 1400, 1930 to **Vallegrande** via **Samaipata**, 5 hrs, US$4.30. Best to book in advance.
From Vallegrande market, a daily bus departs 0815 to **Pucará** (45 km), from where there is transport (12 km) to **La Higuera**.

Taxi A taxi between Vallegrande and La Higuera costs US$25-30.

Camiri *p430*
Bus To **Sucre**, **Emperador** and **Andesbus** run via **Monteagudo** daily, at least 20 hrs, US$20; **Transportes Chaqueña**, Tue and Sat, US$12. To **Santa Cruz**, Transportes Chaqueña runs daily US$6 (*bus cama*), US$4.50 (normal bus). There also several daily minibuses, 7-8 hrs, US$10-12.

⊕ Directory

Samaipata *p426*
Banks No ATMs. The Cooperativa near plaza changes US$ cash at fair rates.
Internet At Entel on the plaza, slow and expensive, US$1.50-2 per hr. **Telephone** Several *cabinas* around the plaza.

The Jesuit Missions

Northeast of Santa Cruz is the region called la Gran Chiquitanía, which includes the provinces of Chiquitos, Ñuflo de Chavéz, Velasco, Angel Sandoval, and German Busch. This is a vast, sprawling, sparsely populated area, mainly used for cattle ranching and of seemingly little interest to the traveller, except perhaps those with a bovine fixation. But this is a part of Bolivia with a fascinating history and a precious heritage. Here lie the six surviving Jesuit Mission churches of San Javier, Concepción, Santa Ana, San Rafael, San Miguel and San José de Chiquitos, all of which became UNESCO World Heritage Sites in 1990. These are perhaps the finest examples of colonial religious art and craftsmanship in the country and will impress even those travellers who would not normally set foot inside a church. ▸▸ *For Sleeping, Eating and other listings see pages 438-440.*

Ins and outs

Getting there and around Access to the mission area is by bus or train from Santa Cruz: a paved highway runs north to San Ramón (139 km) and on north, to San Javier (45 km), turning east here to Concepción (68 km), then, unpaved, to San Ignacio (171 km). One road continues east to San Matías and the Brazilian border (good gravel part of the way); others head south either through San Miguel, or Santa Ana to meet at San Rafael for the continuation south to San José de Chiquitos. By rail, leave the Santa Cruz-Quijarro train at San José and from there travel north. The most comfortable way to visit is by jeep. The route is straightforward and fuel is available.
▸▸ *For transport to the missions, see page 439.*

You should spend at least five days on the Jesuit missions route. The most interesting time to visit is Holy Week or at the end of July when many of the settlements celebrate their patron saint festivals. As rich as the region is in cultural heritage, it is still very much a frontier. This is one of the best regions outside of the Altiplano to sample true Bolivian culture. Tours can also be organized from Santa Cruz.

Tourist information For information on the Chiquitano dry forest contact the **Fundación para la Conservación del Bosque Chiquitano** (**FCBC**) ⓘ *Calle Fortín Platanillos 190, Santa Cruz, T/F03-334 1017,* www.fcbcinfo.org, the website (in Spanish and English) has lots of useful information. A very useful website is www.chiquitania.com, which has extensive historical and practical information. Mancomunidad de Municipios de la Gran Chiquitania, www.mancochiquitana.org, is a non-profit organization dedicated to the economic improvement of the region, including through handicraft workshops.

San Javier → *Colour map 3, B4.*

The little town of San Javier was the first Jesuit mission in Chiquitos, founded in 1691 by the Spaniards Fray José de Arce and Hermano Antonio Ribas. Its **church** ⓘ *US$0.45,* one of the most striking in the region, was designed and built by Father Schmidt between 1749 and 1752. The original wooden structure had survived more or less intact until restoration was undertaken between 1987 and 1993 by Hans Roth. Subtle designs and floral patterns cover the ceiling, walls and carved columns. One of the bas-relief paintings on the high altar depicts Martin Schmidt playing the piano for his indigenous choir. If the main door is closed, enter through the cloister to the right. Also on the Plaza are the **Museo Misiones de Chiquitos** and the **Museo Yaritú** (with displays on the pre-Jesuit Yaritús culture).

The surrounding countryside is excellent for walking or mountain biking. A local fiesta is held on 3 December. Enquire at the town's **Casa de Cultura** ⓘ *in front of the plaza, T03-963 5149,* to find out about events in and around town.

⦂ Arrival of the Jesuits

The Jesuits first arrived in Lima in 1569 and were assigned to the religious instruction of the Aymaras on Lake Titicaca. A separate group later moved to Paraguay and set up an autonomous religious state. It was from there that they expanded northwards to the vast unexplored region of the Eastern Lowlands of Bolivia, reaching Santa Cruz only in 1587.

The Jesuits set about converting the various indigenous communities to Christianity and persuading them to build and then live together in self-sufficient settlements of 2000-4000 inhabitants, known as *reducciones*. These were organized into productive units, led by two or three Jesuit priests.

Politically, the *reducciones* were ruled by the Audiencia de Charcas and ecclesiastically by the Bishop of Santa Cruz, but due to their isolation, they enjoyed a great deal of independence. The internal administration was the responsibility of a council of eight *indígena*, each representing an ethnic group, who met each day to receive the orders of the priests.

In 18th-century terms the *reducciones* were run on remarkably democratic principles. The land was the property of the community and work was obligatory for all able-bodied members. However, the Jesuits' prime concern was to save the souls of the *indígena*, therefore their traditional customs and beliefs were largely suppressed. The Jesuits imposed their Christian values so effectively that little is known about the indigenous cultures of this region. All that remains is the symbolism that was sometimes used in their carvings, replicas of which still decorate the mission churches today.

Despite the destruction of their culture, the *reducciones* brought economic advantages to this previously barren corner of Bolivia. Architects, sculptors and musicians were enlisted to help construct the churches and communities. The Jesuits trained the *indígena* to become great craftsmen in wood and precious metals. The temples they built were the biggest and most beautiful in the Americas. Because of the distances between the settlements, each church is distinctive.

They also formed military units which, for a time, were the strongest and best trained on the continent. These armies provided a defence against the slave-hunting Portuguese in Brazil and the more aggressive native tribes. More important than that, though, was the fact that those who formed part of the *reducciones* were free from the system of *encomiendas*, whereby groups of labourers were sent to the mines of Potosí. For further information see www.chiquitania.com.

Concepción → *Colour map 3, B4. Altitude: 497 m.*

The hot, sleepy colonial town of Concepción, founded by the Jesuit priest Lucas Caballero in 1708, is one of the loveliest and friendliest of the mission settlements. It boasts one of the region's most beautiful plazas, surrounded by covered sidewalks and buildings with red-tiled roofs. The buildings are ornately painted in the style of the beautiful **church** ⓘ *0700-2000, free but donation invited, guided tours at 1000 and 1500, US$1,* which was completed by Martin Schmidt in 1756. It was fully restored between 1975 and 1982 by Hans Roth, whose team of European experts had to recreate the building from the crumbling original. The interior of this architectural gem is mightily impressive with an altar of laminated silver. In front of the church is a bell-cum-clocktower housing the original bells and behind it are well-restored cloisters. Hans Roth used to live here and work with local artisans in the restoration of local churches. In the workshops near the church you can see the remains of the original church. There is a **tourist office** to the right of the church.

⁝ Expulsion of the Jesuits

Despite the economic and religious success of the Jesuit settlements and their role in limiting the territorial ambitions of Portuguese Brazil, in 1767 the missions were dismantled by royal and papal decree and the Jesuits expelled from the continent.

There were various reasons given for the Jesuits' expulsion, some of them less than credible than others. The Spanish Crown believed they had usurped too much power from the state. Furthermore, this was the age of enlightenment and the militant Jesuits were seen as a major obstacle to the progress of reason. Finally, the success of the Jesuits caused considerable jealously among some of the older religious orders, many of whom wanted to establish inroads themselves in the new continent.

Whatever the real motivation, many of the settlements were abandoned and the inhabitants suffered the consequences. The priests who replaced the Jesuits treated the indigenous peoples badly, fomenting war and hatred among the disparate groups while prospering from the livestock that had been introduced to the region. Even after independence

the exploitation of the local people continued during the years of the rubber boom. Scarcely 50 years after the expulsion of the Jesuits, the missions had become shantytowns.

Amazingly, the mission buildings survived this upheaval and the two centuries of isolation that followed. However, the tropical climate had deteriorated them badly. By the 1950s they were well on the way to ruin, although each continued to function as a church. Their salvation came in the form of a Swiss architect, and former Jesuit himself, Hans Roth, who dedicated 27 years of his life to restoring the churches that had been built by his fellow countryman, Father Martin Schmidt. Sadly, he died in 1999, aged 65, and did not live to see the restoration of the final church, Santa Ana de Velasco.

In the past few years, much has been done to carefully promote the heritage of the mission churches and their towns. Biennal music and drama festivals are held in each community, and their sacred art is displayed across the world. For further information, visit the Hans Roth Museum in Concepción (see below), or visit www.chiquitania.com.

On the plaza, **Museo Misional** ① *Mon-Sat 0800-1200, 1430-1830, Sun 1000-1230, US$0.50,* has photographs of the appalling condition of the church before it was restored. It shows a photograph of a central tower, added in 1911 and taken down during restoration, together with its actual clock, which was a gift from Spain. Restoration work is also carried out here and it is possible to talk with the craftsmen and admire their workmanship. The ticket provides entry to the **Hans Roth Museum**, dedicated to the restoration process. Also worth a visit is the **Museo Antropológico de la Chiquitania** ① *16 de Septiembre y Tte Capoblanco, 0800-1200, 1400-1800, free,* which documents the life of the indigenous peoples of the region. It has a café and guesthouse.

San Ignacio de Velasco → *Colour map 3, B5.*

San Ignacio is a hot and dusty commercial centre lying on the main transport route east to Brazil. A series of wide streets made of red earth run from the busy market area down to a large plaza fronted by the church, which is now completely restored.

It was, in fact, a lack of funds for restoration that led to the demolition of San Ignacio's **Jesuit church** in 1948, exactly 200 years after it was built. Hans Roth's replacement is again painted beautifully on the outside with a simple design and is an exact replica of the original, apart from the incongruous concrete bell-tower.

Inside, the pillars are carved but not painted, there is an elaborate high altar and pulpit, paintings and statues of saints. If it is closed at lunch you may be able to get in through the iron gate to the right, the last door on the left. A **museum** in the Casa de la Cultura on the plaza houses a few musical instruments from the old church.

On the outskirts of town, down the road behind the church, is the artificial **Laguna Guapomó**, the source of the town's drinking water. It is good for swimming, boating and fishing. The town hosts a fiesta on 31 July in the Casa de la Cultura, held on the plaza.

San Ignacio is the main starting off point for an overland visit to the **Noel Kempff Mercado National Park**. The park office is on the plaza. For a full description of the park and how to get there, see page 440. A paved road is yet to be finished and, at present, there is only a very rough road running the 200 km north to **La Florida**, which is 25 km west of the park's only vehicular entrance at Los Fierros.

Santa Ana, San Rafael and San Miguel → *Colour map 3, B5.*

The tiny, timeless and peaceful village of **Santa Ana** has its unique original church on one side of a huge plaza where cattle and donkeys graze. Some of the houses still have palm-thatch roofs. The church was built in 1755 and is the only one in the region that has not been fully restored. Nevertheless, this lovely wooden building is in good condition and it is fascinating to see the restoration work in progress. The walls are also interesting for they are covered in *mica*, a natural translucent silver-like substance. To see the restoration work and interior find Señor Luis Rocha who will also explain its history; ask for his house at the shop on the plaza where the bus stops.

San Rafael was founded in 1696 (also by Father Arce, one of the founders of San Javier) and its church was completed by Padre Schmidt between 1740 and 1748. It is beautifully restored with frescoes in beige paint over the exterior. To enter, walk up the right of the church and pull and twist the large wooden knob on the door into the sacristy at the end. Inside, look and listen for the bats nesting in the bamboo-lined roof.

Founded in 1721 by Father Felipe Suárez, **San Miguel** is 40 minutes northwest of San Rafael. Its **church** ① *0800-1800, free entry, donations welcome*, has been completely restored and is considered to be one of the most beautiful of the mission churches. Although it is similar in style to the other churches, its carved and gilded altar is rare. The frescoes on the façade of the church, built in 1754, depict St Peter and St Paul and the interior and exterior walls are covered in brown and yellow designs. The pitched, red-tiled roof blends in with the village architecture. To see it, pass through the gate in the bell-tower and ring the bell of the **Oficina Parroquial**. The mission runs three schools and a workshop. The sisters are very welcoming and will gladly show tourists around. There is a **Museo Etnofolclórico** ① *off the plaza at Calle Betania*; next door is the Municipalidad/Casa de la Cultura, with a **tourist office**, T03-962 4222.

Most traffic from San Ignacio goes via San Miguel, not Santa Ana, to San Rafael. If visiting these places from San Ignacio, it's probably better to go to San Rafael first, then go back via San Miguel. A day-trip by taxi from San Ignacio costs US$35-40.

San José de Chiquitos → *Colour map 3, B5. Population: 12,000.*

San José de Chiquitos, capital of Chiquitos province, lies roughly halfway between Santa Cruz to the west and Puerto Suárez to the east. As the chief settlement between the two, the town is the area's transport hub, cattle-raising centre and oil exploration headquarters, as well as a convenient jumping-off point for tours of the Jesuit Missions circuit. The town is in many ways reminiscent of Santa Cruz 50 years ago. Although it is served by both train and bus, with a partially paved highway that connects it to the region's major towns, San José itself retains the feel of a dusty, frontier town, with its few unpaved streets and even fewer cars. On Monday, members of the local Mennonite colony bring their produce to sell at the market and to buy provisions. The colonies are 50 km west and the Mennonites, who speak German, Plattdeutsch and Spanish, are happy to talk about their way of life.

Mission impossible

The majority of Jesuits sent to 'Upper Peru' came from Spain, but some also came from the countries of northern and central Europe. One of these was Father Martin Schmidt, a Swiss musician and architect, born in 1694.

Father Schmidt began his education with the Jesuits in Lucerne and in 1728 travelled from Cádiz to Buenos Aires. Later he travelled through Bolivia before settling in Santa Cruz. Despite having no formal training, he created all kinds of musical instruments for the

communities and even built organs for the churches. He also taught the *indígena* to play them and wrote music, some of which is still played today.

Furthermore, Father Schmidt also built the churches of San Rafael, San Javier and Concepción and the altars of some others. He even published a Spanish-Idioma Chiquitano dictionary based on his knowledge of the dialects of the region. By the time the Jesuits were expelled in 1767 he was 73 years old. He died in Lucerne in 1772.

The town centre is dominated by the architecturally unique **mission church** and compound, which occupies the whole of one side of the plaza. Founded by the Spanish Jesuits Felipe Suárez and Dionisio de Avila on 19 May 1697, San José was the third of the main missions to be established. The original church, erected in 1696, was replaced by the current one in 1748. This massive neo-baroque structure, although incomplete at the time of the Jesuits' expulsion, was built entirely by hand by the indigenous Chiquitano people using mostly wood and plaster. The mission compound boasts many amazing carvings. It was declared a Patrimony of Humanity by the United Nations in 1992.

The stone buildings are connected by a wall and have a uniform façade, giving the compound an almost military appearance. The buildings consist of the 18th-century chapel, the church, with its triangular façade, the four-storey bell-tower (1748), and the *bóveda* (mortuary), which dates from 1754, with one central window but no entrance in its severe frontage. Weather and age have taken their toll and, as a result, restoration is an ongoing concern. At the time of writing, many of the buildings were closed for repair. Behind are the *colegio* and workshops, which are being transformed into study and practice rooms for the town's young musicians. The **Museo Ayoreo-Chiquitano** ① *across the plaza*, funded by **FCBC** (see page 434) and **Hombre y Naturaleza**, has displays and information on local indigenous culture. The **Oficina Mayor de Cultura y Turismo** ① *on the plaza, T03-972 2084*, provides information. There is an **Entel** office and a hospital.

Excursions from San José A worthwhile trip from San José is to the **Parque Nacional Histórico Santa Cruz la Vieja** ① *4 km south of town on the old Santa Cruz highway, daily, US$2*. The park's heavily forested hills contain much animal and bird life and interesting vegetation, as well as the ruins of the original site of Santa Cruz (circa 1540. It also contains several billion insects, so you are strongly urged to carry repellent. There's a *mirador* giving views over the jungle and, 5 km into the park, a sanctuary.

Perhaps San José's best-kept secret is the **Cascadas del Suruquizo**, an easy 4 km south of Santa Cruz la Vieja National Park. Locals attribute invigorating and healing powers to these three waterfalls and their nearby springs.

Sleeping

San Javier *p434*
D **Gran Hotel El Reposo del Guerrero**, 1½ blocks from plaza, heading from the opposite side to the church, T03-963 5022. Cheaper

Mon-Fri, and with shared bath, includes breakfast; comfortable, restaurant, bar.
D **Hotel Momoqui**, right-hand side of main street before plaza, T03-963 5095,

hotelmomoqui@hotmail.com. Cabins in a pleasant garden, includes buffet breakfast, a/c, large pool, parking, no restaurant.
F-G **Alojamiento Ame Tauna**, on plaza opposite the church, T03-963 5018. Less character but smart and clean, cheaper without bathroom, pet parrot is noisy at dawn.

Concepción *p435*
C **Gran Hotel Concepción**, on the plaza, T03-964 3031, granhotelconcepcion@hotmail.com. Very comfortable, beautiful courtyard garden, excellent service, buffet breakfast, pool, bar. Highly recommended.
D **Apart Hotel Los Misiones**, Calle Luis Caballero, 1 block from church, T03-964 3021. Pleasant rooms around a courtyard, small pool, also an apartment for hire, good value.
E-G **Colonial**, half a block from the plaza, T03-964 3050. Large, clean rooms, hammocks and garden, good value. Breakfast US$0.75.
G **Residencial Westfalia**, 2 blocks from the plaza on same street as the Centro Médico, T03-964 3040. With private bath, US$1.50 cheaper without, German-owned, excellent rooms for the price, nice patio.

San Ignacio de Velasco *p436*
Other hotels (D-G) and places to eat near plaza.
A-B **La Misión**, Plaza 31 de Julio, T03-962 2333, www.hotel-lamision.com. Luxurious, colonial-style with a/c, cable TV and pool, rooms of various standards and prices, includes buffet breakfast, tours arranged.
B **San Ignacio**, Plaza 31 de Julio, T03-962 2283, sanignacio@cotas.com.bo. In a restored former episcopal mansion, non-profit making (funds support local indigenous communities), a/c, hot showers, breakfast.
F **Palace**, Comercio, off the plaza, T03-962 2063. With hot shower, includes breakfast, comfortable, good value.

San José de Chiquitos *p437*
E **Turubó**, on plaza, T03-972 2037. F with fan or shared bath, good location, laundry.
F **Hotel Denise**, Mons Géricke, 4 blocks east of plaza, T03-972 2230. With bath, cheaper with fan, patio, clean and comfortable, good value.
F **La Casona**, half a block south of Plaza Principal, T03-972 2285. Best budget value offerings in town. Safe, quiet and clean. Owner speaks English.

🍴 Eating

San Javier *p434*
🍴 **Ganadero**, San Javier, in Asociación de Ganaderos on plaza. Best restaurant in town with excellent steaks. Others on plaza.

San José de Chiquitos *p437*
🍴 **El Raffa**, between *la tranca* and petrol station on outskirts of town. Highly recommended for *churrasco típico*.
🍴 **El Solar**, on plaza. Hamburgers, *milanesa*, and *salchipapa*.
🍴 **Romanazzi Pizzería**, Bolívar 19. Run by elderly Italian-Bolivian who makes her own pizzas from scratch. Visit at least 2 hrs before you're hungry, very much worth the wait.

✹ Festivals

Jesuit Missions, *p434*
Many towns have their own orchestras that play the Jesuit music on a regular basis.
Mid-Apr The biennial **Festival de Música Renacentista y Barroca Americana**, is celebrated throughout the region.

✈ Transport

San Javier *p434*
Bus *Micros* run to the Terminal Bimodal in **Santa Cruz**: **Línea 31 del Este**, T03-334 9390, 4 hrs, US$2.50, 4 daily 0800-1830; also **Línea 102** and **Jenecherú**, Tue, Thu, Sat. To **Concepción** at 1130, 1830, 1½ hrs, US$0.65.

Concepción *p435*
Bus Santa Cruz-San Ignacio buses pass through about 2400, but drop you at the gas station on the main road, several blocks from plaza; ask around for transport to centre.
Misiones del Oriente, on the plaza, and **Jenecherú**, 2 blocks from plaza, both run buses to **Santa Cruz** and **San Ignacio** (3½ hrs, US$1.25). **31 del Este**, 1 block from plaza, have *micros* to **Santa Cruz** (US$3.10).

San Ignacio de Velasco *p436*
Bus Bus companies are based around the market. Daily buses run to the Terminal Bimodal in **Santa Cruz**: Transbolivia, T03-336 3866, 10 hrs, US$9.50; **Expreso Misiones del Oriente**, T03-337 8782; also **31 del Este**, Trans Velasco, T03-332 5524, and **Jenecherú**.

Flota Chiquitano, Trans Velasco, and several others go to **San Matías** for Brazil, 7 hrs, US$7.50. Some continue to **Cáceres**, 1 hr from San Matías on a paved road. To **San José de Chiquitos**, Transical B, Mon, Wed, Fri, Sat 1430, **Trans Bolivia**, Tue, Thu, Sun at 0700, US$4.25, 4½ hrs. *Micros* to **Santa Ana** (1 daily, none at weekends), **San Rafael** and **San Miguel** (daily) from the market area; also Flota Universal bus, 1430 to **San Miguel**, 1 hr, US$0.65, and Trans Bolivia to **San Rafael** 0700, 1430, 1½-2 hrs, US$0.65.

San José de Chiquitos *p437*
Bus To **San Ignacio**, there are 2 daily buses (at 0700 and 1200), US$3, with **Transical B** and **Trans Bolivia**. Both go via **San Rafael** and **San Miguel**. Overnight bus to **Santa Cruz**, dry season only (May-Oct), US$6 one way. Don't try to drive the unpaved road on this route to Brazil without 4WD, the sandy surface is hell for small cars.

Train Trains run from **Santa Cruz** to **Quijarro** (on the border with Brazil), stopping at San José (8¾ hrs from Santa Cruz), standard: Pullman US$6.50, 1st class US$3.15, 2nd class US$2.50; luxury: *cama* US$24.80, *semi-cama* US$20. To **Quijarro** daily except Sun at 1845; Pullman US$12.25, 1st class US$4. **Ferrobus** Thu, Fri, Mon at 0010; *cama* US$18, *semi-cama* US$15.20. It is possible to reserve seats on either service at the train station up to a week in advance. Trains to San José are usually delayed by an hour or 2. Always reconfirm.

✪ Directory

San Ignacio de Velasco *p436*
Banks Prodem, Velasco, corner with Sucre, T03-962 2099. Cash advances on Visa and MasterCard only (no debit cards), 5% commission, also changes US$ cash.

San José de Chiquitos *p437*
Banks No ATMs, nowhere to change TCs. Banco Unión on main plaza, US$ cash only, fair rates. **Telephone and internet** Several *cabinas* around the plaza.

Eastern Lowlands national parks

Towards Brazil and Paraguay are some of Bolivia's biggest, grandest landscapes. With the road stopping 150 km before the park, the almost completely unexplored Parque Nacional Kaa-Iya del Gran Chaco is an isolated behemoth of a park, the largest in the continent. The diverse Parque Nacional Noel Kempff Mercado is also huge – big enough to make Conan Doyles' Lost World seem still plausible – and covers a striking range of ecosystems, from plateaus to wetlands, forest to mountains. San Matías is another monster park, but little visited. ▸▸ *For Sleeping, activities and transport, see page 444.*

Parque Nacional Noel Kempff Mercado ⊕▲⊕ ▸▸ *p444.*

→ *Colour map 3, B5.*
In the remote northeast corner of Santa Cruz Department, Parque Nacional Noel Kempff Mercado is one of the world's most stunningly diverse natural habitats, with a vast number of animal and plant species. The park is astonishing in every way, especially for its Amazonian forests, spectacular waterfalls and eerie-looking *serranías* (mountain ranges). Recent studies show there may be even more diversity of wildlife here than in Amboró, with some rare aquatic species endemic to the park. There are seven distinct ecosystems within Noel Kempff Mercado, the highest number in any single protected area.

Second only to Amboró in terms of popularity, Noel Kempff Mercado is Bolivia's third-largest protected area, at 15,838 sq km (an area the size of Massachusetts in the USA). It was established in 1979 as 'Parque Nacional de Huanchaca' and changed its name in 1988 in honour of Noel Kempff Mercado, a pioneer of Bolivia's conservation movement who was murdered there two years earlier.

⁝ Discovering the Lost World

The first Westerner to discover the Huanchaca Plateau was the legendary British explorer Colonel Percy Fawcett. He discovered the plateau in 1910 while exploring the Río Verde and demarcating the national boundaries for the Bolivian government.

Colonel Fawcett was the archetypal explorer. Disappearing into the heart of the Amazon on his last expedition in 1925, never to be seen again. His life of jungle exploration was an inspiration to many. It is claimed that Arthur Conan Doyle, who was a friend of the colonel's, wrote *The Lost World* as a result of a conversation about the flat-topped Huanchaca when he was shown photographs of the apparently unscaleable cliffs and imagined an isolated plateau inhabited by dinosaurs. The details and descriptions given in *The Lost World*, match almost precisely the landscape of the park. Despite other theories, it is now generally accepted by most Doyle scholars. For a detailed account of Colonel Fawcett's adventures see *Exploration Fawcett* (Century, 1988).

Access to Noel Kempff Mercado remains limited. While the park's remoteness has helped to preserve its great biodiversity, public transport services are marginal. Several tour operators offer three- to seven-day trips. With a required daily fee of $15 per person per guide, this is Bolivia's most expensive park, but worth every penny.

Ins and outs

Getting there by air The most convenient way of getting to the park is to fly, however this will cost US$300-500. Access by plane from Santa Cruz is to **Flor de Oro**, in the north/central sector, or to **Los Fierros**, the park's headquarters, in the south. Flights also go to smaller places, but are irregular. All flights are operated by the **Fundación Amigos de la Naturaleza (FAN)**, www.fan-bo.org, which has an office in Santa Cruz. There are also an increasing number of air taxi services, most of which land along the banks of the Río Guaporé, which forms the park's eastern border with Brazil.

Getting there by road The only entrance for vehicles is from **La Florida** on the park's southwestern edge. From here a dirt road veers right and enters the park at a guard station at **Los Fierros**, 40 km east. From Santa Cruz, the journey is roughly 700 km and takes an arduous 24 hours; it can only be made by 4WD and in the dry season. This approach is made from either Santa Rosa de la Roca or Carmen Ruiz (the former being the better choice), both located between Concepción and San Ignacio de Velasco along the Jesuit mission road (Route 502). These two roads eventually meet and you enter the park at La Florida, crossing its southwestern border along the Río Paraguá. Another point of entry to the park is **Piso Firme** (181 km further), on the parks' northwestern border, where you can stay at one of several *alojamientos*. After leaving Santa Rosa de la Roca, the rest of the trip is along unmarked roads with no service stations, so bring extra petrol. At Piso Firme, you can charter a boat to **Flor de Oro**. ▸▸ *See Transport, page 444.*

Getting there by river From Piso Firme you can travel by launch up the Río Guapore to **Flor de Oro**; US$250, five to nine hours, depending on the season and the speed of the river's current. A second option is through **Paucerna** (formerly known as Puesto Boca Iténez). Fly first to Flor de Oro and from there go by launch in a westerly direction, reaching Paucerna, which also boats a few places to sleep (five to nine hours).

Tourist Information The best information is from **Proyecto de Acción Climática**, www.noelkempff.com. The park is managed by **Fundación Amigos de la Naturaleza**

(FAN) ① *Km 7.5, Carretera Antigua a Cochabamba, Santa Cruz, T03-354 7383, www.fan-bo.org;* contact Inginiero Gonzalo Peña Bello, gpena@fan_bo.org, or Richard Vaca. Also ask at the **Museo de Historia Natural Noel Kempff Mercado** ① *Av Irala 565, between Velasco y Independencia, Santa Cruz, T03-337 1216, www.museo.sczbo.org.*

Visiting the park

There are two accommodation bases within the park. **Flor de Oro**, a small border town along the Río Guapore, has access to hikes in the pampas and forests, as well as river excursions to the Arco Iris and Federico Ahlfeld falls and to various bays. **Los Fierros**, the park's headquarters, has some of the park's best birdwatching and a few cabañas for lodging. From here you can visit many different habitats and El Encanto falls. Guides can be hired in Flor de Oro. Alternatively, Marcello (the husband of Suzy who runs an information centre in San Ignacio de Velasco; currently closed but hoping to re-open) acts as a guide and can be hired, along with his jeep (five days costs US$250); food and accommodation not included. ▸▸ *For organized trips, see Activities and tours, page 444.*

Around the park

Rising over 500 m above the surrounding plain is the 3000 sq km **Huanchaca Plateau**, which is drained by numerous rivers and streams which merge to form the headwaters of the Verde and Paucerna rivers. Steep cliffs of 200-500 m bound the plateau, creating spectacular waterfalls. Arco Iris and the Federico Ahlfeld Falls on the Río Paucerna are two of the most impressive in the entire continent. An even more stunning waterfall is the 150-m-high **Catarata el Encanto**, about 20 km in from Los Fierros.

The park fee also gives the visitor access to Bolivia's newest reserve, the breathtakingly beautiful **Reserva Biológica Laguna Bahía**, a small area of enormous biological interest and fecundity located within the park's southwest quadrant. Hiking in the park is considered Bolivia's best, and recently park rangers set up a trail that crosses the high plateau. The entire trek takes a week at least, but the scenery along the way is positively breathtaking.

Wildlife

The wildlife count in the park is staggering – so far over 620 bird species have been identified, which is approximately one-quarter of all the birds in the neotropics. These include several types of macaw (blue and yellow, scarlet, golden-collared, and chestnut-fronted), over 20 species of parrots, crimson-bellied parakeets, red-necked aracari, the Amazonian umbrella bird, the pompadour cotinga, helmeted manakin, curl-crested jays, hoatzin and harpy eagles, to name but a few. Among the many large mammals frequently sighted are the tapir, grey and red brocket deer, silvery marmoset, and spider and black howler monkeys. Giant otter and capybara are relatively common along the Iténez and Paucerna rivers, as are jabiru and the maguari stork. Giant anteaters, marsh deer and the rare maned wolf inhabit the western grasslands and the endangered pampas deer roam the dry twisted forest of the Huanchaca Plateau. There's also a chance of seeing jaguars where the narrow Río Paucerna winds its way through dense rainforest on its way to join the Río Iténez.

❧ *Pink river dolphins can be seen in the rivers as well as the black and spectacled caiman.*

Other National Parks in the Eastern Lowlands

Parque Nacional Kaa-Iya del Gran Chaco

The enormous Parque Nacional Kaa-Iya del Gran Chaco, in southeastern Santa Cruz Department, is, at 34,459 sq km, the largest in the country, continent, and the entire hemisphere. This is the ultimate destination for the adventurer or ecotourist, and about as far off the beaten track as one can get. So remote is Kaa-Iya that anthropologists speculate that areas within it have never seen even native tribes, let alone latter-day explorers. The majority of the park is uncharted and unknown except by local peoples, although parts of it were a battleground during the Chaco War between Bolivia and Paraguay. If you're well prepared and have swotted up on the Gran Chaco, you'll find it one of the most rewarding experiences of your life.

Adding to the surreal quality of Kaa-Iya is the fact that it is so difficult to access. Its only feasible access route is by train or road track to **San José de Chiquitos**, still a good 150 km north of the park. From there, it's on foot across the Serranía San José range (or by 4WD in good weather) until the Bañados come into view. Plans are afoot for a road from El Tinto, just west of San José de Chiquitos, but at present nothing exists. There are no facilities of any kind, so careful planning is absolutely essential. Solo travellers to Kaa-Iya too often have a nasty habit of not making it back, as it is very sparsely populated. A compass is essential. Those wishing to make the journey should check with **Servicio Nacional de Areas Protegidas** (SERNAP), www.sernap.gov.bo.

The mysterious **Bañados del Izozog** wetlands are within the park, and it play host to well over 1500 species of birds and animals, including jaguar, panther, and a large number of rare desert-habitat creatures. It also contains a unique desert forest eco-system that has drawn considerable scientific interest.

Otuquis National Park and Integrated Use Nature Area

Carved out of the southern Pantanal in 1979, this large (10,059 sq km) park, along with nearby Kaa-Iya, and Manuripi at the country's other geographical extreme, is Bolivia's most remote habitat. Like Kaa-Iya, Otuquis has no guides, no tours, and no infrastructure. It is virgin wilderness at every turn except for a small enclave near Puerto Suárez, on the border with Brazil.

However, all this is set to change in the near future. Both Bolivia and Brazil are intent on developing Otuquis as a gateway to the Pantanal, and, more insidiously, a big-game hunter's paradise. Travellers who want to see the as-yet-untouched Pantanal's ecosystem, flora, and fauna are advised to visit soon. In a few years much of Otuquis will be well on the way to resembling Amboró and Rurrenabaque. In the Arroyo Concepción region (between Puerto Suárez and Quijarro) there is already one five-star hotel, with others sure to open in the future. The road connecting Puerto Suárez to Puerto Busch via Mutún will soon be completed, opening Otuquis to road traffic, which will likely have a negative effect on the pristine conditions that it currently enjoys.

Otuquis offers everything a trip to the Brazilian Pantanal does, only without any of its better-known counterpart's amenities. For the independent or seasoned wilderness traveller it is a true paradise, however. Wildlife abounds, especially aquatic mammals and reptiles, and the species count is said to rival that of Amboró in some areas. Caimans, tigers, jaguars, otters, egrets, even rare river dolphins have been spotted, along with some of the world's largest flocks of toucans and parrots.

Access to Otuquis is via the rail terminus at Puerto Suárez, then by road to Mutún. You usually can hitch a ride to the park by truck, as several run between Mutún and Puerto Busch. Although the latter lies wholly within Otuquis' boundaries, it is accessible only by river (Río Paraguay) unless you can flag a truck in Puerto Suárez or Mutún. Be sure to take adequate supplies with you: there are no amenities within the park itself and even Puerto Busch has little in the way of supplies.

For further information, contact **SERNAP**'s Otuquis representative, **Luis Marcus** ① *Santa Cruz, T03-355 1971, tucumarcus@hotmail.com.*

San Matías Integrated Use Nature Area

At a staggering 29,185 sq km, San Matías is Bolivia's second-largest park, yet one of its least known, owing to its relative remoteness and infrequent visitors. The flora and fauna of San Matías largely resemble that of Otuquis, as well as that of Noel Kempff Mercado to the north. Visitors will find the climate slightly drier than the southern

Pantanal, but the primary attractions are aquatic fowl and sub-Amazonian animals, including the increasingly rare jaguar. San Matías's three big lakes – Mandiore, Gaiba, and Liberaba – and its Río Curíche Grande are favourites for fishermen.

Access to the park is problematic at best: there are no roads, and only one dirt airstrip at Santo Corazón. Tours may be arranged from Puerto Suárez, and a few visitors have made the trip in a 4WD vehicle from Santiago de Chiquitos during the dry season, but the main attraction of visiting is to see it in the wet season when everything springs to life. An alternate route is a trackless path that heads due south from the border town of San Matías (which has regular air service from Santa Cruz) for approximately 120 km. You'll know you're in the park only if you stop to ask: there are no signs or official entrance posts. For further information, contact the park's overseer (resident in Santa Cruz), **Inginiero Jorge Landivar** ① *Barrio Fleig, Calle Los Limos No 300, corner with Majo, T03-355 1971, sanmatias@latinmail.com.*

Towards Brazil

There are three routes from Santa Cruz: by air to Puerto Suárez, by rail to **Quijarro**, or by road via **San Matías**. Puerto Suárez is near Quijarro and these two routes lead to Corumbá on the Brazilian side, from where there is access to the southern Pantanal. The San Matías road links to Cáceres, Cuiabá and the northern Pantanal in Brazil. For further details, consult the *South American Handbook*.

● Sleeping

Noel Kempff Mercado *p440*
There are 2 lodges in the park. At **Flor de Oro**, there is a renovated ranch with 15 beds and a provisions store. At **Los Fierros**, there are 30 beds in more rustic barrack-style housing (C pp including 3 meals), and *cabañas*. There are lodging options in small towns bordering the park and some camping is available. In all cases, contact **FAN** (see page 441).

▲ Activities and tours

Noel Kempff Mercado *p440*
Tours can be arranged with operators in La Paz, Santa Cruz (see page 428) and San Ignacio de Velasco. Prices for a 7-day/6-night tour range from US$915-1170, not including flights.
Amboró Tours in Santa Cruz, runs trips for US$500 for 6 days all-inclusive travelling by jeep and staying in tents.
International Expeditions Incorporated, One Environs Park, Helena, AL 35080, USA, F205-428 1714, intlexp@aol.com.

Voluntary work
It may be possible to do 3 months' volunteer work in the park. Contact **Dorys Méndez**, Av Irala 565, between Av Velarde and Av Ejército in Santa Cruz, T03-336 6574.

● Transport

Noel Kempff Mercado *p440*
Air All flights are operated by **FAN**, www.fan-bo.com, which has an office in Santa Cruz. Flights from Santa Cruz to **Flor de Oro** in the north of the park (5 hrs), or to **Los Fierros** to the south of the park (2 hrs). There are also flights to **Huanchaca** (2½ hrs), which started life as a drug smuggler's laboratory but is well within the park's borders and sits at the base of the Serranía Negra. This is probably the most convenient option for those short on time – although at more than US$1000, it is certainly not the cheapest. There are occasional flights to nearby **Las Gamas**.

Road
An unpaved track runs north from San Ignacio de Velasco to La Florida. Santa Cruz-San Ignacio 400 km. Santa Cruz-Concepción 300 km. Concepción-San Ignacio 100 km. San Ignacio-La Florida 200 km. Concepción-Piso Firme 367 km. Florida-Los Fierros 40 km.

Bus
From San Ignacio de Velasco, **Trans Carreton** leaves Thu at 1600 (US$9, 24 hrs), **Trans Bolivia** leaves Fri 0800-1000, both to **Piso Firme** on the park's western edge from where you have to charter a boat to Flor de Oro.

Quito and around

Introduction

Few cities have a setting to match that of Quito, the second-highest capital in Latin America. It sits in a narrow valley running north to south, at the foot of the volcano Pichincha (4794 m). Quito is a city of many faces. The Old City, a UNESCO World Heritage Site, is the colonial centre, where pastel-coloured houses and ornate churches line a warren of steep and narrow streets. Following a revitalization programme in recent years, the colonial centre is once again the heart of the city. North of the Old City is modern Quito – or the New City – an altogether different place. Its broad avenues are lined with fine private residences, parks, embassies and villas. Here you'll find Quito's main tourist and business area: banks, tour agencies, airlines, language schools, smart shops and restaurants, bars and cafés, and a huge variety of hotels in the district known as La Mariscal.

Quito's spectacular setting is matched only by the complex charm of the capital's people, the 'Chullas Quiteños', young professionals, office workers and government bureaucrats, conservatively attired and courteous to a fault. You will see them going out for lunch with colleagues during the week, making even a cheap almuerzo seem like a formal occasion. You will also find them in the city's bars and clubs at weekends, letting their hair down with such gusto that they seem like entirely different people.

Quito is surrounded by scenic countryside well worth visiting on day trips or multi-day excursions. There are nature reserves, wonderful thermal baths, mountains to climb, quaint villages and – of course – the monument to the equator, all within easy reach of the city. The western slopes of Pichincha, also close at hand, are covered in beautiful cloud forests where nature lovers can indulge their taste for adventure.

Quito & around

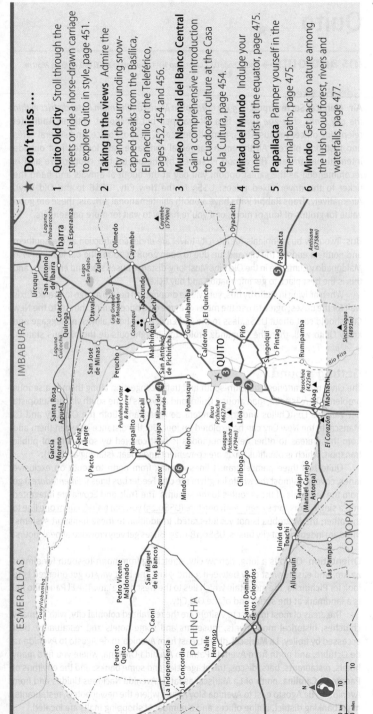

★ Don't miss ...

1 **Quito Old City** Stroll through the streets or ride a horse-drawn carriage to explore Quito in style, page 451.

2 **Taking in the views** Admire the city and the surrounding snow-capped peaks from the Basílica, El Panecillo, or the Teleférico, pages 452, 454 and 456.

3 **Museo Nacional del Banco Central** Gain a comprehensive introduction to Ecuadorean culture at the Casa de la Cultura, page 454.

4 **Mitad del Mundo** Indulge your inner tourist at the equator, page 475.

5 **Papallacta** Pamper yourself in the thermal baths, page 475.

6 **Mindo** Get back to nature among the lush cloud forest, rivers and waterfalls, page 477.

Quito

Ins and outs → *Phone code 02. Colour map 1, A4. Population 2,100,000. Altitude 2850 m.*

Getting there

Air Mariscal Sucre Airport ① *5 km north of La Mariscal, the main hotel district within the city limits, T02-294 4900*, is a bit cramped but functional, with an **Andinatel** telephone office, various ATMs, a small medical clinic, post office, and several cafés and fast-food places. All the main car rental companies are located just outside international arrivals. The airport is served by the airport taxi cooperative and is recommended as the safest option; you pay at the booth at arrivals and hand the ticket to the driver (fixed prices: US$5 to the New City, US$6 to the Old City). Alternatively, **Trans Rabbit Vans** have a booth at international arrivals, these are good value for groups of four or more, or if you're happy to wait for more passengers.

Bus Two new bus terminals for intercity travel are under construction at the southern and northern ends of the city and are due to open 2008 or 2009. The old terminal is at Maldonado y Cumandá in the Old City. Most long-distance buses start and end here, and this is the best place to get information and buy tickets.

When arriving in Quito by bus, you will be dropped off next to a large taxi rank. Taxis wait for the buses; agree to use the meter or agree on a price (during the day to the New City should cost about US$4, less to the Old City). If you have almost no luggage and know Quito well, then the **Cumandá Trole** stop is right outside the old bus station.
▸▸ *See also Transport, page 469.*

Getting around

The city's main arteries run north-south and traffic congestion along them is a serious problem. There is a ring road around Quito, and a bypass to the south via the Autopista del Valle de Los Chillos and the Carretera de Amaguaña. Both the Old City and La Mariscal in the New City can be explored on foot, but the distance between them and from these areas to other neighbourhoods is best covered by some form of public transport, which is plentiful. Taxis are convenient and cheap (starting at US$1).

Quito has three parallel transit lines running from north to south on exclusive lanes, covering almost the whole length of the city. Feeder bus lines (*alimentadores*) go from the terminals of these routes to the suburbs. The **Trole** and **Ecovía** are integrated into a single transport system, with one fare (US$0.25) you can transfer from one line to the other; the **Metrobus** is not yet integrated. In addition to these transport systems, there are independent city buses, US$0.18-0.25. Buses get very crowded at peak hours.

Orientation Quito is a long, narrow city, stretching from north to south for almost 47 km, and east to west only between 3 and 5 km. The best way to get oriented is to look for **Pichincha**, the mountain which lies to the west of the city. The **El Panecillo** hill is a landmark at the south end of the Old City.

The areas of most interest to visitors are the revitalized **colonial city**, with its many churches, historical monuments, museums and some hotels and restaurants, best accessed by trolley; **La Mariscal** district, east from Avenida 10 de Agosto to Avenida 12 de Octubre, and north from Avenida Patria to Avenida Orellana, where you find many hotels, restaurants, bars, discos, travel agencies and some banks; and the environs of **Parque La Carolina**, north of La Mariscal as far as Avenida Naciones Unidas and from Avenida 10 de Agosto east to Avenida Eloy Alfaro, where the newer hotels, restaurants, main banking district, airline offices and a number of shopping malls are located.

⦂ Flying into Quito at night

Quito airport operates 0400-0130. Most flights arrive 1900-2400. If a flight is delayed after midnight, then it may be diverted to Guayaquil. Most airport services close at night, however, you can wait in International Departures (open 24 hours). The information desk at International Arrivals is open until 2400 and the phone office at International Departures until 2300.

The hotels near the airport are poor, so you are better off going into the city. The information desk can find out if they have space. It's best to take a taxi. Try to team up with at least one other traveller and get a taxi voucher in the arrivals area. Insist on being taken to your hotel of first choice. One person can remain with the luggage in the taxi while the other checks out the hotel. It's worth paying a bit more for safe and comfortable accommodation on your first night. It is always intimidating to arrive in a place after dark; but after a good night's sleep you will quickly get your bearings the next morning.

Safety

Efforts by the authorities have improved public safety in parts of the city. However, beware that theft and violent crime are hazards everywhere. Both the Old City, away from a two block core around the Plaza de la Independencia, and the New City including La Mariscal (except for Plaza del Quinde), are dangerous after 2200 and pickpockets are active at all hours. Watch your belongings at all times, avoid crowds, use taxis at night and whenever you carry valuables. Be careful on crowded public transport. Even more caution is required around the Terminal Terrestre and La Marín. Bag slashing can be a problem at bus terminals. City parks should be avoided at night. In the Old City avoid going above Calle Imbabura. The **Policía Nacional de Turismo** ⓘ *T02-254 3983, Mon-Fri 0900-1300, 1500-1830, Sat-Sun 1000-1330-1400-1700*, has information kiosks in La Mariscal (Plaza del Quinde, Avenida Colón, Amazonas y Washington) and one in El Panecillo, brochures, some English spoken. Members of the **Policía Metropolitana**, who patrol the Old City on foot, speak some English and are very helpful.

Walking up to **El Panecillo** is still a risky business, but neighbourhood brigades are patrolling the area and have improved public safety; they charge visitors US$0.25 per person or US$1 per vehicle. However, taking a taxi up is a lot safer than walking. Do not carry valuables and seek local advice before going on foot. ▸▸ *See also Essentials, page 47.*

Tourist information

Corporación Metropolitana de Turismo ⓘ *toll-free T1-800-767767, www.quito.com.ec*, has English-speaking staff, maps, and an excellent website. They also run walking tours of the Old City, see page 465. There are various offices: at the **airport** ⓘ *T02-330 0163, daily 0800-2400*; in the Old City at **Plaza de la Independencia** ⓘ *Venezuela y Espejo, at the Municipio, T02-265 7793, daily 0800-1700*, and **La Ronda** ⓘ *Morales y Venezuela, daily 1000-1600*; in the New City **Museo del Banco Central** ⓘ *Av Patria y 6 de Diciembre, T02-222 1116, Tue-Fri 0900-1700, Sat-Sun 1000-1600*, and **Museo Mindalae** ⓘ *Reina Victoria N26-166 y La Niña, La Mariscal, T02-255 1566, Tue-Sat 0900-1800, Sun 1000-1700*, and **Teleférico** ⓘ *shopping area, Wed-Sun 1000-1900*.

The **Ministerio de Turismo** ⓘ *Eloy Alfaro N32-300, between República and Los Shyris, ground floor, T02-250 7559/560, www.vivecuador.com, Mon-Fri 0830-1700*, has an information counter with brochures for all of Ecuador, English spoken.

For maps, **Instituto Geográfico Militar** ⓘ *Senierges y Telmo Paz y Miño, on top of the hill to the east of Parque El Ejido, T02-254 5090, www.igm.gov.ec, you have to deposit your passport or identification card, Mon-Thu 0800-1600, Fri 0700-1200*, has maps and geographic reference libraries.

Quito orientation

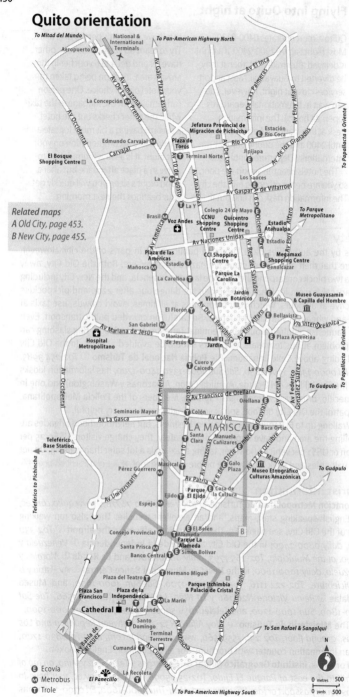

Related maps
A Old City, page 453.
B New City, page 455.

To Mitad del Mundo

National & International Terminals

Aeropuerto

To Pan-American Highway North

Av De La M Prensa

Av Occidental

Av De La Amazonas

La Concepción

Av Galo Plaza Lasso

Av El Inca

Av De Las Palmeras

Edmundo Carvajal M

Carvajal

El Bosque Shopping Centre

Jefatura Provincial de Migración de Pichincha

Plaza de Toros

Terminal Norte

Río Coca

Av De Los Shyris

Av De Los Granados

Av Eloy Alfaro

Estación Río Coca

Jipijapa

To Papallacta & Oriente

La 'Y'

Av 10 de Agosto

Av Amazonas

La Y

Av 6 de Diciembre

Los Sauces

Av Gaspar de Villarroel

Brasil

Av América

Voz Andes

Colegio 24 de Mayo

CCNU Shopping Centre

Quicentro Shopping Centre

Estadio Atahualpa

Av Eloy Alfaro

To Parque Metropolitano

Av Naciones Unidas

Estadio

Megamaxi Shopping Centre

Plaza de las Américas

CCI Shopping Centre

Av Rep del Salvador

Benalcázar

Mañosca

Estadio

Parque La Carolina

La Carolina

Jardín Botánico

Vivarium

Eloy Alfaro

Museo Guayasamín & Capilla del Hombre

El Florón

Av De La República

Bellavista

Vía Interoceánica

San Gabriel

Mariana de Jesús

Plaza Argentina

Av Mariana de Jesús

Hospital Metropolitano

Mariana de Jesús

Mall El Jardín

i

Av Occidental

Cuero y Caicedo

La Paz

To Papallacta & Oriente

Av América

Av Francisco de Orellana

Av Federico González Suárez

To Guápulo

El Panecillo

Av La Gasca

Seminario Mayor

Av 10 de Agosto

Colón

Av Colón

Orellana

Ecovía

Teleférico Base Station

LA MARISCAL

Baca Ortiz

Santa Clara

Manuela Cañizares

Av 6 de Dicie mbre

Telerérico to Pichincha

Pérez Guerrero

Mariscal

Av 10

Av Amazonas

Galo Plaza

Av 12 de Octubre

Av 12 de Madrid

Museo Etnográfico Culturas Amazónicas

To Guápulo

Av Patria

Ejido

Parque El Ejido

Casa de la Cultura

Espejo

B

Consejo Provincial M

El Belén

Santa Prisca M

Alameda

Parque La Alameda

Banco Central

Simón Bolívar

Av Universitaria

Plaza del Teatro

Hermano Miguel

Parque Itchimbía & Palacio de Cristal

Plaza San Francisco

Plaza de la Independencia

La Marín

Av Libertadores

Simón Bolívar

Cathedral

Plaza Grande

Santo Domingo

Terminre Terrestre

A

Av Bahía de Caraquez

Cumandá

Av Cumandá

To San Rafael & Sangolquí

La Recoleta

To Pan-American Highway South

E Ecovía
M Metrobus
T Trole

N

0 metres 500
0 yards 500

Old City

The Centro Histórico, Quito's colonial district, is a UNESCO World Hertiage Site and is a pleasant place to stroll and admire the architecture, monuments and art. At night, the illuminated plazas and churches are very beautiful. The core of the Old City is quite safe with frequent patrols by the Metropolitan Police. On Sundays the area is closed to vehicles (0900-1600) and fills with pedestrians, locals as well as tourists.

Plaza de la Independencia and around

The heart of the colonial city is Plaza de la Independencia or **Plaza Grande**, dominated by the **cathedral** (1550-1562) ① *Mon-Sat 1000-1600, Sun 1000-1400, museum US$2*, with grey stone porticos and green tile cupolas. The portal and tower were only completed in the 20th century. On its outer walls are plaques listing the names of the founding fathers of Quito. Inside, in a small chapel tucked away in a corner, are the tombs of the independence hero, Mariscal Antonio José de Sucre, and other historical personalities. There are many fine examples of the works of the Quito School of Art, including a famous *Descent from the Cross* by the indigenous painter Caspicara. The interior decoration, especially the roof, shows Moorish influence. A former refectory with paintings of all of Quito's archbishops and a display of robes used by priests in the 17th century are shown in a small museum. Beside the cathedral, around the corner, is **El Sagrario** ① *Mon-Sat 0800-1800, Sun 0800-1330, free*.

The colonial **Palacio de Gobierno** or **Palacio de Carondelet** ① *visitors may be allowed in the foyer, ask at the gate*, silhouetted against the flank of Pichincha, is on the west side of the plaza. It was built in the 17th century and remodelled in neoclassical style by Carondelet, president of the Crown Colony and later by Flores, first president of the Republic. Inside are a large mosaic mural of Orellana navigating the Amazon and a painting by Oswaldo Guayasamín, depicting milestones in Latin American history. The ironwork of the balconies looking over the Plaza are from the Tuilleries in Paris.

Facing the cathedral is the **Palacio Arzobispal**, the Archbishop's palace. Part of the building, the Pasaje Arzobispal, houses shops and restaurants around stone courtyards. In the northwest corner, is the **Hotel Plaza Grande**, with an eclectic façade, including baroque columns, it was the first building in the Old City with more than two storeys.

Just southwest of the plaza, at García Moreno y Espejo, is the **Centro Cultural Metropolitano**. It houses the municipal library, several temporary exhibits (free) and the **Museo Alberto Mena Caamaño** ① *T02-295 0272, www.centrocultural-quito.com, Tue-Sun 0900-1700, US$1.50*. This wax museum, well worth a visit, depicts scenes of Ecuadorean colonial history. The scene of the execution of the revolutionaries of 1809 in the original cell is particularly vivid.

One block south of Plaza de la Independencia, on García Moreno, is the fine Jesuit church of **La Compañía** ① *Mon-Fri 0930-1100, 1300-1800, Sat 1000-1600, Sun 1200-1600, US$2*. It has the most ornate and richly sculptured façade and interior. Several of its most precious treasures, including a painting of the Virgen Dolorosa framed in emeralds and gold, are kept in the vaults of the Banco Central and appear only at special festivals. Replicas of the impressive paintings of hell and the final judgement by Miguel de Santiago can be seen at the entrance. A couple of blocks west of Plaza de la Independencia, on Calle Chile, is the church of **La Merced** ① *daily 0630-1200, 1230-1800*.

Many of the heroes of Ecuador's struggle for independence are buried in the monastery of **San Agustín** ① *Flores y Chile, Mon-Fri 0900-1200, 1500-1700, Sat 0900-1200*. The church has beautiful cloisters on three sides, where the first act of independence from Spain was signed on 10 August 1809; it is now a national shrine. The monastery has a large collection of paintings by Miguel de Santiago in its **Museo Miguel de Santiago** ① *Mon-Sat 0900-1200 and Mon-Fri 1500-1730, US$3*.

To the northeast of Plaza de la Independencia, is the **Plaza del Teatro** with the neoclassical 19th-century **Teatro Sucre** ① *Manabí N8-134 y Guayaquil*, a beautiful, small theatre and Quito's main cultural centre. Not far from Plaza del Teatro is **Museo Camilo Egas** ① *Venezuela N9-02 y Esmeraldas, T02-2572012, Tue-Fri 0900-1700, Sat-Sun 1000-1600, US$0.50, Sun free*, housed in a restored 18th-century home. It exhibits the work of the Ecuadorean artist Camilo Egas (1889-1962).

Further north is the large **Basílica del Voto Nacional** ① *Plaza de la Basílica, Venezuela y Carchi T02-228 6063, daily 0930-1730, US$2*, with gargoyles depicting Ecuadorean fauna from the mainland and Galápagos, stained-glass windows with native orchids and fine, bas-relief bronze doors. Underneath is a large cemetery. Construction started in 1926 and took 72 years. It is possible to go up to the towers, where there are great views and a café. If you want to go all the way to the top have your hands free for the upper ladders and walkways (not advisable for those with vertigo).

Plaza de San Francisco and around

Plaza de San Francisco (or **Plaza Bolívar**) is southwest of Plaza de la Independencia. On the west side of this square is the great church and monastery of **San Francisco** ① *Mon-Fri 0900-1300, 1400-1700, Sat 0900-1800, Sun 0900-1200*. Built in 1553 on the site of Inca Huayna Capac's palace, this is Quito's first and largest colonial church. It is here that the famous Quito School of Art was founded. Worth seeing are the fine wood carvings in the choir, a magnificent high altar of gold and an exquisite carved ceiling. The church is rich in art treasures, the best known of which is *La Virgen de Quito* by Legarda, which depicts the Virgin Mary with silver wings. The statue atop Panecillo is based on this painting. There are also some paintings in the aisles by Miguel de Santiago, the colonial mestizo painter. His paintings of the life of Saint Francis decorate the monastery of San Francisco close by. Adjoining San Francisco is the **Cantuña Chapel** ① *daily 0800-1200, 1500-1800*, which has impressive sculptures.

> ● *Of Quito's 86 churches; the star attractions are La Compañía, San Francisco and Santo Domingo.*

In the monastery, the **Museo Franciscano Fray Pedro Gocial** ① *T02-295 2911, www.museofranciscanoquito.com, Mon-Fri 0900-1300, 1400-1700, Sat 0900-1800, Sun 0900-1200, US$2*, has a fine collection of painting and sculpture by artists of the Quito School of Art; there are pieces by many renowned local and European artists. The architecture of the convent is also of interest.

A couple of blocks southeast of Plaza de San Francisco, housed in the restored 16th-century Hospital San Juan de Dios, is the **Museo de la Ciudad** ① *García Moreno 572 y Rocafuerte, T02-228 3882, www.museociudadquito.gov.ec, Tue-Sun 0930-1730, US$2, students US$1.50*. It takes you through Quito's history from pre-Hispanic times to the 19th century. One floor has an interesting wooden parquet mosaic of a city map.

In El Placer, to the west of Plaza de San Francisco, is **Yaku Museo del Agua** ① *El Placer Oe 11-271, T02-257 0359, Thu-Sun 0900-1700, US$2, best reached by taxi*, part of one of Quito's old waterworks now converted into a water museum with interactive displays, good for children and with great city views.

Plaza de Santo Domingo and around

In Plaza de Santo Domingo (or Sucre), to the southeast of Plaza de la Independencia, stands a statue of Mariscal Sucre, pointing to the slopes of Pichincha where he won the decisive battle for the independence of Ecuador. Here, the 17th-century church and monastery of **Santo Domingo** ① *Mon-Sat 0900-1630, Sun 0900-1300*, has a carved Moorish ceiling over its large central nave and rich wood carvings. In the main altar is an impressive silver throne, *El Trono de la Virgen*, weighing several hundred pounds. To the right of the main altar is the remarkable **Capilla del Rosario** ① *daily 0700-1300, 1700-1900*, built on top of the arch of the same name. Santo Domingo housed the Colegio Mayor de San Fernando, where Latin and philosophy were taught in colonial

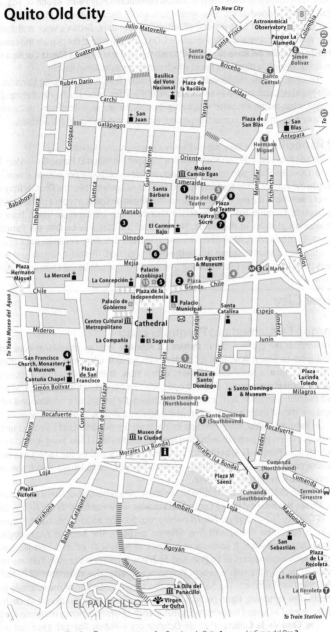

Quito Old City

Sleeping
Guest House **12**
Huasi Continental **8**
Margarita **13**
Patio Andaluz **10**
Plaza del Teatro **5**
Plaza Grande **15**
Relicario del Carmen **9**

San Francisco de Quito **1**
Secret Garden **11**
Viena Internacional **4**

Eating
Café del Teatro **8**
Criollo **7**
Govinda **1**

La Cueva del Oso **2**
La Fuente del
 Conquistador **3**
Mea Culpa **5**
Theatrum **9**
Tianguez **4**
Vista Hermosa **6**

times. Nowadays it houses the fine **Museo Dominicano Fray Pedro Bedón** ① *T02-228 0518, Mon-Sat 0900-1630, Sun 0900-1300, US$2*, named after the friar and painter who created the first brotherhood of indigenous painters, Bedón's work and that of other renowned colonial artists is displayed. On the south side of the plaza is the colonial **Arco de la Capilla del Rosario**. Going through the arch you enter **La Mama Cuchara** (the 'great big spoon'), a dead-end street which conserves its colonial flavour.

Leading off Calle Maldonado, which runs south from Plaza de Santo Domingo, is Calle Morales, better known as **La Ronda**, one of the oldest streets in the city. Refurbished in 2006, it has a narrow cobbled way, wrought-iron balconies, quaint cafés and restaurants. Formerly a rough area, it is much improved, though some caution is still advised.

El Panecillo → *See Safety, page 449, before attempting to climb Panecillo.*

To the south of Plaza de San Francisco is a rounded hill called **El Panecillo** ① *Mon-Thu 0900-1700, Fri-Sun 0900-2100, US$1 per vehicle or US$0.25 per person if walking; entry to the interior of the monument is US$2*. Gazing benignly over the Old City from the top of Panecillo is the impressive statue of the **Virgen de Quito**, a replica of the painting by Legarda found in the San Francisco church. There are excellent views from the observation platform in the statue. Northeast of the statue is **La Olla del Panecillo** ① *Sat-Sun 0900-1800, Mon-Fri on request, donations welcome*, a colonial brick cistern, now housing a small museum run by the neighbourhood. To take a taxi up and down costs US$5 from the Old City, including a wait at the top to admire the spectacular view.

New City

Parque La Alameda to Parque El Ejido

Just north of the colonial city is **Parque La Alameda** with an impressive equestrian monument to Simón Bolívar at its southern tip, various lakes and, at the northwest corner, **El Churo**, a spiral lookout tower with a view. In the centre of the park is the **astronomical observatory** ① *T02-257 0765, Mon-Fri 0900-1200, 1430-1730, US$0.50, ring the bell; also open from 1900 on clear nights for groups of 5 or more and when there are special astral events, US$1*, which houses a display of old instruments.

In **Parque El Ejido**, along Avenida Patria, there are exhibitions of paintings on the weekend, when the park fills with local families. Opposite El Ejido along Avenida 6 de Diciembre is **Parque El Arbolito**, its northern end occupied by the large **Casa de la Cultura** complex, housing a library, several theatres, exhibit halls and museums. Many cultural events are held here.

Parque El Arbolito is also home to the most comprehensive of Quito's museums, the **Museo Nacional del Banco Central del Ecuador** ① *Av Patria y 6 de Diciembre, Casa de la Cultura, T02-222 3259, Tue-Fri 0900-1700, Sat-Sun 1000-1600, US$2, students US$1*. It has three floors, with five different sections. The Sala de Arqueología is particularly impressive. It consists of a series of halls with exhibits and illustrated panels with explanations in English and Spanish. It covers successive cultures from 12000 BC to AD 1534 with excellent diagrams and extensive collections of beautiful pre-Columbian ceramics. The Sala de Oro has a good collection of pre-Hispanic gold objects. The remaining three sections house art collections from colonial to contemporary times. Call ahead for tours in English, French or German. Highly recommended.

The **Casa de la Cultura** ① *12 de Octubre 555 y Patria, T02-222 3392 (ext 321), www.cce.org.ec, Tue-Fri 0900-1300, 1400-1700, Sat 1000-1400, US$2*, operates several museums of its own: **Museo de Arte Moderno**, paintings and sculpture since 1830; **Colección Etnográfica**, a collection of traditional dress and adornments of indigenous groups; **Museo de Instrumentos Musicales**, an impressive collection of musical instruments, said to be the second in importance in the world; and **Museo del Libro**, with works by Ecuador's early explorers.

Quito New City

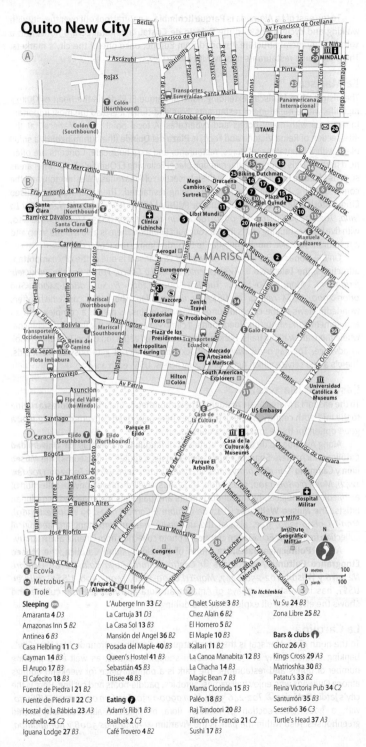

Sleeping 🛏

Amaranta **4** D3
Amazonas Inn **5** B2
Antinea **6** B3
Casa Helbling **11** C3
Cayman **14** B3
El Arupo **17** B3
El Cafecito **18** B3
Fuente de Piedra I **21** B2
Fuente de Piedra II **22** C3
Hostal de la Rábida **23** A3
Hothello **25** C2
Iguana Lodge **27** B3

L'Auberge Inn **33** E2
La Cartuja **31** D3
La Casa Sol **13** B3
Mansión del Angel **36** B2
Posada del Maple **40** B3
Queen's Hostel **41** B3
Sebastián **45** B3
Titisee **48** B3

Eating 🍴

Adam's Rib **1** B3
Baalbek **2** C3
Café Trovero **4** B2

Chalet Suisse **3** B3
Chez Alain **6** B2
El Hornero **5** B2
El Maple **10** B3
Kallari **11** B2
La Canoa Manabita **12** B3
La Chacha **14** B3
Magic Bean **7** B3
Mama Clorinda **15** B3
Paléo **18** B3
Raj Tandoori **20** B3
Rincón de Francia **21** C2
Sushi **17** B3

Yu Su **24** B3
Zona Libre **25** B2

Bars & clubs 🍸

Ghoz **26** A3
Kings Cross **29** A3
Matrioshka **30** B3
Patatu's **33** B2
Reina Victoria Pub **34** C2
Santurrón **35** B2
Seseribó **36** C3
Turtle's Head **37** A3

To the east of La Alameda is **Parque Itchimbía**, a natural lookout over the city with walking and cycle paths and the **Palacio de Cristal**, a cultural centre housed in a 19th-century metal structure imported from Europe, once one of the city's markets. There are some restaurants nearby with lovely views.

La Mariscal

The district of La Mariscal, extending north of Parque El Ejido, is the heart of Quito's nightlife, with a multitude of restaurants, bars and clubs. It is also the most important tourist area with many hotels and cybercafés. A focal point in La Mariscal, at the intersection of Reina Victoria and Foch, is **Plaza del Quinde** (the hummingbird) a small plaza with a fountain, sculptures, restaurants and a 24-hour café. Concerts are often held here and it is a very popular meeting place. Following El Quinde's lead, other areas such as **Plaza de los Presidentes**, at the intersection of Amazonas y Washington, and the corner of Reina Victoria y La Niña, are being revitalized. The latter has the **Museo Etno-histórico de Artesanía del Ecuador** (**MINDALAE**) ⓘ *Reina Victoria N26-166 y La Niña, T02-222 7885, Tue-Sat 0930-1800, Sun 1000-1700, US$3, students US$1.50*, with five halls exhibiting crafts from throughout Ecuador. There is also a crafts shop and a restaurant with live music Thursday to Saturday from 2100 (cover US$4).

On the slopes of Pichincha to the west of La Mariscal is one of the city's important attractions, the **Teleférico** ⓘ *Av Occidental above La Gasca, T1800-835333, www.tele feriqo.com, Mon 1400-2200, Tue-Thu 0900-2200, Fri-Sat 0800-2400, Sun 0800-2000, US$4 regular or US$7 for express line*. The cable car, which offers wonderful views of the city and surrounding mountains, is part of a complex with an amusement park, shops and food courts. It climbs to 4050 m on the flanks of Pichincha, where there are walking trails. Horses can also be hired at the top of the Teleférico (book in advance, T02-245 0508, www.horsebackriding.com.ec). It gets busy at weekends. There's a bus service which runs from luxury hotels, US$1 each way.

East of La Mariscal

To the east of La Mariscal are residential neighbourhoods including **La Floresta** dating to the mid-20th century. Some of the homes here have been converted to lodgings, a good option for those looking for a quiet location.

Along Avenida 12 de Octubre, northeast of Parque El Arbolito, is the **Universidad Católica** which offers Spanish courses and houses a couple of museums. The **Museo Jijón y Caamaño** ⓘ *in the library building, 12 de Octubre 1076 y Roca, T02-299 1700 (ext 1242), Mon-Fri 0800-1300, 1400-1600, US$2*, has a well-displayed private collection of archaeological objects, historical documents and paintings by renowned Ecuadorian artists. The **Museo Weilbauer** ⓘ *12 de Octubre y Carrión, T02-299 1700 (ext 1369), Mon-Fri 0830-1300, free*, also at the university, has an important archaeological collection from many Ecuadorian cultures, a photo collection from Oriente and a library.

At the **Politécnica Salesiana**, north of the Universidad Católica, the **Museo Etnográfico Culturas Amazónicas** ⓘ *Centro Cultural Abya Yala, 12 de Octubre N23-116 y Wilson, T02-250 6247, Mon-Fri 0900-1200, 1400-1600, US$2, children US$1*, has interesting displays of Amazonian flora and fauna, tribal culture and shows the effects of oil exploration and drilling.

La Carolina

To the north of La Mariscal is the large **Parque La Carolina** surrounded by New City's banking district, many of Quito's modern shopping centres, as well as a growing number of hotels and restaurants. The park is a popular place for weekend outings among Quiteños who enjoy ball games, aerobics, paddle-boats and cycling. Here is the city's **Jardín Botánico** ⓘ *T02-246 3197, Mon 0900-1230, Tue-Sun 0900-1700, US$1.50*, with a good cross-section of Andean flora of different altitudes and orchid greenhouses. Also within the park is the **Vivarium** ⓘ *Amazonas 3008 y Rumipamba,*

To2-227 1820, Tue-Sun 0930-1730, US$2.50, children US$1.25, run by **Fundación Herpetológica Gustavo Orces,** an organization striving to protect endangered species through an education programme. They have a large number of South American and other snakes, reptiles and amphibians and run a successful breeding programme. Staff are friendly and explanations are good (English, French and German on request).

The **Parque Metropolitano,** east of Estadio Atahualpa, is the largest park in the city and is good for walking, running or biking through the forest. There are some picnic areas with grills.

Quito suburbs

The beautiful district of **Guápulo,** a colonial town, is perched on the edge of a ravine on the eastern fringe of Quito, overlooking the Río Machángara. It is popular with Quito's bohemian community and a worthwhile place to visit. The **Santuario de Guápulo** ⓘ *Mon-Sat 0900-1200, 1500-1730,* is a lovely 17th-century church, built by indigenous slaves and dedicated to Nuestra Señora de Guápulo. It has many paintings, gilded altars, stone carvings and, above all, a marvellously carved pulpit by Juan Bautista Menacho, one of the loveliest in the whole continent. Next to the Santuario, the **Museo Fray Antonio Rodríguez** ⓘ *Av de los Conquistadores, To2-256 5652, Mon-Fri 0900-1200, 1500-1730,* has three halls with religious art and furniture, from 16th to the 20th centuries. Guided tours (Spanish only) include a visit to the Santuario de Guápulo.

Overlooking the city from the northeast is the grandiose **Capilla del Hombre** ⓘ *Mariano Calvache y Lorenzo Chávez, Bellavista, near the Ecuavisa TV station, To2-244 8492, Tue-Sun 1000-1700, US$3, students US$2 (US$5 if also visiting the Guayasamín museum),* a monument to Latin America conceived by the famous Ecuadorean artist Oswaldo Guayasamín (1919-1999) and completed after his death. The fate of people in this continent is presented through the artist's murals and paintings. A few blocks away is the fine **Museo Guayasamín** ⓘ *Bosmediano 543, To2-245 2938, Mon-Fri 1000-1700, US$3.* As well as the artist's works there is a Pre-Columbian and colonial collection, which is highly recommended. You can buy works of art and jewellery.

The **Valle de los Chillos** lies southeast of the centre of Quito. It is accessed via the Autopista General Rumiñahui, which starts at El Trébol, east of the old Terminal Terrestre. The first suburb you reach in the valley is San Rafael. One block from the main park is **Museo La Casa de Kingman** ⓘ *Portoviejo 111 y Dávila, To2-286 1065, www.fundacionkingman.com, Thu-Fri 1000-1600, Sat-Sun 1000-1700, US$4, students and seniors US$3, includes a guide.* The home of this renowned artist, unchanged from when he lived there, is now open to the public. To get there, take a taxi or a Sangolquí-bound bus from La Marín.

◉ Sleeping

International hotel chains and business hotels Quito is well supplied with these, most are in the New City. They occupy the highest end of the price range and often charge foreign guests more than Ecuadorians. Swissôtel stands out in this group for its opulence and excellent service. Most others are cut from a common mould: large modern buildings, elegant and expensive restaurants and bars, casinos, all services and comforts. They look and feel like big busy hotels anywhere in the world. For details, check the websites: www.hilton.com, www.hojo.com, www.marriotthotels.com, www.mercure.com, www.radisson.com, www.sheraton.com.

Upscale inns Quiteño hospitality excels in this class of select establishments. Scattered throughout the city, they include elegant little places like Relicario del Carmen, Hostal de La Rábida and Villa Nancy (on Muros). Some are in beautifully refurbished private homes. They are expensive, but usually offer a great deal in return: personal service in tasteful, tranquil and comfortable surroundings.

Apart-hotels and suites These furnished apartments are a good choice for longer stays and for families. Some rent by the day. They usually include a living room, fully equipped kitchen, and linnen service. There is a good selection located throughout the New City, with a broad range of prices and facilities.

Old City *p451, map p453*

LL **Plaza Grande**, García Moreno N5-16, Plaza de la Indpendencia, T02-251 0777, www.plazagrandequito.com. Exclusive luxury hotel with an exceptional location. Formerly the **Hotel Majestic**, it is a top-of-the-line version with 15 suites, 3 restaurants including **La Belle Epoque**, gourmet French cuisine and a wine cellar, jacuzzi in all rooms, climate control, mini-spa, Wi-Fi, 110/220V outlets.

AL **Patio Andaluz**, García Moreno N6-52 y Olmedo, T02-228 0830, www.hotelpatio andaluz.com. Self-styled 'boutique hotel' in the heart of the colonial city, exclusive restaurant with Ecuadorean and Spanish cuisine, 5-star comfort and service in a 16th-century house with large arches, balconies and patios. Library and **Folklore Olga Fisch** gift shop.

AL **Relicario del Carmen**, Venezuela 1041 y Olmedo, T02-228 9120, www.hotelrelicario delcarmen.com. Beautifully refurbished colonial house, includes breakfast, good restaurant, cafetería, good rooms and service, no smoking. Opened in 2006.

C **San Francisco de Quito**, Sucre Oe 3-17 y Guayaquil, T02-2287758. Converted colonial building, suites are particularly good value, includes breakfast, sauna, attractive patio but can be noisy at night.

D **Viena Internacional**, Flores 600 y Chile, T02-295 9611. Includes breakfast, good restaurant, nice rooms and courtyard.

E **Plaza del Teatro**, Guayaquil N8-75 y Esmeraldas, T02-295 9462. Nice old hotel, restaurant, private bath, hot water, parking, carpeted rooms, good service and value.

E-F **Huasi Continental**, Flores N3-08 y Sucre, T02-295 7327. Colonial house, restaurant, cheaper with shared bath, hot water, clean and good value.

Parque La Alameda to Parque El Ejido *p454, map p455*

E **L'Auberge Inn**, Colombia 1138 y Yaguachi, T02-255 2912, www.auberge-inn-hostal.com. Spacious clean rooms, restaurant, cheaper with shared bath, excellent hot water, cooking facilities, parking, duvets on beds, lovely garden, terrace and communal area, pool table, includes use of spa, internet, cheap international calls for guests, helpful, good atmosphere. Recommended.

E **Secret Garden**, Antepara E4-60 y Los Ríos, T02-295 6704, www.secretgardenquito.com. Restored old house, lovely roof-top terrace restaurant serves inexpensive breakfast and dinner (vegetarian available), one room with private bath, cheaper in dorm, hot water, nice atmosphere, a very popular meeting place for travellers, Ecuadorean/Australian-run. Recommended.

F **Margarita**, Los Ríos N12-118 y Espinoza, T02-295 0441. Breakfast available, private bath, hot water, parking, good beds, sheets changed daily, great value. Highly recommended.

Apart-hotels and suites

D **The Guest House**, Julio Castro 379 y Valparaíso, T02-222 5644, www.tours-unlimited.com. Rooms with bath for day-by-day or long stays in a nicely restored house, laundry and cooking facilities, good views, friendly and helpful, US$130/month.

La Mariscal *p456, map p455*

AL **Mansión del Angel**, Wilson E5-29 y JL Mera, T02-255 7721, mansion@mansion delangel.com.ec. Beautifully refurbished old building, includes breakfast, parking, very elegant, lovely atmosphere.

A **Hostal de la Rábida**, La Rábida 227 y Santa María, T/F02-222 1720, www.hotel rabida.com. Lovely converted home, good restaurant, parking, bright, comfortable, Italian-run. Recommended.

A **Sebastián**, Almagro N24-416 y Cordero, T02-222 2400, www.hotelsebastian.com. A very good comfortable multi-storey hotel, restaurant, gym, wireless internet, parking.

B **La Cartuja**, Plaza 170 y 18 de Septiembre, T02-252 3577, www.hotelacartuja.com. In the former British Embassy, includes breakfast, good restaurant although menu is limited, beautifully decorated, spacious comfortable rooms, lovely garden, very helpful and hospitable. Highly recommended.

B **La Casa Sol**, Calama 127 y 6 de Diciembre, T02-223 0798, www.lacasasol.com. A small quaint inn with courtyard, includes breakfast, 24-hr cafetería, very helpful, English and

French spoken. Also run **La Casa Sol-Otavalo** (see page 492). Highly recommended.

C **Cayman**, Rodríguez E7-29 y Reina Victoria, T02-256 7616, www.hotelcaymanquito.com. Pleasant hotel, includes breakfast in lovely bright diningroom, cafeteria, parking, rooms a bit small, sitting room with fireplace, garden, very clean and good.

C **Fuente de Piedra I & II**, JL Mera 721 y Baquedano; also at Wilson 211 y Tamayo, T02-290 0323, www.ecuahotel.com. Nicely decorated modern hotels, include breakfast, some rooms are small, nice sitting areas, pleasant and comfortable.

C **Hothello**, Amazonas N20-20 y 18 de Septiembre, T/F02-256 5835, www.hotel othello.com. Small modern hotel, includes good breakfast, café, bright and tastefully decorated rooms, heating, helpful multilingual staff. Recommended.

D **El Arupo**, Juan Rodríguez E7-22 y Reina Victoria, T02-255 7543. Includes breakfast, laundry and cooking facilities, very clean, English and French spoken. Recommended.

D **Posada del Maple**, Rodríguez E8-49 y 6 de Diciembre, T02-254 4507, www.posada delmaple.com. Popular hostel, includes breakfast, restaurant, cheaper with shared bath and in dorm, laundry and cooking facilities, warm atmosphere, free tea and coffee.

D-E **Casa Helbling**, Veintimilla E8-166 y 6 de Diciembre, T02-222 6013, www.casahelbling.de. Cheaper with shared bath, laundry and cooking facilities, parking, helpful, German spoken, family atmosphere, good information, tours arranged. Recommended.

E **Amazonas Inn**, Pinto E4-324 y Amazonas, T02-222 5723, amazonasinn@yahoo.com. Café, private bath, hot water, carpeted rooms, some are sunny, those on 1st floor are best, very clean and friendly. Recommended.

E **El Cafecito**, Cordero 1124 y Reina Victoria, T02-223 4862, www.cafecito.net. Popular with backpackers, vegetarian restaurant, shared bath, hot water, room called 'tomato' has a nice balcony, relaxed atmosphere but can get noisy at night, Canadian-owned.

E **Iguana Lodge**, Calama E4-45 y JL Mera, T02-256 9784, iguanalodge@yahoo.com. Breakfast available, cheaper with shared bath, hot water, large common room makes for a very sociable atmosphere, friendly hosts speak English and French.

E **Queen's Hostel/Hostal De La Reina**, Reina Victoria 836 y Wilson, T02-255 1844, vicent1@interactive.net.ec. Small hotel, popular among travellers and Ecuadoreans, includes breakfast, cafeteria, private bath, hot water, laundry and cooking facilities, sitting room with fireplace. Recommended.

E **Titisee**, Foch E7-60 y Reina Victoria, T02-252 9063, www.hostaltitisee.com. Nice place and owner, cheaper with shared bath, hot water, cooking facilities, large rooms, lounge. Recommended.

Apart-hotels and suites

A **Antinea**, Rodríguez 175 y Almagro, T02-250 6839, www.hotelantinea.com. Includes breakfast, parking, suites and apartments, lovely rooms, from $800/month.

B **Amaranta**, Leonidas Plaza N20-32 y Washington, T02-254 3619. Includes breakfast, good restaurant, parking, comfortable, well-equipped suites, from US$850/month.

East of La Mariscal *p456*

LL **Swissôtel**, 12 de Octubre 1820 y Cordero, T02-256 6497, www.swissotel.com. Superb 5-star accommodation, includes buffet breakfast, Japanese, French and Italian restaurants, also bar, deli and café, state-of-the-art fitness centre, business centre, 3 non-smoking floors and disabled facilities. Recommended.

B **Santa Bárbara**, 12 de Octubre N26-15 y Coruña, T02-222 5121, www.hotel-santa barbara.com. Beautiful refurbished colonial-style house and gardens, sitting room with fireplace, includes breakfast, Italian restaurant, internet connection in rooms, parking, English, French and Italian spoken.

B **Villa Nancy**, Muros 146 y 12 de Octubre, T02-256 2483, www.hotelvillanancy.com. In quiet residential area, includes buffet breakfast, small lobby bar, internet connection in rooms, parking, airport transfers extra, quiet, homey and comfortable, helpful multilingual staff. Recommended.

C-D **Aleida's**, Andalucía 559 y Salazar, T02-223 4570, www.aleidashostal.com.ec. Restored home in a residential area, breakfast available, cheaper with shared

For an explanation of sleeping and eating price codes used in this guide, see inside the front cover. Other relevant information is found in Essentials, see pages 31-35.

bath, internet connection in rooms, nicely decorated with wood, pricier rooms are larger and have better views, garden.

E **Casa de Eliza**, Isabel La Católica N24-679, T02-222 6602, manteca@uio.satnet.net. Laundry and cooking facilities, parking, shared rooms and bath, very popular and homey, no smoking.

E **Casona de Mario**, Andalucía 213 y Galicia, T/F02-223 0129, www.casonademario.com. Popular friendly hostel, shared bath, hot water, laundry facilities, well-equipped kitchen, clean rooms, sitting room, garden, book exchange.

Apart-hotels and suites

A **La Colina Suites**, La Colina N26-119 y Orellana, T02-2234678, www.lacolina suites.com. Includes buffet breakfast, cafeteria, small spa, parking, includes airport pickup or drop-off, from US$1800/month.

C **Apart-Hotel los Quipus**, Lérida E14-55 y Lugo, La Floresta, T02-222 4037, www.aqui pus.com. Rooms and small furnished apartments, meals available, Wi-Fi, parking, small patio and garden, rooms $650/month, flats from US$720.

La Carolina *p456*

AL **Dann Carlton**, República de El Salvador 513 y Irlanda, T02-244 8808, www.hoteles dann.com. Includes breakfast, international restaurant, gym, spa, pool, parking, business centre, wireless internet in rooms.

B **La Pradera**, San Salvador 222 y Pasaje Martín Carrión, T02-222 6833, www.hostal lapradera.com. Nicely decorated converted home in residential area, includes breakfast, restaurant, parking, comfortable rooms, sitting room, nice patio with hammocks, quiet, airport pickup.

B **Sol de Quito**, Alemania N30-170 y Vancouver, T02-254 1773, www.solde quito.com. Lovely converted home with large sitting room and library decorated with antiques, includes breakfast, restaurant, internet connection in rooms, parking, comfortable rooms, suites have beautiful carved doors. Recommended.

C **Hostal La Carolina**, Italia 324 y Vancouver, T02-254 2471, hoscarol@uio.satnet.net. Converted home in residential area, includes breakfast, restaurant, internet connection in rooms, parking, good comfortable rooms,

those in back are quieter, helpful.

Apart-hotels and suites

C **Apartamentos Modernos**, Amazonas N31-75 y Mariana de Jesús, T02-223 3766 ext 800, www.apartamentosmodernos.com.ec. Convenient location near El Jardín Mall and Parque La Carolina, 1- and 2-bedroom flats from US$550 per month, Wi-Fi extra, parking, English spoken, very clean, good value.

Quito suburbs *p457*

A **La Carriona**, Km 2½ vía Sangolquí– Amaguaña, T02-233 1974, www.lacarriona.com. In a beautiful colonial hacienda, includes breakfast, pool and spa, some suites with fireplace, includes horse riding.

A **San Jorge**, Km 4 via old Quito–Nono, to the west of Av Occidental, T02-249 4002, www.hostsanjorge.com.ec. A traditional hacienda on a 80-ha private reserve on the slopes of Pichincha, heated rooms, includes breakfast, full board available, good pricey restaurant, pool, sauna and Turkish bath. Nature reserve has *páramo* and one of the few remnants of native forest near Quito, horse riding and birdwatching, all within easy reach of the city. Recommended.

B **Hostería Sommergarten**, Chimborazo 248 y Riofrío, Urbanización Santa Rosa, Sangolquí, T02-233 0315, rsommer@uio.satnet.net. Comfortable bungalows in nicely kept grounds, includes breakfast, restaurant, pool and sauna, tours and transport available.

● Eating

Many restaurants close on Sun evenings. Those with stickers indicating acceptance of credit cards do not necessarily do so, ask first. In many of the more expensive restaurants 22% tax and service is added to the bill.

Old City *p451, map p453*

♥♥♥ **La Cueva del Oso**, Chile Oe 3-66 y Venezuela, across from Plaza de la Independencia, T02-257 2786, Mon-Sat 1200-2400, Sun 1200-1600. A good place to sample local specialities such as *fritada* or the warming *locro de papas*, in elegant covered courtyard, art deco interior, great atmosphere.

♥♥♥ **Mea Culpa**, Palacio Arzobispal, Chile y Venezuela, T02-2951190, Mon-Sat 1230-

1530, 1900-2300. Mediterranean and international gourmet cuisine, specialities include ostrich in mango sauce. Housed in the 17th- century Palacio Arzobispal, it combines the elegance of colonial decor with opulent gourmet dining. Reservations recommended, formal attire strictly enforced.

Theatrum, Plaza del Teatro, 2nd floor of Teatro Sucre, T02-228 9669, Mon-Fri 1230-1600, 1930-2330, Sat 1930-2330, Sun 1230-1600. Excellent creative gourmet cuisine, try pork medallions in lavender honey. Exclusive dining in the city's most famous theatre.

Café del Teatro, Plaza del Teatro opposite Teatro Sucre, Mon-Wed 1100-2100, Thu-Sat 1100-2400. Ecuadorean and international dishes, good location and atmosphere, live music Thu-Sat from 2000.

Tianguez, Plaza de San Francisco under the portico of the church, Wed-Sat 0830-2400, Sun 0830-2200. International and local dishes, good coffee, snacks, sandwiches, popular with visitors, also craft shop, postcards, run by Fundación Sinchi Sacha.

La Fuente del Conquistador, Benalcázar N7-44 y Olmedo, Sat and Mon-Wed 0730- 1500, Thu-Fri 0730-2100. Good-value set lunch, grill, local and international food à la carte.

Criollo, Flores N7-31 y Olmedo, Mon-Sat 0800-2130, Sun 0800-1700. Good-value set meals (pricier on weekends), tasty chicken and Ecuadorean food à la carte, clean.

Govinda, Esmeraldas Oe 3-115 y Venezuela, Mon-Sat 0800-1600. Vegetarian dishes, good-value set meals and à la carte, also breakfast.

Cafés

Vista Hermosa, Mejía 453 y García Moreno, Mon-Sat 1400-2400, Sun 1200-2100. Drinks, pizza, light meals, live music at weekends, lovely terrace-top views of the Old City.

La Mariscal *p456, map p455*

Chalet Suisse, Reina Victoria N24-191 y Calama, T02-256 2700, daily 1100-1500, 1900-2300. Good steaks, also some Swiss dishes, good quality and service.

Rincón de Francia, Roca 779 y 9 de Octubre, T02-255 4668, www.rinconde francia.com, Mon-Fri 1200-1600, 2000-2300, Sat 1200-1530, 2000-2200. Excellent French food but slow service, reservations essential.

Adam's Rib, Calama E6-16 y Reina Victoria, Mon-Fri 1200-2230, Sat closed, Sun 1030- 2100. Happy hour 1730-2100. Ribs, steaks, good BBQ, great pecan pie, Sun brunch 1030-1300. A popular meeting place for US expats.

Baalbek, 6 de Diciembre y Baquedano. Very good authentic Middle Eastern dishes, great food and atmosphere.

The Magic Bean, Foch 681 y JL Mera, at the hotel, Mon-Sat 1200-1530, 1900-2200, Sun 1200-1530. Specializes in fine coffees and natural foods, more than 20 varieties of pancakes, good salads, large portions, outdoor seating.

Mama Clorinda, Reina Victoria 1144 y Calama, Sun-Mon 1200-1700, Tue-Sat 1200-2100. À la carte and set meals, Ecuadorean cuisine filling, good value.

Paléo, Cordero E5-48 y JL Mera, Mon-Sat 1230-1530 1830-2100. Authentic Swiss cooking with specialities such as *rösti* and *raclette*. Also serve a good economical set lunch, pleasant ambiance, recommended.

Sushi, Calama E5-104 y JL Mera, Mon-Sat 1200-2300, Sun 1200-1600. Sushi bar, pleasant atmosphere with nice balcony, good-value happy hour 1700-1900.

El Hornero, Veintimilla, corner with Amazonas, and several other locations, daily 1200-2300. Very good wood-oven pizza, try one with *choclo* (fresh corn). Recommended.

Chez Alain, Baquedano 409 y JL Mera, Mon- Fri 1200-1600, 1830-2200. French cuisine. Choice of good 4-course set meals at lunch, à la carte in the evening, pleasant and relaxed.

El Maple, Foch E8-15 y Almagro, daily 0730-2330. Strictly vegetarian, varied menu, good meals and fruit juices, covered patio. Recommended.

La Canoa Manabita, Calama y Reina Victoria, daily 1200-2100. Great seafood, very clean.

La Chacha, Foch y JL Mera, Mon-Fri lunch and dinner. Very popular, good Italian food.

Raj Tandoori, Reina Victoria y Wilson. Very good, authentic Indian cuisine, try the coconut nan bread. Recommended.

Yu Su, Almagro y Colón, edificio Torres de Almagro, Mon-Fri 1230-01600, 1800-2000, Sat 1230-1600. Very good sushi bar, clean and pleasant, Korean-run, take-out service.

Zona Libre, Foch y Amazonas, Mon-Fri lunch. A good standard *almuerzo*.

Quito & around Listings

Café Trovero, JL Mera y Pinto, Mon-Fri 1230-2200, Sat 1330-2200. Espresso and sandwich bar, pastries, pleasant atmosphere, nicely decorated with plants.

Kallari, Wilson y JL Mera,. Fair Trade café serving breakfast, snacks, salad and sandwich set lunches, organic coffee and chocolate, also sells native Oriente crafts, run by an association of farmers and artisans from the Province of Napo (www.kallari.com) working on rainforest and cultural conservation.

East of La Mariscal *p456*

¶¶¶ El Galpón, Colón E10-53, in back of Folklore Olga Fisch, T02-254 0209, Sun-Fri 1200-2000. Very good Ecuadorean cooking featuring traditional dishes with innovative twists like lamb in *naranjilla* sauce. Decorated with antiques, pleasant for relaxed dining.

¶¶¶ Fellini, Whymper N29-58 y Coruña, T02-254 5112. Mon-Sat 1230-1530, 1900-2300. Very alternative Italian cuisine with spectacular presentation, delightful ambiance.

¶¶¶ La Choza, 12 de Octubre N24-551 y Cordero, T02-223 0839, Mon-Fri 1200-1600, 1830-2230, Sat-Sun 1200-1630. Traditional Ecuadorean cuisine, good music and decor.

¶¶¶ La Jaiba, Coruña y San Ignacio, T02-254 3887, Mon 1100-1530, Tue-Sat 1100-1600, 1900-2100, Sun 1100-1630. Varied seafood menu, an old favourite at new premises after 36 years, good service.

¶¶¶ Sake, Paul Rivet N30-166 y Whymper, T02-252 4818, Mon-Sat 1200-1530, 1900-2300, Sun 1230-1600. Sushi bar and other Japanese dishes, very trendy, great food, attractive decor.

¶¶¶-¶¶ La Briciola, Toledo 1255 y Salazar, daily 1230-1500, 1900-2300. Extensive menu, excellent Italian food, homey atmosphere, very good personal service.

¶¶ Happy Panda, Isabel la Católica N24-464 y Cordero, daily 1230-2300. Excellent Hunan specialities.

Cafés

Mirador de Guápulo, Rafael León Larrea, off González Suárez, daily 1000-2400. Snacks such as *empanadas*, crêpes, sandwiches, drinks, great views of Guápulo, the Tumbaco valley and Cayambe, portable heaters for outdoor seating at night.

La Carolina *p456*

¶¶¶ Il Risotto, Eloy Alfaro N34-447 y Portugal, T02-224 6850, Mon-Sat 1200-1500, 1900-2200, Sun 1200-1530. Very popular and very good Italian cooking, a Quito tradition.

¶¶¶ La Paella Valenciana, República y Almagro, Tue-Sat 1200-1500, 1900-2300, Sun 1200-1600. Spanish food. Huge portions, superb fish, seafood and paella, an institution.

¶¶¶ Los Troncos, Los Shyris 1280 y Portugal, T02-243 7377, Mon-Sat 1000-2200, Sun 1000-1600. Good Argentine grill, serves beef, chicken, pork, fish, pasta, salads, small and friendly, busy on Sun.

¶¶¶ Rincón de La Ronda, Bello Horizonte 406 y Almagro, T02-254 0459, daily 1200-2300. Very good Ecuadorean and international food, huge Sun buffet, Sun night folklore show. Touristy.

¶¶ Capuletto, Eloy Alfaro N32-544 y Los Shyris, daily 1300-2330. Italian deli serving excellent fresh pasta and desserts, lovely outdoor patio with fountain.

¶¶ Puerto Camarón, 6 de Diciembre y Granaderos, Centro Comercial Olímpico, Sun-Thu 0900-1600, Fri-Sat 0900-1700. Good-quality fish and seafood, recommended.

¶ Las Palmeras, Japón N36-87 y Naciones Unidas, opposite Parque la Carolina, daily 0800-1800. Seafood. Very good *comida Esmeraldeña*, try their hearty *viche* soup, outdoor tables, good value. Recommended.

Bakeries

Cyrano, Portugal y Los Shyris. Excellent pumpernickel and wholewheat breads, outstanding pastries, also a nice atrium café.

Ice cream parlours

Corfú, Portugal y Los Shyris, next to **Cyrano**. Excellent and pricey.

Helados de Paila, Los Shyris, opposite and just north of the grandstands. Good sorbet from local fruits, just like in Ibarra.

⊙ Bars and clubs

Quito's nightlife is largely concentrated in La Mariscal. A municipal ordinance requires all establishments to close by 0300, however this is not strictly enforced. Many of the bars turn into informal discos after 2200. Note that the word 'nightclub' in Ecuadorean usage can mean a brothel.

Bars and clubs are subject to frequent drug raids by police; don't risk it. During a raid, you may be detained for not having your passport. A photocopy of the passport and entry stamp may suffice, depending on the police officer.

For more about Quito's nightlife scene, check www.farras.com.

New City *p454, map p455*
Bars
El Pobre Diablo, Isabel La Católica y Galícia, 1 block north of Madrid, La Floresta, Mon-Sat 1100-0200. Good atmosphere, relaxed, friendly, jazz music, sandwiches, snacks and nice meals, live music some Wed and Thu, a good place to hang out and chill, popular.
Ghoz, La Niña 425 y Reina Victoria, from 1800. Swiss-owned, excellent food, pool, darts, videos, games, music, German book exchange.
Kings Cross, Reina Victoria 1781 y La Niña. Classic rock, good BBQ, best hamburgers, wings. Popular with hippies. Recommended.
Matrioshka, Pinto 376 y JL Mera, Wed-Sat gets started around 2200. Gay and lesbian bar.
Patatu's, Wilson y JL Mera, Mon-Sat 2030-0200. Good drinks, pool table, happy hour all night Mon, loud music. Ideal for those who want to show off their dancing skills.
Reina Victoria Pub, Reina Victoria 530 y Roca, Mon-Sat from 1700. English-style pub, good selection of microbrews and single malt whiskys, moderately priced bar meals, darts, happy hour 1800-2000, relaxed atmosphere, fireplace, popular meeting point for expats.
Santurrón, Calama E4-21 y Amazonas. Good place to hang out, listen to live music (Thu and Sat) and dance, happy hour 1800-2000.
Turtle's Head, La Niña 626 y JL Mera, Mon-Sat 1700-0200, Sun 1200-0200. Microbrews, fish and chips, Sun lunch, pool, darts, fun vibe.

Clubs
Clubs are open Wed/Thu-Sat 2000-0300.
Ramón Antiguo, Mena Caamaño e Isabel la Católica, 2100-0200, live bands Fri-Sat US$5-10. Great for salsa, merengue and other tropical music. Popular with locals.
Santino, Baquerizo Moreno y 12 de Octubre, cover US$8, Thu-Sat 2130-0200. Hip and yuppie place, Latin music, mostly locals.
Seseribó, Veintimilla y 12 de Octubre, Thu-Sat 2100-0100. Caribbean music and salsa, a must for *salseros*, very popular, especially Thu and Fri. Recommended.

⦿ Entertainment

Quito *p448, maps p453 and p455*
For cultural listings consult *El Comercio*, www.elcomercio.com. Also useful are www.quitocultura.com or www.farras.com

Cinema
Multiplex cinemas cost US$2-4, see www.cinemark.com.ec, www.multicines.com.ec.
Cinemateca, at the Casa de la Cultura (see page 454), T02-222 3392 (ext 125), http://cce.org.ec. A film library which has film festivals and shows foreign-language films.
Ocho y medio, Valladolid y Guipuzcoa, La Floresta. Cinema and café, good for art films, programme available from **Libri Mundi**.

Dance lessons
Private or group lessons for US$4-6 per hr.
Son Latino, Reina Victoria 1225 y García, T02-223 4340. Specializes in salsa.
Tropical Dancing School, Foch E4-256 y Amazonas, T02-222 4713. Salsa, cumbia and merengue.
Universal Salsa, Amazonas 884 y Wilson, T02-255 6516. Salsa, capoeira and other dances.

Folk dance shows
Jacchigua, the Ecuadorean folk ballet, **Teatro Demetrio Aguilera Malta**, Casa de la Cultura, 6 de Diciembre y Patria, T02-295 2025. Wed 1930. Entertaining, colourful and touristy, reserve ahead, US$25.
Ballet Andino Humanizarte at Teatro Humanizarte, Leonidas Plaza N24-226 y Baquerizo Moreno, T02-222 6116. Ecuadorean folk ballet every Wed at 1930, US$10.

⦿ Festivals and events

Quito *p448, maps p453 and p455*
For details of national festivals see page 37.
Aug Agosto Arte y Cultura Throughout Aug the municipality organizes cultural events, dancing and music all over the city.
1-6 Dec Día de Quito The city's main festival is celebrated throughout the week ending 6 Dec. It commemorates the founding of the city with parades, bullfights and music in the streets. It is very lively and there is a great deal of drinking. The main events culminate on the evening of 5 Dec, and 6 Dec is the day to sleep it all off; nearly everything closes.

O Shopping

Quito *p448, maps p453 and p455*
Trading hours are Mon-Fri 0900-1900, a few shops close at midday. Most shops close on Sat afternoon and Sun. The Old City is an important commercial area. Otherwise much of the shopping is in malls, see below.

Bookshops

Confederate Books, Calama 410 y JL Mera, open 1000-1900. Excellent selection of second-hand books, including travel guides, mainly in English but German/French also available.
The English Bookshop, Foch y 6 de Diciembre. Second-hand and exchange.
Libri Mundi, JLMera N23-83 y Veintimilla, Mon-Fri 0830-1930, Sat 0900-1400, 1500-1800; also at Quicentro Shopping. Excellent selection of Spanish, English, French and some Italian books. Lots of guidebooks including Footprint titles. Knowledgeable and helpful staff. Highly recommended.
Mr Books, Mall El Jardín, 3rd floor, T02-298 0281, open daily. Excellent bookshop, good selection, many in English including Footprint travel guides. Recommended.

Camping, climbing and trekking gear

Altamontaña, Jorge Washington 425 y 6 de Diciembre, T02-252 4422. Imported climbing equipment for sale and rent, good advice.
The Altar, JL Mera N22-93 y Veitimilla, T02-290 6029. Equipment rental at good prices. Imported and local gear for sale.
Equipos Cotopaxi, 6 de Diciembre N20-50 y Patria, T02-252 6725. Local and imported gear for sale, no rentals.
The Explorer, Reina Victoria E6-32 y Pinto. Reasonable prices for renting or buying, very helpful, will buy US or European equipment.
Los Alpes, Reina Victoria N23-45 y Baquedano. Equipment sale and hire.
Tatoo, JL Mera 820 y Wilson. Quality backpacks, boots, tents and outdoor clothing.

Handicrafts

In the Old City, craft shops are found around the main plazas, especially under the portico of the Palacio de Carondelet. Many craft shops are found in La Mariscal. At **Parque El Ejido** (Av Patria side), artists sell their crafts on weekends. See also under Markets, below.

El Indio, Roca E4-35 y Amazonas. Market, with a wide selection of crafts, coffee shop.
El Quinde, Venezuela y Espejo, at the Municipio. Has a good selection.
The Ethnic Collection, Amazonas N21-63 y Robles, www.ethniccollection.com. Wide variety of clothing, leather, bags, jewellery, balsa wood and ceramic items.
Folklore, Colón E10-53 y Caamaño. The store of the late Olga Fisch. It stocks a most attractive array of handicrafts and rugs, and is distinctly expensive, as accords with the designer's international reputation. Branch stores at **Hilton Colón** and **Patio Andaluz**.
Fundación Sinchi Sacha, Café Tianguez at Plaza de San Francisco and at Museo Mindalae. Cooperative selling select ceramics, arts and crafts from the Oriente. Recommended.
Galería Latina, JL Mera 823 y Veintimilla. Fine selection of alpaca and other handicrafts from Ecuador, Peru and Bolivia.
Hilana, 6 de Diciembre 1921 y Baquerizo Moreno. Beautiful 100% wool blankets in Ecuadorean motifs, excellent quality.
Homero Ortega, Isabel La Católica N24-100. For Panama hats.
Marcel Creations, Roca 766, entre Amazonas y 9 de Octubre. Good selection of Panama hats.
Mercado Artesanal La Mariscal, Jorge Washington, between Reina Victoria and JL Mera, daily 1000-1800. Occupies most of a city block, built to house street vendors.
Museo de Artesanía, 12 de Octubre 1738 y Madrid. Mon-Fri 0900-1900, Sat 0900-1700.
Productos Andinos, Urbina 111 y Cordero, T02-222 4565. An artisans' cooperative selling a great variety of good quality items.
Saucisa, Amazonas 2487 y Pinto, T02-254 3487, and a couple of other locations in La Mariscal. Very good place to buy Andean music CDs and Andean musical instruments.

Malls

There are several modern, smart-looking malls in the New City, with food courts, usually open Mon-Sat 1000-2000 and Sun 1000-1800.
Centro Comercial Iñaquito, known as CCI, Amazonas y Naciones Unidas.
Mall El Jardín, Amazonas between Mariana de Jesús and República.
Quicentro Shopping, Naciones Unidas between Los Shyris and 6 de Diciembre.

▲ Activities and tours

Quito *p448, maps p453 and p455*

City tours
Coches de la Colonia, tickets sold at booth on corner of García Moreno y Sucre, T09-965 2528. For those who would rather ride in style. 25-min tours of the colonial heart on a horse-drawn carriage with an English-speaking guide. Reserve ahead on weekends; daily 1430-2400, US$4, children and seniors US$2, carriage for 4 US$12, carriage for 9 US$24.

Corporación Metropolitana de Turismo, Plaza de la Independencia, Venezuela y Espejo, ground floor of the Municipio, T02-265 7793. Offers *Paseos Culturales*, guided walking tours in the colonial city, daily 0900-1700, 2½-3 hrs, US$12, children and seniors US$6, includes museum entrance fees. Night tours require a minimum of 8 people, 1800-2100, walking tour US$6, bus tours US$15 per person, advance booking required. Tours are led by English-speaking officers of the Policía Metropolitana and include visits to museums, plazas, churches, convents and historical buildings. The night bus tour includes El Panecillo and La Cima de la Libertad lookouts.

Climbing and trekking
Climbs and trekking tours can be arranged in Quito and several other cities. See Essentials, pages 21 and 23, for more information.

The following Quito agencies have been recommended (see under Tour operators for their contact details) all use qualified guides: **Agama Expediciones** (also runs **Albergue Cara Sur** on Cotopaxi, page 507), **Campo Base** (also runs an acclimatization lodge south of Quito), **Campus Trekking**, **Compañía de Guías**, **Pamir Travel** and **Adventures**, **Safari Tours** (also runs a high-altitude glacier school), **Sierra Nevada** and **Surtrek**.

Note that independent guides do not normally provide transport or a full service (ie food, equipment, insurance) and without a permit from the Ministerio del Ambiente, they might be refused entry to the national parks.

Ciclopaseos
Quito has a couple of bike paths, including one around the perimeter of Parque La Carolina. The city organizes a *ciclopaseo*, a cycle day every second Sun. Key avenues are closed to vehicular traffic 0800-1400 and

thousands of cyclists cross the city in 29 km from north to south. The most popular section is from Amazonas y Naciones Unidas in La Carolina to Plaza de la Independencia in the Old City. A great way to tour Quito. See also www.biciaccion.org, for cycling in Ecuador.

Mountain bike tours
There are specialized agencies offering biking tours; a number of other agencies also offer cycling tours or rent bikes.
Aries, Wilson 578 y Reina Victoria, T/F02-290 6052, www.ariesbikecompany.com. 1- to 3-day tours, all equipment provided.
The Biking Dutchman, Foch 714 y JL Mera, T02-254 2806, www.biking-dutchman.com. The pioneers of mountain biking in Ecuador, one-day tours or several days, great fun, good food, very well organized, English, German and Dutch spoken. Recommended.
Safari (see Tour operators, below). Biking tours in small groups, free route planning.

Rafting
The Rio Blanco has some of the best rafting in South America. All agencies in Quito offer 1- to 2-day trips on the Toachi and Blanco rivers.
ROW Expediciones, Pablo Arturo Suarez 191 y Eloy Alfaro, www.rowexpediciones.com.

Tour operators
When booking tours, note that national park fees are rarely included. Many are clustered in the Mariscal district; shop around. Most Quito agencies sell tours to all regions of Ecuador; they may run some of those tours themselves, while they act as sales agents for others. See also pages 283, 559 and 567 for jungle lodges. Choosing a responsible tour operator is very important, not only as a way of getting the best experience for your money, but also to limit impact on areas you will visit and ensure benefits for local communities. See Responsible tourism, page 19. The following companies have all been recommended.
Advantage Travel, El Telégafo E10-63 y Juan de Alcántara, T02-246 2871, www.advantag ecuador.com. Tours to Machalilla and Isla de la Plata. Also operates 4- to 5-day jungle tours on the *Manatee* floating hotel, on the Río Napo.
Agama Expediciones, Washington 425 y 6 de Diciembre, p 2, T02-290 3164, www.cotopaxi-carasur.com. Climbing and

trekking tours, also have a mountain lodge, see Climbing and trekking, above.

Andando Tours, Coruña N26-311 y Orellana, T02-256 6010, www.andandotours.com. Runs the first-class Galápagos vessel *Sagitta* and are agents for the *Beagle* and *Samba*.

Campo Base, T02-2599737, www.campobase turismo.com. Run by Manuel and Diego Jácome, very experienced climbing guides, also trekking and cycling trips and runs an acclimatization lodge south of Quito, near Sincholagua, at 3050 m.

Campus Trekking, Joaquina Vargas 99 y Calderón, Conocoto, Valle de los Chillos, T02-234 0601, www.campustrekking.com. Experienced company specializing in trekking and climbing, also offer cycling and cultural tours, 8 languages spoken.

Compañía de Guías de Montaña, Jorge Washington 425 y 6 de Dicembre, T/F02-250 4773, www.companiadeguias.com. Climbing and trekking specialists, but other tours too.

Dracaena, Pinto 446 y Amazonas, T02-254 6590, dracaena@andinanet.net. Runs very good jungle trips in Cuyabeno.

Ecotours Ecuador, Magnolias n-51 y Crisantemos, La Primavera, Cumbaya, T02-289 7316, www.ecotoursecuador.com. Exclusive booking agent and tour operator for the Napo Wildlife Centre, owned by non-profit conservation group **Eco Ecuador**.

Ecoventura, Almagro N31-80 y Whymper, T/F02-223 1034, www.ecoventura.com. Operate first-class Galápagos cruises and sell tours throughout Ecuador.

Ecuador Adventure, Pasaje Córdova N23-26 y Wilson, T02-222 3720, www.ecuador adventure.ec. Adventure sports and tours in the Andes, Amazon and Galápagos.

Ecuador Journeys, Coruña N27-114 y Orellana p 3, T02-323 8221, www.ecua dorianjourneys.com. Adventure tours to off-the-beaten-path destinations, treks to volcanos including Reventador, jungle trips from Coca and Misahuallí .

Ecuadorian Tours (American Express representative), Av Amazonas 329 y J Washington, several other locations, T02-256 0488, www.ecuadoriantours.com. Tours in all regions and airline tickets.

Equateur Voyages Passion, in L'Auberge Inn (see page 458) Gran Colombia 1138 y Yahuachi, T02-254 3803, www.equateur-voyages.com. Full range of adventure tours. Run a 4- to 5-day jungle tour on the Shiripuno River from Coca. Sell Galápagos cruises.

Galápagos Boat Company, Foch E5-39, T02-2220426, www.safari.com.ec. Broker for about 60 boats in the islands, can find the best deals around.

Galasam, Amazonas 1354 y Cordero, T02-290 3909, www.galasam.com. Has a large fleet of boats in different categories for Galápagos cruises. Full range of tours in highlands, jungle trips to their own lodge on the Río Aguarico. Also city tours.

Green Planet, JL Mera N23-84 y Wilson, T02-252 0570, greenpla@interactive.net.ec. Ecologically sensitive jungle tours in Cuyabeno and the Tena area, friendly staff and guides, good food. Recommended.

Kempery Tours, Ramírez Dávalos 117 y Amazonas, T02-250 5599, www.kempery.com. Good-value tours, 4- to 14-day jungle trips to **Bataburo Lodge** in Huaorani territory, operate Galápagos cruises and the *Jungle Discovery* boat from Coca, multilingual service, recommended.

Quito & around Listings

Klein Tours, Eloy Alfaro N34-151 y Catalina Aldaz, also Shyris N34-280 y Holanda, T02-226 7000, www.kleintours.com. Galápagos and mainland tours, tailor-made, English, French and German spoken.
Metropolitan Touring, República de El Salvador 36-84, T02-298 8200, www.metropolitan-touring.com. A large organization that runs Galápagos cruises, and also arranges climbing, trekking expeditions, as well as city tours of Quito, Machalilla National Park, private rail journeys, jungle camps.
Neotropic Turis, Pinto E4-360 y Amazonas, T02-252 1212, www.neotropicturis.com. Operates the **Cuyabeno Lodge** (see Cuyabeno Wildlife Reserve, page 567), jungle trips and organizes trips in all regions. Recommended.

PalmerVoyages, Alemania 575 (N31-77) y Mariana De Jesus, T02-256 9809, www.palmervoyages.com. Small, specialist company, custom-made itineraries to all areas of Ecuador or Peru. Good rates.

Pamir Travel and Adventures, JL Mera 721 y Ventimilla, T02-254 2605, F2547576. Galápagos cruises, climbing and jungle tours.

Quasar Nautica and Land Services, Brasil 293 y Granda Centeno, edif IACA p 2, T02-244 6996, www.quasarnautica.com. Highly recommeded 7- to 10-day naturalist and diving Galápagos cruises on 8- to 16-berth luxury and power yachts.

Rolf Wittmer, Foch E7-81 y Almagro, T02-252 6938, www.rwittmer.com. Run two first class yachts, *Tip Top III* and *IV*.

Safari Tours, Foch E5-39 y JL Mera, T02-255 2505, www.safari.com.ec. Run by Jean Brown, expat Brit, very knowledgeable and informative. Excellent adventure travel, personalized itineraries, mountain climbing, cycling, rafting, trekking and cultural tours. They also book Galápagos tours, sell jungle trips and run a high-altitude glacier school. Excellent source of travel information. Open daily 0930-1830. Highly recommended.

Sierra Nevada, Pinto E4-150 y Cordero, T02-255 3658, www.sierranevadatrek.com. Specialized adventure tours (climbing, trekking, whitewater rafting) and jungle expeditions.

Surtrek, Amazonas 897 y Wilson, T02-250 0530, T09-973 5448, www.surtrek.com. Climbing and trekking expeditions, birdwatching, river rafting, horse riding, mountain baiking, honeymoon trips, jungle and Galápagos tours, also flights.

Zenith Travel, Juan Leon Mera 453 y Roca, edificio Chiriboga, 2nd fl, T02-252 9993, T09-955 5951 (mob), www.zenith ecuador.com. Good-value Galápagos cruises as well as various land tours in Ecuador and Peru. Land tours include the Devil's Nose train ride and Ingapirca, Papallacta thermal baths, Mindo and surroundings. English and French spoken, knowledgeable helpful staff.

⊙ Transport

Quito *p448, maps p453 and p455*
Air
A taxi to the airport costs US$5 from the New City, US$6 from the Old City. For airport information see Ins and outs,

page 448. Departure tax is US$41 and may increase in 2008.

Note There are often long queues for inter-national departures and airlines recommend you arrive 3 hrs before your flight. You must show your passport and flight ticket (electronic tickets are accepted) to enter the check-in area of international departures.

Domestic airlines Aerogal, Amazonas 607 y Carrión and Amazonas 7797 y Juan Holguín, opposite the airport, T02-292 0495, T1-800-237 6425, www.aerogal.com.ec. **Icaro**, JL Mera N26-221 y Orellana, Shyris N34-108 y Holanda, T02-299 7400, T1-800-883567. **Saéreo**, Indanza 121 y Amazonas, T02-330 2280. **TAME**, Amazonas N24-260 y Colón, 6 de Diciembre N26-112, several others, T02-290 9900 to 909. **VIP**, Foch 265 y 6 de Diciembre, T02-254 6600, T1-800-847847.

International airlines Air France/KLM, 12 de Octubre N26-27 y A Lincoln, edif Torre 1492, No 1103, T02-298 6828. **American**, Amazonas 4545 y Pereira, T02-299 5000. **Avianca**, Coruña 1311 y San Ignacio, T02-255 6715, T1-800-003434. **Continental**, 12 de Octubre y Cordero, World Trade Center, p 11, also Naciones Unidas y República de El Salvador, edif City Plaza, ground floor, T02-225 0905, T1-800-222333. **Copa**, República de El Salvador 361 y Moscú, edif Aseguradora del Sur, ground floor, T02-227 3082. **Delta**, 12 de Octubre y Cordero, edif World Trade Center Torre A, p 8, T02-225 4642, T1-800-101060. **Iberia**, Eloy Alfaro 939 y Amazonas, edif Finandes, p 5, T02-256 6009. **LAN**, Orellana 557 y Coruña and Quicentro Shopping, T02-299 2300, T1-800-101075. **Santa Bárbara**, Portugal 794 y República de El Salvador, T02-225 3972. **TACA**, República de El Salvador N36-139 y Suecia, T02-292 3170, T1-800-008222.

Bus
The old terminal is neither safe nor pleasant, so try to spend as little time here as possible. If going there by taxi, pay the driver a little extra to take you inside directly to the departure platforms, to avoid walking through the station. This is an especially good idea at night or very early in the morning.

Long distance See Ins and outs, page 448, for local bus travel. Several companies have private stations, generally in the New City, buses departing from these stations will also make a stop at the Terminal Terrestre before leaving the city. For the less frequent routes, or at busy times of the year (long weekends or holidays) consider buying your ticket a day in advance.

Flota Imbabura, Manuel Larrea 1211 y Portoviejo, T02-223 6940, for **Cuenca** and **Guayaquil**; Panamericana Internacional, Colón 852 y Reina Victoria, T02-250 1585, for **Huaquillas**, **Machala**, **Cuenca**, **Loja**,

	Ambato	Bahía	Baños	Coca	Cuenca	Esmeraldas	Guaranda	Guayaquil	Huaquillas	Ibarra	Lago Agrio
Ambato	—	xStDom 10h $9	32/day 1h $.80	4/day 10h $12	9/day 7h $8	6/day 8h $8	19/day 2h $2	47/day 6h $6	5/day 8h $8	8/day 5h $5	9/day 10h $10
Bahía	xStDom 10h $9	—	xStDom 11h $10	xQuito 19h $17	xGyquil 10h $10	xStDom 9h $8	xGyquil 11h $9	22/day 6h $5	xGyquil 11h $10	xQuito 12h $10	xStDom 16h $15
Baños	32/day 1h $.80	xStDom 11h $10	—	4/day 9h $11	xAmbto 8h $9	xStDom 8h $8	xAmbto 3h $3	7/day 7h $7	xAmbto 9h $9	xQuito 6h $6	xAmbto 11h $11
Coca	4/day 10h $12	xQuito 19h $17	4/day 9h $11	—	xAmbto 17h $20	xQuito 16h $17	xAmbto 12h $14	4/day 18h $16	xAmbto 18h $20	xQuito 12h $13	23/day 3h $3
Cuenca	9/day 7h $8	xGyquil 10h $10	xAmbto 8h $9	xAmbto 17h $20	—	xGyquil 12h $13	xRbmba 8h $8	65/day 4h $5	8/day 5h $6	xQuito 13h $14	xAmbto 17h $18
Esmeraldas	6/day 8h $8	xStDom 9h $8	xStDom 8h $8	xQuito 16h $17	xGyquil 12h $13	—	xAmbto 10h $10	36/day 8h $8	3/day 12h $10	xQuito 9h $10	xStDom 13h $13
Guaranda	19/day 2h $2	xGyquil 11h $9	xAmbto 3h $3	xAmbto 12h $14	xAmbto 8h $8	xAmbto 10h $10	—	17/day 5h $4	xGyquil 10h $9	xQuito 8h $7	xAmbto 12h $12
Guayaquil	47/day 6h $6	22/day 6h $5	7/day 7h $7	4/day 18h $16	65/day 4h $5	36/day 8h $8	17/day 5h $4	—	22/day 5h $5	9/day 9h $9	3/day 15h $14
Huaquillas	5/day 8h $8	xGyquil 11h $10	xAmbto 9h $9	xAmbto 18h $20	8/day 5h $6	3/day 12h $10	xGyquil 10h $9	22/day 5h $5	—	xQuito 15h $13	xAmbto 18h $18
Ibarra	8/day 5h $5	xQuito 12h $10	xQuito 6h $6	xQuito 12h $13	xQuito 13h $14	xQuito 9h $10	9/day 8h $7	9/day 9h $9	xQuito 15h $13	—	xTulcán 10h $9
Lago Agrio	9/day 10h $10	xStDom 16h $15	xAmbto 11h $11	23/day 3h $3	xAmbto 17h $18	xStDom 13h $13	xAmbto 12h $12	3/day 15h $14	xAmbto 18h $18	xTulcán 10h $9	—
Latacunga	e/10m 1h $1	xQuito 11h $9	xAmbto 2h $2	xQuito 12h $12	xAmbto 8h $9	xQuito 8h $9	xAmbto 3h $3	4/day 7h $7	xAmbto 9h $9	xQuito 5h $4	xQuito 11h $9
Loja	7/day 12h $11	xGyquil 14h $15	xAmbto 13h $12	xQuito 23h $24	22/day 5h $6	xStDom 14h $16	xAmbto 14h $13	10/day 8h $10	6/day 6h $5	xQuito 16h $17	2/day 23h $22
Macas	2/day 7h $7	xGyquil 16h $15	2/day 6h $6	xPuyo 14h $15	15/day 10h $9	xRbmba 14h $13	xRbmba 7h $7	3/day 10h $10	xCuenc 15h $15	xQuito 12h $13	xPuyo 15h $14
Machala	1/day 7h $8	xGyquil 10h $9	xAmbto 8h $9	xAmbto 17h $20	22/day 4h $5	3/day 10h $8	xGyquil 9h $8	48/day 4h $4	72/day 1½h $2	xQuito 13h $13	xAmbto 17h $18
Manta	3/day 11h $8	4/day 3h $3	xAmbto 12h $9	xQuito 20h $20	2/day 8h $9	14/day 10h $8	xGyquil 9h $8	37/day 4h $4	xGyquil 9h $9	xQuito 13h $13	1/day 16h $15
Otavalo	xQuito 5h $5	xQuito 11h $9	xQuito 6h $5	xQuito 12h $12	xQuito 12h $13	xQuito 8h $9	xQuito 7h $7	xQuito 10h $11	xQuito 14h $12	e/5m ½h $.50	xQuito 11h $10
Pto López	xGyquil 10h $10	xManta 6h $6	xGyquil 11h $11	xQuito 20h $22	xGyquil 8h $9	xGyquil 12h $12	xGyquil 9h $8	4/day 4h $4	xGyquil 9h $9	xGyquil 13h $13	xGyquil 19h $18
Puyo	17/day 3h $3	xQuito 14h $12	17/day 1½h $2	6/day 9h $10	xAmbto 10h $11	xQuito 11h $12	xAmbto 5h $5	2/day 9h $9	xAmbto 11h $11	xQuito 8h $8	2/day 10h $9
Quito	e/10m 3h $3	4/day 9h $7	51/day 4h $3	16/day 10h $10	47/day 10h $11	36/day 6h $7	19/day 5h $5	75/day 8h $9	15/day 12h $10	72/day 3h $3	33/day 9h $8
Riobamba	29/day 1h $1	xGyquil 11h $10	28/day 2h $2	11h $13	8/day 6h $6	xGyquil 9h $8	7/day 2h $2	38/day 5h $5	xMchla 9h $8	xQuito 7h $6	xAmbto 11h $11
Sto Domingo	20/day 4h $4	2/day 6h $5	1/day 5h $5	2/day 12h $12	2/day 10h $12	72/day 3h $3	xGyquil 7h $6	72/day 5h $5	xGyquil 10h $10	10/day 6h $5	9/day 10h $10
Tena	21/day 5h $5	xQuito 14h $13	26/day 4h $4	16/day 6h $7	xAmbto 12h $13	xQuito 11h $13	xAmbto 7h $7	1/day 10h $10	xAmbto 13h $13	xQuito 8h $9	1/day 7h $7
Tulcán	xQuito 8h $7	xQuito 14h $11	xQuito 9h $7	xLagAg 10h $10	xQuito 15h $15	xQuito 11h $11	xQuito 10h $9	18/day 13h $13	1/day 16h $15	17/day 3h $2	3/day 7h $7

Guayaquil, **Manta** and **Esmeraldas**; Reina del Camino, Larrea y 18 de Septiembre, T02-258 5697, for **Portoviejo**, **Bahía** and **Manta**; Transportes Ecuador, JL Mera 330 y Jorge Washington, T02-250 3642, for **Guayaquil**; Trans Esmeraldas, Santa María 870 y Amazonas, T02-250 5099, for **Esmeraldas**; Transportes Occidentales, 18 de Septiembre y Versalles, T02-250 2733, for **Esmeraldas**, **Salinas**, **Muisne** and **Lago Agrio**.

Latacunga	Loja	Macas	Machala	Manta	Otavalo	Pto López	Puyo	Quito	Riobamba	Sto Domingo	Tena	Tulcán
/10m 1h $1	7/day 12h $11	2/day 7h $7	1/day 7h $8	3/day 11h $8	xQuito 5h $5	xGyquil 10h $10	17/day 3h $3	e/10m 3h $3	29/day 1h $1	20/day 4h $4	21/day 5h $5	xQuito 8h $7
xQuito 1h $9	xGyquil 14h $15	xGyquil 16h $15	xGyquil 10h $9	4/day 3h $3	xQuito 11h $9	xManta 6h $6	4/day 14h $12	9h $7	xGyquil 11h $10	2/day 6h $5	xQuito 14h $13	xQuito 14h $11
xAmbto 2h $2	13h $12	2/day 6h $6	xAmbto 8h $9	xAmbto 12h $9	xQuito 6h $5	xGyquil 11h $11	17/day 1½h $2	51/day 4h $3	28/day 2h $2	1/day 5h $5	26/day 4h $4	xQuito 9h $7
xQuito 1h $9	23h $24	xPuyo 14h $15	xAmbto 17h $20	xQuito 20h $20	xQuito 12h $12	xQuito 20h $22	6/day 9h $10	16/day 10h $10	xAmbto 11h $13	2/day 12h $12	16/day 6h $7	xLagAg 10h $10
h $9	22/day 5h $6	15/day 10h $9	22/day 4h $5	xQuito 8h $9	xQuito 12h $13	xQuito 8h $9	xAmbto 10h $11	47/day 10h $11	8/day 6h $6	2/day 10h $12	xQuito 12h $13	xQuito 15h $15
xQuito h $9	xStDom 14h $16	xRbmba 14h $13	3/day 10h $8	14/day 10h $8	xQuito 8h $9	xGyquil 12h $12	xQuito 11h $12	36/day 6h $7	1/day 9h $8	72/day 3h $3	xQuito 11h $13	xQuito 11h $11
xAmbto h $3	xAmbto 14h $13	xRbmba 7h $7	xGyquil 9h $8	xGyquil 9h $8	xQuito 7h $7	xGyquil 9h $8	xAmbto 5h $5	19/day 5h $5	7/day 2h $2	2/day 7h $6	xAmbto 7h $7	xQuito 10h $9
/day h $7	10/day 8h $10	3/day 10h $10	48/day 4h $4	37/day 4h $4	xQuito 10h $11	4/day 4h $4	2/day 9h $9	75/day 8h $9	38/day 5h $5	72/day 5h $5	1/day 10h $10	18/day 13h $13
h $9	6/day 6h $5	xCuenca 15h $15	72/day 1½h $2	xGyquil 9h $9	xQuito 14h $12	xGyquil 9h $9	xAmbto 11h $11	15/day 12h $10	xMchla 9h $8	xGyquil 10h $10	xAmbto 13h $13	1/day 16h $15
xQuito h $4	xQuito 16h $17	xQuito 12h $13	xQuito 13h $13	xQuito 13h $13	e/5m ½h $.50	xGyquil 13h $13	xQuito 8h $8	72/day 3h $3	xQuito 7h $6	10/day 6h $5	xQuito 8h $9	17/day 3h $2
xQuito 1h $9	2/day 23h $22	xPuyo 15h $14	xAmbto 17h $18	1/day 16h $15	xQuito 11h $10	xGyquil 19h $18	2/day 10h $9	33/day 9h $8	xAmbto 11h $11	9/day 10h $10	1/day 7h $7	3/day 7h $7
—	xAmbto 13h $12	xAmbto 8h $8	xAmbto 8h $9	xAmbto 12h $9	xQuito 4h $4	xGyquil 11h $11	96/day 4h $4	2h $2	xAmbto 5h $4	xQuito 5h $4	xAmbto 6h $6	xQuito 7h $6
xAmbto h $12	—	xCuenca 15h $15	14/day 6h $6	xGyquil 12h $14	xGyquil 15h $16	xGyquil 12h $14	xAmbto 15h $14	18/day 13h $14	xCuenca 11h $12	1/day 11h $13	xAmbto 17h $16	xQuito 18h $18
xAmbto h $8	xCuenca 15h $15	—	xRbmba 12h $12	xGyquil 14h $14	xGyquil 11h $12	xGyquil 14h $14	22/day 5h $5	13/day 9h $10	6/day 5h $5	xRbmba 10h $10	xPuyo 7h $8	xQuito 14h $14
xAmbto h $9	14/day 6h $6	xRbmba 12h $12	—	xGyquil 8h $8	xQuito 12h $12	xGyquil 8h $8	xAmbto 10h $11	27/day 10h $10	1/day 7h $7	xGyquil 9h $9	xAmbto 12h $13	xQuito 15h $14
xAmbto 2h $9	xGyquil 12h $14	xGyquil 14h $14	xGyquil 8h $8	—	xQuito 12h $12	19/day 3h $3	xAmbto 14h $11	28/day 10h $10	xGyquil 9h $9	37/day 7h $6	xQuito 15h $16	xQuito 15h $14
xQuito h $4	xQuito 15h $16	xQuito 11h $12	xQuito 12h $12	xQuito 12h $12	—	xQuito 12h $14	xQuito 7h $7	72/day 2h $2	xQuito 6h $6	xQuito 5h $5	xQuito 7h $8	xIbarra 3h $3
xGyquil h $11	xGyquil 12h $14	xGyquil 14h $14	xGyquil 8h $8	19/day 3h $3	xQuito 12h $14	—	xGyquil 13h $13	2/day 10h $12	xGyquil 8h $9	xGyquil 9h $9	xGyquil 14h $14	xGyquil 17h $17
xAmbto h $4	xAmbto 15h $14	22/day 5h $5	xAmbto 10h $11	xAmbto 14h $11	xQuito 7h $7	xGyquil 13h $13	—	21/day 5h $5	10/day 4h $4	xAmbto 7h $7	9/day 3h $3	xQuito 10h $9
5/day h $2	18/day 13h $14	13/day 9h $10	27/day 10h $10	28/day 10h $10	72/day 2h $2	2/day 10h $12	21/day 5h $5	—	74/day 4h $4	96/day 3h $3	23/day 5h $6	48/day 5h $4
xAmbto h $2	xCuenca 11h $12	6/day 5h $5	1/day 7h $7	xGyquil 9h $9	xQuito 6h $6	xGyquil 8h $9	10/day 4h $4	74/day 4h $4	—	10/day 5h $5	6/day 6h $6	xQuito 9h $9
xQuito h $4	1/day 11h $13	xRbmba 10h $10	xGyquil 9h $9	37/day 7h $6	xQuito 5h $5	xGyquil 9h $9	xAmbto 7h $7	96/day 3h $3	10/day 5h $5	—	xQuito 8h $9	1/day 8h $8
xAmbto h $6	xAmbto 17h $16	xPuyo 7h $8	xAmbto 12h $13	xAmbto 15h $16	xQuito 7h $8	xGyquil 14h $14	9/day 3h $3	23/day 5h $6	6/day 6h $6	xQuito 8h $9	—	xQuito 10h $10
xQuito h $6	xQuito 18h $18	xQuito 14h $14	xQuito 15h $14	xQuito 15h $14	xIbarra 3h $3	xGyquil 17h $17	xQuito 10h $9	48/day 5h $4	3/day 9h $9	1/day 8h $8	xQuito 10h $10	—

Ormeño Internacional (to **Perú**), office at Los Shyris N34-432 y Portugal, opposite Parque La Carolina, T02-246 0027. They go twice per week to **Lima**, US$70, 36 hrs, **La Paz**, US$150, **Santiago**, US$165, 4 days, and **Buenos Aires**, US$200, 1 week. For these and other South American destinations, it is cheaper to take a bus to the border and change there.

Panamericana Internacional (see Long distance, above) also run an international service: daily to **Bogotá**, changing buses in Tulcán and Ipiales, US$70, 28 hrs; **Caracas**, US$100; to **Lima**, changing buses in Aguas Verdes and Túmbes, US$70, 38 hrs.

Car hire

The main car hire companies have counters at the airport and city offices. For rental prices and procedures, see Essentials, page 30.

Avis, T02-330 0667, Amazonas 4925, T02-2440270, ventas@avis.com.ec. **Bombuscaro**, Amazonas N51-21, T02-330 3304; **Budget**, T02-330 0979; Colón E4-387 y Amazonas, T02-223 7026, www.budget-ec.com. **Expo**, T02-243 3127; Av América N21-66 y Bolívia, T02-222 8688, T1-800-736822; www.exporenta car.com. **Hertz**, T02-225 4257, www.hertz. com.ec. **Localiza**, T02-330 3265, Av Granados E11-26 y 6 de Diciembre, T1-800-562254, www.localiza.com.ec.

To hire 8-14 passenger vans with driver, there are a couple of companies at the airport: **Achupallas Tours**, T02-330 1493; **Trans-Rabbit**, T02-330 1496.

Taxi

To hire a taxi by the hour costs from US$8 in the city, more if going out of town.
Local Taxis are a safe, cheap and efficient way to get around the city. Rides cost from US$1 during the day; there is no increase for extra passengers. You can expect to pay more at night, when taxi meters are not used. During the day, all taxis must have working meters (*taxímetros*) by law, so make sure the meter is running (drivers sometimes say their meters are out of order). If the meter is not running, politely fix the fare before getting in. All legally registered taxis have large numbers prominently displayed on the side of the vehicle and on a decal on the windshield. They are safer and cheaper than unauthorized taxis. Note the registration and the licence

plate numbers if you feel you have been seriously overcharged or mistreated, then complain to the transit police or tourist office. But be reasonable and remember that most taxi drivers are honest and helpful.

At night it is safer to use a radio taxi, there are several companies including: **Taxi Amigo**, T02-222 2222/233 3333, **City Taxi**, T02-263 3333, and **Central de Radio Taxis**, T02-250 0600. Some of these radio taxi companies may use unmarked vehicles; when calling ask the dispatcher exactly what car will pick you up.
Long distance For trips outside Quito, agree taxi tariffs beforehand. Expect to pay US$70-85 a day. Outside the luxury hotels and the airport, cooperative taxi drivers have a list of agreed excursion prices and most drivers are knowledgeable. Arrangements can also be made through the radio taxi numbers listed above. The van companies listed under Car hire also rent vehicles with driver for touring.

Train

Regular passenger service has been discontinued throughout Ecuador. A tourist train runs from Quito to the base of Cotopaxi, Sat-Sun at 0800, US$4.60. Tickets sold at the train station, south of the Old City, T02-265 6142, or at Bolívar 443 y García Moreno in the Old City, T02-258 2930.

❶ Directory

Quito *p448, maps p453 and p455*
Banks The **American Express** representative is **Ecuadorian Tours**, Amazonas 329 y Jorge Washington, T02-256 0488 (ext 451). Replaces lost Amex TCs and sells TCs to some Amex card holders, but does not exchange TCs or sell them for cash, Mon-Fri 0830-1700. **Banco del Austro**, Amazonas y Santa María, Benalcázar N3-21 y Sucre and others. **Banco Bolivariano**, Naciones Unidas E6-99 y Shyris, Amazonas 752 y Veintimilla. **Banco del Pacífico**, Naciones Unidas y Los Shyris, Amazonas y Roca, Mall El Jardín and CC El Bosque. **Pacificard**, Naciones Unidas E7-97 y Shyris, p 2. **Produbanco**, Amazonas N35-211 y Japón (opposite CCI), Amazonas 366 y Robles (also open Sat 0900-1300), Espejo y Guayaquil. *Casas de cambio* all open Mon-Fri 0900-1800, Sat 0900-1300, except at the airport as noted.

Language schools in Quito

Quito is one of the most important centres for Spanish language study in all of Latin America, with over 80 schools. Many people combine language study with opportunities for cross-cultural exposure. Homestays with an Ecuadorean family are often part of the experience. See page 473 for schools that receive consistently favourable recommendations.

If you are short on time then it might be worth making your arrangements from home, either directly with one of the schools or through an agency such as **AmeriSpan Unlimited**. If you have more time and less money, then it's cheaper to organize your studies when you arrive. You can try one or two places without committing for an extended period, although some schools charge a sign-up fee.

Internacional de Español (IE), Pinto E4-358 y Amazonas, T02-256 4910, www.diplomaie.com, trains teachers of Spanish as a second language and maintains a list of schools throughout Ecuador. It provides information, sells course materials and offers advice.

South American Explorers (page 49) sells a list of recommended schools, and may give club members discounts.

Identify your budget and goals for the course: rigorous grammatical and technical training, fluent conversation skills, getting to know Ecuadoreans or just enough basic Spanish to see you through your trip. Visit a few schools to get a feel for what is on offer. Prices vary greatly, from US$4 to US$10 per hour, but you do not always get what you pay for. There is a huge variation in teacher qualifications, infrastructure and resource materials. Emphasis has traditionally been placed on one-to-one teaching, but a well-structured small class can also be very good.

The quality of homestays also varies, with most costing US$12 to US$25 per day including meals. Book one week at first to see how a place suits you, don't be pressed into signing a long-term contract. For language courses and homestays, deal directly with the people who will provide services to you, and avoid intermediaries.

Finally, remember that Quito is not the only place where you can study Spanish. Although some of the best schools are found in the capital, there are good options in Cuenca, Otavalo, Baños, Puerto López, Manta and Canoa, and these are often cheaper.

Euromoney, Amazonas N21-229 y Roca, T02-252 6907. Change cash euros, pounds, soles, pesos colombianos and other currencies. **Mega Cambios**, Amazonas N24-01 y Wilson, T02-2555849. 3% comission for US$ TCs, change cash euros, pounds, Canadian dollars. **Vazcorp**, Amazonas N21- 147 y Roca, T02-252 9212. Good rates and many services, recommended.
Embassies and consulates See Representaciones Diplomáticos y Consulares in www.mmrree.gov.ec. **Emergencies** For all emergencies in Quito call 911.
Internet Quito has very many cyber cafés, particularly in La Mariscal. Rates start at about US$0.60 per hr, but US$1 per hr is more typical. Some places get crowded, smoky and very noisy. Remember that internet access is cheapest and fastest in Quito, Guayaquil and Cuenca, more expensive and slower in small towns and more remote areas. Watch your belongings while in the internet cafés, there have been some reports of theft. **Language schools** See also box, page 473. **Academia de Español Quito**, Marchena Oe 1-30 y Av 10 de Agosto, T02-255 3647, www.academia quito.edu.ec. **Academia Latinoamericana**, Noruega 156 y 6 de Diciembre, T02-225 0946, www.latino schools.com. Also have schools in Peru and Bolivia. **Amazonas**, Washington 718 y Amazonas, edif Rocafuerte, p 3, T02-252 7509, www.eduamazonas.com. Also have a jungle program. **Bipo & Toni's**, Carrión E8-183 y Plaza, T02-250 0732, www.bipo.net. **Cristóbal Colón**, Colón 2088 y Versalles, T02-250 6508, www.colonspanish school.com.

Repeatedly recommended. **Galápagos**, Amazonas 884, T02-256 5213, www.galapagos.edu.ec. **La Lengua**, Colón 1001 y JL Mera, p 8, T02-250 1271, www.la-lengua.com. **Mitad del Mundo**, Patria 640 y 9 de Octubre, edif Patria 1204, T02-254 6827, www.mitadmundo.com.ec. Repeatedly recommended. **Simón Bolívar**, Foch E9-20 y 6 de Diciembre, T02-223 4708, www.simon-bolivar.com. **Sintaxis**, 10 de Agosto 15-55 y Bolívia, edif Andrade, p 5, T02-252 0006, www.sintaxis.net. Repeatedly recommended. **South American**, Amazonas N26-59 y Santa María, T02-254 4715, www.south american.edu.ec. **Superior**, Darquea Terán 1650 y 10 de Agosto, T02-222 3242, www.instituto-superior.net. They also have schools in Otavalo and Galápagos (advanced booking required) and can arrange voluntary work. **Universidad Católica**, 12 de Octubre y Roca, Sección de Español, T02-299 1700 ext 1388, lbvillagomez@puce.edu.ec.

Laundry There are several laundromats around La Mariscal, clustered around the corner of Foch and Reina Victoria, along Pinto and along Wilson. Wash and dry costs about US$0.80 per kg, some deliver pre-paid laundry. Also **Lavandería**, Olmedo 552, in the Old City. **Medical services Doctors** Most embassies have the telephone numbers of doctors who speak non-Spanish languages. The following are recommended. **Dr John Rosenberg**, internist, Med Center Travel Clinic, Foch 476 y Almagro, T02-252 1104, T09-973 9734, internal and travel medicine with a full range of vaccines, speaks English and German, very helpful. **Dr Ernesto Quiñones**, paediatrician, Centro Materno Infantil, Manuel Barreto 167 y Coruña,

T02-223 2956/256 4538. Speaks English and Italian. The following private hospitals are good but pricey, Voz Andes is most economical. **Hospitals Clínica Pichincha**, Veintimilla E3-30 y Páez, T02-256 2296, ambulance T02-250 1565. **Hospital Metropolitano**, Mariana de Jesús y Av Occidental, T02-226 1520, ambulance T02-226 5020. **Hospital Voz Andes**, Villalengua Oe 2-37 y 10 de Agosto, T02-226 2142, out-patient department T02-243 9343. Run by HCJB Christian missionary organization. **Pharmacies Fybeca** is a reliable chain of 35 pharmacies throughout the city. Their 24-hr branches are at Amazonas y Tomás de Berlanga near the Plaza de Toros, and at Centro Comercial El Recreo in the south. Always check expiry dates on any medications and avoid purchasing anything that requires refrigeration in the smaller drug stores. **Police** T101. Report robberies at **Servicio de Seguridad Turística, Policía de Turismo**, Reina Victoria y Roca, T02-254 3983, daily 0800-1900. Also at **Fiscalía de Turismo, Ministerio de Turismo**, Eloy Alfaro N32-300 y Tobar, T02-250 7559 (ext 1014), Public Prosecutors Office, Mon-Fri 0800-1200, 1400-1800. **Post office** See Essentials, page 46, for details of rates, procedures and precautions. There are 23 postal branches throughout Quito, opening times vary but are generally Mon-Fri 0800-1800, Sat 0800-1200. In principle all branches provide all services, but your best chances are at **Colón y Almagro** in the Mariscal district, and at **Japón y Naciones Unidas** opposite Parque la Carolina. **South American Explorers**, see page 49, holds mail for its members. **Useful contacts** Immigration offices See Essentials, page 53.

Around Quito

Despite Quito's bustling big-city atmosphere, it is surrounded by pretty and surprisingly tranquil countryside, with many opportunities for day excursions as well as longer trips. The monument on the equator, the country's best-known tourist site, is just a few minutes away; there are nature reserves, craft-producing towns, excellent thermal swimming pools, walking and climbing routes, and a scenic train ride. To the west of Quito on the slopes of Pichincha is a region of spectacular natural beauty with many crystal-clear rivers and waterfalls, worth taking several days to explore. ▸▸ *For Sleeping, Eating and all other listings, see pages 478-480.*

Mitad del Mundo and around 😊🚗🏔️😊 ▸▸ *pp478-480.*

→ *See Transport, page 480. Colour map 1, A4.*

Some 23 km north of Quito is the **Mitad del Mundo Equatorial Line Monument** at an altitude of 2483 m, near San Antonio de Pichincha. The location of the equatorial line here was determined by Charles-Marie de la Condamine and his French expedition in 1736, and agrees to within 150 m with GPS measurements.

The monument is the focal point of the **Ciudad Mitad del Mundo** ① *T02-239 4806, Mon-Thu 0900-1800, Fri-Sun 0900-1900 (crowded on Sun), US$2, children US$1, includes entry to the pavilions and scale model; parking US$1.50*, a leisure area built as a typical colonial town, with restaurants, gift shops, a post office, travel agency, pavilions of the nations which participated in the expedition and more. There are free live music and dance performances at weekends and holidays. It is all rather touristy but the monument itself contains an interesting **Museo Etnográfico** ① *US$3, including tour in Spanish or English*. A lift takes you to the top, then you walk down with the museum laid out all around with exhibits of different indigenous cultures every few steps. Worth visiting is the interesting **scale model of colonial Quito** ① *daily 0930-1700*, about 10 sq m, with artificial day and night, which took seven years to build, very impressive.

Just north of the complex and a bit difficult to find (200 m north of the roundabout, look for a small sign and lane to your left) is the recommended **Museo Inti-Ñan** ① *T02-239 5122, daily 0930-1730, US$3, English- and German-speaking guides*. It shows fascinating experiments relating to the equator (perhaps aided by a little sleight of hand), as well as exhibits about native life and sun-worshipping peoples.

Pululahua

Five kilometres beyond Mitad del Mundo, off the road to Calacalí, is the **Pululahua crater**, which can be seen from the **Mirador**, a lookout on the rim. It is well worth visiting but try to go in the morning, as there is often cloud later. In the crater, with its own warm microclimate, is the hamlet of Pululahua, surrounded by agricultural land and, to the west of it, the **Reserva Geobotánica Pululahua** ① *US$5*. A track leads down from the Mirador, a half hour walk down, and one hour back up.

Papallacta 😊🚗😊 ▸▸ *pp478-480.*

→ *Colour map 1, A4. Phone code 06. Population 1000. Altitude 3200 m.*

Papallacta is a village 64 km east of Quito, along the Vía Interoceánica, the road between Quito and the Oriente. Perched on a hillside on the eastern slopes of the range, it is an attractive area where you leave the *páramo* for more humid cloudforests. The region has wonderful thermal baths and offers good walking within the **Reserva**

Ecológica Cayambe-Coca ① *Cayambe T02-211 0370, US$10*, which spans the Cordillera Oriental from the high *páramo* to the Amazon lowlands. Abutting the Reserve is **Rancho del Cañón** ① *US$1, guide US$5 per person*, a 250-ha private reserve owned by **Termas de Papallacta** (see below). It follows the Río Papallacta upstream to cloudforest, where there are well-maintained trails.

The **Termas de Papallacta** ① *T02-256 8989 (Quito), daily 0600-2100, you can bathe until 2230, US$6, children under 12 US$3*, are the most attractively developed hot springs in Ecuador. The hot water is channelled into several pools, some large enough for swimming. The baths are crowded at weekends but usually quiet during the week. The view, on a clear day, of Antisana from the Papallacta road or while enjoying the thermal waters is superb. In addition to the pools there is a very clean spa. Access to the complex is along a secondary road branching off the Vía Interoceánica, 1 km west of Papallacta village. From here it is 1 km uphill to the baths.

There are additional pools at the **Hotel Termas de Papallacta** and in the other hotels on the road to the Termas, all for exclusive use of their guests. More springs in this area provide the village of Papallacta with abundant hot water and fill three simple but clean pools at the **Balneario Municipal** ① *daily 0600-1900, US$2, children and seniors US$1*, below the village toward the river.

Noroccidente ⬛🌀❄🔺🔵🔴 ➤ *pp478-480.*

➜ *Colour map 1, A3.*

Despite their proximity to the capital, the western slopes of Pichincha and surroundings are surprisingly wild, with fine opportunities for walking and especially birdwatching. This scenic area has lovely cloudforests, rivers, waterfalls and many nature reserves. Two roads from Quito go north of Pichincha and then down through the area known as the **Noroccidente** (the northwest). The paved **Calacalí–La Independencia** road starts by the Mitad del Mundo Monument, and joins the Santo Domingo–Esmeraldas road at La Independencia. The much older and rougher **Quito–Nono–Mindo** road begins towards the northern end off Avenida Occidental, Quito's western ring road. It is famous for excellent birdwatching and with the growth of nature tourism in the area, this road and its surroundings have been dubbed the **Ecoruta Paseo del Quinde** (route of the hummingbird). There are several connections between the two roads, so it is possible to drive on the paved road most of the way even if your destination is one of the lodges on the Nono–Mindo road. Along the paved Calacalí–La Independencia road, 43 km from Mitad del Mundo, is the small supply town of **Nanegalito**.

Nature reserves

With increased awareness of the need to conserve the cloudforests of the northwest slopes of Pichincha and of their potential for tourism, the number of reserves here is steadily growing. Keen birdwatchers are no longer the only visitors, and the region has much to offer all nature lovers. Infrastructure at reserves varies considerably. Some have upmarket lodges offering accommodation, meals, guides and transport. Others may require taking your own camping gear, food and obtaining a permit.

At 2200 m, **Bellavista** ① *www.bellavistacloudforest.com, Km 68 on the Nono–Mindo road, at the top of the Tandayapa Valley*, is the highest of a mosaic of private protected areas dedicated to conservation. It is the easiest place to see the incredible plate-billed mountain toucan. Over 300 species of bird have been seen in the Tandayapa Valley, including large numbers of hummingbirds drawn to the many feeders at the lodges. The area is also rich in orchids and other cloudforest plants. There are several access routes, the fastest is to take the Calacalí–La Independencia road to Km 52, from where it is 12 km uphill to Bellavista. To get there on your own take a bus to Nanegalito and hire a pickup truck, US$15-20.

Maquipucuna ⓘ *www.maqui.org, US$5, guide US$20 per day for group of 10*, has 4500 ha, surrounded by an additional 14,000 ha of protected forest. The cloudforest, at 1200-2800 m, contains a tremendous diversity of flora and fauna, including over 325 species of bird. Especially noteworthy are the colourful tanager flocks, mountain toucans, parrots and quetzals. There are plenty of trails of varying lengths. To get there, turn right at Nanegalito on the road to Nanegal; keep going until a sign on the right for the reserve (before Nanegal). Pass through the village of Marianitas and it's 20 minutes to the reserve. Past the turn-off for Nanegal the road is poor, especially in the wet season (January to May); 4WD vehicles are recommended. By public transport, take a bus to Nanegalito and hire a truck, US$15-20, or arrange transport with Maquipucuna in Quito, return service from your hotel in Quito US$90 for four, pick up in Nanegalito, US$20.

Reserva Orquideológica El Pahuma ⓘ *www.ceiba.org, day visits 0800-1700, US$3, guide US$1 per person*, at Km 42 on the Calacalí–La Independencia road, is a 600-ha reserve, less than one hour from Quito, with easy access. It is an interesting collaboration between a local landowner and the **Ceiba Foundation for Tropical Conservation**. It features an orchid garden and propagation programme. Trails run from 1900 m to 2800 m. Birds such as mountain toucans, torrent ducks and tanagers are present, and spectacled bears have been seen. To get there, take any bus for Nanegalito or points west.

San Jorge ⓘ *www.hostsanjorge.com.ec*, runs a series of reserves in bird-rich areas. The **Hostería San Jorge**, 4 km from northern Quito along the road to Nono (see Quito Sleeping, page 460) is by the 80-ha **Reserva Ecológica San Jorge**, at 3100 m, a remnant of high-altitude native vegetation near Quito. **San Jorge de Tandayapa** is a 40-ha cloud forest reserve at 1500 m, just below Tandayapa, along the Nono–Mindo road; it has good trails. **San Jorge de Milpe** is a 55-ha upper lowland forest reserve at 900 m, to the north of the Calacalí–La Independencia road. It has nice trails and waterfalls, a new lodge is under construction.

Tandayapa Lodge ⓘ *www.tandayapa.com*, on the Nono–Mindo road, is owned by dedicated birders who can show you practically any of 318 species, even rare birds such as the white-faced nunbird or the lyre-tailed nightjar. Recommended for serious birdwatchers. Access is faster via the Calacali–La Independencia road: take the signed turn-off to Tandayapa at Km 52; it is 6 km from there. At the intersection with the Nono–Mindo road turn right; pickup from Nanegalito US$7.

Mindo and around → *Phone code 02. Colour map 1, A3. Population 2500. Altitude 1250 m.*

The main tourist centre of the Noroocidente, Mindo is a small town surrounded by dairy farms, rivers and lush cloudforest. The most direct access from Quito is along the Calacalí–La Independencia road; at Km 79 to the south is the turn-off for Mindo, from where it is 8 km down a side road to the town. To the west of Mindo is a warm subtropical area where a growing number of reserves and tourist developments are springing up; the main towns here are **San Miguel de los Bancos**, **Pedro Vicente Maldonado** and **Puerto Quito**.

Mindo is an excellent base for many outdoor activities: walking, horse riding, bathing in waterfalls, tubing, canyoning, canopy zip lines, birdwatching and more. A total of 450 species of bird have been identified in the Mindo area; it is one of the best places in the country to see the cock-of-the-rock, the golden-headed quetzal and the toucan-barbet; hummingbirds can be seen by feeders everywhere. Mindo is a popular destination among Quiteños, it gets crowded at weekends and even more-so during holidays.

Some of the area's rich diversity can be admired at several butterfly farms where the stages of metamorphosis are displayed: **Mariposas de Mindo** ⓘ *English spoken, US$3*, is 3 km from town on the road to Mindo Garden; **Mariposas de Colores** ⓘ *US$3*, is 300 m from town on the road to Quito and is also a place to see frogs around sunset; **Nathaly** ⓘ *US$2*, is 100 m from the main park, also has orchids; it is smaller and simpler than the others. A fine collection of the region's orchids can be seen at **Jardín de Orquídeas** ⓘ *2 blocks from church, by the stadium, US$1*, at the eponymous hotel.

Several waterfalls can be visited, all on private land (US$3-5). On the Río Nambillo is the **Cascada de Nambillo**, four hours return. Just nearby is **Santuario de Cascadas**, a series of falls on a tributary of the Nambillo, with the added attraction of a 530-m-long *tarabita* (cable car) to cross the river; if you do not want to use the *tarabita*, you can visit the falls by crossing a bridge; tickets and transport from **Café Mindo** on the main street. **La Isla**, five to six hours return, is a small forest reserve on the Río Saguambi, with a shelter and camping area. Here are three scenic waterfalls, one used for rappelling, guide compulsory, reserve through **César Fiallo** (T09-466 5732). **Canopy**, the latest adventure in Mindo, is available 20 minutes' walk from town on the way to Santuario de Cascadas; the price varies according to the length and steepness of the run.

A very popular activity in the Mindo area is *regattas*, the local name for inner-tubing, floating down a river on a raft made of several inner tubes tied together. The number of tubes that can run together depends on the water level. Several local agencies and hotels offer this activity for US$3-5.

Bosque Protector Mindo-Nambillo Some 19,500 ha around Mindo, ranging in altitude from 1400 m to 4780 m (the rim of the crater of Guagua Pichincha), have been set aside as a nature reserve. The reserve features spectacular flora and fauna, beautiful cloudforest and many waterfalls. Access to the reserve proper is restricted to scientists, but there is a buffer zone of private reserves, which offer good opportunities for exploring.

The environmental group **Amigos de la Naturaleza de Mindo** runs the **Centro de Educación Ambiental (CEA)** ① *office 1½ blocks from the park in Mindo, T02-390 0423, US$1, guide US$20 for up to 10, arrange in advance*, which is located 4 km from town, within a 17-ha buffer zone at the edge of the reserve and has well-maintained trails. Simple lodging is available with shared bath (B with full board, E without meals, use of kitchen facilities US$1.50), and camping US$4 per person. Volunteer programmes can be organized. The group **Acción por la Vida** runs **Hacienda de Desarrollo Sustentable La Esperanza** ① *contact César Fiallo, T09-466 5732*, a 2000-ha reserve, part of a conservation and sustainable development project. Volunteer opportunities available.

Lodges such as **Sachatamia, El Monte, Estación Científica** and **Séptimo Paraíso** run tours on their private reserves.

◯ Sleeping

Mitad del Mundo and around *p475*
AL **El Cráter**, access along the road to the Mirador, T02-243 9254, www.elcrater.com. Lovely luxurious suites set at the rim of Pululahua's crater, includes breakfast, restaurant (see Eating, below), bathtub, heating, parking, stunning views of the crater and towards Mitad del Mundo, pleasant and tranquil, opened in 2005.

Papallacta *p475*
Thermal water is distributed to hotels in Papallacta, in some places it is nice and hot, in others just barely tepid. Try for yourself before checking in.
AL-A **Hotel Termas Papallacta**, T06-232 0622, www.termaspapallacta.com. Part of the Termas complex, good expensive restaurant, thermal pools both indoors and set in a lovely garden, nice lounge with

fireplace, comfortable heated rooms and suites, some rooms have a private jacuzzi, transport service from Quito at extra cost. Recommended.
D **Antisana**, on road to Termas, a short walk from the complex, T06-232 0626. Modern comfortable rooms, restaurant, small thermal pool, a good option among the less expensive places.
D **La Choza de Don Wilson**, at intersection of highway and road to Termas, T06-232 0627. Simple rooms with nice views of the valley, includes breakfast, good restaurant with set meals and à la carte, spa run by physio-therapist, very friendly and attentive owners.

Noroccidente nature reserves *p476*
L **Tandayapa Lodge**, T02-224 1038 (Quito), www.tandayapa.com. Includes full board, 12 very comfortable rooms with private bath

and hot water, some rooms have a canopy platform for observation, large common area for socializing, packages available including guide and transport from Quito.
AL Maquipucuna, T02-250 7200 (Quito), www.maqui.org. Includes full board with private bath, options with shared bath and/or without meals are cheaper.
AL-A Bellavista Cloud Forest Reserve, Bellavista, T02-211 6047; office at Jorge Washington E7-23 y 6 de Diciembre, Quito, T02-290 3166), www.bellavistacloud forest.com. A dramatic dome-shaped lodge perched in beautiful cloudforest, full board (good food, vegetarian on request), cheaper in dorm with shared bath, hot showers, birdwatching and botany, camping US$7 pp. Package tours with guide and transport arranged from Quito, best booked in advance. Recommended.
E El Pahuma, T02-211 6094, www.ceiba.org. Rooms with shared bath, hot water, kitchen, meals on request. Camping possible. Also a very rustic cabin, 2 hrs' climb from entrance, bunk beds, kitchen, take sleeping bag.

Mindo *p477*
With over 60 establishments, there is no shortage of places to stay. However, book ahead for holidays and weekends Jul-Sep.
L El Monte, 2 km from Mindo on road to CEA, then cross river on cable car near the butterfly farm, reserve in advance, T02-255 8881, www.ecuadorcloudforest.com. Includes full board and some excursions, birdwatching, tubing, walking, swimming. Horse riding and English-speaking guide extra.

AL El Carmelo de Mindo, 1 km west of town, T02-390 0409, www.mindo.com.ec. Set in a 32-ha reserve. Cabins, rooms and tree-houses, full board, restaurant, pool and river bathing, camping US$5 pp, excursions, fishing, horse riding, butterfly farm, mid-week discounts.
AL Mindo Garden, 3 km from Mindo on road to CEA, T02-225 2488 ext102 (Quito). Full board. Comfortable tastefully decorated cabins, in a beautiful setting by the river. Good food.
C El Descanso, 300 m from main street, take first right after bridge, T02-390 0443, www.el descanso.net. Attractive house, includes breakfast, cheaper in loft with shared bath, parking, comfortable, friendly. Recommended.
C Hacienda San Vicente, 'Yellow House', 500 m south of the plaza, T02-390 0424. Set in a 200-ha reserve, includes excellent breakfast and dinner, family-run, friendly, pleasant rooms, good walking trails open to non-guests for US$5, refurbished in 2006, good value. Recommended.
E Jardín de los Pájaros, 2 blocks from the main street on side street past the bridge, T02-390 0459. Friendly family-run hostel, private bath, hot water, small pool, parking, large covered terrace, good value, opened in 2006. Recommended.
F Flor del Valle, on lane beside church, T02-390 0469. Shared bath, hot water, small sitting area, basic but clean, good value.

Eating

Mitad del Mundo *p475*
El Cráter, on the rim of the Pululahua crater, access along the road to the Mirador,

T02-239 6399, daily 1200-1600. Popular restaurant in a lovely setting, excellent views. ¶¶¶-¶¶ **Cochabamba**, Mitad del Mundo, daily 0900-1700. Varied Ecuadorean dishes, touristy but hardly surprising considering where it is.

Papallacta *p475*

In addition to restaurants at the hotels, there are several simple *comedores* in Papallacta village and along the road to the Termas complex. Trout is the local speciality.

Mindo *p477*

¶¶-¶ **Fuera de Babilonia**, Las Buganvillas, 1 block from the park, daily 0730-2300. Pleasant, set meals and à la carte, pasta, vegetarian available, **Bar El Nómada** nextdoor.
¶ **El Chef**, Av Quito, daily 0800-2000. Breakfast, good set lunch and à la carte, generous portions. Recommended.
¶ **Panificadora Mindo**, Av Quito, daily 0600-2200. Good bread and sweets, drinks, great pizza, informal sidewalk seating.

❊ Festivals and events

Mindo *p477*

18 May Fiestas de Mindo are held during the weekend closest to 18 May. Celebrations include sport, regattas, masses and partying.

▲ Activities and tours

Mitad del Mundo *p475*

Calimatours, Manzana de los Correos, of 11, at Mitad del Mundo complex, T02-239 4796, calima@andinanet.net. Tours to Pululahua and combined trips to all the local attractions. Also offers general information, very helpful, open daily, English spoken. Recommended.

Mindo and around *p477*

Mindo Bird, Sector Saguambi, on the road to the waterfalls, T02-390 0488, offer regattas, cycling, hiking and other tours.
Vinicio Pérez, T02-390 0412, vinicioperez@andinanet.net, is a recommended birding guide, he speaks some English.

⊖ Transport

Mitad del Mundo *p475*

Bus From Quito take a 'Mitad del Mundo' feeder bus from the Ofelia stop on the

Metrobus, or a Mitad del Mundo bus from Av América y Bolívia. By taxi from the New City US$15. An excursion to Mitad del Mundo by taxi, with a 1-hr wait is about US$25, US$30 if it includes a visit to Pululahua. For **Pululahua** crater rim, at Mitad del Mundo take a bus coming from Quito, the end of the line is just at the turn-off for the Mirador; it is a 30-min walk from there. There is no public transport to the Moraspungo entrance to the reserve.

Papallacta *p475*

Bus and van Many buses a day pass Papallacta on their way to and from Lago Agrio, Coca or Tena (drivers sometimes try to charge full fare). From **Quito**, 2 hrs, US$2. If going to the **Termas**, ask to be let off at the turn-off to the springs before town; it is then a 30-min walk up the hill to the complex. At the turn-off is Restaurante La Esquina, which may offer transport to the Termas, US$0.50-1 pp depending on the number of people. The Termas also offer a van service from their office in Quito and some 5-star hotels, US$30 per person return, minimum 2 passengers. Travelling back to Quito at night is not recommended.

Mindo *p477*

Bus and taxi From **Quito**, Cooperativa **Flor del Valle** (Cayambe), M Larrea N10-44 y Asunción (not from the Terminal Terrestre), T02-252 7495. Mon-Sat at 0800 and 1530, Sat also at 0720, 0900, Sun at 0720, 0800, 0900, 1345, 1645; US$2.50, 2½ hrs. You can also take a bus bound for Esmeraldas, get off at the turn-off for Mindo, from where shared taxis go every 30 mins, US$0.50, US$4 without sharing. To **Quito**, Mon-Fri 0530, 1400, Sat-Sun 0630, 1400, 1500, 1600 (Sun only), 1700. Buses fill quickly on weekends, if fully booked, take a shared taxi to the main highway or a Santo Domingo-bound bus to San Miguel de los Bancos, and transfer there.

❶ Directory

Mindo *p477*

Banks There are no banks or ATMs, take cash. **Internet** On the main street, US$1.50 per hr.

Northern Highlands

Footprint features

Introduction

North from Quito to the border with Colombia is an area of great natural beauty and cultural interest. The landscape is mountainous, with views of Cotacachi, Imbabura, Chiles and glacier-covered Cayambe, interspersed with lakes. This is also a region renowned for its *artesanía*. Countless villages specialize in their own particular craft, be it textiles, hats, woodcarvings, bread figures or leather goods. And, of course, there is Otavalo, with its outstanding market, a must on everyone's itinerary.

The Panamericana, fully paved, runs northeast from Quito to Otavalo (94 km), Ibarra (114 km), and Tulcán (240 km), from where it continues to Ipiales in Colombia. Secondary roads go west from all these cities, and descend to subtropical lowlands. From Ibarra a paved road runs northwest to the Pacific port of San Lorenzo and south of Tulcán a road goes east to Lago Agrio. To the east is the impressive snow-capped cone of Cayambe (5790 m), part of the Reserva Ecológica Cayambe-Coca.

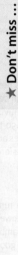

★ Don't miss ...

1 **Parque Arqueológico Tolas de Cochasquí** Admire the pre-Inca pyramids, page 484.

2 **Otavalo market** Take it in with all five senses, page 488.

3 **Laguna Cuicocha** Enjoy a boat ride around the islands, page 491.

4 **Reserva Ecológica El Angel** See the velvet-leaved *frailejones*, page 498.

5 **Tulcán cemetery** The final resting place of Sr José Franco is "so beautiful it invites one to die", page 499.

6 **Sorbet in Ibarra** Savour the delicious *helados de paila*, page 501.

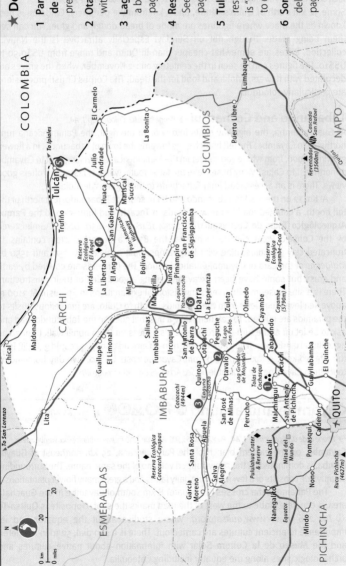

Quito to Otavalo

The Panamericana (Pan-American Highway) runs north from Quito through arid valleys followed by the country's main flower-growing area, before reaching the lake district in the province of Imbabura. ▸▸ *For Sleeping, Eating and other listings, see pages 485-486.*

North of Quito ⊗⊜ ▸▸ *pp 485-486.*

Calderón → *Phone code 02. Colour map 1, A4. Population 97,000. Altitude 2675 m.*
Some 32 km north of Quito's centre, and 5 km from the periphery, Calderón is best known as the place where figurines are made of bread dough and glue. You can see them being made, though not on Sunday. Especially attractive is the Nativity collection. Prices are somewhat cheaper than in Quito and range from US$0.50 to US$10. The figures can be seen in the cemetery on 1-2 November, when the graves are decorated with flowers, drinks and food for the dead. The Corpus Christi processions are particularly colourful.

Tabacundo and Cochasquí → *Phone code 02. Colour map 1, A4.*
At Guayllabamba, the highway splits into two. To the right, the Panamericana runs northeast to Cayambe. The left branch goes towards the town of Tabacundo, in a flower-growing region, from where you can rejoin the Pamamericana travelling east to Cayambe or northeast to Cajas. Many buses take the latter route, which is faster and offers good views. There is an access road from Tabacundo to the Lagunas de Mojanda.

At Km 12 on the road to Tabacundo and 8 km south of Tabacundo, just north of the toll booth, a cobbled road to the west leads to **Tocachi** and further on to the **Parque Arqueológico Tolas de Cochasquí** ① *To2-254 1818, 0830-1630, US$3.* Administered by the Consejo Provincial de Pichincha, the 83.9-ha protected area contains 15 truncated clay pyramids, nine with long ramps, built between AD 950 and 1550 by *indígenas* of the Cara or Cayambi-Caranqui nation. The pyramids are covered by earth and grass but some have been excavated, giving a good idea of their construction. There is a site museum with interesting historical explanations in Spanish. At 3100 m above sea level, the views from the pyramids, south to Quito, are marvellous. Visits to the pyramids are guided. To get there, take a bus that goes on the Tabacundo road and ask to be let off at the turn-off. From there it's a pleasant 8-km uphill walk through an agricultural landscape. If you arrive at the turn-off around 0800, you could get a lift from the site workers. A taxi or pickup from Cayambe costs US$10. Two-day horse-riding tours from Cayambe are available. ▸▸ *See Activities and tours, page 485.*

Cayambe and around ⊜◐●⊗▲⊜◐ ▸▸ *pp 485-486.*

→ *Phone code 02. Colour map 1, A4. Population 55,500. Altitude 2850 m. www.municipiocayambe.gov.ec.*
Cayambe, on the eastern branch of the Panamericana, 25 km northeast of Guaylla bamba, is dominated by the snow-capped volcano of the same name. The surrounding countryside consists of a few remaining dairy farms and a great many flower plantations.

The Panamericana crosses the equator 8 km south of Cayambe in the Guachalá area; a concrete globe to the west of the road marks the spot. Opposite is **Quitsa-To** ① *To2-236 3042, www.quitsato.org*, where studies about the equator and its importance to ancient cultures are carried out. There is a sun dial, 52 m in diameter, and the **Museo de la Cultura Solar** with information about native cultures and archaeologic sites along the equator including Catequilla.

Reserva Ecológica Cayambe-Coca → *Colour map 1, A4.*

ⓘ *Ministerio del Ambiente, Rocafuerte s/n, T02-211 0370, park entry US$10; for Transport information, see page 486.*

Cayambe is a good place to access the western side of the Reserva Ecológica Cayambe-Coca, which spans the Cordillera Oriental and extends down to the eastern lowlands. At 5790 m, **Cayambe Volcano** is Ecuador's third-highest peak and the highest point in the world that lies directly on the equator. It's a technical climb, only for experienced climbers. About 1 km south of Cayambe town is an unmarked cobbled road heading east via Juan Montalvo, leading in 26 km to the Ruales-Oleas- Berge refuge at about 4800 m. The *refugio* costs US$17 per person per night; it can sleep 37 people in bunks, but bring a sleeping bag, as it is very cold. There is a kitchen, fireplace, running water, electric light and a two-way radio.

Northern Highlands Quito to Otavalo Listings

● Sleeping

Cayambe *p484*
B **Hacienda Guachalá**, south of Cayambe on the road to Cangahua, T02-236 3042, www.guachala.com. A colonial hacienda, once a large en*comienda* (slave workshop) producing textiles for Spain. The chapel (1580) is built on top of an Inca structure. Simple rooms in older section (in need of renovation) and fancier ones in newer area, fireplaces, delicious meals at mid-range prices, spring-fed covered swimming pool, parking, attentive service, good walking, horses for rent, excursions to nearby pre-Inca ruins, small museum with historical photos. Recommended.
D **Shungu Huasi**, Camino a Granobles s/n, 1 km northwest of town, T02-236 1847, www.shunguhuasi.com. Comfortable cabins in a 6½-ha ranch, includes breakfast, excellent Italian restaurant, good hot water supply, free internet, heater on request, parking, nice setting, attentive service by owners, offers horse-riding excursions, Italian/Canadian/Ecuadorean-run. Recommended.

● Eating

Cayambe *p484*
There are a number of roadside cafés along the Panamericana serving the local speciality, *bizcochos y queso de hoja* (biscuits and string cheese).
¶¶¶-¶¶ **Shungu Huasi**, at the hotel (see above), daily 1200-2200. Excellent authentic Italian cuisine, in very pleasant surroundings, good service. Recommended.
¶ **Aroma Cafetería**, Bolívar 404 y Ascázubi, open until 2100, Sun until 1800, closed Wed. Large choice of set lunches and à la carte, variety of desserts, very good.

● Festivals and events

Cochasquí *p484*
At Cochasquí festivals take place on the equinoxes and solstices with folk dancing and ceremonies related to the agricultural cycle.

Cayambe *p484*
Mar There is a **fiesta** for the equinox with plenty of local music.
21-29 Jun Inti Raymi during the summer solstice, 21 Jun, blends into the **San Pedro** celebrations around 29 Jun.

▲ Activities and tours

Cayambe *p484*
Shungu Huasi, see Sleeping. Runs horse riding and car tours to all attractions in the area. Horse rentals (US$10/hr), full-day horse-riding tour (US$65), 2-day horse-riding tour to Cochasquí and Mojanda (US$180), an interesting ride, crossing lovely scenery and a couple of microclimates, price includes guide, 1 night's accommodation and meals.

● Transport

Calderón *p484*
Bus From **Quito**, city buses labelled Carapungo leave from La Y on Av 10 de Agosto, near La Y Trole stop.

Tabacundo and Cochasquí *p484*
Bus From **Quito**, Otavalo-bound buses from the Terminal Terrestre go by Tabacundo. For Cochasquí get off at the toll booth along the Guayllabamba-Tabacundo road and walk or take a pickup from Cayambe or Tabacundo.
From **Cayambe**, Libertad y Av Natalia Jarrín, to Tabacundo every 5 mins, US$0.17, 20 mins.

Bus From **Quito**, direct with Flor del Valle, M Larrea y Asunción, every 10 mins, 0400-1900, US$1.25, 1½ hrs. Their Cayambe station is at Montalvo y Junín. To **Otavalo**, from traffic circle at the corner of Bolívar and Av Natalia Jarrín, every 15 mins, US$0.60, 40 mins.

To **Ibarra**, transfer in Otavalo, frequent service, or via Olmedo and Zuleta (see Cayambe to Otavalo, below).

Reserva Ecológica Cayambe-Coca *p485*

Pickup How close to the Volcán Cayambe climbing shelter you will be able to get by vehicle depends on the condition of the road at the time and the type of vehicle. Most can go as far as the **Hacienda Piemonte El Hato** (at about 3500 m) from where it is a 3- to

4-hr walk, longer if heavily laden or if it is windy, but it is a beautiful walk. Regular pickups can often make it to 'la Z', a sharp curve on the road from where it is a 30-min walk to the *refugio*. 4WDs can often make it to the *refugio*. Pickups can be hired by the market in Cayambe, corner Junín y Ascázubi, US$30, 1½-2 hrs. It is difficult to get transport back to Cayambe. A milk truck runs from Cayambe's hospital to the hacienda at 0600, returning between 1700-1900.

❶ Directory

Cayambe *p484*

Banks Banco del Pacífico, Junín y Panamericana. **Post office** Rocafuerte y Sucre, 2nd floor of Centro Comercial.

Otavalo and around

→ *Phone code 06. Colour map 1, A4. Population 56,000. Altitude 2530 m.*

Otavalo is set in beautiful countryside which is well worth exploring. Its enormous Saturday market, featuring a dazzling array of indigenous textiles and crafts, is second to none and is absolutely not to be missed. It's best to travel on Friday, in order to avoid overcrowded buses on Saturday and to enjoy the nightlife. For learning more about how local crafts are made, a visit to surrounding villages is interesting. ▶ *For Sleeping, Eating and other listings, see pages 491-496.*

Ins and outs

Getting there The bus station is at Atahualpa and Ordóñez in the northeast of the city and just off the Panamericana. Through buses going further north drop you at the highway, which is not recommended; **Transportes Otavalo** and **Los Lagos** are the only long-distance companies going into town. There are few hotels around the bus terminal; most are in the centre which is within walking distance (about six blocks); taxis and buses are also available. **Supertaxis Los Lagos** provide shared taxi service from Quito. ▶ *See Transport, page 496, for further details.*

Tourist information Contact **i Tur** ⓘ *Bolívar 8-38 y Calderón, T06-292 1313, sdt@ andina net.net, Mon-Fri 0800-1230, 1400-1730, some Sat 0900-1600*, for local and regional information. The Munipio website, www.otavalo.gov.ec, has information about attractions and services, in Spanish only. **Cámara de Turismo** ⓘ *Sucre y García Moreno, T06-292 1994, www.otavaloturismo.com, Mon-Fri 0830-1230, 1400-1800*, has information and pamphlets.

Safety Otavalo is a generally safe town but beware of pickpockets, especially in crowded markets. Inquire about public safety before walking around **Cuicocha** (see Reserva Ecológica Cotacachi-Cayapas, page 491). Also note that there have been recurring serious public safety problems by the **Lagunas de Mojanda**, and independent visits there is not recommended.

Sights

While most visitors come to Otavalo to meet its native people and buy their crafts, you cannot escape the influence of the outside world here, a product of the city's very success in trade and tourism. The streets are lined not only with small kiosks selling homespun wares, but also with wholesale warehouses and international freight forwarders, as well as numerous hotels, cafés and restaurants catering to decidedly foreign tastes.

In the **Plaza Bolívar** is a statue of Rumiñahui, Atahualpa's general. There was outrage among indigenous residents over suggestions that the monument be replaced with a statue of Bolívar himself, symptomatic of the ongoing rivalry between native Otavaleños and their *mestizo* neighbours.

The **Museo de Tejidos El Obraje** ⓘ *Sucre 608 y Olmedo, T06-292 0261, Mon-Sat 0900-1200, 1500-1800, US$2,* a small private museum run by Luis Maldonado, shows the process of traditional Otavalo weaving from shearing to final products. Traditional weaving lessons are available. There is also a weaving museum in Peguche, see page 489.

Northern Highlands Otavalo & around

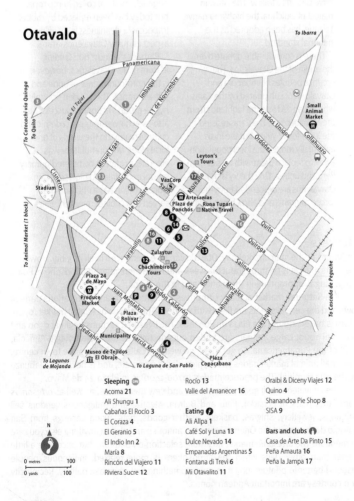

Otavalo

Sleeping	Rocío 13	Oraibi & Diceny Viajes 12
Acoma 21	Valle del Amanecer 16	Quino 4
Ali Shungu 1		Shanandoa Pie Shop 8
Cabañas El Rocío 3	**Eating**	SISA 9
El Coraza 4	Ali Allpa 1	
El Geranio 5	Café Sol y Luna 13	**Bars and clubs**
El Indio Inn 2	Dulce Nevado 14	Casa de Arte Da Pinto 15
María 8	Empanadas Argentinas 5	Peña Amauta 16
Rincón del Viajero 11	Fontana di Trevi 6	Peña la Jampa 17
Riviera Sucre 12	Mi Otavalito 11	

The Otavaleños

In a country where the term *indio* can still be intended as an insult and a very few highland *indígenas* continue to address whites as *patroncito* (little master), the Otavaleños stand out in stark contrast. They are a proud and prosperous people, who have made their name not only as successful weavers and international business-people, but also as unsurpassed symbols of cultural fortitude. Today, they make up the economic elite of their town and its surroundings, and provide an example that other groups have begun to follow. The Otavalo dialect of Quichua, the highland native tongue, has been adopted as the national standard.

There is considerable debate over the origin of the Otavaleños. The pre-Inca peoples of Imbabura and Otavalo were subjugated by the Caras who expanded into the highlands from the Manabí coast. The Caras resisted the Incas for 17 years, but the Incas eventually moved the local population away to replace them with vassals from Peru and Bolivia. One theory is that the Otavaleños are descended from these forced migrants and also Chibcha salt

traders from Colombia, while some current-day Otavaleños prefer to stress their local pre-Inca roots.

Otavalo men wear their hair long and plaited under a black trophy hat. They wear white, calf-length trousers and blue ponchos. The women's clothing consists of embroidered blouses, shoulder wraps and a plethora of gold coloured necklace beads. Their ankle-length skirts, known as *anacos*, are fastened with an intricately woven cloth belt or *faja*. Traditional footwear is the *alpargata*, a sandal whose sole was originally made of coiled hemp rope, but today has been replaced by rubber. Impeccable cleanliness is a striking aspect of many Otavaleños' attire.

Perhaps the most outstanding feature of the Otavaleños, however, is their profound sense of pride and self-assurance. This is aided not only by the group's economic success, but also by achievements in academic and cultural realms. In the words of one local elder: "My grandfather was illiterate, my father completed primary school and I finished high school in Quito. My son has a PhD and has served as a cabinet minister".

Markets

On Saturday, the main market day, Otavalo can be experienced in all its glory. However, the crafts market is on throughout the week and has a more relaxed atmosphere. Polite bargaining is appropriate in the market and in the shops.

The **Saturday market** actually comprises four different markets in various parts of town and the central streets are filled with vendors. The *artesanías* (crafts) market (0700-1800) is based around the Plaza de Ponchos. The livestock sections begin at 0500 and last until 1000. Large animals are traded outside town in the Viejo Colegio Agrícola, west of the Panamericana. To get there, go west on Calle Colón from the town centre. The small animal market trades sheep, pigs, dogs, *cuyes*, etc, and is held on Collahuazo by the bus terminal. The produce market (0700-1400) is in Plaza 24 de Mayo.

The Otavaleños sell goods they weave and sew themselves, as well as *artesanías* from other parts of Ecuador, Peru and Bolivia. Mestizo and indigenous vendors sell paintings, jewellery, shigras, baskets, leather goods, hats, wood carvings from San Antonio de Ibarra and the Oriente, ceramics, antiques and almost anything else you care to mention. The *artesanía* market has more selection on Saturday but prices are a little higher than other days when the atmosphere is more relaxed. Indigenous people respond better to photography if you buy something first, then ask politely. Reciprocity and courtesy are important Andean norms.

Around Otavalo ⊕⊘⊛⊙▲⊜⊕ ⇢ *pp491-496.*

Peguche and other weaving villages → *Colour map 1, A4. Phone code 06.*

The Otavalo weavers come from dozens of communities, but it is easiest to visit the nearby towns of Peguche, Ilumán, Carabuela and Agato which are only 15 to 30 minutes away and have a good bus service. There are also tours going to these villages. Note that the weavers listed are the most famous; many others are also good, so shop around.

In **Peguche**, a few kilometres northeast of Otavalo, are various weaving workshops and stores around the plaza. The Cotacachi-Pichamba family, behind the church has good tapestries. You can also find musical instruments and traditional food. At the entrance to Peguche is **Galería Peguche Huasi** ⓘ *T06-292 2620*, an interesting museum about the native way of life and weaving tradition.

Near the village of Peguche is the **Cascada de Peguche**, a lovely waterfall, a site for ritual purification for the Otavalo people (see Festivals, page 494), now also used by mestizos and foreigners. From Otavalo walk along the railway line (best in groups; don't take valuables) or take an **Imbaburapac** bus from the bus terminal marked Terminal–Cascada–Peguche. There is a small information centre, no entry charge but contributions are appreciated. Climb above the falls for excellent views. From the top of the falls (left side) you can continue the walk to Lago San Pablo (see below).

In **Ilumán**, east of the Panamericana, north of the turn-off for Cotacachi, the Conterón-de la Torre family of **Artesanías Inti Chumbi**, gives backstrap loom weaving demonstrations and sells crafts. There are many felt hat-makers in town who make hats to order and an association of *yachacs* (shamans) who do *limpias* (spiritual cleansing).

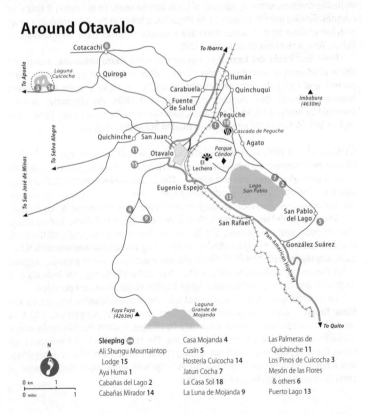

Around Otavalo

Sleeping		
Ali Shungu Mountaintop Lodge 15	Casa Mojanda 4	Las Palmeras de Quichinche 11
Aya Huma 1	Cusín 5	Los Pinos de Cuicocha 3
Cabañas del Lago 2	Hostería Cuicocha 14	Mesón de las Flores
Cabañas Mirador 14	Jatun Cocha 7	& others 6
	La Casa Sol 18	Puerto Lago 13
	La Luna de Mojanda 9	

Northern Highlands Otavalo & around

In **Agato**, northeast of Otavalo, the Andrango-Chiza family of **Tahuantinsuyo Workshop** gives weaving demonstrations and sells textiles.

In **Carabuela**, west of the Panamericana, just south of the road to Cotacachi, many homes sell crafts including hand-knitted wool sweaters. **Carlos de la Torre**, a backstrap weaver, can be found above the Evangelist church.

Lago San Pablo → *Phone code 06. Altitude 2650 m.*

To the southeast of Otavalo, at the foot of Cerro Imbabura and just off the Panamericana is the scenic Lago San Pablo, the largest natural lake in the country. A secondary road circumnavigates the lake. There is a network of old roads and trails between Otavalo and the Lago San Pablo area, none of which takes more than an hour or two to explore. It is worth walking either to or back from the lake for the views. Going in a group is recommended for safety.

The walk via **El Lechero**, a lookout by a large tree considered sacred among indigenous people, is recommended. The trail starts at the south end of Calle Morales in Otavalo. The walk back to Otavalo via the outlet stream from the lake, staying on the right-hand side of the gorge, takes two to three hours, and is also recommended. For a shorter walk, take a bus to the town of San Pablo and walk towards the lake. The views of Imbabura are wonderful. To explore the lake itself, boats can be hired at **Puerto Lago, Cabañas del Lago** or **Jatun Cocha** (see Sleeping, page 492).

On a hill called **Curiloma**, near the community of Pucará Alto, between Otavalo and Lago San Pablo is **Parque Cóndor** ① *T06-292 4429, www.parquecondor.org, Tue-Sun 0930-1700, raptor flight demonstrations at 1100, 1500 and 1600, US$2.75, children US$1.50,* a 17-ha reserve created to rescue and rehabilitate birds of prey, including condors, some 15 species of birds can be seen. To get there, it takes 30 minutes walking from the Cascada de Peguche, 4 km from the Panamericana or 45 minutes walking from Otavalo; there are a couple of buses daily from Otavalo to Pucará Alto; a taxi from Otavalo costs US$3.

From **San Pablo del Lago** it is possible to climb **Cerro Imbabura**, a dormant volcano, at 4630 m and often under cloud – allow at least six hours to reach the summit and four hours for the descent. Navigation is tricky and the final ascent requires technical rock climbing equipment and skills. An alternative access, preferred by many, is from La Esperanza, south of Ibarra (see page 498). Easier, and no less impressive, is the nearby **Cerro Huarmi Imbabura**, 3845 m.

Cotacachi → *Colour map 1, A4. Phone code 06. Population 17,600. Altitude 2440 m.*

West of the Panamericana between Otavalo and Ibarra is Cotacachi, a progressive town where leather goods are made and sold. The **iTur** ① *Casa de las Culturas, Bolívar y 9 de Octubre, T06-2915140, www.cotacachi.gov.ec, Mon-Fri 0900-1300, 1500-1900, Sat-Sun 0900-1700,* has local and regional maps and information and is very helpful.

The **Museo de las Culturas** ① *García Moreno 13-41 y Bolívar, T06-2915945, Mon-Fri 0900-1200, 1400-1700, Sat 1400-1700, Sun 1000-1300, US$1,* off the main plaza, is housed in a nicely refurbished old building with a patio and fountain. It has good displays of Ecuadorean history including maps for different periods, regional crafts (ceramics, basketry, textiles, sisal, silver and leather), regional festivals and traditions, and musical instruments. Some English explanations are provided.

To promote rural and ethno-cultural tourism, the municipality has set up the **Runa Tupari** ① *www.runatupari.com,* or 'meet the natives' programme, which is based in a series of country inns in five nearby villages. Visitors experience life with a native family by taking part in daily activities. The comfortable inns have space for three, fireplace, bathroom and hot shower (US$23 per person including breakfast and dinner and transport from Otavalo). Arrange with **Runa Tupari Native Travel** or other operators in Otavalo, see page 495.

ⓘ *Park entry US$5, payable only if climbing Cotacachi or going beyond Cuicocha; day visit to Laguna Cuicocha including visitor centre US$1.*

To the west of the town of Cotacachi is the scenic Cotacachi-Cayapas reserve which extends from Laguna Cuicocha and the Cotacachi volcano to the tropical lowlands on the Río Cayapas in Esmeraldas. One highland area of the reserve can be easily accessed along a paved road, 15 km from Cotacachi via Quiroga.

The lovely crater lake of **Laguna Cuicocha** sits at the foot of Cotacachi Volcano at an altitude of 3070 m, and is a popular place for a Sunday outing. The visitor centre has good natural history and cultural displays. There is a pier and an *hostería* on the east shore of the lake. Motor boat rides around the islands cost US$1.80 per person for a minimum of eight people.

❗ Do not eat the berries which grow near the lake, as some are poisonous.

There is a well-marked, 8-km path around the lake, which takes four to five hours and provides spectacular views of the Cotacachi, Imbabura and, occasionally, glacier-covered Cayambe peaks. The best views are to be had in the early morning, when condors can sometimes be seen. There is a lookout at Km 3, two hours from the start. It's best to do the route in an anticlockwise direction and take water and a waterproof jacket. The trail ends at the **Hostería Los Pinos de Cuicocha** (meals available) from where you have to walk on the road 4 km back to the park entrance. At **Cabañas Mirador** you can also get a meal and transport back to Quiroga, Cotacachi or Otavalo. There have been occasional holdups of people walking around the lake. Enquire locally before heading out and do not take valuables.

The three-hour walk back from the lake to Cotacachi is beautiful. After 1 km on the road from the park entrance, turn left at the first bend onto the unpaved road. You can also walk to Otavalo, following the paved road to Quiroga and the secondary road from there.

To the north of Laguna Cuicocha and also within the reserve is the ragged peak of **Cotacachi Volcano** (4944 m). This beautiful mountain, often sprinkled with snow, is best admired from the pier side of Cuicocha. The road at the entrance to the park continues from Cuicocha to some antennas on the eastern flank of the mountain; this side is often shrouded in mist. To climb, it is best approached from the ridge to the west. It is a demanding climb and at the top there is dangerous loose rock. Climbing tours to Cotacachi are available through **Cabañas Mirador** and Otavalo agencies.

● Sleeping

Otavalo *p486, maps p487 and p489*

B **Ali Shungu**, Quito y Miguel Egas, T06-292 0750, www.alishungu.com. Tastefully decorated hotel with lovely garden, comfortable rooms, good restaurant with live music on weekends, parking, no smoking, safe deposit boxes, can arrange transport from Quito, credit cards only accepted over the internet using Paypal, surcharge for credit cards and TCs, US-run. Recommended.

B **El Indio Inn**, Bolívar 904 y Calderón, T06-292 2922, hindioinn@andinanet.net. Atractive hotel, includes breakfast, restaurant, parking, carpeted rooms and suites, spotlessly clean, friendly service.

C **El Coraza**, Calderón y Sucre, T/F06-292 1225, www.ecuahotel.com. Modern hotel, includes breakfast,

good restaurant, pleasant rooms, quiet and comfortable. Recommended.

D **Riviera Sucre**, García Moreno 380 y Roca, T06-292 0241, www.rivierasucre.com. Older hotel but still good, ample rooms, good breakfasts, cafeteria, laundry facilities, book exchange, nice garden, friendly, good meeting place.

D-E **Acoma**, Salinas 07-57 y 31 de Octubre, T06-292 6570. A lovely modern hotel built in colonial style, includes breakfast, cafeteria, cheaper with shared bath, parking, nice comfortable rooms, some with balcony, one room with bathtub, one suite with kitchenette in B range. Good value.

E **Cabañas El Rocío**, Barrio San Juan W of Panamericana, near stadium , T06-292 0584, enquire at **Residencial Rocío**. Private bath,

(Northern Highlands Otavalo & around Listings)

hot water, parking. Helpful owners, attractive, gardens, views.

E Rincón del Viajero, Roca 11-07 y Quiroga, T06-292 1741, www.rincondelviajero.org. Very pleasant hostel and meeting place. Simple but nicely decorated rooms, includes a choice of good breakfasts, cheaper with shared bath, hot water, laundry facilities, parking, rooftop hammocks and pool table, sitting room with fireplace, camping, US/Ecuadorean-run, friendly, good value. Recommended.

E Valle del Amanecer, Roca y Quiroga, T06-292 0990. Small rooms around a nice courtyard, includes breakfast, private bath, hot water, popular, mountain bike hire.

E-F Rocío, Morales y Egas, T06-292 0584. Cheaper with shared bath, hot showers, helpful, popular, good value.

F El Geranio, Ricaurte y Morales, T06-292 0185, hgeranio@hotmail.com. Breakfast available, cheaper with shared bath, electric shower, laundry and cooking facilities, quiet, family-run, helpful, popular, also runs economical trips. Good value, recommended.

F María, Jaramillo y Colón, T/F06-292 0672. Modern multi-storey building, private bath, hot water, parking for small car, bright rooms. Very good value, recommended.

Outskirts of Otavalo

L Casa Mojanda, Vía Mojanda Km 3.5, T06-292 2986, www.casamojanda.com. Comfortable cabins set in a beautiful gorge. Includes breakfast and tasty dinner prepared with ingredients from their own organic garden, each room is decorated with its own elegant touch, spa and traditional hot tub with great views, quiet, good library, horse riding. Highly recommended.

AL-A Ali Shungu Mountaintop Lodge, 5 km west of Otavalo by Yambiro village T06-292 0750, www.ranchoalishungu.com. Country inn on a 16-ha private reserve. 4 comfortable, nicely decorated guesthouses with capacity for 6, each with living room and kitchenette. Includes full-course breakfast and dinner, vegetarian available, arrangements through **Hotel Ali Shungu** in Otavalo, 2-night minimum stay in high season.

B Las Palmeras de Quichinche, outside Quichinche, 15 mins by bus from Otavalo, T06-292 2607, www.laspalmerasinn.com. Cabins and rooms with terrace and fireplace in a rural setting, includes breakfast, restaurant, parking, nice grounds and views, pool table and ping-pong, English-owned, friendly.

E-F La Luna de Mojanda, side-road going south off the Mojanda road at Km 4, T09-973 7415, www.hostallaluna.com. Country hostel in nice surroundings, restaurant, hot water, parking, some rooms with fireplace and private bath, others shared, cheaper in dorm, terrace with hammocks, dining room/lounge, camping possible, taxi from Otavalo US$3, bus information on website, excursions arranged. Popular and recommended.

Peguche and other weaving villages *p489, map p489*

B La Casa Sol, near the Cascada de Peguche, T06-269 0500, www.lacasasol.com. Hacienda-style modern hotel perched on a hillside. Rooms and suites with balcony, some with fireplace, includes breakfast and dinner, restaurant, opened in 2006.

D Aya Huma, on the railway line in Peguche, T06-269 0333, www.ayahuma.com. In a country setting between the unused rail tracks and the river. Restaurant, quiet, pleasant atmosphere, live music Sat night, Dutch-run, popular. Highly recommended.

Lago San Pablo *p490, map p489*

AL Cusín, by the village of San Pablo del Lago to the southeast of the lake, T06-291 8013, www.haciendacusin.com. A converted 17th-century hacienda with lovely courtyard and garden, includes breakfast, fine expensive restaurant, 25 rooms with fireplaces sports facilities (pool, horses, mountain bikes, squash court, games room), library, book in advance, British-run, English and German spoken.

A Puerto Lago, just off the Panamericana, on the west side of the lake, T06-292 0920, www.puertolago.com. Modern *hostería* in a lovely setting on the lakeshore, good expensive restaurant overlooking the lake, rooms and suites with fireplaces, very hospitable, a good place to watch the

Northern Highlands Otavalo & around Listings

sunset, includes the use of rowing-boats, pedalos and kayaks, other water sports extra.
B Cabañas del Lago, on northeast shore of the lake, T06-2918001. Cabins on the lakeshore, mid-range priced meals at nice restaurant overlooking the lake, rooms decorated with rustic furniture, some have fireplaces, lovely garden, boats and pedalos, other water sports such as knee boards and water skiing on weekends only (extra), room prices higher Fri and Sat.
B Jatun Cocha, on the east side of the lake, past the village of San Pablo del Lago, T/F06-291 8191, ecuador@ranfturismo.com. Hacienda-style lodge, includes breakfast, restaurant serves set meals and à la carte, mini spa extra, parking, tastefully decorated rooms with fireplaces, water sports include kayaks and windsurfing, bicycles, horses extra.

Cotacachi *p490, map p489*

B Mesón de las Flores, García Moreno 1376 y Sucre, T06-291 6009. Refurbished colonial house in the heart of town, includes breakfast, restaurant in lovely patio, carpeted rooms, live music at lunch Sat-Sun. Recommended.
B Runa Tupari, inns in native communities (see page 490) www.runatupari.com. Price includes breakfast, dinner and transport from Otavalo.
D Sumac Huasi, Montalvo 11-09 y Moncayo, T06-291 5873. Modern pleasant hotel, includes breakfast, adequate rooms and pleasant rooftop terrace.
E Munaylla, 10 de Agosto y Sucre, T06-291 6169. Modern multi-storey building, private bath, hot water, rooms a bit small, friendly, good value.

Reserva Ecológica Cotacachi-Cayapas *p491*

B Los Pinos de Cuicocha, Hacienda Sta Rosa, Km 4 Vía a Intag, T09-900 1516, jorge@lospinosdecuicocha.com. Comfortable heated rooms on a working farm, includes breakfast and horse riding, restaurant serves international dishes, attractive grounds but no views of the lake from rooms, English and German spoken.
C Hostería Cuicocha, Laguna Cuicocha, by the pier, T06-264 8040, www.cuicocha.org. Modern comfortable rooms overlooking the lake, includes breakfast and dinner, restaurant with nice lake views.

E Cabañas Mirador, on a lookout above the Cuicocha pier, follow the trail; or by car follow the road to the left of the park entrance, T08-682 1699, miradordecuicocha@yahoo.com. Simple rooms in a great location, some with fireplace, good economical restaurant, trout is the speciality, private bath, hot water, parking, transport provided to Quiroga (US$4) or Otavalo (US$10), owner Ernesto Cevillano is knowledgeable about the area and arranges trips to the Piñán lakes or to climb Cotacachi.

✪ Eating

Otavalo *p486, map p487*

¶¶ **Ali Shungu**, Quito y Miguel Egas, at the hotel, daily 0700-2100. Good food prepared with mostly organic ingredients, wide choice including vegetarian, ample dining room decorated with native motifs. Recommended.
¶¶ **Fontana di Trevi**, Sucre 12-05 y Salinas, p 2, open 1130-2200. On 2nd floor overlooking Calle Sucre, good pizza and pasta, nice juices, friendly service.
¶¶ **Quino**, Roca 740 y Juan Montalvo, Tue-Sun 1030-2300, Mon 1730-2300. Traditional coastal cooking, speciality is fish, pleasant seating around patio.
¶¶-¶ **SISA**, Abdón Calderón 4-09 y Sucre, daily 1200-2200. Restaurant on 2nd floor serves excellent set meals and à la carte, coffee shop with cappuccino, slow service, also bookstore.
¶ **Ali Allpa**, Salinas 509 at Plaza de Ponchos. Good-value set meals and à la carte, trout, vegetarian and meat. Recommended.
¶ **Mi Otavalito**, Sucre y Morales. Good for set lunch and international food à la carte.
¶ **Oraibi**, Colón y Sucre. Good choice of meals, many vegetarian dishes, salads, quiche, snacks, pleasant courtyard, live music Fri and Sat evenings.

Cafés

Café Sol y Luna, Bolívar 11-10 y Morales, Wed-Sat. Café with a pleasant atmosphere, international and vegetarian dishes.
Dulce Nevado, Sucre y Salinas, no sign, Mon-Fri 0800-2000, Sat-Sun 0700-2000. Breakfast, home made yoghurt, expresso and cappuccino, cakes, ice cream.
Empanadas Argentinas, Sucre, corner with Morales. Very good savoury and sweet *empanadas*.

Shanandoa Pie Shop, Salinas y Jaramillo. Daily 0700-2000. Pies, milk shakes and ice cream, recommended for breakfast, popular and friendly meeting place, book exchange.

Cotacachi *p490*
††-† **La Marqueza**, 10 de Agosto 12-65 y Bolívar, daily 0730-2100. Slightly upscale restaurant, 4-course set lunches and à la carte.
† **El Viejo Molino**, 10 de Agosto 10-65 y Moncayo, daily 0830-2000. Nice set meals and à la carte, good value and quality.

Bars and clubs

Otavalo *p486, map p487*
Peñas are bars which present live folk music; most open Fri and Sat from 2000, entrance US$2.
Casa de Arte Da Pinto, Colón 4-10 y Bolívar. Colourfully decorated, live Latin music at weekends, drinks, pizza and snacks.
Peña Amauta, Morales 5-11 y Jaramillo. Good local bands, varied music, friendly and welcoming, popular with foreigners.
Peña la Jampa, Jaramillo 5-69 y Quiroga, Fri-Sat 1930-0300. Andean and dance music, popular with Ecuadoreans and foreigners.

Festivals and events

Indigenous celebrations overlap with Catholic holidays, prolonging festivities for a week or more. The celebrations take place throughout the Otavalo region and are not restricted to the city. If you wish to visit fiestas in the local villages, ask the musicians in the tourist restaurants, they may invite you; outsiders are not always welcome. The music is good and there is a lot of drinking, but transport back to Otavalo is hard to find.

Otavalo *p486, map p487*
21-29 Jun Inti Raymi celebrations of the summer solstice (21 Jun) are combined with the **Fiesta de San Juan** (24 Jun) and the **Fiesta de San Pedro y San Pablo** (29 Jun). Action takes place in and around Otavalo. The celebration begins with a ritual bath in the Peguche waterfall (a personal spiritual activity, best carried out without visitors and certainly without cameras). There are

bullfights in the plaza and regattas on Lago San Pablo (see Around Otavalo, below, for transport). In Otavalo, indigenous families have costume parties, that at times spill over onto the streets. In the San Juan neighbourhood, near the Yanayacu baths, there is a week-long celebration.
Sep Yamor The **Fiesta del Yamor** and **Colla Raimi** (fall equinox or festival of the moon) are held during the first 2 weeks of Sep. This is the largest festivity in the province of Imbabura, it takes place in several cities and is mainly a mestizo celebration. Events include music, dancing, bullfighting, fireworks and sporting events, including swimming and reed boat races across Lago San Pablo.
Oct Fundación Mojandas Arriba is an annual 2-day hike from Quito over Mojanda to reach Otavalo for the 31 Oct Foundation Day celebrations when Simón Bolívar elevated Otavalo to the status of a city. It is walked by hundreds each year and follows the old trails with an overnight stop at Malchinguí.

Peguche and other weaving villages *p489*
Feb-Mar Pawkar Raimi is a festival held in Peguche during Carnival with much music, food and drinking. It is also a time when many locals who live abroad return for the festivities.

Cotacachi *p490*
21-28 Jun San Juan or **Inti Raymi** festivities of the sun and corn harvest take place during the summer solstice. characters in the parades include the *huarmi tucushca* (a man dressed as a woman), *el capitán* (representing the boss) and *el soldado* (a dancer).
25 Jul Santa Ana festivities in honour of the town's patron saint are held around 25 Jul.
Sep Jora is the celebration of the equinox which takes place during the 3rd week of Sep with sports events, concerts, dances, parades and a *chicha de jora* contest.

Shopping

Otavalo *p486, map p487*
Otavalo can seem like a giant souvenir shop at times. As well as the market, there are countless shops selling sweaters, tapestries and other souvenirs.

Books

The Book Market, Roca y García Moreno. Highly recommended for buying, selling or exchanging books in English, French, German and other languages at cheap prices. Guidebooks, maps, postcards and CDs.
SISA, see Eating, above, has a good bookshop.

Food

Salinerito, Bolívar 10-08. For good cheese and cold cuts.

Cotacachi *p490*

Cotacachi is an important centre for the leather industry. A wide variety of hand- and machine-crafted items can be purchased here. There are nice jackets, purses, belts, wallets, etc. Popular among visitors are the collapsible leather duffle bags which grow to fit all your souvenirs. Some shops accept credit cards, but prices are better for cash.

▲ Activities and tours

Otavalo *p486, map p487*
Climbing and trekking

Otavalo operators offer climbing and trekking tours in the region, including Cotacachi and Imbabura volcanos and Piñán Lakes to the northwest of Ibarra. All about EQ, see below, has been recommended.

Cycling

Some tour operators rent bikes and offer cycling tours (downhill cycling with vehicle for the uphill portions) for US$35-60 a day trip. Mountain bike hire from:
La Tierra craft shop, Salinas 503 y Sucre, Plaza de Ponchos, good equipment.
Deli (see Eating, above).
Taller Ciclo Primaxi, Atahualpa 2-49 y García Moreno and at the entrance to Peguche, good bikes, US$1 per hr. Recommended.
Valle del Amanecer (see Sleeping, above), US$8 per day.

Horse riding

Several operators offer riding tours. Half-day trips to nearby attractions such as El Lechero or artisans' villages cost US$20-25. Full-day trips such as Cuicocha or Mojanda run US$35-40.

Tour operators

All agencies offer similar tours and prices, but there is variation in the duration of the trips, so find out before signing up. Day tours with English-speaking guides to artisans' homes and villages, which usually provide opportunities to buy handicrafts direct from the craftsperson, cost US$20-25 per person. Day trips to Cuicocha or Mojanda, US$25-30.
All about EQ, Colón 4.12 y Sucre in the same office as **Chachimbiro Tours**, T06-292 3633 or contact Iván Suárez T09-993 3148, www.all-about-ecuador.com. Interesting itineraries, trekking and horse-riding tours, climbing, cycling, trips to Intag, Piñán, Cayambe, Oyacachi, rafting and kayaking on the Río Intag. English and French spoken, guides carry radios. Recommended.
Chachimbiro Tours, Colón 412 y Sucre, T06-292 3633, www.chachimbiro.com. Trips to the **Complejo Ecoturístico Chachimbiro** 1 hr northwest of Otavalo (with thermal baths and spa).
Diceny Viajes, Sucre 10-11 y Colón, T06-2921217, zulayviajes@hotmail.com Run by Zulay Sarabino, an indigenous Otavaleña, English and French spoken, native guides knowledgeable about the area and culture, climbing trips to Cotacachi volcano, favourable reports. Recommended.
Ecored Sierra Norte, Jaramillo y Morales, p 2, T06-292 6814, ecored_sierranorte@yahoo.es. Represents 5 community tourism projects in northern Ecuador. Information and bookings.
Leyton's Tours, Quito y Jaramillo, T06-292 2388. Horseback and bicycle tours.
Runa Tupari Native Travel, Sucre y Quiroga, Plaza de Ponchos T/F06-292 5985, www.runatupari.com. Stays with native families in the Cotacachi area, also the usual day tours, trekking, horse riding and cycling trips.
Zulaytur, Sucre y Colón, p 2, T06-292 1176. Run by Rodrigo Mora. English spoken, map of town, slide show, horse riding, interesting day trip to local artisan communities.

Reserva Ecológica Cotacachi-Cayapas *p491*

Ernesto Cevillano at **Cabañas Mirador**, see Sleeping, runs tours around Cuicocha, climbing Cotacachi and other destinations.

⊙ Transport

Otavalo *p486, map p487*
Bus

For main intercity routes see the bus time table, page 470. From **Quito**, Terminal Terrestre, take a **Cooperativa Otavalo** or **Cooperativa Los Lagos** bus, as they are the only ones which go into Otavalo; other companies bound for Ibarra or Tulcán will drop you off on the highway, which is far from the centre and not safe after dark. From the Terminal in Quito, buses go along the Av Occidental and later Av de la Prensa in Cotocollao, where you can also get on. Every 10 mins, US$2, 2½ hrs.

To **Cayambe**, every 10 mins, US$0.75, 45 mins. To **Quiroga** , every 15 mins, US$0.25, 15 mins.

Car

Do not leave your car unattended on the street, especially on Sat. There are public car parks at Juan Montalvo y Sucre, by Parque Bolívar, and on Quito between 31 de Octubre and Jarmillo.

Taxi

A fast and efficient alternative is shared taxis with **Supertaxis Los Lagos** (in Quito at Asunción 3-82, T02-256 5992; in Otavalo at Roca 8-04, T06-292 3203) who will pick you up at your hotel (in the New City only), they continue to Ibarra; hourly Mon-Fri 0700-1900, Sat 0700-1600, Sun 0800-1800, 2 hrs, US$7.50 per person, buy ticket at their office the day before travelling. A regular taxi costs US$50 one way, US$80 return with 3 hrs wait.

Peguche and other weaving villages *p489*
Bus and taxi

For **Peguche**, take an Otavalo city bus along Av Atahualpa, these stop outside the bus terminal and Plaza Copacabana (Atahualpa y Montalvo), every 10 mins, US$0.20. You can also take a taxi or go with a tour. For the other weaving villages buses leave from the terminal.

Lago San Pablo *p490*
Bus and taxi

From **Otavalo** terminal, buses to San Pablo del Lago leave every 25 mins, more often on Sat, US$0.25, 30 mins. A taxi costs US$4.

Cotacachi *p490*
Bus

The bus terminal is at 10 de Agosto y Salinas by the market. To **Otavalo**, every 10 mins, service alternates between the Panamericana and Quiroga roads, US$0.25, 25 mins. To **Quiroga**, every 20 mins, US$0.20, 10 mins. To **Ibarra**, every 15 mins, US$0.45, 45 mins. To **Quito**, transfer in Otavalo.

Reserva Ecológica Cotacachi-Cayapas *p491*
Pickups

To Laguna Cuicocha from **Otavalo** US$10. From **Cotacachi** market or plaza, US$5 one way, US$10 return with 1 hr wait. From **Quiroga** US$4. Return service from the lake available from Cabañas Mirador, same rates.

⊙ Directory

Otavalo *p486, map p487*
Banks Banco del Austro, Sucre y Quiroga. Banco del Pacífico, Bolívar 614 y García Moreno. **Fax Cambios**, Salinas y Sucre, T06-292 0501, Mon-Sat 0745-1900, poor rates for cash, 3% commission on Tcs. Vaz Corp, Jaramillo y Saona, Plaza de Ponchos, T06-292 2926, Tue-Sat 0830-1700. **Internet** Many in town especially along Calle Sucre, US$1 per hr. **Language schools** Instituto Superior de Español, Sucre 11-10 y Morales, p 3, T06-299 2414, www.instituto-superior.net (see also page 473). Mundo Andino Internacional, Salinas 404 y Bolívar, T06-2921864, www.mandinospanishschool.com. Salsa and cooking classes included. Otavalo Spanish Institute, 31 de Octubre 47-64 y Salinas, p 3, T06-292 1404, also offers Quichua lessons. **Laundry** Colón, Colón y Jaramillo, US$0.90 per kg or US$2.50 per machine. New Laundry, Roca y Quiroga, at Hostal Valle del Amanecer. US$1.20 per kg. Tecno Clean, Calle Olmedo 32. Dry cleaning. **Post office** Sucre y Salinas, corner with Plaza de Ponchos, p 1, entrance on Sucre, Mon-Fri 0700-1500, Sat 0800-1200.

Cotacachi *p490*
Banks Banco del Pichincha, Imbabura y Rocafuerte, ATM only. **Internet** US$1 per hr.

Ibarra and north to Colombia

Once a pleasant colonial town (founded in 1606), Ibarra is the main commercial centre of the northern highlands, with an increasingly big city feel. It has many good hotels and restaurants. Prices are lower than Otavalo and there are fewer tourists. ▸▸ *For Sleeping, Eating and all other listings, see pages 499-502.*

Ibarra 🏨🍴🌲❄️🚌🔺🎭🛍️ ▸▸ *pp499-502.*

→ *Phone code 06. Colour map 1, A4. Population 137,000. Altitude 2225 m.*

The city has two fine parks with flowering trees. On **Parque Pedro Moncayo** stand the **cathedral**, with paintings of the Quito School of Art, the Municipio and Gobernación. One block away, at Flores y Olmedo, is the smaller **Parque de la Merced**, named after its church with gilded altar, also known as Parque 9 de Octubre.

Some interesting paintings are to be seen in the church of **Santo Domingo** at the north end of Simón Bolívar. On Sucre, at the end of Avenida A Pérez Guerrero, is the **Basílica de La Dolorosa**, damaged by an earthquake in 1987, and reopened in 1992. A walk down Pérez Guerrero leads to the bustling, large, covered **Mercado Amazonas** on Sánchez y Cifuentes, by the railway station, open daily, busiest at the weekend.

Museo Regional Sierra Norte ① *Sucre 7-21 y Oviedo, T06-260 2093, Mon-Fri, 0830-1700, Sat 1000-1300, 1400-1600, US$1*, run by the **Banco Central del Ecuador**, has interesting displays about the pre-Inca cultures of the northern highlands, the Inca period and a gold display. Explanations are in Spanish and English.

Bosque Protector Guayabillas ① *on the outskirts of town to the east, daily 0900-1730, US$1*, is a 54-ha park on a hill overlooking the city. There are trails and a zoo. To get there, follow Juan de Velasco from the obelisk to Urbanización La Victoria, from where it is 10 minutes' walking, taxi US$2.50; city bus from the obelisk to La Victoria.

The Terminal Terrestre is on Avenida Teodoro Gómez y Avenida Eugenio Espejo, to the southeast of the centre, T06-264 4676. All intercity transport runs from here. City buses go from the terminal to the centre or you can walk in 15 minutes.

The **Ministerio de Turismo** ① *García Moreno 376 y Rocafuerte, T06-295 8547, www.imbabura.gov.ec, Mon-Fri 0830-1300, 1400-1700*, is helpful and provides city maps and leaflets; English spoken. **Cámara Provincial de Turismo de Imbabura** ① *Oviedo y Bolívar, of 102, T06-264 2531, Mon-Fri 0800-1300, 1500-1800*, has regional information in Spanish, helpful. **Dirección Municipal de Turismo** ① *Oviedo y Sucre, corner with del Coco, T06-260 8489, Mon-Fri 0800-1730, Spanish only*.

Around Ibarra 🏨🚲🚌🎭 ▸▸ *pp499-502.*

San Antonio de Ibarra → *Colour map 1, A4. Population 17,000. Altitude 2380 m.*

About 10 minutes south of Ibarra, just off the Panamericana between Otavalo and Ibarra, is San Antonio de Ibarra, a village well known for its wood carvings. The trade is so successful that the main street is lined with galleries and boutiques, and bargaining is difficult. It is worth seeing the range of styles and techniques and shopping around, there are some true works of art. The following workshops are worth visiting: **Moreo Santacruz, Osvaldo Garrido** in the **Palacio de Arte**, **Luis Potosí, Gabriel Cevallos**, and **Juan Padilla**. The latter who has won several prizes for his creations, is in Barrio Bellavista, 2 km from the centre of the village, on the west side of the Panamericana; he has an exhibit of his work, welcomes visitors who are interested in sculpting to join him in his workshop and also offers lodging for them in his home (see Sleeping, below).

To the south, two parallel roads climb out of Ibarra to a scenic area known for its beautiful embroidery work. The women wear very elegant embroidered blouses and matching pleated skirts. They sell blouses and tablecloths from their homes, look for *bordados* signs, some towns also have a community store.

Eight kilometres from Ibarra along the road to Olmedo and Cayambe, which starts at Avenida El Retorno, is **La Esperanza**, a pretty village with a couple of simple lodgings and eateries. Further west, along a road that starts at Avenida Atahualpa, and also 8 km from Ibarra, is the community of **San Clemente**, which has a very good grass-roots tourism project, **Pukyu Pamba**, which offers simple lodging with indigenous families. Visitors become part of the family and participate in the family's daily activities.

South of La Esperanza is the community of **Zuleta**, where beautiful embroidery is done on napkins and tablecloths. There is a Sunday market, a good place to admire the lovely blouses worn by the local women. Nearby is the elegant **Hacienda Zuleta** of former president Galo Plaza, which offers exclusive accommodation (see Sleeping, below). From Zuleta the road continues to Olmedo and Cayambe.

North to Colombia ⬤⬤⬤⬤⬤ » *pp499-502.*

To the north of Ibarra is a land of striking contrasts. Deep eroded canyons and warm subtropical valleys stand side by side with windswept *páramos* and potato fields. The highlight of this area is Reserva Ecológica El Angel, home of the largest stand of *frailejones* (large velvety-leaved plants) in Ecuador. The main city in the region is Tulcán, about 5 km south of the Colombian border.

North of Ibarra, the Panamericana goes past Laguna Yahuarcocha and a turn-off to San Lorenzo on the coast before descending to the hot dry Chota valley. About 30 km north of Ibarra, at Mascarilla, is a police checkpoint (have documents at hand), after which the highway divides.

One branch follows an older route northeast through Mira and El Angel to Tulcán on the Colombian border. This road is paved and in good condition as far as El Angel, but deteriorates rapidly thereafter. The El Angel–Tulcán section is unpaved and in very poor condition but the scenery is beautiful. It is often impassable beyond Laguna El Voladero. The second branch, the modern toll Panamericana, is in excellent shape but with many heavy lorries, runs east through the Chota valley to Juncal, before turning north to reach Tulcán via Bolívar and San Gabriel. A good paved road runs between Bolívar and El Angel, connecting the two branches. A second lateral road, between San Gabriel and El Angel, requires a 4WD vehicle and is often impassable during the rainy season.

El Angel and around → *Colour map 2, A4. Phone code 06.*

The westernmost of the two routes going north towards Tulcán climbs steeply from Mascarilla, 16 km to the town of **Mira** (population 6000, altitude 2400 m). Some of the finest quality woollens come from this part of the country and are sold for export in Otavalo. Locally you can find them up the hill opposite the bus stop.

Beyond Mira, 18 km to the northeast, is **El Angel** (population 6600, altitude 3000 m), a sleepy highland town that comes to life during its Monday market. The **Unidad de Turismo** ⓘ *Municipio de El Angel (the municipality), T06-297 7147,* can provide regional information (including Reserva El Angel), and staff are helpful.

Reserva Ecológica El Angel → *Colour map 1, A4.*

ⓘ *The Ministerio del Ambiente's park office is near the Municipio, T/F06-297 7597. Information and pamphlets are available. Park entry US$10.*

El Angel is the main access point for this reserve which protects 15,715 ha of *páramo* ranging in altitude from 3400 to 4768 m. The reserve contains the southernmost large stands of the velvet-leaved *frailejón* plant, *Espeletia hartwegiana*, also found in the Andes of Colombia and Venezuela. Also here are the spiny *achupallas* a bromeliad with compound flowers. The wildlife includes *curiquingues* (birds of prey), deer, foxes, and a few condors. Many paths criss-cross the *páramo* and it is easy to get lost, so consider taking a guide for longer treks. It can be muddy during the rainy season; the best time to visit is May to August.

The closest place to admire the interesting *frailejón* plants is **El Voladero**, following the poor, direct road between El Angel and Tulcán for 16 km. Here is a ranger station from where a self-guided trail climbs over a low ridge (30 minutes' walk) to two crystal-clear lakes. Camping is possible, but you must be self-sufficient and take great care not to damage the fragile *páramo* . Pickups/taxis can be hired in the main plaza of El Angel for a day trip to El Voladero; US$20 return with a one-hour wait.

Tulcán → *Colour map 1, A4. Phone code 06. Population 63,000. Altitude 2960 m.*

The El Angel road and the Panamericana join at Las Juntas, 2 km south of Tulcán, a commercial centre and capital of the province of Carchi. It is always chilly. East of the city a bypass goes directly to the Colombian border. There is lots of informal trade here with Colombia, and a textile and dry goods fair takes place on Thursday and Sunday.

Unidad de Turismo (Municipio de Tulcán) ⓘ *entrance to the cemetery, T06-298 5760, Mon-Fri 0800-1300, 1500-1800*, Tulcán's main information office, provides local and national pamphlets and maps; they are helpful and speak some English. **i Tur** ⓘ *restored customs house at Rumichaca, the old stone bridge across the border, T06-298 3077, Mon-Fri 0900-1700*, provides local and national information.

North of the centre is the **Tulcán cemetery**, where the art of topiary is taken to incredible, beautiful extremes. Cypress bushes are trimmed into archways and fantastic figures of animals, angels, geometric shapes and so on, in *haut* and *bas* relief. Note the figures based on the stone carvings at San Agustín in Colombia, to the left just past the main entrance. To see the various stages of this art form, go to the back of the cemetery where young bushes are being pruned. The artistry, started in 1936, is that of the late Señor José Franco, now buried among the splendour he created. His epitaph reads: 'In Tulcán, a cemetery so beautiful that it invites one to die!' The tradition is carried on by his sons. At the entrance to the cemetery are a crafts exhibition hall and information centre.

Safety Tulcán and the traditionally tranquil border province of Carchi have seen an increase in tension due to drug trafficking and the *guerrilla* conflict in neighbouring Colombia. Do not travel outside town (except on the Panamericana) without enquiring about current conditions. It is also prudent not to wander about late at night. The area around the bus terminal in Tulcán is unsafe.

⬤ Sleeping

Ibarra *p497*
A Ajaví, Av Mariano Acosta 16-38 y Circunvalación, along main road into town from south, T06-295 5221, h-ajavi@imbanet.net. Slightly upscale hotel, comfortable rooms, includes breakfast, good restaurant serves regional and international cuisine, pool, parking, gets tour groups for Sat lunch.
C Nueva Estancia, García Moreno 7-58 y Sánchez y Cifuentes, Parque La Merced, T06-295 1444, nuevaestancia@andinanet.net. Modern hotel in a central location, includes breakfast, restaurant, parking, small rooms, decoration a bit kitch, opened in 2006.

D Royal Ruiz, Olmedo 9-40 y P Moncayo, T06-264 1999, royalruiz@hotmail.com. Modern hotel, includes breakfast, restaurant, solar-heated water, steam bath, parking, comfortable carpeted rooms.
E El Retorno, Pasaje Pedro Moncayo 4-32 entre Sucre y Rocafuerte, T06-295 7722. Ample rooms, restaurant, cheaper with shared bath, hot water, nice views from terrace. Good value, recommended.
E Hostal Madrid, Olmedo 8-69 y Moncayo, T06-264 4918, rubenmoncayo@hotmail.com. Modern, comfortable rooms, breakfast/lunch available, private bath, hot water, parking.

F **Colón**, Chica Narváez 8-62 y Velasco, T06-295 8695. A friendly basic place, cheaper with shared bath, electric shower, laundry facilities, patio.

Outside Ibarra

B **Hacienda Chorlaví**, Panamericana Sur Km 4, T06-2932222, www.hacienda chorlavi.com. A converted old hacienda with comfortable rooms, includes breakfast, very good, expensive restaurant with excellent *parillada*, set meals and à la carte, pool, parking, popular, busy on weekends, folk music and crafts on Sun.

D-E **Bospas Farm**, in El Limonal, on the road from Ibarra to San Lorenzo on the coast, T06-264 8692, www.bospas.org. A family-run organic fruit farm in a lovely setting. 3 private rooms with terrace and a dorm (cheaper), splendid views of the valley, includes good breakfast with delicious homemade bread, tasty meals available, small pool, camping by the river, treks and horse-riding trips, salsa lessons, excursions to Las Golondrinas, El Angel and to the coast for mangroves, volunteer opportunities. Belgian/Ecuadorean-run, friendly, knowledgeable, recommended.

San Antonio de Ibarra *p497*

E **Casa de Hilario**, Barrio Bellavista, 2 km south of the village of San Antonio, T06-293 2149. Three rooms in the the home of Juan Padilla, a local sculptor. He welcomes people who are interested in learning more about his art, includes breakfast, private bath, hot water, reservations necessary, call after 2000.

Embroidery villages *p498*

LL **Hacienda Zuleta**, by Angochahua, along the Ibarra–Cayambe road, T06-266 2182, T02-222 8554 (Quito), www.zuleta.com. A 2000-ha working historic hacienda, 15 rooms with fireplace, price includes all meals (prepared with organic vegetables, trout and dairy produced on the farm) and excursions. advance reservations required.

B **Pukyu Pamba**, San Clemente, T09-916 1095, manuel_guatemal@yahoo.com. Part of a community-run program. Housing is in cottages on family properties; you are expected to participate in the family's activities. Price includes 3 tasty meals and a guided hike, horses and native guides available for more extended treks.

E **Casa Aída**, La Esperanza village, T06-266 0221. Simple rooms with good beds, breakfast extra, restaurant, shared bath, hot water, clean, room 7 has nice views, friendly, Aída speaks some English, meeting place for Imbabura climbers.

El Angel and around *p498*

AL **Polylepis Lodge**, abutting the reserve, 14 km from El Angel on the road to Socabones, T06-2954009, www.polylepis lodge.com. Rustic cabins with fireplace by a 12-ha polylepis forest, price includes 3 meals (vegetarian on request) and 3 guided walks, jacuzzi.

C **Cotinga Lodge**, 7 km east of Morán along a trail, book through **Hostería El Angel**. A lodge in the cloudforest, includes breakfast, other meals on request, shared bath, cold water.

C **Hostería El Angel**, at the entrance to El Angel, T/F06-2977584, www.ecuador-sommergarten.com. A pleasant inn which caters to groups, includes breakfast, meals available on request, parking, reservations required, contact Quito T02-2330315. Offers trips into reserve and Cotinga Lodge.

F **Paisajes Andinos**, in El Angel, Riofrío, T06-2977557. Adequate hostel, new area with bath, older shared, electric shower; ask for a room in the new section.

Tulcán *p499*

C **Sara Espíndola**, Sucre y Ayacucho, on plaza, T06-2986209. Good hotel with comfortable rooms, includes breakfast, restaurant, spa, parking, helpful staff, best in town.

D **Machado**, Bolívar y Ayacucho, T06-298 4221. Includes breakfast, parking, comfortable.

E **Lumar**, Sucre y Rocafuerte, T06-298 0402. Private bath, hot water, parking, modern, clean and comfortable.

E **Sáenz Internacional**, Sucre y Rocafuerte, T06-298 1916. Private bath, hot water, modern. Good value, recommended.

F-G **Florida**, Sucre y 10 de Agosto, T06-298 3849. Cheaper with shared bath, hot water, modern section at back, good value.

🍴 Eating

Ibarra *p497*

Highly recommended are *helados de paila* (delicious fruit sorbets) made in large copper basins (*pailas*). These are available in many *heladerías* throughout the town, see below.

The upmarket restaurants at **Chorlaví** and **Ajaví** are recommended, but can be crowded with tour buses on Sat and Sun lunchtime.

₸₸₸ El Palacio de Hugo, Moncayo 6-15 y Bolívar, T06-260 0225, Tue-Sat 1300-2100, Sun 1300-1600. Upscale restaurant with seafood and meat specialities.

₸₸ Café Floralp, Av Teodoro Gómez 7-49 y Atahualpa, Mon-Sat 0800-2100, Sun 1700-2000. A variety of crêpes, fondue, good breakfast, bread, yoghurt, cold cuts, excellent coffee, good selection of Chilean wines, the 'in place' to meet and eat. Warmly recommended.

₸₸ Pizza El Horno, Rocafuerte 6-38 y Flores, Tue-Sat 1730-2400, Sun 1800-2300. Good pizza and Italian dishes, live music Sat 2100.

₸ Aroma Gourmet, Sánchez y Cifuentes 8-80 y Oviedo, daily 1200-1600. A very popular place for a good set lunch.

₸ Inti Raymi, Av Pérez Guerrero 6-39 y Bolívar, Mon-Sat 1200-1530. Good simple vegetarian lunches, clean, friendly service.

Cafés

Antojitos de Mi Tierra, Sucre y P Moncayo, at Plazoleta Francisco Calderón, daily in the afternoon. Cafeteria with outdoor seating, serves local drinks and snacks such as *humitas*, *quimbolitos* and *tamales*.

Café Arte, Salinas 5-43 y Oviedo, daily 1700 until late. Café-bar with character, serves drinks, Mexican snacks, sandwiches and some à la carte dishes. Live music Fri and Sat night, good meeting place, publishes monthly cultural calendar.

Ice cream parlours
There are some excellent *heladerías* serving *helados de paila*, homemade fruit sorbets.
Heladería Rosalía Suárez, Oviedo y Olmedo. An Ibarra tradition since 1896, very good, try the *mora* (raspberry) or *guanábana* (soursop) flavours. Highly recommended.
La Bermejita, Olmedo 7-15.

El Angel and around *p498*
₸ El Sabrosón, at the main park. Good value set meals and other dishes, open until 2200.

Tulcán *p499*
There are several *chifas* and many cheap chicken places in town.
₸₸-₸ Sara Espíndola, at the hotel. Set meals and à la carte, fanciest option in town.

₸ Antojitos Express, Sucre y Ayacucho, next door to **Hotel Sara Espíndola**. Set meals and à la carte.
₸ Café Tulcán, Sucre 52-029 y Ayacucho. Good coffee, desserts, snacks and juices, also set lunches.

🍷 Bars and clubs

Ibarra *p497*
At the corner of Bolívar and Oviedo are some cafés, bars and clubs, a popular place locals' hang out, especially Fri and Sat night.
Bar Buda, Sucre y Pedro Moncayo, at Plazoleta Francisco Calderón. Outdoor seating, a good place to meet a friend for a drink in the afternoon.
El Encuentro, Olmedo 9-59. Piano bar, interesting drinks, very popular, pleasant atmosphere, unusual decor.

⊛ Festivals and events

Ibarra *p497*
28 Apr **El Retorno** celebrates the return of the people of Ibarra to their city after 4 years absence following the 1868 earthquake. There are music festivals, bullfights, parades and sporting events.
Sep **Fiesta de los Lagos** is held over the last weekend of Sep, Thu-Sun, to commemorate the foundation of Ibarra. It begins with *El Pregón*, a parade of floats through the city.

🅾 Shopping

Ibarra *p497*
Supermarkets include: **Akí**, Bolívar y Colón; and **Supermaxi**, south of the centre on Eugenio Espejo.

▲ Activities and tours

Ibarra *p497*
Paragliding
Fly Ecuador, Oviedo 9-13 y Sánchez Cifuentes, T06-295 3297, www.flyecuador.com.ec.

Tour operators
EcuaHorizons, Bolívar 4-67 y García Moreno, T06-295 9904, ecuahorizons@andinanet.net. Bilingual guides for regional tours.
Intipungo, Rocafuerte 6-08 y Flores, T06-295 7766. Regional tours.

⊖ Transport

Ibarra *p497*

Bus and taxi **Quito**, frequent service. Shared taxis with **Supertaxis Los Lagos** (in Quito at Asunción 3-81, T02-256 5992; in Ibarra at Flores 924 y Sánchez Cifuentes (**Parque La Merced**, T06-295 5150) who will pick you up at your hotel (New City only), hourly Mon-Fri 0700-1900, Sat 0700-1600, Sun 0800-1800, 2½ hrs, US$7.50 per person, buy ticket at their office the day before travelling. **Cotacachi**, every 15 mins, US$0.45, 45 mins, some continue to **Quiroga**. **Ambato**, CITA goes via El Quinche and bypasses Quito, 8 daily, US$5, 5 hrs. **Baños**, Expreso Baños also bypasses Quito, 2 daily, US$6, 5½ hrs.

San Antonio de Ibarra *p497*

Bus City buses from outside Mercado Amazonas, US$0.18, taxi US$2.50.

Embroidery villages *p498*

Bus To **La Esperanza**, **San Clemente**, and **Zuleta**, buses leave from Parque Germán Grijalva in Ibarra, east of Terminal Terrestre, follow Calle Sánchez y Cifuentes, south from the centre. To **San Clemente** weekdays 0650, 0820, 1000, 1140, 1330, 1530, 1800, Sat 0720, 1100, 1300,1800, Sun 0720, 1100, 1300, US$0.22, 30 mins. To **La Esperanza**, every 20 mins, US$0.22, 30 mins. To **Zuleta**, hourly, US$0.52, 1 hr.

For **Cayambe** via Zuleta, **Coop 24 de Junio**, from the Ibarra Terminal Terrestre, at 0615, 1000, 1225 and 1730 to **Pesillo**, ouside Olmedo, US$0.90, 1½ hrs, from where there is service to Cayambe every 30 mins, US$0.90, 1 hr. Alternative faster route to **Cayambe** take a bus to Otavalo and change there.

Taxi A taxi from Ibarra to **La Esperanza** or **San Clemente** is US$4-5.

El Angel and around *p498*

Bus From **Ibarra** Terminal Terrestre to **Mira**, hourly, US$0.90, 1 hr; to **El Angel**, hourly, US$1.30, 1½ hrs. From El Angel to **Mira**, every 30 mins, US$.50, 20 mins. From El Angel to **Tulcán**, US$1.30, 1½ hrs. From El Angel to **Quito**, US$4, 4 hrs.

Tulcán and around *p499*

Air Tulcán's airport is north along the road to the border; taxi to the airport US$1.50.

TAME, Sucre y Ayacucho, T06-298 0675, flies Mon, Wed and Fri to **Quito**, US$42, and to **Cali**, Colombia, US$91, confirm schedules and prices in advance.

Bus and taxi The Terminal Terrestre is 1½ km uphill, south of the centre. It's best to take a taxi US$1 from Parque Ayora. Beside the terminal is a plaza from where shared taxis and vans leave for nearby destinations such as San Gabriel and Julio Andrade.

There is frequent bus service to **Quito** and **Guayaquil** and destinations along the way.

To **Huaquillas**, on the Peruvian border, with **Panamericana Internacional**, 1 coach a day, US$20. To **Lago Agrio**, 3 a day from Tulcán, US$7, 7 hrs, or take a shared taxi to Julio Andrade and catch the bus originating in Ibarra which passes around noon.

❶ Directory

Ibarra *p497*

Banks Banco del Pacífico, Olmedo y P Moncayo. Banco del Austro, Colón 7-51. **Hospital** Clínica Médica del Norte, Oviedo 8-24, T06-295 5099, private. San Vicente de Paúl, Vargas Torres y Jaime Rivadeneira, T06-295 7272, public. **Internet** Good service at Hostal El Ejecutivo, several more in the centre, for about US$0.75 per hr. **Language schools** Centro Ecuatoriano Canadiense de Idiomas (CECI), Pérez Guerrero 6-22 y Bolívar, T06-295 1911, US$3.50 per hr. **Post office** Flores opposite Parque Pedro Moncayo, p 2. **Useful addresses** Immigration, LF Villamar y Olmedo, T06-295 1712.

Emroidery villages *p497*

Language schools In La Esperanza, Sr Joselo Obando offers Spanish lessons, ask at Casa Aída. In San Clemente, Quichua lessons can be arranged by Pukyu Pamba.

Tulcán *p499*

Banks Banco del Austro, Bolívar y Ayacucho. Bring US$ cash, few places accept credit cards and there is nowhere to change TCs. Street changers at Parque La Independencia deal in Colombian pesos. **Internet** Many in town, US$1. **Post office** Bolívar 53-27. **Useful addresses** Colombian Consulate, Bolívar 368 y Junín, T06-298 7302, Mon-Fri 0800-1300, 1430-1530, visas require up to 20 days.

Central and Southern Sierras

✷ Footprint features

Introduction

South of Quito is some of the loveliest mountain scenery in Ecuador. An impressive roll call of towering peaks lines the route south: Cotopaxi, the Ilinizas, Carihuayrazo and Chimborazo, to name but a few. Naturally, this area attracts its fair share of trekkers and climbers, while the less active can browse through the many markets and colonial towns that nestle among the high volcanic cones.

After you have explored the mountains to your heart's delight, rest up and pamper yourself in Baños, named and famed for its thermal baths. A little further south is Riobamba, dubbed 'corazón de la patria' (cultural heartland of highland Ecuador) and starting point for the country's most spectacular train ride.

The convoluted topography of the southern highlands reveals an ancient non-volcanic past distinct from its northern Sierra neighbours. Here are Ecuador's prime Inca site, two of its most spectacular national parks, and Cuenca – the nation's most congenial city. Cuenca boasts some of the country's finest colonial architecture, and the Cuenca basin is a major *artesanía* centre.

Further south, Loja and Vilcabamba are great bases for trekking and horse riding excursions, with nearby undisturbed *páramo* and cloudforest. They also provide access to the Peruvian border at several different points. An increasing number of travellers are discovering these out-of-the-way crossings, which link Ecuador with interesting areas in the north of Peru.

★ Don't miss ...

1 **Cotopaxi** Climb one of the world's highest active volcanoes, page 507.
2 **Quilotoa Circuit** Hike from inn to inn along this popular route, page 509.
3 **Devil's Nose** Take the train along the high-altitude route from Riobamba to Sibambe, page 522.
4 **Cuenca's architecture** Take a stroll through the colonial past in the heart of the city, page 531.
5 **Parque Nacional Podocarpus** Trek into magical cloud forest, page 543.
6 **Horse riding around Vilcabamba** Give in to the call of the wild in the magnificent scenery around Vilcabamba, page 544.

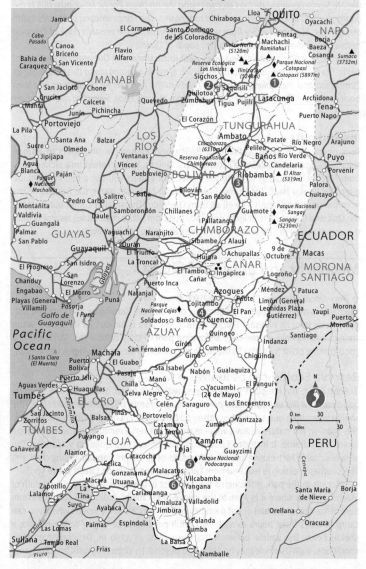

Cotopaxi, Latacunga and Quilotoa

South of Quito, several haciendas offer lodging for visitors who are interested in experiencing farm life. It is a very scenic area dotted with volcanic peaks, well suited to walking and horse riding. Those aiming higher can experience the thrill of climbing one of the peaks of Ilinizas, Rumiñahui or the perfect cone of Cotopaxi. Latacunga, an authentic highland city, is the gateway to the popular Quilotoa Circuit, a loop through several colourful villages. The emerald crater lake of Quilotoa is the jewel of the circuit. This area is also rich in folklore and a number of colourful indigenous markets are well worth a visit.

The Panamericana climbs gradually out of the Quito basin. At Alóag, a road heads west to Santo Domingo de los Colorados and the northern Pacific Lowlands; this is the country's main link between coast and mountains. The Panamericana continues south through the Machachi valley from where it climbs along the western flank of Cotopaxi before descending to Latacunga, 91 km south of Quito.

From Latacunga a scenic road goes west to La Maná and Quevedo on the coastal plain. The loop, known as the Quilotoa Circuit, is made by going along this road as far as Zumbahua and then taking secondary roads to the north as far as Sigchos and then back east to the Panamericana and Latacunga. ‣‣ *For Sleeping, Eating and other listings, see pages 511-517.*

Ins and outs

Tour operators in Quito, Latacunga, Baños and Riobamba offer tours to Parque Nacional Cotopaxi and Reserva Ecológica Los Ilinizas. You can also hire a pickup truck from Machachi or Lasso to go to the parks, but groups without a registered guide might be turned back. Latacunga is well served by buses along the Panamericana from the north and south as well as from Quevedo. The smaller communities along the Quilotoa Circuit have at least one daily bus from Latacunga. Buses returning from the communities to Latacunga often leave very early, before dawn.

Machachi and around ●🏛❄🛏🍴 ‣‣ *pp511-517.*

→ *Phone code 02. Colour map 1, A3. Population 25,000. Altitude 2900 m.*

Machachi is nestled between the summits of Pasochoa, Rumiñahui and Corazón, with good views from its pleasant Parque Central. The area is famous for its mineral water springs and icy cold, crystal-clear **swimming pool** ⓘ *daily 0800-1530*. Machachi is a good starting point for a visit to the northern section of Reserva Ecológica Los Ilinizas

Reserva Ecológica Los Ilinizas → *Colour map 1, B3.*

ⓘ *Entry US$5. The refugio is fully equipped with beds for 18, take a mat and sleeping bag because it fills quickly, US$10 per person, use of stove US$5 (the caretaker locks the shelter when he is out, so check at Hostal La Llovizna in El Chaupi before heading up).*
The 1500-sq-km nature reserve was created to preserve remnants of western slope forest and *páramo*. It includes El Corazón, Los Ilinizas and Quilotoa volcanoes. The area is suitable for trekking and the twin peaks of Iliniza are popular among climbers. The southern section is reached from Latacunga, see Quilotoa Circuit (page 509).

Access to the park is through a turn-off west of the Panamericana, 6 km south of Machachi, from where it is 7 km to the village of **El Chaupi**. A dirt road continues from here to 'La Virgen' (statue) about 9 km beyond. Nearby are some woods where you can camp. It takes three hours to walk with a full pack from 'La Virgen' to the *refugio*, a shelter below the saddle between the two peaks, at 4750 m. Depending on road conditions, a 4WD vehicle may be able to go beyond 'La Virgen'. To walk from El Chaupi to the *refugio* takes seven or eight hours. Horses can be hired (US$15-20) at **Hacienda San José, La Llovizna** or ask around the village.

Iliniza Norte (5105 m), although not a technical climb, should not be under-estimated, a few exposed rocky sections require utmost caution. **Iliniza Sur** (5245 m) is a four-hour ice climb. There are some steep, technical sections on this route, and full climbing gear and experience are absolutely necessary. Beware of falling rock.

Parque Nacional Cotopaxi ○○ ›› *pp511-517.*

→ *Colour map 1, B4.*

The beautiful snow-capped cone of **Volcán Cotopaxi** (5897 m) is at the heart of this lovely national park and is one of the prime tourist destinations in the country. If you only climb one of Ecuador's many volcanoes, then this should be the one. Many agencies run tours here. Note that Cotopaxi is an active volcano; its activity is monitored by the **National Geophysics Institute**, see www.igepn.edu.ec.

There are four access points to Parque Nacional Cotopaxi. The **main access** is 25 km south of Machachi and 6 km north of **Lasso**, along the Panamericana, and is marked by a Parque Nacional Cotopaxi sign. This is the main entrance and it is quicker and easier to follow than the El Boliche route. It leads first to the park gate, then climbs to the plateau and lake of Limpio Pungo. Past Limpio Pungo the road deteriorates and a branch right climbs steeply to a car park at 4600 m, from where a trail continues to the mountain shelter at 4800 m. Walking from the Panamericana to the refuge takes an entire day or more.

The **El Boliche** access, 16 km south of Machachi along the Panamericana, starts at a sign for the Clirsen satellite tracking station, which has a museum. This route goes past Clirsen and the old Cotopaxi railway station, then via **Area Nacional de Recreación El Boliche**. There is a shared entry fee for El Boliche and Cotopaxi; you should only pay once, but enquire beforehand on site. Follow the route for over 30 km along a signposted dirt road to reach the main park gate.

The **Pedregal access** is from the north. Cyclists should consider this approach, rather than the main access, because the latter route is too soft to climb on a bike. From Machachi it is 13 km on a cobbled road, then 2 km of gravel to Santa Ana del Pedregal. A further 5 km of dirt leads to the northern park entrance, then it is 15 km to the car park for the *refugio*. Quito operators run bicycling tours here.

The **Ticatilín** access approaches Cotopaxi from the south. From the Panamericana, 1 km north of Lasso, at a spot known as Aglomerados Cotopaxi (the northern access to Saquisilí) a road goes to the village of San Ramón and on to the community of Ticatilín where a contribution is expected for them to open the chain at the access point (US$1-2 per vehicle). The road leads to the private **Albergue Cotopaxi Cara Sur**.

Attractions and park services

ⓘ *Visitors must register at the main gate, entry US$10, gates 0700-1500, although you can stay until 1800. Note that groups arriving with guides not authorized by the park are turned back at the gate.* The park administration and a small museum (0800-1200 and 1300-1700), are located 10 km from the park gates, just before the plateau of Laguna Limpio Pungo. By the museum are a simple restaurant and shelter (E per person including breakfast, book ahead T09-851 3133, Quito T02-231 4234).

The **Limpio Pungo** plateau (3850 m) with a shallow lake sits between Cotopaxi and **Volcán Rumiñahui** (4712 m) to the northwest. It is a lovely spot from which to observe Cotopaxi and a place to learn about the *páramo* flora and fauna. The hills at the base of Rumiñahui are excellent for birdwatching and it is possible to see several species peculiar to the *páramo*. On the plains watch out for herds of wild horses, llamas and the odd mountain lion or wild bull. This is a very nice area for walking. Just north of Cotopaxi are the peaks of **Sincholagua** (4893 m) and **Pasochoa** (4225 m). To the southeast is the beautiful and elusive **Quilindaña** (4890 m).

From Limpio Pungo a road branches off to climb the north flank of Cotopaxi to a parking area at 4600 m. The road can be covered in snow at times. From here a sandy trail continues to climb to **Refugio José Ribas** (mountain shelter) at 4800 m. It is 30 minutes to an hour on foot; beware of altitude sickness, go slowly. Entry to the refuge costs US$1, or US$16.80 to stay overnight. Facilities include a kitchen, water, and 60 bunks with mattresses. Bring a good sleeping bag and mat, as well as a padlock for your excess luggage when you climb; or use the lockable luggage deposit, US$2.50. In high season the shelter gets very crowded.

On the southwestern flank of Cotopaxi, known as **Cara Sur**, is the private **Albergue Cotopaxi Cara Sur** at 4000 m (see Sleeping, page 512) and four hours from here, at 4800 m, **Campo Alto**, a tent camp run by the same people (F per person). This area offers good walking in the *páramo*, condors are sometimes seen, and you can climb **Morurco** (4881 m) to the base of the rock (the summit is unstable and not recommended).

Climbing Cotopaxi and Rumiñahui

Because of the altitude and weather conditions, Cotopaxi is a serious climb; equipment and experience are required. To maximize your chances of reaching the summit, be sure to acclimatize beforehand. Take a guide if you're inexperienced on ice and snow.

> **For climbing Cotopaxi, a full moon is both practical and magical.**

Agencies in Quito and throughout the central highlands offer Cotopaxi climbing trips. Note that some guides encourage tourists to turn back at the first sign of tiredness, don't be pressured, but be sensible and insist on going at your own pace. The best season is December to April. There are strong winds and clouds from August to December but the ascent is still possible for experienced mountaineers.

To climb the southwestern flank of **Cotopaxi**, the access is from Ticatilín. To reach the summit in one day, you need to stay at **Campo Alto**, a tent camp at 4780 m (see above). The route is reported easier and safer than the north face, but longer. The last hour goes along the rim of the crater with impressive views.

Rumiñahui can be climbed from the park road, starting at Laguna Limpio Pungo from where it takes about 1½ hours to the mountain base. The climb itself is straight-forward and not technical, though it is quite a scramble on the rockier parts and it can be very slippery and muddy after rain. Note that the rock at the summit is unstable.

Latacunga ●❶❷❸❸❸❶ » pp511-517.

→ *Phone code 03. Colour map 1, B3. Population 92,000. Altitude 2800 m.*

The capital of Cotopaxi Province, Latacunga, was built largely from the local light grey pumice and the colonial character of the town has been well preserved. Cotopaxi is 29 km away and dominates the city. Many other mountains can be seen on a clear day and the wind sweeping off them is cold. The architecture, scenery and climate are well complemented by the local people, making Latacunga an authentic highland town.

The Panamericana runs along the western side of town, with the Terminal Terrestre a 10-minute walk to the centre. There are a few simple hotels and restaurants along the highway, with a better selection in the centre, on the other side of the Río Cutuchi. Local and regional information is available from **Cámara de Turismo de Cotopaxi** ① *Sánchez de Orellana y Guayaquil, Plaza de Santo Domingo, T03-281 4968, Mon-Fri 0800-1200, 1400-1700*, Spanish only. The **Oficina de Turismo** ① *Terminal Terrestre, p2, Mon-Fri 0900-1200, 1330-1800, Sat 0900-1600, Sun 0900-1400*, is staffed by friendly high school students studying tourism and has local and some regional information.

The central park, **Parque Vicente León**, is a colourful and beautifully maintained garden with tall palm trees. It is locked at night. The **Casa de los Marqueses de**

Miraflores ① *Sánchez de Orellana y Abel Echeverría, T03-280 1410, Mon-Fri 0800-1200, 1400-1800, free,* is a restored colonial mansion with a lovely inner courtyard and gardens. Some of the rooms have been converted into a modest museum and it includes exhibits about the **Mama Negra** celebrations (see Festivals, page 514), colonial art, archaeology, numismatics and a library. The building itself is worth a visit. It also houses the **Jefatura de Cultura y Turismo del Municipio**.

The **Casa de la Cultura** ① *Antonia Vela 3-49 y Padre Salcedo, T03-813 247, Tue-Fri 0800-1200, 1400-1800, Sat 0800-1500, US$1,* was built around the remains of a Jesuit monastery and incorporates the old Monserrat watermill. The finely designed modern building contains an excellent museum with pre-Columbian ceramics, weavings, costumes and models of festival masks. There is also an art gallery, library and theatre.

Quilotoa Circuit → pp511-517.

→ *Colour map 1, B3. Phone code 03.*

This is a popular route with visitors, yet the many small villages and vast expanses of open countryside preserve an authentic feel. You could easily spend a few days horse riding, hiking, cycling, visiting indigenous markets or just relaxing. A recommended route is from Latacunga to Pujilí, Tigua–Chimbacucho, Zumbahua, Quilotoa, Chugchilán, Sigchos, Isinliví, Toacazo, Saquisilí and back to Latacunga; this circuit can

🕯 *Be prepared for the cold; many places along the loop are above 3000 m.*

be done in two to three days by bus. Some enjoy riding on the roof for the views and thrills, but hang on tight and wrap up well. Accommodation is available in all the villages listed. Note that this is a poor region, watch your belongings.

Latacunga to Zumbahua → *Colour map 1, B3.*

Along the paved road west from Latacunga to Quevedo, 15 km from the city, is **Pujilí** (population 30,000, altitude 2930 m), which has a beautiful church. There is some local ceramic work, a good market on Sunday, and a smaller one on Wednesday. The town has excellent **Corpus Christi** celebrations.

From Pujilí the road climbs steeply to cross the western cordillera. Beyond the pass, it descends through high-rolling country with some lovely views. Ten kilometres from Pujilí is the **Tigua** area where the local people produce interesting crafts. In the

Cotopaxi, Latacunga & Quilotoa

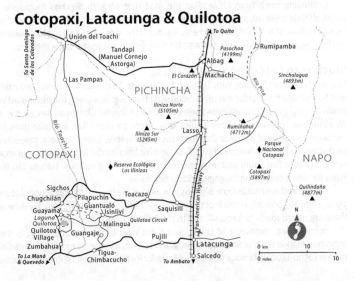

village of **Tigua-Chimbacucho**, by the side of the road, is Alfredo Toaquiza's art gallery where local work can be admired and bought. There are many walking trails in the area including one to Quilotoa.

The indigenous village of **Zumbahua** (population 12,000, altitude 3450 m) lies 500 m north of the main Latacunga–Quevedo road, 65 km from Pujilí. It is quite sleepy for most of the week, but comes alive at weekends, festivals and on market day, Saturday. The market starts at 0600, and is only for local produce and animals, interesting and best before 1000. Friday nights involve dancing and drinking.

Zumbahua to Sigchos → Colour map 1, B3.
Zumbahua is the point to turn off the road to Quevedo, to continue along the Quilotoa Circuit and visit **Quilotoa Crater Lake** ① US$1 entry fee, a spectacular volcanic crater filled by an emerald lake, part of Reserva Ecológica los Ilinizas. The crater rim (3850 m) is reached by a paved road which runs north for 12 km from Zumbahua.

Along the access road to the rim, the small community of Lago Verde Quilotoa, which caters to visitors, has sprung up. A number of the houses are basic lodgings. The limiting factor here is the lack of water, which must be trucked in. There are a number of artists in town and everyone in the village tries to sell the famous *naïf* pictures and carved wooden masks (see Tigua, above). Try to spread your business around as people in this area are very poor.

From the rim of the crater several snow-capped volcanoes can be seen in the distance. During the wet season, the best views are in the early morning. There is a 300-m drop down from the crater rim to the water. The hike down takes about 30 minutes (an hour or more to climb back up). The trail starts to the left of the parking area down a steep, canyon-like cut. You can hire a mule to ride up from the bottom of the crater, but arrange it before heading down. By the lake are a basic community-run hostel (information at **Hostal Princesa Toa**) and kayaks for rent (US$4 per hour), ask for life jackets, the water is very cold.

Beyond Quilotoa the road is unpaved and can be quite poor at times. It is 22 km from Quilotoa to **Chugchilán** (population 7000, altitude 3180 m), a poor, mainly indigenous village in a beautiful setting; market day is Sunday. The area offers good trekking, horse riding and cycling. Horses with a guide for a trip to Quilotoa are available for US$20 per horse. Near town are a cheese factory which welcomes visitors, a carpentry workshop, and further afield an area of nice cloud forest with good birdwatching.

Continuing north from Chugchilán the road runs through **Sigchos** (population 9000, altitude 2880 m), a somewhat larger town, also with a Sunday market. There are beautiful views of both Ilinizas from here. Sigchos is the main starting point for hiking in the Río Toachi Canyon, but this can also be done from other towns along the loop.

Sigchos to Latacunga → Colour map 1, B3.
Two roads connect Sigchos with Toacazo further east. To the north is a cobbled road and further south the older dirt road. Southeast from Sigchos along the older road is **Isinliví** (population 3800, altitude 2960 m), with its colourful Christmas fiestas. It is a pleasant town populated mainly by mestizos. There are nice hikes and bike rides in the area and several *pucarás* (hill fortresses) to explore. There's also a carpentry workshop to visit, and birdwatching. You can hike from Isinliví to Chugchilán, or vice versa, in about five hours and there are many other walking options. Horses can be hired for riding or carrying luggage, US$20 per horse.

The old and new roads from Sigchos join west of the town of **Toacazo** (population 7500, altitude 3060 m), at the foot of Iliniza Sur. There is an inn near town. From here there are paved roads to Saquisilí and to the Panamericana, near Lasso.

Some 16 km southwest of Lasso, and 6 km west of the Panamericana, is the important market town of **Saquisilí** (population 14,000, altitude 2920 m). Its Thursday market (0500-1400) is famous throughout Ecuador for the way in which its seven plazas local *indígenas* with red ponchos and narrow-brimmed felt hats.

The best time to visit the market is between 0900 and 1200, be sure to bargain. The animal market is a little way out of the village and it's best to be there before 0800. There is accommodation in town and a few simple *comedores*.

Cycling around Quilotoa

This is a great area for biking and to get away from traffic, only a few sections are cobbled or rough and there is a choice of routes. Note that riding at this elevation is difficult and you should be in very good physical shape. You can make a four-day circuit or take longer to explore the beautiful surroundings along secondary roads. It's best to start on the Panamericana either from Lasso or Latacunga. On the north side between Toacazo and Sigchos there are two roads. The northern route is mostly cobbled, it hugs the canyon's edge before crossing the Río Toachi. Taking the older southern route via Isinliví avoids most of the cobble, but there's a rough 4-km stretch descending from the pass at Güingopana to Isinliví, the views along this stretch are fantastic. Between Isinliví and Sigchos is another good gravel road.

From the south the road is paved from Latacunga to Quilotoa. Along this route you can take a turn-off to the north between Pujilí and Tigua, at about 4000 m, going to Guangaje, Guantualó and Isinliví, it is good hard-packed earth. Alternatively, you can continue on the paved road to Tigua, Zumbahua, and Quilotoa. From Quilotoa to Chugchilán and on to Sigchos is mostly downhill on gravel. **Black Sheep Inn** in Chugchilán gives 10-15% discounts to those travelling by bicycle.

Trekking around Quilotoa

There are ample opportunities for walking in the Quilotoa Circuit area. There are good day walks from all of the towns along the route and what makes the area special is the number of hostels even in some very small places. An interesting 'hostel-hopping' trek is described in *Trekking in Ecuador* (see Books, page 646).

Quilotoa crater lake is reached in a few hours' walking from Tigua, Zumbahua, Chugchilán and Isinliví (a full day is required from the latter). You can walk right round the Quilotoa crater rim in about six hours; it's very beautiful, but be sure to stick to the rim and don't head down towards the lake as there are cliffs. The path can get slippery and dangerous when the fog rolls in. Enquire locally beforehand and take a stick to fend off dogs. Also be prepared for sudden changes in the weather, and begging kids – don't give them money, buy their crafts instead. Another beautiful walk is from Quilotoa to Chugchilán (11 km, five to six hours) following the crater rim clockwise then descending to the hamlet of **Guayama**, where there are a couple of shops with basic supplies and a hostel, and continuing across the canyon of the Río Sigüi. From Guayama you can also continue to Isinliví, which can also be reached along a road from **Pilapuchín**, on the northeast side of the lake, to **Malingua** and on to **Guantualó**. It is an 8½-hour walk from Quilotoa to Isinliví on either route.

❧ *Bring drinking water as there's none at the top of the crater and the water in the lake is salty and sulphurous.*

⊙ Sleeping

Machachi and around *p506*
C-D La Estación de Machachi, 3 km west of the Panamericana, by railway station outside the village of Aloasí, T02-230 9246, T02-244 7052 (Quito). Rooms in a lovely old home and newer cabins (more expensive), fireplaces, breakfast and set meals, parking, hiking access to Volcán El Corazón, book in advance.

D Chiguac, Los Caras y Colón, 4 blocks from the main park, T02-231 0396, germanimor@punto.net.ec. Small family-run hostel, clean comfortable rooms, includes breakfast, restaurant, shared bath.
E-F Papa Gayo, In Hacienda Bolívia, 500 m west of the Panamericana, T02-231 0002, h_eran@yahoo.com. Chilly old farmhouse,

nice communal area with fireplace and library, restaurant, cheaper in dorm, hot water, parking, homey atmosphere, friendly owner arranges excursions, popular.

Reserva Ecológica Los Ilinizas *p506*
D Hacienda San José del Chaupi, 3 km southwest of El Chaupi, T09-467 1692, haciendasanjosedelchaupi@yahoo.com. Converted hacienda house and wood cabins on a working farm. Shared rooms for 4 and cabins for 6, includes breakfast, meals on request, parking, fireplaces in common areas and cabins, horse riding, visitors can participate in farm activities, reforestation project, horses for hauling gear up to the *refugio*, book ahead.
E La Llovizna, El Chaupi, 100 m behind the church, on the way to the mountain, T09-969 9068. Pleasant hostel, sitting room with fireplace, includes breakfast, restaurant, 4 rooms with bath, others shared, hot water, pool table, table tennis, call in advance to make sure it is open, owned by the guardian of the Iliniza refuge, horse rental.

Parque Nacional Cotopaxi *p507*
LL Hacienda San Agustín de Callo, 2 unpaved access roads off the Panamericana, one just north of the main park access, marked by a painted stone from where it is 6.2 km. The other, just north of Lasso from where it is 4.3 km, T03-271 9160, T02-290 6157 (Quito), www.incahacienda.com. An exclusive inn, the only place in Ecuador where you can sleep and dine in an Inca building. This is the northernmost imperial-style Inca structure still standing. Suites with fireplaces in room and bath. Tasty meals included, also horse rides, treks, bicycles and fishing. The dining room is open to non-guests (US$14-22), visitors pay US$5 to see the courtyard and chapel, US$10 for the interior and a snack.
B Hacienda El Porvenir, between El Pedregal and the northern access to the park, T09-972 7934, T02-223 1806 (Quito), www.tierradel volcan.com. Lodge in a working hacienda at the foot of Rumiñahui. Sitting-room with fireplaces, includes breakfast, set meals available, horses and mountain bikes for hire. Camping **F** per person. Package including full board and transport from Quito available.
C Tambopaxi, at the northern end of the park, along the El Pedregal access (1-hr drive from Machachi) or 4 km north of the turn-off

for the climbing shelter, T02-222 0242 (Quito), www.tambopaxi.com. Straw-bale mountain shelter at 3750 m. 3 double rooms and several dorms, duvet blankets, good restaurant with set meals and Swiss specialities, shared bath with hot shower, camping **G** pp, horse riding and llama trekking with advance notice.
C-D Cuello de Luna, 2 km northwest of the park's main access on a dirt road, T09-970 0330, www.cuellodeluna.com. Comfortable rooms with fireplaces, includes breakfast, meals available, parking, cheaper in dorm (a very low loft). Can arrange transport to Cotopaxi, horse riding and mountain biking.
E Albergue Cotopaxi Cara Sur, southwestern end of the park, at end of the Ticatilín access road, T02-290 3164 (Agama Expediciones, Quito), www.cotopaxi-carasur.com. Mountain shelter at 4000 m. 3 cabins with capacity for 40, meals available with advance notice, use of kitchen, outhouses, hot shower, bunk beds and blankets, transport from Quito and climbing tours available. Campo Alto tent camp US$5 pp, 4 hrs walking from the shelter, horse to take gear to camp US$12.

Latacunga *p508*
D Makroz, Valencia 8-56 y Quito, T03-280 0907. Modern hotel with nicely decorated comfortable rooms, restaurant serves cheap meals (closed Sun), parking. Recommended.
D Rodelú, Quito 16-31, T03-280 0956, rodelu@uio.telconet.net. Comfortable popular hotel, good restaurant (closed Sun), good suites and rooms, except for a few rooms which are small and a bit overpriced.
E Estambul, Belisario Quevedo 6-46 y Padre Salcedo, T03-280 0354. Simple quiet hostel, cheaper with shared bath, popular, tours to Cotopaxi and Quilotoa. Recommended.
E Rosim, Quito 16-49 y Padre Salcedo, T03-280 2172, hotelrosim@hotmail.com. Centrally located, breakfast available, private bath, hot water, carpeted rooms, quiet and comfortable. Discount in low season and for IYHF members.
E Tilipulo, Guayaquil y Belisario Quevedo, T03-281 0611. Comfortable, cafeteria, private bath, hot water, limited parking, ample rooms, popular, helpful owner. Recommended.
F Santiago, 2 de Mayo 7-16 y Guayaquil, T03-280 0899. Pleasant, good value, cheaper with bath outside the room (but not shared), hot water, small but comfortable rooms.

Pujilí

F **Residencial Pujilí**, Rocafuerte, half a block from the highway, T03-272 3648. A simple, small hotel, restaurant downstairs, private bath, hot water.

Tigua-Chimbacucho

C **Posada de Tigua**, 3 km east of Tigua-Chimbacucho, 400 m north of the road, T03-281 3682, laposadadetigua@latinmail.com. Refurbished hacienda house, part of a working dairy ranch. 5 rooms, wood-burning stove, includes breakfast and dinner, tasty home-cooked meals, rooms with bath available, pleasant family atmosphere, horses, trails to river and forest, nice views. Recommended.

Zumbahua

F **Cóndor Matzi**, overlooking the market, T03-281 4611 (at the hospital). Basic but adequate, serves Fri supper (extra cost), other meals on request, shared bath, hot water, one of the better choices in town, reserve ahead.
F **Residencial Oro Verde**, first place on the left as you enter town, T03-2814605, T03-280 2548 (Latacunga). A friendly hotel, provides meals Fri-Sat and or advanced notice, cheaper with shared bath, hot water.

Quilotoa

There are many other basic places to stay.
B **Quilotoa Crater Lake Lodge**, on the main road facing the access to Quilotoa, T09-717 5780, T02-223 8665 (Quito), www.quilotoa lodge.com. Hacienda-style lodge, includes breakfast, restaurant with fireplace and views, electric blankets, homley atmosphere, friendly service, the newest and most upscale place in Quilotoa, opened in 2005. Recommended.
E **Cabañas Quilotoa**, on the left side of the access road, T09-212 5962. Two-storey hostel, includes breakfast and dinner, new rooms with bath, cheaper with shared bath, hot water, wood-burning stoves in rooms. Owned by Humberto Latacunga who will organize treks, he is also a good painter.

Chugchilán

A-B **The Black Sheep Inn**, a few mins below the village on the way to Sigchos, T03-281 4587, www.blacksheepinn.com. An award-winning eco-friendly resort. Lovely private rooms with fireplace, includes excellent vegetarian dinner and breakfast. Composting toilets, book exchange, organic garden, sauna, hot tub, gym and water-slide. Cheaper with shared bath, D pp in dorm. Discounts for ISIC, seniors, SAE members and cyclists. Highly recommended, reservations advised.
C-D **Hostal Mama Hilda**, 100 m from centre of village on the way into town, T03-281 4814. A pleasant family-run hostel, sitting room with stove, large rooms some with fireplace, includes good dinner and breakfast, cheaper with shared bath, F pp in dorm, parking, warm atmosphere, horse riding and walking trips. Good value, highly recommended.
E **Hostal Cloud Florest**, at the entrance to town, 150 m from the centre, T03-281 4808, josecloudforest@gmail.com. Simple but nice family-run hostel, sitting room with stove, includes dinner (good local fare or vegetarian) and breakfast, cheaper with shared bath, hot water, parking, very friendly, helpful owners.

Sigchos

F **Residencial Sigchos**, Carlos Hugo Páez y Rodrigo Iturralde, T03-271 4107. Simple but clean, large rooms, hot water.

Isinliví

E **Llullu Llama** ('baby llama', pronounced zhu-zhu-zhama), T03-281 4790, www.llullu llama.com. Nicely refurbished house, cosy sitting room with wood-burning stove, tastefully decorated rooms, private, semi-private and dorm (G pp), good hearty meals, shared composting toilet with great views, hot water, organic herb garden, relaxing atmosphere, a lovely spot. Recommended.

Toacazo

C **La Quinta Colorada**, 3 km east of Toacazo on the road from Lasso (pickup from Lasso US$3 or bus Saquisilí–Toacazo and walk), T03-271 6122. Hacienda-style house with courtyard and fountain. Most rooms with fireplace, includes breakfast and dinner, tours to Cotopaxi, Ilinizas or Sangolquí market.

Saquisilí

D **Gilocarmelo**, by the cemetery, 800 m from town on the road north to Guaytacama, T09-966 9734, T02-340 0924 (Quito), carlosrlopezc@yahoo.com. Restored hacienda set in 4-ha. Rooms with fireplace, includes breakfast, restaurant, heated pool, sauna, jacuzzi.

🍴 Eating

Machachi and around *p506*

🍴🍴 **El Chagra**, take the road that passes in front of the church, on the right-hand side and it's about 5 km further on. Good local food.

🍴 **El Mesón del Valle**, near the Parque Central. Good food, helpful owner.

Latacunga *p508*

A local speciality is *chugchucaras*, a deep-fried assortment of pork, pork skins, potatoes, corn bananas, popcorn, and *empanadas* – the ultimate high-cholesterol snack. The best are at **Rosita Eloy Alfaro** 31-226 on the Panamericana, very popular.

🍴🍴 **Rodelú**, Quito 16-31 at the hotel, closed Sun. Good breakfasts, steaks and pizzas, popular with travellers.

🍴🍴-🍴 **Los Copihues**, Quito 14-25 y Tarqui, Mon-Sat 1000-2200. Good international food, 4-course set lunch, generous portions.

🍴 **Chifa China**, Antonia Vela 6-85 y 5 de Junio, daily 1030-2200. Good Chinese food, large portions, clean. Recommended.

🍴 **Pizzería Buon Giorno**, Sánchez de Orellana y Maldonado, Mon-Sat 1300-2300. Great pizzas and lasagne. Highly recommended.

Cafés

Café-Libro Volcán, Belisario Quevedo 5-56 y Padre Salcedo. Mon-Fri 1400-2200, Sat 1400-2000. Snacks, tacos, drinks, board games, a place to hang around.

Quilotoa Circuit *p509, map p509*

In **Zumbahua** meals are available at **Residencial Oro Verde** and **Cóndor Matzi** on Fri evening and Sat breakfast and lunch, at other times advance notice is required.

In **Quilotoa**, simple meals are available from **Hostal Pachamama** and **Cabañas Quilotoa**. Note that because of the water shortages, hygiene is often compromised. Drink only bottled water and eat only well-cooked food.

In **Sigchos**, there are several simple *comedores* in town serving set meals.

🍹 Bars and clubs

Latacunga *p508*

Kahlúa Bongo Bar, Padre Salcedo 4-56, on pedestrian mall. Wed-Sat 1900-0100.

🎉 Festivals and events

Machachi and around *p506*

Jul El Chagra, the annual highland rodeo, is held during the 3rd week of Jul.

Latacunga *p508*

23-25 Sep Fiesta de la Mama Negra Latacung's most important festival is held in homage to the Virgen de las Mercedes and the Santísima Tragedia. There is a very well-attended parade in which a man dressed as a black woman, the 'Mama Negra' is the focus of the celebrations. 'She' rides on a horse, carries a doll and changes kerchiefs in every corner. Another character is the 'Shanga', also painted as a black person and carrying a pig, a symbol of abundance. There is dancing in the streets with colourful costumes and masks. This festival is a good example of the syncretism of Andean celebrations: the reverence to the Virgen de la Mercedes, the role of the Santísima Tragedia, the saving force of the survivors of one of the eruptions of Cotopaxi, the celebration of freedom among the black slaves who escaped the plantations and moved to this area, the fight between Christians and Moors imported from Spain and probably much more.

Nov Fiestas de Latacunga Weekend before 11 Nov, these celebrations are similar to those of Mama Negra (see above). The elected officials of the municipality participate in this civic festival.

Quilotoa Circuit *p509, map p509*

Festivals in all the villages are quite lively. Life in these small villages can be very quiet, so people really come alive during their festivals, which are genuine and in no way designed to entertain tourists.

May-Jun Corpus Christi Very colourful celebrations are held in Pujilí for Corpus Christi (Thu after Trinity Sun and on to the weekend) with parades featuring masked dancers (*danzantes*), fireworks, parties, and *castillos*, 5-20 m high poles which people climb to get prizes suspended from the top (including sacks of potatoes and live sheep!). Saquisilí also has colourful Corpus Christi processions.

21 Jun Inti Raymi Festivities for the summer solstice are held in Zumbahua.

⊙ Shopping

Latacunga *p508*
Handicrafts
Regional items include *shigras* (finely stitched colourful straw bags) and 'primitivist' paintings. These are found in the markets, see below.
Azul, Padre Salcedo 4-20, on pedestrian mall, ceramics, bronze and wooden items.
La Mama Negra, Padre Salcedo 4-43, on pedestrian mall, a variety of crafts.

Markets
There is a Sat market on the **Plaza de San Sebastián** at Juan Abel Echeverría. Goods for sale include *shigras*, reed mats, and homespun wool and cotton yarn.
On Calle Guayaquil, between Sánchez de Orellana and Quito, is the **Plaza de Santo Domingo**, where a Tue market is held.

Supermarkets
There are 2 supermarkets: Aki, Av Rumiñahui y Unidad Nacional, southeast of centre; and **Rosim**, Quito 16-37, in the centre.

▲ Activities and tours

Latacunga *p508*
Tour operators
All operators offer day-trips to Cotopaxi and Quilotoa (US$35 pp with lunch and a visit to a market town if on Thu or Sat). Compare services, there have been reports of some tours being no more than transport to the site.
    Climbing trips to Cotopaxi, US$120-130 per person for 2 days (includes equipment, meals, refuge fees), minimum 2 people. Trekking trips to Cotopaxi, Ilinizas, etc, US$30-40 per person, per day.
Neiges, Guayaquil 5-19 y Quito, T/F03-281 1199, neigestours@hotmail.com. Day trips and climbing.
Ruta de los Volcanes, Padre Salcedo 4-55 y Quito, T03-281 2452. Day trips including to Cotopaxi via a more interesting secondary road instead of the Panamericana.
Selvanieve, Padre Salcedo 4-38, T03-281 2895, selvanieve1@hotmail.com. Various tours, climbing, also has an agency in Baños, runs tours throughout Ecuador.
Tovar Expediciones, Guayaquil 5-38 y Quito, T03-281 1333. Climbing and trekking, helpful. Fernando Tovar is a qualified mountain guide.

⊙ Transport

Machachi and around *p506*
Bus Bus stop for **Quito** is at Calle Barriga, 8 blocks south and 2 east of the park – *especiales* go to the Terminal Terrestre, US$0.75, 1 hr; *populares* to El Recreo, 2-3 blocks north of the *Trole* station of the same name, US$0.55, 1 hr. Buses for **Latacunga**, from the obelisk at the Panamericana, US$0.55, 1 hr.

Reserva Ecológica Los Ilinizas *p506*
Bus From Machachi to **El Chaupi**, every 30 mins from Av Amazonas opposite the market, 0600-1930, US$0.30, 30 min.
Pickup From Machachi to 'La Virgen', US$25.

Parque Nacional Cotopaxi *p507*
Bus Note that only vehicles from authorized operators who have a *patente* and take a licensed guide are allowed to take tourists into the park. Other vehicles are turned back.
    To get to the **main park entrance** and **Refugio Ribas** from Quito take a Latacunga bus and get off at the main access point. Don't take an express bus as you can't get off before Latacunga. At the turn-off to the park, Cooperativa Zona Verde vehicles run up to the car park before the refuge, US$25 for up to 5.
    From Machachi, pickups go via the cobbled road to El Pedregal on to Limpio Pungo and the *refugio* car park, US$35. From Lasso, full day trip to the park, US$60 return, arrange at Cabañas los Volcanes. From Latacunga, arrange with tour operators or with Hotel Estambul.
    To get to **Cara Sur** from Quito, **Agama Expediciones** offers transport to Albergue Cara Sur, US$60 per vehicle up to 5 people. Alternatively, take a Latacunga-bound bus and get off at Aglomerados Cotopaxi and take a pickup from there, US$15 per vehicle.

Latacunga *p508*
Bus On Thu many buses to nearby small communities leave from the Saquisilí market instead of Latacunga. The Terminal Terrestre has a tourist office, shops and a restaurant.
    Buses to **Quito**, **Ambato**, **Guayaquil**, **Quevedo** and regional destinations such as **Saquisili**, **Zumbahua**, **Chugchilán** and **Sigchos** leave from the Terminal Terrestre on the Panamericana. Long-distance interprovincial buses which pass through Latacunga, such as **Quito–Cuenca**, **Quito–Riobamba**, etc, do

not go into the terminal. During the day (0600-1700) they go along a bypass road west of the Panamericana. To get on one of these buses during daytime ask for 'Puente de San Felipe', 4 blocks from the terminal. At night the buses go along the Panamericana.

Cooperativa Santa, has its own terminal at Eloy Alfaro 28-57 y Vargas Torres, 3 blocks north of the Terminal Terrestre along the Panamericana, T03-281 1659, serves **Cuenca**, **Loja**, and **Guayaquil** via Riobamba and Pallatanga.

Quilotoa Circuit *p509, map p509*
Bus times are approximate owing to the rough roads. Buses may wait until full before leaving.

Zumbahua

Bus From **Latacunga**, many daily buses on the Latacunga–Quevedo road, 0500-1900, 1½ hrs, US$1.25. Buses on Sat are packed; ride on roof for best views, buy ticket day before.
Pickup From Zumbahua to **Quilotoa** costs US$5-10 depending on number of people; to **Chugchilán** US$30. You can also get a pickup from Quilotoa to Chugchilán, US$25. On Sat mornings many trucks leave the Zumbahua market for Chugchilán and pass Quilotoa.
Taxi Day trip by taxi to **Zumbahua** and **Quilotoa**, return to Latacunga is US$40.

Quilotoa

Bus From Latacunga **Trans Vivero** and **Ilinizas** daily at 1100, 1200, 1300 and 1400, US$2, 2 hrs. Note that this leaves from Latacunga, not Saquisilí market, even on Thu. Return bus to Latacunga around 0300 and 0500. Buses returning around 1300-1600 go only as far as Zumbahua, from where you can catch a Latacunga-bound bus at the highway. In addition to the above, buses going through Zumbahua bound for Chugchilán will drop you at the turn-off, 5 mins from the crater, where you can also pick them up on their way to Zumbahua and Latacunga.

Chugchilán

Bus From Latacunga, daily at 1130 (except Thu) via Sigchos, at 1200 via Zumbahua; on Thu from Saquisilí market via Sigchos around 1130. US$2.50, 3½-4 hrs. Buses return to Latacunga daily at 0300 via Sigchos, at 0400 via Zumbahua. On Sun there are 2 extra buses to Latacunga leaving 0900-1000. There are extra buses going as far as Zumbahua Wed

0500, Fri 0600 and Sun 0900-1000; these continue towards the coast. Milk truck to Sigchos around 0800. From Sigchos, through buses as indicated above, US$0.60, 1-1½ hrs.
Pickup On Sat also pickups going to/from market in Zumbahua and Latacunga. Pickup hire to Quilotoa US$25, up to 5 people, US$5 additional person. To Zumbahua US$30, up to 5 people, US$6 additional person. To Sigchos US$25, up to 5 people, US$5 additional person.
Taxi From Latacunga US$60; Quito US$100.

Sigchos

Bus From **Latacunga** frequent daily service US$1.50, 2-2½ hrs. From **Quito** direct service on Fri and Sun, US$3, 3 hrs.

To Pucayacu off the road to Quevedo, on Wed via Chugchilán, Quilotoa and Zumbahua at 0400, US$3.50, 7 hrs (returns Thu at 0930); and to La Maná on the road to Quevedo, via Chugchilán, Quilotoa and Zumbahua, Fri at 0500 and Sun at 0830, US$3.50, 6 hrs (returns Sat at 0730 and Sun at 1530).

To **Las Pampas**, at 0330 and 1400, US$2.50, 3 hrs. From Las Pampas to **Santo Domingo**, at 0300 and 0600, US$2.50, 3 hrs.

Isinliví

Bus From Latacunga daily (except Thu) at 1215 (14 de Octubre) via Sigchos and 1245 (Trans Vivero) direct, on Thu both leave from Saquisilí market around 1030, on Sat the direct bus leaves at 1030 instead of 1245. US$1.80, 2 hrs. Both buses return to Latacunga at 0330, except Sun 2 at 0700 via Sigchos, 1 at 1200 direct, Mon one at 1430, Wed 1 at 0700.

Buses going through Sigchos can be taken to make a connection to Chugchilán, Quilotoa and Zumbahua. Through buses to Isinliví go by Sigchos around 1300, US$0.60, 45 mins. To check schedules: www.llullullama.com.

Toacazo

Bus from **Latacunga**, every 30 mins via **Saquisilí**, US$0.50, 40 mins. Pickup from **Lasso**, US$3.

Saquisilí

Bus From **Latacunga** every 10 mins, US$0.30, 20 mins. From **Quito**, frequent service 0530-1300, US$2, 2 hrs. Bus tours from **Quito** cost US$45 pp. Buses and trucks to many outlying villages leave 1000 onwards.
Taxi From **Quito** charge about US$60, with 2 hrs wait at market.

● Directory

Latacunga *p508*
Banks Banco de Guayaquil, General Maldonado 720 y Sánchez de Orellana, ATM only. Banco del Austro, Quito y Guayaquil.
Hospital Hospital Provincial General, at southern end of Amazonas y Hermanas Páez, T03-2812505, good service. **Internet** Prices around US$1 per hr. **Laundry** Milenium, Av Rumiñahui y R Coronel, T03-2804486, US$1.50 kg, open daily, pickup service from hotel. **Post office** Belisario Quevedo y Maldonado. **Useful addresses** Immigration office, Juan Abel Echeverría y General Proaño, T03-2802595. **Police**, T101.

Baños and Riobamba

The town of Baños, with its beautiful setting and pleasant subtropical climate, is a major holiday resort. It is bursting at the seams with hotels, residenciales, restaurants and tour agencies. Ecuadoreans flock here on weekends and holidays, and foreign visitors are also frequent; using Baños as a base for trekking, volcano-watching, organizing a visit to the jungle, or just plain hanging out.

Although only 50 km from Baños, Riobamba is a climate-zone apart. This chilly highland city is located at the foot of the magnificent Chimborazo, the highest mountain in the country, and surrounded by other impressive peaks such as El Altar, Tungurahua, Carihuayrazo and Sangay. It is a perfect base from which to explore Parque Nacional Sangay and the Reserva Chimborazo. The famous Devil's Nose train ride also runs through this area and there are a number of indigenous markets worth visiting. ▸▸ *For Sleeping, Eating and other listings, see pages 523-530.*

Ins and outs

Baños is 180 km from Quito via Ambato. There is also a paved road to Baños from Puyo in Oriente. Riobamba is 190 km south of Quito and 250 km north of Cuenca along the Panamericana. In 2007, the direct road from Riobamba to Baños remained closed due to landslides and volcanic activity.

Baños and around ●●●●●●▲●● ▸▸ *pp523-530.*

→ *Phone code 03. Colour map 1, B4. Population 12,000. Altitude 1800 m.*

Baños is Ecuador's most popular highland resort. Situated on the eastern slopes of the Andes, its weather is warmer and more humid than most of the *sierra*. It has a relaxing subtropical feel, but can be cool during the rainy season (May-September). The **Manto de la Virgen** waterfall at the southeast end of town is a symbol of Baños. Other landmarks include the **Parque Central** and the **Parque de la Basílica**, where the **Basílica de Nuestra Señora del Agua Santa** is located. Pilgrims flock to Baños to visit this shrine. The paintings of miracles ascribed to Nuestra Señora are worth seeing.

Baños has a small, central Terminal Terrestre with frequent bus service from Quito, Ambato, Riobamba and Puyo. **i Tur** ① *Municipio, Halflants y Rocafuerte, opposite Parque Central, Mon-Fri 0800-1230, 1400-1730, Sat-Sun 0800-1600,* is helpful and has maps of the area, English spoken. **Cámara de Turismo** ① *16 de Diciembre y Ambato.*

Volcanic activity Baños is nestled between the Río Pastaza and the Tungurahua volcano, and is only 8 km from its crater. In 1999, after over 80 years of dormancy, Tungurahua became active again and has remained so until the present time (2007). The level of activity is variable, the volcano can be quiet for days or weeks. At times it vents steam or ash, and sometimes there are explosive bursts in which incandescent stones and ash are expelled – generally falling on the upper part of the volcanic cone.

The strongest eruptions of the current cycle, in which large amounts of ash and rocks as well as pyroclastic flows (dangerous mixtures of very hot gas and ash) were expelled, occurred in July and August 2006. Small communities on the west flank of the volcano suffered damage, but Baños was unharmed. Baños continues to be a safe and popular destination, and will likely remain so unless the level of volcanic activity greatly increases once again. **Note** When and if activity does increase, the Bascún valley and El Salado thermal baths are especially high risk areas.

Tungurahua is closed to climbers and the road from Baños to Riobamba is impassable because of debris flows, but all else is normal. From time to time, after heavy rains, debris slides down from the volcano and blocks the road from Baños to Ambato; it is usually cleared within a few hours.

Public safety Baños has traditionally been a safe town but there were a handful of incidents in 2006 and 2007, which will hopefully prompt the local authorities to take measures to improve public safety. Enquire with **i Tur** (see above) or at your hotel about the current safety situation in and around town. In particular, be aware that robberies have taken place along the trail to the Bellavista cross and along the cycling route from Baños to Puyo. Also thefts targeting tourists on Quito–Baños buses, take care of your hand-luggage on this route.

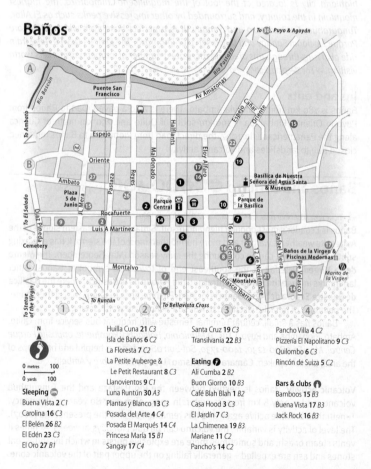

Huilla Cuna **21** *C3*
Isla de Baños **6** *C2*
La Floresta **7** *C2*
La Petite Auberge &
  Le Petit Restaurant **8** *C3*
Llanovientos **9** *C1*
Luna Runtún **30** *A3*
Plantas y Blanco **13** *C3*
Posada del Arte **4** *C4*
Posada El Marqués **14** *C4*
Princesa María **15** *B1*
Sangay **17** *C4*

Santa Cruz **19** *C3*
Transilvania **22** *B3*

Eating
Ali Cumba **2** *B2*
Buon Giorno **10** *B3*
Café Blah Blah **1** *B2*
Casa Hood **3** *C3*
El Jardín **7** *C3*
La Chimenea **19** *B3*
Mariane **11** *C2*
Pancho's **14** *C2*

Pancho Villa **4** *C2*
Pizzería El Napolitano **9** *C3*
Quilombo **6** *C3*
Rincón de Suiza **5** *C2*

Bars & clubs
Bamboos **15** *B3*
Buena Vista **17** *B3*
Jack Rock **16** *B3*

Sleeping
Buena Vista **2** *C1*
Carolina **16** *C3*
El Belén **26** *B2*
El Edén **23** *C3*
El Oro **27** *B1*

Hot springs and spas

The thermal baths which gave Baños its name are a popular attraction and well worth trying. Various sets of baths are located in and around town, of which we list but a few below. On holidays and weekends they can get very crowded. The brown colour of the water is due to its high mineral content. All charge US$1.60 unless otherwise noted.

The **Baños de la Virgen** ① *0430-1700*, are by the waterfall opposite the **Hotel Sangay**. The water in the hot pools is changed daily, and the cold pool is chlorinated. It's best to visit very early before the crowds. Two small hot pools are open in the evenings only (1800-2200, US$2); their water is also changed daily. The **Piscinas Modernas** ① *weekends and holidays only, 0800-1700*, with a water slide, are next door.

The **El Salado baths** ① *0600-1700* (several hot pools with water changed daily, plus icy-cold river water) are 1½ km from the centre, off the Ambato road. If walking from town, take a trail that starts at the west end of Martínez and crosses the Bascún river; the baths are at the top of the road on the west side of the river.

To complement the thermal baths, a growing number of spas are opening. Several hotels have spas and there are also independent spa centres and massage therapists. These offer a combination of the following services: sauna, steam bath, jacuzzi, clay and other types of baths, a variety of massage techniques and more. Some spas, such as the one at **Chalets Bascún**, have medical centres on the premises. ▶▶ *See Activities and tours, page 528.*

Around Baños

There are a number of worthwhile places that can be reached walking from Baños. The **San Martín shrine** is a 45-minute easy stroll from town and overlooks a deep rocky canyon with the Río Pastaza rushing below. Beyond the shrine, crossing the San Martín bridge to the north side of the Pastaza, is the site of the **Ecozoológico San Martín** ① *T03-274 0552, daily 0800-1700, US$1.50*, with a large variety of regional animals, in well-designed enclosures. Recommended.

You can also cross the Pastaza by the **Puente San Francisco** (vehicular bridge), behind the kiosks across the main road from the bus station. On the north side of the river, a series of trails fan out into the surrounding hills, giving great views of Tungurahua from the ridge-tops. A total of six bridges span the Pastaza near Baños, so you can make a round trip.

On the hillside behind Baños, it is a 45-minute hike to **La Virgen**, a statue of the Virgin, with good views of the valley below. Take the trail at the south end of Calle JL Mera, before the street ends, take the last street to the right, at the end of which are stairs leading to the trail. Along the same hillside, starting at the south end of Calle Maldonado, the path to the left leads to the **Bellavista cross**. It's a steep climb (45 minutes to one hour) and there are two cafeterias at the cross, both with unpredictable schedules. **Note** There were robberies along this trail in 2006, enquire before going this way. You can continue from the cross to Runtún.

Just east of Baños is the suburb of **Ulba**, by the river of the same name. Along the eastern bank a road goes up a short distance to the lovely waterfall of **Chamanapamba**, where there are cabins and a café. Trails continue from there along the Ulba.

Volcano watching The positive side of the reactivation of Tungurahua is that volcano watching can be enjoyed from Baños, Patate, Pelileo and several other nearby locations. With clear weather and a little luck, you can experience the unforgettable sight of mushroom clouds being expelled from the crater by day, and occasionally even red-hot boulders tumbling down the flanks of the volcano at night. In town, you can see the volcano from a small bridge over the Río Bascún, accessed from the top (west) end of Calle Ambato, but dangerous when activity is high. Several operators in town offer volcano watching tours, day and night, which take you to viewing spots outside town.

Central & Southern Sierras Baños & Riobamba

The road from Baños to Puyo (58 km) is very scenic, with many waterfalls tumbling down to the Pastaza. This paved road goes through seven tunnels between Baños and Río Negro. The gravel road runs parallel to the new road, just above the Río Pastaza, and is the preferred route for cyclists who, coming from Baños, should only cross one tunnel at Agoyán and then stay to the right avoiding the other tunnels (see Activities and tours, page 528). The area has excellent opportunities for walking and nature observation.

The first town you reach beyond the Agoyán generating station is Río Blanco, beyond which is the hamlet of La Merced with a lookout and a trail with a swing-bridge over the Pastaza going to the base of the lovely **Manto de La Novia waterfall**, on the Río Chinchín Chico. About a kilometre beyond is the *tarabita*, a cable car crossing the Pastaza to the village of San Pedro; it is powered by an old lorry engine, US$1. From the cable car you have nice views of the Pastaza and the **San Pedro waterfall** on the river of the same name. There are several other *tarabitas* along this road.

About 3 km beyond San Pedro and 17 km from Baños is the town of **Río Verde** (population 1070, altitude 1500 m) at the junction of the Verde and Pastaza rivers, with several snack bars, simple restaurants and a few places to stay. The Río Verde has crystalline green water and it is nice for bathing. The paved highway runs to the north of town, between it and the old road used by cyclists, the river was dammed forming a small lake where rubber rafts are rented for paddling. Before joining the Pastaza the Río Verde tumbles down several falls, the most spectacular of which is **El Pailón del Diablo** (the Devil's Cauldron). Cross the Río Verde on the old road and take the path to the right after the church, then follow the trail down towards the suspension bridge over the Pastaza, for about 20 minutes. Just before the bridge take a side trail to the right (signposted) which leads you to **Paradero del Pailón**, a kiosk selling drinks and snacks with viewing platforms above the falls (US$1). The **San Miguel Falls**, smaller but also nice, are some five minutes' walk from the town along a different trail. Cross the old bridge and take the first path to the right, here is **Falls Garden** ① *US$1*, with lookout platforms over both sets of falls and a restaurant.

There are excellent hiking opportunities up the Río Verde. The trail on the west side of the river begins near the **Miramelindo** hotel. This trail makes a good day trip. Some 2 km east of Río Verde is **Machay**, where several more waterfalls can be seen, another lovely area for walking.

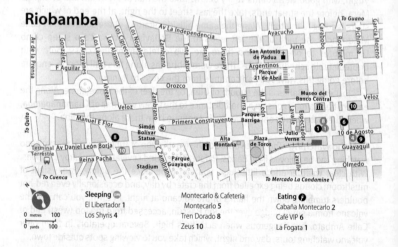

Riobamba

Sleeping 🛏
El Libertador **1**
Los Shyris **4**

Montecarlo & Cafetería
Montecarlo **5**
Tren Dorado **8**
Zeus **10**

Eating 🍴
Cabaña Montecarlo **2**
Café VIP **6**
La Fogata **1**

Riobamba and around ⬛🚲🏃❄🌀⛰🔔ℹ️ ▶ pp523-530.

➔ *Phone code 03. Colour map 1, B3. Population 160,700. Altitude 2754 m.*

Owing to its central location and strong highland traditions, Riobamba and the surrounding province of Chimborazo are known as *Corazón de la Patria*, the heartland of Ecuador. It is a pleasant, friendly city, if somewhat chilly with the breeze blowing down from Chimborazo. The centre has many nice colonial buildings and churches, and magnificent views of five of the great volcanic peaks. On market days (Wednesday and especially Saturday), the city lights up with the bright ponchos and shawls worn by the native people.

Ins and outs In Riobamba, buses from Quito, Guayaquil, Cuenca, Alausí and Ambato arrive at the well-run Terminal Terrestre on Epiclachima y Avenida Daniel León Borja. Buses from Baños and Oriente arrive at the Terminal Oriental, at Espejo y Cordovez. Tourist information is available from **i Tur** ① *Av Daniel León Borja y Brasil, T03-294 7389, Mon-Fri 0800-1230, 1430-1800, Spanish only*. The **Ministerio de Turismo** ① *3 doors from iTur, in the Centro de Arte y Cultura, T/F03-294 1213, Mon-Fri 0800-1300, 1400-1700*, is very helpful and knowledgeable, English spoken.

Sights Riobamba has several attractive plazas and parks. The main plaza is **Parque Maldonado**, with a statue to the local scientist Pedro Vicente Maldonado and some interesting wrought-iron fountains. Around it are the **Santa Bárbara Cathedral**, with a beautiful colonial stone façade and a nice but incongruously modern wooden interior, and the **Museo de la Ciudad** ① *Primera Constituyente y Espejo, T03-295 1906, Mon-Fri 0800-1230, 1430-1800, Sat 0800-1600, free*, in a beautifully restored colonial building with a number of inner patios. There are displays about regional national parks, paintings, photographs and temporary exhibits.

Two blocks north of Parque Sucre, the **Convento de la Concepción** ① *entrance at Argentinos y J Larrea, T03-296 5212, Tue-Sat 0900-1200, 1500-1800, US$2*, has been carefully restored and functions as a religious art museum. The convent takes up an entire block and is a veritable treasure chest of 18th-century religious art. The priceless gold *monstrance* (where the Host, holy sacrament for communion, is kept), **Custodia de Riobamba Antigua**, is the museum's greatest treasure, one of the richest

Mónaco Pizzería **8**
Puro Café **9**
Sierra Nevada **10**

of its kind in South America. It is solid gold and about 1 m high, ornately engraved and decorated with precious stones. The museum is well worth a visit. Guides are friendly and knowledgeable; a tip is expected.

The **railway station**, which was undergoing renovation in 2007, is west of Parque Sucre at Avenida Daniel León Borja y Carabobo. Nearby, is the **Museo del Banco Central** ① *Veloz y Montalvo, T03-296 5501, Mon-Fri 0900-1700, Sat 1000-1600, US$1*, which has interesting, well-displayed exhibits of archaeology and colonial art.

Four blocks northeast of the railway station, the **Parque 21 de Abril**, also known as **La Loma de Quito**, affords an unobstructed view of Riobamba and its five volcanic peaks.

Markets Riobamba is an important market centre where indigenous people from many communities congregate. Saturday is the main market day when the city fills with colourfully dressed *indígenas* from many different parts of the province of Chimborazo, each wearing their distinctive costume; trading overflows the markets and buying and selling go on all over town. Wednesday is a smaller market day. The 'tourist' market is in the small **Plaza de la Concepción** or **Plaza Roja** ① *Orozco y Colón, south of the Convento de la Concepción, Sat and Wed only, 0800-1500.* It is a good place to buy all sorts of local handicrafts and various types of authentic *indígena* clothing.

The main produce market is **San Alfonso** ① *Argentinos y 5 de Junio,* which on Saturday spills over into the nearby streets and also sells clothing, ceramics, baskets and hats. Other markets in the colonial centre are **La Condamine** ① *Carabobo y Colombia, daily, largest market on Fri,* **San Francisco** and **La Merced**, near the churches of the same name, both open daily.

Reserva Faunística Chimborazo → *Colour map 1, B3. See Transport, page 530.*

The most outstanding features of this reserve, created to protect the camelids (vicuñas, alpacas and llamas) which were re-introduced here, are the beautiful snow-capped volcano of **Chimborazo** and its neighbour **Carihuayrazo**. Chimborazo, inactive, is the highest peak in Ecuador (6310 m), and Carihuayrazo is also striking, but, at 5020 m, is dwarfed by its neighbour. Day visitors can enjoy lovely views, a glimpse of the handsome vicuñas and the rarefied air above 4800 m. There are great opportunities for trekking in the area and of course climbing Ecuador's highest peak and its neighbour (from where there are great views of Chimborazo). Horse-riding tours are offered along the Mocha Valley between the two peaks and downhill cycling from Chimborazo is a popular activity. Many agencies run tours here. A good map of the reserve, *Mapa Ecoturístico de los Volcanes Chimborazo y Carihuayrazo,* is published by IGM, see Essentials page 31.

Attractions and park services At the main park entrance from the Vía del Arenal visitors pay an entrance fee of US$10. From the entrance a gravel road climbs steeply for 5 km and gains 440 m in altitude to reach the **Refugio Hermanos Carrel**, a shelter at 4800 m. It has a guard, bunk beds with mattresses for 12, cooking facilities, running water, toilet; bring food and warm gear as it gets very cold at night. In about 45 minutes you can walk up to the **Refugio Edward Whymper**, another shelter at 5000 m; this was once at the foot of the Thielman glacier but it is now receding. The same facilities are available here, with capacity for 45. Do not take unecessary valuables to the mountain.

The access from Riobamba (51 km, paved to the park entrance) is very beautiful. Along the Vía del Arenal past San Juan are a couple of small native communities which grow crops and raise llamas and alpacas. The views are stunning. The *arenal* is a large sandy plateau at 4400 m, to the west of Chimborazo, just below the main park entrance. It can be a harsh, windy place, but it is also very beautiful; take the time to admire the tiny flowers which grow here. This is the best place to see vicuñas, either in family groups: one male and his harem, or lone males which have been expelled from the group. They are very shy so make sure to snap that photo before getting too close to them.

Devil's Nose train ride

① *The train leaves Riobamba on Wed, Fri and Sun at 0700, arrives in Alausí around 1100, reaches Sibambe about 1130-1200, and returns to Alausí by 1330-1400. It stops for a lunch break and returns to Riobamba by about 1800. From Riobamba to Sibambe and back to Alausí costs US$11; Alausí–Sibambe–Alausí US$7.80; Alausí back to Riobamba US$3.40. Tickets are sold the day before departure from 1400 or 1500 (queue up early, they sell out quickly), or the same morning starting around 0600.*

Riding the rails from Riobamba over the Devil's Nose (*La Nariz del Diablo*) is extremely popular with tourists and, increasingly, with Ecuadorean families. It makes a great day trip, the views are lovely, especially between Riobamba and Alausí. Seats are not numbered, so it's best to arrive early. Following a fatal accident in 2007, riding on the roof is currently prohibited but this may change. Never stand on the roof while the train is moving. Also remember that it gets cold early in the morning, so dress warmly. The best views are on the right. On the days when the train is not running, you can walk along the tracks down from Alausí; a pleasant day trip.

The train service has frequent disruptions and timetables often change; it's best to enquire locally about current schedules. During office hours information is available at the **railway administration office** ① *Espejo, next to the post office, T03-296 0115*, or at the **station** ① *T03-296 1909. At times when the tracks are in poor shape due to rain, an autoferro (a motorized rail-car) runs as a replacement for the longer train. Metropolitan Touring (see Tour operators, page 529) operates a private autoferro on the Riobamba–Sibambe route. They require a minimum number of passengers but will run any day and time convenient to the group, US$35 per person.*

Alausí → *Phone code 03. Colour map 1, B3. Population 9400. Altitude 2350 m.*

Some 84 km south of Riobamba along the Panamericana, Alausí sits at the foot of Cerro Gampala on a terrace overlooking the deep Chanchán gorge. From a hill, Loma de Llugchi, a large statue of San Pedro looks over town, there is a lookout here. The area enjoys a temperate climate and, in the heyday of the railroad, it was a popular holiday destination for Guayaquileños wishing to escape the heat. The atmosphere in the town is laid-back and friendly. The colourful Sunday market, in the plaza by the church, just up the hill from the station, draws *campesinos* from the outlying villages. **OMITUR** ① *Av 5 de Junio, opposite Municipio, T03-293 0154 (ext 105), www.sanpedrodealausi.com, Mon-Fri 0900-1600, Sun 1000-1400, helpful*, has pamphlets, maps and runs city tours.

Many tourists join the train in Alausí for the amazing descent to Sibambe, via the famous *Nariz del Diablo* (Devil's Nose), see above. In Alausí, tickets go on sale around 0930 at the train station, T03-293 0126.

⊜ Sleeping

Baños *p517, map p518*
Baños gets very crowded and noisy on public holidays, especially Carnival and Holy Week, when hotels are fully booked and prices rise. The town has lots of accommodation. Cheaper places are found around both parks, and north of Calle Ambato towards the bus terminal.
AL Luna Runtún, Caserío Runtún Km 6, T03-274 0882, www.lunaruntun.com. A classy hotel in a beautiful setting overlooking Baños. Includes dinner and breakfast and use of spa, parking, very comfortable rooms with balconies and superb views, lovely gardens. Excellent service, English, French and German spoken, hiking, horse riding and biking tours, nanny service available.
A Finca Chamanapamba, outside town, a 20-min walk from Ulba on the east shore of Río Ulba, T03-274 2671, chamanapamba@ hotmail.com. 2 nicely finished wooden cabins in a spectacular location overlooking the Río Ulba and just next to the Chamanapamba waterfalls, includes breakfast and dinner, very good café-restaurant serves German food.

A-C Sangay, Plazoleta Isidro Ayora 100, next to waterfall and thermal baths, T03-274 0490, www.sangayspahotel.com. A comfortable hotel and spa (open to non-residents 1600-2000, US$5), includes buffet breakfast, good restaurant specializes in Ecuadorean food, pool, parking, tennis and squash courts, games room, car hire, disco, attentive service, British/Ecuadorean-run. Recommended.
B Chalets Bascún, Vía El Salado, west of town, T03-274 0334, www.hosteriabascun.com. Comfortable cabins for 5, includes breakfast, good restaurant, pool, parking, spa, games.
C La Floresta, Halflants y Montalvo, T03-274 1824, www.lafloresta.banios.com. Pleasant hotel with large comfortable rooms set around a lovely garden, includes excellent breakfast, other meals on request, parking, friendly service. Recommended.
C Posada del Arte, Pasaje Velasco Ibarra y Montalvo, T03-274 0083, www.posadadel arte.com. Cosy inn, includes breakfast, vegetarian restaurant, pleasant sitting room, more expensive rooms have fireplace, terrace.

C-D **Isla de Baños**, Halflants 1-31 y Montalvo, T03-274 0609, islabanos@andinanet.net. Tasteful and comfortable hotel, includes European breakfast and steam bath, internet US$1 per hr, glass-enclosed spa open when there are enough people, pleasant garden.

D-E **La Petite Auberge**, 16 de Diciembre y Montalvo, T03-274 0936, reservation_banos@hotmail.com. Pleasant hotel. Rooms around a patio, some with fireplace, includes breakfast, good French restaurant, parking, quiet.

E **Buena Vista**, Martínez y Pastaza, T03-274 0263. Simple, nice multi-storey hotel, includes breakfast, private bath, hot water, clean, quiet, discounts in low season, helpful, good value.

E **Carolina**, 16 de Diciembre y Martínez, T03-274 0592. Restaurant, private bath, good hot water supply and kitchen facilities, very clean, terrace, discounts for longer stays, friendly, popular. Recommended.

E **El Edén**, 12 de Noviembre y Montalvo, T03-274 0616, hostaleleden@andinanet.net. Pleasant hotel with patio. Restaurant, private bath, hot water, parking, rooms with balconies, pool table, ping-pong. wheelchair-access.

E **El Oro**, Ambato y JL Mera, T03-274 0736. Includes breakfast, private bath, hot water, laundry and cooking facilities, good value, popular. Recommended.

E **Huilla Cuna**, 12 de Noviembre y Montalvo, T03-274 2909, yojairatour@yahoo.com. Good hostel and art gallery, decorated with paintings and antiques. Bright modern rooms, private bath, hot water, patio with fireplace and games.

E **Llanovientos**, Martínez 1126 y Sebastián Baño, T03-274 0682, www.llanovientos.banios.com. A modern breezy hostel with wonderful views. Comfortable rooms, cafeteria, private bath, plenty of hot water, cooking facilities, parking, very clean, nice garden. Recommended.

E **Posada El Marqués**, Pasaje Velasco Ibarra y Montalvo, T03-274 0053, posada_marques@yahoo.com. Private bath, hot water, cooking facilities, spacious, good beds, video room, garden, quiet area, renovated in 2006.

E **Transilvania**, 16 de Diciembre y Oriente, T03-274 2281, www.hostal-transilvania.com. Multi-storey building. Simple rooms, includes breakfast, Middle Eastern restaurant, private bath, hot water, free internet, good views from balconies, large TV and many movies in sitting room, pool table, luggage storage, popular, good value. Recommended.

E-F **Plantas y Blanco**, 12 de Noviembre y Martínez, T/F03-274 0044, option3@hotmail.com. Pleasant, popular hostel with lots of plants, a variety of rooms and prices, cheaper with shared bath and in dorm, hot water, free internet, excellent break-fast, fruit salads and self-service drinks in rooftop cafeteria, steam bath, classic films, bakery, French-run, good value. Repeatedly recommended.

E-F **Santa Cruz**, 16 de Diciembre y Martínez, T03-274 0648, santacruzhostal@yahoo.com. Pleasant modern hotel with 2 colourful buildings, comfortable rooms, breakfast available, private bath, hot water, free internet, cooking facilities, sitting room with fireplace, games, hammocks, book exchange, good value. Recommended.

F **El Belén**, Reyes y Ambato, T03-274 1024, www.hotel-elbelen.com. Good hostel, private bath, hot water, cooking facilities, parking, helpful staff.

F **Princesa María**, Rocafuerte y Mera, T03-274 1035. Clean spacious rooms, private bath, hot water, cheap internet, laundry and cooking facilities, popular budget travellers' meeting place, good value.

East of Baños *p520*

C **Pequeño Paraíso**, 1½ km east of Río Verde, west of Machay, T09-393 7981, www.pequenoparaiso.com. Comfortable cabins in lovely surroundings. Includes breakfast and dinner, small pool, nicely furnished, abundant hot water, vegetarian meals, climbing wall, camping possible.

D **Miramelindo**, outside Río Verde, just north of the paved road, T03-274 0836, www.miramelindo.banios.com. Lovely hotel and spa with pleasant gardens. Nicely decorated rooms, includes breakfast, good restaurant.

Riobamba *p521, map p520*

B **La Andaluza**, 16 km north of Riobamba along the Panamericana, T03-294 9370. An old hacienda with modern facilities, rooms with heaters and roaring fireplaces, includes break-fast, good restaurant, parking, lovely views, good walking in the area. Recommended.

B **Zeus**, Av Daniel L Borja 41-29, T03-296 8036, www.hotelzeus.com.ec. Restaurant, parking, modern, comfortable and nice. Bathtubs with views of Chimborazo.

C **Montecarlo**, Av 10 de Agosto 25-41 between García Moreno and España, T03-296

0557. Attractive house in colonial style, central, includes breakfast, restaurant, parking.

C Rincón Alemán, Remigio Romero y Alfredo Pareja, Ciudadela Arupos del Norte, T03-260 3540, www.rincon-aleman.com. Family-run hotel in a quiet residential area, includes breakfast, laundry and cooking facilities, parking, garden, sauna, fitness room, fireplace, German spoken. Recommended.

E El Libertador, Av Daniel L Borja 29-22 y Carabobo, across from the train station, T03-294 7393. Modern hotel, clean comfortable, ample rooms, private bath, hot water, rooms in back are quieter, opened in 2006.

E Oasis, Veloz 15-32 y Almagro, T03-296 1210. A small, pleasant, family-run hostel in a quiet location, private bath, hot water, laundry facilities. Some rooms with kitchen and fridge and shared kitchen for the others, parking, nice garden, friendly, pickup service from the Terminal. Recommended.

E Tren Dorado, Carabobo 22-35 y 10 de Agosto, near the train station, T/F03-296 4890, htrendorado@hotmail.com. Modern hotel with nice large rooms, early breakfast available in time to catch the train, buffet breakfast when there are enough people, restaurant, private bath, reliable hot water, friendly, very good value. Recommended.

E-F Los Shyris, Rocafuerte 21-60 y 10 de Agosto, T/F03-296 0323, hshyris@yahoo.com. An old-time budget travellers' favourite, cheaper with shared bath, hot water 0600-1000 and 1800-2200, decent rooms, service and value. Rooms at the back are quieter.

Reserva Faunística Chimborazo *p522*

A Chimborazo Base Camp, Totorillas along the Vía del Arenal, T03-296 4915, www.exped iciones-andinas.com. A beautiful lodge in a spectacular secluded valley at the foot of Chimborazo. Includes breakfast and dinner, very comfortable rooms, tasteful decor, heaters. Caters to groups, advance booking necessary.

E Posada de la Estación, Urbina, on the eastern slopes of Chimborazo, T03-294 2215 (Riobamba), aventurag@ch.pro.ec. A pleasant inn located in the converted station of Urbina; at 3619 m this was the highest point of the Ecuadorean railway. Good meals available, shared bath, hot water, clean, cold at night but dining room has a fireplace. Tours and treks can be arranged. Slide shows when the owner is in. Recommended.

E Gampala, 5 de Junio 122 y Loza, T03-293 0138. Restaurant and bar with pool table, private bath, hot water, refurbished in 2006.

E San Pedro, 5 de Junio y 9 de Octubre, T03-293 0089, hostalsanpedro@hotmail.com. Modern hotel with very comfortable rooms, cheaper in older section where rooms are adequate, private bath, hot water, parking, friendly owner, good value, best in town.

E-F Europa, 5 de Junio 175 y Orozco, T03-293 0200. Rooms vary from functional to comfortable, restaurant, cheaper with shared bath, hot water, ample parking.

⓭ Eating

Baños *p517, map p518*
There are restaurants for all tastes and budgets, many close by 2130.

Calle Ambato has several restaurants serving cheap set meals. Also along Calle Ambato between Halflants and 16 de Diciembre are several restaurants intended for foreign visitors, some with outdoor seating, serving international food at mid-range prices.

A local speciality is jaw-sticking toffee (known as *melcocha*) and the less sticky *alfeñique* made in ropes in shop doorways; also *caña de azucar* (sugar cane), sold in pieces or as *jugo de caña* (cane juice).

Ⓣ Le Petit Restaurant, 16 de Diciembre y Montalvo, T03-274 0936, closed Wed. Very good French cuisine, their onion soup is recommended, also vegetarian dishes, fondue, great atmosphere, Parisian owner.

Ⓣ Mariane, Halflants y Rocafuerte. Daily 1600-2300. Excellent authentic Provençal cuisine, large portions, pleasant atmosphere, good value, attentive service. Highly recommended.

Ⓣ Quilombo, Montalvo y 12 de Noviembre, Wed-Sun 1200-2200. Good Argentine grill.

Ⓣ-Ⓣ Buon Giorno, Ambato y Pasaje Ermita de la Virgen west of the market, and at Rocafuerte y 16 de Diciembre, Tue-Sun 1130-2230. Good, authentic Italian dishes, pizza, recommended.

Ⓣ-Ⓣ El Jardín, 16 de Diciembre y Rocafuerte, daily 1200-2200. International and some vegetarian food, juices, large sandwiches, also bar, good atmosphere and attractive garden.

Ⓣ-Ⓣ Pancho Villa, Halflants y Martínez, Mon-Sat 1230-2130. Very good quality Mexican food, good service.

¶¶-¶ **Pizzería El Napolitano**, 12 de Noviembre y Martínez, daily 1200-2400. Good pizza, pasta and antipasto. Also some Ecuadorean dishes. Pleasant atmosphere, pool table.

¶ **Casa Hood**, Martínez between Halflants and Alfaro, Thu-Tue 1000-2200, closed Wed. Largely vegetarian, but also serve some meat dishes, economical set lunches, juices, good desserts, varied menu including Indonesian and Thai. Travel books and maps sold, book exchange, repertory cinema, occasional cultural events. Popular and recommended.

¶ **La Chimenea**, Oriente y 16 de Diciembre, Wed-Mon 1830-2300. Good grilled chicken.

Cafés

Ali Cumba, Maldonado opposite Parque Central, daily 0700-1800. Excellent breakfasts, fruit salads, best coffee in town (filtered , espresso), muffins, cakes, large sandwiches (also take-out), book exchange. Pricey but good, Danish/Ecuadorean-run. Recommended.

Café Blah Blah, Halflants 620 y Ambato, Tue-Sun 0700-1900. Cosy café. Very good breakfast, good coffee, snacks and juices. Good music, popular, friendly meeting place.

Pancho's, Rocafuerte y Maldonado at Parque Central, daily 1500-2200. Hamburgers, snacks, coffee, friendly owner.

Rincón de Suiza, Martínez y Halflants, Tue-Sun 0900-2400. Snacks, drinks, coffee, cappuccino, good cakes and pastries. Pleasant atmosphere, books, games, pool table, ping-pong. Swiss-Ecuadorean run. Recommended.

Riobamba *p521, map p520*

¶¶¶-¶¶ **L'Incontro**, Av Lizarzaburu by the airport, Wed-Mon 1200-1500, 1800-2300. Exclusive Italian restaurant and *peña*, sicilian cuisine, meal of the day and à la carte.

¶¶ **Cabaña Montecarlo**, García Moreno 21-40 y 10 de Agosto, Tue-Sat 1200-2100, Sun-Mon 1200-1500. Set lunch and à la carte. Good food and service, large portions, 'old Riobamba' atmosphere, popular with locals.

¶¶ **Cafetería Montecarlo**, 10 de Agosto 25-45 y García Moreno, daily 0700-1200, 1600-2200 (0500 breakfast can be arranged before train ride). Ecuadorean and international, good breakfasts, snacks and complete meals, pleasant.

¶¶ **Mónaco Pizzería**, Dianiel León Borja y Duchicela, Mon-Tue 1530-2200, Wed-Fri 1400-2200, Sat-Sun 1200-2300. Delicious pizza and pasta, nice salads, very good food, service and value, recommended.

¶¶ **Sierra Nevada**, Primera Constituyente y Rocafuerte, Mon-Sat 0800-2200, Sun 1130-1600. Excellent value set lunch, vegetarian on request. Nice atmosphere, recommended.

¶¶-¶ **Palacio Real**, in the village of Palacio Real near Calpi, 20 mins' drive from Riobamba, 2 km from the Calpi-San Juan road, daily 1130-1500. A country restaurant specializing in llama meat served with quinoa, good food, large portions, they have a small llama museum and walking trails.

¶ **Café VIP**, Rocafuerte entre 10 de Agosto y Primera Constituyente, Mon-Wed and Fri 1200-1500, 1800-2200, Thu until 0100. Economical vegetarian set lunch, café in the evening, live music on Thu.

¶ **La Fogata**, Av Daniel León Borja y Carabobo, opposite the train station, daily 0700-2200. Good economical Ecuadorean food, set meals and breakfast.

Cafés

La Abuela Rosa, Brasil y Esmeraldas, Mon-Sat 1600-2100. Cafeteria in grandmother's house serving *humitas*, *quimbolitos*, and other local snacks. Nice atmosphere and good service.

Puro Café, Pichincha 21-37 y 10 de Agosto, Mon-Sat 0900-1330, 1530-2130. Very nice small European-style coffee shop, good coffee and sandwiches, a good place to hang out.

Alausí *p523*

Alausí is not the culinary capital of Ecuador, but a few places serve decent meals. There are some roadside eateries up by the highway and a good bakery opposite the train station.

¶ **San Pedro**, 5 de Junio at the **Hotel San Pedro**, set meals, breakfast.

🜊 Bars and clubs

Baños *p517, map p518*

Many bars are along Eloy Alfaro between Ambato and Oriente. **Córdova Tours** (see Tour operators below) has a *chiva* (open sided bus) cruising town, playing music, it will take you to different night spots.

Bamboos Bar, Pablo A Suárez y Oriente, at the east end of town, popular for *salsa, live music on weekends, unusual decor*.

Buena Vista, Alfaro y Oriente. A good place for salsa and other Latin music.

Jack Rock, Alfaro y Ambato. Popular traveller hangout, fantastic *piña colada* and juices.
Kasbah, Alfaro y Oriente, open 1900-0200. Latin music, pool table, snacks and pizza.

Riobamba *p521, map p520*
Gens-Chop Bar, Av Daniel León Borja 42-17 y Duchicela. Bar, good music and sport videos, open daily, popular. Recommended.
San Valentín, Av Daniel León Borja y Vargas Torres. A combination restaurant serving good Mexican dishes, pizza, and other snacks, bar and even disco with a mini dance floor. Very popular with locals.

⊛ Festivals and events

Baños *p517, map p518*
Oct Fiestas de Nuestra Señora de Agua Santa Held throughout Oct with several daily processions, bands, fireworks, sporting events and general partying.
Dec Fiestas de Baños Week-long celebrations ending 16 Dec, the town's anniversary, with parades, fairs, sports and cultural events and much partying. On the evening of 15 Dec are the **verbenas** when each barrio hires a band and there are many street parties.

Riobamba *p521, map p520*
Jan Fiesta del Niño Rey de Reyes culminates on 6 Jan after a period of **Pases del Niño**, parades in honour of the baby Jesus, which are carried out throughout Dec and the first week of Jan. On the eve there are fireworks and parties and on the 6th a street parade with floats which gathers thousands of people dressed up in costumes.
Mar-Apr Semana Santa, on the Tue of Holy Week, an impressive, well-attended, solemn procession is held in honour of El Señor del Buen Suceso.
21 Apr Fiestas de Abril, Riobamba's independence day, is celebrated for several days with lively parades, concerts, bullfights and drinking. Hotel prices rise and rooms may be difficult to find during this period.

⊙ Shopping

Baños *p517, map p518*
Book exchange
Casa Hood, Martínez y Alfaro. Rico Pán, Ambato opposite Parque Central and others.

Camping gear
Varoxi, Maldonado 651 y Oriente, quality backpacks, repairs luggage. Recommended.

Handicrafts
There are craft stalls at Pasaje Ermita de la Virgen, between Calle Ambato and Rocafuerte, by the market.
Las Orquídeas, Ambato y Maldonado, also at Halflants y Montalvo (**Hotel La Floresta**), large selection of nice crafts from the area and throughout Ecuador. Also sells some travel and coffee-table books.
Tagua. Nice tagua (vegetable ivory made of palm nuts) crafts can be found at 3 shops on Maldonado between Oriente and Espejo, where you can see how the tagua is carved.
Tucán Silver, Ambato corner Halflants, for jewellery.

Riobamba *p521, map p520*
Camping gear
Some of the tour operators hire camping and climbing gear.
Hobby Sport, 10 de Agosto y Rocafuerte, sleeping bags, tents, fishing supplies.
Protección Industrial, Rocafuerte 24-51 y Orozco, T03-2963017. For waterproof ponchos and suits, fishing supplies, ropes.

Handicrafts
Crafts are sold Wed and Sat, 0800-1500, at Plaza Roja, see Markets, page 522. There are several *tagua* shops on Daniel León Borja near the train station.
Almacén Cacha, Orozco next to the Plaza Roja, Tue-Sat. Cooperative of native people from the Cacha area. Good-value woven bags, wool sweaters and crafts, excellent honey.
Alta Montaña, Av Daniel León Borja y Diego Ibarra. Nice *tagua* carvings and other crafts, you can also see how the *tagua* is carved.
Artesanías Ecuador, Carabobo y 10 de Agosto. Good selection of crafts, ceramics, wood, *tagua*, straw.
Casa de la Cultura, Rocafuerte y 10 de Agosto. Crafts workshops (which you can visit) and store. Wood, knitted garments, and a variety of other crafts.

Supermarkets
Akí, Colón y Olmedo and Costales y Av Daniel León Borja, opposite Parque Guayaquil.
Camari, Av Daniel León Borja y Lavalle, p 1.

▲ Activities and tours

Baños *p517, map p518*

Warning A number of potentially hazardous activities are popular in Baños, including mountaineering and whitewater rafting, as well as adrenalin or extreme sports like canyoning, canopying and bridge jumps. Safety standards vary greatly, there is seldom any recourse in the event of a mishap, and you undertake these activities entirely at your own risk. Also note that some travel insurance policies may not cover such activities.

Canopying

Canopying or canopy zip line is like a Tyrolean traverse. It involves hanging from a harness and sliding from tree-top to tree-top, from tree-top to the ground, or across a gorge.

Canyoning

Canyoning involves rappelling down steep river gorges, above and in the water. Many agencies offer this sport, rates US$25-35.

Climbing and trekking

Possibilities for walking and nature observation near Baños and east towards Oriente are innumerable. Baños operators offer climbing and trekking tours to several destinations. Note that due to the reactivation of the volcano, Tungurahua has been officially closed to climbers since 1999. There is nobody to stop you from entering the area, but the dangers of being hit by flying volcanic bombs are very real. Unless volcanic activity has completely ceased, do not be talked into climbing to the crater or summit.

Cycling

A popular ride is along the scenic road east toward the jungle as far as Río Verde or Puyo. Cyclists have to go through the first tunnel at Agoyán, but not the following tunnels where you stay to the right along the old road at the river's edge; the views are magnificent and you get away from the traffic for those stretches. At Río Verde you can leave your bike at one of the snack bars (tip expected), while you visit the falls. You can continue to Puyo (4-5 hrs cycling from Baños); at any point along the route you can get on a bus to return

to Baños, the bike goes on the roof. **Note** Robberies have taken place along this route, do not take valuables and enquire about safety before heading out. Many places rent bikes but the quality is variable; check brakes and tyres, find out who has to pay for repairs, and insist on a helmet, puncture repair kit and pump. Bicycles from US$4 per day; moped US$5 per hr; motorcycles US$10 per hr.

Carrillo Hermanos, 16 de Diciembre y Martínez. Rents mountain bikes and motorcycles (reliable machines with helmets).

Hotel Isla de Baños (see Sleeping, above). Runs cycling tours with good equipment.

Horse riding

The area around Baños is suited for riding, several tour operators and independent riding guides offer tours. Check the horses are well cared for. Rates average US$5 per hr.

Hotel Isla de Baños (see Sleeping, above). Offers routes outside Baños, 3½ hrs with a guide and jeep transport costs US$25 per person, English and German spoken.

Ringo Horses, 12 de Noviembre y Martínez (Pizzeria El Napolitano). Good horses, offers rides outside Baños.

Massage and spas

Several hotels also have spas.

Chakra, Alfaro y Martínez, T09-355 6698. Swedish massage US$20 full body, US$12 half body, natural facials US$15.

Stay in Touch, Martínez between Alfaro and 16 de Diciembre, T09-920 8000. Massage, various techniques, US$20 per hr.

Puenting

Puenting, or bridge jumps, are similar to bungee jumping, but it is done with a harness attached to the torso and supported by ropes. The jumps are done from different bridges around Baños. Many agencies offer jumps, quality and safety varies. US$10-15 per jump.

Rafting

Note that the Chambo, Patate and Pastaza rivers are all polluted. Fatal rafting accidents have taken place (not with the operator listed). **Geotours**, see below. Half-day US$25-30, US$50 for full day (rapids and calm water in the jungle).

Tour operators

There are many tour agencies in town, some with several offices, as well as 'independent' guides who seek out tourists on the street, or in hotels and restaurants. The latter are generally not recommended. Quality varies considerably; seek advice from travellers who have recently returned from a tour. Most agencies and guides offer trips to the jungle (US$30-50 pp per day in 2007) and 2-day climbing trips to Cotopaxi (about US$130 pp) and Chimborazo (about US$140 pp). There are also volcano-watching, trekking and horse tours, in addition to the day trips and sports mentioned above. The following list is not exhaustive, there are many others.

Córdova Tours, Maldonado y Espejo, T03-274 0923, www.cordovatours.banios.com. Tours on board their *chiva Mocambo*, an open-sided bus to the waterfalls, Puyo, and night tours with music and volcano watching.

Expediciones Amazónicas, Oriente 11-68, T03-274 0506, www.amazonicas.banios.com. Run by Hernán and Dosto Varela, the latter is a recommended mountain guide.

Geotours, Ambato y Halflants, T03-274 1344, www.geotoursecuador.com. Whitewater rafting and other tours.

Rainforestur, Ambato 800 y Maldonado, T/F03-274 0743, www.rainforestur.com.ec. Santiago Herrera, guides are knowledgeable and environmentally conscious.

Riobamba *p521, map p520*

Climbing and trekking

Riobamba is an excellent starting point for trips to Chimborazo, Carihuayrazo, Altar, Tungurahua, Sangay and the Inca Trail to Ingapirca. For organized tours, transport and gear hire see Tour operators, below.

Cycling

There are good cycling routes in the Riobamba area, the most popular is a downhill ride from Chimborazo. Rates from US$10 per day for rentals, from US$35 per day for a tour including transport, guide, meal.

Alta Montaña, Julio Verne (see Tour operators, below).

Pro Bici, Primera Constituyente 23-40 or 23-51 y Larrea (if the bike shop is closed, try at the clothing shop across the street),

T03-295 1759, www.probici.com. Run by guide and mechanic, Galo Brito, bike trips and rental, guided tours with support vehicle, full equipment (Cannondale).

Tour operators

Most companies offer climbing trips (from US$150 pp for 2 days), trekking (from US$50 pp per day) and cycling tours (from US$35 per day). Many hotels also offer tours, but note that guides may not be qualified, they may not have permits and often they offer little more than transport.

Alta Montaña, Av Daniel León Borja 35-17 y Diego Ibarra, T03-294 2215, www.biking spirit.com. Trekking, climbing, cycling, birdwatching, photography and horse riding tours in the highlands, logistic support for expeditions, transport, equipment rental, English spoken. Recommended.

Expediciones Andinas, Vía a Guano, Km 3, opposite **Hotel Abraspungo**, T03-296 4915, www.expediciones-andinas.com. Climbing expeditions, operate Chimborazo Base Camp on south flank of mountain. Run by Marco Cruz, a well-known climber and certified guide of the German Alpine Club, German spoken. Caters for groups, contact well in advance.

Julio Verne Travel, El Espectador 22-25 y Av Daniel León Borja, 2 blocks from the train station, T03-296 3436, www.julioverne-travel.com. Climbing, trekking, cycling, jungle and Galápagos trips, river rafting, transport to mountains, good equipment rental, Ecuadorean/Dutch-run, uses official guides, English spoken, very conscientious and reliable. Recommended.

Metropolitan Touring, Lavalle y Veloz, T03-296 9600, www.metropolitan-touring.com. A branch of the Quito operator, rail tours, air tickets.

◉ Transport

Baños *p517, map p518*

Bus For main intercity routes see the bus timetable, page 470. Note that there have been numerous reports of theft on buses from Quito to Baños, be careful with your hand luggage. Consider taking a bus to Ambato and transferring there.

To **Riobamba**, note that the direct Baños–Riobamba road is closed, buses go via Ambato.

Puyo-bound buses stop at the corner of Av Amazonas (highway) and Maldonado, across Maldonado from the terminal. Some continue from Puyo to **Tena** or **Macas**.
Car hire Córdova Tours, Maldonado y Espejo. 4WD vehicles with driver, US$80 a day.

East of Baños *p520*
Bus From Baños to Río Verde, take any of the buses bound for Puyo from the corner of Amazonas (main highway) y Maldonado, across from the bus terminal, US$0.50, 20 mins. Córdova Tours offer a tour to Río Verde, stopping at several sites along the way, on a *chiva* (see Tour operators, above). For a thrill (not without its hazards), ride on the roof.

Riobamba *p521, map p520*
Bus To **Guayaquil**, goes via Pallatanga, really spectacular for the first 2 hrs. To **Baños** and **Oriente** (including Macas), from the Terminal Oriental. Note that because the direct road to Baños is closed, buses go via Ambato.

Reserva Faunística Chimborazo *p522*
The easiest way to visit the western side of the reserve is on a tour. There are no buses that will take you to the shelters. You can arrange transport with a tour operator or taxi from Riobamba (about US$25 one way). You can also take a bus travelling between Riobamba and Guaranda which goes on the Vía del Arenal (Flota Bolívar 8 daily, 0700-1800; from Riobamba US$0.90, 1 hr). Alight at the turn-off for the refuges and walk the remaining steep 5 km to the first shelter.

Alausí *p523*
Alausí terminals: **Coop Patria**, Colombia y Orozco, 3 blocks up from the main street, **Trans Alausí**, 5 de Junio y Loza. Note many through buses don't go into town, they have to be caught at the highway. To/from the Terminal Terrestre in **Riobamba**, every 30 mins, US$1.50, 1½ hrs. To **Quito**, 5 daily with **Patria** or 3 daily with **Trans Alausí**, US$5, 5 hrs. To **Cuenca**, 6 daily with **Patria** and at 1000 with **Trans Alausí**, US$5, 4½ hrs.

🌐 Directory

Baños *p517, map p518*
Banks Banco del Pacífico, Halflants y Roca-fuerte by Parque Central (no cash advances).

Banco del Austro, Halflants y Rocafuerte, next to Pacífico. **Cooperativa de Ahorros Ambato**, Maldonado y Espejo. TCs, 2% commission, Mon-Fri 0900-1700. **Don Pedro**, Halflants y Martínez, hardware store, open weekends, 3% commission on TCs. Also exchanges euros and other currencies.
Internet Many in town, US$2 per hr (more expensive than in most places in Ecuador). **Language schools** Spanish lessons in 2006 US$5 per hr. **Baños Spanish Center**, Oriente 820 y Julio Cañar, T/F03-274 0632, elizbasc@uio.satnet.net. Elizabeth Barrionuevo, English and German speaking, flexible, salsa lessons. Recommended. **Mayra's Spanish School**, Montalvo y 16 de Diciembre T03-274 2850, www.mayra school.com. **Raíces Spanish School**, Av 16 de Diciembre y Pablo A Suárez, T/F03-274 0090, racefor@hotmail.com.
Laundry Municipal washhouse next to the Virgen baths, US$1 a bundle, or do it yourself for free. Many laundrettes in town, US$0.80-1 per kg, minimum charge per load. Watch the scale. **Post office** Halflants y Ambato across from Parque Central. **Useful addresses** Immigration office, Halflants y Rocafuerte, opposite Parque Central, T03-274 0122. **Police**, T101.

Riobamba *p521, map p520*
Banks Banco del Pacífico, Av Daniel León Borja y Zambrano. **Produbanco**, Veloz y García Moreno esquina. **Hospital Metropolitano**, Junín, between España and García Moreno, T03-294 1930.
Internet Rates about US$1 per hr.
Laundry Donini, Villarroel, between España and Larrea, Mon-Sat 0830-1230, 1500-1800, US$0.40/lb. **Post office** 10 de Agosto y Espejo, esquina. **Travel agents** Diamante Tours, García Moreno y Veloz, T03-296 0124. For airline tickets.
Useful addresses Immigration, Av Leopoldo Freire (Av de la Policía) by the police station, Barrio Pucará, T03-296 4697. **Ministerio del Ambiente**, Av 9 de Octubre y Quinta Macají, at the western edge of town, T03-296 3779, Mon-Fri 0800-1300, 1400-1700. **Police**, T101.

Alausí *p523*
Banks Banco de Guayaquil, 5 de Junio near train station, ATM only. **Internet** US$1 per hr.

Cuenca and around

→ *Phone code 07. Colour map 1, C3. Population 340,000. Altitude 2530 m.*
*Cuenca is capital of the province of Azuay and the third largest city in Ecuador, with
something of a European flavour. The city has preserved much of its colonial ambience,
with many of its old buildings recently renovated. Most Ecuadoreans consider this their
finest city. Its cobblestone streets, flowering plazas and whitewashed buildings with old
wooden doors and ironwork balconies make it a pleasure to explore. In 1999 Cuenca
was designated a World Heritage Site by UNESCO. It remains a rather formal city, loyal
to its conservative traditions. Everything closes for lunch between 1300 and 1500 and
many places are closed on Sunday.* ▸▸ *For Sleeping, Eating and other listings, see pages 536-541.*

Ins and outs

Getting there **Mariscal Lamar airport** ① *Av España, T07-286 2203*, is a 25-minute
walk northeast of the colonial centre (city bus US$0.25, taxi US$2). Also along Avenida
España and five minutes' walk from the airport towards the centre, is the **Terminal
Terrestre** (city bus US$0.25, taxi US$1.50). Note that buses from the centre along Calle
Larga take you to the back of the terminal, which is not a safe area; taking a taxi to the
terminal is a better option. Using a taxi is recommended if arriving at night. The terminal
for local or provincial buses is at the **Feria Libre** on Avenida las Américas. Many city
buses also pass here, but that is also an unsafe area. ▸▸ *For details see Transport, page 541.*

Getting around The colonial centre is fairly compact and flat, making it easy to get
around on foot. The city is bounded by the Río Machángara to the north. The Río
Tomebamba separates the colonial heart from the stadium, universities and newer
residential areas to the south; there are a number of restaurants and night spots along
Avenida Remigio Crespo, a 20-minute walk from the centre. Beyond this district are the
Yanuncay and Tarqui rivers and to the south of them the *autopista*, a multi-lane
vehicular bypass. Avenida las Américas is a ring road to the north and west. Parque
Nacional Cajas can be seen to the west of the city.

Safety Cuenca is safer than either Quito or Guayaquil, but street crime does occur and
precautions are advised. The city centre is deserted and unsafe after 2300; using a taxi
is recommended. Areas where particular caution is advised after dark are, El Puente
Roto (south end of Vargas Machuca), Cruz del Vado (south end of Juan Montalvo), all
around the Terminal Terrestre and around the markets, especially Mercado 9 de Octubre.

Tourist information **Ministerio de Turismo** ① *Sucre y Benigno Malo, on Parque
Calderón next to the Municipio, T07-282 2058, Mon-Fri 0830-1700*. **Cámara de Turismo**
① *Terminal Terrestre, T07-286 8482, Mon-Sat 0830-1200, 1230-1800*. **Asociación
Hotelera de Cuenca** ① *Presidente Córdova y Padre Aguirre, T07-283 6925, Mon-Fri
0830-1300, 1430-1800*, provides a list of hotels but no prices.

Background

From AD 500 to 1480, Cuenca was a Cañari settlement, called Guapondeleg. Owing to
its geographical location, this was among the first parts of what is now Ecuador to come
under the domination of the Inca empire, which had expanded from the south. The Incas
settled the area around Cuenca and called it Tomebamba, which translates as 'Valley of
Knives'. The name survives as one of the region's rivers. Some 70 km north of Cuenca, in
an area known as Jatun Cañar, the Incas built the ceremonial centre of Ingapirca, which
remains the most important Inca site in the country (see page 534). Ingapirca and
Tomebamba were, for a time, the hub of the northern part of the Inca empire.

The city as it is today was founded by the Spanish in 1557 on the site of Tomebamba and named Santa Ana de los Cuatro Ríos de Cuenca. The conquistadors and the settlers who followed them were interested in the working of precious metals, for which the region's indigenous peoples had earned a well-deserved reputation. Following independence from Spain, Cuenca became capital of one of three provinces that made up the new republic, the others being Quito and Guayaquil.

Sights

On the main square, **Parque Abdón Calderón**, are both the Old Cathedral, also known as **El Sagrario**, and the immense 'new' **Catedral de la Inmaculada**. The former was begun in 1557, when modern Cuenca was founded, and was built on the foundations of an Inca structure; some of the Inca blocks are still visible. The New

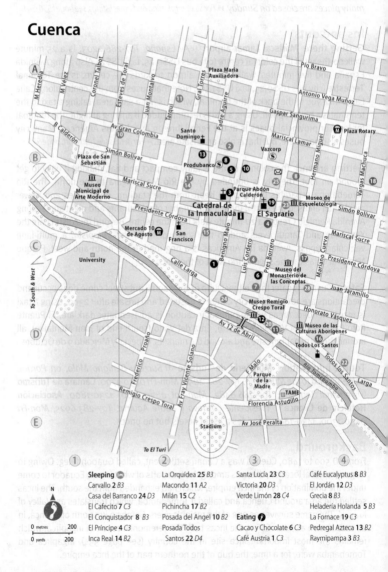

Cuenca

Cathedral was started in 1885 and contains a famous crowned image of the Virgin. It was planned to be the largest cathedral in South America but the architect made some miscalculations with the foundations and the final domes on the front towers could not be built for fear that the whole thing would collapse. Modern stained glass, a beautiful altar and an exceptional play of light and shade inside the cathedral make it well worth a visit. The Sunday evening worship is recommended.

Near the Old Cathedral, the **Museo de Esqueletología** ① *Bolívar y Borrero, Mon-Fri 0900-1330, 1500-1800, US$1,* has a small well-designed collection of bird and animal skeletons, from a hummingbird to an elephant. South of the cathedral and housed in a cloistered convent founded in 1599, the **Museo del Monasterio de las Conceptas** ① *Hermano Miguel 6-33, between Presidente Córdova and Juan Jaramillo, T07-283 0625, Mon-Fri 0900-1730, Sat and public holidays 1000-1300, US$2.50,* has a well-displayed collection of religious and folk art, and an extensive collection of lithographs by Guayasamín.

West of the centre, the **Museo Municipal de Arte Moderno** ① *Sucre 1527 y Talbot, on Plaza San Sebastián, T07-282 0638, mcmartem@etapanet.net, Mon-Fri 0830-1300, 1500-1830, Sat-Sun 0900-1300, free,* has a permanent collection of contemporary art an art library. Some of the exhibits of Cuenca's biennial international painting competition are shown here as well as other cultural activities worth attending.

Along the Río Tomebamba

From the centre, **las escalinatas** (steps) descend towards the river. Along the north shore is **El Barranco**, a bluff with picturesque colonial houses. It can be admired from **Parque de la Madre** and from a linear park along the opposite shore, a pleasant place for a stroll.

The excellent **Museo del Banco Central 'Pumapungo'** ① *Calle Larga y Huayna Capac, entrance on the far left of the building, T07-28 31255, Mon-Fri 0900-1800, Sat 0900-1300, US$3,* is on the southeastern edge of the colonial city, at the actual site of the Tomebamba excavations (see page 531). The ruins can be seen at the **Parque Arqueológico Pumapungo**, part of the museum complex. The **Museo Arqueológico** contains all the Cañari and Inca remains and artefacts found here. Although the Ingapirca ruins are more spectacular, it is believed that Tomebamba was the principal Inca administrative centre in southern Ecuador. There are also several other halls, book and music libraries, and free cultural videos and music events.

Tutto Freddo **10** *B3* Wunderbar **11** *D3*

Bars & clubs 🕐
Café del Tranquilo **4** *C3*
La Mesa Salsoteca **18** *B4*
San Angel **17** *C4*
Tinku **16** *D4*

The **Museo de las Culturas Aborígenes** ⓘ *Calle Larga 5-24 y Mariano Cueva, T07-283 9181, Mon-Fri 0830-1800, Sat 0900-1400, US$2*, the private collection of Dr J Cordero López, has a good selection of pre-Columbian archaeology and is well worth a visit. There are guided tours in English, Spanish and French.

Housed in a beautifully restored colonial mansion, the **Museo Remigio Crespo Toral** ⓘ *Calle Larga 7-27 y Borrero, Mon-Fri*, has various regional history collections, including gold objects from several indigenous cultures. It was undergoing renovations in 2007, but can nonetheless be visited.

Beyond the centre

Located on Calle las Herrerías, or the 'blacksmiths' road, across the river from the Museo del Banco Central, the **Museo de Artes de Fuego** ⓘ *Las Herrerías y 10 de Agosto, Mon-Fri (closed for lunch), Sat am only*, has a display of wrought-iron work and pottery. Also known as **Casa de Chaguarchimbana**, it is housed in a beautifully restored old building. Outside is a sculpture of a volcano and during the **Fiestas de Cuenca** (1-4 November) the god Vulkan, wrapped in flames, emerges from the volcano. There is also a shop.

South of the city, accessed via Avenida Fray Vicente Solano, beyond the football stadium, is **El Turi** church, orphanage and mirador, well worth a visit for the great views; a tiled panorama explains what you see. It's a 40-minute walk from the base to the church or two hours from the colonial city (not safe after dark); or take a taxi. There are good walks along attractive country lanes further south but do not take valuables.

Baños → *Colour map 1, C3.*

There are sulphur baths, 5 km southwest of Cuenca at Baños, with its domed, blue church in a delightful landscape. Water temperatures at the source are measured at 76°C making these the hottest commercial baths in the country, but bathing pools are at various temperatures. There are three complexes: **Rodas**, **Merchán** and **Durán** ⓘ *dawn-2100 or 2200, US$3.50*. The latter are by far the largest and best maintained and, although associated with the **Hostería Durán** (see Sleeping, page 537), the numerous hot pools and tubs and steam baths are open to the public. They are very crowded at weekends. The country lanes above the village offer some pleasant walks. City buses marked 'Baños' go to and from Cuenca; to walk takes 1½ hrs.

Around Cuenca 🚌🚗🚕 »» *pp536-541.*

Cuenca is surrounded by scenic countryside, where you are likely to see the 'chola cuencana' – women dressed in traditional costume, with colourful pleated skirt, lace blouse and Panama hat. To the north is Ingapirca, Ecuador's most important archaeological site. There is also much to explore in beautiful Parque Nacional Cajas, with over 200 lakes only a short ride from the city.

Ingapirca → *Colour map 1, B3. See Transport page 541. Altitude 3160 m.*
ⓘ *Daily 0800-1800, US$6, including museum and guided tour in Spanish 0830-1700.*
Two hours by road from Cuenca, Ecuador's most important Inca site lies just uphill from the village of Ingapirca, where there is an interesting Friday market and a good cooperative craft shop next to the church. Access is from the towns of Cañar or El Tambo, both along the Panamericana and both with poor options for sleeping and eating. If you wish to stay in the area, Ingapirca may be a better bet.

The road from El Tambo is paved and faster, while the Cañar road is recommended for the beautiful four-hour, 16-km walk down from Ingapirca; take water. The site has been administered by the local Cañari community since 2000 and, although still well worth a visit, it is a bit run-down. A small café serves cheap set lunches and llamas graze the grounds. Camping is permitted for free (bathrooms but no showers).

Although it is famed as a classic Inca site, Ingapirca, which translates as 'Wall of the Inca', had probably already been sacred to the native Cañari people for many centuries. It is also known as 'Jatun Cañar' (great Cañar). The Inca Huayna Capac took over the site from the conquered Cañaris when his empire expanded north into Ecuador in the third quarter of the 15th century. Ingapirca was strategically placed on the Royal Highway that ran from Cuzco to Quito and soldiers may have been stationed there to keep the troublesome Cañaris under control.

The site, first described by the French scientist Charles-Marie de la Condamine in 1748, shows typical imperial Cuzco-style architecture, such as tightly fitting stonework and trapezoidal doorways, which can be seen on the **Castillo** and **Governor's House**. The central structure may have been a **solar observatory**. There is considerable debate as to Ingapirca's precise function. From what remains of the site, it probably consisted of storehouses, baths and dwellings for soldiers and other staff, suggesting it could have been a royal *tambo*, or inn. It could also have been used as a sun temple, judging by the beautiful ellipse, modelled on the Qoricancha in Cuzco. Furthermore, John Hemming has noted that the length of the site is exactly three times the diameter of the semi-circular ends, which may have been connected with worship of the sun in its morning, midday and afternoon positions.

A 10-minute walk from the main site is the **Cara del Inca** (face of the Inca), an immense natural formation in the rock looking over the landscape. Nearby is a throne cut into the rock, the **Sillón del Inga** (Inca's chair) and the **Ingachugana**, a large rock with carved channels. This may have been used for offerings and divination with water, chicha or the blood of various sacrificial animals.

Inca trail to Ingapirca → *See Transport page 541.*

The popular three-day hike to Ingapirca on the Inca road starts north of the site at **Achupallas** (altitude 3300 m, one simple hostel), 25 km from Alausí in Chimborazo (see page 523). The route climbs to **Laguna Las Tres Cruces**, then goes past the peak of **Quilloloma**, the shore of **Laguna Culebrillas** and the ruins of **Paredones**. The walk is covered by three 1:50,000 IGM sheets: Alausí, Juncal (the most important) and Cañar. The name 'Ingapirca' does not appear on the latter, so you may have to ask directions near the end. A compass and good camping equipment are essential. Take all food and drink with you as there is nothing along the way. A shop in Achupallas sells basic foodstuffs and on Saturday you can buy fresh vegetables at the market. The trek is offered by tour agencies in Riobamba and Cuenca. You are likely to come across a lot of people begging, especially children, the length of the hike.

Parque Nacional Cajas → *Colour map 1, B/C3. See Transport page 541.*

ⓘ *Park entry is US$10, payable at the entrance gates at Laguna Toreadora, Laguna Llaviuco or Soldados. Information in Cuenca: Presidente Córdova y Luis Cordero, Edif Morejón, p 2, T07-282 9853, www.etapa.com.ec, Mon-Fri 0800-1300, 1500-1800.*

This beautiful national park, located 29 km west of Cuenca, encompasses easily accessible *páramo* and high-elevation forest. It is speckled with over 230 lakes, separated by rocky ridges, and has been a **Ramsar** wetland site since 2002. It is well managed because it is the source of Cuenca's drinking water. The park is relatively small (29,000 ha) but, although hundreds of Cuencanos go there at weekends, it is possible to find solitude, since most tourists do not travel far from the road. The park is a favourite with birdwatchers, trekkers and trout fishermen. Cajas is very rich in birdlife; 125 species have been identified here, including the condor and many varieties of hummingbird.

The park has two access roads. The paved road from Cuenca to Guayaquil via Molleturo goes through the northern section and is the main route for Laguna Toreadora, the visitor centre and Laguna Llaviuco. Skirting the park's southern edge is a poor secondary road, which goes from Cuenca via San Joaquín to the Soldados entrance and the community of Angas.

Travel is largely cross country, along trails or through the *páramo* grasses, so good maps are necessary. The following IGM 1:50,000 maps cover the whole park: Chaucha, Cuenca, San Felipe de Mollerturo and Chiquintad. Access to some drainages on the eastern edge of the park is restricted.

The park ranges in altitude from 3150-4450 m, so there is no permanent snow, but it is cold, especially at night, and it can rain, hail or snow. August and September are the driest months but hiking is possible all year round. The best time is August to January, when you can expect clear days, strong winds, night-time temperatures down to -8°C and occasional mist. From February to July temperatures are higher but there is much more fog, rain and snow. It is best to arrive in the early morning as it can get very cloudy, wet and cool after about 1300.

Attractions and park services **Laguna Toreadora** is in a high *páramo* area at 3870 m, with some attractive polylepis (quinoa) forest fragments around the shore. Along the main road is the **visitor centre** ⓘ *Tue-Sun 0800-1630, also Mon in high season*, the Centro de Interpretación Ambiental, a cafeteria with snacks and warm drinks (it also serves meals at weekends, including local trout) and the *refugio*, a basic shelter with bathrooms but no beds.

Laguna Llaviuco is in a cloud forest area at 3150 m, on the eastern side of the park. Three kilometres off the main road is a camping area, a dock and a cafeteria. There are no facilities at **Soldados**, the southern access point into the park

Trekking in the park For day walks, there are some marked trails near the visitor centre but they tend to peter out quickly. For overnight treks, adequate experience and equipment are necessary. Open fires are not permitted, so take a stove. A very strong hiker with a good sense of direction can cross the park in two days. Groups of eight or more must be accompanied by a naturalist guide, arranged through a Cuenca tour operator. Independent trekkers must register with the rangers, indicate the exact route they are planning and show a GPS and compass.

On the opposite side of Laguna Toreadora from the *refugio* is **Cerro San Luis** (4200 m), which may be climbed in a day; the views are excellent. From the visitor centre go anticlockwise around the lake; after crossing the outflow look for a sign 'Al San Luis', follow the yellow and black stakes to the summit and beware of a side trail to dangerous ledges. Beyond **Laguna Toreadora** on a paved road is the village of **Migüir**, from where you can follow a trail past several lakes and over a pass to **Soldados** (two days). It is also possible to follow the **Ingañán Trail**, an old Inca road that used to connect Cuenca with the coast. It is in ill-repair or lost in places but there are interesting ruins above **Laguna Mamamag**. You can access the Ingañán from the park headquarters or from Migüir, from where it is 2½ days' trekking to **Laguna Llaviuco**. From Llaviuco you might get a ride with fishermen back to Cuenca or you can walk to the main road in an hour.

⊜ Sleeping

Cuenca *p531, map p532*
There are many hotels near the Terminal Terrestre but most cater to short stays and the area is unsafe.
AL **Santa Lucía**, Borrero 8-44 y Sucre, T07-282 8000, www.santaluciahotel.com. Centrally located in an elegantly restored colonial house with 20 comfortable rooms around a patio, includes breakfast, smart Italian restaurant in the central courtyard, fridge, safe deposit box. Comfortable and very pleasant.

A **Carvallo**, Gran Colombia 9-52, between Padre Aguirre and Benigno Malo, T07-283 2063. Combination of an elegant colonial-style hotel and art/antique gallery, includes breakfast, restaurant, comfortable rooms, all have bath tubs, very nice.
A **El Conquistador**, Gran Colombia 665 (also at Sucre 6-78 y Borrero), T07-283 1788, www.hotelconquistador.com.ec. Modern hotel in the heart of the colonial city, includes buffet breakfast, good restaurant,

cafeteria, fridge, includes airport transfers. Avoid back rooms Fri and Sat because of noise from disco, good value.

B Victoria, Calle Larga 6-93 y Borrero, T07-283 1120, santaana@etapaonline.net.ec. Elegant refurbished hotel overlooking the river, includes breakfast, excellent expensive restaurant, comfortable modern rooms, good views, friendly service.

C El Príncipe, J Jaramillo 7-82 y Luis Cordero, T07-284 7287, htprince@etapaonline.net.ec. A refurbished 3-storey colonial house in the centre of town. Comfortable rooms around a pretty patio with plants, includes breakfast, restaurant serves lunch.

C Inca Real, G Torres 8-40, between Sucre and Bolívar, T07-282 3636, incareal@cue.satnet.net. Refurbished colonial house with rooms around patios, includes breakfast, restaurant serves Ecuadorean food, parking, comfortable.

C Nuestra Residencia, Los Pinos 1-100 y Ordóñez Lazo, T07-283 1702, www.nuestra residencia.4t.com. Small hotel in a residential area 10 blocks from the centre, includes breakfast, living room, bar, garden, friendly, good atmosphere.

C Posada del Angel, Bolívar 14-11 y Estévez de Toral, T07-284 0695, www.hostalposada delangel.com. A restored colonial house, includes breakfast, parking, comfortable rooms, sitting area in patio with plants, helpful staff. Recommended.

D Cabañas Yanuncay, Calle Cantón Gualaceo 2-149, between Av Loja and Las Américas (in Yanuncay), 10 mins by car from centre, T07-288 3716. Rustic cabins and rooms in a nice quiet country setting by one of the rivers (there may be mosquitoes), includes good breakfast, home-cooked meals available, ample parking, English spoken, friendly and helpful. Recommended.

D La Orquídea, Borrero 9-31 y Bolívar, T07-282 4511, www.hostalorquidea.com. Refurbished colonial house. Bright rooms, restaurant serves economical set meals, fridge, discounts in low season, good value.

D Macondo, Tarqui 11-64 y Lamar, T07-284 0697, www.hostalmacondo.com. Restored colonial house, includes breakfast, cheaper with shared bath, laundry and cooking facilities, pleasant patio, garden, very popular, US-run. Highly recommended.

E Casa del Barranco, Calle Larga 8-41, between Benigno Malo and Luis Cordero, T07-283 9763, grupobar@etapaonline.net.ec. Refurbished colonial house, some rooms have views over the river, breakfast available, cafeteria, most rooms with private bath, cheaper with shared bath, hot water, parking.

E Milán, Córdova 989 y Padre Aguirre, T07-283 1104, hotmilan@etapaonline.net.ec. Includes breakfast, restaurant, cheaper with shared bath, hot water, laundry facilities, view over market, rooms variable and some are noisy, but clean, popular and good value.

E Posada Todos Santos, Calle Larga 3-42 y Tomás Ordóñez, near Todos Santos Church, T07-282 4247. Nice, clean, tranquil hostel, includes breakfast, very good, friendly.

E Verde Limón, J Jaramillo 4-89 y Mariano Cueva, T07-282 0300, www.verdelimon hostal.com. 3 storey colonial house. Rooms for 1-4, includes basic breakfast, cafeteria-bar in open patio, shared bath, hot water, cooking facilities, sitting room with games and DVDs.

E-F El Cafecito, Honorato Vásquez 7-36 y Luis Cordero, T07-283 2337, www.cafecito.net. Colonial house, restaurant and bar in nice patio, cheaper in dorm, hot water, popular with travellers and noisy.

F Pichincha, Gral Torres 8-82 y Bolívar, T07-282 3868, hpichincha@etapanet.net. Shared bath, hot water, cooking facilities, spacious rooms but a little noisy on the street side. Helpful and recommended.

Apart-hotels and suites
Apartamentos Otorongo, Av 12 de Abril y Guayas, T07-281 8205, pmontezu@az.pro.ec. A 10- to 15-min walk from centre, fully furnished 1- or 2-bedroom apartments with kitchenette, TV, phone, wireless internet, parking. Daily cleaning service included, friendly owners, US$380-480 per month.

Baños *p534*
There are also a few cheap, basic *residencias*.
B Hostería Durán, Km 8 Vía Baños, T07-289 2485, www.hosteriaduran.com. Good hotel in the thermal baths complex. Includes breakfast and use of all facilities. Upmarket restaurant, well maintained and very clean pools (US$4 for non-guets), steam bath, gym, tennis courts.

Ingapirca *p534*
B Posada Ingapirca, 500 m uphill from the archaeologic site, T07-221 5116, T07-283 0064 (Cuenca). A converted hacienda with superb

views, includes typical breakfast with dishes such as *mote pillo* and *morocho*, good expensive restaurant and well-stocked bar, some rooms have fireplace, others have electic heaters, good service.

E **Huasipungo**, in the village. Basic, restaurant, shared bath, hot water on request.

E **Inti Huasi**, in the village, T07-221 5171. Basic, includes breakfast, restaurant serves cheap set meals, private bath, electric shower.

F **Ingañán**, in Achupallas (Chimborazo) at the start of the trek to Ingapirca, T03-293 0652. Private bath, hot water, meals on request, camping possible.

Parque Nacional Cajas *p535*

There is a *refugio* at Laguna Toreadora and camping at Laguna Llaviuco. Other shelters in the park are very primitive.

C **Hostería Dos Chorreras**, Km 14½ vía al Cajas, sector Sayausí, T07-285 3154, doschorreras@etapaonline.net.ec. Hacienda-style inn, outside the park. Carpeted rooms with heating, includes breakfast, restaurant serves trout fresh from the farm, reservations recommended, horse rental (book ahead).

🍴 Eating

Cuenca *p531, map p532*

Dining out in Cuenca can be expensive, but there are cheap *comedores* on the 2nd floor of **Mercado 10 de Agosto**, open all week. Av Remigio Crespo, between the stadium and the coliseum, has a variety of *pizzerías*, *heladerías*, sandwich places, steak houses, bars and discos. The area is popular with local young people and lively at weekends.

A very traditional dish in the Cuenca area is roast *cuy* (guinea pig). In town you can find it in one of the many *salones* along Av Don Bosco between Av Solano and Av Loja. For a more rural setting, go to Ricaurte, a 20-min ride north of Cuenca (bus along Av Sangurima), where many places offer this delicacy, **Mi Escondite** is recommended.

††† **El Jordán**, Calle Larga 6-111, T07-285 0517, www.eljordanrestaurante.com. International and some Middle Eastern dishes. Also serves an economical set lunch. Elegant decor.

††† **La Herradura Grill**, Remigio Romero 3-55 y Remigio Crespo, T07-288 7540. A well-established Cuenca grill. Excellent *parrilladas* and very good service.

††† **Molinos del Batán**, 12 de Abril y Puente El Vado, T07-2811531. Excellent *comida típica Cuencana* in a nice setting by the river.

†† **Café Eucalyptus**, Gran Colombia 9-41 y Benigno Malo, Mon-Fri 1700-2300, Sat 1900-0200. A pleasant restaurant, café and bar in an elegantly decorated 2-storey house. Large menu with dishes from all over the world. British/American-run, popular, recommended.

†† **La Fornace**, Borrero 8-29 y Sucre, Remigio Crespo 5-13 y Imbabura, and other locations. Good pizza and Italian food, attentive service.

†† **Las Tres Caravelas**, Hotel El Conquistador (see Sleeping). Good-value Ecuadorean and international fare. Live Andean music Sat-Sun.

†† **Pedregal Azteca**, Gran Colombia 10-29 y Padre Aguirre, Mon-Sat 1200-1500, 1800-2230. Very good Mexican food. In the **Casa Azul**, a refurbished colonial house with nice patios, live music Fri evenings.

†† **Raymipampa**, Benigno Malo 8-59, Parque Calderón, Mon-Fri 0830-2330, Sat-Sun 0930-2200. Very good international food in a central location, cheap set lunch on weekdays, fast service, very popular, can be hard to get a table.

††-† **Café Austria**, Benigno Malo 5-99 y Juan Jaramillo, daily 0900-2400. A traditional Cuenca café serving international food and great Austrian pastries, pleasant atmosphere, recommended.

††-† **Casa Vieja**, Pres Borrero 5-80 y Juan Jaramillo, Mon-Fri 0930-2400, Sat from 1700. Restaurant and bar serving economical set lunches, snacks and drinks in the evening. Live music Fri and Sat nights.

† **Good Afinity**, Av Ordóñez Lazo y Av Américas, Mon-Sat 1100-1500. Very good vegetarian food, cheap set lunch, pretty garden seating.

† **Grecia**, Gran Colombia y Padre Aguirre, Mon-Sat 1200-1500. Good-quality set lunch.

Cafés and bakeries

Cacao y Chocolate, Juan Jaramillo y Borrero. Chocolate in every imaginable form. Pleasant atmosphere at night.

Heladería Holanda, Benigno Malo 9-51, daily 0930-2000. Yoghurt for breakfast, ice cream, fruit salads, cream cakes. Popular.

Monte Bianco, Bolívar 2-80 y Ordóñez and other locations. Good ice cream and cakes.

Tutto Freddo, Benigno Malo 9-40 y Bolívar and half a block away at corner of Plaza Calderón, daily 0900-2200. Ice cream, pizza and sandwiches, popular.

🌙 Bars and clubs

Cuenca *p531, map p532*
Along Av Remigio Crespo are many night spots. Most bars and clubs open Wed-Thu until 2300, Fri-Sat until 0200.
Café del Tranquilo, Borrero 7-47 y Córdova. Pleasant popular bar, live music US$3 cover.
La Mesa Salsoteca, Gran Colombia 3-36 entre Vargas Machuca y Tomás Ordóñez, no sign. Latin music, very popular among locals and travellers, young crowd.
San Angel, Hermano Miguel 6-88 y Córdova. Popular bar and dance spot, live music, for a mixed-age crowd.
Tinku, Calle Larga y A Jerves. Live music on weekends, US$3 cover.
Wunderbar, entrance from stairs on Hermano Miguel y Calle Larga, T07-2831274, Mon-Fri 1100-0200, Sat 1500-0200. A German café-bar-restaurant, good coffee and food including vegetarian dishes. Nice atmosphere, a popular travellers' hangout, games, book exchange.

🎭 Entertainment

Cuenca *p531, map p532*
Art galleries
Galería Pulla, Jaramillo 6-90. Works by this famous painter, also sculpture and jewellery.
Prohibido Centro Cultural, La Condamine 12-102 in the Cruz del Vado area, T07-282 8094, Mon-Thu 0900-2100, Fri-Sat 0900-2300. Gothic-style gallery and bar. A striking place where artist Eduardo Moscoso presents his paintings of society taboos: sex, death and religion, to the sounds of heavy metal rock.

Dance classes
Cachumbambe, Remigio Crespo 7-79 y Guayas, above **Restaurante Charito**, T07-288 2023, Mon-Thu 1700-1800, 1900-2000, Sat 1400-1600. Salsa, merengue and more.

🎉 Festivals and events

Cuenca *p531, map p532*
Cuenca hosts the internationally famous **Bienal de Cuenca**, a biennial international painting competition. Exhibitions occupy museums and galleries around the city for 3 months starting either during the Apr or Nov festivities. The next *bienal* is due in 2009. Information from Bolivar 13-89, T07-283 1778.

Mar-Apr **Semana Santa**, on Good Fri there is a fine procession through the city and up to the Mirador Turi.
12 Apr **Fundación** is the anniversary of the foundation of Cuenca. Celebrations include fireworks at the Parque Calderón and various exhibits throughout the city including crafts and, on some years, the **Bienal**, see above.
May-Jun **Septenario** is a religious festival in the week leading up to **Corpus Christi**. On Parque Calderón a decorated tower with fireworks attached, known as *'castillo'*, is burnt every night after a mass, *'vacas locas'* or mad cows (people carrying a reed structure in the shape of a cow, with lit fireworks) run across the park, and hundreds of hot-air paper balloons are released. It's a spectacular sight, not to be missed. A traditional drink for this holiday is *rosero*, prepared with *babaco*, *chamburo* (star-fruit) strawberries, *mote*, orange leaves and cloves.
3 Nov **Independencia** celebrates Cuenca's independence, with art exhibitions, street theatre and dances all over the city including the **Puente Roto**, east of the Escalinata.
24 Dec **Pase del Niño Viajero** is probably the largest and finest Christmas parade in all Ecuador. Children and adults from the *barrios* and surrounding villages decorate donkeys, horses, cars and trucks with symbols of abundance. Young children dressed in colourful *indígena* costumes or as biblical figures ride through the streets accompanied by musicians. The parade starts about 1000 at San Sebastián, proceeds along Calle Simón Bolívar, past Parque Calderón and ends at San Blas. On other days around Christmas there are also smaller **Pase del Niño** parades.

🛍 Shopping

Cuenca *p531, map p532*
Camping gear
Apullacta, see Tour operators, hires out camping gear. To buy equipment: **Explorador Andino**, Borrero 7-52 y Sucre, T07-284 7320; and **Tatoo**, Av Solano 4-31 y Florencia Astudillo, T07-288 4809, www.tatoo.ws.

Handicrafts
The Cuenca region is noted for its *artesanía*. Good souvenirs are carvings, leather, basket-work, ceramics, painted wood, onyx, woven stuffs, embroidered shirts and jewellery.

There are many craft shops along Gran Colombia, Benigno Malo and Juan Jaramillo alongside Las Conceptas. There are several good leather shops in the arcade off Bolívar between Benigno Malo and Luis Cordero. At Plaza Rotary (see Markets, below) baskets, pottery and wooden objects are sold.

Artesa, L Cordero 10-31 y Gran Colombia, modern Ecuadorean ceramics at good prices. Several other branches around the city.

Centro Artesanal Municipal 'Casa de la Mujer', Gral Torres 7-33, T07-284 5854. Market with a great variety of handicrafts.

Colecciones Jorge Moscoso, Juan Jaramillo 6-80 y Borrero, T07-282 2114. Weaving exhibitions, ethnographic museum, antiques and handicrafts.

El Barranco, Hermano Miguel 3-23 y Av 3 de Noviembre. Artisans' cooperative selling a wide variety of crafts.

El Tucán, Borrero 7-35. Recommended.

Galápagos, Borrero 6-75. Excellent selection.

Torres, between Sucre y Córdova, or **Tarqui**, between Córdova and the river, for *polleras*, traditional *indígena* women's skirts.

E Vega, on the road up to Turi, T07-288 1407. Good artistic ceramics.

Jewellery

Prices can be high, so shop around.

Galería Claudio Maldonado, Bolívar 7-75. Unusual pre-Columbian designs.

Joyería Turismo, Gran Colombia 9-31. Recommended.

Unicornio, Gran Colombia y Luis Cordero. Good jewellery, ceramics and candelabras.

Markets

Markets sell mostly produce, but some crafts can also be found. Only a few are listed here. Watch your belongings at all markets.

Feria Libre, Av de las Américas y Av Remigio Crespo, west of the centre. The largest market, also has dry goods and clothing. Most activity on Wed and Sat, when people from outlying communities come to trade.

Mercado 9 de Octubre, Sangurima y Mariano Cueva, busiest on Thu. *Limpias*, ritual cleansing by shamans, are carried out here on Tue and Fri, interesting. Crafts are sold nearby at **Plaza** Rotary, Sangurima y Vargas Machuca, best Thu.

Mercado 10 de Agosto, Calle Larga y Gral Torres. A daily produce market with a food and drinks section on the 2nd floor.

Panama hats

Cuenca is a centre of the Panama hat industry. Manufacturers have museums explaining the hat-making process and offer factory tours followed by visits to their showrooms. Note there is a wide range of quality and prices; the finer the fibres used, the more supple and long-lasting the hat, and the higher the price.

Kurt Dorfzaun, Av Gil Ramírez Dávalos 4-34, near the bus terminal, T07-280 7563, www.kdorfzaun.com. A good selection.

Homero Ortega P e Hijos, Hermano Miguel y Córdova, also at Av Gil Ramírez Dávalos 3-86, T07-280 1288, www.homeroortega.com.

▲ Activities and tours

Cuenca *p531, map p532*

Tour operators

All operators offer city tours, trips to Ingapirca (US$35-45), trekking in Cajas (about US$35 pp per day), Gualaceo-Chordeleg crafts towns (US$45), Yunguilla-Girón (US$45).

Apullacta, Gran Colombia 11-02 y Gral Torres, p 2, T07-283 7815, www.apullacta.com. The usual tours, also hires camping equipment.

Ecotrek, Paseo 3 de Noviembre, between Jacarandá and Cedros, 3 blocks from **Hotel** Oro Verde, T07-2834677, ecotrek@cue.sat.net. Manager Juan Gabriel Carrasco specializes in shaman trips and climbing tours.

The Travel Center, Hermano Miguel 5-42, between Honorato Vázquez and Juan Jaramillo, T07-282 3782, www.terradiversa.com. Several tour operators under one roof with lots of useful information, helpful staff, library and bulletin boards. Recommended. **Biking** Adventures, cycling tours, US$43 pp per day. **Montaruna Tours**, horse-riding day-trips and longer tours; US$50 pp per day; **Terra Diversa**, Ingapirca, Cajas and other options, US$39-47 pp per day with fixed departures. Also sell jungle trips, Galápagos tours and flight tickets.

Trekking

There are excellent hiking opportunities in Parque Nacional Cajas (see page 535). Tour operators offer treks for about US$35 per day. **Club Sangay** is a walking and climbing club that meets every Tue at 2000 at Gran Colombia 7-39, p 2E. It organizes outings and welcomes visitors. Contact Victor Hugo Dávila, T07-286 8468, clubsangay@ hotmail.com, or through **Explorador Andino**, see Shopping.

Inca trail to Ingapirca *p535*
Tour operators in Riobamba (see page 529)
offer this 3-day trek for US$200 pp for a
group of 4, everything included. **Sr Gilberto
Sarmiento**, T03-293 0657 in Achupallas can
arrange mules and guides (US$10 per day
for each), but you must provide all the gear
and food for yourself and the muleteer.

Transport

Cuenca *p531, map p532*
Air TAME, Icaro and Aerogal fly from Cuenca
to **Quito**, US$68, and **Guayaquil**, US$49,
several daily, schedules change so ask locally.
    Airline offices Aerogal, Aurelio Aguilar y
Solano; also Av España by airport, T07-286
1041. **American Airlines**, Hermano Miguel
8-63 y Bolívar, T07-283 1699. **Continental**,
Padre Aguirre 10-96 y Lamar, T07-284 7374.
Icaro, Av España 1114, T07-280 2700. **TAME**,
Florencia Astudillo 2-22, also at airport,
T07-288 9581.

Bus For main intercity routes see the bus
timetable, page 470. For destinations around
Cuenca, see page 541. To **Guayaquil**, US$5,
either via Zhud, 5 hrs, or via Cajas and
Molleturo, 4 hrs. There are 2 bus routes to
Gualaquiza, in southern Oriente, either via
Gualaceo (see page 541) and Plan de Milagro,
or via Sígsig.

Car hire Bombuscaro, España y Elia Liut,
by the airport, T07-286 6541. **Localiza**, at the
airport, T07-280 3198, www.localiza.com.ec.

Ingapirca *p534*
Bus There are 2 direct daily buses from
Cuenca, with **Transportes Cañar**, 0900 and
1300, returning 1300 and 1600, US$2.50, 2 hrs.
Also from **Cañar**, corner 24 de Mayo and
Borrero, every 15 mins, 0600-1800, US$0.50,
30 mins; last bus returns from Ingapirca to
Cañar at 1700. The buses from Cañar go
through **El Tambo**, from where it is 20 mins,
US$0.40, to the ruins. If coming from the
north, transfer in El Tambo.

Inca trail to Ingapirca *p535*
Bus From Alausí to **Achupallas**, daily around
1400, US$1, 1 hr, a nice ride; also a truck daily
at 1200. Alternatively, take any bus along the
Panamericana to **La Moya**, south of Alausí, at

the turn-off for Achupallas, and a pickup from
there (best on Thu and Sun). To hire a pickup
from Alausí costs US$15, from La Moya US$10.

Parque Nacional Cajas *p535*
Bus From the **Terminal Terrestre** in Cuenca
take a Guayaquil-bound bus via Molleturo
(not Zhud), US$1-1.50, 30 mins to the
turn-off for **Laguna Llaviuco**, 45 mins to
Laguna Toreadora. Cooperativa Occidental
to **Molleturo** leaves from its own station in
Cuenca, at Lamar y M Heredia, west of the
centre. For the **Soldados entrance**, catch a
bus from Puente del Vado in Cuenca, daily at
0600, US$1.25, 1½ hrs; the return bus passes
the Soldados gate at about 1600.

Directory

Cuenca *p531, map p532*
Banks Banco del Austro, Sucre y Borrero.
Pacificard office at Bolívar y T Ordóñez.
Produbanco, Padre Aguirre 9-72 y Gran
Colombia. Vazcorp, Gran Colombia 7-98 y
Cordero. **Hospitals** Clínica Santa Ana, Av
Manuel J Calle 1-104, T07-281 4068. Hospital
Santa Inés, Av Daniel Córdova Toral 2-113,
T07-281 7888, Dr Jaime Moreno Aguilar speaks
English. Hospital Monte Sinai, Miguel Cordero
6-111 y Av Solano, near the stadium, T07-288
5595, English-speaking physicians. **Language
schools** Spanish classes US$6-10 per hr.
CEDEI (Centers For Interamerican Studies),
Tarqui 13-45 y Pío Bravo, T07-283 9003,
www.cedei.org. Spanish and Quichua, Hostal
Macondo attached, internet. Recommended.
Centro Abraham Lincoln, Borrero 5-18 y
Honorato Vásquez, T07- 282 3898. Small
Spanish language section. Estudio
Internacional Sampere, Hermano Miguel 3-43
y Calle Larga, T07-2841986, samperec@
samperecen.com.ec. Upmarket. Sí Centro de
Español e Inglés, Padre Aguirre 9-43 y Bolívar,
T07-2820429, www.sicentrospanish
school.com. Good teachers, competitive prices,
helpful and enthusiastic. Recommended.
Laundry Fast Klin, Hermano Miguel 4-21 y
Calle Larga. Lavandería, Manuel Vega y Sucre.
Self-service. **Post office** Gran Colombia y
Borrero, T07-283 8311. **Useful addresses**
Emergencies, T911. Immigration, Av Ordóñez
Lazo y Los Cipreces, Edif Astudillo, T07-283
1020. For tourist visa extensions, Mon-Fri
0800-1230, 1500-1830. Police, T101.

Loja and Vilcabamba to Peru

The province of Loja is a land of irregular topography, where the two distinct cordilleras further north give way to a maze of smaller ranges which barely reach 3000 m. Many warm valleys lie between these hills. Beautiful Parque Nacional Podocarpus is the ideal place to visit the cloudforests, which have made Loja famous since colonial days when chinchona, *the bark from which quinine is extracted, was first described here.*

Vilcabamba, once an isolated village although it is only 38 km south of the city of Loja, is today the rainbow at the end of Ecuador's gringo trail. It has an ideal climate and idyllic surroundings which combine to create a special feeling of tranquillity. The town and surroundings are equally popular with Lojanos out on a weekend excursion, with travellers en route from Ecuador to Peru or vice-versa, and with expatriate residents.

Beyond Loja and Vilcabamba are various border crossings, which provide access to different areas in northern Peru. ▸▸ *For Sleeping, Eating and other listings, see pages 548-552.*

Cuenca to Loja 🏨🍴🚲🌐📧 ▸▸ *pp548-552. Colour map 1, C3.*

The road from Cuenca south to Loja is fully paved, though several spots are prone to perennial potholes and landslides. It passes through bare, sparsely populated country and offers lovely views. After crossing the deep canyon of the Río León, it climbs steadily before reaching Saraguro, 130 km south of Cuenca and 70 km north of Loja.

Saraguro → *Phone code 07. Colour map 6, B3. Population 7500. Altitude 2500 m. www.saraguros.com.*

This is a cold town, famed for its weaving and for its distinctive indigenous population, the most southerly Andean group in Ecuador. Saraguros dress all in black and, on special occasions, wear very broad flat-brimmed hard felt hats. The men are notable for their black knee-length shorts, and the women for their pleated black skirts, necklaces of coloured beads and silver *topos*, ornate pins fastening their shawls. Above the altar of the church, with its imposing stone façade, are inscribed the three Inca commandments in Quichua: *"Ama Killa, Ama Llulla, Ama Shua".* Do not be lazy, do not lie, do not steal.

Saraguro is developing community tourism, with a craft fair planned for every second Sunday, and home-stay opportunities including meals and activities with native families. Contact **Fundación Kawsay** ① *18 de Noviembre y Av Loja, T07-220 0331, www.kawsay.org,* or the **Oficina Municipal de Turismo** ① *Calle José María Vivar on the main plaza, T07-220 0100 ext 18, turismosaraguro@yahoo.es, Mon-Fri 0800-1200, 1400-1800.* There is also good birdwatching in the area.

Loja 🏨🍴🏠🌐📧🏔️📷☎️ ▸▸ *pp548-552.*

→ *Phone code 07. Colour map 1, C3 Population 165,000. Altitude: 2060 m.*

This friendly pleasant city, encircled by hills, is the capital of the eponymous province. It is a colonial city, founded on its present site in 1548. The central market is the cleanest in all of Ecuador and Loja has won awards for its beautiful parks and for its recycling programme. For visitors, Loja is an important transportation hub and offers access to Parque Nacional Podocarpus, Vilcabamba and various border crossings to Peru.

Ins and outs

Getting there The city can be reached by air from Quito to **Catamayo** (also known as La Toma), which is 35 km away by paved road. From the airport shared taxis cost US$4 per person to Loja; taxi US$16. Taxi drivers going to the airport are often found outside the **TAME** office in Loja, or arrange the day before (eg with Señor Hugo Martínez, T07-258 1769) and they will pick you up at your hotel.

The well-organized **Terminal Terrestre**, Avenida Gran Colombia e Isidro Ayora, is to the north of the centre. At the terminal are luggage storage, a bus information desk, shops, restaurants, internet and **Pacifictel** office. There are frequent city buses to the centre; a taxi costs US$1. ▸▸ *For further information, see Transport, page 551.*

Tourist information iTur ① *José Antonio Eguiguren y Bolívar, Parque Central, T07-258 1251 ext 220, www.municipiodeloja.gov.ec, Mon-Fri 0800-1300, 1500-1800, Sat 0900-1200*, has local and regional information and maps. The staff are helpful and speak some English. The **Ministerio de Turismo** ① *Bolívar 12-39, between Mercadillo and Lourdes, p 3, Parque San Sebastián, T07-257 2964, fronterasur@turismo.gov.ec, Mon-Fri 0830-1330, 1430-1700*, has information for all of Ecuador, Spanish only.

Sights

Loja has a reasonably preserved centre, bound by the Río Malacatos and Río Zamora. Around the **Parque Central** are the cathedral, with painted interior and carved wooden choir, and the **Centro Cultural Loja**. The latter is housed in a beautifully restored house and is home to the **Museo del Banco Central** ① *10 de Agosto 13-30 y Bolívar, T07-257 3004, Mon-Fri 0900-1300, 1400-1700, US$0.40*, with good displays on archaeology, ethnography, art and history.

The **Parque de San Sebastián**, at Bolívar y Mercadillo, has a tall Moorish clock tower. This square and the adjoining Calle Lourdes preserve the flavour of old Loja. At Puente Bolívar, by the northern entrance to town **La Puerta de la Ciudad** ① *Mon-Fri 0830-2130, Sat-Sun 0900-2130*, is a fortress-like monument and a lookout over the city. It has art exhibits and a small café, a good place to take pictures.

Parque Nacional Podocarpus ● ▸▸ *pp548-552.*

→ *Colour map 1, C3.*

Spanning elevations of 950-3700 m, Podocarpus is one of the most diverse protected areas in the world. It is particularly rich in birdlife, including many rarities; there could be up to 800 species in the park. It also includes one of the last major habitats for the spectacled bear and protects stands of *romerillo* or podocarpus, a large native conifer. The park is divided into two areas, an upper premontane section with spectacular walking country, lush tropical cloudforest and excellent birdwatching, and a lower subtropical section acessed from Zamora (65 km east of Loja on a paved road), with remote areas of virgin rainforest and unmatched quantities of flora and fauna.

Ins and outs

Getting there The park is easily accessed at several points. From Loja, entrance to the upper section of the park is easiest at **Cajanuma**, 8 km south along the road to Vilcabamba, or **San Francisco**, 24 km east along the road to Zamora. For Cajanuma, take a Vilcabamba-bound van (US$1) or *taxiruta* (US$1.20), and get off at the turn-off, from where it is an 8 km uphill walk to the *refugio*. A taxi to the *refugio* from Loja costs about US$10, but may not be feasible after heavy rain. Alternatively, take a tour from Loja.

The southwestern section of the park can also be accessed via trails from Vilcabamba (see page 546). The entrance to the lower subtropical section of the park is at **Bombuscaro**, 6 km from Zamora.

Tourist information Park entry is US$10, valid for five days. Information is provided by the **Ministerio del Ambiente** ① *Sucre 04-55, between Quito and Imbabura, Loja, T07-257 9595, podocam@easynet.net.ec, also Zamora T07-260 6606.*

Valley of the immortals?

At the time a tiny isolated village, Vilcabamba attracted international attention in the 1960s when researchers announced that it was home to one of the oldest living populations in the world. It was said that people here often lived well over 100 years, some as old as 135.

Although doubt was subsequently cast on some of this data, there is still an unquestionably high incidence of healthy, active elders in Vilcabamba. It is not unusual to find people in their 70s and 80s working in the fields and covering several miles a day to get there. Such longevity and vitality has been ascribed to the area's famously healthy climate and excellent drinking water, but other factors must also be involved: perhaps physical activity, diet and lack of stress.

Attracted in part by Vilcabamba's reputation for nurturing a long and tranquil life, a number of outsiders –

both Ecuadoreans and foreigners – settled in the area. Some followed the footsteps of Doctor Johnny Lovewisdom, a California-born ascetic who arrived around 1969 to establish his "Pristine Order of Paradisiacal Perfection". Others just came for a few days and never left.

For a time drugs were in vogue in Vilcabamba, especially a halluci-nogenic cactus extract called *San Pedrillo*. Later, the fashion was UFO sightings, and the most recent trend has been real-estate speculation. Through it all, more and more expatriates continue to arrive, each for their own private reasons. As a group, however, their presence is inevitably changing the town.

Do you think the outsiders will still be able to benefit from the unique serenity of the 'valley of the immortals'? Or have we brought with us the seeds of our own destruction?

Attractions and park services

Both the highland and lowland areas can be quite wet, making rubber boots an asset. There are sometimes periods of dry weather from October to January. The upper section is also very cold, so warm clothing and waterproofs are indispensable year-round.

Cajanuma has cabins with beds and mattresses. This is the trailhead for the eight-hour hike to **Lagunas del Compadre**, 12 lakes set amidst rock cliffs; camping is possible there. At **San Francisco**, the ranger's station offers nice accommodation. This section of the park is a transition cloud forest area at around 2160 m, very rich in birdlife. It is also the best place to see the podocarpus trees. A trail (four hours return) goes from the rangers' station to the small but impressive stand of podocarpus.

At **Bombuscaro**, outside Zamora, are basic facilities at the visitor centre where you can stay or camp, but you must bring your own food, sleeping bag, mosquito protection etc. Halfway from Zamora to the park entrance is **Copalinga**, an 100-ha private reserve with forest, good trails and excellent birdwatching. There are comfortable cabins on site and delicious meals available if arranged in advance. ▸▸ *See Sleeping, page 548.*

Vilcabamba 🚌🚗❄🔲🔺🚪🛈 ▸▸ *pp548-552.*

→ *Phone code 07. Colour map 1, C3. Population 4300. Altitude 1580 m. www.vilcabamba.org.*

Once an isolated village, Vilcabamba has become increasingly popular with *Lojaños* on a weekend excursion as well as foreign visitors and expats. It is a 'must' along the gringo trail from Ecuador to Peru or vice versa. There are many excellent places to stay and several good restaurants. The town has a pleasant well-kept plaza where you can find orchids on the trees. Around it are the church, several open-air cafés and restaurants and well-stocked shops. The area around Vilcabamba is very beautiful and tranquil, with an agreeable climate. There are many great day-walks and longer treks throughout the area, as well as ample opportunities for horse riding. A number of lovely private nature reserves are situated east of Vilcabamba, towards Parque Nacional Podocarpus. Above all, Vilcabamba is a great place to relax, pamper yourself and enjoy nature.

Ins and outs

Vilcabamba is 38 km south of Loja along a paved road and about 150 km on a rough gravel road from the border with Peru at La Balsa (south of Zumba). There are vans and shared taxis from Loja and bus service from Zumba. Tourist information is available from **iTur** ① *Diego Vaca de Vega y Bolívar, corner of the main plaza, T07-264 0090, daily 0800-1300, 1500-1800*, which has various pamphlets; staff are friendly and helpful.

Walks around Vilcabamba

The area around Vilcabamba is splendid for excursions, with crystal-clear rivers that invite you for a dip. Follow any of the roads out of town and discover how the locals stay young in their sugarcane fields, coffee plantations or fruit orchards. You will be rewarded with lovely views and you might stumble onto a working *trapiche*, where you can sample the freshly squeezed cane juice. **Hostería Izhcayluma** (see Sleeping, page 548) has a set of hiking maps and route descriptions. Various operators offer horse riding or walking tours to lookouts and waterfalls near town as well as longer trips to private reserves in the foothills to the east. Trekkers can continue on foot through orchid-clad cloudforests to the

Central & Southern Sierras Loja & Vilcabamba to Peru

Vilcabamba

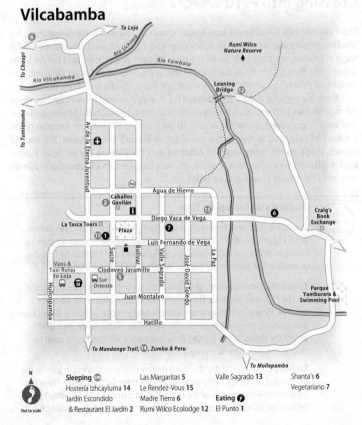

N
Not to scale

Sleeping 🛏
Hostería Izhcayluma **14**
Jardín Escondido
& Restaurant El Jardín **2**

Las Margaritas **5**
Le Rendez-Vous **15**
Madre Tierra **6**
Rumi Wilco Ecolodge **12**

Valle Sagrado **13**

Eating 🍴
El Punto **1**

Shanta's **6**
Vegetariano **7**

high cold *páramos* of **Parque Nacional Podocarpus**. The following private reserves abut Parque Nacional Podocarpus and provide access to it. They all have shelters, but you must make advance arrangements to use them. From north to south they are: **Solomaco**, above Quebrada de Solomaco, information from **El Punto** (see Vilcabamba cafés, below); **Las Palmas**, between Quebrada de Solomaco and Quebrada Las Palmas, run by **Cabañas Río Yambala**; **Los Helechos**, at Cerro Los Helechos on the Capamaco side, run by **La Tasca Tours**, and **Gavin's**, along the Río Capamaco, run by **Caballos Gavilán**. ▸▸ *For further details, see Activities and tours, page 551.*

Rumi Wilco ① *10-min walk northeast of town, take Calle Agua de Hierro towards Calle La Paz and turn left, following the signs from there over the leaning cement footbridge, US$2 valid for the duration of your stay in Vilcabamba*, a 40-ha private nature reserve, has several signed trails. Many of the trees and shrubs are labelled with their scientific and common names. There are great views of town from the higher trails, and it is a very good place to go for a walk. Over 100 species of birds have been identified here. Volunteers are welcome.

Climbing **Mandango** ① *US$1.50, includes bottle of water and bag of panela, local raw sugar,* the 'sleeping woman', is a popular and very scenic half-day walk. Access is signed along the highway, 250 m south of the bus terminal. Although the Vilcabamba area is generally safe, several hold-ups took place on Mandango in 2006-2007. Do not take valuables and ask about the current safety situation with your hotel or the tourist office before climbing. Also be careful on the higher sections when it is windy.

Crossing into Peru ⊟🚲🚌🚏 ▸▸ *pp548-552.*

There are currently five different land border crossings between Ecuador and Peru. For crossing at Huaquillas along the coast, see page 584. For river travel to Peru along the Río Napo in Oriente, see page 568. By far the most efficient and relaxed land border is the scenic route from Loja to Piura via Macará. This is much safer and more pleasant than crossing at Huaquillas, where there are reports of thefts, rip-offs and shake-downs.

There is a regional airport at **Catamayo** (La Toma), due west of Loja city. From here the road divides into two main branches, both of which later subdivide several times. One branch goes west, providing access to the coast, to the western extreme of the province of Loja, and to the border crossings at **Macará** and **Lalamor**. The second branch, partly paved, goes south to **Amaluza** and the **Jimbura** border post. Further east, a different secondary road leads south from Loja through **Vilcabamba** to **Zumba** and on to the border crossing at **La Balsa**.

To Peru via Macará–La Tina

Transport Cars and minivans run from La Tina to Sullana, US$3 per person or US$12 private car, 1½-two hours. From Sullana there is transport to Piura. Direct international buses from Loja to Piura (see page 552) can be boarded in Macará. The bridge over the Río Macará is 2½ km from Macará.

Ecuadorean immigration, open 24 hours, is a few metres from the bridge. On the Peruvian side is **La Tina**, which has a public phone but no other services. **Peruvian immigration** is by the bridge, open 24 hours. After clearing immigration, you must register with the **Policía Nacional de Perú** (PNP) across the street. When leaving Peru (see page 256), there is no need to stop at the PNP, only at immigration.

Exchange During the day there are money changers dealing in *soles* at the bridge, and in Macará at the park where taxis leave for the border. There is a bank on the Peruvian side of the bridge which changes *soles* Monday-Friday 0900-1600. All transactions are US dollars cash only; nowhere to change TCs.

Macará → *Colour map 1, C2. Population 15,000. Altitude 500 m.*

Located 190 kilometers southwest of Loja, this hot noisy border-town has convoluted streets and is the centre of a rice-farming area. Although Macará is growing and sees increasing border traffic, it remains a much more relaxed place to cross to Peru than Huaquillas, with good road connections to Piura on the Peruvian coast.

Vilcabamba to Peru → *Colour map 1, C3.*

South of Vilcabamba the scenery is wild and beautiful, but marred by deforestation. The road, paved at first and then gravel, heads from Vilcabamba to pleasant little village of **Yangana** and then past the **Tapichalaca Reserve** ① *T02-227 2013 (Quito), www.jocotoco.com, day visit US$15,* a beautiful cloudforest area very rich in birdlife and epiphytes. It is run by the **Jocotoco Foundation** and has a few trails and a very nice lodge (see Sleeping, page 549).

Valladolid (population 1500, altitude 1600 m, one basic hotel), is in the next valley. Then comes **Palanda** (population 4050, altitude 1150 m, basic places to sleep and eat), about three hours from Vilcabamba. Beyond Palanda the road deteriorates and crosses several river valleys. After a further two hours, you reach a military control (have your passport at hand) and, just beyond it, **Zumba** (population 7800, altitude 1250 m). Zumba is an end-of-the-road town built around a hillside garrison. Shops are well stocked. Transport leaves from the plaza near the modern church, where several bus companies have offices.

Smaller border crossings

In addition to La Balsa (two hours south of Zumba), there are small border posts at Jimbura and Lalamor. These remote villages are generally relaxed and friendly but facilities and onward transport into Peru are limited. Officials may not always be on hand to stamp passports and there may not be anywhere to change money. Time and patience are required when travelling these back roads.

To Peru via La Balsa–Namballe

A poor dirt road continues south from Zumba towards Peru, with a military control en route. There are two daily *rancheras* from Zumba to the border at **La Balsa** (see page 552) where there are just a few houses on either side of the modern concrete international bridge over the Río Canchis. This is a very small, tranquil crossing.

Ecuadorean immigration (migración) is 80 m from the bridge; it is open 24 hours; knock on the door or ask around for the officer. Entering Peru from Ecuador, passports are stamped at **Peruvian immigration** ① *to the right of the bridge, 0800-1300 and 1500-2000.* Once you have cleared immigration, you must register with the **Policía Nacional del Perú (PNP)**, next door. When leaving Peru (see page 269), there is no need to stop at PNP, only at immigration.

Accommodation and transport There is no accommodation at the border, just a few basic shops. **Namballe**, a small Peruvian village just 15 minutes from La Balsa has basic hotels. Shared taxis wait on the Peruvian side of the bridge. **San Ignacio** is a pleasant town two hours from Namballe, with reasonable hotels and eateries. From San Ignacio there are minivans to **Jaén**, a city with all services. San Ignacio is by far the best place to break a trip between Vilcabamba and **Chachapoyas**. If you leave Vilcabamba on the southbound bus that passes through from Loja around 0630, then you can usually make it to San Ignacio the same day and reach Chachapoyas the following day.

Exchange Shopkeepers in Zumba or the *ranchera* driver will exchange US dollars and *soles*. Once you are in Peru, the **Centro Comercial Unión**, Avenida San Ignacio 393, San Ignacio, changes cash dollars; or there are banks in Jaén.

Although only 4½ hours by bus from Loja, **Amaluza**, is one of the least visited parts of Ecuador. From here a poor road climbs about an hour to **Jimbura**, an authentic village (with basic *residencial* and *comedor*) where time has stood still. About 5 km from Jimbura is a small border crossing to **Espíndola** in Peru.

Ecuadorean immigration is located in Jimbura on the road to the border. Peruvian formalities are at the bridge. To **Ayabaca**, the nearest proper town, a pickup truck leaves Espíndola daily at 0500; if staying in Jimbura, go to Espíndola the day before and let the driver know, he might be able to pick you up in the morning. Ayabaca has places to eat and sleep, and bus service to Piura on the coast of Peru.

Lalamor is a hamlet 21 km along a dirt road from Zapotillo, which is in turn 55 km west of Macará. Lalamor has a tiny not-always-staffed border post. You can cross in a rowboat for US$0.20 or wade across the river which is the frontier. On the Peruvian side you might be able to get a vehicle to **Lancones** and on to **Sullana**, three hours away. There is hardly any traffic.

● Sleeping

Saraguro *p542*

D-E Achik Huasi, on hill above town, contact Fundación Kawsay, T07-220 0331, www.kaw say.org. Community-run *hostería*, improvised but adequate, good views, parking.
F Saraguro, Loja 03-2 y Antonio Castro, T07-220 0286. Clean basic hostel with an attractive little courtyard, cheaper with shared bath, electric shower, family-run and friendly.

Loja *p542*

A La Casa Lojana, París 00-08 y Zoilo Rodríguez, T07-258 5984, casalojanahotel@ utpl.edu.ec. A refurbished residence with colonial decor. Rooms are plain compared to the opulent common areas. Includes breakfast, elegant dining room, parking, lovely grounds and views. Run by the Universidad Técnica Particular and staffed by hotel school students.
B Libertador, Colón 14-30 y Bolívar, T07-257 0344, hlibloja@impsat.net.ec. Very good hotel, central, includes buffet breakfast, good restaurant, indoor pool, and spa, parking, comfortable rooms, suites available.
C Aguilera Internacional, Sucre 01-08 y Emiliano Ortega, T07-257 2894. Comfortable hotel to the north of the centre. Nice rooms, includes breakfast, restaurant and bar, parking, gym, steam bath and sauna.
D América, 18 de Noviembre entre Imba-bura y Quito, T07-257 6593. Modern multi-storey hotel, spacious, comfortable rooms, includes breakfast, restaurant downstairs.
E Metropolitano, 18 de Noviembre 6-31 y Colón, T07-257 0244. Multi-storey building, okay rooms, private bath, hot water, parking.

F Londres, Sucre 07-51 y 10 de Agosto, T07-256 1936. Hostel in a well maintained old house, shared bath, electric shower, basic but very clean, good value.

Parque Nacional Podocarpus *p543*

B-D Copalinga, Km 3 on the road from Zamora to the Bombuscaro entrance of Parque Nacional Podocarpus, T09-347 7013, www.copalinga.com. Comfortable wooden cabins, the more elaborate ones are gorgeous, simpler cheaper ones are also very clean and nice. Lovely setting with balconies overlooking the forest, very good breakfast, other delicious meals available if arranged in advance. Very good birdwatching, English/French spoken, Belgian-run, friendly and attentive. Advance booking advised. Highly recommended.

Vilcabamba *p544, map p545*

You may be approached on arrival by people touting for hotels. For its size, Vilcabamba has one of the best selections of rooms in all of Ecuador, so you are better off looking around and choosing on your own.
B Madre Tierra, 2 km north on road to Loja, then follow signs west, T07-264 0296, www.madretierra1.com. A variety of rooms from ample to small and simple, eclectic colourful decor. Includes breakfast and dinner, vegetarian available, nice grounds, pool, spa (massages and other treatments from US$18), videos, ping-pong. English spoken, US-run.
D-E Hostería Izhcayluma, 2 km south on road to Zumba, T07-264 0095, www.izhcayluma.com. Comfortable rooms and cabins with terrace and hammocks.

Includes very good breakfast, excellent restaurant, cheaper with shared bath, F pp in dorm, nice grounds, pool, dining area with wonderful views, lively bar, billiards, ping-pong and other games. English/German spoken, friendly, helpful. A bit out of the way but bikes to get to town. Highly recommended.

D-E Jardín Escondido, Sucre y Diego Vaca de Vega, T/F07-264 0281, www.vilcabamba. org/jardinescondido.html. A nicely refurbished old house around a lovely patio. Bright, comfortable rooms, includes very good breakfast, excellent restaurant, small pool, jacuzzi extra, limited parking. English spoken.

D-E Rumi Wilco Ecolodge, 10-min walk northeast of town, take Calle Agua de Hierro towards Calle La Paz and turn left, following the signs from there, www.rumiwilco.com. Adobe cabins and a wooden one on stilts (the 'Pole House') located in the Rumi Wilco reserve. Lovely setting on the shores of the river, very tranquil, cheaper with shared bath, laundry facilities, fully furnished kitchens, discounts for long stays, friendly Argentine owners. English spoken, recommended.

E Las Margaritas, Sucre y Clodoveo Jaramillo, T07-264 0051, www.vilcabamba.org/lasmargaritas.html. Small family-run hotel with very comfortable and nicely furnished rooms, private bath, intermittent solar-heated water, pretty garden. Good value.

E Le Rendez-Vous, Diego Vaca de Vega 06-43 y La Paz, T09-219 1180, www.rendezvous ecuador.com. Very comfortable rooms with terrace and hammocks around a lovely garden. Includes good breakfast, private bath, hot water, pleasant atmosphere, friendly service, French-run by Isabelle and Serge, English also spoken. Good value and recommended.

E-F Valle Sagrado, Luis Fernando de Vega y Av de la Eterna Juventud, T07-264 0386, www.vilcabamba.org/vallesagrado.html. Ample grounds, clean basic rooms, cheaper with shared bath, electric shower, laundry and cooking facilities, parking.

Macará *p547*

E El Conquistador, Bolívar y Abdón Calderón, T07-269 4057. Modern, comfortable hotel, includes breakfast, private bath, electric shower, fan, parking.

F Colina, Olmedo y Loja, T07-269 4871. Private bath, some rooms have electric showers, fan, nice, modern and good value.

Vilcabamba to Peru *p547*

L Tapichalaca Reserve, T02-227 2013 (Quito), www.jocotoco.com. Comfortable rooms in a beautiful lodge, with private bath, hot water, nice sitting room with fireplace and a professional cook who prepares great meals. Prices are for full board but do not include guiding.

E-F El Emperador, Colón y Orellana, Zumba, T07-2308063. Newest in town, cheaper with shared bath, cold water, opened in 2006.

Smaller border crossings *p547*

E Guambo Real, Av Chigua y Manuel Enrique Rojas, below the plaza in Amaluza, T07-2653061. Private bath, cold water, small bathrooms, otherwise pleasant and comfortable.

🍴 Eating

Saraguro *p542*

There are several restaurants around the main square, serving economical set meals.

Loja *p542*

Not the culinary capital of Ecuador; local staples, such as *repe* (green banana and dried-pea soup), tend to be rather stodgy. *Tamales lojanos* (corn meal with chicken or pork steamed in *áchira* leaves), however, are quite good. Many restaurants in the city are closed on Sun.

🍴🍴 **Parrilladas Uruguayas**, Juan de Salinas y Av Universitaria. Tue-Sun 1200-0100, Mon 1800-0100. Good grilled meat, helpful Uruguayan owner.

🍴-🍴 **Mi Tierra**, 10 de Agosto 11-14 y Juan José Peña. Economical set lunches and international à la carte.

🍴-🍴 **Pizzería Forno di Fango**, Bolívar 10-98 y Azuay. Tue-Sun 1200-2230. Excellent wood-oven pizza, salads and lasagne. Large portions, friendly service, good value. Recommended.

🍴 **Casa Sol**, 24 de Mayo 07-04 y José Antonio Eguiguren. Daily 0900-2400. Small place serving economical set meals and some à la carte. Pleasant seating on balcony.

🍴 **Diego's**, Colón 14-88 y Sucre, 2nd floor. Mon-Sat 0800-2130, Sun 0800-1530. Pleasant restaurant on the 2nd floor of a colonial house, seating on balconies around a courtyard. Filling set lunches and international à la carte dishes, popular with locals.

¶ **El Paraíso**, Quito 14-50 y Bolívar, daily 0700-2100. Good vegetarian food. Set breakfast, lunch and dinner as well as some à la carte.
¶ **El Tamal Lojano**, 18 de Noviembre e Imbabura, Mon-Sat 0830-2030. Economical set lunches, good *tamales* and other local snacks in the evening.

Cafés

Café Ruskina, Sucre 07-48 y 10 de Agosto, Mon-Sat 0830-1300, 1500-2030. Coffee, cream cakes, other sweets and snacks.

Vilcabamba *p544, map p545*
In addition to the places listed below, there are various simple *comedores* serving economical set meals.
¶¶ **El Jardín**, Sucre y Agua de Hierro, at Jardín Escondido hotel, daily 0800-2000. Excellent authentic Mexican food and drinks (Mexican chef), also international dishes and very good breakfasts. Pleasant atmosphere in a garden setting, attentive service, live music some Sat nights. Highly recommended.
¶¶ **Izhcayluma**, At Hostería Izhcayluma south of town (don´t confuse with **El Molino de Izhcayluma** next door), Mon 1700-2000, Tue-Sun 0800-2000. Excellent international dishes with some German specialities (German chef), good vegetarian options, also serve nice breakfasts. Lovely terrace dining room with wonderful views. Highly recommended.
¶¶-¶ **Shanta's**, 800 m from town on the road to Yamburara, daily 1200-2400. Restaurant and bar, good international food with specialities such as trout and frogs' legs, tasty pizza, nicely decorated rustic setting, pleasant atmosphere, friendly service, recommended.
¶ **Vegetariano**, Valle Sagrado y Diego Vaca de Vega, dpen 0830-2030, closed Sat. Small family-run vegetarian restaurant in a garden setting. Very good 3-course set meals and a few à la carte dishes, also breakfasts.

Cafés

El Punto, Sucre y Luis Fernando de Vega, by the park, pen 0800-2100, closed Tue. A popular meeting place. Breakfast, salads, snacks, sandwiches on home-made bread, good pizza, sweets, coffee and drinks.

Macará *p547*
¶ **Colonial Macará**, Rengel y Bolívar. Set meals and some à la carte dishes.

⊙ Bars and clubs

Loja *p542*
Casa Tinku, Lourdes 14-76 y Sucre. Bar-café, live music on Fri night, also crafts shop.
El Viejo Minero, Sucre 10-76 y Azuay, Mon-Sat 1600-2400. Bar and café, popular with foreigners.

⊛ Festivals and events

Saraguro *p542*
Mar/Apr Interesting Semana Santa celebrations. There are various processions and watchmen stay in the church with the image of Christ from Maundy Thu to Easter Sun.

Loja *p542*
Aug-Sep Fiesta de la Virgen del Cisne, Loja, Catamayo and El Cisne are crowded with religious pilgrims and Ecuadorean tourists during the last 2 weeks of Aug and the first 2 weeks of Sep, when it is very difficult to find a room and all prices rise. The main festival in honour of the Virgen is 15 Aug, when hundreds of pilgrims from Ecuador and Peru gather in El Cisne. On 16-20 Aug, the faithful walk in procession with the image of the Virgin, 74 km from El Cisne to the cathedral in Loja. A religious festival is then held in honour of the Virgin on 8 Sep, with serenades at the cathedral. The image remains in Loja until 1 Nov, after which devotees return the image to El Cisne in another 3-day procession.
17-19 Nov Independencia de Loja, celebrated with dances and parades.

Vilcabamba *p544, map p545*
Feb-Mar Carnival. This is when normally sedate and tranquil Vilcabamba runs riot. The town is crowded, noisy, drunken, and prices go up. Lots of water-throwing.

⊙ Shopping

Loja *p542*
Handicrafts
Regional crafts include Saraguro bead necklaces, *alforjas* (woven saddlebags), ceramics and woodwork. There are several craft shops on Lourdes, near Parque San Sebastián.
Cer-Art, pre-Columbian designs on mostly high-gloss ceramics, which are produced at the Universidad Técnica. Above the university

is the 'Ceramics Plaza', where you can buy directly from the crafts studio.
Patronato Municipal, Bolívar y 10 de Agosto. Varied regional crafts.

Vilcabamba *p544, map p545*
Book exchange
Craig's Book Exchange, Yambura Bajo, follow Diego Vaca de Vega, 1 km from town. Impressive collection, 2500 books in 12 languages, 2 for 1 exchange. Also art gallery and sells great home-made cookies.

Handicrafts
Artesanal Primavera, Diego Vaca de Vega y Sucre, at the main square, Mon-Sat, hours posted. T-shirts and local crafts as well as postage stamps, will mail letters.
Estación 14, Sucre 11-35 on the park, closed Tue. Distinctive locally crafted jewellery.
Pachaferia, a small craft and food fair, is held in front of the church every 2nd Sun morning.

▲▲ Activities and tours

Loja *p542*
Tour operators
Aratinga Aventuras, Lourdes 14-84 y Sucre, T/F07-258 2434, aratinga@loja.telconet.net. Specializes in birdwatching tours, overnight trips to cloud forest, rainforest, dry forest or Tumbesian forest. Pablo Andrade is a knowlegeable guide.
Biotours, 24 de Mayo 08-28 y 10 de Agosto, T07-257 9387, biotours_ec@yahoo.es. City, regional, cycling and jungle tours, flight tickets. Friendly.

Vilcabamba *p544, map p545*
Spas and treatments
Beauty Care, Bolívar y Diego Vaca de Vega, T09-326 1944, daily 1000-1800. Karina Zumba, facials, waxing, Reiki, 1 hr massage US$10.
Shanta's (see Eating, page 550), T08-562 7802, Lola Encalada is a physiotherapist, 1¼ hr therapeutic massage US$11, waxing.

Tour operators
Many operators offer horse riding: US$5 per hour, half day US$16, full day with lunch US$25. Overnight trips cost US$25-35 per day, including meals and lodging. All guides listed below are experienced horsemen. Some have their own shelters in private reserves.

Caballos Gavilán, Sucre y Diego Vaca de Vega, T08-632 3285, gavilanhorse@yahoo.com. Riding with New Zealander Gavin Moore.
Centro Ecuestre, Diego Vaca de Vega y Bolívar. A group of local guides, friendly and helpful.
Las Palmas, at Cabañas Río Yambala, http://www.vilcabamba.cwc.net. Riding tours to their reserve.
La Tasca Tours, Diego Vaca de Vega y Sucre, T09-184 1287. Riding with René León.

⊖ Transport

Saraguro *p542*
Bus Frequent buses to/from **Cuenca**, US$5, 3 hrs, and **Loja**, US$1.75, 2 hrs. Also services to **Quito**, US$12, 12 hrs.

Loja *p542*
Air Aeropuerto Camilo Ponce Enríquez at Catamayo (also called La Toma, 1 hr from Loja) is served by **TAME** and **Icaro**, with 2-4 daily flights to **Quito**, US$70. Flights are sometimes cancelled due to strong winds or fog. For buses to the airport, see below.
　Airline offices TAME, 24 de Mayo y Emiliano Ortega, T07-2570248. Icaro, 24 de Mayo y 10 de Agosto, T07-2585955.

Bus To **Catamayo** (for the airport) every 30 mins, 0600-2000, US$1, 50 mins, take a taxi from the bus station to the airport; none of the buses arrive in Catamayo early enough to connect with the morning flight to Quito.
　There are 3 different routes from Loja to **Machala** on the coast, each with its own bus service; ask for the one you need. They are, from north to south: via Piñas, for **Zaruma** (page 583) unpaved and rough but very scenic; via **Balsas**, fully paved and also scenic; and via **Alamor**, for Puyango petrified forest (page 583), military checkpoints en route.
　To **Vilcabamba**, Vilcabambaturis vans and minibuses from the Terminal Terrestre in Loja, every 15 mins, 0545-2045, US$1, 1 hr; also several bus companies; and *taxirutas* (shared taxis) from Av Pío Jaramillo y Maximiliano Ortega, 0600-2015, US$1.20, 45 mins.
　To **Zumba**, via Vilcabamba, US$7.50, 6-7 hrs, a rough but beautiful ride, prone to landslides with heavy rain, **Sur Oriente**, 0800, 1730, 2130, or **Unión Cariamanga**, 0530, 1200, 1600, 1830, 2330, or **Unión Yantzatza**, 1045, 2145, or **Nambija**, 2400 and 1230.

To **Macará**, frequent service with Transportes Loja and Unión Cariamanga, US$6, 6 hrs.

International buses To **Piura** (Peru), via Macará, Loja Internacional has good service departing 0700, 1300, 2230 and 2300 daily, US$8, 8 hrs including border formalities. Return from Piura at 0930, 1300, 2130, 2230; ample terminal in Piura at Av Sánchez Cerro 1480 y Av Gulman, T073-309407. In Vilcabamba, tickets for Loja to Piura can usually be purchased at the Vilcabambaturis office at the bus station. Unión Cariamanga departs Loja for Piura at 2400 via Catacocha and 0600 via Cariamanga, US$8, 8 hrs. Return from Piura at 1330 via Cariamanga and 2000 via Catacocha; office in Piura at Sánchez Cerro (cuadra 18) y Av Vice.

Car hire Bombuscaro Rent-a-Car, 10 de Agosto y Av Universitaria, T07-257 7021. Localiza, Av Nueva Loja e Isidro Ayora, in El Valle, T07-2581729.

Vilcabamba p544, map p545
Bus and taxi To **Loja**, vans and shared taxis leave from the small terminal behind the market. **Sur Oriente** buses from their office on the main road opposite the market. Buses to **Zumba** pass through Vilcabamba about 1 hr after departing Loja, US$6.50, 5-6 hrs. They stop along the highway, outside the market. Note that some of the buses go only as far as **Palanda**. To **Catamayo airport**, direct taxi US$25, or take a van to Loja, a bus to the centre of Catamayo (see Loja transport, above) and a taxi from there.

Macará p547
Bus To **Loja**, frequent service with Transportes Loja and Unión Cariamanga, US$6, 6 hrs. To **Quito**, US$15, 15 hrs; to **Guayaquil**, US$11, 8 hrs. To the **Peruvian border**, take a taxi (US$0.25 shared, US$1 private) or pick up from the small park near the market. For **Piura**, take the international buses passing Macará about 5 hrs after departure from Loja (see Loja transport above).

Vilcabamba to Peru p547
Zumba
Bus All transport in this area is prone to frequent interruption by landslides after heavy rain. To **Vilcabamba** and **Loja**, 12 a day, US$7.50, 6-7 hrs, see Loja bus transport (page 551). To **Jimbura**, Wed, Sat, Sun, 0700 and 1300, return same schedule, US$6, 5 hrs.
To the border at La Balsa There are 2 daily *rancheras* (open-sided trucks with benches) from Zumba to **La Balsa** border crossing at 0800 and 1430 (from La Balsa to **Zumba** at 1230 and 1700), US$1.75, 1½-2 hrs. Shared taxis from La Balsa to **San Ignacio** (Peru), US$3, 2 hrs."

Smaller border crossings p547
Amaluza
Bus To **Loja**, 8 daily with Unión Cariamanga, US$4.75, 5 hrs. To **Jimbura**, 6 *rancheras* a day, US$1, 1 hr. From Jimbura to **Espíndola** (Peru), US$7 to hire a pickup.

Lalamor
Several daily buses from Zapotillo to **Loja**. Hire a pickup from Zapotillo to **Lalamor**.

ⓘ Directory

Loja p542
Banks Banco del Austro, José Antonio Eguiguren 14-12 y Bolívar. Produbanco, Bernardo Valdivieso y José Antonio Eguiguren, on plaza. Comercial, José Antonio Eguiguren 15-61 y 18 de Noviembre, Mon-Fri 0900-1300, 1500-1800, Sat 0900-1200. Small informal place, changes cash euros and Peruvian soles at poor rates. **Consulates** Peru, Zoilo Rodríguez 03-05, T07-2587330, Mon-Fri 0900-1300, 1500-1700. **Hospital** Clínica San Agustín, 18 de Noviembre 10-72 y Azuay, T07-257 3002. **Internet** US$1 per hr. **Laundry** Lavandería, 24 de Mayo y José Antonio Eguiguren. **Post office** Colón y Sucre.

Vilcabamba p544, map p545
Banks Best to bring cash. There are no banks, just an ATM (sometimes out of order) at Diego Vaca de Vega y Bolívar, next to iTur. If stuck try San Pablo grocery store, Clodoveo Jaramillo, across from the bus station; they may change cash euros and soles and deal with TCs, VISA and Masterard cash advances if the owner is in. **Hospital** Hospital Kokichi Otani, Av Eterna Juventud (highway), T07-264 0188. **Internet** US$1-1.25, Mandango, rooftop terrace, 0900-1900; a couple of others near the park. **Laundry** Lava Listo, Sucre y Diego Vaca de Vega, US$1.25 per kg.

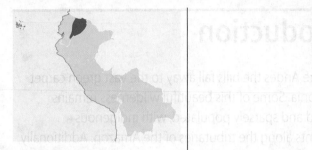

Oriente Jungle

⁑ Footprint features

Introduction

East of the Andes the hills fall away to the vast green carpet of Amazonia. Some of this beautiful wilderness remains unspoiled and sparsely populated, with indigenous settlements along the tributaries of the Amazon. Additionally, the Ecuadorean jungle has the advantage of being relatively accessible and tourist infrastructure here is well developed.

Most tourists love the exotic feeling of the Oriente, and the Oriente needs tourists. Large tracts of jungle are under threat; colonists are clearing many areas for agriculture, while others are laid waste by petroleum exploration or gold mining. The region's irreplaceable biodiversity and traditional ways of life can only be protected if sustainable ecotourism provides a viable economic alternative.

The eastern foothills of the Andes, where the jungle begins, offer the easiest access and a good introduction to the rainforest for those with limited time or money. Further east lie the remaining large tracts of primary rainforest, teeming with life, which can be visited from several excellent (and generally expensive) jungle lodges.

★ Don't miss …

1 **Ecotourism in the jungle** Visit one of the Oriente's excellent lodges or reserves, page 556.
2 **San Rafael Falls** See this stunning cascade, the highest in Ecuador, page 560.
3 **Whitewater rafting** Take the plunge, from Tena, pages 561 and 565.
4 **Misahuallí** Experience the 'near Oriente' from the river-port that time forgot, page 562.
5 **Head downriver** Sail the lower Río Napo from Coca to Iquitos (Peru) and beyond, page 567.

Oriente Jungle

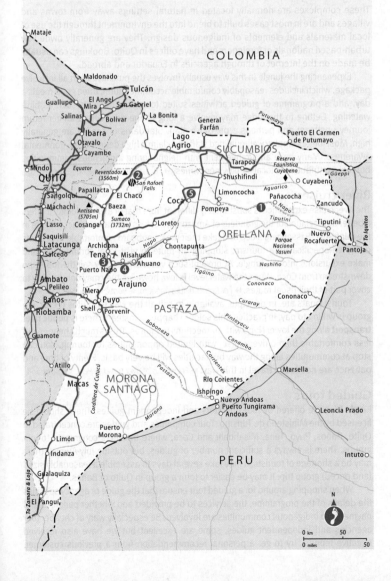

Ecotourism in the Oriente

The Oriente offers an extensive variety of ecotourism services and programmes, which can be divided into four basic types: jungle lodges, river cruises, guided tours, and indigenous ecotourism. A fifth option would be independent jungle travel without a guide, but this is not advisable for your own safety as well as to be a responsible tourist.

Planning your trip

Jungle lodges

These complexes are normally located in natural settings away from towns and villages and are in most cases built to blend into the environment through the use of local materials and elements of indigenous design. They are generally owned by urban-based nationals or foreigners and have offices in Quito. Bookings can usually be made on the internet or through agencies in Ecuador and abroad.

Experiencing the jungle in this way usually involves the purchase of an all-inclusive package, which includes reasonably comfortable accommodation, three good meals a day, and a programme of guided activities suited to special interests such as bird-watching. Getting to the lodge may involve a long canoe ride, with a longer return journey upstream and perhaps a pre-dawn start. Standards of service are generally high. Most lodges employ well-qualified staff and claim a high degree of environmental awareness. Many have an arrangement with neighbouring indigenous communities but their contribution to local employment varies. ▶▶ *For listings, see Jungle lodges, page 559.*

River cruises

The river cruise experience is substantially different from that of a jungle lodge. It offers a better appreciation of the grandeur of Amazonia, but less intimate contact with life in the rainforest. Passengers sleep and take their meals onboard comfortable river boats designed specifically for tourism, stopping en route to visit local communities and make excursions into the jungle. At present such vessels generally sail the Río Napo downstream from Coca. When the water level is low, however, they may only be able to cover part of their usual routes. ▶▶ *For further details about these boats, see page 560.*

Tourist boats are, in principle, available to sail all the way to Iquitos (Peru), if a group is willing to pay. In practice, this seldom happens. Instead, there is **public river transport** along the lower Napo with connections to Iquitos. This is much cheaper and less comfortable than a river cruise, with limited opportunities for touring. You can stop at communities along the way but facilities will be very basic. Plenty of time and patience are needed to travel in this way. ▶▶ *For details of river travel to Peru, see page 568.*

Guided tours

Jungle trips are offered by tour operators and independent guides. These should be licensed by the Ministerio de Turismo. Tour companies and guides are concentrated in Quito, Baños, Puyo, Tena, Misahuallí and Coca, where travellers congregate to join groups. There is always a sufficient number of guides, but outside July-August, there may be a shortage of tourists. It may take several days to assemble a reasonably sized (and priced) group trip. It may be easier to form a group in Quito or Baños.

When shopping around for a guided tour ensure that the guide or agency specifies the details of the programme, the services to be provided and whether park fees and payments to indigenous communities are involved. Be especially wary of cheaper tour agencies and independent guides, some are excellent but we have also received negative reports. Try to get a personal recommendation from a previous customer.

Serious breaches of contract can be reported to the Ministerio de Turismo, but you should be reasonable about minor details. Most guided tours involve sleeping in simple shelters (open-sided raised platforms) or camping in tents or under plastic sheets.

Indigenous ecotourism

A number of indigenous communities and families offer ecotourism programmes in their territories. These are either community operated, or joint ventures between the community and a non-indigenous partner. These programmes usually involve *guías nativos*, who are licensed to guide within their communities. Accommodation is typically in simple native shelters. Local food may be quite good, but keep an eye on hygiene. Bring rubber boots, a light sleeping bag, rain jacket, trousers, long-sleeved shirt for mosquitoes, binoculars, torch (flashlight), insect repellent, sunscreen and hat, water-purifying tablets, and a first-aid kit. Wrap everything in plastic bags to keep it dry.

Choosing a rainforest

A tropical rainforest is one of the most exciting things to see in Ecuador, but it isn't easy to find a good one. The key is to have realistic expectations and choose accordingly. Think carefully about your interests. If you simply want to relax in nature and see some interesting plants, insects, small birds and mammals, you have many choices, including some that are quite economical and easily accessible. If you want to experience something of the cultures of rainforest people, you must go further. If you want the full experience, with large mammals and birds, you will have to go further still and spend more, because large creatures have been hunted or driven out of settled areas.

A visit to a rainforest is not like a visit to the Galápagos Islands. The diversity of life in a good rainforest is far greater, but creatures don't sit around and let themselves be seen. Even in the best forests, your experiences will be unpredictable – none of this 'today is Wednesday, time to see sea lions'. A rainforest trip is a real adventure; the only guarantee is that the surprises will be genuine, and hence all the more unforgettable.

There are things that can increase the odds of really special surprises. One of the most important is a canopy tower. Even the most colourful rainforest birds are mere specks up in the branches, unless you are above them looking down. A good guide is another necessity. Avoid trips that have an emphasis on medicinal plants. This usually means that there isn't anything else to see. If you are interested in exploring indigenous cultures, choose a guide from the ethnic group as the village you will visit.

If you want to see real wilderness, with big birds and mammals, you generally can't go to any lodges you can drive to (an exception is **Gareno Lodge**, see page 559). Expect to travel at least a couple of hours in a motorized canoe. Don't stay near villages even if they are in the middle of nowhere. In remote villages people hunt a lot, and animals will be scarce. Most indigenous groups (except for a very few, such as certain Cofán villages that now specialize in ecotourism) are ruthlessly efficient hunters.

The newest and least well-established lodges offer the best value. A cheaper alternative to a fancy jungle lodge is a canoe camping trip on a remote river like the Cononaco. These trips are a good way to experience real jungle cultures. There are also lodges run directly by the community. An added advantage of this is that your money goes straight to the community, providing an economic incentive for conservation.

Responsible jungle tourism

Some guides will try to hunt meat for your dinner – don't let them, and report such practices to other tourists and to guidebooks. Don't buy anything made with animal or bird parts. Avoid making a pest of yourself in indigenous villages; don't take photographs or videos without permission. In short, try to minimize your impact on the forest and its people. Also remember when choosing a guide, that cheapest is not best. What happens is that guides undercut each other and offer services that are unsafe or harm local communities and the environment. It is your responsibility not to encourage this practice.

Ins and outs

Getting there

There are scheduled commercial flights from Quito to Lago Agrio and Coca. Much of western Oriente is also accessible by roads which wind their way down from the highlands. Quito to Lago Agrio via Baeza, Baños to Puyo and Loja to Zamora are fully paved. The remainder are mostly narrow and tortuous, subject to landslides in the rainy season. Nonetheless, all have regular if rough bus service. Deeper into the rainforest, motorized canoes provide the only alternative to air travel.

Public safety

There are police and military checkpoints in the Oriente, so always have your passport handy. The Oriente is also affected by ongoing armed conflict in neighbouring Colombia. Caution is particularly required throughout the province of Succumbíos, including Reserva Faunística Cuyabeno. Always enquire about public safety before visiting any remote sites north of the Río Napo, and avoid all areas adjacent to the Colombian border. Even when visiting upmarket jungle lodges elsewhere in the Oriente, it is best not to take any unnecessary valuables such as jewellery, credit and debit cards.

Health

A yellow fever vaccination is required. Anti-malaria tablets are recommended (see also Essentials, page 41) and be sure to take an effective insect repellent. A mosquito net may be helpful if you are travelling independently.

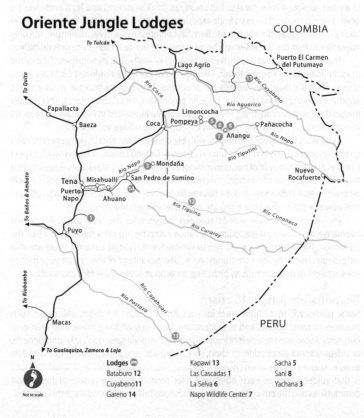

Oriente Jungle Lodges

Lodges		
Bataburo 12	Kapawi 13	Sacha 5
Cuyabeno 11	Las Cascadas 1	Sani 8
Gareno 14	La Selva 6	Yachana 3
	Napo Wildlife Center 7	

Jungle lodges

Unless indicated otherwise, prices are per person for packages including accommodation (generally double occupancy), 3 meals a day and guiding, but not transport from Quito or park fees. All details are subject to change.

Upper Río Napo *p562, map p558*

Listed in order of their distance downriver from Puerto Napo, the closest first.

Gareno, contact Michael Saur, T02-234 4350, or Roeland Van Lede, T02-224 9225 (both in Quito), www.guaponi.com. Set in Huarorani territory, accessible by road. Sightings of nesting harpy eagles reported, and the area is of special interest to birdwatchers. US$55 per night plus a one-off US$20 contribution to the Huaorani community. Recommended.

Yachana, T02-252 3777 (Quito) www.yach ana.com. Located in the village of Mondaña, 2 hrs downstream from Misahuallí. Proceeds go towards supporting community development projects. The comfortable lodge has 14 double rooms and 4 family cabins, all with solar power. US$405 for 4 days. Recommended.

Reserva Faunística Cuyabeno
p567, map p558

Cuyabeno Lodge, run by Neotropic Turis, Pinto E4-360 y Amazonas, T02-252 1212 (Quito), www.neotropicturis.com. Pioneer lodge with cabins in the heart of this fauna-rich reserve. From US$200 for 4 days, including excursions with bilingual guides.

Lower Río Napo *p567, map p558*

The following are listed in order of their distance downriver from Coca, closest first.

Sacha, Julio Zaldumbide 397 y Valladolid, T02-256 6090 (Quito), www.sachalodge.com. An upmarket lodge 2½ hrs downstream from Coca. Very comfortable cabins, excellent meals. The bird list is outstanding; local bird expert, Oscar Tapuy (Coca T06-288 1486), can be requested in advance. Canopy tower and 275-m walkway. Several species of monkey can be seen. Nearby river islands provide access to a distinct habitat. US$645 for 4 days.

La Selva, Mariana de Jesús E7-211 y La Pradera, T02-255 0995 (Quito), www.laselva junglelodge.com. An upmarket lodge, 2½ hrs downstream from Coca on a picturesque lake, surrounded by forest. Bird and animal life is exceptionally diverse. Many species of monkey. A total of 580 bird species have been found. Comfortable cabins and excellent meals. High standards, most guides are biologists. 45-m canopy tower. US$697 for 4 days.

Napo Wildlife Center, T02-289 7316 (Quito), www.ecoecuador.org. Operated by the local Añangu community, 2½ hrs downstream from Coca. Winners of a 2006 responsible tourism award. This area of hilly forest is different from the low flat forest of other sites, and the diversity is slightly higher. There are big caimans and other mammals, including giant otters. Birdwatching is excellent with 2 parrot clay-licks and a 35-m canopy tower. The local guide, Giovanny Rivadeneyra, is one of the most knowledgeable birders in the Oriente. US$650 for 4 days. Recommended.

Sani, Roca 736 y Amazonas, Pasaje Chantilly, T02-255 8881 (Quito), www.sanilodge.com. All proceeds go to the Sani Isla community, who run the lodge. It is located on a remote lagoon which has a 5-m black caiman. The area is rich in wildlife and birds, including scarlet macaw which have disappeared from most other Napo areas. There is good accommodation and a 30-m canopy tower. The lodge is accessible to people who have difficulty walking; it can be reached by canoe (3½ hrs from Coca). US$450 for 4 days. Good value and recommended.

Other locations *map p558*

Bataburo, Kempery Tours, Ramírez Dávalos 117 y Amazonas, Oficina 101, T02-250 5599 (Quito), www.kempery.com. A lodge in Huaorani territory near Parque Nacional Yasuní, on the Río Tiguino, a 3- to 6-hr canoe ride from the end of the Vía Auca out of Coca. Some cabins have private baths, shared shower facilities. Local guides. The birds have been little studied but macaws and other large species are present. The mammal population also appears to be good. US$275 for 4 days.

Kapawi Ecolodge and Reserve, contact T04-228 5711 (Guayaquil), www.canodros.com. A top-of-the-line lodge on the Río Capahuari near its confluence with the Pastaza, in the heart of Achuar territory. Accessible only by small aircraft and motor canoe. The lodge was built in partnership with the Achuar indigenous people and will be turned over to them in 2008. The biodiversity is good, but more emphasis is placed on ethno-tourism.

US$676 for 4 days, plus US$224 for return flight from Quito. Recommended.

Las Cascadas Eco-Lodge, book via Surtrek, Av Amazonas 897 y Wilson, Quito, T02-250 0530/T09-973 5448, www.surtrek.com. First-class accommodation for 20 people, 10 double rooms, private bathroom, hot water, bilingual guide, very welcoming atmosphere, nearby waterfalls. US$570 pp 4 days/3 nights including meals, private guide and transport to/from Quito, excursions, rainboots.

River cruises

Jungle Discovery, Kempery Tours, Ramírez Dávalos 117 y Amazonas, Oficina 101, T02-250 5599 (Quito), www.kempery.com. This 30-passenger vessel sails between Coca and Nuevo Rocafuerte. US$600 for 4 days.
Manatee, Advantage Travel, T02-246 2871 (Quito), www.advantagecuador.com. This 30-passenger vessel sails between Coca and Pañacocha. US$461 for 4 days.

Foothills

The foothills of the Andes are the western boundary of Oriente. Here, where the jungle meets the mountains, are Tena and Puyo, capitals of the provinces of Napo and Pastaza, respectively. Much of the surrounding countryside has been turned into pastureland and primary rainforest is scarce, but this area is nonetheless of interest to visitors. There is convenient road access from highland tourist centres such as Quito and Baños, and enough forest fragments remain to offer an introduction for those tight on time. Among the region's many attractions: Baeza is the gateway to Cascada San Rafael, Ecuador's largest waterfall; whitewater rafting and ethno-tourism flourish around Tena; Misahuallí provides access to the upper Río Napo; and Puyo is surrounded by several small private nature reserves. ▸▸ *For Sleeping, Eating and other listings, see pages 563-566.*

Quito to Lago Agrio 🚍🛈 ▸▸ *pp563-566. Colour map1, A4/5.*

The fully paved road from Quito to Baeza crosses the Eastern Cordillera at the pass of Guamaní (usually called La Virgen), just north of the volcano **Antisana** (5705 m). Then it descends via the small village of **Papallacta**, with wonderful thermal baths (see page 475), to the old mission settlement of **Baeza**.

Baeza → *Phone code 06. Colour map 1, A4. Population 2200. Altitude 1900 m.*

This is a small town in the beautiful setting of the Quijos pass. Baeza is about 2 km from **La "Y"**, the junction of the Quito, Lago Agrio and Tena roads. Buses to and from Tena pass right through town. If arriving on a Lago Agrio bus, get off at La "Y" and walk or take a *camioneta* for US$0.25. Baeza itself is divided in two: a rather faded **Baeza Colonial** (Old Baeza) and **Andalucía** or **Baeza Nueva** (New Baeza), where most hotels, shops and services are located. There are many good hiking opportunities in the area. A one-hour walk is from Old Baeza along the Río Machángara to **La Granja**, an experimental farm with a small zoo and native trees. There are two national park offices under one roof at the **Centro de Comunicación Ambiental** ⓘ *Baeza Colonial, T06-232 0340 (Sumaco-Napo-Galeras), T06-232 0605 (Antisana), Mon-Fri 0800-1300, 1400-1700.* **Municipal tourist office** ⓘ *Baeza Nueva, T06-232 0706, umds@ municipioquijos.gov.ec, Mon-Fri 0730-1200, 1300-1630.*

Baeza to Lago Agrio → *Colour map 1, A4/5.*

The road from Baeza to Lago Agrio has several splendid natural attractions. The access road for **San Rafael Falls** ⓘ *ranger station and dilapidated cabins along the access road, part of Reserva Ecológica Cayambe-Coca, entry US$10,* starts 500 m before the bridge over the Río Reventador (70 km northeast of Baeza) and is signposted. It is a

with stunning views of the thundering cascade. There are several trails to choose
from, including a steep and slippery two-hour descent to the
river. Be careful, a small cross commemorates a Canadian
photographer who got too close to the edge. Interesting birds
can be spotted in the area, including cock-of-the-rock, and also
monkeys and koatimundis.

*The falls are an
impressive 145 m tall,
believed to be the highest
in Ecuador.*

Volcán Reventador (3560 m) is an active volcano which lies on the edge of the
Reserva Ecológica Cayambe-Coca, poking up from the Oriente rainforest. A sudden
eruption in 2002 produced impressive lava flows and a 20-km-high cloud which
covered Quito – 100 km away – in ash. In 2006 the area was again safe and beautiful
for trekking but conditions can change unexpectedly. Always check volcanic activity
updates – www.igepn.edu.ec – and also enquire locally. It is a full day of hard hiking
through lovely forest on frequently muddy trails up to the rim of the volcanic caldera
and back. From the rim, views of the immense caldera filled with steaming blocks of
lava are breathtaking. The trailhead is hard to find, ask at **Hostería El Reventador**. From
Quito, tours are offered by **Ecuador Journeys** (see page 466).

Forty kilometres past the Río Revetador is **El Dorado de Cascales** (population 6000)
with a simple hotel which provides an alternative to sleeping in Lago Agrio. The latter is
only 36 km further east and there is plenty of local transport, so you can reach the
meeting point for Cuyabeno jungle trips early the next day. ▶▶ *See Sleeping, page 563.*

Baeza to Tena 🚌🍴⛰️🚌🏨 ▶▶ *pp563-566. Colour map 1, A/B4.*

The other branch of the road from Baeza heads south to Tena, with a branch off this
road going to Coca via Loreto. The route from Baeza to Tena passes near several
important lodges, reserves and national parks. The first village is **Cosanga** (population
800, altitude 1900), 19 km from Baeza. In the area are **San Isidro**, an excellent birding
lodge and reserve; and **The Magic Roundabout**, a welcoming British-run inn. Sixty-five
kilometers from Baeza is the small colonial town of **Archidona**, and 10 km beyond Tena,
the capital of Napo Province.

Tena → *Phone code 06. See map page 564. Colour map 1, B4. Population 31,000. Altitude 500 m.*
This relaxed and friendly little city occupies a hill above the confluence of the Ríos Tena
and Pano. There are nice views of the Andean foothills, often shrouded in mist. Once an
important colonial missionary and trading post, Tena remains a regional centre and has
become popular with visitors for **whitewater rafting** and ethno-tourism. It makes a
good first stop en route from Quito to points deeper in the Oriente, and a number of
worthwhile excursions can be organized from here. ▶▶ *See Activities and tours, page 565.*

The road from the north passes the airstrip and market and heads through the
town centre as Avenida 15 de Noviembre on its way to the bus station, nearly 1 km
south of the river. Tena is quite spread out. There is a pedestrian bridge and a vehicle
bridge which link the two halves of the town. There are several **tourist information
offices** ① *García Moreno between Calderón and JL Mera, near the river, T06-288
6536, Mon-Fri 0800-1230, 1330-1700,* all under one roof.

Tena to Puyo 🚌🍴⛰️🚌🏨 ▶▶ *pp563-566. Colour map 1, B4.*

From Tena the main highway runs south towards Puyo. Seven kilometers along is the
small town of **Puerto Napo** and a suspension bridge over the Río Napo. On the north
shore a paved road runs 17 km east to Misahuallí. If you are travelling from Puyo to
Misahuallí, you can avoid going into Tena by changing buses here.

⁚ Monkey business in Misahuallí

"Get out the camera, George. The plaza is full of monkeys!" "Sure, Mabel, what are they doing here?"

Misahuallí's experience with white-fronted capuchin monkeys (*Cebus albifrons*) apparently dates back to the 1980s. At the time, the story goes, a pet male monkey named Octavio escaped from his owner, who then tried to lure him back with a female. Instead, she also escaped and the young couple took up residence in a tree by the river.

Among their progeny was Peco, another male who became famous for his mischievous antics with tourists. Peco and his family eventually moved from the outskirts to an abandoned house right on the plaza, where he came to an untimely end in the jaws of a local dog. Peco's troop, however, not only multiplied but also integrated themselves into Misahuallí society.

The monkeys' interaction with humans is a subtle and unusual one, in which both sides appear to benefit. The monkeys have gained a source of food and shelter, and the town has gained an important tourist attraction.

The capuchins have proven amazingly adaptable due to their ability to consume a wide variety of foods, as well as their behavioural complexity which has enabled them to learn how to unscrew the tops off of bottles, unzip tourist luggage, turn doorknobs to get into houses and open refrigerators for a snack.

The symbiotic relationship of Misahuallí's two species of urban primates (those with and those without a camera) has also attracted serious scientific attention. Michelle Field, a PhD candidate in anthropology, is studying them for her dissertation. Enquires may be directed to her at michelleyfield@gmail.com.

Misahuallí → *Phone code 06. Colour map 1, B4. Population 4900. Altitude 400 m.*

This small port at the confluence of the Napo and Misahuallí rivers was once the westernmost access for navigation on the Río Napo, but tourism has since replaced transport as the town's major activity. Today, it is a particularly pleasant and tranquil little place, well suited to those in no hurry. A narrow suspension bridge crosses the Río Napo at Misahuallí and joins the road along the south shore.

Misahuallí is perhaps the best place in Ecuador from which to visit the 'near Oriente', but your expectations should be realistic. The area has been colonized for many years and there is little virgin rainforest. Access is very easy, however, prices are reasonable, and while you will not encounter large animals in the wild, you can see birds, butterflies and exuberant vegetation – enough to get a taste for the jungle. Some Misahuallí operators also offer tours deeper into the jungle, past Coca. There is a fine, sandy beach on the Río Misahuallí, but don't camp on it as the river can rise unexpectedly.

There is a butterfly farm, **mariposario** ① *2 blocks from the plaza, Misahuallí, US$1.50*, with several colourful species that can be observed close up. Interesting and worthwhile. Make arrangements through **Ecoselva**. ▸▸ *See Tour operators, page 565.*

Upper Río Napo → *Colour map 1, B4.*

On the south shore of the Río Napo, a partly paved road with bus service runs from Puerto Napo to **Chontapunta** (also known as Colonia Los Ríos), three hours from Tena and about halfway to Coca. Along the way are several jungle lodges. ▸▸ *For details of jungle lodges on the Upper Napo, see page 559.*

Puyo and around → *Phone code 03. Colour map 1, B4. Population 35,000. Altitude 950 m.*

Some 33 km south of Puerto Napo is **Puyo**, the capital of the province of Pastaza and the largest urban centre in the Oriente. It feels more like a lowland city than a jungle the jungle can also be arranged from Puyo. Sangay and Altar volcanoes can sometimes be seen from town. Puyo is the junction for road travel into the northern and southern Oriente, and for traffic heading to or from Ambato via Baños. Information is available from **Ministerio de Turismo** ① *Francisco de Orellana y General Villamil, Mon-Fri 0830-1230, 1330-1700*; and **Consejo Provincial** ① *145 y 27 de Febrero, ground floor*.

The **Museo Etno-Arqueológico** ① *Atahualpa y General Villamil, 3rd floor*, has displays of the traditional dwellings of various cultures of the province of Pastaza.

Omaere ① *T03-288 7656, daily 0800-1700, US$3, www.omaere.net*, is a 15-ha ethno-botanical reserve located 2 km north of Puyo on the road to Tena. It has three trails with a variety of plants, an orchidarium and traditional native homes.

There are other small private reserves of varying quality in the Puyo area and visits are arranged by local tour operators (see page 566). You cannot, however, expect to see large tracts of undisturbed primary jungle here nor many wild animals.

● Sleeping

Baeza *p560*
E **Bambús**, Av de los Quijos, east end of new town, T06-232 0615. Private bath, hot water, parking, ping-pong, billiards, pleasant, friendly.
F **La Casa de Gina**, Jumandy y Batallón Chimborazo, just off the highway in the old town, T06-232 0471. Private bath, hot water, nicely furnished, clean and good value.

Baeza to Lago Agrio *p560*
E **Hostería El Reventador**, on highway next to bridge over the Río Reventador, T09-357 7143, turismovolcanreventador@yahoo.com. Meals, private bath, hot water, pool, simple rooms, busy on weekends, well located for visiting San Rafael falls and Volcán Reventador.
E **Paraíso Dorado**, El Dorado de Cascales, 250 m from the police checkpoint on the way to Lago Agrio, T09-471 5191. A small clean place, meals on request, private bath, cold water, very friendly and helpful.

Baeza to Tena *p561*
L **Cabañas San Isidro**, Cosanga, T02-254 7403 (Quito), www.ecuadorexplorer.com/sanisidro. A 1200-ha private reserve with rich bird life, comfortable accommodation and warm hospitality. Includes 3 excellent meals. There is an easily accessible cock-of-the-rock lek on the reserve, and feeders make the local hummingbirds easy to see. Reservations required. Recommended.
E **The Magic Roundabout**, turn-off at Las Palmas, just north of Cosanga, T09-934 5264, www.magicroundabout.info. Reservations

advised. Cabins with shared bath and dorms on a hillside. Great views, cosy social area, hiking trails to waterfalls. Good breakfast, other meals available. British-run, very friendly, "the best pub for miles". Recommended.

Tena *p561, map p564*
C **Hakuna Matata**, Vía Chaupi Shungu Km 3.9, off the road between Tena and Archidona, T06-288 9617, www.hakunamat.com. Comfortable cabins in a lovely setting by the Río Inchillaqui. Includes breakfast, other meals available, walks, river bathing and horse riding. Very good food, friendly Belgian hosts, pleasant atmosphere. Warmly recommended.
C **Los Yutzos**, Augusto Rueda 190 y 15 de Noviembre, T06-288 6717, www.uchu tican.com. Comfortable rooms and beautiful grounds overlooking the Río Pano, quiet and family-run. A/c, cheaper with fan, parking, annex next door is cheaper. Recommended.
D **Villa Belén**, on Baeza road (Av Jumandy) near the airport, T06-288 6228. Fan, laundry and cooking facilities, parking, excellent rooms, quiet, friendly. Recommended.
E **Austria**, Tarqui y Díaz de Pineda, T06-288 7205. Includes breakfast, private bath, electric shower, fan, ample parking, spacious rooms, quiet, friendly, good value, popular and often full. Recommended.
E **Brisa del Río**, Malecón y 9 de Octubre, T06-288 6444. One room with private bath, others shared, electric shower, fan, good location, adequate rooms, friendly, helpful, good value.

Oriente Jungle Foothills Listings

E-F **Limoncocha**, Sangay 533, Sector Corazón de Jesús, on a hillside 4 blocks from the bus station, T06-288 7583, limoncocha@ andinanet.net. Concrete house with terrace and hammocks. Café, hot water, fan, laundry and cooking facilities, parking, enthusiastic owners organize tours and change TCs. Out of the way in a humble neighbourhood, nice views, pleasant atmosphere, good value.

Misahuallí p562

C **France Amazonia**, on road to Tena across from the high school, T06-289 0009, www.france-amazonia.com. Includes breakfast, electric shower, pool, parking, nice grounds with river views, cosy rooms (not for very tall people), French-run, very friendly and helpful. Recommended.

C **Hostería Misahuallí**, across the river from town, T06-289 0063, www.misahualli jungle.com. Meals available on request, electric shower, fan, pool and tennis court, cabins for up to 6, nice setting, lovely sunsets.

F **Shaw**, Santander on the plaza, T06-289 0019, www.ecoselva-jungletours.com. Includes breakfast, restaurant downstairs, private bath,

hot water, fan, simple clean rooms, run their own tours, English spoken, very friendly and knowledgeable. Good value. Recommended.

Puyo p562

See also **Las Cascadas Jungle Lodge**, page 560.

B **Flor de Canela**, Paseo Turístico, Barrio Obrero, T03-288 5265. Includes breakfast, restaurant and bar, pool, comfortable cabins, pleasant location but a bit out of the way.

C **Turingia**, Ceslao Marín 294, T03-288 5180, www.hosteriaturingia.com. Restaurant, fan, small pool, parking, comfortable, garden.

D **Casablanca**, 20 de Julio y Bolívar, T03-288 8169. Comfortable rooms, some with balcony, includes breakfast, good restaurant, parking. Recommended.

E **Colibrí**, Calle Manabí, between Bolívar y Galápagos, T03-288 4768, cascada yanarumi@yahoo.es. Private bath, hot water, parking, away from centre, simple but nice, friendly and good value. Recommended.

E **La Palmas**, 20 de Julio y 4 de Enero, 5 blocks from centre, T03-288 4832, www.laspalmas. pastaza.net. Includes breakfast, private bath, hot water, comfortable multi-storey hotel.

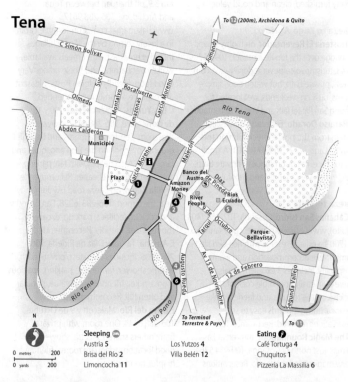

Tena

To 12 (200m), Archidona & Quito

C Simón Bolívar
Sucre
J Montalvo
Rocafuerte
Amazonas
García Moreno
Olmedo
Abdón Calderón
Municipio
JL Mera
García Moreno
Plaza
Malecón
Banco del Austro
Amazon Money
Díaz de Pineda
River People
Ríos Ecuador
3 de Octubre
Tarqui
Parque Bellavista
Av 15 de Febrero
Augusto Rueda
12 de Febrero
Segunda Vallejo
Río Tena
Río Tena
Río Pano
To Terminal Terrestre & Puyo
To 11

N

0 metres 200
0 yards 200

Sleeping
Austria 5
Brisa del Río 2
Limoncocha 11
Los Yutzos 4
Villa Belén 12

Eating
Café Tortuga 4
Chuquitos 1
Pizzería La Massilia 6

🍴 Eating

Baeza *p560*

🍴 **Gina**, Batallón Chimborazo, just off the highway in the old town, daily 0730-2200. Trout is the speciality, friendly and popular.

Tena *p561, map p564*

There are also a couple of *chifas* and various cheap *comedores* in town.

🍴🍴 **Chuquitos**, García Moreno, by the plaza. Good food, à la carte only, seating on a balcony overlooking the river. Pleasant atmosphere, attentive service and nice views. Popular and recommended.

🍴 **Pizzería La Massilia**, Hotel Los Yutzos annex, Good pizza, nice location by the river.

Misahuallí *p562*

🍴 **Doña Gloria**, Arteaga y Rivadeneyra by corner of plaza. Good set meals.

🍴 **Ecocafé**, at Hotel Shaw, on the plaza. Good breakfast, some vegetarian dishes, set meals and à la carte, great atmosphere and service.

Puyo *p562*

🍴🍴 **El Alcázar**, 10 de Agosto 936 y Sucre. Very good restaurant with an unexpectedly Spanish-European flavour. Good-value set meals and varied à la carte. Recommended.

🍴🍴 **El Jardín**, on the Paseo Turístico in Barrio Obrero. Pleasant setting and atmosphere, international food, meat and pasta specialities.

🍴🍴-🍴 **Pizzería Buon Giorno**, Orellana between Villamil and 27 de Febrero. Good pizza, lasagne and salads, good atmosphere, very popular.

🍴 **Casablanca**, 20 de Julio y Bolívar, next to the hotel. Good cheap set lunch, popular.

⛰ Activities and tours

Tena *p561, map p564*

Most Tena hotels and tour operators offer cultural and jungle tours. Rafting and kayaking is especially popular here, US$55-70 per day, but be mindful of safety standards. Avoid touts who try to pick you up on the street. We have received a serious complaint about René Shiguango, working with 'Sachaursay'.

Ricancie, Red Indígena de las Comunidades del Alto Napo para la Convivencia Inter-cultural y El Ecoturismo, Av del Chofer, 2 blocks from bus terminal, T06-288 8479, http://ricancie.nativeweb.org. This local NGO fosters community development through eco/ethnotourism. Kichwa communities may be visited. Also volunteer opportunities.

Ríos Ecuador/Yacu Amu, Tarqui 230 y Díaz de Pineda, Tena, T06-288 6346, www.rios ecuador.com. Highly recommended rafting and kayak trips, and a 4-day kayak school.

River People, 15 de Noviembre y 9 de Octubre, T06-288 8384, www.river peoplerafting ecuador.com. White-water rafting/kayaking.

Misahuallí *p562*

Jungle tours (US$25-50 pp per day) can be also be arranged by most hotels.

Ecoselva, Santander on the plaza, T06-289 0019, www.ecoselva-jungletours.com. Recommended guide Pepe Tapia speaks English and has a biology background.

Selva Verde, Santander on the plaza, T06-289 0165. Guide Luis Zapata speaks English and offers a variety of tours.

Oriente Jungle Foothills Listings

All of the following offer jungle tours.
Trips cost US$25-50 per person per day.
Nave de Santos, at the Terminal Terrestre,
T03-288 3974. Owner, Marco Naveda.
Papangu Tours, 27 de Febrero y Sucre,
T03-288 7684, papangu@andinanet.net.
Operated by the **Organización de Pueblos
Indigenas de Pastaza** (OPIP). Native guides.

⊙ Transport

Tena *p561, map p564*
Air Airport on Av Jumandy, right in town,
T06-288 6808. One flight a week to **Quito**
with **VIP** (T1-800-847847), Thu, US$60.
Not a common route, confirm in advance.
Bus Most local service is from outside
the Terminal Terrestre on 15 de Noviembre,
1 km from the centre (taxi US$1). To
Misahuallí, hourly, US$1, 45 mins. To
Chontapunta, 8 a day, US$3.50, 3 hrs.

Misahuallí *p562*
Bus Local buses run from the plaza. To
Tena, hourly 0700-1800, US$1, 45 mins.
Make long-distance connections in Tena, or
get off at Puerto Napo to catch southbound

buses although you may not get a seat. To
Quito, 1 direct bus a day at 0830, US$6, 6 hrs.
Canoe No scheduled service, but motorized
canoes for 8-10 can be chartered to **Coca**
(5-7 hrs, US$200) or other destinations.

Puyo *p562*
Bus The Terminal Terrestre is on the
outskirts of town, on the Shell and Baños
road in the southwest, a 10- to 15-min walk
from the centre or take a taxi (US$1).

⊙ Directory

Tena *p561*
Banks Banco del Austro, 15 de Noviembre
y Diaz de Pineda. **Amazon Money**, 15 de
Noviembre 422 y 9 de Octubre, p 2, T06-288
8766, 5% commission for TCs, poor rates
for cash Euros. **Hostal Limoncocha** (see
Sleeping, above), 3% commission for TCs.

Puyo *p562*
Banks Casa de Cambios Puyo, Atahualpa y 9
de Octubre, T03-288 3064. 5% commission for
Amex US$ TCs. **Banco del Austro**, Atahualpa,
between10 de Agosto and Dávila. **Laundry**
Lavandería La Mocita, Bolívar y 27 de Febrero.

Downriver

The heart of Ecuador's remaining primary rainforest lies in the east of Oriente, in the provinces of Sucumbíos and Orellana (capitals Lago Agrio and Coca, respectively) as well as eastern Pastaza. Here are two vast national parks, Cuyabeno and Yasuní, as well as the Huaorani Reserve, with many excellent lodges for an unforgettable immersion into life in the rivers, canopy and understorey. Although not cheap, this is Ecuadorean jungle tourism at its best. Despite all the lip-service paid to conservation and ecotourism here, the eastern jungle is also under severe threat from petroleum development and colonization. It is hoped that sustainable tourism can help tip the economic balance in favour of conservation. ▸▸ *For Sleeping, Eating and other listings, see pages 569-570.*

Lago Agrio ⊞⊘▲⊙⊙ ▸▸ *pp569-570.*

→ *Phone code 06. Colour map 1, A5. Population 52,000.*
Despite its importance for tourists as the access for Reserva Faunística Cuyabeno, Lago Agrio is first and foremost an old oil town. It is the capital of the province of Sucumbíos and has close commercial ties with neighbouring Colombia. Lago Agrio has grown in recent years and the infrastructure is adequate, but it remains very much on the frontier. The town's official name is Nueva Loja, owing to the fact that many of the first colonizers were from the southern province of Loja. The name Lago Agrio comes from 'Sour Lake',

the US headquarters of Texaco, the first oil company to exploit the crude reserves beneath Ecuador's rainforest. Avenida Quito is the main street where many hotels and restaurants are located, but there are no street signs. Information is provided by the **Cámara de Turismo de Sucumbíos** ① *Av Quito y Pasaje Gonzanamá, T06-283 2502, Mon-Fri 0830-1200, 1430-1700.*

Safety
Lago Agrio is among the places in Ecuador that has been most severely affected by the armed conflict in neighbouring Colombia. Enquire about public safety before travelling here and enquire again in Lago Agrio before visiting outlying regions of the province of Sucumbíos. Most of town is not safe after 2000. If you do not wish to sleep in Lago Agrio, an alternative is **El Dorado de Cascales** (see page 561).

Reserva Faunística Cuyabeno → *Colour map 1, A6.*
This large tract of rainforest, covering 602,000 ha, is located about 100 km east of Lago Agrio; entry costs US$20. The extensive jungle area is along the Río Cuyabeno, which eventually drains into the Aguarico. In the reserve are many lagoons and a great variety of wildlife, including river dolphins, tapirs, capybaras, five species of caiman, ocelots, 15 species of monkey and over 500 species of bird.

This is among the best places in Ecuador to see jungle animals and the reserve is very popular with visitors. Access is either by road from Lago Agrio, or by river along the Río Aguarico. Within the reserve, transport is mainly by canoe. In order to see as many animals as possible and minimally impact their habitat, seek out a small tour group which scrupulously adheres to responsible tourism practices. Most Cuyabeno tours are booked through agencies in Quito or other popular tourist destinations. ›› *For further details, see Cuyabeno jungle lodges, page 559, and Activities and tours, page 570.*

Warning Armed robberies of tour groups have taken place in and around Reserva Faunística Cuyabeno. Enquire about public safety before signing up for a tour and do not take unnecessary valuables. On no account should you venture into areas directly along the Colombian border.

Coca 🏨🍴🛴🛥️🚌🎒 ›› *pp569-570.*

→ *Phone code 06. See map page 569. Colour map 1, A5. Population 30,000.*

Officially named Puerto Francisco de Orellana, Coca is a hot, bustling and noisy oil town located at the junction of the Ríos Payamino and Napo, just upstream from the confluence of the Coca and Napo. It is the capital of the province of Orellana, and a small monument at the foot of Calle Napo commemorates the passage of Francisco de Orellana through the area in 1542, on his way to discover the Amazon.

The view over the water is nice, and the riverfront can be a pleasant place to spend time, especially around sunset. Hotel and restaurant provision is adequate but electricity and water supply are erratic; better hotels have reserve tanks and generators. Ironically, the petroleum production capital of Ecuador also suffers from occasional gasoline shortages. Although further from the Colombian border and generally safer and more tranquil than Lago Agrio, Coca nonetheless calls for common sense precautions.

Lower Río Napo
Jungle lodges and river cruises Coca is the access point for some of Ecuador's finest jungle lodges, offering one of the best ways to experience the jungle first hand. It is also the starting point for river cruises along the lower Napo, and for the journey downriver to Iquitos, Peru. ›› *For details of lodges and cruises, see page 559.*

Coca to Iquitos (Peru) → *For river transport from Coca to the border, see page 570.*

This river route is increasingly popular but still rough and adventurous, requiring plenty of time and patience. There are at present three different ways to undertake the journey:

1) By far the cheapest option is to take one of the motorized canoes that sail regularly from Coca to Nuevo Rocafuerte on the border (three a week; for schedules see Coca river transport, page 570). They stop en route at **Pañacocha** and other communities depending on passenger demand and the water level, but do no touring.

2) Coca agencies offer jungle tours in motorized canoes, taking in various attractions en route and continuing to Iquitos or closer Peruvian ports from where you can catch onward public river transport. We have received complaints about some of these tours (not with the agencies we list), so ask around carefully, confirm all details in advance and try to pay only half the price up front.

3) River cruise boats offer a much more comfortable and expensive alternative to either of the above, but they seldom sail all the way to Iquitos (see page 556).

Into Peru → *Colour map 1, B6.*

Getting to and crossing the border is relatively straightforward (see border box, below, and Coca River Transport page 570). Tours to **Parque Nacional Yasuní** can be arranged with local guides from Nuevo Rocafuerte, on the Ecuadorean side. The more difficult part of the journey begins in **Pantoja**, Peru, as departure dates of boats to Iquitos are irregular and you could be faced with a long wait. In 2007, the largest and most comfortable *lancha* (riverboat) on the Peruvian Napo was the *Cabo Pantoja* (Iquitos T+51-65-223037), but it sails from Pantoja only once a fortnight. Other more basic vessels include the *Miluska*, the *Victor* (T+51-65-242082), the *Jeisawell* and the *Siempre Adelante* (the latter two have the same owner, T+51-65-266159, T+51-65-961 3049 mob). Most boats only come upriver as far as Pantoja when they have sufficient cargo, so a week or more can go by without any boat calling on the town. Try phoning Iquitos in advance to enquire when the next boat will sail from Pantoja, this information is not available in Coca.

Conditions on some vessels can get crowded and unsanitary. Most have no berths, only deck space to hang your hammock. The four- to six-day trip from Pantoja all the way to Iquitos costs US$30 including basic food, but there are several ways you can shorten or break up the journey. You could sail with the *lancha* only as far as **Santa Clotilde**, about halfway to Iquitos, which has simple places to sleep and eat. From Santa Clotilde there are usually five *rápidos* (speedboats) per week to Mazán (five hours, US$25), which also has simple accommodation and meals. From Mazán, where the lanchas also call, you can cross by motorcycle-taxi to **Indiana** (15 minutes, US$1) and then take another fast boat to **Iquitos** (1½ hours, US$4). So if you are really lucky, you could travel from Coca to Iquitos in about four days, but you must be prepared for a much longer journey. Take a hammock, cup, bowl, cutlery, plenty of extra food and snacks, drinking water or a way to purify it, insect repellent, toilet paper, soap, towel, etc. Cash dollars and soles in small notes are indispensable. Soles are not available in Coca but can usually be purchased from shopkeepers in Nuevo Rocafuerte or Pantoja, although at poor rates.

To Peru via Nuevo Rocafuerte–Pantoja

The Ecuadorian border post at Nuevo Rocafuerte has two simple hotels, and meals can be purchased here. There is an **Ecuadorian immigration** office for exit stamps and boats can be hired for the trip downriver to the Peruvian border town of **Pantoja** (one to three hours depending on the boat, US$30-40 per boat, negotiable). Peruvian entry stamps are given in Pantoja, which has a decent hostal (E Napuruna) and a place to eat next door.

● Sleeping

Lago Agrio p566

B Arazá, Quito 610 y Narváez, T06-283 0223. Quiet location away from centre. Includes breakfast, restaurant, a/c, pool (US$5 for non-residents), fridge, parking, comfortable, clean and nice. Best in town. Recommended.
C Gran Hostal de Lago, Km 1½, Vía Quito, T06-283 2415. Includes breakfast, restaurant, a/c, pool, parking, gardens. Recommended.
D D'Mario, Quito 171, T06-283 0172. Restaurant serves good set meals and pizza in the evening, cheaper with cold water, a/c, small pool, some rooms have fridge, good clean place, helpful owner. Recommended.
E Lago Imperial, Colombia y Quito, T06-283 0453. Private bath, cold water, a/c, cheaper with fan, central location, good value.
F Casa Blanca, Quito y Colombia, T06-283 0181. Private bath, hot water, fan, nice bright rooms, good value.

Coca p567, map p569

B-D El Auca, Napo y García Moreno, T06-288 0600, helauca@ecuanex.net.ec. Restaurant, disco at weekends, cheaper with fan, parking, rooms or mini-suites. Comfortable, garden

with hammocks, English spoken. Popular and centrally located but can get noisy.
B-D La Misión, by riverfront 100 m downriver from the bridge, T06-288 0261, www.hotela mision.com. Restaurant and disco, a/c and fridge, pool and water-slide, parking, good location by the river, English spoken, tours.
C Las Heliconias, Cuenca y Amazonas, T06-288 2010. Restaurant, garden, clean, friendly.
D Amazonas, 12 de Febrero y Espejo, T06-288 0444. Relaxed setting by the river, away from centre, restaurant, a/c, parking, quiet, friendly and good.
D-E San Fermín, Bolívar y Quito, T06-288 0802. A/c, cheaper with fan and cold water, parking, modern and comfortable, good value.
E Oasis, between the bridge and La Misión, T06-288 0206. Private bath, electric shower, a/c, cheaper with fan, parking, quiet, simple.

❼ Eating

Lago Agrio p566

There are decent restaurants at the better hotels. There are also a great many cheap and basic *comedores* along Av Quito.

Coca

Sleeping ●
Amazonas 1
El Auca 4
La Misión 6
Las Heliconias 9
Oasis 7
San Fermín 8

Eating ❼
Ocaso 4
Parrilladas Argentinas 6
Pizza Choza 7

0 metres 50
0 yards 50

Río Napo
To Vía Auca

Several other simple *comedores* in town.
♯ **Parrilladas Argentinas**, Cuenca e Inés
Arango. Argentine-style grill.
♯-♦ **Pizza Choza**, Rocafuerte y Napo.
Good pizza, friendly owner, English spoken.
♦ **Ocaso**, Eloy Alfaro between Napo and
Amazonas. Good-value set meals and à la carte.

▲ Activities and tours

Reserva Faunística Cuyabeno *p567*
For lodges in Cuyabeno, see page 559. The
following Quito agencies also offer tours:
Dracaena, T02-254 6590, dracaena@
andinanet.net, highly recommended.
Green Planet, T02-252 0570,
greenpla@interactive.net.ec.
Kapok Expeditions, T02-255 6348.

Coca *p567, map p569*
A common misconception is that it is easy to
find a cheap jungle tour in Coca. In fact, the
majority of tours out of Coca are booked
through agencies in Quito and other tourist
centres. The quality of Coca agencies varies,
try to get a personal recommendation, prices
are around US$50-60 per person per day.

Tour operators
Ecu-Astonishing, Malecón, by **Hotel Oasis**,
T06-288 0251, juliojarrin@andinanet.net. Julio
Jarrín runs tours to cabins near Pañacocha.
Emerald Forest Expeditions, Quito y Espejo,
T06-288 2309. Luis García offers tours to
Pañacocha, Yasuní and Iquitos, Peru.
Wymper Torres, T06-288 0336. Specializes
in the Río Shiripuno and Pañacocha areas,
also trips to Iquitos, Spanish only.

⊘ Transport

Lago Agrio *p566*
Air The airport is 5 km southeast of the centre.
TAME flies to/from **Quito**, daily except Sun,
US$52 one way. Book 1-2 days in advance and
reconfirm. If there is no space to **Lago Agrio**
then you can fly to **Coca** instead, from where
it is only 2 hrs by bus on a good road.
Bus The Terminal Terrestre is located in the
north of town, but buses for Coca leave from
the market area on Orellana, 3 blocks south
of Av Quito. There are 2 routes from Lago
Agrio to **Quito**: one through El Dorado de

Cascales, the other, slightly longer, through
Coca and Loreto; both have a bus service.

Coca *p567, map p569*
Air The airport is in the north of town. To/
from **Quito**, various daily flights with **TAME**,
Icaro and **VIP**, US$60 one way; reserve as far in
advance as possible and always reconfirm.
Flights in and out of Coca are heavily booked,
oil workers may have priority. **Icaro** office is in
Hotel La Misión, T06-288 0546. **TAME** office
is at Napo y Rocafuerte, T06-288 1078.
Bus Long-distance buses depart from
company offices in town (see map); local
destinations, including **Lago Agrio**, are
served from the terminal a little to the north.
River Boats run down the Río Napo to
Nuevo Rocafuerte on the Peruvian border;
most reliable is **Cooperativa de Transporte
Fluvial Orellana**, at the dock, T06-288 0087,
large motorized canoes with space for 50
passengers Mon and Thu at 0800, 10 hrs,
US$10; returning Wed and Sun at 0530, 12
hrs. Buy tickets a day in advance, be at the
dock early, take food, water, hat, sun-screen.
Another canoe leaves Coca Fri early morning,
returning Tue. An 18-passenger Peruvian
canoe may be chartered for touring and
transport to **Pantoja** (Peru) and beyond,
contact Sra Lilly Valles, T08-630 1047.
There is no regular boat service from
Coca upriver to **Misahuallí** but charters
can be arranged, ask around at the dock.

⊘ Directory

Lago Agrio *p566*
Banks Banco de Guayquil, Quito y 12 de
Febrero; Banco de Pichincha, 12 de Febrero
y Añasco; both for ATM only. *Casa de cambio*,
Quito y Colombia, for Colombian pesos.
These can also be changed in shops.

Coca *p567, map p569*
Banks Banco de Pichincha, Bolívar y 9 de
Octubre, ATM only. Cambiaria Ramírez, Napo
y García Moreno, 4% on TCs (Amex only). No
exchange facilities. **Internet** Prices around
US$1.20 per hr. **Useful addresses**
Immigration, Rocafuerte y Napo, Edificio
Amazonas, p3, T06-288 1594. For travel to or
from Peru by river, passports are normally
stamped at Nuevo Rocafuerte, not Coca, but
you can confirm details here before sailing.

Introduction

The coastal region covers a third of Ecuador's total area. Though popular with Ecuadoreans, who come here in their droves for weekends and holidays, the area receives relatively few foreign visitors, which is surprising given the natural beauty, diversity and rich cultural heritage of the coast. You can surf, watch whales at play, visit ancient archaeological sites, or just relax and enjoy the best food that this country has to offer. The jewel in the coastal crown, Parque Nacional Machalilla, protects a wide variety of wildlife.

The coastal plains are also the agro-industrial heartland of Ecuador. Rice, sugar, coffee, African palm, mango, cacao, and shrimp are produced in these hot and humid lowlands and processed or exported through Guayaquil. The largest and most dynamic commercial centre in the country, Guayaquil is also Ecuador's main port and the city's influence extends along the coast and beyond. Guayaquil has experienced a civic revival in recent years and has some attractions to offer. Trips to Galápagos can be organized from here, and the city is a logical starting point for travels north along the coast.

In the opposite direction, south to the Peruvian border, the land gives the impression of being one giant banana plantation. Machala is the main centre here, and nearby Puerto Bolívar is the port through which the *oro verde* (green gold) is shipped out to the world. Inland from Machala, in the uplands of El Oro, is one of the best hidden treasures of Ecuador – the colonial mining town of Zaruma.

★ Don't miss ...

1 **Malecón 2000** Stroll along Guayaquil's pride and joy, page 575.
2 **Uplands of El Oro** Discover the romance of this seldom-visited colonial gold mining region, page 582.
3 **Parque Nacional Machalilla** Spot birds and marine wildlife on the mainland and on Isla de La Plata, page 587.
4 **Whale watching** Observe migrating humpback whales from Puerto López or other coastal towns, page 592.
5 **Canoa** Be a beach bum or make the most of activities, such as surfing, horse riding and cycling, page 592.

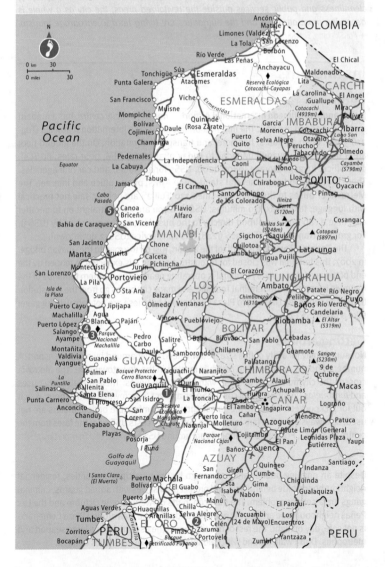

Pacific Coast

Guayaquil

→ *Phone code 04. Colour map 1, B2. Population 2,300,000. Altitude 4 m.*
Ecuador's largest city and the country's chief sea port and industrial and commercial centre lies on the west bank of the chocolate-brown Río Guayas, some 56 km from its outflow into the Gulf of Guayaquil. The city couldn't be more different from its highland counterpart and political rival, Quito. It is hot, sticky, fast-paced, noisy, bold and brash. It may lack the capital's colonial charm, but Guayaquileños are certainly more lively, colourful and open than Quiteños. Since 2000, Guayaquil has cleaned up and 'renewed' some of its most frequented downtown areas, there is a new airport terminal and a new transit system: the Metrovía. Although much remains to be done in terms of safety, cleanliness and public services outside the revitalized areas, the city as a whole is becoming more attractive and the authorities are trying hard to encourage tourism.
▶▶ *For Sleeping, Eating and other listings, see pages 578-582.*

Ins and outs

Getting there
José Joaquín de Olmedo International Airport ① *north of the city centre*, has a modern terminal, opened in 2006. The information booth outside international arrivals (T04-216 9000, open 24 hours) has hotel and transport information. On the ground floor are a **Banco de Guayaquil** (Monday to Friday 0830-1800, ATM, poor rates, no TCs), post office, luggage storage (0800-2200, US$5 for 24 hours) and car hire agencies. There is also a food court, several stand-alone ATMs, phone office and internet. The **Metrovía** or buses to the centre (eg Línea 130 'Full 2') are neither safe nor practical with luggage; take a taxi (10 minutes, US$4). If you are going straight on to another city, take a cab from the airport directly to the bus station, which is close by (US$3). For groups, **Trans Rabbit** (T04-216 9228) has van service (US$12 downtown).

The **Terminal Terrestre** is north of the airport, just off the road to the Guayas bridge. In 2007, this terminal was closed for reconstruction and it is expected to reopen by the end of the year. A temporary terminal is operating nearby. The northern terminus of the Metrovía is opposite the Terminal Terrestre and many city buses go from the bus station to the city centre (eg Línea 84 to Plaza Centenario) but these are not safe with luggage; take a taxi (US$3-4).

Getting around
Not surprisingly for a city of this size, you will need to get around by public transport. A number of hotels, however, are centrally located in the downtown core. The Metrovía crosses the city from north to south with articulated buses. There are also city buses and *furgonetas* (minibuses), all cost US$0.25 and get overcrowded at rush hour; watch out for pickpockets. Taxis are the safest and most comfortable option. Meters are not used, so always agree the fare in advance. Short trips costs US$2.50, the fares from the centre to Urdesa, Policentro or Alborada are around US$3-4. ▶▶ *See also Transport, page 581.*

Safety
Despite an ongoing public safety campaign by the municipal authorities, residential neighbourhoods hide behind bars and protect themselves with armed guards. Criminal gangs are a serious problem. The Malecón, parts of Avenida 9 de Octubre and the Las Peñas neighbourhood are heavily patrolled and safe. The area around Plaza Centenario is not safe, day or night. The rest of the city carries the usual risks of a large seaport and metropolis. Don't walk around with valuables and always take taxis at night.

Centro de Información Turística del Municipio ⓘ *Clemente Ballén y Pichincha, inside Museo Nahim Isaías, T04-232 4182 ext 19, Wed-Sat 1000-1700, English spoken*, has pamphlets and city maps. There is also an information booth on a railway car in Malecón 2000, next to La Rotonda monument. **Ministerio de Turismo** ⓘ *P Ycaza 203 y Pichincha, p 5, T04-256 8764, Mon-Fri 0830-1700 Spanish only*, is friendly and has information about the coastal provinces of Ecuador. Useful websites about Guayaquil and the coast include www.visitaguayaquil.com, www.guayaquil.gov.ec, www.turismo guayas.com and www.guayaquilguides.com.

Sights

Riverfront

A wide, tree-lined avenue, the **Malecón Simón Bolívar** runs alongside the Río Guayas for 2½ km. The riverfront here has been turned into an attractive promenade, known as **Malecón 2000**, where visitors and locals can enjoy the fresh breeze and take in the views. There are lovely gardens, fountains, monuments, upmarket restaurants, cafés and food courts. It is the city's pride and joy.

Guayaquil's second showpiece, the picturesque district of **Las Peñas**, is a vestige of times gone by, built atop **Cerro Santa Ana**, just north of the Malecón 2000. Walk up the hill along a steep stairway amid the brightly painted wooden houses. There are cafés, bars and lovely views from the top. The area is heavily guarded and safe. During the **Fiestas Julianas** (24-25 July), painters exhibit their art here. The entrance to the main street (Numa Pompilio Llona) is guarded by two cannon pointing riverward, a reminder of the days when pirates sailed up the Guayas to attack the city.

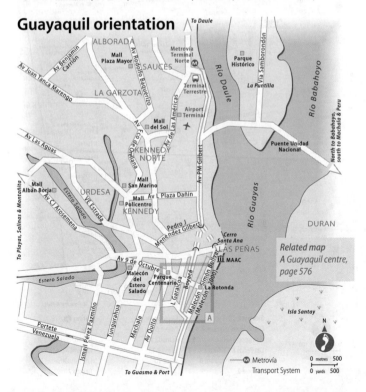

Guayaquil orientation

Related map
A Guayaquil centre, page 576

Metrovía Transport System

0 metres 500
0 yards 500

At the north end of the Malecón 2000, near Cerro Santa Ana, is the **Museo Antropológico y de Arte Contemporáneo (MAAC)** ① *T04-230 9400, Wed-Sat 1000-1730, US$1.50, Sun and holidays 1000-1600, free*, with excellent collections of ceramics, gold from coastal cultures and an extensive modern art collection.

Towards the centre of the Malecón 2000 are a tourist information booth, the Yacht Club and several monuments. Most notable are **La Rotonda**, which marks the meeting between independence leaders Simón Bolívar and José San Martín in 1822, and a **Moorish clock tower**. Further south are the exclusive **Club de la Unión**, a monument to poet and former president José Joaquín de Olmedo, souvenir shops, a shopping mall and the old **Mercado Sur** (prefabricated by Eiffel 1905-1907), now known as **Palacio de Cristal** and used as a gallery for temporary exhibits.

City centre
Opposite the Malecón 2000, between Aguirre and 10 de Agosto, are the imposing **Palacio Municipal** and **Gobernación**. Behind them are the recently created **Plaza de la**

Guayaquil

Pacific Coast Guayaquil

N

0 metres 100
0 yards 100

Ⓜ Metrovía

Sleeping 🛏
Grand Hotel Guayaquil **4**
Hampton Inn Boulevard **5**
Las Peñas & California
  Gourmet Restuarant **8**
La Torre **2**

Malecón Inn **1**
Palace **6**
Ramada **11**
Savoy II **13**
Vélez **10**

Eating 🍴
Asia **5**
La Cruz de Lorena **8**
La Parrilla del Ñato **6**
Los Tres Canastos **3**
Resaca **7**

Administración, with a monument to Sucre, the municipal tourist information office and the **Museo Nahim Isaías** ① *Pichincha y Clemente Ballén, T04-232 4283, Wed-Sat 1000-1700, Sun 1100-1500, US$1.50, free on Sun*, a colonial art museum with a permanent religious art collection and temporary exhibits.

Two blocks further west in the pleasant shady **Parque Bolívar**, stand a monument to Bolívar and the **cathedral**. The park, popularly known as **Parque de las Iguanas**, is filled with large tame iguanas. Near the cathedral are the **Museo Municipal** ① *Sucre y Chile, T04-252 4100, Tue-Sat 0900-1700, tours available, free*, and the **Biblioteca Municipal**, both housed in one building. The museum has paintings, gold and archaeological collections, shrunken Shuar heads, and a section on the history of Guayaquil.

The bustling boulevard 9 de Octubre, the city's main avenue, runs from the Malecón 2000 to the **Estero Salado**, a brackish estuary which flanks the west side of the city centre. Halfway up 9 de Octubre is **Parque Centenario** with its towering monument to the liberation of the city, erected in 1920. Here is **Museo de la Casa de la Cultura** ① *9 de Octubre 1200 y P Moncayo, T04-230 0500, Tue-Fri 1000-1800, Sat 0900-1500. US$0.50, English-speaking guides*, has an impressive collection of prehistoric gold items.

At the west end of 9 de Octubre, along the Estero Salado, is the **Malecón del Estero Salado**, another pleasant waterfront promenade with various monuments, eateries specializing in seafood, rowing boats and pedaloes for hire.

Around Guayaquil

Botanical gardens
① *Av Francisco de Orellana (bus line 63 or furgoneta Orquídeas), T04-289 9689, daily 0800-1600, US$3, English-speaking guides available for about US$5*, are in the Ciudadela Las Orquídeas to the north. There are over 3000 plants, including 150 species of Ecuadorean and foreign orchids.

Bosque Protector Cerro Blanco → Colour map 1, B2.
① *Vía a la Costa, Km 16, entrance beyond the Club Rocafuerte, T04-287 4947, www.bosquecerroblanco.com, US$4, additional guiding fee US$7-12 depending on trails visited, camping US$7 per person, lodge available; reservations required during weekdays and for groups of over 8 people at weekends, and for birders wishing to arrive before or stay after normal opening hours (0800-1530).*

This 6078-ha nature reserve run by **Fundación Pro-Bosque** is set in tropical dry forest along the Río Blanco with an impressive variety of birds (over 200 species), such as the Guayaquil green-macaw (symbol of the reserve), crane hawk and snail kite, and with sightings of howler monkeys, ocelot, puma, jaguar and peccaries, many reptiles, among others. To get there, take a taxi from Guayaquil, US$10-20. The yellow and green 'Chongonera' buses leave every 30 minutes from Parque Victoria and pass the park entrance on the way to Puerto Hondo.

Remember to take water, sun protection and insect repellent on all excursions from Guayaquil.

Reserva Ecológica Manglares-Churute → Colour map 1, B2/3.
① *Entrance to the reserve is at Km 50 of the Guayaquil–Naranjal–Machala road, US$10 per person, basic cabins US$5, camping US$3. Boat tour (2 hrs), US$40 for group up to 15 passengers; arrange several days ahead through the Ministerio del Ambiente in Guayaquil, Av Quito 402 y Padre Solano, p 10, T04-229 3131; or Biólogo Fernando Cedeño, T09-961 9815. Buses (CIFA, Ecuatoriano Pullman, 16 de Junio) leave the Terminal Terrestre every 30 mins, going to Naranjal or Machala; ask to be let off at the Churute information centre. The reserve can also be reached by river.*

About 45 minutes southeast of Guayaquil is Reserva Ecológica Manglares-Churute, part of the national park system, preserving mangroves in the Gulf of Guayaquil and forests of the Cordillera Churute. It is a rich natural area with five different ecosystems. There is a trail through the dry tropical forest (1½ hours' walk) and you can also walk (one hour) to Laguna Canclón or Churute, a large lake where ducks nest. Many waterbirds, animals and dolphins can be seen.

Parque Histórico

ⓘ T04-283 3807, Tue-Sun 0900-1630, US$4.50, www.parquehistorico.com; CISA buses to Samborondón leave Terminal Terrestre every 20 mins, US$0.25.

The Parque Histórico, north of the city in Entreríos, on the way to Samborondón, is a recreation of Guayaquil and its rural surroundings at the end of the 19th century. There is a natural area with native flora and fauna, a traditions section where you can learn about rural life and how crafts are made, an urban section with wooden architecture and an educational farm. It's a pleasant place for a stroll.

Santa Elena and the beaches

Southwest of Guayaquil is the beach resort of Playas and, west of it, the Santa Elena Peninsula, with Salinas at its tip. The resorts of Salinas and Playas are very popular with Guayaquileños. **Playas** is the blue-collar beach and receives huge numbers of day visitors, yet retains something of its former fishing-village atmosphere in the low season. **Salinas** is more highbrow, the place to be seen during 'la temporada'. Both resorts are reached along a paved toll highway from Guayaquil, and are busy and expensive during the high season (Christmas to Easter).

● Sleeping

Guayaquil p574, map p576

Note that we have received numerous negative reports about the hotel **Ecuahogar**.

LL-L Hilton Colón, Av Francisco de Orellana in Kennedy Norte (outside downtown), T04-268 9000, www1.hilton.com. 5 restaurants and bars, 2 pools, largest luxury hotel in town, all facilities, provides airport transfers.

L Hampton Inn Boulevard, 9 de Octubre 432 y Baquerizo Moreno, T04-256 6700, www.hampton.com.ec. Buffet breakfast, restaurant, central location, very good facilities, weekend discounts.

AL Palace, Chile 214 y Luque, T04-232 1080, www.hotelpalaceguayaquil.com.ec. Includes breakfast, 24-hr cafeteria, a/c, modern, traffic noise on Av Chile side, good value for business travellers. Recommended.

A Grand Hotel Guayaquil, Boyacá 1600 y 10 de Agosto, T04-232 9690, www.grand hotelguayaquil.com. Includes buffet breakfast, good restaurants, a/c, pool (US$6 for non-residents), gym and sauna, traditional Guayaquil luxury hotel.

A Ramada, Malecón 606 y Imbabura, T04-256 5555, www.hotelramada.com. Incudes buffet breakfast, a/c, pool, excellent location.

A-D Casa Alianza, Av Segunda 318 y Calle 12, Los Ceibos, T04-235 1261, www.casa alianza.com. Good hostel, far from the centre, a variety of rooms and prices, cafeteria, a/c, cheaper with shared bath and fan, E pp in dorm with a/c, run by a Norwegian NGO.

B Las Peñas, Escobedo 1215 y Vélez, T04-232 3355, www.hlpgye.com. Pleasant hotel in a refurbished part of downtown, includes breakfast, cafeteria, a/c, ample modern rooms, good value. Recommended.

B-C Iguanazú, Ciudadela La Cogra, Manzana 1, Villa 2, off Av Carlos Julio Arosemena, Km 3.5, T04-220 1143, www.iguanazuhostel.com. Lovely suburban guesthouse, includes breakfast, E pp in dorm, pool and jacuzzi, kitchen, parking, terrace with hammocks and views of the city, French spoken, opened in 2006.

C La Torre, Chile 303 y Luque, p 13-15, T04-253 1316, www.latorrehotel.com.ec. Popular hotel in a downtown office building, includes breakfast, cafeteria, a/c, good views, reasonably quiet for where it is, busy, advance booking advised.

C Malecón Inn, Sucre 203 y Pichincha, p 7, 1 block from the Malecón, T04-251 1290, www.maleconinn.com. New hotel occupying a couple of floors in a multi-storey building. Rooms and suites, some with jacuzzi, includes breakfast, restaurant, a/c, gym, parking, opened in 2006.

C **Tangara Guest House**, Manuela Sáenz y
O'Leary, Manzana F, Villa 1, Ciudadela
Bolivariana (a residential area between the
airport and downtown), T04-228 4445. Includes
breakfast, a/c, fridge. Friendly. Recommended.
D-E **Savoy II**, Junín 627 y Boyacá,
T04-2310206. Modern hotel in a central
location, a/c, good value, opened in 2006.
E-F **Vélez**, Vélez 1021 y Quito, T04-253 0356.
Large budget hotel by Plaza Centenario, very
popular and often full, does not take bookings.
Cafeteria, private bath, cold water, a/c, cheaper
with fan, clean and very good value but
occasional reports of theft from rooms.

🍴 Eating

Guayaquil *p574, map p576*
Although not cheap, dining out in Guayaquil
is very good. The main areas for restaurants
are in the centre with many in the larger hotels,
as well as around Urdesa and the residential
and commercial neighbourhoods to the north.
Addresses are a problem outside downtown
but taxi drivers know most of the better
restaurants, ask for them by name. In upmarket
places 22% tax and service is added to the bill.
🍴🍴🍴 **La Trattoria da Enrico**, Bálsamos 504 y
las Monjas, Urdesa, T04-238 7079, Mon-Sat
1230-1530, 1930-1130, Sun 1230-2230.
The best in Italian food and surroundings,
very exclusive, good antipasto.
🍴🍴🍴 **Lo Nuestro**, VE Estrada 903 e Higueras,
Urdesa, T04-238 6398, daily 1100-1530,
1900-2330. Typical coastal cooking.
Great seafood platters, colonial decor.
🍴🍴🍴 **Red Crab**, Estrada y Laureles, Urdesa,
T04-238 0512, daily 1100-2400. Wide variety
of excellent seafood, interesting decor.
🍴🍴🍴 **Tsuji**, VE Estrada 813 y Guayacanes,
Urdesa, T04-288 1183, Tue-Sun 1200-1500,
1900-2300. Wonderful authentic Japanese
dishes, a Guayaquil tradition.
🍴🍴🍴-🍴🍴 **Cangrejo Criollo**, Av Rolando
Pareja, Villa 9, La Garzota, daily 0900-
0100. Excellent, varied seafood menu.
🍴🍴🍴-🍴🍴 **La Parilla del Ñato**, VE Estrada 1219 y
Laureles in Urdesa; Av Francisco de Orellana
opposite the Hilton Colón; Luque y Pichincha
downtown; and several other locations. Daily
1200-2400. Grill with large variety, salad bar.
Good quality, generous portions. Try the
parrillada de mariscos, available only at the
Urdesa and Kennedy locations. Recommended.

🍴🍴🍴-🍴🍴 **Paprika**, Francisco Boloña 715,
opposite Policentro in Kennedy, daily
1100-2400. Good Mediterranean cooking,
belly dancer Thu-Sat from 2100.
🍴🍴 **La Canoa**, Hotel Continental and Mall del
Sol, open 24 hrs. Traditional dishes rarely
found these days, with different specials
during the week.
🍴🍴 **La Vaca Gaucha**, Av Principal y Av Las
Aguas, Urbanor, Tue-Fri 1800-2300, Sat
1200-2000, Sun 1200-1700. Excellent
quality grill, all you can eat for US$10.
🍴🍴-🍴 **Cantonés**, Av G Pareja y Calle 43,
La Garzota, daily 1200-2200. Huge rather
glaring Chinese emporium with authentic
dishes. Very good.
🍴🍴-🍴 **Pizzería Del Ñato**, VE Estrada 1219, Urdesa.
Italian food. Pizza by the metre, good value.
🍴 **Asia**, Sucre 321 y Chile, downtown, daily
1100-2130. Good Chinese food, vegetarian
dishes on request.
🍴 **La Cruz de Lorena**, Junín 417 y Córdova,
downtown, Mon-Sat 1200-1700. Good
economical set lunches and international
dishes à la carte.
🍴 **Ollantay**, Tungurahua 508 y 9 de Octubre,
west of downtown. The best choice for
vegetarian food.

Cafés and snacks
Aroma Café, Malecón 2000 by Tomás
Martínez, daily 1200-2400. Café, also
serves regional food, nice garden setting.
Bopán, VE Estrada y Las Monjas, Urdesa
(Mon-Sat 0800-2400); also at P Icaza y
Malecón, downtown (Mon-Fri 0830-2200).
Excellent sandwiches and local snacks,
salads, coffee, breakfast.
Fruta Bar, Malecón e Imbabura, downtown;
VE Estrada 608 y Monjas, Urdesa. Excellent
fruit juices and snacks, unusual African
decor, good music.
Los Tres Canastos, Chile 126-128 y Vélez
and several other locations. Breakfast, snacks,
safe fruit juices and smoothies.

🍸 Bars and clubs

Guayaquil *p574, map p576*
Guayaquil nightlife is not cheap. Most
clubs charge a cover of around US$5-10 on
weekdays, US$10-15 on weekends and drinks
are expensive. There are clubs, bars and
casinos in most major hotels, as well as in the

northern suburbs, especially at the **Kennedy Mall**. Also pouplar are the Las Peñas/Cerro Santa Ana area and the Zona Rosa, between the Malecón Simón Bolívar and Rocafuerte, and between Calle Loja and Calle Roca. Both these areas are considered reasonably safe.

Bars

El Colonial, Rocafuerte e Imbabura, Mon-Sat from 1600. A traditional bar/restaurant/*peña* in a colonial house, typical dishes, old time music in one hall, modern in another, live music Thu-Sat.

Resaca, Malecón 2000, at the level of Junín, daily 1130-2400. Lovely setting overlooking the river, live tropical music Fri-Sat night. Also serves economical set lunches on weekdays (go early), regional dishes at mid to expensive prices (Mon-Wed, all-you-can-eat crabs and beer US$13) and pricey drinks.

Clubs

Fizz and Santé, Av Francisco de Orellana 769, Kennedy Norte, Thu-Sat 2200-0400. Fizz has an open bar for US$15.

Praga, Rocafuerte 636 y Mendiburo, Tue-Sat from 1830. US$10 cover and live music Fri-Sat. Pleasant atmosphere, several halls with varied music.

Vulcano, Rocafuerte 419 y Padre Aguirre, Fri-Sat from 2230. Cover US$7-8. Popular gay bar which attracts a mixed crowd, varied modern music.

● Entertainment

Guayaquil *p574, map p576*
The **Centro Cívico**, Quito y Venezuela, provides an excellent theatre/concert facility and is home to the Guayaquil Symphony Orchestra which gives free concerts all year.

The **Teatro Centro de Arte**, on the road to the coast, is another first-class theatre complex, with a wide variety of presentations.

● Festivals and events

Guayaquil *p574, map p576*
24-25 Jul Fiestas Julianas, celebrating the foundation of Guayaquil. There are parades and many public events.

9-12 Oct The city's **independence** is commemorated and cultural events take place throughout the month.

○ Shopping

Guayaquil *p574, map p576*

Handicrafts

Albán Borja Mall has El Telar, which is expensive but offers superb quality, especially ceramics, jewellery and embroidery, and Ramayana, for reasonably priced ceramics.

Cerámica Vega, VE Estrada 1200 y Laureles, Urdesa. For brightly painted Cuenca ceramics.

Mall del Sol, has more than 20 crafts shops in the Plaza de Integración section.

Manos, Cedros 305 y Primera, Urdesa. Closes until 1530 for lunch.

Mercado Artesanal del Malecón 2000, at the south end of the malecón, has many small kiosks selling varied crafts.

Mercado Artesanal Guayaquil, Baquerizo Moreno between Loja and J Montalvo. Huge variety, almost a whole block of permanent stalls with good prices.

Malls

Guayaquil is a city of suburban malls, where consumerism flourishes in a/c comfort amid noisy neon-on-plastic surroundings. Here you will find many banks, restaurants, bars, discos, cinemas, cybercafés and shops. See Guayaquil orientation map (page 575) for locations.

▲▲ Activities and tours

Guayaquil *p574, map p576*
Many operators run regional tours to the beaches and whale-watching tours in season (Jun-Sep). A number of the agencies listed operate Galápagos cruises and also have offices in Quito. There are many travel agencies for airline bookings at the Malecón 2000 and in the large shopping centres.

Tour operators

Centro Viajero, Baquerizo Moreno 1119 y 9 de Octubre, No 805, T04-256 2565, T09-235 7745 for 24 hr service, centrovi@ telconet.net. Custom-designed tours to all regions, travel information and bookings, car and driver service, well informed about good-value options for Galápagos. English spoken, very friendly and helpful. Highly recommended.

Ecuadorian Tours, Esmeraldas 816 y 9 de Octubre, p 2, T04-228 6900, www.ecuadorian toursgye.com.ec. Sells land tours and Galápagos cruises. Amex representative.

Galasam, Edificio Gran Pasaje, Av 9 de Octubre 424, ground floor No 9, T04-230 4488, www.galapagos-islands.com. Has a fleet of boats in different categories for Galápagos cruises, city and regional tours, diving trips, also highland and jungle tours. **Metropolitan Touring**, Antepara 915 y 9 de Octubre and at **Hotel Hilton Colón**, T04-232 0300, www.metropolitan-touring.com. High-end land tours and Galápagos cruises.

⊙ Transport

Guayaquil *p574, map p575*
Air
The airport is US$4 by taxi from the centre. International departure tax is US$26.

Airline offices Aerogal, Junín 440 y Cordova, T04-310 346. **American Airlines**, Gen Córdova 1021 y Av 9 de Octubre, edif San Francisco, p 20, T04-259 8800. **Air France/KLM**, at the airport, p 3, T04-216 9070. **Avianca**, Av Francisco de Orellana, mez 111, T04-239 9411, T1-800-003434. **Continental**, 9 de Octubre 100 y Malecón, p 25, T1-800- 222333. **Copa**, 9 de Octubre 100 y Malecón, p 25, T04-230 3211. **Delta**, Av Francisco de Orellana, Galerías Hilton Colón, local 10, T1-800-101060. **Iberia**, Av 9 de Octubre 101 y Malecón, T04-232 9558. **Icaro**, Av Francisco de Orellana, edif World Trade Centre, Torre B, and Malecón y 10 de Agosto, T04-263 0620, T1-800-88356. **LAN**, Av Francisco de Orellana, Galerías Hilton Colón, T04-269 2850, and at the airport, p 2. **Santa Bárbara**, Nueva Kennedy, Calle E y Calle 4 Este, T04-229 0249. **TACA**, 9 de Octubre y Malecón, edif Banco de la Previsora, p 23, T04-256 2950, T1-800- 008222. **TAME**, 9 de Octubre 424, edif Gran Pasaje ground floor , T04-231 0305. **VIP** at the airport, p 2, T04-390 5049, T1-800-847847.

Bus
Local Metrovía (T04-269 1611, US$0.25) is an integrated transport system of articulated buses running on exclusive lanes and *alimentadores* (feeder buses) serving suburbs from the northern and southern terminuses. It runs from the Terminal Río Daule, opposite the Terminal Terrestre, in the north to the Terminal El Guasmo in the south. In the city centre it runs along Boyacá southbound and Pedro Carbo northbound. **City buses** Buses

and *furgonetas* (vans) are only permitted on a few streets in the centre; northbound buses go along Rumichaca, southbound along Lorenzo de Garaicoa or García Avilés, US$0.25.

Regional To Santa Elena Peninsula and beaches Frequent service to all destinations, crowded on weekends and holidays. To **Montañita** and **Olón, CLP** at 0500, 1300, 1630, 3½ hrs, US$5. All leave from Terminal Terrestre.

National For main intercity routes see the bus timetable, page 470. Note that the Terminal Terrestre was being rebuilt in 2007, a temporary terminal was operating nearby. Also, since mid-2006, the bridge to Durán near the bus terminal was closed to long-distance buses. These now have to take an alternate bridge, increasing travel time by 45 mins. To **Quito**, in addition to frequent service from the Terminal Terrestre, **Transportes Ecuador**, Av de las Américas y Hermano Miguel, opposite the new airport terminal, T04-229 4788, has 27 daily buses to its terminal in La Mariscal, US$9, 8 hrs. To **Machala**, in addition to bus service, **Oro Guayas**, Clemente Ballén y Chile, T04-232 0934, and Centro de Negocios El Terminal, by the Terminal Terrestre, has hourly van service, 0600-2000, US$10, 3 hrs.

International To Huaquillas for the **Peruvian border**, direct, US$6, 4½ hrs; or via Machala, 6 hrs. From the Terminal Terrestre, **CIFA**, T04-214 0379, to **Tumbes** 10 daily, US$6, 5½ hrs and **Piura**, at 0720, 1850, 2100 and 2330, US$10 regular, US$12 double-decker bus at 2100, 10 hrs. To **Lima**, Ormeño, Centro de Negocios El Terminal, near the Terminal Terrestre, T04-214 0362, daily at 1130, US$60 includes food, 27 hrs. Also to **Bogotá**, Tue and Fri, US$90, 38 hrs.

Car hire
There are several car hire firms on the ground level of the airport.
Avis, T04-216 9021 (airport), T04-239 5554. **Budget**, T04-216 9026 (airport), T04-228 4559. **Hertz**, T04-216 9035 (airport), T04-288 9789. **Localiza**, T04-390 4523 (airport), T04-239 5236, T1-800-562254.

Taxis and vans
Although not cheap, taxis are a good way of getting around in Guayaquil. Vans for 10-17 passengers are available from **Trans Rabbit**, T04-227 7300. See Getting around, page 574.

❶ Directory

Pacific Coast Guayaquil Listings

Guayaquil *p574, map p576*

Banks **American Express**, Ecuadorian Tours, 9 de Octubre 1900 y Esmeraldas. Replaces lost Amex TCs, but does not exchange TCs or sell them for cash. Mon-Fri 0900-1300, 1400-1800. **Banco de Guayaquil**, at airport. **Banco del Austro**, 9 de Octubre y Boyacá and VE Estrada y Dátiles, Urdesa. **Banco del Pacífico**, P Icaza 200, p 4. **Cambiosa**, 9 de Octubre y Pichincha. **Pacificard**, VM Rendón 415 y Córdova, T04-251 1500. **Produbanco**, Pedro Carbo 604 y Luque , Garaycoa 817 y 9 de Octubre and VE Estrada 206 y Bálsamos, Urdesa. **Medical services** Dr Angel Serrano Sáenz, Boyacá 821 y Junín, T04-256 1785. English-speaking. Hospitals include:**Clínica Kennedy**, Av San Jorge y la 9a, T04-228 9666. The main hospital used by the foreign community and locals

with the means. Also has a branch in La Alborada XII Mz-1227, T04-224 7900. **Clínica Alcívar**, Coronel 2301 y Azuay, T04-258 0030. **Clínica Guayaquil**, Padre Aguirre 401 y General Córdova, T04-256 3555, aging but still the choice downtown (Dr Roberto Gilbert speaks English and German). **Internet** There are many cyber cafés in the centre and suburbs, mainly concentrated in shopping malls, US$1 per hr. **Post office** Main post office, Pedro Carbo y Aguirre. DHL, Malecón 2000, Galería B or 9 de Octubre y P Carbo, edif San Francisco 300, T1-800-989898. **Servientrega**, offices throughout the city, for deliveries within Ecuador and abroad. **Shipping agents** Luis Arteaga, Aguirre 324 y Chile, p 3, T04-253 3592, larteaga@ecua.net.ec. Fast but expensive. **Useful addresses Immigration**, Av Río Daule near the bus terminal, T04-214 0002. For visa extensions.

Guayaquil to Peru

From a travellers' point of view, the area south of Guayaquil to the border with Peru offers some of the best and worst of Ecuador. Here are the lovely and seldom-visited Uplands of El Oro, a tranquil backwater with friendly people, a fresh climate and great scenery. This pleasant hill country has forests and waterfalls, as well as the charming colonial town of Zaruma. On the downside, the sweltering unsafe coastal city of Machala has little to recommend it and nearby beaches are dirty. The border crossing at Huaquillas is likewise hot, frantic and unsafe. Unless you are headed to the Peruvian beaches by Máncora, you are better off using one of the other, more tranquil, border crossings to Peru (see page 546). ▸▸ *For Sleeping, Eating and other listings, see pages 585-586.*

Ins and outs

From Durán, across the river from Guayaquil, an excellent four-lane road heads south to Puerto Inca, Naranjal and on to Machala, centre of Ecuador's most important banana-producing region. At Puerto Inca, one road goes inland to La Troncal, then climbs to Zhud and the Panamericana near El Tambo, a good route to Ingapirca and on to Cuenca. Just south of Puerto Inca another road heads southeast and climbs to Molleturo, goes through Parque Nacional Cajas and on to Cuenca. The latter is the fastest route between Guayaquil and Cuenca. From Machala, roads also run through Pasaje and Girón to Cuenca (188 km), and via Arenillas to Loja. **Warning** The Guayaquil–Machala road has been among the worst in the country for bus hold-ups; never travel at night.

Uplands of El Oro ●❷▲⊟❶❶ ▸▸ *pp585-586.*

This is a beautiful tranquil corner of Ecuador overlooked by most travellers, a great area in which to get off the beaten path. A transition zone between the great coastal plain and the Andes, it has forests (live and petrified), waterfalls, charming colonial cities, gold mines that give the province its name, good walking and a very pleasant climate.

The beautifully conserved town of Zaruma is perched on a hilltop at the heart of a pre-Hispanic gold-mining area. It is reached from Machala by paved road via Piñas, by a scenic dirt road off the main Loja–Machala road, or via Pasaje and Paccha on another scenic dirt road off the Machala–Cuenca road.

Founded in 1549 on the orders of Felipe II to try to control the gold extraction, Zaruma is characterized by steep, twisting streets and painted wooden buildings. The beautiful main plaza faces one of Ecuador's largest and loveliest wooden churches, and Zaruma is a candidate for inclusion in the UNESCO World Heritage Trust.

Many of the noticeably white-skinned inhabitants of direct Spanish stock still work as independent gold miners. On the outskirts of town you can see large *chancadoras*, primitive rock-crushing operations, where miners take their gold-bearing rocks to be crushed then passed through sluices to wash off the mud. It is possible to visit some of the small roadside mining operations and watch the whole process. Agricultural production in this area includes coffee, some of the best in Ecuador – **El Cafetal** shop in Zaruma roasts its own.

The **Oficina de Turismo** ⓘ *in the Municipio, at the plaza, T07-297 3533, www.vive zaruma.org Mon-Fri 0800-1200, 1300-1700, Sat 0900-1600, Sun 0830-1230,* is very friendly and helpful. They can arrange for guides and accommodation with local families. Next door is the small **Museo Municipal** ⓘ *free admission, ask for the key at the tourist office if the museum is closed.* It has a collection of local historical artefacts.

On top of the small hill beyond the market (follow Calle Pichincha) is a public swimming pool (US$1), from where there are amazing views over the nearby valleys. For even grander views, walk up **Cerro del Calvario** (follow Calle San Francisco); go early in the morning as it gets very hot.

Bosque Petrificado Puyango

ⓘ *US$5 includes tour, camping US$5 per person. For further information, try the Dirección Provincial de Turismo, Machala T07-293 2106. For transport, see page 585.*

The 2659-ha Bosque Petrificado Puyango is 110 km south of Machala, west off the Arenillas–Alamor road; the turn-off is at the bridge over the Río Puyango, where there is a military control. A great number of petrified trees, ferns, fruits and molluscs, 65 to 120 million years old, have been found here. A deciduous dry tropical forest at elevations between 270 m and 750 m covers the area. Over 120 species of bird can be seen here, including several endemics.

Machala to the border ⬤⬤⬤⬤ » *pp585-586.*

For many decades this was the preferred overland route to Peru, but it has become particularly unsafe and unpleasant. There are several alternative border points, of which Macará is currently the most popular (see page 546). If you wish to travel along the coast because you are going to Máncora or other beaches in northern Peru, then it is best to take a direct bus with **CIFA** from Machala or Guayaquil, without stopping in Huaquillas.

Machala → *Phone code 07. Colour map 1, C2. Population 270,000.*

The capital of the province of El Oro, this booming agricultural city is the centre of the surrounding banana- and shrimp-producing region. The city is not particularly clean, safe or attractive, but it does have more and better facilities than Huaquillas at the border. **Dirección Municipal de Turismo** ⓘ *9 de Mayo y 9 de Octubre, at the Municipio, 2nd floor, T07-292 0400, Mon-Fri 0800-1230, 1500-1800.*

Warning Machala has serious public safety problems, mind your valuables and avoid deserted areas. Do not leave your hotel late at night.

Huaquillas → *Phone code 07. Colour map 1, C2. Population 50,000.*

This bustling commercial border town is 77 km by road from Machala. It can be a harrowing place, made worse by the crowds and heat. Always watch your belongings carefully. In addition to cheating by money changers and cab drivers, this border is known for its increasingly aggressive shakedowns of travellers (see below). Safer border crossings to Peru are discussed on page 546. Another option is to take a **CIFA** bus from Guayaquil or Machala directly to Tumbes or Piura, Peru, without stopping in Huaquillas. The *ayundantes* (drivers' assistants) are reportedly helpful to travellers during border formalities.

Into Peru: Aguas Verdes and Tumbes

Aguas Verdes is the Peruvian border town, a small place with basic facilities. There are various forms of transport between here and **Tumbes**, the first city 27 km into Peru. Some *colectivos* (shared taxis) leave from right near the international bridge; they charge much higher prices, especially for foreigners. Others leave from further along the main street into Aguas Verdes. Ignore touts offering taxis leaving from side streets; accomplices have been known to jump in the vehicles and trap travellers who are then driven off and robbed. All *colectivos* should stop and wait at the immigration complex in Zarumilla but they are not always willing to do so, ask in advance. There are also *combis* (vans) to Tumbes and mototaxis to Zarumilla. Tumbes has a decent range of hotels, places to eat, and good transport links including flights south down the coast as far as Lima. Coming from Peru into Ecuador, take a bus to Tumbes and a *colectivo* from there to immigration at Zarumilla and on to the border at Aguas Verdes.

To Peru via Huaquillas–Aguas Verdes

The border runs along the Río Zarumilla and is crossed by the international bridge at the western end of Avenida La República. It is a shortish walk from the bus terminals which are mostly on Avenida Teniente Cordovez. Tricycle taxis are available to help with luggage but thefts have been reported. Hang on to your belongings and deal only with border officials or transport staff; avoid all touts and 'helpers' from the street. It is not uncommon to be asked for a small bribe by one of the many officials at the border.

Ecuadorean immigration Passports are stamped 3 km north of Huaquillas along the road to Machala, the office is open 24 hours. Long-distance buses should stop here, have your passport and a pen at hand. Take a taxi (US$1) if you need to go from town back to immigration. To cross to Peru, walk along the main street in Huaquillas and across the international bridge to Aguas Verdes; police may check passports. The bridge is crowded and worked by thieves.

Peruvian immigration Passports are stamped at the Peruvian immigration complex outside Zarumilla, 3 km past the international bridge, open 24 hours. *Colectivos* wait at the bridge or *combis* leave from the market area, US$0.50. They leave passengers at the immigration office. From the border to Zarumillo by mototaxi costs US$0.50 pp. Taxi to Tumbes, including wait at immigration, US$6. It is best to get to Tumbes then a bus south, rather than trying to get a bus from the border. See also Peru, page 257.

Exchange The many street changers, recognized by their black briefcases, deal in *soles* and US dollars cash. Check the rate beforehand on the internet or with people leaving Peru, as there are many tricks and travellers are often cheated. Do not change more dollars than you need to get to Tumbes, where there are reliable *cambios*, but get rid of all your *soles* here as they are difficult to exchange further inside Ecuador. Do your own arithmetic (there have been reports of 'doctored' calculators), count your change carefully and watch out for counterfeit bills. Especially avoid those changers who chase after you.

● Sleeping

Zaruma *p583*

C **Hostería El Jardín**, Barrio Limoncito, 10 mins walk from centre (taxi US$1), T07-297 2706. Lovely palm garden and terrace with views, includes breakfast, comfortable rooms, small zoo, family-run, friendly. Recommended.
D **Cerro de Oro**, Sucre 40, T07-297 2505. Parking, recently renovated, modern, pleasant.
E **Romería**, on the plaza facing the church, T07-297 2173. Old wooden house with balcony, private bath, floors creak a bit but nice and friendly. Recommended.

Machala *p583*

C **Oro Hotel**, Sucre y Juan Montalvo, T07-293 0032, orohotel@oro.satnet.net. Includes breakfast, pricey restaurant and cheaper café downstairs, a/c, fridge, parking, comfortable rooms but those to the street are noisy, helpful staff. Recommended.
D **Ejecutivo**, Sucre y 9 de Mayo, T07-293 3998. Cafetería, electric shower, a/c, parking, modern and good.
E **San Miguel**, 9 de Mayo y Sucre, T07-293 5488. Private bath, hot water, a/c, cheaper with fan, fridge, good value, friendly.

Huaquillas *p584*

E **Hernancor**, 1 de Mayo y Hualtaco, T07-299 5467. Cafetería, private bath, a/c, best in town.

● Eating

Zaruma *p583*

Local specialities often include plantain. Try *tigrillo,* ground plantain fried with eggs, cheese and onions.
♥♥ **Mesón de Joselito**, at the entrance to town from Portovelo. Good seafood.
♥ **Cafetería Central**, on the plaza. Very good local specialities.

Machala *p583*

There are also restaurants in the more upmarket hotels.
♥♥ **Mesón Hispano**, Av Las Palmeras y Sucre. Very good grill, attentive service, outstanding for where it is.
♥ **Chifa Gran Oriental**, 9 de Octubre, between Guayas and Ayacucho. Good food and service, clean place. Recommended.

▲ Activities and tours

Zaruma *p583*

Tours are available to the mines, the Buenaventura nature reserve, Cerro de Arcos, waterfalls and petroglyphs; US$25-40 pp per day. Enquire about local guides at the Oficina de Turismo (see page 583), or contact the following:
Oroadventure, T07-297 2761. Helpful and informative.
Ramiro Rodríguez Pereira, T07-297 2523, T09-249 8623. Speaks English, has his own 4WD vehicle.

● Transport

Zaruma *p583*

Bus Bus companies are along Av Honorato Márquez, some local service goes from Calle Pichincha near Banco del Pichincha. To **Machala**, with **TAC** or **Trans Piñas**, half-hourly, US$3, 3 hrs. To **Piñas**, take a Machala bound bus, US$1, 1 hr. To **Guayaquil**, with **TAC** or **Trans Piñas**, 6 daily, US$6.50, 6½ hrs. To **Quito**, with **TAC** or **Trans Piñas**, 5 daily, US$10, 12 hrs. To **Loja**, with **TAC** or **Trans Piñas**, 4 daily, may have to change at Portovelo, US$5, 5 hrs, sit on the right side for best views. To **Cuenca**, with **TAC** at 0030, **Trans Piñas** at 0315 and **Azuay** at 0730, US$7, 6 hrs. *Rancheras* to **Portovelo**, with **24 de Julio**, every 30 min 0600-1830, US$0.50, 20 mins; taxi US$3, 10 mins.

Bosque Petrificado Puyango *p583*

Bus There are hourly *rancheras* between Arenillas and Alamor. Buses from **Machala**, with **Transportes Loja** at 0930, 1315 and 2130, US$3, 2½ hrs. From **Loja**, with **Transportes Loja** at 0900, 1430 and 1930, US$5, 5 hrs. From **Huaquillas**, with **Transportes Loja** at 0730, US$2, 1½ hrs. Returning to **Machala**, buses pass the bridge about 1100, 1330 and 1700, their final destination may not be Machala, so ask. To **Huaquillas** at about 1000. There are several military checkpoints between Puyango and Machala, have your passport at hand.

Machala *p583*

Air The airport is at the south end of the city, but no flights were operating in 2007.

TAME, Juan Montalvo y Bolívar,
T07-293 0139, 0830-1800.

Bus Most of the bus company offices are quite central, but there is no Terminal Terrestre. Do not take night buses into or out of Machala as they are prone to hold-ups. There are 3 different routes from Machala to **Loja**, with bus service along all of them; ask for the one you need. They are, from north to south: via **Piñas** and **Zaruma**, partly paved and rough but very scenic; via **Balsas**, fully paved and also scenic; and via **Arenillas** and **Alamor**, for **Puyango** petrified forest.

To **Peru**, CIFA to **Piura** at 1100, 1500, 2200 and 2400, US$6, 6 hrs; also to **Tumbes** , 8 daily, US$2, 3 hrs.

Huaquillas *p584*
Bus There is no Terminal Terrestre, each bus company has its own office, many on Teniente Cordovez. If in a hurry to reach Quito or other highland destinations,

it can be faster to change buses in Machala or Guayaquil rather than waiting for the next departure from Huaquillas. There are checkpoints along the road north from Huaquillas to Machala, so keep your passport to hand. To **Machala**, with CIFA (at Santa Rosa y Machala) and **Ecuatoriano Pullman**, direct, 1 hr, US$2, every hr from 0400-2000; via Arenillas and Santa Rosa, 2 hrs, every 10 mins.

Ⓘ Directory

Zaruma *p583*
Banks Banco del Pichincha, Pichincha y Luis Crespo, ATM only. **Internet** US$1.50/hr.

Machala *p583*
Banks Banco del Pacifico, Rocafuerte y Junín. **Consulates** Peru, Urb Unioro, Mz 14, V 11, near Hotel Oro Verde, T07-293 0680. **Internet** Many places, US$1/hr. **Post office** Bolívar y Montalvo.

North along the coast

A four-lane toll highway runs 128 km west from Guayaquil to the Santa Elena peninsula, with its popular urban seaside resorts of Playas and Salinas. From here, the coastal road stretches north for 737 km to Mataje on the Colombian border; along the way are countless beaches and fishing villages, the country's finest coastal national park, and a few important cities. This stretch of coast also has some excellent surfing conditions.
▸▸ *For Sleeping, Eating and other listings see pages 594-602.*

Ruta del Sol: Santa Elena to Manta
🏠🍴🛍️🏖️🔺🚌🎫 ▸▸ *pp594-602.*

The coastal strip is known as the 'Ruta del Sol' as far north as Manta. Seaside resorts are busy and more expensive during the *temporada de playa* (beach season), December to April. The road parallels the shore and provides access to some beautiful beaches. Not all beaches are suitable for bathing however, the surf and undertow can be strong in some places. Between June and September whales may be seen in this area.

Montañita → *Colour map 1, B2. Phone code 04.*
Sixty kilometers north of Santa Elena, Montañita has a good surfing beach and is a popular destination among travellers. The main village has experienced haphazard growth and is crowded with small hotels. There are also restaurants, surfboard rentals, tattoo parlours, craft/jewellery vendors and sundry other services. At the north end of the bay, 1 km away, is another hotel area with more elbow-room, referred to as Montañita Punta, Surf Point or Baja Montañita (after one of the hotels). Between the two is a beach where you'll find some of the best surfing in Ecuador. Various competitions are held during the year and at weekends in season, when the town is

noisy and packed with *Guayaquileños*. There are many street dogs; don't contribute to the problem by feeding them. **Note** Drugs are a problem in Montañita. There are periodic police raids and several people, including foreigners, are serving long sentences in jail.

Ayampe → *Colour map 1, B2. Phone code 04.*

Located 27 km north of Montañita, at the foot of the Cordillera Chongón Colonche, Ayampe is a small, poor village, with friendly people, but no services. Just south of it are a group of hotels offering a good option for those seeking tranquillity. This is a base for trips up to the **Cordillera Chongón Colonche**, which has tropical forest and good birdwatching. The area produces crafts with banana fibres, known as *sapán*.

Alandaluz and around → *Colour map 1, B2. Phone code 04.*

North of Ayampe are the villages of Las Tunas, Puerto Rico and Río Chico; there are places to stay all along this stretch of beach. In **Las Tunas** you can arrange for horse-riding tours with **Kankagua**, opposite **Hotel La Barquita**. Just south of **Puerto Rico** is the **Alandaluz Ecological Centre**, an organization involved in promoting ecologically sound practices in nearby communities. It is also a very good inn (see Sleeping, page 595), which gives working demonstrations of its innovative practices.

Salango → *Colour map 1, B2. Phone code 04. Population 4100.*

Just north of Río Chico and 5 km south of Puerto López is Salango, a commercial fishing port with a fish meal plant. It is worth visiting for its excellent **Presley Norton archaeological museum** ⓘ *towards the north end of town, daily 0900-1200, 1300-1700, US$1*, housing artefacts from the excavations in town, and with a craft shop.

Puerto López → *Colour map 1, B2. Phone code 05. Population 9900.*

This pleasant little fishing town is beautifully set on a turquoise horseshoe bay, with a broad sweep of beach enclosed by headlands. The beach is cleanest at the far north and south ends, away from the fleet of small fishing boats moored offshore. A lookout above the south end of the bay along the main road offers great views.

Tourism is second only to fishing in Puerto López, with a wide array of hotels, restaurants and tour operators catering to the many foreign and Ecuadorean visitors who flock here every year during the *temporada de ballenas* (whale season), approximately mid-June to September. Whale watching is reasonably well organized, but things can get out of hand during the height of the season in July and August, when prices rise and touts await tourists arriving in town. During these peak months, fishermen may offer whale-watching trips for less than authorized tour operators. Such improvised excursions are seldom recommended, your safety may be compromised and the whales can be threatened by boatmen who have not been trained how to approach them. It's best to reserve accommodation and tours in advance during high season. Whales can also be seen from other points along the coast where similar tours are available.

Parque Nacional Machalilla → *Colour map 1, B2.*

ⓘ *Entrance fee for Isla de la Plata, US$15. For mainland part only, US$12. For both mainland and Isla de la Plata, US$20, children and seniors half price. Fee is payable at the park office, Calle Eloy Alfaro y García Moreno, next to the market in Puerto López (open 0800-1200, 1400-1600) or directly to the park rangers (insist on a receipt). The ticket is valid for several days so you can visit the different areas.*

Parque Nacional Machalilla (55,000 ha) is a year-round attraction, which incorporates mainland sites and Isla de la Plata, an offshore island with bird colonies and good snorkelling. The continental portion of the park is divided into three sections which are separated by private land, including the town of Machalilla. It preserves marine ecosystems as well as dry tropical forest and archaeological sites on shore. It is very scenic and recommended for birdwatching, especially in the cloudforest of Cerro San Sebastián. There are also several species of mammals and reptiles. ► *Tours are available from Puerto López, see page 600.*

Isla de la Plata is about 24 km offshore and has nesting colonies of waved albatross (April-November), frigates and three different booby species. A small colony of sea lions also makes its home here and whales can be seen from June to September. As in Galápagos, it is easy to see the bird life – you will walk just by their nests. There is also good diving and snorkelling, and most agencies provide snorkelling equipment. The island must be visited in a day trip, staying overnight is not permitted. Take dry clothes, water, and precautions against sun and seasickness.

Los Frailes beach, 11 km north of Puerto López and and 1 km south of the town of Machalilla, is one of the most stunning on the entire coast. Take a bus bound for Jipijapa (US$0.25) or a pickup (US$5); the beach is a 30-minute walk from the turn-off. Camping is only permitted by the ranger's house where you can get some water, US$5 per tent. The park gates close at 1700. At the north end of the beach is a trail through the forest leading to a lookout with great views. You can continue along this trail to the town of Machalilla. Don't take valuables with you. Bathing at Los Frailes is best at the ends of the bay; in the centre there is a strong undertow.

Five kilometres north of Puerto López, at the settlement of Buena Vista, a road leads 5 km east to the small village of **Agua Blanca**. Set amid hot, arid scrub in the national park, there is a fine, small **archaeological museum** ① *0800-1800, US$3*, containing some fascinating ceramics from the Manteño civilization.

From Agua Blanca, a trip may be made up to **San Sebastián**, 9 km away in tropical moist forest (altitude 800 m), for sightings of orchids, birds and possibly howler monkeys. It is a five-hour trip on foot or by horse. A tour to the forest costs US$30-35 per day including guide, horses and camping (minimum two days).

Manta

Sleeping 🛏
Albatros 1
Barbasquillo 4
Centenario 5

Chávez Inn &
  Chavecito Restaurant 2
Costa del Sol 6
Oro Verde 10

Panorama Inn 11
Vistalmar 12
Yara María 13

0 metres 200
0 yards 200

Manta to Esmeraldas 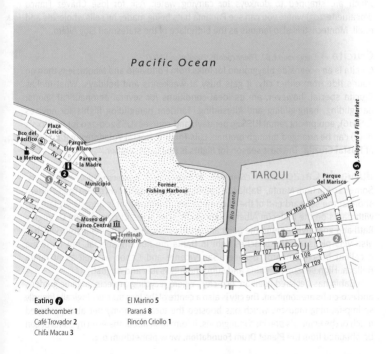 ➤➤ *pp594-602.*

The province of Manabí, located north of Guyaquil and south of Esmeraldas, has many different faces. Manta is a bustling city, a fishing and cargo port with a strategic and controversial US airforce base. North along the coast are countless seaside villages, some half-forgotten, others popular beach destinations. The largest resort area is around Bahía de Caráquez, which has dubbed itself an 'eco-city'. Just beyond Bahía, on the other side of the Río Chone estuary, is the little village of Canoa, boasting some of the finest beaches in Ecuador.

Manta → *Colour map 1, B2. See map page 588. Phone code 05. Population 235,000.*

Manta is the quintessential maritime city. Ecuador's second port after Guayaquil and home to the county's largest fishing fleet, it has hundreds of boats of all sizes moored offshore. This busy lively city has grown and prospered over the past decade. The thriving port and a US air-force base (due to close in 2009) give the city a cosmopolitan flavour and have driven up prices, but not diminished friendliness. Cruise ships call on Manta from time to time.

For information contact: **Ministerio de Turismo** ① *Paseo José María Egas 1034 (Av 3) y Calle 11, T05-262 2944, Mon-Fri 0900-1230, 1400-1700*, very helpful, English spoken. **Cámara de Turismo** ① *Centro Comercial Cocco Manta, Malecón y Calle 23, T05-262 0478, Mon-Fri 0900-1300, 1500-1800*, is helpful and provides a map, English spoken.

A constant sea breeze tempers the intense sun and makes the city's *malecones* pleasant places to stroll. The **Malecón Escénico**, at the gentrified west end of town, has a cluster of bars and seafood restaurants. It is a lively place especially at weekends, when there is good music, free beach aerobics and lots of action. This

Pacific Coast North along the coast

Pacific Ocean

Eating 🍴
Beachcomber **1**
Café Trovador **2**
Chifa Macau **3**

El Marino **5**
Paraná **8**
Rincón Criollo **1**

promenade is built along **Playa Murciélago**, a popular beach with wild surf (enquire locally before bathing, flags are placed on the beach to indicate whether it is safe or not). Surfing is good from December to April. Manta's growing number of upmarket hotels and restaurants are found in the neighbourhoods near Playa Murciélago. Further west is **Playa Barbasquillo**.

The **centre of town**, built on a hill, conserves some older wooden buildings and a bazaar-like atmosphere. Shops, banks, the Terminal Terrestre and a tourist information office are here, but there few hotels and restaurants. The **Museo del Banco Central** ① *Centro Cultural Manta, Av 8 y Calle 7, behind the bus station, T05-262 2956, Tue-Sat 1000-1700, US$1, Sun 1100-1500, free*, has an excellent collection of archaeological pieces from seven different civilizations that flourished on the coast of Manabí between 3500 BC and AD 1530. It is well displayed, with Spanish explanations. There is also a hall for temporary art exhibits.

Two bridges connect the main town with **Tarqui** on the east side of the Río Manta. Many hotels, including most economy ones, are located near the sea here. This is not a safe area at night (take a taxi to your hotel), but a stroll along the Tarqui Malecón can be interesting during the day (do not take valuables). Visit the **fish market** and *astillero* (shipyard) around Calle 110, where large wooden fishing boats are built. At the Malecón y Calle 106 is the **Parque del Marisco**, with many small seafood restaurants. Tarqui Beach is too polluted for swimming and east of Calle 110 it is unsafe at all hours.

Montecristi → *Colour map 1, B2. Phone code 05. Population 50,000*

Located 11 km southeast of Manta, Montecristi is a quiet, dusty town, set on the lower slopes of an imposing hill. It is just high enough to be watered by low cloud which gives the region its only source of drinking water. The town is one of the main centres of Panama hat production and is renowned for high quality. Varied straw crafts and basket-ware is also produced here (much cheaper than in Quito), and wooden barrels which are strapped to donkeys for carrying water. Ask for José Chávez Franco (Rocafuerte 203) where you can see Panama hats being made; he sells wholesale and retail. Montecristi is also famous as the birthplace of the statesman Eloy Alfaro.

Crucita → *Colour map 1, B2. Phone code 05. Population 13,000.*

Crucita is an oceanside playground for folks from Portoviejo and Manta, less than an hour's ride from either city. It gets busy at weekends and holidays. What makes Crucita special, however, are its ideal conditions for several aeronautical sports: paragliding, hang-gliding and kitesurfing. Tandem paragliding flights for novices (US$16), equipment rental (US$25 per day), and courses (US$200-250 for four to six days) can be arranged through brothers Luis Tobar at **Hostal Voladores** or Raul Tobar at **Hostal Cruzita**. The best season for flights is July to December.

Bahía de Caráquez → *Colour map 1, B2. Phone code 05. Population 26,800.*

Some 120 km from Manta, Bahía is a friendly, relaxed resort town set on the southern shore at the seaward end of the Chone estuary. The riverfront is attractively laid out with parks on the Malecón Alberto Santos. This becomes Circunvalación Dr Virgilio Ratti and goes right around the point along the ocean side of the peninsula, which is also very pleasant. The beaches right in Bahía are nothing special, but there are excellent beaches nearby between San Vicente and Canoa as well as at Punta Bellaca. High season for Bahía and surroundings is July and August.

Bahía has declared itself an **'eco-city'**, where recycling projects, organic gardens and eco-clubs are common. The city is also a centre of the less than ecologically friendly shrimp-farming industry, which has boosted the local economy but also destroyed much of the estuary's precious mangroves. Information about the eco-city concept can be obtained from the **Planet Drum Foundation**, www.planetdrum.org.

The Banco Central's **Museo Bahía de Caráquez** ⓘ *Malecón Alberto Santos y Aguilera, Tue-Fri 1000-1700, Sat-Sun 1100-1500, US$1*, has an interesting collection of arcaeological artefacts from various pre-Hispanic coastal cultures.

Near Bahía, the **Río Chone estuary** has several islands with mangrove forest. The area is rich in birdlife, dolphins may also be seen, and conditions are ideal for photographers because you can get really close, even under the mangrove trees where birds nest. The male frigate birds can be seen displaying their inflated red sacks as part of the mating ritual; best from August to January. At **Isla Corazón**, a boardwalk has been built through an area of protected mangrove forest. At the end of the island are a large colony of frigate birds that can only be accessed by boat.

About 10 km north of Canoa, the **Río Muchacho organic farm** ⓘ *reservations necessary, contact Guacamayo Bahía Tours, page 600*, promotes agro-ecology and reforestation in the area, runs an environmental primary school and gives courses in organic farming. A three-day visit to the farm is recommended in order to explore the

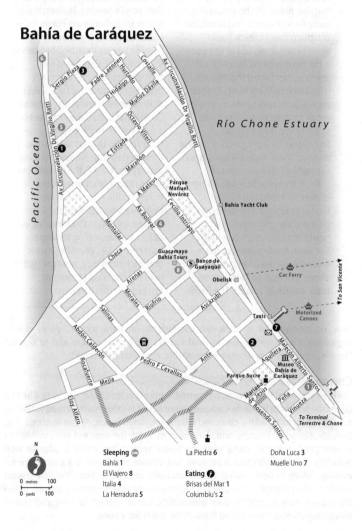

Bahía de Caráquez

Pacific Coast North along the coast

Sleeping
Bahía 1
El Viajero 8
Italia 4
La Herradura 5
La Piedra 6

Doña Luca 3
Muelle Uno 7

Eating
Brisas del Mar 1
Columbiu's 2

⁝ A whale of a time

Whale watching is a major tourist attraction all along the coast of Ecuador. One of the prime sites to see these massive mammals is around Isla de La Plata.

Between June and September, groups of up to 10 humpback whales make the 7200-km trip from their Antarctic feeding grounds to the equator. They head for these warmer waters to mate and calve. Inspired by love, we presume, the gregarious humpbacks become real acrobats. Watching them breach (jump almost completely out of the water) is the most exciting moment of any tour. Not far behind, though, is listening to them 'sing'. Chirrups, snores, purrs and haunting moans are all emitted by solitary males eager to use their chat-up techniques on a prospective mating partner. These vocal performances can last half an hour or more.

Adult humpbacks reach a length of over 15 m and can exceed 30 tonnes in weight. The gestation period is about one year and newborn calves are 5-6 m long. The ventral side of the tail has a distinctive series of stripes which allows scientists to identify and track individual whales. The Pacific Whale Foundation studies some 850 'Ecuadorean' whales; for information, see www.pacificwhale.org.

Humpbacks got their English name from their humped dorsal fins and the way they arch when diving. Their scientific name, *Megaptera novaeangliae*, which means 'large- winged New Englanders', comes from the fact that they were first identified off the coast of New England, and from their very large wing-like pectoral fins. In Spanish they are called *ballena jorobada* or *yubarta*.

These whales have blubber up to 20 cm thick. Combined with their slow swimming, this made them all too attractive for whalers during the 19th and 20th centuries. During that period their numbers are estimated to have fallen from 100,000 to 2500 worldwide. Protected by international whaling treaties since 1966, the humpbacks are making a gradual recovery. Ironically, the same behaviour that once allowed them to be harpooned makes the humpbacks particularly appealing to whale-watchers today. The difference is that each sighting is now greeted with the shooting of cameras instead of lethal harpoons.

area. Accommodation is rustic but comfortable, and the food is good, mainly vegetarian. It's an eye-opener to rural coastal (*montubio*) culture and to organic farming. Volunteer programmes are available. Highly recommended.

Canoa → *Colour map 1, A2. Phone code 05. Rural population 6900.*

The market town of **San Vicente**, on the north side of the Río Chone, can be reached by taking the ferry from Bahía de Caráquez. From here it is 17 km north by road to Canoa, a quiet fishing town, with a clean and relatively isolated beach. At 200 m across, it is the widest beach in Ecuador, and also one of its finest. The choice of accommodation is very good and this, along with the lovely setting, has made it popular with travellers. The beautiful beach between San Vicente and Canoa is a good place for walking, biking or horse riding. Horses and bicycles can be hired through several hotels. Surfing is good, particularly during the wet season, December to April. In the dry season there is good wind for windsurfing. Canoa is good for hang-gliding and paragliding; flights are arranged through the **Hotel Sol y Luna**.

→ *Colour map 1, A2.*

Geographically as well as culturally, Esmeraldas – the northernmost of the coastal provinces – is a unique corner of Ecuador. Here the dry Manabí coastline turns green with palm trees. Inland, the rainforests of Esmeraldas are part of the Chocó bio-geographic region, shared with neighbouring Colombia. And most Esmeraldeños are Afro-Ecuadoreans whose ancestors were brought as slaves to work the cane fields. Mosquitoes and malaria are a serious problem throughout the province, especially in the rainy season (January to May). Take plenty of insect repellent. Most *residenciales* provide mosquito nets (*toldos* or *mosquiteros*), be sure to use them.

Mompiche → *Colour map 1, A2.*

North of Pedernales the coastal highway veers northeast, going slightly inland, then crosses into the province of Esmeraldas near **Chamanga** (San José de Chamanga, population 4300), a thriving little hub with houses built on stilts on the freshwater estuary. This is a good spot from which to explore the nearby mangroves, there is one basic *pensión* to stay at and frequent buses north and south. North of Chamanga is **Portete**, with a pleasant estuary and beach. It is a long walk along an undisturbed beach to **Daule** (popultaion 2200), where a canoe crosses to Cojimies. When there are no passengers, you can hire the canoe for a ride in the estuary (US$10 per hour). Beyond Portete and 7 km from the main road along a poor side road is **Mompiche**, one of Ecuador's best surfing spots (see Footprint's *Surfing the World*). Once a few shacks at the end of the beach, this fishing village surrounded by vegetation is undergoing rapid development. It can also be accessed by boat from Muisne.

Tonchigüe and Punta Galera → *Colour map 1, A2.*

Tonchigüe (population 7500) is a quiet little fishing village with an adequate beach, two hours north from Muisne and 1½ hours southwest of Esmeraldas. There are a couple of simple places to stay, good *comedores* and transportation to Atacames (US$0.70) and Esmeraldas (US$1.50). About 2 km south of Tonchigüe a road goes west and follows the shore to **Punta Galera**; along the way are two very good places to stay, each on its own beach, see page 597.

Súa → *Colour map 1, A2. Phone code 06. Population 3500.*

Fifteen kilometers east of Tonchigüe, Súa is a beach resort set in a beautiful bay with pelicans and frigate birds wheeling overhead when the fishing boats land their catch. Except in the high season (July to September when hotel prices rise) it is a very quiet and friendly little place. Between June and September there are **whale-watching excursions** ⓘ *departures 0800-1100, about US$15 per person,* from Súa. The sighting area is to the south of Punta Galera (see above), 40-60 minutes by boat.

Atacames → *Phone code 06. Colour map 1, A2. Population 12,800.*

Four kilometres east of Súa and 30 km from Esmeraldas, Atacames is one of the main resorts on the Ecuadorean coast. It can become a real 24-hour party town during the high season (July-September) as well as at weekends and national holidays. The beach is none too clean at these times. The west end of Atacames is a little less noisy than the rest and, for those who appreciate peace and quiet, there are much more tranquil alternatives such as Punta Galera further south (see above).

Most hotels are on a peninsula between the Río Atacames and the ocean. The main park, most services and the bus stops are to the south of the river. Information from **Oficina Municipal de Turismo** ⓘ *Av Principal, T06-2731912, Mon-Fri 0800-1230, 1330-1600, municipioatacamesturismo@andinanet.net.*

594

Destruction of the Ecuadorean Chocó

The last coastal rainforests of Ecuador are in grave danger. Despite efforts to provide economic alternatives to logging, deforestation along the Cayapas, Onzole and Santiago rivers remains alarming. A few timber companies buy all the logs from local villagers and there is no control whatsoever by the authorities.

Navigating upriver one meets large rafts of logs floating down to Borbón.

Along the lower parts of the rivers, there are only rare pockets of forest left and you have to go far to find virgin jungle. On the Río Cayapas you must go beyond the village of Zapallo Grande, while on the Río Santiago the forest only starts after Playa de Oro, both approaching the limits of Reserva Ecológica Cotacachi-Cayapas.

Will the destruction stop when it reaches this protected area?

Safety Many assaults on campers and beach strollers have been reported over the years. People walking along the beach from Atacames to Súa have been mugged at all hours; never take valuables. Note also that the sea can be very dangerous; there is a powerful undertow and many people have drowned.

Esmeraldas → *Phone code 06. Colour map 1, A2. Population 95,000.*
Esmeraldas is the provincial capital. The city's main revenue comes from the oil industry: an obsolete polluting refinery and petroleum port at Balao, the end of the oil pipeline from the Oriente. A gaudy show of wealth by a few sharply contrasts with poor living conditions and bad infrastructure on the slopes around town. The city is hot, sticky, suffers from water shortages, and it is not too safe. Some visitors enjoy strolling along the Parque Central or along Las Palmas, the stretch of beach at the west side of town. For information contact the **Ministerio de Turismo** ① *Cañizares, between Bolívar and Sucre, T06-271 1370, Mon-Fri 0830-1215, 1430-1730.*

The area is rich in culture. La Tolita, one of the earliest cultures in Ecuador, developed in this region, and the most important archaeological site is at **La Tolita Island** to the north. This culture's ceramic legacy can be seen at the **Museo del Banco Central** ① *Bolívar y Piedrahita, US$1, displays in English.* At the **Centro Cultural Afro** ① *Malecón y J Montalvo, T06-271 0424, Mon-Fri 0800-1200, 1430-1800, free,* you can see 'La Ruta del Esclavo', an exhibit showing the harsh history of Afro-Ecuadoreans brought as slaves to Ecuador (some English explanations).

On Saturday night, Señora Palma Petite and her marimba group rehearse at **Casa de la Cultura** ① *Av Sucre, T06-271 0738, 1730-2000.* Visitors can attend but should call ahead. There are several other marimba groups in town, enquire at the Ministerio de Turismo for schedules and other details.

The bustling colourful **Mercado Central** is a place to saturate your senses with an impressive array of tropical fruits, spices, cockles and mussels. Don't take any valuables, not even your camera.

Sleeping

Montañita *p586*
B **Baja Montañita**, Montañita Punta, T09-189 8542, www.bajamontanita.com. A small resort off on its own, comfortable, includes breakfast and internet, restaurant, a/c, pool, parking.
C **La Barranca**, on the road north, T04-283 2095. A great hotel in a privileged setting

with lovely views. Spacious rooms, terrace with hammocks, includes breakfast, restaurant, a/c, jacuzzi, very clean.
D-E **Rosa Mística**, Montañita Punta, T09-798 8383, www.hostalrosamistica.com. A small hostel with very attractive cabins

in a quiet location, restaurant, cheaper with shared bath, lovely garden.

E Charo's, Malecón, in town by the beach, T09-319 2222, www.charoshostal.com. Very pleasant hostel, ample rooms, restaurant, private bath, hot water, pretty garden, hammocks, English spoken, very good value.

E-F Tierra Prometida, in town, T09-944 6363, www.thepromisedlandmontanita.com. Café, cheaper with shared bath, hot water, fan, colourful and popular. There are many other places to stay in town, all quite similar.

Ayampe *p587*

L-AL Hotel Atamari, on the headland south of Ayampe, a 15-min walk from the highway, T04-278 0430, www.resortatamari.com. Beautiful cabins with rooms and suites in spectacular surroundings on cliffs above the sea, restaurant with wonderful food, pool, packages available May-Oct.

C-D Hotel Almare, T04-278 0611, hotel almare@yahoo.com. Attractive wooden house with porch, comfortable rooms and suites, fan, English spoken. Fine views especially at sunset.

E Cabañas de la Iguana, T04-278 0605, www.ayampeiguana.com. Ample cabins for 4, restaurant, private bath, hot water, use of kitchen US$2 daily, mosquito nets, quiet, Swiss-Ecuadorian run, family atmosphere, very friendly, helpful and knowledgeable, organizes excursions. Recommended.

Alandaluz and around *p587*

B-D Hostería Alandaluz, part of the ecological center, T04-278 0690, T02-244 0790 (Quito), www.alandaluz.com. Cheaper with shared bath, pool, a variety of cabins ranging from bamboo with thatched roofs and compost toilets to more luxurious with flush toilets, all with private bath. Good home-grown organic food, vegetarian or seafood, bar; all at extra cost. It is a very peaceful place, with a clean beach and attractive botanic garden in the middle of the desert. 10% student discount with ISIC, camping with your own tent **G** pp. Tours to **Cantalapiedra Cabins**, in a lovely forested setting by the Río Ayampe and other locations; not cheap. Often busy, advance bookings required. Friendly and highly recommended.

C Hostería La Barquita, by Las Tunas, 4 km north of Ayampe and 1 km south of

Alandaluz, T04-278 0683, www.labarquita-ec.com. The restaurant and bar are in a boat on the beach with good ocean views, an unusual concept. Separate rooms with fan and mosquito nets, ping pong and billiard, tours, massage, Swiss-run, French, English and German spoken, friendly.

Puerto López *p587*

Puerto López has many hotels, but may nonetheless fill during Jul and Aug. Reserve in advance if you want to stay in a particular establishment at that time.

B Mantaraya Lodge, 3 km south of town on a hill overlooking the ocean, T09-404 4050, www.mantarayalodge.com. Lovely hotel with comfortable rooms, attractive decor, restaurant and bar, pool, lovely views. Horse riding, fishing and diving trips organized. Credit cards and TCs accepted.

C Mandala, Malecón at north end of the beach, T/F05-230 0181, www.hosteria mandala.info. Nice cabins decorated with art and surrounded by a lovely garden, excellent restaurant, fan, mosquito nets, games, music room with several instruments, Swiss/Italian -run, English spoken, owners knowledgeable about the area and whales, TCs accepted with US$5 commission. Recommended.

C-E Pacífico, Malecón y González Suárez, T05-230 0147, hpacific@manta.ecua.net.ec. Pleasant hotel with nice grounds. New rooms with large balcony facing the ocean are comfortable, older ones are good value. Restaurant, a/c, much cheaper in old wing with fan and shared bath but full use of facilities, pool, parking, also run boat tours, friendly and helpful. Recommended.

D La Terraza, on hill north of centre, behind the clinic, T05-230 0235. Meals available on request, 6 cabins with great views over the bay, gardens, spacious. Run by Peter Bernhard, German spoken. Free car service to/from town if called in advance. Highly recommended.

E-F Los Islotes, Malecón 532 y Gen Córdova, T05-230 0108, hostallosislotes@hotmail.com. Modern clean hostel, private bath, fan, **G** pp in dorm, rooftop terrace with ocean views, friendly. Good value, recommended.

F Monte Líbano, southern end of Malecón, T05-230 0231. Breakfast available, cheaper with shared bath, hot water, cooking facilities, very clean, terrace with views, popular, friendly.

Manta *p589, map p588*

Manta's hotels are more expensive than those in other parts of coastal Ecuador.

AL Oro Verde, Malecón y Calle 23, T05-262 9200, www.oroverdehotels.com. Includes buffet breakfast, restaurant, a/c, pool, parking, all luxuries, best in town.

A Vistalmar, Calle M1 y Av 24B, at Playa Murciélago, T05-262 1671, www.vistalmar ecuador.com. Exclusive hotel overlooking the ocean. Ample cabins and suites tastefully decorated with art, a/c, pool, cooking facilities, gardens by the sea. A place for a honeymoon.

A-B Costa del Sol, M1 y Calle 25, T05-262 0025. Includes breakfast, a/c, pool, parking, modern, comfortable, ocean-side rooms with balconies are very pleasant.

B-C Barbasquillo, at Playa Barbasquillo, T05-262 0718. Includes breakfast, restaurant, a/c, pool and gym, fridge, parking, pleasant place with a variety of different rooms at different prices.

D Albatros, Calle 24B y Av M3, by Iglesia del Perpetuo Socorro, T05-262 6423, hostal albatros@yahoo.com. Modern hotel with ample rooms, a/c, pool, parking.

D Yara María, Av 11 y Calle 20, T05-261 3219, yaramariahostal@hotmail.com. Good hostel in a residential area, a/c, jacuzzi, parking, rooms on the top floor are better, terrace, garden, very clean and quiet.

E Centenario, Calle 11 No 602 y Av 5, T05-262 9245, josesanmartin@hotmail.com. Pleasant hostel in a nicely refurbished house in the centre of town, shared bath, some rooms with a/c, cooking facilities, good views, very clean, friendly, in a quiet location.

Tarqui

D Chávez Inn, Av 106 y Calle 106, T05-262 1019. Attractive modern hotel with lovely ample rooms, includes breakfast, restaurant, a/c, very good value, opened in 2006.

D-E Panorama Inn, Calle 103 y Av 105, T05-262 2996, panoramainn@paginasamarilla sec.com. Has 2 sections, a new block with nice modern rooms and an older cheaper section with fair rooms, includes breakfast, restaurant, cold water, a/c, cheaper with fan, pool, parking, friendly and helpful.

Montecristi *p590*

D Orlando, T05-292 2830. Restaurant, a/c, parking.

Crucita *p590*

Most hotels are along the beach.

E Cruzita, at the south end of the beach, T05-234 0068, flyraul2005@hotmail.com. Beautiful hostel with great views right on the beach, restaurant, private bath, cold water, fan, pool, parking, good value. Friendly owner Raul Tobar offers paragliding flights/lessons.

E Hostal Voladores, south end of beach, away from town, T05-234 0200, hvoladores@hotmail.com. Simple but pleasant place, restaurant, cheaper with shared bath, hot water, small pool, sea kayaks available. Friendly owner Luis Tobar offers paragliding flights and lessons.

Bahía de Caráquez *p590, map p591*

B La Piedra, Circunvalación near Bolívar, T05-269 0156, piedraturi@easynet.net.ec Modern hotel with access to the beach and lovely views, good expensive restaurant, a/c, pool, good service, also rents bicycles.

B Saiananda, along the highway, 5 km from the centre of town, T05-239 8331. First-class accommodation in a nature park along the estuary, includes breakfast, very good vegetarian restaurant, fan.

C-E La Herradura, Bolívar e Hidalgo, T05-269 0446. Older hotel but very well maintained, restaurant, a/c, cheaper with fan and cold water, cheaper rooms are good value.

D-E Italia, Bolívar y Checa, T/F05-269 1137. Older comfortable hotel, restaurant, a/c, cheaper with fan.

E Bahía Hotel, Malecón y Vinueza, T05-269 0509. A variety of different rooms, those in back are nicer and quieter, private bath, fan, parking, good value but there have been reports of theft from rooms.

E El Viajero, Bolívar 910 y Riofrío, T05-269 0792. Nicely decorated old house, large rooms, private bath, cold water, fan, pleasant.

Canoa *p592*

B Hostería Canoa, 1 km south, T05-261 6380, ecocanoa@mnb.satnet.net. Comfortable cabins and rooms, includes breakfast, good restaurant and bar, a/c, pool, sauna, whirlpool.

D-E País Libre, 3 blocks from the beach, T05-261 6387. A 'high-rise' by Canoa standards. Spacious rooms, upper floors have pleasant breeze and good views, restaurant, disco in high season, cheaper with shared bath, pool, surf board rentals. Recommended.

E La Vista, on the beach, towards the south end of town, T09-419 6000. Nice hotel, all rooms have balconies to the sea, private bath, cold water, bar, clean, friendly, Norwegian/Ecuadorean-run, good value, opened in 2006.

E-F Bambú, on the beach by town, T05-261 6370. Pleasant location and atmosphere. A variety of rooms and prices, good restaurant including vegetarian options, cheaper with shared bath and in dorm, camping is also possible, hot water, fan, surfing classes and board rentals. Dutch/Ecuadorean-run, very popular and highly recommended.

E-F Coco Loco, on the beach, towards the south end of town, T09-397 2884. Pleasant breezy hotel with nice views, café serves breakfast with home-made bread, also snacks, cheaper with shared bath, **G** pp in dorm, hot showers, cooking facilities, Dutch/Belgian-run, opened in 2006.

Mompiche p593

D Iruña, east along the beach, access only at low tide or by launch, T09-947 2458, www.playa-ecuador.com. A lovely secluded hideaway with 4 nice cabins. Large terraces and hammocks, restaurant, fan, great gardens, very friendly, Spanish-run.

E Gabeal, 300 m east of town, T09-969 6543. Quiet place. Bamboo construction with lovely ocean views, balconies, small rooms and cabins, good restaurant, private bath, friendly. The owner can arrange visits to his private forest reserve, good for birdwatching.

Tonchigüe and Punta Galera p593

D Playa Escondida, 10 km west of Tonchigüe and 6 km east of Punta Galera, T06-273 3106, www.intergate.ca/playa escondida. A charming beach hideaway, set in 100 ha stretching back to dry tropical forest and run by Canadian Judith Barett on an ecologically sound basis. Volunteers are welcome for reforestation. Rustic cabins overlooking a lovely little bay, camping possible, excellent but pricey restaurant, cheaper with shared bath, cold water, good swimming and walking along the beach at low tide. The place is completely isolated and wonderfully relaxing. Recommended.

Súa p593

E Chagra Ramos, on the beach, T06-273 1006. Good restaurant, private bath, fan, great views, friendly, good value.

F Súa, on the beach, T09-535 3825. Simple hostel with 4 rooms, private bath, cold water, fan, reasonably comfortable.

Atacames p593

A Marbella, on the beach, T06-273 1129. Clean rooms for 4-5 people, fan, pool, **D** in low season when it is good value, friendly.

B Cielo Azul, on the beach near the stadium, T06-273 1813, www.hotelcieloazul.com. Rooms with balconies and hammocks,fan, pool, fridge, clean, comfortable and very good.

C Rogers, west end of the beach, T06-273 1041. Restaurant and bar, constant water supply, a/c, cheaper with fan, pool, pleasant and reasonably quiet, good value. Recommended.

D Der Alte Fritz, at the beach, T06-273 1610, www.deraltefritz-ecuador.com. Large bright rooms with ocean views, but can be noisy. Good breakfast included, restaurant serving International food, German and English spoken, discounts for longer stays, owner organizes whale-watching and fishing trips.

D Los Bohíos, 1 block from the beach by the footbridge, T06-273 1089. Pool, simple bungalows, good value. Recommended.

E Las Guadúas, Malecón del Río, 2 blocks from the beach, T06-276 0091, lasguaduas1@ on.net.ec. Quiet hotel on the riverside, private bath, cold water, good value, opened 2006.

Esmeraldas p594

B-C Apart Hotel Esmeraldas, Libertad 407 y Ramón Tello, T06-272 8700, aparthotel esmeraldas@andinanet.net. Includes breakfast, good restaurant, casino, a/c, fridge, parking, excellent quality.

D Hotel del Mar, at the far end of Av Kennedy in Las Palmas, T06-272 3707. A decent breezy hotel in Esmeraldas beach area, restaurant, patio cafeteria, cold water, a/c, parking, good service, friendly. Recommended.

E Galeón, Piedrahita 330 y Olmedo, T06-272 3820. Private bath, cold water, a/c, cheaper with fan, good.

Pacific Coast North along the coast *Listings*

For an explanation of sleeping and eating price codes used in this guide, see inside the front cover. Other relevant information is found in Essentials, see pages 31-35.

🍴 Eating

Montañita *p586*

There are many other small restaurants, all with similar food and prices.

🍴 **Marea Pizzeria Bar**, opposite **Hotel Montañita**. Real wood-oven pizza, very tasty, recommended.

🍴-🍴 **Casa Blanca**, at the hotel. International food with an Asian touch, special.

🍴 **Desde Montanita con Amor**, opposite Hotel Casa Blanca. Good vegetarian.

Puerto López *p587*

🍴 **Bellitalia**, Montalvo y Abdón Calderón, 1 block back from the Malecón and near the river, open from 1800. Excellent Italian food, try their spinach soup. Pleasant garden setting, Italian run. Highly recommended.

🍴 **Flipper**, Gen Córdova, next to **Banco del Pichincha**. Good set meals, friendly. Recommended.

🍴 **The Whale Café**, toward the south end of the Malecón. Good pizza, stir-fried Asian dishes, sandwiches, vegetarian salads, cakes and pies. Nice breakfast, famous for pancakes. US-run, owners Diana and Kevin are very helpful and provide travel information. Recommended.

Manta *p589, map p588*

The upmarket Malecón Escénico has many restaurants, most serve local seafood. A cheaper option for seafood is the Parque del Marisco, at the beach in Tarqui. In general, keep an eye on cleanliness.

🍴 **Chavecito**, Calle 106 y Av 106, Tarqui. Open until 1700. Good *ceviches* and fish. Recommended.

🍴 **El Marino**, Malecón y Calle 110, Tarqui. Classic fish and seafood restaurant, for *ceviches*, *sopa* marinera and other delicacies. Recommended.

🍴-🍴 **Beachcomber**, Calle 20 y Av Flavio Reyes. Set lunch and grill in the evening.

🍴 **Chifa Macau**, Av 15 y Calle 13. Good Chinese food.

🍴 **Paraná**, Malecón y Calle 17 near the port. Excellent quality and value set lunch, also grill in the evening. Highly recommended.

🍴 **Rincón Criollo**, Av Flavio Reyes y Calle 20. Regional cooking, set lunch, a/c.

Cafés

Café Trovador, Av 3 y Calle 11, Paseo José María Egas, closes 2100. Very good cappuccino and other coffees, snacks, sandwiches and economical set lunches.

Fruta del Tiempo, Malecón y Calle 13. Fruit salads, sandwiches, snacks.

Crucita *p590*

🍴-🍴 **Alas Delta 1 & 2**. Both have terrace seating with good ocean views. *Conchas asadas* (grilled shellfish) are the speciality.

🍴-🍴 **Motumbo**. Bar-restaurant with seafood specialities and cocktails, also has bicycles for hire.

Bahía de Caráquez *p590, map p591*

🍴-🍴 **Muelle Uno**, by the pier where canoes leave for San Vicente. Good grill and seafood, lovely setting over the water.Recommended.

🍴 **Brisas del Mar**, Hidalgo y Circunvalación. Good *ceviches* and fish.

🍴 **Columbiu's**, Av Bolívar y Ante. Cheap set meals and à la carte, try the *corvina al pimentón*, good service and value. Recommended.

🍴 **Doña Luca**, Cecilio Intriago y Sergio Plaza, towards the tip of the peninsula. Simple little place serving excellent local fare, *ceviches*, *desayuno manabita* (a wholesome breakfast), and lunches. Recommended.

Canoa *p592*

🍴 **Café Flor**, 100 m behind **Hotel La Vista**, around the corner from the petrol station. Nicely decorated friendly café-restaurant. Best breakfast in town, pizza, crêpes, vegetarian dishes, drinks.

🍴 **El Torbellino**, 4 blocks from the beach along the main street. Good for typical dishes. Set meals and à la carte, popular with locals, huge servings, lunch only.

🍴 **Shamrock**, at the beach in town. Restaurant-bar with international food, snacks, desserts, cocktails.

Mompiche *p593*

🍴 **Alicia**, next to Porta phone cabins. A very simple economical place with very good seafood and set meals, recommended.

🍴 **Kenny**, on the beachfront. Known for its crab dishes.

Súa *p593*
♥ **Kikes**, on the Malecón. Very good set
meals and great variety of seafood.
♥ **La Margarita**, across from the police
station. Pizza and French cuisine, French-run.

Atacames *p593*
The beach is packed with restaurants and
bars, too numerous to list. Most offer seafood
at similar prices: cheap set meals and pricier
à la carte. The best and cheapest *ceviche* is
found at the stands at the west end of the
beach and at the market, but avoid *concha*.
♥♥ **Da Giulio**, on the Malecón. Spanish
and Italian cuisine, good pasta.
♥♥-♥ **Le Cocotier**, Malecón. Very good pizza.
♥ **El Tiburón**, on the beach. Good seafood.

Esmeraldas *p594*
♥♥ **Chifa Asiático**, Cañizares y Bolívar.
A/c, excellent Chinese and seafood.
♥♥-♥ **El Manglar**, Quito y Olmedo. Good
comida esmeraldeña such as *encocado*
and *tapado*, clean and efficient service.
♥ **Tapao.con**, 6 de Diciembre 1717 y
Piedrahita. A popular place for typical dishes
such as *tapado*, *encocado* and *ceviche*.

♠ Bars and clubs

Montañita *p586*
Chief Bar, in the centre of the village.
Very popular bar-pizzeria-restaurant,
good cocktails, nice music.

Puerto López *p587*
La Resaca, on the beach opposite **Whale
Café**, in a converted old fishing boat.

Manta *p589, map p588*
Several bars and clubs are on Av Flavio Reyes.
Cunga, Av 22 y Av Flavio Reyes. Disco, varied
music, occasional shows, mature crowd.
Krug, Av Flavio Reyes, across from **Velboni**
supermarket, Tue-Sun. Bar with varied
music, good atmosphere, very nice place.

Bahía de Caráquez *p590, map p591*
Arena Bar Pizerría, Av Bolívar y Arenas.
Great pizza, snacks, coffee, drinks, cake
and music. Recommended.
Gordon Blues, Arenas y Morales,
good music and atmosphere.

Atacames *p593*
There are more little bars at the beach
than you can count.

Esmeraldas *p594*
By the beach in Las Palmas there's a large
variety of trendy and cool bars blasting
salsa, merengue and regaetón.
Expresiones, Sucre y Manabí, opposite
the cathedral. Bar and gallery displaying
paintings by local artists.

⊛ Festivals and events

Esmeraldas *p594*
Aug 6 Independence festivities starting
on the eve.
Sep 29 Marimba performances at the
Parque Central.

○ Shopping

Puerto López *p587*
There are several craft shops along the
Malecón, including **Palo Santo** for candles.
Yaguarundi, T05-278 0184, is a cooperative,
selling *tagua* (vegetable ivory), cactus fibre
baskets and pottery. They can arrange visits
to homes to see handicrafts being made.

Manta *p589, map p588*
El Paseo Shopping, on Av 4 de Noviembre,
the main road entering town from Portoviejo
(buses run there from the beach end of
town), large mall where you can find
everything from crafts shops and
supermarket to restaurants.
Manicentro, Av Flavio Reyes y Calle 23,
supermarket, restaurant and other shops.

Esmeraldas *p594*
Fauna y Coral, Olmedo y Ricaurte. Crafts
including baskets and musical instruments.
La Barraca, at the Malecón, is a popular
covered market where mosquito nets are sold.

▲ Activities and tours

Montañita *p586*
There are many others offering tours
to Parque Nacional Machalilla.
Machalilla Tours, next to the church,
same service as its Puerto López office.

Montañita Adventures, around the corner from **Hotel Casa Blanca**, kayaks, bicycles, surfing lessons, snorkelling tours.

Puerto López *p587*

Whale watching is possible Jun-Sep or early Oct, and high season is Jul-Aug. There is a good fleet of small boats (16-20 passengers) running excursions, all have life jackets and a toilet; but avoid those boats with a single outboard motor. All agencies offer the same tours for the same price. In high season: US$30 pp for whale watching, Isla de la Plata and snorkelling, including a snack and drinks, US$25 for whale watching only. In low season tours to Isla de la Plata and snorkelling cost US$25 pp, US$20 for whale watching only. These rates don't include the National Park fee (see page 587). Trips start 0800 and return 1700. Operators also offer tours to the mainland sites of the national park.

Tour operators

There are many agencies; not all are listed. **Bosque Marino-Expediciones Oceánicas**, Malecón y Sucre, T05-2604106, T09-337 6505. Experienced guides, some of whom speak English.
Exploramar Diving, Malecón y general Córdova, T05-230 0123, T02-256 3905 (Quito), www.exploradiving.com. French-run outfit based in Quito. They have 2 boats for 8-12 people and their own compressor to fill dive tanks. PADI divemaster accompanies qualified divers to various sites, but advance notice is required, US$85 per person for all-inclusive diving day tour (2 tanks). Also offer diving lessons. Recommended.
Manta Raya, on Malecón Norte, T05-2300233. They have a comfortable and spacious boat. They also have diving equipment and charge US$130 per person, all inclusive.
Sercapez, at the Centro Comercial on the highway, T05-2300173. All-inclusive trips to San Sebastián, with camping, local guide and food run US$30 per person, per day. They also work with **Guacamayo Bahía Tours** and organize trips further north (see Bahía de Caráquez, page 590). Also transport to other cities and the airport Manta/Portoviejo.

Manta *p589, map p588*

Metropolitan Touring, Av 4 y Calle 13, and at **Hotel Oro Verde**, T05-262 3090. Local, regional and nationwide tours (see Quito tour operators, page 468).

Bahía de Caráquez *p590, map p591*

Tours available to the estuary islands and to wetlands inland, near the city of Chone, environmental projects in the area, the Chirije archaeological site, Punta Bellaca dry forest, beaches and whale watching.

Tour operator

Guacamayo Bahía Tours, Av Bolívar y Arenas, T05-269 1412, www.riomuchacho.com. Runs tours, rents bikes, sells crafts and is involved in environmental work in Río Muchacho. Part of tour fees go to community environmental programmes. Discounts for Kiwis and SAE members. Also has a small office at **La Posada de Daniel** in Canoa, where you can be picked up for trips to Rio Muchacho.

⊖ Transport

Montañita *p586*

Bus Montañita is just a few mins south of Olón, from where there are buses to **Santa Elena** or **La Libertad**, US$2.50, 2 hrs. **CLP** have daily direct buses starting in Olón going to **Guayaquil**, at 0500, 1300, 1630, additional at 1500 on weekends (same schedule from Guayaquil), US$5, 3½ hrs; or transfer in Santa Elena. To **Puerto López**, US$1.50, 45 mins.

Puerto López *p587*

Bus To **Santa Elena** or **La Libertad**, every 30 mins, US$2.50, 2½ hrs. To **Montañita** and **Manglaralto**, US$1.50, 1 hr. Pickups for hire to nearby sites, by the market east of the highway.

Manta *p589, map p588*

Air Eloy Alfaro airport is east of Tarqui, along the route to Jaramijó, T05-262 2590. To **Quito**, 4-7 flights daily with **TAME**, Icaro and **Aerogal** US$50-70.

   Airline offices Aerogal, Av 4 No 1251 y Calle 12, T05-261 2588. **American Airlines**, Av 1 y Calle 12, T05-262 2284. **Icaro**, in Hotel Oro Verde, T05-262 7484. **TAME**, Malecón y Calle El Vigía in the centre, T05-262 2006.

Bus The Terminal Terrestre is on Calle 7 y Av 8 in the centre, mind your belongings here. A couple of companies have their own private terminals nearby and run services to their own terminals in Quito. To **Portoviejo**, every 10 mins, US$0.75, 45 mins. To **Jipijapa**, every 20 mins, US$1, 1 hr. To **Pedernales**, 6 daily, US$4.60, 6 hrs. To **Montecristi**, local buses throughout the day from the Terminal Terrestre, US$0.30, 15 min; taxis charge up to US$10, negotiable.

Car hire Avis, Malecón y Circunvalación, CC Cocco Manta, T05-262 6680. Budget, Malecón y Calle 16, T05-262 9919. Localiza, Av Flavio Reyes y Av 21, T05-262 2434.

Bahía de Caráquez *p590, map p591*
Air There is an airport at San Vicente across the estuary, but no commercial flights. For charters contact NICA, T05-269 0332, or AECA, T05-2674198.

Boat Motorized canoes (*lanchas* or *pangas*) cross the estuary to San Vicente, from the dock by the Malecón opposite Calle Ante, by **Muelle 1** restaurant. Frequent service 0615-1800, US$0.29; larger and slower boats make the crossing every 20 mins from 1800-2200, US$0.35, later rent a boat.
　　A car ferry runs from a ramp near the obelisk, next to the Repsol gasoline station, at the end of Calle Ascázubi. It runs every 20 mins or so, 0630-2000, US$2 for small vehicles, US$0.50 for motorcycles, free for foot passengers. Depending on the tide, the steep ramps may be difficult for low-clearance cars.

Bus The Terminal Terrestre is located at the entrance to town. To **Chone**, *ejecutivo*, US$2, 1½ hrs. To **Portoviejo**, US$2, 2 hrs, every 30 mins. To **Puerto López**, go to Manta, Portoviejo or Jipijapa and change buses. To **Quito**, 2 *ejecutivos* daily at 0900 and 2240, US$9, 8 hrs; plus regular service.

Taxi Eco-taxi tricycles are available for short trips during the daytime, US$0.50.

Canoa *p592*
Bus To **San Vicente**, every 30 mins, 0700-1730, US$0.50, 30 mins; taxi US$5. To **Pedernales**, every hour, 0600-1800, US$2.50, 2 hrs.

Mompiche *p593*
Bus To **Esmeraldas**, 5 a day, US$3, 3½ hrs.

Tonchigüe and Punta Galera *p593*
Bus You can take a *ranchera* or bus from Esmeraldas for Punta Galera, 5 a day, US$2, 2 hrs.

Taxi A taxi from Atacames costs US$12; a pickup from Tonchigüe costs US$5.

Atacames *p593*
Bus To **Esmeraldas**, bus every 15 mins, US$0.80, 40 mins. To **Guayaquil**, at 0830 and 2 at night, US$8, 8 hrs. To **Quito**, several companies, about 10 daily, US$8, 6½ hrs.

Taxi A tricycle rickshaw ride costs US$0.50-1.

Esmeraldas *p594*
Air General Rivadeneira Airport is near the town of **Tachina**, on the east shore of the Río Esmeraldas. A taxi to the city centre (30 km) costs US$6. Buses to Esmeraldas go along the road outside the airport about every 30 mins. Daily flights except Sat to **Quito** with TAME, 30 mins, US$40 one way. Check in early as planes may leave 30 mins before scheduled time. Buses to La Tola, Borbón, San Lorenzo or Ibarra pass near the airport so it is not necessary to go into town if northbound.
　　Airline offices TAME, Bolívar y 9 de Octubre, T06-2726863.

Boat The paved road to **San Lorenzo** and the Colombian border runs slightly inland. To reach small villages along the coast, you can take a bus to **La Tola** (see above) from where there are launches to points north.

Bus To **Quito** and **Guayaquil** Panamericana (Colón y Salinas) and **Trans Esmeraldas** (10 de Agosto, Parque Central) run *servicio directo* or *ejecutivo* options, a better choice as they are fancier buses, faster, and don't stop on the side of the road to take passengers.
　　La Costeñita and El Pacífico (both on Malecón) to **La Tola** 8 daily, US$3.75, 3 hrs. To **Borbón**, frequent service, US$3.50, 3 hrs. To **San Lorenzo**, 8 daily, US$4.50, 4 hrs. To **Muisne**, every 30 mins, US$2, 2 hrs. To **Súa**, **Same** and **Atacames**, every 15 mins from 0630-2030, to Atacames US$0.80, 1 hr.

C Directory

Montañita *p586*

Banks No banks in town, there is one ATM (sometimes out of order, bring some cash) Farmacia San José and Hotel Casa Blanca change TCs, 6% commission. **Internet** On street closest to the river, US$2 per hr. **Laundry** Lavandería Espumita, near the church, charges by piece. Several others. **Telephone** Several cell phone cabins. There are problems with regular telephones.

Puerto López *p587*

Banks There are no ATMs, the one bank provides no services, bring cash. **Internet** Several places, US$1.20-1.50 per hr. **Language schools** La Lengua, Abdón Calderón y García Moreno, next to the Municipio, east of the highway, costamar25@ hotmail.com, same school as in Quito, T02-254 3521, www.la-lengua.com. US$6 per hr, can organize homestays.

Manta *p589, map p588*

Banks Banco del Pacífico, Av 2 y Calle 13. **Produbanco**, Malecón y Calle 17. **Hospitals** Clínica Manta, Av 4 de Noviembre, T05-292 1566, is a good private hospital, open 24 hrs, expensive. **Hospital Rodríguez Zambrano**, Vía a San Mateo, T05-261 1849, is a public hospital. **Internet** US$1.20 per hr.

Language schools
Academia Sur Pacífico, Av 24 y Calle 15, Edificio Barre, 3rd floor, T05-261 0838, www.surpacifico.k12.ec. US$4 per hr for group lessons, US$6 for one-on-one. **Shipping agents** The Ministerio de Turismo maintains a list of shipping agents, see Tourist information, page 589.

Bahía de Caráquez *p590, map p591*

Banks Banco de Guayaquil, Av Bolívar y Riofrío, ATM. **Internet** US$1.20-1.50 per hr.

Canoa *p592*

Language schools Canoa Spanish Learning School, at Sundown Inn, on the beach, 3 km from town towards San Vicente, T09-981 5763, www.ecuadorbeach.com

Atacames *p593*

Banks Banco del Pichincha, 1 block from the plaza, VISA ATM, other ATMs at Hotel Lé Castell and Farmacia Sana Sana. Hotel Der Alte Fritz, changes Tcs, 2% commission, and Euros. **Internet** US$1-2 per hr. **Laundry** Zum Tucan, 1 block east of the bridge, on the south side , US$1 per kg.

Esmeraldas *p594*

Banks Banco del Austro, Bolívar 310 y Cañizares. **Produbanco**, Bolívar 415 y Cañizares.

Galápagos Islands

Introduction

A trip to the Galápagos is an unforgettable experience. As Charles Darwin put it: "The natural history of this archipelago is very remarkable: it seems to be a little world within itself". The islands are world renowned for their fearless wildlife but no amount of hype can prepare the visitor for such a close encounter with nature. Here, you can snorkel with penguins and sea lions, watch 200-kg tortoises lumbering through giant cactus forest, and enjoy the courtship display of the blue-footed booby and frigate bird, all in startling close-up.

A visit to the islands doesn't come cheap. The return flight from Quito and national park fee add up to almost US$500; plus a bare minimum of US$100 per person per day for sailing on an economy-class boat. There are few such inexpensive vessels and even fewer good inexpensive ones. Since you are already spending so much money, it is well worth spending a little more to make sure you sign up with a reputable agency on a better cruise, the quality of which is generally excellent.

Land-based and independent travel on the populated islands are also viable alternatives, but there is at present simply no way to enjoy Galápagos on a shoestring. The once-in-a-lifetime Galápagos experience merits saving for, however, and at the same time, high prices are one way of keeping the number of visitors within sustainable levels. The islands have already suffered the impact of rapidly growing tourism and a mechanism is urgently needed to ensure their survival as the world's foremost wildlife sanctuary.

★ Don't miss …

1 **Bartolomé Islet** Let the stunning view of Sullivan Bay take your breath away, page 607.

2 **Lonesome George** Take a wistful look at the last surviving giant tortoise of his sub-species at the Charles Darwin Research Station, page 612.

3 **Male chauvinist sea lions** Watch a male sea lion assert dominion over his beach and harem at Isla Lobos, the ultimate in vociferous machismo, page 614.

4 **Sierra Negra Volcano** Explore the world's largest basaltic caldera, an amazing 10 km in diameter, page 615.

5 **Underwater world** Snorkel or dive to catch a glimpse of the rich and varied underwater life, page 618.

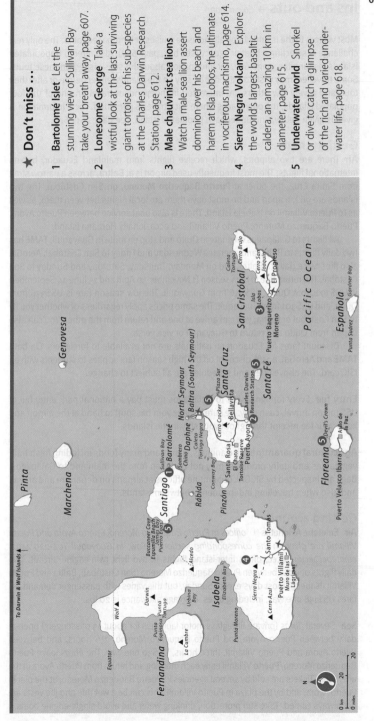

Galápagos Islands

Ins and outs → Colour map 5.

Most visitors to the islands book all-inclusive cruises or land-based tours. The only real challenge is selecting a boat or agency (see box, page 607). Also refer to Unpopulated islands visitor sites, page 607, for information about the sites visited on these tours. Some travellers may wish to extend their stay on the islands, either before or after their tour, and a very few others are interested in independent travel on one of the four populated islands, the only places where such travel is permitted. Local information is given is given below, and under each populated island, see pages 611-620.

Getting there

Air There are two airports, which receive flights from mainland Ecuador, but no international flights. The most frequently used airport is at **Baltra**, across a narrow strait from Santa Cruz, the other at **Puerto Baquerizo Moreno**, on San Cristóbal. The two islands are 96 km apart and on most days there are local flights between them, as well as to Puerto Villamil on Isabela island. There is also boat service between Puerto Ayora, Puerto Baquerizo Moreno, Puerto Villamil and occasionally Floreana island.

All flights to Galápagos originate in Quito and stop en route in Guayaquil. **TAME** has two daily flights to Baltra and operates Wednesday and Friday to San Cristóbal. **AeroGal** also flies twice daily to Baltra, and on Monday, Thursday, Saturday and Sunday to San Cristóbal. The return fare in high season (1 November-30 April and 15 June-14 September) is US$392 from Quito, US$346 from Guayaquil. The low season fare is US$336 from Quito, and US$301 from Guayaquil. The same prices apply regardless of whether you fly to San Cristóbal or Baltra; you can arrive at one and return from the other. You can also depart from Quito and return to Guayaquil or vice versa.

Discount fares for Ecuadorean nationals are not available to foreigners. On both **TAME** and **AeroGal**, a 15% discount off the high season fare applies to students with an ISIC card. The above fares and schedules are all subject to change.

Entry fee Every foreign visitor to Galápagos must pay a national park entry fee of US$100 on arrival, cash only. Be sure to have your passport to hand at the airport and keep your fee receipt throughout your stay in the islands.

Agricultural quarantine Live animals, plants and many foods including fresh fruit, vegetables and dairy products, may not be taken from the mainland to Galápagos. Bags are inspected by SICGAL quarantine officers at airports on departure and arrival, and also when travelling independently between islands.

Getting around

Air Emetebe Avionetas ⓘ *offices in Puerto Baquerizo Moreno, Puerto Ayora and Puerto Villamil are given in the corresponding sections below; in Guayaquil T04-229 2492, emetebe@ecua.net.ec,* offers inter-island flights in two light twin-engine aircraft. Two daily flights operate between Puerto Baquerizo Moreno (San Cristóbal), Baltra and Puerto Villamil (Isabela), most days except Sunday, but this varies with passenger demand. All fares US$158 one way, including taxes. Baggage allowance is 20 lbs.

Sea Several *fibras* (private fibreglass motor launches for about 15 passengers) operate daily between Puerto Ayora and Puerto Baquerizo Moreno, 2½ hours, and between Puerto Ayora and Puerto Villamil, three hours, US$30 one way. The *fibras* leave Puerto Baquerizo Moreno/Puerto Villamil early each morning and return from Puerto Ayora in the afternoon. Tickets are sold by several agencies in Puerto Baquerizo Moreno, at the pier in Puerto Ayora, and by the plaza in Puerto Villamil. This can be a wet ride and life vests are not always carried. Take sun protection, drinking water and avoid single-engine boats.

The islands

→ *Colour map 1.*

Lying on the Equator, 970 km west of the Ecuadorean coast, the Galápagos consist of six main islands: San Cristóbal, Santa Cruz, Isabela, Floreana, Santiago and Fernandina. There are also 12 smaller islands – Baltra and the uninhabited islands of Santa Fe, Pinzón, Española, Rábida, Daphne, Seymour, Genovesa, Marchena, Pinta, Darwin and Wolf – as well as over 40 small islets.

The Galápagos have never been connected with the mainland. Gradually, over many hundreds of thousands of years, animals and plants somehow migrated there across the sea and, as time went by, they adapted themselves to the Galápagos conditions and came to differ more and more from their continental ancestors. Thus many of them are unique: a quarter of the species of shore fish, half of the plants and almost all the reptiles are found nowhere else on earth. In many cases different forms have evolved on the different islands. Charles Darwin recognized this speciation within the archipelago when he visited the Galápagos on the Beagle in 1835 and his observations played a substantial part in his formulation of the theory of evolution. Since no large land mammals reached the islands (until they were recently introduced by man), reptiles were dominant just as they had been all over the world in the very distant past. Another of the extraordinary features of the islands is the tameness of the animals. The islands were uninhabited when they were discovered in 1535 and the animals still have little instinctive fear of man.

The Galápagos have been declared a World Heritage Site by UNESCO and 97% of the land area and 100% of the surrounding ocean are now part of the Galápagos National Park and Marine Reserve. Within the park there are some 60 visitor sites, each with defined trails, so the impact of visitors to this fragile environment is minimized. These sites can only be visited with a national park guide as part of a cruise or tour. → *For Sleeping, Eating and other listings on these islands, see pages 616-620.*

Unpopulated islands visitor sites

Baltra
Once a US Airforce base, Baltra is now a small military base for Ecuador and also the main airport into the islands. Also known as South Seymour, this is the island most affected by human presence. **Mosquera** is a small sandy bank just north of Baltra, home to a large colony of sea lions.

Bartolomé
Bartolomé is a small island located in Sullivan Bay off the eastern shore of Santiago. It is probably the most easily recognized, the most visited and most photographed of all the islands in the Galápagos with its distinctive **Pinnacle Rock**. The trail leads steeply up to the summit, taking 30-40 minutes, from where there are panoramic views. At the second visitor site on the island there is a lovely beach from which you can snorkel or swim and see the penguins.

Daphne Major
West of Baltra, Daphne island has very rich birdlife, in particular the nesting boobies. Because of the possible problems of erosion, only small boats may land here and are limited to one visit each month.

Touring the Galápagos

There are two main ways to travel around the islands: a cruise (also called *tour navegable*), where you sleep on the boat; or land-based tours where you sleep ashore at night and travel during the day. On a cruise you travel at night, arriving at a new site each day, with more time ashore. On a land-based tour you cover less ground and cannot visit the more distant islands. All tours begin with a morning flight from the mainland on the first day and end on the last day with a midday flight back to the mainland.

Cruises

The standard of facilities varies from one tourist vessel to another and you basically get what you pay for in terms of comfort, service and food. Once on shore at the visitor sites, no matter what price you have paid, each visitor is shown the same things. Note however that smaller and cheaper boats may not visit as many or as distant sites. On the other hand, larger vessels may not be allowed to take passengers to some of the more fragile landings such as Daphne Major.

The less expensive boats are normally smaller and less powerful so you see less and spend more time travelling; also the guiding may be mostly in Spanish. The more expensive boats will probably have air conditioning, hot water and private baths. In principle, all boats have to conform to certain minimum safety standards; more expensive boats are better equipped. A water maker (desalinator) can be a great asset. Boats with more than 18 passengers take quite a time to disembark and re-embark people. Smaller boats have a more lively motion, which isn't much fun if you are prone to seasickness.

Each day starts early and schedules are usually full. If you are sailing overnight, your boat will probably have reached its destination before breakfast. After eating, you disembark for a morning on the island. The usual time for snorkelling is between the morning excursion and lunch. The midday meal is taken on board because no food is allowed on the islands. If the island requires two visits, you will return to shore after lunch, otherwise part of the afternoon may be taken up with a sea voyage. After the day's activities, there is time to clean up, have a drink and relax before the briefing for the next day and supper.

Itineraries are controlled by the national park to distribute tourism evenly throughout the islands. All boats must re-provision at Puerto Ayora once a

Española

This is the southernmost island of the Galápagos and, following a successful programme to remove all the feral species, is now the most pristine, with many migrant, resident and endemic seabirds. **Gardner Bay**, on the northeastern coast, is a beautiful white-sand beach with excellent swimming and snorkelling. **Punta Suárez**, on the western tip of the island, has a trail through a rookery. As well as a wide range of seabirds (including blue-footed and masked boobies) there is a great selection of wildlife including sea lions and the largest and most colourful marine iguanas of the Galápagos plus the original home of the waved albatrosses.

Fernandina

Fernadina is the youngest of the islands, at about 700,000 years old, and also the most volcanically active, with eruptions every few years. The visitor site of **Punta Espinosa** is on the northeast coast of Fernandina. The trail goes up through a sandy nesting site for huge colonies of marine iguanas. The nests appear as small hollows in the sand. You can also see flightless cormorants drying their atrophied wings in the sun and go snorkelling in the bay.

week. On the day the boats are in port the passengers visit the Darwin Station and either the highlands or lava tubes or Tortuga Bay. Boats do not put into port just to take off or put on passengers, however some boats do take advantage of the day they are in Puerto Ayora, to change some or all of their passengers.

Price categories

The least expensive boats (economy class) cost about US$100 per person per day; they are usually small and slow, and a few of these vessels are dodgy. For around US$100-250 per day (tourist and tourist superior class) you will be on a better, faster boat which can travel more quickly between visitor sites, leaving more time to spend ashore. Over US$250 per day is entering the first-class and luxury brackets, with far more comfortable and spacious cabins, as well as a superior of service and cuisine. No boat may sail without a park-trained guide.

Most visitors are thoroughly satisfied, but there is the occasional complaint especially at the low end. Remember that all boats look good in brochures, and nothing is more valuable than a personal recommendation by a recent passenger. Note that we have had

repeated complaints about the vessel *Free Enterprise*, sometimes also called *Intrepid* or *Discovery*. The *Gaby I* (also known as *Friendship*) has also been frequently criticized but came under new management in 2006.

Booking a cruise

You can book a Galápagos cruise in lots of different ways: 1) over the the internet; 2) from either a travel agency or though a Galápagos wholesaler in your home country; 3) from one of the many agencies in Ecuador, especially in Quito but also in Guayaquil and elsewhere; or 4) from agencies in Puerto Ayora but not Puerto Baquerizo Moreno. The trade-off is between time and money: booking from home is efficient but expensive, Puerto Ayora is cheapest and most time-consuming, while Quito and Guayaquil are intermediate. Prices for a given boat category do not vary much, however.

To arrange last-minute tours, a highly recommended contact is Jenny Divine at **Moonrise Travel** (see page 619). Note that it is not possible to obtain discounts or find last-minute bookings in high season. Those who attempt to do so in July, August or Christmas/New Year often spend several frustrating weeks in Puerto Ayora without ever sailing the islands.

Genovesa

Located at the northeast part of the archipelago, this is an outpost for many sea birds. It is an eight- to 10-hour all-night sail from Puerto Ayora. Like Fernandina, Genovesa is best visited on longer cruises or ships with larger range.

One of the most famous sites is **Prince Phillip's Steps**, an amazing walk through a seabird rookery that is full of life. You will see tropic birds, all three boobies, frigates, petrels, swallow-tailed and lava gulls, and many others. There is also good snorkelling at the foot of the steps, with lots of marine iguanas. The entrance to **Darwin Bay**, on the eastern side of the island, is very narrow and shallow and the anchorage in the lagoon is surrounded by mangroves, home to a large breeding colony of frigates.

Plaza Sur

One of the closest islands to Puerto Ayora is Plaza Sur. It's an example of a geological uplift and the southern part of the island has formed cliffs with spectacular views. It has a combination of both dry and coastal vegetation zones. Walking along the sea cliffs is a pleasant experience as the swallowtail gull, shearwaters and red-billed tropic birds nest here. This is the home of the **Men's Club**, a rather sad-looking colony of bachelor sea lions

Galápagos tips

Responsible tourism
→ Never touch any of the animals, birds or plants.
→ Do not transfer sand, seeds or soil from one island to another.
→ Do not leave litter anywhere nor take food onto the islands.

Making the most of your trip
→ Always bring some US dollars cash to Galápagos. There is only one
  bank and ATM system, which may not work with all cards.
→ Daytime clothing should be lightweight and even on luxury cruises
  should be casual and comfortable. At night, particularly at sea and
  at higher altitudes, warm clothing may be required.
→ Bring good footwear, soles soon wear out on the abrasive lava terrain.
→ A remedy for seasickness is recommended.
→ A good supply of sun block and skin cream to prevent wind-burn and
  chapped lips is essential, as are a hat and good sunglasses.
→ Be prepared for dry and wet landings. The latter involves wading ashore.
→ Take plenty of memory cards or film. The animals are so tame that you
  will use far more than you expected. An underwater camera is also useful.
→ Snorkelling equipment is particularly useful as much of the sea-life is only
  visible underwater. Few of the cheaper boats provide good snorkelling
  gear. If in doubt, bring your own, rent in Puerto Ayora or buy it in Quito.
→ On most cruises a ship's crew and guides are usually tipped separately.
  The amount is a very personal matter; you may be guided by suggestions
  made onboard or in the agency's brochures, but the key factors should
  always be the quality of service received and your own resources.
→ Raise any issues first with your guide or ship's captain. Additional
  complaints may be made to CAPTURGAL in Puerto Ayora, see page 611.

who are too old to mate and who get together to console each other. There are also lots of blue-footed boobies and a large population of land iguanas on the island.

Rábida
This island is just to the south of Santiago. The trail leads to a salt-water lagoon, occasionally home to flamingos. There is an area of mangroves near the lagoon where brown pelicans nest. This island is said to have the most diversified volcanic rocks of all the islands. You can snorkel and swim from the beach.

Santa Fe
This little island is located on the southeastern part of Galápagos, between Santa Cruz and San Cristóbal, and was formed by volcanic uplift. The lagoon has a large colony of sea lions who are happy to join you for a swim. From the beach the trail goes inland, through a semi-arid landscape of cacti. The island has its own sub-species of land iguana.

Santiago
This large island, also known as James, is to the east of Isla Isabela. It has a volcanic landscape full of cliffs and pinnacles, and is home to several species of marine birds. This island has a large population of goats, one of the four species of animals introduced in the early 1800s.

James Bay is on the western side of the island, where there is a wet landing on the dark sands of **Puerto Egas**. The trail leads to the remains of an unsuccessful salt mining operation. Fur seals are seen nearby. **Espumilla Beach** is another famous visitor site. After landing on a large beach, walk through a mangrove forest that leads to a lake usually inhabited by flamingos, pintail ducks and stilts. There are nesting and feeding sites for flamingos. Sea turtles dig their nests at the edge of the mangroves. **Buccaneer Cove**, on the northwest part of the island, was a haven for pirates during the 1600s and 1700s. **Sullivan Bay** is on the eastern coast of Santiago, opposite Bartolomé Island. The visitor trail leads across an impressive landscape of lava fields formed in eruptions in 1890.

Seymour Norte
Just north of Baltra, Seymour Norte is home to sea lions, marine iguanas, swallow-tailed gulls, magnificent frigate birds and blue-footed boobies. The tourist trail leads through mangroves in one of the main nesting sites for blue-footed boobies and frigates in this part of the archipelago.

Sombrero Chino
This is just off the southeastern tip of Santiago, and its name refers to its shape. It is most noted for the volcanic landscape including sharp outcrops, cracked lava formations, lava tubes and volcanic rubble. This site is only accessible to vessels with capacity for fewer than 12 passengers.

Santa Cruz ⊜⊘⋔⊡⏶⊝⊕ ➻ *pp616-620.*

➻ *pp616-620.*

This is the main inhabited island. Most of the 18,500 inhabitants live in and around **Puerto Ayora**, but there are farming settlements inland at **Bellavista** and **Santa Rosa**. Puerto Ayora is the economic centre of the Galápagos and every cruise visits it for one day anchoring at Academy Bay.

Puerto Ayora → *Phone code 05. Colour map 1. Population 16,000.*
Puerto Ayora, on the south shore of Isla Santa Cruz, is the largest urban area of Galápagos and the main tourist centre. It is a busy prosperous little city, offering a wide range of hotels and restaurants. Most tourist services, including agencies for last-minute cruise bookings, are concentrated along the attractive Malecón Charles Darwin, which also has many shops. If you are travelling independently and choose to arrange a cruise from here, then Puerto Ayora can be a base for several worthwhile excursions. The main streets have bicycle lanes called *ciclovías*.

> ❧ *When looking for a last-minute cruise in Puerto Ayora it is best to pay your hotel one night at a time. Hoteliers may not refund advance payments.*

The 'real town' fills the streets back from the sea and some prices are a little lower here. Although cheap rooms and simple meals can be found in Puerto Ayora, the cost of most goods here and throughout Galápagos is substantially higher than on the mainland. Puerto Ayora has grown rapidly in recent years and lost its former outpost feel as well as its tranquillity. Public safety is a concern late at night.

Ministerio de Turismo ⓘ *Av Charles Darwin y Tomas de Berlanga, T05-252 6174, mturgal@gpsinter.net, Mon-Fri 0800-1230, 1400-1730*, has general information and maps for all of Galápagos, English spoken. The **Dirección Municipal de Turismo (iTur)** ⓘ *next to post office, daily 1000-1700, also at Baltra airport, www.santacruz.gov.ec*, has information about Puerto Ayora and Santa Cruz Island. **CAPTURGAL** ⓘ *Av Charles Darwin y Charles Binford, T05-252 6206, www.galapagostour.org, Mon-Fri 0730-1200, 1400-1730*, is the Galápagos Chamber of Tourism (English spoken). This is the place to present serious complaints about cruise vessels, agencies or tourist services.

ⓘ *Academy Bay, a 20-min walk from the dock at Puerto Ayora, daily 0600-1800.*

In 1959, the centenary of the publication of Darwin's *Origin of Species*, the the Charles Darwin Research Station was established. Collections of several of the rare sub-species of giant tortoise are maintained on the station as breeding nuclei. There is also a tortoise-rearing area where the young can be seen.

Around Puerto Ayora

One of the most beautiful beaches in the Galápagos is at **Tortuga Bay**, 45 minutes' easy walk (2½ km each way) west from Puerto Ayora on an excellent cobbled path through cactus forest. Start at the west end of Calle Charles Binford; further on there is a gate

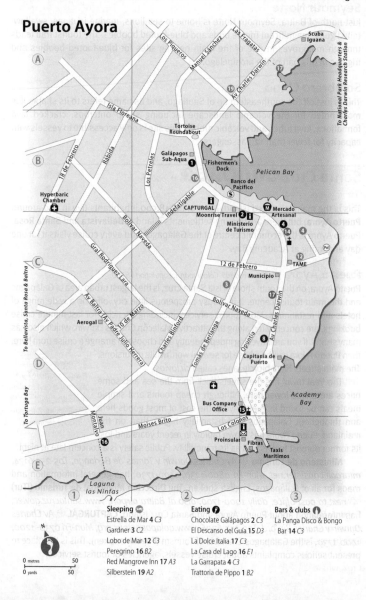

Puerto Ayora

Galápagos Islands The Islands

Sleeping 🛏
Estrella de Mar **4** *C3*
Gardner **3** *C2*
Lobo de Mar **12** *C3*
Peregrino **16** *B2*
Red Mangrove Inn **17** *A3*
Silberstein **19** *A2*

Eating 🍴
Chocolate Galápagos **2** *C3*
El Descanso del Guía **15** *D3*
La Dolce Italia **17** *C3*
La Casa del Lago **16** *E1*
La Garrapata **4** *C3*
Trattoria de Pippo **1** *B2*

Bars & clubs 🍸
La Panga Disco & Bongo Bar **14** *C3*

⦂ Difficult choices for Galápagos

Galápagos is becoming a victim of its own success as a tourist destination. In 2007 UNESCO placed the islands on its list of endangered World Heritage Sites. The main threats are immigration from mainland Ecuador, rapidly growing tourism, ongoing introduction of exotic species of plants and animals, and commercial fishing in the Marine Reserve. The situation raises some difficult questions.

Are the islands first and foremost a sanctuary, a treasure so unique and precious for all mankind as to merit the strictest conservation in the sovereign custody of Ecuador? Or is Galápagos primarily a province of a developing South American republic, with natural resources to be exploited for the enjoyment of visitors and to satisfy the economic needs of residents? And who decides?

where you must register (daily 0600-1800). Take sun screen, drinking water, and beware of the very strong undertow. Camping is not permitted. Do not leave your valuables unattended at the beach. Also, do not walk on the dunes above the beach, which are a marine tortoise nesting area. Ten minutes' walk to the west end of Tortuga Bay brings you to a lovely trail from where it's a further 10 minutes to a mangrove-fringed lagoon. Along the way marine iguanas, blue-footed boobies and pelicans may be seen. The water in the lagoon is calmer and warmer than the sea, and there is nice shade under the mangroves. Kayaks may sometimes be rented here, US$5 per hour.

Las Grietas is a beautiful gorge with a pool at the bottom which is splendid for bathing. Take a water taxi from the port to the dock at Punta Estrada (five minutes, US$0.50). It is a five-minute walk from here to the **Finch Bay Hotel** and 15 minutes further over rough lava boulders to Las Grietas – well worth the trip.

Santa Cruz excursions and visitor sites

Tour operators in Puerto Ayora (see page 618) run excursions to the highland sites for about US$20-30 per person, depending on the number of sites visited and the size of the group. These may include visits to ranches such as Rancho Mariposa, see below.

Bay excursions in glass-bottomed boats visit sites near Puerto Ayora. It involves some walking and you are likely to see sea lions, birds, marine iguanas and marine life including sharks. Snorkelling can be part of the tour. Half-day tours cost around US$25 per person (see page 618). Reservations are strongly recommended in the high season.

At **El Chato Tortoise Reserve**, giant tortoises can be seen in the wild during the dry season. The trail starts at Santa Rosa, 22 km from Puerto Ayora. Near El Chato is the **Butterfly Ranch (Hacienda Mariposa)** ① *beyond Bellavista on the road to Santa Rosa (the bus passes the turn-off, walk 1 km from there), US$2.* Here you can see giant tortoises in the pastures, but only in the dry season. In the wet season the tortoises are breeding down in the arid zone. Camping is possible for $10-15 per person (toilets but no showers) and horse riding is available, enquire at **Moonrise Travel**, see page 619. There are other ranches in the area, agencies in Puerto Ayora can arrange visits.

National park visitor sites on Santa Cruz include **Caleta Tortuga Negra**, on the northern part of the island. Here you can drift by dinghy through the mangrove swamps which are home to marine turtles, white-tipped sharks, spotted eagle rays and yellow cow-nosed rays. Nearby is **Las Bachas**, a swimming beach, also on the north shore. **Conway Bay** is a rarely visited visitor site on the northwest coast, inhabited by a large colony of sea lions. **Whaler Bay** is the site of one of the oldest whaling camps on Santa Cruz. It was to here and the other similar camps that the giant tortoises were brought before being loaded on board the whalers. **Cerro Dragón** is on the north shore of Santa Cruz, where land iguanas and flamingos may be seen.

Galápagos Islands The Islands

San Cristóbal 🔲🔘🔘🔲🔺🔲🔲 ▸▸ pp 616-620.

San Cristóbal is the easternmost island of Galápagos and geologically one of the oldest. The main town, Puerto Baquerizo Moreno, is the capital of the province of Galápagos.

Puerto Baquerizo Moreno → Phone code 05. Population 6600.

Puerto Baquerizo Moreno is a pleasant tranquil place which sees far less tourism than Puerto Ayora. There are beaches nearby, an interesting national park visitor centre and worthwhile excursions to the highlands. Avenida Charles Darwin is a pleasant seafront promenade with a nice **Muelle Turístico** (tourist pier) by Calle Herman Melville.

CATURSAN ① *Malecón Charles Darwin y Española, T05-252 0592, ctcsancrist@ easynet.net.ec, Mon-Fri 0730-1200, 1400-1700*, is the San Cristóbal Chamber of Tourism. **Municipal tourist office** ① *Malecón Charles Darwin y 12 de Febrero, T05-252 1166, www.sancristobalgalapagos.com, Mon-Fri 0730-1230, 1400-1700*, is at the Municipio. Both of the above are helpful and have various pamphlets.

Around Puerto Baquerizo Moreno

To the north of town, opposite Playa Mann, is the Galápagos National Park visitor centre or **Centro de Interpretación** ① *daily 0700-1700, free*. It has an excellent display of the natural and especially the human history of the islands and is highly recommended.

A good trail goes from the Centro de Interpretación to the northeast through scrub forest to **Cerro Tijeretas**, a hill overlooking town and the ocean, 30 minutes away (take drinking water). Along the way are good examples of the arid zone vegetation. There are side trails branch off to lookouts on the cliffs over the sea.

San Cristóbal excursions and visitor sites

From **El Progreso**, 6 km inland from Puerto Baquerizo Moreno, it's a 2½ hour walk to **El Junco lake**, the largest body of fresh water in Galápagos. You can also hire a pickup truck to El Junco, continuing to the beach at **Puerto Chino** on the south side of the island. Along the way is **La Galapaguera** – a man-made tortoise area.

National park visitor sites include **Caleta Tortuga**, on the northwest shore of the island. It's a three-hour hike from from there to **La Galapaguera Natural** where you can see tortoises in the wild. **Isla Lobos** is an islet with a large sea lion colony and nesting site for sea birds northeast of Puerto Baquerizo Moreno. It is also a dive site. **Kicker Rock** (León Dormido), the basalt remains of a crater, is split by a narrow channel and is navigable to the smaller vessels. It is home to a large colony of many seabirds, including masked and blue-footed boobies, nesting in the cliffs rising vertically from the channel. This is also a dive site.

Isabela 🔲🔘🔘🔲🔺🔲🔲 ▸▸ pp 616-620.

The largest of the Galápagos Islands, Isabela is receiving more and more land-based tourism. Several new hotels are under construction and a flurry of development is in the offing, which is a great shame because the island's greatest attraction is precisely its delightfully undeveloped atmosphere and laid-back feeling. Most residents live in Puerto Villamil on the south coast, the main settlement, founded in 1897. The highlands has a cluster of farms known as Santo Tomás.

Puerto Villamil → Phone code 05. Population 2200.

There are several lovely beaches right by town, enquire locally about the best spots for swimming. It is a 2½-hour walk west to **Muro de las Lágrimas**, a gruesome place built by convict labour under hideous conditions. It gets very hot, so start early and

take plenty of water. Along the same road 30 minutes from town is the **Centro de**
Crianza, a man-made breeding centre for giant tortoises surrounded by lagoons with
flamingos and other birds, and pleasant walking trails.

In the opposite direction, 30 minutes east, next to the *embarcadero* (fishing pier)
is **Concha Perla Lagoon**, with a nice access trail through mangroves and a little dock
from which you can go swimming with sea lions and other creatures. **Las Grietas** is a
set of small islets in the harbour where *tintoreras* (white-tipped reef sharks) may be
seen in the still crystalline water; there may also be penguins. A three-hour tour costs
US$20 per person. ▸▸ *See Activities and tours, page 620.*

Isabela excursions and visitor sites

Tours can be arranged to visit **Sierra Negra Volcano**, which has the largest basaltic
caldera in the world, 9 km x 10 km. It is 19 km (one hour) by pickup truck from Puerto
Villamil to the park entrance, take your passport and Galápagos National Park entry
fee receipt. Here you switch to horses for the beautiful 1½-hour ride to the crater rim at
1000 m, where evidence of the spectacular 2005 eruption can easily be seen. It is a
further 1½-hour walk along bare brittle lava rock to **Volcán Chico**, with several
fumaroles and more stunning views. A half-day tour including transport, horses and
lunch costs US$30 per person. ▸▸ *See Activities and tours, page 620.*

National park visitor sites include **Punta Moreno**, on the southwest part of
Isabela, where penguins and shore birds are usually seen. **Elizabeth Bay**, on the west
coast, is home to a small colony of penguins. **Urbina Bay**, at the base of Alcedo
Volcano on the west coast, was the site of a major uplift in 1954, when the land rose
up about 5 m. This event was associated with an eruption of Alcedo volcano. The
coastline rose as far as 1 km out to the sea and exposed giant coral heads. The uplift
was so sudden that lobster and fish were stranded on what is now the shore. **Tagus
Cove** is located on the west coast across the narrow channel from Fernandina island. A
trail leads past **Laguna Darwin**, a large saltwater lake, and then further uphill to a ridge
with lovely views. **Punta Tortuga**, north of Tagus Cove on the west coast of Isabela, is a
bathing beach surrounded by mangroves.

Floreana 🏝 ▸▸ *pp 616-620.*

This is the longest-inhabited of the islands and the site of the mysterious 'Galápagos Affair'
in the 1930s. Most of its 100 inhabitants live in Puerto Velasco Ibarra, by Black Beach.

Puerto Velasco Ibarra → *Phone code 05. Population 88.*

The original settlers came to Floreana to get away from the rest of world. Even today,
unless you come with one of the few cruise boats which land at Black Beach for a few
hours, or make special advance arrangements, it is difficult to get to Floreana and even
more difficult to leave. There is electricity for a few hours each day, telephones and one
small shop with very basic supplies, but you should be as self-sufficient as possible.

Floreana excursions and visitor sites

A vehicle road runs 8 km up into the highlands, where the climate is fresh. You can visit
the natural spring (water supply for the island) at **Asilo de la Paz**, and the nearby cave
where Patrick Watkins, the first inhabitant of Galápagos lived from 1807 to 1809.

National park visitor sites include the **Devil's Crown**, a dramatic snorkelling site
to the north of Punta Cormorant, is an almost completely submerged volcano. Erosion
has transformed the cone into a series of jagged peaks with the resulting look of a
crown. There is usually a wide selection of fish, sharks and turtles easily visible in
about 6 m of water. **Punta Cormorant** is on the northern part of Floreana. The trail
leads to a lake normally inhabited by flamingos and other shore birds and continues

to a beach of fine white-sand particles, an important nesting site for turtles. **Post Office Bay** is west of Punta Cormorant. The Post Office barrel was placed and used in the late 18th century by English whaling vessels and later by the American whalers. It is the custom for visitors to place un-stamped letters and cards in the barrel, and deliver, free of charge, any addressed to their own destinations.

Sleeping

Puerto Ayora *p611, map p612*

LL-AL Red Mangrove Inn, Darwin y las Fragatas, towards the Charles Darwin station, T05-252 7011, www.redmangrove.com. A beautiful hotel with plenty of character. Includes breakfast, restaurant, jacuzzi, deck bar and lovely Japanese dining room. Very tasteful rooms all overlooking the water, ample bathrooms. Owner Polo Navaro offers day tours and diving. Recommended.

AL Silberstein, Darwin y Piqueros, T05-252 6047, www.hotelsilberstein.com. Modern and very comfortable, with lovely grounds and a small pool, buffet breakfast, restaurant and bar, some rooms with a/c, others with fan. Spacious. Recommended.

AL-A Angemeyer Waterfront Inn, by the dock at Punta Estrada, T09-472 4955, tangermeyer@yahoo.com. Gorgeous location overlooking the bay. Very comfortable modern rooms and apartments, some with kitchenettes, opened in 2006.

A Lobo de Mar, 12 de Febrero y Darwin, T05-252 6188, www.lobodemar.com.ec. Modern building with balconies and rooftop terrace, great views over harbour. Includes breakfast, a/c, small pool, comfortable, friendly attentive service. Recommended.

C Estrella de Mar, by the water on a lane off 12 de Febrero, T05-252 6427. Nice quiet location with views over the bay. Includes breakfast, a/c, fan, spacious rooms, sitting area.

D Peregrino, Darwin e Indefatigable, T05-252 6323. Away from the centre of town, includes breakfast, electric shower, a/c, nice rooms, small garden, family-run, homey atmosphere.

D-E Gardner, Berlanga y Naveda, T/F05-252 6108, pensiongardner@yahoo.com. Pleasant and quiet, older rooms are cheaper, cold water, fan, spacious, small sitting area with hammocks and outdoor cooking facilities, popular and good value. Recommended.

Puerto Baquerizo Moreno *p614*

AL Miconia, Darwin y Melville, T05-252 0608, www.miconia.com. Includes breakfast,

restaurant, a/c, pool, gym, modern but small rooms, some with fridge.

C Casablanca, Mellville y Darwin, T05-252 0392, jacquivaz@yahoo.com. Large white house with lovely terrace and views of harbour. Breakfast available, each room is individually decorated by the owner who has an art studio on the premises.

D Mar Azul, Northía y Esmeraldas, T05-252 0139. Newer annex across the street has large modern rooms, electric shower, some with a/c and fridge, cheaper with fan. Both sections are clean, pleasant, friendly and good value. Recommended.

E San Francisco, Darwin y Villamil, T05-252 0304. Private bath, cold water, fan, rooms at the front are nicer, simple but clean, friendly and good value.

Puerto Villamil *p614*

AL-A La Casa de Marita, east end of beach, T05-252 9238, www.galapagosisabela.com. Definitely upscale, even chic. Includes breakfast, other meals on request, a/c and fridge, jacuzzi, very comfortable, each room is a bit different and some have balconies. A little gem. Recommended.

B-D Ballena Azul and Isabela del Mar, Conocarpus y Opuntia, T05-252 9030, www.hosteriaisabela.com.ec. An older wooden building next to modern cabins, both are very nice. Solar hot water, fan, large balcony, pleasant common area and dining room. Swiss-run, friendly and helpful. Recommended.

D-E San Vicente, Cormoranes y Pinzón Artesano, T05-252 9140. Very popular, cold water, a/c, cheaper with fan, use of kitchen/ fridge, meals on request, rooms small but nice, camping possible. Tours and kayak rentals. Family-run, good value. Recommended.

Puerto Velasco Ibarra *p615*

AL Pensión Wittmer, right on Black Beach, , T05-252 9506. Includes 3 delicious meals, fan (when electricity), simple, comfortable, a very special place, reservations required.

❶ Eating

Puerto Ayora *p611, map p612*

¶¶¶ **Angermeyer Point**, across the bay, take a water-taxi from the port, T05-252 7007. Tue-Sat 1800-2200, Sun 1100-1600. Former home of Galápagos pioneer and artist Carl Angermeyer. Gorgeous setting over the water (take insect repellent). Excellent, innovative menu. Reservations advised. Recommended.

¶¶¶ **La Dolce Italia**, Charles Darwin, between Naveda and 12 de Febrero, second location called **Trattoria de Pippo** at Charles Darwin between Indefatigable and Isla Floreana, daily 1100-1500, 1800-2200. Italian, seafood, wine list, a/c, nice atmosphere, attentive owner.

¶¶¶-¶¶ **La Garrapata**, Charles Darwin, between 12 de Febrero and Tomás de Berlanga, Mon-Sat 0830-2200, Sun 1700-2200. Good food, attractive setting and good music, juice bar, sandwiches and set lunch, à la carte at night.

¶¶ **Chocolate Galápagos**, Charles Darwin, between Tomas de Berlanga and Charles Binford, daily 0700-2200. Breakfast, snacks, meals, and desserts, outdoor seating, popular.

¶ **El Descanso del Guía**, Charles Darwin y Los Colonos, near bus company office. Good-value set meals, very popular with locals.

Cafés

La Casa del Lago, Moisés Brito y Juan Montalvo, Barrio Las Ninfas. T09-851 4015, www.galapagos cultural.com, Mon-Sat 0700-2200. Away from the main drag. Drinks, snacks and ice cream, live music, cultural activities. Friendly owners.

Puerto Baquerizo Moreno *p614*

¶¶ **Miconia**, Darwin y Isabela. Good, varied menu, lovely terrace overlooking the harbour.

¶¶-¶ **Rosita**, Ignacio de Hernández y General Villamil, daily from 0730, closed Sun afternoon. Set meals or à la carte, yachtie hangout.

¶ **Deep Blue**, Darwin y Española. *Ceviches* in morning, good set lunch, closed evenings.

Cafés and bakeries

Mockingbird Café, Española y Hernández. Fruit juices, brownies, snacks, internet.

Puerto Villamil *p614*

There are several other simple places to eat.

¶¶-¶ **El Encanto de la Pepa**, Antonio Gil on the Plaza. Set meals and à la carte, lots of character, good food, pleasant outdoor seating.

¶ **Tropical**, Las Fragatas, half a block from Plaza, open daily. Good-quality and value set meals, popular with locals.

❶ Bars and clubs

Puerto Ayora *p611, map p612*

Bongo Bar, Av Charles Darwin y Berlanga, Puerto Ayora, and **La Panga Disco**, upstairs at the same location. Both are popular. See also **La Casa del Lago**, under Cafés, above.

Puerto Baquerizo Moreno *p614*

Calypso, Darwin y Manuel J Cobos, Puerto Baquerizo Moreno, daily 1800-2400. Snacks and drinks, pleasant outdoor seating.

❶ Shopping

Most items can be purchased on the islands, but cost substantially more than on the mainland. Do not buy crafts made of black coral, an endangered species.

Santa Cruz *p611, map p612*

In Puerto Ayora there is an attractive little **Mercado Artesanal** (craft market) at Charles Darwin y Tomás de Berlanga. **Proinsular**, opposite the pier, is the largest and best-stocked supermarket.

San Cristóbal *p614*

There is a good little supermarket, **Dos Hermanos**, at Quito y Juan José Flores.

Handicrafts

In Puerto Baquerizo Moreno, Paintings with Galápagos motifs can be bought. **Fabo Galería de Arte**, Malecón Charles Darwin y Melville, 2nd floor of **Hotel Casa Blanca**. Paintings by the owner Fabricio, and silk-screened T-shirts.

Galápagos Fashion, Av Quito y Juan José Flores, T05-252 0507. Run by local artist Humberto Muñoz who also designs original clothing with local motifs. Recommended.

Isabela *p614*

Isabela is the end of the Galápagos supply line and some items may not be available. Fresh fruits and vegetables are mostly limited to those which grow locally, but shops in Puerto Villamil are well stocked with tins and other non-perishable items.

Galápagos Islands The Islands Listings

▲ Activities and tours

Galacruises Expeditions, N22-118 9 de Octubre y Veintimilla, ground floor, El Trebol Building, Quito, T02-252 3324, www.gala cruises.com. Yachts and catamaramans, cruises and expeditions. Scuba diving, snorkelling, and sea kayaking.

Tambo Tours, 4405 Spring Cypress Rd, Suite #210, Spring, TX, 77388, USA, T1-888-2-GO-PERU (246 7378), T001-281-528 9448, www.2GOPERU.com. Long-established adventure and tour specialist with offices in Peru and USA. Customized trips.

Santa Cruz *p611, map p612*
Cycling
Mountain bikes can be hired from several tour agencies (page 618) and shops along Av Charles Darwin, Puerto Ayora.

Diving
The Galápagos Islands are among the most extraordinary scuba diving destinations in the world, but the water is cold, currents are strong and conditions are difficult. There are 2 options for diving in the Galápagos: live-aboard cruises (often booked many months in advance) and hotel-based day trips. Live- aboard operations usually expect the divers to bring their own equipment, and supply only lead and tanks. The day-trip dive operators supply everything.

There are several diving agencies in Puerto Ayora offering courses, equipment rental, dives within Academy Bay (2 dives for about US$90), dives to other central islands (2 dives, US$140), daily tours for 1 week in the central islands and several-day live-aboard tours.

Safety standards vary considerably; we list only consistently recommended agencies. You are responsible for choosing a reliable operator and having adequate insurance. The hyperbaric chamber in Puerto Ayora charges US$1500 per hr, see Directory, page 620.

Galápagos Sub-Aqua, Av Charles Darwin e Isla Floreana, T05-2526633, www.galapagos-sub-aqua.com, (in Guayaquil: Orellana 211 y Panamá 702, T04-230 5514), Mon-Sat 0800-1230, 1430-1830. Instructor Fernando Zambrano offers full certificate courses up to PADI divemaster level. Consistently recommended.

Scuba Iguana, Charles Darwin near the research station, T05-252 6497, www.scuba iguana.com. Matías Espinoza runs this long-time reliable and recommended dive operator. Courses up to PADI divemaster.

Horse riding
For horse riding, enquire with **Moonrise Travel**, see Tour operators.

Snorkelling
Masks, snorkels and fins can be rented from tour agencies agencies and dive shops, about US$6 per day, deposit required. The closest place to snorkel is by the beaches near the Darwin Station.

Tour operators
Avoid touts who approach you at the airport or in the street offering cheap tours. Also be wary of agencies who specialize in cut-rate cruises, see list of vessels on page 608.
Lonesome George, Av Baltra y Enrique Fuentes, T05-252 6245, lonesomegrg@

yahoo.com. Run by Víctor Vaca. Tours and a variety of gear rentals: bicycles, surfboards, snorkelling equipment and motorcycles. **Moonrise Travel**, Av Charles Darwin y Charles Binford, opposite Banco del Pacífico, T05-252 6348, www.galapagos moonrise.com. Last-minute cruise bookings, day-tours to different islands, bay tours, highland tours, airline reservations. Owner Jenny Divine speaks English, she is very knowledgeable, helpful and reliable. Highly recommended.

San Cristóbal *p614*

Mountain bikes can be hired from several agencies in Puerto Baquerizo Moreno. There are several dive sites around San Cristóbal. The tour operators (below) offer dives. The nearest hyperbaric chamber is in Puerto Ayora (see Directory, below).

Tour operators

Chalo Tours, Española y Hernández, T05-2520953, www.chalotours.com. Bay tours to Kicker Rock and Isla de los Lobos,

boat tours to the north end of the island, highland tours, diving, bike rentals, snorkelling gear, book exchange.
Galakiwi, Española y Darwin, T05-2521562, galakiwi@yahoo.com.au. Owned by New Zealander Tim Cooney. Highland and diving tours, kayaks and other gear rentals.

Isabela *p614*

Hotels in Puerto Villamil arrange visits to local attractions. The tours are mostly operated by Antonio Gil at **Hotel San Vicente** (see page 616), reliable and recommended.
Carapachudo Tours, Escalecias y Tero Real, Puerto Villamil, T08-596 7179, info@cara pachudotours.com. Mountain biking tours, downhill from Sierra Negra and elsewhere, US$42 for a full day including lunch.

⊖ Transport

Santa Cruz *p611, map p612*
Airline offices Aerogal, Padre J Herrera y 10 de Marzo, next to Pacifictel, T05-252 6798, Mon-Fri 0800-1200, 1400-1700, Sat 0900-1300. **Emetebe**, Av Charles Darwin near port, 2nd floor of Ferroinsular hardware store next to Proinsular supermarket, T05-252 6177. **TAME**, Av Charles Darwin y 12 de Febrero, T05-252 6527.
Pickup These may be hired for transport throughout Puerto Ayora, US$1-2, agree the fare in advance. Also for excursions up to the highlands.
Water taxi *Taxis marítimos* are available from the pier to anchored boats and Punta Estrada, US$0.25 per person.

San Cristóbal *p614*
Airline offices Aerogal, at the airport, T05-252 1118. **Emetebe**, at the airport, T05-252 0615. **TAME**, Charles Darwin y Manuel J Cobos, T05-252 1351, Mon-Fri 0830-1230, 1400-1700, Sat 0830-1230. Airport counter T05-252 1089.
Bus 5 buses a day from Puerto Baquerizo Moreno to **El Progreso**, 15 mins, US$0.20.
Pickup You can also hire a pickup truck to the highlands, the road was paved but badly potholed in 2007.

Isabela *p614*
Airline offices Emetebe, Antonio Gil y Las Fragatas, T05-252 9155, Mon-Fri 0700-1230, 1400-1600, Sat 0700-1230.

❶ Directory

Santa Cruz *p611, map p612*
Banks Banco del Pacífico, Av Charles Darwin y Charles Binford, T05-252 6282, Mon-Fri 0800-1530, Sat 0930-1230. US$5 commission per transaction to change TCs, maximum US$500 a day. ATM works with Cirrus, Plus and MasterCard but not Visa; cash advances from tellers on Visa and MasterCard.
Hospital The local hospital on Av Baltra provides first aid and basic care. For anything more serious, locals usually fly to the mainland. **Hyperbaric chamber** 18 de Febrero y Rodríguez Lara, T05-2526911, www.sssnetwork.com. Also has a private medical clinic. Hyperbaric treatment costs US$1500 per hr, 50% discount if your dive operator is affiliated. Confirm in advance whether your diving insurance is accepted and make sure you have adequate coverage.
Internet There are several cybercafés throughout town, US$2 per hr. **Post and couriers** By the port, unreliable; it often runs out of stamps, never leave money and letters. Best take your postcards home with you. DHL courier and **Western Union**, accross the street from Hotel Silberstein. **Useful addresses Immigration**, at police station, 12 de Febrero.

San Cristóbal *p614*
Banks Banco del Pacífico, Charles Darwin, between Española and Melville. Same hours and services as in Puerto Ayora.
Internet Several cybercafés in town, US$2/hr. **Laundry** Lavandería Limpio y Seco, Av Northía y 12 de Febrero. Wash and dry for US$2, daily 0900-2100. **Medical services** The local hospital at Av Northía y Quito offers only basic care. **Dr David Basantes**, Av Northía opposite Hotel Mar Azul, T05-2520126, is a helpful general practitioner. **Farmacia San Cristóbal**, Villamil y Hernández, is the best-stocked pharmacy in town.
Useful addresses Immigration at Police Station, Charles Darwin y Española, T/F05-252 0129, visa extensions up to 90 days.

Isabela *p614*
Banks There are no banks on Isabela, no ATMs, and nowhere to use credit cards or change TCs. You must bring US$ cash.
Internet There are a couple of slow cybercafés in town, US$1.50-2.50 per hr.

Pre-independence history

Earliest settlement

It is generally accepted that the earliest settlers in South America were related to people who had crossed the Bering Straits from Asia and drifted through the Americas from about 50,000 BC. Alternative theories of early migrations from across the Pacific and Atlantic have been rife since Thor Heyerdahl's raft expeditions in 1947 and 1969-1970. The earliest evidence of human presence has been found at various sites: in the Central Andes (with a radiocarbon date between 12,000 and 9000 BC), northern Venezuela (11000 BC), southeast Brazil, south-central Chile and Argentine Patagonia (from at least 10000 BC). After the Pleistocene Ice Age, 8000-7000 BC, rising sea levels and climatic changes introduced new conditions as many mammal species became extinct and coastlands were drowned. A wide range of crops was brought into cultivation and camelids and guinea pigs were domesticated. It was originally thought that people lived nomadically in small groups, mainly hunting and gathering but also cultivating some plants seasonally, until villages with effective agriculture began to appear between 2500-1500 BC. The earliest ceramic-making in the western hemisphere was thought to have come from what is now Colombia and Ecuador, around 4000 BC, but fragments of painted pottery were found near Santarém, Brazil, in 1991 with dates of 6000-5000 BC.

The coast of central Peru was where settled life began to develop most rapidly. But on the evidence of Caral, a city 20 km from the coast in the Supe Valley, dating from about 2600 BC, complex urban society began much earlier than previously thought. It is a monumental construction and appears to be easily the oldest city in South America, flourishing for some 500 years. The city seems to have had a primarily religious, rather than warlike purpose. If these deductions are correct, they also upset some long-held beliefs about city-building worldwide being principally bellicose rather than peaceful. The abundant wealth of marine life produced by the Humboldt Current, especially north of today's Lima, boosted population growth and settlement in this area. Around 2000 BC climatic change dried up the *lomas* ('fog meadows'), and drove sea shoals into deeper water. People turned more to farming and began to spread inland along river valleys. As sophisticated irrigation and canal systems were developed, farming productivity increased and communities had more time to devote to building and producing ceramics and textiles. The development of pottery also led to trade and cultural links with other communities.

The earliest buildings constructed by organized group labour were *huacas*, adobe platform mounds, centres of some cult or sacred power dating from the second millennium BC. During this period a more advanced architecture was being built at Kotosh in the Central Andes, near Huánuco (Peru), for example a temple with ornamental niches and friezes. Pottery found here shows influences from southern Ecuador and the tropical lowlands, adding weight to theories of Andean culture originating in the Amazon.

Andean and Pacific coastal civilizations

Chavín and Sechín For the next 1000 years or so up to around 900 BC, communities grew and spread inland from the north coast and south along the north highlands. Farmers still lived in simple adobe or rough stone houses but built increasingly large and complex ceremonial centres. As farming became more productive and pottery more advanced, commerce grew and states began to develop throughout central and north-central Peru, with the associated signs of social structure and hierarchies.

Around 900 BC a new era was marked by the rise of two important centres; Chavín de Huántar in the central Andes and Sechín Alto, inland from Casma on the north coast, both now in Peru. The chief importance of Chavín de Huántar was not so much in its highly advanced architecture as in the influence of its cult, coupled with the artistic style of its ceramics and other artefacts. The founders of Chavín may have originated in the tropical lowlands, as some of its carved monoliths show representations of monkeys and felines.

The Chavín cult This was paralleled by the great advances made in this period in textile production and in some of the earliest examples of metallurgy. The origins of metallurgy have been attributed to some gold, silver and copper ornaments found in graves in Chongoyape, near Chiclayo, which show Chavín-style features. But earlier evidence has been discovered at Kuntur Wasi (some 120 km east of the coast at Pacasmayo) where 4000-year old gold has been found, and in the Andahuaylas region, dating from 1800-900 BC. The religious symbolism of gold and other precious metals and stones is thought to have been an inspiration behind some of the beautiful artefacts found in the central Andean area.

The cultural brilliance of Chavín de Huántar was complemented by its contemporary, Sechín, with which may have combined forces, Sechín being the military power that spread the cultural word of Chavín. Their influence did not reach far to the south where the Paracas and Tiwanaku cultures held sway. The Chavín hegemony broke up around 500 BC, soon after which the Nazca culture began to bloom in southern Peru. This period, up to about AD 500, was a time of great social and cultural development. Sizable towns of 5000-10,000 inhabitants grew on the south coast, populated by artisans, merchants and government and religious officials.

Paracas-Nazca Nazca origins are traced back to about the second century BC, to the Paracas Cavernas and Necropolis, on the coast in the national park near Pizco in Peru. The extreme dryness of the desert here has preserved remarkably the textiles and ceramics in the mummies' tombs excavated. The technical quality and stylistic variety in weaving and pottery rank them among the world's best, and many of the finest examples can be seen in the museums of Lima. The famous Nazca Lines are a feature of the region. Straight lines, abstract designs and outlines of animals are scratched in the dark desert surface forming a lighter contrast that can be seen clearly from the air. There are many theories of how and why the lines were made but no definitive explanation has yet been able to establish their place in South American history. There are similarities between the style of some of the line patterns and that of the pottery and textiles of the same period. In contrast to the quantity and quality of the Nazca artefacts found, relatively few major buildings belonging to this period have been uncovered in the southern desert. Alpaca hair found in Nazca textiles, however, indicates that there must have been strong trade links with highland people.

Moche culture Nazca's contemporaries on the north coast were the militaristic Moche who, from about AD 100-800, built up an empire whose traces stretch from Piura in the north to Huarmey, in the south. The Moche built their capital outside present day Trujillo. The huge pyramid temples of the Huaca del Sol and Huaca de la Luna mark the remains of this city. Moche roads and system of way stations are thought to have been an early inspiration for the Inca network. The Moche increased the coastal population with intensive irrigation projects. Skilful engineering works were carried out, such as the La Cumbre canal, still in use today, and the Ascope aqueduct, both on the Chicama River. The Moche's greatest achievement, however, was its artistic genius. Exquisite ornaments in gold, silver and precious stones were made by its craftsmen. Moche pottery progressed through five stylistic periods, most notable for the stunningly lifelike portrait vases. A wide variety of everyday scenes were created in naturalistic ceramics, telling us more about Moche life than is known about other earlier cultures, and perhaps used by them as 'visual aids' to compensate for the lack of a written language. A spectacular discovery of a Moche royal tomb at Sipán, made in February 1987 by Walter Alva, director of the Brüning Archaeological Museum, Lambayeque, included semi- precious stones brought from Chile and Argentina, and seashells from Ecuador. The Moche were great navigators.

The cause of the collapse of the Moche Empire around AD 600-700 is unknown, but it may have been started by a 30-year drought at the end of the sixth century, followed by one of the periodic El Niño flash floods (identified by meteorologists from ice thickness in the Andes) and finished by the encroaching forces of the Huari Empire. The decline of the Moche signalled a general tipping of the balance of power in Peru from the north coast to the south sierra.

Huari-Tiwanaku The ascendant Huari-Tiwanaku movement, from AD 600-1000, combined the religious cult of the Tiwanaku site in the Titicaca basin, with the military dynamism of the Huari, based in the central highlands. The two cultures developed independently but they are generally thought to have merged compatibly. Up until their own demise around AD 1440, the Huari-Tiwanaku had spread their empire and influence across much of south Peru, north Bolivia and Argentina. They made considerable gains in art and technology, building roads, terraces and irrigation canals across the country. The Huari-Tiwanaku ran their empire with efficient labour and administrative systems that were later adopted by the Incas. Labour tribute for state projects practised by the Moche were further developed. But the empire could not contain regional kingdoms who began to fight for land and power. As control broke down, rivalry and coalitions emerged, the system collapsed and the scene was set for the rise of the Incas.

Chachapoyas and Chimú cultures After the decline of the Huari Empire, the unity that had been imposed on the Andes was broken. A new stage of autonomous regional or local political organizations began. Among the cultures corresponding to this period were the Chachapoyas in northern highlands (see page 265) and the Chimú. The Chachapoyas people were not so much an empire as a loose-knit 'confederation of ethnic groups with no recognized capital' (Morgan Davis 'Chachapoyas: The Cloud People', Ontario, 1988). But the culture did develop into an advanced society with great skill in road and monument building. Their fortress at Kuélap was known as the most impregnable in the Peruvian Andes. The Chimú culture had two centres. To the north was Lambayeque, near Chiclayo, while to the south, in the Moche valley near present-day Trujillo, was the great adobe walled city of Chan Chán. Covering 20 sq km, this was the largest pre-Hispanic Peruvian city. Chimú has been classified as a despotic state that based its power on wars of conquest. Rigid social stratification existed and power rested in the hands of the great lord *Siquic* and the lord *Alaec*. These lords were followed in social scale by a group of urban couriers who enjoyed a certain degree of economic power. At the bottom were the peasants and slaves. In 1450, the Chimú kingdom was conquered by the Inca Túpac Yupanqui, the son and heir of the Inca ruler Pachacuti Inca Yupanqui.

Cultures of the northern Andes The oldest archaeological artefacts that have been uncovered in Ecuador date back to approximately 10000 BC. They include obsidian spear tips and belong to a pre-ceramic period during which the region's inhabitants are thought to have been nomadic hunters, fishers and gatherers. A subsequent formative period (4000-500 BC) saw the development of pottery, presumably alongside agriculture and fixed settlements. One of these settlements, known as Valdivia, existed along the coast of Ecuador and remains of buildings and earthenware figures have been found dating from 3500-1500 BC.

Between 500 BC and AD 500, many different cultures evolved in all the geographic regions of what is today Ecuador. Among these were the Bahía, Guangalá, Jambelí and Duale-Tejar of the coast; Narrío, Tuncahuán and Panzaleo in the highlands; and Upano, Cosanga and Yasuní in Oriente. The period AD 500-1480 was an era of integration, during which dominant or amalgamated groups emerged. These included, from north to south in the Sierra, the Imbayas, Shyris, Quitus, Puruhaes and Cañaris; and the Caras, Manteños and Huancavilcas along the coast.

This rich and varied mosaic of ancient cultures is today considered the bedrock of Ecuador's national identity. It was confronted, in the mid-15th century, with the relentless northward expansion of the most powerful pre-Hispanic empire on the continent: the Incas.

Southern Andes Although there was some influence in southern Bolivia, northern Chile and northern Argentina from cultures such as Tiwanaku, most of the southern Andes was an area of autonomous peoples, probably living in fortified settlements by the time the Incas arrived in the mid-15th century. The conquerors from Peru moved south to the Río Maule in Chile where they encountered the fierce **Mapuches** (Araucanians) who halted their advance. Archaeological evidence from the Amazon basin and Brazil is more scanty than from the Andes or Pacific because the materials used for house building, clothing and decoration were perishable and did not survive the warm, humid conditions of the jungle. Ceramics have been found on Marajó island at the mouth of the Amazon while on the coast much evidence comes from huge shell mounds, called *sambaquis*. Although structured societies developed and population was large, no political groupings of the scale of those of the Andes formed. The Incas made few inroads into the Amazon so it was the arrival of the Portuguese in 1500 which initiated the greatest change on the Atlantic side of the continent.

Inca Dynasty

The Incas

The origins of the Inca Dynasty are shrouded in mythology. The best known story reported by the Spanish chroniclers talks about Manco Cápac and his sister rising out of Lake Titicaca, created by the Sun as divine founders of a chosen race. This was in approximately AD 1200. Over the next 300 years the small tribe grew to supremacy as leaders of the largest empire ever known in the Americas, the four territories of Tawantinsuyo, united by Cuzco as the umbilicus of the Universe. The four quarters of Tawantinsuyo, all radiating out from Cuzco, were: 1 Chinchaysuyo, north and north-west; 2 Cuntisuyo, south and west; 3 Collasuyo, south and east; 4 Antisuyo, east.

At its peak, just before the Spanish Conquest, the Inca Empire stretched from the Río Maule in central Chile, north to the present Ecuador-Colombia border, containing most of Ecuador, Peru, western Bolivia, northern Chile and northwest Argentina. The area was roughly equivalent to France, Belgium, Holland, Luxembourg, Italy and Switzerland combined (980,000 sq km).

The first Inca ruler, Manco Cápac, moved to the fertile Cuzco region, and established Cuzco as his capital. Successive generations of rulers were fully occupied with local conquests of rivals, such as the Colla and Lupaca to the south, and the Chanca to the northwest. At the end of Inca Viracocha's reign the hated Chanca were finally defeated, largely thanks to the heroism of one of his sons, Pachacútec Inca Yupanqui, who was subsequently crowned as the new ruler.

Inca society

The Incas were a small aristocracy numbering only a few thousand, centred in the highland city of Cuzco, at 3400 m. They rose gradually as a small regional dynasty, similar to others in the Andes of that period, starting around AD 1200. Then in the mid-1400s, they began to expand explosively under Pachacútec, a sort of Andean Alexander the Great, and later his son, Topa. Under a hundred years later, they fell before the rapacious warriors of Spain. The Incas were not the first dynasty in Andean history to dominate their neighbours, but they did it more thoroughly and went further than anyone before them.

Empire building

Enough remains today of their astounding highways, cities and agricultural terracing for people to marvel and wonder how they accomplished so much in so short a time. They seem to have been amazingly energetic, industrious and efficient – and the reports of their Spanish conquerors confirm this hypothesis.

They must also have had the willing cooperation of most of their subject peoples, most of the time. In fact, the Incas were master diplomats and alliance-builders first, and military conquerors only second, if the first method of expansion failed. The Inca skill at generating wealth by means of highly efficient agriculture and distribution brought them enormous prestige and enabled them to 'out-gift' neighbouring chiefs in huge royal feasts involving ritual outpourings of generosity, often in the form of vast gifts of textiles, exotic products from distant regions, and perhaps wives to add blood ties to the alliance. The 'out-gifted' chief was required by the Andean laws of reciprocity to provide something in return, and this would usually be his loyalty, as well as a levy of manpower from his own chiefdom.

Thus, with each new alliance the Incas wielded greater labour forces and their mighty public works programmes surged ahead. These were administered through an institution known as **mit'a**, a form of taxation through labour. The state provided the materials, such as wool and cotton for making textiles, and the communities provided skills and labour.

Mit'a contingents worked royal mines, royal plantations for coca leaves, royal quarries and so on. The system strove to be fair, and workers in such hardship posts as high altitude mines and lowland coca plantations were given correspondingly shorter terms of service.

Organization

Huge administrative centres were built in different parts of the empire, where people and supplies were gathered. Articles such as textiles and pottery were produced there in large workshops. Work in these places was carried out in a festive manner, with plentiful food, drink and music. Here was Andean reciprocity at work: the subject supplied his labour, and the ruler was expected to provide generously while he did so.

Aside from mit'a contributions there were also royal lands claimed by the Inca as his portion in every conquered province, and worked for his benefit by the local population. Thus, the contribution of each citizen to the state was quite large, but apparently, the imperial economy was productive enough to sustain this.

Another institution was the practice of moving populations around wholesale, inserting loyal groups into restive areas, and removing recalcitrant populations to loyal areas. These movements of **mitmakuna**, as they were called, were also used to introduce skilled farmers and engineers into areas where productivity needed to be raised.

Communications

The huge empire was held together by an extensive and highly efficient highway system. There were an estimated 30,000 km of major highway, most of it neatly paved and drained, stringing together the major Inca sites. Two parallel highways ran north to south, along the coastal desert strip and the mountains, and dozens of east-west roads crossed from the coast to the Amazon fringes. These roadways took the most direct routes, with wide stone stairways zig-zagging up the steepest the Andes. The north-south roads formed a great axis which eventually came to be known as **Capaq Ñan** – "Royal, or Principal Road", in Quechua – which exceeded in grandeur not only the other roads, but also their utilitarian concept. They became the Incas' symbol of power over men and over the sacred forces of nature. So marvellous were these roads that the Spaniards who saw them at the height of their glory said that there was nothing comparable in all Christendom.

Every 12 km or so there was a **tambo**, or way station, where goods could be stored and travellers lodged. The tambos were also control points, where the Inca state's accountants tallied movements of goods and people. Even more numerous than tambos, were the huts of the **chasquis**, or relay runners, who sped royal and military messages along these highways.

The Inca state kept records and transmitted information in various ways. Accounting and statistical records were kept on skeins of knotted strings known as **quipus**. Numbers employed the decimal system, and colours indicated the categories being recorded. An entire class of people, known as quipucamayocs, existed whose job was to create and interpret these. Neither the Incas nor their Andean predecessors had a system of writing as we understand it, but there may have been a system of encoding language into quipus.

Archaeologists are studying this problem today. History and other forms of knowledge were transmitted via songs and poetry. Music and dancing, full of encoded information which could be read by the educated elite, were part of every major ceremony and public event information was also carried in textiles, which had for millennia been the most vital expression of Andean culture.

Textiles

Clothing carried insignia of status, ethnic origin, age and so on. Special garments were made and worn for various rites of passage. It has been calculated that, after agriculture, no activity was more important to Inca civilization than weaving. Vast stores of textiles were maintained to sustain the Inca system of ritual giving. Armies and mit'a workers were partly paid in textiles. The finest materials were reserved for the nobility, and the Inca emperor himself displayed his status by changing into new clothes every day and having the previous day's burned.

Most weaving was done by women, and the Incas kept large numbers of 'chosen women' in female-only houses all over the empire, partly for the purpose of supplying textiles to the elite and for the many deities to whom they were frequently given as burned offerings. These women had other duties, such as making *chicha* – the Inca corn beer which was consumed and sacrificed in vast quantities on ceremonial occasions. They also became wives and concubines to the Inca elite and loyal nobilities. And some may have served as priestesses of the moon, in parallel to the male priesthood of the sun.

Religious worship

The Incas have always been portrayed as sun-worshippers, but it now seems that they were mountain-worshippers too. Recent research has shown that Machu Picchu was at least partly dedicated to the worship of the surrounding mountains, and Inca sacrificial victims have been excavated on frozen Andean peaks at 6,700 m. In fact, until technical climbing was invented, the Incas held the world altitude record for humans.

Human sacrifice was not common, but every other kind was, and ritual attended every event in the Inca calendar. The main temple of Cuzco was dedicated to the numerous deities: the Sun, the Moon, Venus, the Pleiades, the Rainbow, Thunder and Lightning, and the countless religious icons of subject peoples which had been brought to Cuzco, partly in homage, partly as hostage. Here, worship was continuous and the fabulous opulence included gold cladding on the walls and a famous garden filled with life-size objects of gold and silver. Despite this pantheism, the Incas acknowledged an overall Creator God, whom they called **Viracocha**. A special temple was dedicated to him at Raqchi, about 100 km southeast of Cuzco. Part of it still stands today.

Military forces

The conquering Spaniards noted with admiration the Inca storehouse system, still well-stocked when they found it, despite several years of civil war among the Incas. Besides textiles, military equipment and ritual objects, they found huge quantities of food. Like most Inca endeavours, the food stores served a multiple purpose: to supply feasts, as provisions during lean times, to feed travelling work parties and to supply armies on the march.

Inca armies were able to travel light and move fast because of this system. Every major Inca settlement incorporated great halls where large numbers of people could be accommodated or feasts and gatherings held, and large squares or esplanades where public assemblies could take place.

Inca technology is usually deemed inferior to that of contemporary Europe. Their military technology certainly was. They had not invented iron-smelting and basically fought with clubs, palmwood spears, slings, wooden shields, cotton armour and straw-stuffed helmets. They did not even make much use of the bow and arrow, a weapon they were well aware of. Military tactics, too, were primitive. The disciplined formations of the Inca armies quickly dissolved into melees of unbridled individualism once battle was joined.

This, presumably, was because warfare constituted a theatre of manly prowess, but was not the main priority of Inca life. Its form was ritualistic. Battles were suspended by both sides for religious observance. Negotiation, combined with displays of superior Inca strength, usually achieved victory, and total annihilation of the enemy was not on the agenda.

Architecture

Other technologies, however, were superior in every way to their 16th-century counterparts: textiles; settlement planning, and agriculture, in particular, with its sophisticated irrigation and soil conservation systems, ecological sensitivity, specialized crop strains and high productivity under the harshest conditions. The Incas fell short of their Andean predecessors in the better-known arts of ancient America – ceramics, textiles and metalwork – but it could be argued that their supreme efforts were made in architecture, stoneworking, landscaping, roadbuilding and in the harmonious combination of these elements.

These are the outstanding survivals of Inca civilization, which still remain to fascinate the visitor: the huge, exotically close-fit blocks of stone, cut in graceful, almost sensual curves; the astoundingly craggy and inaccessible sites encircled by great sweeps of Andean scenery; the rhythmic layers of farm terracing that provided land and food to this still-enigmatic people. The finest examples of Inca architecture can be seen in the city of Cuzco and throughout the Sacred Valley. As more evidence of Inca society is uncovered each year, our knowledge of these remarkable people can only improve: in 2002 alone two new cities in the Vilcabamba region were revealed, as well as the huge cemetery at Purucucho, near Lima, and a mummy at Machu Picchu.

Ruling elite

The ruling elite lived privileged lives in their capital at Cuzco. They reserved for themselves and chosen insiders certain luxuries, such as the chewing of coca, the wearing of fine vicuña wool, and the practice of polygamy. But they were an austere people, too. Everyone had work to do, and the nobility were constantly being posted to state business throughout the empire. Young nobles were expected to learn martial skills, besides being able to read the quipus, speak both Quechua and the southern language of Aymara and know the epic poems.

The Inca elite belonged to royal clans known as panacas, which each had the unusual feature of being united around veneration of the mummy of their founding ancestor – a previous Inca emperor, unless they happened to belong to the panaca founded by the Inca emperor who was alive at the time. Each new emperor built his own palace in Cuzco and amassed his own wealth rather than inheriting it from his forebears, which perhaps helps to account for the urge to unlimited expansion.

This urge ultimately led the Incas to over-stretch themselves. Techniques of diplomacy and incorporation no longer worked as they journeyed farther from the homeland and met ever-increasing resistance from people less familiar with their ways. During the reign of Wayna Cápac, the last emperor before the Spanish invasion, the Incas had to establish a northern capital at Quito in order to cope with permanent war on their northern frontier. Following Wayna Cápac's death came a devastating civil war between Cuzco and Quito and, immediately thereafter, came the Spanish invasion. Tawantisuyo, the empire of the four quarters, collapsed with dizzying suddenness.

Spanish conquest

In 1532 civil war broke out between the two halves of the Inca empire, and Atahualpa secured victory over Huáscar and established his capital in Cajamarca, in northern Peru. In the same year, conquistador Francisco Pizarro set out from Tumbes, on the Peru-Ecuador border, finally reaching Cajamarca. There, he captured the Inca leader and put him to death in 1533. This effectively ended Inca resistance and their empire collapsed. Pizarro claimed the northern kingdom of Quito, and his lieutenants Sebastián de Benalcázar and Diego de Almagro took the city in 1534.

In 1535, wishing to secure his communications with Spain, Pizarro founded Lima, near the ocean, as his capital. The same year Diego de Almagro set out to conquer Chile. Unsuccessful, he returned to Peru, quarrelled with Pizarro, and in 1538 fought a pitched battle with Pizarro's men at the Salt Pits, near Cuzco. He was defeated and put to death. Pizarro, who had not been at the battle, was assassinated in his palace in Lima by Almagro's son three years later.

As Spanish colonization built itself around new cities, the conquistadors set about finding the wealth which had lured them to South America in the first place. The great prize came in 1545 when the hill of silver at Potosí (Bolivia) was discovered. Other mining centres grew up and the trade routes to supply them and carry out the riches were established. The Spanish crown soon imposed political and administrative jurisdiction over its new empire, replacing the power of the conquistadors with that of governors and bureaucrats. The Viceroyalty of Peru became the major outlet for the wealth of the Americas, but each succeeding representative of the Kingdom of Spain was faced with the twofold threat of subduing the Inca successor state of Vilcabamba, north of Cuzco, and unifying the fierce Spanish factions. Francisco de Toledo (appointed 1568) solved both problems during his 14 years in office: Vilcabamba was crushed in 1572 and the last reigning Inca, Túpac Amaru, put to death. For the next 200 years the Viceroys closely followed Toledo's system, if not his methods. The Major Government – the Viceroy, the *Audiencia* (High Court), and *corregidores* (administrators) – ruled through the Minor Government – indigenous chiefs put in charge of large groups of natives: a rough approximation to the original Inca system.

There was an indigenous rising in 1780, under the leadership of an Inca noble who called himself Túpac Amaru II. He and many of his lieutenants were captured and put to death under torture at Cuzco. Another indigenous leader in revolt suffered the same fate in 1814, but this last flare-up had the sympathy of many of the locally born Spanish, who resented their status, inferior to the Spaniards born in Spain, the refusal to give them any but the lowest offices, the high taxation imposed by the home government, and the severe restrictions upon trade with any country but Spain.

Help came to them from the outside world. José de San Martín's Argentine troops, convoyed from Chile under the protection of Lord Cochrane's squadron, landed in southern Peru on 7 September 1820. San Martín proclaimed Peruvian independence at Lima on 28 July 1821, though most of the country was still in the hands of the Viceroy, José de La Serna. Bolívar, who had already freed Venezuela and Colombia, sent Antonio José de Sucre to Ecuador where, on 24 May 1822, he gained a victory over La Serna at Pichincha.

San Martín, after a meeting with Bolívar at Guayaquil, left for Argentina and a self-imposed exile in France, while Bolívar and Sucre completed the conquest of Peru by defeating La Serna at the battle of Junín (6 August 1824) and the decisive battle of Ayacucho (9 December 1824). For over a year there was a last stand in the Real Felipe fortress at Callao by the Spanish troops under General Rodil before they capitulated on 22 January 1826. Bolívar was invited to stay in Peru, but left for Colombia in 1826.

Post-independence history

Peru

After independence

Important events following the ejection of the Spaniards were a temporary confederation between Peru and Bolivia in the 1830s; the Peruvian-Spanish War (1866); and the War of the Pacific (1879-1883), in which Peru and Bolivia were defeated by Chile and Peru lost its southern territory. The 19th and early 20th centuries were dominated by the traditional elites, with landowners holding great power over their workers. Political parties were slow to develop until the 1920s, when socialist thinkers Juan Carlos Mariátegui and Víctor Raúl Haya de la Torre began to call for change. Haya de la Torre formed the Alianza Popular Revolucionaria Americana (APRA), but in the 1930s and 40s he and his party were under threat from the military and the elite.

To the Shining Path

A reformist military Junta took over control of the country in October 1968. Under its first leader, Gen Juan Velasco Alvarado, the Junta instituted a series of measures to raise the personal status and standard of living of the workers and the rural *indígena*, by land reform, worker participation in industrial management and ownership, and nationalization of basic industries, exhibiting an ideology perhaps best described as 'military socialism'. In view of his failing health Gen Velasco was replaced in 1975 by Gen Francisco Morales Bermúdez and policy (because of a mounting economic crisis and the consequent need to seek financial aid from abroad) swung to the Right. Presidential and congressional elections were held on 18 May 1980, and Fernando Belaúnde Terry was elected President for the second time. His term was marked by growing economic problems and the appearance of the Maoist terrorist movement Sendero Luminoso (Shining Path).

Initially conceived in the University of Ayacucho, the movement gained most support for its goal of overthrowing the whole system of Lima-based government from highland *indígena* and migrants to urban shanty towns. The activities of Sendero Luminoso and another terrorist group, Túpac Amaru (MRTA), frequently disrupted transport and electricity supplies, although their strategies had to be reconsidered after the arrest of both their leaders in 1992. Víctor Polay of MRTA was arrested in June and Abimael Guzmán of Sendero Luminoso was captured in September; he was sentenced to life imprisonment (although the sentence had to be reviewed in 2003 under legal reforms). Although Sendero did not capitulate, many of its members in 1994-1995 took advantage of the Law of Repentance, which guaranteed lighter sentences in return for surrender, and freedom in exchange for valuable information. Meanwhile, Túpac Amaru was thought to have ceased operations (see below).

The Fujimori years

The April 1985 elections were won by the APRA party leader Alán García Pérez. During his populist, left-wing presidency disastrous economic policies caused increasing poverty and civil instability. In presidential elections held over two rounds in 1990, Alberto Fujimori of the Cambio 90 movement defeated the novelist Mario Vargas Llosa, who belonged to the Fredemo (Democratic Front) coalition. Fujimori, without an established political network behind him, failed to win a majority in either the senate or the lower house. Lack of congressional support was one of the reasons behind the dissolution of congress and the suspension of the constitution on 5 April 1992. With massive popular support, President Fujimori declared that he needed a freer hand to introduce free-market reforms, combat terrorism and drug trafficking, and root out corruption.

Elections to a new, 80-member Democratic Constituent Congress (CCD) in November 1992 and municipal elections in February 1993 showed that voters still had scant regard for mainstream political groups. A new constitution drawn up by the CCD was approved by a narrow majority of the electorate in October 1993. Among the new articles were the immediate re-election of the president (previously prohibited for one presidential term) and, as expected, Fujimori stood for re-election on 9 April 1995. He beat his independent opponent, the former UN General Secretary, Javier Pérez de Cuéllar, by a resounding margin. The coalition that supported him also won a majority in Congress.

The government's success in most economic areas did not accelerate the distribution of foreign funds for social projects. Furthermore, rising unemployment and the austerity imposed by economic policy continued to cause hardship for many. Dramatic events on 17 December 1996 thrust several of these issues into sharper focus. 14 Túpac Amaru terrorist infiltrated a reception at the Japanese Embassy in Lima, taking 490 hostages and demanding the release of their imprisoned colleagues and new measures to raise living standards. Most of the hostages were released and negotiations were pursued during a stalemate that lasted until 22 April 1997. The president took sole responsibility for the successful, but risky assault which freed all the hostages (one died of heart failure) and killed all the terrorists. By not yielding to Túpac Amaru, Fujimori regained much popularity. But this masked the fact that no concrete steps had been taken to ease poverty. It also deflected attention from Fujimori's plans to stand for a third term following his unpopular manipulation of the law to persuade Congress that the new constitution did not apply to his first period in office. Until the last month of campaigning for the 2000 presidential elections, Fujimori had a clear lead over his main rivals. His opponents insisted that Fujimori that should not stand and local and international observers voiced increasing concern over the state domination of the media. Meanwhile, the popularity of Alejandro Toledo, a centrist and former World Bank official of humble origins, surged to such an extent that he and Fujimori were neck-and-neck in the first poll. Toledo and his supporters claimed that Fujimori's slim majority was the result of fraud, a view echoed in the pressure put on the president, by the US government among others, to allow a second ballot. The run-off election, on 28 May 2000, was also contentious since foreign observers, including the Organization of American States (OAS), said the electoral system was unprepared and flawed, proposing a postponement. The authorities refused to delay. Toledo boycotted the election and Fujimori was returned unopposed, but with minimal approval. Having won, he proposed to "strengthen democracy".

This pledge proved to be worthless following the airing of a secretly-shot video on 14 September 2000 of Fujimori's close aide and head of the National Intelligence Service (SIN), Vladimiro Montesinos, handing US$15,000 to a congressman, Alberto Kouri, to persuade him to switch allegiances to Fujimori's coalition. Fujimori's demise was swift. His initial reaction was to close down SIN and announce new elections, eventually set for 8 April 2001, at which he would not stand. Montesinos, declared a wanted man, fled to Panama, where he was denied asylum. He returned to Peru in October and Fujimori personally led the search parties to find his former ally. Peruvians watched in amazement as this game of cat-and-mouse was played out on their TV screens. While Montesinos himself successfully evaded capture, investigators began to uncover the extent of his empire, which held hundreds of senior figures in its web. Swiss bank accounts in his name were found to contain about US$70 million, while other millions were discovered in accounts in the Cayman Islands and elsewhere. As the search for him continued, Fujimori, apparently in pursuit of his presidential duties, made various overseas trips, including to Japan. Here, on 20 November, he sent Congress an email announcing his resignation. Congress rejected this, firing him instead on charges of being "morally unfit" to govern. An interim president, Valentín Paniagua, was sworn in, with ex-UN Secretary General Javier Pérez de Cuéllar as Prime Minister, and the government set about uncovering the depth of corruption associated with Montesinos and Fujimori. It also had to prepare for free and fair elections.

After Fujimori

In the run-up to the 2001 ballot, the front-runner was Alejandro Toledo, but with far from a clear majority. Ex-President Alan García emerged as Toledo's main opponent, forcing a run-off on 3 June. This was won by Toledo with 52% of the vote. He pledged to heal the wounds that had opened in Peru since his first electoral battle with the disgraced Fujimori, but his presidency was marked by slow progress on both the political and economic fronts. With the poverty levels still high, few jobs created and a variety of scandals, Toledo's popularity plummeted. A series of major confrontations and damaging strikes forced the president to declare a state of emergency in May 2003 to restore order. Nor could Toledo escape charges of corruption being laid at his own door; accusations that he and his sister orchestrated voter fraud in 2000 were upheld by a congressional commission in May 2005 (Toledo was formally charged in December 2006).

The April 2006 elections were contested by Alán García, the conservative Lourdes Flores and Ollanta Humala, a former military officer and unsuccessful coup leader who claimed support from Venezuela's Hugo Chávez and Evo Morales of Bolivia. García and Humala won through to the second round, which García won, in part because many were suspicious, even critical of the "Chávez factor" and the latter's interference in Peruvian affairs. García was anxious to overcome his past record as president and he pledged to hold back public spending despite consistent economic growth from 2005 to 2007. Labour unions complained that Peru's poor were not benefiting from the strong economy, leading to mass demonstrations against García in mid-2007. The Peruvian Congress, meanwhile, approved a trade pact with the United States in 2006, García's support for this being an indication of his willingness to court orthodoxy, rather than the left-leaning model proposed by his Andean neighbours Hugo Chávez and Evo Morales.

All the while, the past continued to dog the present. Since 2002, Montesinos has been convicted of a number of crimes in a series trials and yet more prosecutions are in process. In 2004, prosecutors also sought to charge exiled Fujimori with ordering the deaths of 25 people in 1991 and 1992. This followed the Truth and Reconciliation Committee's report (2003) into the civil war of the 1980s-1990s, which stated that over 69,000 Peruvians had been killed. With attempts to extradite Fujimori from Japan coming to nothing, prosecution could not proceed. Meanwhile Fujimori himself declared that he would be exonerated and stand again for the presidency in 2006. To this end he flew to Chile in November 2005 with a view to entering Peru, but the Chilean authorities jailed him for seven months and then denied him exit from Chile pending the outcome of an extradition request by Peru. In September 2007 the Chilean Supreme Court determined that Fujimori should be sent to Peru to stand trial.

Bolivia

Coups, mines and wars

Bolivian politics have been the most turbulent in Latin America. Although in the 19th century the army was very small, officers were key figures in power-struggles, often backing different factions of the landowning elite. Between 1840 and 1849 there were 65 attempted *coups d'état*. The longest lasting government of the 19th century was that of Andrés Santa Cruz (1829-1839), but when he tried to unite Bolivia with Peru in 1836, Chile and Argentina intervened to overthrow him. After the War of the Pacific (1879-1883) there was greater stability, but opposition to the political dominance of the city of Sucre culminated in a revolt in 1899 led by business groups from La Paz and the tin-mining areas, as a result of which La Paz became the centre of government.

The Bolivian economy depended on tin exports during the 20th century. Railway construction and the demand for tin in Europe and the USA (particularly in wartime) led to a mining boom after 1900. By the 1920s the industry was dominated by three entrepreneurs, Simón Patiño, Mauricio Hochschild and the Aramayo family, who greatly influenced national politics. The importance of mining and the harsh conditions in the isolated mining camps of the Altiplano led to the rise of a militant miners movement.

Since independence Bolivia has suffered continual losses of territory, partly because of communications difficulties and the central government's inability to control distant provinces. The dispute between Chile and Peru over the nitrate-rich Atacama desert in 1879 soon dragged in Bolivia, which had signed a secret alliance with Peru in 1873. Following its rapid defeat in the War of the Pacific Bolivia lost her coastal provinces. As compensation Chile later agreed to build the railway between Arica and La Paz. When Brazil annexed the rich Acre Territory in 1903, Bolivia was compensated by another railway, but this Madeira-Mamoré line never reached its destination, Riberalta, and proved of little use; it was closed in 1972. There was not even an unbuilt railway to compensate Bolivia for its next loss. A long-running dispute with Paraguay over the Chaco erupted into war in 1932. Defeat in the so-called Chaco War (1932-1935) resulted in the loss of three quarters of the Chaco.

Modern Bolivia

The Chaco War was a turning point in Bolivian history, increasing the political influence of the army which in 1936 seized power for the first time since the War of the Pacific. Defeat bred nationalist resentment among junior army officers who had served in the Chaco and also led to the creation of a nationalist party, the Movimiento Nacionalista Revolucionario (MNR) led by Víctor Paz Estenssoro. Their anger was directed against the mine owners and the leaders who had controlled Bolivian politics. Between 1936 and 1946 a series of unstable military governments followed. This decade witnessed the apparent suicide in 1939 of one president (Germán Busch) and the public hanging in 1946 of another

(Gualberto Villarroel). After a period of civilian government, the 1951 elections were won by the MNR but a coup prevented the party from taking office.

The 1952 revolution In April 1952 the military government was overthrown by a popular revolution in which armed miners and peasants played a major role. Paz Estenssoro became president and his MNR government nationalized the mines, introduced universal suffrage and began the break-up and redistribution of large estates. The economy, however, deteriorated, partly because of the hostility of the US government. Paz's successor, Hernán Siles Zuazo (president from 1956 to 1964), a hero of the 1952 revolution, was forced to take unpopular measures to stabilize the economy. Paz was re-elected president in 1960 and 1964, but shortly afterwards in November 1964 he was overthrown by his vice president, Gral René Barrientos, who relied on the support of the army and the peasants to defeat the miners.

Military rule in the 1970s The death of Barrientos in an air crash in 1969 was followed by three brief military governments. The third, led by Gral Torres, pursued left-wing policies which alarmed many army officers and business leaders. In August 1971 Torres was overthrown by Hugo Banzer, a right-wing colonel who outlawed political parties and trade unions. After Banzer was forced to call elections in 1978, a series of short-lived military governments overruled elections in 1978 and 1979 giving victories to Siles Zuazo. One of these, led by Gral García Meza (1980-1981) was notable for its brutal treatment of opponents and its links to the cocaine trade, which led to its isolation by the international community.

Return to democracy In August 1982 the military returned to barracks and Dr Siles Zuazo assumed the Presidency in a leftist coalition government with support from the communists and trade unions. Under this regime inflation spiralled out of control. The elections of 1985 were won again by Víctor Paz Estenssoro, who imposed a rigorous programme to stabilize the economy. In the elections of 1989, Gonzalo Sánchez de Lozada of the MNR (chief architect of the stabilization programme and the wealthiest man in Bolivia) failed to win enough votes to prevent Congress choosing Jaime Paz Zamora of the Movimiento de la Izquierda Revolucionaria (MIR), who came third in the elections, as president in August 1989. Paz had made an unlikely alliance with the former military dictator, Hugo Banzer (of the right-wing Acción Democrática Nacionalista party).

Although Gonzalo Sánchez de Lozada just failed to gain the required 51% majority to win the presidency in the 1993 elections, the other candidates recognized his victory. The main element in his policies was the capitalization of state assets, in which investors agreed to inject fresh capital into a chosen state-owned company in return for a 50% controlling stake. The other 50% of the shares were distributed to all Bolivians over 18 via a private pension fund scheme, known as the *bonosol*. As the programme gained pace, so did opposition to it. In the elections of 1 June 1997, Banzer and the ADN secured 22% of the vote and ADN became the dominant party in a new coalition with three other parties. In his first two years in office, Banzer pursued economic austerity and the US-backed policy of eradicating coca production. In 2000, however, economic hardship in rural areas, together with unemployment and anger at both the coca eradication and a plan to raise water rates led to violent protests and road blocks in many parts of the country. With the country's economic and social problems still severe, President Banzer was forced to resign in August 2001 because of cancer. His replacement, Vice-President Jorge Quiroga, had just a year left of Banzer's term to serve before new elections were held, in which a coalition led by former president Sánchez de Lozada won an extremely narrow victory. The runner-up was the populist candidate Evo Morales, the indigenous leader of the coca growers, who campaigned for a restoration of traditional coca production, a reduction in economic ties with the United States, and an end to free market reforms.

From the outset, Sánchez de Lozada faced economic crisis. In February 2003, mass demonstrations turned into riots over tax increases and the president was forced to flee the presidential palace in an ambulance. A week later, the cabinet resigned, the tax hikes were cancelled, police were awarded a pay rise and Sánchez de Lozada vowed to forego his salary. This failed to ease tension and in September a protest over the sale of Bolivian gas to the US became a national uprising against Sánchez de Lozada's free-market policies. Weeks of violent street protests led to 82 casualties in La Paz and Sánchez de Lozada's resignation on 17 October 2003. Vice president Carlos Mesa took over the presidency, but he managed to survive only until June 2005, when Supreme Court President Eduardo Rodríguez was appointed interim president until new elections on 18 December 2005. Evo Morales of Movimiento al Socialismo (MAS), self-styled "US worst nightmare", managed to beat ex-president Quiroga by a clear majority.

Three main issues precipitated Mesa's demise: the continued opposition to gas sales abroad, linked with demands to renationalize the gas and oil industries; mass protests by the inhabitants of the largely indigenous municipality of El Alto, calling for a more equal society and a new constituent assembly; and pressure from business lobbies in Santa Cruz, Tarija and the Beni, for more autonomy for their regions and a greater share of gas revenues. The first two issues, plus his support for coca growers and insistence on Bolivia freeing itself from 'foreign dominance', precipitated Morales' rise to power. Morales, taking his cue from Venezuela's Hugo Chavez, soon announced elections to a new constituent assembly and, in May 2006, sent troops into the gas fields. This latter move provoked foreign hydrocarbon companies to renegotiate their contracts with Bolivia, but progress in the constituent assembly was nothing like as speedy. From the outset, Morales' party and its allies disagreed with the opposition over the basic voting principles for approving each provision, making an August 2007 completion date an impossibility. This magnified Bolivia's basic division between the indigenous majority and the wealthy eastern lowlands. In late 2006 and early 2007, minor clashes occurred throughout the country over this issue and in Cochabamba *campesinos* confronted wealthy city dwellers and students over the position of the elected mayor, Manfred Reyes Villa's support for regional autonomy from the central government.

Morales has seen his power pase steadily erode as his promises to the predominantly Aymara and Quechua indigenous groups have gone unfulfilled. He has been forced to back down on his promises to levy taxes on foreigners and nationalize their holdings, and his popularity has fallen off considerably as the majority of his reforms have come nothing. All the same, tensions remain high between *collas* (residents of the alitplano) and *cambas* (those of the lowlands), whose anger has been stoked by Morales' threats to hand over much of the Oriente to *campesinos* from the altiplano. In September 2007 the Bolivian constituent assembly was frozen in deadlock. One of the latest issues was the demand by Sucre that it become the real, not only nominal, capital of the nation.

Ecuador

After independence

Ecuador decided on complete independence from the Gran Colombia confederation in August 1830, under the presidency of Juan Flores. The country's 19th century history was a continuous struggle between pro-Church conservatives and anti-Church (but nonetheless devoutly Catholic) liberals. There were also long periods of military rule from 1895, when the liberal Gen Eloy Alfaro took power. During the late 1940s and the 1950s there was a prolonged period of prosperity (through bananas, largely) and constitutional rule, but the more typical pattern of alternating civilian and military governments was resumed in the 1960s and 1970s. Apart from the liberal-conservative struggles, there has been long-lasting rivalry between Quito and the Sierra on one hand and Guayaquil and the Costa on the other.

Following seven years of military rule, the first presidential elections under a new constitution were held in 1979. The ensuing decades of democracy saw an oscillation of power between parties of the centre-right and centre-left. Governments of both political tendencies towed the international economic line and attempted to introduce neoliberal reforms. These measures were opposed by the country's labour organizations and by the indigenous movement, which gained considerable political power. Against a backdrop of this tug-of-war, disenchantment with the political process grew apace with bureaucratic corruption and the nation's economic woes. In 1996 the frustrated electorate swept a flamboyant populist named Abdalá Bucaram to power. His erratic administration lasted less than six months.

Following an interim government and the drafting of the country's 18th constitution, Ecuador elected Jamil Mahuad, a former mayor of Quito, to the presidency in 1998. Mahuad began his term by signing a peace treaty to end the decades-old and very emotional border dispute with Peru. This early success was his last, as a series of fraudulent bank failures sent the country into an economic and political tailspin. A freeze on bank accounts failed to stop landslide devaluation of the Sucre (Ecuador's currency since 1883) and Mahuad decreed the adoption of the US Dollar in a desperate bid for stability.

Less than a month later, on 21 January 2000, he was forced out of office by Ecuador's indigenous people and disgruntled members of the armed forces. The first overt military coup in South America in over two decades, it lasted barely three hours before power was handed to vice-president Gustavo Noboa.

Noboa, a political outsider and academic, stepped into Mahuad's shoes with remarkable aplomb. With assistance from the USA and the International Monetary Fund, his government managed to flesh out and implement the dollarization scheme, thus achieving a measure of economic stability at the cost of deepening poverty. Social unrest diminished, and Ecuadoreans instead attempted to bring about change through the ballot box. In November 2002, Colonel Lucio Gutiérrez, leader of the January 2000 *coup*, was elected president by a comfortable majority. He had run on a populist platform in alliance with the indigenous movement and labour unions, but began to change his stripes soon after taking office. In late 2004, the dismissal of all the supreme court judges by unconstitutional means – and tear gas – drew local and international criticism. This led to mass demonstrations which swept Gutiérrez from office in April 2005. He was the third Ecuadorean president to be deposed in this way in eight years. The latest uprising, like the previous two, was not accompanied by bloodshed and many Ecuadoreans take quiet pride in the country's homespun system of checks and balances. The colonel briefly took asylum in Brazil but soon returned home to again become an active political player. Gutiérrez was replaced by his vice-president, Alfredo Palacio, who led yet another lackluster interim government.

November 2006 elections were won by Rafael Correa, a 43-year-old economics professor and leader of the Alianza País (AP) movement. He immediately called a national referendum to convene a constituent assembly to redraw the constitution and – if all goes the new president's way – shift the nation's foundations toward the political left, echoing processes already taking place in Venezuela and Bolivia. 80% of voters approved Correa's plans in the April 2007 referendum and, in September 2007, his party won an ample majority of seats in the constituent assembly. The assembly is mandated to complete Ecuador's 19th constitution no later than July 2008. Once drafted, the new constitution will be submitted to a referendum and, finally, fresh elections held for president and congress. All this barring the inevitable unforeseens so characteristic of Ecuadorean politics.

The region today

The dominant adjective that links Peru, Bolivia and Ecuador is "Andean", because of the mountain range that is such a massive physical presence and the people, whose historical associations and present-day culture contribute such striking images of the region. But Andean is an imperfect description, as Ecuador and Peru have an extensive Pacific seaboard; a great proportion of national territory is made up of Amazonian lowlands; and Bolivia (62% of which is not geographically Andean at all) has vast lowland areas, such as the Chiqitania, Chaco and Pantanal.

The Spaniards, after conquering the already divided Incas, plundered the riches they found, enslaved the people and deliberately fragmented their society. Neither the conquistadors, however, nor the leaders of the subsequent war of independence from Spain could prevent internal differences tearing their visions apart. The contemporary legacy of this fractured past is mirrored by, for example, the Peruvian-Ecuadorean border disputes which lasted into the 20th century, the rivalry between coast and sierra in Ecuador, or between highlands and eastern lowlands in Bolivia, and pockets of wealth amid areas of extreme poverty. Moreover, there is a general lack of unifying principles in public life, seen most obviously in corruption by those in power. The sense of disillusion in political institutions is not surprising when, for instance, Peruvian President Fujimori's administration was shown to be as corrupt as those he was professing to eradicate (2000), or Ecuador's President Bucaram could only manage six months in office (1996). This is not to downplay the difficulties presidents face, from unpopularity because of unfulfilled promises, to intense international pressures, most obviously in the calls for solidarity in the so-called war against drugs.

Where it would appear that a shared history is failing to hold the region together, there are many issues which cement a common bond. The marginalization of indigenous communities has forged a new drive towards human rights. Indigenous people were instrumental in the overthrow of presidents Bucaram and Mahuad in Ecuador (1997 and 2000) and Sánchez de Lozada in Bolivia (2003). Furthermore, they are major actors in the current socially oriented governments of both countries. This newfound assertiveness is but one aspect of Andean peoples' legendary cultural endurance. Although their customs and beliefs have blended with those imported from Spain and even Africa, these remain as cherished as ever. When you are urged to join a festival parade, be it Corpus Cristi in Pujilí (Ecuador) or Carnaval in Oruro (Bolivia), you can easily see why. And thanks in part to visitors, Andean music, dance and textiles have become part of the world's cultural language.

The mountains and the jungle still hold vast natural resources which perennially promise prosperity. But neither Peru's enormous Yanacocha gold mine, nor Ecuador's reserves of oil, nor Bolivia's natural gas, will contribute to improved social conditions if they only benefit foreign interests. And when, at the other end of the scale, a pittance is paid for produce sweated from precipitous hillsides or extracted from the forest several days' walk from town, it's not surprising that inequality breeds discontent. To make matters worse, the exploitation of natural resources (from minerals, to food crops, to shrimp, to coca) is at times inflicting terrible damage on the natural environment.

Like the Andes themselves, Peru, Bolivia and Ecuador are young and growing. Greater than the deceptions of the past or the challenges of the present are hopes for the future, and sustainable tourism has its part to play. From the local to the global, many travellers embrace the cause of conservation, while others struggle alongside

638 residents to improve life for dispossessed farmers, shanty town dwellers and street kids. And all visitors contribute just by being here. Running a small hotel or tour agency can be a local family's ticket out of poverty. Recognizing this is the first step towards gringos giving something back to the Andes, not plundering like the conquistadors of the past.

In recent times, all three countries are showing divisions within the so-called 'pink tide' that has featured in Latin American politics since Venezuela's Hugo Chávez came to power. While Evo Morales of Bolivia and Rafael Correa of Ecuador side with Chávez to a greater or lesser degree, Peru currently leans more towards the US.

Culture

People

Peru → *Population in 2007 was 28.7 million. Population growth was 1.29%; infant mortality rate 29.96 per 1000 live births; literacy rate 87.7%; GDP per capita US$6400.*

Peruvian society is a mixture of native Andean peoples, Afro-Peruvians, Spanish, immigrant Chinese, Japanese, Italians, Germans and, to a lesser extent, indigenous Amazon tribes. The first immigrants were the Spaniards who followed Pizarro's expeditionary force. Their effect, demographically, politically and culturally, has been enormous. Peru's black community is based on the coast, mainly in Chincha, south of Lima, and also in some working-class districts of the capital. Their forefathers were originally imported into Peru in the 16th century as slaves to work on the sugar and cotton plantations on the coast. Large numbers of poor Chinese labourers were brought to Peru in the mid-19th century to work in virtual slavery on the guano reserves on the Pacific coast and to build the railroads in the central Andes. The Japanese community, now numbering some 100,000, established itself in the first half of the 20th century. Like most of Latin America, Peru received many emigrés from Europe seeking land and opportunities in the late 19th century. The country's wealth and political power remains concentrated in the hands of this small and exclusive class of whites, which also consists of the descendants of the first Spanish families.

The **indigenous population** is put at about three million Quechua and Aymara in the Andean region and 200,000-250,000 Amazonians from 40-50 ethnic groups. In the Andes, there are 5000 indigenous communities but few densely populated settlements. Their literacy rate is the lowest of any comparable group in South America and their diet is 50% below acceptable levels. About two million *indígena* speak no Spanish, their main tongue being Quechua, an Andean language that predates the Incas; they are largely outside the money economy. The conflict between Sendero Luminoso guerrillas and the security forces caused the death of thousands of highland *indígena*. Many idnigenous groups are under threat from colonization, development and road-building projects. Some have been dispossessed and exploited for their labour.

Bolivia → *Population in 2007 was 9.12 million. Population growth was 1.42%; infant mortality rate 50.43 per 1000 live births; literacy rate 86.7%; GDP per capita US$3000.*

Bolivia has the highest percentage of indigenous people of any country in the continent. Of the total population, some two thirds are indigenous, the remainder being *mestizos* (people of mixed Spanish and indigenous origin), Europeans and others. The racial composition varies from place to place: *indígena* around Lake Titicaca; more than half *indígena* in La Paz; three-quarters *mestizo* or European in the Yungas and Cochabamba, Santa Cruz and Tarija, the most European of all. There are also about 17,000 blacks, descendants of slaves brought from Peru and Buenos Aires in 16th century, who now live in the Yungas. Since the 1980s, regional tensions between the 'collas' (*altiplano* dwellers) and the 'cambas' (lowlanders) have become more marked. About two-thirds of the population lives in adobe huts. In the altiplano, less than 40% of children of school age attend school even though it is theoretically compulsory between seven and 14.

The most obdurate of Bolivian problems has always been that the main mass of population is, from a strictly economic viewpoint, in the wrong place, the poor Altiplano and not the potentially rich Oriente; and that the *indígena* live largely outside the monetary system on a self-sufficient basis. Since the land reform of 1952 isolated communities continue the old life but in the agricultural area around Lake Titicaca, the valleys of Cochabamba, the Yungas and the irrigated areas of the south, most peasants now own their land, however small the plot may be. Migration to the warmer and more fertile lands of the east region has been officially encouraged. At the same time roads are now integrating the food-producing eastern zones, with the bulk of the population living in the towns of the Altiplano or the west-facing slopes of the Eastern Cordillera.

The **highland indígena** are composed of two groups: those in La Paz and in the north of the Altiplano who speak the guttural Aymara (an estimated one million), and those elsewhere, who speak Quechua, the Inca tongue (three million – this includes the *indígena* in the northern Apolobamba region). Outside the big cities many of them speak no Spanish. In the lowlands are some 150,000 people in 30 ethnolinguistic groups, including the Ayoreo, Chiquitano, Chiriguano, Garavo, Chimane and Mojo. The **lowland indígena** are, in the main, Tupi-Guaraní. About 70% of Bolivians are Aymara, Quechua or Tupi-Guaraní speakers. The first two are regarded as national languages, but were not, until very recently, taught in schools, a source of some resentment.

The indigenous women retain a traditional costume, with bright petticoats (*polleras*), and in the highlands around La Paz wear, apparently from birth, a brown or grey bowler (locally called a *bombín*). The *indígena* traditionally chew the coca leaf, which deadens hunger pains and gives a measure of oblivion. Efforts to control the cultivation of coca is one of many sources of friction between the indigenous population and the authorities; others include landlessness, and exploitation of labour. On feast days they drink with considerable application, wear the most sensational masks and dance till they drop.

Ecuador → *Population in 2007 was 13.8 million. Population growth was 1.55%; infant mortality rate 22.1 per 1000 live births; literacy rate 91%; GDP per capita US$4500.*

Roughly 50% of Ecuador's people live in the coastal region west of the Andes, 45% in the Andean Sierra and 5% in Oriente. Migration is occurring from the rural zones of both the coast and the highlands to the towns and cities, particularly Guayaquil and Quito, and agricultural colonization from other parts of the country is taking place in the Oriente. There has also been an important flux of mostly illegal migrants out of Ecuador, seeking opportunities in the USA and Spain; 380,000 people (3% of the population) left between 1995 and 2001. Ecuador's national average population density is the highest in South America. Average *per capita* income rose rapidly in the 1970s and 80s, like other oil-exporting countries, but the distribution has become increasingly skewed. A few Ecuadoreans are spectacularly wealthy, while more than 70% of the population lives in poverty. Dollarization, at turn of the millennium, accentuated this imbalance.

There are two to three million Quichua-speaking **highland indígena** and about 70,000 **lowland indígena**. The following indigenous groups maintain their distinct cultural identity: in the Oriente, Siona, Secoya, Cofán, Huaorani, Zápara, Quichua, Shiwiar, Achuar and Shuar; in the Sierra, Otavalo, Salasaca, Puruhá, Cañari and Saraguro; on the coast, Chachi (Cayapa), Tsáchila (Colorado), Awa (Cuaiquer) and Epera. Many indigenous Amazonian communities are fighting for land rights in the face of oil exploration and colonization.

Music and dance

Peru

Peru is the Andean heartland. Its musicians, together with those of Bolivia, have appeared on the streets of cities all over Europe and North America. However, the costumes they wear, the instruments they play, notably the quena and charango, are not typical of Peru as a whole, only of the Cuzco region. Peruvian music divides at a very basic level into that of the highlands ('Andina') and that of the coast ('Criolla'). The highlands are immensely rich in terms of music and dance, with over 200 dances recorded. Every village has its fiestas and each fiesta has its communal and religious dances. Those of Paucartambo and Coylloriti (Q'olloriti) in the Cuzco region moreover attract innumerable groups of dancers from far and wide. The highlands themselves can be very roughly subdivided into some half dozen major musical regions, of which perhaps the most characteristic are Ancash and the north, the Mantaro Valley, Cuzco, Puno and the Altiplano, Ayacucho and Parinacochas.

There is one recreational dance and musical genre, the Huayno, that is found throughout the whole of the Sierra, and has become ever more popular and commercialized to the point where it is in danger of swamping and indeed replacing the other more regional dances. Nevertheless, still very popular among the *indígena* and/or Mestizos are the Marinera, Carnaval, Pasacalle, Chuscada (from Ancash), Huaylas, Santiago and Chonguinada (all from the Mantaro) and Huayllacha (from Parinacochas). For singing only are the mestizo Muliza, popular in the Central Region, and the soulful lament of the Yaravi, originally *indígena*, but taken up and developed early in the 19th century by the poet and hero of independence Mariano Melgar, from Arequipa.

The Peruvian Altiplano shares a common musical culture with that of Bolivia and dances such as the Auqui-Auqui and Sicuris, or Diabladas, can be found on either side of the border. The highland instrumentation varies from region to region, although the harp and violin are ubiquitous. In the Mantaro area the harp is backed by brass and wind instruments, notably the clarinet, in Cuzco it is the charango and quena and on the Altiplano the sicu panpipes. Two of the most spectacular dances to be seen are the Baile de las Tijeras ('scissor dance') from the Ayacucho/Huancavelica area, for men only and the pounding, stamping Huaylas for both sexes. Huaylas competitions are held annually in Lima and should not be missed. Indeed, owing to the overwhelming migration of peasants into the barrios of Lima, most types of Andean music and dance can be seen in the capital, notably on Sunday at the so-called 'Coliseos', which exist for that purpose.

The flood of migration to the cities has meant that the distinct styles of regional and ethnic groups have become blurred. One example is Chicha, a hybrid of Huayno music and the Colombian Cumbia rhythm which comes from the pueblos jóvenes. More recent is Tecno-cumbia, which originated in the jungle region with groups such as Rossy War, from Puerto Maldonado, and Euforia, from Iquitos. It is a vibrant dance music which has gained much greater popularity across Peruvian society than chicha music ever managed.

The 'Música Criolla' from the coast could not be more different from that of the Sierra. Here the roots are Spanish and African. The popular Valsesito is a syncopated waltz that would certainly be looked at askance in Vienna; the Polca has also suffered an attractive sea change, but reigning over all is the Marinera, Peru's national dance, a rhythmic, graceful courting encounter, a close cousin of Chile's and Bolivia's Cueca and the Argentine Zamba, all of them descended from the Zamacueca. The Marinera has its 'Limeña' and 'Norteña' versions and a more syncopated relative, the Tondero, found in the north coastal regions, is said to have been influenced by slaves brought from Madagascar. All these dances are accompanied by guitars and frequently the *cajón*, a resonant wooden box on which the player sits, pounding it with his hands. Some of the great names of 'Música Criolla' are the singer/composers Chabuca

Morochucos and Hermanos Zañartu.

Also on the coast is to be found the music of the small black community, the 'Música Negroide' or 'Afro-Peruano', which had virtually died out when it was resuscitated in the 50s, but has since gone from strength to strength. It has all the qualities to be found in black music from the Caribbean – a powerful, charismatic beat, rhythmic and lively dancing, and strong percussion provided by the *cajón* and the *quijada de burro*, a donkey's jaw with the teeth loosened. Some of the classic dances in the black repertoire are the Festejo, Son del Diablo, Toro Mata, Landó and Alcatraz. In the Alcatraz one of the partners dances behind the other with a candle, trying to set light to a piece of paper tucked into the rear of the other partner's waist. Nicomedes and Victoria Santa Cruz have been largely responsible for popularizing this black music, and Peru Negro is another excellent professional group. The undoubted, internationally famous star, though, is Susana Baca. Finally, in the Peruvian Amazon region around Iquitos, local variants of the Huayno and Marinera are danced, as well as the Changanacui, accompanied by flute and drum.

Bolivia

The heart of Bolivia is the altiplano and it is the music of the Quechua and Aymara-speaking *indígena* of this area that provides the most distinctive Bolivian musical sound. Although there is much that is of Spanish colonial origin in the indigenous dances, the music itself has more Amerindian style and content than that of any other country in South America. It is rare to find an *indígena* who cannot play an instrument and it is these instruments, both wind and percussion, that are quintessentially Bolivian. The clear sounds of the quena and pinkullo, the deeper, breathier notes of the tarka, pututo and sicuri accompanied by huankaré, pululu and caja drums can be heard all over the Altiplano, the charango (a small, G-stringed guitar) being virtually the only instrument of European origin. The indigenous dances are mainly collective and take place at religious fiestas. The dancers wear colourful costumes with elaborate, plumed headdresses and some of them still parody their ex-Spanish colonial masters.

The principal popular dances that can be regarded as 'national' in their countrywide appeal are the Cueca and Huayño. The Bolivian Cueca is a close relative of the Chilean national dance of the same name and they share a mutual origin in the Zamacueca, itself derived from the Spanish Fandango. The Huayño is of indigenous origin and involves numerous couples, who whirl around or advance down the street, arm-in-arm, in a 'Pandilla'. Justly celebrated is the great carnival Diablada of Oruro, with its hordes of grotesquely masked devils, a spectacle comparable to those of Rio in Brazil and Barranquilla in Colombia. The region of Tarija near the Argentine border has a distinctive musical tradition of its own, based on religious processions that culminate with that of San Roque on the first Sunday in September. There are many professional folk groups on record, the best known being *Grupo Aymara, Los Runas, Los Laris, Los Masis, Kolla Marka* and *Bolivia Manta,* some of which have now established themselves in Europe and North America. The music of the Chiquitania – the result of native adaptation of the baroque sacred music handed down from the Jesuits three centuries ago – is an astonishing story in its own right. In recent years there has been an enormous surge of interest in this music and the traditions associated with it.

Ecuador

Culturally, ethnically and geographically, Ecuador is very much two countries – the Andean highlands with their centre at Quito and the Pacific lowlands behind Guayaquil. In spite of this, the music is relatively homogeneous and it is the Andean music that would be regarded as 'typically Ecuadorean'. The principal highland rhythms are the Sanjuanito, Cachullapi, Albaza, Yumbo and Danzante, danced by *indígena* and *mestizo* alike. These may be played by brass bands, guitar trios or groups of wind instruments, but it is the rondador, a small panpipe, that provides the classic Ecuadorean sound, although of late the Peruvian quena has been making heavy inroads via pan-Andean groups and has become a threat to the local instrument. The coastal region has its own song form, the Amorfino, but the most genuinely 'national' song and dance genres, both of European origin, are the Pasillo (shared with Colombia) in waltz time and the Pasacalle, similar to the Spanish Pasodoble. Of Ecuador's three best loved songs, 'El Chulla Quiteño', 'Romántico Quito' and 'Vasija de Barro', the first two are both Pasacalles. Even the Ecuadorean mestizo music has a melancholy quality not found in Peruvian 'Música Criolla', perhaps due to Quito being in the mountains, while Lima is on the coast. Music of the indigenous highland communities is, as elsewhere in the region, related to religious feasts and ceremonies and geared to wind instruments such as the rondador, the pinqullo and pifano flutes and the great long guarumo horn with its mournful note. The guitar is also usually present and brass bands with well worn instruments can be found in even the smallest villages. Among the most outstanding traditional fiestas are Inti Raymi in Cayambe and Ingapirca, the Pase del Niño in Cuenca and other cities, the Mama Negra of Latacunga, carnival in Guaranda, the Yamor in Otavalo, the Fiesta de las Frutas y las Flores in Ambato, plus Corpus Cristi and the Feast of Saint John all over the highlands. Among the best known musical groups who have recorded are Los Embajadores (whose 'Tormentos' is superb) and the Duo Benítez-Valencia for guitar. There is one totally different cultural area, that of the black inhabitants of the Province of Esmeraldas and the highland valley of the Río Chota in Imbabura. The former is a southern extension of the Colombian Pacific coast negro culture, centred round the marimba xylophone. The musical genres are also shared with black Colombians, including the Bunde, Bambuco, Caderona, Torbellino and Currulao dances and this music is some of the most African sounding in the whole of South America. The Chota Valley is an inverted oasis of desert in the Andes and here the black people dance the Bomba. It is also home to the unique Bandas Mochas, whose primitive instruments include leaves that are doubled over and blown through.

Land and environment

Peru → *Land area: 1,285,216 sq km.*

The whole of Peru's west seaboard with the Pacific is desert on which rain seldom falls. From this coastal shelf the Andes rise to a high Sierra which is studded with groups of soaring mountains and gouged with deep canyons. The highland slopes more gradually east and is deeply forested and ravined. Eastward from these mountains lie the vast jungle lands of the Amazon basin.

The **Highlands** (or Sierra), at an average altitude of 3000 m, cover 26% of the country and contain about 50% of the people, mostly *indígena*, an excessive density on such poor land. Here, high-level land of gentle slopes is surrounded by towering ranges of high peaks including the most spectacular range of the continent, the Cordillera Blanca. This has several ice peaks over 6000 m; the highest, Huascarán, is 6768 m and is a mecca for mountaineers. There are many volcanoes in the south. The north and east highlands are heavily forested up to a limit of 3350 m: the grasslands are between the forest line and the snowline, which rises from 5000 m in the latitude of Lima to 5800 m in the south. Most of the Sierra is covered with grasses and shrubs, with Puna vegetation (bunch grass mixed with low, hairy-leaved plants) from north of Huaraz to the south. Here the indigenous graze llamas, alpacas and sheep providing meat, clothing, transport and even fuel from the animals' dung. Some potatoes and cereals (*quinua, kiwicha* and *kañiwa*) are grown at altitude, but the valley basins contain the best land for arable farming. Most of the rivers which rise in these mountains flow east to the Amazon and cut through the plateau in canyons, sometimes 1500 m deep, in which the climate is tropical. A few go west to the Pacific including the Colca and Cotahuasi in the south, which have created canyons over 3000 m deep.

The **coast**, a narrow ribbon of desert 2250 km long, takes up 11% of the country and holds about 45% of the population. It is the economic heart of Peru, consuming most of the imports and supplying half of the exports. When irrigated, the river valleys are extremely fertile, creating oases which grow cotton throughout the country, sugar cane, rice and export crops such as asparagus in the north, grapes, fruit and olives in the south. At the same time, the coastal current teems with fish and Peru has in the past had the largest catch in the world. The **jungle** covers the forested eastern half of the Andes and the tropical forest beyond, altogether 62% of the country's area, but with only about 6% of the population who are crowded on the river banks in the cultivable land – a tiny part of the area. The few roads have to cope with dense forest, deep valleys, and sharp eastern slopes ranging from 2150 m in the north to 5800 m east of Lake Titicaca. Rivers are the main highways, though navigation is hazardous. The economic potential of the area includes reserves of timber, excellent land for rubber, jute, rice, tropical fruits and coffee and the breeding of cattle. The vast majority of Peru's oil and gas reserves are also east of the Andes.

Bolivia → Land area: 1,098,581 sq km.

A study in contrast, much of Bolivia is a harsh, strange land, with a dreary grey solitude except for the bursts of green after rain. Yes in the Oriente, the land is rolling or flat, covered with exuberant, lush vegetation, and amoung the most beautiful anywhere on the continent. Bolivia is the only South American country with no coastline or navigable river to the sea. It is dominated by the Andes and has five distinct geographical areas. The **Andes** are at their widest in Bolivia, a maximum of 650 km. The Western Cordillera, which separates Bolivia from Chile, has high peaks of 5800 m to 6500 m and a number of active volcanoes along its crest. The Eastern Cordillera also rises to giant massifs, with several peaks over 6000 m in the Cordillera Real section to the north. The far sides of the Cordillera Real fall away very sharply to the northeast, towards the Amazon Basin. The air is unbelievably clear – the whole landscape is a bowl of luminous light.

The **Altiplano** lies between the Cordilleras, a bleak, treeless, windswept plateau, much of it 4000 m above sea-level. Its surface is by no means flat, and the Western Cordillera sends spurs dividing it into basins. The more fertile northern part has more inhabitants; the southern part is parched desert and almost unoccupied, save for a mining town here and there. Nearly 70% of the population lives on it; over half of the people in towns. **Lake Titicaca**, at the northern end of the Altiplano, is an inland sea of 8965 sq km at 3810 m, the highest navigable water in the world. Its depth, up to 280 m in some places, keeps the lake at an even all-year-round temperature of 10° C. This modifies the extremes of winter and night temperatures on the surrounding land, which supports a large Aymara indigenous population, tilling the fields and the hill terraces, growing potatoes and cereals, tending their sheep, alpaca and llamas, and using the resources of the lake. The **Yungas** and the **Puna** are to the east of the Altiplano. The heavily forested northeastern slopes of the Cordillera Real are deeply indented by the fertile valleys of the Yungas, drained into the Amazon lowlands by the Río Beni and its tributaries, where cacao, coffee, sugar, coca and tropical fruits are grown. Further south, from a point just north of Cochabamba, the Eastern Cordillera rises abruptly in sharp escarpments from the altiplano and then flattens out to an easy slope east to the plains: an area known as the Puna. The streams which flow across the Puna cut increasingly deep incisions as they gather volume until the Puna is eroded to little more than a high remnant between the river valleys. In these valleys a variety of grain crops and fruits is grown.

The **tropical lowlands** stretch from the foothills of the Eastern Cordillera to the borders with Brazil, Paraguay and Argentina. They take up 62% of the total area of Bolivia, but contain only about 2% of its population. In the north and east the Oriente has dense tropical forest. Open plains covered with rough pasture, swamp and scrub occupy the centre. Before the expulsion of the Jesuits in 1767 this was a populous land of plenty; for 150 years Jesuit missionaries had controlled the area and guided it into a prosperous security. Decline followed but in recent years better times have returned. Meat is now shipped from Trinidad, capital of Beni Department, and from airstrips in the area, to the urban centres of La Paz, Oruro, and Cochabamba. Further south, the forests and plains beyond the Eastern Cordillera sweep down towards the Río Pilcomayo, which drains into the Río de la Plata, getting progressively less rain and merging into a comparatively dry land of scrub forest and arid savanna. The main city of this area is Santa Cruz de la Sierra, founded in the 16th century, now the largest city in Bolivia and its agrobusiness centre.

Ecuador → Land area: 272, 045 sq km.

The Andes, running from north to south, form a mountainous backbone to the country. There are two main ranges, the Central Cordillera and the Western Cordillera, separated by a 400-km long Central Valley, whose rims are about 50 km apart. The rims are joined together, like the two sides of a ladder, by hilly rungs, and between each pair of rungs lies an intermont basin with a dense cluster of population. These basins are drained by rivers which cut through the rims to run either west to the Pacific or east to join the Amazon. Both rims of the Central Valley are lined with the cones of more than 50 volcanoes. Several of them have long been extinct, for example, Chimborazo, the highest (6310 m). At least eight, however, are still active including Tungurahua (5016 m) which had a significant eruption in 2006; Reventador (3560 m) which covered Quito in ash in 2002; Pichincha (4794 m), which expelled a spectacular mushroom cloud in 1999; Cotopaxi (5897 m), which had several violent eruptions in the 19th century; and Sangay (5230 m), one of the world's most active volcanoes, continuously emitting fumes and ash. Earthquakes too are common.

The **sierra**, as the central trough of the Andes in known, is home to about 47% of the people of Ecuador, the majority of whom are indigenous. Some of the land is still held in large private estates worked by the *indígena*, but a growing proportion is now made up of small family farms or is held by native communities, run as cooperatives. Some communities live at subsistence level, others have developed good markets for products using traditional skills in embroidery, pottery, jewellery, knitting, weaving, and carving. The **costa** is mostly lowland at an altitude of less than 300 m, apart from a belt of hilly land which runs northwest from Guayaquil to the coast, where it turns north and runs parallel to the shore to Esmeraldas. In the extreme north is the unique Chocó rainforest, severely endangered by uncontrolled logging. The forests thin out in the more southern lowlands and give way to tropical dry forest. The main agricultural exports come from the lowlands to the southeast and north of Guayaquil. The heavy rains, high temperature and humidity suit the growth of tropical crops. Bananas and mango are grown here while rice is farmed on the natural levees of this flood plain. The main crop comes from the alluvial fans at the foot of the mountains rising out of the plain. Coffee is grown on the higher ground. Shrimp farming was typical of the coast until this was damaged by disease in 1999. The Guayas lowland is also a great cattle-fattening area in the dry season. South of Guayaquil the rainfall is progressively less, mangroves disappear and by the border with Peru, it is semi-arid.

The **Oriente** is east of the Central Cordillera where the forest-clad mountains fall sharply to a chain of foothills (the Eastern Cordillera) and then the jungle through which meander the tributaries of the Amazon. This east lowland region makes up 36% of Ecuador's total territory, but is only sparsely populated by indigenous and agricultural colonists from the highlands. In total, the region has only 5% of the pressure and in the wake of an oil boom in the northern Oriente. There is gold and other minerals in the south. The **Galápagos** are about 1000 km west of Ecuador, on the Equator, and are not structurally connected to the mainland. They mark the junction between two tectonic plates on the Pacific floor where basalt has escaped to form massive volcanoes, only the tips of which are above sea level. Several of the islands have volcanic activity today. Their isolation from any other land has led to the evolution of their unique flora and fauna.

Books

Peru
Reference/trekking
Bartle, Jim *Parque Nacional Huascarán*, a beautiful soft-cover photo collection.
Davis, Morgan *The Cloud People, an Anthropological Survey.*
Muscutt, Keith *Warriors of the Clouds: A Lost Civilization in the Upper Amazon of Peru* (New Mexico Press, 1998; www.chachapoyas.com).
Person, David L and **Beletsky, Les** *Ecotraveller's Wildlife Guide: Peru* (London: Academic Press, 2001).
Sharman, David *Climbs of the Cordillera Blanca of Peru*, (1995). A climbing guide.
South American Explorers publishes a good map with additional notes on the popular Llanganuco to Santa Cruz loop.

Cuzco and Machu Picchu
Bingham, Hiram *Lost City of the Incas*, (available in Lima and Cuzco, new illustrated edition, with introduction by Hugh Thomson, Weidenfeld & Nicolson, London, 2002).
Box, Ben and **Steve Frankham** *Footprint Cuzco and the Inca Heartland* (Footprint).
Frost, Peter *Exploring Cusco*, available in Cuzco bookshops.
Milligan, Max *In the Realm of the Incas* (Harper Collins, 2001). A recommended book with photographs and text.
Thomson, Hugh *The White Rock* (Phoenix, 2002), describes Thomson's own travels in the Inca heartland, as well as the journeys of earlier explorers. *Cochineal Red: Travels through Ancient Peru* (Weidenfeld & Nicolson, 2006), explores pre-Inca civilizations.

The southeastern jungle
MacQuarrie, Kim and **Bartschi, André and Cornelia** *Manu National Park*, an expensive, excellent book, with beautiful photographs.

TReeS *Birds of Tambopata* – a checklist, Mammals, Amphibians and Reptiles of Tambopata, *Ecology of Tropical Rainforesets: a layman's guide* and *Tambopata map guide*, all by TReeS, who also produce tapes of *Jungle Sounds* and *Bird Sounds of southeast Peru*.

History and culture
Hemming, John *The Conquest of t he Incas*, invaluable for the whole period of the Conquest.
Heyerdahl, Thor, **Sandweiss, Daniel H** and **Narváez, Alfredo** *Pyramids of Túcume*, (Thames & Hudson, 1995).
Kendall, Ann *Everyday Life of the Incas*, (Batsford, London, 1978).
Mosely, Michael E *The Incas and their Ancestors: The Archaeology of Peru.*

Travel
Murphy, Dervla *Eight Feet in the Andes* (1983).
Parris, Matthew *Inca-Kola* (1990).
Shah, Tahir *Trail of Feathers* (2001).
Wright, Ronald *Cut Stones and Crossroads: a Journey in Peru* (1984).

Fiction
Alegría, Ciro (1909-67) *El mundo es ancho y ajeno/Broad and Alien is the World* (1941).
Arguedas, José María (1911-1969) *Los ríos profundos/Deep Rivers* (1958).
Mathiessen, Peter *At Play in the Fields of the Lord* (1965).
Matto de Turner, Clorinda (1854-1909) The first writer of 'indigenist' fiction in Peru (see *Aves sin nido*). Others writers listed here followed in attempting to use fiction to address the issues of the ethnic majority.
Roncagliolo, Santiago (1975-), *Abril Rojo* (2006).

Background Books

⁛ Recommended reading

John Hemming, *The Conquest of the Incas* (1970). A masterly account of the events that changed South America for ever.
Matthew Parris, *Inca Kola: A Traveller's Tale of Peru* (1993). A chronicle of Parris and three friends' bizarre adventures in Peru.
Daniel Alarcón, *War by Candlelight* (2005), an excellent collection of short stories, written in English, dealing with contemporary life within and outside Peru.
Mario Vargas Llosa, *Conversation in the Cathedral* (1969). The Peruvian master's complex but compelling novel of life under the Odría dictatorship in 1950s Peru.

Vargas Llosa, Mario (1936-) Peru's best known novelist has written many internationally acclaimed books, eg *La ciudad y los perros/The Time of the Hero* (1962), *La casa verde/The Green House* (1965), *La guerra del fin del mundo/The War of the End of World* (1981), *La fiesta del chivo/The Feast of the Goat* (2000) and *El paraíso en la otra esquina/The Way to Paradise* (2002).
Vallejo, César (1892-1938) Peru's outstanding 20th-century poet: his avant-garde collection *Trilce* (1922) is unlike anything before it in the Spanish language, but his work also has strong political commitment, as in *Poemas humanos* and *España, aparte de mí este cáliz*, both published posthumously.
Wilder, Thornton *The Bridge of San Luis Rey* (1927).

Bolivia
Reference
Meadows, Anne *Digging up Butch and Sundance* (Bison Books, 1996), an account of the last days of Butch Cassidy and the Sundance Kid and the attempts to find their graves.

Trekking
Brain, Yossi *Bolivia – a climbing guide* (The Mountaineers, Seattle, 1999).
Brain, Yossi, **North, Andrew** and **Stoddart, Isobel** *Trekking in Bolivia* (The Mountaineers, Seattle, 1997).
Mesili, Alain *The Andes of Bolivia* (CIMA, La Paz, 2004, www.andes-mesili.com).
Murphy, Alan, **Groesbeck, Geoff**, and **Honnor, Julius** *Footprint Bolivia* (Footprint).

20th-century fiction and poetry
Arguedas, Alcides *Raza de Bronce* (1919); and **Mendoza, Jamie** *El las tierras de Potosí* (1911); both examine the life of the *campesino* in a society dominated by whites.
Céspedes, Augusto *Sangre de mestizos* (1936), a collection of stories on the Chaco War.
Prado de Oropeza, Renato *Los fundadores del alba* (1969), inspired by Che Guevara's campaigns in the 1960s and *Antología del terror político* (1979), which deals with Bolivia under dictatorship.
Zamudio, Adela (1854-1928) Modernist poet.

Ecuador
Hiking trekking and nature
Brain, Y, *Ecuador: A Climbing Guide* (The Mountaineers, Seattle, 2000).
Canaday, C and Jost, L, *Common Birds of Amazonian Ecuador* (Ediciones Libri-Mundi, Quito, 1997).
Kunstaetter, R and D, *Trekking in Ecuador* (The Mountaineers, Seattle, 2002, www.trekkinginecuador.com).
Ridgely, R and Greenfield, P, *Birds of Ecuador* (Cornell University Press, Ithaca, NY, USA, 2001).

Galápagos Islands
Angermeyer, J *My Father's Island* (Anthony Nelson, 1998).
Constant, P, *The Galápagos Islands* (Odyssey, 2000).
Jackson, M H, *Galápagos: A Natural History Guide* (University of Calgary Press, 1985).
Treherne, J, *The Galápagos Affair* (Jonathan Cape, 1983).
Wittmer, M, *Floreana* (Michael Joseph, 1961).

Footnotes

Useful words and phrases

Greetings & courtesies	Spanish	Portuguese
hello/good morning	*hola/buenos días*	*oi/bom dia*
good afternoon/evening/night	*buenas tardes/noches*	*boa tarde/boa noite*
goodbye	*adiós/chao*	*adeus/tchau*
see you later	*hasta luego*	*até logo*
how are you?	*¿cómo está/cómo estás?*	*como vai você?/tudo bem?*
		tudo bom?
I'm fine	*estoy bien*	*tudo bem /tudo bom*
pleased to meet you	*mucho gusto/encantado*	*um prazer*
please	*por favor*	*por favor/faz favor*
thank you (very much)	*(muchas) gracias*	*(muito) obrigado (man speaking)*
		/obrigada (woman speaking)
yes/no	*sí/no*	*sim/não*
excuse me/I beg your pardon	*permiso*	*com licença*
I don't understand	*no entiendo*	*não entendo*
please speak slowly	*hable despacio por favor*	*fale devagar por favor*
what's your name?/	*¿cómo se llama?/me llamo_*	*Qual é seu nome?/ O meu*
I'm called_		*nome é_*
Go away!	*¡Váyase!*	*Vai embora!*

Basic questions		
where is_?	*¿dónde está_?*	*onde está/onde fica?*
how much does it cost?	*¿cuánto cuesta?*	*quanto custa?*
when?	*¿cuándo?*	*quando?*
when does the bus leave/ arrive?	*¿a qué hora sale/llega el autobus?*	*qa que hora sai/chega o ônibus?*
why?	*¿por qué?*	*por que?*
how do I get to_?	*¿cómo llegar a_?*	*para chegar a_?*

Basics		
police (policeman)	*la policía (el policía)*	*a polícia (o polícia)*
hotel	*el hotel (la pensión, el residencial, el alojamiento)*	*o hotel (a pensão, a hospedaria)*
room	*el cuarto/la habitación*	*o quarto*
single/double	*sencillo/doble*	*(quarto de) solteiro*
with two beds	*con dos camas*	*com duas camas*
bathroom/toilet	*el baño*	*o banheiro*
hot/cold water	*agua caliente/fría*	*água quente/fria*
toilet paper	*el papel higiénico*	*o papel higiênico*
restaurant	*el restaurante*	*o restaurante (o lanchonete)*
post office/telephone office	*el correo/el centro de llamadas*	*o correio/o centro telefônico*
supermarket/market	*el supermercado/el mercado*	*o supermercado/o mercado*
bank/exchange house	*el banco/la casa de cambio*	*o banco/a casa de câmbio*
exchange rate	*la tasa de cambio*	*a taxa de câmbio*
travellers' cheques	*los travelers/los cheques de viajero*	*os travelers/os cheques de viagem*
cash	*el efectivo*	*o dinheiro*
breakfast/lunch	*el desayuno/el almuerzo*	*o café da manhã/o almoço*
dinner/supper	*la cena*	*o jantar*
meal/drink	*la comida/la bebida*	*a refeição/a bebida*
mineral water	*el agua mineral*	*a água mineral*
beer	*la cerveza*	*a cerveja*
without sugar/without meat	*sin azúcar/sin carne*	*sem açúcar/sem carne*

Getting around

on the left/right	*a la izquierda/derecha*	*á esquerda/á direita*
straight on	*derecho*	*direito*
bus station	*la terminal (terrestre)*	*a rodoviária*
bus stop	*la parada*	*a parada*
bus	*el bus/el autobus/la flota/ el colectivo/el micro*	*o ônibus*
train/train station	*el tren/la estación (de tren/ferrocarril)*	*o trem*
airport/aeroplane	*el aeropuerto/el avión*	*o aeroporto/o avião*
ticket/ticket office	*el boleto/la taquilla*	*o bilhete/a bilheteria*

Time

What time is it?	*¿Qué hora es?*	*Que horas são?*
at half past two/two thirty	*a las dos y media*	*as duas e meia*
it's one o'clock/ it's seven o'clock	*es la una/son las siete*	*é uma/são as sete*
ten minutes/five hours	*diez minutos/cinco horas*	*dez minutos/cinco horas*

Numbers

1	*uno/una*	*um/uma*
2	*dos*	*dois/duas*
3	*tres*	*três*
4	*cuatro*	*quatro*
5	*cinco*	*cinco*
6	*seis*	*seis*
7	*siete*	*sete*
8	*ocho*	*oito*
9	*nueve*	*nove*
10	*diez*	*dez*
11	*once*	*onze*
12	*doce*	*doze*
13	*trece*	*treze*
14	*catorce*	*catorze*
15	*quince*	*quinze*
16	*dieciseis*	*dezesseis*
17	*diecisiete*	*dezessete*
18	*dieciocho*	*dezoito*
19	*diecinueve*	*dezenove*
20	*veinte*	*vinte*
21	*veintiuno*	*vinte e um*
30	*treinte*	*trinta*
40	*cuarenta*	*quarenta*
50	*cincuenta*	*cinqüenta*
60	*sesenta*	*sessenta*
70	*setenta*	*setenta*
80	*ochenta*	*oitenta*
90	*noventa*	*noventa*
100	*cien, ciento*	*cem, cento*
1000	*mil*	*mil*

Spanish pronunciation

Spanish

The stress in a Spanish word conforms to one of three rules: 1) if the word ends in a vowel, or in n or **s**, the accent falls on the penultimate syllable (*ventana*, *ventanas*); 2) if the word ends in a consonant other than **n** or **s**, the accent falls on the last syllable (*hablar*); 3) if the word is to be stressed on a syllable contrary to either of the above rules, the acute accent on the relevant vowel indicates where the stress is to be placed (*pantalón*, *metáfora*). Note that adverbs such as *cuando*, 'when', take an accent when used interrogatively: *¿cuándo?*, 'when?'

Vowels: a not quite as short as in English 'cat'; **e** as in English 'pay', but shorter in a syllable ending in a consonant; **i** as in English 'seek'; **o** as in English 'cot' (North American 'caught'), but more like 'pope' when the vowel ends a syllable; **u** as in English 'food'; after 'q' and in 'gue', 'gui', u is unpronounced; in 'güe' and 'güi' it is pronounced; **y** when a vowel, pronounced like 'i'; when a semiconsonant or consonant, it is pronounced like English 'yes'; **ai**, **ay** as in English 'write'; **ei**, **ey** as in English 'eight'; **oi**, **oy** as in English 'voice'

Unless listed below **consonants** can be pronounced in Spanish as they are in English. **b**, **v** have an interchangeable sound and both are a cross between the English 'b' and 'v', except at the beginning of a word or after 'm' or 'n' when it is like English 'b'; **c** like English 'k', except before 'e' or 'i' when it is as the 's' in English 'sip'; **g** before 'e' and 'i' it is the same as j; **h** when on its own, never pronounced; **j** as the 'ch' in the Scottish 'loch'; **ll** as the 'g' in English 'beige'; sometimes as the 'lli' in 'million'; **ñ** as the 'ni' in English 'onion'; **rr** trilled much more strongly than in English; **x** depending on its location, pronounced as in English 'fox', or 'sip', or like 'gs'; **z** as the 's' in English 'sip'.

Index → Entries in bold refer to maps.

Advertisers' index

Acknowledgements

Ben Box
Many thanks to Heather MacBrayne at South American Explorers in Cuzco and all the travellers who have written to Footprint's *Peru* and *South American Handbook*.

Geoffrey Groesbeck
This is dedicated to an anonymous little girl I saw only once at the San José de Chiquitos train station. *Te digo que un día no encontraremos otra vez en un lugar mejor; si no es en esta vida, será en la otra.*

Robert and Daisy Kunstaetter
Thanks to Jeaneth Barrionuevo (Cuenca), Jean Brown (Quito), Grace and Marcelo Naranjo (Quito), Michael Resch (Baños), Piet Sabbe (El Limonal), Peter Schramm (Vilcabamba), José Tapia (Misahuallí), Delia Maria Torres (Guayaquil), Popkje van der Ploeg and William Reyes (Riobamba).

Exploring the land of the Incas

We invite you to discover Peru:
the only way, the Orient-Express Way

MIRAFLORES PARK
HOTEL

ORIENT EXPRESS HOTELS
TRAINS & CRUISES

www.mira-park.com
Lima-Perú

MACHU
PICCHU
SANCTUARY LODGE

ORIENT EXPRESS HOTELS
TRAINS & CRUISES

www.sanctuarylodge.net
Machu Picchu-Perú

HOTEL
MONASTERIO

ORIENT EXPRESS HOTELS
TRAINS & CRUISES

www.monasterio.orient-express.com
Cusco-Perú

El Parador del Colca

colca@peruorientexpress.com.pe
Arequipa-Perú

Reservations:
- Hotel Monasterio: res-monasterio@peruorientexpress.com.pe
- Machu Picchu Sanctuary Lodge: res-mapi@peruorientexpress.com.pe
- Miraflores Park Hotel: reservas@peruorientexpress.com.pe
- El Parador del Colca: colca@peruorientexpress.com.pe

Central Call: (511) 610 8300   Fax: (511) 242 3393

Essentials

Essentials

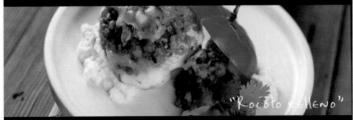

Map symbols

Administration

▫ Capital city
○ Other city, town
International border
Regional border
Disputed border

Roads and travel

Motorway
Main road (National highway)
Minor road
- - - - Track
.... Footpath
Railway with station
✈ Airport
🚌 Bus station
Ⓜ Metro station
- - - - Cable car
Funicular
Ferry

Water features

River, canal
Lake, ocean
Seasonal marshland
Beach, sandbank
Waterfall
Reef

Topographical features

Contours (approx)
▲ Mountain, volcano
Mountain pass
Escarpment
Gorge
Glacier
Salt flat
Rocks

Cities and towns

Main through route
Main street
Minor street

Pedestrianized street
Ϲ Ϲ Tunnel
→ One-way street
Steps
Bridge
Fortified wall
Park, garden, stadium
Sleeping
Eating
Bars & clubs
Building
Sight
Cathedral, church
Chinese temple
Hindu temple
Meru
Mosque
Stupa
Synagogue
Tourist office
Museum
Post office
Police
Bank
Internet
Telephone
Market
Medical services
Parking
Petrol
Golf
A Detail map
A Related map

Other symbols

⊖ Customs
Archaeological site
National park, wildlife reserve
Viewing point
▲ Campsite
Refuge, lodge
Castle, fort
Diving
Deciduous, coniferous, palm trees
Hide
Vineyard, winery
Distillery
Shipwreck
Historic battlefield

Essentials

Map 1 Ecuador

ECUADOR
PERU
BOLIVIA

Pacific Ocean

Ancón
Río Juba
I Sta Rosa
Mataje
Limones (Valdez)
San Lorenzo
La Tola
Las Peñas
Ríoverde
Borbón
Anchayacu
Las Palmas
Atacames
Tonchigüe
Súa
Esmeraldas
ESMERALDAS
Same
Punta Galera
Viche
Esmeraldas
Muisne
Reserva Ecológica Cotacachi-Cayapas
Mompiche
Bolívar
I de Cojimíes
Daule
Rosa Zárate (Quinindé)
Guayllabamba
Apue
Cojimíes
Chamanga
Pedro Vicente Maldonado
Pedernales
Puerto Quito
Caláca
Palmar
La Independencia
San Miguel de los Bancos
Mindo
Nono
Tabuga
Mtas de Chindul
PICHINCHA
Jama
Santo Domingo de los Colorados
Vol Guagua Pichincha (4794m)
El Carmen
Mtas Jama
Machach
Vol El Corazón (4794m)
Canoa
Punta Pasado
Reserva Ecológica Los Ilinizas
Lasso
B Briceño
San Vicente
Volcanes Ilinizas (5126m & 5623m)
Bahía de Caráquez
San Antonio
MANABÍ
Sigchos
Saquisilí
San Clemente
Tosagua
Chone
Chugchilán
Isinliví
Latacunga
San Jacinto
Chone
Zumbahua
Quilotoa
Las Gilces
Rocafuerte
Calceta
Tingo
La Maná
Pilaló
Pijilí
Salcedo
Crucita
Junín
Empalme
Quevedo
COTAPAXI
Manta
Cerro de Hoja
Portoviejo
Santa Ana
El Corazón
Montecristi
La Pila
Sucre
Balzar
Ambato
San Lorenzo
LOS RÍOS
Salasaca
Mocha
Jipijapa
Olmedo
Ventanas
BOLÍVAR
Pelileo
Isla de la Plata
Chimborazo (6310m)
Guano
Puerto Cayo
Agua Blanca
Paiján
Vinces
Pueblo viejo
Riobamba
Penip
Machalilla
Puerto López
Palestina
Guaranda
Cajabamba
Salango
Campozano
Parque Nacional Machalilla
Cascol
Babahoyo
Cebadas
Alandaluz
Pedro Carbo
Salitre
Chillanes
Guamote
Ayampe
Montañita
Dos Ríos
Isidro Ayora
Daule
Samborondón
TUNGURAHUA
Manglaralto
Bosque Protector Cerro Blanco
Palmira
Atillo
Valdivia
Colonche
Yaguachi
Naranjito
Alausí
Tixan
Ayangue
GUAYAS
Durán
Milagro
El Triunfo
Bucay
Sibambe
Achupallas
Monteverde
Guayaquil
Huigra
Chunchi
La Puntilla
Salinas
Ballenita
Zapotal
San Isidro
Reserva Ecológica Manglares-Churute
La Troncal
Zhud
El Tambo
Ingapirca
Santa Elena
La Libertad
El Progreso
Cañar
CAÑAR
Punta Carnero
Anconcito
San Lorenzo
Naranjal
Biblián
Punta Ancón
Chanduy
Molleturo
Azogues
Engunga
El Morro
Parque Nacional Cajas
Sayausí
Paute
Engabao
Canal de Morro
Gualaceo
Playas
Posorja
Puná
Soldados
Baños
Cuenca
Data de Villamil
Chordeleg
Golfo de Guayaquil
Isla Puná
Tarqui
AZUAY
Sígsig
Punta Carnero
Canal Jambelí
Chumblín
Girón
Cumbe
Indanza
I Sta Clara
Machala
El Guabo
San Fernando
Tinajilla Pass (3527m)
Chiquinda
Pasaje
Casacay
Santa Isabel
Nábon
Gima
Aguas Verdes
Sta Rosa
Chilla
Manú
El Progreso
Gualaquiza
Santuario Nacional los Manglares de Tumbes
Huaquillas
EL ORO
Selva Alegre
Oña
Bomboiz
Puerto Pizarro
Zarumilla
Arenillas
Celén
24 de Mayo (Yacuambi)
El Pangui
Tumbes
San Jacinto
Piñas
Saraguro
Los Encuentros
Zorritos
Bosque Petrificado Puyango
Zaruma
Yantzaza
Bocapán
Zona Reserva de Tumbes
Puyango
El Cisne
Chuquiribamba
Nambija
Cumbaratza
Cancas
Cañaveral
TUMBES
Puyango
LOJA
Catamayo
Loja
Zamora
Los Organos
Alamor
Catacocha
ZAMORA-CHINCHIPE
Máncora
Paletillas
Celica
Parque Nacional Podocarpus
Punta Sal
Gonzanamá
Purunuma
Malacatos
Cabo Blanco
Atascadero
Zapotillo
Macará
Colaisaca
Cariamanga
Vilcabamba
Yangana
Parque Nacional Cerros de Amotape
Lalamor
La Tina
Sozoranga
Utuana
Lobitos
PIURA
Suyo
Ayabaca
Amáluza
Valladolid
Talara
Las Lomas
Paimas
Espíndola
Jimbura
Palanda
Negritos
San Jacinto
Tambo Real
Frías
Zumba
La Balsa
Vichayal
Amotape
Sullana

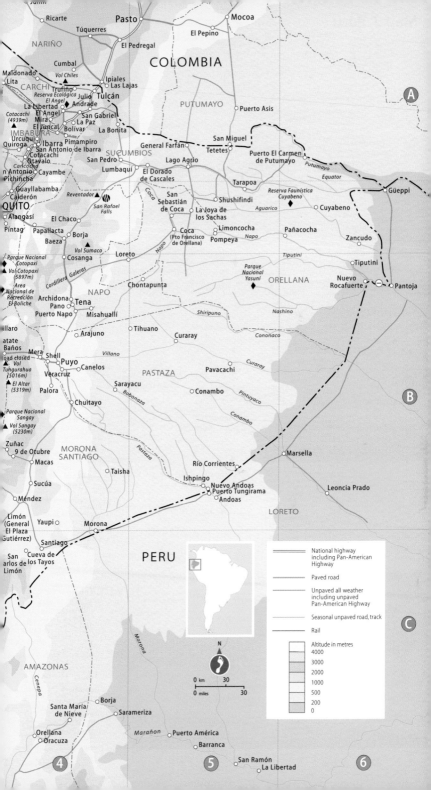

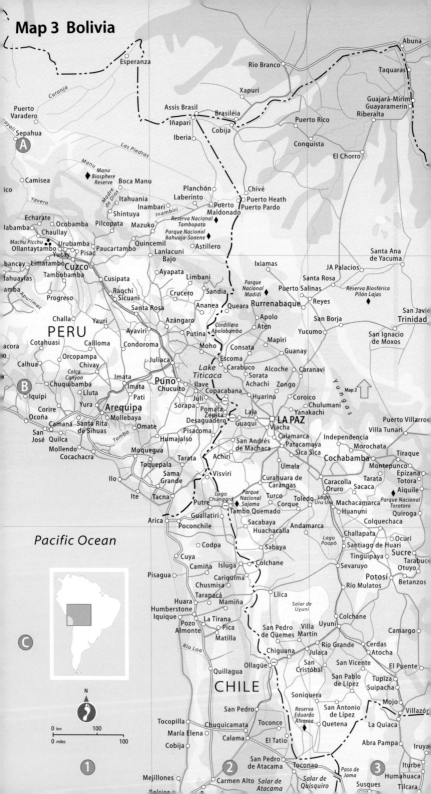

Map 3 Bolivia

Map 4 Urubamba Valley

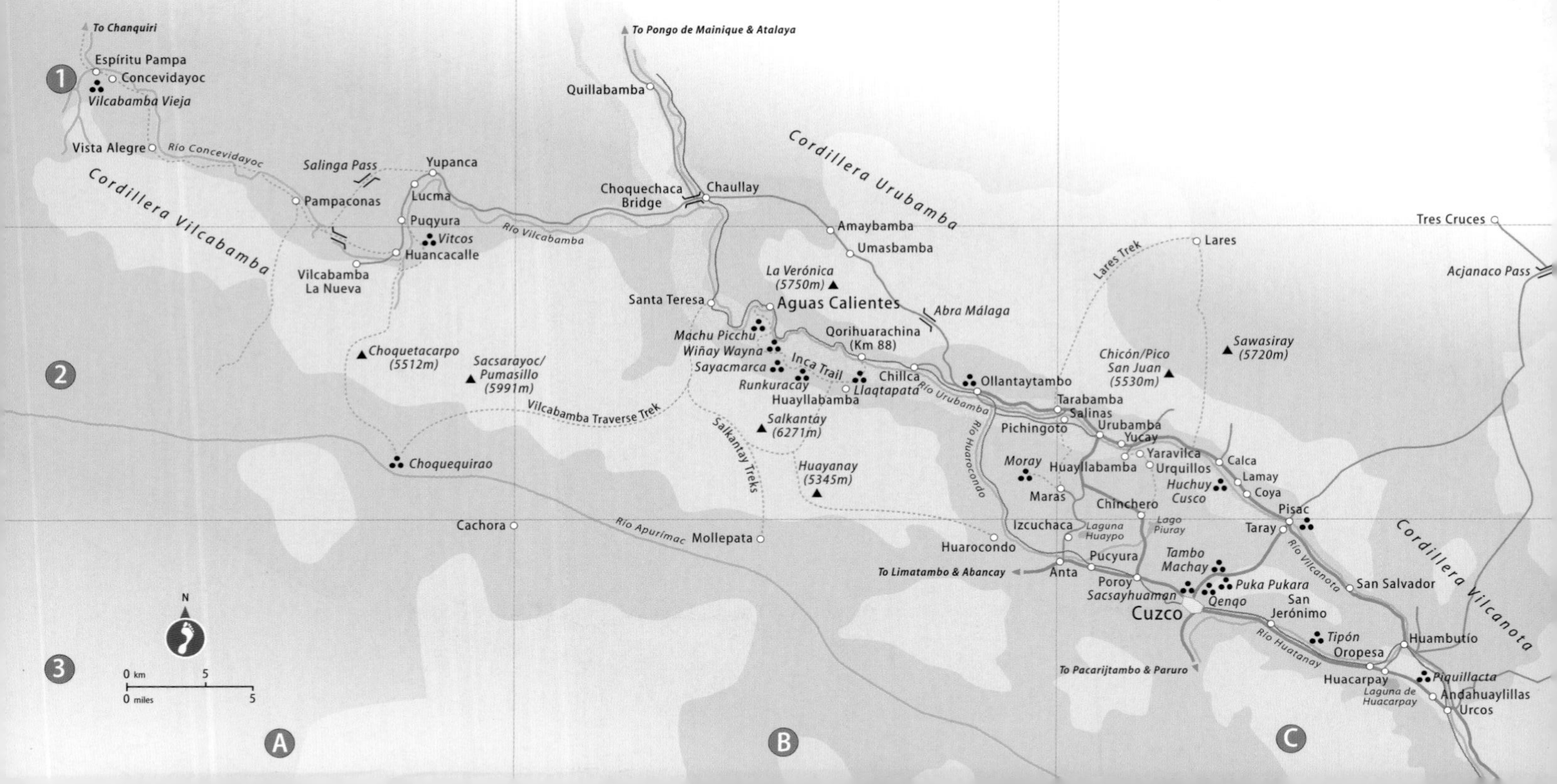

Map labels (north-west to south-east):

To Chaquiri
Espíritu Pampa
Concevidayoc
Vilcabamba Vieja
Vista Alegre
Río Concevidayoc

Yupanca
Lucma
Pugyura
Vitcos
Huancacalle
Salinga Pass
Pampaconas
Vilcabamba La Nueva
Río Vilcabamba

Choquetacarpo (5512m)
Sacsarayoc/Pumasillo (5991m)
Vilcabamba Traverse Trek

Choquequirao

Cachora
Mollepata
Río Apurímac

Quillabamba
To Pongo de Mainique & Atalaya

Choquechaca Bridge
Chaullay

Cordillera Urubamba
Amaybamba
Umasbamba

Santa Teresa
La Verónica (5750m)
Aguas Calientes
Machu Picchu
Wiñay Wayna
Sayacmarca
Runkuracay
Inca Trail
Qorihuarachina (Km 88)
Chilca
Llaqtapata
Huayllabamba
Salkantay (6271m)
Huayanay (5345m)
Salkantay Treks

Cordillera Vilcabamba

Abra Málaga
Río Urubamba
Ollantaytambo
Pichingoto
Río Huarocondo
Huarocondo
Tarabamba
Salinas
Moray
Maras
Izcuchaca
To Limatambo & Abancay

Lares
Lares Trek
Sawasiray (5720m)
Chicón/Pico San Juan (5530m)

Calca
Lamay
Coya
Yucay
Urubamba
Yaravilca
Urquillos
Huchuy Cusco
Chinchero
Laguna Huaypo
Lago Piuray
Pucyura
Poroy
Anta
Sacsayhuamán

Pisac
Taray
Puka Pukara
Tambo Machay
Qenqo
San Jerónimo
San Salvador
Huambutío

Cordillera Vilcanota
Río Vilcanota
CUZCO
Río Huatanay
San Sebastián
Oropesa
Tipón
Huacarpay
Laguna de Huacarpoy
Piquillacta
Andahuayllillas
Urcos
To Pacari/tambo & Paruro

Tres Cruces
Acjanaco Pass

0 km   5
0 miles 5
N

1   2   3
A   B   C

Map 5 Galápagos Islands

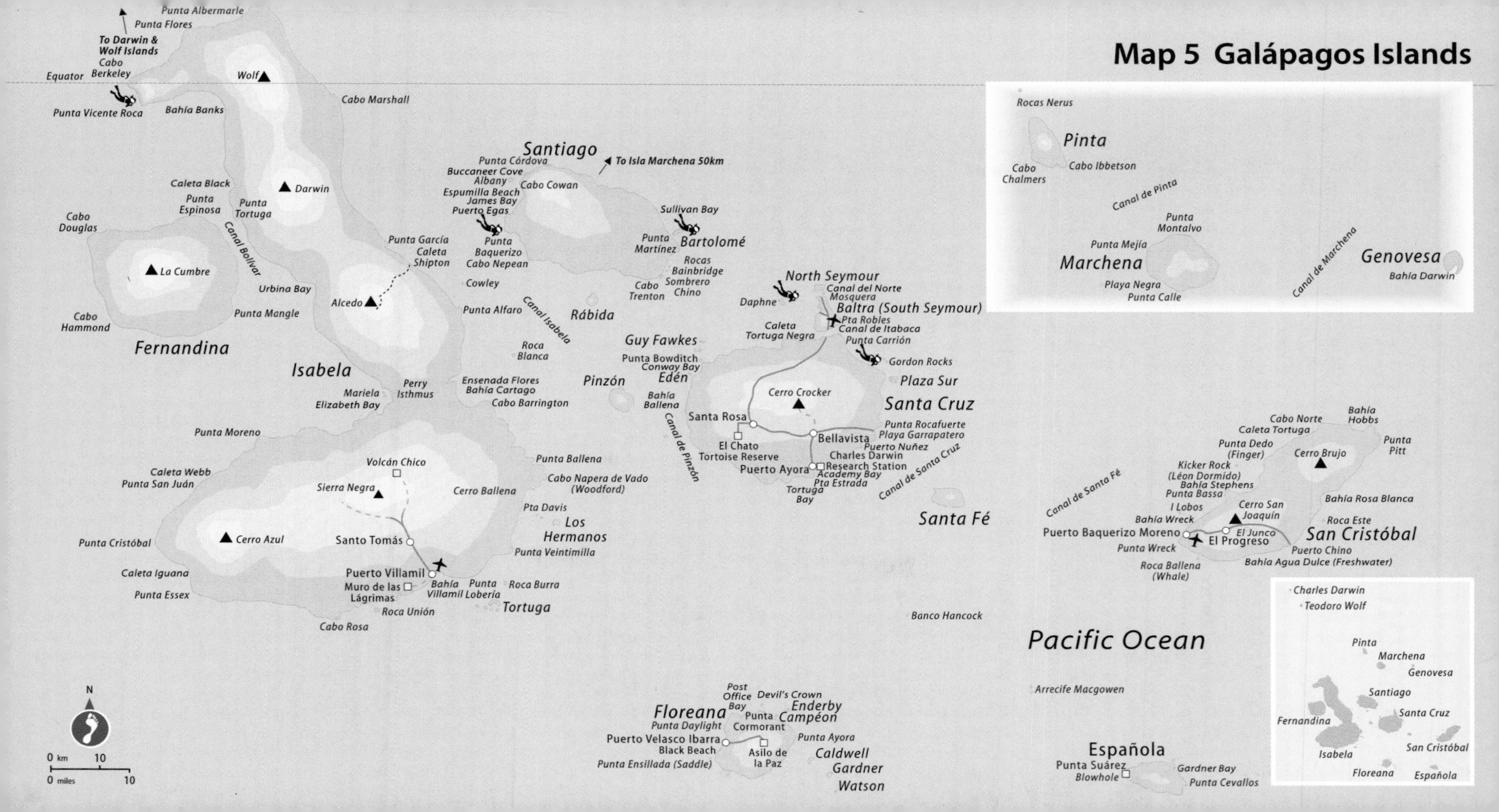

Punta Albermarle
Punta Flores
To Darwin & Wolf Islands
Cabo Berkeley
Equator
Punta Vicente Roca
Bahía Banks
Wolf
Cabo Marshall
Darwin
Caleta Black
Punta Espinosa
Punta Tortuga
Cabo Douglas
Canal Bolívar
La Cumbre
Urbina Bay
Punta Mangle
Cabo Hammond
Fernandina
Isabela
Alcedo
Punta García
Caleta Shipton
Mariela
Elizabeth Bay
Perry Isthmus
Punta Moreno
Caleta Webb
Punta San Juán
Volcán Chico
Sierra Negra
Cerro Azul
Punta Cristóbal
Caleta Iguana
Punta Essex
Santo Tomás
Puerto Villamil
Muro de las Lágrimas
Bahía Villamil
Punta Lobería
Roca Unión
Cabo Rosa
Cerro Ballena
Punta Ballena
Cabo Napera de Vado (Woodford)
Pta Davis
Los Hermanos
Punta Veintimilla
Roca Burra
Tortuga
Santiago
To Isla Marchena 50km
Punta Córdova
Buccaneer Cove
Albany
Espumilla Beach
James Bay
Puerto Egas
Cabo Cowan
Punta Baquerizo
Cabo Nepean
Cowley
Punta Alfaro
Canal Isabela
Roca Blanca
Ensenada Flores
Bahía Cartago
Cabo Barrington
Rábida
Sullivan Bay
Punta Martínez
Bartolomé
Rocas Bainbridge
Sombrero Chino
Cabo Trenton
Guy Fawkes
Punta Bowditch
Conway Bay
Edén
Pinzón
Bahía Ballena
Canal de Pinzón
North Seymour
Canal del Norte
Mosquera
Daphne
Baltra (South Seymour)
Pta Robles
Canal de Itabaca
Caleta Tortuga Negra
Punta Carrión
Gordon Rocks
Plaza Sur
Cerro Crocker
Santa Cruz
Santa Rosa
El Chato Tortoise Reserve
Bellavista
Punta Rocafuerte
Playa Garrapatero
Puerto Nuñez
Charles Darwin Research Station
Puerto Ayora
Academy Bay
Pta Estrada
Tortuga Bay
Canal de Santa Cruz
Santa Fé
Banco Hancock
Floreana
Post Office Bay
Devil's Crown
Enderby
Punta Cormorant
Campéon
Punta Daylight
Puerto Velasco Ibarra
Black Beach
Asilo de la Paz
Punta Ayora
Punta Ensillada (Saddle)
Caldwell
Gardner
Watson
Rocas Nerus
Pinta
Cabo Chalmers
Cabo Ibbetson
Canal de Pinta
Punta Montalvo
Punta Mejía
Marchena
Playa Negra
Punta Calle
Canal de Marchena
Genovesa
Bahía Darwin
Cabo Norte
Bahía Hobbs
Caleta Tortuga
Punta Dedo (Finger)
Punta Pitt
Cerro Brujo
Kicker Rock (Léon Dormido)
Bahía Stephens
Punta Bassa
I Lobos
Cerro San Joaquín
Bahía Rosa Blanca
Roca Este
Bahía Wreck
Canal de Santa Fé
Puerto Baquerizo Moreno
El Junco
El Progreso
San Cristóbal
Punta Wreck
Puerto Chino
Bahía Agua Dulce (Freshwater)
Roca Ballena (Whale)
Pacific Ocean
Arrecife Macgowen
Española
Punta Suárez
Blowhole
Gardner Bay
Punta Cevallos
Charles Darwin
Teodoro Wolf
Pinta
Marchena
Genovesa
Santiago
Santa Cruz
Fernandina
Isabela
San Cristóbal
Floreana
Española
N
0 km 10
0 miles 10

Credits

Footprint credits

Editor: Nicola Gibbs
Map editor: Sarah Sorensen
Picture editor: Robert Lunn

Managing Director: Andy Riddle
Publisher: Patrick Dawson
Editorial: Alan Murphy, Sophie Blacksell,
Nicola Gibbs, Jo Williams
Cartography: Robert Lunn, Kevin Feeney
Design: Mytton Williams
Sales and marketing: Zoë Jackson,
Hannah Bonnell
Finance and administration:
Elizabeth Taylor

Photography credits

Front cover: Jamie Marshall
Back cover: Katarzyna Citko/Shutterstock
Inside colour section: Robert Lunn;
age fotostock/Superstock; South American
Pictures/Tony Morrison; South American
Pictures/Robert Frances; Misha Shiyanov/
Shutterstock; Danny Warren/Shutterstock;
Lorenzo Puricelli/Shutterstock; Jarno Gonzales
Zarraonandia/Shutterstock; Mike Von Bergen/
Shutterstock; Katarzyna Citko/Shutterstock;
Galyna Andrushko/Shutterstock; Ra'id
Khalil/Shutterstock; Chris Howey/Shutterstock;
Brett Atkins/Shutterstock; Joel Blit/Shutterstock;
Yoshio Tomii/Shutterstock; Jose Alberto
Tejo/Shutterstock.

Print

Manufactured in India by Nutech
Pulp from sustainable forests

Footprint feedback

We try as hard as we can to make each
Footprint guide as up to date as possible
but, of course, things always change. If you
want to let us know about your experiences –
good, bad or ugly – then don't delay, go to
www.footprintbooks.com and send in
your comments.

Publishing information

Peru, Bolivia and Ecuador 2nd edition
© Footprint Handbooks Ltd
November 2007

ISBN: 978 1 906098 06 3
CIP DATA: A catalogue record for this book
is available from the British Library

® Footprint Handbooks and the Footprint
mark are a registered trademark of
Footprint Handbooks Ltd

Published by Footprint

6 Riverside Court
Lower Bristol Road
Bath BA2 3DZ, UK
T +44 (0)1225 469141
F +44 (0)1225 469461
discover@footprintbooks.com
www.footprintbooks.com

Every effort has been made to ensure that
the facts in this guidebook are accurate.
However, travellers should still obtain
advice from consulates, airlines etc about
travel and visa requirements before
travelling. The authors and publishers
cannot accept responsibility for any loss,
injury or inconvenience however caused.